The Metaphysical Thought of Thomas Aquinas

Monographs of the Society for Medieval and
Renaissance Philosophy

Number 1

The Metaphysical Thought of Thomas Aquinas

From Finite Being to Uncreated Being

John F. Wippel

The Catholic University of America Press
Washington, D.C.

Copyright © 2000
The Catholic University of America Press
All rights reserved
Printed in the United States of America

The paper used in this publication meets the minimum requirements
of American National Standards for Information Science—Permanence of
Paper for Printed Library materials, ANSI Z39.48-1984.
∞

LIBRARY OF CONGRESS CATALOGING-IN-PUBLICATION DATA

Wippel, John F.
    The metaphysical thought of Thomas Aquinas : from finite being to
uncreated being / John F. Wippel.
        p. cm.—(Monographs of the Society for Medieval and Renaissance
Philosophy: v. 1)
    Includes bibliographical references and indices.
    1. Thomas, Aquinas, Saint, 1225?–1274—Contributions in
metaphysics.   2. Metaphysics—History.   I. Title.   II. Series.
    B765.T54 W487 2000
    110—dc21
    99-053039
    ISBN 0-8132-0982-X (cl. : alk. paper)
    ISBN 0-8132-0983-8 (pbk. : alk. paper)

Contents

Acknowledgments

Initial work on this volume began a number of years ago, but the time required for completing it was extended substantially by my acceptance in January 1989 of a full-time position in the central administration of my University. Only in September 1997 after having fulfilled my administrative responsibilities was I able to return to this manuscript. It is now my pleasant obligation to thank all of those who have assisted me in this undertaking. I would like to begin by expressing my gratitude to the National Endowment for the Humanities for a Fellowship for Independent Study and Research which, joined with a sabbatical leave from The Catholic University of America, first enabled me to take up this project. I must thank the University not only for that leave but for another which allowed me to devote full time to it during the 1997–1998 academic year. I am grateful to The Catholic University of America Press and to the Society for Medieval and Renaissance Philosophy for jointly accepting this book as the first in the Society's monograph series, and again to the Society together with the Billy Rose Foundation for a subsidy which has assisted in defraying the publication costs.

My special thanks are owing to the outside readers selected by the Society and by The Catholic University of America Press for their careful reading of and valuable comments on the text. Although I am not at liberty to disclose all of their names here, I can at least mention Professor Stephen Brown, Chairman of the Society's Committee on Publications. I am deeply grateful to him for the all the time and attention he devoted to my text. I must also thank Dr. David McGonagle, Director of The Catholic University of America Press, for his ever generous cooperation, and Mrs. Susan Needham, also of the Press, for her careful reading and skillful copy editing of the manuscript. I am grateful to a number of professional colleagues who have read one or other part of it over the years, or who have called to my attention certain relevant items in the secondary literature. Although I will not attempt to mention all of them by name, lest I inadvertently omit some, I do wish to single out two who carefully examined major parts of an earlier draft, Dr. Thomas Prufer and Dr. Bonnie Kent.

My special thanks are also owing to my former research assistant, Joseph Brinley, and my present one, Stan Grove, for their generous help in many different ways, and to various staff members of The Catholic University of America's John K. Mullen Library, especially Bruce Miller, for their ever willing cooperation in my seemingly unending search for sources.

Finally, I wish to thank the *Journal of the History of Philosophy*, the American Catholic Philosophical Association, The Catholic University of America Press, and Professor Georg Wieland, Vice-Rector of the Eberhard-Karls-Universität Tübingen in his capacity as an editor together with the Felix Meiner Verlag for permission to use in adapted form articles or portions of articles which had originally appeared in their respective publications: "Thomas Aquinas's Derivation of the Aristotelian Categories," *Journal of the History of Philosophy* 25 (1987), pp. 13–34; "Presidential Address: Substance in Aquinas's Metaphysics," in *Proceedings of the American Catholic Philosophical Association* 61 (1987), pp. 2–22 (Copyright by The American Catholic Philosophical Association); "Thomas Aquinas and Participation," in *Studies in Medieval Philosophy*, J. F. Wippel, ed. (Washington, D.C.: The Catholic University of America Press, 1987), pp. 117–58; "Thomas Aquinas on Substance as a Cause of Proper Accidents," in *Philosophie im Mittelalter. Entwicklungslinien und Paradigmen*, J. P. Beckmann, L. Honnefelder, G. Schrimpf, G. Wieland, eds. (Hamburg: Felix Meiner Verlag, 1987), pp. 201–12.

Abbreviations

AHDLMA	*Archives d'Histoire Doctrinale et Littéraire du Moyen Âge*
CCSL	*Corpus Christianorum. Series Latina*
CSEL	*Corpus Scriptorum Ecclesiasticorum Latinorum*
PG	*Patrologiae cursus completus, Series Graeca,* ed. J. P. Migne
PL	*Patrologiae cursus completus, Series Latina,* ed. J. P. Migne
ST	*Summa theologiae,* Thomas Aquinas
SCG	*Summa contra Gentiles,* Thomas Aquinas

Introduction

In order to set the stage for this study of Thomas Aquinas's metaphysical thought, I would like to recall briefly the essential moments of his life and career. He was born at his family's castle in Roccasecca, Italy in 1224/1225. He received his elementary education at the Benedictine abbey of Monte Cassino, located only a few miles from his family home. In 1239 he began the study of the liberal arts at the newly founded *Studium generale* at Naples and remained there until about 1244. It was undoubtedly there that he received his first formal instruction in philosophy, and it was also there that in 1244 he joined the recently established Dominican Order. This step did not fit in with his family's plans for him. A career with the more prestigious Benedictine Order would have been much more to their liking. So strong was his family's resistance to Thomas's entering the Dominican Order that, upon learning that the Dominicans were sending him to Paris for further studies, his mother arranged to have him intercepted by his brother (or brothers) and some other soldiers in the Emperor's service and detained at the family castle for a year or more. Finally, however, since his resolve remained unbroken, he was permitted to rejoin his Dominican confreres and made his way to Paris in 1245.[1]

At Paris he first came into contact with Albert the Great during the period 1245–1248, and in 1248 he accompanied Albert to Cologne in order to continue his theological formation there. In 1252 he was sent back to Paris to begin working for the highest degree offered by the University there, that of Magister in Theology, and pursued the rigorous academic program required for this until 1256. Not least

---

1. On Thomas's life and writings see J.A. Weisheipl, *Friar Thomas d'Aquino. His Life, Thought and Work*, 2d rev. ed. (Washington, D.C., 1983), and the more recent study by J.-P. Torrell, *Initiation à saint Thomas d'Aquin. Sa personne et son oeuvre* (Fribourg, 1993), English translation, *Saint Thomas Aquinas*. Volume I. *The Person and His Work* (Washington, D.C., 1996). As regards the dating of Thomas's various writings I will follow those proposed in Torrell's study unless otherwise indicated. On this early period in Thomas's life see Weisheipl, pp. 3–36; Torrell, pp. 1–17 (English translation cited here and throughout), and for the events surrounding the intervention of his family, *Albert & Thomas: Selected Writings*, S. Tugwell, ed. (New York–Mahwah, 1988), pp. 204–7.

among his duties during this period was his responsibility to comment on the *Sentences* of Peter the Lombard, and this resulted in the eventual publication of his first major theological writing, his Commentary on the *Sentences*. By 1256 he had completed the requirements for becoming a Master of Theology and in the spring of that year delivered his inaugural lecture as a Regent Master. However, owing to the hostility of a number of secular Masters in the theology faculty against the two recently founded mendicant orders, the Franciscans and the Dominicans, neither Thomas nor his Franciscan counterpart, Bonaventure, was formally admitted into the assembly of Masters until August 1257. They had, however, been lecturing as Masters in their respective religious houses. During this period of preparation at Paris (1252–1256) Thomas also produced two important philosophical treatises, *De principiis naturae* and *De ente et essentia*.[2]

From 1256 until 1259 Thomas carried out the functions of a Master (Professor) of Theology at the University of Paris. These duties included conducting formal disputed questions (resulting in his *Quaestiones disputatae De veritate*) and quodlibetal disputations (where any appropriate question could be raised by any member in the audience, and would ultimately have to be answered by the presiding Master). His Quodlibets 7–11 and his Commentary on the *De Trinitate* of Boethius resulted from this period.[3]

Thomas returned to Italy in 1259 and served there at various Dominican houses of study as Lecturer or as Regent Master, continuing to teach and to write at a rapid pace. During this period he completed his Commentary on the *De anima,* thereby commencing a series of intensive studies of Aristotle which would eventually result in partial or total commentaries on twelve works by the Stagirite. He completed his *Summa contra Gentiles* (1259–1265) and the *Prima Pars* of the *Summa theologiae* (1266–1268). Also dating from this period are his *Exposition on the Divine Names* (of Pseudo-Dionysius), *Disputed Questions on the Power of God (De potentia), Disputed Questions on Spiritual Creatures, Disputed Questions on the Soul,* and many other works of a theological or religious nature.[4]

In late 1268 or early 1269 he returned to Paris to resume his function there as Regent Master of Theology at the University. Various controversies demanded his attention during this period. Certain more conservative theologians, heavily in-

2. On Thomas's time at Paris (1245–1248) see Weisheipl, pp. 36–41; Torrell, pp. 19–24. On the period at Cologne see Torrell, pp. 24–35. On Thomas's first teaching years at Paris as a Bachelor of the Sentences (1252–1256) see Weisheipl, pp. 67–80; Torrell, pp. 36–50. On Thomas's inaugural lecture see Torrell, pp. 50–53. On the complications for Thomas and Bonaventure resulting from the quarrel between the seculars and mendicants see Torrell, pp. 76–79; Weisheipl, pp. 80–96, 113–15.

3. On this period see Weisheipl, pp. 116–39; Torrell, pp. 54–74. For fuller discusion of disputed questions and quodlibetal disputations see B. Bazán, J.F. Wippel, G. Fransen, D. Jacquart, *Les questions disputées et les questions quodlibétiques dans les facultés de théologie, de droit et de médecine* (Turnhout, 1985), Pt. I: "Les questions disputées, principalement dans les facultés de théologie" (Bazán); Pt. II: "Quodlibetal Questions, Chiefly in Theology Faculties" (Wippel).

4. On this period in Italy see Weisheipl, cc. IV–V; Torrell, cc. VI–IX.

spired by the tradition of St. Augustine (although also familiar with Aristotle's thought), were challenging the more Aristotelian version of Christian wisdom Thomas had been developing. To cite but one hotly contested issue, against the prevailing view defended by this group Thomas maintained, as he had throughout his career, that unaided human reason had not proved that the world began to be and, indeed, could not prove this point. Finally, writing in 1270 in his *De aeternitate mundi,* he went so far as to hold that an eternally created world is possible. Like all of his Christian contemporaries, of course, he believed on the grounds of revelation that the world began to be, but for him this was and could be only a matter of religious belief.[5]

During the 1260s and early 1270s a radical form of Aristotelianism was being developed by certain Masters in the Faculty of Arts at Paris (by now really a faculty of philosophy), such as Siger of Brabant, Boethius of Dacia, and others. Often if not accurately referred to as Latin Averroism, this movement was marked by the total dedication of its leaders to the pursuit of the purely philosophical life. At least in some instances, initially they were not particularly concerned if some of their philosophical conclusions happened to be at odds with orthodox Christian belief. So true was this that in December 1270, Stephen Tempier, Bishop of Paris, singled out thirteen propositions for special condemnation, including at least four which Siger had already defended. Aquinas himself, while sharing with these thinkers considerable respect for the thought of Aristotle and for philosophical reasoning, opposed the views of this movement on various points.[6]

Perhaps most notorious was the defense by some members of the Arts Faculty such as Siger himself, at least prior to December 1270, of the Averroistic view of unicity of the possible intellect. According to this position there is only one pos-

5. For discussion and defense of a late September 1268 date for Thomas's return, see Torrell, pp. 181–82, who follows R.-A. Gauthier on this. On the opposition of the conservative theologians to Thomas's views during this period (1268/1269–1272), especially those who might be categorized as belonging to the Neo-Augustinian movement inspired by Bonaventure but really founded by John Pecham, see F. Van Steenberghen, *La philosophie au XIIIe siècle,* 2d rev. ed. (Louvain-la-Neuve, 1991), pp. 398–411. On Thomas's development of his position in his *De aeternitate mundi* see c. VII in my *Metaphysical Themes in Thomas Aquinas* (Washington, D.C., 1984). For references to more recent discussions of Thomas's views on this general topic see Van Steenberghen, p. 405, n. 101. Cf. Torrell, pp. 184–87. As we will see below in Ch. IX, Thomas's defense of unicity of substantial form in human beings was another hotly contested issue.

6. On the rise of this Radical Aristotelian movement at Paris see Van Steenberghen, *La philosophie au XIIIe siècle,* pp. 325–35. On Siger see pp. 335–60; also his *Maître Siger de Brabant* (Louvain-Paris, 1977); *Thomas Aquinas and Radical Aristotelianism* (Washington, D.C., 1980); Wippel, *Mediaeval Reactions to the Encounter between Faith and Reason* (Milwaukee, 1995), pp. 33–59; and most recently, F.-X. Putallaz and R. Imbach, *Profession: Philosophe Siger de Brabant* (Paris, 1997). On Boethius of Dacia see Van Steenberghen, *La philosophie au XIII siècle,* pp. 361–70; Wippel, *Boethius of Dacia. On the Supreme Good. On the Eternity of the World. On Dreams* (Toronto, 1987), pp. 1–23. On the Condemnation of 1270 see Van Steenberghen, *Maître Siger,* pp. 74–79; Wippel, "The Condemnations of 1270 and 1277 at Paris," *Journal of Medieval and Renaissance Studies* 7 (1977), pp. 169–201, esp. pp. 179–85.

sible, i.e., one receiving and spiritual intellect for all human beings, a separate and immaterial substance, which is ultimately responsible for the thinking that each one of us apparently does. Unlike the defense of one separate agent or abstracting intellect for the human race, a view espoused not only by Siger but by various perfectly orthodox thinkers of the time, this Averroistic position undercut the possibility of individual immortality of the human soul and hence of personal reward or punishment in the life to come. In 1270 Thomas directed a well-crafted treatise against this position, his *De unitate intellectus contra Averroistas*. In this work Thomas challenged Siger's interpretation both on historical grounds (it was not the correct reading of Aristotle's *De anima*), and on philosophical grounds (it was not good philosophy). This tightly reasoned work is a lasting testimony to Thomas's philosophical skill and power.[7]

On still another front, the mendicants, including both Franciscans and Dominicans, were again under attack by certain secular Masters in Theology at Paris. Indeed, the very viability of the mendicant way of life was being challenged. Against these dissenting voices Thomas directed the concluding chapters of his *De perfectione spiritualis vitae* and his *Contra doctrinam retrahentium a religione*.[8] Also dating from this period (1269–1272) are many of his commentaries on Aristotle, *Super Librum de causis*, some scriptural commentaries (on Matthew and John), major portions of the *Summa theologiae*, his Disputed Questions *De virtutibus*, Quodlibets 1–6 and 12, and most likely, his Disputed Questions *De malo* and *De unione verbi incarnati*.[9] In the spring of 1272 he was recalled by his religious superiors to Italy and charged with establishing a *studium generale* of theology for his order in Naples. His teaching and writing activities continued until near the end of 1273. Early in 1274 he departed to take part in a general council of the Church at Lyons, but died while on the way at the Cistercian Abbey at Fossanova on March 7, 1274.[10]

Even this brief survey of Thomas's life leaves one with the impression of a vast amount of teaching and writing compressed into a relatively short professional career (a little more than twenty years if we begin with his lectures on the *Sentences* in 1252). At the same time, it is also clear that, so far as his professional teaching

7. On unicity of the possible intellect in Siger and Thomas's reaction see Van Steenberghen, *Thomas Aquinas and Radical Aristotelianism*, "Monopsychism," pp. 29–74; *La philosophie*, pp. 387–97.

8. Cf. Weisheipl, pp. 263–72; Torrell, pp. 182–84.

9. For more details concerning Thomas's writings during this period see Torrell, pp. 196–212. See pp. 211–23 for a series of shorter writings also dating from this time. See pp. 224–36 on the Aristotelian commentaries. For the latest precisions concerning the relative datings of Thomas's Quodlibets see *Sancti Thomae de Aquino Opera omnia*, Leonine ed. (Rome, 1882–), Vol. 25.1, "Avant-Propos," p. ix* (résumé) = Leon. 25.1.ix*, as well as discussion of particular datings in the respective Introductions to various Quodlibets.

10. For details concerning his teaching and writing activities during this final period see Torrell, pp. 247–66. These included lecturing on Paul's Letter to the Romans and continuing his work on the *Tertia Pars* of the *Summa theologiae* and on some of the Aristotelian commentaries (see p. 266). On Thomas's last months and death see Weisheipl, c. VII; Torrell, pp. 289–95.

obligations were concerned, he was a teacher, a professor of theology. And if his writings may be divided into various categories, the majority of them may be described as theological or religious rather than as purely philosophical in character. In short, Thomas Aquinas was a professional theologian.[11]

This point has been especially emphasized by various twentieth-century interpreters of his thought, owing in no small measure to the gradually evolving views developed by Etienne Gilson concerning what he called "Christian Philosophy" and his application of the same to Thomas's philosophical thought. Indeed, Gilson's position concerning this eventually went beyond his earlier claim that we should not study Aquinas's philosophy as a pure philosophy but as a Christian Philosophy, and thereby take into account certain positive influences that it received from Thomas's religious faith. In later writings Gilson emphasized the point that Thomas's original philosophical thought is contained in his theological writings, not in his philosophical opuscula and commentaries. Because it is found in theological writings, it has been transformed into theology and falls under the formal object of theology. Hence we should study it from that perspective, i.e., as transformed into theology, and should not attempt to extract it from its theological home so as to present it as a pure philosophy. By doing this we will thereby gain knowledge of all the philosophy his theology contains.[12]

On other occasions I have examined and critically evaluated this Gilsonian position, and need not repeat that critique here. Suffice it to say that, while I recognize with Gilson that Aquinas never wrote a *Summa philosophiae* or a *Summa metaphysicae,* I am convinced that a well worked out metaphysics existed in his own mind and can be recovered from his various writings. Indeed, his development of this underlying metaphysics was a necessary condition for him to create his highly original speculative theology. The evidence for this is twofold. First, the fundamental elements of his metaphysical thought may be found in his many different kinds of

---

11. See below for my effort to categorize his different kinds of writings.

12. For my presentation of Gilson's developing views on this see *Metaphysical Themes,* c. I, pp. 1–22. A key presentation of Gilson's earlier views on Christian Philosophy may be found in the opening two chapters of his *The Spirit of Medieval Philosophy* (London, 1936; repr. 1950). His later views may be found in his intellectual autobiography, *The Philosopher and Theology* (New York, 1962); *Elements of Christian Philosophy* (Garden City, N.Y., 1960); *Introduction à la philosophie chrétienne* (Paris, 1960), now available in English translation by A. Maurer, *Christian Philosophy. An Introduction* (Toronto, 1993); and other sources cited in my discussion. On the transformation of philosophy into Thomistic theology see *Elements,* p. 282, n. 6; also: ". . . the nature of the doctrine in the *Summa theologiae* should be clear. Since its aim is to introduce its readers, especially beginners, to the teaching of theology, everything in it is theological. This does not mean that the *Summa* contains no philosophy; on the contrary, it is full of philosophy. Since the philosophy that is in the *Summa* is there in view of a theological end, and since it figures in it as integrated with that which is the proper work of the theologian, it finds itself included within the formal object of theology and becomes theological in its own right" (p. 42). Cf. *The Philosopher and Theology,* pp. 102, 198, 211. On the practical consequences Gilson draws for those who would teach Thomas's philosophy today see his "Thomas Aquinas and Our Colleagues," in *A Gilson Reader,* A.C. Pegis, ed. (Garden City, N.Y., 1957), pp. 278–97.

writings, a point to which I shall return below. Second, Thomas has taken the trouble of explaining in considerable detail his views concerning the distinction between philosophy and theology, the different kinds of theoretical philosophy, the distinctive subject of metaphysics, the methodology to be used in metaphysical thinking, and the difference between following the philosophical order and following the theological order. Since all of these elements are present in his writings, they constitute a standing invitation for today's historian of philosophy to take Thomas at his word and to draw upon them in reconstructing his metaphysical thought. It is this that I shall attempt to do in this book.[13]

To return to the point mentioned above, let me now add a word about the different kinds of writings Thomas has left for us. While they may be grouped or divided in various ways, I would propose the following in the interests of simplicity: (1) philosophical commentaries (twelve commentaries on Aristotle and one on the *Liber de causis*); (2) commentaries on sacred scripture; (3) theological commentaries (on the *De Trinitate* and the *De Hebdomadibus* of Boethius, on the *De divinis nominibus* of Pseudo-Dionysius, and on the *Sentences* of Peter Lombard—of these only two are commentaries in the strict sense, i.e., on the *De Hebdomadibus* and on the *De divinis nominibus;* the other two offer brief expositions of the texts of Boethius and of Peter and use them as occasions for much fuller and highly personal disquisitions by Thomas himself); (4) works of theological synthesis *(Summa contra Gentiles, Summa theologiae, Compendium theologiae,* and if one prefers to include it here, the Commentary on the *Sentences* listed above); (5) Disputed Questions and Quodlibetal Questions (resulting from Thomas's functions as a professor of theology); (6) theological opuscula; (7) philosophical opuscula *(De ente et essentia, De principiis naturae, De unitate intellectus, De aeternitate mundi, De substantiis separatis* [the first sixteen chapters, although the second and unfinished part (cc. 17–19) considers separate substances in the light of Catholic teaching and is therefore theological]).[14]

---

13. For my critique of Gilson's position see *Metaphysical Themes*, pp. 22–33. See pp. 23–24 for a qualified way in which I would accept describing a philosophy such as Thomas's as "Christian," i.e., in the moment of discovery but not in the moment of proof. Also see my "The Possibility of a Christian Philosophy: A Thomistic Perspective," *Faith and Philosophy* 1 (1984), pp. 272–90. For a good résumé of his long-running disagreement with Gilson on this issue see Van Steenberghen, "Etienne Gilson, historien de la pensée médiévale," *Revue philosophique de Louvain* 77 (1979), esp. pp. 493–505. For a more recent critique see J. Aertsen, *Medieval Philosophy and the Transcendentals. The Case of Thomas Aquinas* (Leiden, 1996), pp. 3–10. For another version of the tendency to theologism in interpreting Aquinas's philosophical thought see M. Jordan, "Theology and Philosophy," in *The Cambridge Companion to Aquinas,* N. Kretzmann and E. Stump, eds. (Cambridge, 1993), pp. 232–51.

14. This is fundamentally the same classification proposed by Van Steenberghen in his *La philosophie au XIIIe siècle,* pp. 280–83, although I am including under theological opuscula writings he lists under apologetical opuscula, opuscula for the defense of the Mendicants, opuscula on spirituality, and liturgical writings, letters, and sermons. The Catalog in Torrell, prepared by G. Emery, uses the following categories: (1) Theological Syntheses; (2) Disputed Questions; (3) Biblical Commentaries;

In considering possible sources which we may use in recovering Thomas's meta-physical thought, two of these categories of writings, the philosophical commentaries and the philosophical opuscula, stand out since both are clearly philosophical. This notwithstanding, Gilson tended to minimize their importance for any effort to discover Thomas's personal metaphysical thought. According to Gilson, the philosophical opuscula are not all that significant as sources for Aquinas's personal metaphysical thinking, and the commentaries on Aristotle are really only exercises by Thomas in the history of philosophy; in them he writes as the commentator or the *expositor*, not as an original philosopher.[15]

In my view the philosophical opuscula are extremely important sources for our knowledge of Thomas's personal and original philosophical positions. This will become clear below from my citations from them—especially from the *De ente et essentia*, the *De principiis naturae*, and the *De substantiis separatis*—in setting forth some of his most fundamental metaphysical positions. I have already referred to the philosophical significance of Thomas's *De unitate intellectus contra Averroistas* both as a contribution to the study of Aristotle's thoughts on the matter, and as a personal philosophical critique of Siger's views. And for final clarification of his views on the possibility of an eternally created world, I have found his *De aeterni-tate mundi* to be of the utmost importance.[16]

As regards the significance of Thomas's commentaries on Aristotle and the *Liber de causis*, it would be a very strange procedure for us to ignore or minimize their importance for our understanding of his personal philosophical views on a priori grounds. After all, he did devote a considerable amount of time and energy to preparing them. This is especially noteworthy since it was not one of his recognized duties as a professional theologian to write extended literal commentaries on Aristotle's works.[17]

---

(4) Commentaries on Aristotle; (5) Other Commentaries; (6) Polemical Writings; (7) Treatises; (8) Letters and Requests for Expert Opinion; (9) Liturgical Works, Sermons, Prayers. See pp. 330–59.

15. See Gilson, *The Christian Philosophy of St. Thomas Aquinas* (New York, 1956), p. 8. See p. 22: "There is a series of works in which St. Thomas used the philosophical method-the Commentaries on Aristotle and a small number of *Opuscula*. But each *opusculum* gives but a fragment of his thought, and the commentaries on Aristotle . . . only let us suspect imperfectly what might have been the nature of a Summa of Thomistic philosophy organized by St. Thomas himself. . . ." Cf. *Elements of Christian Philosophy*, p. 282, n. 6; *The Philosopher and Theology*, pp. 210–11: "Saint Thomas is only a commentator in his writings on Aristotle. For his personal thinking one must look at the two *Summae* and similar writings. . . . Even in the astonishing tract, *On Being and Essence*, the level of theology is not far from the surface." As I commented in *Metaphysical Themes* (p. 15, n. 41), if in this last text Gilson seems to take the *De ente* more seriously, this is because he here regards it too as a theological writing!

16. See my *Metaphysical Themes*, c. VII, cited above in n. 5.

17. Scholarly opinion is divided concerning Thomas's reasons for writing the Aristotelian commentaries. Weisheipl believes that he saw it as part of his intellectual apostolate to produce reliable guides for young masters in arts which would enable them "to understand Aristotelian philosophy in harmony with the actual text and the guideline of faith, where necessary" *(Friar Thomas*, p. 281; cf. pp. 280–85). Hence he assigns considerable importance to them. For a brief presentation of

Even so, as I have noted on another occasion, I do think that considerable care must be exercised when we consult them as sources for Thomas's personal philosophical thinking. Some twentieth-century interpreters seem to assume that almost any statement made by Thomas in these works should be taken as an expression of his personal thought. Gilson, at the other extreme, would reduce them to mere exercises in and contributions to the history of philosophy. The truth seems to fall somewhere in between. One cannot immediately assume that every position expressed in such a commentary is merely Thomas's understanding of the text on which he is commenting. On many occasions such expositions also seem to represent positions Thomas himself holds. On other occasions Thomas's discussion goes beyond the thought of the text on which he is commenting, and he indicates as much to us. However, when he does not clearly spell this out for us in the commentary itself, we need some kind of control to determine whether Thomas is accepting as his own a particular position he is setting forth in his commentary, or whether he is merely expressing his understanding of the text on which he is commenting. Frequently enough such a control is at hand, either in the Prooemium to a particular commentary itself, where he is more likely to speak in his own name, or in other writings where he deals with the same topic and is clearly expressing his own views. When the views he presents in more independent writings agree with those he exposes in a particular commentary on Aristotle, we may assume that he accepts the latter as his own position as well. When there is disagreement between the two discussions, we should be very hesitant in assigning such a position from one of his commentaries to Thomas himself, unless there is also some evidence pointing to change or development in his thinking on that point.[18]

As for our right to draw upon writings which fall under the other categories we have distinguished above, all of which appear to be theological in some sense, cer-

---

different views concerning whether and to what extent we may use them in reconstructing Thomas's personal thought see Torrell, pp. 237–39. He himself emphasizes the point that in writing them Thomas wishes to determine the mind of Aristotle in the texts on which he comments, but that this desire to discover what Aristotle "wished to say" at times leads Thomas to go beyond the texts themselves in his search for truth. Also cf. J. Doig, *Aquinas on Metaphysics: A historico-doctrinal study of the Commentary on the Metaphysics* (The Hague, 1972), pp. ix–xiv.

18. See my *Metaphysical Themes*, p. 27. I will apply this method in Ch. II below when dealing with Thomas's views on *separatio* and the discovery of the subject of metaphysics. For a useful collection (in Latin and in German translation) of the Prologues (Prooemia) to Thomas's commentaries on Aristotle and on the *Liber de causis* see F. Chevenal and R. Imbach, *Thomas von Aquin. Prologe zu den Aristoteles-Kommentaren* (Frankfurt am Main, 1993). From the Introduction see pp. lvii–lxiv, on the philosophical significance of the Prologues. There (pp. lviii–lix) they offer a helpful corrective to the somewhat exaggerated emphasis placed on the theological character of these commentaries by Gauthier (see Leon. 45.1.288*–94*) and proposed, albeit more tentatively, by J. Owens in his "Aquinas as Aristotelian Commentator," in *St. Thomas Aquinas 1274–1974. Commemorative Studies*, Vol. 1 (Toronto, 1974), pp. 213–38. While one may readily agree with Gauthier and Owens that Thomas saw his writing of these commentaries as contributing ultimately to his theological enterprise by helping him perfect his personal philosophy, he commented on them philosophically, i.e., from the philosophical perspective rather than the theological.

tain distinctions are in order. Van Steenberghen has suggested that at times we find in such writings self-contained philosophical discussions inserted as such into a theological work.[19] For instance, in Chapters I and II below we shall turn to a number of questions and articles from Thomas's Commentary on Boethius's *De Trinitate* where he presents his views on the divisions, subjects, distinctive knowing procedures, and methodologies of the three theoretical sciences, physics, mathematics, and metaphysics. Discussions such as these may and should be used as important sources for recovering his metaphysical thought. Or again, we may find a running series of philosophical discussions joined together as succeeding questions or chapters in works such as the *Summa theologiae* (see the so-called Treatises on God, or on Man, or on Law) or the *Summa contra Gentiles* (see the reliance on arguments based on natural reason throughout Bks I-III), or in the earlier part of the *Compendium theologiae*. We may easily remove such discussions from the general theological context of the writings in which they appear and from the references to Scripture and the Fathers contained in some of their *videtur*s or *sed contra*s and use them as important sources in reconstructing Thomas's metaphysical thought.[20]

On still other occasions we will find similar self-contained philosophical discussions proposed as individual questions within Disputed Questions (see, for instance, the discussion of truth and the associated derivation of the transcendentals in *De veritate*, q. 1, a. 1) or in certain particular questions within his various Quodlibets. These too may easily be removed from their general theological settings and used as important expressions of Thomas's personal thought. Finally, on still other occasions we will find Thomas using philosophical reasoning as an instrument in working out a strictly theological argument. In such cases I would agree with Gilson that the particular philosophical reasoning has here become theological. Nonetheless, we may still examine this underlying philosophical or metaphysical reasoning in order to determine what particular philosophical choice or choices Thomas has made in developing this particular theological argumentation. Because he himself traces diversity in theologies to diversity in their underlying philosophies, we may, if we make appropriate distinctions, use even such texts as additional sources for our effort to recover his metaphysical thought.[21]

---

19. *La philosophie au XIIIe siécle*, p. 318.

20. We can do this because in these cases Thomas has developed his philosophical thinking on these points as part of his philosophical enterprise, by relying on unaided human reason. Because he has done this he can now incorporate such thinking into the broader theological context of the treatise at hand and thereby contribute to his theological goal as well.

21. See *Metaphysical Themes*, p. 28, n. 79, where I offer *De potentia*, q. 3, a. 14, ad 4 as an example of Thomas's incorporation of his personal metaphysics of the essence-*esse* relationship into his theological discussion of the eternal procession of the Son from the Father. For his view that differences between theologians arise from differences in their underlying philosophical positions see *In II Sent.*, d. 14, q. 1, a. 2 *(Scriptum super libros Sententiarum*, P. Mandonnet, ed., [Paris, 1929], Vol. 2, p. 350): "Similiter etiam expositores Sacrae Scripturae in hoc diversificati sunt, secundum quod diversorum

In sum, as regards the different categories of Thomas's writings distinguished above, to the extent that important elements of his thought are contained in any of them, to that extent I will feel free to draw upon those works in presenting his metaphysics. And I will present this as his metaphysics or his metaphysical thought, not as his theology or as his "Christian philosophy."[22]

In this effort I will be guided by Thomas's explicitly stated views concerning the nature and subject of metaphysics, the distinctive processes involved in arriving at metaphysical thinking, the distinction between philosophy and theology, and the difference between following the philosophical order and following the theological order. Before concluding this Introduction, therefore, I wish to consider briefly his views on the distinction between philosophy and theology as well as his understanding of the difference between following the philosophical order and following the theological order.

Thomas deals with the distinction between philosophy and theology on different occasions. He offers perhaps his clearest discussion of this in q. 2, a. 3 of his Commentary on the *De Trinitate* of Boethius. In this particular article he is concerned with determining whether or not it is permissible to use philosophical arguments and authorities in the science of the faith, i.e., in theology. The general setting for this discussion is, therefore, theological, and this is appropriate; conflict between faith and reason should not arise for someone who has no religious faith.[23]

After presenting a series of arguments against the legitimacy of using philosophical arguments and authorities in one's theologizing and then another set of arguments in support of doing this, Thomas offers his solution. The gifts of grace are added to nature in such a way that they do not destroy nature but perfect it. This is an important presupposition on Thomas's part, since it indicates that the gifts of grace, including religious faith, should not be regarded as inimical to or as destructive of nature. As his text continues, the light of faith, which is given to us as a grace, does not destroy the light of natural reason, which is also given to us by God.[24] In saying this Thomas combines something which he accepts only on faith (that the light of faith is divinely given) with something else which he undoubtedly

---

philosophorum sectatores fuerunt, a quibus in philosophicis eruditi sunt." Also see Aertsen, *Medieval Philosophy and the Transcendentals*, p. 7, n. 1, who cites *De malo*, q. 1, a. 2 as an illustration of this. There Thomas indicates that (Pseudo-) Dionysius seems to be following the Platonists when he places the good before being *(Sancti Thomae de Aquino Opera omnia* [Rome, 1882–], Vol. 23, p. 11, lines 159–161=Leon. 23.11:159–161).

22. This is not to deny that Thomas will draw upon his faith as a negative norm in developing his philosophy even in purely philosophical works such as his Commentaries on Aristotle or the philosophical opuscula if and when he finds it necessary to do so. Nor is it to deny that one might refer to his philosophy as Christian in the "moment of discovery" as opposed to the "moment of proof" (see note 13 above).

23. See Leon. 50.96–100.

24. Leon. 50.98:114–118. Note: ". . . unde et lumen fidei, quod nobis gratis infunditur, non destruit lumen naturalis rationis divinitus nobis inditum."

also first accepted on faith but for which he will also argue philosophically (that, like everything else that is distinct from God, the light of natural reason is created by him).[25]

Thomas goes on to explain that while the natural light of human reason is incapable of arriving at knowledge of those things which are made known to us only through faith, i.e., revealed mysteries, it is nonetheless impossible for truths which have been revealed to us by God to be contrary to those instilled in us by nature. This is so, he reasons, because in that eventuality one or the other would have to be false. (Two contradictory propositions cannot both be true simultaneously.) And since Thomas has traced both of these sources of knowledge back to God, this would make God himself the author of falsity, something Thomas rejects as impossible. He adds that, since in imperfect things we find some imitation of those that are perfect, in things we understand through natural reason we find certain likenesses *(similitudines)* of things which are revealed to us through faith.[26]

So far Thomas has been discussing the relationship and lack of opposition or the harmony between faith and reason. Now he goes on to speak explicitly of philosophy and theology. Just as sacred teaching, i.e., theology, is based on the light of faith, so is philosophy grounded on the natural light of reason. Wherefore it is impossible for things which pertain to philosophy to be opposed to those which belong to religious belief, even though the former fall short of the latter. Thomas repeats the point that truths discovered by philosophy contain certain likenesses and, he adds, certain preambles, for those things which are of faith, just as nature itself is a preamble for grace.[27]

However, not being blind to historical realities, Thomas continues. If something is found in the sayings or conclusions of the philosophers that is contrary to faith, this is not really philosophy but an abuse of it that follows from some deficiency on the part of someone's exercise of human reason. Here, therefore, Thomas is assuming that we will remember the point he has just made, that there can be no real contradiction between what we discover through philosophical investigation and what we receive through religious belief. This is because of his conviction that both come to us from God. Hence if an alleged philosophical conclusion contradicts an article of faith, both cannot be true at the same time. Because Thomas is mindful of the possibility that human reason can fall into error, in such a case he assigns greater weight, greater certainty, to revealed truth. He does so because he believes that such truth is given to us directly by God through revelation and is not

25. For the point that all that differs from God is created by him see Ch. XIV below, pp. 579–85.

26. Leon. 50.98:118–99:130. Note: ". . . tamen impossibile est quod ea quae per fidem traduntur nobis divinitus, sint contraria his quae sunt per naturam nobis indita: oporteret enim alterum esse falsum. . . ."

27. Leon. 50.99:131–137. Note: ". . . unde impossibile est quod ea quae sunt philosophiae sint contraria his quae sunt fidei. . . ."

subject to the weaknesses and possible mistakes to which unaided human reason is prone.[28]

Here we have Thomas's justification for the right of the Christian believer to use his or her religious faith as a check, as it were, as a negative norm, with respect to a philosophical conclusion if that conclusion clearly contradicts revealed truth. At the same time, it is interesting to observe that Thomas does not apply this same thinking to a conclusion based on theological reasoning, i.e., to a position a theologian might reach by reasoning about or even from a revealed premise. Presumably this is because Thomas is keenly aware that if human reason when used by philosophers is fallible, it is equally fallible when employed by theologians.[29]

Thomas goes on to draw out an interesting consequence from the point he has just made. In the case of conflict between an (alleged) philosophical conclusion and a revealed truth, it is possible by using the principles of philosophy to refute an error of this kind either by showing that it is altogether impossible or else by showing that it has not in fact been demonstrated. He must allow for these two possibilities because, as he explains, just as those things which pertain to faith (alone) cannot be demonstratively proved, so too, certain things which are opposed to them cannot be demonstratively shown to be false. They can, however, be shown not to be necessary, i.e., not to have been demonstrated.[30] While continuing to defend a real harmony between faith and reason, Thomas is allowing for what we may call revealed mysteries, such as the Trinity or the Incarnation. Because such articles of faith cannot be demonstrated by natural reason, if someone denies such a truth the best the believer can do in responding is to show that the denial itself has not been demonstrated. If Thomas were to allow for the possibility that one could demonstrate that the denial of such a truth is itself false, he would in effect be admitting that the revealed mystery could itself be demonstrated.

Finally Thomas sums up three ways in which one may use philosophy in theological inquiry: (1) to demonstrate what he calls preambles for faith, i.e., truths that should be known by one who believes, such as those that are proved by natural argumentation about God—for instance, the fact that God exists, that God is one—and similar truths which are proved in philosophy about God or about creatures and are presupposed by faith; (2) to manifest through certain likenesses truths

28. Leon. 50.99:137–140: "Si quid autem in dictis philosophorum invenitur contrarium fidei, hoc non est philosophiae, sed magis philosophiae abusus ex defectu rationis. . . ."

29. The right of the Christian believer to use religious faith as a negative norm is granted both by Gilson and his followers in their defense of Christian Philosophy, and by many of his critics who are themselves believing Christians. The point of disagreement rather has to do with the positive influences which Gilson claims to find running from a believer's faith, as in the case of Aquinas, to his philosophizing.

30. Leon. 50.99:141–147: ". . . et ideo possibile est ex principiis philosophiae huiusmodi errorem refellere, vel ostendendo omnino esse impossibile, vel ostendendo non esse necessarium: sicut enim ea quae sunt fidei non possunt demonstrative probari, ita quaedam contraria eis non possunt demonstrative ostendi esse falsa, sed potest ostendi non esse necessaria."

which we know through faith, as Augustine does in his *De Trinitate;* (3) to oppose claims made against faith either by showing them to be false, or else by showing that they are not necessary, i.e., that they have not been demonstrated.[31]

Thomas also identifies two ways in which a believer may fall into error while using philosophy in theology. First, one might employ philosophical conclusions which are opposed to faith and which, he remarks, are not really philosophy but an abuse or corruption of it. Second, one might refuse to accept on faith anything which philosophy cannot demonstrate and, to use a more familiar terminology, fall into rationalism.[32]

In order to fill in one point Thomas has not explicitly developed here, we may turn to his *Summa contra Gentiles* I, cc. 3 and 4. In c. 3 he distinguishes two kinds of truths concerning God which are accessible to us: (1) those which completely surpass reason's ability to discover and which, therefore, can be held only on the grounds of religious belief, such as the Trinity; (2) those which human reason can demonstrate philosophically, such as God's existence or his uniqueness, which, Thomas says, philosophers have demonstrated.[33]

In c. 4 he argues that because there are these two kinds of truths concerning divine things, those which can only be believed (revealed mysteries), and those capable of being demonstrated philosophically, it was fitting for God to reveal both types to us. Rather than develop here Thomas's interesting argumentation to support this claim, it will be enough for us to note that he is now allowing for what we might describe as "mixed truths" concerning God and divine things, i.e., truths which can be demonstrated philosophically, but which are also contained in revelation. It is here that the preambles to faith he mentioned in the text from his Commentary on the *De Trinitate* should be placed.[34] Since these fall within the realm of philosophical investigation, Thomas's discussion of and efforts to demonstrate them will be of great interest to us and an important source in our effort to recover his metaphysical thought about God.

With Thomas's views on the relationship between faith and reason and between theology and philosophy in mind, we may now turn to *Summa contra gentiles* II, c. 4 for some additional guidance concerning the order we should follow in presenting his metaphysics. As he explains there, philosophy studies created things in terms of that which they are in themselves. Christian faith, on the other hand, considers them not as they are in themselves but insofar as they represent God in some way. Thomas returns to this point near the end of the chapter. Because philosophy considers created things as they are in themselves, it begins by studying them and moves on to take up issues concerning God himself only at the end of its investigation. But in theology (the teaching based on faith) one should follow the

---

31. Leon. 50.99:148–161.
32. Leon. 50.99:161–171.
33. See *Summa contra Gentiles* (Editio Leonina manualis = Ed.Leon.man. [Rome, 1934]), p. 2.
34. Ed. cit., pp. 3–4. For more on this text see Ch. X below, Section 1, and notes 7–14.

reverse order, beginning with a study of God, and only subsequently considering creatures insofar as they are ordered and related to God.[35]

Accordingly, after a preliminary discussion in Chapter I of Thomas's views on the subject and the nature of metaphysics as a philosophical science and the relationship of its subject to divine being, in Ch. II we shall consider his account of the way we arrive at knowledge of the subject of this discipline, being as being. Subsequently in our effort to follow the philosophical order as Thomas has described it, we shall devote Parts One and Two to his metaphysical analysis of finite being. Only in Part Three will we move on to consider his philosophical discussion of divine being (God).

Within Part One itself, because of Thomas's defense of being as being as the subject of metaphysics, we will concentrate on certain issues which are as broad in extension as this subject itself, with special emphasis on the role the act of being (esse) plays in his understanding of finite being. Here we will consider his debt to Parmenides in formulating the problem of the One and the Many in the order of being, along with his views on analogy as applied to finite being (Ch. III), his metaphysics of participation in being (Ch. IV), the central role played in his resolution of these issues by his theory of composition of essence and esse in finite beings (Ch. V), and his appeal to a kind of relative nonbeing as part of his response to the issue of the One and the Many in the order of being (Ch. VI).

In Part Two we will shift our emphasis to his explanation of the essence or essential structure of finite being as this is expressed in his general theory of substance-accident composition (Ch. VII) along with certain related issues (Ch. VIII), and then to his understanding of matter-form composition which, against theories of universal hylemorphism, he restricts to material beings (Ch. IX).

In Part Three we will consider in detail his argumentation for God's existence (Chs. X, XI, XII). In Ch. XIII we will examine his highly nuanced views concerning the possibility of quidditative knowledge of God, and will then return to his theory of analogy of being, but this time as applied to divine being. In Ch. XIV we will first complete some additional points which he establishes philosophically about God, and will then revisit certain issues concerning finite being which we had previously considered without assuming God's existence. At this point we will bring this study to a close.

---

35. Ed. cit., pp. 95–96. Note: "Exinde etiam est quod non eodem ordine utraque doctrina procedit. Nam in doctrina philosophiae, quae creaturas secundum se considerat et ex eis in Dei cognitionem perducit, prima est consideratio de creaturis et ultima de Deo. In doctrina vero fidei, quae creaturas non nisi in ordine ad Deum considerat, primo est consideratio Dei et postmodum creaturarum." In his various presentations of Aquinas's "Christian" Philosophy, Gilson would always insist on following the theological order rather than the philosophical. See *The Christian Philosophy of St. Thomas Aquinas*, pp. 21–22, 442–43, n. 33; *Elements of Christian Philosophy*, p. 42 and p. 290, n. 42. For criticisms of Gilson on this point see my *Metaphysical Themes*, pp. 29–33; Aertsen, *Medieval Philosophy and the Transcendentals*, pp. 8–9.

In sum, therefore, in this study I propose to set forth Thomas Aquinas's metaphysical thought, based on his own texts, in accord with the philosophical order, in the way he himself might have done it had he chosen to write a *Summa metaphysicae*. My hope is that it will prove to be of interest to any reader who is interested in exploring that metaphysics.

The Metaphysical Thought of Thomas Aquinas

Aquinas on the Nature of Metaphysics

One of the more notable developments in recent decades in our understanding of Aquinas's metaphysical thought has been a growing appreciation of the distinctive way in which he accounts for our discovery of being as real or as existing and, consequent upon this, for our knowledge of being as being.[1] That this is of importance to anyone interested in his metaphysics goes without saying. According to Thomas, as we shall shortly see in greater detail, metaphysics has as its subject being in general or being as being. Hence in considering his treatment of our discovery of being as being we are really taking up his account of the way in which one gets to the subject of this science or, to put it in other terms, his views concerning the conditions of possibility for metaphysics.

Progress in this area has been facilitated by the recovery and edition of an autograph of one of Thomas's most important discussions of this issue in Questions 5 and 6 of his Commentary *(Expositio)* on the *De Trinitate* of Boethius. This was followed by B. Decker's critical edition of his entire Commentary on that same Boethian treatise and most recently by the Leonine edition of the same.[2] Especially significant for our purposes is a statement made in q. 5, a. 3 of that Commentary, and which appears in other early texts as well. Thomas's point is this: if it is through the intellect's first operation that we discover quiddities or understand what things are, it is only through its second operation that we discover their existence *(esse)*. This second operation is referred to by Aquinas as that whereby the intellect "com-

---

1. Extremely important in this respect is Gilson's *Being and Some Philosophers* (Toronto, 1949; 2d ed. 1952), c. VI, and in the second edition, "Appendix" (pp. 216–32). Here I shall quote from the second edition. Also helpful and widely circulated were certain remarks made by J. Maritain in his *Existence and the Existent* (New York, 1948), especially pp. 22–35. I do not wish, however, to endorse Maritain's views about an intuition of being as an authentic interpretation of Aquinas.

2. See *Thomas von Aquin, In librum Boethii de Trinitate, Quaestiones Quinta et Sexta*, P. Wyser, ed. (Fribourg-Louvain, 1948); *Sancti Thomae de Aquino Expositio super librum Boethii De Trinitate*, B. Decker, ed. (2d ed., Leiden, 1955, repr. 1959); and most recently, *Super Boetium De Trinitate* in Vol. 50 of the Leonine edition, from which I will here cite.

poses or divides" and is better known to us today as judgment.[3] Thomas's appeal to judgment to account for our discovery of the existence of things has been stressed by various writers, but especially so by Etienne Gilson and others who have developed his work in this direction.[4]

Equally important for our appreciation of Thomas's understanding of metaphysics is another point which he makes in q. 5, a. 3 of this same Commentary. There he singles out a special kind of judgment, a negative one which he refers to as *separatio*, which he closely connects with metaphysics and presumably with our discovery of being as being.[5] A number of recent writers have also emphasized the importance of this aspect of Thomas's thought.[6] Before taking up these matters in greater detail, however, it will be to our advantage to consider his views about the place of metaphysics within the division of the theoretical sciences, and his understanding of its proper subject. The present chapter will therefore be devoted to these two issues. The next chapter will examine his account of the way in which we arrive at knowledge of that subject.

1. Division of the Theoretical Sciences and the Place of Metaphysics

In q. 5, a. 1 of his Commentary on the *De Trinitate* of Boethius (ca. 1257–1258 or possibly 1259),[7] Thomas examines a number of questions which Boethius's remarks about the theoretical sciences have raised for him. The first of these is this: Is the division of theoretical science into three parts (natural science, mathematics, and

3. Leon. 50.147:101–105. For discussion and for additional references see the following chapter.

4. See note 1 above. In addition see, for instance, Gilson, *The Christian Philosophy of St. Thomas Aquinas*, pp. 40–45; J. Owens, *An Elementary Christian Metaphysics* (Milwaukee, 1963), pp. 17–42; "Judgment and Truth in Aquinas," *Mediaeval Studies* 32 (1970), pp. 138–58, repr. in his *St. Thomas Aquinas on the Existence of God. The Collected Papers of Joseph Owens*, J. Catan, ed. (Albany, N.Y., 1980), pp. 34–51; "Aquinas on Knowing Existence," *Review of Metaphysics* 29 (1976), pp. 670–90, repr. in *St. Thomas Aquinas on the Existence of God*, pp. 20–33. Also see his *An Interpretation of Existence* (Milwaukee, 1968), esp. c. 2.

5. Leon. 50.148–49.

6. For references to some of these see R. W. Schmidt, "L'emploi de la séparation en métaphysique," *Revue philosophique de Louvain* 58 (1960), pp. 373–93, especially 373–75. Among earlier treatments Schmidt correctly stresses the importance of that by L.-M. Régis, "Un livre: *La philosophie de la nature*. Quelques 'Apories'," *Études et recherches* 1 (1936), pp. 127–56, especially pp. 134–38. Also see J. Owens, "Metaphysical Separation in Aquinas," *Mediaeval Studies* 34 (1972), pp. 287–306; L. Sweeney, *A Metaphysics of Authentic Existentialism* (Englewood Cliffs, N.J., 1965), pp. 307–29 and pp. 307–8, nn. 13, 15, 16, for references to other literature concerning this. Also see the discussions of this in the studies by S. Neumann and L. J. Elders, which are cited below in note 9. Also see H. Weidemann, *Metaphysik und Sprache. Eine sprachphilosophische Untersuchung zu Thomas von Aquin und Aristoteles* (Freiburg-Munich, 1975), pp. 27–32, 43–47, 75–78.

7. On the dating of this work see Torrell, *Saint Thomas Aquinas*, p. 345; the Preface to the Leonine edition (Leon. 50.6–9); D. Hall, *The Trinity. An Analysis of St. Thomas Aquinas' Expositio of the De Trinitate* (Leiden–New York–Cologne, 1992), pp. 38–41.

divine science) a fitting division? As Thomas himself recognizes, the remote ancestry for this threefold division in Boethius is to be found in Aristotle's *Metaphysics,* Bk VI, c. 1.[8]

Thomas begins his full exposition and defense of this division in the corpus of article 1. He comments that the theoretical or speculative intellect is distinguished from the operative or practical intellect by reason of diverse ends. The speculative intellect has for its end the truth which it considers; but the practical intellect orders the truth it considers to operation as its end.[9]

Thomas goes on to distinguish theoretical science from practical science for this same reason. In other words, in a theoretical science one seeks knowledge for its own sake; but in a practical science one seeks knowledge insofar as it can be applied to some action or operation. With this point established Thomas notes that the subject-matter studied by a science must be proportioned to the end of that same science. If this is so, the subject-matter studied in practical sciences should be things which can be made or done by us. The fact that they are made or done by us enables us to order our knowledge of them to some further end, that is, to operation or action. But the subject-matter of theoretical sciences will not be things which are made or done by us. Therefore our knowledge of them will not be ordered to operation as to an end.[10]

To put this in other terms, Thomas is here stating that in theoretical sciences we study things simply as they are in themselves, not things insofar as they are manufactured or manipulated by us for other purposes. Given all of this, Thomas now concludes that the theoretical sciences will be divided or distinguished from one another by reason of differences which apply to things as they are in themselves, and not insofar as they are made or done by us.[11]

Thomas realizes, of course, that we cannot divide the theoretical sciences according to the sheer numerical diversity of the things which are studied therein. Were we to do this, there would be as many theoretical sciences as there are different things to be studied. The possibility of speaking of a subject of a theoretical

8. ". . . primo utrum sit conveniens divisio qua dividitur speculativa in has tres partes: naturalem, mathematicam, et divinam" (Leon. 50.136:1–4). See p. 137:84–87 in the *sed contra,* for Thomas's reference to *Metaphysics* VI, c. 1 (1026a 18–19).

9. ". . . theoricus sive speculativus intellectus in hoc proprie ab operativo sive practico distinguitur, quod speculativus habet pro fine veritatem quam considerat, practicus vero veritatem consideratam ordinat in operationem tamquam in finem" (Leon. 50.137:93–99). Note that he cites Aristotle's *De anima* III, c. 10 (433a 14–15). For other discussions of q. 5, a. 1 of Thomas's Commentary on the *De Trinitate* see S. Neumann, *Gegenstand und Methode der theoretischen Wissenschaften nach Thomas von Aquin aufgrund der Expositio super librum Boethii De Trinitate* (Münster, 1965), pp. 72–74; L. J. Elders, *Faith and Science. An Introduction to St. Thomas' 'Expositio in Boethii De Trinitate'* (Rome, 1974), pp. 91–94; *Tommaso d'Aquino, Commenti a Boezio,* intro. and trans. by P. Porro (Milan, 1997), pp. 23–24; R. McInerny, *Boethius and Aquinas* (Washington, D.C., 1990), pp. 132–36.

10. Leon. 50.137:100–110. Note: ". . . et in II Metaphysicae dicitur quod finis speculativae est veritas, sed finis operativae scientiae est actio." For Aristotle see *Metaphysics* II, c. 1 (993b 20–21).

11. Leon. 50.137:110–138:112.

science, and hence of defending the unity of that science by reason of a unified subject-matter, would be undermined. Instead, notes Thomas, when habits or powers are distinguished by reason of their objects they are divided not by reason of any kind of difference whatsoever, but only by reason of differences which are essential to such objects considered precisely as such.[12] To illustrate this Thomas notes that it is incidental to an object of a sense power whether that object is a plant or an animal. Sense powers are distinguished not by reason of such diversity but by reason of the kind that obtains between color (the specifying object of sight) and sound (the specifying object of hearing). As far as the theoretical sciences are concerned, therefore, they too are to be divided by reason of diversity in objects of theoretical consideration *(speculabilia)* considered precisely as such.[13]

Thomas comments that one aspect belongs to an object of theoretical science insofar as it is considered from the side of the intellective power; and something else belongs to it insofar as it is considered from the side of the habit of science whereby the intellect is perfected.[14] As regards the first point, insofar as something is an object of the intellect, it must be rendered immaterial in some way. This is so because the intellect itself is immaterial. And it also follows, we may add, for Thomas as well as for Boethius, from their commonly shared conviction that whatever is received in something is received in accord with the mode of being or the capacity of that which receives it.[15]

In mentioning the second point Thomas is reminding us that science may be viewed as a virtue and therefore as a habit of the speculative intellect.[16] He reasons that insofar as something is an object of a habit of science it must be rendered necessary in some way; for science deals with that which is necessary. But every

---

12. "Sciendum tamen quod quando habitus vel potentiae penes obiecta distinguuntur, non distinguuntur penes quaslibet differentias obiectorum, sed penes illas quae sunt per se obiectorum in quantum sunt obiecta" (Leon. 50.138:113–117).

13. Leon. 50.138:117–123. Note in particular: ". . . et ideo oportet scientias speculativas dividi per differentias speculabilium in quantum speculabilia sunt."

14. "Speculabili autem, quod est obiectum speculativae potentiae, aliquid competit ex parte intellectivae potentiae et aliquid ex parte habitus scientiae quo intellectus perficitur" (Leon. 50.138:123–126).

15. "Ex parte siquidem intellectus competit ei quod sit immateriale, quia et ipse intellectus immaterialis est . . ." (Leon. 50.138:126–127). For this in Boethius see his *Consolatio philosophiae,* Bk V, Prose 4, in *The Theological Tractates with an English Translation; The Consolation of Philosophy,* trans. H. F. Stewart, E. K. Rand, and S. J. Tester (Cambridge, Mass., 1978), p. 410:75–77: "Omne enim quod cognoscitur non secundum sui vim sed secundum cognoscentium potius comprehenditur facultatem." For Thomas's development of this Boethian theme see, for instance, *In I Sent.,* d. 38, q. 1, a. 2 (Mandonnet ed., Vol. 1, p. 901).

16. See *Summa contra Gentiles* II, c. 60 (Ed.Leon.man.), p. 160: "Sed considerare intelligendo, quod est actus huius habitus qui est scientiae . . . est ipsius intellectus possibilis. . . . Ergo et habitus scientiae non est in intellectu passivo, sed in intellectu possibili." Also see *Summa theologiae* = ST I, q. 14, a. 1, ad 1 (in God, however, science is not a habit or quality). Cf. ST I–II, q. 53, a. 1. See A. Zimmermann, *Ontologie oder Metaphysik? Die Diskussion über den Gegenstand der Metaphysik im 13. und 14. Jahrhundert* (2d rev. ed., Leuven, 1998), pp. 201–7; W. A. Wallace, *The Role of Demonstration in Moral Theology* (Washington, D.C., 1962), pp. 23–25.

necessary thing insofar as it is necessary must be immobile. What is moved is capable of being and of not being, either in the absolute sense, or at least in a qualified sense. Consequently, it follows from all of this that separation from matter and motion or some degree of application to the same will belong to an object of theoretical science considered precisely as such.[17]

At this point, therefore, Thomas has settled on a criterion for dividing the theoretical sciences. They will be distinguished in accord with the degree of freedom from matter and motion of that which they study, that is, of their objects (or subjects) considered precisely as such.[18]

Thomas now begins to apply this criterion. Certain objects of theoretical science depend upon matter to such an extent that they cannot exist apart from it. These in turn are subdivided into those which depend on matter both in order to exist and in order to be understood, and others which, while depending on matter in order to exist, do not depend on sensible matter in order to be understood. (By sensible matter Thomas has in mind matter insofar as it can be perceived by the external senses.) As he explains, sensible matter is included in the very definition of objects of the first kind. This is why such things cannot be understood without sensible matter. In illustration he cites the case of human being. In order for us to understand human being, we must include flesh and bones in our definition. Physics or natural science deals with this kind of object of theoretical science.[19]

Thomas has referred to a second kind of object of theoretical science which depends on matter in order to exist but, unlike the first kind, does not depend on sensible matter in order to be understood. As he explains, by this he has in mind the objects studied by mathematics such as lines and numbers. These cannot in fact exist apart from matter, since, according to Aquinas, they are based on quantity. But they can be understood or defined without any reference to sensible or perceptible matter.[20]

Finally, continues Thomas, there is another kind of object of theoretical science

---

17. *In De Trinitate*, q. 5, a. 1 (Leon. 50.138:128–138). Note in particular: "Sic ergo speculabili, quod est obiectum scientiae speculativae, per se competit separatio a materia et motu vel applicatio ad ea."

18. ". . . et ideo secundum ordinem remotionis a materia et motu scientiae speculativae distinguuntur" (Leon. 50.138:138–140).

19. "Quaedam ergo speculabilium sunt quae dependent a materia secundum esse, quia non nisi in materia esse possunt. Et haec distinguuntur: quia quaedam dependent a materia secundum esse et intellectum, sicut illa in quorum diffinitione ponitur materia sensibilis, unde sine materia sensibili intelligi non possunt, ut in diffinitione hominis oportet accipere carnem et ossa" (Leon. 50.138:141–149). On "sensible matter" see q. 5, a. 3 in this same Commentary: "Unde quantitas potest intelligi in materia subiecta antequam intelligantur in ea qualitates sensibiles, a quibus dicitur materia sensibilis" (Leon. 50.148:191–194). For discussion see S. Neumann, *Gegenstand und Methode*, pp. 63–64.

20. Q. 5, a. 1: "Quaedam vero sunt, quae quamvis dependeant a materia secundum esse, non tamen secundum intellectum, quia in eorum diffinitionibus non ponitur materia sensibilis, sicut linea et numerus; et de his est mathematica" (Leon. 50.138:149–154). On this see A. Maurer, *St. Thomas Aquinas. The Division and Methods of the Sciences*, 4th ed. (Toronto, 1986), pp. xxi–xxii, 38, n. 15; Elders, *Faith and Science*, pp. 96–99.

which does not depend on matter in the order of being *(esse)*. This kind of object can exist apart from matter, either in the sense that it is never present in matter, or else in the sense that in certain cases it is present in matter and in certain cases not. To illustrate the first of these, Thomas singles out God and angels. As examples of the second he cites substance, quality, being *(ens)*, potency, act, the one and the many, and things of this kind.[21]

In other words, objects of the first type are not and cannot be realized in matter because they positively exclude materiality. Hence one may, as I have suggested in another context, describe them as positively immaterial.[22] Objects of the second type do not have to be realized in matter in order to exist, even though they may be. As Thomas puts it, in certain cases they are present in matter, and in certain cases not. Being, for instance, may be realized in matter, as it is in every material being; but it may also be realized without being present in matter, as in immaterial beings. Hence we may describe things of this type as negatively immaterial, meaning thereby that they do not have to be present in matter in order to exist. We may also describe them as neutrally immaterial, meaning by this that they may or may not be present in matter.[23]

Thomas concludes this discussion by noting that divine science deals with all of these, that is, with both types of objects which do not depend on matter in order to exist. He also writes that this science is named theology or divine science because foremost among the things considered in it is God. It is known as metaphysics because it comes after physics in the order of learning. This is so because we must move from a knowledge of sensible things to an understanding of things which are not sensible. This same science is also known as first philosophy insofar as the other sciences take their principles from it and therefore come after it.[24] As I have explained in some detail elsewhere, Thomas does not always offer this same reason for describing metaphysics as first philosophy. In his Commentary on the *Metaphysics* he will say that it is so named because it deals with the first causes of things.[25]

21. "Quaedam vero speculabilia sunt quae non dependent a materia secundum esse, quia sine materia esse possunt, sive numquam sint in materia, sicut deus et angelus, sive in quibusdam sint in materia et in quibusdam non, ut substantia, qualitas, ens, potentia, actus, unum et multa, et huiusmodi" (Leon. 50.138:154–160).

22. See my *Metaphysical Themes in Thomas Aquinas*, c. IV ("Metaphysics and *Separatio* in Thomas Aquinas"), pp. 69–104, especially pp. 72–74, 92–93.

23. Here I have specified my reasons for referring to these as negatively and as neutrally immaterial somewhat more fully than in the reference mentioned in note 22.

24. ". . . de quibus omnibus est theologia, id est scientia divina, quia praecipuum in ea cognitorum est Deus. Quae alio nomine dicitur metaphysica, id est trans physicam, quia post physicam discenda occurrit nobis, quibus ex sensibilibus oportet in insensibilia devenire. Dicitur etiam philosophia prima, in quantum aliae omnes scientiae ab ea sua principia accipientes eam consequuntur" (Leon. 50.138:160–167).

25. See *Metaphysical Themes*, c. III ("'First Philosophy' According to Thomas Aquinas"), pp. 55–67. See *In duodecim libros Metaphysicorum Aristotelis expositio*, M.-R. Cathala and R. Spiazzi, eds. (Turin-Rome, 1950), Prooemium, p. 2. In brief, in the study just cited I have attempted to show how these two reasons do not exclude one another by appealing to Thomas's distinction between synthe-

In the present context Thomas also remarks that it is not possible for there to be things which depend on matter in order to be understood but which do not depend on matter in order to exist. This follows from the immaterial nature of the intellect. An immaterial intellect can hardly impose dependency upon matter in order for objects to be understood if those same objects do not depend on matter in the order of being.[26] This is an important point, since it indicates that in Thomas's eyes the threefold division of theoretical science is exhaustive. There is no fourth distinctive kind of object of theoretical science which might lead one to postulate a fourth theoretical science.

As far as metaphysics is concerned, therefore, q. 5 a. 1 of Thomas's Commentary tells us that it deals with a special kind of object of theoretical knowledge, that is, the kind that does not depend on matter in order to exist. This kind is subdivided into the type of object that cannot exist in matter (the positively immaterial) and the type that may or may not be present in matter (the negatively or neutrally immaterial). Metaphysics deals with both types of objects, though Thomas has not yet indicated how this is possible and how these two types fit together. If he has offered God and angels as illustrations of the positively immaterial, he has listed being *(ens)* and substance along with a number of others as illustrations of the negatively or neutrally immaterial. This reference to being *(ens)* is important since, as we shall shortly see, for Aquinas being as being or being in general is the subject of metaphysics.

Thomas's reply to the sixth objection in this same article merits consideration before we conclude this section. He notes that one may indeed say that the subjects of the other theoretical sciences—physics and mathematics—also enjoy a certain kind of being and can therefore be described as beings. But even though being *(ens)* is the subject of metaphysics, it does not follow from this that these other sciences are themselves parts of metaphysics, as the objection would have it.[27]

Each of these other theoretical sciences examines one part of being (such as mobile being or quantified being), and does so according to its special mode of consideration. The special mode of consideration of any such science is different, continues Thomas, from that whereby the metaphysician studies being. It is because of this that the subject of such a particular science is not a part of the subject of metaphysics. It is not a part of being under that formality whereby being itself is the subject of metaphysics.[28]

---

sis *(via compositionis)* and analysis *(via resolutionis)* and to another distinction he makes between reasoning in terms of intrinsic causes *(secundum rationem)* and in terms of extrinsic causes *(secundum rem).*

26. Q. 5, a. 1 (Leon. 50.138:168–172).

27. For objection 6 see Leon. 50.136–37. For Thomas's reply see Leon. 50.141:322–325: "Ad sextum dicendum, quod quamvis subiecta aliarum scientiarum sint partes entis, quod est subiectum metaphysicae, non tamen oportet quod aliae scientiae sint partes ipsius."

28. ". . . accipit enim unaquaeque scientiarum unam partem entis secundum specialem modum considerandi, alium a modo quo consideratur ens in metaphysica. Unde proprie loquendo subiec-

In short, Thomas is here acknowledging that in a particular theoretical science such as physics one studies a special or restricted kind of being, i.e., mobile being, but not in the way one studies being in metaphysics. In physics one does not study mobile being insofar as it is being, but under some other perspective, that is, insofar as it is mobile.[29] In metaphysics, on the other hand, one studies being taken as such (rather than as restricted to a given kind of being). And one studies it *as* being.

Thomas's discussion in this reply is important, for it suggests that in identifying the subject of a science such as metaphysics it is not enough simply to take into account the kind or range of object studied therein—in the present case, being as such rather than any restricted kind of being. One must also bear in mind the perspective from which such objects are considered, i.e., as being rather than as mobile or as quantified. Moreover, Thomas's answer at least implies that one may examine the same thing, taken materially, from two different formal perspectives and therefore in two different sciences. Thus one and the same material thing may be examined in physics insofar as it is viewed as mobile, and in metaphysics insofar as it is considered as being.[30] With these points in mind we are now in position to turn to the second section of this chapter, where we shall consider Thomas's views concerning the subject of metaphysics.

tum illius non est pars subiecti metaphysicae: non enim est pars entis secundum illam rationem qua ens est subiectum metaphysicae, sed hac ratione considerata ipsa est specialis scientia aliis condivisa" (Leon. 50.141:325–333).

29. See, for instance, Thomas's remarks at the very beginning of his Commentary on the *Physics*, where he again states in succinct fashion his views concerning the different degrees in which things depend on matter, once more arriving at the threefold division of theoretical science. As for physics, he then comments that its subject is *ens mobile:* "Et quia omne quod habet materiam mobile est, consequens est quod ens mobile sit subiectum naturalis philosophiae." See *In octo libros Physicorum Aristotelis Expositio,* P. M. Maggiòlo, ed. (Turin-Rome, 1954), lect. 1, p. 3, n. 3. Also see p. 4, n. 4, where he repeats this point and notes that the subject of physics is *ens mobile* rather than *corpus mobile* because it is in this book (the *Physics*) that one proves that every mobile thing is a body. And he adds: "nulla autem scientia probat suum subiectum."

30. As Thomas spells this out in his Commentary on *Metaphysics* VI, c. 1: ". . . quod licet ad considerationem primae philosophiae pertineant ea quae sunt separata secundum esse et rationem a materia et motu, non tamen solum ea; sed etiam de sensibilibus, inquantum sunt entia, Philosophus perscrutatur." Ed. cit., p. 298, n. 1165. Note that he continues in this text: "Nisi forte dicamus, ut Avicenna dicit, quod huiusmodi communia de quibus haec scientia perscrutatur, dicuntur separata secundum esse, non quia semper sint sine materia; sed quia non de necessitate habent esse in materia, sicut mathematica." In other words, even sensible things may be said to be separate from matter in some sense, that is, when they are considered insofar as they are beings, and hence as falling under that which is negatively or neutrally immaterial. The general reference to Avicenna is probably to the latter's detailed discussion of the subject of metaphysics in his *Liber de Philosophia prima sive Scientia divina,* Bk I, c. 2 (S. Van Riet, ed., Vol. 1 [Louvain-Leiden, 1977], pp. 10–13). See p. 10 where Avicenna argues for the need for a separate science which will consider substance "inquantum est ens vel est substantia, vel de corpore inquantum est substantia. . . ."

2. The Subject of Metaphysics

Something of the Aristotelian (and Boethian) background for Thomas's three-fold division of the theoretical sciences has already been mentioned. Aristotle's presentation and discussion of the science of being as being in his *Metaphysics* evidently exercised considerable influence upon Thomas's development of his own conception of metaphysics. Even so, certain texts in Aristotle's treatise have posed difficulties for commentators down through the centuries, and continue to do so today. One of the most serious of these has to do with the proper relationship, in Aristotle's eyes, between the science of being as being which he presents in *Metaphysics* IV, cc. 1–2, and the divine science or theology to which he refers in the latter part of *Metaphysics* VI, c. 1. Simply put, the question is this: Are these one and the same science? And if Aristotle believes that they are, how can he bring them together?[31]

In brief, in Bk IV, c. 1, Aristotle refers to a science which studies being as being. He contrasts this with more particular sciences which cut off a part of being and study the attributes of that part. They do not treat universally about being as being. The impression is here given that, unlike such sciences, in the science of being as being one does not limit oneself to any given part of being. One rather studies about being universally, taken as being. And if one must seek for principles and causes in any other science, the same will hold here. In this science one must grasp the first causes of being as being.[32] In developing his understanding of being in c. 2 of this same Bk IV, Aristotle assigns primacy to substance. Even though the term "being" is used in different ways, its various meanings are united to some degree because of their relationship to something which is one and first. This first or primary referent for being is substance. Therefore it is of substance(s) that the philosopher—presumably the student of being as being—must grasp the first principles and causes.[33]

---

31. For a brief overview of this controversy in the medieval period see my "Essence and Existence," c. 19 in *The Cambridge History of Later Medieval Philosophy*, N. Kretzmann et al., eds. (Cambridge, 1982), pp. 385–92. For a much fuller treatment see A. Zimmermann, *Ontologie oder Metaphysik? passim*. Also, L. Honnefelder, "Der zweite Anfang der Metaphysik. Voraussetzungen, Ansätze und Folgen der Wiederbegründung der Metaphysik im 13./14. Jahrhundert," in *Philosophie im Mittelalter*, J. P. Beckmann et al., eds. (Hamburg, 1987), pp. 164–86. For some recent interpretations of this issue in Aristotle see I. Düring, *Aristoteles. Darstellung und Interpretation seines Denkens* (Heidelberg, 1966), pp. 594–99; E. König, "Aristoteles' erste Philosophie als universale Wissenschaft von den ΑΡΧΑΙ," *Archiv für Geschichte der Philosophie* 52 (1970), pp. 225–46; J. Owens, *The Doctrine of Being in the Aristotelian Metaphysics*, 3d ed. (Toronto, 1978), esp. pp. xiii–xxvii, 35–67; "The Doctrine of Being in the Aristotelian *Metaphysics*—Revisited," in *Philosophies of Existence, Ancient and Medieval*, P. Morewedge, ed. (New York, 1982), pp. 33–59; and two important and helpful studies by A. Mansion, "L'objet de la science philosophique suprême d'après Aristote, Métaphysique, E, I," in *Mélanges de Philosophie Grecque offerts à Mgr Diès* (Paris, 1956), pp. 151–68; "Philosophie première, philosophie seconde et métaphysique chez Aristote," *Revue philosophique de Louvain* 56 (1958), pp. 165–221.

32. See *Metaphysics* IV, c. 1 (1003a 21–32).

33. Ibid., 1003a 33–1003b 19.

In Bk VI, c. 1, after referring to his investigation of the principles and causes of beings as beings and presumably, therefore, to his science of being as being, Aristotle again contrasts this with more restricted sciences which limit themselves to a given class of being and concern themselves with that rather than with being taken as such and as being.[34] Until this point Aristotle's text presents no insurmountable difficulties for the reader. But after discussing physics or natural philosophy (which studies the kind of substance which has within itself its principle of rest and motion) and mathematics (some parts of which study their objects *as* immutable and separate from matter), Aristotle becomes concerned about the ontological status of the things studied by another science.[35] If there is something eternal and immutable and separate, it belongs to some theoretical science to investigate this. Neither physics nor mathematics will qualify. Therefore there must be a first science which studies things which are both immutable and separate (and which does not merely study them as immutable and separate). This Aristotle refers to as theology (or divine science).[36]

This immediately raises a question for the reader. Has not Aristotle's third theoretical science itself now become a science of a particular kind of being, that is, the immutable and separate and divine? If so, what is the relationship between this third science—theology—and the science of being as being? Until this point Aristotle's emphasis in presenting the science of being as being has been on its nonparticularity and therefore on its universality in scope.[37] Unlike the particular sciences of mathematics and physics, it does not restrict itself to any given kind of being; it studies being taken simply as such, and it studies it as being. Now, however, divine science has been presented as the science of separate entity.

To his credit Aristotle himself saw this difficulty. One might be perplexed, he writes, concerning whether first philosophy is universal, or whether it deals with one given genus or nature. In reply he comments that if there is no other substance apart from those which are composed by nature, physics will be the first science. But if there is some immutable substance, the science which studies this will be prior; it will be first philosophy; it will be universal insofar as it is first; and it will belong to this science to study being as being.[38] In other words, Aristotle wants to identify his divine science or theology with his science of being as being. This much is clear from his text. How he does so and whether he is really successful in this effort is a very different matter, and one which continues to be disputed by commentators.[39] Rather than enter into that question here, it will be enough for us to

---

34. See 1025b 3–10.

35. For his discussion of physics see 1025b 18–1026 a7. On mathematics see 1026a 7–10.

36. See 1026a 10–22.

37. See his presentation in *Metaphysics* IV, cc. 1–2, and in the opening lines of *Metaphysics* VI, c. 1. For the latter see n. 34 above.

38. See 1026a 23–32.

39. See, for instance, the references given above in n. 31.

note that divergent readings of Aristotle concerning this point had surfaced long before the time of Aquinas and that two such interpretations were known to him, that is, those offered by Avicenna and by Averroes.

In his *Metaphysics (Liber de philosophia prima)* Avicenna examines in some detail the claims of different candidates for the title subject of metaphysics. He considers and then rejects the possibility that God might be regarded as the subject of this science. Since no science can demonstrate the existence of its own subject, and since according to Avicenna God's existence can be established in metaphysics and only in metaphysics, he concludes that God cannot be regarded as its subject. Nor will it do to suggest that the causes themselves might be regarded as its subject. Only being as being can serve as the subject of this science.[40]

Against this line of reasoning Averroes argues that it is in physics rather than in metaphysics that one establishes God's existence. Therefore, Avicenna's reasons for rejecting God as the subject of metaphysics must themselves be rejected.[41] While Averroes grants that Aristotle does refer to this as the science which studies "being as being," he notes that in this usage the term "being" really means substance.

40. See his *Liber de Philosophia prima* I, c. 1 (Van Riet ed., pp. 4–6), where he argues that God is not the subject of this science. See pp. 6–9 for his presentation and critique of the view that the causes might serve as the subject of metaphysics, whether taken in the unqualified sense, or insofar as each is a cause according to its proper modality, or in terms of the whole or composite which they constitute. To study them insofar as they have *esse* will rather belong to that science which has as its subject being as being. For further discussion see Zimmermann, *Ontologie oder Metaphysik?* pp. 144–52; J. Doig, "Science première et science universelle dans le 'Commentaire de la métaphysique' de saint Thomas d'Aquin," *Revue philosophique de Louvain* 63 (1965), pp. 73–82; *Aquinas on Metaphysics: A historico-doctrinal study of the Commentary on the Metaphysics,* pp. 23–35; S. Brown, "Avicenna and the Unity of the Concept of Being," *Franciscan Studies* 25 (1965), pp. 117–50, especially pp. 117–19. In citing texts from Avicenna (and Averroes) here and throughout this study, I will use their medieval Latin versions. For discussions based on the Arabic, see A.-M. Goichon, *La distinction de l'essence et de l'existence d'après Ibn Sina (Avicenne)* (Paris, 1937), pp. 3–5; H. A. Davidson, *Proofs for Eternity, Creation and the Existence of God in Medieval Islamic and Jewish Philosophy* (New York–Oxford, 1987), pp. 284–86.

41. See *In I Phys.,* com. 83 in *Aristotelis opera cum Averrois commentariis* (Venice, 1562–1574), Vol. 4, ff. 47rb–48va: "Sed notandum est quod istud genus entium, esse scilicet separatum a materia, non declaratur nisi in hac scientia naturali. Et qui dicit quod prima Philosophia nititur declarare entia separabilia esse peccat. Haec enim entia sunt subiecta primae Philosophiae, et declaratum est in posterioribus Analyticis quod impossibile est aliquam scientiam declarare suum subiectum esse, sed concedit ipsum esse aut quia manifestum per se, aut quia est demonstratum in alia scientia." He immediately launches into a scathing criticism of Avicenna: "Unde Avicenna peccavit maxime cum dixit quod primus Philosophus demonstrat primum principium esse." This critique continues until the end of Averroes's Commentary on Bk I (see f. 47vab) and is resumed in his Commentary on Bk II (see com. 22, ff. 56vb–57ra). There Averroes reads Avicenna as saying that no science can demonstrate the causes of its subject and replies that while this is true of demonstration *simpliciter* and demonstration *propter quid,* it is not true of demonstration *quia.* Therefore Aristotle's demonstration of the first mover is proper to physics and is a demonstration *quia* or, as Averroes also describes it, *per signum.* There he describes Avicenna's way of proving the first principle as the *via loquentium,* i.e., the way of the Muslim theologians *(mutakallimun).* Also see Averroes, *In XII Met.,* com. 5 in *Aristotelis opera cum Averrois commentariis* (Venice, 1562–1574), Vol. 8, ff. 293ra–va. Cf. Davidson, *Proofs for Eternity,* pp. 312–18.

According to Averroes, therefore, one must study substance first and foremost in its primary instance, that is, as realized in that separate substance which serves as the first form and the ultimate end or final cause of everything else.[42] One knows that such a being exists because of one's demonstration of this at the end of *Physics* VIII. Therefore, separate substance or the divine is really the subject of this science.[43] Averroes seems to think that he can safeguard the general or nonparticular character of metaphysics by reasoning that when one studies the first form and ultimate end of all else, one studies all else as well. Whether this solution can do justice to the immediate nonparticularity of the science of being as being as this is set forth by Aristotle in *Metaphysics* IV, c. 1 is highly doubtful, in my opinion.[44]

Be that as it may, here we are interested in Aquinas's position. He agrees with Avicenna that the subject of metaphysics is being as being *(ens inquantum est ens)*, or as he also describes it, being in general *(ens commune)*. This is already at least implied by the text we have examined in q. 5, a. 1, ad 6, of his Commentary on the *De Trinitate*. It is confirmed by remarks Thomas makes in q. 5, a. 4 of this same treatise, as well as in his Commentary on *III Sentences*, d. 27, q. 2, a. 4, sol. 2, and in his Commentary on the *Metaphysics* (Prooemium).[45] At the same time, he offers

42. On this as the science which investigates being as being see *In I Phys.*, com. 83, f. 47vab: "Omne enim de quo loquitur in hoc libro principaliter est propter illud principium; et iste est primus locus in quo naturalis inspicit alium modum essendi ab illo de quo considerat, et apud illum cessat, et dimisit considerationem de eo usque ad scientiam nobiliorem, quae considerat de ente secundum quod est ens." Also see *In IV Met.*, com. 1, f. 64rb (this science investigates being "inquantum est ens"); com. 2, f. 65rb ("Cum autem declaravit quod una scientia debet considerare de ente secundum quod ens est. . . ."); ff. 65rb–66rb (on substance as the primary referent of *ens*). Hence the "Philosopher", i.e., the metaphysician, must study the principles of substance. See *In XII Met.*, com. 5, f. 293rb: "Et dicemus nos quidem quod Philosophus inquirit quae sunt principia substantiae secundum quod substantiae et declarat quod substantia abstracta est principium substantiae naturalis: sed hoc ponendo accepit pro constanti hoc quod declaratum est in naturalibus de principiis substantiae generabilis et corruptibilis, . . . quod declaratum est in Octavo, scilicet, quod movens aeternam substantiam est abstractum a materia. . . ." Also see f. 293va where Averroes notes that in this book, i.e., *Metaphysics* XII, Aristotle makes the point: ". . . quod principium primae substantiae abstractae etiam est substantia et forma et finis, et quod movet utroque modo."

43. See the text from his Commentary on *Physics* I as cited above in note 41. Also see *In XII Met.* (f. 293va) on the respective roles of the first philosopher and the natural philosopher in dealing with separate substance (or substances).

44. Averroes does not bring out this difficulty as clearly as one might wish. His remarks at the end of his Commentary on *Metaphysics* VI, 1 are not very helpful. Cf. Doig, "Science première et science universelle," pp. 53–60; Zimmermann, *Ontologie oder Metaphysik?* pp. 152–54; E. Gilson, *Jean Duns Scot. Introduction à ses positions fondamentales* (Paris, 1952), pp. 77–78. The problem is this. If metaphysics has separate entity and especially the divine as its subject, it, too, seems to deal first, foremost, and immediately with a restricted range of reality and not with being taken universally or as unrestricted to any given class. By studying the cause (first formal and final) of all else one does not immediately and directly study all else, i.e., being as being, but only mediately and indirectly.

45. For the Commentary on the *De Trinitate*, q. 5, a. 1, ad 6, see nn. 27 and 28 above. For q. 5, a. 4, see nn. 51 and 54 below. For *ens commune* as the subject of this science see Thomas's Commentary on the *Metaphysics*, Prooemium, cited below in note 62. See *In III Sent.*, d. 27, q. 2, a. 4, sol. 2 *(Scriptum super Sententiis*, M. F. Moos ed., Vol. 3 [Paris, 1933], pp. 886–87): ". . . sicut philosophia

a new and highly original solution to the issue concerning the relationship between being as being (or being in general) and divine being.

Thus in q. 5, a. 4 of his Commentary on the *De Trinitate,* Thomas continues to defend the view that divine science deals with things which are without matter and motion. In developing this point he explains more fully what he understands by divine science (as Boethius has named it in the text on which Thomas is commenting). If every science studies a given subject-genus, it must also consider the principles of that genus. But principles are of two kinds. Certain principles are complete natures in themselves and at the same time serve as principles for other things. Thus heavenly bodies may be regarded both as complete beings in themselves and as principles of lower bodies; and the same holds for simple bodies in that they are also principles for mixed bodies. If this is so, such principles may be examined in two different sciences, that is, in the science which studies that of which they are principles, and in another science which studies them as complete natures in themselves.[46]

Other principles, however, are not complete natures in themselves but are only principles for other things. It is in this way that a unit functions as the principle of number, a point as the principle of a line, and matter and form as principles of natural body. Such principles are studied in the science which is directed to that of which they are principles; but unlike the first kind of principles, these are not also considered in another science which would treat them as complete natures in themselves.[47]

With these general guidelines established, Thomas goes on to note that any given genus has certain common principles which extend to all the other principles of that genus itself. So it is that all beings, insofar as they share in being, have certain principles which are the principles for every being. Such principles are said to be common in one of two ways, as Avicenna has indicated. They may be common in the order of predication in the sense in which a form is said to be common to all other forms because it can be predicated of each of them. Or they may be common in the order of causality as, for instance, one and the same sun is said to be the principle for all things which are subject to generation. All beings have certain common principles in the first sense, that is, in the order of predication. By this Thomas means that certain names can be predicated of all such principles *secun-*

---

prima est specialis scientia, quamvis consideret ens secundum quod est omnibus commune, quia specialem rationem entis considerat secundum quod non dependet a materia et motu." Though the term "subject" does not appear as such in this passage, the point is clear.

46. *In De Trinitate,* q. 5, a. 4 (Leon. 50.153:80–101). Note in particular: "... et ideo ista non solum considerantur in scientiis ut principia sunt, sed etiam ut sunt in se ipsis res quaedam. Et propter hoc de eis non solum tractatur in scientia quae considerat ipsa principiata, sed etiam habent per se scientiam separatam. . . ."

47. Leon. 50.153:102–107. Note especially: "... unde huiusmodi principia non tractantur nisi in scientia in qua de principiatis agitur."

dum analogiam. But as he points out, beings also have certain principles which are common in the second or causal sense.[48]

To illustrate this point Thomas presents what might be regarded as an outline of an argument for the existence of God. The principles of accidents may be reduced to the principles of substances. And the principles for corruptible substances may be traced back to incorruptible substances, so that all beings are reduced to certain principles according to an ordered gradation. Because that which is the principle of being for all things must itself be being to the maximum degree, principles of this kind (the highest principles for all other beings) must themselves be most perfect and therefore in act to the maximum degree so as to have either a minimum of potentiality or else none at all. This follows from the fact that act is prior to potency, as Aristotle has pointed out in *Metaphysics* IX. Hence these supreme principles will be free from matter (for matter always implies potentiality) and free from motion (the act of that which exists in potency). Divine things are principles of this kind. As Aristotle states in *Metaphysics* VI, "if the divine exists anywhere, it exists in such a nature," i.e., in one that is immaterial and immobile.[49]

After offering this brief argument for the existence of "divine" things or principles, Thomas applies the distinction between the kinds of principles which are also complete natures in themselves and the kinds which are not. Divine things themselves are both complete natures in themselves and the principles for other beings. Therefore they can be studied by two sciences. On the one hand, they can be studied insofar as they are the common principles for all beings. But if such first principles are most intelligible in themselves, they are not most knowable to us. We can arrive at knowledge of them through the light of natural reason only by reasoning from effect to cause, as the philosophers have done. (Here Thomas finds support in the well-known text from *Romans* 1:20: "The invisible things of God are seen, being understood from the things which are made.")[50] Therefore divine things are not studied by the philosophers except insofar as they are the principles of all other things. That is to say, they are considered in that discipline which treats those things which are common to all beings, and which has as its subject being as being *(ens inquantum est ens).* This science, remarks Aquinas, is referred to by the philosophers as divine science.[51]

48. Leon. 50.153:108–124. For Thomas's reference to Avicenna see the latter's *Sufficientia,* I, c. 2 (Venice, 1508), f. 14va. Thomas also refers here to Aristotle's *Metaphysics* XI (i.e., XII) in order to show that certain principles are common in the first way *secundum analogiam.* For this see *Met.* XII, c. 4 (1070a 31–33); c. 5 (1071a 29–35).

49. Leon. 50.153:124–154:143. Thomas introduces this argument with this remark: ". . . ut sint quaedam res eaedem numero existentes omnium rerum principia. . . ." See Aristotle, *Metaphysics* IX, cc. 8 and 9; *Metaphysics* VI, c. 1 (1026a 19–21).

50. Leon. 50.154:143–157. For another and fuller interpretation of Romans 1:20 in this same vein cf. Thomas's Commentary on Paul's Letter to the Romans. See *S. Thomae Aquinatis doctoris angelici in omnes S. Pauli Apostoli Epistolas Commentaria,* Vol. 1 (Turin, 1929), c. 1, lect. 6, pp. 21–22.

51. ". . . unde et huiusmodi res divinae non tractantur a philosophis nisi prout sunt rerum om-

On the other hand, divine things may also be studied as complete natures in themselves rather than as principles of other things. This can happen only insofar as their existence has been made known to us in a nonphilosophical way, that is, through revelation. Therefore, when they are so studied, this must be in a distinct and nonphilosophical discipline. Because of this Thomas concludes that theology or divine science is of two sorts. One kind considers divine things not as the subject of the science, but only as principles of that subject. This is the theology which the philosophers have pursued and which, Thomas comments, is also referred to as metaphysics. Another kind of theology considers divine things for their own sake as its very subject. This is the theology which is based on *(lit.,* "handed down in") sacred Scripture.[52]

Each of these disciplines deals with things which are separate from matter and motion in the order of being *(esse)*, but in different ways. Here Thomas recalls a point he has already made in q. 5, a. 1. Something may be separate from matter and motion in the order of *esse* in such fashion that it is of its very nature not to be present therein. Thomas again has in mind what we have referred to above as the positively immaterial. Once more he illustrates this with God and angels. Or something may be said to be separate from matter and motion in the sense that it is not of its essence to be realized therein; it may exist apart from matter and motion but may also be found therein. Here Thomas has in mind what we have described as the negatively or neutrally immaterial. Again Thomas illustrates this with examples such as being *(ens)*, substance, and potency and act. As he explains, such things are separate from matter and motion in the order of *esse,* and hence differ from mathematicals. While the latter may be understood without sensible matter, they cannot exist apart from such matter.[53]

In concluding this discussion Thomas also offers his solution for the Aristotelian difficulty concerning the relationship between divine science and the science of being as being. Philosophical theology or metaphysics considers things which are separate from matter in the second sense (the negatively or neutrally immaterial) as its subject. It deals with things which are separate from matter and motion in the first and stronger sense (the positively immaterial and hence the divine) only

---

nium principia, et ideo pertractantur in illa doctrina in qua ponuntur ea quae sunt communia omnibus entibus, quae habet subiectum ens in quantum est ens. Et haec scientia apud eos scientia divina dicitur" (Leon. 50.154:157–163).

52. Leon. 50.154:175–182.

53. "Utraque autem est de his quae sunt separata a materia et motu secundum esse, sed diversimode, secundum quod dupliciter potest esse aliquid a materia et motu separatum secundum esse: uno modo sic quod de ratione ipsius rei quae separata dicitur sit quod nullo modo in materia et motu esse possit, sicut deus et angeli dicuntur a materia et motu separati; alio modo sic quod non sit de ratione eius quod sit in materia et motu, sed possit esse sine materia et motu quamvis quandoque inveniatur in materia et motu, et sic ens et substantia et potentia et actus sunt separata a materia et motu, quia secundum esse a materia et motu non dependent sicut mathematica dependebant, quae numquam nisi in materia esse possunt quamvis sine materia sensibili possint intelligi" (Leon. 50.154:182–198).

as the principles of its subject. In other words, the science of being as being can indeed be identified with this kind of divine science, i.e. metaphysics. This is so because one and the same science studies things which are separate from matter and motion in the weaker sense, best illustrated by being *(ens)*, as its subject; and it studies things which are separate from matter and motion in the strong sense (the positively immaterial or divine) only as principles or causes of that which falls under its proper subject.[54]

If we may develop this point a bit more fully, for Aquinas metaphysics is indeed divine science, but philosophical divine science. This does not mean that divine things are the subject of this science, or that they are included within its subject. Thomas will bring this point out even more clearly in the final text to be examined in this chapter. Divine things enter into the metaphysician's field of consideration only indirectly, as principles or causes of its subject, that is, of being as being. By this I take him to mean that divine things are the causes of all that which falls under being as being. A very different kind of theology or divine science, that based on revelation, considers divine things as its very subject. This, of course, is not a philosophical science.[55]

Thomas's solution is much closer to that advanced by Avicenna than to that proposed by Averroes. Still, Avicenna does not seem to have excluded God from being included within the range of being as being which is the proper subject of metaphysics, even though he has refused to admit that God is its subject. Thomas agrees with Avicenna in denying that God is the subject of metaphysics. But in refusing to admit that God is even included within the subject of metaphysics, or that he falls under being as being, Thomas has gone considerably beyond Avicenna. While other Latin medieval participants in this discussion such as Siger of Brabant and Duns Scotus will follow Avicenna on this point, they will not, as Thomas has done, exclude God from being included within the being which serves as the subject of metaphysics.[56] Thomas's position on this pivotal question will have to be

54. "Theologia ergo philosophica determinat de separatis secundo modo sicut de subiectis, de separatis autem primo modo sicut de principiis subiecti" (Leon. 50.154:199–201).

55. ". . . theologia vero sacrae scripturae tractat de separatis primo modo sicut de subiectis, quamvis in ea tractentur aliqua quae sunt in materia et motu, secundum quod requirit rerum divinarum manifestatio" (Leon. 50.154:202–206). On this text also see Aertsen, *Medieval Philosophy and the Transcendentals: The Case of Thomas Aquinas,* pp. 117–21.

56. For this point in Avicenna see three passages which seem to imply this and which have been singled out and interpreted by Zimmermann, *Ontologie oder Metaphysik?* pp. 149–50. As Zimmermann indicates, it was because of passages such as these that Latin medieval thinkers so understood Avicenna. For this in Siger of Brabant and in Duns Scotus see my "Essence and Existence" (cited above in n. 31), pp. 387–90; Zimmermann, pp. 229–34, 294–329; L. Honnefelder, *Der Begriff des Seienden als solchen als Gegenstand der Metaphysik nach der Lehre des Johannes Duns Scotus* (Münster, 1979), pp. 99–132; "Der zweite Anfang," pp. 178–81. As Zimmermann also points out (pp. 186–98), Albert the Great's position on the subject of metaphysics as he develops this in his Commentary on the *Metaphysics* can hardly be reconciled with the view presented in the *Summa theologiae* which is

kept in mind, for it has important implications for other metaphysical positions, for instance, his views concerning analogy of being and participation of beings in *esse*.

Thomas continues to defend this same position in his much later Commentary on Aristotle's *Metaphysics* (ca. 1270–1271/1272?). In the Prooemium, where he is clearly writing in his own name and not merely as the *expositor* of Aristotle, he observes that all sciences and arts are ordered to one end, that is, the perfection and happiness of human beings. Therefore one of these should be director or ruler of the others, and this science will best merit the title wisdom. Such a science must be the one which is most intellectual. And the most intellectual science is that which deals with things which are most intelligible. But things may be described as most intelligible in three different ways.[57]

First of all, something may be described as more intelligible insofar as the intellect attains certainty in knowing it, or as Thomas also phrases it, in terms of the degree *(ordo)* of understanding involved. Since certainty arises in science from the intellect's knowledge of things in terms of their causes, it follows that a knowledge of causes will be most intellectual. Therefore the science which studies the first causes of all things will be best qualified to rule the other sciences.[58]

Secondly, something may be described as most intelligible on the basis of a comparison between the intellect and the senses. While sense perception is directed to particulars, the intellect differs from the senses in that it grasps universals. Therefore that science will be most intellectual which deals with the most universal principles. Such are being *(ens)* and those things which follow upon being, including the one and the many, potency and act, etc. These things should not remain unex-

---

attributed to him. In the Commentary on the *Metaphysics* he is heavily influenced by Avicenna and defends being as being as the subject of this science while denying that God is either its subject or one of its subjects. However, he leaves unclarified the precise relationship between God and this subject although, like Avicenna, he thinks God's existence can be proved in metaphysics itself. See *Physica, Opera omnia* 16.1 (Cologne ed.), pp. 3–5. Zimmermann's presentation should be supplemented by Albert's earlier Commentary on the *Physics*. See T. Noone, "Albert the Great on the Subject of Metaphysics and Demonstrating the Existence of God," *Medieval Philosophy and Theology* 2 (1992), pp. 39–52. There at the end of Bk I Albert refers to the disagreement between Avicenna and Averroes and defends Avicenna's claim that because God and separate substances are inquired after in first philosophy, they cannot be its subject. Only being is. For this see *Opera omnia* 4 (Cologne ed.), Bk I, tr. 3, c. 18, p. 76:37–56. As for Albert's possible influence on Thomas in his Commentary on the *De Trinitate*, of these three sources only the Commentary on the *Physics* could (and may) have been available to Aquinas in time, given its proposed dating by the Cologne edition as ca. 1251/52 and clearly before 1257.

57. Cathala-Spiazzi ed. (Turin-Rome, 1950), p. 1. Note in particular: ". . . ita scientia debet esse naturaliter aliarum regulatrix, quae maxime intellectualis est. Haec autem est, quae circa maxime intelligibilia versatur." For difficulties in dating this Commentary see Torrell, *Saint Thomas,* pp. 232–33, 344.

58. Ibid. Note: "Nam ex quibus intellectus certitudinem accipit, videntur esse intelligibilia magis."

amined, since without them complete knowledge of the things which are proper to any given genus or species cannot be had. At the same time, knowledge of such things cannot be entrusted to any one of the particular sciences; for these universal principles are needed for knowledge of every class of beings and could with equal justification be examined by each particular science. Therefore they should be investigated in one general or universal science which, because it is supremely intellectual, is ruler of the others.[59]

Thirdly, something may be regarded as most intelligible from the standpoint of the intellect's knowledge. Since a thing enjoys intellective power only to the extent that it is free from matter, those things will be most intelligible which are supremely free from matter. This follows because the intellect and its object should be proportioned to one another. But those things are supremely free from matter which abstract not only from designated matter (as do natural forms when they are grasped universally, and with which physics deals), but also from sensible matter entirely. They abstract from sensible matter not only in the order of understanding (as do mathematicals), but also in the order of existence. Such is true of God and intelligences. Therefore the science which studies such things—God and intelligences—seems to be supremely intellectual.[60]

At this point Thomas seems to have identified three different classes of objects which are supremely intelligible: (1) the first causes; (2) that which is most universal, such as being, etc.; (3) God and intelligences. Can he bring these three classes together in some fashion so that all will fall within the scope of a single science?

This he immediately proceeds to do. First of all, he comments, the aforementioned separate substances (God and the intelligences) are the universal and first causes of being. Thus he collapses classes 1 and 3 into one. Moreover, he continues, it belongs to one and the same science to consider the proper causes of a given genus and that genus itself. So it is that the natural philosopher considers the principles of natural body. In like fashion, Thomas continues, it belongs to one and the same science to consider the separate substances and being in general (ens commune). Being in general is the "genus" of which these separate substances are the universal causes. (Thomas does not intend for us to take the term "genus" literally as he uses it here, of course, since he would never admit that being is a genus in the proper sense.) Now he has united the science which has class 2 (being in general) as its subject with the science which studies the principles and causes of that same subject, that is, God and intelligences.[61]

59. Ibid. Note in particular: "Unde et illa scientia maxime est intellectualis, quae circa principia maxime universalia versatur. Quae quidem sunt ens, et ea quae consequuntur ens, ut unum et multa, potentia et actus. . . ."

60. Ibid. See in particular: "Ea vero sunt maxime a materia separata, quae non tantum a signata materia abstrahunt, 'sicut formae naturales in universali acceptae, de quibus tractat scientia naturalis,' sed omnino a materia sensibili. Et non solum secundum rationem, sicut mathematica, sed etiam secundum esse, sicut Deus et intelligentiae."

61. Op. cit., pp. 1–2. "Nam praedictae substantiae separatae sunt universales et primae causae

As Thomas explains, it follows from this that while the science in question studies the three classes of intelligible objects which he has distinguished, it does not consider each of these as its subject, but only one, that is, being in general *(ens commune)*.[62] The subject of a science, continues Thomas, is that whose principles and causes one investigates. The causes of that subject-genus are not themselves the subject of the science. Knowledge of the causes of such a genus is rather the end or goal at which the science's investigation aims. Therefore, while only being in general is the subject of this science, the entire science may be said to deal with things which are separate from matter in the order of being *(esse)* as well as in the order of understanding. Not only are those things said to be separate from matter in this fashion which can never be present in matter; the same is true of those which may or may not be realized there, such as *ens commune*.[63]

At this point, of course, Thomas has once again appealed to his distinction between the two ways in which things may be said to be free from matter and motion in the order of being itself. Both what we have described as the positively immaterial (God and intelligences) and the negatively immaterial (being as such) will be studied by the metaphysician. But it is only the latter, being as such or being in general, which is the subject of this science. God and separate substances are not its subject. Nor is knowledge of such entities presupposed for one to begin metaphysics, at least so far as one can determine from the texts we have examined until now. On the contrary, such knowledge is held out by Thomas as the end or goal of the metaphysician's investigation.[64]

---

essendi. Eiusdem autem scientiae est considerare causas proprias alicuius generis et genus ipsum: sicut naturalis considerat principia corporis naturalis. Unde oportet quod ad eamdem scientiam pertineat considerare substantias separatas, et ens commune, quod est genus, cuius sunt praedictae substantiae communes et universales causae."

62. Op. cit., p. 2: "Ex quo apparet, quod quamvis ista scientia praedicta tria consideret, non tamen considerat quodlibet eorum ut subiectum, sed ipsum solum ens commune." That Thomas also takes it to be Aristotle's view that being as being or being in general is the subject of this science is clear from other passages. See, for instance, *In IV Met.,* lect. 1, p. 150, n. 529: ". . . ideo dicit primo, quod est quaedam scientia, quae speculatur ens secundum quod ens, sicut subiectum, et speculatur 'ea quae insunt enti per se', idest entis per se accidentia." See p. 151, n. 533: ". . . ergo in hac scientia nos quaerimus principia entis inquantum est ens: ergo ens est subiectum huius scientiae, quia quaelibet scientia est quaerens causas proprias sui subiecti." Cf. *In VI Met.,* lect. 1, p. 295, n. 1147. He also agrees with Aristotle in making substance the primary referent for *ens.* See, for instance, *In V Met.,* lect. 7, p. 229, n. 842: "Subiectum autem huius scientiae potest accipi, vel sicut communiter in tota scientia considerandum, cuiusmodi est ens et unum: vel sicut id de quo est principalis intentio, ut substantia." Cf. *In VIII Met.,* lect. 1, pp. 402–3, n. 1682: "Cum enim haec scientia consideret ens commune sicut proprium subiectum. . . ."

63. Ed. cit., p. 2 "Hoc enim est subiectum in scientia, cuius causas et passiones quaerimus, non autem ipsae causae alicuius generis quaesiti. Nam cognitio causarum alicuius generis, est finis ad quem consideratio scientiae pertingit. Quamvis autem subiectum huius scientiae sit ens commune, dicitur tamen tota de his quae sunt separata a materia secundum esse et rationem. Quia secundum esse et rationem separari dicuntur, non solum illa quae nunquam in materia esse possunt, sicut Deus et intellectuales substantiae, sed etiam illa quae possunt sine materia esse, sicut ens commune."

64. See the text cited in the preceding note. This issue will be of importance in our discussion

This suggests 'that in the order of discovery one must first arrive at knowledge of being as being or of being in general in order for metaphysics to have its proper subject established. And this in turn brings us to the issue to be discussed in the following chapter: Precisely how, according to Aquinas, does one go about discovering being as being, the subject of metaphysics?

_____

below of the conditions required for the judgment of separation and hence for one's discovery of the subject of metaphysics.

Our Discovery of the Subject of Metaphysics

Since Aquinas holds that being as being is the subject of metaphysics, it remains for us to determine how he accounts for our discovery of this subject. In order to do this we must first consider his explanation of the way in which we arrive at knowledge of being as real or as existing. As already noted at the beginning of Ch. I, Thomas's most important single discussion of these issues is in q. 5, a. 3 of his Commentary on the *De Trinitate* of Boethius. At the very beginning of the corpus of this article he makes a point which is crucial for our understanding of his view of the way in which one discovers being as existing or as real. Farther on in this same article he offers his fullest account of an operation which he names separation (*separatio*) and which he explicitly connects with metaphysics. In taking up these points, therefore, this text will serve as our focal point.

1. Our Knowledge of Being as Real

Q. 5, a. 3 is explicitly directed to the question whether mathematics considers without matter and motion things which are present in matter. This question itself is raised for Thomas by the Boethian text on which he is commenting.[1]

In setting up his reply Thomas begins by observing that one must understand how the intellect can abstract in its operation. As will become clear from precisions which he introduces into his text at a later point, Thomas is here using the term "abstract" very broadly so as to signify any way in which the intellect distinguishes

---

1. ". . . tertio utrum mathematica consideratio sit sine motu et materia de his quae sunt in materia" (Leon. 50.136:6–7). See Boethius's description of mathematics in c. 2 of his *De Trinitate*: ". . . *mathematica*, sine motu inabstracta (haec enim formas corporum speculatur sine materia ac per hoc sine motu, quae formae cum in materia sint, ab his separari non possunt) . . ." (ed. cit., p. 8:10–14). For Thomas's literal exposition of this passage, before he introduces his more original treatment based on questions and articles, see Leon. 50.134:86–100. As he explains there, while mathematicals can be considered apart from (sensible) matter, they cannot exist apart from it.

or divides. In developing a rather brief remark made by Aristotle in *De anima*, Bk III, Thomas writes that the intellect's operation is twofold. One operation, known as the understanding of indivisibles, is that whereby the intellect knows what a thing is. There is another whereby the intellect composes or divides by forming affirmative or negative statements.[2] In other words, if we may use terminology which will be more familiar to students of a later scholastic tradition, Thomas is here distinguishing between simple apprehension and judgment. By simple apprehension (which must not be confused with sense perception), the intellect simply knows what something is without affirming or denying anything of it. By judgment the intellect composes or divides a predicate and subject and thereby affirms or denies.

Thomas goes on to argue that these two operations correspond to two factors which are present in things. Thus the first operation has to do with the very nature of the thing according to which that thing holds its proper rank among beings. This is true whether that nature is a complete thing, such as a whole, or whether it is only some incomplete thing such as a part or an accident.[3]

The intellect's second operation is directed to the very *esse* of a thing. This *esse*, adds Thomas, results from the union of the principles of the thing in the case of composites, or else accompanies the simple nature of the thing in the case of simple substances.[4] Immediately, of course, the question can be raised: What does Thomas mean by the term *esse* as he employs it in this text?

Aquinas is only too aware that the term *esse* (literally: "to be") can be used with different meanings. For instance, in an early text from his Commentary on I *Sentences* (d. 33, q. 1, a. 1, ad 1), he distinguishes three different meanings for it. As he puts it there, the term *esse* may be taken to signify the very quiddity or nature of a thing, as when we refer to a definition as signifying what a thing's *esse* is; for, as Thomas remarks, a definition signifies the quiddity of a thing.[5] Secondly, *esse* may signify the very act of an essence, meaning thereby not its second act or operation

---

2. ". . . oportet <videre> qua<liter> intellectus secundum suam operationem abstrahere possit. Sciendum est igitur quod secundum Philosophum in III De anima duplex est operatio intellectus: una, quae dicitur intelligentia indivisibilium, qua cognoscit de unoquoque quid est, alia vero qua componit et dividit, scilicet enuntiationem affirmativam vel negativam formando" (Leon. 50.146:87–95). For Aristotle see *De anima* III, c. 6 (430a 26–28).

3. "Et hae quidem duae operationes duobus quae sunt in rebus respondent. Prima quidem operatio respicit ipsam naturam rei, secundum quam res intellecta aliquem gradum in entibus obtinet, sive sit res completa, ut totum aliquod, sive res incompleta, ut pars vel accidens" (Leon. 50.147:96–101).

4. "Secunda vero operatio respicit ipsum esse rei; quod quidem resultat ex congregatione principiorum rei in compositis, vel ipsam simplicem naturam rei concomitatur, ut in substantiis simplicibus" (Leon. 50.147:101–105).

5. Here Thomas is discussing the nature of relations in the Trinity. In responding to an objection he comments: "Sed sciendum, quod esse dicitur tripliciter. Uno modo dicitur esse ipsa quidditas vel natura rei, sicut dicitur quod definitio est oratio significans quid est esse; definitio enim quidditatem rei significat" (Mandonnet ed., Vol. 1, pp. 765–66).

but its first act, i.e., its actual existence. Taken in a third way, *esse* signifies the truth of composition, that is, of judgment, as this is expressed in propositions. In this sense, continues Thomas, the verb "is" is referred to as the copula. When used in this third way *esse* is realized in the full sense in the intellect which composes or divides. Nonetheless, when so used this *esse* itself is grounded in the *esse* of the thing, that is, in the act of its essence (its existence) just as truth is.[6]

Of these three usages the first may strike the reader as somewhat surprising. In many other contexts Thomas is content simply to distinguish between *esse* insofar as it signifies the composition of a proposition which the intellect effects through judgment, and *esse* taken as actual existence or, as Thomas often expresses it, as the *actus essendi* (act of being). In other words, he often limits himself to the second and third meanings he has singled out in the present text. For instance, he appeals to this twofold distinction in *Summa theologiae* I, q. 3, a. 4 in order to meet an objection against his claim that in God essence and *esse* (act of being) are identical.[7]

In our text from Thomas's Commentary on the *De Trinitate* he has distinguished between the nature of a thing to which the intellect looks in its first operation, and the very *esse* of a thing to which the intellect looks in its second operation. In this text it is clear that *esse* cannot mean nature or quiddity; for it is with this that *esse* is here contrasted. It would seem to follow that it must mean either a thing's actual existence, or else that *esse* which is formed by and exists only in the intellect when it judges. But since Thomas has referred here to the very *esse* of the thing *(ipsum esse rei)*, this suggests that he does not here have in mind *esse* simply as it exists in the intellect as expressed in judgment, that is, as the copula. By process of elimination we seem to be left with the remaining alternative: *esse* as used here signifies the actual existence of a thing. It is this which is captured through judgment. Nonetheless, this interpretation is rejected by various Thomistic scholars.[8]

Before pursuing this controverted point in greater detail, it may be useful for us to recall another distinction which Aquinas also makes, and one which Gilson has

---

6. "Alio modo dicitur esse ipse actus essentiae; sicut vivere, quod est esse viventibus, est animae actus; non actus secundus, qui est operatio, sed actus primus. Tertio modo dicitur esse quod significat veritatem compositionis in propositionibus, secundum quod 'est' dicitur copula: et secundum hoc est in intellectu componente et dividente quantum ad sui complementum; sed fundatur in esse rei, quod est actus essentiae, sicut supra de veritate dictum est" (p. 766). Concerning truth cf. *In I Sent.*, d. 19, q. 5, a. 1 (cited below in n. 16).

7. Leon. 4.42. Note: "Ad secundum dicendum quod *esse* dupliciter dicitur: uno modo, significat actum essendi; alio modo, significat compositionem propositionis quam anima adinvenit coniungens praedicatum subiecto." Also see Quodlibet XII, q. 1, a. 1, ad 1: ". . . esse dupliciter dicitur: quandoque enim esse idem est quod actus entis; quandoque significat compositionem enuntiationis et sic significat actum intellectus" (Leon. 25.2.399:34–38). Cf., however, Thomas's remark in *De potentia*, q. 7, a. 2, ad 1: "Ad primum ergo dicendum, quod ens et esse dicitur dupliciter, ut patet V *Metaph*. Quandoque enim significat essentiam rei, sive actum essendi; quandoque vero significat veritatem propositionis. . . ." See *Quaestiones disputatae*, Vol. 2, M. Pession, ed. (Turin-Rome, 1953), p. 191. Also see *In V Met.*, lect. 9, pp. 238–40, nn. 889–896.

8. See the references given below in notes 19, 20, and 21.

highlighted to good effect in various publications, especially in c. VI of his *Being and Some Philosophers.*[9] As Thomas develops this in his Commentary on Aristotle's *De interpretatione,* the verb "is" as it appears in propositions is sometimes predicated in its own right, as when we say: "Sortes *is.*" By this we wish to indicate that Sortes is in reality, i.e., that he actually exists.[10] As Gilson develops this point, the verb "is" often appears in what we may describe as existential judgments, or judgments of existence.[11] But, Thomas continues, on other occasions the verb "is" is not predicated in its own right as if it were the principal predicate, but only as joined to the principal predicate in order to connect it with the subject of a proposition. So it is when we say: "Sortes *is* white." In this case the speaker does not intend to assert that Sortes actually exists, but rather to attribute whiteness to him. As Gilson explains, such judgments may be described as judgments of attribution.[12]

As we return to our text from Thomas's Commentary on the *De Trinitate,* we should recall another point which Thomas makes in the same immediate context. Because truth arises in the intellect from the fact that the intellect is conformed to reality, it follows that in its second operation (judgment) the intellect cannot truthfully abstract what is united in reality. For the intellect to abstract (that is, to distinguish or divide) in this operation is for it to assert that there is a corresponding separation with respect to the thing's very *esse.* For instance, if I am speaking of someone who is actually white and separate human being from whiteness by saying "this human being is not white," my judgment is false.[13]

In other words, Thomas is reminding us that truth in the strict sense arises at the level of judgment. Any composition or division effected by the intellect through judgment must correspond to a composition or division which obtains in reality if that judgment is to be true. While this point appears to be evident enough in itself,

9. Ed. cit., pp. 190–204. Also see his *The Christian Philosophy of St. Thomas Aquinas,* pp. 40–42.

10. ". . . considerandum est quod hoc verbum 'est' quandoque in enunciatione praedicatur secundum se, ut cum dicitur: 'Sortes est', per quod nihil aliud intendimus significare quam quod Sortes sit in rerum natura . . ." *Expositio Libri Peryermenias* II, 2 (Leon. 1*1.88:36–40). This work falls between December 1270 and October 1271 (Leon. 1*1.85*–88*).

11. See *Being and Some Philosophers,* pp. 200–201 as well as the citation and discussion of this text by Régis as reproduced by Gilson in the same source, pp. 218–20.

12. ". . . quandoque vero non praedicatur per se, quasi principale praedicatum, sed quasi coniunctum principali praedicato ad connectendum ipsum subiecto, sicut cum dicitur: 'Sortes est albus': non enim est intentio loquentis ut asserat Sortem esse in rerum natura, sed ut attribuat ei albedinem mediante hoc verbo 'est'" (Leon. 1*1.88:40–46). In the same context Thomas also explains why in this second case *est* is referred to as *adiacens principali praedicato:* ". . . et dicitur esse tertium non quia sit tertium praedicatum, sed quia est tertia dictio posita in enunciatione, quae simul cum nomine praedicato facit unum praedicatum, ut sic enunciatio dividatur in duas partes et non in tres" (48–52). For Gilson on judgments of attribution see *Being and Some Philosophers,* pp. 200, 190–91.

13. Leon. 50.147:105–115. Note: "Et quia veritas intellectus est ex hoc quod conformatur <rei>, patet quod secundum hanc secundam operationem intellectus non potest vere abstrahere quod secundum rem coniunctum est; quia in abstrahendo significaretur esse separatio secundum ipsum esse rei. . . ." Cf. *In V Met.,* lect. 9, p. 239, nn. 895–896.

it is important to keep it in mind in the present discussion. If, as we are suggesting, Thomas holds that the intellect's second operation (judgment) is ordered to the *esse* of things and if this means their actual existence, one might conclude that such is the case only in judgments of existence. Thomas's text indicates that the same holds for judgments of attribution such as "Sortes is white." Even in such judgments there must be some reference to reality or, as Thomas has put it, to the very *esse* of the thing in question. In fact, as Gilson has phrased it, in judgments of attribution "is" has correctly been chosen to serve as a copula "because all judgments of attribution are meant to say *how* a certain thing actually *is*."[14]

Our text from Thomas's Commentary on the *De Trinitate* is more or less paralleled by two others from his Commentary on I *Sentences*. In the first of these, taken from d. 19, q. 5, a. 1, ad 7, Thomas draws the same distinction between the intellect's twofold operation. One of these is named by some "imagination" (that is, concept formation) or "formation" on the part of the intellect, and is referred to by Aristotle as an understanding of indivisibles. The other, which some refer to as belief (*fides*), consists in the composition or division expressed in a proposition. This, of course, is what we mean by judgment. While the first operation grasps the quiddity of a thing, the second has to do with its *esse*. Because truth as such is grounded in *esse* rather than in quiddity, truth and falsity properly speaking are found in this second intellectual operation and in the sign of this same operation, that is, in the proposition.[15]

Thomas has offered a fuller explanation in the corpus of this same article of his point concerning truth. In addition to things which enjoy their complete being (*esse*) outside the mind, and others which exist only in the mind, there are still others which have a foundation in reality outside the mind, but which exist as such (as formally perfected) only in the intellect. Such, for instance, is the nature of a universal or of time. Truth is still another example. While truth has a foundation in extramental reality, it is perfected as such only by an act on the part of the intellect. Moreover, since both quiddity and *esse* are realized in a given thing, truth is based on a thing's *esse* more so than on its quiddity.[16]

---

14. *Being and Some Philosophers*, p. 200.

15. Mandonnet ed., Vol. 1, p. 489. Note: ". . . dicendum, quod cum sit duplex operatio intellectus: una quarum dicitur a quibusdam imaginatio intellectus, quam Philosophus, III *De anima*, text. 21, nominat intelligentiam indivisibilium, quae consistit in apprehensione quidditatis simplicis, quae alio etiam nomine formatio dicitur; alia est quam dicunt fidem, quae consistit in compositione vel divisione propositionis: prima operatio respicit quidditatem rei; secunda respicit esse ipsius." For some helpful comments on the usage of the term *formatio* to designate knowledge by forming a concept see J. Owens, "Aquinas on Knowing Existence," repr. in his *St. Thomas Aquinas on the Existence of God*, p. 24, and n. 10.

16. See ed. cit., Vol. 1, p. 486: "Similiter dico de veritate, quod habet fundamentum in re, sed ratio eius completur per actionem intellectus, quando scilicet apprehenditur eo modo quo est. Cum autem in re sit quidditas eius et suum esse, veritas fundatur in esse rei magis quam in quidditate, sicut et nomen entis ab esse imponitur." See my "Truth in Thomas Aquinas," *Review of Metaphysics* 43 (1989/1990), pp. 296–98, 550–56.

Thomas also writes that it is through that same operation by which the intellect grasps the *esse* of a thing that it completes or perfects the relation of adequation in which truth itself consists.[17] In other words, it is through judgment that one grasps *esse* just as it is through judgment that truth, properly speaking, is realized. Throughout this discussion, therefore, Thomas has contrasted *esse* with nature or quiddity. And throughout this discussion, *esse* is said to be grasped by the intellectual operation we know as judgment. Since *esse* is contrasted with quiddity in this discussion, it seems clear that when it is so used it must signify actual existence. It is this which is grasped through judgment rather than through the intellect's first operation. This being so, it also seems that, as *esse* appears in our text from Thomas's commentary on the *De Trinitate,* there too it means actual existence. It is this which can be grasped only through judgment.[18]

Nevertheless, as we have noted above, this interpretation has frequently been challenged. According to a more traditional reading, well expounded by L.-M. Régis, Thomas does not hold that a thing's existence *(existere)* is directly apprehended through judgment. Against any such reading Régis argues that the direct object of judgment is rather a "composition or synthesis of concepts with which simple apprehension has already enriched the intellect."[19] According to this reading, therefore, and even when we are dealing with an existential judgment, both the nature or essence of a thing and its actual existence will be grasped through the intellect in its first operation, that is, through simple apprehension. Judgment's function will rather be to unite or synthesize the intelligible content already apprehended at the level of the intellect's first operation.[20] Consistent with this interpretation, therefore, Régis cannot admit that in the passages with which we are here con-

---

17. ". . . et in ipsa operatione intellectus accipientis esse rei sicut est per quamdam similationem ad ipsum, completur relatio adaequationis, in qua consistit ratio veritatis. Unde dico, quod ipsum esse rei est causa veritatis, secundum quod est in cognitione intellectus" (ed. cit., p. 486).

18. See the text cited above in n. 4.

19. See L.-M. Régis, *Epistemology,* trans. I. M. Byrne (New York, 1959), pp. 312–13, 322–31. For the text quoted see p. 323.

20. Régis, *Epistemology,* p. 325. He (p. 324) cites the following text from Thomas's Commentary on *Metaphysics* V in support of his interpretation: "Esse vero quod in sui natura unaquaeque res habet, est substantiale. Et ideo, cum dicitur, Socrates est, si ille Est primo modo accipiatur (as signifying that which obtains outside the mind), est de praedicato substantiali. Nam ens est superius ad unumquodque entium, sicut animal ad hominem. Si autem accipiatur secundo modo (as signifying the composition of a proposition), est de praedicato accidentali" (lect. 9, p. 239, n. 896). Régis acknowledges that *est* as used in the first way "expresses the act of the substance it perfects and from which it is distinguished." But he concludes from this that *esse* taken in this sense—as the thing's substantial act of existence—is not grasped through judgment. Only *esse* taken in the second sense—as expressing a composition of concepts—is the direct object of judgment. However, nothing in this text forces one to deny that Thomas holds that *esse* taken as a thing's actual or act of existence is also grasped through judgment. For an extended critique of Gilson's views concerning judgment and existence see J. M. Quinn, *The Thomism of Etienne Gilson: A Critical Study* (Villanova, 1971), pp. 53–91. For the other side see the contributions by J. Owens mentioned above in Ch. I, n. 4.

cerned Thomas intends to signify actual existence by his usage of the term *esse.* He must rather mean thereby a thing's mode of existing.[21]

One remark in the same immediate context from Thomas's Commentary on the *De Trinitate,* q. 5, a. 3, might be taken as support for Régis's reading. After writing that the intellect's second operation looks to the very *esse* of a thing, Thomas adds that this *esse* results from the uniting of the principles of a thing in the case of composites, or accompanies the thing's nature as in the case of simple substances.[22] How can Thomas say that *esse* results from the joining together of the principles of a thing in the case of composites if *esse* means the thing's actual existence? Is it not rather the thing's entire being *(ens)* including its essence and its existence which results from the uniting of its principles, that is, of its matter and its form?[23]

Reinforcement for Regis's reading might also be sought from another parallel text from Thomas's Commentary on I *Sentences* (d. 38, q. 1, a. 3). There, while seeking to determine whether God has knowledge of our individual judgments *(enuntiabilia),* Thomas again distinguishes between a thing's quiddity and its *esse* and correlates these with the same two intellectual operations. If quiddities are grasped by the intellect's first operation (formation, or the understanding of indivisibles), its second operation understands *(comprehendit)* a thing's *esse* through an affirmative judgment.[24] Until this point in the text we would seem to have additional support for the view that it is through judgment that one grasps a thing's existence. But Thomas then adds that the *esse* of a thing composed of matter and form consists of a certain composition of form with matter or of an accident with its subject. How are we to understand *esse* as Thomas uses it here? Must it not be taken to signify the total being of the thing rather than its actual existence?[25]

Militating against any such interpretation, however, is the fact that in this same text Thomas immediately goes on to speak of nature and *esse* in God. Just as God's nature is the cause and exemplar for every other nature, so is his *esse* the cause and

21. For Régis's explicit discussion of our text from *In De Trinitate* and its parallels see pp. 328–31.

22. See n. 4 above for this text. The critical part reads: ". . . quod quidem resultat ex congregatione principiorum rei. . . ."

23. Régis's translation of the final part of this passage strikes me as misleading: ". . . or coincides with the simplicity of nature in spiritual substances" (p. 328). This does not really capture the meaning of the Latin: ". . . vel ipsam simplicem naturam rei concomitatur, ut in substantiis simplicibus" (Leon. 50.147:104–105). A more literal rendering of *concomitatur* as "accompanies" makes it much more evident that *esse* stands for something other than the simple nature itself, and hence that it refers to the thing's actual existence.

24. "Cum in re duo sint, quidditas rei, et esse eius, his duobus respondet duplex operatio intellectus. Una quae dicitur a philosophis formatio, qua apprehendit quidditates rerum, quae etiam a Philosopho, in III *De anima,* dicitur indivisibilium intelligentia. Alia autem comprehendit esse rei, componendo affirmationem . . ." (Mandonnet ed., Vol. 1, p. 903).

25. ". . . quia etiam esse rei ex materia et forma compositae, a qua cognitionem accipit, consistit in quadam compositione formae ad materiam, vel accidentis ad subiectum" (ibid.).

exemplar for all other *esse*. And just as by knowing his essence he knows every other thing, so by knowing his *esse* he knows the *esse* of everything else. But, as Thomas points out, this implies no diversity or composition in God since his *esse* does not differ from his essence, nor does it follow from anything which is composed. Since Thomas has already argued at length elsewhere in this same Commentary on I *Sentences* that essence and *esse* (existence) are not identical in creatures, we can assume that in speaking of the nature and *esse* of a creature in contrast with that of God, he has in mind the creature's nature and its actual existence.[26] Hence it follows that this text also should be taken as implying that the intellect grasps actual existence through judgment.

Still, against this interpretation one may insist: How can Thomas say in the last-mentioned context that the *esse* of a matter-form composite consists of a certain composition of matter and form or of an accident with its subject? And how can he write in q. 5, a. 3 of his Commentary on the *De Trinitate* that the *esse* of a composite results from the joining together of the principles of that composite thing?[27]

The answer, it seems to me, rests on the distinction between different orders of mutual or reciprocal dependency. Thomas's views concerning the distinction and composition of essence and *esse* (act of being) within finite beings will be examined in detail in Ch. V below. Suppose, for the sake of the present discussion, that we concede his theory of real composition and distinction of essence and *esse* within material beings. This will imply that the essence of any such entity is itself composed of matter and form and that if any such being is to exist in actuality, its essence must also be actualized by its corresponding *actus essendi* (act of being).

For Thomas this means, of course, that such a thing's existence must be caused efficiently by some extrinsic agent. But it also means that such a thing's intrinsic act of being must be received by, measured or specified by, and limited by its corresponding essence principle. Only in this way can Thomas account for the fact that it is this kind of being rather than any other kind. Hence in the order of intrinsic dependency, its *esse* (act of being) actualizes its essence. And its essence principle simultaneously serves as a receiving principle for its act of being. Since its act of being is received and limited and specified by its essence, Thomas can say that its

---

26. "Similiter etiam in ipso Deo est considerare naturam ipsius, et esse eius; et sicut natura sua est causa et exemplar omnis naturae, ita etiam esse suum est causa et exemplar omnis esse. Unde sicut cognoscendo essentiam suam, cognoscit omnem rem; ita cognoscendo esse suum, cognoscit esse cuiuslibet rei . . . quia esse suum non est aliud ab essentia, nec est compositum consequens . . ." (ed. cit., pp. 903–4). For earlier discussion and affirmation of the essence-*esse* composition (and therefore distinction) in creatures see, for instance, *In I Sent.*, d. 8, q. 5, a. 1, sol., as well as the second argument in the *sed contra* (ed. cit., pp. 226–27); d. 8, q. 5, a. 2 (pp. 229–30). Also see q. 1, a. 1 of the same distinction, where Thomas writes: "Cum autem ita sit quod in qualibet re creata essentia sua differat a suo esse, res illa proprie denominatur a quidditate sua, et non ab actu essendi . . ." (p. 195).

27. See the texts cited above in nn. 25 and 4 respectively.

esse (taken as its act of being) results from its essence or even that it consists of or is constituted by the union or composition of its matter and its form, that is, of its essence principle.[28]

At this point another distinction should be mentioned, and one which Thomas does not always bring out explicitly. In light of what we have now seen, it is through judgment that we become intellectually aware that things actually exist. But as already noted, in Thomas's metaphysics, if a given substance actually exists, this is owing to the presence within that thing of an intrinsic act principle *(actus essendi)* which actualizes its essence, is distinct from it, and enters into composition with it. According to Thomas the distinction of this intrinsic act of being from its corresponding essence principle is not immediately evident to us, but needs to be justified by philosophical argumentation. This being so, one may ask: In which of these two closely related senses is Thomas using *esse* when he writes that it is grasped through the intellect's second operation (judgment) rather than through its first operation (simple apprehension)? Does he simply intend to signify by *esse* the fact that something actually exists (its facticity)? Or does he also have in mind the thing's distinct intrinsic act of being *(actus essendi)*?[29]

In our texts from Thomas's Commentary on the *De Trinitate,* q. 5, a. 3 and his Commentary on I *Sentences* (d. 19 and d. 38), he has not explicitly distinguished between these two usages of *esse*. And until this point, by using the expression "actual existence" in interpreting these passages, I have attempted to preserve in English something of the ambiguity of the Latin *esse*. In examining this issue, two points should be kept in mind. First of all, if a given thing's intrinsic act of being *(actus essendi)* may be said to be constituted by the principles of its essence insofar as it is measured and limited by that essence, *mutatis mutandis* the same may be

28. For a brief but helpful discussion of this see Owens, "Aquinas on Knowing Existence," p. 28. Also see *In III Sent.,* d. 6, q. 2, a. 2, *responsio,* where, in the course of preparing to address the issue concerning whether there is only one *esse* in Christ, Thomas again notes that *esse* can be used in two different ways, either as signifying the truth of a proposition, i.e., as a copula, or else as that which corresponds *(pertinet)* to the nature of a thing. This second *esse* is found in the thing and is an "actus entis resultans ex principiis rei, sicut lucere est actus lucentis." Thomas again adds that sometimes *esse* is also taken in a third way, as essence. See *Scriptum super Sententiis,* M. F. Moos, ed., Vol. 3, p. 238. For another well-known text see *In IV Met.,* ed. cit., lect. 2, p. 155, n. 558: "Esse enim rei quamvis sit aliud ab eius essentia, non tamen est intelligendum quod sit aliquod superadditum ad modum accidentis, sed quasi constituitur per principia essentiae." This passage should also be interpreted in the way suggested in our text.

29. Owens seems to be uneasy about admitting this distinction, though he raises his doubts in the context of criticizing C. Fabro's way of presenting it: existence as actuality would be distinguished from existence as "result." For Owens see "Aquinas on Knowing Existence," pp. 32–33. For Fabro see his "The Intensive Hermeneutics of Thomistic Philosophy: The Notion of Participation," *Review of Metaphysics* 27 (1974), pp. 449–91, especially p. 470. Also see the sympathetic but critical comments of F. Wilhelmsen in his "Existence and *Esse*," *New Scholasticism* 50 (1976), pp. 20–45. As will be clear from what follows, and without endorsing Fabro's way of presenting it, I regard this distinction as extremely important.

said of its existence *(esse)* when this is taken in the sense of facticity. If this presupposes the presence of an intrinsic act of being *(actus essendi)* in that thing, it also presupposes a corresponding essence principle. The difficulty remains in determining in which of these senses Thomas is using *esse* when he writes that it is grasped though judgment. Secondly, no matter how this particular question may be answered, a philosophically more significant point remains. According to Aquinas, *esse,* when taken as a thing's intrinsic *actus essendi,* cannot be reduced to the status of another quiddity or essence. Any such reduction would destroy its dynamic character as act and would indeed, as Gilson and others have warned, reduce Thomas's metaphysics to another version of essentialism.

In attempting to discern Thomas's answer to our question, we should recall that in his Commentary on Aristotle's *De interpretatione* he has distinguished between what we may call judgments of existence and judgments of attribution. In speaking of judgments of existence in that context he clearly has in mind those judgments whereby we recognize things as actually existing, whether or not we have yet concluded to distinction and composition of essence and *esse* (act of being) within such beings.[30] So, too, as we shall see below in Ch. V, in his *De ente et essentia* he begins to argue for distinction and composition of essence and existence within nondivine beings by starting from the fact that it is different for us to know what something is (i.e., to recognize its quiddity), and to know that it actually exists (presumably through a judgment of existence). If he eventually concludes to composition of essence and an intrinsic act of being *(esse)* within such beings, he can hardly begin with this.[31] Hence in such passages *esse* seems merely to refer to the fact that the thing in question actually exists, i.e., to its actual existence.

On the other hand, in the texts examined above from Thomas's Commentary on I *Sentences* in which he correlates judgment and existence *(esse)*, he can take his theory of intrinsic composition of essence and *esse* within creatures as already given.[32] Hence in these passages he can, if he so wishes, mean by *esse* the intrinsic act of being present within such beings. Thus corresponding to the diversity between intellectual operations whereby we know what something is and recognize that it exists is a composition and diversity within the thing itself, that is, of its essence and its act of being. And it may possibly be this meaning of *esse* that he has in mind in our text from his Commentary on the *De Trinitate,* q. 5, a. 3, though I am less inclined to think so. There the context does not seem to demand this reading, but only that we take *esse* in the sense of actual existence.

---

30. See the text cited above in n. 10.

31. See Ch. V below, pp. 140–50. For another illustration of this usage see ST II–II, q. 83, a. 1, arg. 3, where Thomas refers to Aristotle's distinction between two intellectual operations. Regarding the second Thomas writes: ". . . secunda vero est compositio et divisio, per quam scilicet apprehenditur aliquid esse vel non esse" (Leon. 9.192). While this text appears among the opening arguments, there is no reason to think that Thomas does not accept it as his own view. See his reply to arg. 3 (p. 193).

32. See n. 26 above for references.

Be that as it may, in the order of discovery an intrinsic composition and distinction of essence and *esse* within finite beings is not immediately evident to us in our prephilosophical experience. And since here we wish to develop Thomas's metaphysical thought by following the philosophical order, we need only conclude from the above that according to Thomas it is through judgment that we come to know things as actually existing. We need not and should not yet assume that a distinction and composition of essence and act of being within finite beings has been established. This can only come later, after one has already discovered being as being, the subject of metaphysics. But presupposed for that discovery, I am suggesting, is an initial recognition of being as real or as actually existing. And presupposed for that is an initial judgment of existence.[33]

Another point should be mentioned here. Thomas closely associates *esse* with actuality. In fact, he refers to *esse* as the actuality of every form or nature (ST I, q. 3, a. 4), and in a classic text from the *De potentia* describes it as the "actuality of all acts and because of this [as] the perfection of all perfections."[34] While this understanding of *esse* as actuality takes on its fullest meaning only when it is considered in light of Thomas's theory of composition and distinction of essence and *esse* (act of being) within finite substances, it seems to be available to him prior to his demonstration of that conclusion. Thus he often explains that a thing is or exists by reason of the fact that it has *esse*. The very name being *(ens)* signifies "that which is," or "that which has *esse*."[35] Moreover, as we shall see below in Ch. IV, in his fairly early Commentary on the *De Hebdomadibus* Thomas holds that a being *(ens)* is or exists insofar as it participates in the *actus essendi*.[36] This last-mentioned passage is significant for our purposes since it appears in Thomas's Commentary before

---

33. If I may return to the point of disagreement between Fabro and Owens (see n. 29 above), I would distinguish between the order of discovery and the order of nature. In the order of discovery, what we first know is an existing thing, or a being. To recognize that it exists requires judgment, I would hold, in agreement at least until this point with Gilson and Owens. In the order of nature or reality, on the other hand, according to Thomas's developed metaphysics, any such thing actually exists because of the presence within it of an intrinsic act of being *(actus essendi)* which actualizes its distinct essence principle. This act principle is prior in the order of nature to the thing's actual existence or to its facticity, but not in the order of time.

34. "Secundo, quia esse est actualitas omnis formae vel naturae: non enim bonitas vel humanitas significatur in actu, nisi prout significamus eam esse" (Leon. 4.42). For the *De potentia* see q. 7, a. 2, ad 9: "Quaelibet autem forma signata non intelligitur in actu nisi per hoc quod esse ponitur. . . . Unde patet quod hoc quod dico esse est actualitas omnium actuum, et propter hoc est perfectio omnium perfectionum" (Pession ed., p. 192). For fuller discussion of this see Ch. V below, n. 115.

35. See, for instance, SCG I, c. 22: "Amplius. Omnis res est per hoc quod habet esse." Earlier on in this same chapter he writes: "Esse actum quendam nominat: non enim dicitur esse aliquid ex hoc quod est in potentia, sed ex eo quod est in actu" (ed. cit., p. 24). See ST I–II, q. 26, a. 4: ". . . ens simpliciter est quod habet esse . . ." (Leon. 6.190).

36. *In De Hebdomadibus,* lect. 2: ". . . ita possumus dicere quod ens, sive id quod est sit inquantum participat actum essendi" (Leon. 50.271:57–59). The diversity between *esse* and *id quod est* to which Thomas finds Boethius referring at this point in the text is restricted to the order of intentions (p. 270:36–39). Farther on Thomas turns to their real diversity (p. 273:205–258).

he offers his argumentation for real distinction and composition of essence and *esse* in such participating beings.[37] As he explains in ST I, q. 5, a. 1, ad 1, the term being *(ens)* indicates that something is in act. But act is ordered to potency, he adds. Therefore, something is said to be a being *(ens)* in the unqualified sense insofar as it is distinguished from that which is only in potency. And it is so distinguished by reason of its substantial *esse*.[38]

In his late Commentary on the *De interpretatione* I, 5, while commenting on a doubtful Latin rendering of a passage in Aristotle's text, Thomas remarks that the verb "is" when taken alone "consignifies" composition (judgment), but only by way of consequence and not in its primary meaning. In its primary meaning it rather signifies that which the intellect grasps in the manner of unqualified actuality, since it means "to be in act." The actuality which this verb ("is") signifies is that of any form or act, whether substantial or accidental.[39] But as he had explained in his much earlier Quodlibet 9, q. 2, a. 2, the term *esse* may be taken in one sense as signifying the act of being *(actus entis)* insofar as it is being. By this Thomas has in mind that whereby something is designated as a being in act in the nature of things, that is, as something which actually exists. As he also explains here, in this sense *esse* is properly and truly applied to a thing which subsists in itself, that is, to a subsisting substance.[40]

While frequent reference will be made throughout this study to Thomas's emphasis on *esse* as act and perfection, the point is worth mentioning here for a special reason. In the key passages from his Commentary on I *Sentences* in which he correlates judgment with *esse,* whether or not *esse* signifies a distinct intrinsic *actus essendi,* at the very least it must be taken as referring to actual existence. And it is in this last-mentioned sense that I prefer to take it as it appears in the parallel text from his Commentary on *De Trinitate,* q. 5, a. 3. Moreover, as we have also seen,

---

37. See the texts cited in n. 36 above.

38. Here he is defending his claim that being and goodness are identical in reality, but differ conceptually *(secundum rationem).* Note in particular: "Nam cum ens dicat aliquid proprie esse in actu; actus autem proprie ordinem habeat ad potentiam; secundum hoc simpliciter aliquid dicitur ens, secundum quod primo discernitur ab eo quod est in potentia tantum. Hoc autem est esse substantiale rei uniuscuiusque; unde per suum esse substantiale dicitur unumquodque ens simpliciter" (Leon. 4.56).

39. Leon. 1.*1.31:391–400: "Ideo autem dicit quod hoc verbum 'est' consignificat compositionem, quia non principaliter eam significat, sed ex consequenti: significat enim id quod primo cadit in intellectu per modum actualitatis absolute; nam 'est' simpliciter dictum significat esse actu, et ideo significat per modum verbi. Quia vero actualitas, quam principaliter significat hoc verbum 'est', est communiter actualitas omnis formae vel actus, substantialis vel accidentalis. . . ."

40. Leon. 25.1.94:41–50. There he notes that *esse* can be used in two ways, either as the copula, or: "Alio modo esse dicitur actus entis in quantum est ens, idest quo denominatur aliquid ens actu in rerum natura; et sic *esse* non attribuitur nisi rebus ipsis quae in decem generibus continentur, unde ens a tali esse dictum per decem genera dividitur. Sed hoc esse attribuitur alicui rei dupliciter. Uno modo, sicut ei quod proprie et vere habet esse vel est; et sic attribuitur soli substantiae per se subsistenti. . . ." Note that here Thomas is considering the question whether there is only one *esse* in Christ. Quodlibet 9 dates from the Christmas quodlibetal session of 1257 (Leon. 25.1.ix*).

in other contexts Thomas states or implies that it is through the intellect's second operation (judgment) that we discover that things actually exist.[41] The implication is this. Even at this primitive or prephilosophical level in our understanding of being or of reality, we must understand something as actual if we are to grasp it as existing or as real.

Before concluding this particular section, therefore, I would like to offer a brief account of the steps through which one must pass in discovering being as real or as existing in accord with Thomas's general theory of knowledge. Because Thomas has not spelled out this procedure for us in detail, my account must be regarded as a reconstruction. Others have already attempted to offer such reconstructions in accord with Thomas's thought, and those presented by J. Maritain, by R. Schmidt, and by A. M. Krapiec have proven to be helpful. Nevertheless, my account will differ in various respects from each of theirs, and I must accept full responsibility for any shortcomings that may remain in it.[42]

As is well known, Thomas holds that all of our knowledge begins with sense experience and must in some way be derived from it.[43] Suppose that we have come into contact with one or more objects at the level of external sense perception. In order for perception to occur, in some way one or more external sense power must be acted upon by the object which is to be perceived. That there is a passive element in perception is a point repeatedly made by Aquinas. In reacting to this impression from without, the sense in question will directly perceive the thing insofar as it falls under that sense's proper sense object, that is, insofar as it is something colored, or sounding, or smelling, etc., and hence implicitly something which acts.[44]

---

41. Cf. nn. 10 and 31 above. For still another (anti-"existential") interpretation of *esse* as it is used in the texts from Thomas's Commentary on the *Sentences* see B. Garceau, *Judicium: Vocabulaire, sources, doctrine de saint Thomas d'Aquin* (Montreal-Paris, 1968), pp. 120–29.

42. For these see Maritain, *Existence and the Existent*, pp. 26–30, especially the long note which begins on p. 26; R. W. Schmidt, "The Evidence Grounding Judgments of Existence," in *An Etienne Gilson Tribute*, C. J. O'Neil, ed. (Milwaukee, 1959), pp. 228–44; A. M. Krapiec, "Analysis formationis conceptus entis existentialiter considerati," *Divus Thomas* (Piac.) 59 (1956), pp. 320–50.

43. On this point, of course, Thomas is following Aristotle. It is so central to Aquinas's personal thought that no attempt can be made here to cite all of the texts in which he explicitly states it. For the purpose of illustration, see *In De Trinitate*, q. 6. a. 2: "Principium igitur cuiuslibet nostrae cognitionis est in sensu, quia ex apprehensione sensus oritur apprehensio phantasiae, quae est 'motus a sensu factus' . . . a qua iterum oritur apprehensio intellectiva in nobis, cum phantasmata sint intellectivae animae ut obiecta . . ." (Leon. 50.164:71–76); *De veritate*, q. 12, a. 3, ad 2: "Sed quia primum principium nostrae cognitionis est sensus, oportet ad sensum quodam modo resolvere omnia de quibus iudicamus . . ." (Leon. 22.2.378:379–382); ST II–II, q. 173, a. 2: "Repraesentantur autem menti humanae res aliquae secundum aliquas species: et secundum naturae ordinem, primo oportet quod species praesententur sensui; secundo, imaginationi; tertio, intellectui possibili, qui immutatur a speciebus phantasmatum secundum illustrationem intellectus agentis" (Leon. 10.386).

44. See, for instance, *In II De anima*, 13: "Et ideo aliter dicendum quod sentire consistit in quodam pati et alterari, ut supra dictum est" (Leon. 45.1.120:125–126). See *In II De anima*, 10 (Leon. 45.1.107–9). Cf. *Quodlibet VIII*, q. 2, a. 1: "Sensus autem exteriores suscipiunt tantum a rebus per modum patiendi, sine hoc quod aliquid cooperentur ad sui formationem, quamvis iam formati habeant propriam operationem, quae est iudicium de propriis obiectis" (Leon. 25.1.56:69–73). Note

Going hand in hand with this, according to Thomas, will be recognition by an internal sense power known as the common sense *(sensus communis)* that the external senses are indeed perceiving. At the same time, this internal sense power is required to account for the fact that, even at the level of perception, we can distinguish the proper object of one external sense from that of another, for instance, that which is white from that which is sweet.[45] If these two activities lead Aquinas to defend the need for the common sense as a distinct internal sense, the first of these also suggests that the common sense may play an important role in our discovery of the existence of extramental things. Like the external senses themselves, the common sense presupposes that the external senses are in direct contact with their appropriate objects and, as noted, it also enables one to be aware that one is indeed sensing.[46]

Even at this level there seems to be an implicit awareness of the actual existence of the thing which is perceived by one or more external sense; for in being aware that one is sensing, one is also aware that one's power of sense perception is being acted upon by some object. Strictly speaking, what is perceived is an existent rather than existence as such. Hence such knowledge of existence itself is still only implicit. Existence will not be singled out or isolated as such for consideration at the level of the senses. But the raw material is now at hand for the intellect to advert to the fact that the senses are perceiving some object and for it to judge that the thing in question actually exists.[47]

---

the active and "judging" function assigned by Thomas to the external senses with respect to their proper objects. For discussion see Owens, "Judgment and Truth in Aquinas," pp. 37–42.

45. See *In II De anima*, 13 (Leon. 45.1.120:104–105). Note in particular: ". . . sensu enim communi percipimus nos videre et discernimus inter album et dulce." See *In II De anima,* 26 (Leon. 45.1.178:8–14): ". . . huiusmodi autem actiones sunt duae: una est secundum quod nos percipimus actiones sensuum propriorum, puta quod sentimus nos videre et audire; alia est secundum quod discernimus inter sensibilia diversorum sensuum, puta quod aliud sit dulce, et aliud album." Also see the fuller discussion in cc. 26 and 27 and the opening remark in c. 28 about the twofold activity which he assigns to the common sense (p. 187:1–6). Also see ST I, q. 78, a. 4, ad 2, where Thomas argues that if a particular external sense can judge about its proper sensible object, it cannot distinguish its proper sensible object from those of the other external senses. Nor can it account for the fact that one perceives (literally: "sees") that one is seeing. For both of these activities the common sense is required (Leon. 5.256). Though some of the texts cited above have been taken from Thomas's Commentary on the *De anima,* they clearly reflect his personal position as well. On the relation between the common sense and the particular external senses also see his *Sentencia libri De sensu,* c. 18 (Leon. 45.2.98–99).

46. In addition to the texts cited in the previous note, see his *Sentencia libri De memoria,* c. 2 (Leon. 45.2.109–10). There Thomas follows Avicenna in defending the distinction of the common sense from the imagination and the sense-memory. For the distinction of the four internal senses see the classical text in ST I, q. 78, a. 4 (Leon. 5.255–56).

47. See *In I Sent.,* d. 19, q. 5, a. 1, ad 6 (Mandonnet ed., p. 489): ". . . quamvis esse sit in rebus sensibilibus, tamen rationem essendi, vel intentionem entis, sensus non apprehendit, sicut nec aliquam formam substantialem, nisi per accidens. . . ." In his "The Evidence Grounding Judgments of Existence," Schmidt brings out nicely two points I have in mind: (1) The mere fact that the sense

According to Aquinas's general theory of knowledge, however, other steps are required for this to happen. Still at the level of the internal senses, another internal sense power will produce an image or likeness in which the form of the external object, as appropriately distinguished and organized by the common sense, is preserved. This likeness is known as a phantasm and is produced by the internal sense known as the imagination.[48] This phantasm in turn is submitted to the light of the intellect's active or abstractive power, the agent intellect, which abstracts the potentially intelligible content contained therein from its individuating conditions and renders it actually intelligible. This abstracted intelligible content in turn is impressed on the other intellective power, the possible intellect *(intellectus possibilis)*, and is grasped or apprehended by it. At this point one will have arrived at some kind of general or universal knowledge of the whatness or quiddity of the thing in question, though one will not yet know it intellectually as *this* thing or

---

power is modified and acted upon is not sufficient "for the evidence of sensible being." There must be at the level of the senses an awareness of this modification, or a consciousness that we are sensing. This is delivered by the common sense. (2) Even at this level "existence as such is not directly and properly sensed" (pp. 237–38, 241). In his "Judgment and Truth in Aquinas" (see pp. 38–42), Owens cites a number of texts where Thomas refers to the senses as judging: Quodlibet 8, q. 2, a. 1; *De veritate*, q. 1, a. 11c; ST I, q. 17, a. 2c; ST I, q. 78, a. 4, ad 2. With the possible exception of the text from *De veritate*, q. 1, a. 11, these texts do not state that the senses directly grasp existence as such. Their point rather is that the senses judge or discriminate within the range of their proper sense objects. The text from the *De veritate* appears to say more: ". . . et sic dicitur esse veritas vel falsitas in sensu sicut et in intellectu, in quantum videlicet iudicat esse quod est vel quod non est" (Leon. 22.1.34:56–59). I take this and Thomas's ensuing discussion as meaning that there is truth in the sense when it judges that things are as they are, and falsity when it judges otherwise. See the remark near the end of the corpus about a sense apprehending (not judging) its proper sensible *as it is* (Leon. 22.1.35:120–121).

48. For a helpful description of the role of the imagination in the production of the phantasm, and for the illumination of the phantasm by the agent intellect and the consequent production of species or likenesses in the possible intellect see Quodlibet 8, q. 2, a. 1 (Leon. 25.1.55–57). This article is directed to this question: ". . . utrum anima accipiat species quibus cognoscit a rebus quae sunt extra eam." Here, as in a text cited above in n. 43 (ST II–II, q. 173, a. 2), Thomas's doctrine concerning sensible and intelligible species appears. Species are involved in his account of external sense perception, imagination, and intellection, although evidently in different ways. While a full account of his views on sensible and intelligible species cannot be offered here, one important misconception should be eliminated. For him an intelligible species is not the object which is known, but rather that by means of which some thing is understood by the intellect; the intelligible species is a likeness of that thing and is ultimately required, as Thomas sees it, to account for the presence of the form of the object known in the knowing power. See ST I, q. 85, a. 2, as well as the discussion in the *De spiritualibus creaturis*, a. 9, ad 6, where Thomas discusses both intelligible and sensible species and says as much of each: "Unde species visibilis non se habet ut quod videtur, sed ut quo videtur. Et simile est de intellectu possibili; nisi quod intellectus possibilis reflectitur supra seipsum et supra speciem suam, non autem visus." See *Quaestiones disputatae*, Vol. 2 (Marietti ed., 1953), p. 404. On sensible and intelligible species in Aquinas see J. F. Peifer, *The Concept in Thomism* (New York, 1952), cc. 2 and 3 (helpful but heavily influenced by John of St. Thomas); and a brief presentation by N. Kretzmann in Kretzmann and E. Stump, *The Cambridge Companion to Aquinas* (Cambridge, 1993), pp. 138–42.

as an individual. To put this in other terms, the intellect's first operation—the understanding of indivisibles—will have occurred, whereby the intellect grasps its natural object, the abstracted quiddity of a material thing.[49]

For the intellect to grasp an individual another step is required, which is referred to by Thomas as a kind of *reflexio* or turning back upon the phantasms.[50] Only at this point will one be intellectually aware of this thing or *x* not merely in universal fashion or as *x* but as *this* thing or *this x*. And here, I would suggest, owing to its cooperation with the common sense, the intellect will be in position to judge that the object one is perceiving (and which is acting upon the external senses) actually exists. In short one will now make an initial judgment of existence regarding the particular thing one is perceiving. This may be expressed in explicit terms such as "This *x* is," or "This man is," or perhaps in some other way. In any event, one will now be intellectually aware that the thing in question is real in the sense that it actually exists.[51]

Presumably one will repeat this procedure as one encounters other extramental objects. Corresponding to our perception of these different objects will be a series of individual judgments of existence: "This *x* is"; "This *y* is"; "This *z* is"; etc. At some point, possibly even after one's first existential judgment, perhaps after several have been formulated, one will be in position to reflect upon this procedure and as a consequence to form in some vague and general fashion one's idea of reality,

49. See, for instance, ST I, q. 85, a. 1. Note in particular: "Cognoscere vero id quod est in materia individuali, non prout est in tali materia, est abstrahere formam a materia individuali, quam repraesentant phantasmata. Et ideo necesse est dicere quod intellectus noster intelligit materialia abstrahendo a phantasmatibus." Also see ad 1 (Leon. 5.330). See Quodlibet 8, q. 2, a. 1 for a good exposition of the need for collaboration between the agent intellect and the phantasms for the production of intelligibles in actuality in the possible intellect (Leon. 25.1.56–57). Cf. *De spiritualibus creaturis*, a. 9 (especially for the distinction between the agent intellect and the possible intellect); *Quaestiones disputatae de anima*, q. 4 (on the need to posit the existence of the agent intellect); *De unitate intellectus contra Averroistas*, c. 4 (Leon. 43.309–10); SCG II, c. 73 (against the Averroistic theory of unicity of the possible intellect); c. 76 (on the presence of an individual agent intellect in each human being); c. 77 (for an excellent résumé of the relation between phantasms, agent intellect, and possible intellect in the process of abstraction).

50. See ST I, q. 86, a. 1. There, after denying that our intellect can directly and first know an individual material thing, Thomas writes: "Indirecte autem, et quasi per quandam reflexionem, potest cognoscere singulare . . ." (Leon. 5.347). See *De veritate*, q. 10, a. 5 for an earlier statement of his views concerning our intellectual knowledge of singulars. Note in particular: ". . . et sic mens singulare cognoscit per quandam reflexionem, prout scilicet mens cognoscendo obiectum suum, quod est aliqua natura universalis, redit in cognitionem sui actus, et ulterius in speciem quae est sui actus principium, et ulterius in phantasma a quo species est abstracta; et sic aliquam cognitionem de singulari accipit" (Leon. 22.2.309:73–81). For a much fuller discussion of this and for texts ranging throughout Thomas's career see G. P. Klubertanz, "St. Thomas and the Knowledge of the Singular," *New Scholasticism* 26 (1952), pp. 135–66. Also see F.-X. Putallaz, *Le sens de la réflexion chez Thomas d'Aquin* (Paris, 1991), pp. 118–23; and C. Bérubé, *La Connaissance de L'individuel au Moyen Âge* (Montreal, 1964), pp. 42–64.

51. This procedure would seem to be presupposed for any intellectual awareness on our part of something as real, whether or not we spell this out in so many words by saying "this thing exists."

or being, or whatever term one may use, meaning thereby "that which is." At this point one will have arrived at what I shall call a primitive (meaning thereby a pre-metaphysical) notion of being. One will not yet have reached a metaphysical understanding of being as being. For this another and distinctive kind of judgment will be required, which we shall take up in the final section of this chapter.[52]

Before we turn to this, reference should be made to certain difficulties which remain for interpreters of Thomas's thinking concerning this process whereby we arrive at a primitive understanding of being. First of all, among those who recognize the importance of judgments of existence, some have stressed the role of another internal sense, the cogitative power (vis cogitativa), sometimes also referred to by Thomas as the particular reason. Thus Maritain mentions this power in his account, and Krapiec makes it the center-piece of his description of judgments of existence. Unfortunately, however, the most important text cited by Krapiec in support of this interpretation need not and, in my opinion, should not be taken as assigning a special role to the cogitative power in our discovery of the existence of external objects.[53] While Thomas assigns a function to this power in accounting for our application of general principles to particular actions in practical affairs, that is a very different matter. Because of the immediacy involved in sense perception both at the level of the external senses and at the level of the common sense,

52. It is important to note that this resulting notion of being, "that which is," is complex, and that its complexity is accounted for by appealing to the contributions both of the intellect's first operation (to account for its quidditative side—"that which") and of judgment (to account for its existential aspect—"is"). Hence it should not be regarded as the product of either intellectual operation alone. Cf. G. Klubertanz, *Introduction to the Philosophy of Being* (New York, 1963), pp. 45–52. As I shall do here, he distinguishes between a primitive notion of being and the metaphysical understanding of being required for metaphysics.

53. For Maritain see *Existence and the Existent,* p, 27, n, 13. For Krapiec see his "Analysis formationis conceptus entis . . . ," pp. 331–36. He builds his case in large measure on a text taken from Thomas's Commentary on the *De anima,* Bk II, lect. 13. There, after discussing *per se sensibilia* including both common and proper sensibles, Thomas turns to Aristotle's reference to that which is *sensibile per accidens.* For something to be a *sensibile per accidens,* it must "happen" to that which is a *sensibile per se;* and it must still be apprehended by the sensing being through some other knowing power. If it is something universal, it can only be grasped by the intellect; and if knowledge of it occurs immediately with one's grasp of the *sensibile per se* to which it "happens," then it itself can be called a *sensibile per accidens* (see, for instance, my intellectual awareness that someone whom I see speaking is also living). If the *sensibile per accidens* is something individual, awareness of it is effected in human beings, says Thomas, by the cogitative power (or particular reason), in that it compares particular intentions. In brute animals this is known as the estimative power. He writes: ". . . nam cogitativa apprehendit individuum ut *existentem sub natura communi,* quod contingit ei in quantum unitur intellectivae in eodem subiecto, unde cognoscit hunc hominem prout est hic homo, et hoc lignum prout est hoc lignum" (Leon. 25.1.120–22; citation, p. 122:206; italics mine). Krapiec sees in the words "ut existens sub natura communi" an indication that Thomas assigns a special role to the cogitative power in our knowledge of existence. However, the point of these words is not to assign knowledge of existence as such to the cogitative power, but rather recognition of an individual as individual insofar as it falls under some common nature. On the cogitative power see Klubertanz, *The Discursive Power: Sources and Doctrine of the 'Vis Cogitativa' According to St. Thomas Aquinas* (St. Louis, 1952).

and because it is through the common sense that one is first aware that one is sensing, it seems to me that the contribution of the common sense should be emphasized in accounting for our original judgments of existence, that is, the kind required for us to discover being.[54]

Another difficulty has do to with the issue of priority. The process as I have spelled it out should be taken as implying that there is priority in the order of nature regarding the steps indicated. But when it comes to the intellect's apprehension of an object's quidditative content through the process of abstraction and its judgment that the thing in question actually exists, which is first in the order of time?

Thomas's reference to the one as "first" and the other as "second" might lead us to think that the intellect's first operation—its understanding of indivisibles—is prior to any judgment of existence in the order of time. Another view would hold, however, that these two intellectual operations are simultaneous, with the understanding of indivisibles depending on judgment in the order of formal causality, while judgment would depend on the understanding of indivisibles in the order of material causality.[55]

Though Thomas himself does not explicitly resolve this issue for us so far as I can determine, I am inclined to accept the latter suggestion. The two operations may indeed be simultaneous, but the understanding of indivisibles may be regarded as first in the order of nature from the standpoint of material causality; for it provides the subject for an existential judgment. Such a judgment, on the other hand, may be regarded as prior in terms of formal causality, though again only in the order of nature; for it grasps actual existence, which may be regarded as the actualization of the subject.

A final difficulty should be mentioned. Frequently Thomas refers to being *(ens)* as that which is first grasped or conceived by the intellect, and often enough he

---

54. Here I have in mind another distinction which Thomas makes, for instance in *De veritate*, q. 10, a. 5. We may arrive at knowledge of individuals in two different ways. On the one hand, one may consider the motion of the sensitive power insofar as it terminates in the mind or soul. Here, as already noted, Thomas accounts for this by a process of the mind's turning back to the phantasm produced by the imagination (see the texts cited above in n. 50). On the other hand, one may have in mind knowledge of the singular insofar as such knowledge proceeds from the mind to the sensitive part of the soul, and involves the application of some universal principle which the intellect already knows to a particular and practical situation, that is, to action. Here Thomas calls upon the cogitative power (or particular reason): ". . . universalem enim sententiam quam mens habet de operabilibus non est possibile applicari ad particularem actum nisi per aliquam potentiam mediam [the cogitative power] apprehendentem singulare . . ." (Leon. 22.2.309:90–94). Cf. Klubertanz, "St. Thomas and Knowledge of the Singular," pp. 150–51. Krapiec's text from the Commentary on the *De anima* is intended to account for the second—practical knowledge of the singular.

55. See Maritain, *Existence and the Existent*, p. 26; Owens, "Judgment and Truth in Aquinas," pp. 43–44. Perhaps I should comment here that I find little textual evidence in Aquinas to support Maritain's theory of an intuition of being either as developed in his *Existence and the Existent* or as presented in his later "Reflexions sur la nature blessée et sur l'intuition de l'être," *Revue thomiste* 68 (1968), pp. 5–40. Cf. Gilson's critique in his "Propos sur l'être et sa notion," in *San tommaso e il pensiero moderno*. Studi tomistici 3 (Vatican City, 1974), pp. 7–17.

cites Avicenna as his authority for this. Thus in the Prooemium to his very early *De ente et essentia* he writes that being *(ens)* and essence are first conceived by the intellect, as Avicenna says in Bk I of his *Metaphysics*.[56] In *De veritate* q. 1, a. 1 Thomas writes: "That which the intellect first conceives as most known and into which it resolves all of its conceptions is being, as Avicenna says in the beginning of his *Metaphysics*."[57] The same point reappears in other writings, sometimes with and sometimes without explicit reference to Avicenna.[58]

Moreover, on a number of occasions Thomas draws a parallel between that which is first grasped by the intellect in its apprehending role, i.e., being, and that which is first in the order of principles, i.e., the principle of noncontradiction.[59]

---

56. ". . . ens autem et essentia sunt quae primo intellectu concipiuntur, ut dicit Avicenna in principio suae Metaphysicae . . ." (Leon. 43.369:3–5). For the text from Avicenna see his *Liber de Philosophia prima sive Scientia divina I–IV,* S. Van Riet, ed. (Louvain-Leiden, 1977), tr. I, c. V, pp. 31–32: "Dicemus igitur quod res et ens et necesse talia sunt quod statim imprimuntur in anima prima impressione. . . ." Unlike his usual references to this, here Thomas speaks both of being *(ens)* and of essence as first conceived. One wonders why. First of all, this is consistent with the title and central purpose of this treatise, to develop the meaning of essence and *ens*. Secondly, in other texts, when accounting for the names "being" *(ens)* and "thing" *(res)*, Thomas notes that the first is assigned to something because of its *esse,* and the second because of its quiddity or essence (see, for instance, *De veritate,* q. 1, a. 1c [Leon. 22.1.5:136–139]; *In IV Met.,* ed. cit., lect. 2, p. 155, nn. 553, 558). In the citation from Avicenna, *ens* and *res* are both mentioned, along with *necesse*. This too may have influenced Thomas at this early point in his career.

57. ". . . illud autem quod primo intellectus concipit quasi notissimum et in quod conceptiones omnes resolvit est ens, ut Avicenna dicit in principio suae Metaphysicae" (Leon. 22.1.5:100–104).

58. See *In De Trinitate,* q. 1, a. 3, obj. 3: ". . . quia ens est illud quod primo cadit in cognitione humana, ut Avicenna dicit . . ." (Leon. 50.86:28–30). Thomas's reply indicates that he accepts this part of the objection, and adds a reference to unity: ". . . quamvis illa quae sunt prima in genere eorum quae intellectus abstrahit a phantasmatibus sint primo cognita a nobis, ut ens et unum . . ." (p. 88:174–177). Also see *In I Sent.,* d. 38, q. 1, a. 4, obj. 4: ". . . primum cadens in apprehensione intellectus est ens, ut Avicenna, tract. I *Metaphys.,* cap. vi, dicit . . ." (Mandonnet ed., Vol. 1, p. 905). Thomas replies: ". . . dicendum, quod quidquid cognoscitur, cognoscitur ut ens, vel in propria natura, vel in causa sua, vel in cognitione aliqua . . ." (p. 906). Cf. *De veritate,* q. 21, a. 1: "Cum autem ens sit id quod primo cadit in conceptione intellectus, ut Avicenna dicit. . . . Sic ergo supra ens, quod est prima conceptio intellectus . . ." (Leon. 22.3.593:144–157). See *De potentia,* q. 9, a. 7, ad 15, where Thomas makes the same point in showing how one moves from knowledge of being, to its negation, and then to division, and then to unity, and finally to multitude: "Primum enim quod in intellectum cadit, est ens" (Marietti ed., Vol. 2, p. 244); cf. ad 6 (p. 243). See *In I Met.,* lect. 2, p. 13, n. 46: "Sed dicendum, quod magis universalia secundum simplicem apprehensionem sunt primo nota, nam primo in intellectu cadit ens, ut Avicenna dicit. . . ." Also, ST I–II, q. 55, a. 4, ad 1: ". . . id quod primo cadit in intellectu, est ens: unde unicuique apprehenso a nobis attribuimus quod sit ens . . ." (Leon. 6.353). Also see ST I, q. 5, a. 2, where he supports his assertion that being is first in the intellect's conception by noting that each and every thing is knowable insofar as it is in act (Leon. 4.58). On this cf. Fabro, "The Transcendentality of *Ens-Esse* and the Ground of Metaphysics," *International Philosophical Quarterly* 6 (1966), pp. 407–8, 414; Régis, *Epistemology,* pp. 284–89.

59. For an early illustration of this see *In I Sent.,* d. 8, q. 1, a. 3: "Primum enim quod cadit in imaginatione intellectus, est ens, sine quo nihil potest apprehendi ab intellectu; sicut primum quod cadit in credulitate intellectus, sunt dignitates, et praecipue ista, contradictoria non esse simul vera . . ." (Mandonnet ed., Vol. 1, p. 200). Note that he writes this in order to explain how in the order of meanings *(intentiones)* being is prior even to names such as good, one, and true: "Cuius

Thus he writes in *Summa theologiae* I-II, q. 94, a. 2: "That which first falls under one's apprehension is being *(ens)*, an understanding of which is included in everything else one understands. Therefore the first indemonstrable principle is that 'one cannot simultaneously affirm and deny,' which is based on the notions of being and nonbeing. And upon this every other principle is grounded."[60]

One immediately wonders whether the kind of priority assigned by these texts to our grasp of being in the order of conceptions is to be taken as temporal. If so, does this not imply that we must grasp being intellectually before we can be intellectually aware of anything else, including the abstract quiddity of a material thing? And does not this in turn run counter to my suggestion that even our primitive understanding of being presupposes both simple apprehension (the understanding of indivisibles) and judgment, not merely simple apprehension alone?

I have already suggested that temporal priority need not be assigned either to simple apprehension or to judgment insofar as these two operations are involved in our primitive judgments of existence. Moreover, certain expressions which Thomas uses in referring to being as that which we first understand imply that even in these passages he does not necessarily have in mind temporal priority. For instance, in the text just mentioned from the *De veritate* he refers to being as that into which the intellect "resolves" all its conceptions. And in the text from ST I-II, q. 94, he explains that an understanding of being is included in everything else one may understand. These texts strongly point not to priority in the order of time but to priority in the order of resolution.[61]

For Thomas resolution is a technical expression which can be expressed in English as analysis. As he explains in his Commentary on the *De Trinitate*, q. 6, a. 1, according to this procedure one may move from knowledge of something to knowledge of something else which is implied by the first but not explicitly con-

---

ratio est, quia ens includitur in intellectu eorum, et non e converso." He sets up a similar parallel between propositions which must be "reduced" to principles which are *per se nota* and the order in which we seek to determine "what it is" about each thing in *De veritate*, q. 1, a. 1: ". . . sicut in demonstrabilibus oportet fieri reductionem in aliqua principia per se intellectui nota ita investigando quid est unumquodque, alias utrobique in infinitum iretur . . ." (Leon. 22.1.4:95–5:99). Then the passage cited in note 57 appears. For another clear presentation of this parallelism see *In IV Met.*, lect. 6, pp. 167–68, n. 605.

60. "Nam illud quod primo cadit in apprehensione, est ens, cuius intellectus includitur in omnibus quaecumque quis apprehendit. Et ideo primum principium indemonstrabile est quod *non est simul affirmare et negare*, quod fundatur supra rationem entis et non entis: et super hoc principio omnia alia fundantur . . ." (Leon. 7.169–170).

61. See the texts cited above in nn. 57 and 60. Confirmation for my suggested explanation may also be found in the text cited in n. 59 from *In I Sent.*, d. 8, q. 1, a. 3 and, for that matter, in Thomas's derivation of general and special modes of being in *De veritate*, q. 1, a. 1. Even when dealing with those characteristics or properties which are as broad in extension as being and really convertible with it, primacy is to be assigned to being insofar as it is implied in our understanding of the other transcendentals. A fortiori, being is implied in less extended concepts or in less extended modes of being, as is illustrated by the predicaments or categories. Cf. the important discussion in ST I, q. 5, a. 2 of being's conceptual priority to the good.

tained in it. And this can happen in terms of extrinsic causes *(secundum rem)* as when one reasons from effect to cause. It can happen in terms of intrinsic causes or forms *(secundum rationem)*, when one moves from the more particular to the more universal that is implied therein. Indeed, comments Thomas, the most universal are those things which pertain to all beings. Therefore the terminus of this kind of resolution *(secundum rationem)* is a consideration of being and those things that pertain to being as such. It is with this that divine science or metaphysics is concerned. Hence its consideration is most intellectual.[62]

In similar fashion, I would suggest, Thomas would have us apply this same kind of procedure to those texts in which he refers to being as that which is first in the order of our conceptions. This does not mean that we begin in the order of time with an explicit concept of being. It rather means that whatever it is we may conceive about a given object of our understanding, if we pursue our analysis far enough we will discover that the thing in question must enjoy being, either real being (whether actual or possible) or at least being in the intellect. Otherwise it could not be conceived at all.[63]

62. Thomas's discussion there is far more complicated than my brief summary may suggest. For a fuller discussion see my "'First Philosophy' According to Thomas Aquinas," in *Metaphysical Themes in Thomas Aquinas,* pp. 60–65. In brief, he is concerned with spelling out more fully the difference between the method of intellect *(versari intellectualiter)* and the method of reason *(rationabiliter procedere),* and wishes to correlate these respectively with metaphysics and physics. If rational consideration terminates in intellectual consideration according to the way of resolution (analysis), intellectual consideration serves as a principle for rational consideration according to the process of synthesis (composition). Reason, he notes, can move from knowledge of one thing to knowledge of another in the order of reality *(secundum rem),* as when there is demonstration in terms of extrinsic causes or effects. This will be by composition (synthesis) when one moves from causes to effects, and by analysis when one proceeds from effects to causes. But reason may move from knowledge of one to knowledge of another in the order of reason *(secundum rationem),* as when one proceeds in terms of intrinsic causes. This too may be by composition (synthesis), or by resolution (analysis): ". . . componendo quidem quando a formis maxime universalibus in magis particulata proceditur, resolvendo autem quando e converso, eo quod universalius est simplicius; maxime autem universalia sunt quae sunt communia omnibus entibus, et ideo terminus resolutionis in hac via ultimus est consideratio entis et eorum quae sunt entis in quantum huiusmodi" (Leon. 50.162:374–382). In order to make this final step to the discovery of being as being, however, a special procedure known as *separatio* will be required. See Section 2 of this Chapter. Cf. Régis, "Analyse et synthèse dans l'oeuvre de saint Thomas," in *Studia Mediaevalia in honorem admodum reverendi Patris Raymundi Josephi Martin* (Bruges, 1948), pp. 303–30; S. E. Dolan, "Resolution and Composition in Speculative and Practical Discourse," *Laval théologique et philosophique* 6 (1950), pp. 9–62; J. Doig, *Aquinas on Metaphysics,* pp. 64–76; J. A. Aertsen, "Method and Metaphysics: The *via resolutionis* in Thomas Aquinas," *New Scholasticism* 63 (1989), pp. 405–18; *Medieval Philosophy and the Transcendentals,* pp. 130–36.

63. As Aertsen phrases it: "Being is 'the first known.' But this 'first' becomes explicit, as the beginning of *De veritate* I, 1 makes clear, only on the basis of a resolution." See "Method and Metaphysics," p. 416. However, in his *Medieval Philosophy and the Transcendentals,* Aertsen argues, against "Existential Thomism," that being is grasped at the level of simple apprehension, and that if being signifies "what has being" or "what is," this does not entail a judgment (pp. 179–80). On this point our interpretations differ. Also see *In I Sent.,* d. 19, q. 5, a. 1, ad 5: ". . . de eo quod nullo modo est non potest aliquid enuntiari; ad minus enim oportet quod illud de quo aliquid enuntiatur, sit

Likewise, Thomas's references to being as that which is first in the order of that which we grasp through the intellect's first operation need not be taken as eliminating any role for judgment in our initial discovery of being as real or as existing. On the contrary, what one first discovers through original judgments of existence can be summed up, as it were, under the heading being, or reality, or something similar. Once the intellect makes this discovery, it expresses it in a complex concept or notion, as "that which is." This, I am suggesting, is what Thomas has in mind when he refers to being (ens) as that which is first known. Intellectual awareness of this presupposes both simple apprehension (the intellect's first operation) and judgment and, of course, sense experience.

2. Our Discovery of Being as Being

In the preceding section of this chapter we have attempted to reconstruct the process through which one must pass, according to Thomas's theory of knowledge, in arriving at a primitive or premetaphysical understanding of being. This notion of being is based on our original experience of material and changing beings. While its content is complex—"that which is"—this notion has not yet been freed from restriction to matter and motion. Hence it cannot be identified with our understanding of being as being—the subject of metaphysics.

This is so because, according to Aquinas, metaphysics deals with a special kind of object of theoretical knowledge, that is, the kind that does not depend on matter and motion in order to exist. We have seen him subdividing this kind of object into what we have called the positively immaterial (which cannot exist in matter), and the negatively or neutrally immaterial (which may or may not exist in matter). If the subject of metaphysics—being as being—is immaterial in the second way, that is, negatively or neutrally, how does Aquinas account for our discovery of this? In other words, how does one move beyond a primitive notion of being (as restricted to the material and mobile) to an understanding of being as being?[64]

In order to determine Thomas's answer to this, we shall return to q. 5, a. 3 of his Commentary on the De Trinitate. As we have already seen, there he introduces his discussion by indicating that we must note how the intellect can *abstract* in its operations. In developing this he appeals to the distinction between two intellec-

---

apprehensum; et ita habet aliquod esse ad minus in intellectu apprehendente . . ." (Mandonnet ed., Vol. 1, p. 489). For Thomas's understanding and divisions of the possible see my "Thomas Aquinas, Henry of Ghent, and Godfrey of Fontaines on the Reality of Nonexisting Possibles," in *Metaphysical Themes*, especially pp. 164–73, 189.

64. See our discussions above of q. 5, a. 1 and q. 5, a. 4 from Thomas's Commentary on the *De Trinitate* in Ch. I (pp. 8–9, 17). For some other interpreters of Thomas who also explicitly distinguish between a primitive notion of being and a metaphysical one see H. Renard, "What Is St. Thomas' Approach to Metaphysics?" *New Scholasticism* 30 (1956), p. 73; Krapiec, "Analysis formationis . . . ," pp. 341–44; Klubertanz, *Introduction to the Philosophy of Being*, 2d ed. (New York, 1963), pp. 45–52; R. W. Schmidt, "L'emploi de la séparation en métaphysique," pp. 377–80.

tual operations, one (the understanding of indivisibles) by which we know what something is, and another whereby the intellect composes and divides. While the first has to do with a thing's nature, the second is directed to its *esse*.[65]

As we have also seen, immediately after this Thomas comments that because truth in the intellect results from the fact that it is conformed to reality, in its second operation, that is, in judgment, the intellect cannot truthfully abstract things that are united in reality. In so abstracting (or judging negatively) one would signify that there is a corresponding separation with respect to the thing's *esse*. For instance, if I judge that this individual human being is not white, I state that there is such a separation in reality. If in fact in this given instance human being and whiteness are not separated, my judgment will be false. Therefore, in its second operation, that is, in judging, the intellect can truthfully abstract only things which are separated in reality.[66]

Unlike its second operation or judgment, however, Thomas indicates that through its first operation the intellect can abstract certain things which are not separated in reality.[67] It cannot do this in all cases, however, but only when the intelligibility of that which is abstracted does not depend upon that with which it is united in reality. Only in such instances can the former be abstracted from the latter, whether they are united as part and whole or as form and matter.[68] At this point Thomas introduces some new precisions. As he explains:

Accordingly, through its various operations the intellect distinguishes one thing from another in different ways. Through the operation by which it composes and divides, it distinguishes one thing from another by understanding that the one does not exist in the other. Through the operation, however, by which it understands what a thing is, it distinguishes one thing from another by knowing what one is without knowing anything of the other, either that it is united to it or separated from it. So this distinction is not properly called separation, but only the first. It is correctly called *abstraction*, but only when the things, one of which is known without the other, are one in reality.[69]

65. Cited above in nn. 2, 3, and 4.

66. See n. 13 above for the text. Also note: "Hac ergo operatione intellectus vere abstrahere non potest nisi ea quae sunt secundum rem separata, ut cum dicitur 'homo non est asinus'" (Leon. 50.147:115–118).

67. "Sed secundum primam operationem potest abstrahere ea quae secundum rem separata non sunt, non tamen omnia, sed aliqua" (Leon. 50.147:119–121).

68. Leon. 50.147:119–158. On this see Neumann, *Gegenstand und Methode*, pp. 79–81.

69. As translated by A. Maurer, *St. Thomas Aquinas: The Division and Methods of the Sciences*, 4th ed. (Toronto, 1963), p. 37 (italics mine). For the Latin see Leon. 50.148:159–171: "Sic ergo intellectus distinguit unum ab altero aliter et aliter secundum diversas operationes: quia secundum operationem qua componit et dividit distinguit unum ab alio per hoc quod intelligit unum alii non inesse, in operatione vero qua intelligit quid est unumquodque, distinguit unum ab alio dum intelligit quid est hoc, nihil intelligendo de alio, neque quod sit cum eo, neque quod sit ab eo separatum; unde ista distinctio non proprie habet nomen separationis, sed prima tantum. Haec autem distinctio recte dicitur abstractio, sed tunc tantum quando ea quorum unum sine altero intelligitur sunt simul secundum rem."

Significantly, in this text he substitutes the term "distinguishes" for the term "abstracts." This implies that until this point he has been using "abstract" in an extremely broad sense so as to apply to either way in which the intellect can distinguish. Now, however, he restricts "abstraction" to the way in which the intellect distinguishes through its first operation, that is, simple apprehension. He assigns another technical name to the distinguishing which is effected by the intellect through negative judgment, that is, "separation."

Thomas goes on to propose two subdivisions of abstraction when this is taken strictly in accord with the two modes of union he has already mentioned. Corresponding to the union of part and whole there is what he calls an abstraction of the whole, that is, of the universal from the particular. Corresponding to the union of form (the accidental form of quantity) and its appropriate matter (sensible matter) there is an abstraction of the form.[70] While Thomas's discussion of each of these is too detailed to be presented here, it will be enough for us to note that he correlates these, along with the negative judgment (separation), with his threefold division of the theoretical sciences. It should be stressed that he again refers to these as three ways in which the intellect *distinguishes* in its operations, not three ways in which it *abstracts*.

We conclude that there are three kinds of distinction in the operation of the intellect. There is one through the operation of the intellect joining and dividing which is properly called *separation;* and this belongs to divine science or metaphysics. There is another through the operation by which the quiddities of things are conceived which is the *abstraction* of form from sensible matter; and this belongs to mathematics. And there is a third through the same operation which is the *abstraction* of a universal from a particular; and this belongs to physics and to all the sciences in general, because science disregards accidental features and treats of necessary matters.[71]

Most important for our immediate purposes in this passage is Thomas's singling out of a negative judgment, separation, and his association of this with metaphysics. If he has described judgment as being directed towards a thing's *esse* at the very beginning of this article, he now seems to be thinking of a different kind of judgment. In his earlier reference to judgment and *esse* he seemed to have in mind a positive or affirmative judgment, and one which is best illustrated by judgments of existence when it comes to our discovery of being as real or as existing.[72] In the

---

70. Leon. 50.148:173–179. See pp. 148:180–149:248. Cf. Neumann, *Gegenstand und Methode*, pp. 82–85.

71. Maurer translation, pp. 33–34 (italics mine). For the Latin see Leon. 50.149:275–286: "Sic ergo in operatione intellectus triplex distinctio invenitur: una secundum operationem intellectus componentis et dividentis, quae separatio dicitur proprie, et haec competit scientiae divinae sive metaphysicae; alia secundum operationem qua formantur quidditates rerum, quae est abstractio formae a materia sensibili, et haec competit mathematicae; tertia, secundum eandem operationem, universalis a particulari, et haec competit etiam physicae et est communis omnibus scientiis, quia in omni scientia praetermittitur quod per accidens est et accipitur quod per se est."

72. See above in this chapter, Section 1, pp. 24–27.

present context, however, he is concentrating on negative judgments. This is not surprising, of course, since he now includes separation, along with two forms of abstraction in the strict sense, under the general heading of different ways in which the intellect distinguishes.[73]

If Thomas has now explicitly connected separation with metaphysics, and associated the two kinds of abstraction with the other theoretical sciences, one may wonder why. Just what does separation contribute to metaphysics or to our discovery of its subject? It would be considerably easier for us to answer this question if Thomas had devoted a full article to separation itself. Since he did not do so, we must base our interpretation on the few remarks he makes about it in q. 5, a. 3.

First of all, separation is a judging operation, whereby the intellect distinguishes one thing from another by noting that the one is not found in the other. In other words, it is a negative judgment. Secondly, Thomas also writes within this same article that when we are dealing with things which *can* exist in separation from one another, separation obtains rather than abstraction.[74] Thirdly, he remarks that substance, which he also refers to as the intelligible matter for quantity, can exist without quantity. Therefore to consider substance as such apart from quantity pertains to separation rather than to abstraction.[75]

This third point is especially important because in q. 5, a. 1 of this same Commentary, Thomas has included substance along with being *(ens)* as illustrations of that which is found in matter in certain instances but not in others, that is, of that which is negatively or neutrally immaterial. If it is through separation that one may consider substance as such rather than as quantified (or as material, we may add), so too it is through separation that one may consider being as such or as being rather than as quantified or as material. In sum, it is through separation that one discovers being as being, the subject of metaphysics. This follows both from the fact that Thomas cites substance and being as illustrations of that which is negatively or neutrally immaterial, to use our terminology, and because for Thomas, as for Aristotle, substance is the primary referent of being.[76]

73. See the texts cited above in nn. 69 and 71.

74. For these two points see the text cited above in note 69; and Leon. 50.149:256–258: "In his autem quae secundum esse possunt esse divisa magis habet locum separatio quam abstractio."

75. "Substantia autem, quae est materia intelligibilis quantitatis, potest esse sine quantitate; unde considerare substantiam sine quantitate magis pertinet ad genus separationis quam abstractionis" (Leon. 50.149:270–274).

76. For the text from q. 5, a. 1 see Leon. 50.138:154–160, cited above in Ch. I, n. 21. For the same point in q. 5, a. 4 see Leon. 50.154:182–198, cited above in Ch. I, n. 53. On substance as the primary referent for being see *Metaphysics* IV, c. 2 (1003b 5–19). For Thomas see *In IV Met.*, ed. cit., lect. 1, pp. 152–53, nn. 539–547, and for other texts, Ch. I, n. 62 above. Also see *In VII Met.*, lect. 1, pp. 316–18, nn. 1246–1269. This is not to deny, of course, that being *(ens)* applies intrinsically to the other nine predicaments as well, at least for Thomas (see *In VIII Met.*, lect. 1, pp. 402–3, n. 1682 [after text cited in Ch. I, n. 62]), or that being is broader in extension than substance (see for instance, *De veritate*, q. 1, a. 1).

This also at least suggests why Thomas associates separation with metaphysics and why he does not have recourse to abstraction taken in the strict sense in order to account for our discovery of being as being, the subject of this science. As we shall see in greater detail in the following chapter, for Aquinas being is not a genus, not even the most universal genus of all. In accounting for our discovery of being, therefore, and especially of being as being, the subject of metaphysics, it is important not to exclude anything from its range or scope.[77]

If this notion were reached by a process of abstraction taken in the strict sense, in formulating it one would have to abstract from various characteristics. For instance, one would abstract from existence itself, it would seem; and yet this must be retained in one's understanding of being as "that which is." Moreover, one would abstract from individuating differences, from specific differences, and apparently even from the differences which obtain between the supreme genera or predicaments. Yet all of these must be included in some way in one's understanding of being. Otherwise, they will be relegated to the realm of nonbeing.[78] And while one's abstracted concept of being would be the most general of all, it would also be the emptiest. By appealing to a positive judgment of existence in formulating one's primitive understanding of being, one includes existence within that notion. By appealing to separation in moving from such a primitive notion of being to a metaphysical understanding of being as being, one avoids the unhappy consequences just mentioned which would result if this were achieved only by a more refined kind of abstraction.[79]

To sum this up in other terms, for Thomas separation is the process through which one explicitly acknowledges and asserts that that by reason of which some-

77. This remark should be limited to *ens commune,* the subject of metaphysics. As we have already seen, Thomas does not include God under *ens commune.* Hence it also follows that God will not be included under the notion of being discovered through the separation involved in the discovery of being as being.

78. As we shall see in greater detail in the following chapter, Thomas attributes such reasoning to Parmenides *(In I Met.,* lect. 9, pp. 41–42, nn. 138–139). In brief, as Thomas sees it, Parmenides viewed being as if it were univocal: hence nothing can be added to it from within which might serve to diversify it; nor could anything be added to it from without, since outside being there is only nonbeing. If Thomas's theory of analogy of being will be an important part of his reply to Parmenides, separation as distinguished from abstraction seems to be required to reach an analogical understanding of being. See the helpful remarks by J.-D. Robert in his "La métaphysique, science distincte de toute autre discipline philosophique, selon saint Thomas d'Aquin," *Divus Thomas* (Piac.) 50 (1947), pp. 206–22, especially pp. 214–15 and n. 29. As he explains, the differences which contract being are still included within being according to Thomas, though in a confused way. But specific and individual differences are only potentially and not actually present in non-transcendental concepts. Robert refers the reader to *De veritate,* q. 1, a. 1.

79. Cf. Geiger, "Abstraction et séparation d'après Thomas *In de Trinitate,* q. 5, a. 3," *Revue des sciences philosophiques et théologiques* 31 (1947), p. 28. Note in particular: "Mais dire cela, c'est dire équivalemment que l'être ne peut être abstrait à proprement parler ni de la matière ni des réalités immatérielles, puisque tout cela est de l'être. Finalement c'est donc le caractère transcendental, et avec lui le caractère analogique propre aux données transcendentales qui exige le jugement de séparation. . . ."

thing is recognized as being need not be identified with that by reason of which it is recognized as enjoying a given kind of being, for instance, material being, or changing being, or living being. It may be described as a negative judgment in that through it one denies that that by which something is recognized as being is to be identified with that by reason of which it is a given kind of being. It may be described as separation because through this judgment one distinguishes two intelligibilities, and denies that one is to be identified with or reduced to the other. One distinguishes the intelligibility involved in one's understanding of being from all lesser and more restricted intelligibilities. Thus one negates or eliminates restriction of being to any given kind from one's understanding of being. One judges that being, in order to be realized as such, need not be material, or changing, or quantified, or living, or for that matter, spiritual.[80] Hence one establishes the negatively or neutrally immaterial character of being, and prepares to focus on being as such or as being rather than on being as restricted to this or that given kind.

Through separation one does not deny that beings of this or that kind also fall under being. On the contrary, by denying that being itself must be limited to any one of its actual or possible kinds, one opens the way for considering these, including the differences which are realized in each, within the realm of being, and as being. Even purely material beings can be studied not only insofar as they are material and changing as in physics, but simply insofar as they share in being. This kind of study, of course, will not take place in physics, but in metaphysics, the science of being as being.[81]

Before concluding this discussion, I should mention two points concerning separation which have been disputed by students of Aquinas. First of all, it has been pointed out that his fullest discussion of this appears in a relatively early work, and that his clearly drawn distinction in terminology between abstraction and separation disappears in his later writings. Does this not suggest that Thomas may have given up his earlier view of separation and that in the end he fell back upon abstraction in accounting for our discovery of being as being?[82]

---

80. See, for instance, Thomas's remark about substance in the text cited above in n. 75 as a good illustration of *separatio*.

81. For some additional texts in which Thomas singles out the metaphysician's way of viewing things see *In III Sent.*, d. 27, q. 2, a. 4. sol. 2: "... sicut *philosophia prima* est specialis scientia, quamvis consideret ens secundum quod est omnibus commune, quia specialem rationem entis considerat secundum quod non dependet a materia et motu" (Moos ed., Vol. 3, pp. 886–87); *In IV Met.*, lect. 1, pp. 150–51, n. 530: "Dicit autem 'secundum quod est ens', quia scientiae aliae, quae sunt de entibus particularibus, considerant quidem de ente, cum omnia subiecta scientiarum sint entia, non tamen considerant ens secundum quod ens, sed secundum quod est huiusmodi ens, scilicet vel numerus, vel linea, vel ignis, aut aliquid huiusmodi"; *In VI Met.*, lect. 1, p. 295, n. 1147: "De quolibet enim ente inquantum est ens, proprium est metaphysici considerare"; *In VI Met.*, lect. 1, p. 298, n. 1165: "Advertendum est autem, quod licet ad considerationem primae philosophiae pertineant ea quae sunt separata secundum esse et rationem a materia et motu, non tamen solum ea; sed etiam de sensibilibus, inquantum sunt entia, Philosophus perscrutatur."

82. Thomas was extremely careful in working out this distinction in q. 5, a. 3 of his Commentary

Secondly, in texts cited above from Thomas's Commentary on the *De Trinitate*, at times he writes that through separation we distinguish one thing from another by understanding that the one *need* not be united with the other. But on other occasions he writes that through this judgment we distinguish one thing from another by understanding that the one *is* not united with the other. To apply this to the present issue, in order to begin metaphysics is it enough for us to judge through separation that being, in order to be realized as such, need not be material? Or must we not first already know that in one or more instances being *is* not material?

As for the first point, a lengthy discussion in the *Summa theologiae* (I, q. 85, a. 1) might lead one to conclude that later on in his career Thomas abandoned his earlier views concerning separation. In replying there to the second objection against his contention that our intellect understands material and corporeal things by abstraction from phantasms, Thomas again reviews the kinds of abstraction associated with physics (abstraction from individual sensible matter) and with mathematics (abstraction of quantity from common sensible matter). Certain things, he comments, can be abstracted even from common intelligible matter, i.e., from substance insofar as it is subject to quantity. As illustrations he lists being *(ens)*, the one, potency and act, and other things of this kind. Such things, he adds, can also exist apart from matter, as happens with immaterial substances. Given this, one might maintain that Thomas is now appealing only to abstraction and not to separation in accounting for our knowledge of being as being.[83]

In reacting to this suggestion, one should not overlook Thomas's reply to the first objection in this same article. There he comments that abstraction may take place through the operation whereby the intellect composes and divides, as when we understand that one thing is not in another or that it is separated from it. Or abstraction may occur through that operation whereby the intellect simply understands one thing without understanding anything about another. This Thomas now describes as simple or absolute consideration, and is what we have frequently referred to as simple apprehension or as the understanding of indivisibles. As he had already indicated in his earlier discussion in his Commentary on the *De Trinitate* (q. 5, a. 3), here again he notes that falsity will result if one abstracts in the first

---

on the *De Trinitate*. This is evident not only from the final text itself, but from the fact that his autograph indicates that he began his response to q. 5, a. 3 several times. See Leon. 50.146 for a transcription of these reworkings. For his usage of the language of abstraction to cover negative judgment as well in an earlier redaction see Leon. 50.148, transcription from autograph for lines 159ff. in note: "patet ergo quod triplex est abstractio qua intellectus abstrait. prima quidem secundum operationem operationem (sic) secundam intellectus qua componit et dividit. et sic intellectum abstraere nichil est aliud <quam> hoc non esse in hoc." On the different redactions see Geiger, "Abstraction et séparation," pp. 15–20; Maurer, *St. Thomas Aquinas: The Division and Methods of the Sciences*, pp. xxv–xxvii.

83. Leon. 5.331. Note in particular: "Quaedam vero sunt quae possunt abstrahi etiam a materia intelligibili communi, sicut ens, unum, potentia et actus, et alia huiusmodi, quae etiam esse possunt absque omni materia, ut patet in substantiis immaterialibus."

way, that is, through judgment (composition and division) things which are not separated in reality. This is not necessarily so, however, when one does so in the other way, i.e., through simple apprehension.[84]

In sum, in this reply to the first objection we find the same doctrine as in q. 5, a. 3 of Thomas's Commentary on the *De Trinitate*. It is true that he no longer restricts the term "abstraction" to the process whereby the intellect distinguishes through simple apprehension. Now he uses it broadly so as to apply it in addition to the process whereby the intellect distinguishes by judging, that is, to negative judgments. Even so, he clearly continues to differentiate between these two ways in which the intellect distinguishes. Hence he can and does assume that we will keep this in mind as we read his reply to the second objection.

As we have seen, in his reply to that objection Thomas writes that being, unity, potency and act, etc., can be abstracted from common intelligible matter and that they can also exist apart from matter. He repeats a criticism of Plato which he had already raised in his Commentary on the *De Trinitate*. Plato's failure to differentiate between these two ways in which the intellect can abstract (that is, distinguish intellectually) led him to the mistaken view that every thing which can be abstracted, i.e., distinguished by the intellect, can also be separated in reality.[85] Thomas would have us recall that while this is true of that which the intellect distinguishes through negative judgment, it does not apply to all things which the intellect distinguishes through simple apprehension. If the earlier distinction in terminology between abstraction and separation has now disappeared, the doctrine remains the same. There are two very different ways in which the intellect can distinguish. It arrives at knowledge of being as being through a judging operation, a negative judgment, to be sure; and this is not to be reduced to the level of simple apprehension.[86]

As regards the second disputed point mentioned above, a number of contemporary interpreters of Aquinas insist that one cannot justify separation and thereby discover being as being without having already demonstrated that in at least one case being is realized apart from matter. In other words, one cannot establish the negatively immaterial character of being without already knowing that positively immaterial being exists. Some hold that one must have already demonstrated the

84. Ibid. See in particular: "Ad primum ergo dicendum quod abstrahere contingit dupliciter. Uno modo, per modum compositionis et divisionis; sicut cum intelligimus aliquid non esse in alio, vel esse separatum ab eo. Alio modo, per modum simplicis et absolutae considerationis; sicut cum intelligimus unum, nihil considerando de alio."

85. Ibid., end of reply to obj. 2: "Et quia Plato non consideravit quod dictum est de duplici modo abstractionis, omnia quae diximus abstrahi per intellectum, posuit abstracta esse secundum rem." For a similar criticism in his Commentary on the *De Trinitate* see q. 5, a. 3 (Leon. 50.149:287–290). There Thomas also charges Pythagoras with this same mistake.

86. To repeat a point already made, this becomes clear when one connects Thomas's discussion in replying to objection 2 in the text from ST I, q. 85, a. 1 with his reply to objection 1. Cf. Elders, *Faith and Science*, p. 109.

existence of the First Mover in physics (philosophy of nature). Others require, at the very least, prior knowledge of the spiritual character of the human soul. All of these writers agree that it is only because one already knows that in at least one instance being *is* realized apart from matter that one can validly judge that being in order to be realized as such *need* not be material.[87]

We shall see that certain texts in Thomas's writings, especially in his Commentary on the *Metaphysics,* might be taken as supporting such an interpretation. Other texts, however, suggest a different procedure. As will be recalled from our discussion of Thomas's views concerning the subject of metaphysics, at times he refers to this as *ens commune,* and at times as being as being. In his Commentary on the *De Trinitate* he has indicated that metaphysics treats both of things which are positively immaterial, to use our suggested terminology, and of those which are negatively or neutrally immaterial; but it does not do so in the same way.[88]

Thus in q. 5, a. 4 of that Commentary Thomas writes that philosophical theology (metaphysics) treats of those things which need not be found in matter (the negatively or neutrally immaterial) as its subject, and of that which cannot be found in matter (the positively immaterial illustrated here by divine things) only as the principles of its subject.[89] This should be connected with his earlier remark in that same context to this effect: if every science has a given subject-genus, it belongs to that science itself to study the principles of that subject-genus.[90] Since being as being is the subject of metaphysics, as he also indicates there, it will belong

---

87. See, for instance, A. Moreno, "The Nature of Metaphysics," *The Thomist* 30 (1966), p. 113: "Is the existence of immaterial beings an absolute necessity for metaphysics? If by metaphysics we mean a science specifically different from physics, then, their existence is absolutely necessary"; V. Smith, "The Prime Mover: Physical and Metaphysical Considerations," in *Proceedings of the American Catholic Philosophical Association* 28 (1954), pp. 78–94; *The General Science of Nature* (Milwaukee, 1958), p. 382 (who, while not emphasizing the role of separation, insists that prior knowledge of *immaterial* and *immobile* being [the Prime Mover] is required to establish the possibility of metaphysics); Geiger, "Abstraction et séparation," pp. 24–25 (prior knowledge of the immaterial activity of our intellect and hence of the intellect itself and of the soul is sufficient [and required] for separation and for one to begin metaphysics); Schmidt, "L'emploi de la séparation en mètaphysique," pp. 382–85; J. Weisheipl, "The Relationship of Medieval Natural Philosophy to Modern Science: The Contribution of Thomas Aquinas to Its Understanding," *Manuscripta* 20 (1976), pp. 194–96; also, see his review of my *Metaphysical Themes in Thomas Aquinas,* in *Review of Metaphysics* 38 (1985), pp. 699–700; L. J. Elders, *Faith and Science,* pp. 107–8; "St. Thomas Aquinas' Commentary on the 'Metaphysics' of Aristotle," *Divus Thomas* (Piac.) (1984), pp. 309–10, 312 (who appeals to a demonstration of the immateriality of the human soul as Thomas's justification for his discovery of common being); M. Jordan, *Ordering Wisdom: The Hierarchy of Philosophical Discourses in Aquinas* (Notre Dame, Ind., 1986), pp. 158–60.

88. See my discussions of q. 5, aa. 1 and 4 above in Ch. I (pp. 8–9, 17).

89. Leon. 50.154:199–201. Here we should recall Thomas's description of the negatively or neutrally immaterial: ". . . alio modo sic quod non sit de ratione eius quod sit in materia et motu . . ." (Leon. 50:154:190–191).

90. "Sciendum siquidem est quod quaecumque scientia considerat aliquod genus subiectum, oportet quod consideret principia illius generis, cum scientia non perficiatur nisi per cognitionem principiorum . . ." (Leon. 50.153:82–86).

to the metaphysician to investigate the principles or causes of the subject of that science, that is, of being as being. In no way does this text imply that prior knowledge of positively immaterial being is presupposed for the metaphysician to discover being as being, the subject of his science. On the contrary, it is rather assumed that the metaphysician will take this subject as given, presumably as discovered through the process of *separatio* as described in q. 5, a. 3 of this same Commentary. Only then will he be in position to inquire about the principles of that subject, that is, about divine things or the positively immaterial.[91]

This interpretation is confirmed by Thomas's much later discussion in the Prooemium to his Commentary on the *Metaphysics*. That these remarks appear in the Prooemium is significant since it seems clear enough that here, at least, Thomas is speaking in his own name. Whenever we turn to the body of the Commentary proper, since it is a literal commentary on Aristotle's text, we must constantly ask ourselves whether in explaining the Stagirite's thought, Thomas is also presenting his own. In the Prooemium, at least, he clearly seems to be. This is corroborated by the fact that Thomas's presentation here is in full accord with views he has developed in his Commentary on *De Trinitate*, q. 5, a. 4. One can be confident that Thomas has presented his personal position in that text because he has developed it not in his relatively brief literal exposition of the Boethian text, but in his much fuller and independent discussion through questions and articles.[92]

Reference has been made above to the general context for this discussion in the Prooemium.[93] Here it will be enough for us to concentrate on Thomas's explicit remarks about the subject of metaphysics. "That is the subject in a science whose causes and properties we investigate," he writes. The causes of the subject are not themselves to be identified with the subject of the science. Knowledge of such causes is rather the end or goal at which the science's investigation aims.[94]

Once again, therefore, Thomas's words do not suggest that he would have us presuppose prior knowledge of positively immaterial beings or separate substances

91. On being as being as the subject of this science see Leon. 50.154:161–162: ". . . quae habet subiectum ens in quantum est ens." Cf. the continuing discussion on p. 154.

92. On the problem of determining whether in his Commentary on the *Metaphysics* Thomas is simply presenting Aristotle's thought as he understands it, or whether he uses his Commentary to present his own views, or whether he proceeds in one way at times and in another on other occasions, see J. Doig, *Aquinas on Metaphysics*. For my review see *Speculum* 52 (1977), pp. 133–35. Also see L. Elders, "St. Thomas Aquinas' Commentary on the 'Metaphysics'," pp. 307–26, esp. pp. 324–26; J. Owens, "Aquinas as Aristotelian Commentator," pp. 213–38 (not restricted to Thomas's Commentary on the *Metaphysics*); and additional references cited in my Introduction above, nn. 17 and 18. That the position presented here is Thomas's personal view (1) is clear from the fact that it is in accord with that which he proposes in his Commentary on the *De Trinitate*, q. 5, a. 4, and (2) is also strongly indicated by the self-contained nature of the Prooemium itself. On the significance of the difference between the *expositio* and the *disputatio* in Thomas's Commentary on the *De Trinitate* see J. Aertsen, "Was heißt Metaphysik bei Thomas von Aquin?" in *Miscellanea Mediaevalia* 22.1 (Berlin–New York, 1994), pp. 218–19. For Thomas's *expositio* see Leon. 50.134–35.

93. See Ch. I above, pp. 19–21.

94. Ed. cit., p. 2, quoted above in Ch. I, n. 63.

(God and intelligences), as he here describes them, in order to justify separation or in order to begin metaphysics. On the contrary, it is only after one has discovered the subject of metaphysics—*ens commune*—that one is in a position to inquire about its causes or principles. Since these—separate substances—are the only positively immaterial beings mentioned either here or in the discussion in q. 5, a. 4 from the Commentary on the *De Trinitate,* no support can be found in either text for the claim that Thomas would have us begin with a knowledge of positively immaterial being in order to be enabled to discover being as being.

In confirmation of our interpretation we find Thomas repeating within this same Prooemium a point he had made in his earlier discussion in the *De Trinitate:* it belongs to one and the same science to consider the proper causes of a given genus (or subject) and that genus itself. Thus the natural philosopher considers the principles of natural body.[95] In like fashion, continues Thomas, it belongs to one and the same science to consider *ens commune* and to study separate substances; for *ens commune* is the "genus," that is, the subject of which separate substances are the general and universal causes.[96]

We may develop the analogy which Thomas has drawn between physics and metaphysics. Just as natural philosophy does not presuppose prior knowledge of the causes or principles of its subject (mobile being), neither does metaphysics. In each case knowledge of such principles can come only after one has discovered the subject of the science. Such knowledge is held out as the end or goal of that science's inquiry; it is not presupposed for knowledge of its subject.[97]

In the case of metaphysics, therefore, knowledge of its subject comes first. Only after one has discovered this is one in position to inquire about positively immaterial beings such as separate substances. In fact, in a telling addition to Aristotle's text, Thomas observes while commenting on Bk VI, c. 1 of the *Metaphysics* that even sensible things can be studied insofar as they are beings.[98] That is to say, even

95. Ed. cit., pp. 1–2, quoted above in Ch. I, n. 61.

96. Ibid., p. 2: "Unde oportet quod ad eamdem scientiam pertineat considerare substantias separatas, et ens commune, quod est genus, cuius sunt praedictae substantiae communes et universales causae."

97. Thomas holds that *ens mobile* is the subject of natural philosophy. That mobile being also is corporeal is something which must be shown in physics. See *In I Phys.,* lect. 1, P. M. Maggiòlo, ed. (Turin-Rome, 1954), pp. 3–4, n. 4. Here Thomas cites an underlying principle for his position: ". . . nulla autem scientia probat suum subiectum." However, the analogy he draws in the Prooemium to his Commentary on the *Metaphysics* between the physicist and the metaphysician holds. Each must be concerned with reaching knowledge of the principles of his science's subject-genus. Cf. p. 3, nn. 2–3 in this same context for another brief presentation of the threefold division of the theoretical sciences, and for the distinction between the negatively or neutrally immaterial and the positively immaterial.

98. *In VI Met.,* lect. 1, p. 298, n. 1165 (cited above in n. 81). His immediately following words also merit quotation: "Nisi forte dicamus, ut Avicenna dicit, quod huiusmodi communia de quibus haec scientia perscrutatur, dicuntur separata secundum esse, non quia semper sint sine materia; sed quia non de necessitate habent esse in materia, sicut mathematica."

sensible things can be studied in metaphysics, but only insofar as they are being, not insofar as they are mobile. The latter kind of study of sensible things is proper to physics. This text is interesting for two reasons. It seems to be an expression of Thomas's personal opinion, since he introduces it as a warning to the reader: "Advertendum est autem. . . ." Moreover, simply taken in itself, it does not imply that our investigation of sensible things in metaphysics, i.e., "insofar as they are beings," presupposes prior knowledge of positively immaterial being.

Nonetheless, this reading of Aquinas is rejected by a number of contemporary students of Aquinas. One may wonder why this is so. Two different lines of reasoning seem to converge here, one historical and one philosophical. Since I have devoted an extended discussion to this issue in another context,[99] here I shall briefly summarize and then react to the historical and philosophical evidence which has been offered to support the claim that according to Aquinas, one must have already demonstrated the existence of positively immaterial being in a prior science if one is to discover being as being, the subject of metaphysics.

Much of the historical evidence for this interpretation is drawn from various passages in Thomas's Commentary on the *Metaphysics*. One of the best presentations for this case has been offered by Geiger. Some of the texts he cites are more to the point than others. In fact, one taken from Thomas's Commentary on Bk I of the *Metaphysics* has nothing to do with separation or with our discovery of being, even though it does suggest that Thomas thinks we can demonstrate the existence of some incorporeal reality according to Aristotle's procedure in the *De anima*.[100]

More interesting is a text taken from Thomas's Commentary on *Metaphysics* IV, lect. 5. There Thomas finds Aristotle criticizing the ancient physicists for having busied themselves with an examination of first principles in the order of demonstration. This is understandable, Thomas comments, in light of their view that only corporeal and mobile substance exists. Because of this they thought that they were treating of the whole of nature and therefore of being along with the first principles which follow from being. Against this Thomas counters that they were mistaken, since there is another science which is superior to natural science; for nature is only one class within the totality of being. Not all being is of this kind, he continues (in what appears to be a negative judgment, separation), since it has been proven in *Physics* VIII that there is an immobile being. This being is superior to and nobler than mobile being, which the physicist studies. "And because the consideration of *ens commune* pertains to that science to which it belongs to con-

99. See *Metaphysical Themes in Thomas Aquinas,* c. IV, especially pp. 82–104.

100. See Geiger, "Abstraction et séparation d'après S. Thomas," pp. 24–25, citing *In I Met.,* lect. 12, p. 55, n. 181: "Quia in rebus non solum sunt corporea, sed etiam quaedam incorporea, ut patet ex libro *de Anima.*" Thomas's purpose here is simply to develop and support Aristotle's criticism of the early natural philosophers who reduced everything to one material cause. It is not his purpose here to justify the existence of metaphysics.

sider the First Being, therefore the consideration of *ens commune* also belongs to a science different from natural philosophy."[101]

From this text one might conclude with Geiger that Thomas justifies separation by appealing to the fact that immobile being exists. The existence of metaphysics or the science which studies *ens commune* seems to rest on (1) Thomas's appeal to the demonstration of the existence of immobile being in the *Physics* and (2) his identification of the science which studies *ens commune* with the science which studies the First Being.[102]

Certain arguments may be offered against this interpretation. First of all, the situation in Aristotle's text in the *Metaphysics* is dialectical. There he criticizes the earlier natural philosophers for having restricted reality to the material. Thomas repeats this criticism and in expanding upon Aristotle's text cites a counterfact, the existence of immobile being. This is a perfectly natural reaction, given the immediate context. In developing Aristotle's criticism of the natural philosophers for this restriction and for having identified their science as the highest, he also adds to Aristotle's text the passage just quoted above.[103]

In that passage Thomas identifies the science which studies *ens commune* with the science which studies the First Being. This reflects his understanding of Aristotle's position and, as we have seen, is also a key to his personal resolution of the Aristotelian *aporia* concerning the identity of the science which studies being as such with the science which studies divine being. Even though Thomas seems to move from this identity and from a demonstration in physics of immobile being to the existence of a higher science (metaphysics), there is no indication here that this is the way he would have us proceed in the order of discovery. His purpose is rather to interpret Aristotle's text and to justify Aristotle's claim that the examination of first principles in the order of demonstration does not belong to physics.[104]

Secondly, such an interpretation would run counter to everything we have seen in Thomas's more personal discussions in his Commentary on the *De Trinitate* and in the Prooemium to his Commentary on the *Metaphysics*. Now he would have us first demonstrate the existence of an immobile or first mover in physics and then, because it is identical with the First Being studied in metaphysics, move on to the discovery of the subject of that science through separation. If such were Thomas's recommended procedure, knowledge of such a being would no longer be held out as the end or goal of metaphysical investigation but would be presupposed by it.

101. Ed. cit., p. 164, n. 593. Note in particular: "Non enim omne ens est huiusmodi: cum probatum sit in octavo *Physicorum,* esse aliquod ens immobile. . . . Et quia ad illam scientiam pertinet consideratio entis communis, ad quam pertinet consideratio entis primi, ideo ad aliam scientiam quam ad naturalem pertinet consideratio entis communis. . . ."

102. On this text see Geiger, "Abstraction et séparation," pp. 24–25. Cf. Jordan, *Ordering Wisdom,* p. 160, who cites this text in the course of supporting Geiger's interpretation against my own.

103. For this in Aristotle see *Metaphysics* IV, c. 3 (1005a 31–1005b 1).

104. For Thomas's resolution of the Aristotelian *aporia* see above, Ch. I, Section 2.

Moreover, Thomas's distinction between considering something directly as the subject of a science and considering it only indirectly as a cause or principle of that subject would seem to be endangered. If prior knowledge of separate entity is presupposed for us to discover being as being, the subject of metaphysics, then why not make separate entity itself the subject of this science? This, of course, Thomas has refused to do. Given these considerations, therefore, it seems to me that in this part of his Commentary we have Thomas's explanation of Aristotle's text but not Thomas's personal view concerning the conditions of possibility for the judgment of separation or for the discovery of being as being.[105]

A seemingly more compelling text appears in Thomas's Commentary on the concluding lines of *Metaphysics* VI, c. 1. Here Thomas repeats the question raised by Aristotle himself concerning whether first philosophy studies being taken universally or only some particular genus and nature, that is, the divine.[106] In commenting on Aristotle's reply to this Thomas does little more than repeat the Stagirite's text. If there is no substance apart from those which exist by nature, with which physics deals, physics will be the first science. But if there is some immobile substance, this will be prior to natural substance. Consequently, the philosophy which studies this kind of substance will be first philosophy. Because it is first it will be universal, and it will study being as being. Thomas's concluding remark is not found in Aristotle's text: ". . . for the science of the First Being and the science of *ens commune* are one and the same, as has been indicated at the beginning of Bk IV."[107]

---

105. It is also in this way that I would interpret an interesting remark made by Thomas in SCG I, c. 12, about the order of the sciences. There he is offering a series of brief arguments against the claim that God's existence cannot be demonstrated by reason. Thomas counters that the falsity of this claim can be shown from (1) the art of demonstration which teaches one to reason from effects to causes; (2) ". . . ex ipso scientiarum ordine. Nam, si non sit aliqua scibilis substantia supra substantiam sensibilem, non erit aliqua scientia supra Naturalem, ut dicitur in IV *Metaph.*" (perhaps a reference to *Metaphysics* IV, c. 3, that is, to our passage in Aristotle, as the editors suggest, but certainly not literal); (3) the efforts of the philosophers to demonstrate that God exists; (4) Romans 1:20. (See ed. cit., p. 10.) The last two arguments are clearly based on authority and so, I would suggest, is the second. Moreover, Thomas's purpose here is not to explain the way in which we discover being as being, but to offer some dialectical argumentation and some authorities against those who deny that God's existence can be demonstrated. His philosophical demonstration of his position is yet to come, with his formal presentation of arguments to prove that God exists (in c. 13 and in c. 15, *Amplius*).

106. See *Metaphysics* VI, c. 1 (1026a 23–32). For discussion see Ch. I above, pp. 12–13.

107. See *In VI Met.*, lect. 1, p. 298, n. 1170. Thomas begins by referring to Aristotle: "Secundo solvit. . . ." Note in particular: "Sed, si est aliqua substantia immobilis, ista erit prior substantia naturali; et per consequens philosophia considerans huiusmodi substantiam, erit philosophia prima. Et quia est prima, ideo erit universalis, et erit eius speculari de ente inquantum est ens . . . eadem enim est scientia primi entis et entis communis, ut in principio quarti habitum est." Cf. *In IV Met.*, lect. 1, p. 151, n. 533. There Thomas comments that in this science we are seeking for the principles of being insofar as it is being. Therefore, he continues, being is the subject of this science because every science seeks after the proper causes of its subject. This passage argues for the identity of the

In commenting on the parallel passage from *Metaphysics* XI Thomas adds another remark to his repetition of Aristotle's text: "For the First Beings are the principles of the others." This remark also explains his addition to the text from *Metaphysics* VI. His point seems to be that in studying the First Beings one studies the principles or causes of everything else. Therefore one studies everything else. One should not conclude from this, however, that Thomas himself accepts this position or holds that the First Beings constitute the subject of metaphysics. This would be to impose upon him the Averroistic solution for the Aristotelian *aporia* about the identity of divine science and the science of being as being.[108]

These texts from Thomas's Commentary on *Metaphysics* VI and XI are obviously important for our immediate discussion. If they do reflect his personal position, it will follow that for him the existence of the science of being as being is contingent upon our prior knowledge of the existence of separate entity.[109]

As already indicated, it is very difficult to reconcile this procedure with that implied by Thomas's more independent discussions of the subject of metaphysics. In those contexts knowledge of God or of separate entity is not presupposed for knowledge of being as being or the subject of metaphysics; it is rather proposed as the end or goal of the metaphysician's investigation. Moreover, there can be no question of thinking that Thomas ever made God or separate entity the subject of metaphysics. This can only be being as being or being in general *(ens commune)*.[110]

---

science which seeks after the first and highest principles (hence the first being) and the science of being as being. It does not imply that one must discover the first before the second. On the contrary, just the opposite procedure seems to be indicated. Cf. my remarks about this passage in *Metaphysical Themes*, p. 89.

108. See *In XI Met.*, lect. 7, p. 536, n. 2267. In this text he follows Aristotle's text very closely in writing that if natural substances, which are sensible and mobile substances, are the first among beings, natural science will be first among the sciences. To this he adds: "quia secundum ordinem subiectorum, est ordo scientiarum, ut iam dictum est." In doing so he faithfully interprets Aristotle's reasoning both here and in the corresponding passage in *Metaphysics* VI, c. 1. In these passages, Aristotle's approach is certainly object oriented. Thomas goes on to repeat Aristotle to this effect: "Si autem est alia natura et substantia praeter substantias naturales, quae sit separabilis et immobilis, necesse est alteram scientiam ipsius esse, quae sit prior naturali. Et ex eo quod est prima, oportet quod sit universalis." Then he makes the two additions to Aristotle's text: "Eadem enim est scientia quae est de primis entibus, et quae est universalis. Nam prima entia sunt principia aliorum."

109. For such an interpretation of these passages see Moreno, "The Nature of Metaphysics," pp. 113–15; T. O'Brien, *Metaphysics and the Existence of God* (Washington, D.C., 1960), p. 160 (citing *In VI Met.*, n. 1170); Doig, *Aquinas on Metaphysics*, p. 243, n. 1; p. 303, n. 1; Weisheipl, "The Relationship of Medieval Natural Philosophy to Modern Science," pp. 194–96. Another such passage is found in *In III Met.*, lect. 6, p. 112, n. 398, where Thomas is explaining how Aristotle can assign the study of all substances insofar as they are substance to one science, the science of being as being. After noting that the first substances are immaterial, he comments that a consideration of these belongs properly to the first philosopher, and then refers to *Metaphysics* VI, c. 1: "Sicut si non essent aliae substantiae priores substantiis mobilibus corporalibus, scientia naturalis esset philosophia prima, ut dicitur infra in sexto." While this is his understanding of Aristotle's position in *Metaphysics* VI, c. 1, it does not necessarily follow that it is Thomas's personal position.

110. See above in Ch. I, Section 2, pp. 17–21. Cf. J. Owens, "Metaphysical Separation in Aquinas," pp. 288–91, on the different views of the subject of metaphysics in the Prooemium to Thomas's

Given this, I would offer the same interpretation of Thomas's Commentary on the indicated passages from *Metaphysics* VI and XI as I have for the text from his Commentary on *Metaphysics* IV. In each of these cases we have Thomas's explanation of Aristotle's text, but not Thomas's personal position concerning the conditions of possibility for separation and hence for the discovery of the subject of metaphysics.

It should also be noted, if only in passing, that in none of these texts is there any suggestion that one must have prior knowledge of the spiritual character of the human soul in order to discover being as being. Some writers would require this rather than prior knowledge of separate entity in order to justify separation.[111] But the passages we have just examined from Thomas's Commentary on the *Metaphysics* rather refer to immobile being, meaning thereby the first mover of the *Physics*. It is this which is identified with the First Being studied by first philosophy and hence by metaphysics.[112] So far as Thomas's view is concerned, therefore, if these passages do indeed reflect his personal position, prior knowledge of separate and immobile entity will be required to enable one to discover being as being. Knowledge of the soul's spirituality will not suffice.

In rejecting such passages as expressions of Thomas's personal thought, I do not wish to deny that when he considers the pedagogical issue about the order in which young students should study the various sciences, he recommends that one introduce them to philosophy of nature before attempting to teach them metaphysics. In brief he proposes this sequence: logic, mathematics, natural philosophy, moral philosophy, and finally, metaphysics. In these discussions, however, he is not concerned with the conditions of possibility for metaphysics or for the other sciences but with the gradually developing capacity of young students to learn these different disciplines. Hence such texts can hardly be used to settle the issue now under consideration.[113]

In addition to the historical question, another line of reasoning seems to influ-

---

Commentary on the *Metaphysics* and in his Commentary on the passages in question. On the other hand, J.F.X. Knasas seems to think that for Thomas one may begin metaphysics after discovering being *(ens)* as *habens esse* (apparently what I have described as a primitive notion of being). Then, while practicing metaphysics, one would demonstrate the existence of separate substance and only then discover *ens commune*. See *The Preface to Thomistic Metaphysics* (New York, 1990), pp. 95–113. This approach fails to do justice to Thomas's understanding of the subject of a science, knowledge of which is required for one to begin the science. It also contradicts a principle Thomas accepts from Aristotle to the effect that no science can establish the existence of its own subject.

111. See for instance, Geiger and Elders as cited above in n. 87.

112. See the texts from Thomas's Commentary on *Met*. IV, n. 593; *Met*. VI, n. 1170; and *Met*. XI, n. 2267; cited above in nn. 101, 107, and 108. The last-mentioned passage requires not only a substance which is immobile but one which is *separabilis*. For a discussion of the related but contested point concerning whether for Thomas the First Mover of *Physics* VIII is God, see A. Pegis, "St. Thomas and the Coherence of the Aristotelian Theology," *Mediaeval Studies* 35 (1973), pp. 67–117; J. Paulus, "La théorie du Premier Moteur chez Aristote," *Revue de philosophie*, n.s. 4 (1933), pp. 259–94, 394–424; J. Owens, "Aquinas and the Proof from the 'Physics'," *Mediaeval Studies* 28 (1966), pp. 119–50. Pegis defends this identity, in disagreement with Paulus and Owens.

113. See *Sententia libri Ethicorum* VI, 7 (Leon. 47.2.358:178–359:213); *Sancti Thomae de Aquino*

ence many of those who would rest the possibility of metaphysics on prior knowledge of positively immaterial being. For them it is a necessary philosophical position. As they see it, prior knowledge of the existence of immaterial beings must be presupposed if one is to begin metaphysics. As one recent writer has put it in a generally positive review of an earlier study of mine: "But one may legitimately ask whether mere *possibility* is sufficient to ground the new science of metaphysics? Whence comes this judgment of separability? It is easier to prove the fact of one separated being than to prove its possibility."[114]

Here we have a legitimate difference in philosophical positions. In defending my own interpretation, I would recall certain points. First of all, we are interested in arriving at an understanding of being as being which may serve as the subject of a science of being as being rather than of being as material and changing. Secondly, according to Thomas himself, it is quite possible for us to study material being in metaphysics, not insofar as it is material or mobile, however, but simply insofar as it is being. When it is so viewed it enjoys the negative or neutral kind of immateriality Thomas associates with the subject of metaphysics. Thirdly, in referring to separation in his Commentary on the *De Trinitate*, at times Thomas indicates that what is discovered thereby is without matter and motion. At times he writes that it can be without matter and motion. It is the latter kind of immateriality which he assigns to being as being, the subject of metaphysics.

I would ask the reader evaluating my approach to distinguish two questions and, corresponding to this, two kinds of intelligibilities. One question searches for that by reason of which something is recognized as real or as sharing in being. Another seeks after that by reason of which something enjoys a given kind of being.

Super Librum de causis expositio, H. D. Saffrey, ed. (Fribourg-Louvain, 1954), p. 2. On this see G. Klubertanz, "St. Thomas on Learning Metaphysics," *Gregorianum* 35 (1954), pp. 3–17. Cf. his "The Teaching of Thomistic Metaphysics," *Gregorianum* 35 (1954), pp. 187–205. One might also cite certain texts where Thomas discusses the interrelationship between metaphysics and other speculative sciences. See, for instance, q. 5, a. 1, ad 9 from his Commentary on the *De Trinitate,* where he again suggests that metaphysics should be learned after the natural sciences and after mathematics. He notes that it uses certain things which are explained in natural science such as generation, corruption, motion, etc. As I have indicated in other contexts, in this discussion Thomas is heavily influenced by Avicenna. But what he does not say here is that metaphysics depends on physics (or on mathematics) for knowledge of its subject, being as being. Here too he explains how metaphysics contributes certain things to the other sciences (by proving their principles), and yet borrows certain things from them. See Leon. 50.141:347–381. For discussion see my *Metaphysical Themes,* pp. 97–102, as well as c. II, passim.

114. See Weisheipl's review of my *Metaphysical Themes* as cited above in n. 87. He seems to share this conviction along with all the other authors mentioned in that same note, that is, that their interpretation is also necessary on philosophical grounds. For some more recent discussions which defend on historical grounds the same approach I have presented here see M.-V. Leroy's review of my *Metaphysical Themes in Thomas Aquinas* in the *Revue thomiste,* n.s. 4 (1984), pp. 667–68; Aertsen, "Was heißt Metaphysik . . . ?" pp. 232–33; *Medieval Philosophy and the Transcendentals,* pp. 128–29. Also see Leroy's early discussion of this, "*Abstractio* et *separatio* d'après un texte controversé de saint Thomas," *Revue thomiste* 48 (1948), pp. 328–39, which, he indicates in his review, is in fundamental agreement with the position I am presenting.

If these are two different questions, it seems that one is justified in offering two different answers for them. That intelligible content in a thing by reason of which it is recognized as enjoying reality or being should be distinguished from that intelligible content by reason of which it is recognized as enjoying this or that kind of being. To be material, or living, or mobile is to enjoy a given kind of being, it would seem. Without presupposing that there is any being which is not living and material and mobile, we can still ask why any thing which we experience enjoys being. To ask this is very different from asking what kind of being it enjoys. If these two questions are not identical, it follows that the answer to the one does not have to be identified with the answer to the other. That by reason of which something is recognized as enjoying being need not be identified with that by reason of which it enjoys this or that kind of being. Therefore, we may investigate one and the same physical and changing thing from different perspectives. We may study it insofar as it is material and mobile, or insofar as it is living, or insofar as it is quantified. But we may also study it insofar as it enjoys reality at all, i.e., insofar as it is a being.

An objection might be raised: Is this not to make metaphysics a science of the merely possible? Not at all. To examine something from the standpoint of being is to continue to apply to it the intelligible content contained in our primitive understanding of being as "that which is." As a result of separation we continue to recognize whatever we study in metaphysics as enjoying being, or as an instance of "that which is." We do not abstract from this inclusion of existence in our primitive understanding of being when we apply separation to it. We rather judge that the intelligible content in virtue of which we recognize any thing as a being ("that which is") is not to be restricted to or identified with that intelligible content by which we recognize it as being of this or that kind. Otherwise being could only be one in kind.

At this point I should emphasize that it is not Thomas's distinction and composition of essence and an intrinsic existence principle (act of being) which is discovered through separation. Through separation one simply recognizes the legitimacy of investigating any given thing in terms of its reality or as a being ("that which is") rather than from any other perspective. Investigation of the relationship between essence and existence (esse) can only come later in the order of discovery, and presupposes that one has already discovered being as being.

In concluding this chapter I should add that I do not wish to exclude the possibility that one might proceed in a different way. If one has succeeded in demonstrating the existence of some positively immaterial being in physics, well and good.[115] Then it may be easier for such a person to formulate the negative judgment with

---

115. On this point, Klubertanz takes a very strong position. As he sees it, it is not possible for one to base one's knowledge of being as being on a prior demonstration of the existence of immaterial entity. "Either 'is' is freed from its sensible and changing context (prior to the proof of the existence of immaterial being, and thus is meaningful when we conclude to the existence of such being) or 'is' remains as we first find it immersed in sensibility and change. In the latter case, 'is' means 'is sensible,

respect to being and to conclude that being may be considered not merely as mobile but as being, although in a new and different science. In my opinion, however, such an approach is not required for one to discover being as being through separation and hence to begin metaphysics. And if I may conclude by returning to the historical issue, while such a procedure may have been attributed by Thomas to Aristotle in certain passages, this is simply because in those particular passages Thomas was interpreting Aristotle's texts as best he could. They do not express Thomas's personal approach to discovering being as being.

---

material and changeable', and to assert that 'An *immaterial, immobile* thing is *sensible, material* and *changeable'* is a contradiction" *(Introduction to the Philosophy of Being,* p. 52, n. 28). I would not go quite so far. But I am in full agreement with Klubertanz that such a demonstration is not required for us to speak meaningfully of being as being or to discover the subject of metaphysics.

PART ONE

Aquinas and the Problem of the One and the Many in the Order of Being

III The Problem of Parmenides and
Analogy of Being

As we have now seen in some detail, according to Aquinas metaphysics has as its subject being as being or, as he also puts it, *ens commune.* In Ch. II considerable attention has been directed to his account of the way in which we arrive at knowledge of being as real and then of being as being or of *ens commune.* Now we must take up a problem with which Thomas himself had to come to terms—the seemingly conflicting claims of unity and of multiplicity (and hence of diversity) within being itself.

This problem can be raised at two different levels, but two levels which are closely interconnected. Thus one may ask: What is the nature of a notion or concept which can in some way express both the unity and the diversity which Aquinas assigns to being in general *(ens commune)*? As we shall see, Thomas's answer to this is developed in terms of his theory of analogy of being. But one can also raise this issue at the level of individual beings themselves: How can there be many such beings, given the unity of being as indicated by the fact that each of them shares in being? Thomas's answer to this is complicated, but will include his theory of the participation of beings in being *(esse)*, the composition of essence and *esse* (act of being) which he finds in every participating being, and his defense of the reality of nonbeing in a qualified sense—relative nonbeing, as I shall describe it.

While subsequent chapters will be devoted to each of these issues, in the present chapter we shall first consider the Parmenidean dilemma concerning unity vs. multiplicity of being insofar as this was known to Aquinas. The concluding section of this chapter will be directed to Thomas's answer at the level of our concept or notion of being, that is to say, his theory of analogy of being.

1. The Problem of Parmenides as Formulated by Aquinas

Thomas was primarily dependent on Aristotle for his knowledge of Parmenides and other Pre-Socratic philosophers. He mentions Parmenides by name on a number of occasions, and most frequently in his commentaries on Aristotle. A brief reference in his Commentary on *Metaphysics* XII, lect. 12, is worth noting. There Thomas is explaining a remark in Aristotle's text to the effect that none of the ancient philosophers offered a cause to explain why some beings are corruptible while others are incorruptible.[1]

Some held that all things derive from the same principles, that is, the contraries. Aquinas identifies these as the ancient naturalists. Others maintained that all things derive from nonbeing. Thomas refers to these as the poet-theologians. But since both groups offered the same explanation for all things, they could not account for the distinction between the corruptible and the incorruptible.[2] Finally, continues Thomas, still others maintained that all things are one. They did this in order to avoid either having to hold that all things derive from nonbeing or having to account for the distinction between things. But by so doing they completely eliminated distinction from things, concludes Thomas. He identifies these thinkers as Parmenides and Melissus.[3]

Thomas has considerably more to say about the positions of Melissus and especially of Parmenides earlier on in this same Commentary on the *Metaphysics,* and also discusses their respective views in his Commentary on *Physics* I. Before taking up these texts, however, we should note his reference to the role of nonbeing in accounting for division and hence for multiplicity in a much earlier source, that is, q. 4, a. 1 from his Commentary on the *De Trinitate.* There he is developing a remark made by Boethius to this effect that otherness is the cause of plurality.[4]

Thomas observes that, as Aristotle states in *Metaphysics* X, something is said to be plural (or many) by reason of the fact that it is divisible or divided. If we wish to account for multiplicity, we must turn back to the cause or explanation of division.[5] But the cause of division is not the same in posterior and composite things, on the one hand, and in those which are first and simple, on the other. Thus the

---

1. For Aristotle see *Metaphysics* XII, c. 10 (1075b 13–16). For Thomas see *In XII Met.*, lect. 12, pp. 614–15, n. 2651.

2. See p. 615, n. 2651.

3. "Et ideo alii, ut ad hoc non cogantur, quod scilicet ponant omnia esse ex non ente, vel quod assignent causam distinctionis rerum, posuerunt omnia esse unum, totaliter a rebus distinctionem tollentes: et haec est opinio Parmenidis et Melissi" (ibid.).

4. For this in Boethius see *The Theological Tractates. . . . The Consolation of Philosophy,* ed. cit., c. 1, p. 6: "Principium enim pluralitatis alteritas est; praeter alteritatem enim nec pluralitas quid sit intelligi potest."

5. Leon. 50.120:68–72: "Dicendum, quod sicut dicit Philosophus in X Metaphysicae, plurale dicitur aliquid ex hoc quod est divisibile vel divisum; unde omne illud quod est causa divisionis oportet ponere causam pluralitatis." For Aristotle see *Metaphysics* X, c. 3 (1054a 22–23).

cause (which Thomas identifies as a quasi-formal cause) for the division of things which are posterior and composite is the diversity of that which is simple and prior (or first, depending on one's reading of an ambiguous abbreviation in Thomas's autograph). In illustration he offers two examples, one taken from the order of the accidental, and the other from the order of substances. One part of a line is divided from another part of the same line by reason of the fact that it enjoys a different location *(situs)*. This is the quasi-formal difference of continuous quantity which enjoys position. So too, in the case of substances, a human being is divided from a donkey by reason of the fact that the two have different constituting differences.[6]

This diversity whereby posterior and composite things are divided by reason of prior and simple things itself presupposes a plurality of things which are first (or prior) and simple. Thus human being and donkey enjoy diverse constituting differences precisely because the rational and the irrational are not one but many. As Thomas immediately recognizes, one cannot indefinitely extend this explanation of that which is posterior and composite by appealing to that which is prior (or first) and simpler.[7] Therefore he finds himself compelled to offer another explanation to account for the plurality or division of that which is first and simple. Things of this kind are divided of themselves. But, he continues, being cannot be divided from being insofar as it is being. Nothing is divided from being except nonbeing. Therefore this being is not divided from that being except insofar as in this being there is included the negation of that being.[8]

Rather than pursue Thomas's development of his positive answer to this issue in this same discussion, for the moment it will be enough for us to note the close

---

6. Leon. 50.120:72–84. On Thomas's ambiguous abbreviation, which appears three times in the section from lines 77–91, see Preface, 60.

7. Leon. 50.120:84–92.

8. Leon. 50.120:93–100. Note in particular: ". . . sunt enim huiusmodi secundum se ipsa divisa. Non potest autem hoc esse, quod ens dividatur ab ente in quantum est ens; nihil autem dividitur ab ente nisi non ens, unde et ab hoc ente non dividitur hoc ens <nisi> per hoc quod in hoc ente includitur negatio illius entis." For fuller discussion of this text see below in Ch. VI, as well as my "Thomas Aquinas on the Distinction and Derivation of the Many from the One: A Dialectic between Being and Nonbeing," *Review of Metaphysics* 38 (1985), pp. 563–90. As I indicate in the latter context (p. 563, n. 1), this important article from Thomas's Commentary on the *De Trinitate* has received relatively little attention from contemporary interpreters. For exceptions see H. Weidemann, *Metaphysik und Sprache*, pp. 47–61; "Tradition und Kritik: Zur Auseinandersetzung des Thomas von Aquin mit dem ihm überlieferten Platonismus in der 'Expositio super librum Boethii de Trinitate'," in *ΠΑΡΑΔΩΣΙΣ*: Studies in Memory of Edwin A. Quain (New York, 1976), pp. 99–119. An important part of Thomas's discussion is cited by T. Prufer in his *Sein und Wort nach Thomas von Aquin* (München, 1959), pp. 183–84. Also, passing reference is made to it by G. Rabeau, *Species. Verbum. L'activité intellectuelle élémentaire selon S. Thomas d'Aquin* (Paris, 1938), p. 205. Also see C. Courtès, "L'être et le non-être selon saint Thomas d'Aquin," *Revue thomiste* 66 (1966), pp. 587–88; 67 (1967), pp. 410–11; "Participation et contingence selon saint Thomas d'Aquin," *Revue thomiste* 69 (1969), p. 226; "Cohérence de l'être et Premier Principe selon saint Thomas d'Aquin," *Revue thomiste* 70 (1970), p. 390; L. Elders, *Faith and Science*, pp. 66–69; D. Winiewicz, "A Note on *Alteritas* and Numerical Diversity in St. Thomas Aquinas," *Dialogue* 16 (1977), pp. 693–707; D. Hall, *The Trinity*, pp. 83–84.

connection he draws between division (and therefore multiplicity) and nonbeing. If one thing is different from another, this can only be because the negation of one is in some way included in the other. At the same time, as his later Commentaries on the *Physics* and the *Metaphysics* show, he was well aware of Parmenides' denial that reality can be assigned in any way to nonbeing. And in both of these Commentaries he presents Parmenides as holding that all things are one.[9] As he puts it in commenting on *Metaphysics* I, Parmenides seems to touch on unity in terms of intelligible content, that is to say, from the side of form. Thus Parmenides reasons: whatever is other than being is nonbeing. And whatever is nonbeing is nothing. Therefore, whatever is other than being is nothing. But being is one. Therefore, whatever is other than the one is nothing. That is to say, there is no multiplicity.[10]

In expanding upon Parmenides' reasoning, Thomas comments that he was concentrating on the nature of being itself *(ipsam rationem essendi)*, which seems to be one. This seems to follow because nothing can be conceived which might add to being so as to diversify it. Anything superadded to being would have to be extrinsic to it. And what is extrinsic to being can only be nothingness. Therefore it does not seem that any such factor can diversify being.[11]

Until this point in his text, like Parmenides Thomas himself seems to be concentrating on the nature of being itself. But immediately after this he draws a comparison between being and a genus in order to develop Parmenides' reasoning more fully. The differences which are added to a genus can diversify that genus. But these differences are different from the essence *(praeter substantiam)* of the genus itself; for differences do not themselves participate in a genus. (Otherwise the genus would be included in the essence of the difference and definitions would be frivolous if, after having stated the genus, one then added the difference which already included the genus. Moreover, a difference would then differ in no way from a species.)[12] As Thomas sees it, Parmenides is treating of being as if it were a genus. If being were a genus, those things which are different from the nature of being would have to be nonbeing, just as those things which are different from the nature of a genus must be different from the genus itself. But, he continues in developing Parmenides' position, nonbeing cannot diversify being.[13] Here, therefore, Thomas

---

9. See the texts to be discussed immediately below.

10. "Parmenides enim qui fuit unus ex eis, videtur tangere unitatem secundum rationem, idest ex parte formae. Argumentatur enim sic. Quicquid est praeter ens, est non ens: et quicquid est non ens, est nihil: ergo quicquid est praeter ens est nihil. Sed ens est unum. Ergo quicquid est praeter unum, est nihil." *In I Met.*, lect. 9, p. 41, n. 138.

11. "In quo patet quod considerabat ipsam rationem essendi quae videtur esse una, quia non potest intelligi quod ad rationem entis aliquid superveniat per quod diversificetur: quia illud quod supervenit enti, oportet esse extraneum ab ente. Quod autem est huiusmodi, est nihil. Unde non videtur quod possit diversificare ens" (ibid.).

12. Ibid. Note especially: "Sicut etiam videmus quod differentiae advenientes generi diversificant ipsum, quae tamen sunt praeter substantiam eius. Non enim participant differentiae genus. . . ."

13. "Ea vero quae sunt praeter substantiam entis, oportet esse non ens, et ita non possunt diversificare ens" (ibid.).

begins to formulate Parmenides' problem in terms which seem to refer directly to the nature of our notion or concept of being.

In fact, Thomas immediately criticizes Parmenides for viewing being as if it were one in definition or nature, like a genus. In other words, without using the technical term, Thomas criticizes Parmenides for regarding being as univocal. Against this Thomas immediately protests. Being is not a genus but is said in different ways of different things.[14]

In effect, therefore, Thomas traces back to Parmenides the two levels of the problem of the One and the Many which we have distinguished above. On the ontological level or the level of being itself, it seems that being cannot be divided from being. It cannot be divided from itself by being, since it already is being. Viewed from this perspective, it is simply one. Nor can it be divided from itself by nonbeing, since this is nothingness. Therefore it cannot be divided at all, and all is one. On the level of the concept of being, if being is regarded as univocal in the fashion of a genus, any difference which might serve to divide it will then fall outside one's understanding of being. Therefore any such difference will have to be dismissed as nonbeing and will be unable to differentiate being.

In commenting on Bk I of Aristotle's *Physics* Thomas follows the Stagirite in citing Parmenides and Melissus as holding that there is one immobile principle for nature. Thomas comments that strictly speaking it does not belong to natural science either to reject the position of Parmenides and Melissus or to resolve the argumentation they have offered in support of it. This is so because it does not belong to a given particular science to refute a position which destroys the very principles of that science. For instance, geometry as such need not argue against one who rejects the first principles of geometry. This task will rather fall to another particular science (if geometry itself is subalternated to any other particular science) or else to a general science, that is, logic or metaphysics.[15]

In holding that there is only one being and that all is one and immobile, Parmenides and Melissus have in effect undercut the very meaning of the term "principle." A principle must be a principle of some other thing or things. This presupposes multiplicity. In eliminating all multiplicity they have also rejected all principles.[16] Moreover, Thomas finds Aristotle maintaining that it does not belong

14. "Sed in hoc decipiebantur, quia utebantur ente quasi una ratione et una natura sicut est natura alicuius generis; hoc enim est impossibile. Ens enim non est genus, sed multipliciter dicitur de diversis" (pp. 41–42, n. 139). Immediately thereafter Thomas refers to Aristotle's criticism in *Physics* I of the claim that (all) being is one. For Thomas's commentary on this, see below. For Thomas's repetition of Parmenides' argumentation based on the nature of being, also see p. 42, n. 142. Whatever is other than being is nonbeing. What is nonbeing is to be regarded as nothing. Hence he thought that being is one, and that whatever is other than being is nothingness.

15. See *In I Phys.*, lect. 2, pp. 9–10, nn. 13, 15. Cf. Aristotle, *Physics* I, c. 2 (184b 25–185a 3).

16. See p. 10, n. 15. Note especially: "Sed praedicta positio destruit principia naturae. . . . qui igitur negat multitudinem, tollit principia; non igitur debet contra hanc positionem disputare naturalis."

to a science—physics in the present case—to refute positions which are clearly false or improbable. But such is true of the arguments offered by Parmenides and Melissus. Their arguments fail from the side of their matter by assuming false premises as true; and they fail from the side of their form by not observing the canons of syllogistic reasoning. Both Thomas and Aristotle are especially critical of Melissus along these lines.[17]

In addition, continues Thomas, natural science takes as given the fact that natural bodies, either all or some, are subject to motion. This datum is based on induction. Motion must be presupposed by natural science just as nature itself is; for the definition of nature includes motion. In sum, since the arguments of Parmenides and Melissus do not follow from the principles of physics, they do not have to be refuted in physics.[18]

Nonetheless, Thomas acknowledges that since Parmenides and Melissus were speaking about natural things, it will be useful at this point to criticize their views. Even so, this critique as such does not belong to natural philosophy but to first philosophy.[19]

In *lectio* 3 Thomas finds Aristotle disputing against Parmenides and Melissus as against those who have spoken about nature but not as natural philosophers. As Thomas interprets him, Aristotle concentrates on their assertion that "being is one," and judges it faulty both in terms of their understanding of its subject (being) and its predicate (one). To put this very briefly, Thomas points out that, contrary to their view, being ("that which is") is said in multiple fashion. Hence Thomas asks whether by being they mean substance, or quality, or any of the other supreme genera. In holding that being is one they must apply this statement to substance and accident taken together, or else to accident alone, or else to substance alone. In each case serious difficulties will result for their position.[20]

Moreover, just as being is said in different ways, so is the term "one." This term may be taken as signifying the unity of a continuum such as a line or a body, or the unity of something indivisible such as a point, or unity in intelligible content

17. For Thomas see op. cit., p. 10, nn. 16–17. For Aristotle see *Physics* I, c. 2 (185a 5–12).

18. Ed. cit., pp. 10–11, n. 18.

19. Ed. cit., p. 11, n. 19. Note in particular: ". . . quia etsi non sit scientiae naturalis disputare contra huiusmodi positiones, pertinet tamen ad philosophiam primam."

20. See *In I Phys.*, lect. 3, pp. 13–14, nn. 20–21. Note in particular: "Dicit ergo primo: quod id quod maxime accipiendum est pro principio ad disputandum contra positionem praedictam, est quod id quod est, idest ens, dicitur multipliciter" (n. 21). In brief, Thomas reasons that if by being they mean both substance and accident, then in fact being will not be one only but twofold, i.e., substance and accident. If they have in mind accidental being alone, their position will be impossible; for an accident cannot exist without its subject. And if they have in mind being as substance alone without any accident, it will follow that being is not quantity since quantity itself is an accident. But this eliminates the position of Melissus who held that being is infinite, thereby implying that it must be quantified. For Aristotle see 185a 20–185b 5.

and definition. Thomas follows Aristotle in pointing out inconsistencies which will result on each reading for the positions of Parmenides and Melissus.[21]

Rather than develop each of these here, however, it will be enough for us to note the word of warning issued by Thomas at the end of this *lectio*. Demonstration in the strict sense cannot be offered against one who rejects first principles, but only demonstrations which are based on principles conceded by such an adversary, even if these principles are less evident in themselves. Hence in his dispute with Parmenides and Melissus, Aristotle has fallen back on certain points which are less evident in themselves than is the fact that there are many beings and that being is not merely one.[22] This suggests two points. Much of Aristotle's argumentation against Parmenides and Melissus is dialectical; and for Thomas himself the fact of multiplicity is immediately evident.

In returning to Aristotle's critique of Parmenides' position in *lectio* 6 of this same Commentary on *Physics* I, Thomas recalls the latter's reasoning as Aristotle preserves it for us in *Metaphysics* I and as we have seen Thomas himself developing it in his commentary on that passage. Whatever is other than being is nonbeing. But what is nonbeing is nothingness. Therefore, whatever is other than being is nothingness. But being is one. Therefore, whatever is other than the one is nothingness. Therefore, there is only one being. From this, continues Thomas, Parmenides also concludes that being is immobile. Thomas again judges that in this argumentation Parmenides was concentrating on being in terms of its nature or formal content and therefore that he regarded it as one and finite.[23]

In explaining why Aristotle charges Parmenides with assuming some propositions which are false, Thomas explains that this is because he thought that "that which is," or being, is used in only one way. In fact, however, it is used in different ways. Thus taken in one sense it means substance, and in another accident, and this in turn in still different ways in accord with the different supreme genera or predicaments. But, remarks Thomas, being can also be considered insofar as it is common to both substance and accident.[24]

21. For Thomas see *In I Phys.*, lect. 3, pp. 14–15, nn. 22–24. Cf. Aristotle, 185b 5–25.

22. Note in particular: "Et sic Philosophus in hac disputatione utitur pluribus quae sunt minus nota quam hoc quod est entia esse multa et non unum tantum, ad quod rationes adducit" (ed. cit., p. 15, n. 24).

23. For Thomas see *In I Met.*, lect. 9, p. 41, n. 138 (cited above in n. 11), and p. 42, n. 142. For Aristotle see *Metaphysics* I, c. 5 (986b 27–987a 2). See in *I Phys.*, lect. 6, pp. 23–24, n. 37: ". . . sciendum est quod ratio Parmenides talis erat, ut patet in I *Metaphys.* Quidquid est praeter ens est non ens; sed quod est non ens est nihil; ergo quidquid est praeter ens est nihil. Sed ens est unum; ergo quidquid est praeter unum est nihil; ergo est tantum unum ens. Et ex hoc concludebat quod esset immobile. . . . Ex ipsis autem eorum rationibus patet quod Parmenides considerabat ens secundum rationem entis, et ideo ponebat ens esse unum et finitum. . . ."

24. See *In I Phys.*, lect. 6, p. 24, n. 39. Note in particular: "Dicitur enim ens uno modo substantia, alio modo accidens; et hoc multipliciter secundum diversa genera: potest etiam accipi ens prout est commune substantiae et accidenti."

Hence Parmenides' claim that whatever is different from being is nonbeing is true when being is understood in one way, but false when it is taken in another. If being is understood as that which is common to substance and accident, it is true that what is other than being is nonbeing. Thomas's point here is that if we take being in this sense as applying to all of the predicaments, to negate being is to eliminate everything, leaving only nothingness. But if being is taken as applying only to substance, or only to accident, this conclusion will not follow. Moreover, the claim that being is one is indeed true when said of any given substance or any given accident. But this does not imply that anything apart from that being which is said to be one must be regarded as nonbeing.[25]

Somewhat farther on in this same *lectio* Thomas argues that Parmenides' claim that whatever is other than being is nonbeing should not be applied exclusively to accidental being or exclusively to substance. If one were to apply this claim only to accidental being, it would follow that a substance or substantial subject would be nonbeing. And since an accident is predicated of a subject, and that subject is now relegated to nonbeing, it would follow that being (the accident) would be predicated of nonbeing (the subject). But this would be to imply that nonbeing is being.[26]

Nor should Parmenides' reasoning be applied only to substantial being. Under that supposition any accident which inheres in a substantial subject would itself be nonbeing. And since Parmenides identifies nonbeing with nothingness, it will follow that the accident would not be at all. Yet since an accident is predicated of a subject, nonbeing or nothingness would be predicated of substance, or being. One would imply that being is nonbeing.[27]

Thomas's development of Aristotle's reasoning in this passage should be read in light of his earlier remark about the Stagirite's refutation of Parmenides being based on premises which are less evident than is the fact of multiplicity itself. Moreover, as regards the above argumentation, Parmenides would hardly admit that there is a distinction between substance and accident, and hence that being can be predicated of one and not of the other.[28] At the same time, Thomas's presentation is interesting in that, as he understands Parmenides' reasoning, whatever is other than or different from being is nonbeing in the unqualified sense, absolute nothingness. In other words, Parmenides does not allow for any distinction between absolute

---

25. Ibid.

26. Thomas presents this as a phase in Aristotle's critique of the correctness of Parmenides' reasoning. See *In I Phys.*, lect. 6, pp. 24–25, nn. 41–42. Note in particular: ". . . et ita, cum accidens quod est ens praedicetur de subiecto quod est non ens, sequetur quod ens praedicetur de non ente . . . ergo sequetur quod non ens sit ens" (n. 42).

27. See ed. cit., p. 25, n. 43.

28. Thomas seems to recognize this. See ed. cit., p. 24, n. 40: ". . . non est enim aliud album a susceptibili quia album sit separabile a susceptibili; sed quia alia est ratio albi et susceptibilis. Sed hoc nondum erat consideratum tempore Parmenidis, scilicet quod aliquid esset unum subiecto et multa ratione. . . ."

nonbeing (nothingness) and nonbeing in a qualified sense (relative nonbeing). But as we shall see below in Ch. VI, this distinction is an important part of Thomas's solution to the problem of the One and the Many at the level of being.

Finally, as Thomas remarks, if one admits that being taken strictly applies not only to a subject or substance but to an accident such as whiteness, it will follow that being signifies many different things. But then there will not be merely one being, since a subject and its accident are many in intelligible content. Once again, therefore, without using the technical expression, Thomas is criticizing Parmenides for viewing being as if it were purely univocal.[29]

Thomas has repeatedly sounded this theme in his Commentaries on *Metaphysics* I and *Physics* I. Being is used in many different senses or, to put it in other terms, being is not univocal. While these passages are found in his commentaries on Aristotle, there can be little doubt that in making this point they reflect Thomas's personal position as well as his understanding of Aristotle. And this brings us to the second major section of the present chapter.

2. Thomas's Views concerning the Analogy of Being

As certain recent studies of analogy in Aquinas have shown quite effectively, the problem of analogy of being arises for him on two very different levels. First of all, the issue may be raised at the level of beings insofar as they are given to us through sense experience and fall under *ens commune*—the subject of metaphysics. Certain writers, influenced by the terminology introduced by C. Fabro, refer to this as the predicamental level.[30] Here Thomas is concerned with showing how being can be

---

29. See ed. cit., p. 25, n. 43: "Unde si ad evitandum hoc inconveniens dicamus quod vere ens non solum significat subiectum, sed etiam ipsum album, sequitur quod ens multa significet. Et ita non erit tantum unum ens, quia subiectum et accidens plura sunt secundum rationem."

30. See C. Fabro, *Participation et causalité selon s. Thomas d'Aquin* (Louvain-Paris, 1961), pp. 510–13; 523. For explicit acceptance of this terminology and division of his own treatise in accord with it see B. Montagnes, *La doctrine de l'analogie de l'être d'après saint Thomas d'Aquin* (Louvain-Paris, 1963), pp. 33–40; c. II (pp. 65–114) on transcendental analogy of being. The literature on Thomas's views concerning analogy is extensive. Most helpful for my purposes has been Montagnes' book. For references to many other treatments, see his bibliography. Among these mention should be made of H. Lyttkens, *The Analogy between God and the World: An Investigation of Its Background and Interpretation of Its Use by Thomas of Aquino* (Uppsala, 1952), which is especially helpful for the historical background it offers on analogy prior to Aquinas, though not so reliable in its treatment of the heart of Thomas's metaphysics in itself; G. P. Klubertanz, *St. Thomas Aquinas on Analogy: A Textual Analysis and Systematic Synthesis* (Chicago, 1960), a helpful collection of most of Thomas's texts concerning analogy, with sensitivity to issues of chronology and development in Thomas's thinking concerning this; and Part III, sect. 2 of Fabro's book (pp. 509–37) cited above in this note. Fabro's study is especially important for its contribution to Thomas's theory of participation in being, and his appeal to this to bring out the metaphysical foundations of Thomas's theory of analogy. All of these sources are agreed in rejecting the historical reliability of Cajetan's interpretation as presented in his *De nominum analogia. De conceptu entis*, P. N. Zammit, ed. (Rome, 1934), and of the many later Thomistic interpretations based upon it. For a good and recent restatement of his

applied in analogical fashion to substance and to the other predicaments or accidents. As we have now seen from our review of Thomas's refutation of Parmenides, Aquinas regards it as evident that being is realized in diverse fashion at this level.[31]

Secondly, the problem of analogy of being may be raised at the vertical level or, to use Fabro's terminology, at the transcendental level. In this case Thomas is especially concerned with explaining how being and certain other names can be applied to different kinds of substances and, first and foremost, to God as well as to creatures.[32] It is this dimension of the question which has received the greatest amount of attention from students of Aquinas. Nevertheless, here we are presenting his metaphysical thought according to the philosophical order. Hence in this chapter we shall examine the problem of analogy of being only insofar as it applies to substance and to accidents (the predicamental level, taken strictly) and insofar as it applies to different levels of finite substances (the transcendental level up to a point). Only in a later chapter, after we have considered Thomas's argumentation for the existence of God, will we be in position to take up analogy insofar as it applies to God.[33]

As different writers have pointed out, nowhere in his literary corpus has Thomas presented us with a complete and self-contained exposition of his theory of analogy of being.[34] Hence it is necessary for us to turn to a variety of texts and contexts in order to gather from them the essentials of his thought concerning this sensitive topic. Frequently enough he introduces his discussions of analogy by contrasting it with univocal predication and equivocal predication. Striking similarities appear between his earliest presentation of this in his youthful *De principiis naturae* and his much later discussion in his Commentary on *Metaphysics* IV.[35]

In c. 6 of the *De principiis* Thomas has just turned to the intrinsic principles, matter and form, and wishes to show that such principles will agree with and differ from one another in the same way that the things of which they are principles agree and differ. Certain things are numerically one and the same. Others, while differing numerically, remain the same in species. Still others differ in species but are the same in genus. Finally, some things such as substance and quantity differ even in genus but agree only according to analogy; for they agree only in being (literally:

---

own critique of Cajetan's presentation also see R. McInerny, *Aquinas and Analogy* (Washington, D.C., 1996), pp. 3–29.

31. See Section 1 of this chapter, passim.

32. While most attention is paid by Thomas to analogical predication of being and other names of God as well as of created beings, the issue may also be raised at the level of being insofar as it is predicated of different finite substances when they differ in kind or even when they differ only numerically while falling within the same species. Further reference will be made to this below.

33. See Ch. XIII below.

34. See, for instance, Klubertanz, *St. Thomas Aquinas on Analogy*, p. 3; Ralph M. McInerny, *The Logic of Analogy. An Interpretation of St. Thomas* (The Hague, 1961), p. 1.

35. See Torrell, *Saint Thomas Aquinas,* pp. 48–49, 349. He places the *De principiis naturae* within the period 1252–1256 or possibly even earlier, as has been suggested by the Leonine edition (Leon. 43.6). On the dating of the Commentary on the *Metaphysics* (ca. 1270–1271/2?) see Ch. I, n. 57 above.

"in that which is being [*ens*]"). Being, Thomas goes on to argue, is not a genus, since it is not predicated univocally but only analogically.[36]

In developing the last-mentioned point, Thomas notes that something may be predicated of different things univocally or equivocally or analogically. Something is predicated univocally when it remains the same in name and in intelligible content, that is, in definition. So it is that "animal" is predicated of a human being and of a donkey. Each is said to be an animal, and each is an animated sensible substance, which is the definition of animal.[37]

Something is predicated equivocally of different things when only its name remains the same, but its definition differs in its various applications. It is in this way that the term "dog" may be said of a barking creature as well as of a heavenly body.[38]

Finally, something is predicated analogically when it is applied to things which differ in intelligible content *(ratio)*, but which are related to one and the same thing.[39] To illustrate this Thomas offers an example originally introduced by Aristotle to illustrate the πρὸς ἕν equivocal character of being, i.e., the oft-repeated case of "healthy." Thus the term "healthy" is said of the body of an animal, of urine, and of a potion, but not with entirely the same meaning in each case. It is said of urine as a sign of health, of a body as the subject in which health resides, and of a potion as its cause. Moreover, each of these meanings is related to one and the same end—health.[40]

Thomas goes on to distinguish different orders of causality which may underlie analogical predication. Sometimes such predication is based on the fact that the various (secondary) analogates are ordered to one and the same end, as in the example of health. Sometimes analogy rests on the fact that the secondary analogates are related to one and the same agent, as when the term "medical" is said of the physician who works by means of the art of medicine, and of another who works without that art, such as an elderly woman, and in addition even of instruments used in the practice of medicine. These usages are justified because these secondary analogates are ordered to one agent—the art of medicine itself. Sometimes such

36. Leon. 43.46:1–18. Note in particular: ". . . quaedam autem sunt diversa in genere, sed sunt idem solum secundum analogiam, sicut substantia et quantitas, quae non conveniunt in aliquo genere sed conveniunt solum secundum analogiam: conveniunt enim in eo solum quod est ens, ens autem non est genus, quia non praedicatur univoce sed analogice."

37. "Univoce praedicatur quod praedicatur secundum idem nomen et secundum rationem eandem, idest definitionem, sicut animal praedicatur de homine et de asino . . ." (Leon. 43.46:21–24).

38. "Aequivoce praedicatur, quod praedicatur de aliquibus secundum idem nomen, et secundum diversam rationem . . ." (Leon. 43.46:27–29).

39. "Analogice dicitur praedicari, quod praedicatur de pluribus quorum rationes diversae sunt, sed attribuuntur uni alicui eidem . . ." (Leon. 43.46:33–35). Since Thomas will also apply an analogous *ratio* to things which cannot be defined in any proper sense, the meaning of *ratio* should not be restricted to definition. Hence I will often translate it as intelligible content.

40. Note Thomas's final remark: "Sed tamen omnes istae rationes attribuuntur uni fini, scilicet sanitati" (Leon. 43.46:40–41). For Aristotle see *Metaphysics* IV, c. 2 (1003a 34–1003b 1).

diversity in usage is justified because the various secondary analogates are ordered to one subject, as when being is predicated of substance, of quality, of quantity, and of the other predicaments. Substance and the others just mentioned are not named being according to entirely the same intelligible content; rather the others are so named because they are ordered to substance—their subject.[41]

Given all of this, Thomas also remarks that being is said first and foremost *(per prius)* of substance, and of the others in secondary fashion *(per posterius)*. Therefore being itself is not a genus of which substance, quantity, etc. would be species; for a genus is not predicated of its species according to the prior and the posterior. Hence being is predicated only analogically. It is for this reason that Thomas has written that while substance and quantity, for instance, differ in genus, they are the same by analogy.[42]

With this in mind, Thomas concludes this chapter and this treatise by returning to the issue of the kind of sameness and diversity which obtains between intrinsic principles of different things. The matter and form of things which are themselves numerically identical, of Marcus Tullius and of Cicero, for instance, are themselves numerically identical. In the case of things which are identical only in species, such as Sortes and Plato, their matter and form will also be identical only in species. The principles of things which are alike only in genus will themselves only be generically the same, as is true, for instance, of the body and soul of a donkey and of a horse. The principles of things which are alike only analogically will themselves be the same only according to analogy or proportion. Just as the matter of substance is to substance, so is the matter of quantity to quantity. And just as substance itself is the cause of the other accidents, so are the principles of substance the principles for all the others.[43]

In this discussion of analogy Thomas has closely followed Averroes' Commentary on *Metaphysics* IV, c. 2.[44] At the same time, in Thomas's text we have an inter-

---

41. Leon. 43.46:42–47:55. Note Thomas's remarks concerning being: ". . . aliquando autem per attributionem ad unum subiectum, sicut ens dicitur de substantia, de qualitate et quantitate et aliis praedicamentis: non enim ex toto est eadem ratio qua substantia est ens et quantitas et alia, sed omnia dicuntur ex eo quod attribuuntur substantiae, quod est subiectum aliorum."

42. Leon. 43.47:55–60. Note in particular: "Et ideo ens dicitur per prius de substantia, et per posterius de aliis; et ideo ens non est genus substantiae et quantitatis, quia nullum genus praedicatur per prius et posterius de suis speciebus, sed praedicatur analogice."

43. Leon. 43.47:63–83.

44. See *In IV Met.*, com. 2, *Aristotelis opera cum Averrois commentariis,* Vol. 8, ff. 65rb–va. Averroes takes the example of healthy as illustrating things which are ordered to a common end, and that of medical as illustrating those which are ordered to one and the same agent. He also offers the examples of an elderly woman and of diet (instead of Thomas's *potio*) to illustrate the case of things which are named medical because they are ordered to the action of medicine. (Averroes had already used *potio* as another illustration of the various ways in which health is predicated.) As we have seen Thomas doing, Averroes interprets the case of being as resting upon the ordering of its various applications to one and the same subject, that is, substance. The language of being ordered or related *(attribuuntur, attribuitur, attributiones)* appears even more frequently in Averroes' text than in Thomas's. For more on the similarity between these two texts see Montagnes, *La doctrine*, pp. 178–80.

esting combination of analogy taken as proportion (or proportionality, according to the terminology of the slightly later *De veritate*, q. 2, a. 11), and analogy by reference to a first.[45] In Aristotle himself the term analogy is often taken in the sense of proportion, but when Aristotle so uses it he does not apply it to the case of being. On the other hand, Aristotle must be regarded as the original source for the theory of analogy of being by reference to a first, that is, to substance (οὐσία). At the same time, it should be noted that Aristotle himself never refers to this as a case of analogy. Πρὸς ἕν equivocation is his way of describing it.[46]

If these two aspects of analogy, unity of proportion(ality) and unity by reference to a first, had already been brought together within an earlier philosophical tradition,[47] it is instructive to note how Thomas correlates them in his *De principiis*. On the one hand, in applying his views concerning analogy to intrinsic principles, he has coordinated such principles according to a proportion. Just as the matter of substance stands in relation to substance, so does the matter of quantity in relation to quantity. On the other hand, he has justified this by noting that this proportion holds only because of some causal relationship. As substance itself is the cause of the other predicaments, so are the principles of substance the principles of the other predicaments. And in contrasting analogy with univocity and equivocation, Thomas has strongly emphasized the causal relation which obtains between secondary instances of the analogical perfection and the primary instance. Whether this relation has to do with final causality or efficient causality or the causality of a receiving subject, it is in any event a causal relationship which grounds analogical predication. In the case of being, it is because secondary instances of being, i.e.,

45. As is well known to students of analogy in Aquinas, in *De veritate*, q. 2, a. 11 Thomas eliminates univocal and equivocal predication of names such as *scientia* of God and creatures. Such names can be predicated of God only analogically: ". . . quod nihil est dictu quam secundum proportionem." Thomas notes that such agreement according to proportion can be twofold and accordingly that community according to analogy may also be twofold—the kind that obtains between things which have a direct relation to one another, and the kind which rather rests on the agreement between two relations. Thomas here refers to the first as agreement in terms of proportion, and to the second as agreement in terms of proportionality (Leon. 22.1.79:135–165). The *De veritate* dates from 1256–1259. See Torrell, *Saint Thomas Aquinas*, p. 334.

46. See Montagnes, p. 21, who cites G. L. Muskens in support of the point that the proportion(ality) to which Aristotle appeals in his biological works is never applied to the case of being. For Muskens see his *De vocis ἀναλογίας significatione ac usu apud Aristotelem* (Groningen, 1943), p. 90. Also see Lyttkens, *The Analogy between God and the World*, pp. 29–36 (on analogy in Aristotle's biological and ethical writings), 36–58 (on this in his metaphysics and logic). See pp. 52–58 on Aristotle's use of πρὸς ἕν predication to account for the manifold ways in which being is predicated. The most important source for this, of course, is Aristotle's *Metaphysics* IV, c. 2, for which see below. Cf. McInerny, *Aquinas and Analogy*, pp. 30–47, who also emphasizes the different terminology used by Thomas and Aristotle in referring to the case of being.

47. Montagnes offers the interesting suggestion that these two kinds of unity were brought together under the influence of Boethius's Commentary on the *Categories* (PL 64.166B). There Boethius lists four kinds of equivocals *a consilio*: (1) secundum similitudinem; (2) secundum proportionem; (3) ab uno; (4) ad unum. As Montagnes notes, equivocal terms *a consilio* came to be identified with analogicals. See op. cit., p. 30, n. 13. Cf. p. 24, n. 1.

accidents, depend upon substance as upon their subject that we are justified in also referring to them as being.[48]

More than this, Thomas has also indicated that being is said first and foremost of substance, and of the others only in secondary fashion, presumably because of their dependence upon substance.[49] In sum, as Montagnes has already shown, in this text Thomas makes analogy of proportion dependent upon analogy by reference to a first.[50] From this text we may conclude not only that analogical predication depends upon a unity and diversity which obtains in the order of reality or the order of being; more than this, within the order of reality itself it is because of the causal relation that runs from substance to accident that being is in fact realized in each in diverse fashion and can, therefore, be predicated analogically of each.[51]

Even at the risk of some repetition, it is interesting to turn from this very early text to Thomas's much later Commentary on *Metaphysics* IV, c. 2. There he is commenting on the well-known section in c. 2 where Aristotle writes that being is said in different ways, but always with reference to some one thing and one nature and not purely equivocally.[52] Aristotle introduces the examples both of health and of medicine and subsequently makes the application to the case of being. So too, he explains, being is said in many different ways, but always with reference to some one principle. Thus some things are called beings because they are substances, others because they are the affections of substance, or the path or process towards substance, or corruptions, privations, and qualities of substance, or productive or generative of substance or of things which are related to substance, or even negations, whether of these things or of substance itself. Aristotle's point is that, notwithstanding the manifold ways in which being is predicated, all of these different usages can fall within the scope of a single science. Unity by reference to a first— πρὸς ἕν equivocation—is enough to ensure this.[53]

In commenting on this Thomas repeats Aristotle's statement that being ("that which is," Thomas clarifies) is said in different ways. He then recalls that something may be predicated of diverse things in different ways: sometimes according to an intelligible content *(ratio)* which is completely identical, i.e., univocally; sometimes according to intelligible contents which are completely diverse, i.e., equivocally; and sometimes according to intelligible contents which are partly diverse and partly not diverse.[54] In explaining this third situation Thomas comments that the intelli-

48. Leon. 43.47:50–55, 79–83. Cf. n. 41 above.

49. See n. 42 above.

50. *La doctrine,* pp. 28–30.

51. As we shall see below, this should not be taken as implying that for Thomas being is not intrinsically realized in its secondary analogates, i.e., in accidents.

52. For Aristotle see *Metaphysics* IV, c. 2 (1003a 33–34).

53. Ibid., 1003a 34–1003b 15.

54. "Dicit ergo primo, quod ens sive quod est, dicitur multipliciter. Sed sciendum quod aliquid praedicatur de diversis multipliciter: quandoque quidem secundum rationem omnino eamdem, et tunc dicitur de eis univoce praedicari, sicut animal de equo et bove.—Quandoque vero secundum

gible contents in question are diverse insofar as they imply different relationships, but they are not diverse insofar as these different relationships are ordered to one and the same thing. This, of course, is what it means for something to be predicated analogically, or, as he also puts it, for something to be predicated proportionally. Each of the many things to which the common name is assigned is referred to some one thing because of its particular relationship to that thing.[55]

As Thomas also specifies, that one thing to which the different relationships are ordered in the case of analogy must be numerically one and the same and not merely one in definition or intelligible content *(ratio)* as in univocal predication. This is Thomas's way of explaining Aristotle's remark that though being is predicated in many ways, it is not predicated purely equivocally but with reference to something which is one, that is, some one thing or nature.[56] In developing the examples offered by Aristotle, Thomas again does so in accord with the different orders of causality exemplified thereby, even as he had already presented this in briefer fashion in his *De principiis naturae,* and as Averroes had done in commenting on this same passage from the *Metaphysics.*[57] As Thomas repeats, in offering the example of healthy or healthful Aristotle is showing how many things are related to one single thing as to their end. Thus the name "healthy" is applied to diet insofar as the latter preserves health, to medicine insofar as it produces health, to urine as a sign of health, and to a healthy animal because it receives health. Thomas emphasizes the point that it is one and the same health which the animal receives, which urine signifies, which medicine produces, and which diet preserves.[58]

As Thomas interprets Aristotle's example of medicine, this is intended to show how many things may be related to some one thing which serves as their efficient cause. Thus one who possesses the art of medicine is named "medical" because he is a skilled physician and can exercise that art. Others are so named because they are well fitted to acquire the art of medicine, and may perform certain medical functions by their own ingenuity. Something else is so named because it is needed for the practice of medicine, such as an instrument or the medicine employed by the physician in his healing task.[59]

---

rationes omnino diversas; et tunc dicitur de eis aequivoce praedicari, sicut canis de sidere et animali.—Quandoque vero secundum rationes quae partim sunt diversae et partim non diversae. . . ." See *In IV Met.,* lect. 1, p. 151, n. 535.

55. Ibid. Note especially: ". . . diversae quidem secundum quod diversas habitudines important, unae autem secundum quod ad unum aliquid et idem istae diversae habitudines referuntur. . . ."

56. Ed. cit., pp. 151–52, n. 536: "Item sciendum quod illud unum ad quod diversae habitudines referuntur in analogicis, est unum numero, et non solum unum ratione, sicut est unum illud quod per nomen univocum designatur." Cf. Montagnes, *La doctrine,* pp. 61–62.

57. See above in this chapter, nn. 40, 41, 44.

58. Ed. cit., p. 152, n. 537.

59. Ed. cit., p. 152, n. 538. One might wonder whether in this explanation the prime analogate is the art of medicine, or the physician who possesses that art. One suspects that Thomas has in mind the former. He writes: "Aliquid enim dicitur medicativum, ut qui habet artem medicinae, sicut medicus peritus. Aliquid vero quia est bene aptum ad habendum artem medicinae, sicut homines qui sunt

Thomas finally returns to the case of being. If being is said in different ways, this is always by way of reference to something that is first. In this case the prime referent of being is not an end or an efficient cause, as in the examples of health and medicine, but a subject. Then he paraphrases the Aristotelian text which we have presented above. Some things are called beings or are said to be because they enjoy being *(esse)* in themselves, that is, because they are substances. Hence these are named being in the primary and principal sense. Others are so named because they are *passiones* or properties of substance, such as the *per se* accidents of any substance. Others are so called because they are a process leading to substance, such as generations and motions. Others are named beings because they are corruptions of substance. Since corruption terminates in privation, even privations of substantial forms may be said to be. Again, qualities and certain accidents are named beings because they are productive of substance or of those things which bear any of the aforementioned relationships to substance or any other such relationship. Even negations of those things which are ordered to substance or, for that matter, negations of substance, may be said to be. Thus we say that nonbeing is nonbeing.[60]

In summing up these different kinds of things which may be described as beings, Thomas ranks them in terms of the mode of being enjoyed by each. Weakest of all in their claim upon being are those which exist only in the order of thought, such as negations and privations. Coming immediately after these are generation, corruption, and motion; for these too include some admixture of privation and negation. Third in Thomas's ranking are those which do not include an admixture of nonbeing but still enjoy only a fragile degree of being *(esse debile)*, that is, qualities, quantities and the properties of substance. Fourth and highest in its claim on being is that which is most perfect, that is, substance. Substance enjoys a fixed and solid being and exists in itself. It is to this as to the first and primary instance of being that all the others are related.[61] Thus qualities and quantities are said to be insofar as they inhere in substance; motions and generations insofar as they tend toward substance or toward one of the others already mentioned; privations and negations only insofar as they negate or remove one of the other three kinds or levels.[62]

As already noted above, Aristotle introduced his discussion of the different ways in which being is predicated in order to show that one and the same science

---

dispositi ut de facili artem medicinae acquirant. . . ." In any event, this is clearly the interpretation he had offered in the *De principiis naturae:* ". . . aliquando uni agenti, sicut medicus dicitur et de eo qui operatur per artem et de eo qui operatur sine arte, ut vetula, et etiam de instrumentis, sed per attributionem ad unum agens quod est medicina . . ." (Leon. 43.46–47). Here my reading differs from that offered by Montagnes, p. 28.

60. *In IV Met.*, lect. 1, p. 152, n. 539.

61. Op. cit., p. 152, nn. 540–543. Note Thomas's remarks concerning the fourth class: "Quartum autem genus est quod est perfectissimum, quod scilicet habet esse in natura absque admixtione privationis, et habet esse firmum et solidum, quasi per se existens, sicut sunt substantiae. Et ad hoc sicut ad primum et principale omnia alia referuntur."

62. See n. 543.

can study all of these instances of being.[63] That science—the science of being as being—can do so because what it considers first and foremost is substance. As Thomas interprets this, this science deals primarily with substances and therefore with all instances of being, since it considers that first thing upon which all the others depend for their being (esse) and from which they receive their name. For Thomas as for Aristotle this first thing is substance. Therefore the philosopher who considers all beings, that is to say, the metaphysician, must first and foremost take into consideration the principles and causes of substances. Moreover, as Thomas also explains, all substances insofar as they are beings or substances will fall under this science's field of investigation.[64]

When we compare this discussion of analogy with that presented by Thomas in his De principiis naturae, one slight but interesting development appears. In the earlier treatment Thomas had referred to something as predicated analogically when it is applied to things which have different intelligible contents (rationes), but these rationes are ordered to one and the same thing. In explaining analogical predication in his Commentary on Metaphysics IV, c. 2, Thomas explains that in this case something is affirmed of different things according to rationes which are partly diverse and partly not diverse. Because each of those (secondary) things to which the analogical term is applied is itself related in different fashion to some one thing, the various rationes of these things will differ. But because it is to one thing that the various secondary instances or analogates are ordered, their rationes are partly not diverse or are partly the same. This goes hand in hand with Thomas's insistence that the single thing to which being refers in its other and secondary applications enjoys numerical unity, not merely unity in definition. This implies that all the other qualities and characteristics we find in a given entity may be named being because they bear some ontological relationship to the substance of that very entity.[65]

Thomas frequently repeats the point that the intelligible content (ratio) corresponding to analogical terms is partly the same and partly diverse. For instance, in Summa theologiae I, q. 13, a. 5 he again points out that in the case of things which are said analogically, there is not a single ratio as with univocal terms; nor are the rationes totally diverse, as is the case with equivocal terms. Rather the name which

63. See Metaphysics IV, c. 2 (1003b 11–22).
64. Ed. cit., pp. 152–53, nn. 546–547. Note his concluding remark in n. 547: "Nam omnes substantiae, inquantum sunt entia vel substantiae, pertinent ad considerationem huius scientiae: inquantum autem sunt talis vel talis substantia ut leo vel bos, pertinent ad scientias speciales." This remark should be joined with Thomas's views about God and the subject of metaphysics which we have examined above in Ch. I, and which Thomas has expressed in the Prooemium to his Commentary on the Metaphysics, to the effect that divine being does not fall under the subject of metaphysics—being as being or being in general—but is studied by this science only as the cause or principle of what does fall under its subject.
65. For the De principiis see the texts cited above in nn. 39, 40, and 41. For the texts from the Commentary on the Metaphysics see nn. 54 and 55 above in this chapter.

is predicated analogically signifies different relations (literally: *proportiones*) to some one thing.[66] Or as Thomas explains in commenting on *Metaphysics* XI, c. 3, in the case of analogical predication the same term is applied to different things according to an intelligible content *(ratio)* which is partly the same and partly diverse. This *ratio* is diverse with respect to the different kinds of relations it includes, but the same with respect to that to which the various *relata* are ordered.[67]

Much of what Thomas has to say about analogy occurs in his discussions of our knowledge of and speech about God. While fuller consideration of this part of his theory will be deferred for a later chapter, it may be helpful for us to anticipate that discussion with respect to one point. Frequently in such discussions, especially in mature writings such as *Summa contra Gentiles* I, c. 34; *De potentia,* q. 7, a. 7; or *Summa theologiae* I, q. 13, a. 5, but in some fashion even as early as his Commentary on I *Sentences,* Thomas distinguishes between what we may call the analogy of "many to one" and the analogy of "one to another."[68]

In the first case a name is said to be predicated analogically because of the relationship a number of different things bear to some other single thing. So it is, Thomas writes in SCG I, c. 34, with reference to one and the same health, that the name "healthy" may be predicated of an animal as its subject, of the art of medicine as its efficient cause, of food as that which preserves health, and of urine as a sign of health. In contrast to this analogy of "many to one," on other occasions a term may be predicated analogically of two things simply because one of the analogates is directly related to the other, not because the two of them are related to some third thing. To illustrate this Thomas notes that being *(ens)* is said of substance and of accident analogically insofar as accident is related to substance, not because both substance and accident are related to some third thing. In this context as elsewhere Thomas rejects the analogy of many to one when it comes to analogical

66. "Neque enim in his quae analogice dicuntur, est una ratio, sicut est in univocis; nec totaliter diversa, sicut in aequivocis; sed nomen quod sic multipliciter dicitur, significat diversas proportiones ad aliquid unum" (Leon. 4.147). Here again I would take the analogous *ratio* or intelligible content as including both diversity (in relationships) and unity (in terms of the one to which the secondary analogates are ordered).

67. Ed. cit., p. 519, n. 2197. Note in particular: "In his vero quae praedicto modo dicuntur, idem nomen de diversis praedicatur secundum rationem partim eamdem, partim diversam. Diversam quidem quantum ad diversos modos relationis. Eamdem vero quantum ad id ad quod fit relatio. . . . Et propter hoc huiusmodi dicuntur analoga, quia proportionantur ad unum."

68. See, for instance, *In I Sent.,* Prol., q. 1, a. 2, ad 2: "Creator et creatura reducuntur in unum, non communitate univocationis sed analogiae. Talis autem communitas potest esse duplex. Aut ex eo quod aliqua participant aliquid unum secundum prius et posterius, sicut potentia et actus rationem entis, et similiter substantia et accidens; aut ex eo quod unum esse et rationem ab altero recipit; et talis est analogia creaturae ad Creatorem . . ." (Mandonnet ed., Vol. 1, p. 10). See d. 35, q. 1, a. 4: "Sed duplex est analogia. Quaedam secundum convenientiam in aliquo uno quod eis per prius et posterius convenit; et haec analogia non potest esse inter Deum et creaturam, sicut nec univocatio. Alia analogia est, secundum quod unum imitatur aliud quantum potest, nec perfecte ipsum assequitur; et haec analogia est creaturae ad Deum" (p. 820).

predication of names of God and creatures and allows only for analogy of one to another.[69]

The same distinction between these two types of analogical predication reappears in a later discussion in *De potentia*, q. 7, a. 7, probably dating from 1265–1266. This time, however, both the analogy of many to one and the analogy of one to another are applied to the predication of being at the predicamental level. Thus Thomas writes that something may be predicated analogically of two things by reason of their relation to some third thing, as when being is predicated of quality and of quantity because of their relationships to substance. Here, therefore, we have the analogy of many to one once again, but as applied to predicating being of two accidents because of their relationships to substance. Thomas immediately contrasts this with another kind of analogy whereby something is predicated of two things because of the relationship one of them has to the other. In this way, being is said both of substance and of quantity because of the relationship between quantity and substance, i.e., because quantity depends upon substance for its being. As in SCG I, c. 34, Thomas rejects the first kind of analogy (many to one) and admits only the second (one to another) when it comes to predication of divine names.[70]

Since here we are especially interested in Thomas's views concerning analogy of being at the level of finite being (the predicamental level), it is interesting to see him appealing both to the analogy of many to one and the analogy of one to another in the case of being. It is evidently the ontological situation and relationship—the dependence of an accident upon a substance for its being—which enables one to apply the name being to the accident as well as to the substance and thereby to justify the analogy of one to another. This squares, of course, with the views we have already examined from his Commentary on *Metaphysics* IV and his *De principiis naturae*.[71]

69. "Quod quidem dupliciter contingit. Uno modo, secundum quod multa habent respectum ad aliquid unum. . . . Alio modo, secundum quod duorum attenditur ordo vel respectus, non ad aliquid alterum, sed ad unum ipsorum: sicut ens de substantia et accidente dicitur secundum quod accidens ad substantiam respectum habet, non quod substantia et accidens ad aliquid tertium referantur. Huiusmodi igitur nomina de Deo et rebus aliis non dicuntur analogice secundum primum modum, oporteret enim aliquid Deo ponere prius: sed modo secundo" (ed. cit., p. 34).

70. In *Quaestiones disputatae*, Vol. 2 (Turin-Rome, 1953), P. M. Pession, ed., p. 204. Note in particular: "Huius autem praedicationis duplex est modus. Unus quo aliquid praedicatur de duobus per respectum ad aliquod tertium, sicut ens de qualitate et quantitate per respectum ad substantiam. Alius modus est quo aliquid praedicatur de duobus per respectum unius ad alterum, sicut ens de substantia et quantitate. In primo autem modo praedicationis oportet esse aliquid prius duobus, ad quod ambo respectum habent, sicut substantia ad quantitatem et qualitatem; in secundo autem non, sed necesse est unum esse prius altero. Et ideo cum Deo nihil sit prius, sed ipse sit prior creatura, competit in divina praedicatione secundus modus analogiae, et non primus." For the date see Torrell, *Saint Thomas Aquinas*, p. 335.

71. For the text from the *De principiis* see n. 41 above. For texts from Thomas's Commentary on *Metaphysics* IV see nn. 60, 61, and 62; and for his Commentary on *Metaphysics* XI see n. 67.

Thomas's application of the analogy of many to one to different accidents in the text from the *De potentia* may lead the reader to ask which of these two analogies is prior in the order of nature. If being can be applied both to quantity and to quality because each of them depends upon substance and therefore according to the analogy of many to one, it seems that this analogy rests upon and presupposes a number of direct ontological relationships between accident and substance, each of which may be expressed by an analogy of one to another. In sum, the analogy of many to one presupposes the analogy of one to another. At the same time, in the text under consideration Thomas's purpose in citing the analogy of many to one seems to be to account for the predication of being, not of the secondary analogates (accidents) *and* of the primary analogate (substance), but rather of the various secondary analogates themselves. Being can be predicated of different accidents because of the different relationships they have to being in the primary sense—substance. Presupposed for this, of course, is the possession of being in the full sense by the primary analogate or substance. And to justify predicating being both of any given accident and of substance, Thomas appeals to the analogy of one to another.[72]

As we have already seen, at the predicamental level Thomas admits both of analogy of proportion and of analogy by reference to a first. It is to the latter that he usually assigns ontological priority. One might regard the analogy of many to one and the analogy of one to another as two versions of analogy by reference to a first. If one does so, it will follow that within analogy by reference to a first, priority is to be assigned to analogy of one to another rather than to analogy of many to one.

As an exception to the priority of analogy by reference to a first, a text from Thomas's Commentary on *Ethics* I, c. 6 (1096b 26–30) might be cited. There at the end of *lectio* 7 in his Commentary Thomas is explaining Aristotle's critique of Plato's view of the Good as a separate form or idea. Aristotle has observed that the good takes on different meanings *(rationes)* in its different applications. In commenting on 1096b 26 Thomas finds Aristotle responding to an unexpressed question: How can the different examples of the good which Aristotle has cited all

---

72. See n. 70 above. However, one may compare this with the text cited above in n. 68 from the Prologue to Thomas's Commentary on I Sentences. Unlike the other texts we have examined, there one has the impression that it is because both substance and accident participate in being *(ratio entis)* that each can be described as sharing in being. Also see *In II Sent.*, d. 16, q. 1, a. 1, arg. 3: "Sed quaecumque conveniunt in aliquo uno, habent aliquid prius et simplicius se, sive sit convenientia analogiae, sive univocationis [with Parma]: est enim ens prius substantia et accidente, sicut animal prius homine et equo" (Mandonnet ed., Vol. 2, p. 397). While this text appears in an objection, Thomas's reply implies that he accepts the point that being is prior to substance and accident (see p. 398). Montagnes has noted the difference between these texts as regards the predication of being of substance and accidents, and concludes that this thinking is explicitly rejected by Thomas in SCG I, c. 34 (see the text cited above in n. 69; for Montagnes see *La doctrine*, p. 73 and nn. 17 and 18). Even so, these texts at least foreshadow the later division into the analogy of many to one and the analogy of one to another.

be called good if they have different meanings *(rationes)*? Thomas comments that something may be said of different things according to different *rationes* in two ways, either according to *rationes* which are entirely different and not related to anything that is one (equivocals by chance), or else according to *rationes* which are not completely diverse but which agree in some way. In the latter case the *rationes* may agree (1) by being referred to one principle, i.e., an agent, or (2) by being referred to one end (as in the example of healthy), or (3) either according to diverse relations *(proportiones)* which they have to the same subject (as quality is called being because it is a disposition of being *per se* or substance, and quantity because it is a measure of the same), or according to the same relationship they have to different subjects (thus sight has the same relationship to the body as the intellect has to the soul).[73]

Thomas comments that Aristotle here is stating that the good is said of different goods (1) insofar as all (other) goods depend on one first principle of goodness, or (2) insofar as they are ordered to one end, or (3) more so according to analogy, that is, according to the same relationship *(proportio)* they have to different subjects (thus, just as sight is a good of the body, so is the intellect a good of the soul). Thomas adds that Aristotle prefers this third approach because it has to do with a goodness that is inherent in things, whereas the first two approaches justify naming things good merely because of their relationship to some separate goodness.[74]

In light of this one might object that here Thomas gives priority to analogy of proportion rather than to analogy by reference to a first and, moreover, that he seems to regard analogy of proportion as better suited to safeguard the intrinsic presence of a characteristic such as goodness in all of the analogates. To this Montagnes has rightly pointed out that this passage need not be taken as reflecting Thomas's personal view about whether one should use analogy by reference to a first or analogy of proportion when dealing with the good. Indeed, here we rather have Thomas's effort to explain Aristotle's text which itself, it will be recalled, is part of the Stagirite's refutation of Plato's theory of a separate Form of the Good. To this I would also add that at the beginning of lectio 8, in commenting on Aristotle at 1096b 30–31, Thomas notes that it is necessary here (in the *Ethics*) to set aside this issue concerning how the good may be predicated of different good things according to one or according to different *rationes;* for to establish this with

---

73. *In I Ethic.*, lect. 7 (Leon. 47.1.26:168–27:198).

74. See Leon. 47.1.27:198–213. Note in particular: "Vel etiam dicuntur omnia bona magis secundum analogiam, id est proportionem eandem, quantum scilicet quod visus est bonum corporis et intellectus est bonum animae. Ideo autem hunc tertium modum praefert, quia accipitur secundum bonitatem inhaerentem rebus, primi autem duo modi secundum bonitatem separatam a qua non ita proprie aliquid denominatur." Cf. Montagnes, *La doctrine*, pp. 40–41, for the same view that, for Thomas, analogy by reference to a first is more fundamental at the predicamental level. See pp. 40–43, n. 36, for discussion of this text from Thomas's Commentary on the *Ethics*. For additional discussion of the same see McInerny, *Aquinas and Analogy*, pp. 105–11.

certainty pertains more to another part of philosophy which, Thomas specifies, is metaphysics. Hence Thomas does not find Aristotle offering his final opinion on this metaphysical point here, nor does he here offer his own.[75]

Although a separate chapter will be directed to Thomas's theory of participation of beings in *esse*, it will not be amiss here for us to note that he draws a close connection between his theory of analogy and his metaphysics of participation. This we have already mentioned in passing. And while this connection is much more evident at the transcendental level in conjunction with Thomas's account of analogical predication of divine names, to some extent it enters into his theory of analogy even at the predicamental level. Thus analogy by reference to a first implies a priority and posteriority on the part of the primary analogate and the secondary analogate(s). This also means that a secondary analogate such as an accident may be regarded as sharing in or participating in being from its primary analogate, its substantial subject. Hence even at this level it is the ontological situation, the fact that an accident depends for its being on its substantial subject, that justifies analogical predication of the name being both of it and of its substantial subject.[76]

At the same time, possible confusion could be caused by Thomas's remark in his Commentary on the *De Hebdomadibus* to the effect that a substance participates in its accidents.[77] This is in fact his more usual way of applying participation to the substance-accident relationship. Does this not run counter to the suggestion that accidents participate in being from their substantial subject? Thomas's answer to this would be quite straightforward, I would think. Two different kinds of participation are at issue. An accident may be said to participate in being from its substantial subject to the extent that the former (the accident) shares in being at all. In this case it is participation in being which is at issue. But a substance may be said to participate in its accident, not in order to account for the substantial being of that substance, but in order to account for something else—the kind of accidental

75. For Montagnes see p. 43, n. 36. For Thomas see Leon. 47.1.28:9–13: "Dicit ergo primo quod haec, scilicet qualiter bonum dicatur secundum unam vel diversas rationes de bonis, oportet nunc relinquere, quia per certitudinem determinare de hoc pertinet magis ad aliam philosophiam, scilicet ad metaphysicam."

76. Montagnes (p. 57, n. 93) cites the following texts to illustrate the connection between participation and analogy: SCG I, c. 32, §6; *De pot.*, q. 7, a. 7, ad 2; ST I, q. 4, a. 3, ad 3; *In I Periherm.*, lect. 8, n. 6; *De substantiis separatis*, c. 8. While the first three passages draw this connection between participation and analogy at the transcendental level, the final one brings this out at the predicamental level. See *De substantiis separatis*, c. 8: "Cum enim ens non univoce de omnibus praedicetur, non est requirendus idem modus essendi in omnibus quae esse dicuntur; sed quaedam perfectius quaedam imperfectius esse participant: accidentia enim entia dicuntur, non quia in se ipsis esse habeant, sed quia esse eorum est in hoc quod insunt substantiae" (Leon. 40.D54:109–116). Torrell dates this important but unfinished treatise after the first half of 1271 (op. cit., p. 350). This text implies that accidents participate in *esse* more imperfectly precisely because their *esse* is to inhere in substance.

77. "Similiter etiam subiectum participat accidens et materia formam, quia forma substantialis vel accidentalis, quae de sui ratione communis est, determinatur ad hoc vel illud subiectum." Leon. 50.271:77–80. This important passage will be discussed more fully below in Ch. IV.

being in which the substance shares. There is no contradiction between the two claims.

Before leaving Thomas's discussion of analogy at the predicamental level, we should consider two additional issues: (1) How can Thomas maintain that being can be divided into the various supreme genera or predicaments without falling back into the position he so emphatically rejects—that being is a supreme genus which is divided into its species by *differentiae* which would be added to it from without? (2) Does Thomas apply his theory of analogical predication of being to different substances themselves, especially to different finite substances? This second question may be further refined: Does Thomas apply being analogically to different substances which do not fall within the same species? Does he apply being analogically to different individual substances which do fall within the same species?

As regards the first point, it will be helpful for us to turn to two texts wherein Thomas presents what might almost be regarded as a "deduction" of the ten Aristotelian predicaments. As he observes in his Commentary on *Physics* III, being is not divided into the ten predicaments univocally in the way a genus is divided into its species, but rather in accord with different modes of being.[78] Here, as in a more or less similar development in his Commentary on *Metaphysics* V, Thomas sets up a parallel between different modes of being and different modes of predication. (It would be a mistake to conclude from this that he views the modes of predication as enjoying priority over the modes of being and therefore that analogy is for him primarily a logical doctrine.)[79]

As Thomas explains in commenting on *Metaphysics* V, being is contracted to the different genera or predicaments, but not in the way a genus is contracted to its various species through *differentiae* which fall outside the genus itself. For what is outside being is nothingness, and this could not differentiate being. On the contrary, being is contracted in accord with the different modes of predicating which follow upon different modes of being. Diversity in mode of predication should, therefore, reflect this diversity in mode of being, as Thomas sees things, and, I would add, awareness of these different modes of predicating may assist one in

78. "Ad horum igitur evidentiam sciendum est quod ens dividitur in decem praedicamenta non univoce, sicut genus in species, sed secundum diversum modum essendi." *In III Phys.*, lect. 5, p. 158, n. 322. In terms of context Thomas is commenting on Aristotle's effort to determine whether *actio* and its corresponding *passio* are one and the same motion or distinct motions. He concludes that while the motion involved is one and the same, they constitute two distinct predicaments. Thus *actio* includes in its intelligible content *(ratio)* a reference to its agent, and *passio* a reference to its recipient. See pp. 158–59, nn. 321, 323.

79. For discussion of the passage from *In V Met.* see the following note. In noting that the division of being into the ten predicaments follows upon diverse modes of being which obtain in reality, I am emphasizing the point that Thomas's doctrine of analogy of being is metaphysical. For a different emphasis see R. McInerny, *The Logic of Analogy,* passim, and more recently his *Aquinas and Analogy;* also, D. Burrell, *Aquinas: God and Action* (Notre Dame, Ind., 1979). See Montagnes' brief but perceptive reaction to McInerny's first-mentioned book (op. cit., p. 22, n. 21).

discovering these different modes of being.[80] As Thomas explains in commenting on *Physics* III, these different modes of being are in proportion to the different modes of predication. Thus in predicating one thing of another we are really saying that the one thing is the other.[81] As we shall see more fully in a later chapter, Thomas goes on from this to derive the ten predicaments in each of these passages. Here it will suffice for us to note that in each context he assigns primacy to substance.[82]

For the present, however, we may ask Thomas just how it is that different modes of being may be introduced into the unity of being without being added to it from without and without destroying that unity itself. The well-known text from *De veritate*, q. 1, a. 1 may prove to be helpful concerning this. There, after remarking that all other conceptions on the part of the intellect arise from some addition to being, Thomas writes that things cannot be added to being from without as if they were extraneous to it in the way a difference is added to a genus or an accident to a subject. This will not do in the case of being, since every nature is being essentially, that is to say, intrinsically. Therefore something can be said to add to being only insofar as it expresses a mode of being which is not expressed by the name being itself.[83] But this can happen in two ways, continues Thomas. The mode which is expressed may be some special or more particularized mode of being; or it may be a general mode which follows upon every being.[84]

---

80. As Thomas introduces this division, he finds Aristotle distinguishing different ways in which being is taken *per se* rather than *per accidens*. First among these is the division of being into substance and accident, or into the ten predicaments: "Divisio vero entis in substantiam et accidens attenditur secundum hoc quod aliquid in natura sua est vel substantia vel accidens" *(In V Met.*, lect. 9, p. 238, n. 885). As Thomas describes this in a subsequent paragraph, Aristotle first divides *ens* which is *extra animam* into the 10 predicaments (n. 889). He then draws a parallel between these divisions of being and the supreme figures of predication: "Dicit ergo primo, quod illa dicuntur esse secundum se, quaecumque significant figuras praedicationis. Sciendum est enim quod ens non potest hoc modo contrahi ad aliquid determinatum, sicut genus contrahitur ad species per differentias. Nam differentia, cum non participet genus, est extra essentiam generis. Nihil autem posset esse extra essentiam entis, quod per additionem ad ens aliquam speciem entis constituat: nam quod est extra ens, nihil est, et differentia esse non potest" (n. 889). See n. 890: "Unde oportet, quod ens contrahatur ad diversa genera secundum diversum modum praedicandi, qui consequitur diversum modum essendi. . . ."

81. "Modi autem essendi proportionales sunt modis praedicandi. Praedicando enim aliquid de aliquo altero, dicimus hoc esse illud: unde et decem genera entis dicuntur decem praedicamenta" (ed. cit., p. 158, n. 322, continuing the text cited in n. 78 above).

82. See *In III Phys.*, lect. 5, pp. 158–59, n. 322; *In V Met.*, lect. 9, pp. 238–39, nn. 891–892.

83. "Sed enti non possunt addi aliqua quasi extranea per modum quo differentia additur generi vel accidens subiecto, quia quaelibet natura est essentialiter ens, unde probat etiam philosophus in III Metaphysicae quod ens non potest esse genus; sed secundum hoc aliqua dicuntur addere super ens in quantum exprimunt modum ipsius entis qui nomine entis non exprimitur . . ." (Leon. 22.1.5:106–114). For Aristotle see *Metaphysics* III, c. 3 (998b 22ff.).

84. Thomas's text continues: ". . . quod dupliciter contingit. Uno modo ut modus expressus sit aliquis specialis modus entis. . . . Alio modo ita quod modus expressus sit modus generalis consequens omne ens . . ." (Leon. 22.1.5:114–116, 124–125).

While the second approach leads Thomas to his derivation of what are often called the transcendental properties of being *(res, unum, aliquid, bonum, verum)*, the first is of greater interest for our immediate purposes. According to this approach, every such mode is a more particularized mode of being. There are varying degrees of being, Thomas observes, and in accord with these, different modes of being are realized. And it is in accord with these different modes of being that the different genera (or predicaments) are derived. Here again we should note Thomas's metaphysical approach to the predicaments. They are grounded in different modes of being, and those modes of being in turn reflect different grades or degrees of being.[85]

Thomas cites substance in order to illustrate his point. Substance does not add to being a difference signifying a nature superadded to it (being) from without. Rather, by the name substance a specialized mode of being—a specialized way in which being is realized—is signified, that is, being *per se*. So it is with the other supreme genera.[86] In other words, if being is predicated of substance and of any given accident analogically rather than univocally, this is because the mode of being designated by substance differs from the mode of being designated by the accident.

To say that the mode of being designated by substance differs from that designated by any given accident is to imply that the one is not the other. But is this not to defend the reality of nonbeing and, if Parmenides is correct, to identify any such mode with nothingness? This is to raise the problem of the One and the Many at the more fundamental level already mentioned in the opening page of this chapter, the level of individual beings themselves. Fuller discussion of this will be deferred until the following chapters. As we shall see, Thomas's metaphysics of participation, his theory of real composition of essence and *esse* within finite beings, and his defense of the reality of a kind of nonbeing (relative nonbeing) will all enter into his solution.

At the same time, to anticipate that discussion for a moment, we should note that the text from the *De veritate* makes it abundantly clear that being is realized intrinsically both in substantial being and in accidental being. Hence, unlike Parmenides, Thomas is allowing for a way in which one (substantial being) can be said not to be another (any given accident) and still not fall into absolute nonbeing.[87] And we should remember that Thomas remains faithful to his generally

---

85. ". . . sunt enim diversi gradus entitatis secundum quos accipiuntur diversi modi essendi et iuxta hos modos accipiuntur diversa rerum genera . . ." (5:116–119).

86. ". . . substantia enim non addit super ens aliquam differentiam quae designet aliquam naturam superadditam enti sed nomine substantiae exprimitur specialis quidam modus essendi, scilicet per se ens, et ita est in aliis generibus" (5:119–123).

87. See, for instance the remark cited above in n. 83: "quia quaelibet natura est essentialiter ens." It is important to stress this point because of Thomas's frequent use of Aristotle's example of health to illustrate analogy by reference to a first. If one applies this example too rigidly, one may conclude that just as health is realized intrinsically only in the primary analogate, a living body, so too being is present intrinsically only in the primary analogate for being, substance. This would result in deny-

defended view that if an accident enjoys being in its appropriate way, it does so because it depends upon its substantial subject for that being. It is this ontological dependency which in turn justifies analogical predication of being both of a substance and of its accidents.

This leaves us with our second unanswered question: Does Thomas apply his theory of analogy of being to different finite substances themselves, whether these substances differ in species, or whether they merely differ individually within one and the same species? As regards substances which differ in species, it is well known that Thomas accepts a hierarchical theory of different levels of beings, and hence of substances, within the universe. This point appears as early as his *De ente et essentia* and as late as his *De substantiis separatis*.

In the *De ente* (1252–1256) Thomas intends to explain the meaning of the terms essence and being *(ens)*, and proposes to move from his discussion of being to a consideration of essence. As he notes at the end of c. 1, being is said both of substances *(per prius)* and of accidents *(per posterius et quasi secundum quid)*. Hence essence, too, is realized in substances in the full and proper sense, but only in a qualified way in accidents. Since substances are both simple and composite, and since essence is present in each kind, Thomas considers both types.[88]

He begins with those which are more accessible to us in the order of discovery, that is, with composite substances (see c. 2). His well-known and much-discussed c. 4 is directed to essence as this is realized in separate substances. In c. 5 he sums up his findings regarding the presence of essence in the different levels of substance. In brief, (1) in God essence and *esse* (act of being) are identical; (2) in created intellectual substances essence is distinct from *esse* (act of being), even though the essences of such substances lack matter; (3) in still another way essence is present in matter-form composites.[89] In discussing the second class—essence as realized in

---

ing that being is intrinsically realized in accidents, something Thomas clearly refuses to do. This is also one of the weaknesses in Cajetan's interpretation of analogy of attribution (analogy by reference to a first) as formally extrinsic in contrast with analogy of proportionality, which he takes as allowing for intrinsic realization of the analogous perfection in the various analogates. Here he has unfortunately joined two members of Thomas's threefold division of analogy as found in *In I Sent.*, d. 19, q. 5, a. 2, ad 1—analogy *secundum intentionem tantum et non secundum esse* and analogy *secundum intentionem et secundum esse*—with the analogy of proportion (attribution) and analogy of proportionality distinguished in the troublesome text from *De veritate*, q. 2, a. 11. He has then used this artificial schema to control his understanding of Thomas's many other discussions of analogy. See his *De nominum analogia*, ed. cit. (as well as the English translation by E. Bushinski and H. Koren, Pittsburgh, 1953), nn. 3, 10–11, 17, 21, 23–30. On Cajetan's interpretation see Montagnes, op. cit., pp. 135–50; Klubertanz, *St. Thomas Aquinas on Analogy*, pp. 7–9; Lyttkens, *The Analogy between God and the World*, pp. 205–15; McInerny, *Aquinas and Analogy*, passim.

88. For the dating see Torrell, *Saint Thomas Aquinas*, p. 348. See Prologue: ". . . ideo ex significatione entis ad significationem essentiae procedendum est" (Leon. 43.369:14–15). Also see near the end of c. 1: "Sed quia ens absolute et primo dicitur de substantiis, et per posterius et quasi secundum quid de accidentibus, inde est quod etiam essentia proprie et vere est in substantiis, sed in accidentibus est quodammodo et secundum quid" (Leon. 43.370:53–57).

89. See Leon. 43.378–79. Note especially: "Invenitur enim triplex modus habendi essentiam in

created separate substances—Thomas comments that one such substance will agree with another in being immaterial, but it will differ from another in its degree of perfection according to the extent that it recedes from potentiality and approaches pure act.[90]

The theme of hierarchy underlies much of the *De substantiis separatis* and is brought out especially well in c. 8. There Thomas first observes that because being *(ens)* is not predicated univocally of all things, we do not find the same mode of being *(modus essendi)* in all things which are said to be. Some participate in *esse* more perfectly, and others do so less perfectly. Thus accidents are described as beings not because they enjoy *esse* in themselves, but because their *esse* is to inhere in substance. (Here we have, at least by implication, a reference to analogy on the predicamental level.) Thomas next turns to substances. Not all substances have the same *modus essendi*. Those substances which participate in *esse* most perfectly do not contain anything within themselves which is pure potentiality, i.e., prime matter. Therefore they are known as immaterial substances. Below these are those substances which do contain matter, but in which their matter is so completely actualized by their form that they are not in potency to receive any other substantial form. These are, as Thomas sees it, incorruptible heavenly bodies. Still lower in the hierarchy of being is a third level or grade of substance, that is, bodies which are subject to corruption and which must, therefore, be composed of matter and form.[91]

From these texts it seems to follow that Thomas will not allow for univocal predication of being of these different levels or kinds of substances. This appears to be implied by his remark in the text from the *De substantiis separatis* that because being is not predicated univocally of all things, the same mode of being *(modus essendi)* is not required for all of those things which are said to be. There, after speaking of accidents, he explicitly states that in like fashion the same mode of

---

substantiis. Aliquid enim est sicut Deus cuius essentia est ipsummet esse suum" (378:2–5). "Secundo modo invenitur essentia in substantiis creatis intellectualibus, in quibus est aliud esse quam essentia earum, quamvis essentia sit sine materia" (378:44–47). "Tertio modo invenitur essentia in substantiis compositis ex materia et forma, in quibus et esse est receptum et finitum propter hoc quod ab alio esse habent, et iterum natura vel quidditas earum est recepta in materia signata" (379:131–135).

90. "Una enim substantia separata convenit cum alia in immaterialitate, et differunt ab invicem in gradu perfectionis secundum recessum a potentialitate et accessum ad actum purum" (Leon. 43.379:106–110).

91. See Leon. 40.D54–D55. Note especially D54:109–116, cited above in n. 76 and the following: "Rursumque in substantiis omnibus non est idem modus essendi" (D54:116–117). For a helpful discussion of hierarchy in Aquinas see E. P. Mahoney, "Metaphysical Foundations of the Hierarchy of Being according to Some Late-Medieval and Renaissance Philosophers," in *Philosophies of Existence: Ancient and Medieval,* P. Morewedge, ed. (New York, 1982), pp. 169–82. For an interesting summarizing text wherein Thomas further refines specific diversity within the realm of purely material beings in order to clarify his defense of specific diversity between angels and the human soul see his *Quaestiones disputatae De anima,* q. 7 (Leon. 24.1.59–60). For a full discussion of the dating of these questions see the Préface by the editor, B. C. Bazán (Leon. 24.1.7*–25*). He concludes that they were disputed in Italy between 1266 and 1267.

being is not present in all substances, and goes on to distinguish different grades or levels of substances. Hence his remark that being is not predicated univocally of all things seems to apply not only to the case of substance and accidents, but to the different levels or grades of substance as well. Since he would not accept purely equivocal predication of being of different levels of substances, it seems to follow that he allows only for analogical predication of being of substances that differ in species.

Moreover, Thomas has indicated in the *De ente* (c. 5) that differing degrees of perfection in receiving one and the same kind of form will not result in diversity of species. For example, in the accidental order a more intense and a less intense instance of the color whiteness will both fall within the same species. Hence, such difference in degree does not preclude univocal predication of a specific form or characteristic. But, Thomas continues, differing degrees of perfection between forms or natures themselves do result in different species. From this we may conclude that this kind of diversity does eliminate univocal predication of a specific form or characteristic of such substances.[92] As Thomas also points out in this context, citing a remark from Aristotle's *De historia animalium,* nature proceeds by grades or levels from plants to animals and even through some which are midway between plants and animals.[93] The two texts just mentioned will not suffice to settle the issue about analogical vs. univocal predication of being of substances that differ in kind of form or species. For that we must also use the text from the *De substantiis separatis* (c. 8) discussed above.

As to whether being is predicated univocally or analogically of substances which belong to one and the same species, it is even more difficult to decide this issue on purely textual grounds. Thus John of St. Thomas rejects analogical predication of being in this case.[94] However, the logic of Thomas's own position points to a

92. ". . . gradus enim perfectionis in recipiendo eandem formam non diversificat speciem, sicut albius et minus album in participando eiusdem rationis albedinem: sed diversus gradus perfectionis in ipsis formis vel naturis participatis diversificat speciem . . ." (Leon. 43.379:118–123). Thomas spells this out a bit more fully in a contemporary text, *In I Sent.,* d. 35, q. 1, a. 4, ad 3: ". . . dicendum, quod magis et minus nunquam univocationem vel speciei unitatem auferunt; sed ea ex quibus magis et minus causantur possunt differentiam speciei facere, et univocationem auferre: et hoc contingit quando magis et minus causantur non ex diversa participatione unius naturae, sed ex gradu diversarum naturarum . . ." (Mandonnet ed., Vol. 1, p. 820). For the same point in a later text, see *Quaestiones disputatae De anima,* q. 7, ad 6: ". . . dicendum quod magis et minus est dupliciter: uno modo secundum quod materia eamdem formam diversimode participat, ut lignum albedinem, et secundum hoc magis et minus non diversificat speciem; alio modo secundum diversum gradum perfectionis formarum, et hoc diversificat speciem" (Leon. 24.1.61:383–389).

93. ". . . sicut natura procedit per gradus de plantis ad animalia per quaedam quae sunt media inter animalia et plantas, secundum Philosophum in VII De animalibus" (Leon. 43.379:123–126). For Aristotle see *History of Animals,* Bk VIII, c. 1 (588b 4–13).

94. See his *Cursus Philosophicus Thomisticus, Vol. I: Ars logica,* B. Reiser ed. (Turin, 1930), II. P., q. 13, a. 3, pp. 485–86. As John sees it, when applied to individual members of the same species, being will still be transcendental but not analogical, since such individuals will not be formally but

different conclusion. If individual substances belong to the same species, being may be predicated of them analogically, not univocally. To say anything else would be to run the risk of reducing the differences between any two such beings—their individual differences, if you will—to the realm of nonbeing. If being were predicated of any two substances univocally, their individual and individuating differences would have to be added to being from without.[95]

In addition, as Fabro has pointed out, some textual evidence can also be offered for the interpretation we have just proposed. In his Commentary on I *Sentences*, d. 35, q. 1, a. 4 Thomas notes that something may be common to different things univocally or equivocally or analogically. In support of his contention that nothing can be said univocally of God and of any creature, Thomas reasons that we must take into account both the quiddity or nature of a thing and its *esse*. In things which are common univocally, there must be community in terms of the definition of the nature, but not in terms of *esse*. A given *esse* is present in only one thing. Thus the condition of being human *(habitus humanitatis)* is not realized with the same *esse* in two different human beings. Given this, Thomas concludes that whenever the form signified by a term is *esse* itself, this cannot pertain univocally to different things. Consequently, he continues, being *(ens)* is not predicated univocally.[96] Since he has been discussing *esse* as realized in different human beings, presumably he would apply this conclusion to any two individuals within the same species.

Though Thomas does not spell this out for us in great detail, his reasoning seems to be this: because being *(ens)* itself is complex, including both quiddity and *esse*, and because *esse* is not realized univocally in two different members of the same species, neither is being so realized. It seems to follow, therefore, that for Aquinas, whether being is predicated of substances which differ specifically or of substances which belong to the same species and differ from one another only individually, it must be predicated of them analogically, not univocally.

---

only materially unequal. For discussion see C. Fabro, *La nozione metafisica di partecipazione secondo S. Tommaso d'Aquino*, 2d ed. (Turin, 1950), pp. 171–72.

95. See nn. 13 and 14 above.

96. "Huius ratio est quia cum in re duo sit considerare: scilicet naturam vel quidditatem rei, et esse suum, oportet quod in omnibus univocis sit communitas secundum rationem naturae, et non secundum esse, quia unum esse non est nisi in una re; unde habitus humanitatis non est secundum idem esse in duobus hominibus; et ideo quandocumque forma significata per nomen est ipsum esse, non potest univoce convenire, propter quod etiam ens non univoce praedicatur" (Mandonnet ed., Vol. 1, p. 819). Cf. Fabro, *La nozione metafisica*, p. 172, n. 2.

IV   Participation and the Problem of the One and the Many

During the revival of interest in the philosophical thought of Thomas Aquinas which marked the first six decades or so of the twentieth century, different points have been singled out by Thomistic scholars as offering a key or even *the* key to his metaphysical thought. Thus his theory of real distinction between essence and existence, his metaphysics of act and potency, his views concerning analogy of being, and his stress on the primacy of the act of existence *(actus essendi)*, all have been emphasized in due course. Much more recently J. Aertsen has stressed the importance of the transcendentals in his thought. And each plays an important role within Thomas's metaphysics.[1] But at about the time of the outbreak of World War II, and continuing on within Thomistic studies down to the present, another significant aspect of Aquinas's metaphysical thought has come to be recognized. Important books were produced by C. Fabro, writing in Italy, and then by L. Geiger, writing in France, on the role of participation in Thomas's metaphysics.[2] Shortly thereafter another interesting if not all that reliable study was written

1. For works which have stressed each of these points in turn see, for instance, N. del Prado, *De veritate fundamentali philosophiae christianae* (Fribourg, 1911); G. M. Manser, *Das Wesen des Thomismus*, 3d ed. (Fribourg, 1949); M.T.-L. Penido, *Le rôle de l'analogie en théologie dogmatique* (Paris, 1931), which has been completely superseded by the more recent study by B. Montagnes, *La doctrine de l'analogie de l'être d'après saint Thomas d'Aquin;* and the many studies by Gilson emphasizing the primacy of existence in Thomas's metaphysics including, for instance, *Being and Some Philosophers; The Christian Philosophy of St. Thomas Aquinas; Elements of Christian Philosophy; Introduction à la philosophie chrétienne; Le thomisme*, 6th ed. (Paris, 1965). This line of interpretation has been developed by many of Gilson's followers, especially by J. Owens (see below, Bibliography). For Aertsen see his 1996 study, *Medieval Philosophy and the Transcendentals: The Case of Thomas Aquinas,* and his Bibliography for references to his earlier treatments of this.

2. C. Fabro, *La nozione metafisica di partecipazione secondo S. Tommaso d'Aquino* (Milan, 1939). Here I shall cite from the 2d revised edition (Turin, 1950). L.-B. Geiger, *La participation dans la philosophie de s. Thomas d'Aquin* (Paris, 1942), reissued in 1953. Here I shall use the 1953 edition.

in Ireland by Arthur Little, *The Platonic Heritage of Thomism*. A few years later R. Henle published a collection of texts drawn from Thomas's writings and containing his explicit references to Plato, and W. N. Clarke contributed two important articles on participation in Aquinas. Most recently, R. A. te Velde has published his *Participation and Substantiality in Thomas Aquinas*.[3]

In addressing ourselves to Thomas's views concerning participation, we are also taking up another important part of his solution to the classical problem of the One and the Many. As we have already seen in Ch. III, this problem arises for anyone who, like Aquinas, acknowledges the intelligibility of being and the unity that follows therefrom, and who also wishes to defend the reality of multiplicity or diversity, that is, of the many. One may raise this issue at the level of the concept or notion of being: What is the nature of a notion which, while being sufficiently unified to apply to all that is, or to every being, is also flexible enough to apply to the differences which obtain between beings? Thomas's answer to this is to be found in his theory of analogy of being, and this we have now examined insofar as it applies to the level of finite beings and hence to what falls within the subject of metaphysics. Even more fundamental, however, from the metaphysician's standpoint, is the issue of unity and multiplicity as it obtains within the realm of existing beings themselves. How is one to account for the fact that many different beings do indeed exist, and yet that each of them in some way shares in the perfection of being? It is with this question in mind that we now turn to Thomas's metaphysics of participation.

In examining the meaning and role assigned by Aquinas to participation, I shall attempt: (1) to explain what he understands by participation taken generally, and then what he understands by the most important case of participation for the metaphysician, that of beings in *esse*. (2) Then I shall concentrate on an aspect of Thomas's theory which has received too little attention until now. If, as we shall see, Thomas often refers to finite entities or natures as participating in *esse*, to what does the term *esse* refer as it is used here? Does it mean that they participate in self-subsisting *esse* (God)? Or does it mean that they participate in some general form of being, called *esse commune*? Or does it have some other meaning? (3) Finally, I shall turn to another issue which has divided the two leading specialists on participation in Aquinas, Fabro and Geiger, that is, the relationship between participation, composition, and limitation in finite beings.

3. See A. Little, *The Platonic Heritage of Thomism* (Dublin, 1949). As Little indicates, his book "was projected before the war and written immediately after it" (p. xiv). See the sympathetic but critical review article by W. N. Clarke, "The Platonic Heritage of Thomism," *Review of Metaphysics* 8 (1954), pp. 105–24. Also see R. J. Henle, *Saint Thomas and Platonism: A Study of the "Plato" and "Platonici" Texts in the Writings of Saint Thomas* (The Hague, 1956). For Clarke see "The Limitation of Act by Potency in St. Thomas: Aristotelianism or Neoplatonism?" in *New Scholasticism* 26 (1952), pp. 167–94; "The Meaning of Participation in St. Thomas," *Proceedings of the American Catholic Philosophical Association* 26 (1952), pp. 147–57 (both reprinted in his *Explorations in Metaphysics: Being—God—Person* [Notre Dame, Ind., 1994], pp. 65–88, 89–101, which I shall cite here). For te Velde see *Participation and Substantiality in Thomas Aquinas* (Leiden-New York-Cologne, 1995).

1. The Meaning of Participation

As is generally recognized, there has been considerable difficulty in arriving at a satisfactory definition or even description of participation since the days when such a notion came to be developed in Greek philosophy. We are familiar with Aristotle's obvious impatience with both the Pythagoreans and the Platonists when they appealed to participation and imitation. ". . . for the Pythagoreans," comments Aristotle, "say that things exist by imitation of numbers, and Plato says they exist by participation, changing the name. But what the participation or the imitation of the Forms could be they left an open question."[4] As Geiger has pointed out, Thomas's commentary on this particular passage from *Metaphysics* I is instructive. "The Pythagoreans," writes Aquinas, "while affirming participation or imitation, have not investigated how a common species is participated in by sensible individuals, or imitated by them, which the Platonists taught."[5] Thomas, at least in this text, does not reject every kind of participation nor does he here even directly criticize the Platonists. And Plato himself seems to have recognized this same difficulty, as we can surely conclude from the first part of his *Parmenides*.[6]

In this chapter, however, I shall bypass such questions concerning earlier versions of participation, and concentrate on Thomas Aquinas himself. What does he understand by participation? At times he offers a kind of etymological explanation. "To participate is, as it were, to take a part [of something]." However, already in this same relatively early writing, his Commentary on the *De Hebdomadibus,* he goes considerably beyond this appeal to etymology. "And therefore, when something receives in particular fashion that which belongs to another in universal (or total) fashion, the former is said to participate in the latter."[7] In other words, when

---

4. *Metaphysics* I, c. 6 (987b 11–14), translation from *The Complete Works of Aristotle. The Revised Oxford Translation,* J. Barnes, ed. (Princeton, 1984), Vol. 2, p. 1561.

5. "Sed tamen est sciendum, quod Pythagorici, licet ponerent participationem, aut imitationem, non tamen perscrutati sunt qualiter species communis participetur ab individuis sensibilibus, sive ab eis imitetur, quod Platonici tradiderunt." *In I Met.,* lect. 10, Cathala-Spiazzi ed., p. 46, n. 156. For Geiger see *La participation,* pp. 9–10.

6. Without pausing to go into this issue here, I would simply refer the reader to two excellent studies by R. E. Allen: *Plato's Parmenides: Translation and Analysis* (Minneapolis, 1983); "Participation and Predication in Plato's Middle Dialogues," in *Plato I: Metaphysics and Epistemology: A Collection of Critical Essays,* G. Vlastos, ed. (Garden City, N.Y., 1971), pp. 167–83.

7. "Est autem participare quasi partem capere. Et ideo quando aliquid particulariter recipit id quod ad alterum pertinet universaliter, dicitur participare illud . . ." *(In De Hebdomadibus,* lect. 2, Leon. 50.271:71–73). On the dating see Leon. 50.263–64. It probably is later than the commentary on the *De Trinitate* and therefore after the 1257–1259 period. For other general descriptions of participation see: *In I Met.,* lect. 10, p. 46, n. 154: "Quod enim totaliter est aliquid, non participat illud, sed est per essentiam idem illi. Quod vero non totaliter est aliquid habens aliquid aliud adiunctum, proprie participare dicitur. Sicut si calor esset calor per se existens, non diceretur participare calorem, quia nihil esset in eo nisi calor. Ignis vero quia est aliquid aliud quam calor, dicitur participare calorem"; *In II De caelo,* R. M. Spiazzi, ed. (Turin-Rome, 1952), lect. 18, p. 233, n. 463: ". . . dicit autem *participat,* propter inferiores substantias separatas, quae esse et bonum habent ex alio: nam *partici-*

we find a quality or perfection possessed by a given subject in only partial rather than in total fashion, such a subject is said to participate in that perfection. If in fact other subjects also share in that same perfection, it is because each of them only participates in it. None is identical with it. Thus, appeal to a participation structure is also a way of accounting for the fact that a given kind of characteristic or perfection can be shared in by many different subjects, or of addressing oneself to the problem of the One and the Many.

Thomas immediately goes on to observe that participation can take place in different orders and in different ways. Thus (1) man is said to participate in animal because man does not possess the intelligible content of animal according to its full universality *(secundum totam communitatem)*. So too, Sortes is said to participate in man, and apparently for the same reason. My understanding of Sortes taken as this individual man does not exhaust the intelligible content expressed by man in its full universality. In like fashion, continues Thomas, (2) a subject participates in an accident, and matter in form; for a substantial or an accidental form, while being general or universal in terms of its intelligible content, is restricted to this or that subject in which it is received. Thomas concludes this general description of the kinds of participation by noting (3) that in like fashion an effect is said to participate in its cause, and especially when it is not equal to the power of that cause.[8]

In sum, Thomas has here singled out three major kinds of participation. The first type is represented both by the way a specific notion such as man shares in a generic notion such as animal, and by the way my understanding of an individual such as Sortes shares in my notion of the species of man as such. In each of these examples we are dealing with a less extended intelligibility which is said to share in a more universal or more extended intelligible content. Since in each of these instances we are dealing with the fact that one intelligible content shares in another without exhausting it, we may describe it as a case of participation; but since we are only dealing with intelligible contents, the participation is logical or intentional, not real or ontological.[9]

---

pare nihil aliud est quam ab alio partialiter accipere." Also see Fabro, *La nozione metafisica,* pp. 316–17.

8. ". . . sicut homo dicitur participare animal quia non habet rationem animalis secundum totam communitatem; et eadem ratione Sortes participat hominem. Similiter etiam subiectum participat accidens et materia formam, quia forma substantialis vel accidentalis, quae de sui ratione communis est, determinatur ad hoc vel illud subiectum. Et similiter etiam effectus dicitur participare suam causam, et praecipue quando non adaequat virtutem suae causae, puta si dicamus quod aer participat lucem solis quia non recipit eam in claritate qua est in sole" (Leon. 50.271:74–85).

9. For discussion of this see Fabro, *La nozione metafisica,* pp. 27–28, 145–46, 149–50; Geiger, *La participation dans la philosophie de S. Thomas d'Aquin,* pp. 48–49; te Velde, *Participation and Substantiality,* pp. 76–82. On this second general type of participation also see SCG I, c. 32: "Amplius. Omne quod de pluribus praedicatur univoce, secundum participationem cuilibet eorum convenit de quo praedicatur: nam *species participare dicitur genus,* et *individuum speciem.* De Deo autem nihil dicitur per participationem: nam omne quod participatur determinatur ad modum participati [participantis: seems to be demanded by the sense], et sic partialiter habetur et non secundum om-

The second major division is represented by two examples as well, that of a subject or substance participating in an accident, and that of matter participating in substantial form. In each of these cases, Thomas has indicated, the forms in question, whether substantial or accidental, simply considered in themselves are still common. I take this to mean that, simply viewed in themselves, such forms can be shared in by any number of different subjects or instances of matter. It is only when a given accidental or substantial form is actually received in its appropriate substantial subject or its appropriate matter that it is thereby limited and restricted to the same. Hence the receiving principle, whether matter or a substantial subject, may be said to participate in the received form. In each of these cases the result is a real or ontological composition of a receiving subject and the perfection which is received in that same subject, that is, of substance and its given accident, or of matter and its given substantial form. Hence we may describe this kind of participation as real or as ontological. Here we are no longer dealing merely with a less extended concept which shares in one that is more extended.[10]

Rather than develop the third major kind of participation which he has singled out here (that of an effect in its cause), Thomas immediately returns to the first two. He does this in order to show that in neither of these first two ways can *esse* itself be said to participate in anything.[11] Here it should be noted that Thomas has been commenting on an axiom proposed by Boethius near the beginning of his *De Hebdomadibus* to this effect, that *esse* and "that which is" are diverse. In introducing his commentary on this axiom, Thomas had observed that, as regards being *(ens)*, *esse* itself is to be viewed as something common (universal) and undetermined which may be determined in one way from the side of a subject which has *esse*, and in another way from the side of a predicate that may be affirmed of it. Thus he finds Boethius first considering conceptions (axioms) which are derived from comparing *esse* and "that which is" (its subject). Thomas also observes that at this stage

---

nem perfectionis modum" (ed. cit., p. 33). Thomas's point here is to reject univocal predication of anything of God and other entities. Also note near the end of this same chapter: ". . . de aliis autem praedicationes fiunt per participationem, sicut Sortes dicitur homo non quia sit ipsa humanitas, sed *humanitatem habens*" (italics mine). But compare this with the following remark from *In VII Met.,* lect. 3, p. 329, n. 1328: "Genus autem non praedicatur de speciebus per participationem, sed per essentiam. Homo enim est animal essentialiter, non solum aliquid animalis participans. Homo enim est quod verum est animal." This text seems to deny that a species participates in a genus. For discussion of this difficulty, see below, n. 30. For other texts where Thomas reaffirms the point that an individual may be described as participating in a species see, for instance, ST I, q. 44, a. 3, ad 2: "Licet igitur hic homo sit per participationem speciei, non tamen potest reduci ad aliquid existens per se in eadem specie; sed ad speciem superexcedentem, sicut sunt substantiae separatae" (ed. cit., p. 226); ST I, q. 45, a. 5, ad 1 (cited below in n. 41).

10. Fabro has referred to both of these major kinds of participation as instances of predicamental participation. By this he means that both terms of the participation relationship, the participant and the participated characteristic remain within the field of finite being and finite substance (predicamental). See *La nozione metafisica*, pp. 145ff.

11. "Praetermisso autem hoc tertio modo participandi, impossibile est quod secundum duos primos modos ipsum esse participet aliquid" (Leon. 50.271:85–87).

in his treatise Boethius is not yet discussing diversity that applies to things or that is real, but diversity in the order of intentions.[12]

As Aquinas interprets him, Boethius here distinguishes between *esse* and "that which is" as between that which is signified abstractly, for instance by an expression such as "to run," and the same thing when it is signified concretely, as by an expression such as "one who runs" *(currens)*. Thus while *esse* and "to run" are signified abstractly, like whiteness, "that which is" or being *(ens)* and "one who runs" are signified concretely, like a white thing.[13] Nonetheless, Thomas also finds Boethius spelling out the distinction between these two, that is, between *esse* and "that which is," in three ways, each of which Thomas develops far more fully than does Boethius.

First of all, *esse* is not signified as the subject of being, just as the act of running ("to run") is not signified as if it were the subject which runs. Just as we cannot say that the act of running ("to run") itself runs, neither can we say that *esse* itself exists. And if "that which runs" is signified as the subject of running, so do we signify "that which is" as the subject of being *(subiectum essendi)*. And if we can say of one who runs that he does so insofar as he is subject to running and participates in it, so we can say that a being, or "that which is," exists insofar as it participates in the act of being.[14] Hence in this immediate context, Thomas understands by *esse* the act of being.

Secondly, Boethius states that "that which is" can participate in something, but *esse* itself cannot. It is in explaining this second difference that Thomas introduces

12. Leon. 50.270. Note especially: "Dicit ergo primo, *quod diversum est esse, et id quod est,* quae quidem diversitas non est hic referenda ad res de quibus adhuc non loquitur, sed ad ipsas rationes seu intentiones" (lines 36–39).

13. Leon. 50.270:39–271:45: "Aliud autem significamus per hoc quod dicimus esse et aliud per id quod dicimus id quod est, sicut et aliud significamus cum dicimus currere et aliud per hoc quod dicitur currens. Nam currere et esse significantur in abstracto sicut et albedo; sed quod est, idest ens et currens, significatur in concreto velut album."

14. Leon. 50.271:48–49. Note in particular: ". . . et ideo sicut possumus dicere de eo quod currit sive de currente quod currat in quantum subiicitur cursui et participat ipsum, ita possumus dicere quod ens sive id quod est sit in quantum participat actum essendi." As Fabro points out, Thomas here introduces one of his most original insights into his Commentary on the Boethian text, and one which is completely missing from Boethius himself, that is, his identification of *esse* as it is realized in a finite being as the act of being: ". . . sed id *quod est, accepta essendi forma,* scilicet suscipiendo ipsum actum essendi, *est, atque consistit,* idest in se ipso subsistit" (Leon. 50.271:61–63). For Fabro see *Participation et causalité selon S. Thomas d'Aquin,* p. 270. For different medieval and contemporary ways of understanding the meaning of *esse* in Boethius himself see Fabro, *La nozione metafisica,* pp. 100–103. Also see Geiger, *La participation,* pp. 36–45; P. Hadot, "La distinction de l'être et de l'étant dans le *De Hebdomadibus* de Boèce," *Miscellanea Mediaevalia 2: Die Metaphysik im Mittelalter* (Berlin, 1963), pp. 147–53; G. Schrimpf, *Die Axiomenschrift des Boethius (De Hebdomadibus) als philosophisches Lehrbuch des Mittelalters* (Leiden, 1966). The general (if not universal) consensus is that however Boethius may have understood and contrasted *esse* and *id quod est*—and there is much disagreement concerning this—he did not distinguish them in Thomistic fashion as act of being and essence. However, for a different reading, see R. McInerny, "Boethius and Saint Thomas Aquinas," *Rivista di Filosofia neo-scolastica* 66 (1974), pp. 219–45, and more recently, *Boethius and Aquinas,* pp. 161–253.

the description and divisions of participation we have been considering. Thomas immediately turns from this description of participation to explain why *esse* (the act of being) itself cannot participate in anything else, even though "that which is" or the subject which exists can. Precisely because *esse* is signified in abstract fashion, it cannot participate in anything else in the second general way Thomas has singled out, that is, as a substance participates in its accident or as matter participates in form. This is so, we may presume, because both a substantial subject and matter are signified concretely, and, as we have seen, *esse* is signified abstractly.[15]

Neither, continues Thomas, can *esse* participate in anything else in the first general way, that is, as a less universal concept participates in one which is more universal. (Thomas does acknowledge in passing that in this general way some things which are signified abstractly may be said to participate in others, for instance, whiteness in color.) This kind of participation will not apply in the case of *esse* itself because there is nothing more general than *esse* in which it could participate. *Esse* itself is most universal *(communissimum)*. Therefore *esse* is participated in by other things, but cannot itself participate in anything else.[16] On the other hand, being *(ens)*, even though it too is most universal, is expressed in concrete fashion. Therefore while being cannot participate in anything in the way the less universal participates in the more universal, it does participate in *esse* in the way something concrete participates in something abstract. Thomas comments that this is what Boethius has in mind in another of his axioms to the effect that "what is" can participate in something, but that *esse* itself cannot do so in any way.[17]

We shall pass over Thomas's discussion of the third difference between *esse* and "that which is" as he finds this in Boethius's text. Of greater interest for our immediate purposes is Thomas's acknowledgment that being *(ens)* can participate in *esse* in the way in which something taken concretely participates in something taken abstractly. If we were to stop at this point, we would not yet be justified in thinking that he here defends any kind of real diversity or real composition of *esse* (act of being) and "that which is" within participating beings. We should note that in the following context Thomas writes that for something to be a subject in the unqualified sense, that is, a substance, it must participate in *esse* itself.[18] This is important

---

15. "Non enim potest participare aliquid per modum quo materia vel subiectum participat formam vel accidens quia ut dictum est ipsum esse significatur ut quiddam abstractum" (Leon. 50.271:87–91).

16. "Similiter autem nec potest aliquid participare per modum quo particulare participat universale . . . sed ipsum esse est communissimum, unde ipsum quidem participatur in aliis, non autem participat aliquid aliud" (Leon. 50.271:91–97).

17. See Leon. 50.271:97–105. Note especially: "Sed id quod est sive ens, quamvis sit communissimum, tamen concretive dicitur, et ideo participat ipsum esse, non per modum quo magis commune participatur a minus communi, sed participat ipsum esse per modum quo concretum participat abstractum."

18. "Dicit, quod ad hoc quod aliquid *sit* simpliciter subiectum *participat* ipsum esse. . . . Nam aliquid est simpliciter per hoc quod *participat* ipso *esse;* sed quando iam *est,* scilicet per participatio-

because it indicates that if something is to serve as a subject for an accident, it must itself exist. And in order for it to exist, it must participate in *esse,* or as Thomas has also phrased it, in the *actus essendi* (act of being). Here, then, we find Thomas very deftly inserting his own metaphysics of *esse* taken as act of being into his Commentary on Boethius.[19] This becomes even clearer as Thomas turns to another Boethian axiom: in every composite, *esse* and the composite itself differ. Here Thomas finds Boethius formulating axioms which pertain to the nature of the one *(unum)* rather than of being *(ens),* as had until now been the case. And, comments Thomas, at this point Boethius has shifted from diversity in the order of intentions to diversity in the order of reality. ". . . just as *esse* and 'that which is' differ in the order of intentions, so in composite entities do they differ really [*realiter*]."[20]

In order to support this, Thomas first recalls a point which we have already considered—that *esse* itself does not participate in anything else so that its intelligible content *(ratio)* might consist of different factors. He also recalls another point which until now we have not mentioned—that *esse* does not admit of the addition of anything extrinsic to its formal content. Therefore, he quickly concludes, *esse* itself is not composed. But if it is not, then a composite or composed entity cannot be identified with its *esse* (act of being). Here, then, we seem to have an argument for the real distinction between essence and act of being in composite entities, although not one of Thomas's more usual arguments for that conclusion.[21]

One might immediately ask, however, about finite or caused simple entities. Will essence and *esse* be distinct in them? It seems that some other kind of argumentation will be required to establish this. In apparent anticipation of our query,

---

nem ipsius esse, restat *ut participet* quocumque *alio,* ad hoc scilicet quod sit aliquid" (Leon. 50.272:180–195).

19. In addition to other passages from the Commentary on the *De Hebdomadibus* (see n. 14 above), one may consider a later text such as *Quaestiones disputatae De anima,* q. 6, ad 2: "Ad secundum dicendum quod ipsum esse est actus ultimus qui participabilis est ab omnibus; ipsum autem nihil participat. Unde si sit aliquid quod sit ipsum esse subsistens, sicut de Deo dicimus, nihil participare dicimus. Non est autem similis ratio de aliis formis subsistentibus, quas necesse est participare ipsum esse et comparari ad ipsum ut potentia ad actum" (Leon. 24.1.51:268–275). Here we have in outline form most of the elements of Thomas's mature doctrine of participation of beings in *esse,* and a confirmation of the views expressed in his Commentary on the *De Hebdomadibus: esse* is the ultimate act which can be participated in by all; *esse* itself does not participate in anything; if there is a subsisting *esse*—God—this participates in nothing; other subsisting forms (angels) must participate in *esse* and be related to it (their act of being) as potency to act.

20. Leon. 50.272:196–198. Note: ". . . et est considerandum quod ea quae supra dicta sunt de diversitate ipsius esse et eius quod est, est secundum ipsas intentiones. Hic ostendit quomodo applicetur ad res. . . . Est ergo primo considerandum quod sicut esse et quod est differunt secundum intentiones, ita in compositis differunt realiter" (Leon. 50.272:196–273:206).

21. "Quod quidem manifestum est ex praemissis. Dictum est enim supra quod ipsum esse neque participat aliquid ut eius ratio constituatur ex multis, neque habet aliquid extrinsecum admixtum ut sit in eo compositio accidentalis; et ideo ipsum esse non est compositum; res ergo composita non est suum esse . . ." (Leon. 50.273:206–213). For the point that *esse* admits nothing extrinsic into its formal content see Leon. 50.271:114–272:146. For further discussion of this argumentation see Ch. V below, nn. 80, 81. Cf. McInerny, *Boethius and Aquinas,* pp. 211–15.

Thomas insists that in any simple entity, *esse* and "that which is" are really identical. Otherwise the entity would not really be simple. In explaining this Thomas notes that something is simple insofar as it lacks composition. Since something may lack a given kind of composition without lacking all composition, it may be simple in a qualified sense without being completely simple. Thus fire and water, two of the elements for Thomas and his contemporaries, are called simple bodies because they are not composed of contraries, as are mixtures. But each is still composed both of quantitative parts and of matter and form. Should we find certain forms which do not exist in matter and which are simple in the sense that they lack matter-form composition and quantitative parts, it will not immediately follow that they are perfectly simple. Since any such form must still determine its *esse*, it follows that no such form is *esse* itself. It simply has *esse*.[22]

Here Thomas has introduced one of his favorite ways of expressing the fact that created entities, in this case, created separate substances, participate in *esse* (the act of being). They have *esse*, but are not their *esse* (act of being). By saying that every such form must determine its *esse*, I take Thomas to mean that because every such form enjoys a given kind of being, the determination or specification of its kind of being must come from the side of its form or essence, not from the side of its act of being *(esse)*.

In fact, in an interesting thought experiment, Thomas suggests that even if, for the sake of discussion, we grant with Plato that there are certain subsisting immaterial forms or ideas such as a form for human beings and another for horses, every such form will still be determined with respect to its kind or species. Hence no such subsisting form could be identified with the act of being in general *(esse commune)*. Each such form would only participate in *esse commune*. The same will hold, continues Thomas, if with Aristotle we defend the existence of separate and immaterial substances above the world of sensible things. Each of these, insofar as it is distinct from the others, is a given specific kind of form and therefore participates in *esse*. No such substance, whether it be a Platonic form or an Aristotelian separate substance, will be perfectly simple.[23] Each will be composed of itself— form—and of the *esse* (act of being) in which it participates. There can be only one completely simple being, continues Thomas, and this does not participate in *esse*, but is subsisting *esse*. This, of course, is God.[24]

---

22. See Leon. 50.273:216–235. Note in particular: "Quia tamen quaelibet forma est determinativa ipsius esse, nulla earum est ipsum esse, sed est habens esse. . . ."

23. Leon. 50.273:236–249. Note especially: ". . . manifestum erit quod ipsa forma immaterialis subsistens [a Platonic form], cum sit quiddam determinatum ad speciem, non est ipsum esse commune, sed participat illud . . . unaquaeque illarum [Aristotelian separate substances], in quantum distinguitur ab alia, quaedam specialis forma est participans ipsum esse, et sic nulla earum erit vere simplex."

24. Leon. 50.273:249–258. Note Thomas's reason here for saying that such a being can only be one: ". . . quia, si ipsum esse nihil aliud habet admixtum praeter id quod est esse, ut dictum est, impossibile est id quod est ipsum esse multiplicari per aliquid diversificans. . . ."

This discussion is helpful for a number of reasons. First of all, here Thomas has clearly distinguished between a diversity of *esse* and "that which is" which applies only to the order of intentions, and a real distinction between them. Secondly, he has offered two ways of establishing real distinction between them, one directed to composite entities taken in the usual sense as matter-form composites, and another which applies to finite simple entities such as pure spirits. Even the latter cannot be identified with the act of being taken in general *(esse commune)*, since every such being is a given kind of being and must, therefore, determine and specify the *esse* which it has. In this text, therefore, Thomas has closely connected participation in *esse* with his theory of real distinction between essence and act of being. In fact he has so closely linked them that he immediately moves from the fact that such entities merely participate in *esse* to the conclusion that no such entity is truly simple (which is to say it is composed).[25] This text also tells us that in speaking of participation of beings in being, on some occasions, at least, Thomas means thereby that they participate in the act of being in general or in *esse commune*. With these thoughts in mind, we may now attempt to see how Thomas's understanding of participation of beings in *esse* fits into his earlier threefold division of participation.

We may immediately conclude from the above that the participation of beings in *esse* cannot be reduced to the first kind of participation singled out by Aquinas, whereby a less universal notion or concept participates in one that is more general or universal. Such participation belongs to the logical or intentional order, and does not entail real distinction between the participant and that in which it participates. But, as we have now seen, participation of beings in *esse* clearly does.

What, then, of the second general kind of participation, wherein a subject participates in its accidents, or a given instance of matter participates in substantial form? This, too, evidently involves real participation and real diversity between the participating subject and the participated perfection, that is, between substance and accident, or between prime matter and substantial form. Nonetheless, it seems clear enough that for Thomas, participation of beings in being *(esse)* cannot be reduced to this kind of participation any more than to the first kind.

First of all, in order for a subject to participate in its accidents, Thomas has noted that the subject itself must exist. And it exists only insofar as it participates in *esse*. Participation in *esse* is clearly more fundamental than that of a substance in its accidents. The same may be said of participation of matter in form. Indeed, according to Aquinas, if a matter-form composite is to exist, it must participate in *esse*.[26]

Moreover, in the case where matter is said to participate in form, a third thing *(res)* or a *tertium quid* results, that is, the essence of the material thing which

25. See the texts cited in nn. 22 and 23 above.
26. See n. 14 above. On matter-form composites participating in *esse* see *De substantiis separatis*, c. 8 (Leon. 40.D55:210–218, 225–228). Cf. te Velde, *Participation and Substantiality*, p. 79, and n. 31 (for a reference to my earlier treatment of this).

includes both its form and its matter. However, as Thomas brings out on other occasions—for instance, in his considerably later and very full discussion of participation in Quodlibet 2, q. 2, a. 1 of Advent 1269—it is not in this way that essence and *esse* (act of being) unite in a creature. No *tertium quid* results from their union. Essence and *esse* do not unite in a created separate substance—an angel—as if they were two different parts of the angelic substance. "Thus, therefore, in an angel there is a composition of essence and *esse;* this, however, is not a composition as of parts of substance, but rather as of substance and of that which unites with the substance *(adhaeret substantiae).*"[27] And in replying to the first objection in this same article, Thomas notes that in some cases a third thing *(res tertia)* does result from things which are joined together, as humanity or human being results from the union of soul and body. But on other occasions this is not the case. Rather, something is composed of itself and of something else.[28] Hence, we may conclude, in the case of an angel we have a composition of the angelic essence and of a distinct *esse* (act of being), which itself is neither an essence nor a "thing" nor even a part of an essence.

Still another difference has been pointed out between matter-form composition and the union of essence and *esse* in Thomas's metaphysics,[29] and therefore, one may conclude, between the kinds of participation involved in each. In the case of matter-form union, specification of the kind of being enjoyed by the composite essence, human being or canine being, for instance, is determined by the act principle within the essence, that is, by the substantial form. But in the composition of essence and *esse* within any finite entity, the specification or determination of the kind of being comes not from the side of the act principle—the *actus essendi*— but from the side of the potency principle, that is, from the essence. This is not surprising, of course, since the essence principle itself either is or at least includes a substantial form. While the form is an act principle within the line of essence, in the line of *esse* that same form, either in itself in the case of a separate substance or

27. Quodlibet 2, q. 2, a. 1 is addressed to this question: ". . . utrum angelus substantialiter sit compositus ex essentia et esse." See Leon. 25.2.214–15. Note in particular: "Sic ergo in angelo est compositio ex essentia et esse, non tamen est compositio sicut ex partibus substantiae, sed sicut ex substantia et eo quod adhaeret substantiae" (p. 215:74–76). For the date see Leon. 25.1.ix*. But cf. pp. 111*–112*.

28. The first objection reasons that the essence of an angel is the angel itself. If, therefore, an angel were composed of essence and *esse,* it would be composed of itself and something else. This is rejected by the objection as unfitting (Leon. 25.2.214:13–18). Note from Thomas's reply: ". . . aliquando autem ex his quae simul iunguntur non resultat res tertia . . . et in talibus aliquid componitur ex seipso et alio . . ." (p. 215:81–86).

29. See Geiger, *La participation,* pp. 198–99, n. 2; Fabro, *Participation et causalité,* p. 65. For a general comparison and contrast between the composition of essence *(substantia)* and *esse* and that of matter and form see SCG II, c. 54. There Thomas concludes by noting that the composition of act and potency is broader in extension than that of matter and form. While the latter is restricted to physical *(naturalem)* entity, the former extends to the entire realm of being in general: ". . . potentia autem et actus dividunt ens commune" (ed. cit., p. 147).

together with its matter in the case of a composite entity, is in potency with respect to its act of being.

Another important difference between the first type of participation, that of a species in its genus or of an individual in its species, and other kinds of participation including that of beings in *esse* is brought out in Thomas's Commentary on the *De Hebdomadibus* and in Quodlibet 2, q. 2, a. 1. In *lectio* 3 of the former text Thomas is commenting on a question raised by Boethius concerning whether beings are good by their essence or by participation. Thomas remarks that this question assumes that to be something essentially is opposed to being something by participation. He concedes that this is true according to the second major kind of participation he has distinguished (that of a substance in an accident, or of matter in form). This follows because an accident is not included within the nature of its substantial subject, and form is not included within the nature of matter. But this does not apply to the first major kind of participation he has distinguished, at least not according to Aristotle, although it would apply if, with Plato, we defended distinct forms or ideas, for instance, for man, for biped, and for animal. According to Aristotle, whom Thomas here follows, a man is truly that same thing which is an animal. Because animal does not exist apart from the difference man in this particular illustration, what is said of something by participation in this first major way can also be predicated of it substantially.[30] In other words, man is said to participate in animal in the way a species participates in its genus. But because animal is included within the nature or essence of man, animal may be predicated of man substantially as well. Thomas would deny, of course, that *esse* is predicated of any creature in this way, i.e., substantially or essentially.

In Quodlibet 2, q. 2, a. 1, Thomas explicitly makes this final point. There he has commented that something can be predicated of something either essentially or else by participation. Being *(ens)* is predicated of God alone essentially, and of every creature only by participation; for no creature is its *esse*, but merely has *esse*. Thomas then notes that when anything is predicated of something by participation, something else must be present there in addition to that which is participated. Therefore, in every creature there is a distinction between the creature which has *esse*, and *esse* itself.[31] But something may be participated in two different ways.

---

30. Leon. 50.276:44–63. Note in particular: ". . . sed secundum Aristotelis sententiam qui posuit quod homo vere est id quod est animal, quasi essentia animalis non existente praeter differentiam hominis, nihil prohibet id quod per participationem dicitur etiam substantialiter praedicari." Hence in the troublesome text from *In VII Met.* (cited in n. 9 above) Thomas must be understanding participation only in the second way, with the consequence that the participated characteristic is not included within the essence of the participant. A species does not participate in a genus in this way, but only according to the first general way of participating.

31. Leon. 25.2.214:28–50. Note in particular: "Secundum ergo hoc dicendum est quod ens praedicatur de solo Deo essentialiter, eo quod esse divinum est esse subsistens et absolutum; de qualibet autem creatura praedicatur per participationem: nulla enim creatura est suum esse, sed est habens esse. . . ." Thomas then applies this to goodness as well. While God is said to be good essentially

On the one hand, what is participated may be included within the very essence *(substantia)* of the participant, as when a genus is participated in by its species. But, says Thomas, *esse* is not participated in by a creature in this way. What is included within the essence of a thing falls within its definition. Being *(ens)* is not included within the definition of a creature since being is neither a genus nor a difference. Therefore it *(esse)* is participated in only in the second way, as something which is not included within the essence of the participant. Given this, one must distinguish the question *an est* ("Is it?") from the question *quid est* ("What is it?"). In fact, Thomas even goes so far here as to say that since anything not included within the essence of a thing may be described as an accident, the *esse* which answers to the question *an est* is an accident. He does not mean by this that *esse* (the act of being) is a predicamental accident, but only that it is not part of the essence of any creature. This he clarifies with all desired precision in other contexts, for instance in his Commentary on *Metaphysics* IV and in his Quodlibet 12.[32]

In comparing participation in *esse* with the first two major kinds singled out by Thomas in his Commentary on the *De Hebdomadibus,* we should also note that each of the other kinds allows for univocal predication of the participated perfection. According to Thomas, this is not true of *esse*. It can only be predicated analogically of whatever participates in it. As regards univocal predication of genera and species, Thomas correlates this with participation in an important text from *Summa contra Gentiles* I, c. 32. There he is attempting to show that nothing can be predicated univocally of God and of anything else. "Everything which is predicated of many things univocally pertains to each of those things of which it is predicated [only] by participation. For a species is said to participate in a genus, and an individual in a species."[33] If these are cases of participation, as Thomas has again reminded us here, they are also paradigms for univocal predication.

As Thomas also explains within this same chapter, what is predicated of different things in terms of priority and posteriority is not predicated of them univocally.

---

because he is goodness itself, creatures are said to be good by participation because they have goodness.

32. "Uno modo quasi existens de substantia participantis sicut genus participatur a specie; hoc autem modo esse non participatur a creatura: id enim est de substantia rei quod cadit in eius definitione, ens autem non ponitur in definitione creaturae, quia nec est genus neque est differentia. Unde participatur sicut aliquid non existens de essentia rei, et ideo alia quaestio est 'an est' et 'quid est'; unde, cum omne quod est praeter essentiam rei dicatur accidens, esse, quod pertinet ad quaestionem 'an est', <est> accidens" (Leon. 25.2.214:51–215:63). Cf. Thomas's reply to objection 2: ". . . esse est accidens, non quasi per accidens se habens, sed quasi actualitas cuiuslibet substantiae . . ." (Leon. 25.2.215:88–90). Cf. Quodlibet 12, q. 4, a. 1: "Et sic dico quod esse substantiale rei non est accidens, sed actualitas cuiuslibet formae existentis, sive sine materia sive cum materia. . . . Et ad id quod Hilarius dicit, dico quod accidens dicitur large omne quod non est pars essentiae, et sic est esse in rebus creatis, quia in solo Deo esse est eius essentia" (Leon. 25.2.404:27–37). Cf. *In IV Met.,* lect. 2, p. 155, n. 558.

33. Ed. cit., p. 33, cited above in n. 9.

Thus, as we have already seen, being *(ens)* is not predicated univocally of substance and of accidents. And as Thomas continues, nothing can be said of God and other things as if they were on the same level, but only according to priority and posteriority. Therefore, while names such as being *(ens)* and good are said of God essentially, they are predicated of all else only by participation. Hence, Thomas concludes once more, nothing can be said univocally of God and of other things.[34]

Before leaving this general discussion of Thomas's understanding of participation, reference should be made to another aspect of his theory. Participation evidently entails distinction and composition in the participant of a receiving and participating principle, and of that which is received and participated. This has already emerged from our analysis of Thomas's Commentary on the *De Hebdomadibus,* and is reinforced by his discussion in Quodlibet 2. But in cases of real or ontological participation, the participating principle or subject is related to the participated perfection as potency to act. The participated perfection is the act of the principle or subject which receives it as its corresponding potential principle. As Thomas explains in ST I, q. 75, a. 5, ad 1: "A potency, however, since it receives act, must be proportioned to its act. But received acts, which proceed from the first and infinite act and are certain participations of it, are diverse."[35]

Very frequently Thomas also applies this thinking to the participation of beings in *esse.* That essence is related to the act of being *(esse)* as potency to act in every finite being is a position he defends from his earliest writings, and even in contexts where he is not using the language of participation, as for instance, in certain passages in his Commentary on I *Sentences,* or in c. 4 of his *De ente et essentia.*[36]

The importance of this conjoining of the potency-act relationship between essence and *esse* with the metaphysics of participation can hardly be overstated. Without this, the intrinsic and essential unity of a participating being would not be assured.[37] One may recall the following text from SCG II, c. 53: "Everything which participates in something is related to that which is participated as potency to act.

34. Ibid. See in particular: "Adhuc. Quod praedicatur de aliquibus secundum prius et posterius, certum est univoce non praedicari. . . ."

35. "Potentia autem, cum sit receptiva actus, oportet quod actui proportionetur. Actus vero recepti, qui procedunt a primo actu infinito et sunt quaedam participationes eius, sunt diversi" (Leon. 5.202).

36. See, for instance, *In I Sent.,* d. 8, q. 5, a. 2: "Et quia omne quod non habet aliquid a se, est possibile respectu illius; huiusmodi quidditas cum habeat esse ab alio, erit possibilis respectu illius esse, et respectu ejus a quo esse habet, in quo nulla cadit potentia; et ita in tali quidditate invenietur potentia et actus, secundum quod ipsa quidditas est possibilis, et esse suum est actus ejus. Et hoc modo intelligo in angelis compositionem potentiae et actus, et de 'quo est' et 'quod est', et similiter in anima" (Mandonnet ed., Vol. 1, pp. 229–30). In the *De ente* it is only after having completed his argumentation for the essence-*esse* distinction in non-divine simple entities and after having reasoned from their caused character to the existence of God that Thomas establishes act-potency composition within them. See Leon. 43.377:147–152. For discussion see Ch. V below.

37. See W. N. Clarke, *Explorations in Metaphysics,* pp. 79–82, 95–97.

Through that which is participated the participant becomes actually such. But it has been shown above that God alone is being essentially, and that all others participate *ipsum esse.* Therefore every created essence [*substantia*] is related to its *esse* as potency to act."[38] Here we have the general point that whatever participates in something is related to that in which it participates as potency to act. And this is followed by the particular application to created essences as participating in and as related to their acts of being as potency to act.

If the act-potency relationship applies to the participation of beings in *esse,* it also holds in other instances of real participation. According to Aquinas, matter participates in form and is related to it as potency to act. A substance participates in its accidents and is related to them as a receiving potency to its received albeit secondary acts. But most important for our purposes is Thomas's repeated application of this to participation in *esse.* As he puts it in his even later *De substantiis separatis:* "Everything which is has *esse.* Therefore, in everything apart from the first, there is both *esse* itself as act, and the substance of the thing which has *esse* as the potency which receives this act which is *esse.*"[39]

At this point it may be helpful for us to sum up the various features of Thomas's understanding of the participation of beings in *esse* which have so far emerged from our discussion. The participation of beings in *esse* is more fundamental than the other kinds of participation, for it alone accounts for the fact that a given entity

38. "Item. Omne participans aliquid comparatur ad ipsum quod participatur ut potentia ad actum: per id enim quod participatur fit participans actu tale. Ostensum autem est supra quod solus Deus est essentialiter ens, omnia autem alia participant ipsum esse. Comparatur igitur substantia omnis creata ad suum esse sicut potentia ad actum" (ed. cit., p. 146). The whole of c. 53 is devoted to proving that there is act-potency composition in created intellectual substances, that is, of *substantia* and *esse.* In c. 52 Thomas had offered a series of arguments to prove that there is diversity of *quod est* (essence) and *esse* in such entities.

39. On the relationship between a subject or substance and its accidents see, for instance, Thomas's *De virtutibus in communi,* a. 3, in *Quaestiones disputatae,* Vol. 2 (Turin-Rome, 1953), p. 715, and ST I, q. 77, a. 6, and ad 2 (on the soul and its powers). Also see Ch. VIII below, Sections 3 and 4. On the act-potency relationship between prime matter and substantial form see Ch. IX below, Sections 1 and 2. For the passage cited in our text from the *De substantiis separatis* see: "Omne autem quod est esse habet; est igitur in quocumque praeter primum et ipsum esse tamquam actus et substantia rei habens esse tamquam potentia receptiva hujus actus quod est esse" (Leon. 40.D55:183–187). Also see *Quodlibet* 3, q. 8, a. 1: "Oportet igitur quod quaelibet alia res sit ens participative, ita quod aliud sit in eo substantia participans esse et aliud ipsum esse participatum. Omne autem participans se habet ad participatum sicut potentia ad actum. Unde substantia cuiuslibet rei creatae se habet ad suum esse sicut potentia ad actum" (Leon. 25.2.277:37–46). Here Thomas is rejecting matter-form composition in the human soul. Also see *De spiritualibus creaturis,* a. 1, where Thomas is rejecting matter-form composition of spiritual substances. Note the passage cited below in n. 62. Also see *In VIII Phys.,* lect. 21, where Thomas is criticizing Averroes for rejecting true matter-form composition in heavenly bodies. Even if one conceded this position to Averroes, there would still be a potency for being *(potentia essendi)* in heavenly bodies (p. 615, n. 1153). Quodlibet 3 dates from Easter 1270 (Leon. 25.1.ix*); *De substantiis separatis* after the first half of 1271 (Torrell, p. 350); *De spiritualibus creaturis,* between November 1267 and September 1268 (Leon. 24.1.22*, 24*); *In Phys.,* ca. 1268–1269 (Torrell, p. 342). All are relatively late works. Also see W. N. Clarke, *Explorations in Metaphysics,* pp. 89–101, esp. pp. 95–97.

actually exists. No *tertium quid* or third thing results from the union of the participating principle (essence) and that in which it participates *(esse)*. The participated perfection—*esse*—cannot be predicated univocally of the various subjects which participate in it, but only analogically. The participating principle, or essence, specifies the kind of *esse* which is received, and therefore also establishes the kind of entity which results from this participation. The participating principle also limits *esse*, although as yet we have not developed this point. The participated perfection is not included in the nature or essence which participates in it, but is really distinct from that essence. Therefore essence and *esse* can only enter into composition with one another. While *esse* may be described as accidental insofar as it is not included within the essence of the participating subject, it is not to be regarded as if it were a predicamental accident. The participated perfection *(esse)* unites with the participating subject as act with potency, so as to result in a being that is not merely accidentally but essentially one, an *unum per se*. Finally, as we shall see below in Section 3 of this chapter, neither the participating principle *(essence)* nor the participated principle *(esse)* can exist without the other.

Granting all of this, however, one may still wonder how Thomas's view of the participation of beings in *esse* can be fitted into his threefold division of participation. Since it is not reducible either to logical participation or to the kind of real participation whereby matter participates in form or a subject participates in its accidents, what remains? As we have seen above, in his Commentary on the *De Hebdomadibus* Thomas notes that being *(ens)* participates in *esse* in the way something concrete participates in something abstract. However, he has not identified participation of the concrete in the abstract with any of the three divisions. Hence it seems that the only possible remaining member of that division is that wherein an effect participates in its cause, and especially if it is not equal to the power of its cause. As is well known, Thomas often refers to beings other than God as participating in *esse*. On some occasions he means by this that they participate in *esse commune*, as we have seen from his Commentary on the *De Hebdomadibus*.[40] On other occasions, however, he seems to mean that creatures participate in self-subsisting *esse*, or in God. How are we to understand each of these usages, and can we fit them together? This also presents us with a certain difficulty in our effort to follow what Thomas himself calls the philosophical order in presenting his metaphysical thought. In his theological writings he can follow the theological order and either take God's existence as given on the grounds of religious belief, or offer philosophical argumentation for his existence early on in these works (see ST I, q, 2, a. 3; SCG I, c. 13; *Compendium theologiae*, c. 3). He can then view created reality from the perspective of God, as it were. But were he to follow the philosophical

40. See n. 17 above for the text. Cf. te Velde, *Participation*, p. 79, although I would not want to suggest, as he does, that participation of the concrete in the abstract is a new and fourth mode. Cf. L. Dümpelmann, *Kreation als ontisch-ontologisches Verhältnis. Zur Metaphysik der Schöpfungstheologie des Thomas von Aquin* (Freiburg-Munich, 1969), pp. 24–27.

order in presenting his metaphysical thought, he would not be justified in assuming that God exists until he had offered philosophical evidence for this. He has proposed such knowledge as the end or goal of the metaphysician's inquiry rather than as its beginning. Consequently, to the extent that we find Thomas referring to created beings as participating in divine *esse,* we shall regard these references as based on the putative existence of God, which still remains to be demonstrated and which we will take up in later chapters. With this in mind, we may now turn to the next major section of this chapter.

2. Participation in *Esse*

In an interesting passage in *Summa theologiae* I, q. 45, a. 5, ad 1, Thomas draws a comparison between the way an individual participates in human nature, and the way any created being participates in the "nature of being." "Just as this human being participates in human nature, so does any created being *(ens)* participate, if I may so speak, in the nature of being, because God alone is his *esse.*"[41] His qualifying remark suggests that we should not simply identify the "nature of being" *(natura essendi)* with another abstract and universal concept. Nor should we identify it with God *(esse subsistens),* who is here introduced in contrast with all else which only participates in *esse.* It must, therefore, refer to *esse commune.*

In fact, as Thomas explains in *Summa contra Gentiles* II, c. 52, *esse* is not divided in the way a genus is divided by differences into its species. If *esse* were so divided, it would already follow from this that there can only be one self-subsisting *esse.* But *esse* is rather divided by reason of the fact that it is received in this or in that subject. Hence it follows with even greater force that *esse subsistens* or any separate *esse* can only be one.[42] (I would note that this claim holds even if one does not yet assume that God in fact exists. At most there can only be one *esse subsistens.*) For our immediate purposes, the point to be stressed is this: Thomas is keenly aware of the difference between *esse commune* and any abstract and universal generic or specific notion.[43]

41. "Sed sicut hic homo participat humanam naturam, ita quodcumque ens creatum participat, ut ita dixerim, naturam essendi: quia solus Deus est suum esse, ut supra dictum est" (Leon. 4.470). In this article Thomas is addressing the question: "Utrum solius Dei sit creare."

42. "Sic igitur, si hoc ipsum quod est esse sit commune sicut genus, esse separatum per se subsistens non potest esse nisi unum. Si vero non dividatur differentiis, sicut genus, sed per hoc quod est huius vel illius esse, ut veritas habet; magis est manifestum quod non potest esse per se existens nisi unum" (ed. cit., p. 145). By way of contrast, Thomas concludes that nothing other than God can be its own *esse.*

43. Thomas makes the point that *esse* is not divided like a genus through differences in many different contexts, some of which will be noted below. Here one is also reminded of his procedure in the *De ente,* c. 4, in what I will call the second phase of his complex argumentation for real distinction of essence and *esse* in separate entities other than God. There he distinguishes three ways in which something can be multiplied in his effort to show that at most there can be one self-

Still, one might be tempted to identify *esse commune* with self-subsisting being or God as one recent writer, K. Kremer, has done.[44] Thomas strongly rejects any such suggestion. For instance, in *Summa contra Gentiles* I, c. 26, he attempts to show that God is not the formal *esse* for other things, or the *esse* whereby each of them exists.[45] One of his arguments runs this way. What is common to many things does not exist as such apart from the many except in the order of thought. Thus animal is not something which exists apart from Socrates and Plato and other animals except in the intellect. The intellect can grasp the form of animal by abstracting it from all individuating and specifying characteristics. Much less, continues Thomas, is *esse commune* to be regarded as something which exists apart from individual existent things, except in the order of thought. If, Thomas concludes, God were to be identified with *esse commune,* then God too would exist only in the order of thought or in the intellect.[46]

It is important to bear this in mind lest one misinterpret a passage such as the following, taken from Thomas's late *De substantiis separatis,* c. 8. There he is attempting to show against Avicebron that one need not postulate matter-form composition in nondivine separate substances (angels) in order to avoid identifying them with God. Some potency is present in such substances precisely because they are not *ipsum esse* but only participate in *esse.* Thomas then reasons that there can only be one subsisting *esse,* just as any form, when it is considered in itself and as separate, can only be one. So it is that things which differ in number are one in species, since the nature of the species simply considered in itself is one. If such a specific nature could exist in itself, then it would also be one in the order of reality. The same holds, continues Thomas, for a genus in reference to its species, until we reach *esse* itself, which is most common. That is, if any genus could exist apart from its species, it could only be one. But in the case of *esse,* Thomas implies, there is a

subsisting *esse* (Leon. 43.376:103–377:126). While he does not there explicitly refer to *esse commune,* the similarity in procedure is worth noting. For discussion see Ch. V below, Section 1, and n. 37.

44. *Die Neuplatonische Seinsphilosophie und ihre Wirkung auf Thomas von Aquin* (Leiden, 1966), especially pp. 357–72. For a long and critical review see Fabro, "Platonism, Neo-Platonism and Thomism: Convergencies and Divergencies," *New Scholasticism* 44 (1970), pp. 69–100, especially from p. 80 onward. For another critical reaction to Kremer's interpretation see Aertsen, *Medieval Philosophy and the Transcendentals,* pp. 388–90.

45. This entire chapter bears reading, for it offers a host of arguments against any such pantheistic understanding of God, and concludes by considering and criticizing a series of reasons or motives which may have led some to accept it. One interesting possible source for such is a misinterpretation of a remark in c. 4 of Pseudo-Dionysius's *De caelesti hierarchia:* "Esse omnium est super-essentialis divinitas." For Thomas any attempt to interpret this as implying that God is the formal *esse* of all things is offset by the text itself, for then God would not be *above (super)* all things but in *(inter)* all things or even something of all things *(aliquid omnium).* See ed. cit., p. 28.

46. Ed. cit., p. 27. Note: "Multo igitur minus et ipsum esse commune est aliquid praeter omnes res existentes nisi in intellectu solum. Si igitur Deus sit esse commune, Deus non erit aliqua res nisi quae sit in intellectu tantum."

self-subsisting *esse*. Therefore he concludes that this self-subsisting *esse* can only be one, and that in addition to it no other subsisting entity can be pure *esse*.[47]

One should not infer from this, however, either that Thomas regards *esse commune* as another genus, albeit the most general one, or that he is identifying *esse commune* with God. His purpose is rather to show that if, *per impossibile,* a genus or species could subsist in itself, it could only be one. So too, we may reason in following the philosophical order, if there is a self-subsisting *esse,* it can only be one.

In other contexts Thomas brings out the difference between *esse commune* and self-subsisting *esse* in still another way. For instance, in *De potentia,* q. 7, a. 2, ad 4, he explicitly makes the point that the divine *esse* which is identical with the divine essence *(substantia)* is not *esse commune* and is distinct from every other instance of *esse*. Hence through his very *esse* God differs from every other being. And in replying to the sixth objection Thomas acknowledges that being in general *(ens commune)* is such that nothing is added to it, but not in such a way that no addition could be made to it. On the other hand, the divine *esse* is such that nothing is added to it and nothing can be added to it. Therefore, he concludes, the divine *esse* is not *esse commune*.[48] In other words, being in general is neutral with respect to such addition. Self-subsisting *esse* excludes the possibility of any kind of addition.[49]

In *Summa theologiae* I, q. 3, a. 4, ad 1, Thomas makes this very same point. To be without addition in the sense that all addition is positively excluded is true of the divine *esse*. To be without addition in the neutral sense is true of *esse commune*. The only difference between the two discussions is that in the text from the *Summa* Thomas speaks of *esse commune* rather than of *ens commune,* as he does in his reply to objection 6 in the text from the *De potentia*. Even in the *De potentia,*

47. For such a misinterpretation see Kremer, op. cit., pp. 370–71. For Thomas see Leon. 40.D55:164–187. Note in particular: ". . . inde est enim quod ea quae sunt diversa numero sunt unum specie quia natura speciei secundum se considerata est una: sicut igitur est una secundum considerationem dum per se consideratur, ita esset una secundum esse si per se existeret. Eademque ratio est de genere per comparationem ad species, quousque perveniatur ad ipsum esse quod est communissimum." In contrast with the unique *ipsum esse subsistens,* Thomas concludes that in everything else there is both *ipsum esse,* as act, and the substance (or essence) of the thing, which has *esse* and receives it as potency.

48. "Ad quartum dicendum, quod esse divinum, quod est eius substantia, non est esse commune, sed est esse distinctum a quolibet alio esse." Also: "Ad sextum dicendum, quod ens commune est cui non fit additio, de cuius tamen ratione non est ut ei additio fieri non possit; sed esse divinum est esse cui non fit additio et de eius ratione est ut ei additio fieri non possit; unde divinum esse non est esse commune . . ." (ed. cit., Vol. 2, p. 192).

49. To illustrate the kind of "neutrality" he is here assigning to *ens commune* (and then, apparently, to *esse commune*), Thomas concludes his reply to objection 6 by drawing a comparison with animal taken in general *(animal commune)*. If animal considered as such does not include the difference rational, neither does it exclude the possibility of its being added to animal. One should not conclude from this that Thomas has therefore identified *ens commune* as another albeit most universal genus. Given Kremer's identification of *esse commune* and *esse subsistens,* he understandably finds this text and its parallels difficult (op. cit., p. 361).

however, he then also refers to *esse commune* just as he had done in his reply to objection 4.[50]

In his late Commentary on the *Liber de causis* of 1271–1272 Thomas finds its unknown author considering the following objection. Someone might argue that if the first cause is pure *esse (esse tantum)*, it is *esse commune* which is predicated of all things; therefore it is not something existing individually and distinct from all others. That which is common is not rendered individual except by being received in something. Since the first cause is, in fact, something individual and distinct from all others, it seems necessary to conclude that it has *yliatim*, that is, something which receives its *esse*.[51]

Thomas comments that to this the *Liber de causis* replies that the very infinity of the divine *esse*, insofar as it is not restricted by any receiving principle, plays the role in the first cause which *yliatim* exercises in other things. This is so because the divine goodness and the divine *esse* are rendered individual by reason of their very purity, that is, by reason of the fact that they are not received in anything else. Thomas explains that something is said to be an individual because it is not its nature to be found in many things. But this may happen in two ways. It may be owing to the fact that the thing in question is determined to some one subject in

50. For ST I, q. 3, a. 4, ad 1, see Leon. 4.42: "Ad primum ergo dicendum quod *aliquid cui non fit additio* potest intelligi dupliciter. Uno modo, ut de ratione eius sit quod non fiat ei additio. . . . Alio modo intelligitur aliquid cui non fit additio, quia non est de ratione eius quod sibi fiat additio. . . . Primo igitur modo, esse sine additione, est esse divinum: secundo modo, esse sine additione, est esse commune." Here he is answering an objection which would identify God with *esse commune* or *ens commune* if one maintains that in God essence and *esse* are the same. Thomas's reply to objection 6 in *De potentia*, q. 7, a. 2 is addressed to essentially the same objection. Cf. *In I Sent.*, d. 8, q. 4, a. 1, ad 1, where a similar objection and Thomas's reply are expressed in terms of *ens commune* (Vol. 1, p. 219). For the same distinction see SCG I, c. 26, "Secundum" (ed. cit., p. 28).

51. "Posset enim aliquis dicere quod, si causa prima sit esse tantum, videtur quod sit esse commune quod de omnibus praedicatur et quod non sit aliquid individualiter ens ab aliis distinctum; id enim quod est commune non individuatur nisi per hoc quod in aliquo recipitur. Causa autem prima est aliquid individualiter distinctum ab omnibus aliis. . . . Ergo videtur quod *necesse* sit dicere causam primam habere *yliatim*, id est aliquid recipiens esse." See *Sancti Thomae de Aquino super Librum de causis expositio*, H. D. Saffrey, ed. (Fribourg-Louvain, 1954), pp. 64–65. Thomas has greatly expanded upon a brief statement of this objection by the author of the *Liber de causis* (see Prop. 9), and seems to have read into it his own concern about not identifying the first cause with *esse commune*. The original objection reads: "Quod si dixerit aliquis: necesse est ut sit <habens> *yliatim*, dicemus . . ." (p. 57). Thomas had attempted an etymological explanation of the rather mysterious expression *yliatim* in the immediately preceding context, by tracing it back to the Greek term for matter: "Nam intelligentia habet *yliatim*, id est aliquid materiale vel ad modum materiae se habens; dicitur enim *yliatim* ab *yle*, quod est materia" (p. 64). In fact, the Arabic original from which the corrupted Latin transliteration was taken can mean "ornament," "attribute," "quality," "state," "condition," "appearance," or "form." See R. Taylor, "St. Thomas and the *Liber de causis* on the Hylomorphic Composition of Separate Substances," *Mediaeval Studies* 41 (1979), pp. 510–13. Nevertheless, as Taylor also points out, while being mistaken in thinking that *yliatim* is derived from the Greek term for matter, Thomas "was quite correct in maintaining that in the *De causis* the intelligences do not have matter." On the general accuracy of Thomas's Commentary see C. d'Ancona, *Recherches sur le Liber de causis* (Paris, 1995), pp. 229–58. Cf. pp. 118–19.

which it is received. Or it may simply be owing to the fact that the thing in question is not of such a nature as to be received in something, and therefore is an individual of itself. Thus, if there were a separated whiteness which could exist apart from any receiving subject, it would be individual of itself. This kind of individuation in fact obtains in the case of created separate substances which are forms which have *esse*. In other words, such entities are not individuated by being received in matter. This explanation also applies, concludes Thomas, to the first cause which is subsisting *esse* itself. Most important for our immediate purposes, however, is Thomas's continuing refusal to identify *esse commune* with *esse subsistens*.[52]

If this is granted, it must also be acknowledged that there are other passages where Thomas refers to beings or to created beings as participating in (or from) self-subsisting *esse* or in (or from) their cause. How is this to be reconciled with his view that finite entities participate in *esse commune*? An extremely important discussion is contained in Thomas's Commentary on the *Divine Names*, c. V, lect. 2, dating either from 1261–1265 or from 1265–1268. Here Thomas finds Pseudo-Dionysius (=Dionysius) drawing out certain implications from his conclusion that God is the universal cause of being, that is, by showing that he is the cause of all particular beings including the various levels or degrees of beings. These levels include, continues Thomas, angelic substances in their various degrees; substances which are not bodies but are united to bodies, i.e., souls; corporeal substances themselves; accidents insofar as they fall into the nine supreme genera or predicaments; and finally, things which do not exist in the nature of things but only in thought and which are called beings of reason *(entia rationis)*, such as genera, species, mental states (here illustrated by opinion), and others of this kind.[53]

Shortly thereafter Dionysius shows that God is the cause of *esse commune* itself. As Thomas interprets this, Dionysius first shows that *esse* is common to all things; then he explains how *esse commune* stands in relation to God. Granted the diversity in levels of beings, Thomas concludes his own discussion of the first step by noting that nothing can be described as an existent unless it has *esse*. This is what Thomas

---

52. Saffrey ed., pp. 65–66. Note in particular: "Sed ad hoc respondet quod ipsa *infinitas* divini *esse,* in quantum scilicet non est terminatum per aliquod recipiens, habet in causa prima vicem *yliatim* quod est in aliis rebus . . . ita divina *bonitas* et esse individuatur ex ipsa sui puritate per hoc scilicet quod ipsa non est recepta in aliquo. . . ."

53. *In librum beati Dionysii De divinis nominibus expositio,* C. Pera, ed. (Turin-Rome, 1950), c. V, lect. 2, p. 244, n. 655. On the dating see Torrell, p. 346. Earlier in his Commentary (see c. V, lect. 1) Thomas had commented on Pseudo-Dionysius's view that God is the universal cause of being. See in particular p. 234, n. 629, where Thomas explains that all things other than God have "esse receptum et participatum et ideo non habent esse secundum totam virtutem essendi, sed solus Deus, qui est ipsum esse subsistens, secundum totam virtutem essendi, esse habet." See pp. 234–35, n. 630, where he warns that Pseudo-Dionysius's statement about God's being the *esse* for existents *(ipse est esse existentibus)* should not be taken to mean that God himself is the formal *esse* of existents, but rather in a causal sense; p. 235, n. 631, where Thomas comments: "*et iterum omnia Ipso participant,* sicut forma exemplari; *et* non solum est causa quantum ad fieri rerum, sed et quantum ad totum esse et durationem. . . ."

means, therefore, by referring to *esse* as common. It is that intrinsic principle, that act of being, found in every existing entity, that is, every substance, which accounts for the fact that it actually exists. As regards the second step, Thomas comments that *esse commune* is related to God and to other existents in very different fashion. In fact, Thomas spells out three such differences.[54]

First of all, other existents depend on *esse commune,* but God does not. Rather, *esse commune* itself depends on God. If we wonder how this can be, this becomes clearer as Thomas develops the second and third differences. Secondly, therefore, all other existents are contained under *esse commune* itself, but God is not. *Esse commune* itself rather falls under God's power. For God's power is more extended than is created *esse.* By this Thomas must mean that God can create many things which he does not actually create and to which *esse commune* does not actually extend.[55]

As a third difference Thomas explains that all other existents participate in *esse* (*esse commune,* we may assume), but that God does not. On the contrary, created *esse* is a kind of participation in God and a likeness of God. This is Thomas's way of explaining Dionysius's statement that *esse commune* "has" God. He means that it, i.e., the entities that fall under it, participate in a likeness of God. And in saying that God does not "have" *esse,* he means that God does not participate in it. So understood, Thomas does not here contradict his claim in his Commentary on the *De Hebdomadibus* that *esse* itself does not participate in anything else, although being *(ens)* does. Thomas goes on to explain that God is an existent before every other substance and every other being and before every *aevum,* not only in terms of duration or order, but also in terms of causality. God is the cause of existence *(causa subsistendi)* for all other things, and their principle of being *(principium essendi).* He is also the end to which all things tend.[56]

Two questions might be raised about this passage: How do other existents depend upon *esse commune*? And how does *esse commune* itself depend on God? As

54. See p. 245, n. 658: ". . . ostendit quod Deus est causa ipsius esse communis; et circa hoc, duo facit: primo, ostendit quod ipsum esse est omnibus commune; secundo, ostendit qualiter ipsum esse commune se habeat ad Deum. . . ." Also see nn. 659–660. Note especially: "Et licet huiusmodi *dignitates essendi* superioribus tantum substantiis conveniant, tamen hoc ipsum quod est *esse, ab omnibus existentibus* non *derelinquitur,* quia nihil potest dici existens nisi habeat esse. . . ."

55. ". . . primo quidem, quantum ad hoc quod alia existentia dependent ab esse communi, non autem Deus, sed magis esse commune dependet a Deo; et hoc est quod dicit quod ipsum *esse* commune *est ipsius Dei,* tamquam ab Ipso dependens, *et non ipse* Deus *est esse,* idest ipsius esse communis, tamquam ab ipso dependens. Secundo, quantum ad hoc quod omnia existentia continentur sub ipso esse communi, non autem Deus, sed magis esse commune continetur sub eius virtute, quia virtus divina plus extenditur quam ipsum esse creatum . . ." (p. 245, n. 660).

56. Ibid. Note in particular: "Tertio, quantum ad hoc quod omnia alia existentia participant eo quod est esse, non autem Deus, sed magis ipsum esse creatum est quaedam participatio Dei et similitudo Ipsius; et hoc est quod dicit quod *esse* commune *habet Ipsum* scilicet Deum, ut participans similitudinem Eius, *non* autem *ipse* Deus *habet esse,* quasi participans ipso esse." Cf. the texts from Thomas's Commentary on the *De Hebdomadibus* cited above in nn. 15, 16, and 17. Cf. F. O'Rourke, *Pseudo-Dionysius and the Metaphysics of Aquinas* (Leiden–New York–Cologne, 1992), pp. 141–43.

regards the first question, Thomas has indicated both that other existents are contained under *esse commune,* and that they participate in it. Here, then, we return
to a theme we have already considered in other texts—other existents are said to
participate in *esse commune.* This accounts for the fact that they are said to have
esse, but are not identical with the *esse* (act of being) which they have or in which
they participate. This should not be taken to imply, of course, that *esse commune*
actually subsists as such apart from individual existents. It rather means that every
individual created existent may be viewed as only sharing in or participating in *esse,*
with the consequence that the *esse* (act of being) which is intrinsic to it is only a
partial sharing in the fullness of *esse commune* when the latter is simply considered
in itself.

As for our second question, in saying that *esse commune* depends upon God,
Thomas has commented that it falls under God's power. I take him to mean by
this that every individual existent exists only insofar as it is caused by God. Moreover, created *esse* has also now been described as a likeness of God. Hence, in participating in the *esse* which is efficiently communicated to it by God, the creature may
also be said to participate in some way in God, that is, in his likeness. God is its
exemplar cause as well as its efficient cause and its final cause.

With this we have rejoined the third member of Thomas's earlier division of
participation in his Commentary on the *De Hebdomadibus,* that whereby an effect
may be said to participate in its cause, and especially if it is less perfect than its
cause. Even so, I would suggest that participation of beings in *esse commune* should
also be placed under this same third part of Thomas's division, both because it does
not fall under either of the first two members, and because it is closely associated
with participation in *esse subsistens.* In the case where a caused being participates in
God, its first cause, it is clear enough that the effect is less perfect than the cause.
It is also worth noting that Thomas often draws a close connection between being
by participation and being caused. Thus in *Summa theologiae* I, q. 44, a. 1, he
comments that if "something is found in some thing by participation, it must be
caused in that thing by that to which it belongs essentially." He recalls that earlier
in the *Summa* he has already shown that God is self-subsisting being (I, q. 3, a. 4),
and that *esse subsistens* can only be one. Therefore all things other than God are not
identical with their *esse,* but participate in *esse.* But things which differ according
to varying degrees of participation in *esse,* so as to be more or less perfectly, are
caused by one first being, which is in most perfect fashion.[57] In replying to the first
objection within this same article, Thomas comments that it follows from the fact

---

57. Leon. 4.455. Note in particular: "Si enim aliquid invenitur in aliquo per participationem,
necesse est quod causetur in ipso ab eo cui essentialiter convenit. . . . Relinquitur ergo quod omnia
alia a Deo non sint suum esse, sed participant esse. Necesse est igitur omnia quae diversificantur
secundum diversam participationem essendi, ut sint perfectius vel minus perfecte, causari ab uno
primo ente, quod perfectissime est."

that something is a being *(ens)* by participation that it is caused by something else.[58] This is important if we would follow the philosophical order in presenting Thomas's metaphysics of participation. In the order of discovery one may move from one's discovery of individual beings as participating in *esse commune* to the caused character of such beings, and then on to the existence of their unparticipated source *(esse subsistens)*. Once this is established, one can then speak of them as actually participating in *esse subsistens* as well.

Thomas makes a similar point in c. 3 of his *De substantiis separatis,* where he is bringing out some points of agreement between Plato and Aristotle concerning separate substances: "Everything which participates [in] something receives that which it participates from that *from* which it participates, and with respect to this that from which it participates is its cause."[59] This text is interesting because it makes three points: (1) something may participate (in) some perfection (accusative case); (2) it then participates in that *from* something else (ablative case); (3) the source is identified as the cause which accounts for the presence of the participated perfection in the participant.[60]

On other occasions Thomas refers even more directly to the participant as participating in its source or in God rather than in *esse commune*. In these cases he is dealing with what he at times refers to as an analogical cause or agent, and at times as one that is equivocal. His point is that the divine agent is not univocal with any creature.[61] As will be recalled, in the major text taken from his Commentary on the *Divine Names,* if a creature is said to participate in the divine *esse,* this is because a likeness or similitude of the divine is in some way produced in the creature.

58. According to the objection, a relationship of effect to cause does not seem to be included in the intelligible content *(ratio)* of beings. Certain things can be understood without this relation, and therefore they can exist without it. To this Thomas replies that while relationship to a cause is not included in the definition of a being which is caused, it does follow from what is included in its intelligibility: ". . . quia ex hoc quod aliquid per participationem est ens sequitur quod sit causatum ab alio" (Leon. 4.455).

59. ". . . omne autem participans aliquid accipit id quod participat ab eo a quo participat, et quantum ad hoc id a quo participat est causa ipsius: sicut aer habet lumen participatum a sole, qui est causa illuminationis ipsius" (Leon. 40.D46:11–15). It is true that Thomas is here presenting this as Plato's opinion, but also as one with which Aristotle agrees. But there can be no doubt that it is also Thomas's personal view, in light of the texts we have seen, and in light of the fuller discussion in c. VIII of this same treatise.

60. In this text the participated perfection is described as being in the participating subject. As will be seen below, this is one way in which Thomas refers to things other than God as participating (in) *esse,* i.e., in the *actus essendi* which is intrinsic to them. As will be noted, however, at times it is difficult to determine whether Thomas is referring explicitly to the *esse* which is intrinsically present in the participating entity or to *esse commune* when he refers to something as participating in *esse*.

61. For this distinction in Thomas's Commentary on the *Sentences* see Montagnes, *La doctrine de l'analogie de l'être,* pp. 47–49. For this in some later writings see Fabro, *Partecipazione e causalità* (Turin, 1960), p. 452, n. 2. See especially *Summa theologiae* I, q. 13, a. 5, ad 1 (quoted by Fabro); and *De potentia,* q. 7, a. 7, ad 7.

We have an interesting illustration of this in a text taken from Thomas's Disputed Question *De spiritualibus creaturis*, a. 1, of 1267–1268:

Everything which comes after the first being [*ens*], since it is not its *esse*, has an *esse* which is received in something by which the *esse* itself is limited; and thus in every creature the nature of the thing which participates *esse* is one, and the participated *esse* itself is something other. And since every thing participates in the First Act by assimilation insofar as it has *esse*, the participated *esse* in each thing must be related to the nature which participates [in] it as act to potency.[62]

In this text Thomas appeals to diversity of essence and *esse* (act of being) in everything other than God. (Thomas has argued for this on the ground that there can at most be one self-subsisting being which is unlimited act and which contains within itself the fullness of being.) From this diversity of essence and *esse* in other beings he concludes that in each of them *esse* (the act of being) is received by a distinct principle which limits that *esse*. This, of course, is its nature or essence. Here another important part of Thomas's views on participation of beings in *esse* is introduced, that is, that the participating and receiving principle limits the participated act of being or *esse*.[63] Now Thomas goes on to express this diversity of nature and received *esse* in terms of participation. The nature which participates *esse* is one, and the participated *esse* something other. Until this point he has been speaking of the nature of the thing as participating (in) *esse* where *esse* is expressed by the accusative case. But he goes on to explain that everything participates in the First Act (also in the accusative case) by imitation insofar as it has *esse*, and then applies act-potency composition to the participated *esse* and the participating nature.[64]

This is a helpful summarizing passage because here we find two usages of participation: (1) The essence or nature of the creature participates *esse*, taken here, apparently, as the *actus essendi* which is realized within this particular individual. (2) It participates in the First Act or God by imitation. Hence both composition and imitation are involved in participation. We shall return to this point below.

62. "Omne igitur quod est post primum ens, cum non sit suum esse, habet esse in aliquo receptum, per quod ipsum esse contrahitur; et sic in quolibet creato aliud est natura rei quae participat esse, et aliud ipsum esse participatum. Et cum quaelibet res participet per assimilationem primum actum in quantum habet esse, necesse est quod esse participatum in unoquoque comparetur ad naturam participantem ipsum, sicut actus ad potentiam." See *Quaestiones disputatae*, ed. cit., Vol. 2, p. 371. Here Thomas is again rejecting matter-form composition of spiritual substances. For the date see Torrell, pp. 335–36.

63. This point is extremely important in connection with Thomas's understanding of the relationship between essence and *esse* in finite beings. Its importance will also emerge in the following section of this chapter when we turn to the issue of participation by composition and participation by assimilation. Surprisingly, te Velde expresses doubt that Thomas really held that *esse* is limited by the essence or nature of a finite being, and, in my opinion, misinterprets (on this point) the text we have cited above in n. 62. See *Participation and Substantiality*, pp. 151–54.

64. As I shall point out below, it seems that in this text Thomas does not explicitly refer to the nature of the creature as participating in *esse commune*, but in the *esse* which is intrinsic to the creature and received and limited by the nature of the creature.

Similar language appears in c. 8 of Thomas's *De substantiis separatis*. There he notes that things which participate *esse* (accusative case) from the first being (ablative case) do not participate *esse* according to the universal mode of being, i.e., the fullness of being, as it is present in the first principle, but in particular fashion according to the determined mode of being which pertains to this genus or species.[65] And he observes that each and every thing is adapted to one determined mode of being in accord with the mode of its substance (essence). Thus the mode for a substance composed of matter and form will be in accord with its form by which it belongs to its given species. Therefore a thing composed of matter and form participates *esse* itself through its form, from God, according to its proper mode.[66]

Here again Thomas refers to things as participating *esse* from the first cause. I conclude from this that the *esse* in which they participate according to this passage is not the divine *esse* but the act of being insofar as it is realized in particular fashion in the given participants. They participate *esse* from the first being, as Thomas phrases it this time. Again he singles out the important role assigned to essence, or to the form principle within the essence of a matter-form composite, that is, to determine the essence's appropriate mode or way of receiving *esse*. Shortly thereafter he refers to matter when it is simply considered in itself as having *esse* only in potency, and this, he continues, belongs to it because of its participation in [literally: of] the first being. Simply viewed in itself, matter lacks a form through which it participates in *esse* in actuality according to its proper mode.[67]

In another text from Quodibet 12, q. 4, a. 1 (dating from Easter 1272), Thomas refers to the fact that something which is in potency is actualized in that it participates in a higher act. And something is rendered fully in act by reason of the fact that it participates by likeness in the First and Pure Act (accusative case). This Thomas immediately identifies as *esse subsistens*. In short, here he is referring to a creature as participating by likeness or by imitation in subsisting *esse* or God.[68]

---

65. "Sed considerandum est quod ea quae a primo ente esse participant non participant esse secundum universalem modum essendi, secundum quod est in primo principio, sed particulariter secundum quendam determinatum essendi modum qui convenit vel huic generi vel huic speciei" (Leon. 40.D55:199–204). Here Thomas is refuting a series of arguments offered by Avicebron in favor of matter-form composition of spiritual substances.

66. Leon. 40.D55:205–212. Note especially: ". . . sic igitur res composita ex materia et forma per suam formam fit participativa ipsius esse a Deo secundum proprium modum."

67. ". . . non enim est esse rei neque forma eius neque materia ipsius, sed aliquid adveniens rei per formam. Sic igitur in rebus ex materia et forma compositis materia quidem secundum se considerata secundum modum suae essentiae habet esse in potentia, et hoc ipsum est ei ex aliqua participatione primi entis, caret vero secundum se considerata forma per quam participat esse in actu secundum proprium modum . . ." (Leon. 40.D55:216–225).

68. On the date see Leon. 25.1.158*–160*. For the text see Leon. 25.2.404:16–25: "Sciendum ergo quod unumquodque quod est in potentia et in actu, fit actu per hoc quod participat actum superiorem; per hoc autem aliquid maxime fit actu, quod participat per similitudinem primum et purum actum; primus autem actus est esse subsistens per se. . . ." The text continues: ". . . unde completionem unumquodque recipit per hoc quod participat esse. Unde esse est completivum omnis formae, quia per hoc completur quod habet esse, et habet esse cum est actu. . . ." Here again Thomas refers

On some occasions Thomas describes this kind of participation, that of creatures in God, by reversing his perspective, that is, by looking at things from the side of God. For instance, in his Commentary on the *Divine Names,* within a theological context, he contrasts the way in which the second and third persons of the Trinity proceed from the Father and the way creatures come forth from God. In the procession of divine persons the divine essence itself is communicated to the persons which proceed; and so there are different persons which possess one and the same divine essence. But in the procession of creatures the divine essence itself is not communicated to the creatures which proceed from God. To admit this, of course, would be to fall into a pantheistic understanding of creation. The divine essence itself remains uncommunicated, continues Thomas, or as he also phrases it, unparticipated; but its likeness, through those things which it communicates to creatures, is propagated and multiplied in creatures. In this way, therefore, divinity may be said to proceed into creatures and to be multiplied in them, that is, by likeness but not by its very essence.[69]

Thomas is evidently much concerned in this context about avoiding any semblance of a pantheistic interpretation of the procession of creatures from God. In fact, as he has implied, if one were to understand participation as meaning that the divine essence itself is communicated to creatures, this would involve a kind of pantheism. What Thomas does admit is that a likeness of the divine essence is communicated to creatures and multiplied in them. In fact, a bit farther on in this same Commentary he harks back to this same passage and explains that there he has shown that God is participated in by creatures in such fashion that he still remains unparticipated with respect to his own substance (or essence). In other words, God does not communicate his own substance or essence to creatures.[70]

In sum, it seems that Thomas refers to beings other than God as participating in *esse* in three different senses. (1) At times he means thereby that they participate in *esse commune.* This is to say that each finite being merely shares in, without possessing in its fullness, the perfection signified by the term *esse.* Every such entity exists only insofar as it possesses its particular act of being. To say that it participates in *esse commune*—the act of being viewed in general—is not to imply that there is some kind of subsisting universal *esse commune* of which each particular entity's *esse*

---

within the same context to something as participating in *esse subsistens* (God), and then as participating in *esse,* where *esse* is that which perfects the thing's form, in other words, the intrinsic *actus essendi.*

69. See c. II, lect. 3, p. 51, n. 158.

70. See lect. 4, pp. 56–57, n. 178: "Ostensum est autem supra, quod Deus ita participatur a creaturis per similitudinem, quod tamen remanet imparticipatus super omnia per proprietatem suae substantiae." In this same context (n. 177) Thomas has referred to Dionysius's remark that divine things are known to us only by participations. Thomas comments that this participation is twofold: one insofar as our intellect participates in the intellectual power and the light of divine wisdom; another insofar as things which can be grasped by our intellect themselves participate in the divine, as things are good by participating in divine Goodness, and things are existent and living "per participationem divini Esse seu Vitae."

(act of being) would simply be a piece or a part. *Esse commune* does not exist as such apart from individual existents, except in the order of thought. (2) On other occasions Thomas refers to such entities as participating in the First Act, or the First *Esse,* or the First Being, and as he often adds, by similitude or by imitation. This does not imply that they have a part of God's being. It rather means that in every finite substantial entity there is a participated likeness or similitude of the divine *esse,* that is, an intrinsic act of being *(esse)* which is efficiently caused in it by God. (3) On still other occasions, when Thomas refers to such entities (or natures) as participating in *esse,* he seems to have in mind immediately the *esse* which is realized within such entities as their particular acts of being *(actus essendi).* While this usage may strike Thomas's reader as unusual, it may be helpful to recall that frequently in such contexts Thomas uses "participate" *(participare)* as a transitive verb with *esse* as its direct object.[71]

Even so, for Thomas to speak in this third way is also for him to indicate, at least by implication, that any finite substance simply has or participates in *esse commune* without exhausting it. The first usage, whereby such substances or natures participate in *esse commune,* whether explicitly expressed or implied by the third usage, does not exclude the second major usage, whereby they participate in self-subsisting *esse.* In fact, as we shall suggest below, in the order of philosophical discovery, the first usage should ultimately lead to the second. In the order of nature, on the other hand, the second usage is the ultimate metaphysical foundation for the first. If finite natures or substances do in fact participate in *esse commune,* this is ultimately because they participate in *esse subsistens.*[72]

71. For an early explicit text which first suggested this reading to me see *In I Sent.,* d. 19, q. 5, a. 2 (Mandonnet ed., Vol. 1), p. 491: ". . . quaelibet res participat suum esse creatum, quo formaliter est, et unusquisque intellectus participat lumen per quod recte de re judicat. . . ." For other examples see ST 1, q. 44, a. 1 (cited above in n. 57: ". . . omnia alia a Deo non sint suum esse, sed participant esse"); *De spiritualibus creaturis,* a. 1 (see n. 62 and the English translation in my corresponding text, and n. 64 for discussion); *De substantiis separatis* (cited in nn. 65, 66, 67). While the passage cited in n. 65 might leave one in doubt as to whether Thomas has in mind *esse commune* or the participant's intrinsic *actus essendi,* the latter interpretation is strongly suggested by the remainder of the text as quoted in nn. 66 and 67. Also see Quodlibet 12, q. 4, a. 1 (see n. 68).

72. It is not always easy to determine which of these three usages of *esse* Thomas has in mind, and on occasion it is especially difficult to decide between the first and the third usages, i.e., between participating in *esse commune* and in *esse* taken as the *actus essendi* which is realized intrinsically within the participant. See, for instance, *Quaestiones disputatae De anima,* q. 6, ad 2: ". . . dicendum quod ipsum esse est actus ultimus qui participabilis est ab omnibus; ipsum autem nihil participat. Unde si sit aliquid quod sit ipsum esse subsistens sicut de Deo dicimus, nichil participare dicimus. Non est autem similis ratio de aliis formis subsistentibus, quas necesse est participare ipsum esse et comparari ad ipsum ut potentia ad actum" (Leon. 24.1.51:268–275). The first reference to *ipsum esse* would make one think of *esse commune;* but the final usage of *ipsum esse* may refer to the subsisting form's intrinsic *actus essendi.* This usage is more evidently intended in the corpus of Thomas's reply: ". . . nam materia ex hoc quod recipit formam participat esse. Sic igitur esse consequitur ipsam formam, nec tamen forma est suum esse, cum sit eius principium. . . . Et ita in formis per se subsistentibus invenitur et potentia et actus, in quantum ipsum esse est actus formae subsistentis, quae non est suum esse" (Leon. 24.1.51:232–247). Also see SCG I, c. 22 (ed. cit., p. 24): "Amplius. Omnis res

This brings us to still another important difference between participation of beings in *esse* and the other major kinds of participation singled out by Thomas in his Commentary on the *De Hebdomadibus*. Not only do finite entities participate in *esse commune;* this ultimately leads him to posit the existence of a source which is self-subsisting *esse*.[73] In other cases of real participation, Thomas will not permit us to conclude to the existence of a self-subsisting accidental form in which particular substances participate, or a self-subsisting substantial form in which individual instances of matter would participate. While Thomas stoutly resists any suggestion that *esse commune* subsists as such outside the mind apart from individual existents, self-subsisting *esse* does exist. It is his distinction between *esse commune* and self-subsisting *esse* which permits him to maintain this view, and yet to avoid any Platonic theory of subsisting universal forms.[74]

This also nicely fits together with another distinctive position of Aquinas, his refusal to include God within the subject of metaphysics. As we have already seen in Ch. I, for Thomas the subject of metaphysics is what he sometimes describes as *ens commune* (being in general), and sometimes as being as being or *ens inquantum ens*. He stands out among his contemporaries for refusing to admit that God himself falls under this notion of being which is the very subject of metaphysics. God can and indeed should be studied by the metaphysician, but only as the principle or cause of *ens commune* or of that which falls under *ens commune*. God himself is not included within *ens commune*.[75] If we may assume that *esse commune* is coterminous in extension with *ens commune,* then we may conclude that the subject of metaphysics is limited to the kinds of being which participate in *esse,* and that this

---

est per hoc quod habet esse. Nulla igitur res cuius essentia non est suum esse [*actus essendi,* presumably], est per essentiam suam, sed participatione alicuius, scilicet ipsius esse [*esse commune* or *actus essendi?*]. . . ." For two other references to participation in *esse* in the sense of the *actus essendi* see Quodlibet 3, q. 8. a. 1 (cited above in n. 39); and *In VIII Phys.*, lect. 21, p. 615, n. 1153: "Necesse est enim quod omnis substantia simplex subsistens, vel ipsa sit suum esse, vel participet esse. . . . Omnis ergo substantia quae est post primam substantiam simplicem, participat esse. Omne autem participans componitur ex participante et participato, et participans est in potentia ad participatum."

73. See, for instance, ST I, q. 44, a. 1, as cited above in n. 57; *De substantiis separatis,* c. 8, as cited above in nn. 65, 67; Quodlibet 12, q. 4, a. 1, as cited in n. 68; *Quaestiones de anima,* q. 6, ad 2 (cited in n. 72). Arguments for God's existence based on participation also make this same point. See ST I, q. 2, a. 3 for the fourth way. It is also clearly implied by the three arguments offered in *De potentia,* q. 3, a. 5, to show that there can be nothing apart from God which is not created by him. See ed. cit., p. 49, especially arguments 2 (the way of Aristotle) and 3 (the way of Avicenna). See Clarke, "The Meaning of Participation in St. Thomas," *Explorations in Metaphysics,* pp. 94–95, 97.

74. Cf. the texts cited above from SCG I, c. 26 (n. 46); *De potentia,* q.7, a. 2, ad 4 and ad 6 (n. 48); ST I, q. 3, a. 4, ad 1 (n. 50).

75. See *In De Trinitate,* q. 5, a. 1, ad 6 (Leon. 50.141:323–324, 330–331), where *ens* is twice identified as the subject of metaphysics; q. 5, a. 4 (Leon. 50.154:161–162), where this subject is referred to as *ens in quantum est ens,* and where *res divinae* are identified not as the subject of metaphysics, but as principles of the subject (p. 154:176–178); Prooemium to his Commentary on the *Metaphysics* (ed. cit., p. 2), where he identifies this subject as *ens commune* and refuses to include separate substances within it. These (God and intellectual substances) are rather studied by metaphysics as causes of its subject, i.e., *ens commune*. Also see *In IV Met.*, lect. 1, p. 151, n. 533. Being *(ens)* is the subject.

subject includes the *esse commune* in which they participate, but not the *esse subsistens* in which they also participate. As we have already seen from the important text from Thomas's Commentary on the *Divine Names,* there he excludes God from *esse commune.* As one would expect, if God does not fall under *ens commune,* the subject of metaphysics, no more does he fall under *esse commune.*[76]

Perhaps a word should be said here about the precise relationship between *ens commune* and *esse commune.* Are they completely identical? As Thomas indicates in his Commentary on the *De Hebdomadibus, ens* and *esse* are both most universal, and hence, I have suggested, equal in extension. But he had also noted there that while *esse* may be participated in by other things, *ens* may not be. When Thomas describes the subject of metaphysics as *ens commune* or as *ens inquantum est ens,* he is using *ens* in such fashion as to include both the essence principle and the *(esse)* principle, the act of being, found within any finite substance. Hence, strictly speaking, the subject of metaphysics for Aquinas is not existence or even the act of being *(esse)* but being *(ens),* which includes both essence and the act of being *(esse).*[77] But, as we have now seen in many different contexts, Thomas constantly refers to finite entities as participating in *esse.* Since he has denied that *ens* can be participated in, and since he has correlated the *esse* in which they participate with their nature or essence as act and potency, it seems clear that *esse commune* also signifies the act principle *(actus essendi)* which is required for any concrete entity *(ens)* to be realized in actuality; but it signifies this act principle considered universally and in its fullness of perfection rather than as received in any given participant. It follows from this that while *ens commune* and *esse commune* are equal in extension, and while God does not fall under either of them, they are not completely identical and are not perfectly convertible with one another.[78]

---

76. See above, n. 55, for the text from the Commentary on the *Divine Names.* For an unsuccessful attempt to include God within Thomas's understanding of *esse commune* see J. de Vries, "Das 'esse commune' bei Thomas von Aquin," *Scholastik* 39 (1964), pp. 163–77. For well taken critiques see Aertsen, *Medieval Philosophy and the Transcendentals,* pp. 390–94; te Velde, *Participation and Substantiality,* pp. 187–94.

77. In addition to the texts just cited (see n. 75), see *In IV Met.,* lect. 2, p. 155, n. 553. There Thomas makes the point that if the name *res* is taken from quiddity, the name *ens* is taken from the *actus essendi.* Both designate the same reality, however, as Thomas repeats in n. 558: "Et ideo hoc nomen Ens quod imponitur ab ipso esse, significat idem cum nomine quod imponitur ab ipsa essentia." In short, both *res* and *ens* are convertible insofar as they designate the concrete entity, including both its essence and its *esse.* For the same see *De veritate,* q. 1, a. 1 (Leon. 22.1.5:131–139), where Thomas offers his derivation of the transcendental properties of being. For the point that *ens* is that which has *esse,* see, for instance, ST I–II, q. 26, a. 4: "Sicut enim ens simpliciter est quod habet esse, ens autem secundum quid quod est in alio . . ." (Leon. 6.190). Also see *In XII Met.,* lect. 1, p. 567, n. 2419: "Nam ens dicitur quasi esse habens, hoc autem solum est substantia, quae subsistit." For references both to *esse* and to *ens* as *communissimum* see *In De Hebdomadibus,* cited above in nn. 16 and 17.

78. Thus while one can say that *ens commune* is the subject of metaphysics, one should not say this of *esse commune.* This is because *esse* here signifies the *actus essendi* rather than "that which is," which *ens* signifies and which therefore *ens commune* also signifies.

At the same time, it should also be noted that *esse* has been applied by Thomas to self-subsisting *esse* or God, in which creatures participate. When used in this way, of course, as *esse subsistens*, it is no longer included within *esse commune* nor, for that matter, within *ens commune*. Additional confirmation for this is found in Thomas's Commentary on Prop. 6 of the *Liber de causis*. There he is trying to explain what certain Platonists had in mind by stating that the First Cause is above being *(supra ens)*. Rightly understood, says Thomas, this means that the First Cause is above being *(ens)* insofar as it (the First Cause) is unlimited or infinite *esse*. Being *(ens)*, continues Thomas, is restricted to that which participates in *esse* in finite fashion. This, in turn, is proportioned to our intellect, whose object is quiddity *(quod quid est)*, as is said in Bk III of the *De anima*. Therefore that alone can be grasped by our intellect which has a quiddity that participates in *esse*. Because God's quiddity is his very *esse*, he is beyond our understanding; that is, we cannot know him as he is in himself.[79] While Thomas is here commenting on a highly Neoplatonic source, he certainly agrees that we cannot arrive at quidditative knowledge of God in this life. This is consistent with his refusal to include self-subsisting *esse* within *ens commune*. Whether he would deny that being *(ens)* taken in some other way can be applied analogically to God is a point we shall defer for consideration in our discussion of analogical predication of divine names.[80]

3. Participation, Composition, Limitation

With this we come to an issue which has divided Fabro and Geiger from the time when their two books on participation first appeared.[81] How does one ultimately account for the fact that finite beings are indeed finite or limited? Is it by appealing to the intrinsic composition within any such being of an essence principle which limits the *actus essendi* which it receives? Or is it rather by appealing to the fact that the *esse* of every such being is only a limited and deficient imitation of the divine being? In other words, when it comes to the ultimate explanation for the limitation of the many within the order of being, is this owing to what Geiger

79. *Sancti Thomae de Aquino super Librum de causis expositio,* Saffrey ed., p. 47. Note in particular: "Sed secundum rei veritatem causa prima est supra ens in quantum est ipsum esse infinitum, ens autem dicitur id quod finite participat esse, et hoc est proportionatum intellectui nostro cuius obiectum est quod quid est ut dicitur in III° *De anima,* unde illud solum est capabile ab intellectu nostro quod habet quidditatem participantem esse; sed Dei quidditas est ipsum esse, unde est supra intellectum." For Aristotle see *De anima* III, c. 4 (429b 10 ff.).

80. For fuller discussion of this, see Ch. XIII below.

81. Fabro's *La nozione metafisica di partecipazione secondo S. Tommaso d'Aquino* first appeared in 1939 (Milan: Vita e pensiero, 1939). Here I have used the second edition (Turin: Società editrice internazionale, 1950). Geiger's *La participation dans la philosophie de s. Thomas d'Aquin* (Paris: Vrin, 1942) was reissued by the same publisher in 1953 (the edition I am using here). Geiger notes at the end of his Introduction that his work was completed when the first edition of Fabro's book became available to him. He did manage to incorporate various references to Fabro in the notes of his work, including points of agreement and disagreement.

calls participation by composition or to what he calls participation by similitude or formal hierarchy? In accounting for the limited character of finite beings, Fabro assigns primacy to participation by composition, though he refuses to separate composition and imitation as sharply as he believes Geiger has done. Geiger, on the other hand, assigns primacy to participation by similitude in accounting for this. If the *esse* of a given being is limited, this is first and foremost because it imitates its divine source only to a limited degree, not because it is limited by the essence which receives it. Limitation is prior in nature to composition.[82]

This disagreement in interpretation centers in large measure on what Fabro calls transcendental participation rather than predicamental participation. By predicamental participation he means that all the participants have in themselves the same formality in terms of its essential content, and that the participated characteristic does not exist as such apart from its participants.[83] Here one has to do with "univocal formalities, such as genera with respect to species, and species with respect to individuals."[84] In other words, Fabro here has in mind the first two major kinds of participation distinguished by Thomas in his Commentary on the *De Hebdomadibus*—logical participation and real participation, whether of matter in form or of a substance in its accidents. By transcendental participation he rather means that the participants have in themselves only a lesser likeness or similitude of the participated perfection, which does exist in itself either as a property of a higher entity, or in the pure state as a pure and subsisting formality in full possession of itself. In the last-mentioned case we are dealing with the participation of beings in *esse,* with the consequence that the participated perfection can only be predicated analogically of the participants, not univocally.[85]

Geiger, on the other hand, distinguishes two different systems of participation, that is, participation by composition and participation by similitude. In the first case, participation is based upon a duality of a receiving subject and an element which is received. Here the fundamental element is composition. To participate is

82. For an overview of this controversy see Helen James John, *The Thomist Spectrum* (New York, 1966), pp. 88–97, 108–18. For a good résumé of Fabro's personal reactions to Geiger's approach see Fabro, *Participation et causalité selon s. Thomas d'Aquin,* pp. 63–73.

83. See *La nozione metafisica,* pp. 317–18.

84. See Fabro, "The Intensive Hermeneutics of Thomistic Philosophy," *Review of Metaphysics* 27 (1974), pp. 471–73.

85. See *La nozione metafisica,* p. 318. As Fabro also writes: "La partecipazione *analoga,* in concreto, è quella della creatura dal Creatore che, essendo l'essere per essenza, in sè riassume . . . tutte le altre perfezioni, *formalmente* se sono perfezioni pure, *virtualmente* se miste." For support he cites two interesting texts: *In II Sent.* d. 16, q. 1, a. 1, ad 3 (Mandonnet ed., Vol. 2, p. 398): ". . . convenientia potest esse dupliciter: aut duorum participantium aliquod unum, et talis convenientia non potest esse Creatoris et creaturae . . . ; aut secundum quod unum per se est simpliciter, et alterum participat de similitudine ejus quantum potest . . . et talis convenientia esse potest creaturae ad Deum . . . ;" *De veritate,* q. 23, a. 7, ad 10: ". . . creatura non dicitur conformari Deo quasi participanti eandem formam quam ipsa participat, sed quia Deus est substantialiter ipsa forma cuius creatura per quandam imitationem est participativa . . ." (Leon. 22.3.672:336–340).

to possess something one has received. It is also the case that if the receiving subject is less perfect than the received perfection, the subject will limit that perfection. Hence limitation is also present in almost all instances of participation. Nonetheless, philosophies which adopt this kind of participation derive limitation from composition. Composition is prior in the order of nature. Geiger proposes this as a definition of participation by composition: it is the reception and consequently the possession of an element, which has the role of form, by a subject which has the role of matter. If limitation also results therefrom, this is owing to the imperfection of the receiving subject; but composition is essential.[86]

By participation by similitude or formal hierarchy, on the other hand, Geiger has in mind more or less perfect states of one and the same form and their hierarchical ordering; this ordering is based on their unequal degrees of perfection. In this case participation immediately expresses a diminished and particularized state of an essence each time it is not realized in the absolute fullness of its formal content. According to this approach, the many, when contrasted with the unity of the first principle, is explained first and foremost not by intrinsic composition but by formal inequality. If X and Y both imitate a common source for their perfection, this is because X does so only to its given degree, and Y does so only to its given degree. Composition may also enter in here. Hence the distinction between the two kinds of participation does not rest on the presence or absence of composition, but on the relationship between composition and limitation. If composition accounts for limitation, we have participation by composition. If limitation is prior in the order of nature to composition, we have participation by similitude or formal hierarchy.[87]

According to Geiger, Thomas found himself faced with the problem of the One and the Many, and with these two different ways of accounting for multiplicity. While Geiger argues that they are indeed two complete systems of participation, he denies that Thomas simply chose one over the other.[88] Nonetheless, on Geiger's account, in developing his highly original metaphysics of participation, including that of beings in *esse,* Thomas assigns primacy to participation by similitude or formal hierarchy.[89]

86. Geiger, *La participation,* pp. 27–28.
87. *La participation,* pp. 28–29.
88. On the two systems as Thomas was faced with them, see pp. 63–73. On Thomas's refusal simply to choose one or the other see p. 31.
89. P. 47. There he concentrates on Thomas's solution for the problem faced by Boethius in his *De Hebdomadibus:* How are creatures good—substantially or by participation? Geiger finds Thomas substituting for participation by composition "la participation par similitude ou par hiérarchie formelle, où la participation n'exclut pas, bien plus où elle *implique l'identité* entre l'essence de ce qui est par participation et ce qu'on lui attribue." For continued insistence on Thomas's assigning of primacy to participation by similitude see pp. 49–55. See pp. 60–61, n. 3, where Geiger maintains the same when it comes to the case of essence as participating in *esse.* He insists that if a being is this kind of being by reason of its essence, and real by reason of its existence, one must account for the diversity and inequality which arise from the side of the essence. Here one must appeal to participation by formal hierarchy. The essence "which participates in [*à*] existence is itself a participation of

Geiger acknowledges that participation by composition is implied in the second main division from Thomas's text from his Commentary on the *De Hebdomadibus*. But he notes that participation by an effect in its cause (the third main division) falls on a different level. Even so, it is in terms of the note of formal inequality (of the participated perfection in the participants) that this kind of participation bears some similarity with the first two types. An effect does not receive in all its fullness that which its cause is capable of producing.[90] This is also true when we are dealing with *esse* as it is realized in finite beings. According to Geiger, participation by composition does not play a fundamental role in Thomas's account of the participation of beings from the First Being. Geiger acknowledges that in finite beings existence *(esse)* is always conjoined with a distinct essence principle. But this composition of essence and *esse* does not of itself account for the fact that *esse* is present in such entities in limited fashion. Rather, both essence and *esse* are to be regarded as participations with respect to the First Being and therefore as limited. However, in a note he does acknowledge, if somewhat begrudgingly, that Thomas usually explains the finite character of a creature by appealing to the "limits" of its *esse*, which themselves depend on the finite character of the creature's nature or essence. But he sees in this an implicit affirmation by Thomas of the primacy of participation by formal limitation (similitude). Because of this, Fabro (and Nicolas) charge that Geiger has in effect undermined the ultimate justification for defending real composition and distinction of essence and *esse* in creatures.[91]

In reacting to this, I would first recall that neither the division of participation proposed by Fabro between transcendental and predicamental participation nor that offered by Geiger between participation by composition and participation by formal similitude appears as such with these exact titles in Thomas's texts. Nonetheless, as we have seen from his Commentary on the *De Hebdomadibus* and from various other supporting texts, elements of each of the above can be found there. If I may now bypass the first member of Thomas's threefold division, logical participation, and concentrate on the remaining two, I would recall that under the second division Thomas has offered two examples that clearly involve real composition between a participant and a participated perfection—that of matter in form, and

---

[*de*] the First Perfection, of which it expresses only a limited and fragmentary aspect." Also see pp. 64–65, 67, 217, and especially 392–98.

90. Pp. 49, 78.

91. Pp. 392–93; 394, n. 2. Geiger seems to have some difficulty in dealing with Thomas's view that act is limited by a distinct potency (see p. 394, n. 1, and n. 2). The text he analyzes in n. 1, p. 396 (from *De spiritualibus creaturis*, a. 1) also seems to work against his stress on the primacy of participation by similitude. Indeed, he himself comments that composition appears as an a priori condition for the existence and possiblity of a finite being. Cf. J.-H. Nicolas, "Chronique de Philosophie," *Revue thomiste* 48 (1948), pp. 555–64. Fabro has referred to this as the most decisive and radical critique of Geiger's conclusions. For the charge that Geiger's approach undermines the ultimate reason for defending the real distinction of essence and *esse* in creatures, see Fabro, *Participation et causalité*, p. 64, where he is quoting (with approval) from Nicolas, p. 561.

that of a subject in its accidents. But I have also concluded from analyzing his texts that one should not place Thomas's account of the participation of beings in *esse* under this member of Thomas's division. I have rather suggested that it should fall under the third major division, that whereby an effect participates in its cause, especially when the cause is of a higher order than the effect. However participation in *esse* may be understood by Thomas in a particular context—whether as participation in *esse commune*, or in a finite being's own *actus essendi*, or in *esse subsistens*—it seems to me that it should still be placed under this third division.

It should also be noted that if the examples of participation offered by Thomas in the second division (whether of matter in form or of a subject in its accident) involve real distinction and composition of participant and participated perfection, one should not automatically assume that all of the other conditions realized in these two instances must also apply to other cases where participation involves composition. As we have now seen in various contexts, composition is involved in Thomas's account of the participation of beings in *esse*. A participant is united with that in which it participates *(participatum)* as potency and act. Within any participating being, its essence enters into composition with its act of being *(esse)*. In addition to this, although I have not yet stressed this point, Thomas insists that act as such is not self-limiting. If one finds limited instances of act, especially of the *actus essendi*, this can only be because in every such case the act principle *(esse)* is received and limited by a really distinct potency principle. Hence composition with essence is necessary if one is to account for the limitation of *esse* within a given entity. On this point Fabro is surely correct.[92]

It is also true, of course, that according to Aquinas, the essence principle and the act of being *(actus essendi)* of any creature are both created by God simultaneously, since the entire being is created, including both.[93] Hence, at least within

92. For discussion see Nicolas, "Chronique de Philosophie," pp. 561–62; Wippel, *Metaphysical Themes,* pp. 157–61, and Ch. V below; J.-D. Robert, "Le principe: 'Actus non limitatur nisi per potentiam subjectivam realiter distinctam,'" *Revue philosophique de Louvain* 47 (1949), pp. 44–70. For some texts where Thomas accepts and uses the principle that act as such or *esse* is not self-limiting, see *In I Sent.,* d. 43, q. 1, a. 1 (Mandonnet ed., Vol. 1, p. 1003); *In I Sent.,* d. 8, q. 2, a. 1 (p. 202); *In I Sent.,* d. 8, q. 5, a. 1, sed contra (p. 226); SCG I, c. 43; ST I, q. 7, a. 1; *Compendium theologiae,* c. 18 (Leon. 42.88:7–8). See *De spiritualibus creaturis,* a. 1. Note especially: ". . . habet esse in aliquo receptum, per quod ipsum esse contrahitur" (cited above in n. 62). Cf. n. 63 above and te Velde, *Participation and Substantiality,* pp. 153–54, who refuses to see in texts such as these Thomas's acceptance of the view that *esse* is limited by a receiving principle. His remark on p. 154 indicates that he believes that to admit this would commit Thomas to holding that the received nature would already exist "before" it received *esse*. No reputable interpreter of Aquinas would accept this consequence, of course, but I do not think that acceptance of this central axiom in Thomas's metaphysics (that unreceived act or *esse* is unlimited) commits one to any such position. For a more extensive examination of the textual evidence pointing to the presence of this axiom in Aquinas's metaphysics see my "Thomas Aquinas and the Axiom That Unreceived Act Is Unlimited," *Review of Metaphysics* 51 (1998), pp. 533–64.

93. See, for instance, *De potentia,* q. 3, a. 5, ad 2: "Ad secundum dicendum, quod ex hoc ipso quod quiddati esse attribuitur, non solum esse, sed ipsa quidditas creari dicitur: quia antequam

Thomas's perspective, there is little justification for Geiger's fear that appeal to participation by composition might lead to the defense of some kind of preexisting subject or essence which would be independent from God and would wait for existence to be created and poured into it at some subsequent point in time. Any such reading of Aquinas would, of course, be a caricature, but one not too far removed from an interpretation actually imputed to a more traditional Thomism by some, such as William Carlo. Such a fear also seems to haunt Geiger's discussions of this issue. Perhaps this is because he has assumed without justification that an application of what he understands by participation by composition to the case of *esse* will carry with it unacceptable consequences which were part of certain theories of participation prior to Aquinas, or which may apply to participation of matter in form or of a subject in its accidents, but not to participation of beings in *esse*.[94]

Moreover, some such misunderstanding seems to have led te Velde to the mistaken view that if one holds that essence receives and limits its corresponding act of being *(esse)*, it must be produced by God before its act of being and only subsequently actualized by its act of being, which God also produces.[95] Such an interpretation would lead to the absurd consequence that essences would preexist (taken temporally) before receiving their acts of being, something that Thomas would, of course, never have admitted. It seems to me, however, that both Geiger and te Velde have failed to see (1) that here Thomas is applying in an appropriately adapted way the adage that causes can be causes of one another simultaneously according to different causal lines, or in this case, that principles can be mutually dependent on one another according to different lines of dependency, and (2) that priority in the order of nature does not necessarily imply priority in the order of time. Thus, while the act of being actualizes the corresponding essence principle of a given entity and

---

esse habeat, nihil est, nisi forte in intellectu creantis, ubi non est creatura, sed creatrix essentia" (ed. cit., p. 49). Cf. *De potentia*, q. 3, a. 1, ad 17: "Ad decimum septimum dicendum, quod Deus simul dans esse, producit id quod esse recipit: et sic non oportet quod agat ex aliquo praeexistenti" (p. 41). Also see J. Owens, "The Accidental and Essential Character of Being in the Doctrine of St. Thomas Aquinas," in *St. Thomas Aquinas on the Existence of God*, J. Catan, ed. (Albany, N.Y., 1980), pp. 91–92.

94. In addition to the texts cited above, see Geiger, *La participation*, pp. 64–65, 393, and 393 n. 1. For discussion and refutation of this way of viewing things see Fabro, *Participation et causalité*, pp. 69–71; Nicolas, "Chronique," pp. 561–62. For Carlo see his "The Role of Essence in Existential Metaphysics," in J. Rosenberg, ed., *Readings in Metaphysics* (Westminster, Md., 1963), pp. 278–81, which originally appeared in *International Philosophical Quarterly* 2 (1962), pp. 584–89; and *The Ultimate Reducibility of Essence to Existence in Existential Metaphysics* (The Hague, 1966), especially pp. 103–5. This is in connection with Carlo's insistence, along with a number of other Thomists today, that essence for Aquinas, when rightly interpreted, is reducible to the given degree or mode of existence possessed by a given finite entity. For discussion and criticism of this reading see my "Thomas Aquinas on the Distinction and Derivation of the Many from the One," pp. 586–90, and Ch. VI below, pp. 190–92.

95. For te Velde see the reference in n. 92 above. Cf. pp. 82–83 (his general concern, shared with Geiger, about referring to essence and being [*esse*] as composed); p. 87 ("pre-existent subject of participation"); p. 89 (according to Fabro's account essence would be created as potency and subsequently endowed with actuality).

makes that entity actually exist, simultaneously the essence principle receives and limits the act of being. Neither preexists as such apart from the other, and each enjoys its appropriate priority in the order of nature (not in the order of time) with respect to its particular ontological function within a given entity.

Even so, one may still ask about the essence principle itself of any finite being. It is only by appealing to the essence principle of any such being that one can account for the fact that the being is of this kind rather than of any other kind and participates in *esse* to its given and limited degree. But what about the essence itself? A metaphysical explanation must also be offered for it.

Here, it seems to me, Geiger has a certain point in his favor. As we have seen, both the essence and the *esse* of any finite being are created, according to Thomas. If we ask why this given being has this essence principle rather than any other, Thomas's ultimate explanation is that this is because its essence imitates its appropriate divine idea and depends upon it as upon its formal exemplar cause and because God, acting as an efficient cause, has actually created it in accord with its divine idea together with its act of being in creating this individual being. According to Aquinas a divine idea is nothing but a given way in which God understands himself as capable of being imitated by a creature. Hence the essence of any existing creature is an expression of a particular way in which the divine idea can be imitated and in fact is imitated.[96] At this point it seems that participation by composition within an existing creature entails causal dependency, not only in the order of efficient causality, but also in the order of extrinsic formal or exemplar causality. In other words, participation by composition, as it is expressed in the intrinsic structure of any created entity, receives its final explanation in the order of extrinsic causality by leading one to recognize God not only as the first efficient cause but also as the extrinsic formal or exemplar cause of every participant. And this, it seems to me, is to bring in the element of participation by assimilation or formal hierarchy, as Geiger would have it.[97]

96. For a general discussion of Thomas's views concerning divine ideas and his reasons for appealing to them see Geiger, "Les idées divines dans l'oeuvre de S. Thomas," in *St. Thomas Aquinas 1274–1974. Commemorative Studies,* A. Maurer et al., eds. (Toronto, 1974), Vol. 1, pp. 175–209; Wippel, "Thomas Aquinas on the Divine Ideas," *Etienne Gilson Series* 16 (Toronto, 1993); V. Boland, *Ideas in God according to Saint Thomas Aquinas: Sources and Synthesis* (London–New York–Cologne, 1996). For Thomas see ST I, q. 15, a. 1, ad 3: "Unde idea in Deo nihil est aliud quam Dei essentia" (ed. cit., p. 90); ST 1, q. 15, a. 2: "Sic igitur inquantum Deus cognoscit suam essentiam ut sic imitabilem a tali creatura, cognoscit eam ut propriam rationem et ideam huius creaturae" (p. 91); *In I Sent.,* d. 36, q. 2, a. 2: "Unde cum hoc nomen 'idea' nominet essentiam divinam secundum quod est exemplar imitatum a creatura . . ." (Mandonnet ed., Vol. 1, p. 842); *De veritate,* q. 3, a. 2: ". . . unde essentia sua est idea rerum non quidem ut essentia sed ut est intellecta . . ." (Leon. 22.1.104:202–204).

97. For a somewhat different way of bringing together in complementary fashion participation by composition and by similitude see J.-D. Robert, "Note sur le dilemme: 'Limitation par composition ou limitation par hiérarchie formelle des essences,'" *Revue des sciences philosophiques et théologiques* 49 (1965), pp. 60–66.

In sum, both composition and assimilation or imitation are involved in Thomas's explanation of the participated structure of creatures. For the philosopher, I would suggest, who must begin with finite beings and only eventually reason from what he finds in them to knowledge of God as their cause, participation in *esse commune* comes first in the order of discovery. Along with this comes recognition of one way of reasoning to the distinction and composition of essence and *esse* (act of being) within such entities—although, as we shall see in the next chapter, other ways may also be found in Thomas's texts. (As I read Aquinas, demonstration of real distinction between essence and *esse* within finite beings need not presuppose prior knowledge of the existence of God.)[98]

Explicit recognition of the radically caused character of any such being easily follows from the recognition of the distinction of essence and act of being therein, and with this, a metaphysical basis for an eventual demonstration of the existence of God. After one has demonstrated God's existence, one will then be justified in speaking of participation in *esse subsistens* as distinguished from participation in *esse commune*. Appeal to God as the formal exemplar cause as well as the efficient cause of any existing finite being is necessary to complete the picture. Only then will one be in position to recognize such a being as a created imitation and assimilation of the divine being. Hence, if with Geiger one wishes to speak of participation by assimilation or formal hierarchy, such enters in only at this point. That is to say, it comes later in the order of discovery. But it does seem to enjoy priority in the order of nature, although not in the order of time insofar as explanation in terms of exemplar causality is concerned. Creatures actually exist because God wills them to exist and efficiently causes them. But God can will a creature of a certain kind to exist only if it can exist. And it can exist only if it is viewed by God as a possible way of imitating the divine essence.[99]

To this I would add, in order to forestall any possible misunderstanding, that this is not to imply that the creaturely essence enjoys any actual reality in itself apart from the divine essence prior to its actual creation in an existing entity together with its corresponding act of being. The actual creation of any such an entity, including both its essence and its act of being, also requires the simultaneous exercise of divine efficient causality.

98. See my *Metaphysical Themes*, cc. 5 and 6, as well as Ch. V below.
99. For discussion of this see *Metaphysical Themes*, c. 6, especially pp. 163–71.

Essence-*Esse* Composition and
the One and the Many

In the previous chapter, while considering various statements by Aquinas to the effect that finite beings participate in *esse,* we eventually concluded that these statements may be interpreted in three different ways. At times he means thereby that particular entities or natures participate in *esse commune* (the act of being considered in general). At times he means that they participate in *esse subsistens* (God). And on other occasions he simply wishes to indicate that each finite nature participates in the *esse* which it receives, that is, in its own act of being *(actus essendi).* When Thomas speaks in this third way, he is also assuming, at least by implication, that particular beings participate in *esse commune.* This follows because for him to refer to a particular entity as participating in its own *esse* or its own act of being is by implication to contrast its *esse* with that in which it merely participates but which it does not exhaust, i.e., *esse commune.* As we have also noted, if finite substances may be described as participating in *esse* in either of these ways, this will ultimately be because they participate in *esse subsistens.* The most important contrast, therefore, is between participation in *esse subsistens,* on the one hand, and participation in *esse commune* (or in the finite being's particular act of being), on the other.[1]

Even so, when it comes to the philosophical order of discovery, we have already suggested that recognition of finite entities as participating in self-subsisting *esse* comes later.[2] And since here we are committed to presenting Thomas's metaphysical thought according to the philosophical order as he himself has defined it, we now wish to explore the evidence he offers to show that such entities really do participate in *esse.* This means that we should first examine the evidence he offers

1. See above, pp. 120–21.
2. See Ch. IV above, p. 131.

to show that they participate really rather than merely logically or in a purely mind-dependent way in *esse commune* and/or in their own *actus essendi*. Only subsequently will it be appropriate for us to take up Thomas's evidence for their participating in *esse subsistens,* that is, after we have considered his philosophical argumentation for God's existence. In the present chapter, therefore, we shall concentrate on the first point; in later chapters the second issue will be examined.[3]

As regards participation by particular entities or natures in *esse commune* and, following from this, in their own act of being, what philosophical evidence does Thomas offer for this? If this kind of participation is going to be recognized as real and not merely as logical or notional in the way one concept may be said to participate in another, it seems that it will have to be based on real reception by a participating subject or principle of a participated perfection, i.e., *esse*. But as we have now seen in some detail, for Aquinas this entails real diversity and composition within the participant of a participating principle and a participated or received perfection.[4] In other words, recognition of such participation as real is closely conjoined with Thomas's well known if much contested views concerning real composition and distinction of essence and *esse* in every participating entity or substance.[5]

If Thomas frequently identifies the participated principle in nondivine entities as *esse,* his terminology when referring to the principle which participates in *esse* is much less fixed. As we have already seen from various texts analyzed in Ch. IV, on different occasions he refers to the participating and receiving principle as being *(ens),* or as "that which is," or as quiddity (or essence), or as substance, or as form, or as a creature, or as a thing *(res),* or as nature, or simply as that which participates *(participans).*[6] His meaning will usually be captured if we simply employ the terms "essence" or "nature" to express this, as he himself also does.[7] Nonetheless, if

3. In other words, as already noted above, until philosophical evidence for God's existence has been presented, one is entitled to speak of non-divine natures or entities as participating in self-subsisting *esse* only in a putative or hypothetical fashion. On God's existence see Chs. X, XI and XII below.

4. See, for instance, in Ch. IV the discussion and references to texts from Thomas's Commentary on the *De Hebdomadibus* (nn. 20, 21, 22, 23), and Quodlibet 2, q. 2, a. 1 (n. 27). Also see the discussion in Section 3 of that chapter.

5. See n. 91 of the preceding chapter for Fabro's stress on the close connection between these. As I see it, the best way of determining whether or not participation is real is to examine the structure of the participant. Real composition therein of a participating and receiving principle, on the one hand, and of a received and participated perfection, on the other, points to real rather than merely logical or intentional participation.

6. For illustrations see in Ch. IV, nn. 14 *(ens* and *id quod est, In De Hebd.);* 79 *(ens* and *quidditas, In De causis,* Prop. VI); 39 *(substantia,* Quodl. 3, q. 8, a. 1); 22 and 23 *(forma, In De Hebd.);* 72 *(forma, Quaestiones disp. De anima,* q. 6); 31 *(creatura,* Quodl. 2, q.2, a. 1); 62 *(res* and *natura, De spirit. creaturis,* a. 1); 66 *(res, De subs. sep.,* c. 8); 39 *(participans,* Quodl. 3, q. 8. a. 1). Also see *In VIII Phys.,* lect. 21, p. 615, n. 1153: *substantia.*

7. See, for instance, *De veritate,* q. 21, a. 5: "Ipsa autem natura vel essentia divina est eius esse; natura autem vel essentia cuiuslibet rei creatae non est suum esse sed est esse participans ab alio" (Leon. 22.3.606:137–141).

Thomas is to justify his claim that nondivine entities really do participate in *esse commune* and therefore in their own *esse* (act of being), it will be incumbent upon him to establish the reality of such diversity and composition of a participating principle or essence and of a participated perfection *(esse)* within such beings.

This brings us back to the issue of Thomas's views concerning the relationship between essence and *esse* (act of being, or existence, as it is often referred to) in creatures. A definitive history of the general thirteenth-century controversy concerning the essence-existence relationship in created entities remains to be written. The same is true of the history of the more remote origins of any theory that defends real distinction between essence and existence in such entities.[8] For our immediate purposes it will be enough to recall that this issue arises in large measure from efforts by various medieval thinkers to account for the radically contingent or caused character and for the nonsimple or composite character of beings other than God. To the extent that the second point is emphasized, appeal to real composition and distinction of essence and existence in such entities is also a way of responding to the problem of the One and the Many.

Avicenna has often been cited, both by thirteenth-century writers and by twentieth-century scholars, as an early defender of real distinction between essence and existence in such beings. Thus thinkers as diverse in metaphysical outlook as Thomas himself, Siger of Brabant, and James of Viterbo, basing themselves on the medieval Latin translation of his *Philosophia prima,* all criticized Avicenna for having defended an extreme version of this theory. Not only had he distinguished between essence and existence in such entities; he had mistakenly treated existence as if it were superadded to essence almost like an accident. Averroes was also known to each of these writers and their contemporaries for his criticisms of Avicenna on this very point. Shortly after the death of Aquinas in 1274, a running controversy broke out between Henry of Ghent and Giles of Rome. Giles had used the language of thing and thing *(res* and *res)* in defending real distinction between essence and

8. For helpful introductions to this issue, especially in terms of its more remote sources, see M.-D. Roland-Gosselin, ed., *Le 'De ente et essentia' de s. Thomas d'Aquin* (Paris, 1948; originally appeared in 1926), pp. 137–205; J. Paulus, *Henri de Gand. Essai sur les tendances de sa métaphysique* (Paris, 1938), pp. 260–91; A. Forest, *La structure métaphysique du concret selon saint Thomas d'Aquin,* 2d ed. (Paris, 1956), pp. 128–65. On thirteenth-century (and later) controversies concerning this see Gilson, *History of Christian Philosophy in the Middle Ages* (New York, 1955), pp. 420–27; M. Grabmann, "Doctrina S. Thomae de distinctione reali inter essentiam et esse ex documentis ineditis saeculi XIII illustratur," in *Acta Hebdomadae Thomisticae Romae celebratae 19–25 Novembris 1923 in laudem S. Thomae Aquinatis* (Rome, 1924), pp. 131–90; R. Imbach, "Averroistische Stellungnahmen zur Diskussion über das Verhältnis von *esse* und *essentia.* Von Siger von Brabant zu Thaddaeus von Parma," in *Studi sul XIV secolo in memoria di Anneliese Maier,* A. Maierù and Paravicini Bagliani, eds. (Rome, 1981), pp. 299–339; and Wippel, "Essence and Existence," c. 19 in *The Cambridge History of Later Medieval Philosophy,* pp. 392–410; "The Relationship between Essence and Existence in Late-Thirteenth-Century Thought: Giles of Rome, Henry of Ghent, Godfrey of Fontaines, and James of Viterbo," in *Philosophies of Existence, Ancient and Medieval,* P. Morewedge, ed. (New York, 1982), pp. 131–64.

existence, and however he may have intended for this to be understood, sharp criticism was directed against his version of this theory by Henry, and then by Godfrey of Fontaines and by many other late thirteenth- and early fourteenth-century thinkers. Against Giles, Henry rejected any real distinction between essence and existence and held that they are only "intentionally" distinct. While agreeing with Henry in eschewing any kind of real distinction between them, Godfrey also rejected Henry's claim that they are intentionally distinct. For him there is only a distinction of reason between them.[9]

Aquinas himself was familiar with earlier discussions of the relationship between essence and *esse*. As we have already seen in Ch. IV, he seems to find support for his own theory in the *De Hebdomadibus* of Boethius and, for that matter, also in the *Liber de causis*.[10] Whether or not he really believed that his own understanding of the essence-*esse* relationship had been defended by these sources is a matter for conjecture. Be that as it may, his understanding of the essence-*esse* relationship cannot be reduced to that of Avicenna or, for that matter, to that of Boethius or the *Liber de causis* or any other earlier thinker, at least in my judgment. On the other hand, some twentieth-century scholars have gone to the opposite extreme and have denied that Thomas himself ever defended any such theory. While some dispute may be possible about the best way of expressing in English Thomas's understanding of this diversity or distinction, there can be no doubt, in my opinion,

---

9. In addition to explicit discussions of Avicenna's position in the studies by Roland-Gosselin, Paulus, and Forest cited in the previous note, see Thomas Aquinas's critique of the Avicennian position in his *In IV Met.,* lect. 2, Cathala-Spiazzi ed., p. 155, nn. 556–558. For Siger of Brabant see *Quaestiones in Metaphysicam,* W. Dunphy, ed. (Louvain-la-Neuve, 1981), *Introductio,* q. 7, pp. 45–46, 47 (Munich ms.); *Quaestiones in Metaphysicam,* A. Maurer, ed. (Louvain-la-Neuve, 1983), *Introductio,* q. 7, pp. 30, 32, 34 (Cambridge ms.); *Introductio,* 2, p. 398 (Paris ms.). Note that in the first two contexts Siger associates Avicenna's view with that of Albert the Great. For James see *Jacobi de Viterbio, O.E.S.A., Disputatio prima de quolibet,* E. Ypma, ed. (Würzburg, 1968), q. 4, pp. 46, 53–54, 55:402–403. For Avicenna see his *Liber de Philosophia prima sive Scientia divina I–IV,* Bk I, c. 5, pp. 34–35, and *Liber de Philosophia prima V–X* (Louvain-Leiden, 1980), Bk V, c. 1, p. 233. For Averroes' understanding and critique of Avicenna see *In IV Met.,* ed. cit., Vol. 8, fol. 67rab–67va. On Thomas's interpretation of and reaction (both positive and negative) to Avicenna see my "The Latin Avicenna as a Source for Thomas Aquinas's Metaphysics," *Freiburger Zeitschrift für Philosophie und Theologie* 37 (1990), pp. 65–72. For defenses of Avicenna based on the Arabic text of his metaphysics against the charge that he had viewed existence as if it were an accident see F. Rahman, "Essence and Existence in Avicenna," *Mediaeval and Renaissance Studies* 4 (1958), pp. 1–16; "Ibn Sina," in M. M. Sharif, ed., *A History of Muslim Philosophy,* Vol. 1 (Wiesbaden, 1963), pp. 483–86; P. Morewedge, "Philosophical Analysis and Ibn Sina's 'Essence-Existence' Distinction," *Journal of the American Oriental Society* 92 (1972), pp. 425–35. On the controversy between Henry, Giles, and Godfrey of Fontaines, see in addition to the two references in the preceding note to other studies of mine, my *The Metaphysical Thought of Godfrey of Fontaines: A Study in Late-Thirteenth-Century Philosophy* (Washington, D.C., 1981), pp. 39–99.

10. See the texts cited in nn. 20–23 in the preceding chapter from Thomas's Commentary on Boethius's *De Hebdomadibus.* For different interpretations of the meaning of *id quod est* and *esse* in Boethius see n. 14 of the same chapter. Also see nn. 51 and 52 for references to Thomas's Commentary on the *Liber de causis.* For discussion of the latter see Roland-Gosselin, *Le "De ente et essentia,"* pp. 146–49. For Thomas's citation of the *De causis* in his *De ente,* c. 4 see Leon. 43.376:36–40.

that he defended real as opposed to merely mind-dependent or logical composition of essence and *esse* in every finite entity. And while he speaks more frequently of their composition or of their being composed than of their being really distinguished or diverse, he does at times use the latter terminology. A number of texts which point to this conclusion have already been examined in Ch. IV, and more will now be considered.[11]

As we turn again to Thomas's texts, an important question of methodology arises. As we have already suggested, one can establish the participated character of nondivine beings in two of the senses distinguished above before taking up the question of God's existence. But does Thomas think that recognition of real composition and distinction of essence and *esse* in such beings is possible without prior knowledge that God exists?

On this point contemporary interpreters of Thomas's thought differ. As I have argued elsewhere and will again attempt to show here, not all of Thomas's arguments for the essence-*esse* distinction or composition presuppose knowledge of God's existence. Many of them surely do.[12] Consequently, in this chapter I shall single out for consideration those arguments for such distinction and composition which do not, in my opinion, presuppose such knowledge. Presentation of these will be sufficient to show that Thomas can speak of nondivine entities as participating in *esse* in the two ways singled out for consideration here. For the sake of completeness, other arguments which do presuppose God's existence will be mentioned in a later chapter. These will be treated separately in order to emphasize (1) that such arguments are not required for Thomas the philosopher to speak of real par-

---

11. For some who have denied that Aquinas defends real distinction between essence and *esse* see M. Chossat, "Dieu," *Dictionnaire de théologie catholique*, Vol. 4, pt. 1, col. 1180; "L'Averroïsme de saint Thomas. Notes sur la distinction d'essence et d'existence à la fin du XIIIᵉ siècle," *Archives de philosophie* 9 (1932), pp. 129[465]–177[513]; F. Cunningham, "Distinction according to St. Thomas," *New Scholasticism* 36 (1962), pp. 279–312; "Textos de Santo Tomás sobre el *esse y esencia*," *Pensamiento* 20 (1964), pp. 283–306; "The 'Real Distinction' in John Quidort," *Journal of the History of Philosophy* 8 (1970), pp. 9–28; and finally his large volume *Essence and Existence in Thomism: A Mental vs. The "Real Distinction"?* (Lanham, Md., 1988). For some who do find this position in Aquinas see N. del Prado, *De veritate fundamentali philosophiae Christianae*, pp. 23–79; C. Fabro, "Un itinéraire de saint Thomas. L'établissement de la distinction réelle entre essence et existence," originally published in *Revue de philosophie* 39 (1939), pp. 285–310, repr. in his *Esegesi tomistica* (Rome, 1969), pp. 89–108; *La nozione metafisica di partecipazione*, pp. 212–44; E. Gilson, *History of Christian Philosophy*, pp. 420–27; *Being and Some Philosophers*, 2d ed. (Toronto, 1952), pp. 171–78; M. Grabmann, "Doctrina s. Thomae de distinctione reali, " pp. 131–90; J. de Finance, *Être et agir dans la Philosophie de Saint Thomas*, 2d ed. (Rome, 1960), pp. 94–111; L. Sweeney, "Existence/Essence in Thomas Aquinas's Early Writings," *Proceedings of the American Catholic Philosophical Association* 37 (1963), pp. 97–131; J. Owens, "Quiddity and Real Distinction in St. Thomas Aquinas," *Mediaeval Studies* 27 (1965), pp. 1–22, esp. 19–22; *Aquinas on Being and Thing* (Niagara, N.Y., 1981); "Stages and Distinction in *De ente*: A Rejoinder," *The Thomist* 45 (1981), pp. 99–123; "Aquinas' Distinction at *De ente et essentia* 4.119–123," *Mediaeval Studies* 48 (1986), pp. 264–87; Wippel, "Aquinas's Route to the Real Distinction: A Note on *De ente et essentia*, c. 4," *The Thomist* 43 (1979), pp. 279–95; *Metaphysical Themes in Thomas Aquinas*, cc. 5 and 6 (pp. 107–61).

12. See the last two items mentioned in the preceding note.

ticipation of beings in *esse,* so long of course as we do not mean thereby participation in *esse subsistens,* and (2) that after philosophical argumentation for God's existence has been offered, Thomas can revisit the issue of participation of finite beings in *esse subsistens* from a purely philosophical perspective and reinforce his defense of the distinction and composition of essence and act of being in such entities.

While Thomas's arguments for distinction and composition of essence and *esse* in beings other than God have been classified in different ways by different scholars, here I shall consider them under the following headings: (1) what is often referred to as the *intellectus essentiae* argument, especially as this is presented in the *De ente et essentia,* but together with what I have elsewhere referred to as the second phase of the argumentation in the *De ente;* (2) other arguments based on the impossibility of there being more than one being in which essence and *esse* are identical; (3) what Leo Sweeney has called the "genus" argument; (4) arguments based on participation; (5) argumentation based on the limited character of individual beings.[13]

1. The *Intellectus Essentiae* Argument

This argumentation, especially as it is presented in c. 4 of Thomas's early *De ente et essentia* (ca. 1252–1256), has occasioned considerable controversy. The points of disagreement have to do not only with the validity of the argument considered in itself, but also with the proper understanding of Thomas's purpose in developing it.[14] The first phase or stage of the argumentation in this chapter has often been removed from its context and presented as a complete argument in itself which should stand on its own merits. For that matter, shortly after Aquinas's death, one finds an interesting variation of this argument offered by Giles of Rome in support of real distinction of essence and existence in creatures, and roundly criticized by others such as Godfrey of Fontaines.[15]

13. For other attempts to classify Thomas's arguments see Fabro, *La nozione metafisica,* pp. 212–44; de Finance, *Être et agir,* pp. 94–111; and Sweeney, "Existence/Essence in Thomas Aquinas's Early Writings," esp. pp. 105–31. My own classification is most indebted to that offered by Sweeney.

14. For discussion see Fabro, *La nozione metafisica,* pp. 218–20; "Un itinéraire de saint Thomas," *Esegesi Tomistica,* pp. 94–108; U. Degl'Innocenti, "La distinzione reale nel 'De ente et essentia' di S. Tommaso," *Doctor Communis* 10 (1957), pp. 165–73; J. Bobik, *Aquinas on Being and Essence* (Notre Dame, Ind., 1965), pp. 162–70; A. Maurer, *St. Thomas Aquinas: On Being and Essence* (Toronto, 1968), pp. 21–4; F. Van Steenberghen, *Le problème de l'existence de Dieu dans les écrits de s. Thomas d'Aquin* (Louvain-la-Neuve, 1980), pp. 33–51; S. MacDonald, "The *Esse/Essentia* Argument in Aquinas's *De ente et essentia,*" *Journal of the History of Philosophy* 22 (1984), pp. 157–72; Owens and Wippel, as cited in n. 11 above.

15. In his "Essence/Existence in Thomas," Sweeney considers the *intellectus essentiae* argument as a distinctive argument while examining a number of early Thomistic texts in which it appears (pp. 105–9). But he also takes up the version presented in the *De ente* under the general heading of "God-to-creatures" argumentation (pp. 115–17), and thereby seems to recognize it as the first stage of a larger and more complicated argument. MacDonald objects to the description of the first part of the *De ente* argumentation as an *intellectus essentiae* argument, arguing that the claim that "whatever is not part of an essence is other than the essence" does not enter into Thomas's argumentation there.

If interpreters differ today concerning the connection of this stage of the argument with the subsequent part of Thomas's discussion in c. 4 of the *De ente,* they also disagree about the relationship between Thomas's argumentation for the essence-*esse* distinction in that chapter and the argument for God's existence which also appears there.[16] Since I have had occasion elsewhere to consider some of these divergent interpretations, and especially one by J. Owens which would make the argumentation in the *De ente* (and apparently any other possible argumentation) for real composition and distinction of essence and *esse* dependent on prior knowledge of God's existence, I shall not repeat the details of that discussion here.[17] Instead I shall simply present the argument in the way in which I believe it should be interpreted in light of Thomas's text, examine it critically, and then briefly address some of the differences in interpretation that remain between Owens and myself.

The general background for Thomas's argumentation in c. 4 is well known. There he is attempting to determine how essence is realized in separate substances, that is, in the soul, in intelligences, and in the First Cause (God).[18] While the simplicity of the First Cause is generally granted, observes Thomas, some defend matter-form composition in the soul and in intelligences. Thomas identifies Avice-

---

He also comments that this would not allow for the possibility that, in one case, *esse* and essence are identical ("The *Esse/Essentia* Argument," p. 162). While the label "*intellectus essentiae*" argument is not a major concern, I would question MacDonald's way of reformulating Thomas's opening remark in the argument. "Whatever belongs to a thing," as MacDonald correctly adds, and "is not part of its essence" does not quite capture the point of Thomas's Latin: "Quicquid enim non est de intellectu essentiae vel quidditatis . . ." (cited below in n. 25). Moreover, if one interprets this as meaning "Whatever is not included in the *understanding* (or notion) of an essence . . . ," as I would, then the statement does allow for the possibility that in one case essence and *esse* are identical. In that one case *esse* would be included in the notion or understanding of that being's *essence* if someone could adequately grasp it. Hence, with Owens ("Quiddity," pp. 5–7) and Sweeney, I will continue to refer to this as the *intellectus essentiae* argument. For Giles of Rome's variation on this see his *Quaestiones disputatae de esse et essentia,* q. 11. There he had listed six truths which cannot be maintained without the real distinction between essence and existence. The first of these is this, that the essence of every creature can be understood with the opposite of its *esse* ("cum opposito ipsius esse") i.e., as not existing. But since nothing can be understood with the opposite of itself, he concludes that whatever is understood with the opposite of a given thing must really differ from that thing. Therefore essence really differs from *esse* (Venice, 1503), fol. 24vb. Cf. f. 20va. For discussion see my "The Relationship between Essence and Existence in Late-Thirteenth-Century Thought," p. 138. And for Godfrey's exposition and critique of this see my *The Metaphysical Thought of Godfrey of Fontaines,* pp. 48–9, 60. See Godfrey's Quodlibet 3, q. 1, in *Les Quatre premiers Quodlibets de Godefroid de Fontaines,* ed. M. de Wulf and A. Pelzer, Les Philosophes Belges, Vol. 2, pp. 158, 302 (short version), and 171, 305 (short version). Giles's version, by stating that one can understand the essence of a thing as not existing, goes farther than Thomas's *De ente.*

16. See, in particular, the discussions by J. Owens and myself cited above in n. 11, and the article by MacDonald cited in n. 14.

17. In addition to the references mentioned in the preceding note, see Gilson, "La preuve du 'De ente et essentia'," *Acta III Congressus Thomistici Internationalis: Doctor communis* 3 (Turin, 1950), pp. 257–60; "Trois leçons sur le problème de l'existence de Dieu," *Divinitas* 5 (1961), pp. 26–28.

18. "Nunc restat videre per quem modum sit essentia in substantiis separatis, scilicet in anima, intelligentia et causa prima" (Leon. 43.375:1–3).

bron's *Fons vitae* as the apparent original source for this view, which is often referred to as universal hylemorphism.[19]

Thomas comments that this position is generally rejected by philosophers. Their strongest reason for denying that there is matter-form composition in separate substances and souls is their conviction that such would be incompatible with the intelligent nature of such entities. Forms are not rendered actually intelligible except insofar as they are separated from matter and its conditions; nor are they rendered actually intelligible except by the power of an intelligent substance insofar as they are received in that substance and acted on by it. Hence every intelligent substance must be completely free from matter, so much so that such a substance cannot include matter as a part of itself, nor can it be a form which is impressed upon matter as material forms are.[20]

Someone might counter, observes Thomas, that it is only corporeal matter that impedes intelligibility, and not every kind of matter. Presumably he has in mind those who would defend the presence of an incorporeal or spiritual matter in such entities. Against these he replies that since matter is described as corporeal only insofar as it falls under a corporeal form, it would then follow that matter's impeding intelligibility is owing to its corporeal form. This cannot be, protests Thomas, because even a corporeal form is intelligible once it is abstracted from matter. Therefore, he insists, there is no matter-form composition in the soul or in intelligences, though there is composition of form and *esse*. He cites from the *Liber de causis* (Proposition 9, Commentary) in support of this claim: "An intelligence is that which has form and *esse*." According to Thomas, form as it appears in this text stands for a quiddity or simple nature itself.[21]

In support of this claim Thomas reasons that when things are so related to one another that one is the cause of the other, that which serves as cause can exist without the other, but not vice versa. The relationship between matter and form is such that form gives *esse* (existence) to matter. Therefore, while it is not possible for matter to exist without any form, it is not impossible for some form to exist

<hr />

19. Leon. 43.375:3–8. For some background on thirteenth-century defenders and opponents of universal hylemorphism and on Avicebron see E. Kleineidam, *Das Problem der hylomorphen Zusammensetzung der geistigen Substanzen im 13. Jahrhundert, behandelt bis Thomas von Aquin* (Breslau, 1930); O. Lottin, *Psychologie et morale au XIIe et XIIIe siècles,* Vol. 1 (Louvain-Gembloux, 1942), pp. 427–60; Wippel, *The Metaphysical Thought of Godfrey of Fontaines,* pp. 275–77 (see nn. 51, 53, 57 for additional references); and J. Weisheipl, "Albertus Magnus and Universal Hylomorphism: Avicebron," in *Albert the Great Commemorative Essays,* ed. F. J. Kovach and R. W. Shahan (Norman, Okla., 1980), pp. 239–60, esp. pp. 250–60.

20. Leon. 43.375:8–376:22.

21. Leon. 43.376:23–40. For Thomas's reference to the *Liber de causis* see: "Sed est ibi compositio formae et esse; unde in commento nonae propositionis libri De causis dicitur quod intelligentia est habens formam et esse: et accipitur ibi forma pro ipsa quidditate vel natura simplici." Cf. *Le Liber de causis,* A. Pattin, ed., published separately by the *Tijdschrift voor Filosofie* (Leuven, 1966), p. 69: "Et intelligentia est habens *yliathim* quoniam est esse et forma." On the meaning of the term *yliathim* in this context see Ch. IV above, n. 51.

without matter. Form insofar as it is form need not depend on matter. And if some forms can exist only in matter, this is not because they are forms but because of their great distance from the first principle which is the First and Pure Act. Hence the essence of a composite substance differs from that of a simple substance. While the essence of a composite includes both matter and form, the essence of a simple substance is a pure form.[22]

If one grants this to Aquinas, one may still ask about nondivine simple substances or forms. If they do exist, as Thomas here takes as given, how will they differ from God?[23] It seems that, like God, they too will be perfectly simple. It is in responding to this difficulty that Thomas introduces his argumentation for distinction and composition of essence and *esse* in all such entities.

Even though such substances are pure forms and lack matter according to Aquinas, he refuses to admit that they are so simple in themselves as to be identified as pure actualities. He insists that they do include some degree of potentiality. It is important for the reader to note this point, since it indicates that if Thomas is to achieve his objective in developing the argumentation which follows, he will have to establish some kind of real and ontological, as distinguished from any purely mind-dependent or logical, act-potency composition or admixture within such beings.[24]

Thomas immediately presents what I shall describe as phase one of his argument. Whatever is not included within the notion or understanding *(intellectus)* of an essence or quiddity comes to it from without and joins in composition with it. In proof he comments that no essence can be understood without those things which are parts of that essence itself. Then he continues: but every essence or quiddity can be understood without anything being understood about its *esse* (existing). In proof Thomas notes that I can understand what a human being is, or what a phoenix is, and nevertheless not know whether such a thing exists in reality. Thomas immediately draws his conclusion. Therefore it is evident that *esse* (act of being) differs from (literally: "is other than") essence or quiddity in such entities.[25]

---

22. Leon. 43.376:41–65. Thomas then develops two other differences which follow from this. First, the essence of a composite substance can be signified as a whole or as a part, but the essence of a simple entity, i.e., its form, can only be signified as a whole. Second, the essences of composites, since they are received in designated matter, are multiplied in accord with divisions of such matter and can, therefore, be multiplied within one and the same species. Because the essence of a simple form is not received in matter, it cannot be multiplied numerically within a species (Leon. 43.376:65–89).

23. See, for instance, Thomas's remarks at the end of c. 1 of the *De ente* to the effect that some substances are simple and some are composite (Leon. 43.370:58–60). In other contexts Thomas does offer philosophical argumentation for the existence of created separate substances, i.e., angels. See J. Collins, *The Thomistic Philosophy of the Angels* (Washington, D.C., 1947), pp. 16–41.

24. "Huiusmodi autem substantiae, quamvis sint formae tantum sine materia, non tamen in eis est omnimoda simplicitas nec sunt actus purus, sed habent permixtionem potentiae; et hoc sic patet" (Leon. 43.376:90–93).

25. "Quicquid enim non est de intellectu essentiae vel quidditatis, hoc est adveniens extra et faciens compositionem cum essentia, quia nulla essentia sine hiis quae sunt partes essentiae intelligi

If one were to take this as an independent argument in its own right, that argument would end here. Immediately, however, certain questions may be raised about the force of the argument until this point. It seems to move very quickly from its recognition of the distinction between knowing what something is and knowing that it is to the conclusion that there is a corresponding extramental (i.e., real) distinction of an essence principle and an *esse* principle within any such being. And if the argument is to achieve its objective—to establish a real or ontological composition of act and potency in such entities—it seems that the *esse* which has now been shown to be distinct from essence must be taken as signifying the act of being, not merely the fact that something exists. But Thomas himself has warned against the danger of moving too quickly from distinctions which obtain in the order of thought (conceptual distinctions) to distinctions within the order of reality, or real distinctions. This, in fact, is one of his chief criticisms of Platonism.[26]

Or to put this same objection in other terms, does not the argument move illegitimately from its recognition of the distinction between what is grasped by the intellect in its first operation (essence) and what is grasped by it in its second operation (existence) to a corresponding real distinction between essence and *esse* (act of being) within the existing thing? Thomas, of course, distinguishes between the intellect's first operation whereby it knows what something is, and its second operation whereby it judges that something is. But of itself this is hardly sufficient to justify without additional evidence the conclusion that there are corresponding really distinct principles in an extramental entity.[27]

More than this, the argument also seems to presuppose that if our intellect does not include something such as actual existence in its grasp of the quiddity of a

---

potest. Omnis autem essentia vel quidditas potest intelligi sine hoc quod aliquid intelligatur de esse suo: possum enim intelligere quid est homo vel phoenix et tamen ignorare an esse habeat in rerum natura; ergo patet quod esse est aliud ab essentia vel quidditate" (Leon. 43.376:94–103).

26. For instance, in his Commentary on the *De Trinitate* of Boethius, q. 5, a. 3, Thomas connects the Pythagorean and Platonic defense of separate mathematicals and universals with the failure on the part of these thinkers to distinguish between the intellect's abstracting operations (whether abstraction of the whole or abstraction of the form) and its operation of judging negatively, i.e., *separatio*. See Leon. 50.149:287–290. Cf. ST I, q. 85, a. 1 ad 2. Also see *De substantiis separatis*, c. 2, where after a detailed exposition in c. 1 of the hierarchical structure of reality as envisioned by Plato, Thomas comments: "Huius autem positionis radix invenitur efficaciam non habere. Non enim necesse est ut ea quae intellectus separatim intelligit separatim esse habeant in rerum natura . . ." (Leon. 40.D43:2–D44:5).

27. Cf. Owens, "Quiddity and Real Distinction in St. Thomas Aquinas," pp. 8–14; "Stages and Distinction in *De ente*," pp. 107–8. While I agree with him that the argument in this first stage only establishes conceptual distinction between essence and *esse*, we differ with respect to the argument's second stage. See below. On the other hand, Fabro has attempted to defend the argument even in this first stage, or what he calls the logical argument. See "Un itinéraire de saint Thomas," pp. 94–97. For other defenses of it as concluding to an ontological or real distinction at this stage see Bobik, *Aquinas on Being and Essence* pp. 163–69; L. Dewan, "Saint Thomas, Joseph Owens, and the Real Distinction between Being and Essence," *Modern Schoolman* 61 (1984), pp. 145–56; W. Patt, "Aquinas's Real Distinction and Some Interpretations," *New Scholasticism* 62 (1988), pp. 1–29.

given entity, that factor is not really included within the essence itself. But Thomas's restrictions on our capacity to arrive at quidditative knowledge of separate substances, including created separate substances, are well known. Not quite so well known, perhaps, are the restrictions he places upon our ability to reach quidditative knowledge of most corporeal things. Still, as Owens has pointed out, merely generic knowledge of a given entity may be all that Thomas requires for this part of his argumentation to be verified if it is intended to establish only a conceptual distinction between essence and *esse;* and Thomas does grant such generic knowledge of material things to us.[28]

Still another criticism has been raised by F. Van Steenberghen. Thomas seems to shift in his usage of the term *esse* within the argument itself. Thus he reasons that any essence or quiddity can be understood without anything being known about its *esse.* Here, as we have already suggested above in presenting this text, *esse* stands for existence in the sense of facticity, the fact that something exists. The proof offered by Thomas to support this claim is our ability to understand what a human being is, or what a phoenix is, without our knowing whether or not it exists in reality. But then the argument immediately concludes that *esse* differs from essence or quiddity in such beings. Here *esse* seems to refer not to mere facticity, but to an intrinsic principle, an act of being as we have rendered it, present in all such beings. That it must be taken in this sense is confirmed, in my judgment, by the very next lines, which initiate what I shall describe as phase two of the argument: "Unless, perhaps, there is some thing whose quiddity is *esse* itself." For Van Steenberghen this shift in the meaning of *esse* renders the entire argument invalid.[29]

28. See *Super Boetium De Trinitate,* q. 6, a. 3, where Thomas denies that we can have *quid est* knowledge of God or of other separate substances; nor can we even reach any obscure quidditative knowledge of them in terms of their genus and accidents (Leon. 50.167:94–97; 168:155–168). On our difficulty in reaching knowledge of essential differences in sensible entities (and in immaterial substances) see *De ente,* c. 5, (Leon. 43.379:76–84). For a listing of texts ranging throughout Thomas's career where he maintains this reserved attitude with respect to our knowledge of essential differences in sensible things, see Roland-Gosselin, *Le "De ente,"* p. 40, n. 2. For Owens see "Quiddity and Real Distinction," pp. 6–7; "Stages and Distinction," p. 106. In the first-mentioned source Owens sets this part of the argument against the background of Thomas's earlier discussion, in c. 3 of the *De ente,* of the different ways in which a nature may be considered, i.e., absolutely or in itself, or in terms of its *esse* whether in the mind or in individual things. As Owens interprets it, this phase of the argument concentrates on quiddity or essence in its absolute consideration (see pp. 2–3).

29. See *Le problème de l'existence de Dieu dans les écrits de s. Thomas d'Aquin,* pp. 37–38, 40–41. Van Steenberghen also offers other criticisms, somewhat similar to those already mentioned. He does not concentrate on the argument's second phase which, we shall suggest, is considerably more promising. For Thomas's text see "Nisi forte sit aliqua res cuius quidditas sit ipsum suum esse . . ." (Leon. 43.376:103–104). As regards possible sources for Thomas's *intellectus essentiae* argument, Avicenna's general influence has been recognized (see Roland-Gosselin, p. 187; A. Forest, op. cit., pp. 148ff.; Van Steenberghen, p. 41). William of Auvergne's influence has also been noted (Roland-Gosselin, p. 187; Maurer, *On Being and Essence,* pp. 23–24). As I have noted in *Metaphysical Themes* (p. 111, n. 12), Algazel's *Logica* is still another likely source. See *"Logica Algazelis,* Introduction and Critical Text," C. Lohr, ed., *Traditio* 21 (1965), p. 247:26–33. Both human being and phoenix are cited in this text as examples to show that "esse accidentale est omnibus quae sunt."

Given these and similar difficulties which have been raised against this part of Thomas's argumentation, one will not be surprised to find that an increasing number of his interpreters today suggest that it is a mistake to extract this part of his reasoning from its context and to present it as an independent argument for real distinction of essence and *esse*. Some, including myself when writing elsewhere, have suggested that Thomas may not even have intended for this part of the argument to stand alone.[30] Be that as it may, since I am personally persuaded that the argument as it appears in phase one does not in fact establish any such real distinction and composition of essence and *esse,* I shall simply regard it as an introduction to the next phase, and as an introduction which will not stand on its own without that phase. Whether or not Thomas himself would have wished it to be presented as a valid argument in its own right for anything more than a conceptual distinction remains, in my opinion, an open question. The fact that he seems quietly to abandon such an argument in his later writings, while not decisive in itself, at least suggests that he may have had some reservations about it.[31]

In phase two Thomas introduces a general kind of argumentation which we shall see reappearing with some modifications in later writings. So true is this that we have reserved a special heading for consideration of those later presentations— "arguments based on the impossibility [of] there being more than one being in which essence and *esse* are identical." In phase two of the *De ente* argumentation Thomas reasons as follows. If perhaps *(forte)* there is some thing whose quiddity is its very *esse* (act of being), such a thing can only be one and first. This is so because multiplication of something can occur in only three ways: (1) by the addition of some difference, as the nature of a genus is multiplied in its species; or (2) by the reception of a form in different instances of matter, as the nature of a species is multiplied in different individuals; or (3) because one instance of a thing is absolute

30. See my *Metaphysical Themes,* p. 113; Owens, "Quiddity and Real Distinction," pp. 17ff., who also regards the argument from "quidditative content" as "but a stage in a larger demonstration." Cf. "Stages and Distinction," p. 108; MacDonald, "The *Esse/Essentia* Argument," passim.

31. For other passages from early works where the *intellectus essentiae* argument is also to be found see Sweeney, pp. 105–9. These include *In I Sent.,* d. 8, Expositio Primae Partis Textus (Mandonnet ed., Vol. 1, p. 209): ". . . et ita cuilibet quidditati creatae accidit esse, quia non est de intellectu ipsius quidditatis; potest enim intelligi humanitas, et tamen dubitari, utrum homo habeat esse"; d. 8, q. 4, a. 2 (p. 222): ". . . potest enim cogitari humanitas et tamen ignorari an aliquid homo sit," where it is incorporated into what we shall call the "genus argument," for which see below; *In II Sent.,* d. 1, q. 1, a. 1 (Mandonnet ed., Vol. 2, p. 12): ". . . ita tamen quod ipsarum rerum naturae non sunt hoc ipsum esse quod habent: alias esse esset de intellectu cuiuslibet quidditatis, quod falsum est, cum quidditas cuiuslibet rei possit intelligi etiam non intelligendo de ea an sit," where Thomas concludes from this to the caused character of every such being and then to the existence of God, and ultimately to God's unicity; *In II Sent.,* d. 3, q. 1, a. 1 (p. 87): "Quaedam enim natura est de cuius intellectu non est suum esse, quod patet ex hoc quod intelligi potest esse cum hoc quod ignoretur an sit, sicut phaenicem, vel eclipsim, vel aliquid huiusmodi," where Thomas ultimately concludes to a composition of quiddity and *esse* as of potency and act in angels while rejecting their matter-form composition. Sweeney also cites *De veritate,* q. 10, a. 12, but acknowledges that it moves in the opposite direction (see "Existence/Essence," p. 106).

and all others are only received in something else. Thomas illustrates this third possibility with a hypothetical example. If there were such a thing as a completely separate heat, it would be different from all instances of nonseparated heat by reason of its very separation. This is to say, precisely because it was not received in anything else, it would differ from all other instances of heat which are received in something else which is heated.[32]

Suppose, continues Thomas, that there is a thing which is nothing but *esse* (act of being) so as to be subsisting *esse*. Such a thing cannot be multiplied by the addition of any difference; for then it would not be pure *esse* but *esse* plus the differentiating form. So much, therefore, for possibility one. To appeal to it in order to account for many instances of subsisting *esse* would be self-refuting. In every case, with one possible exception, we would have *esse* plus a form which differentiates it. In no case would we have pure subsisting *esse*.[33]

What, then, of the second possible way of multiplying something? Thomas finds this even less satisfactory when one attempts to use it to multiply instances of pure *esse*. In all such cases, with our one hypothetical exception, we would no longer have pure *esse*, but *esse* plus the particular matter which receives and multiplies it.[34]

Wherefore, continues Thomas, it follows that there can only be one such thing which is its very *esse* (act of being). One may immediately ask, of course, what about the third possible way of multiplying something? By implication Thomas is telling us that to appeal to it is, in effect, to concede his point. For then there would indeed be only one pure and subsisting *esse*. In everything else there would be a combination of *esse* and a subject which receives *esse*, just as, if a pure and separated heat could exist, it would be distinct from all instances of received heat and would therefore be unique.[35] Wherefore, continues Thomas, since there can only be one such thing which is its very *esse* (act of being), in every other thing its *esse* (act of being) and its quiddity or nature or form differ (literally: "are other"). And if this is so, he can also conclude that in intelligences there must be *esse* in addition to (*praeter*) form, or form and *esse*. This follows because in every being, with this one possible exception, *esse* and form differ.[36] With this, phase two of Thomas's argumentation comes to an end.

32. Leon. 43.376:103–377:113. Note his description of the third possibility: ". . . vel per hoc quod unum est absolutum et aliud in aliquo receptum . . ." (110–111).

33. "Si autem ponatur aliqua res quae sit esse tantum ita ut ipsum esse sit subsistens, hoc esse non recipiet additionem differentiae quia iam non esset esse tantum sed esse et praeter hoc forma aliqua . . ." (Leon. 43.377:113–117).

34. ". . . ut multo minus reciperet additionem materiae, quia iam esset esse non subsistens sed materiale" (Leon. 43.377:117–119).

35. "Unde relinquitur quod talis res quae sit suum esse non potest esse nisi una . . ." (Leon. 43.377:119–121).

36. ". . . unde oportet quod in qualibet alia re praeter eam aliud sit esse suum et aliud quidditas vel natura seu forma sua; unde oportet quod in intelligentiis sit esse praeter formam, et ideo dictum est quod intelligentia est forma et esse" (Leon. 43.377:121–126). See his earlier reference to the *Liber de causis* (376:36–39).

In my judgment, this part of Thomas's argumentation is much more interesting and promising than phase one. Phase two also rests on certain presuppositions, of course. First of all, there is the fact of multiplicity. If multiplicity of intelligences is admitted, in such intelligences essence and *esse* must differ. The reason for this is that at most there can be one thing in which essence and *esse* are identical. At the same time, it seems to me that this argument, if valid, will apply as soon as multiplicity of substantial entities of any kind is admitted. If two or more things exist— which for Aquinas is an undeniable datum of sense experience—in none of them with the one possible exception can essence and *esse* be identified. This is so because there cannot be more than one being which is its very *esse*. Hence, this argument may also be regarded as an early attempt on Thomas's part to address himself to the problem of the One and the Many.

Secondly, the argument seems to rest on the exhaustive character of the three possible ways of accounting for multiplicity which it distinguishes. Is there no other way of accounting for the multiplication of beings? At least as of this writing Thomas thinks that there is not. Moreover, as we shall see below when considering the next class of his arguments, he eventually seems to have concluded that this threefold way of accounting for multiplicity could be reduced to two fundamental types: (1) multiplication by the addition of a difference (cf. possibility one as proposed in the *De ente*); (2) multiplication by reception in different subjects (joining possibilities two and three of the *De ente*, apparently).[37]

Owens has maintained that Thomas's argumentation in the *De ente* presupposes and must presuppose that God's existence has already been established before it can conclude to a real distinction between essence and *esse* in other entities. Owens and I continue to differ on this issue. On my reading, until this point in the argumentation, God's existence has entered in only as an hypothesis. At most there can be one being in which essence and *esse* are identical. In all other beings they must

---

37. See Fabro, "Un itinéraire de saint Thomas," p. 99. To illustrate the more common appeal to two ways of accounting for multiplication, Fabro cites *Compendium theologiae*, c. 15: ". . . duplex est modus quo aliqua forma potest multiplicari: unus per differentias, sicut forma generalis, ut color in diversas species coloris; alius per subiecta, sicut albedo" (Leon. 42.87:22–25). Here Thomas is attempting to show that there is only one God. His argument continues to this effect: if a form cannot be multiplied by the addition of differences, and if it is not a form that exists in a subject, it can only be one. But such is true of the divine essence which is identical with the divine *esse*. It should be noted that Fabro also warns here against separating the three arguments of the *De ente*. He regards the present one, which he calls metaphysical, as the prolongation and natural complement of the first one, which he refers to as logical (pp. 98–99). Fabro cites *In I Sent.*, d. 8, q. 4, a. 1, ad 2 as a contemporary version of the threefold division of the *De ente*. There Thomas writes that among created things something may be determined so as to be *aliquid* either (1) by the addition of a difference, or (2) because a common nature is received in something, or (3) by the addition of an accident. None of these will apply to God, whose simplicity Thomas is here defending. However, while the first two divisions more or less parallel the first two in the *De ente*, the third member of the division in *In I Sent.* finds no parallel in the *De ente*. And their purposes are not the same. See ed. cit., Vol. 1, pp. 219–20.

differ. But if God's existence enters in at this point only as a working hypothesis, this does not mean that the conclusion itself is only hypothetical. On the contrary, Thomas's point is to show that it is impossible for there to be more than one being in which essence and *esse* are identical. If we grant the fact of multiplicity, then in all existing things, with this single possible exception, essence and *esse* must differ. Nor is this to reason from possibility to actuality. It is rather to reason from the impossibility of there being more than one thing in which essence and *esse* are really identical to the conclusion that in all other things, with this one possible exception, essence and *esse* are not identical. It is only in what I shall call phase three of Thomas's argumentation that he attempts to prove that God does in fact exist. But at the end of phase two Thomas has concluded that in all things, with the single possible exception, *esse* differs from ("is other than") quiddity or nature or form. He immediately applies this to intelligences, as we have seen, and finds confirmation in this for his earlier citation from the *Liber de causis*—an intelligence includes both form and *esse*. He had cited that text as an authority in introducing his overall argumentation to show that there is composition of form and *esse* in intelligences.[38]

Owens and I do agree that Thomas defends real distinction of essence and *esse* by the end of phase three of his general argument. According to Owens, however, Thomas does not establish this distinction as real rather than as merely conceptual until after he presents his argument for God's existence in that same phase three. In phase two he would have established nothing more than the conceptual distinction already argued for in phase one, but would now have extended its application to intelligences. In support he also comments that Thomas introduces nothing in his argumentation in phase two to indicate that he is there attempting to establish a real distinction.[39]

To this I would first point out that Thomas does not use the terminology of real distinction or of conceptual distinction between essence and *esse* anywhere in the

38. See the text cited above in n. 21.

39. For these various interventions in chronological order see Owens, "Quiddity and Real Distinction," *Mediaeval Studies* 27 (1965), pp. 1–22; Wippel, "Aquinas's Route to the Real Distinction," *The Thomist* 43 (1979), pp. 279–95; Owens's reply: "Stages and Distinction in *De ente*," *The Thomist* 45 (1981), pp. 99–123; Wippel's reply: *Metaphysical Themes in Thomas Aquinas,* pp. 120–32 (see pp. 107–20 for a reprint of "Aquinas's Route to the Real Distinction"); Owens, "Aquinas' Distinction at *De ente et essentia* 4.119–123," *Mediaeval Studies* 48 (1986), pp. 264–87. Also see MacDonald's "The *Esse/Essentia* Argument," *Journal of the History of Philosophy* 22 (1984), pp. 157–72; W. Patt, "Aquinas's Real Distinction," *New Scholasticism* 62 (1988), pp. 1–29. Only after I had completed this book and submitted it for publication did a recent study by A. Maurer become available, entitled "Dialectic in the *DE ENTE ET ESSENTIA* of St. Thomas Aquinas," in *Roma, magistra mundi. Itineraria culturae medievalis.* Mélanges offerts au Pére L. E. Boyle à l'occasion de son 75e anniversaire, J. Hamesse, ed. (Louvain-la-Neuve, 1998), pp. 573–83. While I cannot devote to it here the attention it deserves, I would simply note that Maurer argues that in the *De ente* Thomas only intended to offer dialectical argumentation, not metaphysical demonstrations, either for the real distinction or composition of essence and *esse* in creatures, or for the existence of God. Suffice it to say that my interpretation differs greatly from such a reading.

argumentation in *De ente* c. 4, even though, as Owens himself has pointed out, this issue would become important shortly after Aquinas's death, and even though it is important for us. On a few other occasions Thomas does refer to the distinction or composition of essence and *esse* as real. But in the *De ente* he leaves it to his reader to discern what kind of distinction he has in mind. Even so, it seems clear enough that throughout phase two Thomas is arguing for a distinction that does not depend on our way of thinking about it, and hence for what we understand as a real distinction between them. Thus he opens phase two with the transition clause: "Unless perhaps there is some thing whose quiddity is *esse* itself." Here he surely means that, if such a thing does exist, its quiddity is really, not merely conceptually, identical with its *esse*. Such a being could only be one and first, he continues to argue, and he attempts to prove this by introducing three ways in which something might be multiplied. As we have seen, he quickly eliminates the first and second proposed ways of multiplying supposed instances of subsisting *esse* as self-refuting and concludes that in every other thing, apart from this one possible exception, *esse* differs from the nature or form or essence of that thing. Since he wants to show that there is or can be only one thing in which essence and *esse* are really identical, it follows that he here is making the point that in all other things they are not really identical. But this is to say that they are really, not merely conceptually distinct.[40]

Moreover, as supporting evidence for my interpretation, I would recall the example Thomas uses to illustrate the third possible way of multiplying something, whereby one instance of it is separate and all other instances are received in something. Presumably in each of these nonseparate instances, what receives must be distinct, and really distinct, from that which is received. As an example Thomas offers the case of heat. If there were a pure and separate heat, it would be different from all instances of heat that are not separate, i.e., that are received in something else. And in all these other cases, the heat would presumably be distinct, and really distinct, from the subject that receives it. So too, Thomas would have us reason, if there is such a thing that is subsisting *esse* itself, by reason of its separation it will be different from all instances of *esse* that are not separate, that is to say, that are received in something. From this we may conclude that in such things that which

---

40. On Aquinas's lack of concern in most contexts about identifying explicitly as real or as conceptual the distinction he was defending between essence and existence see Owens, "Quiddity and Real Distinction," pp. 19–22; "Stages and Distinction," p. 104; "Aquinas' Distinction at *De ente*," pp. 265–66. Owens has singled out five passages in Thomas's writings where he actually refers to this distinction (or composition) as real: *In I Sent.,* d. 13, q. 1, a. 3 (Mandonnet ed., Vol. 1, p. 307): "Ad hoc enim quod sit universale et particulare, exigitur aliqua diversitas realis . . . quidditatis communicabilis, et esse quod proprium est;" *In I Sent.,* d. 19, q. 2, a. 2, sol. (p. 471): "Actus autem qui mensuratur aevo, scilicet ipsum esse aeviterni, differt ab eo cuius est actus re quidem . . ."; *De veritate,* q. 27, a. 1, ad 8 (which will be discussed below under Section 3 of this chapter); *In De Hebdomadibus,* lect. 2, Leon. 50.272:196–273:207 (cited above in Ch. IV, n. 20); ibid., 273:219–220: "Si enim esset aliud realiter id quod est et ipsum esse, iam non esset simplex sed compositum" (discussed below in this chapter). For Owens see "Aquinas' Distinction," pp. 266–73.

receives (essence, or nature, or form) is distinct, and really distinct, from that which is received (*esse,* or the act of being).

Hence there is no reason, so far as I can determine, to think that in phase two Thomas is limiting himself to a purely conceptual or logical distinction. Indeed, if he did not think that he had now demonstrated that in all other things, including intelligences, essence and *esse* are not really identical (and therefore are really distinct), he would have failed to achieve one of his stated objectives in phase two of his argumentation, i.e., to prove that there is at most one thing in which essence and *esse* are identical. Proof of that objective was necessary for him to establish his main conclusion, that in everything else, and therefore in intelligences, they are (really) distinct.

What about phase three in Thomas's argumentation? Why has Thomas introduced it, if it is not a necessary step in his demonstration of real distinction between essence and *esse* in things other than God? As I interpret the text, Thomas takes the conclusion of phase two, real otherness of essence and *esse,* as his point of departure for his argument for God's existence in phase three.[41] This makes it most unlikely that he would again prove this same point at the conclusion of his argumentation for God's existence. But what he does add in phase three to our understanding of the relationship between essence and *esse* in intelligences is the point that they unite with one another as potency and act.

Though this argument for God's existence will be considered in greater detail in a subsequent chapter, certain parts of it should be mentioned here. It begins by noting that whatever belongs to a thing is caused by the principles of that thing's nature (as is true of risibility, a proper accident, in a human being), or comes to it from some extrinsic principle (as light is present in air owing to the influence of the sun). But, continues Thomas, *esse* itself cannot be caused (efficiently) by the very form or quiddity of a thing, for that thing would then cause itself and produce its own existence, something which Thomas rejects as impossible. Therefore, in any thing in which nature (essence) and *esse* differ, that thing must receive its *esse*

41. While Owens denies that real distinction between essence and *esse* has been established by Thomas either at the end of phase one or at the end of phase two of the argumentation in the *De ente,* he maintains that the conceptual distinction which has then been established is sufficient for Thomas to conclude to the efficiently caused character of any such being, and therefore, to begin his argumentation for God's existence. See "Quiddity and Real Distinction," p. 16; "Being and Natures in Aquinas," *Modern Schoolman* 61 (1984), pp. 160–61. Whether the argument based on inspection of essence or quidditative content is sufficient to establish the efficiently caused character of any such being is another difficult and contested point. For discussion and criticism see Van Steenberghen, *Le problème de l'existence de Dieu,* pp. 39–40. Whatever the validity of such an approach, my contention is that Thomas does not follow this procedure in the *De ente,* but rather reasons from real distinction of essence and *esse* in all existing beings, with only one possible exception, to the efficiently caused character of such beings. For another who finds Thomas arguing for real distinction at what I am calling phase two of the argument, see MacDonald, "The *Esse/Essentia* Argument," pp. 167–68.

from something else, or must be efficiently caused. Here Thomas uses the conclusion established in phase two as the point of departure for his argument for God's existence; for he grounds the radically caused or contingent character of all beings, with one possible exception, on the distinction within them of essence and *esse*.[42]

After completing his argument for God's existence Thomas observes that this First Cause is the cause of *esse (causa essendi)* for all other things by reason of the fact that it is pure *esse*. He again notes that an intelligence is form and *esse* (see the conclusion of phase two), but now goes on to show that form and *esse* are related as potency and act.[43] That which receives something from another is in potency with respect to that which it receives, and that which is received in it is its act. Hence the quiddity or form (or essence) which is an intelligence is in potency to the *esse* it receives from God, and its *esse* is received as its act. In other words, only now has Thomas completed his general effort in this chapter to show not only that essence and *esse* are really distinct in all nondivine beings and therefore in intelligences, but also that they are united in intelligences as potency and act. His text shows that he is again using *esse* to signify the intrinsic act of being of any such being. "Because . . . the quiddity of an intelligence is the intelligence itself, therefore its quiddity or essence is identical with that which it is, and its *esse,* which it receives from God, is that whereby it subsists in reality."[44]

Thomas also comments that for this reason substances of this kind are said to be composed of *quo est* and *quod est,* or as Boethius puts it, of *quod est* and *esse*. Though Thomas has not used the term "real" to describe the diversity and composition of essence and *esse* which he has argued for in this chapter, he will use such terminology a few years later in interpreting the Boethian couplet in his Commentary on the *De Hebdomadibus*. This we have already seen in the previous chapter. But it is worth mentioning again, since it suggests that the kind of diversity

42. Leon. 43.377:127–137. Note the concluding remark: "Ergo oportet quod omnis talis res cuius esse est aliud quam natura sua habeat esse ab alio." By this statement Thomas has considered and eliminated a third possibility, i.e., that something which belongs to a thing is simply identical with that thing itself. He eliminates it by concentrating on beings in which nature and *esse* really differ. In all such beings their *esse* must be given to them from without, which is to say, they must be efficiently caused.

43. For the continuation of the argument for God's existence see Leon. 43.377:137–146. Note in particular: ". . .oportet quod sit aliqua res quae sit causa essendi omnibus rebus eo quod ipsa est esse tantum . . ." He then joins the conclusion from phase two with this: "Patet ergo quod intelligentia est forma et esse, et quod esse habet a primo ente quod est esse tantum, et hoc est causa prima quae Deus est."

44. "Omne autem quod recipit aliquid ab alio est in potentia respectu illius, et hoc quod receptum est in eo est actus eius; ergo oportet quod ipsa quidditas vel forma quae est intelligentia sit in potentia respectu esse quod a Deo recipit, et illud esse receptum est per modum actus. Et ita invenitur potentia et actus in intelligentiis, non tamen forma et materia nisi aequivoce. . . . Et quia, ut dictum est, intelligentiae quidditas est ipsamet intelligentia, ideo quidditas vel essentia eius est ipsum quod est ipsa, et esse suum receptum a Deo est id quo subsistit in rerum natura . . ." (Leon. 43.377:147–163).

and composition he has in mind here is real, not merely conceptual or mind-dependent.[45]

A final observation is in order here. If my interpretation of Thomas's procedure in this chapter from the *De ente* is correct, Thomas does not rest his case for real distinction or otherness of essence and *esse* on prior knowledge of God's existence. But he does introduce the argumentation for God's existence before he correlates essence and *esse* as potency and act. Does this not mean that his conclusion that essence and *esse* are composed as potency and act presupposes knowledge of God's existence, even if his case for a real distinction between them does not?

While I grant that in the *De ente* Thomas has correlated essence and *esse* as potency and act only after he has completed his argument for God's existence, I would suggest that he would not have to proceed in this way. Simply by reasoning from real diversity of essence and *esse* in all beings with one possible exception, he can and does establish the efficiently caused character of such beings. At this point he could, if he wished to do so, immediately establish the fact that in each of them essence and *esse* unite as potency and act. He could do this merely by appealing to the principle that what is received by something from without unites with that thing as an act with its receiving potency, the same principle he has employed in the *De ente*.[46] In short, the actual argumentation for God's existence could have been omitted. Thomas has not introduced it as a step in his demonstration of real diversity of essence and *esse* in nondivine entities. And he could have established the point that essence and *esse* unite as potency and act in such entities without inserting the argument for God's existence. That he has in fact proceeded otherwise here is perfectly natural, since he has stated at the beginning of *De ente,* c. 4 that he wishes to indicate how essence is realized in separate substances including the soul, intelligences, and the First Cause. Rather than continue to speak in hypothetical fashion about the First Cause or God, it was quite appropriate for Thomas to complete his account at this point by demonstrating God's existence.[47]

2. Arguments Based on the Impossibility of More Than One Being in Which Essence and *Esse* Are Identical

In addition to the particular version of this argumentation which we have seen in phase two of Chapter 4 of the *De ente,* Thomas frequently enough has recourse to a somewhat similar procedure in other contexts. In these other contexts he almost always takes God's existence as given or as already established, and reasons from this to distinction or composition of essence and *esse* in other beings. This is

---

45. ". . . et propter hoc a quibusdam dicuntur huiusmodi substantiae componi ex quo est et quod est, vel ex quod est et esse, ut Boethius dicit" (Leon. 43.377:163–166). See Chapter IV, n. 20, for the citation from the Commentary on the *De Hebdomadibus,* and n. 40 above in the present chapter.

46. See the text from the *De ente* cited above in n. 44.

47. See the text cited above in n. 18.

understandable because of the theological nature or because of the particular structure of the works in which such argumentation appears. But in some of these cases, Thomas would not have to assume God's existence as already given in order for his argumentation to retain its force. Hence I shall regard these last-mentioned cases as illustrations of arguments which need not presuppose God's existence, even though in presenting them Thomas usually assumes this as given.[48]

Already in his Commentary on Bk I of the *Sentences* Thomas reasons from the uniqueness of that Being in which essence and *esse* are identical to composition of essence and *esse* in every other being. But since these arguments do seem to require prior knowledge of God's existence for their validity, I will defer consideration of them for a later chapter.[49] Instead I will now turn to one of Thomas's more mature works, *Summa contra Gentiles* II, c. 52. There again, while he rejects matter-form composition of created intellectual substances, he wishes to show that they do not equal the divine simplicity. There is another kind of composition in such entities, that of *esse* and *quod est*. His first three arguments will illustrate the kind of reasoning I have in mind.[50]

In the first argument Thomas reasons that if there is such a thing as subsisting *esse*, nothing else can be found in it in addition to its *esse*. Even in the case of a thing which is not subsisting *esse*, whatever is present in it in addition to its *esse* will unite with the existing entity but not with its *esse* except *per accidens*. Such will happen insofar as there is a single subject which has both *esse* and something which is different from *esse*. Thus in a subject such as Sortes, something such as whiteness may be present in addition to his substantial *esse*. In this case, of course, the whiteness of Sortes is distinct from his substantial *esse*, i.e., his act of being.[51]

If, therefore, *esse*, the act of being, is not present in a subject, nothing else can be united with it. *Esse* insofar as it is *esse* cannot be diversified. It can only be diversified by something that is other than *esse*. So it is that the *esse* of a stone is different from the *esse* of a human being. (By this Thomas means that it is because the essence of a stone is different from the essence of a human being that the act of being of the former is different from the act of being of the latter. At the same time

48. In other words, it is because I regard prior knowledge of God's existence as unnecessary for the inner workings of such arguments that I classify them here rather than under arguments which do presuppose his existence.

49. See *In I Sent.*, d. 8, q. 5, a. 1, sol. (Mandonnet ed., Vol. 1, pp. 226–27), and q. 5, a. 2 (pp. 229–30); *In II Sent.*, d. 3, q. 1, a. 1 (Mandonnet ed., Vol. 2, pp. 87–88) as analyzed below in Chapter XIV, Section 1.

50. The chapter heading reads: "Quod in substantiis intellectualibus creatis differt esse et quod est." But in his introductory remarks Thomas writes: "Invenitur enim in eis aliqua compositio ex eo quod non est idem in eis esse et quod est." It would seem, therefore, that he would move from diversity of *esse* and *quod est* to their composition. In fact, he concentrates on the first point in c. 52, and in c. 53 goes on to correlate them as act and potency. See ed. cit., p. 145.

51. Note in particular: "Quia etiam in his quorum esse non est subsistens, quod inest existenti praeter esse eius, est quidem existenti unitum, non autem est unum cum esse eius, nisi per accidens, inquantum est unum subiectum habens esse et id quod est praeter esse . . ." (ed. cit., p. 145).

he is implying that the essence of each differs from the act of being of the same, since he has reasoned that *esse* can only be divided by something that is different from *esse*.) Therefore, concludes Thomas, *esse subsistens* can only be one. But he has already shown (see Bk I, c. 22) that God is his own subsisting *esse*. Therefore nothing other than God can be its *esse* (act of being). Consequently, in every other substance, the act of being and the substance (essence) differ.[52]

In this argument Thomas can take God's existence as established (for this see Bk I, c. 13). Nonetheless, the argument itself does not turn upon the fact that God or self-subsisting being exists, but on the impossibility of there being more than one instance of self-subsisting *esse*, or more than one being which is identical with its act of being. Hence, if more than one being actually exists, one may conclude that in every such being, with one possible exception, essence and act of being differ. Also central to the argument is the point that *esse* (the act of being) is not self-dividing and can only be divided by something other than itself, i.e., by essence.

Thomas's second argument begins with the observation that any common nature, if it is simply considered in itself as separate, can only be one. This is so even though there may be many individuals which share in that nature. If the nature of animal, for instance, could subsist in itself and as separate, it would not include those things which are proper to species such as human being or ox. When the differences which constitute species are removed, the nature of the genus remains as undivided. This follows because the very same differences which serve to constitute species also serve to divide the genus. If, therefore, *esse* itself were common in genus-like fashion, there could only be one separate and subsisting *esse*. And if in fact *esse* is not divided by differences like a genus but rather because it pertains to this or to that subject, as is indeed the truth of the matter, it follows with even greater reason that there can be only one case of subsisting *esse*. Since God is subsisting *esse*, nothing other than God can be its own *esse* (act of being).[53]

While Thomas naturally assumes God's existence in this argument because he has already demonstrated it, that assumption is not required for the validity of the argument. Once again the argument rests on the impossibility of there being more than one case of self-subsisting *esse*. If many different beings do exist in fact, in each of them, with this single possible exception, essence and *esse* must differ.

---

52. Note in particular: "Esse autem, inquantum est esse, non potest esse diversum: potest autem diversificari per aliquid quod est praeter esse; sicut esse lapidis est aliud ab esse hominis. Illud ergo quod est esse subsistens, non potest esse nisi unum tantum. Ostensum est autem quod Deus est suum esse subsistens. Nihil igitur aliud praeter ipsum potest esse suum esse. Oportet igitur in omni substantia quae est praeter ipsum, esse aliud ipsam substantiam et esse eius" (ibid.).

53. Ibid. Note the concluding part of the argument: "Sic igitur, si hoc ipsum quod est esse sit commune sicut genus, esse separatum per se subsistens non potest esse nisi unum. Si vero non dividatur differentiis, sicut genus, sed per hoc quod est huius vel illius esse, ut veritas habet; magis est manifestum quod non potest esse per se existens nisi unum. Relinquitur igitur quod, cum Deus sit esse subsistens, nihil aliud praeter ipsum est suum esse."

A third argument is based on the impossibility of there being more than one completely infinite *esse*. Completely infinite *esse* embraces the total perfection of being. Therefore, if such infinity were realized in two different beings, there would be no way in which one such being could be distinguished from another. But subsisting *esse* must be infinite, continues Thomas, because it is not limited by any receiving principle. (Here he has introduced another important principle for his metaphysics already noted in our preceding chapter, i.e., that act, especially the act of being, is unlimited unless it is limited by a receiving principle.) Apart from this one case, therefore, there can be no other subsisting *esse*. Though Thomas does not spell this out for us, it follows because otherwise there would be two infinite cases of subsisting *esse*, something which he has just rejected as impossible. Presumably he would also have us draw the unexpressed conclusion: therefore in every other being essence and *esse* (act of being) differ.[54]

Like the two previous arguments, this one apparently also takes God's existence as already established. But also like the other two arguments, its inner logic does not require that one make this assumption. Because there cannot be two infinite beings, there cannot be two beings in which essence and act of being are identical. Therefore, if many beings do in fact exist, in each of them, with one possible exception, essence and act of being are not identical.

Thomas offers another version of this kind of reasoning in his relatively late *De spiritualibus creaturis*, a. 1 (1267–1268). There again he rejects matter-form composition of created spiritual substances.[55] Nonetheless, he continues, two factors are present in any created spiritual substance, one of which is related to the other as potency to act. Thomas notes that the first being or God is infinite act, having in himself the fullness of being, a fullness which is not restricted to the nature of any genus or species. From this it follows that God's *esse* is not instilled, as it were, into any distinct nature which is not identical with his *esse;* for if it were, it would be limited to that nature. Hence we can say that God is his very *esse*. But, continues Thomas, this is true of no other being. Thus if whiteness could exist in separation apart from every subject or receiving principle, this separate whiteness would only be one. So too, it is impossible for there to be more than one subsisting *esse*. Therefore, everything which comes after the first being, since it is not its *esse*, must have an *esse* which is received in something else by which that *esse* is limited.[56]

Then, as we have already seen in Ch. IV above, Thomas goes on to compare the receiving principle or nature of any such being with the *esse* which it receives

---

54. Note in particular: "Esse autem subsistens oportet esse infinitum: quia non terminatur aliquo recipiente. Impossibile est igitur esse aliquod esse subsistens praeter primum" (ibid.).

55. Ed. cit. (Calcaterra-Centi), pp. 370–71.

56. Ibid. Note in particular: ". . . sed si esset albedo separata ab omni subiecto et recipiente, esset una tantum; ita impossibile est quod sit ipsum esse subsistens nisi unum tantum. Omne igitur quod est post primum ens, cum non sit suum esse, habet esse in aliquo receptum, per quod ipsum esse contrahitur. . . ."

as participant and participated. In every creature the nature of the thing which participates *esse* is one, and the participated *esse* something other. The participated *esse* is related to the nature which participates in it as act to potency.[57]

Most important for our immediate purposes, however, is Thomas's claim that it is impossible for there to be more than one subsisting *esse*. He has introduced this argument by stating that God is infinite act and has in himself the fullness of being. In other words, Thomas is taking God's existence as given. Even so, if the argument is intrinsically sound, it will hold whether or not one already knows that God exists. For the argument rests on the impossibility of there being more than one self-subsisting *esse*. In all other beings with this single exception, whether or not it is realized in actuality, essence and *esse* must differ. Or as Thomas puts it, the nature which participates in *esse* is one *(aliud)*, and the participated *esse* is other *(aliud)*.[58]

As another interesting illustration of this procedure one may turn to Thomas's Commentary on Bk VIII of Aristotle's *Physics* (ca. 1268–1269). This time the argument appears within the broader context of a discussion of the presence or absence of matter-form composition in heavenly bodies. After Thomas himself argues for matter-form composition in such bodies, he comments that even if we were to concede that there is no such composition there, some kind of potency would still be present in them, i.e., a potency for being *(potentia essendi)*. Every simple subsisting substance must either be identical with its *esse*, or else participate in *esse*. But there can only be one simple substance which is subsisting *esse* itself, just as, if whiteness could subsist in itself, it could only be one. Therefore every substance which comes after the first and simple substance participates in *esse*. But, continues Thomas, every participant is composed of that which participates and that in which it participates; and the participating principle is in potency to that in which it participates. Therefore, in every substance, however simple it may be, with the exception of the First Substance, there is a potency for *esse*.[59]

---

57. See Ch. IV above, n. 62.

58. Ed. cit., p. 371: ". . . et sic in quolibet creato aliud est natura rei quae participat esse, et aliud ipsum esse participatum." In order to support his claim that *esse subsistens* can only be one, Thomas has this time drawn an analogy with a hypothetical subsisting whiteness. His point is that just as whiteness can be multiplied only by being received in different subjects, so it is with *esse*. If we find different instances of *esse*, in every case with one single (and possible) exception, *esse* will have to be received by a distinct principle which limits it. After again correlating the nature of a created spiritual substance with its *esse* as potency and act, Thomas adds an important qualification: ". . . adhuc comparabitur ad suum esse ut potentia ad actum: non dico autem ut potentiam separabilem ab actu, sed quam semper suus actus comitetur." Hence there can never be an actually existing nature without its act of being.

59. See *In VIII Phys.*, lect. 21, p. 615, n. 1153. Note in particular: "Substantia autem simplex quae est ipsum esse subsistens, non potest esse nisi una, sicut nec albedo, si esset subsistens, posset esse nisi una. Omnis ergo substantia quae est post primam substantiam simplicem, participat esse. Omne autem participans componitur ex participante et participato, et participans est in potentia ad participatum. . . ."

As in the argument from *De spiritualibus creaturis,* so in this one as well Thomas joins his case for composition of things other than God with his metaphysics of participation. And like the previously considered arguments, this one also rests on the impossibility of there being more than one substance which is its very *esse.* The by-now familiar parallel with whiteness is again drawn. If whiteness could subsist in itself, it could only be one. If *esse* does subsist in itself, it too can only be one. Once more, therefore, the argument would not have to assume that there is such a thing as self-subsisting *esse.* The impossibility of there being more than one case of this would be enough for Thomas to conclude to nonidentity of essence and act of being and, according to the present argument, to the composition of potency and act, in every other substance.

Our final text in this section is taken from Thomas's very late *De substantiis separatis,* c. 8 (1271 or later). There he again argues against Avicebron that there is no need to hold that created separate substances are composed of matter and form in order to avoid identifying them with God. Some potency is present in them since they are not *esse* itself but only participate in it.[60]

Thomas again insists that there can only be one subsisting thing that is *esse* itself. In support he reasons that if any other form is considered as separate, it can only be one. Just as a species is one in the order of thought when it is simply considered in itself, a specific nature would be one in reality if it could exist in itself as such. The same may be said of a genus in relation to its species. Just as it is one in the order of thought when it is considered in itself rather than as realized in its species, so too a genus would be one in the order of reality if it could subsist in itself. By applying similar reasoning we finally come to *esse* itself which, says Thomas, is most universal *(communissimum).* Therefore, he quickly concludes, *esse subsistens* is only one. His point again is that since *esse* does subsist as such and in itself, subsisting *esse* can only be one. Once more he contrasts this with everything else. Everything which exists has *esse.* Therefore in everything apart from the First Being there is both *esse* as its act and the substance of the thing which has *esse* and is a receiving potency for that act.[61] Like the previously considered arguments, this one does in fact take God's existence as granted. But like the others, it would not have to do so in order to remain valid. It, too, rests on the impossibility of there being more than one being which is its very *esse.*

Before concluding this particular section, some remarks should be made about the different ways in which Thomas attempts to show that there can only be one thing in which essence and *esse* (act of being) are identical, or only one case of *esse subsistens* and hence, by contrast, that essence and act of being differ in every-thing else.

60. Leon. 40.D55:164–169.
61. Leon. 40.D55:169–187.

At times he draws an analogy between *esse* and less extended specific or generic natures. If a given specific or generic nature could subsist in itself and apart from anything else, it could only be one. Therefore, since *esse* does subsist apart from anything else in one instance, subsisting *esse*, it too can only be one. Thomas does not want us to forget the difference between *esse* and any generic or specific nature; nor does he want us to make the mistake of identifying *esse subsistens* with *esse commune*. This we have already seen.[62]

The point of his analogy rather is that if such a specific or generic nature could subsist in itself, it would only be one. One may ask why this is so. As regards a genus, Thomas spells this out more fully in the second argument from *Summa contra Gentiles* II, c. 52. If a generic nature could subsist in itself, it would lack the differences which constitute its species and which serve to divide the genus. Therefore, nothing would remain which could divide the genus. But what about a specific nature? If such were to subsist in itself apart from different receiving subjects, it too would lack any principle for division into numerically distinct individuals. In fact, if specific forms are multiplied in individuals, this is because in each of them the form is received and individuated by a distinct receiving and individuating principle, that is, matter as designated by quantity.[63]

As regards *esse*, Thomas has argued that if it could be multiplied by differences in the way a genus is, then, if it subsisted in itself, it could only be one. This would follow because it too would lack any such differences which could divide it. But Thomas holds that in fact *esse* is not a genus and is not divided or multiplied in this way. It can only be multiplied by being received in this or that subject, that is, in this or that nature or essence.[64] Since subsisting *esse* is not received by any distinct nature or subject, it cannot be multiplied. In everything else, on the other hand, *esse* and that which receives and divides *esse* must differ.

On other occasions Thomas draws an analogy between *esse* and accidental forms such as heat or whiteness. If any such form could exist in itself apart from a receiving subject, it would only be one. This is because this kind of form is multiplied by reason of diversity in the subjects which receive it. So too, reasons Thomas, if *esse* can subsist in itself apart from any receiving subject or principle, such subsisting *esse* can only be one. And if *esse* is multiplied in other cases, this can only be by reason of different principles or essences which receive it and render it many.[65]

---

62. See above in Ch. IV, Section 2.

63. This will be discussed below in our consideration of the principle of individuation in Ch. IX, Section 4.

64. See SCG II, c. 52, 2d argument, as cited above in n. 53. This corresponds to the third possible way of multiplying subsisting *esse* which was considered in c. 4 of the *De ente*. If subsisting *esse* cannot be multiplied even in that way, nonsubsisting *esse* can be.

65. Thomas has, of course, drawn the analogy with heat in c. 4 of the *De ente*. For the analogy with whiteness see the arguments just considered from *De spiritualibus creaturis*, a. 1; Commentary on *Physics* VIII, lect. 21.

Thus we see that in these later texts Thomas has reduced the major ways in which something can be multiplied from the three mentioned in the *De ente* to two. As he puts this in his *Compendium theologiae,* c. 15, a form can be multiplied in one of two ways: (1) by the addition of differences, as a generic form is multiplied in its species; or (2) by being received in different subjects. Since the divine essence is *esse* itself, it can be multiplied in neither of these ways, and Thomas goes on to conclude that it can only be one.[66] By implication he is also telling us that since *esse,* taken as the *actus essendi* which is intrinsic to every existing substance, cannot be multiplied in the first of these ways, it can only be multiplied in the second way. It can only be multiplied by being received in different receiving and dividing principles, that is, in distinct essences or natures. He does not mean to imply that such essences or natures actually preexist before they receive their respective acts of being, as we have previously pointed out.

3. The "Genus" Argument

Thomas appeals to this kind of argumentation in texts which range in time from his Commentary on I *Sentences* until as late as *Summa theologiae* I; and it appears in somewhat different form in his *Compendium Theologiae.*[67] Frequently he uses it as a step in his effort to prove that God does not fall into any genus; for whatever is included in a genus has a quiddity that differs from its act of being. On one occasion, in the *De veritate,* he develops a fuller version of this argument within a very different setting. As we shall see, in none of these contexts does the inner force of the argument rest on prior knowledge that God exists.

A version of the first kind of argumentation appears in his Commentary on I *Sentences,* d. 8, q. 4, a. 2. There Thomas is attempting to show that God does not

---

66. See note 37 of this chapter for references and discussion. Note that here again in c. 15 he draws an analogy with whiteness to illustrate multiplication by reason of reception in different subjects: "Omnis ergo forma quae non potest multiplicari per differentias, si non sit forma in subiecto existens, impossibile est quod multiplicetur; sicut albedo, si subsisteret sine substantia, non esset nisi una tantum" (Leon. 42.87:25–29).

67. The argument appears in *In I Sent.,* d. 8, q. 4, a. 2 (ca. 1252–1256); *De veritate,* q. 27, a. 1, ad 8 (1258–1259); SCG I, c. 25 (1259–1265); *De potentia,* q. 7, a. 3 (1265–1266); ST I, q. 3, a. 5 (1266–1268); *Compendium theologiae,* c. 14 (ca. 1265–1267). In the last-mentioned text Thomas appeals to it to show that God himself is not a species which is predicated of various individuals; for the different individuals which fall within a given species differ in terms of their *esse,* but agree in sharing in a single (specific) essence. Therefore, within individual members of a given species, essence and *esse* differ (literally: "are other and other") (see Leon. 42.87:122–129). In addition to these, Sweeney has also singled out four other texts from Thomas's Commentary on the *Sentences* where this type of argumentation appears: *In I Sent.,* d. 19, q. 4, a. 2, sol. (Vol. 1, p. 483); *In II Sent.,* d. 3, q. 1, a. 1, ad 1 (Vol. 2, p. 88); ibid., a. 5 (pp. 99–100); ibid., a. 6 (pp. 102–3). See L. Sweeney, "Existence/Essence in Thomas Aquinas's Early Writings," p. 109. In none of these texts, however, does Thomas attempt to prove that membership in a genus entails diversity of essence and *esse.* Hence we need not delay over them here.

fall into any genus. As his third argument in support of this claim Thomas offers an approach which he describes as more subtle and as taken from Avicenna.[68] Everything which is included in a genus has a quiddity which differs from its *esse*, as is true, for instance, of human being. Actual existence *(esse in actu)* is not owing to humanity simply insofar as it is humanity. In proof Thomas appeals to a version of the *intellectus essentiae* approach. One can think of humanity without knowing whether a particular human being exists. Thomas then develops his reason for holding that whatever falls into a genus has a quiddity that differs from its *esse* (act of being). The common factor which is predicated of all those things which belong to a genus is asserted of them in quidditative fashion; for genus and species are predicated of anything in terms of its quiddity. But the act of being *(esse)* does not belong to a quiddity except by reason of the fact that the quiddity is received in this or in that individual. Therefore the quiddity of a genus or species is not communicated in terms of a single act of being *(esse)* to all members of the class, but only in terms of the common intelligible content *(ratio)*. From this Thomas draws the conclusion that the *esse* (act of being) of any such thing is not identical with its quiddity.[69]

Thomas appeals to similar argumentation in *Summa contra Gentiles* I, c. 25; *De potentia*, q. 7, a. 3; and in *Summa theologiae* I, q. 3, a. 5. In each of these cases he is attempting to make the same point once more, that is, to show that God is not included in any genus. He phrases the argument in this way in SCG I, c. 25. Whatever is included in a genus is different from other members of that genus in terms of its *esse*. Otherwise the genus would not be predicated of many. But things which belong to the same genus must agree in terms of the quiddity of that genus. In proof Thomas again comments that this is so because the genus is predicated of its members in quidditative fashion. Therefore, he concludes, the *esse* (act of being) of each thing which exists in a genus is different from its quiddity. Since such is not possible in the case of God, God is not included in any genus.[70]

---

68. "Tertia ratio subtilior est Avicennae, tract. V *Metaph.*, cap. iv, et tract. IX, cap. i." Ed. cit., Vol. 1, p. 222. Sweeney has commented on the difficulty of finding this argument explicitly presented as such in Avicenna, notwithstanding Thomas's fairly frequent ascriptions of it to Avicenna (especially in Thomas's earlier presentations and references to it). See Sweeney, "Existence/Essence," p. 110, n. 21, where he cites a text from Avicenna's *Metaphysica*, tr. VIII, c. 4, but which, as Sweeney recognizes, does not really contain the genus argument. For Thomas's text see ed. cit., Vol. 1, p. 222.

69. "Omne quod est in genere, habet quidditatem differentem ab esse, sicut homo; humanitati enim ex hoc quod est humanitas, non debetur esse in actu; potest enim cogitari humanitas et tamen ignorari an aliquis homo sit. Et ratio huius est, quia commune, quod praedicatur de his quae sunt in genere, praedicat quidditatem, cum genus et species praedicentur in eo quod quid est. Illi autem quidditati non debetur esse nisi per hoc quod suscepta est in hoc vel in illo. Et ideo quidditas generis vel speciei non communicatur secundum unum esse omnibus, sed solum secundum unam rationem communem. Unde constat quod esse suum non est quidditas sua" (ibid.). Thomas goes on to note that since God's *esse* is his quiddity, God cannot belong to a genus. For another equally early employment of this line of reasoning, see *De ente*, c. 5 (Leon. 43.378:8–14).

70. "Item. Quicquid est in genere secundum esse differt ab aliis quae in eodem genere sunt; alias genus de pluribus non praedicaretur. Oportet autem omnia quae sunt in eodem genere, in quidditate generis convenire: quia de omnibus genus *in quod quid est* praedicatur. Esse igitur cuiuslibet in genere

Fundamentally the same reasoning reappears in *De potentia,* q. 7, a. 3, in Thomas's first argument there to show that God is not included in a genus.[71] We find this repeated in its essentials in ST I, q. 3, a. 5. In his third argument there to show that God is not in any genus, Thomas reasons that all things which are included in a given genus share in the quiddity or essence of that genus; for the genus is predicated of them in quidditative fashion. But they differ in terms of their *esse.* Thus the *esse* of a human being is not identical with that of a horse nor, for that matter, is the *esse* of this human being identical with the *esse* of another human being. Therefore, in all things which fall into a genus, *esse* (act of being) and *quod quid est,* or essence as Thomas also specifies, differ. But they do not differ in God.[72]

As I have already indicated, in none of these arguments does Thomas appeal to God's existence in order to make his point about essence and *esse.* On the contrary, he rather argues that if something belongs to a genus, essence and *esse* (act of being) differ in that thing. Since essence and *esse* (act of being) do not differ in God, he cannot belong to any genus. Moreover, appeal to any version of the *intellectus essentiae* approach has disappeared from these later presentations.

Before examining this line of reasoning more critically, it will be helpful to turn to the version offered in *De veritate,* q. 27, a. 1, ad 8. There Thomas is considering the question whether grace is something positive which is created in the human soul. In defending his affirmative reply, Thomas must meet this objection: Only things which are composed can belong to a genus. Grace, being a simple form, is not composed. Therefore grace is not present in any genus. But since everything which is created belongs to a genus, grace is not something created.[73]

While the context for this objection is theological, Thomas's reply is of considerable philosophical interest. He begins by agreeing with the objection, but only in part: if something belongs to the genus substance, he specifies, it must be composed, and by real composition, he adds. In support he reasons that whatever falls within the predicament substance subsists in its own *esse.* Therefore its *esse* (act of being) must be different from that thing itself. Otherwise, such a thing could not differ in terms of its *esse* from all other things with which it agrees in quidditative content. Such agreement in quidditative content is required for things to belong to a given predicament. Therefore, he concludes, everything which is included directly within the predicament substance is composed, at least of *esse* and *quod quid est,* that is, of act of being and essence. On the other hand, he continues, something does not have to be composed by real composition in order to belong to an acciden-

---

existentis est praeter generis quidditatem. Hoc autem in Deo impossibile est. Deus igitur in genere non est" (ed. cit., p. 26).

71. Ed. cit., p. 193. Note: "Primo quidem, quia nihil ponitur in genere secundum esse suum, sed ratione quidditatis suae; quod ex hoc patet, quia esse uniuscuiusque est ei proprium, et distinctum ab esse cuiuslibet alterius rei; sed ratio substantiae potest esse communis. . . ."

72. Leon. 4.44. Note the conclusion: "Et sic oportet quod quaecumque sunt in genere, differant in eis esse et *quod quid est,* idest essentia. In Deo autem non differt. . . ."

73. Leon. 22.3.790:51–55.

tal predicament. Logical composition of genus and difference will suffice. Such is true of grace. With this he meets the theological difficulty.[74]

For our purposes the important point is Thomas's claim that whatever belongs to the genus substance must be really composed of essence and *esse* (act of being). Other versions of the argument have claimed that in such things essence and *esse* (act of being) must differ. The heart of his argumentation for this seems to be the following. If such a thing belongs to the predicament substance, it must subsist in itself and therefore with its own *esse*. To admit this, of course, is not yet to acknowledge that the essence of such a thing really differs from its intrinsic *actus essendi* or is really composed with it. But Thomas reasons that such a distinction must obtain. Otherwise, because such a thing is identical in definition or in quidditative content with the other members of its genus, it cannot really differ from them at all unless its *esse* principle is really different from its essence. In his conclusion he has in mind a distinction and composition of the thing's individual essence and its individual *esse*. Hence he also concludes that whatever is directly included within the category or predicament of substance is really composed of its essence and its *esse,* as he explicitly states in the last text.

The "genus" argument as it is proposed by Thomas, and especially in this text from the *De veritate,* has its strong points and its weak points. To concentrate on the first for a moment, the argument makes it quite clear that Thomas intends to reason to real composition (and by implication, real distinction) of essence and *esse* in members of a genus, that is, of the genus substance. Secondly, to repeat a point already made, in none of the formulations we have considered does the argument itself presuppose knowledge of God's existence. Thirdly, the argument assumes that if things fall into the same genus, they must agree in quidditative content with other members of that genus. At the same time, if one is dealing with substances, every such substance must differ from all others by reason of its individual *esse*.

At the same time, serious questions may be raised about the argument's validity. It seems to move very quickly from the order of logic and conceptual distinction to the order of real composition and distinction. One may readily grant with Aquinas that some common intelligible content must be present in the different members of a genus such as substance or in the different members of the same species. And one may also grant that the various members of the generic or specific class differ in some way. As Thomas sees it, they differ in terms of their *esse*.

But at the beginning of the argument, to what does the term *esse* refer? In the argument's conclusion, of course, *esse* signifies the particular *actus essendi* which is

---

74. Leon. 22.3.792:221–231: "Ad octavum dicendum, quod omne quod est in genere substantiae, est compositum reali compositione; eo quod id quod est in praedicamento substantiae est in suo esse subsistens, et oportet quod esse suum sit aliud quam ipsum, alias non posset differre secundum esse ab illis cum quibus convenit in ratione suae quidditatis; quod requiritur in omnibus quae sunt directe in praedicamento: et ideo omne quod est directe in praedicamento substantiae, compositum est saltem ex esse et quod est."

present within every particular substance (excluding God) and which is really distinct from the individual essence of that same substance. But as it first appears in the argument, *esse* may signify nothing more than a particular actually existing member of a generic or specific class, that is, a particular concrete existent. One cannot yet assume what remains to be proved, i.e., that *esse* already signifies an act principle which is really distinct from the essence principle of each particular substance. Hence, at the beginning of the argument, the contrast rather seems to be between a general or universal quidditative content which is shared in by all members of the class, on the one hand, and actually existing particular instantiations of the same, on the other hand. Thomas himself would not allow for real distinction between a universal intelligible content and a particular instantiation of the same. Nor would he allow for real distinction between a genus and the various species which share in it. As we have seen, if a species participates in its genus, it does so in such fashion as to include the genus in which it participates within its essence. Merely conceptual or logical distinctions obtain in these cases.[75]

But if this is so, it is difficult to see how Thomas can so readily conclude to real composition and distinction of an essence principle and an *esse* principle within each existing substance within a genus (or species) on the strength of this argumentation. That he does draw this conclusion is evident enough. Whether he can justify this conclusion simply by appealing to the "genus" argument is not so clear. It seems that the argument needs to be reinforced by the addition of other metaphysical considerations. But as soon as one does this, one may no longer have the "genus" argument as such, but a combination of it with some other and more metaphysical approach.[76] As I see things, the "genus" argument simply taken in itself is not sufficient for Thomas to draw his intended conclusion.

4. Arguments Based on Participation

As Fabro has shown in great detail, Thomas frequently reasons from the participated character of particular beings to composition of essence and *esse* (act of being) within them. Fabro finds Thomas appealing to "vague" formulations of this approach in his earlier writings, especially those dating from his first teaching period

75. If Thomas does not allow for real distinction between a generic or specific nature and an individual instance of that nature, he does base multiplication of individuals within a species on a real composition and distinction within the essence of a material being, that is, of matter as designated by quantity, and form. See Ch. IX below. But as Sweeney and de Finance point out, the "genus" argument is not restricted to material substances. See Sweeney, "Existence/Essence," pp. 111–12; de Finance, *Être et agir dans la philosophie de Saint Thomas*, pp. 95–96. However, neither Sweeney nor de Finance really manages to salvage this argument (cf. Sweeney, p. 130). For the point that there is no real distinction between a specific nature and an individual see Owens, "Quiddity and Real Distinction in St. Thomas Aquinas," pp. 9–10; "Aquinas' Distinction," p. 268.

76. For an effort to do this see Sweeney, p. 112, especially n. 23. Also see my comments in *Metaphysical Themes*, pp. 138–39.

at Paris, and becoming much more explicit in using this procedure in his mature works. As Fabro sees it, Thomas simplifies his approach to the essence-*esse* issue in these later works, and comes to rely ever more heavily on argumentation based on participation.[77]

Limitations of space will not permit me to examine all such texts in this section. Hence I shall concentrate on arguments based on participation only to the extent that they do not (or at least need not) presuppose prior knowledge of God's existence. Moreover, it should be noted that at times Thomas moves from the essence-*esse* distinction or composition of particular beings to their participated character.[78] On other occasions he rather reasons from their participated character to their essence-*esse* composition or distinction. It is this second approach which will be of interest here.

One of the best illustrations of this procedure is offered within a context already examined in Chapter IV, that is, in *lectio* 2 of Thomas's Commentary on the *De Hebdomadibus* of Boethius. As will be recalled, Thomas has now reached the point in his Commentary where he finds Boethius moving from diversity between *esse* and "that which is" in the order of intentions to such diversity in the order of reality: ". . . just as *esse* and 'that which is' differ in the order of intentions, so in composite entities do they differ really."[79] Thomas then offers two versions of argumentation based on participation to make his point.

The first argument rests on the claims (1) that *esse* does not participate in anything else; and (2) that it does not admit of the addition of anything extraneous to its formal content. Given these two points which he has already developed in his Commentary, Thomas concludes that *esse* itself is not composed. And if *esse* itself is not composed, Thomas then quickly concludes that a composite thing cannot be identified with its *esse*. And he immediately adds, since he is commenting on a Boethian axiom: "And therefore [Boethius] says that in every composite *esse* is one (thing) and the composite itself which is by participating in esse *(ipsum esse)* is something other."[80] This may be regarded as an argument which is based on partic-

---

77. For his collection of both vague and explicit texts see Fabro, *La nozione metafisica*, pp. 222–43. For his other remarks, see p. 217.

78. For a good illustration of both procedures see Quodlibet 2, q. 2, a. 1, and my discussion of this below in the present chapter.

79. See Leon. 50.272:196–273:206, cited above in Chapter IV, n. 20.

80. Leon. 50.273:206–213, cited above in Ch. IV, n. 21. For the concluding remark see 273:213–215: "et ideo dicit quod in *omni composito aliud est* esse [ens] et *aliud* ipsum compositum quod est participando *ipsum esse.*" Brackets mine. In interpreting this passage I have omitted the term *ens* since in the immediately preceding and following context Thomas compares and contrasts *esse* and *quod est,* and the omission of *ens* seems to be required by the philosophical sense of the text. Owing to the hospitality of Fr. J. F. Hinnebusch of the Washington, D.C. Leonine Commission, C. Bazán, K. White, and I were recently able to review the microfilms of the manuscripts containing this part of Thomas's treatise which are housed here in Washington. While the vast majority of the nine manuscripts we could consult do include *ens* and therefore support the Leonine reading, two of them, each constituting an independent witness in the manuscript tradition, omit *ens* (L⁴ = Leipzig,

ipation at least to some extent because of the first claim: *esse* itself does not participate in anything else even though, as Thomas has shown earlier in this same *lectio*, "that which is" or being *(ens)* does participate in *esse*.[81]

Thomas's recognition that this kind of argumentation is restricted to matter-form composites may account for his immediate introduction of a second approach which is more directly based on participation. And it could be that he realized that the first argument needs some reinforcement. Be that as it may, he first distinguishes between things which are simple in the absolute sense so as to lack all composition, and things which are simple in a qualified sense. If there are certain forms which do not exist in matter, every such form will be simple insofar as it lacks matter and quantity. If such forms subsist, it does not immediately follow from this that they are perfectly simple. Suppose for the sake of discussion that one admits the existence either of subsisting and separate forms or ideas in the Platonic sense or of Aristotle's separate entities; in either case any such form will determine *esse* with respect to its kind of being. No such form will be identical with *esse commune* itself, but each will only "have" *esse*. Each, insofar as it is distinguished from other separate forms, will be a specific form that participates in *esse*. None will be simple in the unqualified sense; but each will be composed, we may conclude, of its form or essence, on the one hand, and of the *esse* (act of being) in which it participates, on the other.[82]

Thomas moves from this to the conclusion that the only perfectly simple being is one which does not participate in *esse* but is subsisting *esse*. Again he reasons that such a being can only be one; for if *esse* insofar as it is *esse* admits of nothing extrinsic to itself, that which is subsisting *esse* cannot be multiplied by any diversifying principle. This unique being, of course, is God.[83]

These two arguments are of considerable interest to our present discussion, first because in introducing them Thomas has explicitly distinguished between diversity

---

Universitätsbibliothek 482, f. 99ra, 14th century; and V⁶ = Vatican Library 808, f. 44va, early 15th century). But the strongest evidence pointing to omitting *ens* is, in my opinion, philosophical and contextual. For the point that *esse* admits of nothing extraneous to its intelligible content see Leon. 50.271:114–272:146. In brief Thomas bases this on the fact that *esse* is considered abstractly.

81. McInerny denies that Thomas intends for this to be a demonstration of a real distinction between *esse* and *quod est*. It is true that one might expect Thomas to introduce another step after writing that *esse* itself is not composed, i.e., that *esse* itself cannot be identified with any composite thing, and then by conversion reach the conclusion that a composite thing is not *esse*. But as McInerny notes, Thomas writes that a composite thing is not *its* esse. See McInerny, *Boethius and Aquinas*, pp. 213–14. I would suggest, however, that Thomas reasons as follows: If *ipsum esse* cannot be identified with any composite thing because *esse* itself is not composed, then no composite can be identified with *esse*, whether it *(esse)* is taken abstractly or as realized in a concrete existing composite entity.

82. Leon. 50.273:221–249. Note in particular lines 236–249 as cited above in Ch. IV, n. 23. Thomas had introduced this discussion with this remark: "Si enim esset aliud realiter id quod est et ipsum esse, iam non esset simplex, sed compositum" (219–220). For more discussion see Ch. IV above, nn. 22, 23, and the corresponding text.

83. Leon. 50.273:249–258. See Ch. IV above, n. 24.

which applies only to the order of intentions and real diversity. It is the latter kind of diversity (and composition) between "that which is" *(quod est)* and *esse* (act of being) which he here intends to establish. Secondly, neither argument presupposes God's existence. Each rather rests on certain observations about *esse*. According to the first argument, *esse* itself is not composed because it does not participate in anything else and because it admits of nothing extrinsic to itself. According to the second argument, any subsisting form, whether Platonic or Aristotelian, enjoys only a restricted kind of being. Because of this it cannot be identified with *esse* taken as such, or as Thomas here puts it, with *esse commune*. Hence it only participates in *esse*.[84] Given this, Thomas has concluded that no such being is perfectly simple. His point is that any such being is composed of essence or form and of a really distinct or diverse act of being. In this second argument Thomas reasons from participation in *esse commune* to distinction and composition within the participant of its essence and its intrinsic act of being. More will be said below about this move.[85]

This line of argumentation reappears in *Summa theologiae* I, q. 75, a. 5, ad 4. There Thomas is meeting an objection to the effect that unless the human soul is composed of matter and form, as a pure form it will be pure and infinite act just as God is. In reply Thomas comments that every participated characteristic is related to that which participates in it as its act. Whatever created form is held to subsist must itself participate in *esse*. Even life itself, or whatever else may be so expressed, participates in *esse*, as Dionysius holds. But participated *esse* is limited to the capacity of that which participates in it. Therefore God alone, who is his very *esse* itself, is pure and unlimited act. In finite intellectual substances there is composition of act and potency, not indeed of matter and form, but of (pure) form and the participated *esse*. Wherefore such substances are said by some to be composed of *quo est* and *quod est*, or of *esse* and *quod est*, since, as Thomas explains, *esse*, (the act of being) is that whereby something exists.[86]

This text is illuminating in that it begins with the fact that any created subsisting form must participate in *esse* (the act of being). Though Thomas does not spell this out for us here, his reason for saying this must be the same as that offered in

---

84. See n. 82 above.

85. For discussion of this move from participation in *esse commune* to real distinction between the participating nature of essence and its own *actus essendi*, see the remaining arguments in this section of this chapter.

86. See in particular: "Quaecumque autem forma creata per se subsistens ponatur, oportet quod participet esse: quia etiam *ipsa vita*, vel quidquid sic diceretur, *participat ipsum esse*, ut dicit Dionysius, 5 cap. *de Div. Nom.* Esse autem participatum finitur ad capacitatem participantis. Unde solus Deus, qui est ipsum suum esse, est actus purus et infinitus. In substantiis vero intellectualibus est compositio ex actu et potentia; non quidem ex materia et forma, sed ex forma et esse participato. Unde a quibusdam dicuntur componi ex *quo est* et *quod est*: ipsum enim esse est *quo* aliquid est" (Leon. 5.202). Also see Thomas's Commentary on this passage from Dionysius *(In De divinis nominibus*, c. V, lect. 1, pp. 235–36, n. 635): ". . . per hoc quod *quaecumque* participant aliis participationibus, primo *participant* ipso *esse*. . . ."

the second argument from his Commentary on the *De Hebdomadibus*. Precisely because any such form enjoys only a given kind of being, it cannot be identified with the act of being in general *(esse commune)*. But the argument introduces a new factor. Participated *esse* is limited to the capacity of that which participates in it. Here we have at least a trace of what I shall consider below as a separate kind of argumentation: because unreceived *esse* is unlimited, appeal to some distinct receiving and limiting principle in the participant will be required to account for the limited presence of *esse* in that participant. Though Thomas also notes that God alone is pure and unlimited act, this reference to God does not appear to be necessary for the argument to function. In every intellectual substance which only participates in *esse*, there must be a composition of potency and act, that is, of its form and its participated *esse* (act of being).[87]

For fuller development of this final point, but still within the context of participation, one may turn to Thomas's later Commentary on the *Liber de causis* (1272). In Proposition 4 the anonymous author writes that the first of created things is *esse*, and that nothing else is created before this. Thomas suggests that the author does not here have in mind some universal separated *esse*, as did the Platonists. Nor is the anonymous writer thinking of *esse* insofar as it is participated in universally, that is to say, by all existents, as Dionyius held. Rather he seems to be speaking of *esse* insofar as it is participated in at the first (and highest) level of created being, the level of intelligence and soul.[88]

Thomas attempts to explain the author's meaning when he writes that this first created *esse* is multiplied only insofar as it is composed of the finite and the infinite. As Thomas sees it, the author is singling out the possibility of accounting for multiplication at this level—the level of intelligence(s)—by appealing to diversity on the side of essence. If a given pure form or nature is completely separate and simple, it cannot be multiplied. Once more Thomas appeals to the familiar example of a hypothetical separate whiteness. If such could exist, it would only be one. So too, if the first created *esse* were something separate *(abstractum)* as the Platonists held, it could not be multiplied. It would only be one. But because this first created *esse* is participated in by the nature of intelligence(s), it can be multiplied in accord with diversity on the part of the participants. In other words, there can be multiplicity at this level only because different intelligent natures or essences participate in *esse*.[89]

87. That Thomas here has in mind real composition of form and *esse* is implied both by the context—to prove that there is act-potency composition in intellectual substances—and by his reference to the formula *quo est et quod est.*

88. "Videtur tamen non esse eius intentio ut loquatur de aliquo esse separato, sicut Platonici loquebantur, neque de esse participato communiter in omnibus existentibus, sicut loquitur Dionysius, sed de esse participato in primo gradu entis creati, quod est esse superius" (Saffrey ed., p. 29). Cf. p. 28 for Thomas's descriptions of the views of the "Platonists" and of Dionysius.

89. For the text from the *Liber de causis* see Saffrey edition, p. 26: "Et ipsum quidem non est factum multa nisi quia ipsum, quamvis sit simplex et non sit in creatis simplicius eo, tamen est compositum ex finito et infinito." For Thomas's commentary see pp. 29–30. Note: "Sic igitur, si esse

Thomas develops this final point. If something should have an infinite power for being in such fashion that it did not participate in *esse* from anything else, it alone would be infinite. Such is true of God. But if something has an infinite power for being by reason of an *esse* which it participates in from something else, insofar as it participates in *esse* it is still finite. This is so because what is participated is not received in the participant according to its full infinity, but only in partial fashion (*particulariter*). Therefore an intelligence is composed of the finite and of the infinite insofar as the nature of the intelligence is said by the anonymous author to be infinite in terms of its potency for infinite duration; but the *esse* which it receives is finite. Hence at the level of intelligence *esse* can be multiplied insofar as it is participated *esse*. And this, Thomas concludes, is what the author has in mind by saying that an intelligence is composed of the infinite and the finite.[90]

In sum, Thomas has applied his own theory of nature or essence as participating in *esse* to the composition of the finite and the infinite which the *Liber de causis* assigns to the level of intelligence. He had already offered a somewhat similar reading of the *Liber de causis* as early as c. 5 of his *De ente et essentia*, but this time he sets his interpretation within the framework of his metaphysics of participation.[91] At the same time, he has introduced some interesting ways of strengthening his argumentation from participation for such composition.

Thus, if *esse* is to be multiplied, this can only be owing to diversity on the part of that which participates in it. This means that if different beings are to participate in *esse* there must be different natures or essences in each of them. Still, if we were to stop here, we might wonder whether this is enough to establish real diversity

---

creatum primum esset esse abstractum, ut Platonici posuerunt, tale esse non posset multiplicari, sed esset unum tantum. Sed quia esse creatum primum est esse participatum in natura intelligentiae, multiplicabile est secundum diversitatem participantium."

90. Ed. cit., p. 30. Note in particular: "Si autem aliquid sic haberet infinitam virtutem essendi quod non participaret esse ab alio, tunc esset solum infinitum; et tale est Deus. . . . Sed, si sit aliquid quod habeat infinitam virtutem ad essendum secundum esse participatum ab alio, secundum hoc quod esse participat est finitum, quia quod participatur non recipitur in participante secundum totam suam infinitatem sed particulariter. In tantum igitur intelligentia est composita in suo esse ex finito et infinito, in quantum natura intelligentiae infinita dicitur secundum potentiam essendi; et ipsum esse quod recipit, est finitum." On Thomas's interpretation of the infinite as a capacity for infinite duration as it appears in this text, see p. 30:12–14. For confirmation see his Commentary on Prop. 5 (p. 39:16–20). In this interpretation he is influenced by Proclus's *Elementatio theologica*, Prop. 89. See p. 30:9–14.

91. Leon. 43.378:44–56. Note: "Unde esse earum non est absolutum sed receptum, et ideo limitatum et finitum ad capacitatem naturae recipientis; sed natura vel quidditas earum est absoluta, et non recepta in aliqua materia. Et ideo dicitur in libro De causis quod intelligentiae sunt infinitae inferius et finitae superius; sunt enim finitae quantum ad esse suum quod a superiori recipiunt, non tamen finiuntur inferius quia earum formae non limitantur ad capacitatem alicuius materiae recipientis eas." Note that Thomas's reason for describing such intelligences as infinite from below differs from that which we have just considered in his Commentary on the *Liber de causis*, probably owing to his usage there of Proclus (see n. 90 above).

and composition between the nature and the act of being which is intrinsic to each of these entities. Would it not be enough to say that each of these different natures or entities participates in the act of being viewed in general *(esse commune)* and is therefore merely conceptually distinct from *esse commune* in the way an individual instance of human nature as realized in Sortes is only conceptually distinct from the human species in which he participates?

Thomas evidently thinks that a merely conceptual distinction between nature or essence and act of being will not be enough to account for participation of beings in *esse*. In fact, the present text suggests two additional reasons for this. The first is not fully developed, but runs something like this. If *esse* (the act of being) is to be multiplied, this can only be owing to diversity on the part of that which participates in it. Therefore, because different natures or entities participate in it, it is realized in different fashion in each of them. Not only does this require real diversity between one participating nature or entity and another; it also requires real diversity within every such being between something which receives and diversifies *esse* (the act of being) and the received and diversified act of being itself. One may ask why. This follows because *esse* as such is not self-dividing or self-diversifying. As Thomas has explained in a number of other contexts, *esse* insofar as it is *esse* is not divided. It can only be divided by something that is different from itself, that is, by a nature or essence which receives and diversifies it. If the *esse* (act of being) of this human being is different from the *esse* (act of being) of that human being or that stone, this is because in each of them the nature or essence which receives and diversifies *esse* is distinct from the *esse* which it receives and diversifies.[92]

The second reason is more directly suggested by our text and will be developed in the following section of this chapter. It follows from Thomas's oft-repeated claim that act, especially the act of being *(esse)*, is not self-limiting. But if *esse* is participated in by a subject or participant, it is present in that subject only in partial or limited fashion. This follows from the very nature of participation, as Thomas understands it. If one is to account for the limitation of that which is not self-limiting, one must postulate within such a participant an intrinsic principle which receives and limits *esse* (the act of being), and a really distinct act of being which is received and limited. Hence for both of these reasons, appeal to a merely logical or conceptual distinction between essence and act of being will not be sufficient to account for the fact that given beings actually and really do participate in *esse*. Real

92. This notion is already implied by Thomas's Commentary on the *De Trinitate* of Boethius, q. 4, a. 1, although there it is applied to *ens:* "Non potest autem hoc esse, quod ens dividatur ab ente in quantum est ens; nihil autem dividitur ab ente nisi non ens" (Leon. 50.120:96–98). It becomes much more explicit in SCG II, c. 52, within the first argument for composition of *esse* and *quod est* in created intellectual substances, where it is applied to *esse* (see n. 52 above for the text). It is confirmed by a remark in *De potentia,* q. 7, a. 2, ad 9: "Et per hunc modum, hoc esse ab illo *esse* distinguitur, in quantum est talis vel talis naturae" (Pession ed., p. 192).

diversity and composition of essence and *esse* (act of being) within every participating entity will be required if such participation is to be regarded as real rather than as merely logical or conceptual.

With this we may turn to a similar approach based on participation which also presupposes God's existence, but would not have to do so. In Quodlibet 3, q. 8 of 1270, Thomas is attempting to show that while there is no matter-form composition properly speaking in the human soul, there is potency-act composition. God alone is his *esse*, in that his *esse* is identical with his substance. This can be said of nothing else since there can only be one subsisting *esse*, just as, if whiteness could subsist in itself, it could only be one. Therefore, every other thing is a being by participation, so that within it its substance which participates in *esse* is one, and its participated *esse* something other.[93]

Here Thomas moves quickly from the observation that every being other than God merely participates in *esse* to otherness or distinction in such beings of substance (essence) and *esse* (act of being). He goes on to correlate the substance and act of being of any such being as potency and act because "every participant is related to that in which it participates as potency to act." He also uses the Boethian terminology of *quod est* and *esse* in contrasting them, thereby leaving little doubt again that he has in mind real diversity and composition.[94]

Even so, the argument begins with the assumption that God alone is his *esse*. Does the argument not presuppose God's existence for its validity? It does not seem so. The point of introducing God is to show that there can at most be one being which is its very *esse* (act of being) just as if, *per impossibile,* there were a subsisting whiteness, it too could only be one. Whether or not one knows that God does exist in fact, the impossibility of there being more than one such being is enough to justify the conclusion that no other being is its *esse*. Here, therefore, Thomas has combined argumentation based on the impossibility of there being more than one subsisting *esse* with an approach which rests on participation.[95]

A very interesting approach appears in the slightly earlier Quodlibet 2, q. 2, a. 1 of 1269, in a text we have already examined above in our discussion of participation.[96] This text is equally important for our present concern, since in it we have a combination of two possible directions in which one may move. Here Thomas is

---

93. "... manifestum est enim quod solus Deus est suum esse, quasi essentialiter existens, in quantum scilicet suum esse est eius substantia, quod de nullo alio dici potest; esse enim subsistens non potest esse nisi unum, sicut nec albedo subsistens posset esse nisi una. Oportet ergo quod quaelibet alia res sit ens participative, ita quod aliud sit in eo substantia participans esse et aliud ipsum esse participatum" (Leon. 25.2.277:32–40).

94. Leon. 25.2.277:40–48. Note: "Omne autem participans se habet ad participatum sicut potentia ad actum. Unde substantia cuiuslibet rei creatae se habet ad suum esse sicut potentia ad actum."

95. For another argument in which Thomas joins these two approaches see that taken from his Commentary on *Physics* VIII, lect. 21 (see n. 59 above).

96. See Ch. IV, nn. 27, 28, 31, 32.

attempting to show that an angel is composed substantially of essence and act of being *(esse)*. He begins by contrasting two ways in which one thing may be predicated of another—essentially or else by participation. Being *(ens)* is predicated of God alone essentially, since the divine *esse* is subsisting and absolute. Being is predicated of every creature by participation. If one were to stop here, one would assume that Thomas makes this statement because he is contrasting every such being with God. But the very next sentence suggests a different reason: "For no creature is its *esse* but is that which has *esse*."[97] In other words, here Thomas appeals to the fact that a creature is not its act of being in order to show that it participates in being. Hence he moves from the essence-*esse* distinction within the creature to its participated character. And though he does not spell this out here, he seems to base his evidence for this distinction on the fact that God alone is subsisting *esse* and, therefore, that essence and *esse* (act of being) must differ in everything else.

Shortly thereafter, however, Thomas reverses his procedure. When some characteristic is predicated of something else by participation, there must be something in the participant in addition to that which is participated. In other words, participation entails composition within the participant of a participating principle or subject and of that in which it participates. Here, therefore, we have the basic argument which moves from participation to composition. And lest there be any doubt about Thomas's intention, he immediately applies this reasoning to the case at hand: "And therefore in every creature, the creature which has *esse* is one, and its very *esse* is something other." Again he appeals to Boethius's formula as found in his *De Hebdomadibus,* thereby indicating to us once more that he has in mind real diversity between such a thing's essence and its act of being *(esse)*.[98]

From this text we may conclude that, as we see in its first part, one may reason from the essence-*esse* distinction or composition within any being to the conclusion that it participates in *esse*. On the other hand, the second part of this text suggests that one may move in the opposite direction. There Thomas has appealed to a more general principle: predication of a perfection by participation points to distinction between the participant and that in which it participates. This leads him to the conclusion that in the case of any creature, because the creature merely participates in *esse,* it is distinct from its *esse* (act of being). Thomas apparently sees no incompatibility between these two approaches. It is simply a matter of where one begins. If one has already established the essence-*esse* composition or distinction within any finite being by some other means, one can quickly conclude to its participated character. If, on the other hand, one begins with the fact that every such

97. Leon. 25.2.214:28–38. See Ch. IV above, n. 31, for part of the text. Note in particular: ". . . nulla enim creatura est suum esse, sed est habens esse."

98. "Quandocumque autem aliquid predicatur de altero per participationem, oportet ibi aliquid esse praeter id quod participatur, et ideo in qualibet creatura est aliud ipsa creatura quae habet esse, et ipsum esse eius. Et hoc est quod Boetius dicit in libro De hebdomadibus, quod in omni eo quod est citra primum, aliud est esse et quod est" (Leon. 25.2.214:44–50).

being merely participates in *esse (commune)* without exhausting its fullness, one may conclude to real diversity and composition of its essence and its act of being. This second route, of course, is the one followed by Thomas in most of the other texts examined in this section.

5. Argumentation Based on the Limited Character of Individual Beings

Reference has already been made in the preceding section of this chapter to this way of establishing an essence-*esse* distinction and composition within finite beings (substances). If this approach incorporates principles which recur repeatedly throughout Thomas's career, it appears very rarely in his writings as a distinct argument for the real distinction. In fact, to the best of my knowledge, it is offered in explicit fashion as an argument for this conclusion only in Thomas's Commentary on Bk I of the *Sentences,* d. 8, q. 5, a. 1. Even in that context it appears in the *sed contra* rather than in the *corpus* of his discussion. This notwithstanding, it draws on principles which Thomas frequently uses and it supports the conclusion for which he there argues. Hence we seem to be justified in assuming that he accepts the argument as his own.[99]

In this particular article Thomas is attempting to determine whether any creature is simple. In rejecting the claim that some creature is perfectly simple, Thomas offers two arguments for the contrary position before presenting his reply in the *corpus.* The first argument simply cites from Boethius's *De Trinitate,* c. 2: "In everything apart from the First (Being) 'that which is' and 'that whereby it is' differ." But every creature is different from the First Being; therefore it is composed of *esse* and *quod est.*[100]

The second argument for the contrary is of greater interest to us here. It runs this way. Every creature has a finite *esse.* But *esse* which is not received in something is not finite but unrestricted *(absolutum).* Hence every creature has an *esse* which is received in something. Therefore it must consist of at least these two, that is, of *esse* and of that which receives *esse.*[101]

---

99. For a brief presentation and discussion of this argument see also my *Metaphysical Themes,* pp. 157–61. For Thomas's text see Mandonnet ed., Vol. 1, pp. 226–27.

100. Ed. cit., p. 226: "Contra, Boetius, I *De Trinitate,* cap. II: 'In omni eo quod est citra primum, differt et quod est et quo est.' Ergo est composita ex esse et quod est." For the text from Boethius see *The Theological Tractates,* p. 10:29–37. This is not an exact citation: "Sed divina substantia sine materia forma est atque ideo unum et est id quod est. Reliqua enim non sunt id quod sunt. Unum quodque enim habet esse suum ex his ex quibus est, id ex partibus suis, et est hoc atque hoc . . . igitur non est id quod est."

101. Ed. cit., p. 226: "Praeterea, omnis creatura habet esse finitum. Sed esse non receptum in aliquo, non est finitum, immo absolutum. Ergo omnis creatura habet esse receptum in aliquo; et ita oportet quod habeat duo ad minus, scilicet esse, et id quod esse recipit."

This argument begins with the fact that creatures only have finite or limited *esse*. This fact would be so evident to Aquinas that it would hardly need justification. Nonetheless, he also formally argues elsewhere that there cannot be two completely infinite beings. Thus in SCG II, c. 52, he reasons that completely unlimited *esse* would embrace the total perfection of being. Hence if such infinity were to be assigned to two different beings, there would be no way in which one could be distinguished from the other.[102]

As for the argument in Thomas's Commentary on I *Sentences,* this reasoning assumes that if *esse* were not received in any subject, it would be unlimited. In other words, it is not self-limiting. Because *esse* is found in limited fashion in every creature, it must be received by some limiting principle in every such being. Otherwise we could not account for the limitation of that which is not self-limiting. (In light of what Thomas says in the *corpus* of this article, the argument and its conclusion should be restricted to the level of complete beings or substances. Complete beings or substances fall short of the divine simplicity by being composed. And since in God alone is there identity of quiddity and *esse,* in every creature one must find both its quiddity or nature and its *esse* which is given to it by God. And so it is composed of quiddity or nature and of *esse.* This is not true of what we might call incomplete beings or principles of being, such as prime matter, or a given form, or even a universal.)[103]

As we have noted, the argument in the *sed contra* rests on the presupposition that unreceived *esse* is unlimited. The view that act as such or, as in this case, that *esse* as such is not self-limiting appears frequently enough in Thomas's writings, from the earliest to the latest. He often uses it as a working principle to establish other points, for instance, divine infinity.[104] When it comes to Thomas's reasons

102. Ed. cit., p. 145: "Adhuc. Impossibile est quod sit duplex esse omnino infinitum: esse enim quod omnino est infinitum, omnem perfectionem essendi comprehendit; et sic, si duobus talis adesset infinitas, non inveniretur quo unum ab altero differret."

103. Ed. cit., pp. 226–27. Note in particular: "Dico ergo quod creatura est duplex. Quaedam enim est quae habet esse completum in se, sicut homo et huiusmodi, et talis creatura ita deficit a simplicitate divina quod incidit in compositionem. Cum enim in solo Deo esse suum sit sua quidditas, oportet quod in qualibet creatura, vel in corporali vel in spirituali, inveniatur quidditas vel natura sua, et esse suum, quod est sibi acquisitum a Deo, cuius essentia est suum esse; et ita componitur ex esse, vel quo est, et quod est." Here Thomas moves from identity of essence and *esse* in God to distinction of the same in complete creatures or substances. This does not imply that the argument based on limitation which he presents in the *sed contra* rests on the same assumption.

104. For some representative texts see *In I Sent.,* d. 8, q. 2, a. 1 (ed. cit., Vol. 1, p. 202): ". . . et hoc modo solum divinum esse non est terminatum, quia non est receptum in aliquo, quod sit diversum ab eo"; *In I Sent.,* d. 43, q. 1, a. 1 (p. 1003), where Thomas first applies this to form, and then to *esse:* "Et ideo illud quod habet esse absolutum et nullo modo receptum in aliquo, immo ipsemet est suum esse, illud est infinitum simpliciter"; SCG I, c. 43 (p. 41), where it is used to prove divine infinity: "Actus igitur in nullo existens nullo terminatur . . ."; SCG II, c. 52 (cited above in n. 54), where it is again used to establish divine infinity; ST I, q. 7, a. 1 (to prove divine infinity); *Compendium theologiae,* c. 18, to prove divine infinity: "Nullus enim actus invenitur finiri nisi per potentiam quae est eius receptiva . . ." (Leon. 42.88:7–8).

for accepting this principle, however, I must acknowledge that I have been unable to find any attempted demonstration of it in his works.

One might suspect that it is because of his conviction that God is infinite that Thomas can conclude that *esse* as such is not self-limiting. Otherwise *esse* would have to be limited even in God. This explanation will not do, however, since Thomas often uses the notion that act and therefore that *esse,* the act of being, is not self-limiting in order to establish divine infinity. Therefore he can hardly appeal to God's infinity in order to justify this principle without falling into circular reasoning.[105]

At times I have considered connecting this principle with Thomas's theory of separation. As will be recalled from Ch. II above, through this negative judgment Thomas would have us discover being as being by noting that we need not identify the intelligibility by reason of which something is recognized as being with that by which it enjoys a given kind of being. To be finite, one might reason, is to enjoy a given kind of being. Therefore, being, in order to be realized as such, need not be finite.

While this approach is tempting, it now seems to me that it will not suffice to ground the principle at issue. First of all, separation directly applies to the subject of metaphysics; but as we have seen, this is not *esse* but being *(ens)*. Even more fatal to this approach is the fact that the principle in question makes a stronger claim: *esse* as such *is* not self-limiting. The process of separation would at best leave us with the conclusion that *esse need* not be limited.[106]

Hence it seems to me that a more promising avenue is to conclude that for Aquinas this is a self-evident axiom. It is important to qualify this suggestion as I have done ("for Aquinas") because acceptance of this axiom presupposes a certain way of understanding *esse,* that is, as the actuality of all acts and the perfection of all perfections. Reference has already been made to this in an earlier chapter.[107] If this is one's understanding of *esse,* and it surely is Aquinas's, it will only be reason-

---

105. See the texts cited in the preceding note. Also see L. Sweeney, "Presidential Address: Surprises in the History of Infinity from Anaximander to George Cantor," *Proceedings of the American Catholic Philosophical Association* 55 (1981), pp. 11–12; and in the same, D. L. Balas, "A Thomist View on Divine Infinity," pp. 91–98. Cf. Sweeney, "Bonaventure and Aquinas on the Divine Being as Infinite," c. 19 in his *Divine Infinity in Greek and Medieval Thought* (New York, 1982), especially pp. 432–37. On the importance of this axiom (that unreceived act is unlimited) in Thomas's metaphysics see de Finance, *Être et agir,* pp. 51–56; W. N. Clarke, "The Limitation of Act by Potency," pp. 65–88; Nicolas, "Chronique de Philosophie," pp. 561–64; Fabro, *Participation et causalité,* pp. 64ff. Cf. Ch. IV above, nn. 91, 92. Also see Robert, "Le principe: 'Actus non limitatur nisi per potentiam subjectivam realiter distinctam'," pp. 44–70. Though he does not find Thomas reasoning explicitly from the limitation of act by potency to the essence-*esse* distinction, he grants that the essential elements for such an approach are present in his texts, including the limitation principle itself (pp. 51, 53ff.).

106. For a discussion of separation and its rôle in one's discovery of the subject of metaphysics see above, Ch. II, Section 2.

107. See Ch. II above, pp. 33–34, and nn. 34–39.

able for him to conclude that *esse* is not self-limiting. To say anything else would be to account for the limitation and imperfection (negation of further perfection) of a being by appealing to that which is its ultimate principle of actuality and perfection. For Thomas, actuality and perfection go together.[108]

At times Thomas refers to a "power of being," a *virtus essendi,* or a *potestas essendi* that he assigns to the act of being. Thus in *Summa contra Gentiles* I, c. 28 he notes that if there is something to which the total power of being *(virtus essendi)* belongs, no nobility or perfection will be lacking to that thing. And then he refers to that thing which is identical with its act of being, i.e., God, as possessing *esse* according to the total power of being *(potestas essendi).* To illustrate this he appeals to his favorite example of whiteness. If there were a separate (subsisting) whiteness, nothing of the power *(virtus)* of whiteness would be lacking to it. In fact, however, something of the power of whiteness is lacking to particular white things because of some deficiency on the part of the subjects in which whiteness is received; for any such subject receives whiteness according to its particular (and limited) mode.[109] In commenting on Prop. 4 of the *Liber de causis* he remarks that if something should possess the infinite power of being in such fashion that it did not participate *esse* (the act of being) from something else, it and it alone would be infinite. In fact such is true of God. But, he continues, if something possesses the infinite power to exist *(infinitam virtutem ad essendum)* only according to an act of being that is participated in from something else, insofar as it participates in the act of being *(esse)*, it is finite; for what is participated is not received in the participant according to its total infinity, but only in partial, i.e., finite fashion.[110] And in his Commentary on the *Divine Names,* Thomas writes that because things other than God have an *esse* that is received and participated, they do not possess it according to the total power of being.[111]

Fabro is well known for having emphasized the importance of what he refers to as intensive *esse* in Aquinas. And in a recent book F. O'Rourke stresses this very strongly along with Thomas's debt to Pseudo-Dionysius in developing this

108. See the text from *De potentia,* q. 7, a. 2, ad 9, cited below in n. 115.

109. Ed. cit., pp. 29–30: "Igitur si aliquid est cui competit tota virtus essendi, ei nulla nobilitatum deese potest quae alicui rei conveniat. Sed rei quae est suum esse, competit esse secundum totam essendi potestatem: sicut, si esset aliqua albedo separata, nihil ei de virtute albedinis deesse posset; nam alicui albo aliquid de virtute albedinis deest ex defectu recipentis albedinem, quae eam secundum modum suum recipit, et fortasse non secundum totum posse albedinis. Deus igitur, qui est suum esse, ut supra probatum est, habet esse secundum totam virtutem ipsius esse. Non potest ergo carere aliqua nobilitate quae alicui rei conveniat."

110. Ed. cit., p. 30. For the Latin see n. 90 above.

111. See *In De divinis nominibus,* c. V, lect. 1, p. 234, n. 629: ". . . omnis forma, recepta in aliquo, limitatur et finitur secundum capacitatem recipientis. . . . Sed si esset albedo separata, nihil deesset ei quod ad virtutem albedinis pertineret. Omnia autem alia, sicut superius dictum est, habent esse receptum et participatum et ideo non habent esse secundum totam virtutem essendi, sed solus Deus, qui est ipsum esse subsistens, secundum totam virtutem essendi, esse habet."

theme.[112] By these references to the "power" of being Thomas appears to have in mind a fullness of being and of perfection which is found in the notion of *esse* when it is simply considered in itself, and which is in fact fully realized only in God, self-subsisting *esse*. Other existents only participate in *esse* in limited fashion. And since Thomas has associated his example of whiteness with this theme, his point in so doing seems to be this: When whiteness is considered in itself, it contains nothing but the notion of and the power of whiteness. If whiteness could exist as such apart from any receiving and limiting subject, it would be nothing but whiteness, and it would be unique. For there would be nothing within it to prevent the fullness of whiteness from being realized therein, as Thomas points out in SCG I, c. 43, for instance.[113] Thomas frequently goes on to draw a parallel with *esse*. Simply considered in itself, *esse*, the act of being, includes nothing but actuality or perfection, the total power of being. And it is actually realized in this way in that unique case where it subsists apart from any receiving subject, i.e., in God. In every other case it is received by a subject that simultaneously limits it, thereby preventing it from being realized in its unlimited fullness.[114]

With this we may return to *De potentia*, q. 7, a. 2, ad 9. In analyzing any given form, Thomas writes, we may consider it (1) only insofar as it exists within the potentiality of matter. Or we may consider it (2) insofar as it is contained within the active power of an agent which could bring it into actual existence. Or we may consider it (3) insofar as it simply exists in the mind as an object of thought. Finally (4), he remarks, it is by reason of its *esse*, its act of being, that it enjoys actual existence. Given this, Thomas concludes that what he calls *esse* is the actuality of all acts and the perfection of all perfections.[115]

112. For Fabro see, for instance, *Participation et causalité,* p. 195, where he refers to this intensive notion of *esse* as "le véritable fondement de la métaphysique thomiste de la participation." Also see p. 229 where he identifies Pseudo-Dionysius as the principal source for the Thomistic notion of intensive *esse*. For O'Rourke see his *Pseudo-Dionysius and the Metaphysics of Aquinas,* pp. 155–87. See pp. 174–80 for his discussion of the meaning of *esse intensivum* in Aquinas, and pp. 180–85 for his stress on Dionysius in developing this. Also see pp. 156–74 where he emphasizes a distinction made by Thomas between dimensional quantity and virtual quantity, for instance in *De veritate,* q. 29, a. 3, and elsewhere, in order to stress Aquinas's application of the notion of virtual quantity to *esse*. Here some caveats are in order, since not all of the texts he cites have to do with the intensive *esse* of the act of being but, in some cases, with the capacity or power of certain beings to exist forever; and that is a very different matter. See, for instance, SCG I, c. 20 (ed. cit., pp. 20–21) and O'Rourke's discussion on pp. 167–71.

113. Ed. cit., p. 41. "Amplius. Omnis actus alteri inhaerens terminationem recipit ex eo in quo est: quia quod est in altero, est in eo per modum recipientis. Actus igitur in nullo existens nullo terminatur: puta, si albedo esset per se existens, perfectio albedinis in ea non terminaretur, quominus haberet quicquid de perfectione albedinis haberi potest. Deus autem est actus nullo modo in alio existens. . . . Relinquitur igitur ipsum esse infinitum."

114. See, for instance, the texts cited in nn. 109, 111, and 113.

115. *De potentia,* q. 7, a. 2, ad 9: "Ad nonum dicendum, quod hoc quod dico *esse* est inter omnia perfectissimum: quod ex hoc patet quia actus est semper perfectio<r> potentia. Quaelibet autem forma signata non intelligitur in actu nisi per hoc quod esse ponitur. Nam humanitas vel igneitas

If one agrees with Thomas that what he calls *esse* (the act of being) is indeed the actuality of all acts and the perfection of all perfections, wherever one finds it realized in only limited fashion, one must account for its actual realization, to be sure, but one must also account for its limitation, for the fact that it is not realized according to its full power or plenitude in this particular instance. For Thomas, appeal to an extrinsic cause is necessary but not sufficient to account for this. He is convinced that a distinct intrinsic limiting principle is also required, in order to account for the limitation of that which is not self-limiting.[116]

Closely connected with this issue is another question: Does this argument for a real distinction and composition of essence and *esse* in finite beings presuppose knowledge of God's existence? Recognition of its starting point, the fact that limited beings exist, clearly does not. But what about its appeal to the axiom that unreceived *esse* is unlimited? Does not this presuppose knowledge that God exists? I have suggested that acceptance of this axiom rests on Thomas's particular way of understanding *esse*. Does not his understanding of *esse* as the actuality of all acts and the perfection of all perfections presuppose the Judeo-Christian revelation of God as subsisting *esse* as implied in Exodus 3:14?[117]

As I see things, it does not. If Thomas understands by *esse* that principle within any given substantial entity which accounts for the fact that it actually exists, this is because the distinction between an actual existent and a merely possible existent is something which we can discover within the realm of our own experience and reflection upon the same. As he remarks in the text from the *De potentia* cited in a previous paragraph, it is by reason of its *esse* (act of being) that a given form (or entity) enjoys actual existence. Given his recognition of this, Thomas then concludes immediately that what he calls *esse* is the actuality of all acts and the perfection of all perfections.[118] This well-known text does not give the impression that Thomas depends upon prior knowledge of God's existence for his understanding of *esse* as actuality and perfection. Hence neither does his acceptance of the axiom that unreceived *esse* is unlimited.

---

potest considerari ut in potentia materiae existens, vel ut in virtute agentis, aut etiam ut in intellectu: sed hoc quod habet *esse*, efficitur actu existens. Unde patet quod hoc quod dico *esse* est actualitas omnium actuum, et propter hoc est perfectio omnium perfectionum" (ed. cit., p. 192). Thomas then immediately adds that *esse* cannot be determined by anything else that would be more formal and would be added to it as act to potency. Hence *esse* is not determined by something else in the way potency is determined by act, but rather in the way act is determined, i.e., limited, by potency.

116. For fuller discussion of this principle see my "Thomas Aquinas and the Axiom That Unreceived Act Is Unlimited," and Ch. IV, n. 92 above.

117. For this suggestion see Gilson, *Elements of Christian Philosophy*, pp. 130–32; and for background, pp. 119–24; also see his *Introduction à la philosophie chrétienne*, pp. 45–58, and for difficulties involved in any purely philosophical approach to establishing the essence-existence distinction, pp. 98–109. As Gilson views the matter, this would be a fine illustration of Thomas's preference for the theological order rather than the philosophical, as well as an example of what Gilson understands by Thomas's Christian Philosophy.

118. *De potentia*, q. 7, a. 2, ad 9, cited in n. 115 above.

Finally, if the above analysis of this kind of argumentation is correct, one may ask why Thomas does not have recourse to this approach to establishing the distinction between essence and *esse* more frequently, and especially in his later writings. In attempting to answer this I can only speculate. Often enough in these later writings, as we have seen, Thomas reasons either from the participated character of creatures to their essence-*esse* composition, or else from the claim that there can only be one subsisting *esse* to this same conclusion. These approaches are not surprising in light of the theological contexts in which they usually appear, even if, as I have argued, certain formulations of them do not have to presuppose knowledge of God's existence. Since the argument based on limitation seems to follow the philosophical order more directly than an approach which moves from knowledge of God to such distinction in creatures, Thomas would have relatively little occasion to have recourse to it in any of his theological writings. At the same time, passing remarks in a number of different contexts strongly suggest that he never rejected or abandoned it.[119]

---

119. See my remarks in the preceding section of this chapter about ST I, q. 75, a. 5, ad 4; and Thomas's Commentary on the *Liber de causis,* Prop. 4. Also see *In De divinis nominibus,* c. V, lect. 1 (cited in n. 111 above). Also see *De spiritualibus creaturis,* a. 1, ad 15: ". . . dicendum quod esse substantiae spiritualis creatae est coarctatum et limitatum non per materiam, sed per hoc quod est receptum et participatum in natura determinatae speciei. . . ." (ed. cit., p. 373).

Relative Nonbeing and the
         One and the Many

We have now considered major parts of Thomas's answer to the problem of the
One and the Many in the order of being. Many individual beings may exist without
doing violence to the unity of being because each of them merely participates in
being *(esse commune)*; no one of them is identical with it. In order to be assured
that the kind of participation at issue here is not merely logical or conceptual, we
have also followed Thomas's argumentation for real composition and distinction
of essence and act of being in every participating entity. Precisely because the act
of being *(esse)* is received in and limited by a distinct essence principle within every
such being, we can say that such beings participate in *esse* really rather than in
merely logical fashion; for in each of them there is a composition and distinction
of a principle that participates (essence, nature, substance) and a participated principle, the act of being. Moreover, as we shall see in a subsequent chapter, Thomas's
account of participation as well as his doctrine of analogy of being take on fullest
meaning once he has established the existence of a subsisting and unparticipated
source of all other being, that is, the existence of God. But for the present, I would
like to consider one more facet of Thomas's solution to the problem of Parmenides
as he works this out at the level of finite being.

1. Relative Nonbeing

As will be recalled from our introduction of the problem of the One and the
Many in Ch. III, as Thomas understands him, Parmenides maintains that multiplicity must be rejected because there is no sense in which nonbeing may be said
to be or to be real. For Thomas the evidence pointing to multiplicity is undeniable.
Even so, he grants the basic Parmenidean insight to this effect, that multiplicity
and therefore diversity do presuppose in some way the reality of nonbeing. It re-

mains for us to determine whether—and, if so, to what extent—Thomas himself admits of any kind of real nonbeing.

In order to ascertain Thomas's answer to this, it will be helpful for us to return to a text we had begun to examine above in Ch. III, that is, q. 4, a. 1 of his Commentary on Boethius's *De Trinitate*.[1] As will be recalled, there Thomas is attempting to identify the ultimate foundation for plurality or for multiplicity. If this is otherness, as Boethius states, what is the ultimate explanation for otherness? Taking his cue from Aristotle's *Metaphysics* X, Thomas has argued that something is plural or many only insofar as it is divisible or divided.[2] Wherefore it follows that the cause of division will also be the cause of plurality. And if one may account for the division of things which are posterior and composite by appealing to a diversity of things which are simple and first, one must still explain division at the level of that which is simple and first. In attempting to do this, Thomas reasons that the cause (which he here identifies as a quasi-formal cause) for the division of things which are posterior and composite is the diversity of that which is simple and prior (or first).[3] To illustrate this he offers two examples: one part of a line is divided from another part of that same line because it enjoys a different position. In this case, taken from the order of accidents, position serves as a quasi-formal difference for continuous quantity. Or in the order of substance, a human being is divided from a donkey because the two have different constituting differences. To develop the second example more fully, human being and donkey enjoy diverse constituting differences precisely because the rational and the irrational are not one but many.[4]

As Thomas immediately recognizes, we cannot extend this process to infinity and thereby in every case account for the division of that which is posterior and composite by postulating a further division of the prior and simpler. Hence he concludes that things which are primary and simple are divided of themselves. In supporting this he uses language which is reminiscent of Parmenides. Being *(ens)* cannot be divided from being insofar as it is being. Nothing is divided from being except nonbeing. Therefore this being is not divided from that being except insofar as in this being there is included the negation of that being.[5] Unlike Parmenides, however, Thomas apparently admits that in some way the negation of this being is included in that being. In other words, Thomas is willing to admit that in some way nonbeing is. How he does so remains to be seen.

In the text at hand Thomas briefly turns from the ontological order to what we today might call the epistemological order, that is, from a consideration of being

---

1. See above in Ch. III, Section 1 and n. 8 for references to secondary literature concerning this text. Also see Aertsen, *Medieval Philosophy and the Transcendentals,* pp. 222–23.

2. Leon. 50.120 (cited above in Ch. III, n. 5).

3. Leon. 50.120:72–77. Note in particular: "In posterioribus namque et compositis causa divisionis quasi formalis, id est ratione cuius fit divisio, <est> diversitas simplicium et pri(m)orum."

4. Leon. 50.120:78–89.

5. Leon. 50.120:89–100. See above, Ch. III, n. 8.

to a consideration of first principles in the order of thought. He notes that in the case of first terms (and principles, I would add), negative propositions are immediate. This is so because the negation of one term is, as it were, included in one's understanding of the other.[6] Though Thomas immediately shifts from this reference to first terms and principles back to the ontological order, his intent is clear enough. I take him to mean by this that in the order in which we discover first principles, the principle of noncontradiction comes first, and not, for instance, the principle of identity. As he indicates in other writings, we first come to a knowledge of being and then, by negating being, to a knowledge of nonbeing. When we compare these two notions we immediately see that being is not nonbeing.[7]

In our passage from his Commentary on the *De Trinitate*, however, Thomas immediately returns to the ontological order. He notes that when the very first creature is considered together with its cause, plurality is thereby introduced into the realm of being. Such a first creature does not attain to its first cause. Apparently with some sort of a Neoplatonic emanation scheme in mind, Thomas observes that some would introduce plurality into the realm of being by arguing that from the One only one thing can proceed (immediately). This very first effect, taken together with its cause, would constitute a many or a plurality. And from this first effect two things would proceed—one from the first creature when it is simply considered in itself; and another from that same first creature when it is viewed in relation to its cause.[8]

6. ". . . unde in primis terminis propositiones negativae sunt immediatae, quasi negatio unius sit in intellectu alterius" (Leon. 50.120:100–102).

7. As Courtès points out, some twentieth-century interpreters of Aquinas have defended the priority of the principle of identity rather than that of noncontradiction. He cites J. Maritain and R. Garrigou-Lagrange to this effect. See his "L'être et le non-être selon saint Thomas d'Aquin," pp. 584–87. As regards the order of discovery, this is clearly not Thomas's view. See, for instance, *In I Sent.,* d. 8, q. 1, a. 3, Mandonnet ed., Vol. 1, p. 200: "Primum enim quod cadit in imaginatione intellectus, est ens, sine quo nihil potest apprehendi ab intellectu; sicut primum quod cadit in credulitate intellectus sunt dignitates, et praecipue ista, contradictoria non esse simul vera. . . ." Also see *Summa contra Gentiles* II, c. 83 (ed. cit., p. 200): "Naturaliter igitur intellectus noster cognoscit ens, et ea quae sunt per se entis inquantum huiusmodi; in qua cognitione fundatur primorum principiorum notitia, *ut non esse simul affirmare et negare,* et alia huiusmodi." Especially significant is the following text from ST I–II, q. 94, a. 2 (Leon. 7.169–70): "In his autem quae in apprehensione omnium cadunt, quidam ordo invenitur. Nam illud quod primo cadit in apprehensione, est ens, cuius intellectus includitur in omnibus quaecumque quis apprehendit. Et ideo primum principium indemonstrabile est quod *non est simul affirmare et negare,* quod fundatur supra rationem entis et non entis: et super hoc principio omnia alia fundantur, ut dicitur in IV *Metaphys.*" Weidemann offers other examples where negative propositions are based immediately on primitive terms because the negation of one is included in the other, such as those involving the "one" and the "other," or the "one" and the "many", or the "same" and the "diverse." See *Metaphysik und Sprache,* pp. 52–53. Granting this, however, it seems to me that Thomas's point in the immediate context (q. 4, a. 1 of his Commentary on the *De Trinitate*) is best brought out by the opposition between being and nonbeing as formulated in the principle of noncontradiction.

8. Leon. 50.120:104–110.

Here one is reminded of a slightly more complicated emanation scheme defended by Avicenna in his *Philosophia prima,* and certainly well known to Thomas and his contemporaries. According to this approach, which owes a deep debt to Neoplatonism, from the First Being only one being, the First Intelligence, proceeds immediately. Indeed, it does so necessarily and eternally, although that is another issue. Insofar as this First Intelligence turns back to and understands its source, the First Being, it (the First Intelligence) produces a Second Intelligence. Insofar as it understands itself as an intelligence, this First Intelligence also produces the soul of the first (outermost) heavenly sphere. And insofar as it understands itself as a possible being in itself, the First Intelligence produces the body of the first heavenly sphere. Thomas presents this theory very accurately in his *De substantiis separatis,* c. 10, with only slight variation from Avicenna's text.[9]

It seems likely, however, that in our text from his Commentary on the *De Trinitate,* Thomas is following Algazel's more simplified presentation of this Avicennian emanation scheme. Thus Algazel's *Metaphysics* manifests the same concern to show how from the First Being only one effect proceeds immediately, but that from this second being (the first effect), which is the First Intelligence, two other things proceed, i.e., the Second Intelligence and the outermost heavenly sphere. Here Algazel does not introduce the further distinction between the emanation of the soul and the emanation of the body of the first heavenly sphere.[10]

In any event, it is this kind of emanation scheme that Thomas has in mind and which he here as always firmly rejects. He argues that there is another way of introducing plurality into the realm of reality. While his discussion understandably takes God's existence as established, it also casts light on his view of the role of nonbeing in accounting for differentiation of being from being, and hence for multiplicity. As he puts it, one first effect can imitate the First Being in a way in which another falls short of that First Being; and it can fall short of the First Being in a way in which the other effect imitates it. In this way, reasons Thomas, there can be many first effects; that is to say, many effects which are immediately produced by the one First Being. In each of these first and immediate effects there will be a negation of the First Cause and of any other effect.[11] By saying this, of course,

---

9. For Avicenna see *Liber de Philosophia prima sive Scientia divina V–X,* tr. IX, c. 4, pp. 481–84, especially p. 483. For Thomas's presentation of this theory see, for instance, *De substantiis separatis,* c. 10 (Leon. 40.D59:4–27), where he attributes it to Avicenna and, with less certainity, to the *Liber de causis.* Cf. my "The Latin Avicenna as a Source for Thomas Aquinas's Metaphysics," pp. 74–78. For my critique of Weidemann's attempt to show that in this text *(In De Trinitate,* q. 4, a. 1) Thomas has the *Liber de causis* in mind, see my "Thomas Aquinas on the Distinction and Derivation of the Many from the One," p. 567, n. 9. For Weidemann see "Tradition und Kritik," pp. 103–5.

10. See *Algazel's Metaphysics,* J. T. Muckle, ed. (Toronto, 1933), pp. 20–21.

11. "Quod dicere non cogimur, cum unum primum possit aliquid imitari in quo alterum ab eo deficit, et deficere in quo alterum imitatur; et sic possunt inveniri plures primi effectus, in quorum quolibet est negatio et causae et effectus alterius secundum idem, vel secundum remotiorem distantiam etiam in uno et eodem" (Leon. 50.120:110–121:117).

Thomas has returned to the issue of nonbeing. In some way we may say that non-being is present within a given effect or entity insofar as that entity is not identical with the First Cause or with any other effect.

In the present context Thomas explains that this negation may occur either by reason of one and the same thing, or else perhaps by reason of the greater distance which is present in one and the same thing. Presumably by the first of these explanations he means that some factor is found in a given effect. This same factor accounts both for the way in which that effect imitates and falls short of the First Being, and for the way in which it differs from other immediate effects of the First Being. By the second proposed explanation he seems to mean that by reason of its given degree of perfection, a particular immediate effect of the First Being will be more "distant" or farther removed from the First Being than another immediate effect which imitates the First Being more perfectly. To repeat a point already made, according to either explanation one may say that the effect is not the First Cause, and that it is not any other effect.[12]

But one may still ask: In a given first and immediate effect of the First Cause, or for that matter and to broaden the issue, in any given being we may experience or discover, how can there be a negation of the First Cause and of any (and every) other effect? In seeming anticipation of our query, Thomas develops more fully the themes of negation and affirmation, and the opposition between being and nonbeing. As he now puts it, the first (in the sense of ultimate) principle or explanation for plurality or division arises from negation and affirmation. In order to account for the origins of plurality, being and nonbeing must first be understood. Those first things which are divided from one another are constituted of these, that is, of being and nonbeing. It is because of this that they themselves form a plurality or a many.[13]

12. See the final part of the text cited in the preceding note. For a similar interpretation of this passage see Weidemann, "Tradition und Kritik," pp. 113–14. However, Weidemann takes *secundum remotiorem distantiam* in the second explanation as meaning that in terms of a given aspect a particular first effect would be more distant from another effect than from its creator. I rather take it to mean that one creature would be more distant from God than would another creature which imitates the First Being in that respect. On the "infinite distance" which always remains between God and creatures see *De veritate*, q. 2, a. 3, ad 16; q. 2. a. 11, ad 4; q. 23, a. 7, ad 9. On the transfer of the term "distance" from the realm of the spatial and quantitative to the metaphysical in Aquinas, see E. P. Mahoney, "Metaphysical Foundations of the Hierarchy of Being," pp. 170–71, and the references given there in nn. 34 and 44. Also see pp. 209–12. As Montagnes points out *(La doctrine de l'analogie de l'être,* p. 89), Thomas uses this metaphor of the infinite distance between creatures and God in his early works (see n. 48 for additional references). Cf. the later *De potentia,* q. 7, a. 7, ad 1, even though the spatial reference is not explicit there: ". . . talis autem mensura non est Deus, cum in infinitum omnia excedat per ipsum mensurata" (ed. cit., p. 204). Also cf. ST I, q. 13, a. 5, sed contra 2, cited by Montagnes, p. 89, n. 47.

13. Leon. 50.121:118–123: "Sic ergo patet quod prima pluralitatis vel divisionis ratio sive principium est ex negatione et affirmatione, ut talis ordo originis pluralitatis intelligatur, quod primo sint intelligenda ens et non ens, ex quibus ipsa prima divisa constituuntur, ac per hoc plura. . . ."

Whence, Thomas continues, just as the one is discovered immediately after being insofar as being is viewed as undivided from itself, so too after the division between being and nonbeing a plurality of prior (or first) and simple things is immediately given. Diversity rests upon and follows from this plurality, continues Thomas, insofar as there remains within this plurality the power of its cause, that is, the power of the opposition between being and nonbeing. Therefore, one of many things is said to be diverse when it is compared to another because it is not the other.[14] (Again, therefore, we find Thomas stressing this original opposition between being and nonbeing as the ultimate explanation for a plurality of created things which are primary and simple. This plurality in turn accounts for the diversity of the same, that is, of created things which are primary and simple.)

Lest there be any misunderstanding, Thomas reemphasizes his point. Because a second cause cannot produce its effect except by the power of its first cause, the plurality of things which are primary cannot account for the division and plurality of things which are secondary and composed unless there remains within the latter plurality the force or power of the original opposition. The causality he has in mind, it will be recalled, is what he has described as quasi-formal causality. And the original opposition to which he is referring is that which obtains between being and nonbeing, as he again reminds us. Because of this opposition between being and nonbeing, the original diversity between things which are first and simple arises. And in this way the diversity of things that are primary produces a plurality of those that are secondary.[15]

At this point in his discussion Thomas returns to the Boethian dictum which gave rise to this particular article—otherness is the principle of plurality. Thomas takes this to mean that otherness is found in certain things insofar as they are

---

14. ". . . unde sicut post ens in quantum est indivisum statim invenitur unum, ita post divisionem entis et non entis statim invenitur pluralitas pri(m)orum simplicium. Hanc autem pluralitatem consequitur ratio diversitatis, secundum quod manet in ea suae causae virtus, scilicet oppositionis entis et non entis; ideo enim unum plurium diversum dicitur alteri comparatum, quia non est illud" (Leon. 50.121:123–131). This derivation of (transcendental) unity, based as it is on the denial that being is divided from itself, reminds one of Thomas's procedure in *De veritate,* q. 1, a. 1. See Section 5 below in this chapter. Also see *In IV Met.,* lect. 3, Cathala-Spiazzi ed., p. 158, n. 566. There again Thomas writes that the kind of one or unity which is convertible with being *(ens)* implies the absence of formal division by opposites; the ultimate foundation *(prima radix)* for such division is the opposition between affirmation and negation: "Nam illa dividuntur adinvicem, quae ita se habent, quod hoc non est illud." Thomas then spells out this sequence: "Primo igitur intelligitur ipsum ens, et ex consequenti non ens, et per consequens divisio, et per consequens unum quod [di]visionem privat, et per consequens multitudo, in cuius ratione cadit divisio sicut in ratione unius indivisio. . . ." Hence, just as indivision is included in the intelligible content of the one, so is division (of one thing from another) included in the intelligible content of the many. Cf. *In I Sent.,* d. 24, q. 1, a. 3, ad 1, ad 2, ad 3 (Mandonnet ed., vol. 1, pp. 583–84).

15. ". . . et quia causa secunda non producit effectum nisi per virtutem causae primae, ideo pluralitas primorum non facit divisionem et pluralitatem in secundis compositis, nisi in quantum manet in ea vis oppositionis primae, quae est inter ens et non ens, ex qua habet rationem diversitatis. Et sic diversitas primorum facit pluralitatem secundorum" (Leon. 50.121:131–138).

diverse from one another. Hence we might say that diversity is the principle or cause of plurality in such things. But now he introduces a further precision by distinguishing between division and diversity. In accord with the theory he has just presented, division is presupposed for the plurality of things which are prior (or first); but diversity is not. This is because division does not require that each of the things which are so distinguished must enjoy being, since it arises from affirmation and negation. Unlike division, however, diversity presupposes that both of the things that are distinguished enjoy being. Therefore, diversity presupposes plurality, and plurality presupposes division. Or to reverse our perspective, division gives rise to plurality, which in turn gives rise to diversity. Hence, reasons Thomas, diversity cannot be regarded as the cause or explanation for the plurality of things which are first unless one takes diversity as equivalent to division. Therefore he concludes that the Boethian dictum applies to the plurality of composites. In the case of composites, the cause of plurality or multiplicity is otherness, i.e., the diversity of things which are first and simple.[16]

Of greatest interest to us here is Thomas's appeal to the opposition and division between being and nonbeing in his effort to account for any kind of plurality or multiplicity within the realm of being. This most fundamental opposition between being and nonbeing will be enough for him to distinguish a first created effect from God, the uncreated cause. And it will also be required for him to distinguish any given creature from any other. If we concentrate on one such effect, we may say that it is or enjoys being, presumably because it exists, and yet that it is not (or includes nonbeing) in some other way, since it is not its divine cause and is not any other effect. And if we can refer to a plurality or multiplicity of such primary and simple things—effects immediately produced by God—this is because the power of the original opposition between being and nonbeing is preserved in each of them.[17]

2. Distinction of Any Finite Being from Other Beings

If we grant Aquinas all of this, we may still wonder what it is within the structure of any such prior and simpler being which accounts for the fact that it is not God and that it is not to be identified with any other primary and simple creature. It seems that in some way Thomas is going to have to defend the reality of some kind of nonbeing if he is to account for this. Moreover, we may wonder whether these primary and simple effects to which he has referred in our text are complete beings in themselves, or perhaps something still more fundamental. I shall now turn to these two issues, although in reverse order.

---

16. Leon. 50.121:138–151. Note in particular: ". . . quamvis autem divisio praecedat pluralitatem pri(m)orum, non tamen diversitas, quia divisio non requirit utrumque condivisorum esse ens, cum sit divisio per affirmationem et negationem, sed diversitas requirit utrumque esse ens, unde praesupponit pluralitatem."

17. See n. 15 above.

As regards the second of these, there are indications in the text just analyzed which suggest that Thomas is willing to take these first and simple effects in either sense, that is, either as complete beings, or as referring to something more fundamental which is found only as an intrinsic principle in such beings. On the one hand, in noting that one cannot indefinitely extend one's account of composite entities by saying that they are composed of prior and simpler entities *ad infinitum,* Thomas appealed to constituting differences to illustrate such prior and simple factors, namely, the different positions enjoyed by continuous quantity in the case of a line, and the constituting differences present in a human being and in a brute animal. In each of these cases, in referring to that which is first (or prior) and simple he seems to have in mind something less than complete entities or substances.[18]

On the other hand, Thomas then considered and rejected a Neoplatonic account of how many effects might derive from one first being. Against this theory he offered his own explanation, and this time, it would seem, at the level of complete beings. One first being may be immediately created by God and still differ from him because it both falls short of him and imitates him in some way; and it may also differ from any other immediately created effect by imitating God in a way in which that other effect does not and by not imitating him in a way in which that other immediately created effect does.[19]

For additional light concerning this we may a turn to an earlier text, d. 8, q. 5, a. 1 of Thomas's Commentary on Bk I of the *Sentences.* There he considers an issue which is related to our present concern—whether any creature is perfectly simple.[20] In his reply Thomas comments that whatever proceeds from God so as to differ in essence from him must fall short of his simplicity. But Thomas then introduces an important qualification. For something to fall short of the divine simplicity it need not itself be composed. For instance, for something to fall short of supreme goodness, it need not itself include any kind of evil. Accordingly, Thomas distinguishes two situations, or what he refers to as two kinds of "creatures." There is a kind of creature which enjoys complete being *(esse)* in itself, such as a human being or anything of this sort. Such a creature falls short of the divine simplicity by being composed. Since quiddity and *esse* are identical only in God, it follows that in every such creature, whether corporeal or spiritual, there must be its quiddity or nature and its *esse* (act of being). Consequently, every such creature, i.e., every created substance, is composed of *esse* (act of being) or *quo est* and of essence *(quod est).* Here, of course, we have another argument for the essence-*esse* composition of creatures, and one which presupposes God's existence.[21]

18. See Leon. 50.120:78–84.
19. See Leon. 50.120:110–121:117. See n. 11 above.
20. Mandonnet ed., Vol. 1, p. 226: "Utrum aliqua creatura sit simplex."
21. Mandonnet ed., pp. 226–27 (cited above in Ch. V, n. 103).

More interesting for our immediate purposes, however, are Thomas's remarks about the other kind of creature—the kind that does not enjoy complete being in itself. He now explains more fully what he understands by such creatures. These do not exist in themselves but only in something else. In illustration he cites prime matter, or any form, or a universal.[22] In the first two cases he has in mind what are often referred to within the Thomistic tradition as principles of being. Neither prime matter nor any (corporeal) form, whether substantial or accidental, is a complete being in its own right; each is only a principle or intrinsic constituent of a complete being or substance. (And not being a Platonist concerning this point, Thomas certainly rejects any doctrine of subsisting universal forms.) In what sense, therefore, can one say that "creatures" of this type are not simple? Thomas comments that such creatures do not fall short of the divine simplicity by being composed.[23]

Immediately, of course, we wonder how this can be. How can such a creature, or such a principle of being, fall short of the divine simplicity without itself being composed? We are reminded of Thomas's distinction in q. 4, a. 1 of his Commentary on the De Trinitate between accounting for plurality and diversity of things which are composite, on the one hand, and those which are first and simple, on the other. In the present discussion he seems to be dealing with the latter kind—those which are first and simple (simple in the sense that they are not composed of something that is still prior and simpler). If so, how do they fall short of the perfect simplicity of God?

In reply to our question Thomas suggests that such a creature (or principle) can fall short of the perfect simplicity of the First Principle in one of two ways. It may do so because it is potentially divisible or divisible per accidens. Such is true of prime matter, of form, and of a universal. Or it may be that it can enter into composition with something else (componibile alteri). This, comments Thomas, could never be admitted of the divine simplicity, since God could never enter into composition with anything else.[24]

Thomas's discussion in this article from his Commentary on I Sentences is helpful because of his distinction between "creatures" which enjoy complete being in themselves, and others which do not. As regards the first type, they are not perfectly simple because at the very least every such entity is composed of essence and esse. This we have seen not only from the present text but in many other contexts as

22. "Est etiam quaedam creatura quae non habet esse in se, sed tantum in alio, sicut materia prima, sicut forma quaelibet, sicut universale . . ." (p. 227).

23. ". . . et talis creatura non deficit a simplicitate, ita quod sit composita" (ibid.).

24. "Unde oportebit devenire ad aliquid quod non est compositum, sed tamen deficit a simplicitate primi: et defectus iste perpenditur ex duobus: vel quia est divisibile in potentia vel per accidens, sicut materia prima, et forma, et universale; vel quia est componibile alteri, quod divina simplicitas non patitur" (ibid.).

analyzed in our Ch. V above. By this kind of entity he also seems to have in mind the kind of beings—the "composite" entities—whose multiplicity he accounts for in his Commentary on the *De Trinitate* by holding that they are composed of that which is first (or prior) and simple.[25]

As regards "creatures" of the second type—those which do not enjoy complete being in themelves—he has now accounted for the fact that they are not perfectly simple by suggesting either that they are potentially divisible or divisible *per accidens,* or else that they can enter into composition with something else. For instance, prime matter, as it enters into Thomas's account of individuation, is capable of being divided only insofar as it is subject to quantity or designated by quantity. A given substantial form can be divided or distinguished from other forms of the same type or species by being received in different instances of quantified matter.[26] A universal is potentially divisible or divisible *per accidens* in that it can be shared in or participated in by different intellects. An accidental form can be divided from other accidental forms of the same kind by being received in different substantial subjects. Moreover, prime matter and substantial form enter into composition with one another.

But, one may ask, what about a creature whose essence is not composed of matter and form, such as an angel? As we have seen, Thomas will reply that the essence principle of such a being enters into composition with its corresponding act of being and vice versa.[27] Hence according to this explanation both essence and the act of being *(esse)* fall short of the divine simplicity because each enters into composition with the other. But neither the act of being nor, in the case of a separate entity, the essence itself is composed of prior and simpler elements.

3. Essence as Relative Nonbeing

In light of all of this, we may now return to the point raised by Thomas in his discussion in q. 4, a. 1 of his Commentary on the *De Trinitate.* We are to account for the division and multiplicity of things which are first and simple by holding that in them there is some opposition between being and nonbeing. As we have now seen, complete entities or substances are distinguished from God at least by being composed of essence and act of being. But may we not pursue this line of reasoning still farther? Should not the very possibility of distinguishing between essence and *esse* within complete beings itself rest upon the fundamental opposition

25. As I am using the term "composite" here, it will apply not only to matter-form composites but also to entities which are not so composed but which are composed of essence and *esse.*

26. For fuller discussion of Thomas's account of the individuation of material substances, see Ch. IX, Section 4 below. For the present it will suffice to note that an excellent introduction to his theory can be found in this same Commentary on the *De Trinitate,* in q. 4, a. 2 (Leon. 50.125:194–213).

27. See Ch. V above for Thomas's argumentation for the essence-*esse* distinction and composition.

between being and nonbeing? This brings us back to the first of the two problems distinguished above at the beginning of Section 2 of this chapter. Does Thomas defend in some way the reality of nonbeing?[28]

On more than one occasion Thomas does use the language of nonbeing when referring to creatures. For instance, in replying to an objection in his *De veritate,* q. 2, a. 3 he comments that the more a creature approaches to God the more it has of being *(esse).* And the more it recedes from God the more it has of nonbeing *(non esse).* He continues that because a creature approaches to God only insofar as it participates in *esse* to a finite degree and because it remains infinitely distant from him, it may be said to have more of nonbeing *(non esse)* than of being *(esse).*[29] By *esse* as he uses it here he has in mind the act of being. Hence nonbeing *(non esse)* as he employs it here is really the negation of the act of being.

Additional light is cast on this by a remark Thomas makes in *Summa contra Gentiles* II, c. 52. As we have already seen, in this text he offers a series of arguments to show that in created intellectual substances the act of being *(esse)* and essence *(quod est)* differ. In one of these arguments he comments that *esse* insofar as it is *esse* cannot be diverse. It can only be diversified by something which is other than *esse.* Thus the *esse* of a stone is other than the *esse* of a human being.[30] This text is interesting because it indicates that there is something within any such finite being which is different from *esse* (the act of being) and which can therefore diversify or divide it. This diversifying principle, of course, is essence. In the examples cited it is the essence of a stone, in the one case, and the essence of a human being, in the other, which diversifies the *esse* of each. Because Thomas has here referred to such a principle as that which is other than *esse,* he could also, it would seem, describe this principle—essence—as nonbeing. Nonbeing when so used would not be absolute nothingness, of course, but nonbeing in a relative sense—the negation of the act of being.

This clearly appears to be the meaning of the expression nonbeing *(non ens)* as it appears in Thomas's *De potentia,* q. 3, a. 4, ad 4. There he is replying to an objection against the possibility that any being might proceed from another from eternity and therefore that the Son can eternally proceed from the Father within the Trinity. While Thomas's concern here is ultimately theological, the objection and his reply are also philosophical. As he explains, whatever receives *esse* from another is said to be nonbeing when it is considered in itself if it is distinct from

28. See above, p. 183.

29. "Ad sextum decimum dicendum quod esse simpliciter et absolute dictum de solo divino esse intelligitur, sicut et bonum. . . . unde quantum creatura accedit ad Deum tantum habet de esse, quantum vero ab eo recedit tantum habet de non esse; et quia non accedit ad Deum nisi secundum quod esse finitum participat, distat autem in infinitum, ideo dicitur quod plus habet de non esse quam de esse . . ." (Leon. 22.1.54).

30. For the full text see Ch. V above, n. 52. Note especially: "Esse autem, inquantum est esse, non potest esse diversum: potest autem diversificari per aliquid quod est praeter esse . . ." (ed. cit., p. 145).

the *esse* it receives from the other. But if it is identical with the *esse* it receives from another, then, considered in itself, it cannot be regarded as nonbeing. Nonbeing cannot be found within *esse* itself, but it can be found in that which is other than *esse*. In support he cites from Boethius's *De Hebdomadibus* to the effect that "that which is" can admit of some admixture within itself, but *esse* cannot. In light of this distinction Thomas concludes that the first situation is that of a creature, but that the second is that of the Son of God.[31] This is so because, according to Christian belief, within the Trinity each divine person is identical with the divine nature and therefore with the divine *esse*. In creatures, however, nonbeing is present precisely because there is some principle within the creature which is different from, i.e., not identical with, its act of being *(esse)*. This principle, the creature's essence, may be described as nonbeing because it is not the creature's act of being. Hence we may refer to the creature's essence as relative nonbeing.

Finally, such an interpretation of Thomas's thinking is confirmed when one turns to his late *Treatise on Separate Substances*. There he notes that the expression "nonbeing" may be employed in different ways. In using this expression we may negate nothing but a given (finite) substance's act of being *(esse in actu)*. If so, what remains within the structure of such a being may then be described as nonbeing *(non ens)*, writes Thomas. This would be its form, and in the case of a separate substance, its essence. Hence essence may be described as nonbeing *(non ens)*. Thomas also comments that when we are dealing with a material being, in addition to its act of being we may negate the form by means of which it participates in *esse*. If we describe what remains as *non ens*, the expression "nonbeing" will now refer only to matter.[32]

For our present purposes, Thomas's explicit reference to the form or essence of such an entity as nonbeing is helpful. It suggests that when he appealed to the opposition between being and nonbeing in his Commentary on the *De Trinitate* to introduce division and ultimately to introduce multiplicity into the universe of being, he may have had this same point in mind. In every complete finite entity or substance there is a composition of essence and *esse*. But more than this, because *esse* is not divided by itself, it can only be divided by something that is distinct from itself, i.e., by essence or real nonbeing. Here we see both the strength and the

---

31. See *De potentia*, q. 3, a. 13, ad 4: "Ad quartum dicendum, quod illud quod habet esse ab alio, in se consideratum, est non ens, si ipsum sit aliud quam ipsum esse quod ab alio accipit; si autem sit ipsum esse quod ab alio accipit, sic non potest in se consideratum, esse non ens; non enim potest in esse considerari non ens, licet in eo quod est aliud quam esse, considerari possit. Quod enim est, potest aliquid habere permixtum; non autem ipsum esse, ut Boëtius dicit in libro *De Hebdomadibus*. Prima quidem conditio est creaturae, sed secunda est conditio Filii Dei" (ed. cit., p. 79).

32. "Si igitur per hoc quod dico 'non ens' removeatur solum esse in actu, ipsa forma secundum se considerata est non ens sed esse participans. Si autem 'non ens' removeat non solum ipsum esse in actu sed etiam actum seu formam per quam aliquid participat esse, sic materia est non ens; forma vero subsistens non est non ens, sed est actus, qui est forma participativus ultimi actus qui est esse" (Leon. 40.D55:236–D56:244).

weakness of the Parmenidean argumentation. Being cannot be divided from itself by itself, to be sure; it can only be divided by something that is different from itself. But this does not mean that what is different from *esse* must be identified with absolute nothingness or absolute nonbeing. Thomas is defending an alternative—relative nonbeing. Therefore in every complete finite being or substance there is a composition of and distinction between its intrinsic principle of relative nonbeing (essence) and its act of being *(esse)*. Viewed from the side of the finite being, this composition of essence and *esse*—of relative nonbeing and an act of being—is necessary if Thomas is to distinguish any such being from God or from any other finite being.[33]

So long as we remain at the level of finite being, therefore, Thomas's answer to Parmenides is to be found here. By adapting to his own purposes a distinction which goes back as far as Plato's *Sophist* (to which Thomas did not have direct access), he meets the dilemma posed by the Eleatic thinker by distinguishing between absolute nonbeing, on the one hand, and qualified or relative nonbeing, on the other.[34] He grants the need for some principle which is different from being *(esse)* if being itself is to be divided. But he refuses to admit that this necessarily leads to the identification of any such principle with absolute nonbeing or nothingness. For him essence is the principle of relative nonbeing within every finite being which is required to account for the fact that its *esse* and therefore its total being is different from that of any other entity.

At this point we can appreciate how closely Thomas's answer to Parmenides is connected with his defense of real composition and distinction of essence and *esse* in finite beings. As we have also seen, this in turn fits together very nicely with his theory of participation of beings in *esse*. If particular beings can participate in *esse*, this is because in no such being is there identity of the participating principle and subject, its essence, and the perfection in which it participates, its intrinsic act of being *(esse)*. And if this is so, we may indeed say that within every such being there is both a principle of being *(esse* = act of being) and a principle of relative nonbeing

33. Although in some of the texts we have just considered Thomas is concerned with the distinction between finite beings and God, the logic of his position applies to his explanation of any multiplicity of beings. Even without presupposing God's existence one must account for the fact that one being is not another, and is not to be identified with the totality of being. In order to do this, Thomas proposes a composition within every finite substance of an *esse* principle, and of that which is distinct from *esse* and can therefore diversify it, that is, essence or relative nonbeing.

34. See Plato's discussion of the other (or difference) as he singles this out and uses it within the general context of the ways in which forms or ideas combine and do not combine with one another. This, of course, is part of his effort to show against Parmenides that in a certain sense we can say that being (that which is) is not, and that nonbeing (that which is not) is. See 252E through 259B, and especially 255Eff., along with the important summarizing statement running from 258E:6 to 259B:6, and the introductory remark at 241D:5–7. For some discussion of this passage see W. Beierwaltes, *Identität und Differenz* (Frankfurt am Main, 1980), pp. 12–23. If, as I am suggesting, Thomas's thinking about nonbeing may have been ultimately indebted to Plato's discussion in the *Sophist*, any such influence could be only indirect. The *Sophist* was not then available in Latin translation.

(essence). Hence the act of being *(esse)* is not divided from itself by itself, but by that which is nonbeing in a qualified or relative sense, i.e., essence.[35]

4. A *Caveat*

In concluding this discussion of relative nonbeing, I would like to emphasize the point that for Aquinas essence is not to be identified with absolute nonbeing or nothingness. Because essence is not identical with the act of being of a given entity, it may be described as relative nonbeing. But this is not to imply that it enjoys no formal or positive content in itself. According to Aquinas's metaphysics, an essence can never be realized as such apart from its corresponding act of being *(esse)* within a given substantial entity. Strictly speaking, it is neither essence nor the act of being that exists as such in finite beings; it is rather the concrete subject or substance which exists by reason of its act of being. This same concrete subject is what it is by reason of its essence. This presupposes that the essence principle has its own formal content, and is an intrinsic constituent of the existing entity.[36]

This being so, here I would like to distance my understanding of essence as nonbeing from certain recent interpreters of Aquinas who have so emphasized this aspect of essence that they would reduce it to nothing but a given mode of existence.[37] If I understand them correctly, by this they mean that the essence of any finite being is nothing but the degree of existence which it enjoys. As I see things, to reduce essence to a mode or degree of *esse* would be to rob the essence principle of a finite substance of any formal or positive content in distinction from that of

35. Cf. the text cited in n. 32 above from Thomas's *De substantiis separatis.*

36. See, for instance, *In III Sent.,* d. 2, q. 2, a. 3 (Moos ed., Vol, 3, p, 85): "Dicendum quod nulla natura habet esse nisi in supposito suo. Non enim humanitas esse potest nisi in homine." Also see ST I, q. 45, a. 4: "Unde illis proprie convenit fieri et creari, quibus convenit esse. Quod quidem convenit proprie subsistentibus: sive sint simplicia, sicut substantiae separatae; sive sint composita, sicut substantiae materiales. Illi enim proprie convenit esse, quod habet esse; et hoc est subsistens in suo esse" (Leon. 4.468). Also see *De potentia,* q. 3, a. 5, ad 2; q. 3, a. 1, ad 17 (both cited above in Ch. IV, n. 93).

37. For statements of this position see G. B. Phelan, "The Being of Creatures," in J. Rosenberg, ed., *Readings in Metaphysics* (Westminster, Md., 1963), pp. 265–72, especially p. 270; W. N. Clarke's commentary on this, "Commentary on the 'Being of Creatures'," ibid., pp, 273–76; and especially W. E. Carlo, "The Role of Essence in Existential Metaphysics," ibid., pp. 278–81. The first two articles originally appeared in *Proceedings of the American Catholic Philosophical Association* 31 (1957), pp. 118–25, 128–32, and the third in *International Philosophical Quarterly* 2 (1962), pp. 584–89. The Rosenberg anthology also contains an interesting excerpt from J. Owens, *St. Thomas and the Future of Metaphysics* (Milwaukee, 1957), pp. 69–74. See *Readings in Metaphysics,* pp. 276–78. Owens strongly defends the positive content of essence. For a fuller statement of Carlo's position see his *The Ultimate Reducibility of Essence to Existence in Existential Metaphysics,* pp. 99–105. Also note the preface by W. N. Clarke, pp. vii–xiv. For a later statement of Clarke's view see his "What Cannot Be Said in St. Thomas' Essence-Existence Doctrine," *New Scholasticism* 48 (1974), pp. 35–38. However, for some still later reservations and qualifications see Clarke, *Explorations in Metaphysics,* pp. 14–15, and especially n. 7, p. 29. Also see Dümpelmann, *Kreation als ontisch-ontologisches Verhältnis. Zur Metaphysik der Schöpfungstheologie des Thomas von Aquin,* pp. 27–30.

its act of being. This in turn would seriously compromise the meaning of and even eliminate the need for one of Thomas's most central metaphysical positions—real composition and distinction of essence and act of being *(esse)* in finite substances.[38] Moreover, such an interpretation seems to undermine a number of crucial roles assigned by Aquinas to the essence principle of finite substances.

First of all, as will become clear from the immediately following chapters of this study, Thomas turns to the essence of any given substantial entity in order to account for the determination or specification of the kind of being it enjoys. It is because its essence receives and specifies its act of being that a given substance is of this kind rather than of any other kind, for instance, a human kind of being rather than a canine kind. To the extent that we may connect the structure of a given substance with the determination of its kind of being, structure too is conferred on that substance by its essence. This follows because within a given substance its essence principle receives and limits, to be sure, but also determines and specifies its correlative act of being. If essence is equated with absolute nonbeing, or even if it is viewed as nothing but a given mode or degree of existence, Thomas's way of accounting for the essential structure of particular beings will be severely compromised.[39]

Secondly, as we have already seen in Ch. V in some detail, according to Aquinas act as such is not self-limiting and therefore the act of being is not self-limiting. If we do encounter finite instances of being and therefore of the act of being, this is because in every finite substance its act of being is received and limited by its correlative essence principle. While differing from the act of being, therefore, essence must enjoy some positive content if it is to receive and limit the act of being of any given entity.[40] Essence will be unable to fulfill this function either if it is reduced to absolute nonbeing or if it is regarded as nothing but a mode or degree of existence.

Thirdly, my interpretation in this chapter has concentrated on Thomas's explanation of division and multiplicity within the realm of being. In this order of ex-

38. Clarke, for one, is aware of this difficulty. See his Preface to Carlo's book as cited in the previous note, pp. xii–xiv; also see his "What Cannot Be Said . . . ," pp. 37–38.

39. See, for instance, *In De Hebdomadibus,* lect. 2: "Quia tamen quaelibet forma est determinativa ipsius esse, nulla earum est ipsum esse, sed est habens esse . . ." (Leon. 50.273:234–236). Also see SCG I, c. 26, especially the following: "Relinquitur ergo quod res propter hoc differant quod habent diversas naturas, quibus acquiritur esse diversimode" (ed. cit., p. 27). Cf. SCG II, c. 52 (cited in Ch. V above, n. 52); *De potentia,* q. 7, a. 2. ad 5, and ad 9. Note in the last-mentioned passage: "Et per hunc modum, hoc esse ab illo esse distinguitur, in quantum est talis vel talis naturae" (ed. cit., p. 192). At least according to my interpretation, the individuation of material substances must also come from the side of essence rather than from the side of existence, as will be seen in Ch. IX below. Finally, as both Geiger and Fabro have recognized, the composition of essence and *esse* differs from that of matter and form in terms of the specifying principle in each case. While matter (the potential principle) is specified by form, it is *esse* (the act principle) which is specified by the essence or potency in which it is received. For references to Geiger (pp. 198–99, n. 2) and to Thomas see Fabro, *Participation et causalité,* p. 65.

40. For some representative texts and for discussion see Ch. V, Section 5 above, and my "Thomas Aquinas and the Axiom That Unreceived Act Is Unlimited," passim.

planation he has appealed to the division and opposition between being and non-being. This account remains incomplete, of course, until one joins it with his metaphysics of participation. To reduce the essence principle within finite beings to absolute nonbeing, or even to regard it as nothing but a mode or degree of existence, will seriously compromise Thomas's understanding of participation. To put this in summary fashion, the essence principle within a given substance receives and limits that same substance's *esse* and thereby enables the substance to participate in *esse,* to receive it in particular fashion, without being identical with it. It is difficult to understand how an essence which is either nothing but a given mode or degree of existence *(esse)* or which is understood as absolute nonbeing can fulfill this function.[41]

5. Derivation of the Transcendentals

Before concluding this chapter, I wish to consider another point that is closely connected with Thomas's understanding of being as such, i.e., his derivation of certain characteristics or properties that follow upon being and that are as broad in extension as being itself. These would come to be known in the scholastic tradition as transcendentals, and are occasionally referred to by Thomas himself as *transcendentia.* His best-known derivation of them occurs in his *De veritate,* q. 1, a. 1. As will be recalled from our discussion above in Ch. III, there Thomas argues that nothing can be added to being from without in the way a difference is added to a genus or an accident to a subject. As we have seen, this is because if anything were added to being in such fashion, it would not fall under being itself.[42]

From this Thomas goes on to reason that something can be added to being in the sense that it expresses a mode not expressed by the name being itself. This may happen in two fundamentally different ways. It may be that the mode which is thereby expressed is some more particularized or restricted mode of being. Corresponding to such more particularized modes of being are the ten supreme genera or predicaments, which we will discuss more fully in the immediately following chapters.[43] Or it may be that something is said to add being simply because it expresses a mode which is not more restricted or particularized in extension, but which follows upon every being.[44]

Thomas maintains that there are five distinct modes which are as broad in extension as being itself, or which follow upon every being. As he explains, such a general

41. This also seems to be a fundamental weakness in Geiger's attempt to assign priority to participation by similitude or formal hierarchy over participation by composition.

42. For Thomas's use of the term *transcendentia* (on fourteen occasions) see Aertsen, *Medieval Philosophy and the Transcendentals,* p. 91 and n. 52. For the context in *De veritate,* q. 1, a. 1 see Ch. III above, p. 88. For the text itself see Leon. 22.1.5:106–111.

43. Leon. 22.1.5:114–123.

44. "Alio modo ita quod modus expressus sit modus generalis consequens omne ens . . ." (Leon. 22.1.5:124–125).

mode may follow upon any being insofar as that being is in itself, or else insofar as that being is related to something else. If the mode in question follows upon every being insofar as it is in itself, it may express something about being either positively or negatively. If it does so positively, that which is said in affirmative fashion of every being is its essence, in accord with which it is said to be. Accordingly, the name (1) "thing" *(res)* is imposed on it.[45] In other words, viewed from this perspective every being may be referred to as a thing, and this by reason of its essence principle. If the mode expresses something negatively that follows upon every being, this indicates that it is undivided from itself and may, therefore, be described as (2) "one" *(unum)*.[46]

On the other hand, if the mode follows upon every being insofar as it is related to something else, this also may happen in two different ways. The mode may follow upon each and every being insofar as it is divided from every other being. Accordingly, we may refer to it as (3) "something" *(aliquid)*, indicating thereby that it is, as it were, another "what." Thomas explains that just as a being is described as one insofar as it is undivided from itself, so it is said to be something insofar as it is divided from all others.[47] On the other hand, the mode may follow upon every being insofar as it stands in agreement or in conformity with something else. This, reasons Thomas, can happen only by reason of something to which it belongs to be in conformity with everything else, i.e., the soul. Here he has in mind Aristotle's reference to the soul as being in a certain fashion all things.[48] As Thomas points out, in the soul there is both a cognitive and an appetitive power. If we consider any being insofar as it is conformed to the soul's appetitive power, we may refer to it as (4) "good" *(bonum)*. If we consider it insofar as it is conformed to the soul's intellective power, we may describe it as (5) "true" *(verum)*.[49]

This, then, is Thomas's often-quoted derivation of the transcendental properties of being. It implies that wherever we find him speaking of being, we may also assume that whatever is entitled to that title may also be described (1) as a thing,

45. Leon. 22.1.5:126–139. Note: "Non autem invenitur aliquid affirmative dictum absolute quod possit accipi in omni ente nisi essentia eius secundum quam esse dicitur, et sic imponitur hoc nomen res. . . ."
46. Leon. 22.1.5:139–142. Note: ". . . nihil aliud enim est unum quam ens indivisum."
47. Leon. 22.1.5:142–150. For the background in Avicenna's *Liber de philosophia prima* I, c. 5 for *res* and *aliquid* see Aertsen, p. 102.
48. Leon. 22.1.5:150–155. For Aristotle see *De anima* III, c. 8 (431b 21).
49. Leon. 22.1.5:155–160. On this and on Thomas's two other derivations of the transcendentals in *De veritate*, q. 21, a. 1 and *In I Sent.*, d. 8, q. 1, a. 3 see Aertsen, pp. 97–103. *Res* and *aliquid* are not included in these two texts. As Aertsen brings out (pp. 100–101), and as these two texts also specify, the transcendentals can only add something conceptual to being, not something that is really distinct from being. For the first see Leon. 22.3.592:124–593:178; for the second see Mandonnet ed., Vol. 1, pp. 199–201. In the latter text Thomas points out that while *ens, bonum, unum,* and *verum* are convertible in terms of the subject in which they are realized *(secundum suppositum)*, in terms of their intelligible content being is prior to the others; for it is included in our understanding of each of the others, whereas the converse is not the case.

(2) as one (as not divided from itself), (3) as something (i.e., as divided and distinguished from everything else), (4) as ontologically good, and (5) as ontologically true (as intrinsically intelligible in itself). We should remember that these properties or attributes of being are not themselves really distinct from being, but only conceptually *(secundum rationem),* and therefore do not imply the addition of any really distinct attribute or property to being. Indeed, when we view them as existing concretely, i.e., as subjects, we may say that they are convertible with being.[50]

50. See the references given in n. 49.

PART TWO

The Essential Structure of Finite Being

Substance-Accident Composition

We have now completed our analysis of Aquinas's solution to the problem of the One and the Many at the level of finite being considered simply as being. There can be different beings because each of these merely shares in or participates in the perfection of being *(esse)*. No one of them can simply be identified with this perfection. The act of being *(esse)* is not self-limiting. The individual beings we experience are obviously limited. The need to account for this leads to or at least reinforces Thomas's conviction that in every such being there is a composition of an essence or quidditative principle, on the one hand, and an intrinsic act of being, on the other.

If we would cast this problem in Parmenidean terms we may, as we have already suggested, appeal to Aquinas's distinction between nonbeing in a qualified sense *(non esse)*, or relative nonbeing as I have styled it, and nonbeing in the absolute sense *(non ens)*. Thomas agrees with Parmenides that being cannot be divided from being simply insofar as it is being, or to put it in Aquinas's language, that *esse* is not divided from itself by itself. He also refuses to defend the reality of nonbeing in the absolute sense. It does not follow from this, however, that all beings are one. The act of being is limited and diversified within each finite being by an intrinsic principle that is really distinct from it, that is, by essence, or by Thomas's candidate for real nonbeing in the qualified sense indicated in the preceding chapter.

Even so, there are other facets of finite being which must be examined by the student of being as being. For instance, not only do we discover many different beings within the unity of being; we also find that individually different entities may share in essentially or specifically the same kind of being. How is one to account for this? As we shall see in a subsequent chapter, Thomas appeals to the Aristotelian theory of matter-form composition to explain this.[1] And in the case of purely spiritual created beings—the angels of the Christian tradition—he simply

1. See Ch. IX below.

denies that individuals are multiplied within species. Each angel is a distinct species in and of itself.[2]

There is still another and even more extended aspect of finite being which must be taken into account. Within the finite beings we experience, there is need to distinguish between that which makes each of them a being, a center of existence in itself, and other aspects present within such beings which do not exist in themselves but only in something else. Aquinas also holds that this situation applies to angelic beings.

In coming to grips with this issue Thomas develops his personal views concerning substance and accidents and their interrelationship. In doing so he depends heavily upon Aristotle but at the same time goes considerably beyond the Stagirite. This is not surprising, of course, since Thomas must incorporate Aristotle's thinking on substance and accident into his own general metaphysics of essence and *esse*.

Because substance-accident composition is broader in extension than matter-form composition, at least according to Aquinas's thinking, we shall consider these two metaphysical compositions in terms of their decreasing generality. That is to say, because matter-form composition is less universal in application, a subsequent chapter (Ch. IX) will be directed to the metaphysical consideration of this in material entities. The two prior chapters will be devoted to Thomas's views on substance and accidents. In the present one we shall consider: (1) Thomas's general understanding of substance and accident; (2) his derivation or deduction of the ten Aristotelian predicaments or categories; (3) his precisions concerning the "definitions" of substance and accident. In Ch. VIII we shall take up certain questions relating to substance, accidents, and *esse*.

1. General Understanding of Substance and Accident

In Chapter II above we attempted to reconstruct Thomas's understanding of the way one arrives at knowledge of being as real or as existing. Without repeating that account in detail, it will be helpful for us to recall that according to his think-

---

2. Thomas defended this position from the beginning to the end of his career. See, for instance, *De ente et essentia*, c. 4 (Leon. 43.376:83–89). It follows from his denial that there is matter-form composition in angels or in pure spirits of any kind. For more on this and for his association of this theory—universal hylomorphism—with Avicebron see also: *In II Sent.*, d. 3, q. 1, a. 1 (Mandonnet ed., Vol. 2, pp. 86–88); ST I, q. 50, a. 2; *De substantiis separatis*, cc. 5–8. For discussion and additional references see J. Guttmann, *Das Verhältniss des Thomas von Aquino zum Judenthum und zur jüdischen Litteratur* (Göttingen, 1891), pp. 16–30; M. Wittmann, *Die Stellung des hl. Thomas von Aquin zu Avencebrol (Ibn Gebirol)*, Beiträge zur Geschichte der Philosophie des Mittelalters 3, 3 (Münster, 1900), esp. pp. 33–55; E. Kleineidam, *Das Problem der hylomorphen Zusammensetzung der geistigen Substanzen im 13. Jahrhundert, behandelt bis Thomas von Aquin*; A. Forest, *La structure métaphysique du concret selon saint Thomas d'Aquin*, pp. 109–20; J. Collins, *The Thomistic Philosophy of the Angels*, pp. 42–74; F. Brunner, *Platonisme et Aristotélisme. La critique d'Ibn Gabirol par saint Thomas d'Aquin* (Louvain-Paris, 1965), pp. 33–61. Also see J. Weisheipl, "Albertus Magnus and Universal Hylomorphism: Avicebron," in *Albert the Great Commemorative Essays*, pp. 239–60, esp. 245–60.

ing what one first discovers are concrete material existing entities. This discovery presupposes that at the level of external sense experience we have encountered at least one extramental existent and, then, owing to the collaboration of the internal senses, intellectual abstraction and judgment, have recognized such an entity as actually existing, that is, as a being.[3]

We have also considered Thomas's repeated claim that what the intellect first conceives, and that to which it reduces all its other conceptions, is being. We have taken this priority as referring to the order of resolution (analysis). This means that whatever we may grasp through intellectual awareness about a given object or thing, fuller analysis will eventually enable us to recognize it explicitly as a being. Within the realm of finite being *(ens commune)* we were then in position to follow Thomas as he accounted for the unity and diversity we find therein. But also within the range of finite being, Thomas would have us recognize a fundamental distinction between that which exists in itself, on the one hand, and that which exists only in something else, on the other, or to use more technical language, the distinction between substance and accidents.[4]

As will be recalled from our discussion of analogy of being, Thomas, following Aristotle, regards substance as the prime referent of being, even though both thinkers acknowledge that the term "being" is used in different ways. Aristotle accounts for this by his theory of the πρὸς ἕν equivocation of being, and Thomas uses this same notion as part of his justification for developing his doctrine of analogy of being. As Thomas puts this while commenting on Aristotle's *Metaphysics* IV, c. 2, if being is predicated in different ways, every being is so named by reference to something that is one and first. This single principle is not to be regarded as an end or as an efficient cause but as a subject for other and secondary instantiations of being. Thus some things are described as beings or are said to be because they enjoy being in themselves *(per se)*. These, of course, are substances. Therefore substances are beings in the principal and primary sense.[5]

After following Aristotle in listing a number of other ways in which things are named beings, Thomas sums this up in his own way. The aforementioned modes of being may be reduced to four kinds. One of these is the weakest in its claim

---

3. See Ch. II above, pp. 35–39.

4. According to the interpretation I am offering, one does not first explicitly discover accidents or accidental being and then reason from them to infer the existence of substantial reality by applying the principle of causality. One first discovers being as such, and only thereafter is one in a position to distinguish therein between substance and accident. More will be said below about this.

5. For discussion see our Ch. III, pp. 80–81. From Thomas's Commentary note in particular: "Sed tamen omne ens dicitur per respectum ad unum primum. Sed hoc primum non est finis vel efficiens sicut in praemissis exemplis, sed subiectum. Alia enim dicuntur entia vel esse, quia per se habent esse sicut substantiae, quae principaliter et prius entia dicuntur" *(In IV Met.,* lect. 1, Cathala-Spiazzi ed., p. 152, n. 539). Earler in this same *lectio* Thomas explicitly makes the point that it belongs to one science to study being as being, including both substances and accidents: ". . . ergo omnia entia pertinent ad considerationem unius scientiae, quae considerat ens inquantum est ens, scilicet tam substantias quam accidentia" (p. 151, n. 534).

upon being and exists only in the order of thought, that is to say, negations and privations. A second class is closest to it in the weakness of its claim upon being, because its members still include some admixture of negation and privation. Here Thomas has in mind generation, corruption, and motion. Thirdly, still others are described as beings not because they share in nonbeing but because they enjoy only a weakened kind of being and do not exist in their own right *(per se)* but only in something else. Thomas lists qualities, quantities, and the properties of substance. Finally, there is the most perfect class, which both exists in reality without including privation and enjoys what Thomas refers to as a firm and solid being *(esse)*. This kind of being exists in its own right or *per se* and is, of course, identified by Thomas once again as substance.[6]

For our present purposes we are especially concerned with Thomas's third and fourth divisions, that is, with the kinds of beings which do not exist in themselves but only in something else, and with others which exist in themselves. Although Thomas has only mentioned qualities, quantities, and properties as members of this third class, we may assume that he wishes to include therein accidents in general. In short, in his third and fourth classes he has introduced the fundamental distinction between accidental being and substantial being.[7]

As we have mentioned above in our discussion of analogy, in his Commentary on *Metaphysics* V Thomas offers what may be regarded as a derivation or kind of deduction of the ten supreme categories or predicaments into which being itself is divided. Since this issue will be taken up in detail in the following section of the present chapter,[8] we need not delay over it now. It will be enough for us to note that Thomas develops this deduction or derivation in the course of commenting on Aristotle's treatment of the mode of being *per se*. Of three precisions Thomas finds Aristotle applying to this mode of being, the first is the Stagirite's division of extramental being into the ten predicaments.[9] Within the predicaments them-

6. Ed. cit., p. 152, nn. 540–543.

7. See n. 542: "Tertium autem dicitur quod nihil habet de non ente admixtum, habet tamen esse debile, quia non per se, sed in alio, sicut sunt qualitates, quantitates et substantiae proprietates." Also see n. 543: "Quartum autem genus est quod est perfectissimum, quod scilicet habet esse in natura absque admixtione privationis, et habet esse firmum et solidum, quasi per se existens, sicut sunt substantiae." Cf. lect. 4, p. 162, n. 587: ". . . illa scientia non solum est considerativa substantiarum, sed etiam accidentium, cum de utrisque ens praedicetur. . . ."

8. See below, Section 2.

9. See *In V Met.*, lect. 9, p. 238, n. 889. The other two precisions have to do with the distinction between being which exists only in the mind and being which exists extramentally, and the division of being in terms of potency and act. As Thomas has already mentioned at the beginning of this *lectio*, Aristotle introduces c. 7 of Bk V by distinguishing between being *(ens)* which is said *secundum se* and being which is said *secundum accidens*. That division is not to be confused with the division of being into substance and accident. The first division is concerned with whether something is predicated *per se* or *per accidens*. The second is based on the fact that something is in its nature either a substance or an accident. This is why the first member *(ens secundum se)* of the first division is itself divided into substance and the nine accidents. See pp. 237–38, n. 885: "Unde patet quod divisio entis secundum se et secundum accidens, attenditur secundum quod aliquid praedicatur de aliquo per se

selves, substance is, of course, first. In this context Thomas writes that in the case of substance the predicate (predicament) is said to signify (that is, to be predicated of) "first substance." First substance is identified as the particular or individual substance, of which all else is predicated. For instance, if I say "Socrates is an animal," the predicate animal is predicated of the individual or first substance, i.e., Socrates.[10]

In the immediately following *lectio* 10 of this same Commentary on *Metaphysics* V, Thomas finds Aristotle singling out four different modes of substance. Thomas, following Aristotle, reduces these to two modes. As Thomas reports this, the first mode is that according to which individual substances are said to be substances: for instance, simple bodies (earth, fire, water, etc.); and even mixed bodies when the parts of which they are constituted are similar, for instance, a stone, flesh, blood; and also living beings such as animals which consist of these, along with their parts.[11] All such things are said to be substance, not because they are predicated of another subject, but because other things are predicated of them. With an explicit reference to Aristotle's distinction between first substance and second substance in the *Categories*, Thomas comments that this is the way first substance is described there.[12]

As a second mode Thomas lists that which is called substance insofar as it is the intrinsic formal cause of such substances, that is to say, the substantial form of the same.[13] As a third mode Thomas, still following Aristotle, mentions the parts of such substances which limit them and render them divisible. In particular he lists surfaces, lines, points, and especially numbers, which some view as the substance of all things. (Thomas will reject this as a legitimate application of the term substance, since it confuses the properties of things with their substance.)[14] As a fourth mode Thomas and Aristotle single out the quiddity of a thing which is signified

---

vel per accidens. Divisio vero entis in substantiam et accidens attenditur secundum hoc quod aliquid in natura sua est vel substantia vel accidens."

10. See *In V Met.*, lect. 9, p. 238 n. 891: "Et hoc praedicatum dicitur significare substantiam primam, quae est substantia particularis, de qua omnia praedicantur."

11. Ibid., lect. 10, p. 241, n. 898. Note his remark concerning animals: "Et iterum animalia quae constant et [read: ex] huiusmodi corporibus sensibilibus, et partes eorum, ut manus et pedes et huiusmodi. . . ." For Aristotle see *Metaphysics* V, c. 8. Thomas is evidently somewhat perplexed by Aristotle's inclusion of "demons" *(daemonia)* under this mode of substance in the same context, and suggests that Aristotle may have in mind pagan idols, or perhaps certain living entities such as those defended by the "Platonists."

12. Ibid. "Haec enim omnia praedicta dicuntur substantia, quia non dicuntur de alio subiecto, sed alia dicuntur de his. Et haec est descriptio primae substantiae in praedicamentis." Cf. Aristotle, *Categories*, c. 5.

13. Ed. cit., p. 241, n. 899: "Dicit quod alio modo dicitur substantia quae est causa essendi praedictis substantiis . . . non quidem extrinseca sicut efficiens, sed intrinseca eis, ut forma."

14. Ibid., n. 900. For Thomas's rejection of this as a true mode of substance see nn. 901 and 905. In n. 901 he also remarks that those who identify number with substance have failed to distinguish between the one which is convertible with being (transcendental unity) and the one which is a principle of number (unity based on quantity).

by that thing's definition. This is an important usage because, so far as Thomas is concerned, the quiddity signified thereby includes not only the substantial form but the entire essence of the thing. In other words, for Thomas although not for Aristotle, prime matter is included within the quiddity or essence of a material thing. Thomas also comments that it is according to this mode that genus and species are said to be the substance of the thing of which they are predicated.[15]

With Aristotle, Thomas quickly reduces these four usages of substance to two. The first is that according to which a substance is the ultimate subject of a proposition, and in such fashion that it is not predicated of anything else. This is first substance, as Thomas points out, and he adds that this is a particular something (*hoc aliquid*) which subsists in itself (*per se*) and which is separate in the sense that it is distinct from all other things and incapable of being communicated to many things.[16]

This, of course, is the primary realization of substance and, Thomas reminds us, this first or particular substance differs from substance when it is taken universally in three ways: (1) a particular substance is not predicated of anything else, as is universal substance; (2) universal substance does not subsist except by reason of an individual substance which, as we have seen, alone exists in itself; (3) universal substance is realized in many different individuals, but individual substance is not. It is distinct and separate from everything else.[17]

In completing his reduction of the original fourfold division to two, Thomas quickly eliminates the third mode, as has already been mentioned. He combines the second (substance as form) and the fourth (substance as quiddity). In justifying this final reduction, Thomas comments that essence and form agree in this that

---

15. Ibid., n. 902: "Dicit quod etiam quidditas rei, quam significat definitio, dicitur substantia uniuscuiusque. Haec autem quidditas sive rei essentia, cuius definitio est ratio, differt a forma quam dixit esse substantiam in secundo modo, sicut differt humanitas ab anima. Nam forma est pars essentiae vel quidditatis rei. Ipsa autem quidditas vel essentia rei includit omnia essentialia principia. Et ideo genus et species dicuntur esse substantia eorum de quibus praedicantur, hoc ultimo modo. Nam genus et species non significant tantum formam, sed totam rei essentiam." As Thomas uses the term "form" here, he has in mind what he sometimes names the form of the part (*forma partis*) rather than the form of the whole (*forma totius*). The latter includes both matter and form in material substances; not so the former, since it does not include prime matter. For this see *De ente et essentia*, c. 2 (Leon. 43.373:283–289). Also see *In VII Met.*, lect. 9, pp. 358–59, nn. 1467–1469, especially n. 1469, where Thomas attributes this distinction (which he accepts) to Avicenna, and where he rejects Averroes' identification of essence with form. On the difference between Aristotle's text and Thomas's interpretation of it on this point, see A. Maurer, "Form and Essence in the Philosophy of St. Thomas," *Mediaeval Studies* 13 (1951), pp. 165–76, repr. in his *Being and Knowing. Studies in Thomas Aquinas and Later Medieval Philosophers* (Toronto, 1990), pp. 3–18.

16. *In V Met.*, lect. 10, p. 242, n. 903: "Reducit dictos modos substantiae ad duos; dicens . . . quod substantia duobus modis dicitur: quorum unus est secundum quod substantia dicitur id quod ultimo subiicitur in propositionibus, ita quod de alio non praedicetur, sicut substantia prima. Et hoc est, quod est hoc aliquid, quasi per se subsistens, et quod est separabile, quia est ab omnibus distinctum et non communicabile multis."

17. Ibid.

each of these is said to be that *by which* something is. I take him to mean by this, that neither is, properly speaking, that which exists. This is true only of the subject or *suppositum*. But they differ in that form is directly ordered to the (prime) matter which it actualizes, while quiddity is ordered to the subject (or *suppositum*) which is signified as that which has such an essence or quiddity. In effect, substance taken as form is subsumed under substance taken as essence or quiddity.[18]

That Thomas accepts this twofold division of substance as his own is evident not only from his references to it in his Commentary on the *Metaphysics* but from his appeal to it in other contexts where he is clearly writing in his own name. For instance, in *Summa theologiae* I, q. 29, a. 1, he writes that if both the universal and the individual are present in all genera, it is in a special way that an individual is included in the genus substance. Substance is rendered individual by itself (that is, we may assume, by principles found within itself). Accidents are rendered individual through their subject or substance. Therefore individual instances of substance are given a special name such as *hypostases* (from the Greek) or first substances.[19] And as Thomas writes in a. 2 of this same q. 29, according to Aristotle in *Metaphysics* V, substance is used in two ways. It may mean (1) the quiddity of a thing which its definition signifies (οὐσία in Greek, and *essentia* in Latin, as Thomas clarifies); or (2) the subject or *suppositum* which subsists within the genus substance.[20]

In *Summa theologiae* III, q. 17, a. 1, ad 7, Thomas again comments that substance is said not only of nature but of the subject *(suppositum)*, as is stated in *Metaphysics* V.[21] Or as he puts this in q. 2, a. 6, ad 3 of the same *Tertia Pars,* substance, as is clear from *Metaphysics* V, is expressed in two ways: as essence or nature, and as the subject *(suppositum* or *hypostasis).*[22]

Thomas makes the same point in *Summa contra Gentiles* IV, c. 49, and adds an important clarification. According to Aristotle, writes Thomas, substance is used in two ways, that is, as subject *(suppositum)* within the genus substance, which is

18. Ibid., n. 904. Note: "Sed forma refertur ad materiam, quam facit esse in actu; quidditas autem refertur ad suppositum, quod significatur ut habens talem essentiam. Unde sub uno comprehenduntur 'forma et species', idest sub essentia rei."

19. ". . . licet universale et particulare inveniantur in omnibus generibus, tamen speciali quodam modo individuum invenitur in genere substantiae. Substantia enim individuatur per seipsam, sed accidentia individuantur per subiectum, quod est substantia: dicitur enim haec albedo, inquantum est in hoc subiecto. Unde etiam convenienter individua substantiae habent aliquod speciale nomen prae aliis: dicuntur enim *hypostases*, vel *primae substantiae*" (Leon. 4.327).

20. ". . . dicendum quod, secundum Philosophum in V *Metaphys.*, substantia dicitur dupliciter. Uno modo dicitur substantia *quidditas rei,* quam significat definitio, secundum quod dicimus quod *definitio significat substantiam rei:* quam quidem substantiam Graeci *usiam* vocant, quod nos *essentiam* dicere possumus.—Alio modo dicitur substantia *subiectum vel suppositum quod subsistit in genere substantiae*" (Leon. 4.330). For Aristotle see *Metaphysics* V, c. 8 (1017b 23–26).

21. "Substantia autem dicitur non solum natura, sed etiam suppositum, ut dicitur in V *Metaphys.*" (Leon. 11.220). In terms of context, a. 1 asks: "Utrum Christus sit unum vel duo" (p. 219).

22. "Substantia autem, ut patet V *Metaphys.*, dupliciter dicitur: uno modo, essentia sive natura; alio modo, pro supposito sive hypostasi" (Leon. 11.37). This article asks: "Utrum humana natura fuerit unita Verbo Dei accidentaliter" (p. 36).

also known as *hypostasis;* and as quiddity *(quod quid est)* which Thomas identifies with the nature of a thing. As a clarification he adds that the parts of a given substance are not described as particular substances in such a way as to imply that they subsist in themselves; they subsist only in the whole substance. Therefore such parts cannot be called subjects or *hypostases.* Otherwise it would follow that in a human being there would be as many subjects as there are parts.[23] This clarification is helpful, since it indicates that we should not take Thomas's references to the parts of animals as substances (see his Commentary on *Metaphysics* V) as implying that such parts are to be regarded as existing in their own right or in themselves. They are rather parts of the subsisting whole—the subsisting subject or first substance.[24]

When we turn back to a much earlier text from Thomas's Commentary on I *Sentences,* d. 25, q. 1, a. 1, ad 7, we find a somewhat different division of substance. There Thomas is defending the Boethian definition of a person as "an individual substance of a rational nature."[25] In meeting the seventh objection, Thomas comments that substance is spoken of in four ways: (1) insofar as it is identified with essence (in this sense substance is found in all of the genera, just as is essence); (2) as an individual within the genus substance, i.e., as first substance or *hypostasis;* (3) as second substance; (4) in general fashion insofar as it abstracts from first substance and from second substance. It is in the fourth sense, comments Thomas, that the term "substance" is used as it appears in Boethius's definition of person. Of greater interest to us, however, are the second and third usages of substance, that is, as first substance and as second substance.[26]

As this text indicates, Thomas was already familiar with Aristotle's distinction in the *Categories* between substance in the primary sense or first substance and second substance. Substance taken in its strictest and primary meaning is that which is neither said of a subject nor in a subject, that is, this individual human being or this individual horse. The species in which such first substances are realized are called second substances, as are the genera of those species. Thus an individual human being (first substance) belongs to the human species (second substance), and this in turn to the genus animal (second substance).[27]

23. Ed. cit., p. 504. For the clarification, note: "Sed neque partes alicuius substantiae sic dicuntur particulares substantiae quasi sint per se subsistentes, sed subsistunt in toto." Here Thomas is showing that one cannot move from the fact that Christ's human nature (or substance, when used in one way) is individual to the conclusion that it is a subject or *hypostasis.*

24. See the text cited in n. 11 above.

25. See *In I Sent.,* d. 25, q. 1, a. 1: "Utrum definitio personae posita a Boetio sit competens" (Mandonnet ed., Vol. 1, pp. 600–606).

26. See p. 605. The first usage is interesting in that it means that when substance is taken in this sense—as essence—even accidents may be described as "substances." This follows because they, too, have essences or quiddities: ". . . et hoc significatur, cum quaeritur: Quid est albedo? Color."

27. See *Categories,* 5 (2a 11–19). For some interesting studies on Aristotle's understanding of substance in the *Categories* and in later works and for additional references, see: L. Kosman, "Aristotle's First Predicament," in M. L. O'Hara, ed., *Substances and Things: Aristotle's Doctrine of Physical Substance in Recent Essays* (Washington, D.C., 1982), pp. 19–42; C. Georgiadis, "Two Conceptions of

From the texts we have just considered some question might be raised about Thomas's understanding of the relationship between first substance and essence or quiddity, on the one hand, and first substance and second substance, on the other. Are these two correlations the same? Or to put it another way, may substance taken as quiddity, essence or nature be identified with second substance? One might be inclined to think that this is so in light of Thomas's remark in his Commentary on *Metaphysics* V about substance taken as essence or quiddity: it is in this way that genus and species are said to be the substance of those things of which they are predicated. As we have just seen, in the *Categories* Aristotle holds that both genera and species are substances taken in the secondary sense, that is, second substances.[28] Other texts, however, indicate that we would be ill-advised to conclude that Thomas identifies substance taken as essence or quiddity with second substance.

Thomas presents a fuller discussion of this in his *De potentia,* q. 9, a. 1. There he is considering the relationship between person, on the one hand, and essence, subsistence, and *hypostasis,* on the other. He begins his response by recalling that Aristotle holds that substance is used in two ways: (1) as the ultimate subject which is not predicated of anything else, that is, an individual within the genus substance; (2) as the form or nature of a subject.[29]

The reason for this distinction, Thomas continues, is the fact that many subjects may share in a given nature, for instance, many men in human nature. Therefore we must distinguish between that which is one and that which is multiplied. The common nature is signified by the definition which indicates what the thing is. Therefore this common nature is known as essence or quiddity. Whatever is in a thing and belongs to its common nature is included within the meaning or definition of its essence. However, not everything that is present within an individual substance or subject is of this kind. Otherwise there could be no distinction between individual substances which share in one and the same nature. What is present in an individual substance in addition to the common nature is the individual matter which serves as its principle of singularity, and therefore the individual accidents which determine such matter. Therefore, continues Thomas, essence is related to an individual substance as a formal part of the latter. It is in this way that humanity is related to Socrates. Hence in matter-form composites an essence is not

Substance in Aristotle," op. cit., pp. 172–87; J. A. Driscoll, "EIΔH in Aristotle's Earlier and Later Theories of Substance," in *Studies in Aristotle,* D. J. O'Meara, ed. (Washington, D.C., 1981), pp. 129–59.

28. See *In V Met.,* lect. 10, n. 902, cited above in n. 15. A close reading of the last two sentences of this text as quoted there suggests, however, that Thomas's point is to show that genus and species do not signify form alone, but the entire essence of a thing, and that they have this in common with substance when it is taken as essence or quiddity. This does not necessarily mean that substance taken as essence or quiddity can be identified with genus or species, or with second substance.

29. "Dicendum quod Philosophus ponit substantiam dupliciter dici: Dicitur enim uno modo substantia ipsum subiectum ultimum, quod non praedicatur de alio: et hoc est particulare in genere substantiae; alio modo dicitur substantia forma vel natura subiecti" (ed. cit., p. 226).

totally identical with its subject. Consequently, the essence cannot be predicated of the subject. We cannot say that Socrates is humanity.[30]

In simple substances, that is, substances not composed of matter and form, on the other hand, there is no distinction between an essence and its subject since there is no matter in them to individuate the common nature. In them essence and subsistence are identical, continues Thomas. For support he turns to Aristotle and to Avicenna. The latter states in his *Metaphysics* that the quiddity of a simple entity is the simple entity itself.[31]

Thomas goes on to explain that substance taken as subject has two characteristics. First of all, it needs no extrinsic foundation or support, but is sustained in itself. For this reason it is said to subsist, that is, to exist in itself and not in some other subject. Secondly, it is the foundation and support for accidents. Hence it is said to stand under them. Insofar as the substance or subject subsists in itself it is known as οὐσιώσις in Greek, or as *subsistentia* in Latin, (subsistence in English translation). Insofar as it stands under accidents it is known as *hypostasis,* according to the Greeks, or as first substance *(substantia prima),* according to the Latins. From this it follows that *hypostasis* and substance taken as subject differ in reason or conceptually, but are one and the same in reality.[32]

In sum, as realized in material entities, essence is not identical with those things, nor is it totally distinct from them. It is related to them as a formal part to a whole. But in immaterial entities the two are completely identical in reality, though they differ in reason. Person, Thomas remarks, adds to hypostasis a determined kind of nature, since a person is nothing other than the *hypostasis* (individual subject) of a rational nature. Perhaps we should note here, if only in passing, that this view about the identity of nature and the individual subject *(suppositum)* in spiritual entities is difficult to reconcile with the position defended by Thomas in his somewhat later Quodlibet 2, q. 2, a. 2 of December 1269. There he states that nature and *suppositum* differ not only in material entities but also in created spirits.[33]

30. Ibid., p. 226. Note in particular: "Et ideo in rebus, ex materia et forma compositis, essentia non est omnino idem quod subiectum; unde non praedicatur de subiecto: non enim dicitur quod Socrates sit una humanitas."

31. Ibid. Note in particular: ". . . et per Avicennam, qui dicit, in sua *Metaphysica,* quod quidditas simplicis est ipsum simplex." For Avicenna see his *Liber de philosophia prima sive scientia divina V–X,* tr. 5, c. 5, p. 274: "Quidditas autem omnis simplicis est ipsummet simplex: nihil enim est ibi receptibile suae quidditatis."

32. Ed. cit., p. 226. Note in particular: "Substantia vero quae est subiectum, duo habet propria: Quorum primum est quod non indiget extrinseco fundamento in quo sustentetur, sed sustentatur in seipso; et ideo dicitur subsistere, quasi per se et non in alio existens. Aliud vero est quod est fundamentum accidentibus substentans ipsa; et pro tanto dicitur substare. Sic ergo substantia quae est subiectum, in quantum subsistit, dicitur οὐσιώσις vel subsistentia; in quantum vero substat, dicitur hypostasis secundum graecos, vel substantia prima secundum latinos. Patet ergo quod hypostasis et substantia different ratione, sed sunt idem re."

33. "Essentia vero in substantiis quidem materialibus non est idem cum eis secundum rem, neque penitus diversum, cum se habeat ut pars formalis; in substantiis vero immaterialibus est omnino

In the discussion in the *De potentia,* the important distinction for our purposes is that between substance taken as the ultimate subject within the genus substance, that is, first substance, and substance taken as the form or nature of the subject. This reminds us again of the twofold division of substance in *Metaphysics* V (and in Thomas's Commentary on the same) into first substance and substance as quiddity or nature. In neither context is the contrast between first substance and second substance.[34]

As Thomas has indicated in his discussion in the *De potentia,* substance taken as quiddity cannot be completely identified with and cannot be predicated of substance taken as subject. We cannot say that Socrates is humanity. But second substance can be predicated of first substance. We can say that Socrates is a man. If we may repeat our conclusion, second substance, or substance taken as genus or species, is not to be reduced to or identified with substance taken as nature or quiddity. To me it is clear that the latter distinction, that between substance as subject and substance as nature or quiddity, is of greater importance for Thomas's metaphysics. Moreover, it is not reducible to a purely conceptual distinction. The former distinction, that between first substance and second substance, is of greater concern to logic than to metaphysics. Moreover, in Thomas's eyes it is only a distinction of reason.[35]

Thus in replying to the sixth objection in *De potentia,* q. 9, a. 2, Thomas comments that when substance is divided into first substance and second substance, this is not a division of a genus into its species. Nothing is contained under second substance which is not also present in first substance. It is rather a division of a genus according to different modes of being. Second substance signifies the absolute nature of the genus taken in itself. First substance signifies this same generic nature but as subsisting individually. Hence, Thomas adds, this is more a division of something analogous than of a genus.[36] By this I take him to mean that this is really a division by reason of diversity in modes of being rather than the division of a genus into its species by specific differences.

Finally, we may turn to Thomas's Commentary on *Metaphysics* VII, c. 3. Here he is following Aristotle's well-known preliminary division of substance into four modes according to which something is said to be substance: (1) the quiddity, essence, or nature of a thing, here styled its *quod quid erat esse,* is said to be its substance; (2) the universal is regarded as a substance according to Thomas by those who hold that the ideas (forms) are universal species and the very substance of

---

idem secundum rem, sed differens ratione" (ibid.). For Quodlibet 2, q. 2, a. 2 see Leon. 25.2.216–17. For discussion see Ch. VIII below, Section 1.

34. See the text cited above in n. 29.

35. In other words, it is only a distinction between an individual (first substance) and a universal (genus or species) of which that individual is a member. The distinction between substance as subject and substance as nature or quiddity, on the other hand, is that which obtains between a whole and a formal part.

36. Ed. cit., p. 228. Note especially: ". . . sed est divisio generis secundum diversos modos essendi. . . . Unde magis est divisio analogi quam generis."

individuals; (3) the primary genus seems to be the substance of each thing for those who hold that unity and being are the substance of all things; (4) the subject, i.e., the particular substance of which other things are predicated but which is not itself predicated of anything else, is called a substance.[37]

Thomas comments that as the term subject is used here, it is identical with first substance as Aristotle understands this in his *Categories*. As Aristotle there explains, first substance is such in the proper, primary, and maximum way, and is that which stands under all else, that is, under species, genera, and accidents. But second substances as they are understood in the *Categories,* that is, genera and species, stand under accidents alone. And they do so only by reason of first substance. Thus man (second substance) is white only insofar as *this* man (first substance) is white.[38]

Aristotle has mentioned the universal and the genus in the second and third members of his division in *Metaphysics* VII, c. 3. Given this, Thomas correlates these with second substance as this is understood in the *Categories*. But the first member of the division in *Metaphysics* VII, i.e., quiddity or essence or nature *(quod quid erat esse)*, does not appear in the division in the *Categories*. Thomas accounts for this by noting that quiddity, taken as such, does not enter into the division of the categories (predicaments) except insofar as it serves as a principle for each of them. By this he means that quiddity itself is not a genus or species or individual; it is only a formal principle for each of these.[39]

In sum, the second member of the twofold division offered in *Metaphysics* V and so often repeated elsewhere by Thomas, that is to say, nature or quiddity or essence, is missing from the division in the *Categories* into first substance and second substance. From this it follows once more that we should not identify nature or quiddity or essence with second substance. And we should regard the division into substance as subject and substance as nature (or quiddity) as of primary importance to Thomas's metaphysics.

2. Derivation of the Predicaments

The distinction between substance and accidents is often presented as an answer to the problem of becoming at the nonessential or nonsubstantial level. Various

---

37. *In VII Met.*, lect. 2, pp. 320–21, nn. 1270–1274. For Aristotle see 1028b 33–36. Regarding the first mode, Thomas writes: ". . . primus est secundum quod 'quod quid erat esse', idest quidditas, vel essentia, sive natura rei dicitur eius substantia." As A. Maurer indicates, as early in his career as his *De ente,* c. 1, Thomas had identified essence, quiddity, and *quod quid erat esse,* and had attributed this identification to Aristotle (see Leon. 43.369:27–34). But as Maurer points out, for Aristotle the concept of "what the thing is" is not completely identical with his understanding of *quod quid erat esse.* See "Form and Essence in the Philosophy of St. Thomas," in *Being and Knowing,* pp. 13–14.

38. See p. 321, nn. 1273–1274. Note in particular: "Patet autem, quod subiectum hic dicitur, quod in *Praedicamentis* nominatur substantia prima, ex hoc, quod eadem definitio datur de subiecto hic, et ibi de substantia prima" (n. 1273).

39. See n. 1275.

Neoscholastic interpreters of Aquinas favor this approach.[40] Moreover, Aristotle's discussion of the principles of becoming in *Physics* I, c. 7 seems to offer some warrant for this. There he draws an analogy between less fundamental kinds of change and a more radical type—change in substance.

Now in all cases other than substance it is plain that there must be something underlying, namely, that which becomes. For when a thing comes to be of such a quantity or quality or in such a relation, time, or place, a subject is always presupposed, since substance alone is not predicated of another subject, but everything else of substance.[41]

Just as an underlying subject (and a form and privation) must be postulated to account for these less radical changes, so must one postulate a subject (matter), form, and privation to account for the more fundamental or substantial kind of change. In the former case the underlying subject is the substance itself, the form an accident, and the privation the absence of the accidental form which is to be acquired.[42]

While one may grant all of this, one may still ask whether this is the most fundamental way of getting at the distinction between substance and accident and in particular, whether this is a metaphysical or only a physical approach to that distinction.

In a different context, while commenting on *Metaphysics* VII, c. 3, Thomas first remarks that matter itself cannot be known sufficiently except through motion. Because of this, the investigation of matter seems to belong primarily to natural philosophy. Here, that is, in the *Metaphysics,* Aristotle takes from physics what has already been established there about matter, in particular, that considered in itself it is "neither a quiddity (that is, not a substance), nor a quality, nor any of the other genera by which being is divided or determined."[43] But Thomas then comments

---

40. See, for instance, C. A. Hart, *Thomistic Metaphysics. An Inquiry into the Act of Existing* (Englewood Cliffs, N.J., 1959), pp. 173–75; L. De Raeymaeker, *The Philosophy of Being* (St. Louis–London, 1954), pp. 170–77; J. B. Lotz, *Ontologia* (Barcelona, 1963), pp. 302–5; G. Klubertanz, *Introduction to the Philosophy of Being*, pp. 91–96, 245–50.

41. *Physics* I, c. 7 (190a 33–190b 1). Translation from *The Complete Works of Aristotle,* J. Barnes, ed., Vol. 1, p. 325.

42. Ibid., cc. 7–9. See in particular c. 7 (191a 8–15). Also see Thomas, *In I Phys.*, ed. cit., lect. 12, p. 54, n. 107. There he refers to Aristotle's effort in Bk I, c. 7 to show that there must be a subject in every natural production (see the passage quoted in our text). Thomas comments that in this context Aristotle establishes this only by induction, since to do so *per rationem* rather pertains to the metaphysician. This, he says, Aristotle does in Bk VII of the *Metaphysics* (see *lectio* 6 from Thomas's Commentary on the *Metaphysics* [p. 343, n. 1388]). Cf. *In I Phys.*, lect. 12, p. 54, n. 107: "In his igitur quae fiunt secundum quid, manifestum est quod indigent subiecto: nam quantitas et qualitas et alia accidentia, quorum est fieri secundum quid, non possunt esse sine subiecto; solius enim substantiae est non esse in subiecto."

43. See *In VII Met.*, lect. 2, p. 322, n. 1285: "Unde et Philosophus accipit hic [i.e., in the *Metaphysics*] de materia, quae in physicis sunt investigata, dicens: Dico autem materiam esse 'quae secundum se', idest secundum sui essentiam considerata, nullatenus est 'neque quid', idest neque substantia, 'neque qualitas, neque aliquid aliorum generum, quibus ens dividitur, vel determinatur'."

that Aristotle does not establish the distinction of matter from all forms, substantial and accidental, by appealing to motion (the proof from natural philosophy), but by appealing to the order of predication. This, Thomas observes, is proper to logic.[44]

Given this, we might also expect Thomas to hold that one establishes the distinction between substance and accidents not by appealing to motion (the way of natural philosophy), but by having recourse to the order of predication. In this passage from his Commentary on *Metaphysics* VII, Thomas justifies his appeal to logic on the part of the metaphysician by noting the close affinity between the two, an affinity, he adds, which Aristotle has mentioned in *Metaphysics* IV.[45] By this I take Thomas to mean that logic and first philosophy have this in common, that they are not restricted to a particular kind of being in their respective inquiries, as are the philosophy of nature and mathematics. As he explains elsewhere in his Commentary on *Metaphysics* VII (lect. 17), the logician considers the mode of predication but not the existence of a thing. The metaphysician, of course, must consider the existence of things, because he studies them insofar as they are being.[46]

These remarks are interesting because, as we shall now see, Thomas frequently appeals to the difference between that which exists in itself and that which does not but only in something else in order to establish the distinction between substance and accident. This approach to the substance-accident distinction does not seem to be based on change or becoming. It does, however, fit rather nicely with our earlier remarks concerning Thomas's view of being as that which we first discover.[47]

Thus our recognition of substance as such and accident as such presupposes that we have already discovered one or more beings and formulated a notion, at least a primitive notion, of being. Once we arrive at explicit awareness of the difference within the realm of being between that which exists in itself and that which does not, we would seem to have discovered the distinction between substance and accident.

Moreover, as we shall shortly observe in detail, Thomas appeals to diverse modes of predication in order to derive and justify, one might even say "deduce," the ten Aristotelian categories or predicaments. In his Commentary on *Metaphysics* V he does this while reminding us that these diverse modes of predication correspond

44. See n. 1287: "Attamen diversitatem materiae ab omnibus formis non probat Philosophus per viam motus, quae quidem probatio est per viam naturalis Philosophiae, sed per viam praedicationis, quae est propria Logicae, quam in quarto huius dicit affinem esse huic scientiae." Cf. *In IV Met.*, lect. 4, p. 160, n. 574. Note especially: "Et ideo subiectum logicae ad omnia se extendit, de quibus ens naturae praedicatur. Unde concludit, quod subiectum logicae aequiparatur subiecto philosophiae, quod est ens naturae."

45. See n. 44 above.

46. See *In VII Met.*, lect. 17, p. 396, n. 1658. Note: "Logicus enim considerat modum praedicandi, et non existentiam rei. . . . Sed philosophus qui existentiam rerum quaerit. . . ." Also see *In VII Met.*, lect. 3, p. 327, n. 1308: "Sicut enim supra dictum est, haec scientia habet quandam affinitatem cum Logica propter utriusque communitatem."

47. See n. 4 above.

to and reflect diverse ways in which being itself is realized, or what he calls diverse modes of being *(modi essendi)*. In other words, this diversity in the order of predication follows from and depends upon diversity in the order of being.[48]

As I interpret this, Thomas would have us appeal not to motion and to the philosophy of nature but to diversity in modes of predication in order to render explicit the distinction between substance and accident in general, and also to derive the nine supreme classes of accidents. Since he grounds this diversity in the order of predication on diversity in the order of being, he assigns this justification to the science of being as being, that is to say, to metaphysics. If it is not a physical approach, neither is it a purely logical approach. It is metaphysical, i.e., the employment in metaphysics of a logical technique.[49]

In connection with this we might recall another point Thomas makes at the beginning of his Commentary on *Metaphysics* VII. The mode or way in which words signify does not immediately follow upon the mode of being of such things, but only as mediated by the way in which such things are understood. To put this another way, words are likenesses or signs of thoughts, and thoughts themselves are likenesses of things, as Thomas recalls from Bk I of Aristotle's *De interpretatione*.[50]

Nonetheless, the point we have been stressing remains. As Thomas sees things, supreme and diverse modes of predication (as expressed in the predicaments) ultimately follow from and depend upon supreme and diverse modes of being. It is for this very reason that Thomas thinks we can discover these supreme modes of being by proceeding in the opposite direction, as it were, that is, by beginning with diversity in the order of predication.

As we approach this issue, we should bear in mind another point which Thomas mentions in the same context. We cannot automatically assume that every distinction introduced by the intellect in its thinking and expressed by us in speech follows from and points to a corresponding real diversity in the order of being. In fact, Thomas often criticizes the Platonists for making this mistake.[51] This awareness does not prevent Thomas from appealing to the different ways in which we assign predicates to subjects in order to justify the division of being into ten supreme categories or predicaments.

48. See *In V Met.*, lect. 9, p. 238, n. 890. Cf. above, Ch. III, n. 80.

49. See nn. 44 and 46 above for Thomas's remarks about the affinity between logic and metaphysics.

50. "Licet modus significandi vocum non consequatur immediate modum essendi rerum, sed mediante modo intelligendi; quia intellectus sunt similitudines rerum, voces autem intellectuum, ut dicitur in primo *Perihermenias*." *In VII Met.*, lect. 1, p. 317, n. 1253. See *De interpretatione*, c. 1 (16a 3–4). For Thomas's commentary on this see *Expositio Libri Peryermenias*, I, 2 (Leon. 1*.1.10:95–11:112).

51. *In VII Met.*, lect. 1, n. 1254. "Licet autem modus essendi accidentium non sit ut per se sint, sed solum ut insint, intellectus tamen potest ea per se intelligere, cum sit natus dividere ea quae secundum naturam coniuncta sunt." Thomas makes these points within the more general context of distinguishing between two ways in which accidents can be signified, abstractly and concretely. See nn. 1252–1255. For one of many references to the Platonists' mistake in this respect see *In De Trinitate*, q. 5, a. 3 (Leon. 50.149:287–290).

As he takes up this topic in his Commentary on *Metaphysics* V, Thomas follows Aristotle in singling out being as it exists outside the mind and is divided into the ten predicaments. (He distinguishes being considered in this way both from being as it exists only in the mind, and from being as it is divided in terms of act and potency.)[52] Thomas begins with the observation that according to Aristotle those things are said to be in the proper sense *(secundum se* rather than only *per accidens)* which signify different figures of predication. In terms which are familiar to us, Thomas reminds us that being itself cannot be restricted to any determined predicament in the way a genus is contracted by differences to species. A difference is not included within the essence of a genus; but nothing can fall outside the essence of being which might be added to it so as to divide it into species. What is outside being is absolute nothingness, and this cannot serve as a difference. And as we have seen, being itself is not a genus.[53]

Therefore, Thomas continues, being is contracted to its various genera according to the different modes of predication which follow upon different modes of being. As we have already suggested, in making this point Thomas is also acknowledging that in the order of discovery we may be led to recognize these different modes of being by appealing to diverse modes of predication. Because of this, Thomas can agree with Aristotle that in whatever ways being is predicated, in so many ways is *esse* signified, that is, in so many ways is something signified to be.[54]

This also accounts for the fact that we name those classes into which being is first divided "predicaments"; these predicaments are distinguished according to different modes or ways of predicating. Of those names which are predicated, continues Thomas, some signify what something is, that is to say, substance. Some signify how it is (quality), and others how much there is (quantity), and so on. Therefore, in accord with each of these supreme modes of predicating, *esse* must signify the same thing, i.e., what something is, or what kind it is, or how much there is, etc. For instance, when we say that man is an animal, the term "is" signifies substance. When we say a man is white, the verb "is" signifies quality. Perhaps we should comment here that these propositions express what we, following Gilson, have called judgments of attribution. In these the verb "is" takes its meaning from the term which is affirmed of a subject. In this discussion Thomas is not primarily concerned with judgments of existence.[55]

52. *In V Met.*, lect. 9, p. 238, n. 889.
53. Ibid. Cited above in Ch. III, n. 80.
54. Ibid., n. 890: "Unde oportet, quod ens contrahatur ad diversa genera secundum diversum modum praedicandi, qui consequitur diversum modum essendi; quia 'quoties ens dicitur', idest quot modis aliquid praedicatur, 'toties esse significatur', idest tot modis significatur aliquid esse."
55. Ibid. Note in particular: "Quia igitur eorum quae praedicantur, quaedam significant quid, idest substantiam, quaedam quale, quaedam quantum, et sic de aliis; oportet quod unicuique modo praedicandi, esse significet idem. . . ."

At this point Thomas offers a derivation or a kind of deduction of the ten su-preme genera or categories.[56] As he puts this, a predicate may be related to a subject in three different ways. In one way, the predicate is really identical with that which serves as the subject as, for instance, when we say "Socrates is an animal." Here Socrates is that very thing which is an animal. Hence the predicate "animal" is affirmed of (literally: "said to signify") the subject Socrates. And the term "Socrates" is said to signify first substance—the individual substance of which all else is predi-cated.[57]

56. For discussions see S. Breton, "La déduction thomiste des catégories," *Revue philosophique de Louvain* 60 (1962), pp. 5–32; Hart, *Thomistic Metaphysics,* pp. 179–81; A. Krempel, *La doctrine de la relation chez saint Thomas* (Paris, 1952), pp. 79–83 (see below on his denial that the last six categories also signify for Thomas ontological divisions of being); H. M. Baumgartner, G. Gerhardt, K. Kon-hardt, and G. Schönrich, "Kategorie, Kategorienlehre. 4: Thomas von Aquin," in *Historisches Wör-terbuch der Philosophie,* J. Ritter and K. Gründer, eds., Band 4 (Basel-Stuttgart, 1976), cols. 722–723 (which credits Thomas with being the first to attempt a systematic deduction of the Aristotelian categories). Cf. Breton, pp. 8ff. However, W. E. McMahon maintains that Thomas's views on the categories are "obviously derived from those of Albert." See his "Albert the Great on the Semantics of the Categories of Substance, Quantity, and Quality," *Historiographia Linguistica* 7:1/2 (1980), pp. 145–57, esp. p. 146; "The *Liber sex principiorum,* A Twelfth-Century Treatise in Descriptive Meta-physics," *Studies in the History of Linguistics.* Vol. 20: *Progress in Linguistic Historiography,* K. Koerner, ed. (Amsterdam, 1980), pp. 3–12, esp. p. 8, where he credits Albert with an attempt to systematize discussion of the *sex principia* in the *Liber sex principiorum* itself (see n. 98 below), and refers to Aquinas's derivation in his Commentary on the *Metaphysics* as involving only minor modi-fications of Albert's discussions. In the first-mentioned article McMahon cites three (or four?) deriva-tions in Albert, i.e., his paraphrase of the *Categories* = *Liber de praedicamentis,* I, c. 7 (A. Borgnet ed., Vol. 1, pp. 163–65); VII, cc. 1–2 (pp. 270–72); and his paraphrase of the *Liber de sex principiis* = *De sex principiis,* I, c. 1 (Borgnet ed., Vol. 1, pp. 305–7); and I, c. 6 (pp. 315–16). Estimates concerning the dating of Albert's logical commentaries vary considerably. See Weisheipl, "The Life and Works of St. Albert the Great," in *Albertus Magnus and the Sciences. Commemorative Essays 1980,* J. A. Weis-heipl, ed., (Toronto, 1980), p. 27 (on the difficulty and variation in proposed datings for these works), and p. 40 (where he dates the logical paraphrases before 1264). In sum, Thomas could have had access to both Albertine sources. Cf. Leon. 25.2.452 ("Index") where ca. 1261 is proposed as the date for Albert's *Praedicamenta,* and Thomas's Quodlibet III, q. 3, a. 2, where descriptions of *situs* from the *Liber de sex principiis* itself and from our two commentaries by Albert are cited as (possible) sources for Thomas's own description there of this category (Leon. 25.2.250:38–39). Be that as it may, McMahon should be given credit for singling out Albert's derivations of the categories and for suggesting that they are prior in time to those developed by Thomas. On the other hand, my own comparison of Albert's derivation of the categories with those proposed by Thomas does not support the view that Thomas simply derived his approach from Albert. While there are some obvious simi-larities, e.g., with respect to substance, quantity, and quality and with respect to descriptions of some other predicaments, some of these may go back to Aristotle himself, and others to the *Liber de sex principiis.* I am more impressed with the differences between Thomas's treatments and Albert's, especially as regards the *sex principia* (the last six), and view Thomas's derivations, especially in his Commentary on the *Metaphysics,* as superior from the standpoint of metaphysics, while acknowledg-ing that Albert's derivations appear in logical writings.

57. *In V Met.,* lect. 9, p. 238, n. 891. "Sciendum enim est quod praedicatum ad subiectum triplici-ter se potest habere. Uno modo cum est id quod est subiectum, ut cum dico, Socrates est animal. Nam Socrates est id quod est animal. Et hoc praedicatum dicitur significare substantiam primam, quae est substantia particularis, de qua omnia praedicantur." In interpreting this I take *hoc praedica-*

In a second way, a predicate may be taken from something which is *in* the subject. If the predicate is taken from something which is in the subject considered absolutely—that is, when the subject is simply viewed in itself—and which follows upon the matter of that subject, we have (2) the predicament quantity. If the predicate is taken from something which is in the subject in this absolute way but which follows from its form, we have (3) the predicament quality. But if the predicate is taken from something which is in the subject only when the subject is considered in relation to something else, (4) the predicament relation results.[58]

In a third major way, a predicate may be derived from something which is realized outside the subject, and this in turn in two ways. It may be that the predicate is taken from something which is realized entirely outside the subject, and in such fashion that it does not in any way serve to measure the subject. In this case we have (5) the predicament *habitus.* If we bear in mind the medieval way of referring to the distinctive garb worn by a member of a religious community as a religious habit, this usage will not be quite so puzzling to us today. Thomas himself offers two examples: Socrates is wearing shoes; Socrates is wearing clothes.[59]

In short, what Thomas has in mind is the distinctive mode of being which results from the fact that a subject, e.g., Socrates, is considered in relation to something else which is ontologically distinct and separate from that subject, and which does not serve as a measure of that subject. The mode of being which results from this, being clothed, for instance, justifies a distinctive way of referring to that subject. Why Thomas singles this out as a distinct predicament will become clearer when we consider his parallel derivation of the categories in his Commentary on *Physics* III.[60]

It may happen that the predicate in question is taken from something which is entirely outside the subject but which does in some way measure that subject. If that from which the predicate is taken measures the subject in terms of time, the subject is said to be in time and we have the corresponding predicament (6) "time when."[61]

If that from which the predicate is derived measures the subject in terms of place but without any reference to the way the parts of the subject are distributed in that

---

tum in the last sentence as referring to *animal* directly. "Animal" can be said to signify first substance only in the sense that it is predicated of "Socrates," the first substance.

58. "Secundo modo ut praedicatum sumatur secundum quod inest subiecto: quod quidem praedicatum, vel inest ei per se et absolute, ut consequens materiam, et sic est quantitas: vel ut consequens formam, et sic est qualitas: vel inest ei non absolute, sed in respectu ad aliud, et sic est ad aliquid" (*In V Met.*, lect. 9, pp. 238–39, n. 892).

59. "Tertio modo ut praedicatum sumatur ab eo quod est extra subiectum: et hoc dupliciter. Uno modo ut sit omnino extra subiectum: quod quidem si non sit mensura subiecti, praedicatur per modum habitus, ut cum dicitur, Socrates est calceatus vel vestitus" (p. 239, n. 892).

60. See n. 87 below in this chapter.

61. "Si autem sit mensura eius, cum mensura extrinseca sit vel tempus vel locus, sumitur praedicamentum vel ex parte temporis, et sic erit quando . . ." (p. 239, n. 892).

place, we have (7) the predicament "place where" *(ubi)*. Here it may be helpful to recall the Aristotelian view that place is the first immobile surface of the surrounding medium. The predicament Thomas has in mind is not place itself but the mode of being which applies to a subject insofar as that subject is in place, or enjoys what we might call location.[62]

If that from which the predicate is taken measures the subject in terms of place and also in terms of the way the parts of the located body are ordered to one another, still another predicament results: (8) position *(situs)*. This may be illustrated by statements such as "Socrates is sitting," or "Socrates is standing."[63]

Finally, it may happen that what the predicate is taken from is not completely external to the subject, but partly present in the subject. If this mode of being is present in the subject insofar as the subject itself is a principle of acting, the predicament (9) action results. In other words, the principle of action is in the subject itself.[64] On the other hand, that from which the predicate is derived may not be totally external to the subject for the opposite reason; it may be present in the subject insofar as the subject itself is the terminus of and receives the action in question. If so, we have (10) the final predicament—"to be acted upon" *(passio)*.[65]

In this derivation we have Thomas's answer in advance to a criticism raised centuries later by Kant against Aristotle's list of ten categories or predicaments. According to the *Critique of Pure Reason* (A 81/B 106–107), Aristotle relied on sheer induction in arriving at his haphazard list. He did not develop it systematically from any common principle.[66] Whatever the merits of this criticism when leveled

62. ". . . vel ex loco, et sic erit ubi, non considerato ordine partium in loco . . ." (ibid.). For Aristotle on place see *Physics* IV, c. 4 (212a 20–21).

63. ". . . quo considerato erit situs" (ibid.). For brief but helpful discussions of *ubi* ("place where"), *situs* (position), and *quando* ("time when") see J. Owens, *An Elementary Christian Metaphysics*, pp. 204–8.

64. "Alio modo ut id a quo sumitur praedicamentum, secundum aliquid sit in subiecto, de quo praedicatur. Et si quidem secundum principium, sic praedicatur ut agere. Nam actionis principium in subiecto est" (ed. cit., p. 239, n. 892).

65. "Si vero secundum terminum, sic praedicabitur ut in pati. Nam passio in subiectum patiens terminatur" (ibid.). The later scholastic tradition distinguishes between immanent action and transitive action. If, as F. A. Blanche has pointed out, Thomas does not use this precise terminology, he does distinguish between the kind of action which "remains within" and the kind which "passes over" to a recipient ("Sur la langue technique de saint Thomas d'Aquin," *Revue de philosophie* n. s. 1 [1930], pp. 7–30, esp. p. 15). See, for instance, *De veritate*, q. 8. a. 6 (Leon. 22.2.238:104–111); ST I, q. 18, a. 3, ad 1 (Leon. 4.228); ST I, q. 23, a. 2, ad 1 (Leon. 4.273): "actiones in exteriorem materiam transeuntes . . . actiones in agente manentes;" ST I, q. 34, a. 1, ad 2 (Leon. 4.366): "non enim intelligere significat actionem ab intelligente exeuntem, sed in intelligente manentem"; ST I, q. 56, a. 1 (Leon. 5.62). Cf. G. Langevin, "L'action immanente d'après s. Thomas d'Aquin," *Laval théologique et philosophique* 30 (1974), pp. 251–66; M. Kelly, "Action in Aquinas," *New Scholasticism* 52 (1978), pp. 261ff.; M. Miller, "The Problem of Action in the Commentary of St. Thomas Aquinas on the *Physics* of Aristotle," *Modern Schoolman* 23 (1945–1946), pp. 140–46; J. Owens, *An Elementary Christian Metaphysics*, pp. 193–94, n. 4.

66. See Kant's remark about Aristotle: "It was an enterprise worthy of an acute thinker like Aristotle to make search for these fundamental concepts. But as he did so on no principle, he merely

against Aristotle, it does not seem to apply fully to Aquinas. As he sees things, there is a kind of principle to account for the fact that there are ten and only ten categories or predicaments. This principle is complex. It rests upon the difference between three major ways in which a predicate may be related to a subject, i.e., (1) as identical with the subject; or (2) as derived from something that is present in the subject; or (3) as derived from something that is outside the subject. Thomas's application of this in turn rests on a point we have already made, i.e., that we can arrive at knowledge of the major ways in which being is realized by attending to the major ways in which predicates are affirmed of a subject. For Thomas's very non-Kantian theory of knowledge, of course, this presupposes that the order of thought is based upon the order of reality and reflects it. Because words in turn reflect thoughts, by attending to distinctive modes of predication we may ultimately discern different modes of being.

At the same time, Thomas was aware that Aristotle did not always list ten predicaments or categories. In fact, in the passage upon which Thomas is here commenting, Aristotle only lists eight. "To be clothed" *(habitus)* and position *(situs)* are omitted. Nonetheless, Thomas seems to regard the listing of ten categories in Aristotle's *Categories* as normative, and it is this ten-part division that he here attempts to justify. We shall return to this point below.[67]

Thomas offers an additional clarification in the same context. One might think that because the verb "is" does not explicitly appear in each of the predicaments, such predications really do not fall under the predication of being. For instance, when we say "a man walks," the verb "is" does not appear. According to Thomas, Aristotle wards off this objection by arguing that in each of these predications something is signified to be. In support Thomas observes that every verb may be resolved *(resolvitur)* into the verb "is" and a participle. To say that someone convalesces amounts to saying that person *is* convalescing. To say that a man walks is really to say that he *is* walking.[68]

Whether or not one accepts this grammatical point, Thomas's claim seems to be sound enough on metaphysical grounds.[69] To walk, to act, to be acted upon, to

picked them up as they came his way, and at first procured ten of them, which he called *categories* (predicaments)." *Immanuel Kant's Critique of Pure Reason,* N. Kemp Smith, trans. (London, 1964), p. 114.

67. Aristotle lists ten predicaments in *Categories,* c. 4 (1b 25–27) and *Topics* I, c. 9 (103b 20–23). Krempel comments that these are works of his youth and that elsewhere, even when he envisions a complete number, he omits position and *habere (habitus).* See *Post. Anal.* I, c. 22 (83b 16–17); *Physics* V, c. 1 (225b 5–9); and our present passage, *Metaphysics* V, c. 7 (1017a 24–27). See *La doctrine de la relation,* p. 82.

68. *In V Met.,* lect. 9, p. 239, n. 893: ". . . ideo consequenter hoc removet, dicens quod in omnibus huiusmodi praedicationibus significatur aliquid esse. Verbum enim quodlibet resolvitur in hoc verbum Est, et participium. Nihil enim differt dicere, homo convalescens est, et homo convalescit, et sic de aliis. Unde patet quod quot modis praedicatio fit, tot modis ens dicitur." Cf. n. 54 above.

69. For some apparent reservations about admitting this grammatical point, see Gilson, *Being and Some Philosophers,* pp. 191–92, 196–97.

be clothed, etc., such predications signify distinct modes of being, or distinct ways in which being is realized in a subject. Hence these too must ultimately fall within the range of being itself. Consequently the terms we use to signify them should be reducible to being in some way. This follows from Thomas's repeated insistence that being *(ens)* is that which the intellect first conceives and into which it resolves all other conceptions. Whatever idea or concept one has formed about any reality, eventual analysis *(resolutio)* will lead one to recognize it as enjoying being in some way.[70]

In assessing Thomas's procedure in commenting on this particular text in Aristotle, it will be helpful for us to turn once again to his discussion in *De veritate,* q. 1, a. 1. In this relatively early but extremely important work Thomas was clearly writing in his own name. If the thinking we find there supports the procedure he has employed in his Commentary on the *Metaphysics,* this will strongly suggest that in the latter context as well he is expressing his own position and not merely explaining Aristotle's text.

As will be recalled, in *De veritate,* q. 1, a. 1, Thomas stresses the primacy enjoyed by being in the order of resolution. There too he remarks that nothing can be added to being from without which might divide it in the way a genus is divided into its species; for being is not a genus. Therefore, certain things may be said to add to being only insofar as they express a mode that is not expressed by the name being itself. This happens in one way when the mode expressed is something special, that is, some more restricted mode of being. As Thomas puts this, there are different degrees of entity, and different modes of being *(essendi)* correspond to these. The different genera (read: predicaments) are taken from these different modes of being.[71]

Substance, for instance, does not add to being a difference which signifies some nature that would be superadded to being. The name substance rather signifies a special mode of being—being in itself *(per se)*. And so it is, continues Thomas, with the other genera. Each of them also expresses a special mode of being.[72]

In both texts, therefore, we find Thomas emphasizing the close relation between these supreme genera (predicaments) and the supreme modes of being *(modi es-*

70. See Ch. II above, pp. 40–44. I am assuming that in the text cited in n. 68 Thomas does not have in mind judgments of existence. On the difficulty of reducing them to judgments of attribution see Gilson, *Being and Some Philosophers,* pp. 192–93, 201.

71. ". . . unde probat etiam Philosophus in III *Metaphysicae* quod ens non potest esse genus; sed secundum hoc aliqua dicuntur addere super ens in quantum exprimunt modum ipsius entis qui nomine entis non exprimitur, quod dupliciter contingit. Uno modo ut modus expressus sit aliquis specialis modus entis; sunt enim diversi gradus entitatis secundum quos accipiuntur diversi modi essendi et iuxta hos modos accipiuntur diversa rerum genera." See Leon. 22.1.5:100–119. On the primacy of being *(ens)* in the order of resolution see Ch. II above, nn. 57–60.

72. Leon. 22.1.5:119–123, cited above in Ch. III, n. 86. Immediately after this Thomas presents his derivation of those general modes which follow upon every being, i.e., the transcendentals. Cf. Ch. VI above, Section 5.

sendi). In the text from the *De veritate* he explicitly mentions the point that the supreme modes of being correspond to supreme degrees or levels of entity *(entitas)*. While the reference to supreme modes of predicating is made more explicit in the Commentary on the *Metaphysics* and while it is there that Thomas goes on to derive all the categories, the underlying thinking in the two texts is essentially the same. We may assume, therefore, that in developing his derivation of the categories in his Commentary on the *Metaphysics* Thomas is presenting his personal views.[73]

Thomas offers another derivation and justification for the division of being into ten predicaments in his Commentary on *Physics* III, lect. 5. In this context he is following Aristotle's effort to work out the appropriate relationship and distinction between motion, on the one hand, and the predicaments action and passion on the other. Thomas defends Aristotle's claim that while the motion of a mover and a receiver are one and the same in reality, two distinct predicaments, action and passion, are involved. A first objection against this urges that if action and passion are one and the same motion and differ only in definition, it does not seem that they can constitute two distinct predicaments; for predicaments are supreme genera of things.[74]

Thomas recalls that being is not divided into the ten predicaments univocally as a genus into its species, but rather according to diverse modes of being. These modes of being correspond to (literally: "are proportional to") different modes of predication. In support Thomas remarks that when we predicate one thing of another, we say that the latter *is* the former. Hence, because of this correspondence between these modes of being and the modes of predication, Thomas concludes that the ten supreme genera of being are referred to as ten predicaments.[75]

As in his Commentary on the *Metaphysics,* Thomas remarks that predication may take place in three ways. The first mode is that where something which belongs to the essence of a subject is predicated of it, for instance, when I say "Socrates is a man," or "man is an animal." It is according to this mode that we derive (1) the predicament substance. In each of these examples, that which is expressed by the predicate is included within the essence of the subject.[76]

---

73. As we shall indicate again below, this also applies to Thomas's defense of ten predicaments or categories.

74. *In III Phys.*, lect. 5, ed. cit., pp. 157–58, nn. 310–320. For this difficulty or objection see n. 321: ". . . si actio et passio sint unus motus, et non differunt nisi secundum rationem, ut dictum est, videtur quod non debeant esse duo praedicamenta, cum praedicamenta sint genera rerum."

75. See p. 158, n. 322: ". . . sciendum est quod ens dividitur in decem praedicamenta non univoce, sicut genus in species, sed secundum diversum modum essendi. Modi autem essendi proportionales sunt modis praedicandi. Praedicando enim aliquid de aliquo altero, dicimus hoc esse illud: unde et decem genera entis dicuntur decem praedicamenta."

76. "Unus quidem modus est, quando de aliquo subiecto praedicatur id quod pertinet ad essentiam eius, ut cum dico *Socrates est homo,* vel *homo est animal;* et secundum hoc accipitur praedicamentum *substantiae*" (ibid.).

A second mode of predication arises when something which is not included within the essence of a subject but inheres in it is predicated of that subject. If this arises from the side of the matter of the subject, we have (2) the predicament quantity (for quantity follows upon matter). If this happens from the side of the form of the subject, we have (3) the predicament quality. From this it follows, remarks Thomas, that qualities are based on quantity. Thus color (a sensible quality) pre-supposes a surface, and configuration *(figura)*, another quality, presupposes lines or surfaces.[77]

Or it may be that something is predicated of a subject only insofar as the latter is ordered to something else. This results in (4) the predicament relation. For instance, if I say "a man is a father," nothing absolute is predicated of that man simply considered in himself, but only a relationship in him to something extrinsic.[78]

Until this point, therefore, there are no major differences between the procedure indicated by this text and that presented in the Commentary on the *Metaphysics.* But in introducing the third major mode of predication, Thomas explains that this arises when something extrinsic is predicated of a subject by way of "denominating." By this Thomas means that a name, based on a mode of being, is assigned to a subject by reason of something extrinsic to that subject. It is in this way that extrinsic accidents are predicated of substances. We should not take Thomas to mean by this that such accidents exist apart from and in separation from their subjects. He rather means that that from which the name of such accidents is taken is extrinsic to the subject of the accidents. He goes on to note that one way of being named from something extrinsic applies to (material) things taken generally; but another way of being so named is restricted to human beings.[79]

Something may be named from something which is extrinsic to it in the first and general way either on the basis of causation, or else because it is measured by that other thing. As regards denominations based on causality, Thomas quickly sets aside predications based on material and formal causality. Because both mate-

---

77. See n. 322, p. 158. Note in particular: "Alius autem modus est quo praedicatur de aliquo id quod non est de essentia eius, tamen inhaeret ei." In his remark about quality's being based on quantity, Thomas is restricting himself to qualities as realized in material entities. He also defends certain spiritual powers of the soul, i.e., intellect and will, which continue to inhere therein when the body is destroyed (see ST I, q. 77, a. 8). He identifies powers of the soul as belonging to the second species of quality (ST I, q. 77, a. 1, ad 5). For more on the four species of quality see ST I–II, q. 49, a. 2.

78. ". . . aut se habet per respectum ad alterum, et sic est praedicamentum *relationis* (cum enim dico *homo est pater,* non praedicatur de homine aliquid absolutum, sed respectus qui ei inest ad aliquid extrinsecum)." Ed. cit., pp. 158–59 n. 322. For more on Thomas's views on relation see M. G. Henninger, *Relations: Medieval Theories 1250–1325* (Oxford, 1989), c. 2.

79. "Tertius autem modus praedicandi est, quando aliquid extrinsecum de aliquo praedicatur per modum alicuius denominationis. . . . Denominari autem ab aliquo extrinseco invenitur quidem quodammodo communiter in omnibus, et aliquo modo specialiter in iis quae ad homines pertinent tantum" (p. 159, n. 322).

rial and formal causes are intrinsic to the essence of the subject or substance itself, predications based on these fall under the predicament substance. A final cause cannot exercise its causality apart from an agent, since an end can serve as a cause only by moving an agent.[80]

From this it follows that something may receive its name from something else by being caused only in the order of efficient causality. In this case we have (5) the predicament "being acted upon" *(passio)*. Or something may be named an efficient cause by reason of an effect which it produces. Here the effect itself is extrinsic to the subject. In this case we assign (6) the predicament action *(actio)* to the subject which acts.[81]

As regards modes of predicating which are based on something else which serves as a measure of a subject, such measures may be extrinsic or intrinsic. By intrinsic measures Thomas has in mind the particular length, width, and depth of a given thing. In this case the thing is so named, for instance, as being so long or wide or deep, from something which inheres in it intrinsically. This does not result in a distinct mode of predicating or in a distinct predicament, but is included under the predicament quantity.[82]

As extrinsic measures Thomas lists time and place. Insofar as something is named from time, that is, from the time in which it is realized, (7) the predicament "time when" *(quando)* results. Insofar as something is named from place, the predicaments (8) "place where" *(ubi)* and (9) position *(situs)* result. As in his Commentary on *Metaphysics* V, Thomas here explains that the predicament position adds to the predicament "place where" the note that the parts of the located body are ordered to one another.[83] He also now comments that this subdivision into "place where" and position does not apply to the predicament "time when." An ordering of parts within time is already implied by the definition of time itself. Time, Thomas reminds us, is the numbering of motion according to the before and the after.[84]

Finally, he returns to the case where a given kind of subject, a human being, is named from something which is extrinsic to it. There is something unique about human beings, he explains. Nature has sufficiently equipped other animals with all

---

80. Ibid. Thomas's remark here about matter and form squares with his earlier explanation of the first way in which something is predicated of something else, i.e., as belonging to its essence and hence as pertaining to the predicament substance (see n. 76 above).

81. "Sic igitur secundum quod aliquid denominatur a causa agente, est praedicamentum *passionis,* nam pati nihil est aliud quam suscipere aliquid ab agente: secundum autem quod e converso denominatur causa agens ab effectu, est praedicamentum *actionis,* nam actio est actus ab agente in aliud . . ." (ibid.).

82. ". . . ab his ergo denominatur aliquid sicut ab instrinseco inhaerente; unde pertinet ad praedicamentum quantitatis" (ibid.).

83. Ibid.

84. Ibid. Note Thomas's final remark concerning these: "Sic igitur aliquid dicitur esse *quando* vel *ubi* per denominationem a tempore vel a loco."

that is necessary for the preservation of life, for instance, with horns for self-defense, a thick and hairy skin, hooves so as to walk without being harmed, etc. To refer to such animals as being armed or clothed or shod (i.e., equipped with hooves) is not to name them from something extrinsic but simply from their proper parts. Therefore, when such names are applied to them, they will fall within the predicament substance. This is to say, I take it, that such properties follow from their essence or nature as a given kind of animal.[85]

A human being is more complicated because of the subtle way in which his material part is formed and because of the many different kinds of deeds he can perform by using his reason. Because of this, nature could not fit him with instruments which could be accommodated to all his varying needs. Instead, human beings have been endowed with reason, which they may use to prepare extrinsic instruments for performing many and varied tasks, including those for which animals are fitted by their natural and intrinsic parts.[86]

It is for this reason, continues Thomas, that there is a distinct (10) predicament, *habitus,* which applies only to human beings. For instance, when we say that someone is wearing armor, or is clothed, or is wearing shoes, we name him from something which is extrinsic to him and not related to him so as to cause or measure his being.[87]

At the end of this derivation of the predicaments, Thomas returns to his discussion of motion, action and passion. In replying to the objection already mentioned,[88] he comments that if a given motion is ontologically one, two different predicaments may result. This is because the two different predicamental names are taken from two distinct things which are external to the subject. If the external thing by reason of which we ascribe the motion (i.e., being moved) to a subject is itself the agent, we say that the subject is being acted upon. This justifies our assigning the predicament passion to that subject. But if the external thing by reason of which we ascribe the motion to a subject is itself a receiver of that motion, we rather speak of the subject as acting. Hence we assign the predicament action to that subject.[89]

---

85. Ibid. See in particular: "Unde hoc refertur in his ad praedicamentum substantiae: ut puta si diceretur quod homo est *manuatus* vel *pedatus.*"

86. "Sed huiusmodi non poterant dari homini a natura, tum quia non conveniebant subtilitati complexionis eius, tum propter multiformitatem operum quae conveniunt homini inquantum habet rationem, quibus aliqua determinata instrumenta accomodari non poterant a natura . . ." (ibid.).

87. Ibid. Note in particular: ". . . unde est speciale praedicamentum, et dicitur habitus." *Habitus* as it is used in this context should not be confused with "habit" insofar as it is a species of quality (see ST I–II, q. 49, a. 1, for both of these usages of *habitus,* as well as a third one for the infinitive *habere,* i.e., taken as one of the postpredicaments). On the predicament *habitus* cf. I. Valbuena, "De significatione specialis praedicamenti 'habitus' apud philosophum et divum Thomam," *Angelicum* 22 (1945), pp. 172–77.

88. For the text see n. 74 above.

89. "Sic igitur patet quod licet motus sit unus, tamen praedicamenta quae sumuntur secundum motum, sunt duo, secundum quod a diversis rebus exterioribus fiunt praedicamentales denominati-

For our present purposes, however, other points are more important. First of all, as in the parallel passage from his Commentary on *Metaphysics* V, in the present context Thomas justifies the derivation of the predicaments by concentrating on different modes of predication. But as he has made abundantly clear in his Commentary on the *Metaphysics,* and as he also states here albeit more briefly, these different modes of predicating ultimately arise from and depend upon different modes of being, or different ways in which being is realized. As he puts it in the present context, the modes of being are in accord with the modes of predication. And he justifies this with the comment that when we predicate something of something else, we say that the latter *is* the former.[90]

Moreover, there are interesting points of similarity and diversity between the two derivations of the predicaments. Most important is the primacy given to substance in each. This is only fitting, of course, in light of Thomas's (and Aristotle's) view that substance is the primary referent and primary instantiation of being. Again, each division results in ten predicaments. Finally, the order in which Thomas has derived the predicaments is essentially the same for the first four predicaments— substance, quantity, quality, and relation. From that point on, however, there is considerable diversity in the order Thomas follows in the two passages.[91]

According to both texts, the third general way of predicating something of a subject arises from the fact that the name of the predicate is taken from something which is in fact extrinsic to that subject. This is spelled out more fully in the Commentary on the *Physics,* as we have just seen. One addition there has to do with the distinction between two situations. A name may be taken from something which is extrinsic to the subject in such fashion that it can be applied to all material subjects. Or the name may be taken from something which is extrinsic in such fashion that it can be applied only to human subjects.[92]

In the Commentary on the *Metaphysics* Thomas has immediately gone on to derive the predicaments (5) *habitus,* (6) time when, (7) place where, (8) position and finally (9) action and (10) passion. In the Commentary on the *Physics* he follows a different order for the last six predicaments: (5) passion, (6) action, (7) time when, (8) place where, (9) position, and finally (10) *habitus.* Perhaps Thomas's im-

---

ones. Nam alia res est agens, a qua sicut ab exteriori, sumitur per modum denominationis praedicamentum passionis: et alia res est patiens a qua denominatur agens" (p. 159, n. 323).

90. See the text cited above in n. 75.

91. See Krempel, *La doctrine,* pp. 79–83, for a presentation of the two derivations in parallel columns. In his Commentary on *Metaphysics* V Thomas does not follow Aristotle's text in listing action and passion immediately after the first four predicaments. In this respect, the order he follows in commenting on *Physics* III is closer to that followed by Aristotle in *Metaphysics* V, c. 7. Though Thomas's listing in his Commentary on *Metaphysics* V also differs somewhat from that followed by Aristotle in *Categories,* c. 4, the two agree in naming action and passion as numbers 9 and 10. Action and passion also appear as numbers 9 and 10 in *Topics* I, c. 9. In the incomplete listings in *Posterior Analytics* I, c. 22 and *Physics* V, c. 1, action and passion are placed respectively immediately after relation and in the last two positions.

92. See n. 79 above.

mediate concern in his Commentary on the *Physics,* to clarify the nature of action and passion, has led him there to introduce these as predicaments 6 and 5 rather than as 9 and 10 as in his Commentary on the *Metaphysics.*

There is another interesting difference between his discussion of these in the two Commentaries. In his Commentary on the *Metaphysics* he has indicated that in such modes of predication, that from which the name is derived is partly intrinsic to the subject of which it is affirmed. In other words, it is not to be regarded as purely extrinsic. Thus in the case of action, that from which the name is taken is said to be intrinsic to the subject insofar as the subject is viewed as a principle: "for the principle of action is in the subject." And in the case of being acted upon (passion), that from which the name is taken is in some way intrinsic to the subject which is acted upon: "for *passio* has as its terminus the receiving subject." This is important, it would seem, since it explains why in the first case we can assign action to a given subject, as when we say "Socrates is making a table." At the same time we can say that the corresponding *passio* is realized in the material subject from which the table is being made, as is implied when we say "A table is being made by Socrates."[93]

In the Commentary on the *Physics,* however, Thomas is content simply to include action and passion under the general mode of predication according to which a name is assigned to a subject by reason of something extrinsic. If this extrinsic point of reference is an agent which acts upon the subject being named, we have the predicament passion. If the extrinsic point of reference is rather that upon which the subject being named exercises efficient causation, we assign the predicament action to that subject.[94]

While this difference in nuance between the two derivations of action and passion should not be exaggerated, it should at least be noted. The approach offered in the Commentary on the *Metaphysics* appears to me to be more precise, and also serves better to set action and passion apart from the other predicaments which are applied to a subject by reason of something extrinsic.[95]

While there is no substantial disagreement between these two attempts on Thomas's part to derive the ten predicaments, we may wonder which comes later in time. It is as difficult to answer this question with certainty as it is to determine whether the Commentary on the *Metaphysics* is prior to the Commentary on the *Physics,* or perhaps vice versa. In fact, Weisheipl suggested that Thomas may have been working on the two commentaries at approximately the same time—the *Physics* (at Paris from 1270 to 1271) and the *Metaphysics* (at Paris, and possibly at

93. For the texts see nn. 64 and 65 above.
94. See n. 81 above.
95. In saying that the approach in the Commentary on the *Metaphysics* appears to be more precise, I have in mind the point that it explicitly justifies Thomas's claim that the principle of action is found in the subject (in the case of the predicament action), while *passio* is received in the subject being acted upon.

Naples, from 1269 to 1272). As Weisheipl also warns, we should not assume that Thomas composed his Commentary on the *Metaphysics,* at least in its final version, in the order in which we number its books today. While accepting this final point, Torrell places the Commentary on the *Physics* during the earlier part of Thomas's second teaching period at Paris, ca. 1268–1269. Although he acknowledges the uncertainties surrounding the dating of the Commentary on the *Metaphysics,* he suggests that its beginning may date from the academic year 1270–1271, with the Commentary on Bks VII–XII falling after mid-1271 but before 1272–1273. Since Torrell has been able to take into account more recent research concerning this, he should be followed on this point. Consequently, it now appears that Thomas's derivation of the predicaments in his Commentary on the *Metaphysics* expresses his most mature thought on this issue.[96]

From another standpoint, Thomas's emphasis on the point that the different modes of predication follow upon and reflect different modes of being, while present in both derivations, is developed more fully in the passage from the Commentary on the *Metaphysics.* This is important if we are to view the ten predicaments not as purely logical categories but as of importance for the science of being as being. This emphasis on being is what one would expect in a Commentary on the *Metaphysics.* Somewhat more surprising is the fact that Thomas devoted so much attention to deriving all ten predicaments in his Commentary on the *Physics,* and especially in this particular context. This full derivation of the predicaments hardly seems necessary there for him to clarify Aristotle's understanding of action and passion and defend the claim that they constitute two different predicaments.[97]

Before concluding this section, we should raise another question about Thomas's derivation of the ten predicaments, in particular about the last six—the *sex principia* as they were often referred to by medieval thinkers. Did Thomas regard his derivation or deduction of them as definitive? It seems that he did, although doubt would be expressed by others in the thirteenth and fourteenth centuries concerning whether they really are ten and irreducible. Thus thinkers such as Henry of Ghent, and in the fourteenth century, William of Ockham, would sharply reduce the list. And even someone as sympathetic to Thomas's views on substance and accidents as Godfrey of Fontaines did not regard the number of the

---

96. Weisheipl, *Friar Thomas d'Aquino,* pp. 375–76 (as corrected), 379; Torrell, *Saint Thomas Aquinas,* pp. 231–33, 342, 344.

97. It is true that Thomas had raised a second difficulty in introducing his derivation of the predicaments in his Commentary on the *Physics,* concerning whether motion is also found in substance, quality, quantity, and *ubi,* if it is an action or passion (ed. cit., p. 159, n. 321). For Thomas's answer see n. 324, where he distinguishes between motion as it is realized in extramental reality *(in rerum natura)* and in terms of what is required for its full intelligible content *(ratio).* If Thomas's brief reply to this objection would hardly require the detailed derivation of the predicaments which he offers here, his fuller discussion of Aristotle's restriction of motion to quality, quantity and *ubi* in Bk V, cc. 1–2 does assume the theory of 10 predicaments. See *In V Phys.,* lect. 3, pp. 328–32, esp. nn. 661ff.

predicaments as certainly demonstrated to be ten, even though he was willing to accept this number in practice.[98]

One may put this question another way: Did Thomas regard the last six predicaments as corresponding to and naming distinct modes of being—modes which cannot be reduced to the first four categories? Thomistic interpreters have also been divided concerning this. Some have argued that the last six predicaments could be accounted for either in part or totally by reducing them to some combination of the first four. For instance, it might seem that a combination of relation and quantity could be used to account for predicaments such as "time when," "place where," position, and *habitus*. Others disagree.[99]

It seems to me that in every case Thomas regards the mode of being which justifies a distinct predicamental name as a distinct and irreducible mode of being.

98. This usage—*sex principia*—seems to go back to the *Liber sex principiorum*, written by an unknown twelfth-century Latin, which deals with the last six Aristotelian predicaments. It enjoyed considerable authority and was often joined with the corpus of Aristotle's logical writings, though it was recognized by Thomas's time that the work was not by Aristotle. Some have attributed it to Gilbert of Poitiers, but this seems to be incorrect. For such an attribution see Krempel, *La doctrine*, p. 426, n. 1. On this work see B. G. Dod, "Aristoteles latinus," in *The Cambridge History of Later Medieval Philosophy*, N. Kretzmann et al., eds. (Cambridge, 1982), pp. 48, 50; W. E McMahon, "The *Liber sex principiorum*," pp. 3–12; and for the text *Aristoteles Latinus* I.6–7, L. Minio-Paluello, ed. (Bruges-Paris, 1966). Insofar as the predicaments are regarded as supreme divisions or classes of things (and not as supreme genera of our concepts), Henry of Ghent reduces them to three: substance, quantity, and quality. See his Quodlibet V, q. 6 (Paris, 1518), f. 161v. Note in particular: "... in tota universitate creaturae non sunt nisi tria genera rerum, videlicet substantia, qualitas, quantitas." For discussion and references see J. Paulus, *Henri de Gand*, pp. 158–63. See Paulus's remarks about Henry's *de facto* difference from Aristotle (and Aquinas and others) on this, and similarities with Boethius (pp. 162–63). Though not regarded as a distinct *res* in its own right, relation is extremely important in Henry's account of the categories (see Paulus, pp. 164–72). On Ockham's refusal to admit that, from the viewpoint of natural reason, the ten categories signify distinct and irreducible kinds of entity *(res)* with the exception of substance and quality see E. A. Moody, *The Logic of William of Ockham* (New York, 1965), pp. 131–72; M. McCord Adams, *William of Ockham*, Vol. 1 (Notre Dame, Ind., 1987), cc. 5–8. For Godfrey on this see my *The Metaphysical Thought of Godfrey of Fontaines*, p. 175.

99. For the view that Thomas regards the last six predicaments as purely extrinsic and as implying no new and distinct reality in the subject which is so named, see P. Hoenen, *Cosmologia*, 5th ed. (Rome, 1956), pp. 74–94 (with special emphasis on *ubi*); cited with approval concerning this point by Krempel, p. 430, n. 3. Krempel is hard pressed to find explicit justification in Thomas for this position (the texts he cites on pp. 429–30 about local motion prove nothing about the reality of "being in place" so far as the located subject is concerned). He offers a questionable explanation based on the inappropriate intellectual climate at the time and suggests that for this reason Thomas preferred to refer to the *sex principia* as being named from without rather than to describe them explicitly as purely logical categories (pp. 431–32). See pp. 437–40 for his appeal to relation to account for four of the last six predicaments (excluding action and passion), and pp. 441–50 for his discussion of action and passion. In the first discussion Krempel moves, mistakenly it seems to me, from a remark by Thomas to the effect that the four predicaments in question follow upon relation rather than cause it *(In V Met.,* lect. 17, p. 266, n. 1005) to the conclusion that they are reducible to relation. For a different interpretation regarding the *sex principia*, see Owens, *An Elementary Christian Metaphysics*, pp. 191–209. Even he seems to have some doubts concerning whether *situs*, though clearly real, should be regarded as a distinct category or merely as a specification of *ubi* (p. 206).

No exceptions are made to this in his derivations of the predicaments in his Commentaries on the *Metaphysics* and the *Physics*. Moreover, in another context, *Summa theologiae* I–II, q. 49, a. 1, obj. 2, he states that in order for a predicament to be a predicament, it must be irreducible to another (literally: "not contained under another"). Since he has proceeded to derive ten predicaments in the passages we have just examined, and since in other contexts such as, for instance, *De ente*, c. 1, he states that the predicaments are ten, we should conclude that he regards them as real, as distinct, and as irreducible. As he sees things, something distinctive does happen to a material subject by reason of the fact that it is present in place, for example, and something which cannot be accounted for merely by appealing to that subject's quantity, the quantity of the surrounding medium, and relation. To be in place also involves a distinctive accidental determination or mode of being on the part of the body which is said to be in place.[100]

Today we might prefer to account for such predicaments, and even more so, perhaps, for position and *habitus,* by reducing them to some combination of the first four predicaments. As a philosophical position, something might be said for such efforts. But any such reduction should not be represented as Thomas's personal position. And as regards action and passion, it is even clearer that he regards these as distinct predicaments and as implying distinctive modes of being on the part of the subject which is said to act or to be acted upon. Thomas maintains this view even while holding with Aristotle that the motion involved in such an action and its corresponding passion is one and the same. This does not imply that the action and the passion themselves are not real, or not really distinct from one another.[101]

As regards action, an additional difficulty should at least be mentioned here, though limitations of space will preclude full discussion of it. According to a classical interpretation within Thomism, immanent action falls within the predicament quality, but transitive action does not.[102] While it is clear that immanent action

---

100. ST I–II, q. 49, a. 1, obj. 2: "Sed unum praedicamentum non continetur sub alio. Ergo habitus non est qualitas." While this appears in an objection, Thomas's reply indicates that he accepts the principle invoked in the objection, i.e., that one predicament is not contained under another (Leon. 6.309–10). See *De ente*, c. 1: "Sciendum est igitur quod, sicut in V Metaphysicae Philosophus dicit, ens per se dupliciter dicitur: uno modo quod dividitur per decem genera. . . . Sed primo modo non potest dici ens nisi quod aliquid in re ponit . . ." (Leon. 43.376:1–12).

101. See the text cited in n. 89 above.

102. See Y. Simon, *Introduction à l'ontologie du connaître* (Paris, 1934), p. 97, n. 1, who acknowledges that he cannot cite explicit texts from Thomas to prove that he viewed immanent action as a quality. Nonetheless, Simon is convinced that this must be granted if one is to do justice to Thomas's theory of knowledge. For additional historical notes on a long tradition within Thomism to this same effect, see Owens, *An Elementary Christian Metaphysics,* pp. 194–95, n. 5. Owens himself does not fully subscribe to this view (see pp. 197–98, 202). Krempel, in line with his reductionist effort, includes *both* immanent and transitive action in the category quality (p. 441). Miller distinguishes between the predicament action (where she places transitive action) and immanent action, which she too regards as a quality (see "The Problem of Action," pp. 144–46).

must reside in the agent of such action, what about transitive action? Texts can be cited where Thomas writes that transitive action or operation is in the recipient.[103] But other texts seem to state that action, including transitive action, is in the agent.

An easy solution would be to suggest that only immanent action resides in the agent as in its subject. But Thomas does not restrict this claim to immanent action. For instance, in *Summa contra Gentiles* II, c. 9, he writes:

An action which is not identical with the substance of an agent is present in it as an accident in a subject. Wherefore, action too is counted as one of the nine predicaments of accident.[104]

And in *De potentia*, q. 8, a. 2, he remarks:

. . . nothing prevents something from inhering even though it is not signified as inhering, just as action also is not signified as being in an agent but as from an agent, and nonetheless it is clear that action is in an agent.[105]

Both of these remarks seem to apply to transitive action. The second implies that if action is signified as being from an agent, this is not to deny that it also inheres in that agent.

In attempting to resolve this dilemma we should recall that Thomas accepts Aristotle's view that one and the same motion is involved in both action and passion.[106] Given this, we can understand why Thomas often writes that transitive action or operation is in the recipient. But we should also bear in mind that for Thomas action is a distinct predicament from passion. Hence it must involve a distinctive accidental mode of being. If so, we can also understand why Thomas refers to it as inhering in the agent as in its subject. This mode of being—action—is not reducible to the motion which is produced by the acting agent. Perhaps it is this aspect that Thomas has in mind when he refers to operation as an actuality of

103. For some of these see *De potentia*, q. 10, a. 1: "Est autem duplex operatio: Quaedam quidem transiens ab operante in aliquid extrinsecum, sicut calefactio ab igne in lignum; et haec quidem operatio non est perfectio operantis, sed operati . . . Alia vero est operatio non transiens in aliquid extrinsecum, sed manens in ipso operante, sicut intelligere, sentire, velle, et huiusmodi. Hae autem operationes sunt perfectiones operantis . . ." (ed. cit., p. 254). Also see: *In IX Met.*, lect. 8, p. 447, n. 1863 (". . . quia ipsa actio est in facto, ut aedificatio in eo quod aedificatur"); *In III Phys.*, lect. 4, p. 153, n. 303 ("et sic manifestum est quod actus motus est in mobili, cum sit actus mobilis, causatur tamen in eo a movente"); ibid., n. 325; *In II De anima*, c. 16 (Leon. 45.1:180:146–184). For discussion see Krempel, *La doctrine*, pp. 442–46; Miller, "The Problem," pp. 200–226; F. X. Meehan, *Efficient Causality in Aristotle and St. Thomas* (Washington, D.C., 1940), pp. 213–17; Owens, *An Elementary Christian Metaphysics*, pp. 196–202.

104. "Actio quae non est substantia agentis, inest ei sicut accidens subiecto: unde et actio unum inter novem praedicamenta accidentis computatur" (ed. cit., p. 98).

105. "Unde dicendum est, quod nihil prohibet aliquid esse inhaerens, quod tamen non significatur ut inhaerens, sicut etiam actio non significatur ut in agente, sed ut ab agente, et tamen constat actionem esse in agente" (ed. cit., p. 217). Compare with the text from *De potentia*, q. 10, a. 1 (see n. 103 above). This suggests that we cannot solve the difficulty by holding that Thomas changed his mind.

106. See the text cited above in n. 89.

an operative power, or as an ultimate act or second act or second perfection of an agent.[107]

This in turn is closely connected with another distinctive view defended by Aquinas—that any created agent or substance can act or operate only by means of really distinct powers. These powers fall within the predicament quality (its second species) and are related to their substantial subject as acts to potency. An action, including a transitive action, I would suggest, may in turn be viewed as a second act which directly inheres in and informs its corresponding operative power.[108] From this perspective it will again follow that action, including transitive action, resides in the acting subject by means of that subject's operative power. Viewed from the side of the motion which is produced by the acting agent, of course, Thomas can continue to say that action is present in the recipient as in its subject.[109]

3. "Definitions" of Substance and Accident

Though Thomas's derivation or deduction of the predicaments is interesting, still more significant is the fundamental distinction he draws between that which exists in itself (substance) and that which exists in something else (accident). He does not appear to hold that we first discover accidents as such and then reason from them to knowledge of substance as their cause. What we first discover are

---

107. Certain texts concerning operation might be cited to support this reading, for instance, *De spiritualibus creaturis*, a. 11: "Sicut autem ipsum esse est actualitas quaedam essentiae, ita operari est actualitas operativae potentiae seu virtutis" (ed. cit., p. 412); ST I–II, q. 3, a. 2: "Manifestum est autem quod operatio est ultimus actus operantis; unde et actus secundus a Philosopho nominatur, in II *De anima* . . ." (Leon. 6.27); SCG II, c. 46: "Amplius. Perfectio secunda in rebus addit supra primam perfectionem" (ed. cit., p. 139); ST I, q. 54, a. 1: "Actio enim est proprie actualitas virtutis; sicut esse est actualitas substantiae vel essentiae" (Leon. 5.39). In all of these contexts, however, with the possible exception of the first text, Thomas may be referring only to immanent action or operation, and not to transitive action. In the first text he may have both in mind, since he subsequently goes on to argue for the specific point that the powers of the soul are distinct from the soul's essence. On most of these texts see Meehan, *Efficient Causality*, pp. 216ff., and on the first Owens, *An Elementary Christian Metaphysics*, p. 197, n. 16.

108. See the continuation of the text from *De spiritualibus creaturis* as cited in the previous note. Also on this general issue see ST I, q. 54, a. 1 ("Utrum intelligere angeli sit eius substantia"); ST I, q. 77, a. 1 ("Utrum ipsa essentia animae sit eius potentia"); Quodlibet X, q. 3, a. 1 (Leon. 25.1.130–31); *Quaestiones de anima*, q. 12 (Leon. 24.1.109–10). For a very early treatment see In I *Sent.*, d. 3, q. 4, a. 2 (Mandonnet ed., Vol. 1, pp. 116–17). For discussion see P. Künzle, *Das Verhältnis der Seele zu ihren Potenzen. Problemgeschichtliche Untersuchungen von Augustin bis und mit Thomas von Aquin* (Freiburg, Switzerland, 1956), pp. 171–218. For more on this see Ch. VIII, Section 4 below.

109. Meehan attempts to resolve this apparent dilemma by suggesting that when Thomas refers to transitive action as the perfection of the thing acted upon he is using the term "perfection" in the sense of efficient causality. And when he refers to such action as a perfection of the acting subject he is taking the term "perfection" in the sense of formal causality. This is to say that action when so viewed formally perfects the acting subject, though it does so as an accidental or secondary formal cause. See pp. 214–16. Promising though Meehan's suggestion is, it is an interpretation rather than a solution that can be found in Thomas's texts.

beings. Once we have formulated the general notion of being ("that which is"), we are in position to distinguish therein between that which exists in itself, and that which exists in something else. This has been discussed above.[110]

Given this, we might think that Thomas would be content to define substance, to the extent it can be defined, as that which exists in itself, and accident as that which exists in something else. Thomas in fact refers to substance in this way frequently enough, as in some passages already considered.[111] Nonetheless, as Gilson has pointed out in an interesting article, almost from the beginning of his career Thomas repeatedly returns to a point which he also attributes to Avicenna: being in itself *(per se)* is not the definition of substance.[112]

At first sight, this claim is surprising. It is easy enough to understand why theological considerations concerning Eucharistic transubstantiation might lead Aquinas to qualify the definition of accident. Instead of referring to an accident as that which exists in something else, such concerns might lead him to qualify this so as to read: an accident is that to which it belongs to exist in something else. This will leave open the possibility that certain accidents might be kept in existence by divine power even when their original and proper subject no longer exists, as in the Eucharist. But such concerns would not seem to require any corresponding modification of the definition of substance.[113]

In rejecting "being in itself *(per se)*" as a definition of substance and in citing Avicenna as his authority for this rejection, Thomas has created two problems for his readers. First of all, it is difficult if not impossible to find this exact quotation in the Latin translation of Avicenna's *Metaphysics*. Secondly, Thomas's reasons for rejecting this definition should be explored, as well as his views concerning the proper way of defining or at least of describing substance.

---

110. See above in this chapter, n. 4. Here my interpretation of Thomas differs to some extent from that proposed by B. F. Brown: "The knowledge of substance, therefore, is *per accidens*—accidental in the most literal sense. The *per* in this case means that a substance is known through its accidents, in the way in which a cause is known through its effects. Our knowledge of material substance and essences is the result of an inference *a posteriori:* from the posterior effect to its prior cause." See his *Accidental Being: A Study in the Metaphysics of St. Thomas Aquinas* (Lanham, Md., 1985), pp. 82–83. The texts cited there by Brown illustrate how cautious Thomas was in attributing to us any direct knowledge of the essential (or substantial) differences between material forms. They do not imply that Thomas thinks we first come to an explicit (and intellectual) knowledge of accident and then infer the existence of some underlying subject (substance).

111. See, for instance, the texts cited above in notes 5, 7, 16, 23, 32, 51, 72.

112. "Quasi Definitio Substantiae," in *St. Thomas Aquinas 1274–1974: Commemorative Studies,* ed. A. Maurer et al. (Toronto, 1974), Vol. 1, pp. 111–29. Here as throughout this chapter I prefer to render the Latin *ens per se* as being *in* itself rather than more literally as being *through* itself. My reasons for so doing are twofold: (1) because when applied to substance this is surely what Thomas means by so describing substance, i.e., as that which exists in itself (and not in something else), or as that which exists in its own right; (2) because to translate it as being *through* itself mightly possibly lead to the mistaken interpretation that Thomas regards substances (finite) as beings which do not depend on something else for their existence, i.e., as uncaused.

113. See the final part of this chapter for more on the definition of accident.

As regards the first difficulty, after considerable effort Gilson has managed to show that there is some foundation in the Latin translation of Avicenna's *Metaphysics* for Thomas to attribute this view to him. Even for this attribution to be successful, one must concede that "not to be in a subject" (or better, "to be not in a subject") can be identified with "to be in itself." Gilson's identification and interpretation of this particular passage from Avicenna is highly plausible.[114] If correct, it is another illustration of how likely Thomas was to quote a difficult and possibly confusing text from the Latin Avicenna *ad sensum* rather than *ad litteram.*

Of greater concern to us here is the second issue: Why does Thomas reject this as a definition of substance, and what does he substitute for it? In what appears to be his earliest explicit discussion of this, d. 8, q. 4, a. 2 from his Commentary on I *Sentences,* Thomas considers an argument in support of the claim that God is included in the predicament substance. According to objection 2, substance "is that which is not in a subject, but which is a being in itself [*per se*]." Since this description is especially true of God, it follows that God is included within the genus substance.[115]

In replying to this argument, Thomas counters that, as Avicenna tells us, substance cannot be defined as "that which is not in a subject." Being, reasons Thomas, is not a genus. And the negative part of the proposed definition—"not in a subject"—posits nothing. Therefore, when I speak of "being which is not in a subject," I am not referring to any genus.[116]

If we wonder why this is so, Thomas appeals to a point we have already seen him make in other contexts: whatever is included in a genus must signify a quiddity which does not include the act of being *(esse)* in its intelligible content. In fact, the term being *(ens)* does not signify quiddity but rather the act of being *(actus essendi)*. Therefore it does not follow that if something is not in a subject, it is included in the genus substance. What does follow is this. If something has a quiddity to which it belongs to exist not in a subject, then it is included within the genus substance. But this (to have a quiddity to which it belongs to exist not in a subject) is not true of God. Therefore God does not fall within the genus substance.[117]

114. Gilson, "Quasi Definitio Substantiae," pp. 112–14. For the text from the Latin Avicenna see *Liber de philosophia prima,* Vol. 2, tr. VIII, c. 4 (pp. 403–4). Also see A. Judy, "Avicenna's *Metaphysics* in the *Summa contra gentiles* (III)," *Angelicum* 53 (1976), pp. 201–8; H. Hoping, *Weisheit als Wissen des Ursprungs. Philosophie und Theologie in der "Summa contra gentiles" des Thomas von Aquin* (Freiburg im Breisgau, 1997), p. 153, n. 171.

115. "Praeterea, substantia est quod non est in subiecto, sed est ens per se. Cum igitur Deo hoc maxime conveniat, videtur quod ipse sit in genere substantiae" (Mandonnet ed., Vol. 1, p. 221).

116. Ibid., pp. 222–23: ". . . ista definitio, secundum Avicennam . . . , non potest esse substantiae: substantia est quae non est in subiecto. Ens enim non est genus. Haec autem negatio 'non in subiecto' nihil ponit; unde hoc quod dico, ens non est in subiecto, non dicit aliquod genus. . . ."

117. See pp. 222–23: ". . . quia in quolibet genere oportet significare quidditatem aliquam, ut dictum est, de cuius intellectu non est esse. Ens autem non dicit quidditatem, sed solum actum essendi, cum sit principium ipsum; et ideo non sequitur: est non in subiecto, ergo est in genere

Certain points should be singled out in this reasoning. First of all, Thomas supports the claim which he attributes to Avicenna, that substance cannot be defined as "that which is not in a subject," because Thomas is convinced that being is not a genus. Although in the present context he does not spell out his reasons for denying that being is a genus, we have seen some of these elsewhere.[118] We shall return to this issue below. Secondly, the proper description of substance is this, "to have a quiddity *to which it belongs* to exist not in a subject." Finally, because this cannot be said of God, God does not fall within the genus substance.

If we ask Thomas why the last-mentioned claim is true, he will reply that it follows from the fact that God's essence is identical with his act of being *(esse)*. As Thomas has already reasoned in the corpus of this same article, for something to be included in a genus, it must have a quiddity that differs from its act of being. Here the reader may recall his argumentation for the essence-*esse* distinction based on membership in a genus or species.[119]

In another passage taken from his Commentary on Bk IV of the *Sentences,* Thomas succinctly sums up these views concerning the definition of substance. To exist in itself is not the definition of substance; for this description does not indicate the quiddity of substance but its *esse*. The definition or quasi-definition of substance is this: "a thing which has a quiddity to which it is given or belongs to exist not in something else."[120]

In order to appreciate more fully Thomas's reasons for holding this position concerning the definition of substance, we shall now turn to some passages from his more mature writings. One of the most interesting appears in *Summa contra Gentiles* I, c. 25. There again he is attempting to show that God is not contained in any genus. His fourth argument in support of this reminds us of the reasoning we have just seen in his Commentary on the *Sentences,* but now it is spelled out in greater detail.[121]

According to this argument, a thing is included in a genus by reason of its quiddity, since a genus is predicated in quidditative fashion *(in quid)*. But God's quiddity is identical with his act of being *(esse)*, as Thomas has shown in c. 22. We cannot say that God is present in a genus by reason of his act of being *(esse)*, contin-

---

substantiae; sed oportet addi: est habens quidditatem quam consequitur esse non in subiecto; ergo est in genere substantiae. Sed hoc dictum Deo non convenit, ut dictum est."

118. See Ch. III above, Section 1, pp. 68–71.

119. Ed. cit., p. 222. Thomas introduces this argument: "Tertia ratio subtilior est Avicennae." For the text see Ch. V above, n. 69.

120. See *In IV Sent.*, d. 12, q. 1, a. 1, ql. 1, ad 2 (Moos ed., Vol. 4, p. 499): ". . . sicut probat Avicenna in sua *Meta.*, per se existere non est definitio substantiae; quia per hoc non demonstratur quidditas eius, sed esse eius. Et sua quidditas non est suum esse; alias non posset esse genus, quia esse non potest esse commune per modum generis, cum singula contenta in genere differant secundum esse. Sed definitio vel quasi definitio substantiae est res habens quidditatem, cui acquiritur esse vel debetur non in alio."

121. C. 25 is directed to this topic: "Quod Deus non est in aliquo genere" (ed. cit., p. 26).

ues Thomas, for then being *(ens)*, which signifies the act of being, would itself be a genus.[122] Thomas's point here is that given the identity of essence and act of being in God, we cannot say that God is present in a genus by reason of his essence without implying that he is included therein by reason of his act of being *(esse)*. And this would be to make *esse* and therefore being *(ens)* a genus.

In order to prove that being *(ens)* is not a genus, Thomas refers to Aristotle's procedure. If being were a genus, we would have to identify a difference which would restrict being to its particular species. But no difference participates in a genus in such a way that the genus is included within the intelligible content of the difference; for then a genus would be twice included within the definition of the species.[123] (For instance, if the difference rational already includes the genus animal in its intelligible content, to define man as a rational animal would really be to define him as a "rational animal animal.")

Therefore a difference must be something in addition to the intelligible content of the genus. But nothing, and therefore no difference, can fall outside the intelligible content of being, since being is included within the intelligibility of all those things of which it is predicated. Therefore being cannot be contracted by any difference. It follows from this that being is not a genus and in turn from this that God is not present in any genus.[124]

Thomas then poses an objection for himself. Someone might argue that while the name "substance" cannot properly apply to God for the reason that God does not stand under accidents, the reality signified by the name substance does apply to God. Therefore God is in the genus substance. This follows because a substance is a being in itself *(per se)*, and to be such is also true of God.[125]

To this Thomas replies that "being in itself" is not the definition of substance. He has already shown that being *(ens)* is not a genus. The "in itself" part of the proposed definition seems to imply nothing but a pure negation, that is, the fact that something does not exist in something else. And a pure negation cannot serve as a genus. It follows from this that substance should rather be understood as a thing to which it belongs to exist not in a subject. The name "thing" *(res)* is taken from the substance's quiddity, and the name "being" *(ens)* from its act of being *(esse)*. Hence implied in the meaning of substance is that it have a quiddity to which it belongs to exist not in something else. And this, Thomas contends, cannot be said of God.[126]

---

122. "Amplius. Unumquodque collocatur in genere per rationem suae quidditatis: genus enim praedicatur *in quid est.* Sed quidditas Dei est ipsum suum esse. Secundum quod non collocatur aliquid in genere: quia sic ens esset genus, quod significat ipsum esse" (ibid.).

123. Ibid. Note in particular: "Nulla autem differentia participat genus, ita scilicet quod genus sit in ratione differentiae, quia sic genus poneretur bis in definitione speciei. . . ." For Aristotle see *Metaphysics* III, c. 3 (998b 22–27).

124. Ed. cit., p. 26.

125. Ed. cit., p. 27.

126. Ibid. Note in particular: "Oportet igitur quod ratio substantiae intelligatur hoc modo, quod

The reader may again ask: Why cannot this be said of God? Once more Thomas's denial follows from his identification of essence and act of being *(esse)* in God and his distinction of these in everything else. As Thomas has explained, a substance is a thing to which it belongs to exist not in a subject. The term thing *(res)* implies that it has an essence, while the term being is taken from its act of being. Apparently Thomas is convinced that this formulation also implies that the two, essence and act of being, must be distinct in everything that meets the definition of substance.[127]

Thomas spells out this thinking more succinctly and perhaps more clearly in his still later *De potentia,* q. 7, a. 3.[128] According to the fourth objection, the definition of substance, to exist in itself, applies to God to the maximum degree. Thomas writes:

To the fourth objection it must be said that being in itself is not the definition of substance, as Avicenna says. For being cannot be a genus for anything, as the Philosopher proves, since nothing can be added to being which does not participate in it; but a difference should not participate in its genus. But if substance can be defined, notwithstanding the fact that it is the most general genus, this will be its definition: "substance is a thing [*res*] to whose quiddity it belongs to be not in something (else)." Thus the definition of substance will not apply to God, who does not have a quiddity in addition to his *esse.* Therefore God is not in the genus substance but is above every substance.[129]

Not only does Thomas again reject "being in itself" as a definition of substance and propose a substitute. This time he implies that this substitute is not a definition in the proper sense. If substance can be defined, its definition will be "a thing to whose quiddity it belongs to be not in something (else)." As will be recalled, already in his Commentary on IV *Sentences* he had referred to this as a definition or quasi-definition.[130]

If we wonder why substance cannot be defined in the proper sense, the reason is suggested by the text. Substance itself is the most general genus. Therefore, there can be no more general genus of which it would be a species. By having denied

---

substantia sit res cui conveniat esse non in subiecto; nomen autem rei a quidditate imponitur, sicut nomen entis ab esse. . . ."

127. Ibid. "Hoc autem Deo non convenit: nam non habet quidditatem nisi suum esse." Also see arguments two and three in this same c. 25. Both maintain that what falls in the genus cannot be identified with its *esse* (see p. 26).

128. "Tertio quaeritur utrum Deus sit in aliquo genere" (Pession ed., pp. 193–94).

129. "Ad quartum dicendum, quod ens per se non est definitio substantiae, ut Avicenna dicit. Ens enim non potest esse alicuius genus, ut probat Philosophus, cum nihil possit addi ad ens quod non participet ipsum; differentia vero non debet participare genus. Sed si substantia possit habere definitionem, non obstante quod est genus generalissimum, erit eius definitio: quod substantia est res cuius quidditati debetur esse non in aliquo. Et sic non conveniet definitio substantiae Deo, qui non habet quidditatem suam praeter suum esse. Unde Deus non est in genere substantiae, sed est supra omnem substantiam" (p. 194).

130. See the text as cited above in n. 120.

that being is a genus, Thomas has in effect concluded that substance itself is the most general genus of all.

Thomas repeats the essentials of this reasoning once again in his still slightly later treatment in *Summa theologiae* I, q. 3, a. 5, ad 1. As before his purpose in this article is to show that God is not contained within any genus. In responding to the first objection, Thomas continues to reject the possibility of simply defining substance as "being in itself" *(ens per se)*. However, here he does not explicitly dismiss but appears to admit the possibility of describing substance in another way, that is, as an "essence to which it belongs to exist in itself."[131]

From these texts we may draw the following conclusions. According to Thomas: (1) "being in itself" is not an appropriate definition of substance; (2) if substance could be defined in the strict sense, its definition would be "a thing to whose quiddity it belongs to exist not in something else"; (3) even this is not a definition of substance in the strict sense but only a quasi-definition.

With these conclusions in mind we may now turn to a related issue, the definition of accident. In the continuation of a text from his Commentary on IV *Sentences* (d. 12, q. 1, a. 1, ql. 1, ad 2) which we have examined above, Thomas not only makes the point that the quasi-definition of substance is a thing to whose quiddity it belongs to exist not in something else; he comments that "to be in a subject" is not the definition of accident. An accident is rather a "thing to which it belongs to be in something else." This can never be separated from the nature of an accident. By reason of its quiddity, it will always be that kind of thing.[132]

But as Thomas also explains, divine power may bring it to pass that an accident actually does exist apart from and without its substantial subject, as in the Eucharist. This does not do violence to Thomas's proposed definition of an accident. Even such an accident will be that to which it belongs to exist in something else.[133]

Within this same context Thomas has considered another objection. If the *esse* of a thing should be separated from that being, that being would be nonbeing. Since God cannot make two contradictories true at one and the same time, not even he can separate the *esse* of a thing from that being. But the *esse* of an accident

---

131. Leon. 4.44. Note that he adds the point that the *esse* of a being that falls within the genus substance differs from its essence: ". . . dicendum quod substantiae nomen non significat hoc solum quod est per se esse. . . . Sed significat essentiam cui competit sic esse, idest per se esse: quod tamen esse non est ipsa eius essentia." Note too that here he substitutes "an essence to which it belongs . . . to exist in itself" for "an essence to which it belongs to exist not in something else" as we have seen in the other passages.

132. "Et similiter esse in subiecto non est definitio accidentis, sed e contrario res cui debetur esse in alio. Et hoc nunquam separatur ab aliquo accidente, nec separari potest; quia illi rei quae est accidens, secundum rationem suae quidditatis, semper debetur esse in alio" (Moos ed., Vol. 4, p. 499). For the immediately preceding text see n. 120 above.

133. Ibid. "Sed potest esse quod illud quod debetur alicui secundum rationem suae quidditatis, ei virtute divina agente non conveniat. Et sic patet quod facere accidens esse sine substantia, non est separare definitionem a definito."

is to inhere *(inesse)*. Therefore God cannot bring it to pass that an accident does not inhere in a subject.[134]

In replying to this objection, Thomas comments that to inhere *(inesse)* does not describe the *esse* of an accident in unqualified fashion, but rather the mode of being which pertains to it insofar as it is ordered to the proximate cause of its *esse*. (By the proximate cause of its *esse* we may assume that he has in mind the substantial subject which stands under the accident and serves as its cause, at least as its material cause.) But when the ordering of an accident to its proximate cause is removed, the accident may continue to be ordered to its first cause. According to its ordering to its first cause, an accident's mode of being is to be *from* another, not *in* another. Because of this, Thomas concludes that God can cause an accident to exist and yet not to inhere in a subject. In this case the *esse* of the accident will not be eliminated, but only its mode of being in or existing in another.[135]

From these two replies we may draw the following conclusions. So far as Thomas is concerned, the mode of being which is proper to an accident is to inhere in something else, that is, in a substantial subject. This mode of being is known as its "existing in" or inhering *(inesse)*.

Secondly, by divine power this mode of being, existing in, can be removed from an accident without militating against the fact that the accident still depends upon something else as the first cause of its *esse,* and without doing violence to its nature as an accident. It continues to be a quiddity to which it belongs to exist in something else.

Finally, this precision regarding the appropriate definition of an accident would probably not have occurred to Thomas or to other Christian thinkers but for their belief in Eucharistic transubstantiation. In order to account for this they maintained that the species of bread and wine (Aristotelian accidents as they saw things) can remain after the substance of bread and wine has been changed into Christ's body and blood.[136] It is interesting to observe that a number of propositions that denied that accidents can be kept in existence apart from their substantial subject were included among the 219 condemned by Stephen Tempier, Bishop of Paris, in 1277.[137]

In Quodlibet 9, q. 3, a. 1 dating from Christmas 1257 and therefore from Thomas's first teaching period as a Master in theology at Paris, he develops this same

134. Ed. cit., p. 496 (obj. 1).

135. Ed. cit., p. 499.

136. See Gilson, "Quasi Definitio Substantiae," pp. 122–24. Cf. B. Brown, *Accidental Being,* pp. 111–14.

137. See propositions 196–199 (according to the Mandonnet numbering). For discussion see R. Hissette, *Enquête sur les 219 articles condamnés à Paris le 7 mars 1277* (Louvain-Paris, 1977), pp. 287–90. See his discussion there of an anonymous commentary on the *Physics* as a possible source for some of these. Cf. A. Zimmermann, ed., *Ein Kommentar zur Physik des Aristoteles aus der Pariser Artistenfakultät um 1273* (Berlin, 1968), pp. xxvii–xxviii.

thinking once more. This time an objection was raised by a participant at the quod-libetal disputation against the possibility that in the Eucharist accidents can continue to exist without their substantial subject. According to the second objection, of whatever a definition is predicated, so is that which is defined also predicated. But the definition or description of substance is a "being in itself." If after Eucharistic transubstantiation accidents remain in themselves without their substance, it follows that these accidents themselves will then be substances.[138]

Thomas begins his reply by recalling that, according to Avicenna, *esse* cannot be included in the definition of a genus or species. This follows because, while all individuals have in common the generic or specific definition, the genus or species is not realized in the individual members according to a single act of being *(esse)*. Thomas quickly rejects the description of substance as "that which exists in itself" or of accident as "that which exists in something else." These are only circumlocutions for the correct descriptions. A substance is a "thing to whose nature it belongs to exist not in something else." An accident is a "thing to whose nature it belongs to exist in something else."[139]

In light of this, Thomas concludes that if miraculously, i.e., through divine power, an accident does not exist in a subject, it does not thereby meet the definition of substance. In other words, it will not thereby be turned into a substance. It will still not be owing to its nature not to exist in something else. Nor does such an accident cease to be defined as an accident; its nature will still be such that it belongs to it to exist in something else.[140] Finally, near the end of his career, Thomas makes these same points once again in *Summa theologiae* III, q. 77, a. 1, ad 2.[141]

These passages are important because they reinforce the point that Thomas refuses to define substance as being in itself, or to define accident as that which exists in something else. But they are interesting for another reason. In the texts we had previously considered, strictly philosophical concerns accounted for Thomas's refusal to define substance as that which exists in itself. These concerns followed from

138. Leon. 25.1.97–98. Note in particular: ". . . si ergo in sacramento altaris accidentia sunt per se, non in subiecto, sequitur quod sint substantiae. . . ." Also see the note to lines 15–16 for a valuable set of references to earlier and contemporary usages of *ens per se* to define substance, including Alexander of Hales, the *Summa fratris Alexandri*, Albert, and Bonaventure. The Leonine editor (Gauthier) comments that this definition is not really found in Aristotle but seems to derive from John Damascene's *Dialectica* in its translation by Robert Grosseteste.

139. Leon. 25.1.99:78–90. Note especially: "Et ideo haec non est vera definitio substantiae: 'Substantia est quod per se est', vel <accidentis>: 'Accidens est quod est in alio', sed est circumlocutio verae descriptionis, quae talis intelligitur: 'Substantia est res cuius naturae debetur esse non in alio'; 'Accidens vero est res, cuius naturae debetur esse in alio'."

140. Leon. 25.1.99:90–95.

141. This article asks: "Utrum accidentia remaneant in hoc Sacramento sine subiecto" (Leon. 12.193). See p. 194 for the reply to objection 2. After rejecting the faulty definitions of substance and accident Thomas substitutes: "sed quidditati seu essentiae substantiae competit habere esse non in subiecto; quidditati autem sive essentiae accidentis competit habere esse in subiecto."

his philosophical conviction that substance is not to be regarded as a species of a still higher genus, i.e., being, and that membership in the predicament substance implies distinction between the essence and the act of being *(esse)* of any such being. These points in turn led Thomas to deny that God falls in the genus substance.

The texts just considered show that this general theory dovetails with another and strictly theological concern. Far from admitting that the accidents of bread and wine which survive after Eucharistic transubstantiation have become substances, Thomas responds that they both fail to meet his proposed "quasi-definition" of substance and continue to fall under the definition of accidents. They continue to be natures or quiddities to which it belongs to exist in something else.

Substance, Accidents, and *Esse*

In the previous chapter we have examined Thomas's views concerning the general nature of substance and accident, the deduction or derivation of the predicaments, and the appropriate "definitions" of substance and accident. With this background in mind we are now in position to concentrate on certain more particular issues which are especially characteristic of his metaphysics of substance and accident. Because of his emphasis on the role of the act of being *(esse)* within the metaphysical structure of finite beings, we may now ask how Thomas correlates this with his views on substance and accident. Regarding finite substances, what is the precise relationship between substance (especially when taken as the individual subject or supposit) and *esse*? Regarding accidents, does each accident enjoy its own act of being *(esse)* in addition to and in distinction from that of its substantial subject? Moreover, some interesting questions arise concerning Thomas's views on the causal relationship between substance and accidents and, in particular, on the relationship between the soul and its powers.

With these issues in mind, we shall divide the present chapter into four parts: (1) *esse* and the individual subject *(suppositum)*; (2) accidents and accidental *esse;* (3) the causal relationship between substance and accidents; (4) the relationship between the soul and its powers.

1. *Esse* and the Individual Subject *(Suppositum)*

As we have seen in the preceding chapter, Thomas frequently distinguishes two important senses in which substance may be understood: (1) as essence or nature or quiddity; (2) as the individual subject *(suppositum)*. If we cannot identify essence or nature or quiddity as he uses it in this division with second substance, we can identity the individual subject *(suppositum)* with first substance as Aristotle explains the latter in the *Categories*. Our findings so far have shown that Thomas correlates the individual subject or supposit and nature as whole and as formal part. This is clear at least in his discussions of material entities. In such beings there is some kind of distinction between the individual subject (supposit) and nature, and one that is not merely mind-dependent or logical.[1]

In the present discussion we shall concentrate on the metaphysical structure of first substance or the subject (supposit). In so doing we shall be especially interested in the role Thomas assigns therein to the act of being *(esse)*. Because many of his statements concerning this arise from discussions having to do with the relationship between nature and supposit (i.e., the individual subject), we shall begin with such passages. Even metaphysicians who reject a real distinction between essence and *esse* may find it necessary to distinguish in some way between essence or nature and the existing or subsisting subject. This need would seem to be heightened for Christian thinkers because of their belief that the human nature of Christ, while being individuated, is not thereby constituted as a distinct person (or intellectual supposit). And the possibility of distinguishing between nature and supposit would seem to be greater for Aquinas precisely because he defends a real distinction between essence and act of being *(esse)*.[2]

As will be recalled from our previous discussion, Thomas, following Aristotle, holds that a first substance is the ultimate subject, that is, that which serves as a subject in propositions in such fashion that it is not predicated of anything else. He refers to it as a particular something *(hoc aliquid)* which subsists in itself and is separate because it is distinct from all else and cannot be communicated to anything else. This description appears in his Commentary on *Metaphysics* V and, therefore, in a strictly philosophical context.[3] At the same time, by noting that it is distinct from all others and cannot be communicated to anything else, Thomas has singled out important characteristics of the individual subject or supposit. To put it another way, because of these characteristics it is separate, i.e., it is that which exists in itself rather than in something else.[4]

---

1. See Ch. VII, above, Section 1.

2. For discussion of different ways in which a number of later thirteenth-century thinkers— Henry of Ghent, Giles of Rome, and Godfrey of Fontaines—approached this topic see my *The Metaphysical Thought of Godfrey of Fontaines,* pp. 227–45. Of these only Giles of Rome defended a real distinction between essence and existence.

3. See *In V Met.,* lect. 10, p. 242, n. 903, as cited above in Ch. VII, n. 16.

4. For more on the incommunicability which Thomas associates with a person (i.e., an intellectual supposit or subject), see *In III Sent.,* d. 5, q. 2, a. 1, ad 2: ". . . triplex incommunicabilitas est de ratione personae: scilicet *partis,* secundum quod est completum; et *universalis,* secundum quod est subsistens: et *assumptibilis,* secundum quod id quod assumitur transit in personalitatem alterius et non habet personalitatem propriam" (Moos ed., Vol. 3, p. 200). Here Thomas is arguing that it was fitting for a divine person (the Word) to assume a human nature. Nonetheless, we may assume that, *mutatis mutandis,* he would assign these three ways in which a person cannot be communicated to any individual subject or supposit, i.e., a supposit cannot be communicated to something else in the way (1) a part is assumed by a whole, or (2) a universal is in some way communicated to individuals, or (3) a given nature might be assumed by another supposit so as not to subsist in its own right.

As we have seen Thomas indicating in his *De potentia* q. 9, a. 1, substance taken as subject has two characteristics. First of all, it needs no extrinsic foundation which would support it; it is sustained in itself and is therefore said to subsist. This means that it exists in itself and not in something else. Secondly, it serves as the foundation for accidents. Insofar as we wish to emphasize the first characteristic, the fact that it subsists in itself, Thomas notes that we may describe it in Greek as οὐσίωσις and in Latin as *subsistentia*. Insofar as we stress the second characteristic, we refer to it in Greek as *hypostasis* and in Latin as *prima substantia* (first substance).[5] Hence if *hypostasis* and first substance differ in name, they are one and the same in reality.[6]

In his attempt to account for that which distinguishes an individual subject or supposit from its essence or nature or quiddity, two possibilities seem to be open to Thomas. On the one hand, he might simply appeal to the difference between the individuating characteristics which are present in concrete material subjects or substances, and the nature which is realized in each of them. He often turns to this in accounting for the diversity between the two, as in our passage from *De potentia*, q. 9, a. 1. Since according to Thomas there is no matter in angelic substances, it will follow from this approach that in them there is no real distinction between nature and the individual subject or supposit.[7]

On the other hand, Thomas might appeal to his theory of real composition and distinction of essence and act of being *(esse)* in all finite substances. If we include the act of being in our understanding of the subject or supposit, it will follow from this approach that in every finite substance, angels included, the subject or supposit will differ from its essence or nature. Thomas reasons in this way in Quodlibet 2, q. 2, a. 2, as we shall shortly see.[8] Puzzling, however, is the fact that he usually does not speak this way. More frequently he holds that nature and supposit are identical in created spirits or angels.

For instance, in his early Commentary on Bk III of the *Sentences* (d. 5, q. 1, a. 3), Thomas is concerned with showing that in Christ there is only one person. He observes that in certain cases nature and person differ really and in other cases only conceptually *(secundum rationem)*. By nature he has in mind the quiddity of a thing which is signified by its definition. By person he rather means this particular something *(hoc aliquid)* which subsists in its given nature. If we bear in mind that for Thomas a person is a rational or intellectual supposit, we can easily see that here

---

5. Ed. cit., Vol. 1, p. 226; cited in Ch. VII above, n. 32.

6. On this identification of the individual substance as first substance or *hypostasis* see ST I, q. 29, a. 1. Cf. *In I Sent.*, d. 23, q. 1, a. 1 (Mandonnet ed., Vol. 1, pp. 553–57), especially: "Ideo aliter dicendum est, secundum Boetium, ut sumatur differentia horum nominum, 'essentia, subsistentia, substantia,' secundum significationem actuum a quibus imponuntur, scilicet esse, subsistere, substare" (pp. 554–55). Also see *In VII Met.*, lect. 2, nn. 1270–1274, and the text cited in Ch. VII above, n. 38.

7. Ed. cit., p. 226. See Ch. VII, n. 33.

8. See n. 22 below.

he is going to allow for a real distinction between nature and the individual subject or supposit in certain instances.[9]

As Thomas goes on to explain, in simple beings which lack matter, the simple being is identical with its quiddity.[10] But the quiddity of a composite being is not identical with that composite being. Humanity, for example, cannot be identified with a human being. To support this final claim, Thomas reasons that the meaning of humanity (or quiddity or nature) includes only the principles essential to human being taken as human being. Those things which apply only to the determination of matter whereby nature is rendered individual are not contained within the meaning of human being. They are included in the meaning of Socrates. This is to say, they are included in that whereby Socrates is this individual and divided from other individual human beings. Therefore, because humanity (quiddity) is taken as a part, it does not include in its meaning the whole which is realized in the subsisting subject. And because it is only the composite whole which subsists, while a part is merely had by its whole, humanity itself does not subsist. Socrates, this individual human being, subsists as that which has humanity.[11]

On the other hand, the expression "human being" signifies both that which is essential to human being as such and individuating characteristics. It signifies the essential characteristics in a determined fashion, and the individuating notes in an undetermined fashion, whether they are these or those. Because human being, unlike humanity, is taken as a whole, it can be predicated of Socrates. Socrates is the subject which has humanity, and we can say that Socrates is a human being. Human being taken universally does not subsist, but this human being, to whom the meaning of person applies, subsists.[12]

In sum, it belongs to a person (and therefore a supposit) to be something distinct which subsists in itself and includes all that is found in a thing. Nature includes only the essential principles. In the case of simple beings nature and person (or supposit) do not really differ. In them nature is not received by any matter which would individuate it; a nature subsists in itself. Insofar as we consider the

9. Moos ed., Vol. 3, p. 196. Note in particular: "Natura enim, secundum quod hic loquimur, est quidditas rei quam significat sua definitio. Persona autem est hoc aliquid quod subsistit in natura illa."

10. "In simplicibus autem quae carent materia . . . ipsum simplex est sua quidditas." Ibid. Thomas had already made the same point in his *De ente*, c. 4. See Leon. 43.376:77–79. In both texts Thomas attributes this position to Avicenna. For this see his *Liber de Philosophia prima V–X*, Van Riet ed., Bk V, c. 5, p. 274:57–58: "Quidditas autem omnis simplicis est ipsummet simplex: nihil enim est ibi receptibile suae quidditatis."

11. Moos ed., p. 196. Note in particular: "Et ideo, quia humanitas non includit in sua significatione totum quod est in re subsistente in natura, cum sit quasi pars, non praedicatur; et quia non subsistit nisi quod est compositum, et pars a suo toto habetur, ideo humanitas non subsistit, sed Socrates, et ipse est habens humanitatem."

12. Ibid. Note: "Homo autem significat utrumque, et essentialia et individuantia, sed diversimode; quia essentialia significat determinate, individuantia vero indeterminate, vel haec vel illa. Et ideo homo, cum sit totum, potest praedicari de Socrate et dicitur habens humanitatem. . . ."

essential principles of such a thing, we may speak of its nature; insofar as we think of it as subsisting, we may describe it as a person, and hence as a supposit. In brief, in this discussion Thomas holds that nature and person (and therefore supposit) differ really in material beings, and that they do not in simple substances. While he does not explicitly speak of *created* simple entities, the context makes it clear that he also has these in mind, and not merely God.[13]

This same reasoning is implied by a brief remark in the later *Summa contra Gentiles* IV, c. 55, where Thomas is defending the fittingness of the Incarnation: "Human nature was more fittingly assumed than angelic nature, because in man nature and person differ, since man is composed of matter and form; (this is) not so in an angel, which is immaterial."[14] Of interest to us is the brief observation that, because man is composed of matter and form, in him nature and person (and therefore supposit) differ. Because an angel is not so composed, in an angel nature and person (or supposit) do not differ. Presumably Thomas means by this that they do not really differ in angels, although they do so in human beings.

Thomas defends essentially the same position in later writings. For instance, in *De potentia*, q. 9, a. 1 (1265–1266) he writes that in simple substances there is no distinction between their essence and the subsisting subject (supposit) because there is no matter therein to individuate a common nature. In such substances, therefore, essence and subsistence are identical.[15] In his *De spiritualibus creaturis*, a. 5, ad 9 (1267–1268), Thomas holds that in things composed of matter and form the individual adds to the nature of the species the designation of matter and individual accidents. But in separate substances the individual does not add anything real to the nature of the species; in such beings essence is identical with the subsisting individual.[16] And in his Commentary on Bk III of the *De anima* (1267–1268),

13. Ibid., pp. 196–97. Note in particular: "In simplicibus autem non differt [omit: *esse*] re natura et persona; quia natura non recipitur in aliqua materia per quam individuatur, sed est per se subsistens. . . ." See his earlier remark about simple beings which lack matter, as cited in n. 10 above. There is no reason to think that here he is restricting this to the divine being.

14. "Convenientius igitur assumpta est hominis natura quam angelica: quia in homine aliud est natura et persona, cum sit ex materia et forma compositus; non autem in angelo, qui immaterialis est" (ed. cit. pp. 515–16). This is Thomas's second reason for rejecting a fourth argument against the fittingness of the Incarnation. For that argument see c. 53 (p. 510). The objection reasons that because angelic nature is closer to and more like God than human nature, it was not fitting for God to assume a human nature rather than an angelic nature.

15. See ed. cit., p. 226. Also see the text cited above in n. 33 of Ch. VII. Also see *De potentia*, q. 7, a. 4, ed. cit., p. 195. Note: "In angelis enim quodlibet suppositum est sua natura. . . ."

16. ". . . dicendum quod in compositis ex materia et forma, individuum addit supra naturam speciei designationem materiae et accidentia individualia. Sed in formis abstractis non addit individuum supra naturam speciei aliquid secundum rem, quia in talibus essentia eius est ipsummet individuum subsistens, ut patet per Philosophum in VII Metaph." See *Quaestiones disputatae*, Vol. 2, Calcaterra-Centi ed., p. 390. Against the editors' note 9 on p. 390, it is clear to me that Thomas is again identifying the essence or nature of a created spiritual entity with the *subsisting* individual, i.e., with the subject or suppositum. Cf. O. Schweizer, *Person und hypostatische Union bei Thomas von Aquin* (Freiburg, Switzerland, 1957), pp. 83–84.

Thomas comments that in matter-form composites a thing *(res)* and its quiddity *(quod quid est)* are not entirely the same. But in simple forms (separate entities) a thing and its quiddity cannot differ. If we identify thing *(res)* as it is used here with the subsisting individual or supposit, we have the same position.[17]

In *Summa theologiae* I, q. 3, a. 3 (ca. 1266–1268) Thomas develops the same position in some detail in the course of his effort to show that God is identical with his essence or nature. Thomas notes that nature or essence differs from the subsisting subject (supposit) in material things for the reason we have already seen. Essence or nature includes within its meaning only those things which fall under the definition of the species and not, therefore, individual matter with all the accidents which serve to individuate it. For instance, humanity includes in itself all those things which fall within the definition of human being, since it is by reason of these that a human being is a human being. But this flesh and these bones and things of this type are not included within the definition of human being and, therefore, are not included within humanity as such. Because of this Thomas concludes that a human being and humanity are not completely the same, but that humanity is signified as a formal part of a human being. Because subsisting forms, i.e., angels, are not composed of matter and form and not individuated by matter, these forms themselves are subsisting supposits. Therefore in them nature and supposit do not differ.[18]

In Quodlibet 2, q. 2, a. 2 of Christmas 1269, a change occurs, at least in Thomas's way of expressing himself. In this important text Thomas has been asked to determine whether in angels the subsisting subject (supposit) and nature differ. As he explains here, while the term "nature" is used in different ways, in one sense it refers to the substance of a thing, that is, insofar as substance itself is taken to signify the essence or quiddity of a thing. By supposit he understands an individual within the genus substance. This is also known as an *hypostasis* or as a first substance. Because sensible substances are better known to us, he first turns to them in order to determine the relationship between essence or nature and the subsisting subject.[19]

After referring to and criticizing a view which would identify the form of the part with the form of the whole, Thomas reiterates a point we have already seen.

---

17. *In III De anima*, c. 2 (Leon. 45.1:63–91). Note in particular: "In his vero quae non habent formam in materia sed sunt formae simplices, nihil potest esse praeter essentiam speciei, quia ipsa forma est tota essentia, et ideo in talibus non possunt esse plura individua unius speciei nec potest in eis differre res et quod quid est eius."

18. Leon. 4.39–40.

19. Leon. 25.2.216. Note in particular: "Natura autem, quamvis multipliciter dicatur, tamen uno modo dicitur natura ipsa *substantia* rei, ut dicitur in V Metaphysicae, secundum quod substantia significat essentiam vel quidditatem rei vel quod quid est; illud ergo significatur nomine naturae, prout hic loquimur de natura, quod significat definitio. . . . Suppositum autem est singulare in genere substantiae, quod dicitur hypostasis vel substantia prima." For Aristotle see *Metaphysics* V, c. 4 (1015a 10–11).

In matter-form composites, essence or nature is not restricted to the substantial form alone, but includes both matter and form. Given this, Thomas asks whether in such entities the subject (supposit) or individual natural being *(individuum naturale)* is identical with its essence or nature. He refers to Aristotle's *Metaphysics* VII where he finds the Stagirite holding that in things which are predicated *per se,* a thing *(res)* and its quiddity *(quod quid est)* are the same. This is not true of things which are predicated *per accidens.* For instance, continues Thomas, man is nothing other than what it is to be a man, since man signifies a two-footed animal capable of walking. A white thing, on the other hand, is not altogether identical with what it is to be white; for while the quiddity white signifies a quality, a white thing is a substance which has that quality.[20]

Given all of this, Thomas develops this working principle. If a thing is such that something else can "happen" to it which is not included in the definition *(ratio)* of its nature, that thing *(res)* and its "what it is" *(quod quid est)*, or that subject and its nature differ. This follows because the meaning or definition of nature includes only that which belongs to its specific essence. But an individual subject includes not only this but other things which "happen" to that essence. For this reason the subject (supposit) is signified as a whole, and its nature or quiddity as a formal part. This point, of course, is consistent with Thomas's earlier remarks concerning nature and supposit in material entities. They are related as part and whole, and they differ from one another.[21]

In this text, however, Thomas makes no exceptions for created spiritual beings. Only in God are there no accidents in addition to his essence, and this is because the divine essence and the divine act of being are identical. It follows from this that in God the subsisting subject and nature are completely identical. But in angels

---

20. Leon. 25.2.216:43–217:84. Note in particular: "Restat ergo considerandum, cum suppositum vel individuum naturale sit compositum ex materia et forma, utrum sit idem essentiae vel naturae. Et hanc quaestionem movet Philosophus in Libro VII Metaphysicae, ubi inquirit, *utrum sit idem unumquodque, et quod quid est eius.* Et determinat quod in his quae dicuntur per se, idem est res et quod quid est rei, in his autem quae dicuntur per accidens, non est idem: homo enim nihil est aliud quam quid est hominis, nihil enim aliud significat 'homo' *quam animal gressibile bipes;* sed res alba non est idem omnino ei quod quid est album, quod scilicet significatur nomine albi: nam *album nihil significat* nisi *qualitatem,* . . . res autem alba est substantia habens qualitatem" (p. 217:69–84). For Aristotle see *Metaphysics* VII, c. 6, especially 1031a 15–1031b 28. There Aristotle is discussing the identity or nonidentity of a thing with its τὸ τί ἦν εἶναι, which Thomas here renders as its *quod quid est.* In his Commentary on Metaphysics VII, lect. 5, he refers to this as a thing's *quod quid erat esse,* which is, of course, a literal translation from the Greek. There, too, he follows Aristotle in holding that in things which are predicated *per se,* the thing must be identified with its *quod quid erat esse* (nn. 1362, 1371), although not so in things which are said *per accidens,* such as a "white man" (n. 1372). See n. 1377 for the same. Also see Thomas's explanation in nn. 1378–1379. Compare with our earlier remark above in Ch. VII, n. 37 about Thomas's usual identification of essence, quiddity and *quod quid erat esse.*

21. Leon. 25.2.217:85–93. Note in particular: "Secundum hoc ergo, cuicumque potest aliquid accidere quod non sit de ratione suae naturae, in eo differt res et quod quid est, sive suppositum et natura. . . ."

nature and the subsisting subject are not completely the same. Something additional does "happen" to an angel apart from that which follows from the intelligible content of its species. Thus the act of being *(esse)* of an angel is "added" to its essence or nature, along with other things which "happen" to it, i.e., accidents. (By these accidents Thomas must have in mind angelic operations and operative powers.) These pertain to an angelic subject or supposit, but are not included within its essence or nature.[22]

In sum, in this discussion from Quodlibet 2, and in apparent opposition to the other texts we have considered, Thomas holds that nature and supposit differ in angels and not merely in matter-form composites. His most fundamental reason for defending this position is the composition and distinction of essence and act of being in such entities.

In this same article, while replying to the first objection,[23] Thomas distinguishes two ways in which something may be present within a given thing without being included in its essence or definition. It may be that what is added to a thing's essence determines some essential principle of that thing in some fashion—in the way, for instance, that rational determines the essence of animal. Or it may be that it does not do so—for instance, in the way whiteness is accidental to human being. In matter-form composites both of these situations obtain. For instance, to be composed of body and soul follows from the definition of the human species. But the determination to be composed of *this* body and *this* soul is accidental to human being taken as such, although not to this individual human being. If this individual human being could be defined, to be composed of this body and this soul would follow from his or her essence.[24]

Thomas's point here is that the individuating characteristics which make human being to be this human being determine the essential principles of human being in some fashion. On the other hand, many other characteristics are present in matter-form composites which are neither included in their specific definition nor

22. Leon. 25.2.217:93–102. Note in particular: "In angelo autem non est omnino idem, quia aliquid accidit ei praeter id quod est de ratione suae speciei, quia et ipsum esse angeli est praeter eius essentiam seu naturam et alia quaedam ei accidunt, quae omnia pertinent ad suppositum, non autem ad naturam." This does not mean, of course, that Thomas regards *esse* as a predicamental accident. Cf. Quodlibet 12, q. 4, a. 1: ". . . esse substantiale rei non est accidens, sed actualitas cuiuslibet forma existentis . . ." (Leon. 25.2.404:27–29). As he goes on to explain in responding to the *sed contra*, to refer to *esse* as an accident is to use the term "accident" broadly so as to make the point that *esse* is not a part of a creature's essence (lines 34–36).

23. Leon. 25.2.215:4–10. This objection reasons that it is because the subject (supposit) adds individual matter to nature that supposit and nature differ in matter-form composites. If there is no matter-form composition in angels, suppositum and nature will not differ therein.

24. For Thomas's reply see Leon. 25.2.217:103–218:133. Note that Thomas introduces his reply by reaffirming the position he has developed in the corpus: "Ad primum ergo dicendum quod non solum in compositis ex materia et forma invenitur aliquod accidens praeter essentiam speciei, sed etiam in substantiis spiritualibus . . . et ideo in utrisque suppositum non est omnino idem quod natura."

determine their essential principles. It is in this way that an accident such as whiteness is related to a material entity.[25]

In created spiritual substances, however, Thomas allows only for the second possible way in which something not included in the definition of its species may be added to a thing's essence, that is, without determining that thing's essential principles. According to Thomas, because angelic natures are subsisting forms, they are not individuated by matter but simply of themselves; hence they cannot be multiplied in different individuals within their species or admit of anything added to their essence which might determine them in that fashion. But because no angel can be identified with its act of being *(esse)*, something does "happen" to an angel in addition to its essence or nature, that is, *esse* and certain other accidents which are attributed to an angelic subject or supposit although not included within its essence or nature. Because of this, in them nature and supposit are not entirely the same.[26]

Thomas makes basically the same point in replying to the second objection. He acknowledges that the act of being is not included within the definition of a supposit, as the objection points out. But because the act of being does belong to the supposit and because it is not included in a created thing's nature, Thomas concludes that nature and supposit are not completely identical in those things in which essence *(res)* and act of being *(esse)* differ.[27]

This discussion leaves us with some unanswered questions. First of all, has Thomas now rejected his earlier defense of identity of nature and supposit in created spirits? At first sight, at least, it would seem so, since he now holds that even in these nature and supposit differ. Moreover, in light of this text and the earlier ones, what is the precise relationship between the act of being and the supposit in creatures? To put this another way, does a created individual subsisting subject or supposit include its act of being within its formal structure, even though its nature or essence does not?

As regards these questions, various attempts have been made to reconcile Thomas's earlier discussions with the text in Quodlibet 2. Thus L. De Guzman Vicente regards the treatment in Quodlibet 2 as decisive. There Thomas defends a real

---

25. Leon. 25.2.218:133–135.

26. Leon. 25.2.218:136–149. See in particular: "Sed quia non est suum esse, accidit ei aliquid praeter rationem speciei, scilicet ipsum esse, et alia quaedam quae attribuuntur supposito et non naturae. Propter quod suppositum in eis non est omnino idem cum natura." See Schweizer, *Person und hypostatische Union*, pp. 86–87; J. Winandy, "Le Quodlibet II, art. 4 de saint Thomas et la notion de suppôt," *Ephemerides theologicae Lovanienses* 11 (1934), pp. 10–11. However, Winandy there mistakenly identifies nature as second substance.

27. The objector goes on to conclude that supposit will not differ from nature by reason of its *esse*. See Leon. 25.2.215–216 (objection) and 218:150–58 (reply). From Thomas's reply note: ". . . et ideo, licet ipsum esse non sit de ratione suppositi, quia tamen pertinet ad suppositum, et non est de ratione naturae, manifestum est quod suppositum et natura non sunt omnino idem in quibuscumque res non est suum esse." See Schweizer, pp. 87–88; Winandy, pp. 11–13.

distinction between nature and supposit in all creatures, including angels, because in all of them *esse* taken as the act of being is included in the supposit in some way. As for those texts where Thomas seems to say the opposite and to identify nature and supposit in created spirits, De Guzman Vicente suggests that if in these texts Thomas speaks of simple substances taken in general, what he really has in mind is the divine substance. In God, of course, nature and supposit are identical.[28] Interesting though this proposed solution is, it will not resolve our difficulty. Consultation of each of the passages we have considered above wherein Thomas identifies nature and supposit in nonmaterial beings shows that explicitly in a number of them and by implication in others Thomas has in mind created spiritual entities, not merely God.[29]

A second solution has been offered by O. Schweizer. According to this approach, at times Thomas takes the term supposit as signifying an individual substantial nature which is viewed as completed in itself. At other times, and especially in Quodlibet 2, q. 2, a. 2, he uses it in a broader sense so as to include not only the individual substantial nature but its act of being *(esse)*. When taken in this broader sense as including the act of being (and other accidents, I would add), the subject or supposit will differ from nature in all creatures, not merely in material beings. When taken in the narrower sense, since it does not then include the act of being, the subject or supposit will not really differ from nature in created spirits.[30]

Rather than think that Thomas has rejected his earlier position, Schweizer suggests that in Quodlibet 2 he has given another and broader meaning to the term

28. See "De notione subsistentiae apud sanctum Thomam," *Divus Thomas* (Piac.) 71 (1968), pp. 418–19. See p. 419: "Ad textus autem inductos pro contraria sententia dicendum est quod in illis S. Thomas agit de substantiis simplicibus in communi, ac praesertim de Deo, ut quis facile comperire potest."

29. See *De ente*, c. 4 (Leon. 43.376:51–60), where Thomas makes it perfectly clear that he is speaking of subsisting forms other than God. He describes them as being closest to the First Principle. Forms of this type are intelligences, he continues, and their essences or quiddities need not be other than the forms themselves. Hence, as we have seen in n. 10 above, he writes that the quiddity of (such a) simple being is that simple being itself (p. 376:77–78). For the same in *In III Sent.*, d. 5, q. 1, a. 3, see nn. 10 and 13 above. As we have indicated in the last-mentioned note, if Thomas does not here explicitly mention angels, there is no reason to think that he restricts identity of nature and person to God. See n. 14 for the citation from SCG IV, c. 55, where Thomas explicitly states that nature and person differ in man, but not in an angel. In *De potentia*, q. 9, a. 1, Thomas states that in simple substances there is no difference between essence and the subject because they lack matter which would individuate a common nature. That he is including angels here seems to be implied by the immediately following reference to Avicenna—that the quiddity of a simple being is that simple being itself (see ed. cit., p. 226). He had already explicitly identified nature and supposit in angels in q. 7, a. 4 (see n. 15 above). *De spiritualibus creaturis*, a. 5, ad 9, is explicitly directed to created spirits, i.e. angels (see n. 16 above for the text). The text from *In III De anima* speaks of things which do not have a form in matter, such as simple substances (see n. 17 above). Again no effort is made to restrict this to God. The same is true of ST I, q. 3, a. 3 (see n. 18 above).

30. *Person und hypostatische Union*, pp. 85–89. See p. 88 where he remarks that when we take supposit in this broadened sense, we name nature without existence "nature" and nature with existence "supposit."

supposit. In some way *esse* is now included within his understanding of a subsisting subject (supposit). Yet, as Thomas indicates in replying to the second objection, this does not imply that the definition of a subject or supposit includes *esse*.[31]

Schweizer cites another interesting text from *Summa theologiae* III, q. 2, a. 2, dating from ca. 1271/1272–1273. Here Thomas raises a strictly theological issue concerning whether the hypostatic union is a union in person or in nature. In defending union in person, Thomas again examines the meanings of person and nature. Nature signifies the essence of the species, that which is expressed by a definition. If nothing else could be added to those things which fall under this specific meaning, there would be no need to distinguish nature from an individual supposit in which that nature is realized; for an individual subject (supposit) is that which subsists within such a nature. Hence every individual which subsists within a given nature would be totally identical with its nature.[32]

In certain subsisting things, however, something is present which is not included within the specific meaning of that thing, namely, accidents and individuating principles. This is most evident in matter-form composites. Therefore, in such entities nature and supposit really differ. This does not mean that they are completely separate from one another, but that the nature of the species is contained within the supposit, along with certain other things which are not included within the specific content of that nature. Therefore the subject or supposit is signified as a whole, which includes the nature as a formal part.[33]

If there is something in which nothing whatsoever is present in addition to the intelligible content of its nature, supposit and nature will not really differ in that being. Such is true of God. In such a being supposit and nature will differ only in the order of thought, i.e., conceptually. It will be referred to as a nature insofar as it is a given essence, while this same nature or essence will be described as a supposit insofar as it subsists.[34]

Does this text support the position presented in Quodlibet 2, q. 2, a. 2 in distinguishing nature and supposit in created spirits? Schweizer seems to think so, even though Thomas has not explicitly referred here to angels. He has reasoned that in those subsisting things in which something is present which is not included within

31. See Schweizer, pp. 88–89. For Thomas's text see n. 27 above.

32. Leon. 11.25. Note especially: "Et si quidem his quae ad rationem speciei pertinent nihil aliud adiunctum inveniri posset, nulla necessitas esset distinguendi naturam a supposito naturae, quod est individuum subsistens in natura illa: quia unumquodque individuum subsistens in natura aliqua esset omnino idem cum sua natura."

33. Ibid. Note in particular: "Contingit autem in quibusdam rebus subsistentibus inveniri aliquid quod non pertinet ad rationem speciei, scilicet accidentia et principia individuantia: sicut maxime apparet in his quae sunt ex materia et forma composita. Et ideo in talibus etiam secundum rem differt natura et suppositum, non quasi omnino aliqua separata. . . ."

34. "Si qua vero res est in qua omnino nihil est aliud praeter rationem speciei vel naturae suae, sicut est in Deo, ibi non est aliud secundum rem suppositum et natura, sed solum secundum rationem intelligendi: quia natura dicitur secundum quod est essentia quaedam; eadem vero dicitur suppositum secundum quod est subsistens" (ibid.). Cf. his reply to obj. 1.

the specific content of their nature, nature and supposit differ. And he has remarked that this is especially evident in matter-form composites. Does this last remark not imply that he also allows for such diversity in angels, even though there it may be less evident?[35] On the other side, Thomas has mentioned individuating accidents and principles in this context. He does not have to assign distinct individuating principles to angels, since for him each is a species in and of itself. However, in this text he does not explicitly refer to the presence of a distinct act of being in angels or in other creatures. At best, therefore, this text seems to be noncommital regarding the relationship between nature and supposit in angels. It does not tell us, as does Quodlibet 2, that in everything in which essence and act of being differ, nature and supposit also differ.[36] Nor does it exclude that view.

We may still ask whether in Quodlibet 2, q. 2, a. 2, Thomas has changed his position regarding the relationship between nature and supposit in created spiritual beings. And if he has, which position better accords with his general metaphysical principles? Schweizer's suggested way of reconciling this text with Thomas's earlier discussions has considerable merit. If correct, this explanation simply means that at the time of Quodlibet 2 Thomas broadened his understanding of the subject or supposit so as to include therein not only what is contained within a thing's essence or nature along with its individuating notes, but also and especially the act of being which is joined with that nature in a subsisting subject or supposit. Once this understanding of the subject or supposit is introduced, of course, it will follow that even in angels nature and supposit differ and differ really; for even in them there is a real distinction and composition of nature or essence and act of being *(esse)*.[37]

Another way of approaching this is to recall that frequently enough Thomas uses Boethian language in referring to the distinction or composition of essence and act of being in created beings. This is to say, he often describes it as a distinction or composition of "that which is" *(quod est)* and of *esse*. When Thomas speaks this way, we should understand him to be emphasizing not the "is" *(est)* but the "that which" *(quod)* in this expression. It is because of this emphasis on the quidditative aspect of a concrete entity that Thomas can say that such a concrete being ("that which is") is other than and enters into composition with its act of being *(esse)*.

---

35. See the text cited in note 33 above: "sicut maxime apparet. . . ." For Schweizer, see p. 98. While Thomas does not explicitly mention angels here, reasons Schweizer, by stressing the point that God alone is perfectly simple, he implies that a distinction between nature and supposit is to be recognized in angels.

36. See the texts cited above in nn. 22, 26 and 27.

37. H. Degl'Innocenti puts this point another way, by distinguishing between the supposit taken *materialiter* (as synonymous with the individual), and *denominative* (as meaning the individual which has *esse*, or is united with *esse*, or stands under *esse*). It is in the first way *(materialiter)* that he finds Thomas using the term supposit in Quodlibet 2, q. 2, a. 2. See his "De nova quadam ratione exponendi sententiam Capreoli de constitutione ontologica personae," *Divus Thomas* (Piac.) 53 (1950), pp. 325–26.

Even in a created spiritual entity, its "that which is" when so understood will not include its act of being.[38]

For instance, in *De spiritualibus creaturis,* a. 1, ad 8, Thomas explains that to be composed of "that which is" *(quod est)* and that "whereby it is" *(quo est)* is not the same as to be composed of matter and form. While form may be described as that "whereby something is," matter cannot, properly speaking, be referred to as "that which is." "That which is" *(quod est)* is that which subsists in the order of being. In corporeal substances this is the composite of matter and form; in incorporeal substances, i.e., angels, it is the simple form itself. In contrast, that "whereby it is" is the participated act of being *(esse)* itself, for a thing exists only insofar as it participates in *esse.* Because of this, concludes Thomas, Boethius writes in his *De Hebdomadibus* that in things other than the first being, "that which is" *(quod est)* and *esse* are not the same.[39] It is because of this usage that Thomas can distinguish between "that which is" and *esse* as between essence and act of being.[40]

Mutatis mutandis, we might say much the same of Thomas's understanding of supposit in his more frequent comparisons of this with nature. Just as the expression "that which is" may be taken as signifying a concrete subject which exists, but with an emphasis on its quidditative aspect, so the term "supposit" may be taken as signifying this same subject with this same quidditative emphasis along with the additional implication that the subject is ontologically complete and incommunicable. In this usage the individuated nature or essence is viewed as related to the subject or supposit as a formal part to a concrete whole. Since in material entities the concrete whole or subject includes individuating characteristics in addition to the specific essence, Thomas always defends real distinction between nature and

---

38. See, for instance, *De ente et essentia,* c. 4: ". . . et propter hoc a quibusdam dicuntur huiusmodi substantiae componi ex quo est et quod est, vel ex quod est et esse, ut Boetius dicit" (Leon. 43.376:163–166); *In I Sent.,* d. 8, q. 5, a. 1 (Mandonnet ed., Vol. 1, p. 227): ". . . et ita componitur ex esse, vel quo est, et quod est"; *De veritate,* q. 27, a. 1, ad 8 (cited above in Ch. V, n. 74); ST I, q. 75, a. 5, ad 4 (cited in Ch. V, n. 86), where he holds that in created intelligences there is a composition of form and participated *esse,* or as some say, of *quo est* and *quod est.* Also see the whole of SCG II, c. 52, which is directed to proving that in created separate substances there is distinction and composition of *esse* and *quod est* (or *substantia*). Also see Quodlibet 2, q. 2, a. 1: ". . . et ideo in qualibet creatura est aliud ipsa creatura quae habet esse, et ipsum esse eius. Et hoc est quod Boetius dicit . . . quod in omni eo quod est citra Primum, *aliud est esse* et quod est" (Leon. 25.2.214:46–50). Cf. Quodlibet 3, q. 8, a. 1 (Leon. 25.2.277:44–48).

39. "Ad octavum dicendum quod non idem est componi ex quod est et quo est, et ex materia et forma. Licet enim forma possit dici quo aliquid est, tamen materia non proprie potest dici quod est, cum non sit nisi in potentia. Sed quod est, est id quod subsistit in esse, quod quidem in substantiis corporeis est ipsum compositum ex materia et forma, in substantiis autem incorporeis est ipsa forma simplex; quo est autem, est ipsum esse participatum, quia in tantum unumquodque est, in quantum ipse esse participat. Unde et Boëtius sic utitur istis vocabulis in libro *de Hebdomad.,* dicens, quod in aliis praeter primum, non idem est quod est et esse." Ed. cit., p. 372.

40. See the texts cited above in nn. 38 and 39. For the text from Boethius's *De Hebdomadibus* see *The Theological Tractates,* p. 40, Axiom 2; p. 42, Axioms 7 and 8.

supposit in such beings. And since such added individuating characteristics are unnecessary in created subsisting forms or angels, Thomas can identify nature and supposit in such beings when he understands supposit in this way, that is, when he concentrates on its quidditative aspect.

On the other hand, we might emphasize the "is" *(est)* in the expression "that which is." We could then argue that the concrete existing entity, which we may still identify as a supposit, includes its act of being *(esse)* in addition to its nature or essence. So understood, the subject or supposit will differ really from its nature or essence even in created spirits, not merely in material beings. This will follow because in each case the existing supposit includes the act of being in addition to its essence or nature.[41] In fact it is in this way that Thomas understands the supposit in Quodlibet 2, q. 2, a. 2. Without necessarily implying a substantive change in doctrine, this text surely does point to a change in usage.

This shift in usage is significant, for it brings out more forcefully the role of *esse* or the act of being within the ontological structure of any subsisting subject. If we may repeat the point just made, when the concrete existing subject is viewed as a whole and in the second way just indicated, it must include the act of being as well as essence or nature. This is not to say, of course, that the definition *(ratio)* of the supposit actually includes the act of being.[42] A definition taken as such will be restricted to the quidditative side of the subsisting subject or supposit. But one's full understanding of the concrete subject or supposit should also include reference to its act of being.

Much has been written within the Thomistic tradition about the principle which formally constitutes an individual nature as a supposit or, in the case of an intelligent nature, as a person. Does Thomas here appeal to some kind of real substantial mode in the line of essence which would seal, as it were, the nature and render it ontologically incommunicable? This view is usually associated with the later Cajetan, and is defended by his followers as the correct reading of Aquinas.[43] Or does Thomas rather appeal to existence itself as the formal constituent of the subsisting subject or supposit? This view has long been attributed to Capreolus

---

41. The comparison we have suggested here between *id quod est* and *esse*, on the one hand, and nature and supposit, on the other, should not be taken to imply that Thomas identifies *esse* and supposit. On the contrary, when supposit is used in the second way we have suggested, it will involve both nature (essence) and its corresponding act of being.

42. See the text from Quodlibet 2, q. 2, a. 2, ad 2 cited above in n. 27.

43. See T. U. Mullaney, "Created Personality: The Unity of Thomistic Tradition," *New Scholasticism* 29 (1955), pp. 377–85; Schweizer, *Person und hypostatische Union*, pp. 29–31 (with a list of names and references of those who have followed him). For a later thirteenth-century treatise which appeals to a mode to distinguish supposit from nature see Giles of Rome's *De compositione angelorum*, q. 5, partially edited by D. Trapp in his "Aegidii Romani de doctrina modorum," *Angelicum* 12 (1935), pp. 449–501. For discussion and criticism by Godfrey of Fontaines see my *The Metaphysical Thought of Godfrey of Fontaines*, pp. 232–36.

and in more recent times has especially been defended by Billot.[44] Still more recently, however, another reading of Capreolus has been proposed: he did not really hold that it is existence *(esse)* itself, but rather an ordering to existence on the part of an individual thing's nature which serves as the formal constituent of the supposit.[45]

It is not my purpose here to enter into the controversy concerning the views of Cajetan, Capreolus, and Billot about this. It seems to me that when the problem is stated in these terms it is difficult if not impossible to find an answer in Thomas's texts. This is because he usually casts the issue in other terms, having to do with the relationship and distinction between nature and supposit. It will be enough for us to recall that at least in Quodlibet 2 Thomas includes the act of being *(esse)* within the ontological structure of the individual subject or supposit. This suggests that the act of being plays an important role in Thomas's mind within the structure of any existing subject or supposit. It reminds us again that for Thomas the act of being *(esse)* is the actuality of all acts and the perfection of all perfections within a given being.[46] This is not to say, however, that Thomas has explicitly raised or answered the question concerning the formal constituent of the supposit or person. It is to suggest that if one wishes to answer that question within Thomas's metaphysics, an important role should to be assigned to the act of being *(esse)*.

Reference to the act of being raises some other points. Thomas is convinced that there can only be one substantial act of being in a given subject or supposit, at least in the natural order. The act of being with which he deals in Quodlibet 2, q. 2, a. 2 is, of course, substantial *esse,* not accidental *esse.* Whether accidents also enjoy distinctive acts of being *(esse)* is an issue we shall take up in the following section of this chapter. As regards substantial *esse,* Thomas's conviction that there can only be one substantial act of being in a given supposit or subject assists him in meeting other questions. For instance, he usually appeals to this in addressing a

44. On this see Schweizer, pp. 23–28 (on Capreolus and for some who would deny that he makes existence the formal constitutent); 32–34 (Billot and his followers). Also see J. Hernandez-Pacheco, *Acto y substancia. Estudio a través de Santo Tomás de Aquino* (Seville, 1984), pp. 144–54.

45. For efforts in this direction see F. Muñiz, "El constitutivo formal de la persona creada en la tradición tomista," *La Ciencia tomista* 68 (1945), pp. 5–89; 70 (1946), pp. 201–93; E. Quarello, "Il problema scolastico della persona nel Gaetano e nel Capreolo," *Divus Thomas* (Piac.) 55 (1952), pp. 34–63; "Discussioni nell'interpretazione di Capreolo sul problema della persona," *Salesianum* 18 (1956), pp. 297–310; Mullaney, "Created Personality," pp. 385–91. For criticism of Muñiz and Quarello see Degl'Innocenti, "De nova quadam ratione," pp. 321–38; "Capreolo d'accordo col Gaetano a proposito della personalità?" *Euntes docete* 7 (1954), pp. 168–203. For agreement with the view that Capreolus did defend the existence theory see Schweizer, p. 27. Note that Schweizer himself ultimately concludes that Thomas defended none of these theories, but espoused the theory of "pure union" and therefore held that what makes an individual nature a person is not something positive but something negative, i.e., the absence of union with another supposit (passim, and especially pp. 114–17).

46. See *De potentia,* q. 7, a. 2, ad 9.

strictly theological issue concerning unity or plurality of *esse* in Christ.[47] Here we shall not pause to examine this theological question. Again, Thomas turns to this same thinking in defending a position which would be subject to considerable controversy shortly after his death—unicity of substantial form in human beings. This will be discussed in the following chapter.

2. Accidents and Accidental Being

In the preceding section of this chapter we have concentrated on Thomas's understanding of the individual subsisting subject (supposit) and its relationship to its act of being *(esse)*. Underlying much of that discussion is Thomas's general theory of distinction and composition of essence and act of being in all finite substances. At the same time, in certain passages he distinguishes between substantial *esse* and accidental *esse*.[48] If there can only be one substantial act of being *(esse)* in a given subject or suppositum, what does Thomas have to say about accidental *esse*? Are there accidental acts of being which correspond to each accidental essence and which are distinct from the substantial act of being of their subject? If so, does Thomas defend a distinction of accidental being *(esse)* from accidental essence which parallels in some way the distinction between a substantial act of being and substantial essence? As we shall see, an affirmative answer to the second question just raised does not necessarily entail an affirmative answer to the last question.

In one of the passages examined in Ch. VII we found Thomas distinguishing between the "being in" or "existing in" *(inesse)* of an accident and its being *(esse)*. If an accident loses its "being in" owing to Eucharistic transubstantiation, Thomas there reasons that because of divine power the accident still retains its accidental being *(esse)*. Again one wonders about his understanding of this accidental *esse*.[49]

---

47. While Thomas usually assigns only one substantial *esse* to Christ, that of the Divine Word, one of his texts poses a special problem. In his Disputed Question *De unione verbi incarnati* he seems to defend a different position in that he assigns to Christ not only the Word's eternal *esse*, but another and human *esse* as well which, while not being accidental, is described as *secundarium*. See a. 4: "Est autem et aliud esse huius suppositi, non in quantum est aeternum, sed in quantum est temporaliter homo factum. Quod esse, etsi non sit esse accidentale . . . non tamen est esse principale sui suppositi, sed secundarium" (Calcaterra-Centi ed. [Turin-Rome, 1953]), p. 432. On this see P. Bayerschmidt, *Die Seins- und Formmetaphysik des Heinrich von Gent in ihrer Anwendung auf die Christologie* (Münster i. W., 1941), pp. 54–63; A. Patfoort, *L'unité d'être dans le Christ d'après s. Thomas* (Tournai, 1964), pp. 85–106. For other important texts in Thomas see *In III Sent.*, d. 6, q. 2. a. 2; Quodlibet 9, q. 2, a. 2; ST III, q. 17, a. 2; *Compendium theologiae* I, c. 212. For discussion see Bayerschmidt, pp. 46–54, 63–65; Patfoort, pp. 33–84, 107–89.

48. See *De unione verbi incarnati*, a. 4, as cited in the preceding note for his distinction between *esse suppositi* and *esse accidentale*. More of these passages will be considered below.

49. See *In IV Sent.*, d. 12, q. 1, a. 1, ql. 1, ad 2 and ad 1 as cited above in Ch. VII, nn. 132 and 135 and discussed in my text.

Regarding this issue there is considerable diversity of opinion within the Thomistic tradition concerning Thomas's position. At least as far back as Capreolus in the early fifteenth century, leading commentators may be found who hold that Thomas assigns an existence or *esse* to accidents which is distinct from that of their substantial subject.[50] This reading continues to have its defenders down to the present day, and includes many twentieth-century interpreters of Aquinas.[51]

On the other hand, Bañez seems to have begun by rejecting this reading of Aquinas, only to shift his interpretation at a later point in his career.[52] And among twentieth-century scholars, many deny that Thomas assigns distinct acts of existing to accidents.[53] Most recently, however, Barry Brown has devoted a book-length study to this same question. After offering many precisions and clarifications, he

50. See his *Defensiones theologiae Divi Thomae Aquinatis* (Turin, 1900), Vol. 2, p. 122b. On this see B. F. Brown, *Accidental Being*, p. 10 and n. 12. For a helpful treatment of Capreolus's life and work see J. Hegyi, *Die Bedeutung des Seins bei den klassichen Kommentatoren des heiligen Thomas von Aquin. Capreolus—Silvester von Ferrara—Cajetan* (Pullach bei München, 1959), pp. 9–15. As Brown points out, this interpretation is also defended by Silvester of Ferrara in his Commentary on Thomas's *Summa contra Gentiles* IV, c. 14 (Leon. 15.61b–63b); Cajetan, *In De Ente et essentia D. Thomae Aquinatis commentaria*, M.-H. Laurent, ed. (Turin, 1934), p. 227 (where he also holds that the *esse actualis existentiae* of an accident is really distinct [*distinguitur realiter*] not only from the *esse subjecti actualis* but also from the essence of the accidental form from which it comes); see also his Commentary on *Summa theologiae* I, q. 28, a. 2 (Leon. 4.322–23); John of St. Thomas, *Cursus philosophicus*, Vol. 1, p. 513a.

51. See, for instance, N. Del Prado, *De veritate fundamentali philosophiae christianae*, pp. 133, 136 (where he also distinguishes the *esse actualis existentiae* of an accident from the *esse subjecti actualis* and from the essence or nature of the accident); J. Maritain, *Distinguish to Unite or The Degrees of Knowledge*, trans. G. B. Phelan (New York, 1959), pp. 436–37; C. A. Hart, *Thomistic Metaphysics*, pp. 175–78; J. Owens, *An Elementary Christian Metaphysics*, pp. 159–61 (where he also defends, though cautiously, real distinction of accidental existence from accidental essence); F. E. McMahon and J. Albertson, "The Esse of Accidents: A Discussion," *The Modern Schoolman* 31 (1953–1954), pp. 125–32 (with Albertson dissenting); McMahon and G. B. Phelan, "The *Esse* of Accidents," *New Scholasticism* 43 (1969), pp. 143–48; B. F. Brown, "Accidental *Esse*: A Confirmation," *New Scholasticism* 44 (1970), pp. 133–52; A. Patfoort, *L'unité d'être dans le Christ d'après s. Thomas*, pp. 229–33. Cf. L. De Raeymaeker, *Metaphysica generalis* (Louvain, 1931), Vol. 1, pp. 141–42, who later seems to have changed his mind (see n. 53 below).

52. For Bañez see his *Scholastica Commentaria in Primam Partem Summae Theologicae S. Thomae Aquinatis* (Madrid-Valencia, 1934; repr. Dubuque, Iowa, n.d.), p. 144b (where he also refers to the common opinion, which "seems to be that of D. Thomas," according to which the *inesse* of any accidental form is really distinct from the essence of the accident and from the *esse* of the subject), pp. 158b–160b (where he notes that he had at one time regarded as more probable the view which denies that accidents have a proper existence which is really distinct from the existence of their substance, but now regards as *multo probabilior* the affirmative position).

53. See, for instance, L. De Raeymaeker, *The Philosophy of Being*, pp. 180–81; Gilson, "La notion d'existence chez Guillaume d'Auvergne," AHDLMA 15 (1946), p. 89, n. 1; J. de Finance, *Être et agir*, pp. 248–50 (who seems to favor this reading, but who acknowledges certain difficulties in interpreting Thomas; he himself distinguishes between the situation of proper accidents, operations, and those introduced by an extrinsic cause, thereby leading Brown to classify him under "The Middle Way" in his *Accidental Being*, p. 13); J. Albertson, "The *Esse* of Accidents according to St. Thomas," *Modern Schoolman* 30 (1953), pp. 265–78; Fabro, *Participation et causalité*, pp. 299–302, esp. p. 301. For others see Brown, *Accidental Being*, pp. 11–12.

concludes that according to Aquinas "accidents are actuated by their own being, which is really distinct from their essence and from the being and essence of their substance."[54]

When one turns to the texts of Aquinas, one readily understands why there has been so much controversy concerning his personal view. Passages can be cited which seem to point to distinctive acts of being *(esse)* for accidents. Others, however, might be taken as arguing against such a conclusion. Perhaps most difficult to justify for those who follow the first line of interpretation is the additional claim defended by some to the effect that accidental *esse* is also really distinct from accidental essence or quiddity. As noted above, it is one thing to admit that Thomas distinguishes between substantial *esse* and accidental *esse*. It is something else to conclude from this that he also distinguishes, and distinguishes really, between the essence or quiddity of a given accident and its corresponding accidental act of being *(esse)*.[55]

If we may begin with some of his earliest texts, in *De ente*, c. 6, Thomas writes that accidents admit only of an incomplete definition; for they can be defined only if their subject is included in their definition. This in turn follows from the fact that they do not enjoy existence *(esse)* in themselves and apart from their subject. Just as a substantial act of being *(esse)* results from the composition of matter and form, an accidental being *(esse)* results from the union of an accident and its subject.[56]

As Thomas also observes, that to which an accident comes is a complete being in itself which subsists with its own act of being *(esse)*. This act of being is prior in nature to the accident which is added to it. Because of this, the supervening accident does not cause the act of being in which the thing or subject subsists and through which it is a being in its own right, an *ens per se*. Rather, when an accident joins with its subject, the accident causes a certain secondary being.[57] This in turn means that something essentially one does not result from the union of an accident with its subject, but only something accidentally one. From all of this it follows that an accident is neither a complete essence nor a part of a complete essence. Just as it is a being *(ens)* only in a qualified sense, so it has an essence in a qualified sense.[58]

While Thomas's stated purpose in this chapter is to clarify how essence is realized in accidents, his remarks concerning accidental or secondary being *(esse)* are

54. See *Accidental Being*, passim, and p. 281 for the quoted text.

55. Brown defends both points, as the reader can determine from the passage cited in the preceding paragraph. We shall return to this issue near the end of this Section.

56. Leon. 43.379:6–380:13. Note in particular: ". . . et hoc ideo est quia non habent esse per se absolutum a subiecto, sed sicut ex forma et materia relinquitur esse substantiale quando componuntur, ita ex accidente et subiecto relinquitur esse accidentale quando accidens subiecto advenit."

57. Leon. 43.380:33–40. See in particular: "sed causat quoddam esse secundum. . . ."

58. Leon. 43.380:42–49. Note in particular: ". . . sicut est ens secundum quid, ita et essentiam secundum quid habet." For different discussions of this passage see Albertson, "The *Esse* of Accidents," pp. 277–78; Brown, *Accidental Being*, pp. 150–52.

of greatest interest to us here. By saying that such an accidental being *(esse)* results from the union of a subject and its accident, I take him to mean that the accident in some way causes (as a secondary formal or determining cause) this accidental being in its subject. As he puts it in the second passage just analyzed, the supervening accident does not cause a thing's substantial act of being, but a certain secondary being *(esse)*. We are still very much in the dark concerning Thomas's understanding of this secondary being *(esse)*. But at least this much is clear from Thomas's remarks in the *De ente*. He distinguishes between a thing's substantial act of being and a superadded secondary or accidental *esse*.

In this discussion Thomas does not indicate how this secondary or accidental being *(esse)* stands in relation to the accidental form or essence. Are the two really distinct from one another? He does state that the accidental form causes this secondary being.[59] One might be tempted to conclude that this is enough to show that Thomas really distinguishes between them as between an accidental form and the being *(esse)* which it causes. This, however, would be to take too much from this text. If the causality in question is of the formal order, as it clearly must be, we should remember that a formal cause exercises its causality by communicating itself as a determining principle. Even if the accidental form is really identical with the accidental being it is said to cause, that form could still be described as a formal cause of the accidental being *(esse)* within a given substance.

In his equally early *De principiis naturae*, c. 1, Thomas distinguishes between two kinds of existence *(esse)*—the substantial or essential existence of a thing, as for a man to be, which is existence in the unqualified sense; and an accidental existence *(esse)*, as for a man to be white, which is to be in a qualified way *(esse aliquid)*.[60] Shortly thereafter he comments that a (substantial) form gives existence *(esse)* to matter, whereas a subject gives existence to its accidents. In other words, a substantial subject does not derive its substantial existence from its accidents.[61]

If we were to stop at this point in Thomas's text, we might suspect that here he rejects his claim in the *De ente* that an accident or accidental form gives an accidental and secondary being *(esse)*. This is not the case, however, as Thomas soon clarifies. What produces substantial existence in actuality is substantial form. What produces accidental existence *(esse)* in actuality is an accidental form. Again, therefore, he refers to an accidental *esse* which is caused by an accidental form, and which he distinguishes from the substantial existence of the underlying subject. Whether

---

59. See the text cited in n. 57.

60. "Sed duplex est esse, scilicet esse essentiale rei sive substantiale, ut hominem esse, et hoc est esse simpliciter; est autem aliud esse accidentale, ut hominem esse album, et hoc est esse aliquid" (Leon. 43.39:4–8).

61. See Leon. 43.39:20–35. Note in particular: "Unde simpliciter loquendo forma dat esse materiae, sed subiectum accidenti. . . ." In this context Thomas does not clearly distinguish between *esse* taken as a substantial *actus essendi* and as the factual existence which results therefrom. Hence I have here chosen the neutral term "existence" to express it in English.

this accidental *esse* is also really distinct from the accidental form which serves as its formal cause remains undetermined.[62]

In his also early Commentary on III *Sentences,* d. 6, q. 2, a. 2, Thomas distinguishes different ways in which the verb *esse* may be used. After speaking of it insofar as it signifies the truth of a proposition, he notes that in another way it may be taken to mean that *esse* which belongs to the nature of a thing, and according to which there is a division into the ten predicaments. Here Thomas identifies this *esse* as the act of a being *(actus entis)* which results from a thing's principles, just as to shine is the act of a shining body.[63]

While Thomas's major concern in this discussion is with the substantial act of being, he has here referred to a division into the ten predicaments by reason of *esse* when this is understood as real rather than as purely mental. This might be interpreted as indicating that he assigns corresponding acts of existing or being to each of the predicaments, not merely to substance. At least it does not exclude that reading. At the same time, however, a little farther on in this same context he cautions against our thinking that the nature of a thing exists, or its parts, or its accidents, when that term is taken in the strict sense, that is, as signifying the act of a being. Only the complete subject exists in this sense.[64]

In a slightly later text which still dates from Thomas's first teaching period in Paris, Quodlibet 9, q. 2, a. 2 of Christmas 1257, he develops the last-mentioned point. One of those present at this public disputation had raised the theological issue already mentioned in the preceding section of this chapter: Is there only one act of being *(esse)* in Christ?[65] Once again Thomas distinguishes two ways in which *esse* may be understood—either as the verbal copula which signifes the composition of a judgment produced by the soul; or as the act of a being insofar as it is a being, i.e., that whereby something is designated as a being in act in the nature of things. Thomas comments that when *esse* is taken in this second way—as the act of a being—it can only be attributed to things that fall within the ten predicaments. Therefore, insofar as the name being *(ens)* is derived from *esse* when understood in this way, being itself is divided into the ten predicaments.[66]

62. Leon. 43.39:43–46: ". . . quod autem facit actu esse substantiale est forma substantialis, et quod facit actu esse accidentale dicitur forma accidentalis."

63. Note that this article is concerned with the question whether in Christ there is only one *esse.* See in particular: "Alio modo dicitur esse quod pertinet ad naturam rei, secundum quod dividitur secundum decem genera. Et hoc quidem esse in re est, et est actus entis resultans ex principiis rei, sicut lucere est actus lucentis" (Moos ed., Vol. 3, p. 238). Note also that immediately following this text is one of those relatively rare passages in which Thomas indicates that *esse* can also be taken in a third way so as to signify the essence of a thing.

64. See pp. 238–39. See in particular: "Unde nec natura rei nec partes eius dicuntur proprie esse, si esse praedicto modo accipiatur; similiter autem nec accidentia, sed suppositum completum est, quod est secundum omnia illa."

65. See Leon. 25.1:93–95. Cf. n. 47 above.

66. Leon. 25.1.94:31–46. When taken in the first sense, *esse* does not exist in the nature of things, Thomas points out, but only in the act of the soul which judges ("tantum in actu animae compo-

When *esse* is used in this second sense—as the act of a being—it in turn may be attributed to something in two different ways. Thus in one way it is assigned to that which enjoys existence *(esse)* or is in the strict sense. When so used it is attributed to substance alone as to that which subsists in itself. Hence that which truly exists is called a substance.[67] In a second way it may be assigned to things which do not subsist in themselves but only in another and with another, whether they be accidents, or substantial forms, or parts. Thus *esse* (taken as act of being) is not assigned to any of them in the sense that they themselves truly exist, but only in the sense that each of them is that *by which* something is. For instance, whiteness may be said to be, not in the sense that it subsists in itself, but because by means of whiteness something else enjoys white being *(esse album)*.[68]

At this point the reader may ask whether Thomas is still defending a twofold *esse* within a given entity, or whether he is simply saying that one and the same act of being (substantial *esse)* is assigned to substance as to that which exists and to any accident as to that whereby a substance is in a given way. Thomas goes on to offer some additional precisions. He repeats the point that *esse* is truly and properly attributed to a thing which subsists in itself, that is, to a subsisting subject. But a twofold *esse* is assigned to such a subject. One *esse* results from those things by which the unity of the subsisting subject is completed. This is the subject's proper and substantial act of being. Another kind of being *(esse)* is assigned to the subject in addition to all those factors which complete it as a subsisting subject. Thomas describes this as a superadded or accidental being *(esse)*. For instance, when we say "Sortes is white," we assign "being white" to him.[69] Thomas applies this reasoning to the theological question at issue. In Christ there is only one substantial act of being, that of the divine supposit; but in him there is also a manifold accidental being *(esse)*.[70]

From all of this we may conclude that Thomas will also hold that in any created substantial subject there is only one substantial act of being. But in any such created subject there may also be a multiplicity of instances of accidental being *(esse)*. Hence, in spite of the contrary impression given by the first part of this discussion,

nentis et dividentis"). As for *esse* when taken in the second way: ". . . esse dicitur actus entis in quantum est ens, id est quo denominatur aliquid ens actu in rerum natura; et sic esse non attribuitur nisi rebus ipsis quae in decem generibus continentur. . . ."

67. "Sed hoc esse attribuitur alicui dupliciter. Uno modo sicut ei quod proprie et vere habet esse vel est; et sic attribuitur soli substantiae per se subsistenti, unde quod vere est, dicitur substantia . . ." (Leon. 25.1.94:47–50).

68. "Omnibus vero quae non per se subsistunt sed in alio et cum alio, sive sint accidentia sive formae substantiales aut quaelibet partes, non habent esse ita quod ipsa vere sint, sed attribuitur eis esse alio modo, idest ut quo aliquid est . . ." (ibid., lines 51–56).

69. Leon. 25.1.94:58–95:65: "Esse ergo proprie et vere non attribuitur nisi rei per se subsistenti. Huic autem attribuitur esse duplex. Unum scilicet esse quod resultat ex his ex quibus eius unitas integratur, quod est proprium esse suppositi substantiale. Aliud esse est supposito attributum praeter ea quae integrant ipsum, quod est esse superadditum, scilicet accidentale. . . ."

70. Leon. 25.195:67–86.

here again Thomas continues to defend multiplicity of *esse* in created subjects, one substantial and others which are accidental.[71]

At the same time, Thomas has insisted that whether *esse* is taken as substantial act of being or as accidental being, it is truly and properly assigned only to the subsisting thing or subject. We are not surprised that he says this of the substantial act of being. As regards accidental being *(esse)*, in this discussion he would have us assign this to the substantial subject as that by which the subject enjoys being of a given kind, not being without qualification. Thomas's concern here seems to be to prevent anyone from concluding that an accident such as whiteness exists in its own right or, if you will, that it is a substance. Thus to say that Sortes is white is not to assign independent being *(esse)* to whiteness. It is rather to say that his whiteness is that whereby Sortes, the substantial subject, enjoys being in a given way, that is, "being white."[72]

This text and others like it should not be taken as implying that Thomas does not distinguish between a substantial act of being and accidental *esse*.[73] But it continues to leave unclarified his answer to our other question: What is the exact relationship between an accident and its corresponding accidental *esse*—for instance, between the accident whiteness and *being* white? Are they really one and the same, or are they really distinct? Either position, it seems, can be reconciled with Thomas's assigning both substantial *esse* and accidental *esse* to the subsisting subject in the two different ways he has indicated.

Frequently enough Thomas speaks in a similar vein in other texts. For instance, in *Summa theologiae* I, q. 90, a. 2, he writes that an accident does not have *esse*. Rather it is by means of an accident that something is in a given way, and it is for this reason that an accident may be described as a being. For instance, whiteness is said to be a being because by means of it something is white. Hence an accident is more properly said to be "of a being" than "a being."[74] This text likewise need not be read as implying that Thomas has rejected his earlier doctrine that accidental *esse* is distinct from substantial *esse*. Again his purpose is to convey the point that accidents do not subsist in their own right.

In ST I–II, q. 110, a. 2, Thomas makes the same point. While replying there to the third objection he comments that the being *(esse)* of an accident is "to be in"

---

71. See above, n. 68.

72. ". . . ut esse album attribuitur Sorti cum dicimus: Sortes est albus" (Leon. 25.1.95:65–66, in continuation of the text cited above in n. 69).

73. For such an interpretation see Albertson, "The *Esse* of Accidents," pp. 272–74.

74. Leon. 5.386. In this article Thomas is asking whether the soul is produced through creation. He replies that this is necessarily the case for the rational soul. In developing this point he draws a parallel between the way something is brought into being and the way being *(esse)* pertains to it. But that is said to be in the proper sense which has existence and subsists in itself; hence only substances are named beings in the strict and proper sense. Then he turns to accidents, as we have indicated in our text: "Accidens vero non habet esse, sed eo aliquid est, et hac ratione ens dicitur. . . . Et propter hoc dicitur in VII *Metaphys.*, quod accidens dicitur *magis entis quam ens.*" For Aristotle see *Metaphysics* VII, c. 1 (1028a 18–20).

(inesse). Therefore an accident is not described as a being because it has *esse,* but rather because by means of the accident, something is. Hence it is better described as "of a being" than as "a being."[75]

In his Commentary on *Metaphysics* XI, lect. 3, Thomas mentions the different ways in which being is said. That is described as being in the unqualified sense *(ens simpliciter)* which enjoys existence in itself, that is to say, that which is a substance. Other things are described as beings because they pertain to that which exists in itself. Such is true, for example, of a *passio* or a habit or anything of this kind. Thus a quality is not said to be a being because it has *esse* but because a substance is disposed in a certain way by that quality. So it is with the other accidents. It is for this reason that they are said to be "of a being."[76] Thomas makes the same point in his Commentary on *Metaphysics* XII, lect. 1. There he adds that accidents and privations differ from one another in this respect, that by reason of accidents a subject enjoys some kind of being *(esse aliquale),* while by reason of a privation it does not but rather lacks a certain being *(esse).*[77]

None of these passages should be read as implying that Thomas is now denying that there is an accidental being in distinction from the substantial act of being in a given subject. His purpose repeatedly is to guard against the mistaken impression that an accident has existence in its own right, or that it subsists in itself, or that it is a substance. Only substances are beings in the unqualified sense.[78]

Thomas had already made this point, but with an interesting precision in terminology, in ST I, q. 45, a. 4. There he attempts to show that accidents and forms and other things of this sort which do not subsist are more properly said to be concreated than created. Only things which subsist are created, strictly speaking. To justify this conclusion he reasons that to exist belongs properly to that which has being, i.e., that which subsists in its own act of being. Forms and accidents and other things of this kind are not described as beings as if they themselves exist, but rather because by means of them something is in a given way. Thus whiteness is said to be a being because by means of it a subject is white. Therefore, an accident is more properly said to be "of a being" than a being. And things of this type which do not subsist are more "coexistents" than beings and hence more properly

---

75. Here Thomas is defending the point that one kind of grace—habitual or what is often known as sanctifying—is a quality of the soul. In replying to objection 3 he comments: ". . . accidentis esse est inesse. Unde omne accidens non dicitur ens quasi ipsum esse habeat, sed quia eo aliquid est. Unde et magis dicitur *entis* quam ens . . ." (Leon. 7.313).

76. Ed. cit., p. 519, n. 2197. See in particular: "Non enim qualitas dicitur ens, quia ipsa habeat esse, sed per eam substantia dicitur esse disposita."

77. See p. 567, n. 2419: "Nam ens dicitur quasi esse habens, hoc autem solum est substantia, quae subsistit. Accidentia autem dicuntur entia, non quia sunt, sed quia magis ipsis aliquid est." For the comparison with privations see n. 2420.

78. Also see *De potentia,* q. 3, a. 8, ed. cit., p. 62: ". . . sicut et accidentia dicuntur entia, quia substantia eis est vel qualis vel quanta. . . ."

concreated than created.[79] By referring to accidents, etc., as coexistents more so than as beings Thomas is once more making the point that they do not subsist in their own right; they are not substances. They exist in substances, which alone are beings in the proper sense of the term.

That Thomas defends an accidental being that is distinct from the substantial act of being of finite substances is confirmed by passages where he distinguishes between the kinds of *esse* given respectively by substantial forms and by accidental forms. The notion that an accidental form gives or communicates an accidental being is already present in his earliest works, as we have seen in the *De ente* and the *De principiis naturae*.[80] While this doctrine is defended by Thomas throughout his career, here we shall limit ourselves to a few additional texts.

In the *Summa contra Gentiles* I, c. 23, Thomas remarks that the subject of an accident is related to that accident as potency to act. This is so because an accident is a certain kind of form which produces being in actuality according to an accidental *esse*.[81]

In ST I, q. 77, a. 6, Thomas spells this out more fully. Substantial forms and accidental forms have something in common in that both are acts and by reason of each a thing enjoys actuality in some fashion. But they also differ. A substantial form produces the act of being in the unqualified sense *(esse simpliciter)*, and the subject of such a form is being only in potency, i.e., prime matter. An accidental form does not produce *esse simpliciter* but only being in a qualified sense—for instance, being of such a kind, or so much being, etc. And the subject of an accidental form is a being in act, i.e., a subsisting subject.[82]

While more texts of this type could be cited, these will suffice to show that Thomas continues to distinguish between the act of being which is given to a subject by its substantial form, and being in a qualified sense which is given by an accidental form.[83] These passages simply confirm the point we have been making: as Thomas distinguishes between substance and accident, so does he distinguish between substantial *esse* and accidental *esse*.

Before concluding this discussion of accidental *esse*, however, we must return again to Thomas's understanding of the relationship between an accident and the

---

79. Leon. 4.468. Note in particular: "Sicut igitur accidentia et formae, et huiusmodi, quae non subsistunt, magis sunt coexistentia quam entia; ita magis debent dici concreata quam creata. Proprie vero creata sunt subsistentia." Cf. *De potentia*, q. 3, a. 3, ad 2 (ed. cit., p. 43).

80. See above nn. 56, 57, and 62.

81. Ed. cit., p. 25: ". . . eo quod accidens quaedam forma est faciens esse actu secundum esse accidentale."

82. Leon. 5.246. See in particular: "Forma autem accidentalis non facit esse simpliciter; sed esse tale, aut tantum, aut aliquo modo se habens: subiectum enim eius est ens in actu."

83. See *Quaestiones disputatae de anima* (Leon. 24.1.79:145–80:150): "Est autem hoc proprium formae substantialis quod det materiae esse simpliciter. . . . Non autem per formas accidentales habet esse simpliciter, sed esse secundum quid, puta esse magnum vel coloratum vel aliquid tale."

corresponding accidental being. Are they distinct from one another or are they in fact identical? From the texts we have examined until now, the issue remains unresolved.

Certain texts may be cited in support of the view that Thomas distinguishes between an accident and its corresponding accidental *esse*, for instance between the quiddity of an accident such as whiteness as it is realized in a given subject, and the *esse* of that same whiteness which the accident contributes to its substantial subject.

For instance, in *Summa contra Gentiles* IV, c. 14, Thomas is engaged in a theological discussion of subsisting relations within God in connection with the eternal generation of the Word. He contrasts relation as it is realized in God and in creatures. In creatures relations have a dependent being, since their *esse* is distinct from the act of being of their subject or substance. Wherefore they enjoy the mode of being which is proper to their nature just as do other accidents. Because all accidents are certain forms which are superadded to a substance and caused by the principles of that substance, it follows that their *esse* is superadded to the *esse* of their substance and dependent upon it.[84]

Here Thomas appears to draw a parallel between accidents and their accidental *esse* and the substance and its act of being to which the accidents are added and upon which they depend. This account is at least open to the view that Thomas distinguishes between an accidental form and its corresponding being just as he distinguishes between a substantial form and its corresponding act of being *(esse)*. Even so, this passage can hardly be said to prove beyond all doubt that this is Thomas's position. Even if he identifies accidental form and accidental being *(esse)*, he can still hold that the being of an accident is superadded to and dependent upon the act of being of its substantial subject. And he clearly distinguishes here once again between accidental being and a substance's act of being.

Brown appeals to a number of passages where Thomas defends difference or otherness of quiddity and *esse* in things which fall into genera. We have already seen some of these in our discussion in Chapter V of the distinction between substantial essence and act of being. Brown, however, argues that there is no reason to think that Thomas restricts this reasoning to presence in the genus or predicament substance. As he sees things, Thomas rather is implying that presence in any genus, including the various predicamental accidents, requires a distinction between the essence and *esse* of that which falls therein.[85]

---

84. Ed. cit., p. 454: "In nobis enim relationes habent esse dependens, quia earum esse est aliud ab esse substantiae: unde habent proprium modum essendi secundum propriam rationem, sicut et in aliis accidentibus contingit. Quia enim omnia accidentia sunt formae quaedam substantiae superadditae, et a principiis substantiae causatae; oportet quod eorum esse sit superadditum supra esse substantiae, et ab ipso dependens. . . ." On this text see Brown, *Accidental Being*, pp. 219–22.

85. Brown cites *In I Sent.*, d. 19, q. 4, a. 2; *In II Sent.*, d. 3, q. 1, a. 1, ad 1; *In De Trinitate*, q. 6, a. 3; SCG I, c. 25; and *In I Sent.*, d. 8, q. 4, a. 2. For Brown see pp. 245–46. For discussion of some of these and other similar passages see Ch. V above, Section 3.

This is an interesting approach, but one that is not without its difficulties. First of all, in none of these passages does Thomas explicitly say that presence in any of the accidental predicaments entails distinction of essence and *esse* on the part of the accident in question. Against this criticism, Brown counters that in two of them Thomas wishes to show that God is not included in any genus, whether substance or accident. Hence he must mean that the presence of something in any predicament implies the distinction in it of essence and *esse*.[86]

Thus in his Commentary on the *De Trinitate* (q. 6, a. 3), Thomas remarks in passing that we cannot arrive even at confused knowledge of what God is by moving from some proximate or remote genus to knowledge of him; for God is not in any genus, since he does not have a quiddity which is distinct from his *esse*. But such otherness or distinction is required for membership in all genera.[87] However, it does not necessarily follow from this text that Thomas holds that membership in an accidental predicament requires distinction of essence and *esse* on the part of that accident. The more natural reading is simply to assume that Thomas is speaking of membership on the part of any substance in a proximate or remote genus.[88]

Brown also argues from a text taken from *Summa contra Gentiles* I, c. 25, and one we have analyzed above.[89] As Brown points out, in the immediately preceding paragraph Thomas has shown that God cannot be either in the genus substance or in the genus accident. Therefore, reasons Brown, when Thomas concludes that the *esse* of whatever belongs to a genus is other than its quiddity, he must be thinking of accidents as well as of substance.[90]

What Brown fails to mention, however, is the fact that in the text which he cites, Thomas has offered one argument to show that God is not in the genus accident and another to show that he is not in the genus substance. God cannot be an accident because he is the first being and the first cause. He cannot fall into the genus substance because a substance which is (in) a genus is not identical with its act of being; otherwise every substance would be identical with its act of being and would not be caused by something else. Because God is identical with his act of being, he is not in any genus.[91] Again, therefore, all signs indicate that Thomas is restricting his "genus argument" for a distinction of essence and act of being to members of the genus substance. He does not appear to apply it to accidents.

86. See Brown, p. 246.

87. Leon. 50.168:133–137: "Hoc autem non potest esse per cognitionem alicuius generis proximi vel remoti, eo quod Deus in nullo genere <est>, cum non habeat quod quid est aliud a suo esse; quod requiritur in omnibus generibus. . . ."

88. That Thomas is restricting this claim to substances is also especially clear in the second text cited by Brown, that is, *In II Sent.,* d. 3, q. 1, a. 1, ad 1 (Mandonnet ed., Vol. 2, p. 88).

89. Ed. cit., p. 26 "Item." See Ch. V above, n. 70 and my corresponding text.

90. Brown, p. 246. For Thomas see ed. cit., p. 26, first "Amplius."

91. Ed. cit., p. 26: "In genere etiam substantiae esse non potest: quia substantia quae est genus, non est ipsum esse. . . ."

Finally, militating strongly against Brown's interpretation is a text from *De veritate*, q. 27, a. 1, ad 8. As will be recalled from our consideration of this text in Ch. V above, there Thomas analyzes the ontological character of grace in the soul. An objector had reasoned that only things which are composed can belong to a genus. Grace, as a simple form, is not composed and therefore is not present in a genus. But everything created belongs to some genus. Hence grace is not something created.[92]

In replying to this objection Thomas agrees with it in part, that is, only insofar as it applies to substances. If something falls directly within the genus substance, it must be composed and really composed of an act of being *(esse)* and "what it is" (essence). But something need not be so composed in order to belong to an accidental predicament. A merely logical composition of genus and difference will suffice, and this is the situation with respect to grace, which Thomas places under the first species of quality.[93] Brown attempts to interpret this text so as to make it consistent with his claim that membership in any genus or category, including accidents, entails distinction or otherness (but not composition) of essence and *esse*. His interpretation strikes me as a valiant effort but as somewhat forced.[94] In any event, none of the texts examined so far proves that Thomas defended a real distinction between an accident or accidental quality and a corresponding accidental *esse*. And the present text strongly suggests that he rejected this position at the time of *De veritate*, q. 27, a. 1, ad 8.

On the other hand, Thomas makes an interesting if passing reference in his Commentary on III *Sentences*, d. 1, q. 1, a. 1. There he has identified four ways in which different things might be united with one another by being conjoined with something that is one: (1) numerically, or (2) in species, or (3) in genus, or (4) by analogy or proportion. It is in the last-mentioned way that substance and quality are one in being, that is, by analogy or proportion. As a substance is with respect to the being owing to it, so is a quality with respect to the being *(esse)* which is appropriate to its genus. From this text one might easily conclude that, just as Thomas distinguishes really between a substance and its act of being, so does he distinguish really between a quality and the accidental act of being *(esse)* which corresponds to it.[95]

92. See Leon. 22.3.790:51–55.

93. See Leon. 22.3.792:221–244. For the first part of this text see Ch. V. above, n. 74 and my corresponding text. Also note: "Similiter accidentia, quia non subsistunt, non est eorum proprie esse; sed subiectum est aliquale secundum ea; unde proprie dicuntur magis entis quam entia. Et ideo ad hoc quod aliquid sit in praedicamento aliquo accidentis non requiritur quod sit compositum compositione reali...." See q. 27, a. 2, ad 7 (p. 795:192–202) on grace as falling within the first species of quality as a kind of *dispositio*.

94. See Brown, pp. 247–51.

95. "... vel unum analogia seu proportione, sicut substantia et qualitas in ente: quia sicut se habet substantia ad esse sibi debitum, ita et qualitas ad esse sui generis conveniens" (Moos ed., Vol. 3, p. 8).

In addition, a text from Thomas's Commentary on IV *Sentences* (d. 12, q. 1, a. 1, sol. 3, ad 5) seems to make the same point. There Thomas is speaking of the accidents of bread and wine which remain after Eucharistic transubstantiation. According to an objection to this claim, if these accidents remain without their substantial subjects, they will approach the divine simplicity more closely than do angels. For angels are at least composed of *esse (quo est)* and of "that which is" *(quod est)*. To this Thomas responds that because such accidents have their *esse* and their proper essence, and since the two are not identical in them, it follows that in accidents they are distinct and composed with one another. In other words, like angels, such accidents are composed of essence and act of being *(esse)* and moreover, unlike angels, also of quantitative parts.[96]

These two texts point more strongly than any others we have examined to the conclusion that, at least at some point in the mid-1250s, Thomas did distinguish between accidental quiddity or essence and accidental *esse*. Unfortunately, however, I have been unable to find similar explicit defenses of that position in Thomas's later writings. While some of the later texts we have seen are at least open to such an interpretation, none is sufficiently pointed to show that Thomas continued to defend this position to the end of his career. On the contrary, the text from *De veritate*, q. 27, strongly suggests that shortly after completing his Commentary on III and IV *Sentences* he abandoned this view, at least for a time.[97]

In sum, it seems clear enough that Thomas consistently defended the reality of an accidental being *(esse)* which is distinct, and really distinct, from the substantial act of being of its subject. He always clearly distinguished between substance and accident when the latter is taken in its quidditative sense. Concerning whether he also defended a real distinction between an accidental quiddity and a corresponding accidental *esse,* my findings are less conclusive. As mentioned in the preceding paragraph, it seems that he did so at least during the early to mid-1250s, at the time of his Commentary on Bks III and IV of the *Sentences.* Whether he eventually returned to this as his final position remains, in my opinion, highly questionable. So far as I can determine, he can account for the various characteristics he assigns to accidents under either alternative, whether by assigning distinctive acts of being to each of them, or by identifying their essence with their *esse* and then appealing to the substantial act of being of their respective substantial subjects to account for their own existential actuality.

96. For obj. 5 see Moos ed., Vol. 4, p. 498. For Thomas's reply see pp. 503–4: "Ad quintum dicendum quod cum ista accidentia habeant esse et essentias proprias, et eorum essentia non sit eorum esse, constat quod aliud est in eis esse et quod est. Et ita habet compositionem illam quae in angelis invenitur, et ulterius compositionem ex partibus quantitatis quae in angelis non invenitur."

97. I am assuming that Thomas's Commentary on III and IV *Sentences* dates from the latter part of the period from 1252–1256, i.e., ca. 1255–1256, and that q. 27 of the *De veritate* was disputed in the 1258–1259 academic year. See Weisheipl, *Friar Thomas d'Aquino,* pp. 358–59, 362–63; Torrell, *Saint Thomas Aquinas,* pp. 332, 334.

3. The Causal Relationship between Substance and Accidents

Everything we have seen until this point concerning Thomas's views about substance and accidents indicates that in the purely natural order an accident does not exist in its own right apart from its substantial subject. Whether or not one assigns an act of being to an accident in addition to its quiddity, this point still holds. According to Aquinas accidents depend upon their substantial subject for whatever reality they enjoy. This is also brought out by the "quasi-definition" Thomas has proposed for accidents. An accident is that to which it belongs to be in something else. Even the accidents of bread and wine which survive Eucharistic transubstantiation continue to meet this definition, as Thomas sees things.

Our discussion in Ch. VII above has shown that Thomas regards a substantial subject as a receiving principle for the accidents which inhere in it. In fact, while commenting on *Metaphysics* IV he specifies that the substantial subject is not an end or an efficient cause but a subject for other and secondary instances of being, including especially, of course, accidents.[98] This is to say that the substantial subject exercises a material and receiving causality with respect to the accidents which inhere in it, and that it stands in potency with respect to them. The accidents themselves, as secondary forms or actualities, correspondingly exercise a determining or formal causality with respect to their substantial subject, but only in a secondary sense, of course.

There are other texts, however, in which Thomas is not content to restrict the kind of causality which a substance exercises with respect to some of its accidents to the order of material or receiving causality. When dealing with proper accidents, those which must be found wherever a given kind of being or substantial essence is realized, he often speaks of them as "flowing" or "emanating" or "following" from the essence of their subject. Immediately, of course, we wonder about the kind of causality he then has in mind. Is something more than material causality implied?

Before pursuing this issue, it will be helpful to recall that Thomas distinguishes different ways in which accidents stand in relation to their substantial subject. In one of his earliest discussions, his Commentary on I *Sentences,* d. 17, q. 1, a. 2, ad 2, he observes that a subject is related in diverse fashion to different kinds of accidents. There are certain natural accidents which are "created" from the principles of their subject. This in turn can happen in two different ways. Some accidents are caused from the principles of the species of the subject. These, says Thomas, are proper accidents *(passiones)* which follow upon the entire species. By this he means that such accidents must be realized in all substances which belong to a given species. Other accidents are also caused from the principles of their subject, but only as an individual insofar as they follow from its individual principles. By these

98. See *In IV Met.,* lect. 1, p. 152, n. 539, cited in Ch. VII above, n. 5.

Thomas has in mind certain accidents which must be realized wherever this given individual is realized, but which need not be present in every member of that same species.[99]

In contrast to the two classes of accidents which are caused from the principles of their subject, Thomas notes that others are introduced into a subject from without. This may be by violence, in the way heat, for instance, is introduced into water. Such accidents are opposed to the principles of the subject that receives them. Still other accidents are also introduced into a subject from without, but without being opposed to the principles of the subject that receives them. Rather such accidents perfect the principles of their receiving subject. It is in this way that light is received by air, and it is also in this way that charity is received in the soul from without.[100]

Thomas concludes this discussion by observing that a subject is in some fashion a cause of all the accidents which are sustained within the being of that same subject. Presumably by this he means that all accidents depend upon their subject as upon a receiving or material cause. But he also adds that not all accidents are educed from the principles of their subject.[101] If we may return to the fourfold division he has just proposed, only accidents of the first two types may be so described, that is, those which are proper in the sense that they follow from principles which are essential to a given species, and those which follow from principles which must be realized in a given individual. What he means by saying that such accidents are educed from the principles of their subject remains to be determined.[102]

Thomas returns to this issue in his much later *Quaestiones disputatae De anima*, q. 12, ad 7, dating from 1266–1267, as we have seen. There he continues to defend his view that the soul cannot be identified with its powers. In replying to the seventh objection, he observes that there are three kinds (genera) of accidents. Some are caused from the principles of a thing's species, and are described as proper accidents. In illustration Thomas cites the capacity of human beings to laugh. In other

99. In this question Thomas asks whether charity is an accident. According to the second objection, every accident is caused by its substance. But charity is not caused by the principles of the soul in which it is present. Therefore it seems that it is not an accident. See Mandonnet ed., Vol. 1, p. 397 for this objection, and pp. 398–99 for Thomas's reply to the same. From that reply note the following: "Quaedam autem sunt accidentia naturalia quae creantur ex principiis subiecti; et hoc dupliciter: quia vel causantur ex principiis speciei, et sic sunt propriae passiones, quae consequuntur totam speciem; vel ex principiis individui, et sic sunt communia consequentia principia naturalia individua" (p. 398). Thomas is using *creantur* broadly in the first part of the quoted text so as to be equivalent to *causantur.*

100. Ibid.

101. "Tamen sciendum, quod omnibus accidentibus, communiter loquendo, subiectum est causa quodam modo, inquantum scilicet accidentia in esse subiecti sustentantur [with Parma ed.; see Busa ed., Vol. 1, p. 45/Mandonnet: substantificantur]; non tamen ita quod ex principiis subiecti omnia accidentia educantur" (ibid., pp. 398–99).

102. See n. 99 above for the text.

words, wherever human beings are found, this capacity or accidental property must also be present.[103]

Other accidents are caused from the principles of an individual, and this in two different ways. Some of these accidents have a permanent cause in their subject and are, therefore, inseparable accidents. Such is true of masculine and feminine and other things of this type. In other words, accidents of this kind, while not present in all members of a species, follow from the individual principles of a particular being and must therefore always be found wherever that particular being is realized.[104]

Other accidents are also caused from the principles of an individual but do not always have a permanent cause in their subject. Because of this they may or may not be present in that subject and are therefore known as separable accidents. As illustrations Thomas mentions the acts of sitting and walking.[105]

Thomas also remarks that it is common to every accident not to be included within a thing's (substantial) essence, and hence not to fall within its definition. Because of this, we can understand the substantial quiddity of such a thing without understanding or thinking of its accidents. On the other hand, a species cannot be understood to exist without those accidents which follow from a principle of its species; but it can be understood to exist without accidents of the second type he has distinguished, those which are caused from principles of the individual considered as such. Indeed, this is true even if such accidents are inseparable. Finally, both a species and an individual can be realized (literally: "can exist") without their separable accidents. Thomas concludes this discussion by noting that the powers of the soul are accidents taken in the first sense, that is, properties or proper accidents. Hence what the soul is, i.e., its essence, can be understood without them; but it is neither thinkable nor possible for the soul to exist without them.[106]

Common to the three kinds of accidents Thomas has distinguished in this discussion is the fact that they are caused in some way by principles which are intrinsic to their receiving subject. This applies to proper accidents, to inseparable accidents which follow from the principles of an individual (such as male and female), and even to separable accidents such as walking or sitting. In each case, of course, these accidents inhere in their substantial subject. Therefore their subject serves as their

---

103. The seventh objection in q. 12 argues that an accident can be present and absent without entailing the corruption of its subject. But the powers of the soul cannot be absent (from the soul). Hence they are not accidents of the soul. For this objection see Leon. 24.1.106:42–45. For Thomas's reply see p. 111:265–287. From his reply note in particular: ". . . quaedam enim causantur ex principiis speciei et dicuntur propria, sicut risibile homini . . ." (lines 266–268).

104. ". . . quaedam causantur ex principiis individui, et hoc dupliciter: quia vel habent causam permanentem in subiecto, et haec sunt accidentia inseparabilia, sicut masculinum et femininum et alia huiusmodi . . ." (Leon. 24.1.111:268–272).

105. Leon. 24.1.111:272–274.

106. Leon. 24.1.111:275–287. Note in particular: "Sine separabilibus vero esse potest non solum species, sed etiam individuum."

receiving or material cause. In the third case—operations—the subject is to be regarded as the efficient cause of the accidents in question. But what of the first and second types? In addition to serving as their material or receiving cause, is their substantial subject also an efficient cause of such accidents?[107]

That Thomas has something more in mind than mere receiving or material causality by a subject of its inseparable accidents is already suggested by different passages from earlier writings. As will be recalled from his Commentary on I *Sentences*, d. 17, there he holds that a subject is a cause of all its accidents insofar as they are sustained in being by the being of the subject, but not in the sense that all the accidents are "educed" from the principles of the subject.[108] The implication is that some accidents—those that follow either from the principles of the subject's species, or from its principles as an individual—are educed or caused or "created" from the principles of the subject, and that this involves more than material or receiving causality.[109]

Something similar is suggested by a remark Thomas makes in his Commentary on the *De Trinitate,* q. 5, a. 4, ad 4. Certain accidents, such as shape in a heavenly body, are naturally and perpetually conserved in their subjects; for they follow upon a substance as upon their cause, and their subject is related to them not merely as a passive potency but in some way as an active principle.[110]

107. In *De ente,* c. 6 Thomas offers a somewhat different classification. Substance, as enjoying being in the primary sense, must be the cause of accidents. The essence of a material thing is composed of matter and form. Certain accidents primarily follow upon a thing's form, and others upon its matter. But one kind of form—the intellective soul—does not depend upon matter to exist. Therefore, among accidents which follow upon a form, one kind does not share in matter in any way, for instance, the act of understanding. Other accidents which follow upon a thing's form do share in matter, such as perceiving, etc. On the other hand, no accident follows upon matter without having something in common with form. Among the latter some accidents follow upon matter according to the order it bears to a specific form, such as male and female in animals. Hence when the form of the animal is removed, such accidents do not remain except in an equivocal sense. Other accidents follow upon matter insofar as it is ordered to a generic form. When the specific form is removed, these accidents remain, such as an Ethiopian's darkness of skin which remains after his death. Accidents which follow upon matter are said to be accidents of the individual, while those which follow upon form are known as properties of the genus or species (such as a human being's ability to laugh). Thomas also remarks that accidents are sometimes caused so as to be completely actualized by the principles of their subject, as heat in fire. Others are only caused as aptitudes by their subject's principles, and require intervention by some external agent if they are to be fully realized in the subject; e.g., transparency *(diaphaneitas)* in air which is perfected by an external luminous body. See Leon. 43.380:54–381:104. Rather than attempt to force this division into that offered in q. 12 of the *Quaestiones disputatae De anima,* it will be enough for us to note that the issue of the efficient causation of intrinsically caused accidents can be raised about those accidents which follow either from a thing's form or from its matter and which reside in that thing.

108. See nn. 99 and 101 above.

109. See especially the text cited in n. 101. To be educed from the principles of the subject is restricted to some accidents.

110. Leon. 50.155:277–156:286. Note especially: ". . . quia figura et omnia accidentia consequuntur substantiam sicut causam, et ideo subiectum se habet ad accidentia non solum ut potentia passiva, sed etiam quodammodo ut potentia activa. . . ."

A number of passages dating from Thomas's more mature writings also point to the same conclusion. For instance, a text we have already considered from *Summa contra Gentiles* IV, c. 14 (dating from ca. 1264–1265) is at least open to this interpretation. There Thomas remarks that all accidents are certain forms which are superadded to their substance and caused by the principles of the substance. In this text, however, he does not indicate in what way accidents are caused by their substance's principles, whether only in the order of receiving causality, or in other orders as well.[111]

In the *De potentia*, q. 7, a. 4 (dating from 1265–1266), Thomas offers a series of arguments to show that there are no accidents in God. In his second argument he reasons that since an accident is extrinsic to the essence of its subject and since things which are diverse can only be united through some cause, to admit that an accident is present in God would require a cause. No extrinsic cause could be admitted to account for this; for something would then be prior to God. Nor will appeal to an intrinsic cause suffice in the case of God, although this situation does obtain in the case of *per se* or proper accidents. They do have a cause within their subject. But a subject cannot serve as a cause of its accident by reason of that whereby it receives the accident; for no potency can move itself to act. Therefore a subject must receive an accident under one aspect and serve as the cause of that accident under another aspect. This is to say that the subject must be composed in some way, as is true of those subjects which receive an accident by reason of their matter and cause the same accident by reason of their form.[112]

This is an interesting text for a number of reasons. In it Thomas appeals to his general theory of act and potency to make the point that a subject cannot receive an accident under the same aspect in which it causes the accident; for no potency can reduce itself to act. We shall see more of his thinking concerning this when we take up his argumentation from motion for God's existence in ST I, q. 2, a. 3.[113] But Thomas's remark again suggests that, at least when he is dealing with proper accidents, he assigns some kind of causation to their substantial subject which is distinct from material or receiving causality. We would still like to learn more about this nonreceiving kind of causality.

This text is also important because in it Thomas anticipates a possible objection against the claim that a substantial subject can both receive and actively produce one and the same accident. He attempts to meet this objection by distinguishing within the subject between that by means of which it receives and that by means

111. See n. 84 above.

112. Ed. cit., pp. 195–96. Note in particular: "Similiter etiam non potest esse ex causa intrinseca, sicut est in per se accidentibus [for: per se in accidentibus], quae habent causam in subiecto. Subiectum enim non potest esse causa accidentis ex eodem ex quo suscipit accidens, quia nulla potentia movet se ad actum. Unde oportet quod ex alio sit susceptivum accidentis, et ex alio sit causa accidentis, et sic est compositum; sicut ista quae recipiunt accidens per naturam materiae, et causant accidens per naturam formae."

113. See Ch. XII, Section 1, "The First Way."

of which it actively causes an accident. In material substances he can appeal to the presence of matter and form to account for this. But what is he to say of the proper accidents of spiritual substances, such as the powers of intellect and will? As he sees things, these powers inhere in the soul itself rather than in the matter-form composite, and the human soul itself is not composed of matter and form. We shall return to this shortly.[114]

Not long after the time of his *De potentia,* Thomas touches on this theme in different passages from the *Prima Pars* of the *Summa theologiae.* Thus in q. 3, a. 4 he makes a pertinent observation in the course of his first argument to show that God is identical with his act of being *(esse).* Whatever is present in a thing in addition to its essence must be caused either by the principles of the thing's essence or by something extrinsic. It is in the first way that proper accidents which follow upon the species are caused, such as the capacity of human beings to laugh. This is to say, proper accidents are caused by a thing's essential principles. Thomas contrasts this with the kind of thing which is caused by an extrinsic principle, such as heat which is produced in water by fire. Since in the latter case he clearly has in mind efficient causation, one strongly suspects that this is true of the former case as well, i.e., that proper accidents which follow upon a thing's species are caused efficiently by that thing's essential and intrinsic principles.[115] At the very least, something more than receiving or material causality is intended.

Farther on in this same *Prima Pars,* Thomas spells out his position more fully. Q. 77 is directed to the powers of the soul. As we will see in the final section of this chapter, in a. 1 Thomas strongly insists that the essence of the soul cannot be identified with its powers. In a. 6 he asks whether the powers of the soul flow from the soul's essence. As noted above, in this discussion he compares and contrasts substantial forms and accidental forms. Because that which is first in a genus serves as a cause, a substantial form causes the actual being of its subject. (Here, of course, Thomas is not thinking of efficient causality.) Conversely, he continues, actuality is present in the subject of an accidental form before (at least in the order of nature) it is found in the accidental form itself. Therefore, the actuality of an accidental form is caused by the actuality of its subject. Hence the subject, insofar as it is in potency, receives an accidental form; but insofar as the subject is in act, it produces the accidental form. Thomas immediately adds that in saying this he has in mind only proper and *per se* accidents. As regards any extrinsic accident, i.e., one produced by some external agent, the subject is only a receiving principle. The productive principle for such an accident is the extrinsic agent.[116]

---

114. See below pp. 272–75.

115. Leon. 4.42. See in particular: ". . . quia quidquid est in aliquo quod est praeter essentiam eius, oportet esse causatum vel a principiis essentiae, sicut accidentia propria consequentia speciem, ut risibile consequitur hominem et causatur ex principiis essentialibus speciei. . . ."

116. Cf. n. 82 above. For Thomas's discussion in a. 6 see Leon. 5.246. Note in particular: ". . . unde actualitas formae accidentalis causatur ab actualitate subiecti. Ita quod subiectum, inquan-

Important for our present purpose is Thomas's remark that insofar as a subject is in act, it produces its proper accidents. As he makes clear in the following lines, even those powers of the soul which reside in the soul alone (rather than in the matter-form composite) flow from the soul's essence as from their productive principle. He comments that a (proper) accident is caused by its subject insofar as the subject is in actuality, and is received by that subject insofar as it is in potency. In this case, of course, he cannot account for this dual causal role on the part of the subject by appealing to matter-form composition of the soul itself. Nor does he judge it necessary to do so. Simply insofar as the soul is in potency in some way, he has remarked, it can be the subject or receiving principle for those accidents which reside in it. Though Thomas does not develop this point here, we may recall that, as the form or act principle of a human essence, the human soul is still in potency with respect to the act of being which it receives and communicates to its correlative matter. This, apparently, is enough for it to be in potency in a second way as well, as the receiving principle of its accident. And if we wonder why the soul is in act (and therefore productive of its proper accidents), this must ultimately follow from the fact that it is actualized by its corresponding act of being.[117]

In replying to the second objection in this same article, Thomas spells out his thinking more fully. The objection maintains that the essence of the soul cannot be called a cause of its powers, as anyone can see by running through the different genera of causes. Therefore the powers of the soul do not flow from its essence. Thomas counters that a subject is a cause of its proper accidents in three ways, i.e., as a final cause, in a certain way *(quodammodo)* as an active cause, and also as a material cause. It is a material cause insofar as it receives the accidents. He concludes from this that the essence of the soul is a cause of all its powers by serving as their end (final cause) and as their active principle. It causes some of them as their receiving cause.[118] He makes this last qualification in accord with a point he

---

tum est in potentia, est susceptivum formae accidentalis; inquantum autem est in actu, est eius productivum. Et hoc dico de proprio et per se accidente: nam respectu accidentis extranei, subiectum est susceptivum tantum. . . ." Cf. ST I, q. 77, a. 1, ad 5.

117. "Unde manifestum est quod omnes potentiae animae, sive subiectum earum sit anima sola, sive compositum, fluunt ab essentia animae sicut a principio: quia iam dictum est quod accidens causatur a subiecto secundum quod est actu, et recipitur in eo inquantum est in potentia" (Leon. 5.246). On the unique status of the human soul as a form which possesses being *(esse)* in its own right and can, therefore subsist, unlike purely material or corporeal forms, see, for instance, *De unitate intellectus contra Averroistas* (Leon. 43.298:622–653). On this see F. Van Steenberghen, *Thomas Aquinas and Radical Aristotelianism*, pp. 64–66; *Maître Siger de Brabant*, pp. 356–57. Van Steenberghen stresses the point that for Thomas the human soul is indeed a form of matter but not a material form. Cf. B. C. Bazán, "La corporalité selon saint Thomas," *Revue philosophique de Louvain* 81 (1983), pp. 386–87. See p. 383 on Thomas's refusal to regard the human soul as an hypostasis or a person.

118. Leon. 5.246: ". . . dicendum quod subiectum est causa proprii accidentis et finalis, et quodammodo activa; et etiam ut materialis, inquantum est susceptivum accidentis. Et ex hoc potest accipi quod essentia animae est causa omnium potentiarum sicut finis et sicut principium activum; quarundam autem sicut susceptivum."

had already developed in the corpus of this same article. While the soul alone is the subject of some of its powers, i.e., the purely spiritual ones, the composite of soul and body serves as the subject for other powers, i.e., those that depend upon the body as well.[119]

While we can easily understand why Thomas describes the soul as the receiving principle for some of its powers, and also as the final cause for all its powers, we may still wonder what he means by referring to it as in a certain way their active or productive principle. In replying to the third objection in this same context, Thomas remarks that the emanation of proper accidents from a subject does not take place through any kind of change but simply through what he calls a natural "resulting," or according to other manuscript readings, a natural "concomitance" or "consequence." By this he seems to mean that one thing, a property, naturally results from another, a subject, in the way color naturally results from light.[120] He makes the same point in replying to the first objection in the following article, and in the corpus of that article again remarks that the essence of the soul is related to its powers as an active principle, as a final principle, and as a receiving principle.[121]

In his later writings Thomas continues to defend the point that the powers of the soul are caused by its essential principles. For instance, in his *De spiritualibus creaturis,* a. 11 (dating from 1267–1268), he distinguishes once more between the powers of the soul and its essence. In the corpus and in his reply to the fifth objection he notes that the powers of the soul can be called essential principles, not in the sense that they are parts of the soul's essence, but in the sense that they are caused by its essential principles and naturally follow from its essence.[122]

In his still later Disputed Question *De virtutibus in communi,* a. 3 (Paris, 1271–1272), Thomas considers the question whether a power of the soul can be the sub-

---

119. Ibid. Also see ST I, q. 77, a. 8: "Utrum omnes potentiae animae remaneant in anima a corpore separata" (Leon. 5.248–49).

120. Ibid. "Ad tertium dicendum quod emanatio propriorum accidentium a subiecto non est per aliquam transmutationem; sed per aliquam naturalem resultationem, sicut ex uno naturaliter aliud resultat, ut ex luce color."

121. See q. 77, a. 7: "Ad primum ergo dicendum quod, sicut potentia animae ab essentia fluit, non per transmutationem, sed per naturalem quandam resultationem, et est simul cum anima. . . ." From his reply note: "Sed quia essentia animae comparatur ad potentias et sicut principium activum et finale, et sicut principium susceptivum, vel seorsum per se vel simul cum corpore . . ." (Leon. 5.247). By saying that powers are related to the soul as to their final principle Thomas means that the soul is in some way completed or perfected through its powers (and their operations). See, for instance, q. 77, a. 6c: ". . . sed e converso, forma accidentalis est propter completionem subiecti" (p. 246).

122. Calcaterra-Centi ed., in *Quaestiones disputatae,* Vol. 2, p. 414: "Ad quintum dicendum quod potentiae animae dici possunt proprietates essentiales, non quia sint partes essentiae, sed quia causantur ab essentia; et sic non distinguuntur ab accidente quod est commune novem generibus: sed distinguuntur ab accidente, quod est accidentale praedicatum et non causatur a natura speciei." By this he means that a power of the soul is indeed a predicamental accident, but not a predicable accident. In other words, it is a property. For this see the corpus of his reply, p. 413. As he points out there, powers of the soul fall under the second species of quality.

ject of a virtue. In preparing his answer he first notes that a subject is related to an accident in three ways: (1) by sustaining or supporting the accident, since an accident does not exist in its own right apart from a subject; (2) as potency to act (thus a subject stands under an accident as a certain potency for something active; for this reason the accident is related to it as a form); (3) as a cause to its effect, since the principles of the subject are the principles of a *per se* (or proper) accident.[123]

Rather than explain more fully how a substance may be said to cause its proper accidents, Thomas goes on to examine if and to what extent one accident may stand in similar relationships to other accidents.[124] But since he has referred to a substance in one way as sustaining or supporting an accident, and in the third way as causing it in some fashion, the kind of causality he has in mind seems once more to be distinct from material or receiving causation.

In sum, we have seen that throughout his career Thomas holds that a substance serves as a receiving or material cause for the accidents which inhere in it. Hence the subject is in potency to such accidents, and the accidents may be regarded as its secondary acts or secondary forms. In itself this poses no great difficulty. But Thomas refers to certain accidents as being "created" or "caused" from or by the principles of their substantial subject, or as being "educed" or "flowing from" or "resulting from" the same. This is repeatedly said to be true of proper accidents, i.e., those which follow from a thing's essential or specific principles, though some texts suggest that it applies to other accidents which follow from a thing's individual principles—but only, I would suggest, if those accidents are inseparable from that individual.[125]

Thomas has also indicated that a subject may be regarded as a productive principle or cause of its proper accidents. This follows from the fact that the subject is in actuality in some way. In the case of a composite substance, Thomas has traced this producing role back to the substantial form of that subject. In the case of a simple form such as the human soul, the form itself is in act insofar as it is actualized by its corresponding act of being, although it is in potency to any accidental forms which inhere in it. Thomas has noted that a subject is a cause of its proper accidents in three ways, i.e., as a final cause, in a certain way as an active cause, and as a material cause. And in the last text we have examined *(De virtutibus,* a. 3), he has remarked that a subject is related to its proper accident as a cause to its effect; for the principles of the subject are also principles for such an accident.[126]

---

123. A. Odetto, ed., in *Quaestiones disputatae,* Vol. 2, p. 715: ". . . subiectum tripliciter comparatur ad accidens. Uno modo, sicut praebens ei sustentamentum; nam accidens per se non subsistit, fulcitur vero per subiectum. Alio modo sicut potentia ad actum; nam subiectum accidenti subiicitur, sicut quaedam potentia activi; unde et accidens forma dicitur. Tertio modo sicut causa ad effectum; nam principia subiecti [conjectural correction for: subiecta] sunt principia per se accidentis."

124. Ibid.

125. For texts where Thomas applies this to accidents which follow from a thing's individual principles see nn. 99 and 104 above.

126. See n. 123 above.

One might wish that Thomas had spelled out more fully what it means for the soul or for a substantial subject to serve "in a certain way" as an active or productive or efficient cause of its proper accidents. For some reason he has not seen fit to do so. What he seems to mean by this is the following. As regards the kind of accidents which necessarily follow from the essence of a given substance, once that substance is brought into being by its extrinsic efficient cause, its proper accidents are also automatically given. The substantial subject need not be prior to them in time, but only in nature. But since Thomas regards them, and especially the powers of the soul, as distinct from the essence of the substance or soul, he holds that the subject may be regarded as their proximate cause, and even as their proximate active or efficient cause in some sense. To view the subject or soul as a mere receiving cause of such accidents is not sufficient.

And if the subject or soul serves as a proximate efficient cause for the coming into being of such accidents or powers, it fulfills this same function in accounting for their continuing existence. Perhaps we can best express this by saying that the subject or soul exercises a kind of instrumental efficient causality regarding such proper accidents. As Thomas sees things, they, like their substantial subject, will continue to depend on some extrinsic principal efficient cause as well, as least upon God, for their continuing existence.

4. The Relationship between the Soul and Its Powers

Because so much of Thomas's discussion of the causal relationship between a subject and its proper accidents is set within the context of the relationship between the soul and its powers, we shall conclude this chapter by turning to that issue. On this point Thomas defends a position which was by no means universally accepted in his time.[127] He denies that the soul is to be identified with its powers and distin-

127. For a helpful overview of earlier positions concerning this in the thirteenth century see P. Künzle, *Das Verhältnis der Seele zu ihren Potenzen*, pp. 97–170 ("Die Hochscolastik"). On p. 140 he sums up his treatment of the earlier Franciscan School: "Mit Ausnahme des Richardus Rufus lehnen also alle Franziskaner die Identität ab, aber ebensosehr und zusehends stärker die *konsequente* Realunterscheidung, die den Potenzen nur akzidentelles Sein zuerkennen kann." See pp. 144–58 on Albert who, concludes Künzle, regards the powers of the soul as accidents but, unlike Aquinas, makes the soul the subject of all the powers (see p. 158). Not too long after Thomas's death Henry of Ghent would deny that the spiritual powers of the soul are things *(res)* which are really distinct from the soul itself. They are rather relationships *(respectus)* on the part of the soul itself. Though not really distinct from the soul, Henry holds that they are "intentionally" distinct from it, applying thereto an intermediary kind of distinction for which he would become noted. Against Henry, Godfrey of Fontaines argued strongly for real distinction between the soul and its powers as between a substance and its accidents. On Henry see R. Macken, "Les diverses applications de la distinction inten-tionnelle chez Henri de Gand," *Miscellanea Mediaevalia* 13.2 (Berlin, 1981), p. 770; "La volonté humaine, faculté plus élevée que l'intelligence selon Henri de Gand," *Recherches de Théologie ancienne et médiévale* 42 (1975), pp. 23–30; "Heinrich von Gent im Gespräch mit seinen Zeitgenossen über die menschliche Freiheit," *Franziskanische Studien* 59 (1977), p. 156. For Godfrey see my *The Metaphysical Thought of Godfrey of Fontaines*, pp. 202–7.

guishes between them as between that which falls into the category of substance (the soul) and that which falls into the accidental category of quality (powers of the soul). As we shall see, he defends this position, at least in its essentials, from the beginning of his teaching career. Some years ago, however, a surprising claim was advanced by E.-H. Wéber. Owing to his philosophical "dialogue" with Siger of Brabant at Paris around the year 1270, Thomas would have eventually abandoned this position and ended by identifying the human soul with what he had previously regarded as a distinct power—the intellect.[128] In order to detect any such possible historical development in Thomas's position, therefore, we shall begin with his earliest texts. Only after having considered the relevant texts will we be in position to react to Wéber's claim.

In Bk I of his Commentary on the *Sentences* (d. 3, q. 4, a. 2), Thomas asks whether the powers of the soul are (identical with) its essence.[129] After offering a number of arguments for and against this claim, he presents his personal solution. He builds this upon a more general metaphysical position—that an immediate and proper effect must be proportioned to its cause. Because of this, if a thing's proximate principle of operation falls within the genus substance, that thing's operation itself must be its substance. But this is true only of God. Because God's operation and substance are identical, God is the only agent who does not act by means of an intermediary power which differs from his substance. The operations of other agents are accidents. Therefore the proximate principles for such operations must also be accidents.[130]

Thomas then draws an analogy between fire, on the purely corporeal level, and the human soul. Just as the substantial form of fire can operate only by means of active and passive qualities which are, as it were, its powers and potencies, so too the soul, being a substance, can perform no operation except by means of a power. (He adds that a perfect operation cannot be produced except by means of a habit which, we may assume, will inform such a power.)[131]

Thomas goes on to observe that these powers flow from the essence of the soul. Certain ones do so in such fashion that they are perfections of parts of the body,

128. *La controverse de 1270 à l'Université de Paris et son retentissement sur la pensée de s. Thomas d'Aquin* (Paris, 1970), cc. 3–6 (pp. 47–220); "Les discussions de 1270 à l'Université de Paris et leur influence sur la pensée philosophique de s. Thomas d'Aquin," *Miscellanea Mediaevalia* 10: *Die Auseinandersetzungen an der Pariser Universität im XIII Jahrhundert* (Berlin, 1976), pp. 285–316. For lengthy critical reactions to Wéber's thesis see C. Lefèvre, "Siger de Brabant a-t-il influencé saint Thomas? Propos sur la cohérence de l'anthropologie thomiste," *Mélanges de science religieuse* 31 (1974), pp. 203–15; and especially, B. Bazán, "Le dialogue philosophique entre Siger de Brabant et Thomas d'Aquin. A propos d'un ouvrage récent de E. H. Wéber, O.P.," *Revue philosophique de Louvain* 72 (1974), pp. 53–155.

129. Mandonnet ed., Vol. 1, p. 115.

130. Ed. cit., p. 116. Note especially: "In omnibus autem aliis operatio est accidens; et ideo oportet quod proximum principium operationis sit accidens. . . ."

131. Ibid. Note especially: "Similiter dico, quod ab anima, cum sit substantia, nulla operatio egreditur, nisi mediante potentia: nec etiam a potentia perfecta operatio, nisi mediante habitu."

i.e., those which operate by means of the body (sense, imagination, etc.). Others do so in such fashion that they inhere in the soul itself. These are those powers which do not require the body for their operations, i.e., intellect and will.[132] Finally, in describing these powers as accidents, Thomas does not intend to say that they are common accidents but rather that they are proper accidents, properties, we may say, which follow from a thing's specific essence and are found, therefore, wherever this specific kind of being is realized.[133]

A number of things are clear from this very early text (ca. 1252). Already Thomas refuses to identify the soul with its powers. Powers of the soul are accidents, but proper accidents or properties. These properties are said to flow from the essence of the soul, although Thomas does not here attempt to elucidate the particular kind of causal relationship that obtains between the soul and its powers. His purpose is rather to show that the soul and its powers are not to be identified.

As for his argument to show this, it rests upon his conviction that a proper and immediate effect must be proportioned to its cause. Therefore, if a thing's proximate principle of operation falls within the genus substance, the operation itself must also be a substance. If we grant this, the conclusion quickly follows simply by denying the consequent. The operation of a creature is not a substance, since it is only something accidental. (For Thomas this would be evident enough from the fact that the soul is not always performing all of its operations.) Therefore the proximate principle for such an operation does not fall within the predicament substance and can only be something accidental. Even so, we might ask whether the overriding presupposition for this argument is immediately evident, i.e., that if a thing's proximate principle of operation falls within the genus substance, the operation itself must also be a substance. Others had and would acknowledge that a thing's operations may indeed be accidental, but maintained that the proximate principle for such operations need not be a really distinct accidental power, but the substance of the soul itself insofar as it is ordered to those operations. Fuller justification seems to be needed for this part of Thomas's argumentation.[134]

In *De veritate*, q. 10, a. 1 (ca. 1257–1258) Thomas makes some interesting remarks about the powers of the soul, even though he is not here concerned with establishing the distinction between the soul and its powers. He simply takes this distinction for granted. Article 1 is directed to determining whether mind *(mens)*, insofar as it

132. Ibid. Note: "Hae autem potentiae fluunt ab essentia ipsius animae. . . ."

133. Ibid. ". . . non quod sint communia accidentia . . . ; sed sicut propria accidentia, quae consequuntur speciem, originata ex principiis ipsius. . . ."

134. Thus Bonaventure, without defending unqualified identity between the soul and its powers, holds that they do not differ sufficiently from the soul so as to fall into a distinct and accidental genus; they fall within the genus substance *per reductionem*. See, for instance, his *In I Sent.*, d. 3, p. 2, a. 1, q. 3, resp. (cited and discussed by Künzle, *Das Verhältnis der Seele*, pp. 129ff.). And for Henry of Ghent see above, n. 127. For some interesting remarks about historical antecedents for the five arguments cited by Thomas in favor of identity of the soul with its powers see Künzle, pp. 171–72. On this argument in Thomas see Künzle, p. 174.

is viewed as an image of the Trinity within the soul, is to be taken as the essence of the soul or as a power.[135]

In developing his reply, Thomas notes that the term "intellect," insofar as it is expressed in relationship to the act of (understanding), designates a power of the soul. Such a *virtus* or power is intermediate between the essence of the soul and its operation. Farther on Thomas remarks that the human soul includes the highest level of powers of the soul. And from this highest level of power the human soul receives its name. Thus it is known as the intellective soul, or sometimes simply as the intellect or mind, since this power (intellect or mind) naturally flows from the human soul itself.[136] Given this, Thomas concludes that the term "mind" expresses that in our soul which is highest as a power. And since the divine image is found in us according to that which is highest within us, the image of the Trinity will not belong to the essence of the soul except by reason of "mind," its highest power. In other words, insofar as the image of the Trinity is expressed by the term "mind" *(mens)*, it refers not to the essence of the soul but to its highest power. Or if it does refer to the soul's essence, this is true only insofar as the power of mind flows from the soul's essence itself.[137]

In this discussion and in replies to certain objections in this article Thomas takes as given the distinction between the soul and its powers. Important for our later consideration of any eventual evolution in his position is his remark that the soul is known as the intellective soul, but also as the intellect or mind. This suggests that we must carefully determine when Thomas uses the term "intellect" to signify a power of the soul, and when he uses it to designate the intellective soul itself.[138]

In the only slightly later Quodlibet 10, q. 3, a. 1 of 1258, Thomas again responds to the question whether the soul is identical with its powers. In replying he notes that we may speak of the soul in two ways, either (1) insofar as it is a certain substance, or (2) insofar as it is a certain potential whole.[139]

When taken in the first way—as a certain substance—the soul cannot be identified with its powers, and this for two reasons. First of all, it is impossible for one

---

135. "Et primo quaeritur utrum mens, prout in ea est imago Trinitatis, sit essentia animae, vel aliqua potentia eius" (Leon. 22.2.295:2–5). With Weisheipl I am assuming that Thomas disputed q. 10 during his second year as Regent Master (see *Friar Thomas d'Aquino*, pp. 362ff.).

136. Leon. 22.2.296:107–297:139. Note: ". . . sed anima humana pertingit ad altissimum gradum inter potentias animae et ex hoc denominatur, unde dicitur intellectiva et quandoque etiam intellectus, et similiter mens inquantum scilicet ex ipsa nata est effluere talis potentia, quod est sibi proprium prae aliis animabus" (297:133–139).

137. Leon. 22.2.297:140–149. Note: ". . . vel si nominat essentiam, hoc non est nisi inquantum ab ea fluit talis potentia."

138. See our discussion below of Wéber's claim that Thomas eventually abandoned his theory of real distinction between the soul and its powers. Note that in his reply to objection 2 Thomas explains that the term "mind" can be used so as to include both the intellect and the will, in that it then signifies a certain genus of powers of the soul, i.e., those that completely transcend matter and the conditions of matter in their operation (Leon. 22.2.298:212–219). Cf. his replies to objections 7 and 8.

139. See Leon. 25.1.130–31: ". . . primo utrum anima sit suae potentiae."

and the same thing, insofar as it is one and the same, to be the principle for many things which are (specifically) distinct from and even, as it were, opposed to one another. But through its different powers the soul serves as the principle for acts which differ from one another in species and which are, as it were, opposed to one another. Therefore, it is impossible for the essence of the soul, which is one, to function immediately as the principle for such diverse acts. Consequently, one must posit in the soul, in addition to its substance (essence), natural powers which are the immediate principles for its acts or operations.[140]

This argument, which Thomas regards as directed to the soul itself rather than to all finite being, is based on a question of fact—that diverse kinds of operations are performed by the soul—and a question of principle—that one and the same soul cannot, insofar as it is one and the same essence, serve as the proximate principle for such diverse operations. Only by postulating distinct powers within the soul can one account for such diversity in operations.

Thomas offers a second argument which he applies to the soul and to every created substance. In no created substance are act of being *(esse)* and operation identical. Such identity obtains in God alone. But an essence is a principle for the act of being, while a power is a principle of operation. Therefore, since from one principle only one thing can follow by nature, no substance, with the exception of the divine, is identical with its operative power.[141]

This argument reminds one of that offered in Thomas's Commentary on I *Sentences,* though it is phrased somewhat differently. In no creature can act of being *(esse)* and operation be identified. The reason for this, we may presume, is that if this were not the case, to operate would be to change and even to destroy the substantial act of being of the agent in question. But an essence is a principle for a thing's act of being since, as we have seen, it is related to its act of being as potency to act. A power, on the other hand, is a principle for its operation. If we grant to Thomas that a creature's act of being *(esse)* cannot be identified with its operation, it will follow, he reasons, that the principle for a thing's act of being—its essence—cannot be identified with the principle for its operations—its operative powers. We may wonder why this follows. Thomas's answer is that from one principle only one thing (or kind of thing, we should add) follows by nature. Because operation differs from act of being, the principle for a thing's operations must differ from the principle for its act of being, i.e., its essence.[142]

---

140. Leon. 25.1.130:37–131:50. Note in particular: ". . . unde impossibile est quod ipsa essentia animae, quae est una, sit immediate horum principium. . . ."

141. ". . . in nulla enim substantia creata est idem esse et operatio, hoc enim solius Dei est; essentia autem est essendi principium, potentia vero operationis; unde, cum ab uno naturaliter non sit nisi unum, nulla substantia, nisi divina, est sua potentia"(Leon. 25.1.131:52–57).

142. See the final part of the text cited in n. 141. It is important to stress the term *naturaliter* in this passage. By this Thomas has in mind naturally determined agents or principles as distinguished from those which act freely. For the argument from *In I Sent.* see n. 130 above.

In what may be a bow to Albert the Great, Thomas concludes his response in
Quodlibet 10 by returning to the second way in which one may speak of the soul,
i.e., insofar as it is a certain potential whole. When we understand the soul in this
way, we may regard its various powers as parts of the same potential whole. Although this will involve an "abuse of predication," Thomas notes that in this sense
the term "soul" may be predicated of its powers or vice versa in the way a completed
whole may be said of its parts or vice versa. He adds that the abuse of language
involved in such speech is less egregious when we are dealing with a potential whole
than with a completed whole.[143]

For the moment we shall bypass Thomas's discussion in *Summa contra Gentiles,*
Bk II, and turn to three later and chronologically very close works where he continues to argue for a distinction between the soul and its powers: ST I, q. 77; *De
spiritualibus creaturis,* a. 11; *Quaestiones disputatae De anima,* q. 12, dating respectively, as will be recalled, ca. 1266–1268 (ST I), 1266–1267 *(Qu. disp. De anima),*
and between November 1267 and September 1268 *(Qu. disp. De spiritualibus creaturis).* In his critical edition of the *Qu. disp. De anima,* Bazán has developed a strong
case for placing the disputation of this work in Italy and slightly before the other
two works to be considered. He is fully aware of various efforts by some to place it
after the other two. Without attempting to resolve any remaining disagreements
about the relative chronology of these three works, but simply to facilitate ease in
presenting the various arguments found in each, I will begin with ST I, followed
by *Qu. disp. De spiritualibus creaturis,* and then *Qu. disp. De anima.*[144]

The whole of q. 77 of ST I is devoted to the powers of the soul taken in general.
Article 1 is explicitly directed to our problem: whether the essence of the soul is
(identical with) its power. Consistent with all the texts we have seen until now,
Thomas flatly states that it is not possible to hold that the essence of the soul is
identical with its power, even though some have proposed this. He immediately
offers two arguments in support of his position.[145]

143. Leon. 25.1.131:61–69. Note in particular: ". . . et sic diversae potentiae sunt partes eius, et ita
anima praedicatur de potentiis vel e converso, abusiva praedicatione, sicut totum integrale de suis
partibus vel e converso. . . ." Cf. from his Commentary on I *Sentences,* d. 3, q. 4, a. 2, end of corpus:
"[potentiae] simul tamen sunt de integritate ipsius animae, inquantum est totum potentiale, habens
quamdam perfectionem potentiae, quae conficitur ex diversis viribus" (Mandonnet ed., Vol. 1,
p. 116). For references to and discussion of Albert's view of the soul as a potential whole, especially
when he is rejecting theories that would identify the soul and its powers, see Künzle, *Das Verhältnis
der Seele,* pp. 146–51. This view is present in Albert's very early works including his *Summa de homine*
and his Commentary on *I Sent.,* d. 3, a. 34.

144. For these datings see Torrell, *St. Thomas Aquinas,* p. 333 (ST I); Bazán, Préface, Leon.
24.1.7*–25*. See p. 23* for his discussion of an interesting proposal by K. White which, based on the
superiority of the presentation in q. 9 of the *Qu. disp. De anima,* would place it after ST I, *Qu. disp.
De spiritualibus creaturis,* and *Sententia libri De anima.* For White see "Aquinas on the Immediacy
of the Union of Soul and Body," in *Studies in Thomistic Theology,* P. Lockey, ed. (Houston, 1995),
pp. 209–80.

145. Leon. 5.236: "Respondeo dicendum quod impossibile est dicere quod essentia animae sit
eius potentia. . . ."

In his first argument Thomas explicitly appeals to his understanding of potency and act. Because potency and act divide being and every genus of being, a potency and its corresponding act must belong to the same genus. Therefore, if a given act does not fall within the genus substance, the potency which is ordered to that act cannot be within that genus. But an operation of the soul is not in the genus substance, since in God alone are substance and operation identical. Therefore, the potency which serves as God's principle of operation is his very essence. Such cannot be said of the soul or of any creature, Thomas continues, as he has already shown above when dealing with angels.[146] In other words, in creatures powers of operation can only be accidents.

Here, therefore, Thomas continues to hold that no created substance is immediately operative. This time he supports that claim by explicitly making the point that a potency and its corresponding act must belong to the same genus. In order to complete his argument, however, he would have us turn back to his earlier discussion of this in angels. In ST I, q. 54, a. 3 he argues that neither in an angel nor in any creature is an operative power identical with that creature's essence. In proof he reasons that since potency is ordered to act, potencies must be diversified in accord with diversity of acts. It is for this reason, he explains, that a proper act is said to correspond to its proper power. But in every creature essence differs from act of being and is related to it as potency to act. But the act to which an operative power is ordered is an operation. In an angel an act of understanding cannot be identified with that angel's act of being; for in no creature is any operation to be identified with that creature's act of being *(esse)*. Therefore, the essence of an angel is not identical with its intellective power, nor is the essence of any creature identical with its powers of operation. The reader will immediately note the close similarity between this reasoning and the second argument we have just considered from Quodlibet 10, even though in ST I, q. 77, a. 1 Thomas has more explicitly appealed to the point that a potency and its corresponding act must belong to the same genus.[147]

In sum, in these two texts (q. 77, a 1; q. 54, a. 3) Thomas connects his argumentation for a distinction between the soul and its powers with his metaphysics of act and potency; and he applies the latter to the essence-*esse* relationship, and then to the relationship of a power to its operations. In a creature essence is related to act of being *(esse)* as potency to act. Because a creature's act of being is distinct from any of that creature's operations, the potency which is ordered to its act of being, i.e., its essence, cannot be identified with any potency which is ordered to its operation.[148]

146. Ibid.

147. See Leon. 5.47. For the point that the action of an angel or of any other creature cannot be identified with that creature's *esse* see q. 54, a. 2 (Leon. 5.45).

148. Wéber's presentation of this argumentation in ST I, q. 77, a. 1 and q. 54, aa. 1–3, could be considerably strengthened by bringing out explicitly Thomas's appeal to the essence-*esse* distinction.

In q. 77, a. 1 Thomas offers a second argument which is immediately directed to the human soul rather than to created being in general. With obvious reference to Aristotle's description of the soul in the *De anima* and his own view that the human soul is a substantial form, Thomas remarks that according to its essence the soul is an act. If the essence of the soul were its immediate principle of operation, one who always possessed a soul in actuality would also always actually perform all its vital operations. Thomas also observes that insofar as the soul is a form, it is not an act which is ordered to any further act; rather it is the ultimate terminus of the process of generation. For the soul to be in potency to additional acts does not belong to its essence insofar as it is a form, therefore, but only by reason of some potentiality. And insofar as the soul is subject to such potentiality, it is referred to as a first act which is ordered to a second act. In fact, however, we observe that someone who has a soul does not always perform all the soul's vital operations. From this it follows that the essence of the soul cannot be identified with its potency for operation.[149]

While this argument is cast in different terms from any we have seen so far, in it Thomas again appeals to a general principle and to a fact which can be discovered by introspection and by observation of other human agents. The principle assumes that the soul is an act in the line of essence and, because of this, that if the soul were the immediate principle of its operations, whenever it existed it would also perform those operations. Introspection and observation reveal, however, that the soul does not always perform those operations. Hence it is not the immediate principle of its operations. To account for these, and to account for the fact that the soul is in potency to other acts, one must appeal to powers of operation which are distinct from the soul's essence. Presumably those who reject Thomas's conclusion would reject the principle on which the argument rests.[150]

In *Summa theologiae* I, q. 79, a. 1 Thomas repeats a version of the first argument we have just considered. There he asks whether the intellect is a power of the soul. In supporting his affirmative reply, he again reasons that the immediate principle of an agent's operation can be its essence only if that agent's operation is identical with its act of being *(esse)*. Just as a potency is related to its operation as to its act,

---

See *La controverse*, pp. 91–93. Wéber does mention this point in passing in n. 51, p. 107. He also stresses the influence on Thomas of a statement from Pseudo-Dionysius's *Celestial Hierarchy*, c. 11, cited in ST I, q. 77, a. 1 ("sed contra"), according to which heavenly spirits are divided into essence, power, and operation (pp. 89–91).

149. Leon. 5.236–37. Note that he connects his observation that one who has a soul does not always perform all its vital operations with Aristotle's description of the soul in *De anima* II, c. 1, as "the first actuality of a natural body which has life in potency" (412a, 27–28). "Et sic ipsa anima, secundum quod subest suae potentiae, dicitur *actus primus*, ordinatus ad actum secundum.— Invenitur autem habens animam non semper esse in actu operum vitae. Unde etiam in definitione animae dicitur quod est *actus corporis potentia vitam habentis*, quae tamen potentia *non abiicit animam*." Cf. *De anima* II, c. 1 (412b 25–26).

150. On this argument see Künzle, *Das Verhältnis der Seele*, pp. 211–14; Wéber, *La controverse*, pp. 93–97 (whose interpretation differs considerably from mine).

so an essence is related to its corresponding act of being. But in God alone are act of understanding and act of being identical. Therefore in God alone are intellect and essence identical. Because they cannot be identified in intellectual creatures, in them the intellect is a certain power of the one who understands.[151]

Before leaving this discussion in the *Summa theologiae,* we should note that in q. 77, a. 1, ad 5, Thomas again spells out his understanding of a power of the soul insofar as it is distinguished from substance. If by an accident we have in mind that which is distinct from substance, a power of the soul is indeed an accident, and falls into the second species of quality *(potentia et impotentia).* And when an accident is understood in this way, there is no intermediary between substance and accident. But if we take the term "accident" as signifying one of the predicables, there is an intermediary between substance and accident, that is, a property. A property is not included within a thing's substantial essence, but is caused by the essential principles of its species. So understood, powers of the soul may be said to be intermediary between substance and accident, since they are natural properties of the soul.[152] In other words, powers of the soul are accidents (qualities), if by this we mean predicamental accidents. But when we refer to the predicables, powers of the soul are properties rather than predicable accidents.

In his Disputed Question *De spiritualibus creaturis,* a. 11, Thomas again faces this question. Once more he denies that the powers of the soul can be identified with its essence. He offers two types of argumentation to support his case. As in ST I, q. 77, a. 1, one is general in its application, and the other is restricted to the human soul.

The first reminds us of the first argument we have considered from ST I (q. 77, a. 1; q. 54, a. 3). It is impossible for the essence of any created substance to be identical with its operative powers, Thomas begins. Different acts belong to different subjects of these acts, since an act is always proportioned to that of which it is the act. But just as the act of being *(esse)* is an actuality of an essence, so is an operation the actuality of an operative power. Therefore, just as operation and act of being cannot be identified in any creature, but only in God, it follows that the operative power of a creature cannot be identified with the creature's essence. Only God's essence is identical with his power.[153]

In his second argument Thomas concentrates on the soul itself, and this reminds us of his procedure in ST I, q. 77, a. 1, although the kind of argumentation he offers here is quite different. Identity between the soul and its operations is impossible, he

---

151. Leon. 5.258: "Utrum intellectus sit aliqua potentia animae."

152. Leon. 5.237. For more on the species of quality see ST I–II, q. 49, a. 2. Cf. Aristotle, *Categories,* c. 8.

153. See Calcaterra-Centi ed., in *Quaestiones disputatae,* Vol. 2, pp. 412–13. Note in particular: "Sicut autem ipsum esse est actualitas quaedam essentiae, ita operari est actualitas operativae potentiae seu virtutis. Secundum enim hoc, utrumque eorum est in actu: essentia quidem secundum esse, potentia vero secundum operari. Unde, cum in nulla creatura suum operari sit suum esse, sed hoc sit proprium solius Dei, sequitur quod nullius creaturae operativa potentia sit eius essentia. . . ."

maintains, for three reasons. First of all, while the essence of the soul is one, multiplicity of powers must be maintained in the soul because of the diversity of the operations (and of the objects of the operations) performed by the soul. This follows because powers must be diversified in accord with their acts; for potency is ordered to actuality.[154] Though he states this in different terms here, once more Thomas appeals to the observable fact that the soul performs different operations and different kinds of operations, and to the principle that because potency is ordered to actuality, essential diversity of operations points to diverse powers.

Secondly, Thomas appeals to a distinction between powers of the soul themselves, an appeal which he had already made in his Commentary on *I Sent.*, d. 3, q. 4, a. 2. Some powers are acts of certain parts of the body, that is to say, they inform or inhere in the body. Such is true, for example, of the powers of the sensitive and nutritive parts of the soul. Other powers do not inhere in any part of the body but only in the soul, as is true of the intellect and will. But such diversity could not obtain between the powers themselves unless they are distinct from the soul's essence. One and the same thing cannot be both an act of the body and something separate from the body unless by reason of diverse factors, i.e., powers.[155] In short, if one admits this fundamental distinction in kind between powers of the soul, Thomas also holds that one must distinguish such powers (or at least some of them, I would add) from the soul itself. This argument, if simply taken by itself, would not seem to be sufficient to prove that *all* the powers of the soul, including the intellect and will, are distinct from the soul's essence.

Thirdly, the same conclusion follows from the way the powers of the soul are related to one another. Thus we find that one power moves another. For instance, reason moves the irascible and concupiscible appetites, and the intellect moves the will. This would not be possible if all the powers were identical with the essence of the soul; for one and the same thing cannot move itself under the same aspect.[156] By this Thomas means that one and the same thing cannot move and be moved at the same time and in the same respect. If the soul and its powers are not really distinct from one another, to say that the intellect moves the will would be to imply that the soul moves itself. As we shall see below in Chapters XI and XII, the principle that one and the same thing cannot move and be moved at the same time and in the same respect will play an important role in Thomas's argumentation from motion for the existence of God, based as that argumentation is on the axiom that "whatever is moved is moved by something else."

---

154. Ed. cit., p. 413.

155. Ibid. For the reference to *In I Sent.* see Mandonnet ed., Vol. 1, p. 116.

156. Ibid. Note that Thomas concludes his response by explaining again that a power of the soul is an accident (predicamental) and falls within the second species of quality, though it is not a predicable accident but a property. Also see ad 2 on the difference between a universal whole, an integral whole *(totum integrale)*, and a potential whole (pp. 413–14). Cf. n. 143 above.

Reference has been made above to a dispute concerning whether Thomas's *Quaestiones disputatae De anima* should be regarded as dating from the same period as his *Quaestio disputata De spiritualibus creaturis* or else as slightly earlier, as its Leonine editor, B. C. Bazán, maintains. However that may be, q. 12 of the first-mentioned work is directed to determining whether the soul is identical with its powers.[157]

Thomas introduces his response by noting that some identify the soul with its powers, while others reject this and hold that the powers are certain properties of the soul. Thomas comments that a power is nothing other than a principle for some operation, whether that operation is an action or a passion. By this he does not have in mind the principle which is the acting or receiving subject itself, but rather that principle by means of which an agent does something or a recipient receives something. Thus the art of building is a power or potency in a builder by means of which he builds; and heat is a potency in fire by means of which the fire heats. Those who hold that the soul is identical with its powers mean thereby that the very essence of the soul is the immediate principle for all its operations. Thus a human being would understand, sense, etc., through the soul's essence, even though the soul will receive different names from the different operations it performs. For instance, we would refer to the soul as a sense power insofar as it performs some act of perceiving, and as the intellect insofar as it performs an act of understanding.[158]

In rejecting this position Thomas first argues that each and every thing acts insofar as it actually is that which it effects. For instance, fire does not heat insofar as it is actually bright, but insofar as it is actually hot. Accordingly, every agent produces something that is like itself. (Here Thomas cites another broader principle from his metaphysics which, as will be seen in Ch. XIII below, also plays an important role in his justification of analogical predication of the divine names.) In order to identify the principle for an action, therefore, we should examine that which is effected; for the two must be similar to one another. For support Thomas cites *Physics* II to the effect that the form (of the thing produced) and the generating principle are the same in species.[159]

In developing this argument, Thomas observes that if what is effected or produced by an agent does not belong to that agent's substantial act of being, it is not

157. On the issue of the relative chronology see n. 144 above. For the text see Leon. 24.1.105: "Duodecimo quaeritur utrum anima sit suae potentiae."

158. Leon. 24.1.108:118–140. Note especially: ". . . sciendum est quod potentia nihil aliud est quam principium operationis alicuius, sive sit actio sive passio. . . ."

159. Leon. 24.1.108:143–109:152. Strictly speaking, this applies to agents and effects which are the same in kind or species or, as Thomas sometimes puts it, which are univocal. Agents which are higher in level of being than their effects need not formally possess the effect which they produce; they must at least possess it virtually, i.e., have the power to produce it. See, for instance, ST I, q. 4, a. 2 (and my remarks below in Ch. XI, n. 59 with respect to the argument from motion for God's existence). For Aristotle see *Physics* II, c. 7 (198a 24–27).

possible for the principle by means of which it is produced to be part of the agent's essence. In other words, in such a case the agent is not immediately operative. For support Thomas turns to natural agency. In the case of substantial generation, a natural agent acts by changing matter with respect to the form that informs it. In other words, the agent introduces a new substantial form into the matter. This happens only insofar as the matter is first properly disposed for that form. Only then will the matter actually receive the form. Thus generation (the introduction of the new substantial form) is the terminus of alteration (in this case, a change in the previous dispositions of the matter). Hence in such natural changes it is necessary that what acts immediately from the side of the agent be an accidental form. Only such a form will correspond to the disposition introduced into matter. In other words, because the disposition which is introduced into matter by an agent is an accident, the proximate principle which introduces that disposition must itself also be an accident.[160]

Thomas also remarks that such an accidental form can act only in virtue of a substantial form and as its instrument. Otherwise the accidental form would be incapable of inducing a substantial form into the matter through its action. For instance, in the case of the elements the only evident principles of action are active and passive qualities, which themselves act in virtue of substantial forms. It is for this reason that such actions terminate not only in accidental dispositions, but also in substantial forms. The only agent which can produce a substance directly and immediately through its own essence or substance is one that acts through its essence; in such an agent there will be no distinction between its essence and its active power. For Thomas, of course, God alone is such an agent.[161]

Until this point Thomas's argument has concentrated on the need for a distinct active power in every case where what is done or produced is something accidental. He now includes passive powers. It is evident that a passive potency which is directly ordered to a substantial act is in the genus substance, though by reduction. And a passive power which is in potency to an accidental act must be in the genus accident, but by reduction once again. This follows because every genus is divided by potency and act. But it is clear that the powers of the soul, whether active or passive, are not so named because they are directly ordered to something substantial but rather because they are ordered to something accidental. For instance, to understand in act or to sense in act involves not substantial being but accidental being; and it is to this accidental being that the powers of intellect and sense are respectively ordered.[162]

---

160. Leon. 24.1.109:152–163. Note in particular: "Quando igitur id quod agitur non pertinet ad esse substantiale *rei,* impossibile est quod principium quo agitur sit aliquid de essentia *rei*" (italics mine).

161. Leon. 24.1.109:164–182. Thomas also remarks that Avicenna said the same of his separate Agent Intellect.

162. Leon. 24.1.109:183–197.

Thomas's point is that because there must be a proper and proximate potency which corresponds to such accidental acts, such powers or potencies cannot be identified with the soul's essence. He acknowledges that the powers of generation and nutrition are ordered to substance, whether to produce or to preserve it, but points out that they do this only by introducing some change (and hence some accidental disposition) into matter. Therefore such actions, like the actions of other natural agents, are performed by a substance only by means of some accidental principles or powers. He concludes that it is clear that the essence of the soul is not the immediate principle for its operations. The soul operates only by means of distinct accidental principles or powers. Such powers of the soul are not its essence, therefore, but properties or proper accidents.[163]

With this Thomas's first argument comes to an end. Since it is fairly long and involved, we may sum up its essentials in this way:

1. Each and every thing acts insofar as it actually is that which it effects or produces. Therefore, to identify the principle for such action, one must examine that which is produced; for the two must be conformed to one another. This reflects the broader metaphysical principle that every agent produces something that is like itself.[164]

2. When that which is done or produced does not belong to an agent's substantial act of being, the (proximate) principle by means of which it is effected or produced cannot be part of the essence of the agent. Thomas has turned to natural agency in the process of generation to support his point.[165]

3. But it is evident that powers of the soul, whether active or passive, are directly ordered not to something substantial but to something accidental.[166]

4. Therefore, it follows that the essence of the soul is not the immediate principle for its operations, and that it operates by means of accidental principles or powers.[167]

Thomas's second argument is the by now familiar one based on the evident diversity in the soul's operations. These operations differ in genus and therefore cannot be

163. Leon. 24.1.109:199–110:209.

164. Leon. 24.1.108:143–109:150. See n. 159 above. Cf. Künzle's discussion and reconstruction of this argument, pp. 193–97.

165. See nn. 160 and 161 above. This step reminds one of other arguments where Thomas moves from the distinction between substantial *esse* and operation to a distinction between the principles for each, i.e., essence and accidental powers. Admittedly, the thrust here is somewhat different. See above for Quodlibet 10, q. 3, a. 1 (2d argument), cited above in n. 141; ST I, q. 54, a. 3 (see n. 147 above); ST I, q. 79, a. 1 (see n. 151 above); *De spiritualibus creaturis*, a. 11, arg. 1 (see n. 153 above).

166. Leon. 24.1.109:183–197.

167. See n. 163 above. With respect to the relative chronology of this treatment and those found in *Qu. disp. De spiritualibus creaturis* and ST I (see n. 144 above), it seems to me that the argumentation in the latter two sources is more clearly and effectively presented than that found in the *Qu. disp. De anima*. Hence it does not appear to me that the discussion of this particular issue in the *Qu. disp. De anima* is superior and more mature.

reduced to one and the same immediate principle; for some of them are actions and some passions, and they also differ in other ways. Therefore they must be attributed to diverse principles. And since the essence of the soul is one, it cannot serve as the immediate principle for all its operations. It must rather have a multiplicity of powers which correspond to its diverse operations. To seal this argument, as it were, Thomas reminds us that potency is ordered to actuality. Therefore there must be diverse powers in order to correspond to such diversity in kind of operation.[168]

From all the texts we have examined until this point, it is clear that Thomas consistently denies that the soul can be identified with its powers. This squares with his more general conviction that no created substance can be immediately operative. If other created substances can operate only by means of distinct and accidental powers, the same applies to the human soul. Even though he usually does not refer to the distinction between the soul and its powers as a real distinction, this is clearly what he has in mind. In distinguishing between them as between substantial essence and (predicamental) accident or property, he is saying the same thing. The soul and its powers are indeed distinct, and by a real distinction rather than by one that is merely conceptual or mind-dependent. Moreover, in one early discussion *(In I Sent.,* d. 7, q. 1, a. 1, ad 2), he does note that between an essence and an operation there is an intermediary power *(virtus)* which differs from them both—*really,* in the case of creatures, and only conceptually *(ratione)* in the case of God. A creature's operative power, therefore, really differs both from the essence of that creature and from the operation it performs by means of that power.[169]

At the beginning of this Section, I made a passing reference to an interpretation proposed by E.-H. Wéber to the effect that, owing to his philosophical dialogue with Siger of Brabant around the year 1270, Thomas abandoned his theory of real distinction between the soul and its powers, at least and especially as regards the intellect. From that time onward Thomas would no longer have distinguished between the essence of the soul and the intellect as between a substantial essence and an accident, but would have regarded the two as really identical. More than this, this change in position is reflected by "retouchings" which Thomas would have introduced into Bk II of the *Summa contra Gentiles,* beginning with c. 56, and into

---

168. Leon. 24.1.110:210–222. Note that Thomas concludes by citing Aristotle's *Nicomachean Ethics* VI, c. 1 (1139a 6–15), to the effect that the scientific part of the soul, which deals with the necessary, and the calculative part, which deals with the contingent, are different powers because the necessary and the contingent differ in genus (p. 110:222–226). In his Commentary on the *Ethics* Thomas recognizes that this text poses a problem since the possible intellect is a single power. He resolves it by suggesting that in referring here to a part of the soul that deals with the contingent, Aristotle really is thinking of the cogitative power, i.e., that internal sense which is sometimes called *ratio particularis.* See *Sententia libri Ethicorum* (Leon. 47.2.333:150–334:214).

169. "Egreditur etiam ab essentia alius actus, qui est etiam actus habentis essentiam sicut agentis, et essentiae, sicut principii agendi: et iste est actus secundus, et dicitur operatio: et inter essentiam et talem operationem cadit virtus media differens ab utroque, in creaturis etiam *realiter,* in Deo *ratione tantum* . . ." (italics mine). Mandonnet ed., Vol. 1, p. 177.

the *Prima Pars* of the *Summa theologiae* at q. 76. This new position also clearly appears in Thomas's *De unitate intellectus contra Averroistas* of 1270.[170]

In my opinion, Wéber's strongest evidence for this alleged shift in position is to be found in a number of passages where Thomas refers to the intellect as the form of a human being.[171] While Thomas always regarded the intellective soul as a human being's substantial form, how could he so describe the intellect if he viewed it as a power which is distinct from the essence of the soul?

For instance, in ST I, q. 76, a. 1, Thomas writes that it must be said that the intellect "which is the principle of intellectual operation, is the form of the human body; for that by which something first operates is the form of that to which the operation is attributed."[172] Wéber also quotes the following from this same context: "Therefore this principle by which we first understand, whether it is called the intellect or the intellective soul, is the form of the body."[173] Wéber reads the second text as implying that the intellect and the intellective soul are one and the same. Hence in this text Thomas would have renounced his earlier formulations which distinguish between the intellect (taken as a distinct power) and the intellective soul. Wéber also argues that this particular text (along with articles 2 and 3) must be placed after ST I, qq. 77 and 79 and must therefore date from about 1270. They would have been added to the earlier *Prima Pars* at that time.[174]

In the *De unitate intellectus contra Averroistas* of 1270 Wéber finds Thomas holding that the powers of the soul are not really distinct from the soul, although in a first reference to this issue Thomas sees Aristotle as setting aside the case of the intellect. Farther on Thomas writes that Aristotle was of the view that "that by which we understand is the form of the physical body."[175] Wéber does acknowledge

---

170. See Wéber, *La controverse*, pp. 115–27, 154–56; "Les discussions de 1270," pp. 298–304.

171. See *La controverse*, pp. 124–26; "Les discussions," pp. 299–300.

172. "Respondeo dicendum quod necesse est dicere quod intellectus, qui est intellectualis operationis principium, sit humani corporis forma. Illud enim quo primo aliquid operatur, est forma eius cui operatio attribuitur . . ." (Leon. 5.208).

173. "Hoc ergo principium quo primo intelligimus, sive dicatur intellectus sive anima intellectiva, est forma corporis" (ed. cit., p. 209). For Wéber's citation of this text and that quoted in n. 172 see *La controverse*, p. 124; "Les discussions de 1270," p. 299 and n. 59.

174. See *La controverse*, pp. 124–25; p. 123, n. 16; "Les discussions,"pp. 303–4.

175. See Wéber, *La controverse*, p. 124, n. 21, where he cites the following text to show that, according to Thomas, Aristotle holds that the powers are not really distinct from the soul, even though he (Aristotle) does not yet state his position concerning the intellect: ". . . supra enim quaesitum est, utrum una pars animae ab alia separata sit ratione solum, aut et loco. Hic dimissa quaestione illa quantum ad intellectum, de quo nihil hic determinat, de aliis partibus animae dicit manifestum esse quod non sunt separabiles, scilicet loco, sed sunt alterae ratione" (Leon. 43.293:178–184). Wéber's interpretation here is surprising. To say that the other parts of the soul are not separable (from one another) in place is not to say that they are not really distinct from one another. In fact, in this context, for Thomas to say that they are distinct from one another *ratione* is to state that they differ in definition and hence in essence. In another text dating from 1267–1268, in commenting on this same expression taken from the Latin translation of the *De anima* ("Ratione autem quod alterae, manifestum est"), Thomas says as much: ". . . ostendit quod sint separabiles ratione. Cuiuslibet enim

that more frequently in this treatise Thomas is concerned with showing that the intellect belongs to the soul. In fact, Thomas states that it is a "power of the soul."[176]

Wéber cites various texts from *Summa contra Gentiles* II, cc. 56–90, to support his reading. These too would have been retouched around 1270 in order to incorporate Thomas's new position. For instance, in c. 59 Thomas writes that "the intellect is the soul of man, and consequently his form."[177] In c. 70 Thomas attempts to show that, according to Aristotle, "according to its substance the intellect is united to some body as a form."[178] As regards c. 70, it should be noted that Thomas there presents Aristotle as arguing that the heaven has an intellect but does not possess a sensitive soul. Therefore it lacks the sensitive powers of the soul. So too, continues Thomas, it is Aristotle's view that an intellect is not united to the heaven by phantasms but according to its substance as a substantial form. In like fashion, an intellectual substance is united to the human body, not by means of phantasms as Averroes would have it, but as the form of the body.[179] In these texts, therefore, Thomas evidently uses the term "intellect" to signify the intellective soul. But this does not imply that he has abandoned his view that the term "intellect" may also be used to designate a really distinct power of the soul. On the contrary, in the immediately following c. 71 he remarks that the soul performs its operations by means of its powers.[180]

---

potentiae ratio est secundum ordinem ad actum; unde necesse est, si actus sint diversi secundum speciem, quod potentiae habeant diversam rationem speciei. . . ." *In II De anima,* c. 4, commenting on 413b 29 (Leon. 45.1.84:120–125). For the passage just quoted in our text see: "Fuit ergo sententia Aristotelis quod id quo intelligimus sit forma corporis physici" *(De unitate intellectus* [Leon. 43.293:210–212]). See Wéber, *La controverse,* p. 125, n. 24; "Les discussions," p. 299.

176. See *La controverse,* p. 125, n. 24, citing *De unitate intellectus:* "Vult ergo [Aristoteles] quod intellectus sit potentia animae quae est actus corporis" (Leon. 43.294:229–231). This text, however, along with those cited in the preceding note, makes perfect sense if we take Thomas to be maintaining that Aristotle defended real distinction between the soul and its powers. Moreover, in ST I, q. 76, a. 2, supposedly another reworked text according to Wéber, while refuting unicity of the possible intellect, Thomas writes: "Similiter etiam patet hoc esse impossibile, si, secundum sententiam Aristotelis, intellectus ponatur pars, seu potentia, animae quae est hominis forma" (Leon. 5.216).

177. Note that here Thomas is presenting a series of arguments against the Averroistic theory of unicity of the possible intellect. He reasons that where there is a higher kind of vital operation, there must be a higher kind of life. But in human beings there is a higher vital operation than in other animals, i.e., intellection. Therefore a human being enjoys a higher species of life. But life comes through the soul. Therefore a human being will have a higher soul by which he lives: "Nulla autem est altior quam intellectus. Est igitur intellectus anima hominis. Et per consequens forma ipsius" (ed. cit., p. 157). See Wéber, "Les discussions de 1270," p. 299.

178. ". . . ostendendum restat quod necesse est dicere, secundum opinionem Aristotelis, intellectus secundum suam substantiam alicui corpori uniri ut formam" (ed. cit., p. 169). See Wéber, "Les discussions de 1270," p. 299; cf. *La controverse,* pp. 82–83.

179. Ed. cit., pp. 169–70. Note in particular: "Sic igitur et corpori humano . . . secundum intentionem Aristotelis substantia intellectualis unitur non per aliqua phantasmata, sed ut forma ipsius" (p. 170).

180. In c. 71 Thomas is defending the view that the soul is united to the body immediately rather than by any intermediary. Note in particular: "Anima enim omnes operationes suas efficit per suas potentias . . ." (p. 170).

Rather curiously, Wéber cites Bk II, c. 69 in order to show that Thomas there argues that Aristotle is not opposed to his (Thomas's) view that the possible intellect is the substantial form of a human being. But the text cited by Wéber speaks not of the possible intellect but of the "intellective substance."[181] Moreover, elsewhere in this same c. 69, Thomas explains that Aristotle's reference to the intellect as separate need not be taken as implying the Averroistic position, or that the "substance of the soul of which the intellect is a power, or the intellective soul, is not the act of the body as a form which gives *esse* to such a body."[182] Here we have a clear statement of Thomas's usual view that the intellect is a power of the soul and that this soul—the intellective soul—is the form of the body.

On the other hand, at times Thomas does refer to the possible intellect as the form of the body. For instance, in the *Summa contra Gentiles* II, c. 98 he is discussing the knowledge enjoyed by separate substances, and proceeds to contrast this with our knowledge. To facilitate this contrast he draws an analogy with heavenly bodies. The matter of a heavenly body is perfected by its form in such fashion that there remains in it no potentiality to receive any other form. In like fashion, as regards its natural knowledge, the intellect of a separate substance is totally perfected by its intelligible forms. On the other hand, "our possible intellect is related in proportional fashion to the corruptible bodies to which it is united as a form; for it actually has certain intelligible forms in such fashion that it remains in potency to others."[183] Is this not for Thomas to say that the possible intellect unites with the body as its substantial form, and therefore that there can be no real distinction between the possible intellect and the intellective soul which informs the body? Not necessarily, as we shall shortly see.

---

181. Wéber, *La controverse de 1270*, p. 125, where he cites from SCG II, c. 69: "Verba enim Aristotelis quae dicit de intellectu possibili . . . non cogunt confiteri quod *substantia intellectiva* non sit unita corpori ut forma dans esse. Unde patet quod nec demonstratio Aristotelis hoc concludit, quod *substantia intellectiva* non uniatur corpori ut forma" (italics mine). See ed. cit., p. 169.

182. "Et per hoc dicitur intellectus esse *separatus:* non quin substantia animae cuius est potentia intellectus, sive anima intellectiva, sit corporis actus ut forma dans tali corpori esse" (p. 168). See p. 169: ". . . [Aristoteles] non intendat excludere ipsum esse partem sive potentiam animae quae est forma totius corporis. . . ."

183. "Intellectus autem possibilis noster proportionaliter se habet corporibus corruptibilibus, quibus unitur ut forma: sic enim fit actu habens quasdam formas intelligibiles quod remanet in potentia ad alias" (ed. cit., pp. 222–23). Cited by Wéber, "Les discussions," p. 299. There (see n. 58) Wéber also cites c. 73: "Intellectus enim possibilis, sicut et quaelibet substantia, operatur secundum modum suae naturae. Secundum autem suam naturam est forma corporis" (ed. cit., p. 175). For discussion of similar passages see Bazán, "Le dialogue philosophique," pp. 84ff. As Bazán points out, in refuting the Averroistic theory of a separate agent intellect and a separate possible intellect, Thomas notes that what he himself regards as the intellective soul is viewed by Averroes as a separated substance and referred to by him as the "intellect." In contesting this view, Thomas adopts the terminology of Averroes and refers to the (possible) intellect as the act (or form) of the body. But Bazán rightly insists that this in no way compromises the point that Thomas continues to regard the intellect as a power of the soul, as is clear from Thomas's continuing reference to the intellect as a *virtus, pars,* or *potentia animae* (p. 85).

Wéber also cites passages from the *Compendium theologiae*. In c. 85 Thomas writes: "The intellect, therefore, by which a human being understands, is the form of this human being. . . ." Farther on in that same chapter, he remarks: "The intellective soul, from the nature of its species has this (characteristic), that it be united to some body as a form. . . ."[184] In c. 87 Thomas states: "It is therefore necessary for the agent intellect and the possible intellect to come together in the single essence of the soul." But this passage should be read in context. Earlier in c. 87 Thomas has argued that since the agent intellect and the possible intellect are formally united to us, it remains to indicate that they come together in one and the same essence of the soul. For what is formally united to a thing is united to it either after the manner of a substantial form, or after the manner of an accidental form. In the latter case, each will be an accident of the soul. In either case, he reasons, the same conclusion will follow, namely, that they come together in the essence of the soul.[185]

Since Wéber's thesis has been effectively challenged by others and in considerable detail, here I shall limit myself to a few observations.[186] First of all, the texts we have seen so far can be given a much simpler interpretation. As Thomas has already reminded us as early as his *De veritate*, one may use the term "intellect" to refer to the intellective potency or power of the soul, and hence to a power that is distinct from the soul. Or one may take it as a way of designating the intellective soul itself. This is confirmed by the remark from ST I, q. 76, a. 1, cited above.[187]

184. ". . . intellectus igitur quo homo intelligit, est forma huius hominis . . ." (Leon. 42.109:55–56). Note that Thomas is here again arguing against anyone who would defend the separated character of the possible intellect. Also note from near the end of this chapter: "Anima enim intellectiva ex natura suae speciei hoc habet ut uniatur alicui corpori ut forma . . ." (p. 110:158–160). See Wéber, "Les discussions," p. 300 for citation of the first of these passages. However, he should have also cited the second one; for it shows how easily Thomas moves from speaking of the *intellect* as the form of this individual man to referring to the *intellective soul* as the form which is united to a body.

185. "Oportet igitur quod intellectus agens et possibilis in una essentia animae convenient" (Leon. 42.111:17–19). Cited by Wéber, "Les discussions," p. 300. For Thomas also see the first part of this chapter (pp. 110–111). In c. 88 Thomas explains how these two, the agent and the possible intellect, come together in the single essence of the soul. He notes that it is not unfitting for one and the same intellective soul to be "in potentia respectu ad omnia intelligibilia, prout ponitur in ea intellectus possibilis, et comparetur ad ea ut actus, prout ponitur in ea intellectus agens" (p. 111:33–36). As he explains, the potency by reason of which the single intellective soul receives intelligible species is called the possible intellect. The potency by which it abstracts intelligible species from phantasms is called the agent intellect (lines 51–58). He goes on in c. 89 to apply this to all the powers of the soul, noting that all are in a certain way "rooted in the soul" ("in anima radicantur"). Some, such as the powers of the vegetative and sensitive part, are in the soul as in their principle and in the composite as in their subject. Others, such as the powers of the intellective part, are in the soul both as in their principle and as in their subject (Leon. 42.112). These texts do not give the impression that Thomas has now identified the soul with its powers.

186. See n. 128 above for references to Lefèvre and Bazán. Also see *Rassegna di letteratura tomistica* 5 (1973), pp. 65–72; F. Van Steenberghen, *Maître Siger de Brabant* (Louvain-Paris, 1977), pp. 357–60, 412–14.

187. For the text from *De veritate*, q. 10, a. 1, see n. 136 above. For that from ST I, q. 76, a. 1, see n. 173.

Hence in the passages just considered, when Thomas refers to the intellect (or even to the possible intellect as in SCG II, c. 98) as the form of the body, he simply means thereby the intellective soul. Such expressions should not be taken as implying that Thomas is now giving up his theory that the powers of the soul, including the intellect, are really distinct from the intellective soul.[188]

Moreover, other passages which date from Thomas's second Parisian teaching period and apparently, therefore, after the time of his encounter with Siger of Brabant, clearly presuppose the distinction between the soul and its powers. This is true of discussions both in *Summa theologiae* I–II, q. 50, a. 2 and in Thomas's *De virtutibus in communi,* a. 3. In each case Thomas is seeking to determine whether habits inhere in the soul by means of powers of the soul.

In ST I–II, q. 50, a. 2, the second objection reasons that there cannot be an accident of an accident, i.e., an accident that inheres in another accident. But a habit is an accident, and powers of the soul also belong to the genus accident, as has been stated in the *Prima Pars* (for which see ST I, q. 77, a. 1, ad 5). Therefore a habit cannot inhere in the soul by means of its powers.[189]

In reply to this Thomas comments that an accident, simply taken in itself *(per se),* cannot be the subject for another accident. But there is a certain order among accidents. Insofar as the substantial subject stands under one accident, it (the substantial subject) can also be understood as the subject for another accident. In this way we can say that one accident is the subject for another, for instance, that a surface is the subject for the accident color. It is in this way, Thomas concludes, that a power of the soul can be the subject of a habit, or to put it in other terms, that one accident can serve as the subject for another. The implication is clear that powers of the soul are accidents and that habits can inhere in those powers.[190] In a. 4 Thomas holds that the habit science inheres in the possible intellect. He reasserts this point in his reply to the first objection: the possible intellect is the subject of intellectual habits.[191] Torrell dates the *Prima-Secundae* in 1271.[192]

Thomas develops this same thinking in a. 3 of his Disputed Question *De virtutibus in communi.* According to Torrell, this work dates from 1271–1272.[193] Thomas sets the stage for his explanation of how a power of the soul can be the subject for

188. Cf. n. 183 above.

189. Q. 50, a. 2 is directed to determining whether the soul is the subject of a habit "secundum suam essentiam, vel secundum suam potentiam." For this and for objection 2 see Leon. 6.318. Note the opening words of the objection: ". . . accidentis non est accidens."

190. Leon. 6.318–19. Note in particular: "Et sic dicitur unum accidens esse subiectum alterius: ut superficies coloris. Et hoc modo potest potentia esse subiectum habitus." For the same point cf. ST I–II, q. 56, a. 1, ad 3 (Leon. 6.355).

191. Leon. 6.321. In the corpus Thomas argues against the position which denies that habits are in the (possible) intellect on the grounds that it is against the mind of Aristotle, and it is untrue. From his reply to objection 1 note: "Unde intellectus possibilis est subiectum habituum intellectualium."

192. See *Saint Thomas Aquinas,* p. 333.

193. See *Saint Thomas Aquinas,* p. 336.

accidents by clarifying three ways in which a substantial subject stands in relationship to its accidents. This we have already seen in Section 3 of the present chapter.[194] Consistent with his discussion in ST I–II, q. 50, a. 2, Thomas continues to hold that if one accident cannot serve as the ultimate substratum for another, the underlying substantial subject can receive one accident by means of another. Because of this, i.e., because it is supported by its substantial subject, a power of the soul can serve as the subject for habits.[195] Once more he identifies powers of the soul as accidents and, we may therefore infer, continues to regard them as really distinct from the essence of the soul, their substantial subject.

In conclusion, we may turn to a still later work, the *Tertia Pars* of the *Summa theologiae* (ca. 1271–1273).[196] Wéber cites q. 9, a. 1 to support his claim that Thomas revised his position. There, in the course of a strictly theological discussion about the presence of human knowledge in Christ's human nature, Thomas remarks that the soul, considered in itself, is in potency to know intelligibles. Wéber takes this as a clear identification by Thomas of the soul with the possible intellect.[197] But such an interpretation is not justified by the immediately following context. There Thomas cites Aristotle's *De anima* to the effect that the soul is like a *tabula* on which nothing is written, and adds that something can be written on it "because of the possible intellect."[198] In short, he maintains the distinction between the intellective soul and one of its powers—the possible intellect. In a. 3 he states quite clearly that the possible intellect is in potency to all intelligibles.[199] In a. 4 he notes that in human nature God has instilled an agent intellect and a possible intellect.[200] These passages do not convey the impression that Thomas has now abandoned his earlier doctrine of a distinction between the soul and its powers. Hence when he writes in a. 1 that the soul considered in itself is in potency to know intelligibles, he is simply assigning to the soul a function which belongs to it by reason of one of its powers, the possible intellect.[201] In sum, therefore, Thomas consistently defended the distinction between the soul and its powers from the beginning to the end of his career.

194. See *Quaestiones disputatae*, Vol. 2, p. 715 (cited above in n. 123).

195. Ibid. Note in particular: "Non quod unum accidens possit alteri accidenti sustentamentum praebere; sed quia subiectum est receptivum unius accidentis altero mediante. Et per hunc modum dicitur potentia animae esse habitus subiectum."

196. See Torrell, *Saint Thomas Aquinas*, p. 333.

197. "Anima enim, secundum se considerata, est in potentia ad intelligibilia cognoscenda . . ." (Leon. 11.138). See Wéber, "Les discussions," p. 300, and n. 63.

198. ". . . est enim *sicut tabula in qua nihil est scriptum;* et tamen possibile est in ea scribi, propter intellectum possibilem . . ." (Leon. 11.138). For Aristotle see *De anima* III, c. 4 (429b 31–430a 2).

199. "Intellectus autem possibilis humanus est in potentia ad omnia intelligibilia" (Leon. 11.142).

200. "Manifestum est autem quod in humana natura Deus plantavit non solum intellectum possibilem, sed etiam intellectum agentem" (Leon. 11.144). Thomas goes on to conclude from this that we must therefore hold that in the soul of Christ there was not only a possible intellect, but also an agent intellect.

201. See n. 197 above.

ı x   Prime Matter and Substantial Form

Having now completed our examination of Thomas's views concerning substance and accidents, we may turn to his understanding of a more restricted area of finite being, i.e., the metaphysical structure of material or corporeal entities. According to Thomas, finite being includes both material entities and spiritual ones within its scope. The first two great compositions we have now examined, essence and act of being, substance and accident, apply to all finite substances, whether material or immaterial. But as we shall now see, Thomas holds for another kind of composition in purely material entities, a composition within their very essence, i.e., that of matter and form.

Following Aristotle, Thomas sometimes appeals to what is often referred to as substantial change in order to establish the matter-form composition of such entities. This approach is taken from Aristotle's texts, some of which we have already mentioned when examining Thomas's views about the distinction between substance and accident. In that context we have argued that for Thomas there is another and more metaphysical approach to the substance-accident distinction. Now we shall suggest that for Thomas there is also another and more metaphysical approach to the distinction between prime matter and substantial form.

After examining these approaches in the first section of this chapter, we shall next consider a series of questions relating to Thomas's understanding of prime matter. For instance, is prime matter pure potentiality? Can it be kept in existence without any substantial form whatsoever? How do we come to an understanding of it? In the third section of the chapter we shall concentrate on his understanding of the nature of substantial form, and pay particular attention to his contested position concerning unicity of substantial form. The final section of the chapter will consider his explanation of the individuation of material substances.

1. The Distinction between Matter and Form

Before taking up Thomas's physical and metaphysical approaches to the distinction between matter and form, it may be helpful for us to turn to one of his earliest overall discussions of these two principles. This is to be found in his *De principiis naturae,* and has the additional advantage of being presented in an independently written work, not in a commentary on Aristotle.[1]

This treatise begins with an explanation of the distinction between potency and act. That which can exist but does not is said to exist in potency. That which already exists is said to exist in actuality. But there are two kinds of existence *(esse)*—the essential or substantial existence of a thing, as for a human being to exist (this is to exist without qualification [*esse simpliciter*]); and accidental existence, as for a human being to be white (this is to be in a qualified sense [*esse secundum quid*]).[2]

Corresponding to these two ways in which existence *(esse)* may be realized, i.e., as substantial and as accidental, are two ways in which something may be in potency. For instance, something may be in potency to be a human being, such as sperm or menstrual fluid. Or something may be in potency to be white, such as a human being. Both that which is in potency to substantial existence and that which is in potency to accidental existence may be described as matter, but with this difference. The kind of matter which is in potency to substantial existence is referred to as matter "from which" *(ex qua),* while the matter which is in potency to accidental existence is rather known as matter "in which" *(in qua).* Strictly speaking, the kind of matter which is in potency to accidental existence is known as a subject, while that which is in potency to substantial existence is known as matter in the proper sense. Thus we note that accidents are said to be in, i.e., to inhere in their subject, but that substantial form is not described in this way.[3]

Presumably by this final remark Thomas wants to avoid assigning to matter when compared with substantial form the kind of ontological priority substance enjoys with respect to its accidents. Thus, he continues, a subject does not derive its existence from that which "comes" to it, i.e., from its accidents; but matter does receive existence from that which "comes" to it, since in itself it only has incomplete being *(esse).* Hence while substantial form may be said to give existence *(esse)* to

1. As will be recalled, this work was written during Thomas's time as a Bachelor of the Sentences at Paris (1252–1256), or possibly even earlier. See Torrell, *Saint Thomas Aquinas,* p. 349. On the question of matter and form it anticipates much of the thinking we shall see in Thomas's later works, including his Commentaries on the *Physics* and the *Metaphysics.*

2. "Nota quod quoddam potest esse licet non sit, quoddam vero est. Illud quod potest esse dicitur esse potentia, illud quod iam est dicitur esse actu" (Leon. 43.39:1–8). For the continuation of this text see Ch. VIII above, n. 60.

3. Leon. 43.39:9–26.

matter, it is rather the substantial subject which gives existence to its accidents.[4] Nonetheless, Thomas notes that we sometimes substitute one for the other, that is, matter and the substantial subject. Thus we may describe anything which is in potency as "matter," speaking loosely, of course. And we may likewise refer to that from which something receives existence, whether substantial or accidental, as a form. The kind of form which produces substantial existence in act is substantial form, and that which produces accidental existence is an accidental form.[5]

At this point Thomas brings in the issue of change. Because generation is a motion towards a form, corresponding to the two kinds of forms he has just distinguished are two kinds of generation. Generation in the unqualified sense (substantial change) is ordered to a substantial form, while generation in the qualified sense is ordered to an accidental form. As Thomas also explains, when a substantial form is introduced, something is said to be made in the unqualified sense; when an accidental form is introduced, something is said to be made this or that. And corresponding to these two kinds of generation are two kinds of corruption—corruption in the unqualified sense (substantial change), and corruption in the qualified sense. While generation and corruption in the unqualified sense are restricted to the genus substance, accidental generations and corruptions occur in the other genera.[6]

Thomas goes on to introduce privation as the third principle required for generation and corruption. While generation is a certain change from nonexistence or nonbeing to existence or being *(esse vel ens)*, corruption rather involves a change from existence to nonexistence. But it is not from any kind of nonexistence *(non esse)* whatsoever that generation proceeds, but from the kind of nonbeing *(non ens)* which is being in potency. Hence for generation to occur three principles are required: being *(ens)* in potency or matter; nonexistence *(non esse)* in actuality or privation; that by which something is made to be in actuality, or form.[7]

In c. 2 Thomas explains more fully these three principles of nature. One of them, form, is that toward which generation proceeds. The other two fall on the side of that from which the generation proceeds. Because of this, matter and privation are one and the same in subject, but differ in nature *(ratione)*. For instance, bronze lacks any configuration before this form is introduced; but it is described as bronze under one aspect and as lacking configuration under another. Hence this lack or privation is described not as a principle *per se* but only as a principle *per*

4. Leon. 43.39:27–33. Note in particular: ". . . quia subiectum est quod non habet esse ex eo quod advenit, sed per se habet esse completum . . . sed materia habet esse ex eo quod ei advenit, quia de se habet esse incompletum."

5. Loc. cit., lines 34–46.

6. Leon. 43.39:47–40:61. Note in particular: ". . . generatio vero et corruptio simpliciter non sunt nisi in genere substantiae, sed generatio et corruptio secundum quid sunt in aliis generibus."

7. Leon. 43.40:62–74. Note especially: "Ad hoc ergo quod sit generatio, tria requiruntur; scilicet ens potentia, quod est materia; et non esse actu quod est privatio; et id per quod fit actu, scilicet forma."

accidens, since it befalls matter.[8] To say that privation is only a principle *per accidens* for motion or change is not to imply that it is not required for such to occur. In this context the expression "per accidens" simply means that the privation happens to be joined with this subject in this case, much in the way the art of medicine happens to be joined with a builder in a given individual. It is accidental (or incidental) to the builder qua builder that he also happens to be a physician.[9]

Matter is always subject to some privation. While it is informed by one form, it lacks another, and vice versa. Thus in the element fire there is the privation of air, and in the element air there is the privation of fire. In other words, privation is the absence of a form which could be present in a given subject, or to put it another way, the absence of a form in an appropriate subject. It is not a mere negation. Thus we do not say of a stone that it undergoes a privation because it cannot see. But we do assign blindness as a privation to a subject which is designed by nature to see.[10]

Thomas also singles out another point of difference between matter and form, on the one hand, and privation, on the other. Both matter and form serve as principles in the order of being as well as in the order of becoming. Thus if a statue is to be made, the matter or bronze must be at hand, and subsequently the figure (form) of the statue. But privation serves only as a principle in the order of becoming. In order for a statue to be made, it must first not be a statue. Once the statue is made, however, there is no longer a privation of that statue (or its form).[11]

Thomas distinguishes between two kinds of matter. One kind of matter is itself composed of matter and form, for instance, the bronze which serves as the matter for a statue. This is not prime matter. Prime matter does not include any form or privation in its nature, but serves as the ultimate subject for form and privation. In other words, there is no other matter which might serve as the subject for prime matter. Because all definition and understanding are in terms of form, it follows from this that this most fundamental kind of matter—prime matter—cannot be known or defined simply in itself but only by means of a kind of analogy with what is often referred to as second matter, matter taken in the less fundamental sense as composed matter. It is prime matter which stands in relation to all forms and privations in the way bronze does to the form of a statue and the absence of such a form. Prime matter is matter in the unqualified sense.[12]

---

8. C. 2, beginning (Leon. 43.40:1–10).

9. Ed. cit., lines 11–13. Cf. Aristotle, *Physics* I, c. 8 (191a 34–191b 10).

10. Leon. 43.40:18–33. For some interesting remarks concerning privation see K. Schmitz, "Analysis by Principles and Analysis by Elements," in *Graceful Reason. Essays in Ancient and Medieval Philosophy Presented to Joseph Owens, CSSR,* L. P. Gerson, ed. (Toronto, 1983), pp. 320–22.

11. Leon. 43.40:39–41:52. At the end Thomas repeats the point that privation is a principle *per accidens,* whereas the other two (matter and form) are principles *per se.*

12. Leon. 43.41:70–85. Note especially: "Ipsa autem materia quae intelligitur sine qualibet forma et privatione, sed subiecta formae et privationi, dicitur materia prima, propter hoc quod ante ipsam non est alia materia: et hoc etiam dicitur yle."

Thomas notes that prime matter is said to be numerically one in all things. As he explains, something may be said to be numerically one in two different senses: (1) as that which has numerically one and the same form, e.g., Sortes; (2) as that which in itself lacks those dispositions which make things numerically distinct. It is only in the second way that prime matter may be regarded as numerically one. And if when considered in itself prime matter does not include any form or privation, it never exists in the real order without some form and privation. Of itself it is only potency. In other words, Thomas is in effect saying that prime matter is pure potency.[13]

With this general introduction in mind from Thomas's *De principiis naturae*, we may now turn to his more explicit efforts to establish the reality of the distinction between matter and form. If Thomas had allowed only for a purely physical approach to matter-form composition, we might well have omitted this chapter from our study of his metaphysics. But since he, following Aristotle's lead, devotes a considerable amount of attention to matter and form in metaphysical contexts, we may anticipate that he will also offer a more metaphysical approach to this same topic. If we remember that he regards matter and form as intrinsic principles of material beings, and that even material beings are to be studied in the science of being as being, we will not be surprised at this.[14] Hence we shall first turn to his more obviously physical approach to matter-form composition. Even this appears in his mind to need to be completed by a more logical and metaphysical procedure based on predication. Subsequently we shall consider what is a still more strictly metaphysical approach, developed from his answer to the problem of the One and the Many on the side of essence.

In Bk I of the *Physics* Aristotle argues for matter, form, and privation as the principles of changing being. He does so by setting up a kind of parallel or analogy which moves from more obvious cases to the less obvious, that is, from the principles required for nonessential or accidental change, on the one hand, to those required to account for change in substance, on the other. Following immediately upon a passage from Bk I, c. 7 quoted in Ch. VII above,[15] Aristotle continues:

But that substances too, and anything that can be said to be without qualification, come to be from some underlying thing, will appear on examination. For we find in every case something that underlies from which proceeds that which comes to be.[16]

---

13. Leon. 43.41:98–119. Note: "Sed per se nunquam potest esse, . . . sed est solum in potentia; et ideo quicquid est actu non potest dici materia prima" (114–119). On prime matter as pure potency see Section 2 in the present chapter.

14. See *In VI Met.*, lect. 1, p. 298, n. 1165, and our discussion of this above in Ch. I, n. 30. For his view that the subject of physics or natural philosophy is *ens mobile*, see *In I Phys.*, lect. 1, p. 3, n. 3, cited in our Ch. I, n. 29.

15. See Ch. VII, Section 1, p. 209 above, and n. 41.

16. See *Physics* I, c. 7 (190b 1–4). For the English translation see *The Complete Works of Aristotle*, J. Barnes, ed., Vol. 1, p. 325.

After pointing out that the principles of change are two in one sense, i.e., if we take them as the contraries, and three in another sense, i.e., if we include the contraries and that which underlies, Aristotle continues:

We have now stated the number of the principles of natural objects which are subject to generation, and how the number is reached; and it is clear that there must be something underlying the contraries, and that the contraries must be two. . . . The underlying nature can be known by analogy. For as the bronze is to the statue, the wood to the bed, or the matter and the formless before receiving form to any thing which has form, so is the underlying nature to substance, i.e., the 'this' or existent.[17]

In commenting on the final part of the second passage, Thomas remarks that according to Aristotle prime matter cannot be known in itself, since whatever is known is known by means of its form; but prime matter is regarded as standing under every form. But prime matter is known by analogy, that is, Thomas explains, according to a proportion. Thus we know that wood is different from the form of a bench and from the form of a bed because the wood is now subject to one form, and now to another. So too, when we see that what is air now becomes water, we must conclude that something which existed under the form of air is now subject to the form of water. Therefore, just as wood is different from the form of a bench and from the form of a bed, we conclude that the underlying subject is different from the form of water and from the form of air. Hence this underlying subject is related to natural substances in the way bronze is related to a statue and wood to a bed, and anything material and unformed to a form. This underlying subject, Thomas concludes, is called prime matter.[18]

Thomas also remarks that prime matter is one principle of nature, although it is not one in the same way as is a determined individual which enjoys a form and unity in actuality. Prime matter is said to be one (and to enjoy being) insofar as it is in potency to form. Thomas also comments that form (or *ratio*) is another principle, and that the privation which is contrary to the form is a third. He refers back to his earlier explanation in this *lectio* of the ways in which these principles may be regarded as two and as three.[19]

---

17. See 191a 3–12; English trans., p. 326.

18. See *In I Phys.,* lect. 13, p. 59, n. 118. Note in particular: "Sed scitur secundum analogiam, idest secundum proportionem. . . . Quod igitur sic se habet ad ipsas substantias naturales, sicut se habet aes ad statuam et lignum ad lectum, et quodlibet materiale et informe ad formam, hoc dicimus esse materiam primam." Cf. *De principiis naturae,* c. 2 (Leon. 43.41:78–85). As A. Forest has pointed out, Thomas would have us arrive at a knowledge of matter by following two routes: (1) by knowing it in terms of the form which actualizes it; and (2) by analogy or proportion *(La structure métaphysique du concret,* p. 212). For reference to both of these ways see *In De Trinitate,* q. 4, a. 2 (Leon. 50.123:94–100): ". . . uno modo per analogiam sive per proportionem, ut dicitur in I Physicorum . . . alio modo cognoscitur per formam, per quam habet esse in actu. . . ." Cf. q. 5, a. 3 (147:128–130) for the second way. Cf. *De veritate,* q. 10, a. 5 (Leon. 22.2.309:44–45).

19. *In I Phys.,* lect. 13, p. 59, n. 118.

In connection with this last point, Thomas had previously observed that form and the subject are principles *per se* of that which is produced according to nature; but privation (or the contrary of the form) is a principle *per accidens*, since it "happens" to a subject. He also notes that prime matter is never realized in fact without privation; for when matter has one form, it is joined with the privation of another. As we have just seen, he had already made these points in his *De principiis naturae*. He now concludes that, according to Aristotle, privation is not to be regarded as an aptitude for a form, nor as the beginning stage *(inchoatio)* of the form, nor as some imperfect active principle, as some hold. It is rather the very absence of the form or the contrary of that form, which "happens" to the subject.[20] (This remark is important, for it is another way of emphasizing Thomas's personal view that prime matter is pure potency. The new substantial form which is to be introduced into it in a given case does not preexist in any actual way in the matter, not even as an *inchoatio* or incipient actuality as Albert the Great had maintained.)[21]

These observations permit Thomas to explain that when Aristotle notes that the principles of change may be regarded as two, he is concentrating on principles *per se*, i.e., matter and form. But if one also includes the principle *per accidens* along with the two principles *per se*, one may say that the principles are three.[22]

Throughout this discussion, therefore, Thomas (and Aristotle) appeal to privation, matter, and form in order to account for change, and to prime matter in order to account for that radical kind of change we know as substantial, for instance, that

20. See lect. 13, p. 58, nn. 112–113. Note in particular: "Patet ergo secundum intentionem Aristotelis quod privatio, quae ponitur principium naturae per accidens, non est aliqua aptitudo ad formam, vel inchoatio formae, vel aliquod principium imperfectum activum, ut quidam dicunt, sed ipsa carentia formae vel contrarium formae, quod subiecto accidit" (n. 113).

21. For another reference to this theory see *In VII Met.*, lect. 8, p. 352, n. 1442. For helpful background concerning different efforts to reconcile the view that forms might be thought to preexist in incipient fashion in matter with Aristotle's understanding of matter see B. Nardi, "La dottrina d'Alberto Magno sull' 'inchoatio formae'," in *Studi di filosofia medievale* (Rome, 1960), pp. 69–101. Nardi points out the Augustinian antecedents for this (see his theory of seminal reasons), and Bonaventure's contribution to the discussion (see pp. 77–79) along with others. For Albert's position see pp. 79–100. Nardi insists that his position cannot be identified with that of Aquinas (see pp. 87ff.; 92, where he cites Thomas's *In II Phys.*, lect. 1, n. 143, p. 74). For confirmation of Thomas's divergence from Albert on this see B. Geyer, "Albertus Magnus und die Entwicklung der scholastischen Metaphysik," *Miscellanea Mediaevalia* 2 (1963), pp. 10–11. Also see passing references in J. A. Weisheipl, "The Concept of Matter in Fourteenth Century Science," in *The Concept of Matter in Greek and Medieval Philosophy*, E. McMullin, ed. (Notre Dame, Ind., 1965), pp. 151–52; B. M. Ashley, "St. Albert and the Nature of Natural Science," in *Albertus Magnus and the Sciences: Commemorative Essays 1980*, J. A. Weisheipl, ed. (Toronto, 1980), p. 82 and n. 48. But for a very different reading of Albert concerning this see S. C. Snyder, "Albert the Great, *Incohatio Formae* and the Pure Potentiality of Matter," *American Catholic Philosophical Quarterly* 70 (1996), pp. 63–82.

22. See *In I Phys.*, lect. 13, p. 58, n. 114: "Et concludit ex praedictis quod quodammodo dicendum est esse duo principia, scilicet per se; et quodammodo tria, si coassumatur principium per accidens cum principiis per se." Cf. n. 112 (on form and the subject as principles *per se*, and privation as a principle *per accidens*); n. 113 as cited in note 20; n. 115.

of air into water, or that of a nonman into a man. Moreover, when commenting on *Metaphysics* VII, c. 3, Thomas remarks that matter cannot be known sufficiently except through motion.[23] Because of this, the investigation of matter seems to belong first and foremost to natural philosophy or to physics. Thus in the *Metaphysics* Aristotle takes from physics what he has already established about matter, that is, that considered in itself it is "neither a quiddity (that is, not a substance), nor a quality, nor any of the other genera by which being is divided or determined."[24] In that context Thomas goes on to observe that this is especially evident from motion; for the subject of change and of motion must differ from each of the terms of motion, as Aristotle has proved in *Physics* I. Therefore, since matter is the first subject which stands under motions in terms of quality, quantity, and the other accidents but also under changes in terms of substance, matter differs in essence from all substantial forms and their privations; that is to say, it differs from the *termini* of substantial generation and corruption. It is not enough, therefore, merely to say that it differs from quantity, quality, and the other accidents.[25]

Next, as we have also seen above, Thomas remarks that Aristotle does not here in the *Metaphysics* establish the difference of matter from all forms by appealing to motion, the path of natural philosophy. He turns to predication, a procedure which is proper to logic. And logic, as Aristotle has stated in Bk IV of the *Metaphysics,* is closely related to metaphysics. For there must be something of which all the aforementioned (forms) are predicated, so that the subject of which they are predicated is different in essence from each of the things predicated of it. Thomas explains that here Aristotle is not thinking of univocal predication whereby genera are predicated of species. In such cases the definition of the species, e.g., "rational animal," includes the genus, e.g., "animal." He rather has in mind predication by denomination whereby the other supreme genera are predicated of substance. For instance, when white is predicated of a human being, the quiddity of the white differs from that of the human being. Thomas finds Aristotle holding that it is in this same denominative way that substance is predicated of matter.[26]

To illustrate this Thomas explains that just as we can say "a human being is white" but not "a human being is whiteness" or "humanity is whiteness," so we can

---

23. See *In VII Met.,* lect. 2, p. 322, n. 1285.

24. Ibid., quoted in part in Ch. VII above, n. 43.

25. *In VII Met.,* lect. 2, pp. 322–23, n. 1286. Note: ". . . oportet, quod materia sit alia secundum sui essentiam ab omnibus formis substantialibus et earum privationibus, quae sunt termini generationis et corruptionis; et non solum quod sit aliud a quantitate et qualitate et aliis accidentibus."

26. Loc. cit., p. 323, n. 1287, partially cited above in Ch. VII, n. 44. See my discussion there. For a part of the text which is not quoted there note: "Dicit ergo, quod oportet aliquid esse, de quo omnia praedicta praedicentur; ita tamen quod sit diversum esse illi subiecto de quo praedicantur, et unicuique eorum quae de 'ipso praedicantur', idest diversa quidditas et essentia." For the continuation of Thomas's reasoning, see n. 1288. Note especially: "Unde subiungit, quod alia genera praedicantur hoc modo de substantia, scilicet denominative, substantia vero praedicatur de materia denominative."

say "this enmattered thing *(materiatum)* is a human being," but not "matter is a human being" or "matter is humanity." Hence this kind of concrete denominative predication shows that just as substance is different in essence from accidents, so is matter different in essence from substantial forms. Hence it follows that that which is the ultimate subject speaking *per se* is not a "what," that is, not a substance, nor is it a quantity or anything else by which something is included in a given genus of being. It is matter. In sum, Thomas has appealed to predication by denomination in order to show that matter cannot be identified with any form, whether substantial or accidental.[27]

If we were to come to a stop at this point, we would conclude that Thomas first appeals to change and therefore to natural philosophy in order to establish the need for matter, form, and privation as the principles of change. But in order to prove that matter is distinct from every form, both substantial and accidental, Thomas now finds Aristotle turning in the *Metaphysics* not to change or motion but to predication by denomination. We have already recalled Thomas's association of this procedure with logic, and his remark that logic bears an affinity with metaphysics. Hence the physical approach to the distinction between matter and form needs to be completed within metaphysics, by one's having recourse to an analysis of predication by denomination.[28]

We may now turn to what we shall regard as a strictly metaphysical approach to the distinction and composition of matter and form. We have seen that Thomas addresses the Parmenidean problem of the One and the Many within the order of being by appealing to a real composition and distinction of essence and act of being *(esse)* in every finite being. If the act of being is realized in different fashion and degree in different beings, this is because the essence principle of one being receives

27. Loc. cit., n. 1289. Note: ". . . ita haec est vera: hoc materiatum est homo, non autem haec: materia est homo, vel materia est humanitas. Ipsa ergo concretiva, sive denominativa praedicatio ostendit, quod sicut substantia est aliud per essentiam ab accidentibus, ita per essentiam aliud est materia a formis substantialibus." Note that here (nn. 1285–1289) Thomas has been commenting on *Metaphysics VII*, c. 3 (1029a 20–25). Thomas also agrees with Aristotle that one cannot conclude from all of this that matter alone is substance (see nn. 1291–1292).

28. See Ch. VII above, nn. 44, 46. For an interesting comparison of Aristotle's procedure in this section of Bk VII, c. 3, and Thomas's Commentary, see J. Doig, *Aquinas on Metaphysics. A historico-doctrinal study of the Commentary on the Metaphysics* (The Hague, 1972), pp. 317–19. Doig comments that "in the long run, Aquinas' exposition does not deviate" from Aristotle's goal, i.e., to show that we must study the form of sensible things in our investigation of substance. But he also remarks: "It is true that he [Thomas] sees a metaphysical proof of the distinction of matter and form where there was none" (p. 319). Elsewhere Doig is critical of Forest for not having mentioned this proof based on predication when he considers Thomas's argumentation for the distinction between matter and form. As Doig indicates, few students of Thomas have singled out this particular argument. In fact, the sole exception Doig has found is C. Hart, *Thomistic Metaphysics: An Inquiry into the Act of Existing*, p. 122. See Doig, p. 280, n. 1. Even for Hart this argument from predication is not Thomas's major metaphysical argument for the reality of the matter-form distinction. That is rather based on the fact of multiplicity of individuals within species (see Hart, pp. 117–20), an argument which we shall develop below.

and limits its act of being differently from the way the essence principle of another being receives and limits its act of being. In short, this explanation accounts for diversity in the order of being by appealing to different kinds of essences.[29]

Well and good, one may counter, but what are we to say about different beings which share in specifically or essentially the same kind of being—many human beings, for instance, or many animals which enjoy essentially the same type of being? In such cases appeal to composition of essence and act of being will not be sufficient. One must now also account for the fact that there can be distinct instances of essentially the same kind of being. If we would cast this issue in terms of the problem of the One and the Many, we may ask how it is that many (numerically) distinct beings can share in essentially the same kind of being. Apparently each enjoys the same kind of essence, since each can be defined in the same way; and yet each is numerically distinct from the others.

As we have also seen, Thomas's metaphysics of participation plays a central role in his solution to the problem of the One and the Many in the order of being.[30] We may now ask whether the metaphysics of participation also enters into his solution to the present problem. As will be recalled from his Commentary on the *De Hebdomadibus,* he there distinguishes different kinds of participation. Man (a species) may be said to participate in animal (a genus), and Socrates (an individual) in man (a species). If these fall on the side of what we have called logical participation, Thomas also points to instances of real participation. Thus a subject participates in an accident and matter participates in form because the accidental or substantial form, being common of itself, is determined (limited) to this or to that subject. Hence his metaphysics of participation is intended to apply to his understanding of the matter-form composition of material entities.[31]

If we may develop this a bit, according to Thomas it is the substantial form of a material entity which accounts for the fact that the latter enjoys this kind of being rather than any other. Hence its form accounts for its belonging to its given species and, therefore, for that which it has in common with other members of the same species. At the same time, no such entity exhausts its kind of being. If it did, there could be no other beings of the same type. To account for the fact that this particular being only shares in but does not exhaust its specific kind of being, Thomas appeals to another principle within its essence, its matter. It is matter which receives and limits or restricts the form principle to this particular subject.[32]

---

29. See above, Ch. V, Section 1 (phase 2 of the *De ente* arg.); Section 2; Section 4 passim; and especially Section 5.

30. See Ch. IV above, passim.

31. See Thomas's Commentary on the *De Hebdomadibus,* lect. 2 (Leon. 50.271:74–85), quoted above in Ch. IV, n. 8.

32. See *In De Hebdomadibus,* lect. 2 (Leon. 50.271:78–80): ". . . quia forma substantialis vel accidentalis, quae de sui ratione communis est, determinatur ad hoc vel ad illud subiectum." Also see below.

Support for this approach can be found in other texts. For instance, in the *Summa theologiae* I, q. 11, a. 3, Thomas observes: "That by which Socrates is a human being can be communicated to many; but that by which he is this human being can be communicated only to one."[33] In other words, here Thomas distinguishes between what accounts for the fact that an individual enjoys its given or specific kind of being, and what accounts for the fact that it is only this individual instance of that kind of being. If it is substantial form which explains the first, it is prime matter which accounts for the second. As Thomas also points out in this text: ". . . if Socrates were a human being by that whereby he is this human being, just as there cannot be many Socrateses, so too there could not be many individual human beings."[34]

In presenting Thomas's solution to the problem of the One and the Many in the order of being, we also found him correlating the principle which receives and limits (essence) and the principle which is received and limited (the act of being) as potency and act. He says much the same of matter and form. For a helpful passage we may turn to his Disputed Question *De spiritualibus creaturis*, a. 1. There he is attempting to refute universal hylemorphism, i.e., the view that assigns matter-form composition to spiritual entities as well as to those that are corporeal. Thomas notes that because potency and act divide being and every genus of being, prime matter is generally taken as potency within the genus substance. It is understood to be different from every species and form, and even different from privation; for it receives both forms and privations. So understood, matter cannot be present in spiritual beings.[35]

As he continues to develop his argument against the presence of prime matter in separate substances, Thomas eventually appeals to their intellectual operation. This he had done from the beginning of his career, as in *De ente*, c. 4.[36] He argues that there must be a potency in spiritual substances which is fitted to receive intelligible forms: "The potency of prime matter is not of this sort, since prime matter

33. Here Thomas is making the point that what accounts for the fact that some given thing is this individual thing cannot be communicated to many. He continues: "Illud enim unde Socrates est homo, multis communicari potest: sed id unde est hic homo, non potest communicari nisi uni tantum" (Leon. 4.111).

34. "Si ergo Socrates per id esset homo, per quod est hic homo, sicut non possunt esse plures Socrates, ita non possent esse plures homines" (ibid.).

35. Ed. cit., p. 370. Note: ". . . id communiter materia prima nominatur quod est in genere substantiae, ut potentia quaedam intellecta praeter omnem speciem et formam, et etiam praeter privationem; quae tamen est susceptiva et formarum et privationum. . . ."

36. Ibid. Before turning to the intellectual operations of spiritual substances, Thomas builds another argument upon the claim that what is prior does not depend on what is posterior, though the converse obtains. Thus there is one case of a pure and first act which is totally free from potentiality; but there is never found in reality a potency which is not perfected by some act. Hence some form is always present in prime matter. Thomas then appeals to a principle of hierarchy according to which all other beings are caused by the First Being according to a certain order. Since no caused being enjoys the fullness of perfection, the more perfect a given (created) act is, the closer it is to God. Among creatures, spiritual substances most closely approach God. Hence the principle of hierarchy or order in no way requires that spiritual substances should include prime matter within their

receives a form by limiting [*contrahendo*] it to individual existence. An intelligible form is present in the intellect without being limited in this way."[37]

Thomas's remark is interesting because it indicates that prime matter not only receives but restricts or limits the form it receives. This squares, of course, with his much earlier statement in his Commentary on the *De Hebdomadibus* to the effect that matter participates in form insofar as it determines (limits) the form to this or that subject.[38] It also indicates that Thomas continues to maintain that act as such, and hence that form as such, is not self-limiting. If a form is present in a given material entity in a limited and restricted fashion, this can only be because it is received by a distinct limiting principle, i.e., prime matter.

Thomas clarifies this a bit more fully in his reply to the second objection. There he notes that form may be limited in two different ways. In one way, the form of a species is limited to an individual member of that species. This kind of limitation takes place by means of matter. This he contrasts with another way in which the form of a genus is limited to the nature of a given species. This kind of limitation, which we may view as a kind of determination, does not take place by means of matter. It happens by means of a more determined form, from which a difference derives. When added to the genus this difference contracts it to this species.[39]

Thomas concludes his discussion in the corpus of this same article by noting that in corporeal entities matter does not directly participate in the act of being *(esse)*, but does so only by means of substantial form. It is the form which informs matter which makes the latter exist in actuality. Therefore in composite entities there is a twofold potency-act composition. First of all, matter is potency with respect to its substantial form, and the form is the act of matter. Secondly, every nature or essence which is composed of matter and form is itself potency with respect to its act of being.[40]

In order to deepen our appreciation of this approach to matter-form composition, it may be helpful for us to consider some other passages where Thomas

---

being, since it is the most imperfect *(incompletissimum)* among all beings. For his appeal to the intellectual operation of spiritual substances in the *De ente*, see c. 4 (Leon. 43.375:11–376:34).

37. "Talem igitur potentiam oportet in substantiis spiritualibus requirere, quae sit proportionata ad susceptionem formae intelligibilis. Huiusmodi autem non est potentia materiae primae: nam materia prima recipit formam contrahendo ipsam ad esse individuale; forma vero intelligibilis est in intellectu absque huiusmodi contractione" (ed. cit., p. 370).

38. See n. 32 above.

39. Objection 2 reasons that every created form is limited and finite. But a form is limited by matter. Therefore every created form is present in matter, and no created substance is a form without matter (p. 367). For Thomas's reply see p. 371. Note in particular: "Una quidem secundum quod forma speciei limitatur ad individuum, et talis limitatio formae est per materiam. Alia vero secundum quod forma generis limitatur ad naturam speciei; et talis limitatio formae non fit per materiam, sed per formam magis determinatam, a qua sumitur differentia; differentia enim addita super genus contrahit ipsum ad speciem." Only the second kind of limitation of forms occurs in spiritual substances, in that each is a form of a determined species.

40. Ed. cit., p. 371.

speaks of form as limited by matter. Interesting texts are already to be found in his Commentary on I *Sentences*. For instance, in d. 8, q. 2, a. 1, Thomas distinguishes different ways in which *esse* may be said to be limited. As the third of these ways he notes that *esse* may be terminated, i.e., limited by the subject (suppositum) in which it is received, just as every other form, which is universal *(communis)* of itself, insofar as it is received in something is limited to that which receives it.[41] If matter receives form, as it surely does for Aquinas, it follows from this that the form is limited to the matter which receives it.

In d. 43, q. 1, a. 1 of this same Commentary on I *Sentences,* Thomas is attempting to prove that God's power is infinite. He singles out different ways in which something may be limited. He notes that form, which in itself can perfect different parts of matter, is limited by the matter in which it is received. It is by the negation of any such limit that the divine essence is said to be unlimited. For any form taken in its proper nature, if it is considered abstractly, that is, apart from its reception in a subject, enjoys infinity. For instance, when we consider whiteness in the abstract, the essence of whiteness is not limited to any subject, even though the nature of color and the nature of being are restricted in whiteness to its determined species of color. In other words, color is a restricted instance or kind of being, and whiteness is still more restricted, since it is only a species of color. Thomas concludes from this that what enjoys *esse* without qualification and whose *esse* is not received in anything else must itself be infinite in the unqualified sense. For Thomas, of course, this is God. Important for our immediate purpose, however, is Thomas's remark that form is limited by the matter in which it is received. And underlying the entire argument is the notion that what is received in something is limited according to the capacity of that which receives it.[42]

Thomas brings out the same point in *De veritate*, q. 2, a. 2. In replying to the fifth objection he comments that every form which is received in something is limited according to the mode of that which receives it. He concludes that because the divine being *(esse)* is not received in something else, it is unlimited (and so is the divine essence).[43] Again we also have the statement that a form which is received in something is limited according to the mode of that which receives it.

41. ". . . vel ratione suppositi in quo esse recipitur: esse enim recipitur in aliquo secundum modum ipsius, et ideo terminatur, sicut et quaelibet alia forma, quae de se communis est, et secundum quod recipitur in aliquo, terminatur ad illud . . ." (Mandonnet ed., Vol. 1, p. 202). See our earlier discussion of Thomas's usage of the principle that unreceived *esse* is unlimited in Ch. IV, n. 92; Ch. V, nn. 104, 105.

42. Mandonnet ed., Vol. 1, p. 1003. Note in particular: ". . . et similiter forma, quae, quantum in se est, potest perficere diversas partes materiae, finitur per materiam in qua recipitur. Et a negatione talis finis essentia divina infinita dicitur. Omnis enim forma in propria ratione, si abstracte consideretur, infinitatem habet. . . ."

43. Here Thomas is making the point that God is not said to be infinite when that term is taken in the sense of a privation *(privative)*, but only when it is taken negatively, i.e., as the negation of limitation: "Sed Deus dicitur infinitus negative, quia scilicet eius essentia per aliquid non limitatur: omnis enim forma in aliquo recepta terminatur secundum modum recipientis, unde, cum esse di-

In *Summa contra Gentiles* I, c. 43, Thomas notes that every act which inheres in something receives its termination (limitation) from that in which it inheres; for what is in another is present in it in accord with the mode of the receiver. And since it receives its limitation from that in which it inheres, we may assume that it is limited by that which receives it. He confirms this by stating that an act that exists in nothing else is limited by nothing. He goes on to apply this to God, who is an act which is not received in anything else and is, therefore, infinite.[44]

Another application of this reasoning appears in Thomas's Commentary on the *De divinis nominibus*, c. 5. Every form which is received in something is limited according to the capacity of that which receives it. Thus this white body does not possess the whole of whiteness according to the total force or power of whiteness. But if there were such a thing as a separate whiteness, nothing would be lacking to it of that which pertains to the power of whiteness as such.[45] In *Summa theologiae* I, q. 4, a. 2, the example of heat is used instead of that of whiteness. If there could be a self-subsisting heat, nothing would be lacking to it of the power of heat.[46]

In q. 7, a. 1 of ST I this general thinking once more enters into Thomas's effort to establish divine infinity. He writes that matter is limited by form insofar as before receiving form, matter is in potency to many forms. In other words, by receiving a given form matter is thereby determined by that form. And form is limited by matter, Thomas continues, insofar as a form, simply considered in itself, is open to inform many instances of matter. By being received in this matter the form becomes the form of this given thing and is thereby limited or restricted to it. Thomas comments that while matter is perfected by the form by which it is limited, i.e., determined, form is not perfected by the matter which receives and limits it. Rather the fullness of a form is limited or contracted by the matter.[47]

Finally, there is an excellent statement of Thomas's thinking concerning this in his *Compendium theologiae*, I, c. 18. No act is limited except by a potency which receives it; for we see that forms are limited in accord with the potency of the matter which receives them. As on so many other occasions, Thomas goes on to conclude from this that God is infinite.[48]

---

vinum non sit in aliquo receptum, quia ipse est suum esse, secundum hoc esse suum non est finitum . . ." (Leon. 22.1.46:262–268).

44. Ed. cit., p. 41: "Amplius" (cited above in Ch. V, n. 113). Also note that he again uses the example of whiteness.

45. *In De divinis nominibus* V, 1 (ed. cit., p. 234, n. 629), cited above in Ch. V, n. 111.

46. Leon. 4.52, as part of his second argument to show that God contains the perfections of all things within himself. Since God is self-subsisting *esse,* nothing of the perfection of being can be lacking to him, and hence no perfection. Cf. Thomas's earlier appeal to the example of heat in *De ente,* c. 4, to illustrate one of three ways in which something may be multiplied (Leon. 43.377:112–113).

47. Leon. 4.72. Note in particular: "Forma vero finitur per materiam, inquantum forma, in se considerata, communis est ad multa: sed per hoc quod recipitur in materia, fit forma determinate huius rei."

48. Leon. 42.88:7–13. "Nullus enim actus invenitur finiri nisi per potentiam quae est eius receptiva: invenimus enim formas limitari secundum potentiam materiae." Here again Thomas indicates

In Ch. V above we discussed the metaphysical presupposition or principle which underlies the thinking reflected in these texts, i.e., that unreceived act is unlimited. There we considered different possible explanations for Thomas's ready acceptance of that principle.[49] Our purpose here is different. We are interested in his understanding of matter and form and have now seen that, according to him, matter both receives and limits its corresponding substantial form. We might add that recent research indicates that this is one more illustration of a nonAristotelian element which Thomas has introduced into an Aristotelian context. There is no evidence to indicate that Aristotle regarded unreceived forms or actualities as unlimited, and therefore, that he needed to appeal to matter as a distinct and limiting potential principle.[50] Thomas's adoption of this position strengthens what we are calling his metaphysical approach to matter-form composition. Because of his understanding of form and of actuality, he must conclude to the presence of a corresponding potency principle which receives and limits forms in all cases where numerical multiplication of individuals within species occurs.

As another element in Thomas's solution to the problem of the One and the Many in the line of being, I have suggested that there he applies the notion of relative nonbeing. Essence may be regarded as relative nonbeing in the sense that it is distinct from the act of being *(esse)* which it receives and limits.[51] We may now ask whether Thomas also applies some understanding of nonbeing to matter.

Indeed he does, as is well illustrated by a text from his *De Substantiis separatis.* He there writes that if by nonbeing I negate only the act of being *(esse in actu)*, the form itself (of a simple substance) may be described as (relative) nonbeing, which participates in the act of being. But if by nonbeing I negate not only the act of being but even the act or form by which something participates in *esse,* then what still remains may be regarded as nonbeing. In this sense, therefore, matter may be described as (relative) nonbeing.[52]

---

that infinity taken negatively is to be assigned to God, but not infinity in the sense of privation which is rather something which follows upon quantity.

49. See Ch. V, Section 5 above, pp. 172–76. There I concentrated on Thomas's reasons for accepting the principle as it applies to *esse,* i.e., *esse* is not self-limiting, or unreceived *esse* is unlimited. I suggested that because of Thomas's view that *esse* is the actuality of all acts and the perfection of all perfections, he probably regarded this principle as self-evident. *Mutatis mutandis* I would suggest that the same applies to his view that unreceived form is unlimited. Since he regards form as act and as a principle of perfection in the line of essence (though not in the line of existence), and since he regards limitation of form as a restriction and imperfection, he can hardly regard form as self-limiting; for this would be to appeal to a principle of perfection (form) in order to account for imperfection (limitation of form). Hence form is not self-limiting. As Thomas writes in Quodlibet 7, q. 1, a. 1, ad 1: ". . . forma non limitatur nisi ex hoc quod in alio recipitur, cuius modo commensuratur . . ." (Leon. 25.1.9:147–153).

50. See in particular W. N. Clarke, "The Limitation of Act by Potency in St. Thomas," pp. 66–69, 72–75.

51. See Ch. VI above, Section 3.

52. Leon. 40.D55:236–D56:244, cited above in Ch. VI, n. 32.

As Thomas had already explained in this same context, in a composite substance there is a twofold ordering: (1) that of matter to form; (2) that of the composite thing (i.e., essence) to the act of being in which it participates. Therefore, in a matter-form composite matter may be regarded as having being only in potency; simply taken in itself, it lacks the form whereby it participates in the act of being according to its proper mode. And when we consider a composite thing in terms of its entire essence, it now includes form as well as matter but still participates in its act of being through its form.[53] As Thomas goes on to observe, potency as realized in purely spiritual substances applies to their essences insofar as the latter are ordered to their respective acts of being. But in a composite entity, the potency of matter is ordered to its form, and then to its act of being.[54]

As Thomas had already pointed out as early as his *De ente et essentia*, here again he notes that a material substance may be said to be finite in two directions, as it were, i.e., from the side of its form which is received in matter (and thereby limited), and from the side of its act of being in which it participates according to its particular (and limited) mode. Hence it is finite from above and finite from below. A created spiritual substance is finite or limited from above, insofar as it participates in the act of being according to its proper mode from the first principle (God). This is so, of course, because its act of being is limited by its essence. But such a created spiritual substance is unlimited from below, since it, i.e., its form, is not in turn participated in by another receiving subject, i.e., by matter.[55]

At this point we may sum up the different elements of what we are calling Thomas's strictly metaphysical argument for matter-form composition of material entities and for his solution to the problem of the One and the Many in the order of essence. It is true that he has not joined all of these elements together as one argument in any single text. Nevertheless, it is, I trust, a faithful reconstruction of his thinking.

Thomas begins with what is for him an undeniable fact, that many individual entities may and do share in essentially or specifically the same kind of being. Because of this, we must assume that they have the same kind of essence, and that this accounts for their unity in species. At the same time, each of them differs numerically from the others. Hence each of them possesses its specific kind of being in restricted or limited fashion. No one of them exhausts the possibilities marked out by its specific kind of being. Otherwise, for one individual to enjoy this kind

---

53. Leon. 40.D55:213–228.

54. Leon. 40.D56:244–249. Note especially: ". . . potentia vero materiae secundum ordinem et ad formam et ad esse."

55. Leon. 40.D56:254–271. Note especially: "Nam materiales substantiae finitae quidem sunt dupliciter, scilicet ex parte formae quae in materia recipitur et ex parte ipsius esse quod participat secundum proprium modum, quasi superius et inferius finita existens. . . ." Cf. *De ente*, c. 5 (Leon. 43.378:47–56). Intelligences are infinite from below and finite from above: ". . . non tamen finiuntur inferius quia earum formae non limitantur ad capacitatem alicuius materiae recipientis eas." See p. 379:131–138 (composite substances are finite from above and from below).

of being would be for it to exhaust the possibilities of that species. There could be no other members. As Thomas has put it, if that whereby Socrates is a human being were identified with that whereby he is this individual human being, then just as there cannot be many Socrateses, there could not be many individual human beings.[56]

Accordingly, Thomas finds it necessary to distinguish between that whereby a given material being belongs to its kind or species, and that whereby it is only an individual instance of that kind or species. As he sees things, the first point is accounted for by a principle of actuality within such a thing's essence—its substantial form. The second finds its explanation in the presence of a distinct principle of potentiality within the same essence—prime matter. Because the receiving and potential principle limits the form or act principle, we may also say that the former, the matter, participates in the latter, the form. Moreover, insofar as prime matter is not to be identified with its form, we may, if we wish, refer to it as a kind of relative nonbeing in the sense just explained.[57]

This, therefore, is what I am referring to as Thomas's strictly metaphysical approach to the matter-form composition of material entities. As is well known, Thomas holds that where such composition and distinction are lacking, there can be no multiplicity of individuals within species. Since he steadfastly rejects matter-form composition of purely spiritual entities throughout his career, he eliminates the very possibility of numerical multiplication of such entities (angels) within species. Every angel is a species in and of itself. No two angels can belong to the same species.[58] This position was to appear among the 219 propositions condemned by

---

56. See nn. 33, 34 above.

57. See the text from *De substantiis separatis*, c. 8, as quoted above in Ch. VI, n. 32. Reference has been made above (see n. 28) to Hart's appeal to this kind of argumentation to establish the distinction of matter and form. For versions of this offered by L. De Raeymaeker see his *Metaphysica generalis*, Vol. I (Louvain, 1931), pp. 119–25; *The Philosophy of Being*, pp. 155–62.

58. See *De ente*, c. 4 (Leon. 43.376:83–89): "Sed cum essentia simplicis non sit recepta in materia, non potest ibi esse talis multiplicatio; et ideo oportet ut non inveniantur in illis substantiis plura individua eiusdem speciei, sed quot sunt ibi individua tot sunt ibi species, ut Avicenna expresse dicit." For Avicenna see his *Liber de philosophia prima sive scientia divina* V, c. 2 (Van Riet ed., pp. 239:74–240:83). Thomas would continue to defend this position throughout his career. See, for instance, SCG II, c. 93, especially: "Adhuc. . . . Substantiae autem separatae non habent omnino materiam, neque quae sit pars earum, neque cui uniantur ut formae. Impossibile est igitur quod sint plures unius speciei" (ed. cit., p. 216). Also see ST I, q. 50, a. 4 (see a. 2 for Thomas's rejection of matter-form composition in angels); *De spiritualibus creaturis*, a. 8 (ed. cit., pp. 397–98), especially the first argument. For discussion see J. Collins, *The Thomistic Philosophy of the Angels*, pp. 95–102. For additional discussions of Thomas's critique of universal hylemorphism see the references given in my *The Metaphysical Thought of Godfrey of Fontaines*, pp. 275–76, and n. 57 (for discussions of this in other thirteenth-century thinkers). There is a troublesome passage from Thomas's *De unitate intellectus*, c. 5 (Keeler ed., sect. 105, pp. 67–68/Leon. 43.311:96–117), which has been taken by some as indicating that Thomas did not really regard it as metaphysically impossible for separate substances to be multiplied in their species. Others, and rightly so in my opinion, reject this interpretation. See Keeler himself (pp. 67–68, note); R. Hissette, *Enquête sur les 219 articles condamnés à Paris le 7 mars 1277*, pp. 83–84; Collins, pp. 100–101, n. 37 (with references to other discussions); de Fi-

Bishop Stephen Tempier of Paris on March 7, 1277. Whether Thomas himself was directly targeted by any of the condemned propositions continues to be disputed today. It is my view that he was. But that is another story.[59]

2. The Nature of Prime Matter

In this section we shall explore more fully Thomas's views concerning prime matter. Some of the texts we have already considered anticipate his answers to three questions about prime matter which we shall now examine, and which we raised in our introductory remarks at the beginning of this chapter: (1) Is prime matter pure potentiality? (2) If so, can it be kept in existence, at least by divine power, apart from any substantial form? (3) How can prime matter be known or understood?[60]

Perhaps most fundamental is Thomas's answer to the first question. During the thirteenth and fourteenth centuries there was considerable disagreement concerning this issue. The view that prime matter enjoys some actuality in itself and, following from this, the conviction that God could keep matter in existence apart from any corresponding substantial form, was fairly widespread. As Allan Wolter has observed, this is especially so among Franciscans from the English province. For instance, in Thomas's time this position had been proposed by John Pecham. Not too long after Thomas's death, it would again be represented by Richard of

---

nance, *Être et agir*, pp. 56–57, n. 59. The text continues to pose some problems for interpreters, must be read in context, and deserves fuller examination on another occasion.

59. Among the 219 propositions condemned in 1277 by Bishop Tempier see 81/43: "Quod, quia intelligentiae non habent materiam, Deus non posset facere plures eiusdem speciei;" 96/42: "Quod Deus non potest multiplicare individua sub una specie sine materia" (with the *Chartularium* numbering listed first, followed by Mandonnet numbering; also listed by Hissette, *Enquête*, p. 82). Since these views were also defended by Boethius of Dacia and Siger of Brabant, Hissette thinks that not Thomas himself but the latter were the primary targets of these condemned propositions (pp. 84–87). For a review and restatement of his general claim that Thomas himself was not a direct target of the 1277 condemnation, also see Hissette's "Albert le Grand et Thomas d'Aquin dans la censure parisienne du 7 mars 1277," in *Miscellanea Mediaevalia* 15 (Berlin–New York, 1982), pp. 226–46. Others, myself included, disagree with Hissette concerning this claim. I find it difficult to imagine that Masters of Theology charged with drawing up the list of condemned propositions, including those such as Henry of Ghent, who knew full well that Thomas and some Masters from the Arts Faculty had taught certain propositions such as these, did not intend to condemn Thomas's teaching of the same along with the Masters of Arts. See my *Mediaeval Reactions to the Encounter between Faith and Reason*, pp. 26–27; "Thomas Aquinas and the Condemnation of 1277," *Modern Schoolman* 72 (1995), pp. 239–48. Cf. pp. 246–48 on Godfrey of Fontaines' discussion of these and other condemned propositions which, he says in his Quodlibet XII of 1296/1297, seem to be taken from Thomas's writings. Cf. S. Brown, "Godfrey of Fontaines and Henry of Ghent: Individuation and the Condemnation of 1277," in *Société et Église. Textes et discussions dans les universités d'Europe centrale pendant le moyen âge tardif*, ed. S. Wlodek (Brepols, 1995), pp. 193–207. For a recent defense of his position see Hissette, "L'implication de Thomas d'Aquin dans les censures parisiennes de 1277," *Recherches de théologie et philosophie médiévales* 44 (1997), pp. 3–31.

60. See above, p. 295.

Middleton, and somewhat later by William of Ware, John Duns Scotus, and William of Ockham.[61] Among secular Masters in Theology at Paris, it would find a forceful defender in Henry of Ghent. And somewhat earlier, at the beginning of the 1250s, Bonaventure had developed an understanding of matter that assigns a greater degree of reality to it in its own right than Aquinas would. As R. Macken has observed in his study of matter in Bonaventure, the Franciscan Master distances himself from Thomas's view that matter is pure potency; he also differs with Thomas's reading of Aristotle concerning this.[62] Moreover, although Bonaventure is not so explicit about this as others such as Henry of Ghent and John Pecham would subsequently be, Macken believes that Bonaventure also thought that, owing to special divine intervention, matter could be kept in existence without any form.[63]

That prime matter is nothing but pure potentiality is at least suggested by certain passages in Thomas we have already investigated. For instance, in the *De principiis naturae* he stresses the point that prime matter is in potency to substantial existence. He distinguishes it from what we might call second matter in that prime matter is the ultimate subject of form and of privation. Considered in itself prime matter includes neither form nor privation in its nature. This is to imply that it includes no determination or actuality in itself.[64] This is also why Thomas concludes in the *De principiis* and elsewhere that prime matter cannot be known directly in itself. It can only be known by analogy or proportion, or by means of the form that actualizes it.[65] Thomas obviously finds his view that prime matter is pure potentiality confirmed by Aristotle's description of it as neither "a quiddity (that is, not a substance), nor a quality, nor any of the other genera by which being is divided or determined."[66]

In addition to such passages, there are many others in which Thomas refers to prime matter as being only in potency, or as pure potency. One way in which he

---

61. See his "The Ockhamist Critique," in *The Concept of Matter in Greek and Medieval Philosophy*, E. McMullin, ed. (Notre Dame, Ind., 1965), pp. 131–34 for additional references and for discussion. Among these note especially R. Zavalloni, *Richard de Mediavilla et la controverse sur la pluralité des formes* (Louvain, 1951), pp. 303–7.

62. See R. Macken, "Le statut de la matière première dans la philosophie d'Henri de Gand," *Recherches de Théologie ancienne et médiévale* 46 (1979), pp. 130–82, esp. pp. 140–56; "Subsistance de la matière première selon Henri de Gand," in *San Bonaventura, Maestro di Vita Francescana e di Sapienza Cristiana (Atti del Congresso internazionale per il VII centenario di San Bonaventura da Bagnoregio)*, Vol. 3 (Rome, 1976), pp. 107–15; "Le statut philosophique de la matière selon Bonaventure," *Recherches de Théologie ancienne et médiévale* 47 (1980), pp. 188–230, esp. pp. 200–202, 209, 219. See p. 188, n. 4 of the last-mentioned article for references to other studies of matter in Bonaventure.

63. "Le statut philosophique de la matière selon Bonaventure," pp. 219, 229–230 (see n. 133 for references to the views of others concerning Bonaventure's position). Note in particular Henry's *Quodlibet I*, R. Macken, ed. (Leuven-Leiden, 1979), q. 10, pp. 66–67 (dating from Christmas 1276); and Pecham's Quodlibet 4, q. 1 in *Quodlibeta Quatuor*, G. Etzkorn, ed. (Grottaferrata, 1989), pp. 174–76.

64. Leon. 43.41:74–80. See n. 12 above.   65. Leon. 43.41:80–86. Also see n. 18 above.

66. See n. 24 above and Ch. VII, n. 43.

makes this point is by stressing the fact that prime matter in itself lacks every form and determination. For instance, in his Commentary on II *Sentences,* d. 12, q. 1, a. 4, Thomas writes that prime matter does not include any form as part of its essence. As he explains, prime matter is that with which the resolution of natural bodies must come to a halt. In itself it must be devoid of any form since every subject which has a form can be divided into the form and the subject of that form. (Here too he observes that, because all knowledge is in terms of form, prime matter can be known only by analogy, as Aristotle explains in I *Physics.*) While prime matter includes no form within its essence or nature, it is never realized in fact apart from some form.[67]

Other passages are still more explicit. For instance, in his Commentary on I *Sentences,* d. 39, q. 2, a. 2, ad 4, Thomas distinguishes three grades or levels among natural entities. One kind enjoys being only in actuality, in the sense that it can undergo no deficiency (or loss) in being. Thomas has in mind heavenly bodies which he, along with his contemporaries, regarded as incorruptible. There is a second level of natural entity which enjoys being only in potency. This is prime matter. Finally, there is a third level which always includes some mixture of act and privation, i.e., things which are subject to generation and corruption.[68] Most important for our immediate purposes, of course, is his remark that prime matter is being only in potency.

In his Commentary on II *Sentences,* d. 34, q. 1, a. 4, Thomas remarks that substantial form is the first perfection of a subject which exists only in potency, i.e., prime matter. Insofar as prime matter is an incomplete being and in potency, it is also subject to the privation of a substantial form.[69]

As we move forward through Thomas's career, explicit references to prime matter as pure potency or as being only in potency appear more frequently. For instance, in *De veritate* (1256–1259), q. 8, a. 6, he refers to gradations of act and potency among beings in that there is something which is in potency only *(potentia tantum),* i.e., prime matter; something else which is in actuality only, i.e., God; and still something else which is in act and potency, i.e., intermediary entities.[70] In

67. "Secundum quod importat ordinem naturae, materia prima est illud in quo ultimo stat resolutio corporum naturalium, quod oportet esse absque omni forma . . . et quamvis materia prima sic accepta non habeat aliquam formam partem essentiae suae, nunquam tamen dividitur ab omni forma" (Mandonnet ed., Vol., 2, p. 313).

68. ". . . aliquid autem est quod est tantum in potentia sicut materia prima, et hoc semper habet defectum, nisi removeatur per aliquod agens reducens eam in actum . . ." (Mandonnet ed., Vol. 1, p. 934).

69. "Est autem quaedam perfectio prima ut forma substantialis, subiectum cuius est in potentia tantum, scilicet materia prima, quae sicut est ens incompletum et in potentia, et ipsa etiam subiicitur privationi substantialis formae . . ." (Mandonnet ed., Vol. 2, p. 884).

70. ". . . sicut enim est gradus actus et potentiae in entibus, quod aliquid est potentia tantum ut materia prima, aliquid actu tantum ut deus; aliquid actu et potentia ut omnia intermedia, sic est in genere intelligibilium . . ." (Leon. 22.2.238:148–153).

q. 21, a. 2, while replying to objection 3, Thomas comments that just as prime matter is being in potency and not in actuality, so it is perfect and good only in potency, not in actuality.[71]

In *Summa contra Gentiles* I, c. 17, Thomas writes that God and prime matter are distinguished from one another in this respect, that while God is pure actuality, prime matter is pure potency.[72] In c. 43 Thomas notes that among things we find something which is nothing but potency *(potentia tantum)* i.e., prime matter, and something else which is nothing but actuality, i.e., God.[73] (These texts confirm our assumption until now that for Thomas to refer to prime matter as potency only or as nothing but potency [*potentia tantum*] is the same as for him to refer to it as pure potency.)[74] In *Summa contra Gentiles* II, c. 16, Thomas reasons that prime matter is in some fashion because it is being in potency. But God is the cause of all things which are. Therefore God is the cause of prime matter.[75] In addition to reaffirming the point that prime matter is being in potency, this text is interesting because it indicates that even prime matter is caused in some way by God. This will reappear in some other texts we have yet to examine.

In the *De potentia* (1265–1266), q. 1, a. 1, ad 7, Thomas accepts the objection's contention that just as prime matter is pure potency, so God is pure actuality. Thomas responds that this argument succeeds in showing that there is no passive potency in God, a point which he grants. It does not prove that there is no active potency in God.[76] In q. 3, a. 2 Thomas refers to the subject of substantial form as prime matter which, he comments, is not being in actuality.[77] In q. 3, a. 5 he considers an argument which is intended to show that prime matter is not created by God. Every action terminates in some kind of act. But prime matter is pure potency. Therefore the act of the creator cannot terminate in it. Thomas replies that

71. Here Thomas is defending the view that being and goodness are convertible. An objection maintains that not every being enjoys perfection, since prime matter does not. Therefore not every being is good. To this Thomas responds: ". . . sicut materia prima est ens in potentia et non in actu, ita est perfecta in potentia et non in actu, bona in potentia et non in actu" (Leon. 22.3.597:117–120).

72. Here Thomas is refuting what he describes as the *insania* of David of Dinant, who dared to say that God and prime matter are identical. Thomas traces this back to his failure to distinguish between difference *(differentia)* and diversity *(diversitas)*. The former applies to things which agree in some respect, e.g., in genus. The latter obtains between things which are diverse of themselves. "Sic etiam Deus et materia prima distinguuntur, quorum unus est actus purus, aliud potentia pura, in nullo convenientiam habentes" (ed. cit., p. 17).

73. Here he notes again that there is still something else which is both in act and in potency, i.e., other things. For his reference to God and prime matter see: "Adhuc. In rebus invenitur aliquid quod est potentia tantum, ut materia prima; aliquid quod est actus tantum, ut Deus . . ." (p. 41).

74. See above nn. 68, 69, 70.

75. "Item. Materia prima aliquo modo est: quia est ens in potentia. Deus autem est causa omnium quae sunt. . . . Deus igitur est causa materiae primae" (p. 103).

76. For the objection see Pession ed., p. 8: "Praeterea, sicut materia prima est pura potentia, ita Deus est purus actus." For Thomas's reply see p. 9.

77. "Formae enim substantialis et privationis subiectum est materia prima, quae non est ens actu . . ." (ed. cit., pp. 41–42).

this argument shows that prime matter is not created alone *(per se)*; but it does not follow from this that it is not created under its appropriate form.[78]

In the *Prima Pars* of the *Summa theologiae* (1266–1268), similar expressions occur. For instance, in q. 5, a. 3, ad 3 Thomas notes that just as prime matter is being only in potency, so it is good only in potency. He also comments that according to the Platonists it can be said that prime matter is nonbeing *(non ens)* because of the privation which is joined with it.[79] In q. 7, a. 2, ad 3 he writes that prime matter does not exist in reality in itself (that is, apart from some form), since it is not being in actuality but only in potency. Hence it is more properly said to be concreated than created. By this Thomas means that it is a constituent or principle of the composite entity which is created.[80] In *Summa theologiae* I, q. 44, a. 2, ad 3 Thomas again answers an argument against his view that prime matter is created by God. The argument, which is based on the claim that prime matter is only in potency, does not show that it is not created at all, but that it is not created without some form.[81]

In ST I, q. 48, a. 3 Thomas refers to prime matter as being in potency in the unqualified sense.[82] In q. 77, a. 1 he considers an argument against the distinction between the soul and its powers. The soul is nobler than prime matter. But prime matter is identical with its potency. Therefore, much more so is the soul. To this Thomas replies (ad 2) that the act to which prime matter is in potency is substantial form. Therefore the potency of matter is not distinct from its essence. This is an important point, as we shall see, since it indicates that there is no distinction between prime matter and its potency.[83]

In q. 115, a. 1, ad 2 Thomas notes that prime matter is pure potency, just as God is pure act. In replying to the fourth objection, he comments that what is farthest removed from God is prime matter, since it is an agent in no way; for it is only in

78. See objection 3 (ed. cit., p. 48). Note in particular: "Sed materia prima est pura potentia." For Thomas's reply see p. 49: ". . . ratio illa probat, quod materia prima per se non creatur; sed ex hoc non sequitur quod non creetur sub forma; sic enim habet esse in actu."

79. Again Thomas is here concerned with showing that every being is good. Note from his reply to objection 3: ". . . materia prima, sicut non est ens nisi in potentia, ita nec bonum nisi in potentia" (Leon. 4.59).

80. ". . . materia prima non existit in rerum natura per seipsam, cum non sit ens in actu, sed potentia tantum: unde magis est aliquid concreatum, quam creatum" (Leon. 4.74).

81. Objection 3 argues that everything which is made must in some way be in act, whereas prime matter is only in potency. Note from Thomas's reply: ". . . illa ratio non ostendit quod materia non sit creata, sed quod non sit creata sine forma" (Leon. 4.458).

82. Thomas remarks that the subject of privation and the subject of form are one and the same, i.e., *ens in potentia*. This applies: ". . . sive sit ens in potentia simpliciter, sicut materia prima, quae est subiectum formae substantialis et privationis oppositae; sive sit ens in potentia secundum quid . . ." (Leon. 4.493).

83. For objection 2 see Leon. 5.235. For Thomas's reply see p. 237: "Ad secundum dicendum quod actus ad quem est in potentia materia prima, est substantialis forma. Et ideo potentia materiae non est aliud quam eius essentia."

potency.[84] And in his Disputed Questions *De anima,* (1266–1267), q. 12, while replying to objection 12, Thomas comments that prime matter is in potency to substantial act (substantial form); it is for this reason that its potency is identical with its essence.[85] In replying to objection 5 in q. 18, Thomas notes that prime matter stands in relation to substantial forms in one of two ways—either in pure potency, presumably when it is simply considered in itself, or in pure act, that is, as actualized by a given form.[86] And in his Disputed Questions *De malo,* q. 1, a. 2, Thomas again notes that prime matter is described as being only in potency.[87]

Finally, if we may conclude this survey of texts by returning to Thomas's Commentary on the *Metaphysics,* in commenting on Bk XI, lect. 9, he writes that according to Aristotle, being is divided in terms of act and potency. Thus among beings a certain one is in act (the first mover or God), while another is in potency only (prime matter), and still another kind is in potency and in act (all intermediary entities).[88]

In sum, it is clear that from the beginning to the end of his career Thomas defends the view that prime matter includes no form or actuality within its nature, since it is the first or ultimate subject both for form and for privation. Frequently enough he refers to prime matter as potency (or as "in potency") only. This is really equivalent to his other way of describing it—as pure potency. In both cases he wishes to stress the point that it neither is nor contains any actuality in and of itself, and yet that it is not sheer nothingness. Nor is it reducible to privation. On the contrary, it is a real intrinsic principle which must be present in every corporeal being both to account for the fact that such a being is capable of undergoing substantial change and to allow for the possibility that a given kind of being can be multiplied in numerically distinct individuals which belong to the same species.

As we shall see in greater detail below when taking up Thomas's defense of unicity of substantial form, that position is closely connected with his conviction that prime matter is pure potentiality. If one were to assign even some minimum

---

84. Leon. 5.539 (ad 2). See Thomas's reply to objection 4: "Sed id quod maxime distat a Deo, est materia prima; quae nullo modo est agens, cum sit in potentia tantum" (ibid.).

85. Here Thomas is meeting an argument which would identify the intellective soul with its powers on the grounds that just as prime matter is in potency to sensible forms, so is the intellective soul in potency to intelligible form. Because prime matter is identical with its potency, so is the intellective soul identical with its potency (power). Thomas responds: "Ad duodecimum dicendum quod materia prima est in potentia ad actum substantialem qui est forma; et ideo ipsa potentia est ipsa essentia eius" (Leon. 24.1.III:306–309).

86. "Ad quintum dicendum quod materia prima non se habet ad formas nisi dupliciter: vel in potentia pura, vel in actu puro . . ." (Leon. 24.1.159:397–399).

87. On the dating, perhaps 1269–1271, see Torrell, *Saint Thomas Aquinas,* p. 336. For q. 1, a. 2 see Leon. 23.II:164–166: ". . . quia materia prima non dicitur ens nisi in potentia. . . ."

88. "Et hoc est quod dicit, quod entium quoddam est actu, sicut primum movens, quod Deus est; quoddam potentia tantum, ut materia prima, quoddam potentia et actu, sicut omnia intermedia" (ed. cit., p. 544, n. 2289). This is one of two ways in which he thinks Aristotle's text may be interpreted, but it implies again that for Thomas prime matter is pure potency.

degree of actuality to prime matter, one would thereby compromise the essential unity of a matter-form composite. For instance, as Thomas puts this in his Commentary on *Metaphysics* VIII, lect. 1, if prime matter included any proper form in and of itself, it would enjoy some actuality by reason of that form. When another substantial form was introduced, matter would not receive unqualified or substantial being from that form, but only some kind of accidental being.[89] Hence, we may infer, the matter-form composite would not be essentially one.

Before ending this discussion of prime matter as pure potentiality, we should refer to another point. In many of the texts we have now examined, Thomas identifies prime matter with potentiality. He seems to allow for no distinction between prime matter, on the one hand, and its potentiality, on the other. By its very nature it is a potency to substantial being or form.[90] However, there is a difficult passage in his Commentary on I *Sentences* (d. 3, q. 4, a. 2, ad 4). There he is meeting an objection against his defense of distinction between the soul and its powers. According to objection 4, prime matter is identical with its potency. But just as passive potency follows upon prime matter, so does active potency follow upon form. Therefore a substantial form such as the essence of the soul must be identified with its active potency or power.[91]

In replying to this objection, Thomas introduces a distinction. If by passive potency one has in mind the relation of matter to form, matter is not identical with its potency; for the essence of matter is not a relation. But if one simply has in mind potency insofar as it is a principle within the genus substance in the sense that potency and act are principles for every genus, one may identify matter with its potency. Hence when potency is taken in this second sense, one may say that prime matter as a receiving principle is identical with its passive potency just as God is identical with his active power *(potentia)*. As Thomas points out against the original objection, the potency of matter is not ordered to operation but to receive a form.[92]

While this may be an effective reply to the opposing argument, it raises some question about Thomas's earliest understanding of prime matter as ordered to form. The distinction he has introduced implies that if by passive potency we have

89. Here he finds Aristotle turning to substantial generation and corruption in order to arrive at some knowledge of prime matter. Then Thomas continues: "Si enim materia prima de se haberet aliquam formam propriam, per eam esset aliquid actu. Et sic, cum superinduceretur alia forma, non simpliciter materia per eam esset, sed fieret hoc vel illud ens. Et sic esset generatio secundum quid et non simpliciter" (ed. cit., p. 404, n. 1689).

90. See, for instance, the texts cited above in nn. 82, 83, 84, 85, and 87.

91. Mandonnet ed., Vol. 1, p. 115.

92. Mandonnet ed., Vol. 1, p. 117. Note especially: "Ad quartum dicendum, quod si per potentiam passivam intelligatur relatio materiae ad formam, tunc materia non est sua potentia, quia essentia materiae non est relatio. Si autem intelligatur potentia, secundum quod est principium in genere substantiae, secundum quod potentia et actus sunt principia in quolibet genere . . . sic dico, quod materia est ipsa sua potentia. . . ."

in mind the ordering or relationship of matter to form, matter is not identical with its potency. Thomas's reason for saying this is that the essence of matter is not a relation. In later writings he does not find it necessary to distinguish prime matter from its potency or from its ordering or relationship to form.[93] In these passages, when he identifies prime matter with its potency, he does not exclude the relationship of matter to form from his understanding of it as passive potency. At the same time, he will never admit that prime matter, by reason of its passive potentiality, falls into the genus or category of relation. For instance, in his Commentary on I *Physics*, lect. 15, he states that the potency of (prime) matter is not a property which is superadded to matter's essence. According to its essence *(secundum suam substantiam)* (prime) matter is a potency to substantial being.[94] As he writes while commenting on Bk II, matter is included among those things which are ordered to something else; for it is ordered to form. In other words, he is saying that matter is correlative by its very nature, but not that it falls within the genus relation.[95] He could not admit that it does, of course, without undercutting matter's role as an intrinsic constituting principle of the composite substantial essence itself.

In his later writings, therefore, Thomas seems to have concluded that prime matter is pure potentiality of its very nature (as he apparently always held), and that this potentiality is or entails an ordering or relationship to substantial form. This ordering or relationship is not to be regarded as something superadded to matter, as it would be if it belonged to the category relation. But he no longer finds it necessary to distinguish two meanings for the passive potentiality of matter. Matter is now regarded as identical with its potentiality and with its relationship

93. For discussion of this issue see A. Forest, *La structure métaphysique du concret*, pp. 214–16. As Forest points out, in this very same Commentary on I *Sentences*, d. 8, q. 5, a. 1, Thomas refuses to distinguish prime matter (or substantial form) from the relations whereby they are ordered to one another. He argues that "creatures" such as prime matter, any form, or a universal do not exist in themselves, and do not fall short of the divine simplicity by being composed. It will not do to say that they are composed of their own nature and the relations by which they are ordered to God or to that with which they enter into composition: "Si enim dicatur, quod componitur ex ipsa sua natura et habitudinibus quibus refertur ad Deum vel ad illud cum quo componitur, item quaeritur de illis habitudinibus . . ." (Mandonnet ed., Vol. 1, p. 227). Cf. Ch. VI above, nn. 22–24, and our discussion of these texts.

94. In this immediate context Thomas is trying to clarify the meaning of the potency of matter. He notes that it must be held that act and potency divide every genus of beings. Just as the potency for quality does not fall outside the genus quality, so the potency for substantial being does not fall outside the genus substance. He continues: "Non igitur potentia materiae est aliqua proprietas addita super essentiam eius; sed materia secundum suam substantiam est potentia ad esse substantiale" (Maggiòlo ed., p. 67, n. 131). Hence in speaking of matter here, he is referring to prime matter.

95. Here he is commenting on and agreeing with Aristotle's claim that it belongs to one and the same natural science to consider both matter and form. He reasons that one science deals with those things which are ordered to something *(ad aliquid)*: "Sed materia est de numero eorum quae sunt ad aliquid, quia dicitur ad formam. Quod non ideo dicitur quasi ipsa materia sit in genere relationis, sed quia cuilibet formae determinatur propria materia . . ." (see lect. 4, ed. cit., p. 88, n. 174). Here also he has in mind prime matter, since he is treating of the matter (and form) of natural things. See n. 173 (at end) and n. 175.

to form.[96] Interestingly, in the early 1270s at Paris, Siger of Brabant seems to have made and defended a distinction much like Thomas's earlier view concerning the potency of matter.[97] And some years thereafter, Godfrey of Fontaines refers to and employs a similar distinction.[98]

If prime matter is pure potentiality, completely devoid in itself of any form or determination or actuality, one might wonder whether it can be kept in existence without any substantial form, even by God. Reference has already been made to other thirteenth- and fourteenth-century thinkers who, in addition to rejecting prime matter as pure potentiality, thought that divine power could keep it in existence apart from any substantial form.[99] Some of the passages we have now considered already indicate that Thomas will not allow for any such possibility.[100] Others are still more explicit, though they are often joined with his discussion of the way in which God knows prime matter, or to be more specific, the question whether there is a divine idea for prime matter. Even though discussion of both of these issues anticipates our presentation of Thomas's philosophical argumentation for

96. Many Thomistic interpreters have expressed this by saying that matter is transcendentally related to form, and form to matter. They do so in order to express the point that there is no predicamental (or accidental) relation which is added to matter and relates it to its form. De Raeymaker describes this well in its general application to principles of being. Each principle "is identified entirely with the relation which binds it to its co-principle, and it does not contain anything which is not referred to this other principle" (*Philosophy of Being*, p. 105; see n. 5 as well). However, in recent times, doubt has been raised concerning whether Thomas himself defended the classical "Thomistic" doctrine of transcendental relation. See Krempel, *La doctrine de la relation chez saint Thomas*, pp. 174–79, 361–68, and especially pp. 583–96 (where he denies that Thomas admits of any kind of transcendental relation of matter to form, and concludes that there is only a logical relation between individual matter and its substantial form, and an accidental relation between the body and the soul). While I would grant that the terminology "transcendental relation" is missing from Thomas's texts, I am not convinced by Krempel's interpretation. To me it is clear that Thomas defends the view that a principle of being such as matter is related in objective or extramental fashion, i.e., really rather than merely logically, by its very nature or essence to its correlative principle, i.e., its substantial form and vice versa. On the union of soul and body see K. White, "Aquinas on the Immediacy of the Union of Soul and Body," passim; and M. Schulze, *Leibhaft und Unsterblich: Zur Schau der Seele in der Anthropologie und Theologie des Hl. Thomas von Aquin* (Freiburg, Switzerland, 1992), pp. 139–44, for a good critique of Krempel and others.

97. See his *Quaestiones in Physicam*, Bk I, qq. 1–2, in *Écrits de logique, de morale et de physique*, B. Bazán, ed. (Louvain-Paris, 1974), pp. 149–50, esp. 150:31–36. Bazán dates this work ca. 1268–1271, and as probably in 1269 or 1270. Cf. Siger's *Quaestiones in Metaphysicam*, W. Dunphy, ed. (Louvain-la-Neuve, 1981), Munich Ms., Bk V, q. 5, pp. 247–48. On the problem of dating the different *reportationes* of Siger's *Quaestiones in Metaphysicam* see Dunphy, pp. 20–25. He proposes placing them between 1271–1272 and 1275–1276. For brief discussion of these two texts see Van Steenberghen, *Maître Siger de Brabant*, p. 327.

98. See Quodlibet 10, q. 9, *Le huitième, Le neuvième, Le dixième Quodlibet*, J. Hoffmmans, ed., Les Philosophes Belges (Louvain, 1924, 1928, 1931), p. 341. Cf. Quodlibet 9, q. 12, pp. 251–52 and, for discussion, my *The Metaphysical Thought of Godfrey of Fontaines*, p. 270. Godfrey's Quodlibets 9 and 10 may be dated in the academic years 1293/1294 and 1294/1295 respectively (pp. xxvii–xxviii).

99. See above in this chapter, Section 1, nn. 61–63.

100. See *In II Sent.*, d. 12, q. 1, a. 4 (cited above in n. 67); ST I, q. 7, a. 2, ad 3 (see n. 80); ST 1, q. 44, a. 2, ad 3 (see n. 81).

God's existence, his assumption of God's existence in these texts enables him to clarify more fully his understanding of prime matter. The conclusions he draws concerning prime matter will hold if one takes God's existence only as putatively established at this point in our exposition.

Thus in his Commentary on I *Sentences,* d. 36, q. 2, a. 3, ad 2, Thomas writes that since prime matter comes from God, there must be an idea for such matter in God in some way. To put this another way, to the extent that being *(esse)* is attributed to matter, to that extent there must be a divine idea for it. But complete being *(esse perfectum)* does not belong to matter in itself but only insofar as it is realized in a composite. In itself it enjoys only imperfect being according to the lowest degree of being, i.e., being in potency. Therefore, a perfect divine idea corresponds to matter only insofar as it is realized in a composite. When it is considered in itself, the nature of a divine idea corresponds to matter only imperfectly.[101]

As Thomas clarifies while replying to objection 3, particular things have their proper ideas in God. Hence the divine idea of Peter differs from the divine idea of Martin, even as do the ideas for human being and for horse. But since the diversity between human being and horse, specific diversity, is in terms of form, there are diverse divine ideas in the perfect or complete sense for these. The distinction of individuals within one and the same species is according to matter. And Thomas has just asserted that prime matter does not admit of a divine idea in perfect or complete fashion. Therefore, the distinction of divine ideas which corresponds to different species is more perfect than is that which corresponds to different individuals within the same species. As Thomas quickly adds, the imperfection in question refers not to the divine essence itself which is imitated, but only to the things which imitate that essence.[102]

Thomas again addresses himself to this question in *De veritate,* q. 3, a. 5. He reasons that since we hold that matter is caused by God, we must also hold that in some way there is a divine idea for prime matter. Whatever is caused by God retains some likeness of him. But if we would speak of a divine idea in the strict sense, we cannot hold that there is an idea in God for prime matter which is distinct from the idea of the form or the composite. This is so because a divine idea in the strict sense applies to a thing insofar as it can be produced in being. But matter cannot be brought into being without form, nor can the converse obtain. Strictly speaking,

---

101. Mandonnet ed., Vol. 1, pp. 844–45. Note especially: ". . . et ideo perfectam rationem ideae non habet nisi secundum quod est in composito, quia sic sibi a Deo esse perfectum confertur; in se vero considerata, habet in Deo imperfectam rationem ideae. . . ." On the divine ideas in general see my *Thomas Aquinas on the Divine Ideas,* The Etienne Gilson Series 16 (Toronto, 1993). On divine ideas and matter see pp. 42–44. Also cf. V. Boland, *Ideas in God according to Saint Thomas Aquinas,* pp. 227–29.

102. ". . . dicendum, quod particularia habent proprias ideas in Deo; unde alia est ratio Petri et Martini in Deo, sicut alia ratio hominis et equi. Sed tamen diversimode . . . et ideo perfectior est distinctio rationum respondentium diversis speciebus quam diversis individuis . . ." (p. 845). Cf. my *Thomas Aquinas on the Divine Ideas,* pp. 40–42.

therefore, a divine idea does not correspond to matter alone or to form alone. There is one divine idea for the composite whole, and it serves as a productive principle for the entire composite, including both its matter and its form. However, he adds that we may also take a divine idea in a broader sense as signifying a similitude. According to this usage things may have distinct divine ideas if they can be considered distinctly even though they cannot exist separately. When taken in this broader sense, one may grant that there is a divine idea for matter considered in itself.[103]

In replying to the third objection in this same article, Thomas once more remarks that matter cannot exist in itself, i.e., apart from form. Nonetheless, it can be considered in terms of itself *(secundum se)* and to that extent can have a divine likeness or idea.[104] (Thomas's remark about matter's being considered in terms of itself will have to be kept in mind below when we return to the question of how we know prime matter. He does not mean to imply that we have any direct intellectual grasp of it.) But for the moment, it will be enough for us to note that here Thomas insists that prime matter is not realized in actual existence except in a composite, a point which he reiterates in replying to the first objection for the contrary position. He also offers an interesting clarification while replying to the second objection for the contrary position: strictly speaking, prime matter does not itself have an essence; it is a part of the essence of the composite whole.[105]

In *Summa contra Gentiles* II, c. 43, Thomas is arguing against the view of "certain modern heretics" who say that God created the matter of all visible things, but that it was then differentiated through the agency of an angel by different forms. In one of his arguments against this position he reasons that prime matter could not have preexisted in itself before all formed bodies, since it is nothing but potency; all being in actuality comes from some form.[106] In another argument he reasons that the first introduction of form into matter cannot be produced by an agent which operates only through motion; for every motion to a form is from a determined form to a determined form. But matter cannot exist without some form and therefore some form must be presupposed as present in the matter.[107] Again, therefore, even though the context is very different, Thomas simply accepts as a given that matter cannot exist without some form. And as he indicates in the first argument we have just considered, this follows from his conviction that matter is nothing but potency.

---

103. Leon. 22.1.112:35–55. Note: "Sed tamen si proprie de idea loquamur, non potest poni quod materia prima habeat per se ideam in deo distinctam ab idea formae vel compositi, quia idea proprie dicta respicit rem secundum quod est producibilis in esse. . . ."

104. Leon. 22.1.112:68–71. Note: ". . . quamvis materia secundum se esse non possit, tamen potest secundum se considerari et sic potest habere per se similitudinem." Again Thomas is speaking of a divine idea for matter only in the broad sense.

105. Leon. 22.1.112:76–82.

106. Ed. cit., p. 134 "Amplius. Materia autem prima non potest praefuisse per seipsam ante omnia corpora formata: cum non sit nisi potentia tantum; omne enim esse in actu est ab aliqua forma."

107. Ibid. ("Item").

In *De potentia,* q. 4, a. 1, Thomas considers the question whether the creation of unformed matter was prior in duration to the creation of particular things. He notes that interpreters of Scripture have differently understood the beginning of *Genesis,* especially the verse which states that the earth was empty and void. Some take this as indicating that matter was unformed in the sense that it is understood without any form but as existing in potentiality to all forms. Thomas comments that matter taken in this sense cannot exist in reality without being informed by some form. For whatever exists in reality exists actually; and matter does not enjoy actual existence except through form, its act. Moreover, since something can be contained in a genus only by reason of a difference which determines it to its species, matter cannot be realized in being without being determined to some specific mode of being. But this happens only through form.[108]

As noted above, in *Summa theologiae* I, q. 7, a. 2, ad 3, Thomas remarks that prime matter does not exist in reality in and of itself, since it is not being in act but only in potency. Hence it is more concreated than created.[109] In q. 15, a. 3, Thomas again examines the question whether there is a divine idea for matter. In replying to objection 3 he comments that because Plato, according to some, held that matter is not created, he did not defend an idea for matter. Since "we" hold that matter is created by God, although never without some form, Thomas concludes that there is an idea for matter in God. But this idea is not distinct from the divine idea for the composite. Matter neither exists in itself (i.e., apart from form), not is it knowable in that fashion. In sum, he now seems to have quietly abandoned his earlier notion of an imperfect idea for matter considered in itself, or an idea for matter taken in the broad sense.[110]

In q. 66, a. 1 of the *Prima Pars* Thomas once more asks whether matter existed in time before form was introduced into it. He notes that Augustine held that the unformed character of corporeal matter did not precede its actually being informed in the order of time but only in the order of nature. Augustine also understood matter's lack of being informed as implying the absence of every form. If we do take it that way, comments Thomas, it will be impossible for us to hold that matter existed in time before it was actually informed. Thus if matter did preexist before it received any form, it would have already existed in actuality. For the terminus of creation is a being in actuality. But that which is actuality is form. Therefore, to say that matter preexisted without form would be to describe it as being in actuality without any actuality, something which implies contradiction.[111]

---

108. Pession ed., p. 105. For an interesting discussion of this issue see M. McGovern, "Prime Matter in Aquinas," in *The Metaphysics of Substance: Proceedings of the American Catholic Philosophical Association* 61 (1987), pp. 221–34, esp. pp. 226ff. Cf. my *Thomas Aquinas on the Divine Ideas,* p. 44.

109. Cited above in n. 80.

110. Leon. 4.204. Note: "Nam materia secundum se neque esse habet, neque cognoscibilis est."

111. Leon. 5.154. Note in particular: "Ipsum autem quod est actus, est forma. Dicere igitur materiam praecedere sine forma, est dicere ens actu sine actu: quod implicat contradictionem."

This is perhaps Thomas's most forceful statement among the texts we have examined so far. To say that prime matter could preexist without some form would be to defend something self-contradictory. It would be to say that matter was being in actuality (since it existed) and not in actuality (since it is pure potentiality). In replying to the third objection in this same article, Thomas makes an interesting observation. Since an accident is a form, it is a kind of act; but matter is being in potency. Therefore it is more repugnant for matter to exist in actuality without form than for an accident to exist without its subject.[112] Here he has neatly turned the tables in dealing with an argument based on the theology of the Eucharist. According to that argument as Thomas formulates it in the third objection, matter is more powerful than any accident, since it is part of a substance. But God can bring it to pass that an accident exists without its subject, as happens in the Eucharist. Therefore he could bring it to pass that matter would exist without any form. This is of historical interest since it focuses on one reason for the refusal of others, such as Henry of Ghent, William de la Mare, and John Pecham, to deny that God could keep prime matter in existence without any form. If God could not do this, how could he keep accidents in existence without their substantial subject in the Eucharist?[113]

Finally, in Quodlibet 3, q. 1, a. 1 (Easter, 1270), this very question was put to Thomas at a public disputation: "Can God make matter exist without any form?" In answering this question, Thomas offers in summary fashion an excellent statement of his views concerning divine power. Because God is self-subsisting being, it is clear that the nature of being pertains to him infinitely without any limitation or contraction. (Here we have another at least implicit application of the principle that unreceived act is unlimited.) Therefore God's active power extends in infinite fashion to every (actual) being and to every possible being, i.e., to that which can share in the nature of being. That alone is excluded from divine power which is repugnant to the nature of being. And this is owing not to any deficiency in divine

---

112. Leon. 5.155: ". . . accidens, cum sit forma, est actus quidam: materia autem secundum id quod est, est ens in potentia. Unde magis repugnat esse in actu materiae sine forma, quam accidenti, sine subiecto."

113. Leon. 5.154. See *Henrici de Gandavo Quodlibet I*, R. Macken, ed. (Leuven-Leiden, 1979), p. 62:9–14, for an opening argument in support of the claim that matter could exist without form based on a comparison with an accident which can subsist without its subject, as in the Eucharist: "Multo fortius ergo et materia potest per se subsistere." Henry's presentation of this argument bears close similarities with that in Thomas's text (q. 66, a. 1). For Henry's acceptance of this argument see the conclusion of the corpus (p. 67:3–8). On Henry's general position concerning prime matter see R. Macken, "Subsistance de la matière première selon Henri de Gand," "Le statut de la matière première dans la philosophie d'Henri de Gand" (both as cited above in n. 62). Also see my *The Metaphysical Thought of Godfrey of Fontaines*, pp. 263–65, 273. As I indicate in the latter context, William de la Mare argues in similar fashion against Thomas (and against ST I, q. 66, a. 1) in his *Correctorium Fratris Thomae*. See *Le Correctorium Corruptorii "Quare"*, P. Glorieux, ed. (Le Saulchoir, Kain, 1927), p. 114. Henry's Quodlibet I dates from 1276, and William's *Correctorium* ca. 1278. For more on this see my "Bishop Stephen Tempier and Thomas Aquinas: A Separate Process against Aquinas?" *Freiburger Zeitschrift für Philosophie und Theologie* 44 (1997), pp. 127–29. For Pecham see Quodlibet 4, q. 1 (in *Quodlibeta Quatuor*, pp. 174–76).

power but to the fact that what is proposed simply cannot be realized as a being and therefore cannot be done. But it is repugnant to the nature of being for it to be nonbeing at the same time and in the same respect. Therefore, for something to be and not to be at the same time and in the same respect cannot be brought about by God, nor can anything which implies contradiction. But for matter to exist in actuality without form implies contradiction.[114]

To prove this final point, Thomas reasons that what is in act is either act itself, or a potency which participates in act. To be an act is repugnant to the nature of matter, because by its nature matter is being in potency. It follows therefore that matter cannot be in act except insofar as it participates in act. But an act which is participated in by matter is nothing other than a form. Therefore, it is one and the same thing to say that matter is in act and that matter has a form. Consequently, to hold that matter is in act without any form is to say that contradictories are realized simultaneously. Therefore this cannot be brought to pass, not even by God.[115]

In sum, in Quodlibet 3 we have what I regard as Thomas's finest metaphysical statement of his reasons for denying that matter can be kept in existence without some form. This follows from his conviction that not even God can do that which is self-contradictory or, to put it in metaphysical terms, that which is repugnant to the nature of being. To say that something can be and not be at the same time and in the same respect is repugnant to the nature of being. And if prime matter is indeed pure potentiality, as Thomas maintains, to say that it could actually exist without any form would be to say that it is in act (and therefore participates in form) and not in act (since according to the hypothesis it does not participate in form) at one and the same time. Because this is intrinsically contradictory, it cannot be done, not even by God.[116]

In concluding this discussion of prime matter we shall return to Thomas's explanation of the way in which it can be known. His stress on matter's purely potential character seems to create some difficulty both for his account of God's knowledge of prime matter and for his account of our knowledge of it.

---

114. Leon. 25.2.241:39–242:53. Note especially: "Repugnat autem rationi entis non ens, simul et secundum idem, existens: unde quod aliquid simul sit et non sit, a Deo fieri non potest, nec aliquid contradictionem includens. Et de huiusmodi est materiam esse actu sine forma. . . ."

115. Leon. 25.2.242:55–64. Note in particular: "Dicere ergo quod materia sit in actu sine forma, est dicere contradictoria esse simul; unde a Deo fieri non potest." In again meeting an objection based on an alleged parallel with accidents in the Eucharist, Thomas here stresses the difference between the two cases. An accident depends for its being upon its subject as upon a cause which sustains it. Because God can produce the effects of second causes without those second causes themselves, he can preserve an accident in being without its subject. But matter depends upon a form for its actual being insofar as the form is the very act of matter. Hence there is no parity between the two cases. (See lines 65–73.)

116. For some other texts where Thomas reasons from the absolutely impossible character of something (because it is intrinsically contradictory) to the conclusion that it cannot be done by any agent, including God, see De potentia, q. 3. a. 14 (ed. cit., p. 80); ST I, q. 25, a. 3 (Leon. 4.293–94); De aeternitate mundi (Leon. 43.85:46–86:49); Quodlibet 5, q. 2, a. 1 (Leon. 25.2:367:29–37).

As will be recalled from the texts we have now examined, in his Commentary on I *Sentences* (d. 36, q. 2, a. 3), Thomas appears to hold that there is a kind of divine idea for prime matter. There is a perfect divine idea for prime matter only insofar as it is realized together with its appropriate form in a given composite. This is because perfect being pertains to matter only insofar as it is so realized. But what Thomas there describes as a divine idea in the imperfect or incomplete sense would correspond to prime matter considered in itself. This is because prime matter taken in itself enjoys only imperfect or incomplete being.[117]

Subsequently in *De veritate*, q. 3, a. 5, Thomas notes that to the extent that prime matter is caused by God, there must be a divine idea for it. But if we take a divine idea in the strict and proper sense, we can say only that it is one and the same idea which corresponds to the composite essence—including both matter and form—and which also serves as a productive principle for that composite. In other words, strictly speaking, there is not a distinct divine idea for the matter of a composite essence, or even for its form, but only one divine idea for the whole. However, in this context Thomas also speaks of a divine idea in the broad sense. Taken in this way, there are distinct divine ideas for things which can be considered in distinction from one another even though they cannot exist in separation from one another. In this broad sense, therefore, Thomas here acknowledges that there can be a divine idea for prime matter itself.[118] In *Summa theologiae* I, q. 15, a. 3, Thomas reiterates the first part of this solution. There is a divine idea for matter, but not one that is distinct from the divine idea for the composite. As we have already noted, here he no longer speaks of a distinct divine idea for matter when that term is taken in the imperfect sense or broadly.[119]

As for human knowledge of prime matter, Thomas holds, as we have seen, that we cannot know it in and by itself. This follows from his conviction that it is pure potency and therefore completely undetermined in and of itself. As he explains in q. 5, a. 3 of his Commentary on the *De Trinitate*:

For, since everything is intelligible insofar as it is in act, as the *Metaphysics* says, we must understand the nature itself or the quiddity of a thing either inasmuch as it is a certain act (as happens in the case of forms themselves and simple substances); or through that which is its act (as we know composite substances through their forms); or through that which takes the place of act in it (as we know prime matter through its relation to form).[120]

---

117. Mandonnet ed., Vol. 1, pp. 844–45. See above, nn. 101, 102, and my corresponding text.

118. Cited above in n. 104.

119. Leon. 4.204, p. 92. See n. 110 above.

120. "Cum enim unaquaeque res sit intelligibilis secundum quod est in actu, ut dicitur in IX Metaphysicae, oportet quod ipsa natura sive quidditas rei intelligatur vel secundum quod est actus quidam, sicut accidit de ipsis formis et substantiis simplicibus, vel secundum id quod est actus eius, sicut substantiae compositae per suas formas, vel secundum id quod est ei loco actus, sicut materia prima per habitudinem ad formam . . ." (Leon. 50.147:121–130). English translation from Maurer, *Thomas Aquinas: The Division and Methods of the Sciences* (4th ed., Toronto, 1986), pp. 35–36.

According to this text, therefore, we can know prime matter through the form which actualizes it. But as we have also seen, in other contexts Thomas writes that we can know prime matter by a kind of analogy or proportion: prime matter is related to all forms and privations in the way bronze is related to a statue and to the lack of configuration.[121] In another text from this same Commentary on the *De Trinitate* (q. 4, a. 2) Thomas explicitly distinguishes these two approaches. There he writes that prime matter can be known in two ways: (1) by analogy or proportion, as is stated in I *Physics* (thus we say that matter is that which is related to natural things as wood is related to a bed); (2) by reason of the form through which it enjoys being in actuality; for each and every thing is knowable insofar as it is in act, not insofar as it is in potency, as is stated in *Metaphysics* IX.[122]

Since these two approaches are not mutually exclusive, we conclude that according to Thomas we can know prime matter in both ways—by analogy or proportion, and by reason of the form which actualizes it. Because of its purely potential character, we cannot know it directly in and of itself. In and of itself it possesses no form or actuality which would render it intelligible to us.

3. Substantial Form and Its Unicity

Something of Thomas's understanding of the nature of substantial form has already emerged from our discussion of his views concerning prime matter. Thus in the *De principiis naturae*, c. 1 he writes that prime matter receives its existence *(esse)* from form. To put this another way, substantial form is said to give substantial existence to matter.[123] This notion, that substantial form gives *esse* to matter, appears frequently in Thomas's other writings—for instance, in the *De ente* and the Commentary on the *Sentences,* to mention but two early works, and in mature writings such as *Summa theologiae* I and the *De substantiis separatis*. At times he applies this to *esse* in the sense of existence, but on other occasions also applies it to *esse* taken as the act of being.[124]

121. See *De principiis naturae,* c. 2, as cited above in n. 12; *In I Phys.,* lect. 13, p. 59, n. 118, cited above in n. 18.

122. Leon. 50.123:94–102. See n. 18 above. The text continues: ". . . unumquodque enim cognoscitur secundum quod est in actu et non secundum quod est in potentia, ut dicitur in IX Metaphysicae." For Aristotle see *Metaphysics* IX, c. 9 (1051a 29–32).

123. Leon. 43.39:20–44. Note: ". . . quod vero est in potentia ad esse substantiale dicitur proprie materia. . . . Unde, simpliciter loquendo forma dat esse materiae. . . . Et quia forma facit esse in actu, ideo forma dicitur esse actus; quod autem facit actu esse substantiale est forma substantialis. . . ."

124. See *De ente et essentia,* c. 2 (Leon. 43.370:31–35); c. 4 (p. 376:45–47); c. 6 (p. 380:64); *In I Sent.,* d. 23, q. 1, a. 1 (Mandonnet ed., Vol. 1, p. 555): "Similiter dico, quod cum esse consequitur compositionem materiae et formae, quamvis forma sit principium esse, non tamen denominatur aliquod ens a forma, sed a toto . . ."; *In II Sent.,* d. 12, q. 1, a. 4 (Mandonnet ed., Vol. 2, p. 314): "Sed hanc positionem Avicenna improbat, quia omnis forma substantialis dat esse completum in genere substantiae"; *In III Sent.,* d. 6, q. 2, a. 2, ad 1 (Moos ed., Vol. 3, p. 239): ". . . dicendum quod forma facit esse; non ita quod illud esse sit materiae aut formae, sed subsistentis"; *De veritate,* q. 28, a. 7

Also in the *De principiis* Thomas comments that generation is a motion towards a form. Generation in the unqualified sense is ordered to a substantial form, while generation in the qualified sense is ordered to an accidental form. When a substantial form is introduced, something is said to be made in the unqualified sense.[125]

Frequently enough Thomas refers to substantial form as the act of matter, for instance in *De spiritualibus creaturis,* a. 1, as cited above. At the same time, he holds that form is limited by matter.[126] This is another application of his conviction that unreceived act is unlimited. If we find a substantial form in limited fashion in a particular entity, this is because its corresponding principle—prime matter—receives and limits it.[127]

For Thomas substantial form plays a primary role within the metaphysical structure or essence of any being, including corporeal entities. A thing's type or kind (species) is determined by its essence. Within the essence of corporeal entities, a thing's specific kind of being is determined by its substantial form. In the case of created spiritual entities—angels—a thing's substantial form is identical with its substantial essence.[128]

As has already been noted at least in passing, Thomas maintains that both matter and form are included within the essence of a corporeal entity. Accordingly, each must be included within the definition of such a thing. At the same time, he was aware that the view that matter is included within a thing's essence had been controverted, and that Aristotle's mind concerning this was also subject to dispute. Thus in his Commentary on *Metaphysics* VII, c. 10, Thomas refers to two major opinions concerning the definitions and essences of things.[129]

Some hold that the entire essence of a species is the form itself, just as they hold that a human being's entire essence is to be identified with the soul. For this reason they also maintain that the "form of the whole" *(forma totius)* as signified by a term such as "humanity" is to be identified with the "form of the part" *(forma partis),* as illustrated, for instance, by the name "soul." Defenders of this view acknowledge that the two differ conceptually *(secundum rationem).* Thus the name "form of the part" is applied to a substantial form insofar as the latter is viewed as perfecting

---

(Leon. 22.3.840:146–150): ". . . similiter materia est causa formae aliquo modo in quantum sustinet formam, et forma est aliquo modo causa materiae in quantum dat materiae esse actu"; SCG II, c. 55 (ed. cit., p. 147): ". . . per formam enim substantia fit proprium susceptivum eius quod est esse"; ST I, q. 14, a. 2, ad 1 (Leon. 4.168): "Forma enim, inquantum perficit materiam dando ei esse, quodammodo supra ipsam effunditur . . ."; *De substantiis separatis,* c. 8: "Quia igitur materia recipit esse determinatum actuale per formam, et non e converso . . ." (Leon. 40.D55:228–230). In the last three texts, at least, *esse* refers to the act of being.

125. See above in this chapter, p. 297 and n. 6.

126. Ed. cit., p. 371. See above in this chapter, n. 37.

127. See nn. 37 and 39 above.   128. See *De ente,* c. 4 (Leon. 43.376:61–89).

129. *In VII Met.,* lect. 9, p. 358, n. 1467.

prime matter and making it exist in actuality. But this very same substantial form is known as the "form of the whole" insofar as we mean thereby that it is by reason of the form that the composite whole is placed in its appropriate species. Given this, defenders of this position maintain that no parts of matter should be included in the definition which indicates a thing's species, but only the formal principles of the species. Thomas comments that this view seems to be that of Averroes and some of his followers.[130]

If this is indeed the position espoused by Averroes, there are passages in Aristotle's *Metaphysics*, especially in Bk VII, which strongly suggest that it was also the Stagirite's view. For instance, in c. 10 Aristotle is discussing the parts of which substance (οὐσία) consists.

> If then matter is one thing, form another, the compound of these a third, and both the matter and the form and the compound are substance, even the matter is in a sense called part of a thing, while in a sense *it* is not, but only the elements of which the formula of the form consists.[131]

To illustrate this Aristotle observes that flesh, a given kind of matter, is not part of the form concavity, though it is a part of snubness, another kind of form. Or again, bronze is a part of a particular statue, but not of the statue taken as form. And he immediately comments that each thing must be referred to by "naming its form, and as having form, but never by naming its material aspect as such."[132]

In the ensuing discussion Aristotle goes on to distinguish between two kinds of parts, or even three kinds. There are certain parts of which a thing is composed not as parts of their essence (οὐσία) but only as parts of matter, for instance, the halves of a line. On the other hand, there are other parts—parts of the form—to which the definition (λόγος) refers. The former—parts of matter—are not included in the definition of a thing, while parts of the form are so included. Hence the parts of the definition (λόγος) into which the λόγος is divided are prior to the definition (either all are, or at least some).[133]

> And since the soul of animals (for this is the substance [οὐσία] of living beings) is their substance according to the formula, i.e., the form and the essence of a body of a certain

---

130. Ibid. On this passage and those that follow see A. Maurer, "Form and Essence in the Philosophy of St. Thomas," pp. 165–76, repr. in his *Being and Knowing*, pp. 3–18, which I shall cite here. For this in Averroes see his *In VII Met.*, com. 34, ed. cit., Vol. 8, fol. 184r. Note especially: ". . . si igitur hoc nomen substantia dicitur simpliciter de materia substantiae compositae ex materia et forma, et de forma eius, et de composito, tunc forma substantiae dicetur esse substantia rei, cum ipsa declaret essentiam illius. Materia vero dicitur secundum considerationem ad substantiam compositam ex materia et forma esse pars substantiae. Secundum considerationem vero ad substantiam declarantem essentiam rei non dicitur esse pars substantiae. . . ." For Thomas on the distinction between parts of the form and parts of the whole also see *In De Trin.*, q. 5, a. 3 (Leon. 50.148:204–149:237).

131. See 1035a 1–4. English trans., p. 1634.   132. See 1035a 5–9. English trans., p. 1634.
133. See 1035a 10–1035b 14.

kind, . . . therefore the parts of soul are prior, either all or some of them, to the concrete animal, and similarly in each case of a concrete whole.[134]

As Aristotle summarizes shortly thereafter, a part may be a part (1) of the form (i.e., the essence), or (2) of the compound of the form and the matter, or (3) of the matter itself. "But only the parts of the form are parts of the formula (λόγος) and the formula is of the universal."[135] In this passage he identifies the form with essence (τὸ τί ἦν εἶναι). And in the previously cited text he refers to the soul, i.e., the form of animals as the substance (οὐσία) of living things and notes that this form is their substance according to their definition, i.e., the form and the essence of a body of a certain kind. In short, Aristotle identifies form with οὐσία when we take the latter as the quiddity or essence of a material thing.[136]

As A. Maurer and J. Owens have pointed out, this is not to deny that in answering the question "What is a material entity?" Aristotle will point to the matter-form composite. It is rather to affirm that when it comes to identifying the essence of a corporeal substance, Aristotle restricts this to form. Matter is not included within such a thing's essence.[137]

If Thomas himself identifies this reading of Aristotle with that proposed by Averroes, he goes on to distinguish another position. According to this second view, followed by Avicenna, the form of the whole, i.e., the quiddity of the species, differs from the form of the part just as a whole differs from its part. Hence the quiddity of the species is itself composed of matter and form, although not of this individual form and this individual matter. Only an individual composite is composed of the latter. Again, while Thomas is correct in attributing this position to Avicenna,[138] he is not content to stop with this. He goes on to state that the Avicennian view is that of Aristotle himself and suggests that in this particular chapter of the *Metaphysics* Aristotle appeals to it in order to refute Plato's theory of ideas. By holding that sensible matter is a part of the species for natural entities, Aristotle also shows that it is impossible for the species of such things to exist without sensible matter; but this

---

134. 1035b 14–20. English trans., p. 1635.

135. 1035b33–1036a 1. English trans., p. 1635.

136. See Maurer, "Form and Essence," pp. 6–7. Cf. J. Owens, *The Doctrine of Being in the Aristotelian Metaphysics*, pp. 360–65; G. Verbeke, "Substance in Aristotle," *Proceedings of the American Catholic Philosophical Association* 51 (1987), pp. 35–51, esp. pp. 44–47. Cf. A. C. Lloyd, *Form and the Universal in Aristotle* (Liverpool, 1981), pp. 30–41.

137. See Maurer, pp. 6–7, and his acknowledged debt to Owens in making this distinction. He cites from Owens, *The Doctrine of Being*, pp. 185–87.

138. *In VII Met.*, lect. 9, pp. 358–59. Note: ". . . nam quidditas speciei, est composita ex materia et forma, non tamen ex hac forma et ex hac materia individua." For Avicenna see his *Liber de Philosophia prima sive Scientia divina V–X*, S. Van Riet, ed., tr. V, c. 5, p. 275:62–75: "Ergo forma est unum eorum quae conveniunt in hac compositione, quidditas vero est ipsa compositio complectens formam et materiam. . . ." For discussion see Maurer, "Form and Essence," p. 9. Maurer comments that the "expressions *forma partis* and *forma totius* do not seem to appear in the Latin translation of Avicenna's works."

would be required by Plato's view that the species or forms of things exist separately without such matter.[139]

Earlier on within this same general context Thomas had rejected the view of Averroes as being contrary to the mind *(contra intentionem)* of Aristotle. Thomas recalls a passage from *Metaphysics* VI where Aristotle writes that natural things include sensible matter in their definition and that in this respect they differ from mathematicals. But if this is granted, it can hardly be said that natural substances are defined by something which is not part of their essence. Substances do not admit of this kind of definition by addition *(ex additione)*. Only accidents do. Therefore it follows that sensible matter is a part of the essence of natural substances. And this applies not only to concrete individuals, but even to their species; for definitions are offered not for individuals but for species.[140]

Thomas's remarks make two points clear. First of all, he is convinced of the truth of the claim that the essence of matter-form composites must include both prime matter and substantial form. Secondly, in commenting on certain passages from Aristotle's *Metaphysics* VII, c. 10 which seem to state the opposite, Thomas interprets them so as to confirm his personal position. As Maurer has pointed out in detail, in so reading these texts Thomas seems to force some of them.[141]

As for Thomas's personal position, the view he defends in this late work—his Commentary on the *Metaphysics*—is consistent with that which he maintained throughout his career. This applies both to the truth of the matter as Thomas sees it and to his appeal to Avicenna for support. For instance, this doctrine is clearly presented as early as *De ente*, c. 2. There Thomas remarks that neither matter taken alone nor form taken alone can be identified with the essence of a composite substance. That matter alone is not the essence of such a thing is evident from the fact that a thing is knowable through its essence and placed thereby in its appropriate genus or species. But matter in itself is not a principle whereby something is knowable, or determined to its genus or species.[142]

Nor can essence be identified with the form of a composite entity, continues Thomas, although some have defended this view. He recalls that, as he has indicated in c. 1, the essence is signified by the definition of a thing. But the definition of natural substances includes matter as well as form. Otherwise there would be no difference between physical and mathematical definitions. Nor will it do to counter that matter is included in the definition of a natural substance only as something added to its essence, or as something that falls outside its essence. This way of

---

139. See n. 1469.

140. See p. 358, n. 1468. For the text from *Metaphysics VI*, c. 1, see 1025b 30–1026a 6. For Thomas's commentary on this see *In VI Met.*, lect. 1, pp. 296–97, nn. 1155–1161. Cf. Maurer, pp. 5–6, 8–9.

141. See Maurer, pp. 11–14.

142. See Leon. 43.370:2–10. Note: ". . . sed materia neque cognitionis principium est, neque secundum eam aliquid ad genus vel speciem determinatur. . . ."

defining applies to accidents, Thomas responds, since they do not enjoy complete essences in themselves but must include in their definitions the subject which receives them. But, he implies, this way of defining does not apply to substantial essences.[143]

Thomas also briefly considers and dismisses another position which would hold that the essence signifies a relation between matter and form or something superadded to them. This would be an accident, he counters, and therefore extrinsic to the thing itself. And the thing would not be known by means of any such factor. But, as he has just pointed out, a thing is rendered knowable by its essence.[144] Along with others, Thomas cites Avicenna as holding that the quiddity of composite substances involves the composition of both form and matter.[145]

Thomas finds this view supported by reason as well. The *esse* of a composite substance is not merely that of its form alone or that of its matter alone but the *esse* of the composite itself. And the essence of a thing is that in accord with which the thing is said to exist. Therefore the essence by reason of which a thing is named a being *(ens)* should be identified not with its form alone or with its matter alone, but with both. Thomas does acknowledge that it is the form that causes such *esse* in accord with its appropriate mode, i.e., by serving as its formal cause.[146] As Maurer has pointed out, throughout his career Thomas would continue to insist that matter is included within the essence of corporeal substances—as late, for instance, as in his *Compendium theologiae*, c. 154, of ca. 1265–1267. And of

---

143. Leon. 43.370:10–25. Note Thomas's concluding remark: "Patet ergo quod essentia comprehendit et materiam et formam."

144. Ed. cit., p. 370:26–31.

145. Leon. 43.370:40–371:50. Again the Avicennian reference appears to be to his *Liber de Philosophia prima*, i.e., his *Metaphysica* (see above, n. 138). Thomas also refers to Boethius's Commentary on the *Predicaments* (". . . ubi dicit quod usya significat compositum . . ."), although as Maurer (op. cit., p. 15) and Roland-Gosselin *(Le "De ente et essentia,"* p. 8, n. 1) have pointed out, this alleged Boethian dictum is not to be found in that work by Boethius. Interestingly, Thomas also cites Averroes accurately in support of his reading: "Natura quam habent species in rebus generabilibus est aliquod medium, id est compositum ex materia et forma." For Averroes see *In VII Met.,* c. 27, ed. cit., Vol. 8, f. 177ra. However this is not for Averroes to say that the essence of a composite includes both matter and form.

146. "Huic etiam ratio concordat, quia esse substantiae compositae non est tantum formae neque tantum materiae, sed ipsius compositi; essentia autem est secundum quam res esse dicitur: unde oportet ut essentia qua res denominatur ens non tantum sit forma, neque tantum materia, sed utrumque, quamvis huiusmodi esse suo modo sola forma sit causa" (p. 371: 50–57). One wonders whether Thomas here has in mind the act of being when he uses the term *esse.* If so, he would be anticipating the argumentation for composition and distinction of essence and *esse* which he presents later in the *De ente* (in c. 4), and this reading lends greater strength to the argument. Perhaps the safest course is to suggest that he deliberately leaves this unspecified in c. 2, being content for us to take *esse* as signifying that something exists. Once he has established to his own satisfaction in c. 4 the distinction of essence from *esse,* he will be in position to apply *esse* taken as the act of being to his present remarks. On form as the formal cause of *esse* see J. Aertsen, *Nature and Creature: Thomas Aquinas's Way of Thought,* trans. H. D. Morton (Leiden–New York–Cologne, 1987), pp. 331–36.

course the Commentary on the *Metaphysics* is still later, probably dating after mid-1271.[147]

The notion that form causes or in some way gives *esse* to matter and hence to the composite requires some further precisions concerning the relationship between form and matter, on the one hand, and substantial *esse* (the act of being), on the other. If form gives the act of being to matter, form cannot be identified with that act of being; for form falls on the side of a thing's essence and, as we have now seen, is regarded by Thomas as intrinsic to that essence. But he also holds that *esse* when taken as the act of being is distinct from essence. Hence it is also distinct from form.

As we have already seen in this chapter, Thomas spells out these two relationships in different contexts, but perhaps nowhere more clearly than in his *De spiritualibus creaturis,* a. 1. In things composed of matter and form, he explains, there is a twofold actuality and a twofold potentiality. At one level prime matter is a potency with respect to form, and its corresponding form serves as the act of matter. But at another level the essence (nature) composed of matter and form itself serves as a potency in relationship to its act of being *(esse)*. This follows, of course, from Thomas's view that the composite essence or nature receives its act of being.[148] Thomas goes on in this context to contrast this situation (that of a composite of matter and form) with that of a pure spirit. Though not composed of matter and form, the created spirit's form or essence stands in potency to its own act of being.[149] Or as Thomas puts this in c. 8 of his *De substantiis separatis,* a thing composed of matter and form participates in its act of being from God through its form according to its proper mode. And as he has just explained in the same context, the mode of any substance composed of matter and form is in accord with its form by reason of which it belongs to its given species.[150]

With this we may now turn to Thomas's views on unicity of substantial form. Surely no other name in thirteenth-century philosophy is more closely associated with this theory than that of Aquinas. As he repeatedly makes clear in his mature writings, if form in some way communicates the substantial act of being *(esse)* and if a thing's unity follows upon its being, there can be only one substantial form in any given substance. Otherwise there would be more than one substantial act of

---

147. See Maurer, p. 10, n. 33. For the *Compendium theologiae* see Leon. 42.140:55–88. While this text is directed to determining whether it is only by divine power that the soul can be reunited with numerically one and the same body at the resurrection, in it Thomas gives another excellent statement of his view that the essence, for instance of a human being, includes both matter and form. For the date of the Commentary on *Metaphysics* VII see Torrell, *Saint Thomas Aquinas,* p. 344.

148. Ed. cit., p. 371.

149. Ibid.

150. Leon. 40.D55:205–212. Note especially: ". . . sic igitur res composita ex materia et forma per suam formam fit participativa ipsius esse a Deo secundum quendam proprium modum." He immediately goes on to distinguish the relationship of matter to form, and that of the composite essence to its participated *esse*.

being and therefore more than one substantial unit or substance. Even so, it has been suggested that Thomas's adoption of this position in his earliest writing was more hesitant, and that at the time of his Commentary on the *Sentences* he also allowed for a second kind of substantial form in corporeal entities, a form of corporeity. Since this claim is contested by other scholars, we shall now consider a number of Thomas's discussions from earlier and from later texts. Only then will we be in position to return to the question of any possible evolution in his thinking concerning this.[151]

In his Commentary on Bk II of the *Sentences,* d. 12, q. 1, a. 4, Thomas considers the question whether prime matter might ever have existed without any substantial form. He notes that prime matter cannot include any form as part of its essence; nor does it ever exist apart from all form. When it loses one form it acquires another. He also writes that it was not possible for prime matter when taken in a temporal sense as "first matter" to have existed even at the dawn of creation without some form.[152] Even so, he acknowledges diversity of opinion both among the ancients and among modern thinkers, i.e., his contemporaries. Some of the ancients held the whole of matter to be subject to one form by making one of the elements (or something falling between them) the prime matter for everything else. From this all other things would be generated by a process of rarefaction and condensation. Other ancients held that matter did exist under many forms, but only as mixed together in confused fashion. These would then have been ordered to and distinguished from one another by the work of some "creative principle."[153]

Since Thomas judges that Aristotle has sufficiently refuted such theories in Bk I of his *Physics,* he quickly turns to the view of the moderns. Here again he finds two fundamentally different approaches. Some hold that prime matter was originally subject to one form. But this form was not one of the four elements but something which is only *in via* with respect to the elements, much in the way the form of an embryo stands in relation to a complete animal. Militating against this view is the fact that the first aptitude of matter is for the form of an element, and that there is no intermediary form between prime matter and the form of an element. Moreover, if one accepted this theory, even now when elements are generated

---

151. See especially R. Zavalloni, *Richard de Mediavilla et la controverse sur la pluralité des formes,* pp. 261–66, esp. p. 266, and his references there to others, including G. Théry, A. Forest, and M.-D. Roland-Gosselin. According to Théry, Thomas grasped the implications of his doctrine of unicity of substantial form from the very beginning. See his "L'Augustinisme médiévale et le problème de l'unité de la forme substantielle," in *Acta Hebdomadae Augustinianae-Thomisticae* (Rome, 1931), pp. 144–200, esp. 169–70. Zavalloni himself rejects this and argues for some evolution on Thomas's part. Forest *(La structure,* pp. 190–93) and Roland-Gosselin *(Le "De ente,"* pp. 104–5, n. 1) are more cautious about this.

152. "Utrum prima materia fuerit informis" (Mandonnet ed., Vol. 2, p. 312). See p. 313: ". . . et quamvis materia prima sic accepta non habeat aliquam formam partem essentiae suae, nunquam tamen dividitur ab omni forma. . . ." Also see pp. 313–14.

153. Ed. cit., p. 314.

one would have to recognize another form in matter before the form of any given element. This runs counter to sense experience, objects Thomas, unless perhaps one agrees with Avicebron that there is one primary form and that this common corporeal form was first introduced into matter, followed by distinct specific forms.[154] Undermining this, comments Thomas, is Avicenna's argument. Because every substantial form gives complete *esse* within the genus substance, whatever comes to a thing after it exists in actuality can only be an accident. All other natural forms would only be accidents, and the process of substantial generation would be reduced to the level of accidental change, i.e., alteration. Hence Avicenna concludes that it is through one and the same form that fire is fire, and that it is a body and a substance.[155]

Given this Avicennian rejection of plurality of forms, Thomas resolves the issue by following another modern view, which he refers to as the way of other *sancti*. Prime matter was originally created under many substantial forms (for the different parts of prime matter), and all the substantial forms for the essential parts of the world were created at the beginning. However, Thomas proposes that the active

154. Ed. cit., pp. 314–15. Note especially: ". . . nisi forte dicatur, secundum positionem libri *Fontis vitae*, esse unam primam formam, et sic in materia primo inductam fore formam corporalem communem, et postmodum formas speciales distinctas." Here as throughout his literary corpus Thomas assigns responsibility for the origination of the theory of plurality of forms to Avicebron. On the origins of the controversy concerning unicity vs. plurality of substantial form see, in addition to Théry (as cited in n. 151), D. A. Callus, "The Origins of the Problem of the Unity of Form," in *The Dignity of Science*, J. A. Weisheipl, ed. (Washington, D.C., 1961), pp. 121–49. After citing Avicenna (pp. 127–28) and Dominic Gundissalinus as channels for transmitting the Avicennian position (which focuses more on unity of soul than on unity of form) to the Latins (pp. 128–33), Callus refers to Avicebron "as the main true source from which the pluralist theory has come down to the Schoolmen" (p. 134). If Avicenna is cited as an early source for the unicity theory by Callus and by Théry ("L'augustinisme," pp. 146–49), Zavalloni sees in him an important source for the opposed plurality theory (pp. 423–28). But, as Van Steenberghen has pointed out, Zavalloni seems to understate Avicebron's influence in the development of the plurality position among the Latins *(La philosophie au XIIIe siècle*, pp. 429–30).

155. Ed. cit., pp. 314–15. Note: "Sed hanc positionem Avicenna improbat, quia omnis forma substantialis dat esse completum in genere substantiae. Quidquid autem advenit postquam res est in actu, est accidens: est enim in subiecto quod dicitur ens in se completum. Unde oporteret omnes alias formas naturales esse accidentia. . . ." Cf. *In II Sent.*, d. 18, q. 1, a. 2: "Et praeterea, cum omnis forma det aliquod esse, et impossibile sit unam rem habere duplex esse substantiale, oportet, si prima forma substantialis adveniens materiae det sibi esse substantiale, quod secunda superveniens det esse accidentale: et ideo *non est alia forma qua ignis est ignis, et qua est corpus,* ut Avicenna vult, *Suffic.*, lib. II, cap. iii" (italics mine). Ed. cit., p. 452. The italicized text is cited by A. Forest to support his claim that Avicenna indeed defended unicity of substantial form (as Thomas thought). See *La structure métaphysique*, p. 178. Cf. pp. 193ff. Zavalloni (p. 427) refers to A.-M. Goichon's lack of success in finding the particular passage in question in Avicenna himself. See her *La distinction de l'essence et de l'existence d'après Ibn Sina (Avicenne)*, pp. 435–36, n. 6. Zavalloni (p. 428) concludes that Avicenna's understanding of corporeal form, his views concerning the permanence of elements in a mixture, and his theory of a hierarchy of souls suggest that he is a true precursor of the theory of plurality of forms, frequent reference to him as a defender of unicity of form by Thomas and other thirteenth-century thinkers notwithstanding. For another thirteenth-century witness see Giles of Rome's *Errores philosophorum*, J. Koch, ed. (Milwaukee, 1944), pp. 24–26, 34.

and passive powers were not yet conferred on the various parts of the world in the way they would subsequently be distinguished and ordered. He argues that this suggestion is possible if one accepts Avicenna's view that elements remain in a mixture in terms of their substantial forms as regards their primary *esse* even though they are changed in terms of their secondary *esse*, i.e., in terms of their active and passive powers. Therefore, he suggests, it is also possible for matter to be subject to a given substantial form without possessing the corresponding active and passive powers in perfect fashion.[156]

In d. 18, q. 1, a. 2 of this same Commentary on II *Sentences* Thomas wonders whether and to what extent the notion of seminal reasons is acceptable. He notes that some hold that the form of a species is not received in matter except by means of a generic form. Hence that form by reason of which fire is fire is numerically distinct from that form whereby fire is a body. Some would refer to this incomplete generic form as a seminal reason, because it leaves an inclination in matter to receive specific forms. Thomas rejects this approach because every form which comes to something after its substantial being *(esse)* can only be an accidental form. If such a form can be added to something which already enjoys substantial being, when that form is removed the individual substance will still remain.[157] In short, here again, as in our first text, Thomas rejects a theory which would defend plurality of substantial forms.

Thomas also offers a second version of this argument against plurality of substantial forms. Since every form gives *esse*, and since it is impossible for one and the same thing to have two substantial acts of being *(esse)*, it follows that if the first substantial form coming to matter gives a substantial act of being to it, any second and superadded form can only contribute an accidental *esse*. Therefore, and once again with Avicenna, he concludes that it is by reason of one and the same form that fire is fire and fire is a body.[158]

As we move forward a few years to the *De veritate*, in q. 13, a. 4 we find Thomas writing that for the soul to be united to the body no additional factor *(intentio)* is required; for this union does not depend upon the will of the soul but on nature. The soul is not united to the body as a form by means of its powers but by its essence, since there is no intermediary between form and matter. Thomas goes on to observe that it does not follow from this that the human soul is united to the body in such fashion as to be totally dependent upon the bodily condition.[159] But of greater interest to us here is his claim that there is no intermediary between form and matter. Hence there is no intermediary substantial form between the primary substantial form and the matter of a given substance.

---

156. Mandonnet ed., vol. 2, p. 315: "Note: "Unde possibile est materiam esse sub forma substantiali sine hoc quod habeat qualitates activas et passivas in sui complemento. . . ."

157. Ed. cit., pp. 451–52.   158. Ed. cit., p. 452, cited above in n. 155.

159. Leon. 22.2.428:109–429:121.

This same general thinking is also present in Thomas's reply to objection 13 of *De veritate*, q. 16, a. 1. There he argues that there are not two forms in the human soul but only one, which is its essence. Hence it is through its essence that the human soul is a spirit and through that same essence that it is the form of the body.[160]

In *Summa contra Gentiles* II, beginning with c. 56, Thomas examines the relationship between and the union of soul and body. In c. 56 he considers a number of unacceptable proposals, and ends by turning to the possibility that soul and body are united in such fashion that the soul is the form of the body. While this is a somewhat different issue from that of unicity vs. plurality of substantial form, Thomas's views concerning unicity of substantial form heavily influence his position on the soul's union with the body.[161]

In subsequent chapters Thomas considers a number of earlier attempts to resolve this problem, such as those offered by Plato (cc. 67–68), Averroes (cc. 69–71), Alexander of Aphrodisias (c. 72), Galen (c. 73), Empedocles (c. 74), and certain ancients who held that the soul is a body (c. 75) or that it does not differ from the senses (c. 76) or that it is to be identified with the imagination (c. 77). After concluding that all these efforts have failed, he offers his own solution in c. 78: the intellectual human soul is united to the body as a substantial form. If something is to serve as the substantial form of something else, two conditions must be met. First of all, it must be the principle of substantial being for that of which it is the form. By this he means that it must be the formal principle, not the productive principle, by reason of which something exists and is named a being. Secondly, the form and the matter must have one single act of being *(esse)*. (This second condition does not obtain in the case of an efficient cause when it gives existence to something else; for both an efficient cause and its effect have distinct acts of being.) And it is by reason of this single act of being *(esse)* that the composite substance subsists.[162]

Thomas goes on to argue that there is nothing to prevent an intellectual substance, by reason of the fact that it subsists, from serving as the formal principle of being for matter by communicating its act of being to matter. It is not unfitting for the act of being in which the composite subsists to be identical with that whereby the form itself subsists.[163]

It might be objected that an intellectual substance cannot communicate its own act of being to corporeal matter in such a way that there is only one act of being

---

160. Leon. 22.2.506:405–507:410. While showing that the soul itself is not composed of two forms, this argument taken alone does not necessarily eliminate plurality of forms, e.g., the soul and a form of corporeity, in a human being.

161. Ed. cit., pp. 150–51.

162. Ed. cit., p. 167. Note: "Quorum unum est, ut forma sit principium essendi substantialiter ei cuius est forma: principium autem dico, non factivum, sed formale, quo aliquid est et denominatur ens. Unde sequitur aliud, scilicet quod forma et materia conveniant in uno esse. . . ."

163. Ibid.

for the intellectual substance and the corporeal matter. Thomas counters that this objection might hold if the single act of being belonged both to matter and to the intellectual substance in the same way. But this is not the case. The act of being pertains to corporeal matter as to that which receives it and which is subjected to something higher; but it belongs to the intellectual substance as to its (formal) principle. Hence there is nothing to prevent that intellectual substance which is the human soul from being the form of the human body.[164]

After attempting to show in c. 70 against Averroes that Aristotle holds that the intellect is united to some body as its form, in c. 71 Thomas argues that the human soul is immediately united to the body. No intermediary should be postulated in order to account for such union, whether this be a phantasm, or the powers of the soul itself, or some kind of corporeal spirit. Thomas's position follows, he urges, from his conclusion that the soul is united to the body as its form. A form is united to matter without any intermediary. It pertains to a form to be the act of the body *per se* and not by means of something else. If, as Thomas here maintains, there is no intermediary between soul and body in the order of being, the implication again is that there is no place for an intermediary form of corporeity which might inform prime matter and itself be informed by the intellective soul.[165]

While Thomas's primary concern throughout this discussion in the *Summa contra Gentiles* is with the human soul, constantly presupposed is his theory of unicity of substantial form. As he puts this in c. 58:

Moreover, the principle of a thing's unity is the same as that of its being [*esse*]; for one is consequent upon being [*ens*]. Therefore, since each and everything has being [*esse*] from its form, it will also have unity from its form. Consequently, if several souls, as so many distinct forms, are ascribed to man, he will not be one being, but several.[166]

While Thomas is here refuting the view that there are many souls in human beings, he builds his case upon unicity of substantial form in any given substance. His argumentation for this is consistent with what we have previously seen. But he introduces it by appealing to the transcendental nature of the one and its convertibility with being. As will be recalled from *De veritate*, q. 1, a. 1, the one follows upon being *(ens)* insofar as being is considered in itself and negatively, that is, as not divided from itself. Therefore, just as a thing's *esse* follows upon its form, so

---

164. Ibid. Note: "Nihil igitur prohibet substantiam intellectualem esse formam corporis humani, quae est anima humana."

165. Ed. cit., p. 170. For some interesting remarks about a possible misunderstanding which might be drawn from Thomas's frequent reference to the soul as the form of the *body* rather than the form of matter, see F. Van Steenberghen, *Thomas Aquinas and Radical Aristotelianism*, pp. 73–74.

166. See *On the Truth of the Catholic Faith*, J. F. Anderson, trans. (Garden City, N.Y., 1956), p. 174. For the Latin see ed. cit., p. 154: "Ab eodem aliquid habet esse et unitatem: unum enim consequitur ad ens. Cum igitur a forma unaquaeque res habeat esse, a forma etiam habebit unitatem. Si igitur ponantur in homine plures animae sicut diversae formae, homo non erit unum ens, sed plura."

does its oneness. If there are many forms in a given entity, there will be more than one act of being and hence more than one center of ontological unity. Therefore there will be more than one substance.[167]

While we should distinguish the issue of plurality of souls from that of plurality of forms, in this text Thomas shows that if one defends unicity of substantial form, one should defend unicity of the soul. The converse, however, might not follow. One might defend unicity of the human soul and still hold for plurality of forms, for instance, by postulating a form of corporeity in addition to the soul in a human being. But this Thomas does not do, at least not in any text examined so far.[168]

In SCG IV, c. 81, while considering a number of objections against the resurrection of the body, Thomas refers to corporeity. He distinguishes two ways in which this term is used. It may simply mean the substantial form of a body insofar as the latter falls within the genus substance. When so understood the corporeity of a given body is nothing other than its substantial form. It is by reason of this form that it falls into its genus and species, and from this it belongs to a corporeal thing to have three dimensions. Thomas again remarks that there are not different substantial forms in one and the same thing, by one of which it would be placed in its supreme genus, e.g., substance, and by another in its proximate genus, e.g., body or animal, and by still another in its species, e.g., horse or human being. Against such a theory Thomas counters that if the first form made the substance exist, all subsequent forms would be added to that which is a given something in actuality *(hoc aliquid)* and which subsists, i.e., an existing substance. Because of this, subsequent forms would not constitute it as this substance but would merely inhere in a subsisting subject or substance; hence they would only be accidental forms.[169]

In sum, if corporeity is taken in the first way Thomas has distinguished—as the substantial form of a body—in the case of a human being it is nothing other than the rational soul insofar as it requires matter to have the three dimensions. Thomas notes that corporeity may also be taken in a second way, as an accidental form in terms of which a body belongs to the genus quantity. So understood, corporeity is

---

167. See, for instance, the two arguments considered above from his *In II Sent.*, d. 18 (see nn. 157, 158). See Aertsen, *Medieval Philosophy and the Transcendentals*, pp. 233–34, for discussion of a similar approach in *Qu. disp. De spiritualibus creaturis*, a. 3.

168. On the distinction between these two issues see Callus, "The Origins of the Problem of Unity of Form," pp. 123–25.

169. Ed. cit., pp. 546–47. Note especially: "Corporeitas autem dupliciter accipi potest. Uno modo, secundum quod est forma substantialis corporis, prout in genere substantiae collocatur. Et sic corporeitas cuiuscumque corporis nihil est aliud quam forma substantialis eius, secundum quam in genere et specie collocatur, ex qua debetur rei corporali quod habeat tres dimensiones. Non enim sunt diversae formae substantiales in uno et eodem. . . . Quia si prima forma faceret esse substantiam, sequentes formae iam advenirent ei quod est hoc aliquid in actu et subsistens in natura: et sic posteriores formae non facerent hoc aliquid, sed essent in subiecto quod est hoc aliquid sicut formae accidentales." On the meaning of the expression *hoc aliquid* in a similar context *(Quaestiones disp. De anima,* q. 1) see B. C. Bazán, "The Human Soul: Form and Substance? Thomas Aquinas' Critique of Eclectic Aristotelianism," AHDLMA 64 (1997), pp. 97–101.

nothing other than the three dimensions which form the nature *(ratio)* of a body.[170] In this text we again have a strong defense of unicity of substantial form. No place is left for any kind of distinctive substantial form of corporeity which might be superadded to or stand under other substantial forms in a given entity.

In *Summa theologiae* I, q. 76, Thomas devotes a series of articles to the human soul. In a number of these he appeals to or introduces his theory of unicity of substantial form. For instance, in a. 3 he considers and rejects any theory of plurality of souls in human beings (and by implication, in other living beings). While Thomas's arguments in this context are once more directed against plurality of souls rather than plurality of substantial forms, the first two also apply to theories of plurality of forms. The first argument returns to a by now familiar theme. If there were many souls in an animal, that animal would not enjoy ontological unity in the unqualified sense. Nothing is one in the unqualified sense except through one form by which the thing itself enjoys its existence. This again follows from Thomas's conviction that it is by reason of one and the same ontological principle that a thing is a being and is one. In other words, being and the one are convertible. Therefore things which take their name from different forms, such as a white man, are not one in the unqualified sense. So too, if a human being derives the fact that it is a living thing from one form (the vegetative soul) and the fact that it is an animal from another form (the sensitive soul), and the fact that it is a human being from still another (the intellective soul), it would not be one in the unqualified sense. Thomas turns to Aristotle's *Metaphysics* VIII and to *De anima* I for additional support for this argument.[171]

Thomas's second argument approaches the problem from another side—the way in which we predicate. Those things which are derived from diverse forms are predicated of one another either (1) *per accidens,* if the forms are not ordered to one another, as when we say something white is sweet, or (2) *per se,* if the forms are ordered to one another, but only according to the second mode of *per se* predication. As Thomas explains here, and as he develops more fully in his Commentary on the *Posterior Analytics,* in this second mode of *per se* predication a subject is included in the definition of a predicate. This is unlike the first mode of *per se* predication wherein a predicate is included in the definition of a subject.[172]

---

170. Ed. cit., p. 547: "Alio modo accipitur corporeitas prout est forma accidentalis, secundum quam dicitur corpus quod est in genere quantitatis. Et sic corporeitas nihil aliud est quam tres dimensiones, quae corporis rationem constituunt."

171. Note that Thomas introduces all three of these arguments in this way: "Sed si ponamus animam corpori uniri sicut formam, omnino impossibile videtur plures animas per essentiam differentes in uno corpore esse." For this and the first argument see Leon. 5.221. For Aristotle see *Metaphysics* VIII, c. 6 (1045a 14–20); *De anima* I, c. 5 (411b 5–14).

172. Leon. 5.221. Cf. *Expositio libri Posteriorum* I, 10 (Leon. 1*.2.39:25–67). As Thomas explains, the first mode of *per se* predication occurs when what is attributed to something else pertains to its form. But the second mode of *per se* predication points to a relationship based on material causal-

Thomas's argument continues. If it is by reason of one form that something is called an animal and by reason of another that it is called a human being, it will follow that one of these ("animal") cannot be predicated of the other ("human being") except *per accidens* if the two forms are not ordered to one another. If the forms are ordered to one another so that one is presupposed for the other, one term could be predicated of the other only according to the second mode of *per se* predication. But neither of these alternatives can be accepted. In fact animal is predicated of human being *per se* rather than *per accidens*. Moreover, human being is not included in the definition of animal; rather animal is included in the definition of human being. And to say "a human being is an animal" is to employ not the second mode of *per se* predication (where the subject is included in the definition of the predicate) but the first (where the predicate is included in the definition of the subject). Since a theory of plurality of forms cannot allow for this, Thomas again concludes that it is rather through one and the same form that something is both an animal and a human being.[173]

In a. 4 Thomas specifically asks whether in a human being there is any other form in addition to the human soul. This, too, is germane to our inquiry because, as we have suggested above, one might grant to Thomas that there is numerically only one soul in a human being but still hold that there is at least one other substantial form—a form of corporeity. Thomas replies that a substantial form differs from an accidental form in a fundamental respect. An accidental form does not grant the act of being *(esse)* in the unqualified sense but only *esse* of a given kind—accidental *esse*. Because of this, when an accidental form is introduced into a substance, something is said to be made or to be generated only in a qualified sense, not in the unqualified sense. So too, when an accidental form departs, something is said to be corrupted not in the unqualified sense but only in a qualified sense *(secundum quid)*.[174]

Thomas recalls that only substantial form gives the act of being in the unqualified sense (substantial *esse*) and that it is only through the acquisition or loss of this that something is generated or corrupted in the unqualified sense. Therefore, if in addition to the intellective soul some other substantial form were present in matter by reason of which the subject in which the soul inheres enjoys being in actuality, the soul itself would not give the substantial act of being. This would in turn imply that the soul itself is not really a substantial form.[175] Hence Thomas remains stead-

---

ity—that to which something is attributed serves as the proper subject and as matter for what is predicated.

173. Leon. 5.221. Note: "Ergo oportet eandem formam esse per quam aliquid est animal, et per quam aliquid est homo: alioquin homo non vere esset id quod est animal, ut sic animal per se de homine praedicetur."

174. Leon. 5.224.

175. Ibid.

fast in his view that no other substantial form is present in a human being in addition to the intellective soul. Just as the intellective soul contains virtually the sensitive and nutritive souls, so does it contain in virtual fashion all lower forms. By this Thomas means that the intellective soul can account for whatever less perfect forms explain in less perfect substances.[176]

In a. 6 Thomas reasons that if the intellective soul is indeed united to the body as a substantial form, no intermediary accidental disposition can fall between the soul and the body, nor, for that matter, between any substantial form and its matter. This follows from the fact that matter is in potency to different acts according to a certain order. That which is first among acts must be understood in matter before other acts. But the first of all acts is *esse* (the act of being). Therefore matter cannot be understood to be hot or quantified before it exists in actuality. And it exists in actuality through a substantial form which gives it the act of being in the unqualified sense.[177] As Thomas maintains in a. 7, it also follows from this that the soul cannot be united to the body by means of any other body. Again he builds his case upon the ontological claim that a thing enjoys unity insofar as it enjoys being. Form of itself makes a thing exist in act, since form of its essence is actuality. Therefore form does not grant *esse* to matter through any intermediary. Indeed, the very unity of a matter-form composite comes to it through its form which unites with its matter as the act of matter.[178]

Similar argumentation is to be found in a number of Thomas's other works. Especially helpful are his discussions in his Disputed Questions *De anima* (1266–1267) and his Disputed Question *De spiritualibus creaturis* (1267–1268).[179]

In two questions from his Disputed Questions *De anima* Thomas once more takes up the issue of unity vs. plurality of substantial form. In q. 9 he asks whether the soul is united to corporeal matter through an intermediary.[180] In replying Thomas recalls that the act of being *(esse)* pertains more immediately and more intimately to things than does anything else. Since matter has actual being through a form, that form which gives the act of being to matter must be understood as informing matter before anything else and more immediately so than anything else. But it is proper to substantial form to give the act of being in the unqualified sense to matter, since it is through its substantial form that a thing is what it is. A thing does not have the act of being in this unqualified sense from an accidental form but only *esse* in a qualified sense. Therefore any form which comes to matter

---

176. "Unde dicendum est quod nulla alia forma substantialis est in homine, nisi sola anima intellectiva; et quod ipsa, sicut virtute continet animam sensitivam et nutritivam, ita virtute continet omnes inferiores formas, et facit ipsa sola quidquid imperfectiores formae in aliis faciunt" (ibid.).

177. Leon. 5.229. Note in particular: "Primum autem inter omnes actus est esse. Impossibile est ergo intelligere materiam prius esse calidam vel quantam, quam esse in actu. Esse autem in actu habet per formam substantialem, quae facit esse simpliciter. . . ."

178. Leon. 5.231.

179. For these dates see Bazán, in Leon. 24.1.25*.

180. "Nono quaeritur utrum anima uniatur materiae corporali per medium" (Leon. 24.1.75:1–2).

which already exists in actuality through some other form cannot be a substantial form.[181]

On this basis Thomas reasserts his long-standing view that there can be no intermediary substantial form between prime matter and its substantial form and therefore that plurality of substantial forms must be rejected. Only the first form would make a substance exist in actuality and hence only the first would in fact be a substantial form. All others would be accidental. Thomas concludes that it is by numerically one and the same form that a thing is a substance and is placed in its proximate species and in all intervening genera.[182]

In Question 11 Thomas examines the closely related question concerning whether in a human being the rational soul, the sensible soul, and the vegetative soul are one and the same substance.[183] In criticizing a theory of plurality of souls (which he here assigns to Plato), Thomas again marshals a series of arguments against plurality of forms. The first is the argument based on predication that we have already seen in ST I, q. 76, a. 3.[184] The second reasons that a theory of plurality of forms (or souls) will be unable to safeguard the essential unity of a human being. Though similar to earlier versions of this argument considered above, in the present text Thomas reasons that under the hypothesis of plurality of forms, some intrinsic binding or connecting principle would be required to account for a human being's essential unity. But none would be at hand. Therefore, because a human being would not be one in the unqualified sense but only by aggregation, it would not be a being in the unqualified sense; for each and everything enjoys being to the extent that it enjoys unity.[185] The last argument again contends that under the theory of plurality of souls, the final or intellective soul would not give substantial existence but only some type of accidental existence. Hence it would not really be a substantial form at all and would not confer specific being.[186]

---

181. Leon. 24.1.79:139–80:154.

182. Leon. 24.1.80:155–72.

183. "Undecimo quaeritur utrum in homine anima rationalis, sensibilis et vegetabilis sit una substantia" (Leon. 24.1.95:1–3).

184. Leon. 24.1.99:194–217. Since this argumentation has not always been correctly interpreted, it may be helpful to summarize it again as it appears here. If certain things are predicated of a given subject by reason of different forms, one of these things can be predicated of the other only per accidens. So if Sortes is said to be a man and an animal by reason of different (substantial) forms, it will follow that the statement "man is an animal" involves predication only per accidens, not per se, and hence that man is not truly that which is an animal. If these different forms in a subject are ordered to one another, Thomas acknowledges that per se predication of a sort will result. But this will not be per se predication of the first type since in this case the predicate is not included in the definition of the subject; rather the subject is included in the definition of the predicate. Hence it would follow that animal is not predicated per se of man, but that man is predicated per se of animal. Cf. nn. 172 and 173 above and my corresponding text for this argument in ST I, q. 76, a. 3.

185. Leon. 24.1.99:218–100:230. Note especially: "Ex pluribus enim actu existentibus non fit unum simpliciter nisi sit aliquid uniens et aliquo modo ligans ea ad invicem."

186. Leon. 24.1.100:231–245.

In replying to objection 9 of a. 1 of his Disputed Question *De spiritualibus crea-turis* Thomas succinctly sums up his position. He notes that something may fall under something which is general or common in one of two ways: (1) as an individual falls under its species; (2) or as a species falls under its genus. In order to account for the presence of many individuals within the same species, Thomas here appeals to individual matter. This is something added to a thing's specific nature. To account for the presence of many species within the same genus, however, he argues that it is not necessary for the forms by which the species differ from one another to be really distinct from the common generic form. It is rather through one and the same form that a given individual entity *(hoc individuum)* is placed in the genus substance, in the genus body, and so on down to its proximate species. If it were by reason of a special form that this individual entity is a substance, all other super-added forms by which it is placed in lower genera and species could only be accidental.[187]

In support Thomas again appeals to the difference between an accidental form and a substantial form. If a substantial form accounts for the fact that a thing is this particular something *(hoc aliquid)*, i.e., a substance, an accidental form presupposes that a thing is constituted as an existent. If, therefore, the first form by which it is placed in its genus makes it a given entity or substance, all other forms which are superadded to this subsisting individual can only be accidental. And from this it would follow that the gain or loss of such subsequent forms would not be generation or corruption in the unqualified sense but only in an accidental sense. From this Thomas goes on once more to reject the view of Avicebron, whom he continues to regard as defending plurality of forms.[188]

Article 3 of this same Disputed Question is explicitly addressed to the issue whether a spiritual substance, i.e., the human soul, is united to the body through a medium. As we have previously seen, Thomas rejects any such suggestion. In the course of doing this he also opposes any theory of plurality of substantial forms and again singles out Avicebron as a primary target of his critique. Against any such view he offers three arguments which follow from what he calls the true principles of philosophy which Aristotle considered.[189]

First and foremost, on such a view no individual substance would be one in the unqualified sense. Something which is one in the unqualified sense does not arise

187. *De spiritualibus creaturis*, ed. cit., p. 372.
188. Ibid.
189. Ed. cit., pp. 380–81. Note that at the beginning of his response Thomas writes that if one holds that the soul is united to the body as a form, the soul must be immediately united to the body. If one holds that the soul unites with the body only as a mover, one may well posit many intermediaries between soul and body. This in turn leads him to distinguish between the theory of plurality of substantial forms and that which defends unity. After noting close similarities between Plato's view and that of Avicebron, he comments: "Sed haec positio, secundum vera philosophiae principia, quae consideravit Aristoteles, est impossibilis" (pp. 381). Cf. White, "Aquinas on the Immediacy of the Union of Soul and Body," pp. 230–38.

from two things in actuality but from potency and act insofar as something in potency is actualized by its appropriate act. This is why a white man is not one in the unqualified sense, whereas a two-footed animal is. But if animal and two-footed were in fact separate within an individual human being, such a being would not be one but many. So, too, if substantial forms were multiplied in a given substance, that substance would not be one in the unqualified sense but only in accidental fashion, in the way a white man is one.[190]

Secondly, it is of the nature of an accident to exist in a subject, and in such fashion that by a subject we understand a being in actuality, not one that exists only in potency. Accordingly, a substantial form does not inform a substantial subject but matter. (This precision should be kept in mind when we interpret texts where Thomas refers to the human soul as the form of the body. He really means that it informs matter.) To return to his argument, he observes that if a given form presupposes a being in actuality as its subject, that form is an accident. But every substantial form makes and constitutes a being in actuality. (This, of course, is the major presupposition in Thomas's argument.) Therefore only the first form which informs prime matter directly is substantial. All subsequent forms are accidental.[191] Nor will it do, as some attempt, to say that the first substantial form is in potency to the second. Against this Thomas reasons that every subject is related to its accidents as potency to act. Under such a hypothesis, therefore, the form of a body which gives the capacity for life would be more complete than one which does not. If, therefore, the form of an inanimate body makes it a subject, much more so would the form of a body that has life in potency make it to be a subject. But then the superadded human soul would itself only be a form that inheres in a subject, and this would be to reduce it to the level of an accident.[192]

Thirdly, under the hypothesis of plurality of forms, acquisition of the final form would not be generation in the unqualified sense but only in a qualified or accidental sense. In other words, a seeming substantial change would really only be accidental. Because generation is a change from nonbeing *(nonesse)* to being *(esse)*, that alone is generated in the unqualified sense which becomes a being in the unqualified sense after having enjoyed nonbeing in that same sense. But what already preexists in actuality does not become a being in the unqualified sense but only this or that kind of being, for instance, white, or great, etc. Once more, therefore, Thomas reasons that because a prior form when present in matter gives a substantial act of

190. Ed. cit., p. 381. Note especially: "Non enim fit simpliciter unum ex duobus actibus, sed ex potentia et actu, in quantum id quod est potentia fit actu. . . ."

191. "Secundo vero, quia in hoc consistit ratio accidentis quod sit in subiecto, ita tamen quod per subiectum intelligatur aliquod ens actu, et non in potentia tantum; secundum quem modum forma substantialis non est in subiecto sed in materia" (ibid.).

192. Ibid. Note especially: ". . . unde si forma corporis inanimati facit ipsum esse subiectum, multo magis forma [corporis: according to projected Leonine ed., courtesy of J. Cos, O.P.] potentia vitam habentis facit ipsum esse subiectum: et sic anima esset forma in subiecto, quod est ratio accidentis."

being, subsequent forms cannot do so. They can only contribute a qualified kind of being. It was for fundamentally this same reason that those ancients who identified first matter with something in actuality, for instance, fire or air or water or something intermediary, concluded that to become or to be made was really to undergo nothing but alteration, a change in quality. Aristotle overcame their difficulty by maintaining that matter is only in potency and by making it the subject of unqualified generation and corruption.[193]

In these three arguments, therefore, Thomas has summed up most of his earlier reasoning against the theory of plurality of substantial forms. The first is his oft-repeated claim that the theory of plurality of forms would make it impossible to defend the substantial unity of the resulting substance. The second is slightly different in cast from those previously considered, since it argues that a substantial form cannot exist in any being or subject that itself exists in actuality. To view a substantial form in such a way would in effect make of it another accidental form. The third argument is familiar enough, being based on the claim that under the theory of plurality of forms, acquisition of all subsequent and allegedly substantial forms would not be unqualified generation but only the gain of something accidental. Not present in this series of three arguments is the one based on the need to account for *per se* predication of the first type which we have seen from ST I, q. 76. But as already noted, that argument is present in Thomas's Disputed Questions *De anima*. It is interesting to observe how Thomas quickly sums up three arguments in his very late Quodlibet 12, q. 6, a. 1 (Easter 1272). There is only one substantial form in any body because (1) if there were many, the following forms would not be substantial (which gives *esse* in the unqualified sense), but only accidental; (2) the acquisition of a substantial form would not be generation in the unqualified sense; and (3) the composite of soul and body would not be one in the unqualified sense, but only *per accidens*. Again, all the essentials are there, with the exception of the argument based on predication.[194]

At the beginning of our discussion of Thomas's views concerning unicity of substantial form, reference was made to the claim by some that at the time of his

193. Ibid.

194. For Quodlibet 12 see Leon. 25.2.406:12–21. I should also mention that in his Commentary on Bk II of the *De anima* (ca. 1267–1268) Thomas repeats central parts of his case against plurality of substantial forms. In the course of explaining Aristotle's definition of the soul as the first act of a physical body which has life in potency, he finds Aristotle eliminating the possibility of holding that the soul is act in the way an accidental form is. Aristotle writes that the soul is act in the way a substance is, i.e., as form. Thomas immediately recalls that a substantial form differs from an accidental form precisely because the latter does not make something a being in act in the unqualified sense. Only substantial form does this. Therefore, a substantial form does not come to a subject which already preexists in actuality but only to one that exists in potency, i.e., prime matter. Hence he concludes that it is impossible for many substantial forms to be present in one and the same substance. Only the first would give being in actuality in the unqualified sense. All others would come to a subject which already exists in actuality and would unite with it only in accidental fashion. See *In II De anima*, Leon. 45.1.70:235–288.

Commentary on the *Sentences* he seems to have allowed for the presence of a second kind of substantial form in corporeal entities—a form of corporeity. If so, it would seem that in spite of everything we have seen until now, Thomas did not defend unicity of form in this very early period. Moreover, some have suggested that his early views concerning the permanence of the forms of elements in mixtures and his hesitancy about the issue of undetermined dimensions also point to the same conclusion.[195]

As one sign of this, Zavalloni cites Thomas's Commentary on I *Sentences,* d. 8, q. 5, a. 2. There Thomas considers and criticizes the view that the soul itself is composed of matter and form. Against this he appeals to Avicenna who writes that something is possessed of intellect insofar as it is free from all matter. Therefore prime matter, when viewed as lacking all form, is not diversified. Nor is it rendered diverse through certain accidents prior to the arrival of a substantial form, since accidental being is not prior to substantial being. But to one thing which is capable of being perfected, one perfection is owing. Therefore a thing's first substantial form perfects the whole of matter. But the first form which is received in matter is corporeity, and matter is never freed from this. Therefore the form of corporeity is present in all of matter and so matter will be found only in bodies.[196] Does this not imply that Thomas here accepts a form of corporeity which would militate against his espousing unicity of substantial form?[197]

Not necessarily, or so it seems to me. Thomas's intent here is to argue against matter-form composition of the soul. In holding that the first substantial form must perfect the whole of matter and that the first form received in prime matter is corporeity, he may simply mean that it is the first and ultimate substantial form found in a corporeal entity. Hence it is that which accounts for the fact that such a being is corporeal. His statement need not be taken as implying that other sub-

---

195. See n. 151 above.

196. Mandonnet ed., Vol. 1, pp. 228–29. Note especially: "Et propterea materia prima, prout consideratur nuda ab omni forma, non habet aliquam diversitatem, nec [with Parma-Busa ed./Mandonnet: sed] efficitur diversa per aliqua accidentia ante adventum formae substantialis cum esse accidentale non praecedat substantiale. Uni autem perfectibili debetur una perfectio. Ergo oportet quod prima forma substantialis perficiat totam materiam. Sed prima forma quae recipitur in materia, est corporeitas, a qua nunquam denudatur." See Zavalloni, *Richard de Mediavilla,* p. 263. But see I. Klinger, *Das Prinzip der Individuation bei Thomas von Aquin* (Vier-Türme, 1964), pp. 39–41, for the opposite interpretation. On p. 41 Klinger cites this text apparently from the Mandonnet edition; but without alerting the reader, he substitutes "nec" for "sed" just as I have done. See *S. Thomae Aquinatis opera omnia,* R. Busa, ed., Vol. 1, p. 266.

197. See Zavalloni, *Richard de Mediavilla,* p. 263; M. Wittmann, *Die Stellung des hl. Thomas von Aquin zu Avencebrol (Ibn Gebirol),* p. 74; E. Kleineidam, *Das Problem der hylemorphen Zusammensetzung,* p. 63; Roland-Gosselin, *Le "De ente et essentia,"* pp. 104–5. He observes that regarding unity of substantial form in man, Thomas's thought is perfectly fixed in his Commentary on I *Sentences* (d. 8, q. 5, a. 3). But he comments: "Cependant, nous l'avons remarqué déjà, la manière dont saint Thomas parle à plusieurs reprises au premier livre et au deuxième, de la corporéité première forme substantielle, l'indécision qu'il paraît garder tout d'abord à l'égard de Gebirol, laissent dans l'esprit du lecteur quelque hésitation" (pp. 110–11).

stantial forms might also be present in the same body at the same time in addition to corporeity. And Thomas may here be anticipating a point we have seen him making in *Summa contra Gentiles* IV, c. 81 to the effect that when corporeity is taken in one way it is nothing other than the substantial form of a body.[198] Hence this text in itself does not necessarily indicate that Thomas originally defended a form of corporeity which would be prior to other substantial forms within the given body or corporeal entity.

As we have also seen, in his Commentary on Bk II of the *Sentences* (d. 12, q. 1, a. 4) Thomas explicitly rejects the view of Avicebron according to which there is a common corporeal form along with additional specific forms in a given substance. He cites Avicenna to support his own claim that such superadded forms would have to be accidental. Hence, as of this writing there is no sign of hesitation; he clearly defends unicity of substantial form.[199]

Nonetheless, as another sign of his alleged hesitation about unicity of substantial form, reference is sometimes made to his varying reactions to the question concerning the continuing presence of the forms of elements in mixed bodies. In other words, when earth, air, fire, and water unite in some corporeal entity, do their substantial forms continue to exist in the resulting mixed body? If so, and if this mixed body itself enjoys substantial unity, Thomas's theory of unicity of substantial form would again seem to be compromised.

As we have also noted, in this same text from his Commentary on II *Sentences* (d. 12, q. 1, a. 4), Thomas proposes that from the dawn of creation various parts of prime matter existed under different substantial forms in the different parts of the universe. But the active and passive powers corresponding to such substantial forms were not yet conferred on all of these distinct parts in the beginning. To support the plausibility of this suggestion, Thomas refers to Avicenna's view that elements

---

198. See nn. 169, 170 above. In his discussion in d. 8, q. 5, a. 2 from the Commentary on I *Sentences,* Thomas notes that someone might suggest that the very quiddity of a substance is the first form received in matter. Thomas replies that his position still stands. It is not from the substantial quiddity that matter receives its division but from corporeity. And the dimensions of quantity follow from such corporeity (ed. cit., p. 229). Since the dimensions of quantity are here said to follow upon corporeity, it again seems that corporeity itself, or the form of corporeity, is simply taken by Thomas as referring to substantial form, and to the unique substantial form in a given substance.

199. See Mandonnet ed., Vol. 2, p. 314, cited above in n. 155. As Zavalloni observes, in d. 3, q. 1, a. 1 of this same Commentary on II *Sentences* Thomas still uses the expression *forma corporeitatis.* For Zavalloni see p. 264, n. 6. There Thomas is refuting matter-form composition in angels. He writes: "Sed ante corporeitatem non potest intelligi aliqua diversitas quia diversitas praesupponit partes, quae non possunt esse nisi praeintelligatur divisibilitas quae consequitur quantitatem, quae sine corporeitate non est. Unde oportet quod tota materia sit vestita forma corporeitatis; et ideo si aliquid est incorporeum oportet esse immateriale" (Mandonnet ed., Vol. 2, pp. 86–87). Again I would suggest that the *forma corporeitatis* as Thomas is using it here is identical with the substantial form of a corporeal substance. The text of itself does not imply plurality of substantial forms. See Quodlibet 12, q. 6, a. 1 for a late reference to two ways in which *corporeitas* may be understood, either as the three dimensions (and this is not a substantial form), or as the specific substantial form from which the three dimensions will follow (Leon. 25.2.406:22–27).

remain present in a mixture in terms of their substantial forms with respect to the primary being *(esse)* of such forms, but not as regards their secondary being. Is this not for Thomas to allow for plurality of substantial forms in mixed bodies?[200]

One might read this text in this way, but it does not strike me as the better interpretation. Thomas simply cites the Avicennian distinction between the primary and secondary being of substantial forms in order to develop his own point. If, as Avicenna suggests, the substantial forms of elements remain present in mixtures in terms of their primary being though not in terms of their secondary being (their active and passive qualities), so too, Thomas reasons, the substantial forms of the various parts of created being were present from the beginning; but the active and passive powers corresponding to such forms were not yet conferred on the various parts of the universe. This text need not be taken as implying that according to Aquinas the substantial forms of elements are actually present in mixtures. Thomas could reasonably expect his reader to remember that he had in fact excluded plurality of substantial forms in the immediately preceding context.[201]

At the same time it should be noted that not too much later, in his Commentary on the *De Trinitate* of Boethius (q. 4, a. 3, ad 6), Thomas again refers to the Avicennian view. He now acknowledges that Avicenna's theory implies that elements remain in a mixed body by reason of their substantial forms. Thomas denies that this results in their constituting many distinct bodies in actuality. Otherwise no mixed body would be truly one. In fact, he continues, a mixed body is one in actuality although potentially many. But now he comments that the view defended by Averroes in his Commentary on Bk III of the *De caelo et mundo* seems to be more probable. Averroes rejects the Avicennian view and argues that the forms of elements do not continue to be present in a mixed body. Yet these forms are not totally corrupted. Out of them one intermediary form is produced insofar as they admit of greater and lesser degrees. But, comments Thomas, it is disturbing *(absonum)* to say that substantial forms admit of greater or lesser degrees in themselves. Therefore, it seems that Averroes must be understood as meaning that the forms of elements admit of greater or lesser degrees not in themselves but only insofar as they remain in virtual fashion in the qualities of those elements. It is from these qualities that a new intermediary quality is constituted.[202]

200. Cf. Zavalloni, p. 264. For Thomas's text see Mandonnet ed., Vol. 2, p. 315.

201. Cf. P. Denis, "Le premier enseignement de saint Thomas sur l'unité de la forme substantielle," AHDLMA 21 (1954), pp. 143–44.

202. Leon. 50.130:261–280. For Averroes see *In III De caelo et mundo,* com. 67, *Aristotelis opera cum Averrois commentariis* (Venice, 1562–1574), Vol. 5, f. 227r. Cf. Denis, pp. 144–45; Zavalloni, pp. 264–65. For a similar discussion Zavalloni refers to *In IV Sent.,* d. 44, q. 1, a. 1, ad 4: ". . . ita forma mixtionis, quae est forma resultans ex qualitatibus simplicibus ad medium venientibus, non est substantialis forma corporis mixti, sed est accidens proprium, et dispositio per quam materia fit necessaria ad formam. Corpus autem humanum praeter hanc formam mixtionis non habet aliam formam substantialem nisi animam rationalem . . ." (Busa ed., Vol. 1, p. 635c). Note that in this text Thomas explicitly denies that the intermediary form of a mixture is its substantial form.

In still later discussions, however, Thomas rejects the position of Averroes as even less acceptable than that of Avicenna. The Averroistic theory implies that a substantial form itself can be changed essentially, i.e., that it can undergo intensification and remission (or admit of greater and lesser degrees in itself). For Thomas's discussions one may consult Quodlibet 1, q. 4, a. 1, ad 3; ST I, q. 76, a. 4, ad 4; Disputed Questions *De anima*, q. 9, ad 10. In these texts Thomas concludes that the forms of the elements do not remain actually present in mixtures but only virtually. In other words, they remain insofar as the power of their respective substantial forms remains in a mixture in the quality of the element, though in weakened degree and, as it were, approaching an intermediary level.[203]

Of more immediate interest to us here, however, is Thomas's steadfast refusal to allow for the actual presence of the substantial forms of elements in mixed bodies. If he was willing in the first of these discussions to entertain the Avicennian distinction between the primary and the secondary being of elementary substantial forms, he did not then regard this admission as militating against his defense of unicity of substantial form in mixed bodies. Subsequently he rejected both this Avicennian approach and the Averroistic solution (after being at one point more sympathetic to the latter). In preference to either of these, he developed his own view about the continuing virtual presence in mixtures of the qualities of the elements. His apparently changing view about the role of determinate vs. indeterminate dimensions in his explanation of individuation will be examined in the final part of this chapter. If I may anticipate that discussion, I will only comment here that his position(s) concerning such dimensions never implied that he was defending a plurality of substantial forms.

Hence one may safely conclude that from the beginning to the end of his career Thomas defended unicity of substantial form in all substances. If he was willing to speak of a form of corporeity in some early texts, his usage of this terminology does not imply his acceptance of plurality of substantial forms. It may well be that his terminology concerning this became more precise as time went on and that he became more sensitive to the possible misunderstanding to which some of his earli-

203. ST I, q. 76, a. 4, ad 4. After rejecting both the Avicennian and Averroistic positions, Thomas writes: "Et ideo dicendum est, secundum Philosophum in I *De Generatione,* quod formae elementorum manent in mixto non actu, sed virtute. Manent enim qualitates propriae elementorum, licet remissae, in quibus est virtus formarum elementarium" (Leon. 5.224). Cf. Quodlibet 1, q. 4, a. 1, ad 3 where, after rejecting the views of Avicenna and Averroes, Thomas comments: "Et ideo aliter dicendum, secundum Philosophum in I De generatione, quod formae miscibilium non manent in mixto actu, sed virtute, prout scilicet virtus formae substantialis manet in qualitate elementari, licet remissa, et quasi ad medium redacta: qualitas enim elementaris agit in virtute formae substantialis . . ." (Leon. 25.2.185:144–151). For *Qu. disp. De anima,* q. 9, ad 10 see Leon. 24.1.85:451–467. For Aristotle see *On Generation and Corruption* I, c. 10 (327b 29–31). For additional discussion of Thomas's changing views concerning the problem of mixtures see Denis, pp. 160–64. Denis does not find Thomas's hesitations concerning this in any way implying that he ever wavered concerning unicity of substantial form (see pp. 150, 159, 164).

est terminology might lead. So too, his original sympathetic reading of the Avicennian theory of surviving elementary forms in mixtures did not at that time in his own mind compromise his defense of unicity of substantial form in material substances. If he subsequently rejected the Avicennian solution and turned briefly to that of Averroes, this may in part be owing to his growing awareness that the Avicennian view could too easily be taken as implying plurality of substantial forms. And if he subsequently abandoned the Averroistic approach, this abandonment never led him to entertain seriously the theory of plurality of forms. Rather than return to the Avicennian view, Thomas developed his own theory of the virtual presence of the qualities of elements in mixed bodies.[204]

4. The Individuation of Material Substances

In Section 1 of this chapter we noted that Aquinas appeals to matter-form composition of material entities to resolve two different issues: first, the fact that such substances can undergo substantial change; and second, the fact that many individual material entities may share in specifically the same kind of being. We have referred to this second issue as the problem of the One and the Many in the line of essence. As we have also seen, in resolving this second problem Thomas has assigned an important role to prime matter. There can be different individual members in the same class or species only if each of them possesses the same kind of form. This of itself does not account for what distinguishes these individuals from one another. But because prime matter receives and limits form, it seems well equipped to exercise this individuating function.

Before we conclude too quickly that prime matter is the principle of individuation, however, we should also bear in mind Thomas's claim that prime matter is pure potentiality. This seems to pose a problem for him: How can a purely potential principle individuate? To distinguish or divide one individual from another seems to imply some kind of determination. But such a role seems to be foreign to prime matter, if it is indeed purely potential. In the present section of this chapter, therefore, we shall turn to a number of texts where Thomas addresses the problem

---

204. In addition to Denis as cited in the preceding note, see Schneider, *Die Einheit des Menschen. Die anthropologische formel "anima forma corporis" in sogennanten Korrektoriumstreit und bei Petrus Johannis Olivi* (Münster, 1973), pp. 16–17; also B. Bazán, "La corporalité selon saint Thomas," pp. 396–98. For confirmation one may also consult Thomas's *De mixtione elementorum*. Once dismissed by some Thomistic scholars as nothing but an extract from lect. 24 of Thomas's Commentary on the *De generatione et corruptione*, with some borrowed material from his Commentary on the *Physics* and ST I, this work has been restored by the Leonine editors to its place as a late and independent treatise. See Leon. 43.135–36 for discussion, and for the text pp. 155–57, especially pp. 156–57. If Mandonnet had proposed 1269–1272 as a possible dating for this opusculum, the Leonine edition suggests that it might be better to place it before the apparent challenge to Thomas's theory of unicity of substantial form in 1270. Cf. Torrell, *Saint Thomas Aquinas*, p. 355.

of individuation. To state this problem in simple terms, what intrinsic principle (or principles) accounts for the fact that one individual material substance is numerically distinct from other members of the same species?

As is evident even in Thomas's earliest discussions of this, prime matter does indeed play an important role in his explanation of individuation. For instance, near the beginning of his Commentary on Bk I of the *Sentences* (d. 2, q. 1, a. 1), he presents some opening arguments against the possibility of there being many Gods. The second part of one of these arguments rests on the claim that whatever belongs to the same species is not divided numerically except according to a division of matter or of some potentiality. While this text appears in an opening argument, there is no reason to think that Thomas does not accept it.[205]

In d. 8, q. 5, a. 2 of his Commentary on Bk I, Thomas considers and rejects matter-form composition of the human soul. As we have seen above, there he argues that something is intelligible to the extent that it is freed from matter. And, he continues, prime matter, insofar as it is considered without any form, does not admit of any diversity. Nor is it rendered diverse by certain accidents before the arrival of a substantial form, since accidental *esse* does not precede substantial *esse* in any given substance.[206] This passage is helpful because it points to the need for something else in addition to prime matter if prime matter itself is to be rendered diverse and capable of diversifying and individuating substantial form. But this text also touches on a possible difficulty in this line of explanation. Thomas cannot admit that in any given substance accidental being is prior to substantial being.

Thomas then reasons that one perfection corresponds to one thing that is capable of being perfected. Because the first (substantial) form received in matter is corporeity, corporeity informs the whole of matter. Therefore matter is present only in bodies, not in the human soul. He notes that someone might counter that

---

205. The argument has just refuted any claim that many Gods might differ from one another in species or genus. If the difference which distinguishes such Gods is the same in species but numerically different, the argument continues, ". . . quidquid est eiusdem speciei, non dividitur secundum numerum, nisi secundum divisionem materiae vel alicuius potentialitatis. Ergo si illa differentia est eadem secundum speciem, sed differens numero, oportebit ergo quod in Deo sit aliquid potentiale . . ." (Mandonnet ed., Vol. 1, p. 60). For discussion see J. Owens, "Thomas Aquinas: Dimensive Quantity as Individuating Principle," *Mediaeval Studies* 50 (1988), p. 282. For other discussions of individuation in Aquinas see Roland-Gosselin, *Le "De ente et essentia,"* pp. 104–34; U. Degl'Innocenti, "Il pensiero di San Tommaso sul principio d'individuazione," *Divus Thomas* (Piac.) 45 (1942), pp. 35–81; J. Bobik, "Dimensions in the Individuation of Bodily Substances," *Philosophical Studies* (Maynooth) 4 (1954), pp. 60–79; "La doctrine de saint Thomas sur l'individuation des substances corporelles," *Revue philosophique de Louvain* 51 (1953), pp. 5–41; J. Rosenberg, *The Principle of Individuation: A Comparative Study of St. Thomas, Scotus, and Suarez* (Ph.D. dissertation: The Catholic University of America, Washington, D.C., 1950); I. Klinger, *Das Prinzip der Individuation bei Thomas von Aquin;* Owens, "Thomas Aquinas (b. ca. 1225; d. 1274)," in J.J.E. Gracia, ed., *Individuation in Scholasticism: The Later Middle Ages and the Counter Reformation* (Albany, N.Y., 1994), pp. 173–94; K. White, "Individuation in Aquinas's *Super Boetium De Trinitate,* Q. 4," *American Catholic Philosophical Quarterly* 69 (1995), pp. 543–56.

206. See d. 8, q. 5, a. 2 (Mandonnet ed., Vol. 1, p. 228, cited above in n. 196).

instead of corporeity, the first form received in matter is rather the substantial quiddity. This will lead to the same conclusion, he replies; for it is not by reason of a substantial quiddity that matter is divided but by reason of corporeity. Quantitative dimensions insofar as they are realized in actuality follow from this same (substantial) form, corporeity. Moreover, it is only because matter is divided and therefore subject to different positions *(situs)* or locations that it can receive different forms.[207]

This text indicates, therefore, that in addition to matter something else is necessary if matter is to be diversified and rendered capable of individuating substantial forms. This additional factor will be an accident rather than a substance or substantial principle, and, as we shall see in other texts, Thomas will identify it as quantity or quantitative dimensions. Moreover, he has introduced location or position as playing a role in the division of matter, although much is left unexplained in this passage.[208] And a possible objection to Aquinas's position could be raised in light of this discussion: How can he avoid reducing the distinction between different substances within the same species to the accidental level, since he now appeals to something accidental in order to explain how matter is diversified? We shall return to this issue below.

A passing reference in a theological discussion of the Father and the Son in d. 9, q. 1, a. 2 simply indicates that a species of substance is multiplied in individuals in accord with the division of matter.[209] In d. 23, q. 1, a. 1, Thomas attempts to clarify the relationship between the terms "essence," "subsistence," "substance," and "person," especially as they are said of God. He notes that since the act of being *(esse)* follows upon the composition of matter and form, even though form is a principle of *esse,* a given being does not receive its name from its form alone but from the whole. Therefore the essence of a composite being is not merely its form but includes both matter and form. Such an essence may also be referred to as a thing's quiddity or nature, as Boethius states. But when nature is so understood, even though it does indicate a matter-form composite, it does not yet imply a composite of this "given" *(demonstrata)* matter standing under determined *(determinatis)* accidents in which matter the form is individuated. It is this given matter which, as it were, receives the common nature. Here, as Owens points out,

207. Mandonnet ed., Vol. 1, pp. 228–29. Note: "Ergo forma corporeitatis est in tota materia, et ita materia non erit nisi in corporibus . . . quia ex quidditate substantiae materia non habet divisionem, sed ex corporeitate, quam consequuntur dimensiones quantitatis in actu; et postea per divisionem materiae, secundum quod disponitur diversis sitibus, acquiruntur in ipsa diversae formae." Cf. Owens, "Thomas Aquinas: Dimensive Quantity," p. 285.

208. On this see Klinger, *Das Prinzip der Individuation,* pp. 40–41. Assuming that Thomas already has in mind the distinction between the two meanings of corporeity we have seen from SCG IV, c. 81 (see nn. 169 and 170 above), substantial form and the three dimensions, here he is using it in the first sense, i.e., as substantial form.

209. ". . . sicut species substantiarum multiplicantur per individua, secundum divisionem materiae" (Mandonnet ed., pp. 248–49).

Thomas is viewing the common nature against an Avicennian background as if it were received in a determined portion of matter.[210] Noteworthy in this text are Thomas's references to matter (1) as given *(demonstrata)*, i.e., as that at which one can point; and (2) as standing under determined accidents as a result of which the matter can, as it were, receive and individuate the common nature. Both of these features will reappear in some of his fuller discussions of individuation.[211]

Additional light is cast on Thomas's usage here of the expression "given" *(demonstrata)* by his reply to the first objection. There he writes that an individual signifies a composite of a given *(demonstrata)* matter and form. But in the case of composites, a universal signifies a composite of matter and form, to be sure, but not of matter and form which are given. Thus human being taken universally signifies a composite of soul and flesh and of the act of being, but not of *this* flesh and *these* bones.[212] To refer to matter (and form) as given, therefore, is to refer to them as *this* or as *these,* that is to say, as individuated. But the reader may still wonder what it is that renders matter (and form) this matter and this form.

Slightly different language appears in d. 25, q. 1, a. 1, ad 3. There Thomas comments that in the case of composites a designated nature *(natura signata)* implies in addition to the nature itself a given matter *(materia demonstrata)*. It is through this that the common nature is individuated.[213] Here Thomas evidently draws a close connection between a nature and the given matter contained therein.

---

210. Mandonnet ed., Vol. 1, p. 555. Note in particular: "Sed ista natura sic considerata, quamvis dicat compositum ex materia et forma, non tamen ex hac materia demonstrata determinatis accidentibus substante, in qua individuatur forma. . . . Haec autem materia demonstrata est sicut recipiens illam naturam communem." See Owens, "Thomas Aquinas: Dimensive Quantity," p. 287.

211. For further discussion of this text and its context see Klinger, *Das Prinzip der Individuation,* pp. 34–36.

212. ". . . quia particulare significat compositum ex materia et forma demonstrata, sed universale in substantiis compositis significat etiam compositum ex materia et forma, sed non demonstrata, sicut homo ex anima, et carne, et esse, non tamen ex his carnibus et ex his ossibus" (Mandonnet ed., p. 557). Roland-Gosselin cites an interesting text from Boethius's second Commentary on the *Isagoge* as a possible source for the expression *demonstrata.* See Le *"De ente et essentiae,"* p. 58, and for Boethius, *In Isagogen Porphyrii Commenta,* S. Brandt, ed., CSEL Vol. 48 (Vienna, 1906), pp. 233:21–234:9. Note: "Individua enim maxime ostendi queunt, si vel tacito nomine sensui ipsi oculorum digito tactive monstrentur. . . ."

213. In this article Thomas is discussing the Boethian definition of a person as an "individual substance of a rational nature." In his reply to objection 3 he notes that essence or nature can be signified either as a part (e.g., by a term such as "humanity"), or as a whole (e.g., by the concrete name "man"). As the term "nature" appears in this definition, it signifies in the first way. Thomas continues: ". . . natura autem *signata* in rebus compositis etiam realem differentiam habet ad personam, inquantum scilicet naturae fit additio alicuius ut materiae *demonstratae,* per quam natura communis generis vel differentiae individuatur" (Mandonnet ed., p. 604). Italics mine. Note the term *signata* in this text, although as Degl'Innocenti observes, here it is applied to nature and not yet to matter. See his "Il pensiero di San Tommaso," p. 39. Roland-Gosselin cites a number of texts from the Latin Avicenna where the term *signatum* appears or some version thereof *(designatum, signatio, assignatio, designatio, signare, designare).* See Le *"De ente et essentia,"* pp. 59–60.

In replying to objection 6 of this same article Thomas distinguishes two features of individuation insofar as this is realized in composites: (1) the cause of individuation, which he here identifies as matter; (2) the notion of individuation when this is taken as incommunicability in the sense that one thing is not divided into many, nor predicated of many, nor even divisible into many.[214] The issue of incommunicability is raised here because of the general context, Thomas's defense of the Boethian definition of a person as an "individual substance of a rational nature."[215]

In d. 34, q. 1, a. 1, ad 4, Thomas makes another passing reference to species as individuated by matter. In d. 35, q. 1, a. 5 he refers to the fact that God's essence cannot be described as universal or as particular, because the principle of the particular, i.e., the individual, is either matter or something else which serves as matter.[216] In d. 36, q. 1, a. 1, while defending God's knowledge of singulars, Thomas describes matter as individuating and as the principle of individuation. In q. 2, a. 3, ad 3 of this same d. 36, he observes that the distinction of individuals within the same species is in terms of matter.[217]

In his Commentary on Bk II of the *Sentences* (d. 3, q. 1, a. 1), Thomas is arguing against matter-form composition of angels. He attempts to show that if something is incorporeal it must also be completely immaterial. He reasons that one perfection is owing to one thing that can be perfected. In prime matter taken as such there is no diversity. Therefore any form, prior to which diversity can neither be present nor be understood in matter, must itself inform the whole of the matter. But corporeity is such a form, since before it is present in matter, no diversity can be understood therein; for diversity presupposes parts. And parts cannot be present unless divisibility is presupposed. Divisibility presupposes and follows upon quantity. And quantity itself presupposes corporeity. Hence the form of corporeity must inform the entire matter. Again I take the form of corporeity as used here as the substantial form. Thomas concludes that if something is incorporeal, it must also be immaterial.[218]

---

214. Mandonnet ed., pp. 604–5. Note especially: ". . . est duo considerare: primum scilicet, individuationis causam quae est materia . . . et secundum, scilicet rationem individuationis quae est ratio incommunicabilitatis. . . ."

215. For this definition in Boethius see his *Contra Eutychen et Nestorium*, III, in *The Theological Tractates*, p. 84: ". . . reperta personae est definitio: 'naturae rationabilis individua substantia'."

216. For the first text see Mandonnet ed., p. 790: ". . . sicut . . . et species per materiam individuatur." In the second text Thomas writes: "Id autem quo Deus cognoscit quasi medio est essentia sua, quae non potest dici universale, quia omne universale additionem recipit alicuius per quod determinatur; et ita est in potentia, et imperfectum in esse; similiter non potest dici particularis, quia particularis principium materia est, vel aliquid loco materiae se habens . . ." (p. 822).

217. For a. 1 see Mandonnet ed., p. 832: "Et ideo cum materia sit principium individuationis . . . unde non tantum cognoscit res secundum naturas universales, sed secundum quod sunt individuatae per materiam. . . ." In the second text Thomas defends, with certain qualifications, divine ideas for particulars. See p. 845.

218. Mandonnet ed., Vol. 2, pp. 86–87. Note: ". . . cum enim uni perfectibili debeatur una perfectio, et in materia prima non sit ulla diversitas, oportet quod omnis forma ante quam non potest

According to this text, therefore, we have the following sequence. Matter is undivided of itself. Diversity in matter presupposes parts. The presence of parts in matter presupposes divisibility. Divisibility presupposes quantity. Quantity presupposes corporeity, i.e., the substantial form that confers corporeity or the three dimensions. Therefore diversity in matter presupposes all of these. Hence, we may conclude, so does the individuation of form by matter. There can, of course, be no temporal priority involved here, only priority in the order of nature. Moreover, if I may anticipate another point to be developed below, different lines of causality exercised simultaneously are at work here. One line has to do with the material and receiving causality exercised by matter, once it is diversified, with respect to form. The other is the formal and determining causality exercised by form with respect to matter and the accidents, especially quantity, that follow therefrom.

In his reply to the third objection in this same article, Thomas again refers to form as individuated by matter.[219] And in a. 3, ad 1 of the same question Thomas distinguishes two kinds of unity—the unity which is convertible with being (transcendental unity) and the unity which serves as the principle of number (numerical unity). He identifies the latter with discrete quantity, which itself is caused by the division of matter or of the continuum.[220]

Already in his Commentary on Bk I (d. 8, q. 5, a. 2), Thomas had introduced the notion of dimensions. To the extent that quantitative dimensions are actually realized they follow upon and presuppose corporeity, i.e., the form of corporeity.[221] This notion is developed more fully in connection with individuation in the Commentary on Bk II, in the *De ente et essentia,* and in other texts. At the same time, a textual problem arises, because at times Thomas refers to these dimensions as *terminatae,* at times as *determinatae,* and at other times as *interminatae.*

In his Commentary on Bk II, d. 3, q. 1, a. 4, Thomas comments that it is not possible for us to think of different parts in matter unless we presuppose as present in such matter dimensive quantity, at least indeterminate *(interminata)* dimensive quantity, by which matter is divided, as Averroes maintains. If quantity were removed from any substance, its matter would remain indivisible. In terms of general context, Thomas is here refuting theories that would admit that more than one

---

in ea esse ulla diversitas, nec intelligi, investiat eam totam. Sed ante corporeitatem non potest intelligi aliqua diversitas quia diversitas praesupponit partes, quae non possunt esse nisi praeintelligatur divisibilitas quae consequitur quantitatem, quae sine corporeitate non est. Unde oportet quod tota materia sit vestita forma corporeitatis; et ideo si aliquid est incorporeum, oportet esse immateriale" (Mandonnet ed., Vol. 2, pp. 86–87). The parallel between this text and that from *In I Sent.,* d. 8, q. 5, a. 2 is quite striking (see nn. 206 and 207 above).

219. ". . . materia enim prima recipit formam non prout est forma simpliciter, sed prout est hoc, unde per materiam individuatur" (pp. 88–89).

220. Mandonnet ed., Vol. 2, p. 94. Thomas would always defend the distinction between these two types of unity and is highly critical of Avicenna for having failed to do so. See, for instance, *In IV Met.,* lect. 2, pp. 155–56, nn. 556–560.

221. See n. 207 above.

angel could belong to the same species, even if, against Thomas's metaphysics, such angels were composed of matter and form.[222] But more important for our purposes is his reference to the need for dimensive quantity, at least indeterminate dimensive quantity, if matter itself is to be divided into parts and therefore rendered capable of receiving different forms of the same kind.

Later on in this same Commentary on Bk II (d. 30, q. 2, a. 1), Thomas again refers to division as taking place in matter only insofar as matter itself is considered as subject to dimensions, at least to indeterminate ones *(saltem interminatis);* for if quantity were to be removed, the substance would be indivisible. There too he notes that when we speak of matter as it exists in an individual thing we are not considering matter absolutely, i.e., without reference to its mode of existence, but only insofar as it is subject to dimensions.[223] Again he assigns an important role to matter, but only insofar as it is divided into parts. And now he has written that matter can be so divided only insofar as it is subject to dimensions, at least those that are indeterminate. Hence, from these texts we conclude that in order for matter to be rendered divisible and to exercise its individuating function with respect to a given substantial form, it must be subject at least to indeterminate dimensions.

On the other hand, in his Commentary on Bk III of the *Sentences* (d. 1, q. 2, a. 5, ad 1), Thomas explicitly states that the "principle of individuation is matter considered in some way under determinate *(terminatae)* dimensions." Here he is discussing the theological issue of the assumption by one divine Person of two natures in the hypostatic union. In replying to the first objection he notes that it is by reason of one and the same thing that a nature is individuated and divided. Because the principle of individuation is matter considered in some way under determinate dimensions, it is from the division of matter that human nature itself

222. Mandonnet ed., Vol. 2, p. 97. Note: "Sed impossibile est in materia intelligere diversas partes, nisi praeintelligatur in materia quantitas dimensiva ad minus *interminata,* per quam dividatur ut dicit Commentator in libro *De substantia orbis,* cap. 1, et in I *Physic.,* quia separata quantitate a substantia remanet indivisibilis . . ." (italics mine). For Averroes see *In I Phys.,* com. 63, *Aristotelis opera cum Averrois commentariis* (Venice, 1562–1574), Vol. 4, ff. 37vb–38rb; *De substantia orbis,* c. 1, ed. cit., Vol. 9, ff. 3vb–4vb. See Klinger, *Das Prinzip,* pp. 28–30. For the Hebrew edition, an English translation, and helpful notes see *Averroes' De substantia orbis,* by A. Hyman (Cambridge, Mass. and Jerusalem, 1986). See his Introduction for discussion of Averroes' understanding of the indeterminate three dimensions, which Hyman finds him identifying with the corporeal form, but distinguishing the latter from substantial forms that give existence in actuality to prime matter (pp. 30–31). Also see p. 41, n. 7. Thus Averroes holds that prime matter receives first (in the order of nature) the indeterminate three dimensions, then the substantial form, and finally the determinate dimensions that follow from the substantial form (Hyman, p. 53, n. 36). This is not to imply that Averroes thinks that prime matter ever exists with indeterminate dimensions but without any substantial form or determinate dimensions (see p. 62, text corresponding to note 65).

223. "Divisio autem non accidit materiae, nisi secundum quod consideratur sub dimensionibus saltem interminatis: quia, remota quantitate, ut in I *Physic.,* text. 15, dicitur, substantia erit indivisibile. Unde consideratio materiae huius rei est consideratio non materiae absolute, sed materiae sub dimensione existentis" (Mandonnet ed., pp. 781–82). See Owens, "Thomas Aquinas: Dimensive Quantity," pp. 288–89, n. 19.

is divided and multiplied.[224] Of immediate interest to us is Thomas's reference here to matter considered in some way under determinate dimensions as the principle of individuation.

Compounding the difficulty, at least as regards terminology, is Thomas's discussion in the *De ente et essentia*. In c. 2 he writes that it is not matter taken in any way whatsoever which is the principle of individuation but only designated matter *(materia designata)*. He immediately explains that by designated matter he has in mind matter insofar as it is considered under determined *(determinatis)* dimensions.[225]

Frequently enough interpreters of Aquinas assume that the expression "determined" *(determinatae)* is identical with "determinate" *(terminatae)* when applied to dimensions. In order to avoid prejudging that issue, here I shall translate them differently. If we do this, we now have three ways in which Thomas refers to dimensions as playing a role in individuation, i.e., as: (1) determinate *(terminatae)*; (2) indeterminate *(interminatae)*; and (3) determined *(determinatae)*.[226]

In this same context Thomas spells out the difference between designated *(signata)* and undesignated *(non signata)* matter. Undesignated matter is included in the definition of human being taken universally because flesh and bones are contained therein, although not this flesh and these bones. On the other hand, if we could define an individual human being such as Sortes, this flesh and these bones would be included in that definition. This is what Thomas means by designated matter, which he has also now identified as matter considered under determined dimensions. Designated matter is the kind of matter at which one can point and which one can grasp through the external senses, or to put it another way, the kind that is realized in actually existing individuals.[227]

Concerning the role of dimensions in individuation, therefore, there appears to be some difference between Thomas's position in the *De ente* and in the passages

224. "Ad primum ergo dicendum quod natura ab eodem habet ut individuetur et dividatur. Unde cum principium individuationis sit materia aliquo modo sub dimensionibus terminatis considerata, ex eius divisione natura humana dividitur et multiplicatur" (Mandonnet ed., Vol. 3, p. 45). Owens sees no discrepancy between this approach and that found in the Commentary on Bk II. See "Dimensive Quantity," pp. 289–90. As will become clear below, in my judgment the discrepancy is real.

225. "Et ideo sciendum est quod materia non quolibet modo accepta est individuationis principium, sed solum materia signata; et dico materiam signatam quae sub determinatis dimensionibus consideratur" (Leon. 43.371:73–77).

226. On the other hand, Owens holds that for Thomas determined dimensions may be either determinate or indeterminate or, to use his proposed terminology, definite or undefined. See "Thomas Aquinas: Dimensive Quantity," pp. 297–99, and pp. 295–96, n. 29; also, "Thomas Aquinas (b. ca. 1225; d. 1274)," pp. 182–84.

227. "Haec autem materia in definitione quae est hominis in quantum est homo non ponitur, sed poneretur in definitione Sortis si Sortes definitionem haberet. In definitione autem hominis ponitur materia non signata . . ." (Leon. 43.371:77–81).

already considered from his Commentary on Bk II of the *Sentences*. It is true that in his Commentary on Bk I of the Sentences (d. 23, q. 1, a. 1) he has referred to this given *(demonstrata)* matter as standing under determined *(determinatae)* accidents in which matter a form is individuated. If this text does not speak explicitly of determined dimensions but of determined accidents, it still seems to be in fundamental agreement with *De ente*, c. 2.[228] And in his Commentary on Bk III of the *Sentences* (d. 1, q. 2, a. 5, ad 1), Thomas has stated that the principle of individuation is matter considered in some way under determinate *(terminatis)* dimensions. But in his Commentary on Bk II, at d. 3, q. 1 a. 4 and again at d. 30, q. 2, a. 1 he has written that we cannot think of different parts or of division in matter without presupposing dimensive quantity or dimensions that are at least indeterminate *(interminatae)*.[229]

Two difficulties immediately appear. There seems to be opposition between the reference to determined *(determinatae)* dimensions in the *De ente* and to indeterminate *(interminatae)* dimensions or quantity in the texts from the Commentary on Bk II of the *Sentences*. Moreover, there seems to be still greater opposition between the second text from Bk II of the Commentary on the *Sentences*, on the one hand, and that just cited from the Commentary on Bk III, on the other hand, that is, between Thomas's appeal to indeterminate *(interminatae)* dimensions and to determinate *(terminatae)* dimensions. Complicating this issue is the fact that both the *De ente* and the Commentary on the *Sentences* are usually dated from 1252–1256. Guided in large measure by such terminological differences between the *De ente* and the Commentary on Bks I and II of the *Sentences*, Roland-Gosselin concluded that the *De ente* should be dated from about the time Thomas was commenting on Bk I, d. 25 of the Commentary on the *Sentences*. But this effort to arrive at greater chronological precision may or may not be accurate. Nonetheless, I would suggest that the *De ente* may be prior to the commentary on Bk II, d. 3.[230]

228. Cited above in n. 210.

229. See nn. 224, 222, and 223 above.

230. For the dating of the Commentary on the *Sentences* see Weisheipl, *Friar Thomas d'Aquino*, pp. 358–59. Note his citation of Tocco to the effect that Thomas was still writing this work "at the beginning of his career as master," that is to say, after his inception as Master in the spring of 1256. On the *De ente*'s dating see p. 386. Since this was written before Thomas became a Master, it must antedate at least the final written part of the Commentary on the *Sentences*. Also see Leon. 43.319–20, for discussion; Roland-Gosselin *Le "De ente et essentia,"* pp. xxvi–xxviii. He finds less precision on Thomas's part in dealing with the issue of individuation in the first 24 distinctions of the Commentary on Bk I of the *Sentences* than in the *De ente*, and he notes that the term *signatum*, so central to the discussion *De ente*, c. 2, appears for the first time at d. 25, q. 1, a. 1, ad 2, in the Commentary. He also points to the introduction of the term *interminata* in d. 3, q. 1, a. 4 of Bk II as going beyond the thinking of the *De ente*. Note that he dates the Commentary on the *Sentences* from 1254–1256 rather than from 1252–1256. Torrell is content to date the *De ente* from 1252–1256, and the Commentary (the fruit of his teaching from 1252–1254) as not yet completed in written form when Thomas incepted as Master in 1256 *(Saint Thomas Aquinas,* pp. 348–49, 332).

Thomas's fullest statement of his views on individuation appears in his Commentary on the *De Trinitate* of Boethius. While this work is some times dated between 1252 and 1259 and perhaps more frequently between 1255 and 1259, both Torrell and the Leonine edition now place it in 1257–1258 or possibly in early 1259.[231] Accordingly, I will regard it as subsequent to both the *De ente* and the Commentary on the *Sentences*. In q. 4, a. 2 Thomas addresses himself to the broader question concerning whether difference in accidents produces numerical diversity and plurality (of subjects). He begins his reply by observing that in a composite substance three factors are present—matter, form, and the composite. He goes on to connect diversity in genus with diversity in matter, diversity in species with diversity in form, and numerical diversity partly with diversity of matter and partly with diversity of accidents.[232]

As regards individuals within the same species, Thomas develops this explanation. If the parts of a genus and a species are matter and form, the parts of an individual are *this* matter and *this* form. Hence it is this matter and this form that account for numerical diversity within species. But no form insofar as it is a form is this form (or individual) of itself. (He explains that he has added "insofar as it is a form" because of the rational soul. In a way it is this individual something [*hoc aliquid*] of itself, but not insofar as it is a form.)[233] He also notes that our intellect can attribute to many things any form which can be received in something as in matter or a subject. But this ability to be predicated of many is contrary to the nature of an individual. Therefore, form becomes this form or individual by being received in matter. But matter is indistinct in and of itself. Hence it cannot individuate the form it receives unless it is rendered divisible. This follows, Thomas explains, because a form is not individuated simply because it is received in matter. It is individuated only insofar as it is received in *this* matter which is distinct and determined to the here and now. And matter is rendered divisible only through

---

231. Weisheipl dated this in 1258–1259 in the first edition of his *Friar Thomas* (p. 381), but in the second edition changes this to 1252–1259 (pp. 482–83); on p. 469 he is more specific ("anytime between 1253–58"). See Ch. I, n. 7 above for references to Torrell, and the Leonine ed.

232. ". . . secundo utrum varietas accidentium faciat diversitatem secundum numerum" (Leon. 50.119:4–5). Thomas begins his response by noting that Boethius has referred to a threefold diversity (generic, specific, numerical), and indicates his intention to identify the cause for each (p. 139). Here, of course, we are interested in his explanation of numerical diversity. "Sciendum est ergo quod diversitas secundum genus reducitur in diversitatem materiae, diversitas vero secundum speciem in diversitatem formae, sed diversitas secundum numerum partim in diversitatem materiae, partim in diversitatem accidentis" (Leon. 50.123:77–89). His explanation of the causes of the first two types of diversity is considerably more complicated than this brief introductory remark indicates, but I shall bypass that discussion here.

233. Leon. 50.125:188–198. Note: ". . . ita diversitatem in numero facit haec forma et haec materia. Nulla autem forma inquantum huiusmodi est haec ex se ipsa;—dico in quantum huiusmodi propter animam rationalem, quae quodammodo ex se ipsa est hoc aliquid, sed non in quantum forma." The human soul is an individual of itself, in a way, because according to Thomas it not only gives *esse* to matter but has *esse* in its own right.

quantity. In other words, it is only by reason of quantity that matter can be divided into parts and rendered subject to the here and now. Therefore, Thomas continues, matter is rendered *this* and designated only insofar as it is subject to dimensions.[234]

Thomas takes it as evident that if something is determined to the here and now, i.e., to this place and this time, it must be individual. The unexpressed presupposition is that quantity, insofar as it is determined to the here and now, is self-individuating. As such it can individuate matter and enable matter to individuate form.

We may still ask what it is about quantity that renders it determined to the here and now. It is at this point that Thomas brings dimensions into the discussion. Dimensions may be considered in two ways. In one way, they are considered in terms of their termination, that is, according to their determined *(determinatam)* measure and configuration. When they are so considered, they fall into the genus quantity as enjoying complete or perfected being, a being which is accidental, of course, rather than substantial. However, Thomas continues, when dimensions are considered in this first way, they cannot serve as the principle of individuation. The particular dimensions of a given individual may vary considerably during its period of existence. If dimensions when understood in this way were to serve as the principle of individuation, when a material substance's dimensions changed it would no longer be numerically one and the same individual.[235]

Moved by this reasoning, Thomas turns to the second way in which dimensions may be viewed, that is, without any such determination but only insofar as they are dimensions. He immediately adds that they will never exist in fact without also enjoying a given determination, that is to say, a given measure and shape. Nonetheless, they may be thought of without any such determination, and when so considered, they also fall into the genus quantity, but only as something imperfect and incomplete. It is such indeterminate *(interminatae)* dimensions which render matter "this" or individual and designated, and thus enable it to individuate form and to cause numerical diversity within the same species.[236]

---

234. Leon. 50.125:198–213. Note especially: ". . . unde forma fit haec per hoc quod recipitur in materia. Sed cum materia in se sit indistincta, non potest esse quod formam receptam individuet nisi secundum quod est distinguibilis: non enim forma individuatur per hoc quod recipitur in materia, nisi quatenus recipitur in hac materia distincta et determinata ad hic et nunc. Materia autem non est divisibilis nisi per quantitatem; unde Philosophus dicit in I Physicorum quod subtracta quantitate remanebit substantia indivisibilis; et ideo materia efficitur haec et signata secundum quod subest dimensionibus." For Aristotle see *Physics* I, c. 2 (185b 16), although the citation is not literal.

235. "Dimensiones autem istae possunt dupliciter considerari. Uno modo secundum earum terminationem;—et dico eas terminari secundum determinatam mensuram et figuram, et sic ut entia perfecta collocantur in genere quantitatis—et sic non possunt esse principium individuationis, quia cum talis terminatio dimensionum varietur frequenter circa individuum, sequeretur quod individuum non remaneret semper idem numero" (Leon. 50.125:214–222).

236. "Alio modo possunt considerari sine ista determinatione, in natura dimensionis tantum, quamvis numquam sine aliqua determinatione esse possint, sicut nec natura coloris sine determinatione albi et nigri; et sic collocantur in genere quantitatis ut imperfectum, et ex his dimensionibus

Until this point I have attempted to preserve in English the difference between the three Latin terms Thomas applies to dimensions, i.e., "determinate" *(terminatae)*, "indeterminate" *(interminatae)*, and "determined" *(determinatae)*. In the present text, however, the distinction between determinate *(terminatae)* and determined *(determinatae)* seems to have broken down, at least by implication. Now we read that when dimensions are considered without any determination *(determinatio)* of their dimensions and hence, one assumes by implication, as undetermined *(indeterminatae)*, they may be described as indeterminate *(interminatae)*. This invites us to take indeterminate as equivalent to undetermined. And it also invites us to take as the opposite of the indeterminate not only the determinate *(terminatae)* but also the determined *(determinatae)*. Hence I find it difficult to agree with those recent interpreters who see no real difference between Thomas's appeal to determined (or determinate) dimensions and his appeal to those that are indeterminate (or undetermined). If he has turned to indeterminate or undetermined dimensions in the present text, he has done so deliberately and, as we may gather from other passages, with awareness of his debt to Averroes' terminology in making this choice.[237] If he will eventually drop this terminology and return to determinate or determined dimensions in accounting for individuation, this, too, will point to a real shift, not merely to a change in his way of expressing himself.

In the following lines of this text Thomas points out that matter taken in itself is not the principle of specific or numerical diversity; but just as it is a principle for diversity in genus insofar as it is subject to a common form, so is it a principle for numerical diversity insofar as it is subject to indeterminate *(interminatis)* dimensions. He acknowledges that such dimensions are accidents, and therefore, that numerical diversity is sometimes reduced to diversity of matter, and sometimes to diversity of accidents by reason of these (indeterminate) dimensions. Thomas apparently accepts both explanations when appropriate qualifications are added. This implies that for him the principle of individuation is matter, but not merely matter. Indeterminate or undetermined dimensions also serve as another and secondary principle of individuation.[238] Thomas also adds in a noteworthy comment that accidents other than such dimensions are not themselves the principle of indi-

---

interminatis materia efficitur haec materia signata, et sic individuat formam. Et sic ex materia causatur diversitas secundum numerum in eadem specie" (Leon. 50.125:223–31).

237. See, for instance, L. J. Elders, *Faith and Science* (Rome, 1974), pp. 75–77, 80–81; Owens, "Thomas Aquinas: Dimensive Quantity," pp. 289–90, 293–94, 301–3; Bobik, "Dimensions in the Individuation of Bodily Substances," pp. 69–72; "La doctrine de saint Thomas," pp. 29–38. For the Latin Averroes' terminology in *De substantia orbis* see n. 222 above.

238. Leon. 50.125:231–242. Note: ". . . ita est principium diversitatis secundum numerum prout subest dimensionibus interminatis. Et ideo, cum hae dimensiones sint de genere accidentium, quandoque diversitas secundum numerum reducitur in diversitatem materiae, quandoque in diversitatem accidentis, et hoc ratione dimensionum praedictarum." Cf. the text from *In IV Sent.*, d. 12, cited below in n. 245.

viduation, even though they do enable us to recognize distinct individuals.[239] If we may put this another way, Thomas is well aware that all of the accidents found in one individual substance differ numerically from those present in another. And he is equally cognizant of the difference between individuating, on the one hand, and rendering distinct individuals discernible to a human knower, on the other. According to this text, therefore, among accidents, only indeterminate dimensions can qualify for the role of secondary principle of individuation in the causal and ontological sense just described, although other accidents enable us to recognize individuals.

In his Commentary on Bk II of the *Sentences,* Thomas had stated that the quantity or dimensions involved in the division of matter (and hence in individuation, we may presume) must be considered as *at least* indeterminate. At the time of his writing q. 4, a. 2 of the Commentary on the *De Trinitate,* any such hesitation has disappeared from his mind. It is only when dimensions are considered as indeterminate that they can serve to divide matter and thereby contribute to the individuation of material substances.

Thomas's firmness in this conviction is confirmed by his reply to objection 3. There he observes that it is of the nature *(ratio)* of an individual to be undivided in itself and divided from other things by an ultimate division. (By this reference to an ultimate division he means that an individual cannot be further divided without losing its essential identity.) Among accidents, only quantity has within itself the proper explanation for its division from others. This is because dimensions contain in themselves the reason for their individuation as a result of their position; and position itself is a quantitative difference. Dimensions therefore share in individuation in two ways: first, by reason of their subjects, since, like other accidents, they derive their individuation from their substantial subjects; and second, by reason of themselves, insofar as they have position. Therefore matter can individuate substantial forms precisely because it is subject to an accidental form which has within itself the explanation for its own individuation, that is to say, quantity as subject to indeterminate dimensions.[240]

In fact, Thomas explains, like other accidents even determinate dimensions, grounded as they are in a subject which enjoys complete or perfected being, are themselves in some way individuated from matter. This matter itself is individuated by the indeterminate dimensions which are preunderstood in that matter.[241]

---

239. "Alia vero accidentia non sunt principium individuationis, sed sunt principium cognoscendi distinctionem individuorum. Et per hunc modum etiam aliis accidentibus individuatio attribuitur" (Leon. 50.125:242–246).

240. Leon. 50.125:258–126:270. Note: "Nullum autem accidens habet ex se propriam rationem divisionis nisi quantitas; unde dimensiones ex se ipsis habent quandam rationem individuationis secundum determinatum situm, prout situs est differentia quantitatis."

241. Leon. 50.126:270–277: "Et ideo recte materiae convenit individuare omnes alias formas, ex hoc quod subditur illi formae quae ex se ipsa habet individuationis rationem, ita quod etiam ipsae

This final remark is interesting, for it attributes the individuation of determinate dimensions to individuated matter, and the individuation of the latter to indeterminate dimensions. In his reply to objection 5 Thomas makes the same point. While complete accidents presuppose the existence of substantial form in matter, indeterminate dimensions, which are preunderstood in matter before the coming of that form, do not. And, he adds, an individual cannot be understood without these indeterminate dimensions.[242]

Here we should mention a possible objection to Thomas's explanation of individuation. Does this solution not presuppose that indeterminate dimensions pre-exist in matter before a given substantial form does? And must this not be so if the prime matter of a substantial subject is to be divided and rendered individual and therefore capable of individuating a substantial form?

In responding to this we should recall a point Thomas has already made. Dimensions may be thought of as indeterminate; but they can never exist without also enjoying a given measure and configuration.[243] Hence we should likewise not assume that in reality prime matter is first informed only by indeterminate dimensions and then subsequently in the order of time divided and rendered individual so as to be able to individuate its appropriate substantial form. In the order of causal explanation, while indeterminate dimensions render matter divisible and individual and capable of individuating a substantial form, the substantial form simultaneously gives being to matter and hence to all the accidents, including the determined dimensions, which actually inhere in that substance.

As we have also mentioned above, Thomas would have us remember that distinct lines of causality are at work in this explanation, i.e., material or receiving, and formal or actualizing. Moreover, we should recall that causes can cause one another simultaneously according to different orders of causality. If we may apply this to the present case, according to the thinking in Thomas's Commentary on the *De Trinitate,* q. 4, a. 2, matter is rendered divisible and designated insofar as it is informed by indeterminate dimensions. As so divided it simultaneously exercises receiving and material causality with respect to the substantial form which it individuates while the substantial form actualizes and determines the matter and joins with it to constitute the substantial essence of a composite. From this essence the proper accidents of the composite essence flow, including in particular its quantity as subject to dimensions. But insofar as we now think of it as an actually existing substance, these dimensions are in reality determinate, not merely indeterminate. And finally, presupposed for such a composite substance to exist is its actualization

---

dimensiones terminatae, quae fundantur in subiecto iam completo, individuantur quodammodo ex materia individuata per dimensiones interminatas praeintellectas in materia."

242. Leon. 50.126:287–292.

243. See q. 4, a. 2 (Leon. 50.125:224–227, cited in n. 236 above). Thomas makes this observation in the same context where he appeals to designated matter under indeterminate dimensions as that which individuates substantial form.

in the existential order by its act of being. This is a complicated explanation of individuation, to be sure, and one that can easily be misunderstood. Perhaps Thomas himself came to realize this. If so, that realization might account at least in part for his eventual abandonment of the terminology of indeterminate dimensions in later discussions.[244]

In his Commentary on Bk IV of the *Sentences,* Thomas speaks in fundamentally the same fashion. Thus in d. 12, q. 1, a. 1, sol. 3, ad 3 he writes that two things are implied in the notion of an individual. It must be a being in actuality, either in itself or in something else. And it must be divided from others which are or can be members of the same species, and exist in undivided fashion in itself. Therefore he identifies matter as the primary principle of individuation, whereby being in actuality pertains to any such form whether substantial or accidental. And he now indicates that dimension serves as the secondary principle of individuation, since it is from dimension that matter is rendered capable of being divided.[245]

If Thomas does not specify in this immediate context whether these dimensions are determinate or indeterminate, he does so shortly thereafter. Still within the same general discussion of Eucharistic theology, he again refers to two texts from Averroes' *De substantia orbis* and his Commentary on *Physics* I. He does this while noting that in the matter of things subject to generation and corruption we must first think of indeterminate dimensions before the arrival of substantial form. Otherwise the division of matter into different parts and the presence of different substantial forms in these parts could not be properly understood. After the substantial form is present, such dimensions enjoy a being that is determinate and complete. So here again he refers both to determinate and to indeterminate dimensions. But as in his Commentary on the *De Trinitate*, q. 4, a. 2, he attributes the division of matter into parts and hence the individuation of substantial form to indeterminate dimensions, not to those that are determinate.[246]

---

244. The same misunderstanding could easily arise from the two texts from Thomas's Commentary on Bk IV of the *Sentences,* which we shall now consider. We should also bear in mind Thomas's warning in his Commentary on Bk I of the *Sentences,* d. 8, q. 5, a. 2, that accidental *esse* does not precede substantial *esse* in any given substance (see n. 196 above).

245. See Moos ed., Vol. 4, p. 503. Note in particular: "Et ideo primum individuationis principium est materia, qua acquiritur esse in actu cuilibet tali formae sive substantiali sive accidentali. Et secundarium principium individuationis est dimensio, quia ex se habet materia quod dividitur."

246. See *In IV Sent.*, d. 12, q. 1, a. 2, sol. 4. The particular question at issue here is whether anything can be generated from the Eucharistic species which remain after transubstantiation. Thomas reasons that after transubstantiation, just as these species by reason of the fact that they subsist are capable of doing whatever they could have done when the substances of bread and wine existed, so too they can be converted into whatever the preexisting substances could have been converted into. In explaining this he writes: "Sicut enim Commentator dicit in I *Phys.* (text 63) et in lib. *De substantia orbis* (cap. 1), in materia generabilium et corruptibilium oportet intelligere dimensiones interminatas ante adventum formae substantialis; alias non posset intelligi divisio materiae, ut in diversis partibus materiae diversae formae substantiales essent. Huiusmodi autem dimensiones post adventum formae substantialis accipiunt esse terminatum et completum. Quidquid autem intelligitur in materia ante adventum formae substantialis, hoc manet *idem numero* in generato et in eo ex

In his Commentary on d. 44, q. 1, a. 1a, ad 3, Thomas once more refers to and accepts the Averroistic notion of indeterminate dimensions. This time he does so in supporting his claim that in some way the same body will be reunited with the soul at the time of the resurrection. Thomas writes that what is understood in matter before form remains in the matter after the substance has been corrupted. As Averroes says in his Commentary on *Physics* I and in his *De substantia orbis,* we must think of indeterminate *(non terminatae)* dimensions as present in the matter of things subject to generation and corruption before their substantial form. It is according to these dimensions that matter is divided so as to be able to receive different forms in its different parts. Therefore, continues Thomas, after the separation of a substantial form from matter, these dimensions still remain the same. Hence whatever form matter may receive, when the matter exists under such dimensions it has a closer identity with something that was generated from it than it has with some other part of matter existing under any other form.[247] Of most immediate interest to us is Thomas's appeal once more to the Averroistic notion of indeterminate dimensions as required and apparently as sufficient to divide matter and enable its parts to receive different substantial forms.

We have already referred to the difference between this approach and that offered in the *De ente,* c. 2, where Thomas appeals to designated matter, or matter under determined *(determinatae)* dimensions, as the principle of individuation. It has been suggested that this apparent dilemma can be resolved in one way or another, for instance, if we refuse to identify determined dimensions with determinate *(terminatae)* dimensions and acknowledge that determined dimensions may be either determinate or indeterminate.[248] But this solution seems to be precluded by Thomas's statement in his Commentary on Bk III of his Commentary on the *Sentences* (d. 1, q. 2, a. 5, ad 1) that the principle of individuation is matter considered in some way under determinate *(terminatae)* dimensions. Even if we grant a distinction between determined and determinate dimensions, determined dimensions themselves would then be either determinate or indeterminate. According to this text the principle of individuation is not matter considered under indeterminate dimensions, as the texts from the Commentary on Bks II and IV of the *Sentences* and q. 4, a. 2 of the Commentary on the *De Trinitate* would have it. It is

---

quo generatur, quia remoto posteriori oportet remanere prius" (italics mine). Moos ed., Vol. 4, pp. 513–14. The similarity between the first part of this text and q. 4, a. 2 of the Commentary on the *De Trinitate* is evident. For the references to Averroes see above, n. 222. The last sentence just quoted could create some difficulty. I take Thomas to mean by this that the indeterminate dimensions we preunderstand as being present in matter "before" the new substantial form are not really or ontologically distinct from the determinate dimensions that follow upon or "after" that substantial form, and not that numerically the same accidents pass from one substance to another in the natural order.

247. For q. 1, a. 1a, ad 3 see Busa ed., Vol. 1, p. 635c. Cf. q. 1, a. 2, ad 3, Busa ed., p. 638b: "Ad tertium dicendum. . . ." On this text see Owens, "Thomas Aquinas: Dimensive Quantity," p. 292.

248. See the references given in n. 237 above.

matter considered under determinate dimensions.[249] Even if we carried our investigation of Thomas's texts no farther, it seems clear that we should admit that his thinking about the role of determinate and indeterminate dimensions did change. At the same time, Thomas's more fundamental claim—that matter itself is in some way a principle of individuation, and that quantitative dimensions also are in a secondary way—remains constant.

Before concluding this investigation, we shall now turn to some other texts. Thomas's De veritate is usually dated from 1256–1259. It should be slightly after the Commentary on the Sentences, since it is the work of a Master of Theology, not a Bachelor. In De veritate, q. 2, a. 6, ad 1, Thomas refers in passing to matter and all the material conditions which are principles of individuation. He does this in the course of explaining that the human intellect directly knows universals rather than individuals. In replying to the first objection he writes that there are two kinds of matter from which one may abstract—intelligible matter and sensible matter. Both types may be taken either as designated or as not designated. By designated matter he here means matter insofar as it is considered with a determination of its dimensions, i.e., with these or those given dimensions. Matter is not designated when it is considered without any determination of its dimensions. And he then comments that designated matter is the principle of individuation from which the intellect abstracts when it is said to abstract from the here and now.[250]

This statement that designated matter, or matter insofar as it is subject to a determination of its dimensions, is the principle of individuation agrees with the views Thomas had expressed in De ente, c. 2, and in his Commentary on Bk III of the Sentences. At the same time, it is difficult to reconcile this passage with those texts where Thomas proposes indeterminate dimensions rather than determinate dimensions as accounting for the division of matter into parts and for its ability to individuate a substantial form.[251]

---

249. For the text from the Commentary on III Sentences see n. 224 above.

250. On the dating of the De veritate see Weisheipl, Friar Thomas d'Aquino, p. 362. He suggests that questions 1–7 were disputed in the 1256–1257 academic year, and questions 8–20 in 1257–1258. Torrell limits himself to dating them from 1256 to 1259 (see Saint Thomas Aquinas, p. 334). For the text see Leon. 22.1.66:101–111. Note especially: ". . . et dico signatam secundum quod consideratur cum determinatione dimensionum harum scilicet vel illarum, non signatam autem quae sine determinatione dimensionum consideratur. Secundum hoc igitur sciendum est quod materia signata est individuationis principium a qua abstrahit omnis intellectus secundum quod dicitur abstrahere ab hic et nunc. . . ."

251. If we may date this text after the Commentaries on Bk IV of the Sentences and on the De Trinitate, we will not be surprised to find that appeal to indeterminate dimensions in accounting for individuation does not reappear in subsequent works. Whether the De veritate was actually written after the Commentary on the De Trinitate is more difficult to state with certainty; in support of that likelihood it should be noted that some time could pass between a Master's oral determination of a set of Disputed Questions such as the De veritate and his submission of his definitive written version to the University stationer.

That this is indeed Thomas's view in *De veritate,* q. 2, a. 6 is supported by a similar statement in q. 10, a. 5. There Thomas writes that it is not matter viewed in universal fashion that serves as the principle of individuation, but rather matter insofar as it is considered in an individual, that is to say, designated matter as it exists under determined *(determinatis)* dimensions.[252]

In Quodlibet 7, q. 4, a. 3 (Easter 1256), Thomas was asked whether God can make whiteness and some other corporeal quality exist without quantity, just as he makes quantity exist in the Eucharist without a substantial subject. In discussing this he distinguishes between the nature of a quality such as whiteness and its individuation as this sensible whiteness in distinction from any other sensible whiteness. He concludes that it is not possible for this individuated sensible whiteness to exist without quantity, even though it is possible for individuated quantity to exist by divine power without a substantial subject, as in the Eucharist. This is because quantity is individuated not merely by its subject (as are other accidents), but also from its position, which is included in the notion of dimensive quantity.[253] Although this text casts no light on the respective roles of determined and undetermined dimensions in individuation, it shows that dimensions and position continue to play an important role in accounting for the self-individuating character of quantity.

In Quodlibet 9, q. 6, a. 1 (Christmas 1257), Thomas faces another theological question—whether charity may be increased in terms of its essence. In considering this he draws a parallel with changes involving increase in quantity. He notes that in the case of corporeal growth the essence of quantity is not destroyed, since indeterminate dimension remains. But insofar as the quantity receives different limits *(terminationes)*, it changes from smaller to greater. So too, he concludes, the virtue of charity is not destroyed in its essence if its limits or degree change.[254] While this text does not address the application of indeterminate or determinate dimensions to the issue of individuation, it does once again illustrate Thomas's willingness to distinguish between them at this point in his career.

In later texts Thomas makes passing references to the issue of individuation, but usually without manifesting any preference for determinate or indeterminate dimensions. For instance, in *Summa contra Gentiles,* Bk IV, c. 65 (ca. 1264–1265), he is again discussing the Eucharist. Once more he writes that it is peculiar to dimensive quantity among all the accidents to be individuated of itself. This is because dimensive quantity includes position, the ordering of parts in a whole, within its intelligible content. Because dimensive quantity alone is self-individuating, the

---

252. Here Thomas considers whether the human mind can know material things as individual. He comments that when it is viewed universally ". . . materia non est individuationis principium, sed secundum quod consideratur materia in singulari quae est materia signata sub determinatis dimensionibus existens: ex hac enim forma individuatur . . ." (Leon. 22.2.309:48–53).

253. Leon. 25.1.23:52–83.

254. Leon. 25.1.114:40–63.

ultimate foundation for numerical multiplication appears to arise from dimensions. So it is that in the genus substance, multiplication takes place in accord with the division of matter, a division which can be accounted for only insofar as matter is considered under dimensions.[255] And in c. 81, while defending the resurrection of numerically the same body, he comments that none of a human being's essential principles falls into nothingness at death. The soul remains; the matter which was a subject for the soul which informed it also remains, and under the same dimensions by which it was rendered individual.[256]

In q. 9, a. 1 of the *De potentia* (1265–1266), Thomas refers to individual matter as the principle of singularity, and notes that in simple substances there is no individual matter which would individuate a common nature. He makes basically the same point in a. 2, ad 1. This singular or individual is individuated through this matter, and that individual through that matter. In the *Summa theologiae* I, q. 75, a. 4, Thomas refers to designated matter as the principle of individuation. And in q. 119, a. 1, he mentions individual designated matter and describes form as individuated through this kind of matter.[257]

Two texts stand out as exceptions in these later writings, however. In his Commentary on Bk II of the *De anima*, c. 12, Thomas writes that the individuation of a common nature in corporeal and material things results from corporeal matter insofar as it is contained under determined *(determinatis)* dimensions. This work dates from 1267–1268.[258]

In his Disputed Questions *De anima* (1266–1267), q. 9, one of the preliminary arguments (arg. 17) notes that this body is *this* body because it is subject to determinate *(terminatae)* dimensions. Therefore the soul is united to the body by means of determinate dimensions. In replying to this argument, Thomas does not challenge the reference to determinate dimensions. Rather he counters that dimensions cannot be thought of in matter unless the matter is understood as already constituted by its substantial form in its substantial and corporeal being. In the case of a human being this substantial form is the human soul. Therefore, dimensions of this kind (determinate dimensions, we may assume) are not understood as present

255. Ed. cit., pp. 528–29. Note: "Et quia sola quantitas dimensiva de sui ratione habet unde multiplicatio individuorum in eadem specie possit accidere, prima radix huiusmodi multiplicationis ex dimensione esse videtur: quia et in genere substantiae multiplicatio fit secundum divisionem materiae; quae nec intelligi posset nisi secundum quod materia sub dimensionibus consideratur. . . ."
256. Op. cit., p. 546. Note especially: ". . . materia etiam manet, quae tali formae fuit subiecta, sub dimensionibus eisdem ex quibus habebat ut esset individualis materia." For further discussion of this and additional texts see E. Sweeney, "Individuation and the Body in Aquinas," in *Miscellanea Mediaevalia* 24 (1996), esp. pp. 189–94.
257. For the texts from the *De potentia* see Pession ed., pp. 226 (q. 9, a. 1); 228 (q. 9, a. 2, ad 1). For the *Summa* see Leon. 5.200 (q. 75, a. 4); Leon. 5.571 (q. 119, a. 1): ". . . ad veritatem autem naturae in hoc particulari consideratae, pertinet materia individualis signata, et forma per huiusmodi materiam individuata."
258. Leon. 45.1.115:83–86: "Individuatio autem naturae communis in rebus corporalibus et materialibus est ex materia corporali sub determinatis dimensionibus contenta. . . ."

in matter prior to the soul without qualification, but only as prior to the soul's higher degrees of perfection.[259] This text implies that Thomas does not reject the claim that it is only insofar as the body is subject to determinate dimensions that it individuates. But he also makes it clear that one need not presuppose or view dimensions of this kind as being in matter before the soul itself is. And he makes no reference in either of these texts to indeterminate dimensions.[260]

When we turn to other later texts, explicit reference to determinate or indeterminate dimensions in connection with individuation does not appear. It is enough for Thomas to refer to dimensions or to dimensive quantity or else to designated sensible matter. For instance, in the *Compendium theologiae* (ca. 1265–1267 for the first part), c. 154, Thomas again discusses the numerical identity of the risen body. The matter of a resurrected human body will remain numerically the same by divine power, insofar as it is understood as existing under those dimensions by reason of which matter can be called and is the principle of individuation. Thomas here gives no indication concerning whether these dimensions are determinate or indeterminate, but presumably has in mind determinate dimensions.[261]

In his Commentary on the *De caelo et mundo*, Bk I, lect. 19 (probably dating from 1272–1273), Thomas comments that even though natural forms cannot be understood without, i.e., abstracted from, common sensible matter, they can be understood without or abstracted from designated sensible matter, which he here identifies as the principle of individuation and singularity.[262]

In *Summa theologiae* III (winter 1271/72–1273), q. 77, a. 2, Thomas writes that it belongs to the notion of an individual not to be capable of existing in many things. But this may come to pass in two ways: in one way, because it is not of the nature of the thing to be in something else, as is true of immaterial separate forms; or in another way, because it is of the nature of a substantial or accidental form to inhere in some one thing or subject but not in many. As regards being an individual in the first way, matter is the principle of individuation for all forms which inhere in it. By being received in matter, which itself is not present in something else, a form of this kind is likewise rendered incapable of existing in something else. As regards being an individual in the second way, the principle of individuation is

259. Leon. 24.1.79:117–121 (for the preliminary arg.): "Sed hoc corpus est per hoc quod est sub aliquibus dimensionibus terminatis." For Thomas's reply see pp. 85:513–86:522. For confirmation see the corpus of a. 9, cited in n. 260 below.

260. Cf. our discussion of indeterminate dimensions in n. 246 above. And note the following from the corpus of a. 9: "Sicut ex hoc quod materia constituitur in esse corporeo per formam, statim consequitur ut sint in ea dimensiones per quas intelligitur materia divisibilis per diversas partes, ut sic secundum diversas sui partes possit esse susceptiva diversarum formarum" (Leon. 24.1.81:212–217).

261. "Quae quidem materia eadem numero manet, in quantum intelligitur sub dimensionibus existens secundum quas haec materia dici potest et est individuationis principium" (Leon. 40.140:37–40).

262. ". . . possunt tamen intelligi sine materia sensibili signata, quae est individuationis et singularitatis principium . . ." (Spiazzi ed., p. 93, n. 187).

dimensive quantity. Insofar as something is undivided in itself and divided from everything else, it belongs to it to exist in only one subject. But it is by reason of quantity that division pertains to a substance. It follows that dimensive quantity is a certain principle of individuation for forms of this type insofar as numerically diverse forms are received in different parts of matter. And dimensive quantity enjoys a certain individuation of itself—or, as we have phrased it, it is self-individuating.[263]

In sum, therefore, Thomas remains faithful to his earlier view that designated matter is to be regarded as the principle of individuation for corporeal entities and that in a secondary way dimensive quantity also contributes to this. In these later texts he normally does not distinguish between determinate and indeterminate dimensions. However, in two passages we have found him referring to individuation as resulting from corporeal matter insofar as it is contained under determined dimensions, or from body insofar as it is subject to determined dimensions.

In spite of efforts on the part of some to prove that Thomas never changed his mind concerning the kind of dimensions involved in individuation, it seems clear from the texts we have examined that he did, and more than once. If he defends designated matter as considered under determined dimensions as the principle of individuation in the De ente, he just as clearly allows for this function to be fulfilled by matter considered at least under indeterminate dimensions in his Commentary on Bk II of the Sentences. In his Commentary on Bk IV of the Sentences and especially in his Commentary on the De Trinitate he defends this second view without any such hesitation or qualification. And his Quodlibet 9, q. 6, a. 1 may allow for this. But in his Commentary on Bk III of the Sentences he states that the principle of individuation is matter considered in some way under determinate dimensions. The expression "in some way" might be taken as pointing to some hesitation in his mind at this point in his career. Be that as it may, in later texts, beginning with the De veritate, when the issue of the kind of dimensions is raised at all, Thomas opts for determinate or determined dimensions. This appears to be his final position.[264]

---

263. Leon. 12.196–197. The context is theological, concerning whether after Eucharistic transubstantiation the accidents of bread and wine which remain inhere in dimensive quantity as in their subject. Note: "Quantum autem ad secundum, dicendum est quod individuationis principium est quantitas dimensiva. Ex hoc enim aliquid est natum esse in uno solo, quod illud est in se indivisum et divisum ab omnibus aliis. Divisio autem accidit substantiae ratione quantitatis. . . . Et ideo ipsa quantitas dimensiva est quoddam individuationis principium huiusmodi formis, inquantum scilicet diversae formae numero sunt in diversis partibus materiae."

264. Hence, without agreeing with them in every detail, my conclusion supports the views of Roland-Gosselin and Klinger rather than those of Degl'Innocenti, Bobik, and Owens, who maintain that Thomas's position on the role of determinate and indeterminate dimensions in individuation did not shift during his career. For references to their studies see n. 205 above. I have not here taken into account two opuscula whose Thomistic authorship is at best very doubtful, De natura materiae and De principio individuationis. For fuller discussion of their authenticity and content see Klinger, Das Prinzip, pp. 85–121. Torrell simply mentions them, along with many others, under a list of "unauthentic works or works of doubtful authenticity" (Saint Thomas Aquinas, pp. 360–61).

If this is correct, one may still ask how Thomas can reconcile his appeal to determinate dimensions as a secondary principle of individuation with the objection he himself raised against this in his Commentary on the *De Trinitate,* q. 4, a. 2. As will be recalled, there he pointed out that when dimensions are considered as terminated, they cannot serve as the principle of individuation. This is because the particular dimensions of a given material entity may vary considerably during the course of its existence. Hence, if dimensions when considered as determinate were to serve as the principle of individuation, when a material thing's dimensions changed, it would lose its numerical identity.[265]

I have not found an explicit answer to this objection in those later contexts where Thomas appeals to determinate dimensions or simply to dimensions or dimensive quantity in referring to the individuation of material substances. Hence my proposed answer will be somewhat conjectural. First of all, I would note that it is not to determinate dimensions alone that he appeals to account for individuation but to matter insofar as it is designated or insofar as it is subject to such dimensions. This is important, because it enables him to meet another frequently raised objection to his solution, namely, that he has appealed to an accident or to accidental principles to account for the individuation of material substances. According to Thomas matter itself is an intrinsic and essential principle of corporeal essences. And while matter taken alone cannot account for individuation, once matter has been rendered this matter or designated matter by quantity and hence by being subject to the three dimensions, it is matter itself, a substantial or essential principle, that both receives and individuates its appropriate substantial form.

In addition, I would suggest that Thomas may also have come to recognize that just as the intension or remission of an accidental quality need not destroy the numerical identity of that same quality, so too, so long as changes in a material entity's dimensions remain within the limits marked out for it to be a given type of being, such changes will likewise not prevent the matter of that entity from continuing to be numerically the same matter. Hence it will continue to individuate its substantial form and both will retain their numerical identity. Although Thomas does not there apply this thinking to our specific problem, and indeed was then still maintaining a distinction between determinate and indeterminate dimensions, in Quodlibet 9, q. 6, a. 1 he had drawn this parallel between increases in quantity and increases in charity, i.e., in quality. Beginning with his *De veritate* and in subsequent works he no longer seems to have been concerned about this particular issue. It may also be that, because he realized that dimensions never actually exist in a given material entity without being determined, he concluded that it was not helpful to fall back upon them considered as indeterminate in order to account for individuation. In any event, he certainly was aware that a corporeal

---

265. See n. 235 above for the text.

entity's given determinations may change within certain limits without destroying that thing's numerical identity and its individuation.

In this discussion we have until now restricted our analysis to Thomas's explanation of the individuation of material substances. Indeed, that is the very title of this section of Ch. IX. Nonetheless, Thomas does at times refer to the individuation of separate substances. As he puts it in a text we have just examined (ST III, q. 77, a. 2), an individual may not be capable of being multiplied in different entities or subjects simply because it is not of its nature to exist in something else: "And in this way immaterial separate forms, which subsist in themselves, are also individuals of themselves."[266] According to Thomas's metaphysics, of course, all such entities, with the exception of God, are composed of an essence and a distinct act of being. God's essence is identical with his act of being. God is undivided in himself and distinct from everything else by his very essence, as Thomas makes clear, for instance, in his Commentary on I *Sentences*, d. 8, q. 4, a. 1, ad 1, and in *De potentia*, q. 8, a. 3.[267] As he points out in ST I, q. 29, a. 4, and as we have already seen from other texts, an individual is that which is indistinct (or undivided) in itself and distinct (or divided) from everything else. Prompted by these and similar texts, J. Owens has recently proposed that existence may be called "the cause of individuality" according to Thomas's philosophical thinking.[268]

This is not for Owens to deny that Thomas also assigns an important role to matter and dimensions in accounting for the individuation of corporeal entities. Owens concludes by suggesting that Thomas uses two sequences and deals with two orders in explaining individuation. One sequence has to do with the order of being, and here, according to Owens, Thomas assigns primacy to existence in individuation not only in God and in angels, but in material substances as well. But he maintains that Thomas also follows a reverse sequence which applies to our understanding of the notion *(ratio)* of individuation. In this order of concepts, quantity alone individuates by itself, and this accounts for matter's ability to do so, which in turn serves to account for the individuation of form or essence, and ultimately of the act of being which is received by essence. But, Owens insists, "in the real order the basic cause of individuality is existence."[269]

In another recent study, J. Aertsen has drawn upon Thomas's Commentary on the *Liber de causis,* proposition 9, in order to arrive at somewhat similar if not

266. Leon. 12.196: "Et hoc modo formae immateriales separatae, per se subsistentes, sunt etiam per seipsas individuae."

267. See Mandonnet ed., Vol. 1, p. 219 *(In I Sent.)*: "Ita etiam divinum esse est determinatum in se et ab omnibus aliis divisum, per hoc quod sibi nulla additio fieri potest." For *De potentia* see Pession ed., p. 220: "Deus enim per essentiam est aliquid in se indivisum, et ab omnibus quae non sunt Deus, distinctum."

268. See his "Thomas Aquinas (b. ca. 1225; d. 1274)," p. 175. For Thomas's text from ST I see Leon. 4.333.

269. See Owens, pp. 186–87. For the text quoted see p. 188.

identical conclusions. As Aertsen notes (and as we have seen above in Ch. IV), the medieval Latin translation of a term from the Arabic text of this work as *yliatim* posed a problem for Thomas.[270] The Latin text of the *Liber de causis* indicates that an intelligence has *yliatim* because it is *esse* and form, and that in like fashion the soul has *yliatim* and so does nature. But the First Cause does not. Thomas mistakenly thinks that this term comes from the Greek term for matter (*yle*, in its medieval Latin transcription), when in fact the Arabic original rather signifies form or something like it. Nonetheless, Thomas adapts this meaning sufficiently so as to fit it into his own thinking. He interprets it broadly as signifying either matter or something that behaves like matter, that is, something potential or receiving. Thus he can agree with the *Liber de causis* that the quiddity of a (created) separate entity or intelligence, being a subsisting form and not being identical with its *esse,* is related to the *esse* in which it participates as potency to act. So too, the soul may be said to have *yliatim* not merely in the sense that it has (or is) a form (which is in potency to *esse),* but also in the sense that it has a body of which it is the form. In like fashion nature (or a natural entity) has *yliatim* since it is really composed of form and matter. Not having any participated *esse,* the First Cause in no way has *yliatim* but is pure *esse* and, adds Thomas, pure goodness.[271]

In developing this point, Thomas notes that something may be said to be an individual by reason of the fact that it is not suited to be in many things, as is a universal. But something may not be suited to be in many things in two different ways. First of all, this may be because it is determined to the single subject in which it is present. Thus this whiteness, precisely because it is received in this subject, cannot be present in another. Because this method of explanation cannot proceed to infinity, Thomas concludes that one must arrive at something whose very nature it is not to be received in something else, and which is individuated of itself. This, he says, is prime matter which in corporeal things is a principle of singularity for them. And this leads him to the second way in which something is not suited to be multiplied in other things, namely because it is not of its nature to be in something else. It is in this way that individuation occurs in separate substances, which are forms which have *esse,* as well as in the First Cause, which is subsisting *esse* it-

---

270. See "Die Thesen zur Individuation in der Verurteilung von 1277, Heinrich von Gent und Thomas von Aquin," in *Miscellanea Mediaevalia* 24 (Berlin–New York, 1996), pp. 249–65, especially pp. 259–60. See our remarks concerning this in Ch. IV, n. 51.

271. For the Latin text of the *Liber de causis* see *Sancti Thomae de Aquino super Librum de causis expositio,* Saffrey ed., p. 57. For Thomas's Commentary see p. 64. Note especially: "Nam *intelligentia habet yliatim,* id est aliquid materiale vel ad modum materiae se habens; dicitur enim *yliatim* ab *yle,* quod est materia." For discussion see R. Taylor, "St. Thomas and the *Liber de causis*" (as cited in Ch. IV, n. 51 above); Aertsen, "Die Thesen," pp. 259–60; A. Speer, "*Yliathin quod est principium individuandi.* Zur Diskussion um das Individuationsprinzip im Anschluss an prop. 8[9] des 'Liber de causis' bei Johannes de Nova Domo, Albertus Magnus und Thomas von Aquin," in *Miscellanea Mediaevalia* 24 (1996), pp. 271–72, 282–85.

self. In other words, both separate substances and God are individuated of themselves.[272]

The reader will undoubtedly note the similarity between this text and the one from ST III, q. 77, a. 2 which we have analyzed above. In both passages Thomas distinguishes the same two ways in which something may not be suited to be multiplied in different subjects. And in each text he describes immaterial separate forms (ST III, q. 77, a. 2), or separate substances and God (in the present text), as incapable of being multiplied in different subjects by their very nature or, as we have also phrased it, as self-individuating.[273]

In reacting to the studies by Aertsen and Owens I would agree with both that Thomas discusses the issue of individuation not only at the level of corporeal entities but also at the level of created separate substances and of God. I also acknowledge that Owens is correct in emphasizing the important role Thomas assigns to the act of being within the ontological structure of every substance and level of substance, including material substances. However, I have not found him explicitly referring to existence or the act of being as the principle of individuation for corporeal substances. Moreover, it seems to me that Thomas's appeal to designated matter or to matter as subject to dimensions in accounting for the individuation of corporeal entities is intended to apply to the real order or the order of being, not merely or even primarily to the order of concepts. Hence I do not think one should refer to the act of being or to existence as the principle of individuation in corporeal entities—even though Thomas clearly does hold that, without the presence of the act of being within a given corporeal entity, there would be no actually existing entity and no individuation.

272. See Saffrey ed., pp. 64:27–65:15.
273. Saffrey ed., pp. 65:16–66:7. Note especially: "Unde oportet quod omne quod non est natum esse in aliquo, ex hoc ipso sit individuum; et hic est secundus modus quo aliquid non est natum esse in multis, quia scilicet non est natum esse in aliquo. . . ." Cf. Aertsen, pp. 261–62. Note the comparison he draws with Thomas's *De ente,* c. 5, and Thomas's reference there to prop. 9 of the *Liber de causis* in discussing individuation in God.

PART THREE

From Finite Being to Uncreated Being

Argumentation for God's Existence

Introductory Remarks

We have now completed our presentation of Thomas's metaphysical under-standing of finite being, both at the level of being in Part I and at the level of essence in Part II. At the level of being we have found him defending an essence-*esse* composition that applies to every finite being. At the level of essence he defends a less fundamental composition of substance and accident that also is realized in all finite beings, and a composition of matter and form that applies only to material beings.

In the preceding chapters of this study we have seen numerous texts wherein Thomas takes God's existence as granted, whether on the grounds of reason or revelation. In attempting to present his metaphysical thought according to the philosophical order as he has defined it, until this point we have regarded these references to God's existence as anticipatory or as putative rather than as philosophically established. This is because until now we have not yet considered in detail his formal presentation of argumentation for this conclusion. Even so, we have often found Thomas's references to God, even when considered only as a working hypothesis, to be quite useful in enabling him to clarify his metaphysical thinking concerning finite being. We have now reached the point where it is appropriate to consider his explicit philosophical argumentation for the existence of such a being. As will be recalled, for Thomas the subject of metaphysics is being as being, or *ens commune*. But he has also indicated that it is the goal or end of metaphysics to arrive at knowledge of the cause or the principle of this subject. And with that in mind, we now turn to the issue of God's existence.

As is well known, Thomas Aquinas frequently offered philosophical argumenta-tion in support of the claim that God exists. The secondary literature concerning

his "five ways" and some of his other approaches to God's existence is extensive.[1]
While many of these more recent studies have proved helpful to me in preparing
the present chapter and those that immediately follow, here I will make no attempt
to refer to all of them or, for that matter, even to cite every text in which Thomas
argues for God's existence. An excellent survey and critical analysis of Thomas's
texts along with frequent reference to much of the secondary literature is available—F. Van Steenberghen's *Le problème de l'existence de Dieu dans les écrits de s.
Thomas d'Aquin* of 1980.[2] In Chapters XI and XII I shall present in their essentials
the major ways of arguing for God's existence which Thomas proposes in a number
of his writings. Before doing this, however, it will be necessary in the present chapter to determine more precisely Thomas's views concerning the possibility of demonstrating God's existence.

1. Faith, Reason, and the Issue of God's Self-Evidence

In q. 2, a. 3 of his Commentary on the *De Trinitate* Thomas offers what is
perhaps his finest exposition of his views concerning the proper relationship between faith and reason. As we have already seen, there he argues that there can be
no conflict between faith rightly interpreted and reason when it is rightly exercised
(or between faith and philosophy) because both ultimately derive from one and
the same source, God himself.[3] In summing up the ways in which the student of
theology *(sacra doctrina)* may legitimately employ philosophy in his theological
task, Thomas mentions as a first illustration of this the demonstration of what he
calls preambles to faith. By these he has in mind certain truths which the believer
must know, such as those which are proved by natural reason about God. Thomas
mentions our demonstration that God exists, and then points such as God's

1. Here I will limit myself to mentioning but a few: *L'existence de Dieu,* Cahiers de l'actualité
religieuse 16 (Tournai-Paris, 1961); D. Bonnette, *Aquinas' Proofs for God's Existence. St. Thomas Aquinas on: "The Per Accidens necessarily implies the Per Se"* (The Hague, 1972); L. Charlier, "Les cinq voies
de saint Thomas. Leur structure métaphysique," in *L'existence de Dieu,* pp. 181–227; L. J. Elders, *The
Philosophical Theology of St. Thomas Aquinas* (Leiden, 1990); R. Garrigou-Lagrange, *God: His Existence and His Nature,* Vol. 1 (St. Louis-London, 1949); M. L. Guérard des Lauriers, *La preuve de Dieu
et les cinq voies* (Rome, 1966); A. Kenny, *The Five Ways: St. Thomas Aquinas' Proofs of God's Existence*
(Notre Dame, Ind., 1980); J. Maritain, *Approaches to God* (London, 1955); T. O'Brien, *Metaphysics
and the Existence of God;* J. Owens, *St. Thomas Aquinas on the Existence of God: The Collected Papers
of Joseph Owens,* J. Catan, ed. (Albany, 1980); E. Sillem, *Ways of Thinking about God: Thomas Aquinas
and the Modern Mind* (New York, 1960). As the titles of some of these works indicate, not all are
equally historical in their approach to Aquinas's texts. For an effort to collect Thomas's own texts in
their chronological order see J. A. Baisnée, "St. Thomas Aquinas's Proofs of the Existence of God
Presented in Their Chronological Order," in *Philosophical Studies in Honor of the Very Reverend Ignatius Smith, O.P.,* ed. J.K.Ryan (Westminster, Md., 1952), pp. 29–64.
2. Louvain-la-Neuve, 1980. See pp. 359–66 for bibliography.
3. Leon. 50.98:114–99:137. Cf. my discussion above in the Introduction, pp. xxii–xxiv.

uniqueness or unicity, and other things of this kind. These, he explicitly states, are proved in philosophy and are presupposed by faith.[4]

Certain comments should be made about this important passage. To begin, Thomas lists as first among the preambles to faith that are to be demonstrated the proof that God exists. There can be no doubt, therefore, that Aquinas was convinced that God's existence can be proved or demonstrated in philosophy. Secondly, he remarks that truths such as God's existence or God's uniqueness—preambles to faith—are proved or demonstrated in philosophy and presupposed by faith. One should not conclude from this either that one cannot believe in God unless one has already demonstrated his existence, or that it is an easy matter to work out a valid demonstration of God's existence.[5] What Thomas is rather setting forth here is an ideal for the adult mind whereby one would move from philosophically demonstrated conclusions (that God exists and other truths of this kind) to a mature act of faith in divinely revealed truth concerning God. The demonstration that God exists would not of itself be sufficient to establish the truth of revelation for the religious believer. For this an act of faith would also be required.[6]

If we may develop more fully one point just made in the preceding paragraph, while Thomas was convinced that unaided human reason can demonstrate God's existence, he did not regard this as a simple matter. In fact, in *Summa contra Gen-*

---

4. "Sic ergo in sacra doctrina philosophia possumus tripliciter uti: primo ad demonstrandum ea quae sunt praeambula fidei, quae necesse est in fide scire, ut ea quae naturalibus rationibus de Deo probantur, ut Deum esse, Deum esse unum, et alia huiusmodi vel de Deo vel de creaturis in philosophia probata, quae fides supponit" (Leon. 50.99:148–154). Since Thomas does not give a complete list of other things of this kind which human reason can demonstrate about God, one must turn to his writings to determine this in particular cases. See, for instance, my effort to show that omnipotence is one of these truths in "Thomas Aquinas on Demonstrating God's Omnipotence," *Revue internationale de philosophie* 52 (1998), pp. 227–47. And for a detailed examination of those truths about God which Aquinas attempts to establish by philosophical reasoning in SCG I see N. Kretzmann, *The Metaphysics of Theism: Aquinas's Natural Theology in Summa Contra Gentiles I* (Oxford, 1997).

5. Without wishing to enter into a theological analysis of Thomas's understanding of the act of faith, it will be enough here for us to recall his brief remarks in *De veritate*, q. 10, a. 12, and 3: ". . . dicendum quod veritas supra ens fundatur; unde sicut ens esse in communi est per se notum, ita et etiam veritatem esse. Non est autem per se notum nobis esse aliquod primum ens quod sit causa omnis entis quousque hoc vel fides accipiat, vel demonstratio probet; unde nec est per se notum omnem veritatem ab aliqua prima veritate esse. Unde non sequitur quod deum esse sit per se notum" (Leon. 22.2.341:206–214). More will be said below about Thomas's views concerning whether God's existence is self-evident. Also see Thomas's reply to arg. 4 (lines 215–220). On the difficulties involved in demonstrating God's existence see below for our discussion of SCG I, c. 4.

6. On the need for the will to enter into the act of faith see, for instance, *De veritate,* q. 10, a. 12, reply to arg. 6 *in contrarium* (Leon. 22.2.342:289–302). Note: ". . . quod enim credens assentit his quae credit, non provenit ex hoc quod eius intellectus sit terminatus ad illa credibilia virtute aliquorum principiorum, sed ex voluntate, quae inclinat intellectum ad hoc quod illis creditis assentiat. . . ." Also see *De veritate,* q. 14, a. 1 (Leon. 22.2.436–38, esp. 437:129–149). Cf. J. F. Ross, "Aquinas on Belief and Knowledge," in *Essays Honoring Allan B. Wolter,* W. A. Frank and G. J. Etzkorn, eds. (St. Bonaventure, N.Y., 1985), pp. 245–69.

tiles I, c. 4 he pursues a line of thinking which should always be kept in mind when one evaluates his various attempts to demonstrate God's existence. In this particular chapter Thomas is reflecting back upon the two different kinds of truths concerning God that are available to human beings which he has just distinguished in the preceding chapter. Certain truths concerning God completely surpass the capacities of unaided human reason. A prime illustration is the doctrine of the Trinity. If we are to accept such truths, it can only be because we believe that God has revealed them to us. Other truths concerning God can be discovered by natural reason, such as his existence and his uniqueness, etc. Thomas comments that the philosophers, guided by the light of natural reason, have succeeded in demonstrating such truths.[7]

This being so, one might ask whether it was fitting for God to reveal to us truths of the last-mentioned type. If unaided human reason can demonstrate them, there would seem to be no need for God to reveal them. It is to this issue that Thomas turns explicitly in c. 4. There he argues that it was indeed fitting for God to reveal even those truths concerning himself which unaided human reason can establish. If God had not done so, three major unhappy consequences *(inconvenientia)* would have resulted for the human race.[8]

First of all, few would in fact arrive at knowledge of God. In supporting this rather pessimistic analysis of the human condition, Thomas singles out three factors which would prevent most human beings from reaching such knowledge on purely philosophical grounds. Some are incapable of succeeding in such an effort because they lack the natural ability for philosophical inquiry. By no amount of effort could they arrive at this highest level of human knowing which consists in knowledge of God.[9] Others would be prevented from reaching knowledge of God's

---

7. SCG I, c. 3: "Quaedam namque vera sunt de Deo quae omnem facultatem humanae rationis excedunt, ut Deum esse trinum et unum. Quaedam vero sunt ad quae etiam ratio naturalis pertingere potest, sicut est Deum esse, Deum esse unum, et alia huiusmodi; quae etiam philosophi demonstrative de Deo probaverunt, ducti naturalis lumine rationis" (Ed. Leon. man., p. 2).

8. Ed. cit., pp. 3–4. Note in particular: "Sequerentur autem tria inconvenientia si huiusmodi veritas solummodo rationi inquirenda reliqueretur" (p. 4).

9. Ed. cit., p. 4. As Thomas puts this last-mentioned factor: "Quidam siquidem propter complexionis indispositionem, ex qua multi naturaliter sunt indispositi ad sciendum. . . ." In referring to *complexionis indispositionem* Thomas may be following an Avicennian theme according to which proper cognitive functioning depends to a considerable degree upon an appropriate balance of bodily humors and a balanced temperament. Thus within a more general discussion of dreams and their reliability, Avicenna remarks that the dreams of human beings of a temperate *complexio* are more reliable than those of a dry or humid or hot or cold *complexio*. See *Liber de Anima seu sextus de naturalibus: IV–V,* S. Van Riet, ed. (Louvain-Leiden, 1968), IV, c. 2, pp. 32:47–33:57. On the other hand, Thomas may have simply taken this directly from Moses Maimonides, to whom he is largely indebted in this general discussion, and who lists this under the fourth of his five causes which prevent one from beginning instruction with divine science. See n. 13 below for more on this. See in particular from the Latin version of Maimonides' *Guide, Dux seu Director dubitantium aut perplexorum* (Paris, 1520; repr. Frankfurt, 1964) I, c. 33, f. 13r: "Sunt autem multi in quibus est complexio naturalis, cum qua nullo modo convenit perfectio intellectus. . . ."

existence by the demands of practical life, that is, by their need to devote full time and attention to practical affairs or, in today's idiom, to earning a living.[10] Still others would fail in this effort because they are too lazy. Thomas comments that many things are presupposed for successful rational investigation about God. In fact, as he sees it, almost the whole of philosophy is in some way ordered to knowledge of God; it is for this reason that metaphysics, which deals with divine things, comes last among the parts of philosophy in the order of learning. (The reader will recall our remarks above in Ch. II about Thomas's views concerning the appropriate pedagogical order for learning metaphysics.) If this is so, considerable effort is required for such an undertaking. In Thomas's judgment, few would be willing to expend so much effort simply for the love of knowing.[11]

As a second unhappy consequence, Thomas observes that even those few individuals who did manage to arrive at natural knowledge of God would do so only after a long period of time had passed. This would be required because of the depth of the truth at issue, which human reason can grasp only after the intellect has been properly prepared through long practice, and because of the many things such knowledge presupposes. Moreover, during one's youth one is not in a good position to succeed in such an investigation, because one's soul is still too subject to the movements of the passions.[12]

As if this were not enough, Thomas singles out a third unhappy consequence which would follow if God had not chosen to reveal himself to human beings. Considerable falsity would be intermingled with human reason's findings concerning this issue because of the weakness of our intellects and because of what Thomas calls a mixing of phantasms. By this I take him to mean that because our knowledge begins with sense experience, and because images formed by the imagination, i.e., phantasms, are required for the intellect to perform its proper activities, it is easy for us to be deceived by these phantasms and to mistake such images for higher realities. This is especially likely when we are dealing with a subject which cannot be imagined adequately, i.e., a spiritual reality and an infinite one at that. Moreover, remarks Thomas, even truths which had been correctly demonstrated would remain in doubt for many, since they would fail to grasp the force of the demonstration and since they would see different things being taught by others who are generally thought to be wise. In other words, the scandal generated by disputes between philosophers would deter many from accepting what was truly demonstrated. And

10. Ed. cit., p. 4.

11. Ibid. Note in particular: "Ad cognitionem enim eorum quae de Deo ratio investigare potest, multa praecognoscere oportet: cum fere totius philosophiae consideratio ad Dei cognitionem ordinetur; propter quod metaphysica, quae circa divina versatur, inter philosophiae partes ultima remanet addiscenda."

12. Ibid. Thomas expresses the final point in the following terms: "Tum etiam propter hoc quod tempore iuventutis, dum diversis motibus passionum anima fluctuat, non est apta ad tam altae veritatis cognitionem, sed *in quiescendo fit prudens et sciens,* ut dicitur in VII *Physic.*" See *Physics* VII, c. 3 (247b 11–12).

among truths which had been demonstrated, falsity might still be intermingled with truth in that something might be thought to have been demonstrated when in fact it had been established only by probable or even by sophistical argumentation.[13]

Thomas concludes, therefore, that it was most fitting for divine providence to reveal such truths to human beings so that all might easily arrive at knowledge of God, and this without hesitation and error.[14] In making this statement, of course, Thomas is writing as a believer in the Christian revelation. But in holding that unaided human reason *can* demonstrate God's existence, even though it succeeds in doing so only relatively rarely, he is surely speaking as a philosopher as well.

With these two sources in mind we may now turn to other contexts where Thomas explicitly attempts to show that it is possible for us to prove or to demonstrate that God exists. The final proof of this, of course, will be the force of the philosophical argumentation he can muster for this conclusion. At the same time, he frequently judges it necessary to eliminate certain objections which might be raised in advance, on a priori grounds, as it were, against this possibility. From his earliest consideration of this in his Commentary on I *Sentences* until his mature treatments of the same, he always rejects what he regards as two extreme positions—agnosticism concerning our knowledge of God's existence, and any view which would hold that such a demonstration is impossible for the opposite reason, that is, because God's existence is self-evident to us.

In his Commentary on Bk I of the *Sentences* Thomas addresses this issue in commenting on distinction 3. Because this is a commentary, the general organiza-

---

13. As Thomas puts the first point: "Tertium inconveniens est quod investigationi rationis humanae plerumque falsitas admiscetur, propter debilitatem intellectus nostri in iudicando, et phantasmatum permixtionem" (ed. cit., p. 4). For an interesting study of Thomas's evident usage of Maimonides' *Guide of the Perplexed* I, c. 34, in developing his own treatment in SCG I, c. 4 and in parallel texts, see P. Synave, "La révélation des vérités naturelles d'après saint Thomas d'Aquin," in *Mélanges Mandonnet,* Vol. 1 (Paris, 1930), pp. 327–70. For Maimonides see the translation by S. Pines (Chicago, 1963), pp. 72–79. For the medieval Latin version see *Dux seu Director dubitantium* I, c. 33, ff. 12v–13v. In the chapter in question Maimonides lists and develops at length five causes that prevent one's beginning instruction with divine science, indicating things literally as they are, and presenting this to the many. While Thomas's treatment in SCG I, c. 4 involves considerable reorganization and reworking of the Maimonidean presentation, he was even more dependent upon Rabbi Moses in earlier treatments of this in *In III Sent.*, d. 24, a. 3, "ad primam quaest." (Moos ed., Vol. 3, pp. 773–74); *In De Trinitate*, q. 3, a. 1 (Leon. 50.108:131–163); and *De veritate*, q. 14, a. 10 (Leon. 22.2.467:184–201). At the same time, the treatment in SCG I, c. 4 strongly influences the summarized presentations he offers in ST I, q. 1, a. 1, and ST II–II, q. 2, a. 4. Synave mistakenly thought that the 1520 Latin version was translated only at that time by Agostino Giustiniani. But, as W. Dunphy points out, the first Latin translation was produced in the 1230s from the second Hebrew translation of the Arabic original. It was this thirteenth-century Latin version that Giustiniani edited and which was published in 1520. See his "Maimonides and Aquinas on Creation: A Critique of Their Historians," in *Graceful Reason: Essays in Ancient and Medieval Philosophy Presented to Joseph Owens, CSSR,* L. Gerson, ed. (Toronto, 1983), p. 363, n. 7.

14. "Salubriter ergo divina providit clementia ut ea etiam quae ratio investigare potest, fide tenenda praeciperet: ut sic omnes de facili possent divinae cognitionis participes esse, et absque dubitatione et errore" (SCG I, c. 4, p. 4).

tion of Thomas's discussion is at least in part controlled by the text of the Lombard. In his division of the first part of the text of distinction 3, Thomas finds Peter establishing the unity of the divine essence by natural arguments, although not the Trinity of Persons.[15] He notes that Peter first cites St. Paul's Letter to the Romans (1:20): "The invisible things of God are seen, being understood by the creature *(creatura)* of the world through those things which have been made, his everlasting power and divinity."[16] Thomas next finds the Lombard offering proof or argumentation for this point, i.e., the unity of the divine essence, and in fact Thomas breaks this down into four arguments. He correlates these four arguments with the three-fold Dionysian approach to knowledge of God based on (1) the way of causality; (2) the way of negation; and (3) the way of eminence. Then, having completed his division of the Lombard's text, Thomas opens q. 1 of his Commentary on this distinction with the comment that Peter is here showing how one arrives at knowledge of God through vestiges which are present in creatures.[17] Thomas himself subdivides the discussion concerning our knowledge of God into four articles, and by doing so sets the stage for his more personal examination of the kind of knowledge we can have of God by reasoning from creatures.

In q. 1, a. 1 Thomas simply asks whether God can be known by a created intellect. Various arguments are offered as objections against this possibility, and Thom-

15. Mandonnet ed., Vol. 1, p. 88: ". . . in prima ostendit unitatem essentiae per rationes naturales. . . ."

16. For the text as cited by Peter see p. 80: "Apostolus namque ait ad Rom., I, 20, quod *invisibilia Dei, a creatura mundi per ea quae facta sunt, intellecta conspiciuntur, sempiterna quoque virtus eius et divinitas.*" This text poses a problem concerning the meaning of the phrase *a creatura mundi,* a problem of which both Peter and Thomas are aware. As Peter interprets it, it means "man," either because he can view the invisible things of God by means of his intellect or because he can do so by means of other creatures. For Thomas's citation of the same text in an opening argument, which he accepts, see d. 3, q. 1, a. 3 (p. 95). There the argument repeats Peter's identification of *creatura* as "man." But for this reading along with another which is in accord with the accepted translation of the passage today ("For *since the creation* of the world his invisible attributes are clearly seen . . .") see Thomas's Commentary on Paul's *Letter to the Romans* in *S. Thomae Aquinatis doctoris angelici in omnes S. Pauli Apostoli Epistolas Commentaria,* Vol. I, c. 1, lect. 6, p. 22. There Thomas observes that the phrase *a creatura mundi* may be taken to refer to man or even to the whole of creation. But he then notes that instead of referring to that which has been created *(ipsa res creata),* it may rather be referred to *rerum creatio* so as to mean "from the creation of the world."

17. As Thomas presents Peter's reasoning here, the being *(esse)* of any creature derives from another. Hence we are led from a creature to that cause from which the creature's being comes. But this may be pursued either with respect to that which is received (the way of causality) or with respect to the mode or way in which it is received, since it is received imperfectly. This second alternative in turn can be followed according to the mode of negation, whereby we deny imperfection of God, or according to the mode of eminence whereby that which is received in a creature is more perfectly realized in the Creator. Thomas applies the threefold Dionysian way to the four kinds of argumentation he finds in Peter: (1) an argument based on causality; (2) an argument based on the presence of imperfection in creatures (the way of negation) and the need to conclude to the existence of something which is perfect; (3) an argument based on eminence as applied to being; (4) another argument based on eminence but as applied to knowledge (op. cit., pp. 88–89). For discussion see Van Steenberghen, *Le problème de l'existence de Dieu,* pp. 13–17. For Thomas's text of d. 3, q. 1 see ed. cit., p. 90.

as's replies to some of these are worth noting. Before turning to these, however, we should mention a point made in his solution. In this discussion Thomas is not concerned with showing that God can be known by us immediately in his essence, but only with whether we can know him in any way at all. Thomas's answer as he sets it forth here is that God can be known by us, but not in such fashion that we can grasp or comprehend his essence. Here we see foreshadowed a position Thomas will often defend in subsequent discussions: we can know that God is, and what God is not, but not what God is.[18]

According to the second objection, God is more distant from any intelligible object which is accessible to us than is an intelligible object from an object of the senses. But no sense power can grasp an intelligible object. Therefore God cannot be known by the human intellect. In replying to this Thomas admits that in terms of his nature God is more distant from any other intelligible object than is such an object from an object of the senses. Nonetheless, from the standpoint of knowability there is greater agreement between God and any other intelligible object than there is between the latter and an object of the senses. For what is separate from matter can be known as an intelligible object. But what is material is known as something sensible. Hence, while Thomas does not spell this out in detail, he is eliminating an argument against his view that God is knowable in some way by the human intellect. He does not yet indicate how and to what extent.[19]

In replying to the third objection, Thomas makes a somewhat puzzling remark. The objection points out that all knowledge occurs through some kind of species. By means of such a species the knower is rendered like the thing known. But no species can be abstracted from God, since he is most simple; therefore, God is not knowable. Thomas replies that any such species by means of which knowledge takes place is present in a knowing power according to the mode of that knowing power. When the intellect knows objects which are more material than the intellect itself, the intelligible species of such objects in the intellect are simpler than are the material objects themselves which are known. Hence such objects are known by the process of abstraction. But God and angels are simpler than the human intellect. Therefore any species produced in the human intellect by means of which it knows God or an angel is less simple than the object known thereby. Given this, we are not said to understand such objects by abstraction but by an "impression" of the objects themselves upon our intelligences. Thomas does not explain here what he understands by this "impression," and it sounds surprisingly like certain language used by Augustine in developing his own doctrine of illumination.[20]

---

18. "Et ideo dicimus quod Deus cognoscibile est; non autem ita est cognoscibilis, ut essentia sua comprehendatur" (ed. cit., p. 91). For fuller discussion see Ch. XIII, Section 1 below.

19. Ed. cit., p. 90 (obj. 2); pp. 91–92 (reply).

20. See p. 90 (obj. 3); p. 92 (reply). For the troubling passage see p. 92: "Unde non dicimur cognoscere ea per abstractionem, sed per impressionem ipsorum in intelligentias nostras." Van Steenberghen refers to the Neoplatonic "touch" of this passage and notes the difficulty in determin-

Additional light is cast on this by Thomas's reply to the fifth objection. This objection appeals to Aristotle's *De anima* to the effect that phantasms are related to the intellect as colors to sight. Since corporeal vision cannot see anything without color, our intellect cannot understand anything without phantasms. Because no phantasm can be formed of God, it seems that God cannot be known by our intellect.[21]

In replying to this Thomas comments that Aristotle is speaking of the kind of intellectual knowledge which is connatural to us during the present life. In terms of such knowledge, Thomas agrees that God is not known to us except by means of phantasms. Any such phantasm will not be a phantasm of God himself but of some effect by means of which we move on to knowledge of him. But this is not to deny that there can be another kind of intellectual knowledge which is not natural to us and which is given to us in a higher way. Since such knowledge is given through the influence of the divine light, Thomas concedes that phantasms will not be necessary for it. In introducing this theme, Thomas must have in mind a kind of knowledge which differs not only from our natural knowledge, but even from that given to us through revelation. For as he implies elsewhere, even revealed knowledge depends on phantasms.[22] In light of this reply, I would suggest that it

---

ing precisely what Thomas has in mind and what particular historical influence he is reflecting. See *Le problème de l'existence de Dieu*, p. 20. Augustine sometimes refers to notions such as wisdom or happiness as impressed upon our minds, presumably through the process of illumination. See, for instance, *De libero arbitrio*, Bk II, 9, 26, 103 (CCSL Vol. 29, p. 254): "Sicut ergo antequam beati simus mentibus tamen nostris impressa est notio beatitatis—per hanc enim scimus fidenterque et sine ulla dubitatione dicimus beatos nos esse velle—, ita etiam priusquam sapientes simus, sapientiae notionem in mente habemus impressam, per quam unus quisque nostrum, si interrogetur velitne esse sapiens, sine ulla caligine dubitationis se velle respondet." However, here Augustine seems to be speaking of natural illumination while, as we shall suggest, Thomas's text appears to envision some higher kind of knowing. For some brief but pertinent remarks concerning this in Augustine see R. A. Markus, "Augustine: Reason and Illumination," in *The Cambridge History of Later Greek and Early Medieval Philosophy*, A. H. Armstrong, ed. (Cambridge, 1967), pp. 365–68.

21. Ed. cit., pp. 90–91. The objection's citation from Aristotle, *De anima* III, text 1, is not literal.

22. Ed. cit., p. 92. Here Thomas refers to Aristotle, *De anima* III, text 30, for which see c. 7 (431a 14–17). Note in particular: "Sed per hoc non removetur quin cognitio aliqua possit esse intellectus, non per viam naturalem nobis, sed altiorem, scilicet per influentiam divini luminis ad quam phantasma non est necessarium." See *In De Trinitate*, q. 6, a. 3. There Thomas is making the point that in this life we cannot arrive at quidditative knowledge of God or of other separate substances through our natural way of knowing or through revelation. Even revelation must be in accord with the way or mode in which we know, i.e., by means of likenesses taken from sensible things. See Leon. 50.167:99–113. Also see q. 1, a. 2, which closely parallels in more structured fashion much of the thinking of d. 3, q. 1, a. 1 of the Commentary on *I Sent*. Note that there, too, Thomas rejects the view that God cannot be known by us in any way in this life, but, as we will see below in Ch. XIII, he denies that we can attain quidditative knowledge of God during our earthly sojourn (Leon. 50.84–85). There he also refers to two ways in which something might be known by means of a form derived from that thing, i.e., either by abstraction, or because the form of the thing known is "impressed" on the knower by the object known, as Avicenna maintains we understand intelligences by their *impressiones* on us (p. 84:52–63). Thomas also observes there that the human mind can be strengthened in its knowledge of God by a new illumination such as the light of faith and the gift of wisdom and understanding (p. 85:118–124).

is to this kind of higher knowledge that Thomas was also referring in his reply to the third objection. Presumably he wants at least to leave open the possibility for the kind of knowledge involved in mystical experience, and perhaps also in prophetic revelation.

In a. 2 Thomas asks whether God's existence is self-evident *(per se notum)*. In the corpus of his reply he introduces an important distinction. In discussing our knowledge of anything we may speak of that thing simply as it is in itself, or insofar as it is with respect to us. If we are speaking of God as he is in himself, his existence is self-evident even as he is intelligible of himself and not by being rendered intelligible in the way we make material things actually intelligible through the process of abstraction.[23]

But if we are speaking of God in relation to us, an additional distinction is in order. By his existence we may have in mind nothing other than a created likeness or participation of God as we find this in creatures. If this is what we mean, we can say that his existence, i.e., the existence of his likeness in creatures, is known *per se* or self-evident. Nothing is known except through its own truth which depends upon God as its exemplar. That truth exists is self-evident, Thomas maintains, and this we discover, he implies, in knowing creatures.[24]

On the other hand, we may have in mind God as he subsists in himself as something incorporeal and not merely as he is expressed by the creatures which imitate him. Taken in this way, and this is the normal understanding for today's reader, God's existence is not self-evident to us. In fact, remarks Thomas, many have denied that God exists, such as those philosophers who did not admit the existence of a supreme efficient cause. He mentions Democritus and others, relying for this information on Aristotle's *Metaphysics* I. This is so, Thomas continues, because those things which are self-evident to us are immediately based on our sense experience. For instance, once we have experienced a whole and a part, we immediately know that any whole is greater than its part. We know such principles as soon as we understand their terms. But upon seeing sensible objects we do not arrive at knowledge of God unless we reason from effect to cause.[25]

---

23. Ed. cit., pp. 93–94. Note in particular: "Loquendo igitur de Deo secundum *seipsum, esse est per se notum, et ipse est per se intellectus, non per hoc quod faciamus ipsum intelligibile,* sicut materialia facimus intelligibilia in actu" (p. 94). After noting the apparent problem with the part of the text italicized here, Van Steenberghen proposes the following conjectural corrections: "Loquendo igitur de Deo secundum *se, ipsum esse est per se notum, et ipse est per se intelligibilis,* non per hoc quod faciamus ipsum *intelligibilem* . . ." *(Le problème,* p. 21, n. 8). I have followed Van Steenberghen's proposed emendation.

24. Ed. cit., p. 94: "Aut secundum suam similitudinem et participationem; et hoc modo ipsum esse, est per se notum; nihil enim cognoscitur nisi per veritatem suam, quae est a Deo exemplata; veritatem autem esse, est per se notum."

25. Ibid. Note in particular: "Aut secundum suppositum, id est, considerando ipsum Deum, secundum quod est in natura sua quid incorporeum; et hoc modo non est per se notum. . . ." For Aristotle's reference to Democritus see *Metaphysics* I, c. 4 (985b 4–20).

Here we have in its essentials the position Thomas will continue to defend throughout his career, even if he presents it somewhat more simply and clearly in later writings. God's existence is self-evident in itself because his essence is his act of being *(esse)*. But God's existence is not self-evident to us since, as Thomas puts this in *Summa contra Gentiles* I, c. 11, God's essence or what God is remains unknown to us. As he explains there, the proposition that a whole is greater than its part is self-evident in itself. But it would remain unknown to anyone who could not understand the notion of a whole. It is within this general context of showing that God's existence is not self-evident to us that Thomas also turns to Anselm's argumentation in his *Proslogion*.[26]

Not only does Thomas follow this procedure in the *Summa contra Gentiles;* he operates in similar fashion in replying to objection 4 in our text from his Commentary on I *Sentences* (d. 3, q. 1, a. 2); in a brief reference in his Commentary on the *De Trinitate* (q. 1, a. 3, ad 6) though there he is rather attempting to show that God is not the first thing we know; in the corpus and in his reply to objection 2 in *De veritate*, q. 10, a. 12; and in the well-known discussion from *Summa theologiae* I, q. 2, a. 1, ad 2. While Thomas's discussion of Anselm's argumentation has understandably received some attention, it is important for the reader to remember that in none of these contexts does Thomas single it out for its own sake by addressing a specific article or question to it. In each case he presents and then criticizes the Anselmian approach as one illustration of a more general position which he is rejecting.

As Thomas explains in *De veritate* q. 10, a. 12, some have held that God's existence is not self-evident and that it cannot be demonstrated. It can only be accepted on faith. Thomas quickly rejects this position as false, and comments that God's existence has in fact been proved by philosophers with irrefutable arguments. Others, such as Avicenna, hold that God's existence is not self-evident but that it can be demonstrated. Still others such as Anselm think that God's existence is self-evident insofar as no one can truly think within himself that God does not exist, even though he may utter the words externally and even internally think of the words by which he states this. Thomas himself finds some truth in each of the two last-mentioned positions. Again he distinguishes between that which is self-evident in itself and that which is self-evident to us. That God exists is self-evident only in the first way, but not in the second. Therefore, if this truth is to be known philosophically it must be demonstrated, and by reasoning from effect to cause.[27]

26. Ed. Leon. man., p. 9. Note: "Nam simpliciter quidem Deum esse per se notum est: cum hoc ipsum quod Deus est, sit suum esse. Sed quia hoc ipsum quod Deus est mente concipere non possumus, remanet ignotum quoad nos. Sicut omne totum sua parte maius esse, per se notum est simpliciter: ei autem qui rationem totius mente non conciperet, oporteret esse ignotum." Here Thomas is responding to an argument offered in c. 10 (p. 8) in support of the claim that God's existence is self-evident, which incorporates reasoning from Anselm's *Proslogion*, c. 2.

27. Leon. 22.2.340:122–143. Note his remark concerning the first position: "Prima quidem opinio manifeste falsa apparet: invenitur enim hoc quod est Deum esse, demonstrationibus irrefragabilibus

As he explains, for a proposition to be self-evident in itself, nothing more is required than that its predicate be included within the intelligible content of its subject. Given this, one cannot understand the subject without also seeing that the predicate is contained therein. But for such a proposition to be self-evident to us, the intelligible content *(ratio)* of the subject must be known to us. Thus certain propositions are self-evident to all: this is because their subjects are such that an understanding of them is given to everyone. So it is that everyone knows what a whole is and what a part is, and hence understands that every whole is greater than its part. But some propositions are self-evident only to the wise, since they alone can grasp the intelligible content of the terms of these propositions.[28]

Thomas next turns to Boethius's *De Hebdomadibus* for additional support for the distinction he has just made. According to Boethius certain conceptions are common or general in the sense that they are available for everyone. If you take away equals from equals, equals remain. Other conceptions are accessible only to the learned, such as, for instance, the statement that incorporeal things are not present in place. Only the learned will grasp this, because the uneducated will be unable to rise above the level of the imagination so as to understand the meaning of the incorporeal.[29]

As Thomas sees things, existence *(esse)* is included within the essence of no creature since the act of being *(esse)* of any creature is distinct from its quiddity. (Here we have the converse of the reasoning reflected in his *intellectus essentiae* argument for the real distinction as presented in his *De ente et essentia*.) Given this, the existence of no creature can be said to be self-evident, not even in itself. God's existence *(esse)* is included within the intelligible content of his essence, since in him the act of being and essence *(esse* and *quod est)* are identical. This is why God's existence is self-evident in and of itself. But since God's quiddity remains unknown to us, his existence is not evident to us but needs to be demonstrated. On the other hand, in the life to come those who enjoy the beatific vision will see the divine essence. God's existence will then be much more self-evident to them than is the principle of noncontradiction to us here and now.[30]

By so reasoning Thomas has also offered his reply to another argument in support of the claim that God's existence is self-evident to us. As Thomas presents this argument in his later discussion in *Summa contra Gentiles* I, c. 10, because God's essence is his *esse,* the answer to the question "What is God?" is identical with the answer to the question "Does God exist?" In the statement "God is," the predicate

etiam a philosophis probatum. . . ." As regards his own position, note: "Est enim dupliciter aliquid per se notum, scilicet secundum se et quoad nos. Deum igitur esse secundum se est per se notum, non autem quoad nos; et ideo nobis necessarium est ad hoc cognoscendum demonstrationes habere ex effectibus sumptas" (p. 340:141–149).

28. Leon. 22.2.340:149–341:164.

29. Leon. 22.2.341:164–178. For Boethius see his *De Hebdomadibus* in *The Theological Tractates,* p. 40. For Thomas's Commentary on this see *In De Hebdomadibus,* I (Leon. 50.269:124–185).

30. Leon. 22.2.341:174–189.

is identical with the subject or at least included within it. Therefore, that God exists is self-evident. In replying to this Thomas repeats the point that for those who directly see the divine essence, it is self-evident that God exists. But since we do not enjoy such knowledge in this life, we must move to knowledge of him by reasoning from his effects.[31] Thomas makes fundamentally the same point in *Summa theologiae* I, q. 2, a. 1c. Again he concludes that the proposition "God exists" is self-evident in itself but not to us, since we do not know what God is.[32]

2. Aquinas and the Anselmian Argumentation

Highly influential on the subsequent history of philosophical discussion of God's existence was the reasoning developed by St. Anselm in his *Proslogion,* cc. 2 and 3. Since Thomas refers to this line of reasoning in each of the five passages already mentioned, it may be of interest here for us to turn briefly to his treatment of the Anselmian approach. Even before doing so, we can easily anticipate his re-action. As we have now seen him arguing repeatedly, God's existence is not self-evident to us but must be demonstrated by reasoning from effect to cause. Whether or not one agrees with Thomas's inclusion of Anselm among those who regard God's existence as self-evident, one can hardly reduce the argumentation of the *Proslogion* to a procedure that reasons from effect to cause. At the same time, in rejecting any kind of a priori approach to God's existence, and in rejecting Anselm's argumentation, Thomas will be forced almost by process of elimination to adopt ways which move from effect to cause.

Thomas's presentation and critique of Anselm's argumentation has sometimes been criticized for not distinguishing between the procedures used in cc. 2 and 3 respectively of the *Proslogion.* This same point is made by others who contend that Thomas did not appreciate or take into account sufficiently the distinctively modal approach followed by Anselm in *Proslogion,* c. 3. On the other hand, Thomas's treatment of the Anselmian argumentation has its defenders.[33] Here we shall be

---

31. Ed. cit., p. 8, arg. 3. For Thomas's reply see c. 11 (p. 9): "Nam sicut nobis per se notum est quod totum sua parte sit maius, sic videntibus ipsam divinam essentiam per se notissimum est Deum esse, ex hoc quod sua essentia est suum esse. Sed quia eius essentiam videre non possumus, ad eius esse cognoscendum non per seipsum, sed per eius effectus pervenimus."

32. Leon. 4.27–28. Note: "Dico ergo quod haec propositio, *Deus est,* quantum in se est, per se nota est: quia praedicatum est idem cum subiecto; Deus enim est suum esse, ut infra patebit. Sed quia nos non scimus de Deo quid est, non est nobis per se nota. . . ."

33. For reference to some of this literature as well as for a sympathetic investigation of Thomas's own texts concerning Anselm see M. R. Cosgrove, "Thomas Aquinas on Anselm's Argument," *Review of Metaphysics* 27 (1974), pp. 513–30. Among this literature the reader may consult G. Matthews, "Aquinas on Saying That God Doesn't Exist," *The Monist* 47 (1963), pp. 472–77 (while critical of Thomas's appeal to the distinction between the two types of self-evident propositions in criticizing Anselm's reasoning, Matthews finds another criticism in SCG I, c. 11 more telling); C. Hartshorne, *Anselm's Discovery: A Re-Examination of the Ontological Proof for God's Existence* (La Salle, Ill., 1965, repr. 1991), pp. 154–64 (an extremely negative evaluation of Aquinas's critique). Also see the disserta-

guided by Thomas's own texts, and shall examine them according to their chronological sequence.

In his Commentary on I *Sent.*, d. 3, q. 1, a. 2, Thomas cites Anselm while considering a fourth argument in support of the claim that God's existence is self-evident. That is self-evident (known *per se*) which cannot be thought not to exist. But God cannot be thought not to exist. Therefore God's existence is self-evident. The middle is proven from Anselm's *Proslogion*. God is that than which a greater cannot be thought. But that which cannot be thought not to exist is greater than that which can be thought not to exist. Therefore God cannot be thought not to exist.[34] Thomas notes that this same point can be argued for in another way. Nothing can be understood without its quiddity, for instance, human being without rational mortal animal. But God's quiddity is his existence *(esse)* as Avicenna maintains. Therefore God cannot be thought not to exist.[35]

In replying to this line of argumentation, Thomas comments that Anselm's reasoning should be interpreted in the following way. After we understand God, we cannot think both that God exists and that he is thought not to exist. But from this it does not follow that someone cannot deny his existence or think that God does not exist. For someone may think that nothing of this kind exists, that is, that than which no greater can be thought. Hence Anselm's argument operates under the presupposition that there is indeed something than which no greater can be thought. In other words, the argument succeeds only if we already presuppose God's existence.[36]

---

tion by W. Bassler, published in *Franziskanische Studien* 55 (1973), pp. 97–190; 56 (1974), pp. 1–26, under the title "Die Kritik des Thomas von Aquin am ontologischen Gottesbeweis" (favorable to Aquinas); and K. Flasch, "Die Beurteilung des Anselmianischen Arguments bei Thomas von Aquin," *Analecta Anselmiana* IV, 1 (1975), pp. 111–25 (with additional bibliography, pp. 111–12, n. 1). Flasch, too, is critical of Thomas's appreciation and evaluation of Anselm's argument.

34. Mandonnet ed., Vol. 1, p. 93. Note in particular: "Probatio mediae est per Anselmum, *Proslog.* (cap. xv . . .): Deus est quo maius cogitari non potest. Sed illud quod non potest cogitari non esse, est maius eo quod potest cogitari non esse. Ergo Deus non potest cogitari non esse." The explicit reference to the *Proslogion* is missing from the Parma ed. (for which, see Busa ed., Vol. 1, p. 10c). That edition adds to the last sentence we have quoted: "cum sit illud, quo nihil maius cogitari potest." In any event, the correct reference should be to *Proslog.*, c. 3, for which see Anselm, *Opera omnia*, F. S. Schmitt, ed. (Stuttgart-Bad Canstatt, 1968), T. I, vol. 1, pp. 101–2 (cc. 2–3).

35. Mandonnet ed., p. 93. There a reference is given in the text to the Pseudo-Avicennian *De intelligentiis*, c. 1, though this reference is missing from the Parma ed. (Busa ed., Vol. 1, p. 10c). For discussion of a work announced under this title but also referred to as *Liber Avicennae de primis et secundis substantiis* in the 1508 Venice ed. see R. de Vaux, *Notes et textes sur l'Avicennisme latin aux confins des XIIe–XIIIe siècles* (Paris, 1934), c. 7. There he notes the difficulty of finding even in his critical edition of this apocryphal work the texts to which Thomas refers in his Commentaries on I and II *Sentences* and concludes that it is not the work cited by Thomas (pp. 64–65).

36. Mandonnet ed., p. 94: "Ad quartum dicendum, quod ratio Anselmi ita intelligenda est. Postquam intelligimus Deum, non potest intelligi quod sit Deus, et possit cogitari non esse; sed tamen ex hoc non sequitur quod aliquis non possit negare vel cogitare, Deum non esse; potest enim cogitare nihil huiusmodi esse quo maius cogitari non possit; et ideo ratio sua procedit ex hac suppositione, quod supponatur aliquid esse quo maius cogitari non potest."

In presenting Anselm's argument in this context, Thomas has reported him as concluding that God cannot be thought of as not existing. If we may distinguish Anselm's procedure in *Proslogion,* c. 3 from that which he follows in c. 2, as certain recent interpreters insist we should, here it is the version from c. 3 which is represented. Hence even in this earliest treatment Thomas was aware of the version from c. 3 and apparently even of its modal character (if we mean thereby that it concludes that God cannot even be thought of as not existing and, therefore, that he exists necessarily).[37] At the same time it is clear that Thomas does not accept this as a valid way of demonstrating God's existence, or of showing that God's existence is self-evident to us (which, it will be recalled, is Thomas's primary purpose in considering it here).

A very brief reference to this line of argumentation appears in q. 1, a. 3 of his Commentary on the *De Trinitate.* As part of the sixth argument in support of the claim that God is the first thing known by the human mind, Thomas again presents Anselm as holding that God cannot be thought not to be. Once more, therefore, we have a reference to the thinking from Anselm's *Proslogion,* c. 3, even though in this context Thomas is content merely to mention this as Anselm's position without reproducing his argumentation for it.[38] In replying to this, as we have already seen, Thomas observes that God's existence is indeed self-evident in itself, since his essence is his *esse;* and, he adds, in what appears to be an accommodated reading, this is what Anselm had in mind. But, he concludes, it is not self-evident to us. We lack knowledge of the divine essence during the present life.[39]

In *De veritate* q. 10, a. 12 Thomas presents the following as a second argument in support of the claim that God's existence is self-evident to us. God is that than which no greater can be thought, as Anselm holds. But that which cannot be thought not to exist is greater than that which can be thought not to exist. Therefore God cannot be thought not to exist. Here again, therefore, we have a reference to Anselm's formulation as he presents it in c. 3 of the *Proslogion,* and, albeit in summarized fashion, to the heart of the argument rather than merely to its conclusion.[40]

---

37. See Hartshorne, *Anselm's Discovery,* pp. 85–108, for a good statement of the philosophical significance of the version in *Proslogion,* c. 3. For more on recent discussions of Anselm's argument see A. C. McGill, "Recent Discussions of Anselm's Argument," in *The Many-Faced Argument,* J. H. Hick and A. C. McGill, eds. (New York, 1965), pp. 33–110. Also see J. Hopkins, *A Companion to the Study of St. Anselm* (Minneapolis, 1972), pp. 67–89.

38. ". . . nec potest Deus cogitari non esse, ut dicit Anselmus. Ergo Deus est primum quod a nobis cognoscitur" (Leon. 50.86:56–58).

39. Leon. 50.88:198–202: "Ad sextum dicendum, quod Deum esse, quantum est in se est per se notum, quia sua essentia est suum esse—et hoc modo loquitur Anselmus—non autem nobis, quia eius essentiam non videmus."

40. "Praeterea, 'Deus est id quo maius cogitari non potest', ut Anselmus dicit; sed illud quod non potest cogitari non esse est maius illo quod potest cogitari non esse; ergo Deus non potest cogitari non esse" (Leon. 22.2.339:10–14). Not explicitly stated but implied is the point that if that than which no greater can be thought could be thought of as not existing, it would not be that than which no greater can be thought. See Anselm, *Proslogion,* c. 3 (ed. cit., p. 102:9–10).

Thomas replies that one might reason in this way if it were true from God's standpoint that his existence is not self-evident. In fact, Thomas continues, it is rather from our standpoint that God can be thought not to exist. (In other words, as Thomas has already established in the corpus of this article, God's existence is self-evident in itself but not to us.) Thomas explains that this is owing to the fact that we fall short in knowing things which are most knowable in themselves. This is why the fact that God can be thought not to exist does not militate against the fact that God is that than which no greater can be thought.[41] In other words, against the heart of Anselm's claim in c. 3 of the *Proslogion,* Thomas maintains that it is not contradictory for us to say that that than which no greater can be thought can itself be thought of as not existing. This is because God's existence is self-evident in itself (hence viewed in himself he is that than which no greater can be thought) and yet it is not self-evident to us (hence we can think of him as not existing).

In *Summa contra Gentiles* I, c. 10 Thomas offers two versions of the Anselmian argument in support of the more general claim that it is self-evident that God exists. The first of these follows the reasoning of *Proslogion,* c. 2. By the name God we understand something than which no greater can be thought. This understanding is formed in the intellect by anyone who hears and understands the name of God. Therefore it is clear that God exists at least in that person's intellect. But God cannot exist in the intellect alone; for what exists both in the intellect and in reality is greater than that which exists in the intellect alone. But the very meaning of the name God shows that nothing is greater than God. Therefore, that God exists is self-evident, as is clear from the meaning of his name—that than which no greater can be thought.[42]

As a second argument to prove that God's existence is self-evident, Thomas presents a version that depends heavily on *Proslogion,* c. 3. It can be thought that there is something which cannot be thought not to exist. Such a thing is clearly greater than that which can be thought not to exist. If God could be thought not to exist, something could be thought of which is greater than God. Therefore, since

---

41. "Ad secundum dicendum quod ratio illa procederet si esset ex parte ipsius quod non est per se notum; nunc autem quod potest cogitari non esse est ex parte nostra qui sumus deficientes ad cognoscendum ea quae sunt in se notissima. Unde hoc quod Deus potest cogitari non esse, non impedit quin etiam sit id quo maius cogitari non possit" (Leon. 22.2.341:198–205). Here my reading differs considerably from that implied by Hartshorne's comment: ". . . however, *where he* [Thomas] *is explicitly rejecting* the *Proof* (in the two *Summas*) he mentions only Prosl. II . . ." (*Anselm's Discovery,* p. 155).

42. "Nam nomine Dei intelligimus aliquid quo maius cogitari non potest. Hoc autem in intellectu formatur ab eo qui audit et intelligit nomen Dei: ut sic saltem in intellectu iam Deum esse oporteat. Nec potest in intellectu solum esse: nam quod in intellectu et re est, maius est eo quod in solo intellectu est; Deo autem nihil esse maius ipsa nominis ratio demonstrat. Unde restat quod Deum esse per se notum est, quasi ex ipsa significatione manifestur" (Ed. Leon. man., p. 8).

this would be opposed to the very meaning of the name God, i.e., that than which no greater can be thought, the argument concludes that it is self-evident that God exists.[43]

In criticizing the first formulation (based on *Proslogion*, c. 2), Thomas counters that it is not evident to all who grant God's existence that God is that than which no greater can be thought. Thus many of the ancients identified the world with God. Nor is this meaning included among the interpretations offered for the name God by John Damascene in his *De fide orthodoxa*.[44] Moreover, if for the sake of discussion we grant that by the name God everyone understands that than which no greater can be thought, it does not follow from this that such a being actually exists in reality. A thing which is named and the meaning of its name must be posited in the same way. Thus from the fact that the mind conceives what is expressed by this name God, it does not immediately follow that God exists in any way except in the intellect. In other words, Thomas is reasoning that because the meaning of the name God is posited in the intellect, the thing signified thereby cannot be assumed to exist in any other way except in the intellect. Nor will it be necessary for that than which no greater can be thought to exist except in the intellect. It will not follow from this that something than which no greater can be thought exists in reality. Indeed, whatever may exist in reality or in the mind, it is not unfitting to admit that something still greater can be thought except for someone who already grants that there exists in reality something than which no greater can be thought.[45]

Against the second formulation based on *Proslogion*, c. 3 Thomas counters that it does not follow that something can be thought to be greater than God if God himself can be thought not to exist. The fact that God can be thought not to exist does not arise from any imperfection or lack of certitude in his own being, since his existence is most evident in itself; it arises from the weakness of our intellect

---

43. "Cogitari quidem potest quod aliquid sit quod non possit cogitari non esse. Quod maius est evidenter eo quod potest cogitari non esse. Sic ergo Deo aliquid maius cogitari posset, si ipse posset cogitari non esse. Quod est contra rationem nominis. Relinquitur igitur quod Deum esse per se notum est" (ibid.).

44. SCG I, c. 11 (p. 9). See *De fide orthodoxa: Versions of Burgundio and Cerbanus,* E. M. Buytaert, ed. (St. Bonaventure, N.Y., 1955), c. 9, pp. 48–50.

45. "Deinde quia, dato quod ab omnibus per hoc nomen Deus intelligatur aliquid quo maius cogitari non possit, non necesse erit aliquid esse quo maius cogitari non potest in rerum natura. Eodem enim modo necesse est poni rem, et nominis rationem. Ex hoc autem quod mente concipitur quod profertur hoc nomine *Deus,* non sequitur Deum esse nisi in intellectu. Unde nec oportebit id quod maius cogitari non potest esse nisi in intellectu. Et ex hoc non sequitur quod sit aliquid in rerum natura quo maius cogitari non possit. Et sic nihil inconveniens accidit ponentibus Deum non esse: non enim inconveniens est quolibet dato vel in re vel in intellectu aliquid maius cogitari posse, nisi ei qui concedit esse aliquid quo maius cogitari non possit in rerum natura" (ed. cit., p. 9). For an interesting discussion of this passage from SCG I, c. 11, see Matthews, "Aquinas on Saying That God Doesn't Exist," pp. 474–77.

which cannot see God in himself but can only be led by reasoning from his effects to knowledge of him as their cause.[46]

Thomas's final treatment of the Anselmian argument appears in the *Summa theologiae* I, q. 2, a. 1 and once more within the broader context of an effort to determine whether God's existence is self-evident. The second argument in support of this claim reasons that those propositions are said to be self-evident which are known immediately once their terms are understood. Once we understand what the name God signifies, we must recognize immediately that God exists. For by this name is signified that than which no greater can be signified. But to exist in reality and in the intellect is greater than to exist in the intellect alone. Therefore, once the name God is understood, it immediately exists in the intellect; given this, it must also exist in reality. Therefore it is self-evident that God exists.[47]

In the corpus of his reply, as we have mentioned above, Thomas once more has recourse to the distinction between that which is self-evident in itself but not to us, and that which is self-evident both in itself and to us. As regards the statement "God exists," this is self-evident in itself since its predicate is identical with its subject. This is so because God is identical with his *esse*. Since we do not know of God "what he is," his existence is not self-evident to us but must be demonstrated by beginning with that which is better known to us even though less knowable in the order of nature, i.e., his effects.[48] In replying to the second argument Thomas presents in briefer fashion the first point from his critique in *Summa contra Gentiles* I, c. 11. Not everyone understands by the name "God" that than which no greater can be thought, since some held that God was a body. And even if everyone did understand the name "God" in this way, it would not follow from this that what is signified by this name actually exists in the nature of things, but only that it is present in the intellect. Nor can it be argued that it exists in reality unless it is granted that there exists in reality a being than which no greater can be thought. This will not be admitted by those who do not grant God's existence.[49]

Departing from his earlier treatments, in *Summa theologiae* I, q. 2, a. 1 Thomas bypasses the version of Anselm's argument offered in *Proslogion*, c. 3. Why he does so is a matter for conjecture; perhaps the fact that he has written this great work

46. Ibid. On Thomas's discussion of this in SCG, see H. Hoping, *Weisheit als Wissen des Ursprungs*, pp. 123–25.

47. Leon. 4.27. Note in particular: "Sed intellecto quid significet hoc nomen *Deus*, statim habetur quod Deus est. Significatur enim hoc nomine id quo maius significari non potest: maius autem est quod est in re et intellectu, quam quod est in intellectu tantum: unde cum, intellecto hoc nomine *Deus*, statim sit in intellectu, sequitur etiam quod sit in re. Ergo Deum esse est per se notum." As Thomas presents the argument in this context, the term *significari* has been substituted for *cogitari*. Nonetheless, for the purposes of the argument Thomas seems to regard them as equivalent. To this same effect see Cosgrove, "Thomas Aquinas on Anselm's Argument," p. 518.

48. Leon. 4.27–28. See the text cited above in n. 32.

49. Ed. cit., p. 28.

for "beginners" in theology is enough to account for this.[50] In any event, in this text as in the earlier ones Thomas's primary concern is not so much to refute Anselm as to reject the more general position which regards God's existence as self-evident. His earlier discussions show clearly enough that he was familiar with the versions presented both in *Proslogion*, c. 2 and in c. 3, and in three of these contexts he has in fact given preference to the formulation taken from c. 3 (see *In I Sent.*, *De veritate, In De Trinitate*). In the rather full discussion in SCG I, cc. 10–11, both versions are presented as distinct arguments. Nonetheless, it has also been suggested that we need not necessarily conclude that Thomas had access to the entire text of the *Proslogion*. If he did not, of course, his knowledge of Anselm's text would have been limited to the excerpts or perhaps the summary version(s) available to him.[51]

Several times we have noted that Thomas joins his presentation (and refutation) of Anselm's argumentation with the broader issue concerning whether God's existence is self-evident (known *per se*). That Thomas closely connects these two concerns will not be so surprising if we recall that the issues of the indubitability of God's existence and Anselm's argumentation had already been conjoined by others before and during his time. Thus, as J. Châtillon has shown, earlier thinkers in the thirteenth century such as Richard Fishacre and Alexander of Hales had already maintained that God's existence is grasped by the human mind in such a way that one cannot truly understand or think that God does not exist.[52]

But the more likely immediate target of Thomas's discussion appears to be St. Bonaventure. In his Commentary on I *Sentences,* in d. 8, p. 1, a. 1, q. 2 (dating 1250–1252), Bonaventure asks whether the divine existence *(esse)* is so true that it cannot be thought not to exist. The first of a series of opening arguments he offers in support of this proposition explicitly refers to Anselm by suggesting, with an unacknowledged nod to a notion taken from Boethius's *De Hebdomadibus,* that in

---

50. See the frequently quoted Prologue to the *Summa theologiae* and his references there to instructing beginners *(incipientes)*. See Leon. 4.5. It has often been assumed that in Thomas's day beginners in theology, at least at the University level, were presumed to have already completed the equivalent of an arts program whether at the University or in a religious house of studies or therefore to have a solid philosophical formation behind them. More recently, however, L. Boyle has challenged the assumption that Thomas directed the *Summa theologiae* to such students and argues that he probably rather intended it for not so sophisticated Dominican students such as those present at their house of studies in Rome in 1266. See Boyle, *The Setting of the Summa Theologiae of Saint Thomas,* Étienne Gilson Series 5 (Toronto, 1982), esp. pp. 17–20. Cf. Torrell, *Saint Thomas Aquinas,* pp. 142–45; Thomas F. O'Meara, *Thomas Aquinas: Theologian* (Notre Dame, Ind., 1997), pp. 51–53.

51. Such a suggestion seems to be implied by B. Davies, *The Thought of Thomas Aquinas* (Oxford, 1993), p. 25, n. 17.

52. J. Châtillon, "De Guillaume d'Auxerre à saint Thomas d'Aquin: l'Argument de saint Anselme chez les premiers scolastiques," in his *D'Isidore de Séville à saint Thomas d'Aquin* (London, 1985), pp. 209–31, esp. pp. 219–21. As Châtillon also points out, this does not mean that for them and for Bonaventure God's existence should not be demonstrated.

accord with a "common conception of the soul," God is that than which nothing greater can be thought. But that which cannot be thought not to exist is greater than that which can be thought not to exist. Therefore, since nothing can be thought to be greater than God, the divine existence exists in such fashion that it cannot be thought not to exist. In other words, Bonaventure here uses the thinking of *Proslogion,* c. 3 to support his view that the divine existence is so true that it cannot be thought not to exist. This does not mean that Bonaventure will not offer additional argumentation to support this claim, or that he does not recognize that some in fact may deny that God exists. They can do so with an inner assent, he maintains, only if they fail to understand what the name God signifies.[53]

And in his slightly later Disputed Questions *De mysterio Trinitatis,* q. 1, a. 1 (dating from 1254), Bonaventure asks whether God's existence is a truth that cannot be doubted. He begins by offering three "ways" in which this can be shown to be the case. In the third of these "ways" he argues that every truth that is so certain that it cannot be thought not to be is an indubitable truth. He then shows with a series of arguments that God's existence is such a truth. Among the arguments he offers in support of this, the first four are drawn from Anselm. The first of these cites *Proslogion,* c. 4, where Anselm now recognizes that, owing to God's illumination, even if he did not want to believe that God exists, he could not fail to understand this to be the case. The second argument recalls *Proslogion,* c. 3, while the third reproduces thinking taken from c. 2. The final argument appeals to a principle Anselm himself uses in the second part of the *Proslogion,* beginning in c. 5, to support his derivation of various divine attributes, to the effect that, as Bonaventure phrases it, God alone is whatever it is better to be than not to be. But, Bonaventure continues, truth that cannot be doubted is better than truth that can be doubted. Therefore, indubitable existence must be assigned to God rather than existence that can be doubted.[54]

Also within this same "third way" Bonaventure presents an argument to the effect that no proposition can be truer than that wherein the same thing is predicated of itself. But in saying "God exists" we predicate of God that which is entirely identical with him, i.e., his *esse.* Hence, as a proposition that expresses identity, it cannot be thought to be false or be doubted. And still another argument reasons that a proposition such as "The best is the best" is true. But the best is what is most complete. And what is most complete, by reason of that very fact, exists. Therefore, if the best is the best, it exists. So too, if God is God, God exists.[55]

53. See *In Primum Librum Sententiarum, Sancti Bonaventurae opera omnia,* Vol. 1 (Quaracchi, 1882–), pp. 153–54. Note from his conclusion (p. 155): "Concedendum est igitur, quod tanta est veritas divini esse, quod cum assensu non potest cogitari non esse nisi propter ignorantiam cogitantis, qui ignorat, quid est quod per nomen Dei dicitur."

54. See *Opera omnia,* Vol. 5, pp. 45, 47 (nn. 22–24). For the dating of these two works see J. G. Bougerol, *Introduction à Saint Bonaventure* (Paris, 1988), pp. x–xi.

55. Ed. cit., p. 48 (nn. 28–29).

In his solution Bonaventure again concedes that someone may in fact deny that God exists. And he also argues in other ways for God's existence, especially in presenting ten self-evident presuppositions in his "second way" and then reasoning from them to this conclusion. Even so, he still maintains that a human intellect that fully understands the meaning of the name "God" cannot doubt that God exists and cannot think of him as not existing. Bonaventure concludes that the arguments (which he has presented) proving this are to be granted.[56]

In light of Bonaventure's discussions, therefore, we may more easily understand why Thomas himself did not hesitate to place Anselm's argumentation within the broader context of arguments offered in support of the claim that God's existence is self-evident or, to use Thomas's terminology, known *per se*. The fact that Thomas did so, however, does not of itself imply that he failed to appreciate the force of Anselm's argumentation for God's existence before subjecting it to criticism. Thomas has pointed out that because God's essence is to exist, such argumentation would succeed, or at least God's existence would be evident to us, if we enjoyed direct knowledge of the divine essence or quiddity. According to Thomas's theory of knowledge, no such knowledge is available to us within the present life, at least within the natural order. Hence he cannot justify any immediate movement from our understanding of God as that than which no greater can be thought to his actual existence. Given this, only one route remains open for the philosopher who would arrive at knowledge of God. One must reason from effects which are accessible to us to knowledge of God as their unseen cause.

56. Ed. cit., pp. 49–50. For Bonaventure's discussion of the ten "manifest and evident presuppositions" (which he uses to reason from creatures to God) see pp. 46–47 (nn. 11–20). For more on Bonaventure's argumentation for God's existence, especially in the two texts we have been considering, see Gilson, *La philosophie de Saint Bonaventure,* 3d ed. (Paris, 1953), pp. 101–18.

XI

Argumentation for God's Existence
in Earlier Writings

From what we have seen in the preceding chapter, it is clear that Aquinas thinks it possible for us to demonstrate God's existence by reasoning from effect to cause. As anyone who is even slightly familiar with Thomas's thought well knows, he has distinguished a number of different ways in which this can be done. Each of the "five ways" developed in the *Summa theologiae* is based on some kind of causality, whether efficient or formal (exemplar) or final. The same holds for the different arguments offered for this conclusion in Thomas's many other discussions of this issue. In the present chapter I shall concentrate on a number of these presentations taken from writings prior to the *Prima Pars* of the *Summa theologiae*. The following chapter will be devoted to the five ways themselves. Here I shall begin with Thomas's earliest treatment, that offered in distinction 3 of his Commentary on I *Sentences*. This is at best a rough foreshadowing of some of the more formalized kinds of argumentation that will emerge in his subsequent writings.

1. *In I Sent.,* d. 3

As already noted, in his division of the first part of the text of distinction 3, Thomas finds Peter the Lombard establishing the unity of God, i.e., of the divine essence, by rational argumentation. Thomas discerns four distinct arguments in Peter's text and correlates them with the threefold Dionysian way in which we can arrive at knowledge of God.[1] Since these arguments for divine unity are in effect arguments for God's existence as well, each will now be considered in turn.

The first argument, says Thomas, is taken from the way of causality (the first Dionysian way) and may be formulated as follows. Whatever has being *(esse)* after

1. See Ch. X, n. 17 above.

having not been, literally, "after nothingness" *(ex nihilo)*, must derive from some-thing (else) from which its being has come. But all creatures have being after having not been. This is evident from their imperfection and their potentiality. Therefore they must derive from some one and first principle, i.e., God.[2]

As I have already intimated, this argument is presented by Aquinas in rudimen-tary fashion, almost in outline form. On the positive side, it has the merit of being based on causality, and on efficient causality at that. Hence it foreshadows a route which he will exploit to considerable advantage in his subsequent writings. On the negative side, certain assumptions in the argument as it stands need fuller justifica-tion, and there is at least one difficulty in interpreting it.

The first assumption is the claim that whatever has being from nothingness *(ex nihilo)* must depend on something (else) from which its being comes. One may take the expression *ex nihilo* as it appears here in the temporal sense, as we have just done. So understood, the premise means that if something enjoys existence after having not existed, it must receive its existence from something else. This is a version of the principle of causality as applied to the level of being or existence itself, but not necessarily the most universal and most fundamental expression of that principle.[3]

On the other hand, one might take the expression *ex nihilo* as implying cre-ation—that something has its being from no preexisting subject. Then the claim would be that anything which has its being from no preexisting subject depends on something else for its being. So understood, it would seem to say more than Thomas intends. God does not have his being from any preexisting subject, but this does not imply that he is caused.[4] Against this objection one might counter that the verb "has" *(habet)* implies that the subject in question merely participates in being. While this is certainly true for Aquinas in his more formal discussions of participation, he has hardly justified or developed this point within the present context. It seems, therefore, that the expression as it is employed here should rather be understood in the temporal sense.[5]

2. "Prima ergo ratio sumitur per viam causalitatis, et formatur sic. Omne quod habet esse ex nihilo, oportet quod sit ab aliquo [Parma/Busa: *alio*] a quo esse suum fluxerit. Sed omnes creaturae habent esse ex nihilo: quod manifestatur ex earum imperfectione et potentialitate. Ergo oportet quod sint ab aliquo uno primo, et hoc est Deus" (Mandonnet ed., Vol. 1, p. 88; Busa ed., Vol. 1, p. 10a).

3. What I have in mind is the possibility, admitted by Thomas, that something might have never begun to be and still be caused. See my remarks below about his views concerning the possibility of an eternally created world (n. 6). The way in which he expresses the principle of causality in the *De ente*, c. 4 is more satisfactory. For this see the next section of the present chapter.

4. Admittedly, this objection may be forcing Thomas's text somewhat. Strictly speaking, the text states that everything which has its *esse* from/after nothing must depend on something (else) from which its *esse* flows. Instead of saying that God has his *esse* from nothing, Thomas would prefer to state that God does not have his *esse* from something; he is his own *esse*.

5. The emphasis in the present text does not seem to be on this ("has") but on *ex nihilo*. For another who prefers to interpret it in a temporal sense see Van Steenberghen, *Le problème de l'exis-tence*, p. 14. As he sees it, the expression *ex nihilo* cannot designate the origin or source of beings

More difficult to establish philosophically, in my opinion, is the minor: all crea-tures have being after having not existed *(ex nihilo)*. This is justified by an appeal to the imperfection and potentiality of creatures. As Van Steenberghen has pointed out, Thomas's usage of the term "creature" here is unfortunate, since it seems to assume what remains to be proved, that such beings are indeed created. Presumably the term is here being used loosely. One should substitute for it something else such as "all finite beings." Secondly, if we take *ex nihilo* in the temporal sense, as I have argued we should, it is difficult to reconcile this statement with Thomas's repeated insistence that one cannot demonstrate that the world began to be. Thomas defends this position as early as his Commentary on II *Sentences,* that is, perhaps a year after the present text.[6]

Nonetheless, if we take *ex nihilo* as meaning that finite beings have their being from no preexisting subject, the argument remains incomplete; for it must be shown that this is the case. Can one establish the fact that such beings do not have their being from some subject (and therefore are created) by arguing from the implications which follow from their imperfection and potentiality? Will such an approach be able to establish anything more than the changeable character of such entities? If so, it seems that considerable metaphysical reinforcement and some intermediate steps will be required.[7] In sum, while this first argument suggests an interesting avenue for demonstrating God's existence, on either reading of *ex nihilo* as it stands it is neither a finished nor a fully satisfying proof.

The Platonic-Neoplatonic inspiration of the three following arguments is evi-dent. While Thomas connects argument two with the negative way of Pseudo-Dionysius, as he himself presents it, it is an argument for God's existence. It is not simply a way of rendering more precise our knowledge of God once we have already established his existence by an argument based on efficient causality. As Thomas formulates it, beyond all that is imperfect there must be something that is perfect, free from any admixture of imperfection. But any body is imperfect because it is finite and restricted in its dimensions and because it is mobile. Therefore, beyond all bodies there must be something which is not a body. Moreover, every change-

---

since the text concludes that this is God, not nothingness; and nothing can proceed or flow from nothingness. Hence it must be given the temporal meaning (as we have done), or a purely negative reading—not from a preexisting subject. Van Steenberghen regards the former as the more prob-able reading.

6. See Van Steenberghen, op. cit., p. 17. For Thomas see *In II Sent.,* d. 1, q. 1, a. 5 (Mandonnet ed., Vol. 2, pp. 32–33). For more on Thomas's views concerning the possibility of an eternally created universe see my *Metaphysical Themes,* c. 8 (pp. 191–214).

7. For instance, one might reason from the imperfection and potentiality of such beings to their finite or limited character, and from this to the distinction in them of essence and *esse.* See above in Ch. V, Section 5 for this way of arguing for the essence-*esse* distinction, that is, the argument based on limitation. One would then conclude that such beings, because their *esse* is really distinct from their essence, receive their *esse* from something else, i.e., that they are caused. However, no such reasoning is offered by the present text.

able incorporeal thing is imperfect of its nature. Therefore, beyond all natures which are subject to change, such as souls and angels, there must be some incorporeal and immobile being which is completely perfect. This is God.[8]

One immediately wonders how we are to establish the overriding Platonic principle, as it appears both in the first and in the second stage of the argument: wherever we find something imperfect, there must also be something which is perfect. Thomas himself does not attempt to justify this principle in the present context. Rather than explore this question more fully here, we shall defer discussing it until we take up the fourth way as it is presented in *Summa theologiae* I, q. 2, a. 3.[9]

While Thomas associates the third and fourth arguments taken from Peter's text with the Dionysian way of eminence, as he recasts them they are both arguments for God's existence. As Thomas sees things, the third argument is based on the way of eminence as it applies to being *(esse)*. The good and the better are so named in comparison with that which is best. But among substances a body is good, and a created spirit is better, though it does not possess goodness of itself. Therefore there must be some best from which the goodness of body and the goodness of spirit derive.[10]

The fourth argument is also based on the way of eminence, but as applied to the order of knowledge. Where one discovers a more and a less beautiful, one must also find a principle of beauty. It is in terms of its proximity to this principle that something else is said to be more beautiful than another. But we find that bodies are beautiful with a sensible kind of beauty, and that spirits are more beautiful with an intelligible kind of beauty. Therefore there must be something from which these things derive their beauty, and which created spirits approach more closely than do bodily things.[11]

In these two arguments we again have the claim that where there is a more and a less, or where we recognize a more and a less, there must be some supreme principle which lesser instances only approximate in varying degrees. It remains to be determined what philosophical justification Thomas can offer for this claim. He

---

8. "Secunda ratio sumitur per viam remotionis, et est talis. Ultra omne imperfectum oportet esse aliquod perfectum, cui nulla imperfectio admisceatur. Sed corpus est quid imperfectum. . . . Item, omne incorporeum mutabile de sui natura est imperfectum. Ergo ultra omnes species mutabiles, sicut sunt animae et angeli, oportet esse aliquod ens incorporeum et immobile et omnino perfectum, et hoc est Deus" (Mandonnet ed., Vol. 1, pp. 88–89).

9. See below in Chapter XII.

10. Ed. cit., p. 89. Note: "Tertia ergo sumitur ratio per viam eminentiae in esse, et est talis. Bonum et melius dicuntur per comparationem ad optimum. Sed in substantiis invenimus corpus bonum et spiritum creatum melius, in quo tamen bonitas non est a seipso. Ergo oportet esse aliquod optimum a quo sit bonitas in utroque."

11. "Quarta sumitur per eminentiam in cognitione, et est talis. In quibuscumque est invenire magis et minus speciosum, est invenire aliquod speciositatis principium, per cuius propinquitatem aliud alio dicitur speciosius. Sed invenimus corpora esse speciosa sensibili specie, spiritus autem speciores specie intelligibili. Ergo oportet esse aliquid a quo utraque speciosa sint, cui spiritus creati magis appropinquant" (ibid.).

does not attempt to do so here. Once more, therefore, we shall defer further discussion of this for our treatment of his fourth way in the *Summa theologiae.*

It is interesting to compare these four approaches to God's existence with Thomas's later treatments. The first argument stands out in that it is based on efficient causality. The other three resemble one another in that they are Platonic-Neoplatonic in inspiration and, as noted, seem to anticipate Thomas's "fourth way" from the *Summa theologiae.* In terms of their inner metaphysical structure, these four arguments really reduce to two major lines of argumentation, one based on efficient causality, and the other on the presence of varying degrees of perfection at the level of finite being. None of these should be regarded as a complete or fully satisfying proof as presented in this early text; nor is there any reason to think that Thomas regarded it as his task in this context to offer such finished and satisfying argumentation.[12]

2. *De ente et essentia,* c. 4

As we move beyond this early discussion to treatments in Thomas's *De ente et essentia,* his *De veritate,* and especially his *Summa contra Gentiles,* we note that his argumentation for God's existence has become considerably more sophisticated from the philosophical standpoint. Van Steenberghen has suggested that already by the time of the *De ente* the philosophical climate for the still-youthful Thomas had changed and that he was then more aware of and conversant with the world of the philosophers.[13] Perhaps one reason for this display of increased philosophical sophistication on Thomas's part, at least in the *De ente,* is the fact that in writing it he seems to have had in mind a strictly philosophical work, and one which may have been intended to help round out the philosophical formation of his young Dominican colleagues at St. Jacques in Paris. As noted in chapter IX above, there is general agreement that this treatise was written during the period 1252–1256 and, therefore, at the time Thomas was also commenting on the *Sentences.* It seems likely to have been written after Thomas had commented on the first part of Bk I of the *Sentences* and, we have suggested, perhaps before he commented on Bk II, distinction 3.[14] It is more important to remember, however, that in commenting on the *Sentences,* Thomas was fulfilling an official duty as a Bachelor in theology. And in preparing his *De veritate* he was carrying out one of the official functions of a Master in theology, that is, to preside over solemn academic disputations. Be

---

12. It will be recalled that in this part of his Commentary, Thomas is offering his division of a particular part of Peter's text. One could hardly expect his account in this immediate context to be anything but sketchy, and so it proves to be.

13. See *Le problème,* p. 33.

14. See our Ch. IX above, n. 230. Also see Weisheipl, *Friar Thomas d'Aquino,* pp. 78, 386 (it was written for Thomas's *confrères* at St. Jacques in Paris); Van Steenberghen, *Le problème,* p. 33; Torrell, *Saint Thomas Aquinas,* pp. 47–48, 348 (who dates it from 1252–1256).

that as it may, it is interesting to note that in the *De ente,* when it comes to citations of earlier authorities, Christian writers, so much in evidence in the Commentary on I *Sentences,* have given way to non-Christian philosophers, especially Aristotle, Avicenna, the *Liber de causis,* and Averroes.[15]

The general orientation for the reasoning presented by Thomas in *De ente,* c. 4 has already been indicated above in our Ch. V. There we have presented what we have described as phases one and two of his argumentation for real distinction of essence and *esse* in substances other than God. If my interpretation is correct, in completing phase two of his argument Thomas has already established the real and not merely conceptual character of this distinction, and he has done this without presupposing the existence of God. It is in stage three that what I regard as an argument for God's existence is introduced. The conclusion from this argument ultimately enables Thomas to show that essence and *esse* are related as potency and act in substances other than God. For our present purposes, however, it is the argument for God's existence that is of special interest.[16]

As Thomas presents this argument, everything which belongs to a given thing is either caused in it by the principles of that thing's nature or comes to it from some extrinsic principle. Thomas appeals to a human being's capacity to laugh to illustrate the first situation, and to the presence of light in air owing to the influence of the sun to illustrate the second. *Esse* cannot be caused by the form or quiddity of a thing, Thomas continues, and immediately specifies that he has in mind efficient causality. This is so because something would then be its own efficient cause and would bring itself into existence *(esse).* This he rejects as impossible. Therefore every thing whose *esse* is other than its nature or essence must receive its *esse* from something else.[17]

With this the first part of the argument for God's existence concludes. It is interesting for a number of reasons. First of all, there has been considerable disagreement concerning whether Thomas's arguments for God's existence, and especially his five ways, are properly speaking physical arguments or metaphysical arguments. The reader will recall the controversy between Avicenna and Averroes about

15. See Van Steenberghen, *Le problème,* p. 33.

16. See Ch. V, Section 1 above. As will be clear from what is to follow, I do regard this as an argument for God's existence. For Gilson's apparent later denial that this is intended by Thomas to be an argument for God's existence see his "Trois leçons sur le problème de l'existence de Dieu," *Divinitas* 5 (1961), pp. 26–28. Cf. his "La preuve du 'De ente et essentia'," pp. 257–60. For Owens's effort to show that this shift does not mean that Gilson really rejected the cogency of the argument see his "Stages and Distinction in *De ente:* A Rejoinder," pp. 110–17. Cf. my *Metaphysical Themes,* p. 125, n. 46.

17. "Omne autem quod convenit alicui vel est causatum ex principiis naturae suae, sicut risibile in homine, vel advenit ab aliquo principio extrinseco, sicut lumen in aere ex influentia solis. Non autem potest esse quod ipsum esse sit causatum ab ipsa forma vel quidditate rei, dico sicut a causa efficiente, quia sic aliqua res esset sui ipsius causa et aliqua res se ipsam in esse produceret: quod est impossibile. Ergo oportet quod omnis talis res cuius esse est aliud quam natura sua habeat esse ab alio" (Leon. 43.377:127–137).

whether it belongs to metaphysics (Avicenna) or to physics (Averroes) to demonstrate God's existence. There can be no doubt about the argument offered in the *De ente*. It builds upon a highly metaphysical conclusion, real distinction between essence and *esse* in all beings with one possible exception, and moves from this to the conclusion that the *esse* of every such being must be caused by something else.[18]

Secondly, the argument is explicitly based on efficient causality, not on any other kind. In fact, it is in the case of efficient causality that it is clear that a given being cannot be the cause of its own existence. One might argue, for instance, that a given thing's essence does exercise another kind of causality, formal causality, with respect to its *esse* (act of being) by determining and specifying the latter; but it cannot efficiently cause its own existence. For then the thing in question would exist insofar as it communicates existence (to itself) and yet, ontologically viewed, would not exist insofar as it receives its existence (from itself, according to the hypothesis). This appears to be the reason why Thomas rejects the possibility that a given thing could be the efficient cause of its own *esse*.[19]

Thirdly, as regards the causal explanation of a thing's *esse*, Thomas has considered two possibilities. Either that thing's *esse* is caused by its nature, or its *esse* comes to it from without. One might suggest a third possibility. Perhaps the thing's *esse* is identical with its essence. Thomas anticipates and eliminates this, however, by writing that when we are dealing with a thing whose *esse* is other than its nature or essence, it must receive its *esse* from something else. Hence we are not dealing with a being in which essence and *esse* are identical. Moreover, as already noted, we cannot account for the *esse* of such a thing by appealing to some principle within its essence from which its *esse* would follow as a necessary property (as the ability to laugh follows from the essence of human beings). In the case of *esse* such a suggestion would imply that the thing in question was its own efficient cause and that it brought itself into existence. In short, what Thomas has offered is a promising way of establishing the radically contingent character of all beings with one

---

18. See above in Ch. I, nn. 40–42, for references to the controversy between Avicenna and Averroes. Here, of course, I am following the conclusion for which I have already argued above in Ch. V, Section 1, that at the end of phase two in the argumentation in c. 4 of the *De ente* Thomas has already established real distinction between essence and *esse* in all beings with one possible exception. On the other hand, Owens maintains that even at the end of phase one of the argumentation, and so too, apparently, at the end of phase two, Thomas has established only a conceptual distinction between essence and *esse* in such beings, but that this is enough for him to show that they are efficiently caused. See his "Quiddity and Real Distinction in St. Thomas Aquinas," especially pp. 15–17. However, one may question whether the fact that I can know what a given thing is without knowing that it exists is enough to prove that its existence is efficiently caused.

19. Cf., for instance, *Summa contra Gentiles* I, c. 18 (ed. cit., p. 17, "Amplius"). There, within a series of arguments aimed at showing that there is no composition in God, Thomas reasons that if God were composed, he would require someone to render him composed, since nothing can cause itself; for it would then be prior to itself. Therefore God would be efficiently caused. Note: ". . . non enim ipse seipsum componere posset, quia nihil est causa sui ipsius; esset enim prius seipso, quod est impossibile."

possible exception. Precisely because the *esse* of any such being is really distinct from its essence, we must conclude that in every such case the thing's *esse* is communicated to it from without, that is, that the thing in question is efficiently caused.[20]

Before moving on to the second part of Thomas's argumentation for God's existence in the *De ente,* we should mention a point already raised in our Ch. V. In what sense is Thomas using the term *esse* in this argumentation? Does it simply signify a thing's facticity, the mere fact that it exists? Or does it signify the thing's intrinsic act of being *(actus essendi)*? As we pointed out there, in phase one of the argumentation for a distinction between essence and *esse* in this same chapter from the *De ente,* Thomas has shifted in his usage of this term.[21] Even so, this does not appear to be true of phase two where he attempts to show that in all beings, with one possible exception, essence and *esse* are not identical. This follows because *esse* cannot be multiplied except by being received in a distinct subject (essence). In other words, in that part of his argumentation Thomas is taking *esse* as an intrinsic principle (act of being) of every nondivine being.

If this is correct, *esse* must also be taken in this same sense when it serves as the starting point for phase three of the general argumentation for the real distinction and at the same time as the point of departure for the demonstration of God's existence. However, when Thomas reasons that a thing's *esse* cannot be caused efficiently by its form or quiddity, because that thing would then bring itself into existence *(esse),* he does seem to be using *esse* in two different ways. As I interpret this, the term refers to actual existence in the last-mentioned usage, but to an intrinsic principle of being *(actus essendi)* in the previous one.

At this point in the argument, this shift in usage is legitimate. Because Thomas has already shown that within any such being essence and *esse* (intrinsic principle) are distinct, he can conclude that its *esse* (taken as intrinsic act of being) and its existence (facticity) must be given to it from without. Were this not so, it would then be the efficient cause of its own *esse* (existence). This is so because, as he sees things, *esse* taken as the act of being also accounts for the fact that the thing exists.[22]

---

20. Needless to say, the validity of the argument in its immediate context as I am interpreting it depends upon the success of Thomas's effort in phase two to show that essence and *esse* are really distinct in all beings with the single possible exception. On the other hand, if one prefers, one could substitute one of Thomas's other ways of establishing such real distinction between essence and *esse* in nondivine beings and then go on from there.

21. See Ch. V above, Section 1 and n. 29.

22. See *In De divinis nominibus,* C. Pera, ed., p. 245, n. 659: ". . . quia nihil potest dici existens nisi habeat esse." For context and discussion see Ch. IV above, n. 54 and my corresponding text. Also see *In I Sent.,* d. 19, q. 5, a. 2 (Mandonnet ed., Vol. 1, p. 491): ". . . quaelibet res participat suum esse creatum, quo formaliter est;" SCG I, c. 22 (ed. cit., p. 24): "Amplius. Omnis res est per hoc quod habet esse. Nulla igitur res cuius essentia non est suum esse, est per essentiam suam, sed participatione alicuius, scilicet ipsius esse;" *De potentia,* q. 7, a. 9, ad 2 (cited more fully in Ch. V above, n. 115): ". . . sed hoc quod habet *esse,* efficitur actu existens." For some other interesting texts and for brief discussions see Gilson, "Éléments d'une métaphysique thomiste de l'être," AHDLMA 40 (1973), pp. 8–13.

As Thomas will eventually show after completing his proof of God's existence, this *esse* (act of being) unites with essence in all nondivine beings as act with potency.

With this we come to the second major part of this argument for God's existence. Here Thomas moves quickly. He has just concluded that anything whose essence is distinct from its *esse* (act of being) must receive its *esse* from something else. In other words, it must be caused efficiently. Because that which depends on something else for its *esse* (or which is *per aliud*) is reducible to that which does not depend on anything else (or which is *per se*) as its first cause, there must be some thing which is the cause of *esse* for all other things in that it itself is pure *esse*. Otherwise, continues Thomas, we would regress to infinity in caused causes, because, as he repeats, anything which is not pure *esse* depends on something else as the cause of its *esse*.[23]

The most critical phase in this step in Thomas's argument is his elimination of the possibility of one's appealing to an infinite regress of caused causes of *esse*. He will develop his reasons for maintaining this position more fully in other contexts—for instance, in his discussion in *Summa contra Gentiles* I, c. 13, or in his treatment of the first and second of his five ways. However, as I shall indicate more fully below, his primary concern in those contexts is not to eliminate the possibility of every kind of infinite series of caused causes. He rather wants to establish the impossibility or at least the insufficiency of an infinite series of caused causes in which the simultaneous existence and exercise of causal activity by all members of the series is required for the final member to be caused. As is well known, Thomas does not think it possible to demonstrate that there cannot be a series of moved movers (or caused causes of motion) extending into a beginningless past. In such a case, however, the exercise of causality by all prior members would not be required here and now for the causal activity of a subsequent member. This reasoning is part and parcel of his denial that one can demonstrate that the world began to be.[24]

In the *De ente* Thomas is discussing efficient causation of *esse*. If we may anticipate his later and more fully developed discussions of the regress to infinity, in the present case also he seems to have in mind a regress involving caused causes of *esse*, each of which would have to act simultaneously in order for any given and final effect to receive *esse*. This he rejects, apparently because he is convinced that admission of this kind of series would be tantamount to denying that there is any self-sufficient source of *esse* and hence any real explanation for the caused sources of *esse*

23. "Et quia omne quod est per aliud reducitur ad illud quod est per se sicut ad causam primam, oportet quod sit aliqua res quae sit causa essendi omnibus rebus ex eo quod ipsa est esse tantum; alias iretur in infinitum in causis, cum omnis res quae non est esse tantum habeat causam sui esse, ut dictum est" (Leon. 43.377:137–143).

24. See n. 6 above. Also see discussion of this issue below in connection with the argumentation in SCG I, c. 13, and the references in n. 63.

presupposed by the hypothesis. In other words, as he sees things, appeal to such a series would explain nothing.[25]

At the same time, one might interpret Thomas as not necessarily wishing to reject a possibly infinite sequence of caused causes so long as one admits the existence of some uncaused cause of *esse* upon which all the other causes will depend for their very *esse*. This is not to say that he admits that such a series is possible, but that at times he expresses doubts about the success of any and all efforts to prove that there could not be an actual infinite multitude of beings, or—as this hypothesis would imply when placed within the context of the *De ente*—of simultaneously existing and acting causes of *esse*. His point rather seems to be that such a suggestion is irrelevant to the present discussion. Unless we grant the existence of an uncaused source of *esse,* the *esse* of every caused being remains unexplained. Multiplying caused causes of *esse* to infinity will not resolve anything.[26]

---

25. In this text Thomas has reasoned that that which is *per aliud* must be traced back *(reducitur)* to that which is *per se* as its first cause; if one does not acknowledge the existence of such a first cause, one will fall into an infinite regress. Some writers conclude from this that it is the claim that the *per aliud* demands the existence of the *per se* that is most important here, and that Thomas regards this as a necessary proposition. See J. Bobik, *Aquinas on Being and Essence,* pp. 175–82. In his *Aquinas' Proofs for God's Existence,* D. Bonnette follows Bobik on this point and explicitly states that it is from this principle rather than from his refutation of a regress to infinity that Thomas concludes to the existence of a first cause (see pp. 62–63). Both writers argue that within the context of the *De ente* that which is *per aliud* is understood by Thomas to depend completely on something else for its existence. But in the following statement, it seems to me that they claim too much: "And it is to be noticed that 'completely dependent on an extrinsic source' means not only that the *per aliud* cannot depend on the extrinsic source for more than its existence . . . , but also that the extrinsic source is *all* that the *per aliud* depends on" (Bobik, pp. 177–78, cited by Bonnette, p. 63). While Thomas would agree that a being in which essence and *esse* differ must receive its *esse* (and hence its entire being) from something else, and that it is therefore completely dependent in this sense, this does not immediately justify the conclusion that the extrinsic source is "all that the *per aliud* depends on." Thomas also here considers and rejects the possibility of falling back upon an infinite series of caused causes of *esse* as an adequate explanation.

26. For a later presentation of this view see *In II Met.,* lect. 3, pp. 86–87, nn. 302–304. See below, n. 85, for Thomas's reference to this position in his SCG I, c. 13. Thomas's view concerning the possibility of an actual infinity of created entities, at least of spiritual entities, seems to have shifted during his career. See, for instance, his outright rejection of this possibility in ST I, q. 7, a. 4 (Leon. 4.79) or in his much earlier Quodlibet 9, q. 1, a. 1 (Leon. 25.1.89–90), dating from 1266–1268 and 1257 respectively. Compare this with the uncertainty he expresses about this in a well-known text from *De aeternitate mundi* ("Et praeterea non est adhuc demonstratum quod Deus non possit facere ut sint infinita actu" [Leon. 43.89:306–308]), dating from ca. 1271. Also see the important distinction between number and multitude which he applies in criticizing argumentation against the possibility of an actual infinite multitude based upon its being identified with number, argumentation which he had accepted in ST I, q. 7, a. 4 *(In III Phys.,* lect. 8, p. 175, nn. 351–352). Note in particular: "Similiter qui diceret aliquam multitudinem esse infinitam, non diceret eam esse numerum, vel numerum habere. Addit enim numerus super multitudinem rationem mensurationis: est enim numerus multitudo mensurata per unum. . . ." From this he concludes that number is a species of discrete quantity, but that multitude pertains to the transcendental ("est de transcendentibus"). Cf. *In X Met.,* lect. 10, p. 551, n. 2329 for the same.

As I have indicated above, in the *De ente* Thomas moves from his demonstration of God's existence to the relationship of essence and act of being within nondivine intelligences. He has already shown (in phase two of his general argumentation for the essence-*esse* distinction) that essence and act of being are distinct in such entities. He now makes the point that because every such intelligence receives its *esse* from that first being which is pure *esse* and the first cause (God), such an intelligence is in potency to the *esse* it receives from its cause. That which receives something from something else is in potency with respect to that which it receives, and that which is received is present in it as its act. Hence the quiddity or essence of an intelligence is in potency with respect to the *esse* it receives from God, and its *esse* is received as its intrinsic act. Thus potency and act are present in intelligences, although not matter and form, he insists, unless one uses the latter pair of terms equivocally.[27] It is only at this point that Thomas completes his effort to show that in such creatures essence and act of being are related to one another as potency and act. It is also clear at this stage, as throughout phase two and most of phase three of his general argumentation, that the term *esse* is being used to signify not mere facticity but a principle within every finite substance which serves as its intrinsic act of being *(actus essendi)* and which accounts for the fact that it exists.

3. *De veritate,* q. 5, a. 2

As we move forward a few years in Thomas's career to the time of his *De veritate* (1256–1259), we find there much more than a foreshadowing of another of his five ways, the argument based on final causality. As this reasoning appears in q. 5 of the *De veritate,* it is part of Thomas's effort to show that the world is directed by providence. In fact, however, that general effort leads him to develop what is an argument for God's existence.

As Thomas has just explained in q. 5, a. 1, providence in general has to do with a practical knowledge of means insofar as they are ordered to an end, and therefore in God includes both knowledge and will; nonetheless, it remains essentially in the order of knowledge, but practical knowledge.[28] In a. 2 he explicitly asks whether the world is ruled by providence. After presenting the usual series of opening arguments against providence and then a number in defense of it, Thomas begins his reply by turning back to the early days of Greek philosophy. As he notes, any one who rejects final causality must also reject providence. Among the ancients there

---

27. "Omne autem quod recipit aliquid ab alio est in potentia respectu illius, et hoc quod receptum est in eo est actus eius; ergo oportet quod ipsa quidditas vel forma quae est intelligentia sit in potentia respectu esse quod a Deo recipit, et illud esse receptum est per modum actus. Et ita invenitur potentia et actus in intelligentiis, non tamen forma et materia nisi aequivoce" (Leon. 43.377:147–154).

28. Leon. 22.1.139:175–181.

were two schools of thought which did in fact leave no place for final causality. Some allowed for nothing but a material cause. Since these thinkers were unable even to arrive at knowledge of efficient causes, they could not discover final causality; for an end does not function as a cause except insofar as it moves an agent. Other later thinkers defended the existence of some kind of efficient cause, but said nothing about any final cause. According to both positions, therefore, all things happen out of necessity in that they necessarily result from prior causes (whether these are merely material causes, or whether they are efficient causes).[29]

Thomas comments that philosophers themselves have rejected this position. While appeal to a material cause and to an efficient cause may enable one to account for the existence of a given effect, such an approach will not explain the presence of goodness in that effect. By this Thomas means that such an explanation will be unable to tell us why a given effect is fitting in itself so as to be able to survive and at the same time be of benefit to other things by offering support for them.[30] Seizing upon an example drawn from the world of everyday experience, he notes that heat taken simply in terms of its own nature dissolves things. But it is not always good for things to be dissolved and is so only within certain limits and in an appropriate manner. Thus if there were no other cause but heat (an efficient cause) and other agents of this kind within nature, we could not account for the fact that things in nature happen in good and fitting fashion.[31] In other words, mere appeal to material causes and blindly acting efficient causes would result in the chaotic destruction of things, not in their preservation and harmonious collaboration.

This in turn would force one to turn to chance to account for the fact that things do work out in good and fitting manner within nature; for that which has no determined cause happens by chance. Thomas attributes such a position to Empedocles. According to him, it happens by chance through friendship, i.e., the cosmic force love, that the parts of animals are fitted together in such fashion that the animal can be preserved, and this occurs frequently.[32]

Against any explanation based on chance Thomas counters that those things which happen through chance occur only infrequently *(in minori parte)*. But the fitting and beneficial occurences in nature which he has been citing take place either always or at least in the greater number of cases *(in maiori parte)*. Therefore they cannot result from chance but must follow from the pursuit of an end. But

---

29. Leon. 22.1.143:120–134.

30. "Causa enim materialis et agens inquantum huiusmodi sunt effectui causa essendi. Non autem sufficiunt ad causandum bonitatem in effectu secundum quam sit conveniens et in seipso ut permanere possit et aliis ut eis opituletur . . ." (Leon. 22.1.143:136–141).

31. Leon. 22.1.143:141–148. Note: ". . . unde nisi poneremus aliam causam praeter calorem et huiusmodi agentia in natura, non possemus assignare causam quare res convenienter fiant et bene."

32. Leon. 22.1.143:148–156.

anything which lacks intellect or knowledge cannot tend to an end in the sense of being directed toward it unless the end is assigned to it and it is directed to that same end by some kind of knowledge.[33] Since natural things themselves lack knowledge, some intellect must preexist which orders them to an end in the way an archer gives a certain motion to an arrow so that it tends to a particular end. And just as the impact of the arrow is said to be effected not merely by the arrow but also by the archer, so too every work of nature is said by the philosophers to be a work of intelligence (and not merely of some noncognitive agent). Hence the world must be governed by the providence of an intellect which has instilled in nature the aforementioned ordering to an end.[34]

Thomas likens this supreme providence whereby God governs the world to that of the head of a household (economic providence) whereby someone governs a family, or to that of a state (political providence) whereby someone governs a state or kingdom. In each case it is through providence that someone orders the actions of others to an appropriate end. Thomas concludes with the observation that God cannot exercise providence with respect to himself, since all that is present in God is an end, not a means to an end.[35]

While the stated purpose of this article is to show that the world is governed by divine providence, in it Thomas has presented what will later become one of his five ways of demonstrating God's existence—the argument based on final causality. The essentials of his reasoning may be summed up as follows. There is evidence of finality in nature on the part of things which lack intelligence. Mere recourse to material and efficient causes and to chance cannot account for the behavior one finds among natural agents and the way in which so many varied natural agents and forces repeatedly work together so as to produce beings which remain in existence themselves and contribute to the existence and well-being of others. Therefore finality in nature points to the influence of intelligence upon such agents. Since these agents themselves lack understanding, there must be some intelligence which transcends the beings of nature and which accounts for the fact that each acts for an end.[36]

Central to this argument is its starting point, the fact that noncognitive agents repeatedly act and cooperate so as to produce that which is beneficial for themselves

---

33. Leon. 22.1.143:156–144:166. Note: "Sed id quod intellectu caret vel cognitione, non potest directe in finem tendere nisi per aliquam cognitionem ei praestiutuatur finis, et dirigatur in ipsum. . . ."

34. Leon. 22.1.144:166–177. Note: "Et sic oportet quod per providentiam illius intellectus qui ordinem praedictum naturae indidit, mundus gubernetur."

35. Leon. 22.1.144:177–185.

36. Van Steenberghen sums up the heart of the argument in the following way: *Major.* Finality reveals the action of an intelligence. *Minor.* There is finality in beings of nature which lack intelligence. *Conclusion.* Therefore this finality reveals the action of an intelligence which transcends the beings of nature. For this and for fuller discussion see *Le problème*, pp. 62ff.

and for other natural things. Central too is Thomas's claim that such regular behavior cannot be accounted for by appealing to chance and must, therefore, be owing to intelligence. Whether this argument succeeds in showing that there must be one supreme intelligence to account for all such behavior is another matter, but one we shall defer for fuller discussion in our consideration of the fifth way from *Summa theologiae* I, q. 2, a. 3. Care should be taken not to confuse this approach with the more popular argument for God's existence based on the wonderful order and design of the universe. Here Thomas is rather reasoning from the presence of finality in noncognitive nature.[37]

4. *Summa contra Gentiles* I, cc. 13, 15

In *Summa contra Gentiles* I, cc. 10–12, Thomas considers and rejects two extreme positions concerning our knowledge of God's existence—one which holds that his existence is self-evident to us, and one which maintains that God's existence cannot be demonstrated in any way but can only be based on religious belief.[38] In c. 13 he turns to his positive presentation of formal argumentation for the existence of God. He proposes to do this by offering arguments by which both philosophers and Catholic teachers have proved that God exists. Even though he presents these as arguments already developed by others, there can be little doubt that as of this writing he accepts them as valid and hence as his own as well.[39] In fact he sets forth four arguments taken from Aristotle, two of which are based on motion, along with a fifth derived from John Damascene.

The arguments based on motion occupy by far the greater part of Thomas's presentation in c. 13. The first one runs as follows. Everything which is moved is moved by something else. But that something is moved is evident to us from sense experience and, in accord with the accepted geocentric theory of his time, Thomas offers the sun as an example. Therefore it is moved by some other mover. But either that mover is itself moved or it is not. If it is not moved we have established the conclusion that there is some immobile mover. And this we call God. If, however, that other mover is itself moved, then it too is moved by something else. Either one must regress to infinity with moved movers, or one must arrive at some im-

---

37. For discussion of some of these points see Van Steenberghen, pp. 68–71. However, he seems convinced that our discovery of finality in nature today is in effect restricted to the realm of living things. As he sees it, the material universe taken as a whole does not point to finality but to order which leads to a different approach to God's existence, not to one based on finality (see p. 70, n. 19).

38. Ed. Leon. man., c. 10: presentation of arguments, including Anselm's, that God's existence is self-evident (pp. 8–9); c. 11: refutation of these arguments (pp. 9–10); c. 12: presentation and critique of view that God's existence cannot be demonstrated but can only be believed (p. 10).

39. "Ostenso igitur quod non est vanum niti ad demonstrandum Deum esse, procedamus ad ponendum rationes quibus tam philosophi quam doctores Catholici Deum esse probaverunt" (ed. cit., p. 10).

mobile mover. But one cannot regress to infinity with moved movers. Therefore one must conclude that there exists some first immobile mover.[40]

As Thomas himself immediately points out, central to this proof are two propositions which remain to be established *(probandae)*: (1) that every thing which is moved is moved by something else; (2) that one cannot regress to infinity with movers and things which are moved.[41] Thomas's effort to establish each of these is fairly lengthy and, as one would expect, heavily indebted to Aristotle.

As regards the first proposition, there is some disagreement among interpreters of Aquinas concerning how its subject is to be translated. The difficulty arises from a certain ambiguity in Latin usage concerning the verb *movere*. When it is taken in its present passive form *(movetur)*, it can be translated into English either passively ("whatever is moved") or intransitively ("whatever is in motion"). When Thomas repeats this proposition in listing it as one of two premises which must be proved, he uses the passive participle: "every moved thing *(motum)* is moved by something else."[42] Nonetheless, some commentators reason that if the subject is taken in a strictly passive sense, the proposition will beg the question. In effect it will state that whatever is moved (by something else, as implied by the passive) is moved by something else.[43]

Others such as Van Steenberghen reject this charge, arguing that when we are dealing with something which is being moved, two alternatives must still be considered. Either it is moved by itself, or it is moved by something else. It is only by excluding the first that Thomas establishes the second and thereby the truth of the proposition itself.[44] Weisheipl has written an interesting study of this same principle in Aquinas though, as one would expect, he concentrates on its justification and application in physics (natural philosophy). He too strongly insists that the

40. "Omne quod movetur, ab alio movetur. Patet autem sensu aliquid moveri, utputa solem. Ergo alio movente movetur.—Aut ergo illud movens movetur, aut non. Si non movetur, ergo habemus propositum, quod necesse est ponere aliquod movens immobile. Et hoc dicimus Deum.—Si autem movetur, ergo ab alio movente movetur. Aut ergo est procedere in infinitum: aut est devenire ad aliquod movens immobile. Sed non est procedere in infinitum. Ergo necesse est ponere aliquod primum movens immobile" (ed. cit., pp. 10–11). Cf. Aristotle's *Physics* VII, c. 1.

41. "In hac autem probatione sunt duae propositiones probandae: scilicet, quod *omne motum movetur ab alio;* et quod *in moventibus et motis non sit procedere in infinitum*" (p. 11).

42. Cf. the texts cited above in notes 40 and 41. For the Greek text in Aristotle see *Physics* VII, c. 1 (241b 34). Note that Thomas's term *motum* literally translates the Greek κινούμενον.

43. See G. Verbeke, "La structure logique de la preuve du Premier Moteur chez Aristote," *Revue philosophique de Louvain* 46 (1948), p. 153. A. Kenny also appears to take it in this way. See his *The Five Ways*, pp. 6, 8, 11–13.

44. See *Le problème*, pp. 114–15. As Van Steenberghen points out, it would be disturbing to find Thomas shifting from the intransitive meaning to the passive meaning so quickly within the same sentence if one were to accept the other reading, especially in the oft-repeated formula: "quidquid movetur, ab alio movetur," or as he has first phrased it here: "Omne quod movetur, ab alio movetur" (see n. 40 above). Moreover, the second clause is intended to be a precision of the first. There can be no doubt that in the second case *movetur* must be given a passive interpretation. Hence, he concludes, the same must be true of the first usage.

term *movetur* must be understood in the passive sense. Weisheipl adds the following remark: "Nor did St. Thomas—or Aristotle, for that matter—ever maintain that everything that is in motion must be here and now moved by something, as some imagine. This interpretation is grammatically impossible and philosophically absurd."[45]

For my part, it seems clear enough to me that the verb *movetur* and the participle *motum* as they appear in Thomas's text indicate that the subject of the principle is to be understood in the passive voice and not intransitively. Accordingly, the subject of the proposition is "whatever is moved" or "every moved thing." At the same time, Thomas does not regard the proposition as a mere tautology; nor does he think it so evident as not to need proof. In fact he follows Aristotle in offering three different ways of proving it.[46]

As Thomas phrases the first way of establishing this principle, if something moves itself, it must contain within itself the principle of its own motion. Otherwise, of course, it would be moved by something else (and the principle that whatever is moved is moved by something else would be granted). Moreover, Thomas takes this as implying that our alleged self-mover must also be that which is moved primarily. By this he means that it must be moved by reason of itself taken as a whole and not merely by reason of one of its parts, in the way, for instance, an animal is moved by the motion of its foot. In the latter case our alleged self-mover would not be moved by itself but only its part would be moved, and this by another part. Finally, Thomas adds that the alleged self-mover must be divisible and have parts, since whatever is moved is divisible according to Aristotle in *Physics* VI.[47]

---

45. "The Principle *Omne quod movetur ab alio movetur* in Medieval Physics," *Isis* 56 (1965), pp. 26–45; repr. in his *Nature and Motion in the Middle Ages*, W. E. Carroll, ed. (Washington, D.C., 1985), pp. 75–97 (which will be cited here). See p. 78. For others who take it in the passive sense see J. Owens, "The Conclusion of the *Prima Via*," in *St. Thomas Aquinas on the Existence of God*, pp. 143–44, 154–55; also, "The Starting Point of the *Prima Via*," in the same source, pp. 171–72; S. MacDonald, "Aquinas's Parasitic Cosmological Argument," *Medieval Philosophy and Theology* 1 (1991), pp. 123–24 and n. 6. For an overview of the medieval background and usage of this principle around and after the time of Aquinas see R. Effler, *John Duns Scotus and the Principle "Omne quod movetur ab alio movetur"* (St. Bonaventure, N.Y., 1962), pp. 1–21. Also for another who took this principle very seriously and argued that it allowed for no exceptions see my "Godfrey of Fontaines and the Act-Potency Axiom," *Journal of the History of Philosophy* 11 (1973), pp. 299–317.

46. Though he is aware that Thomas says in our passage from SCG I, c. 13 that the principle must be proved, Weisheipl suggests that we can perhaps say it is not "demonstrated strictly speaking. Rather it seems to be an axiom, or principle *per se notum sapientibus,* requiring sense experience and a careful analysis of the terms." See his "The Principle *Omne quod movetur,*" p. 78. This is not Thomas's assessment of the situation, as we shall shortly see.

47. "Si aliquid movet seipsum, oportet quod in se habeat principium motus sui: alias, manifeste ab alio moveretur.—Oportet etiam quod sit primo motum: scilicet quod moveatur ratione sui ipsius, et non ratione suae partis, sicut movetur animal per motum pedis; sic enim totum non moveretur a se, sed sua pars, et una pars ab alia.—Oportet etiam ipsum esse divisibile, et habere partes: cum omne quod movetur sit divisibile, ut probatur in VI *Physic.*" (ed. cit., p. 11). For Aristotle see *Physics* VI, c. 4 (234b 10–20); c. 10 (240b 10–241a 26).

With these preliminaries in mind, Thomas continues, let us suppose that that which is alleged to be moved by itself is also that which is moved primarily. If any part of this self-mover is at rest, the whole will be at rest. (Otherwise, if one part of it were moved while another was at rest, the whole itself would not be moved primarily. Only that part which was moved while another part was at rest would be so moved.) But if something is at rest only because something else is at rest, it cannot be regarded as moved by itself. If its rest depends upon the rest of something else, continues Thomas, its motion must also depend upon the motion of that other thing. Therefore it will not be moved by itself. Hence we must conclude that whatever is moved (including our alleged self-mover) is moved by something else.[48]

In his later Commentary on *Physics* VII Thomas presents fundamentally the same interpretation of Aristotle's argument, though in more extended fashion. There, as in our present text, he also wards off a possible objection to Aristotle's reasoning, an objection which he attributes to Avicenna. Someone might counter that a part of that which is said to move itself cannot be at rest, or again, that we cannot speak of the rest or motion of a part of a true self-mover except *per accidens*. Hence Aristotle's argument is based upon an impossible hypothesis. Against this Thomas replies that Aristotle's argument does not presuppose that a given part of a self-mover is in fact at rest, but only this: *if* a part should be at rest, the whole would then be at rest. As Thomas views the matter, if something does move itself primarily and *per se* (and not simply in the sense that one of its parts moves another), its motion cannot depend on anything else. But the motion of anything that is divisible, like its very being, depends upon that of its parts. Therefore no such thing can move itself primarily and *per se*.[49]

As it appears in Aristotle's text, this argument is known for its difficulty. Thomas himself is aware of objections which have been raised against it as he indicates both

48. SCG I, c. 11 (p. 11). Note: "Nihil autem quod quiescit quiescente alio, movetur a seipso: cuius enim quies ad quietem sequitur alterius, oportet quod motus ad motum alterius sequatur; et sic non movetur a seipso. Ergo hoc quod ponebatur a seipso moveri, non movetur a seipso. Necesse est ergo omne quod movetur, ab alio moveri."

49. Cf. *In VII Phys.*, lect. 1, pp. 449–50, nn. 885–886. Note that in the Latin text on which Thomas is commenting Aristotle states that everything which is moved must be moved by something. Thomas takes Aristotle as meaning by this that it must be moved by something *else* ("Proponit ergo primo quod necesse est omne quod movetur, ab aliquo *alio* moveri," n. 885). Is Thomas therefore forcing Aristotle's text so as to arrive at a stronger conclusion? It does not seem so since the whole point of the Stagirite's argument is to refute the claim that if something is moved as a whole and not by anything external to itself, it is therefore moved by itself. See *Physics* VII, c. 1 (241b 34–242a 49, especially 241b 39–41). For the objection taken from Avicenna and for Thomas's reply see SCG I, c. 13, p. 11 ("Nec obviat huic rationi. . . ."); *In VII Phys.*, lect. 1, pp. 450–51, nn. 888–889. In the latter text Thomas credits Averroes for the central part of his own reply to this objection. A conditional proposition can be true even if its antecedent and its consequent are impossible, such as this: if a man is a donkey, he is an irrational animal. So too in the present case: if a part of a self-moving mover is at rest, the whole is at rest. See p. 451, n. 889. For Avicenna see his *Sufficientia*, Bk I, c. 1, f. 24r. For Averroes see *In VII Phys.*, ed. cit., Vol. 4, f. 308ra.

in his succinct presentation in SCG I, c. 13 and in his Commentary on *Physics* VII.[50] Even so, he seems to think that these objections can be met. One of the argument's assumptions is that anything that is moved must be divisible. Thomas seems satisfied that Aristotle has established this in *Physics* VI.[51] Another is the claim that if something depends for its rest upon something else, its motion must depend upon the motion of that other thing. Therefore it is not truly moved by itself. In his Commentary on *Physics* VII, Thomas notes that Aristotle accepts this as if it were self-evident. In other words, because the motion of the alleged self-mover—the whole—depends upon the motion of one of its parts, the whole is not moved by itself. But the dependency upon which this argument turns appears to be in the order of material causality, not in the order of efficient causality, as Silvester of Ferrara noted long ago. We may wonder whether this argument shows that any alleged self-mover must be moved by another efficient cause if it is to be moved at all.[52]

One may also be concerned about the presupposition that whatever is moved must be divisible and therefore consist of parts in some sense. Might not one postulate an unextended and indivisible self-mover in order to account for the observable and physical motion which serves as the argument's point of departure?

Thomas anticipates this concern after presenting this argument in his Commentary on *Physics* VII and after presenting all three arguments in support of the general proposition (whatever is moved is moved by another) in SCG I, c. 13. He writes that Plato used the term "motion" more broadly than did Aristotle and could

50. In addition to the objection just mentioned in the preceding note, see Thomas's reference to another raised by Galen. See *In VII Physic.,* p. 450, n. 887. W. D. Ross argues that Aristotle uses the notion of "depending upon" equivocally when he argues that the motion of a whole depends upon that of a part. While the motion of a whole "logically implies the motion of the part," it is not necessarily causally dependent upon it. See his *Aristotle's Physics* (Oxford, 1936), p. 669, commenting on 242a 38. Kenny agrees with this criticism and also charges that the argument "equivocates between being a necessary condition and being a sufficient condition" *(The Five Ways,* p. 19). His point is that if a part's being at rest is a sufficient condition for the whole's being at rest, it will follow that the motion of the part is a necessary condition for the whole's motion, but not that it is a sufficient condition or a cause of that motion.

51. See the references given above in n. 47.

52. "Omne quod movetur a seipso, non quiescit a suo motu per quietem cuiuscumque alterius mobilis. Et hoc accipit quasi per se notum. Ex hoc autem ulterius concludit, quod si aliquod mobile quiescit ad quietem alterius, quod hoc movetur ab altero. . . . Sed supra habitum est, quod si aliquid quiescit et desinit moveri ad quietem alterius, hoc ab altero movetur" (ed. cit., p. 450, n. 886). See Owens for discussion of objections to this raised by Simplicius and Ross, as well as the point that the dependence of the whole upon its part(s) for its motion is in the order of material causality ("The Conclusion of the Prima Via," p. 264, n. 24). There Owens cites from Silvester of Ferrara's Commentary on *Summa contra Gentiles* I, c. 13 (Leon. 13.34) for the same point. He does not appear to regard this as a telling objection against the argument. It does seem, however, that something more is needed to support the transition to efficient causality with which the principle is concerned. This objection could be met by joining to this argument the third one offered by Thomas in SCG I, c. 13 in support of this same principle, that is, the one based on potentiality and actuality which will be considered below.

therefore say that every mover is moved. Aristotle takes the term strictly, limiting it to the act of that which is in potency insofar as it is in potency. So understood, continues Thomas, motion applies only to divisible and corporeal things. Plato's self-mover is not a body, since he was using motion broadly enough so as to apply also to acts of understanding and thinking. Even Aristotle uses similar language in *De anima* III, c. 7. Because of his broader usage Plato could hold that the first mover moves itself because it understands and loves itself. On this point, Thomas concludes, there is only a verbal difference between Aristotle and Plato.[53]

This is an important admission on Thomas's part, for it leaves open the possibility that the immobile mover at which the argument from SCG I, c. 13 arrives is not God but some lesser self-moving mover (an intelligence, perhaps) which is the efficient cause of the observable physical motion of things in this world.[54]

Finally, however one may personally assess the force of this physical way of supporting the claim that whatever is moved is moved by something else, it is interesting to see Aquinas disputing Averroes' claim that it is only a demonstration of the fact *(quia)* and not a demonstration of the reasoned fact *(propter quid)*. According to Thomas it seems to be a demonstration of the reasoned fact *(propter quid)*, because it includes the cause which shows why it is not possible for any moved thing to move itself.[55]

In *Summa contra Gentiles* I, c. 13, Thomas next turns to Aristotle's *Physics* VIII, c. 4 for a second way of proving this principle. This time the argument is explicitly said to be based on induction. Things which are moved *per accidens* are clearly not moved by themselves but owing to the motion of something else, i.e., by being a

---

53. SCG I, c. 13, ed. cit., pp. 11–12 ("Sciendum autem quod Plato . . ."). Note in particular: "Secundum Platonem autem movens seipsum non est corpus: accipiebat enim motum pro qualibet operatione, ita quod intelligere et opinari sit quoddam moveri. . . ." See *In VII Phys.*, lect. 1, p. 451, n. 890. Cf. Aristotle, *De anima* III, c. 7 (431a 4–7).

54. This will be discussed more fully below. But if the argumentation considered so far only reaches this kind of mover, that mover will not necessarily be completely and totally immutable. Then one will have to ask whether or not it too depends upon something else for its being moved, i.e., changed. The justification offered so far for this general principle—that whatever is moved is moved by something else—would not enable one to apply it to such an incorporeal self-mover, it would seem. On the other hand, the argumentation based on potentiality and actuality (see Thomas's third way of justifying his principle) may.

55. See *In VII Phys.*, p. 451, n. 889: ". . . sed videtur dicendum quod non sit demonstratio *quia*, sed *propter quid*; continet enim causam quare impossibile est aliquod mobile movere seipsum." For Averroes see *In VII Phys.*, f. 307vb. On this see Owens, "The Conclusion of the *Prima Via*," pp. 145–46. As Owens points out, Thomas immediately offers a fuller justification for this. For something to move itself is for it to cause its own motion. But that which causes something in itself must possess that which it causes in the primary sense; for that which is first in a given genus is the cause of those things which come after it (thus fire which causes heat in itself and in others is the primary instance of heat [*primum calidum*]). But in motion there is nothing which is primary in this sense, whether in terms of time, or magnitude, or the mobile thing itself, since all of these are divisible. Hence there cannot be a primary mobile thing whose motion does not depend upon something prior, i.e., the motion of its parts.

part of or attached to something else that is moved. The same holds for those which are moved by violence. Not even things which are moved by nature *of* themselves *(ex se)*, i.e., animals, are moved *by* themselves *(a seipso)*; for they are moved by their souls. Neither are those things moved by themselves which are moved by nature, in the way heavy bodies tend to go down and light bodies tend to rise. Such bodies are rather moved by the cause which generated them and by any other cause which removes an obstacle preventing them from so acting. Thomas then turns to a classification of the different ways in which something can be moved. Everything which is moved is moved either *per se* or *per accidens*. If a thing is moved *per se*, this is either by violence or by nature. If it is moved by nature, it is either moved of itself, as in the case of animals, or not of itself, as is true of the heavy and the light. But as Thomas has now shown, in all of these cases the thing in question is moved by something else. Therefore, he concludes, everything which is moved is moved by something else.[56]

As this line of reasoning appears in Aristotle's text, it is part of his more general effort to show that while some things are so constituted as to be capable of being in motion or at rest, others are always in motion, and still others are always at rest. In his Commentary on this same chapter of the *Physics,* Thomas carefully explains Aristotle's text. But as he has indicated in the text from SCG I, c. 13, this particular argument is based on induction. It also presupposes that the proposed classification and division of ways in which something can be moved is exhaustive. Can one be certain that the induction and classification are indeed complete? Again, possible counterexamples such as projectile motion and gravity are often raised, which we will defer for consideration in connection with the first way in the following chapter. Finally, this argument would hardly justify our applying the motion principle to a possible kind of self-mover of which we have no direct experience, that is, an immaterial or spiritual self-mover. To put this another way, this argument, like the first one, is limited to the motion of corporeal and divisible things.[57]

---

56. SCG I, c. 13, p. 11.

57. For Aristotle see *Physics* VIII, c. 3 (254b 1–6); c. 4, passim, but especially 255b 31–256a 3. For Thomas's commentary see *In VIII Phys., lectiones* 7–8. In lect. 7 he divides things which are said to move or to be moved *per accidens* into: those which are said to move or be moved insofar as they are present in a mover or in what is moved; and others which are said to move or be moved because they move or are moved as a part of something else (see p. 535, n. 1022). Also note that in this context, in contrast with SCG I, c. 13, he does refer to animals as being moved *by* themselves (or as self-movers), i.e., by their souls, instead of being moved *of* themselves. See n. 1023. With Aristotle he insists that in these something is moved by something else, although there may be difficulty in determining which part moves and which is moved. See nn. 1023, 1024. See the important summarizing passage in lect. 8, p. 542, n. 1036. Note his comment concerning the rise and fall of light and heavy bodies: "Sed causa huius est, quia habent naturalem aptitudinem ad talia loca. Hoc enim est esse leve, habere aptitudinem ad hoc quod sit sursum: et haec est etiam ratio gravis, habere aptitudinem ad hoc quod sit deorsum. Unde nihil est aliud quaerere quare grave movetur deorsum, quam quaerere quare est grave. Et sic illud idem quod facit ipsum grave, facit ipsum moveri deorsum" (p. 541, n. 1034).

Thomas takes his third argument from *Physics* VIII, c. 5. This time he casts it in terms of the distinction between actuality and potentiality. One and the same thing cannot be simultaneously in act and potency with respect to the same thing. But everything which is moved, insofar as it is moved, is in potency. This follows from the definition of motion as the act of that which is in potency insofar as it is in potency. But what moves does so insofar as it is in act, since nothing acts except insofar as it is in act. Therefore nothing can be both mover and moved with respect to one and the same motion, which is to say that nothing can move itself.[58]

While this argument is taken from Aristotle's *Physics,* as it appears there and especially as Thomas formulates it in SCG I, c. 13, it appeals to the broader notions of potentiality and actuality in order to support the narrower claim that whatever is moved is moved by something else. To that extent it seems to be transposed from the level of the purely physical to the metaphysical plane, as Owens has pointed out. Interesting, too, is the fact that by the time of *Summa theologiae* I, q. 2, a. 3, Thomas quietly omits the first two (and clearly physical) ways of establishing the narrower claim and presents again in somewhat greater detail the argument based on potentiality and actuality. We shall also reserve fuller discussion of this for our consideration of the first way in ST I, q. 2, a. 3.[59]

For the present it will be enough for us to note that because this argumentation is based on potentiality and actuality, it seems far more likely than either of the other two approaches to admit of universal application to all kinds of change, and not merely to the motion of things which are corporeal and divisible. Hence it leaves open the possibility of being applied even at the level of a "self-moving"

---

58. "Tertio, probat sic. Nihil idem est simul actu et potentia respectu eiusdem. Sed omne quod movetur, inquantum huiusmodi, est in potentia: quia motus est *actus existentis in potentia secundum quod huiusmodi.* Omne autem quod movet est in actu, inquantum huiusmodi: quia nihil agit nisi secundum quod est in actu. Ergo nihil est respectu eiusdem motus movens et motum. Et sic nihil movet seipsum" (SCG I, c. 13, p. 11).

59. For this argument in Aristotle see *Physics* VIII, c. 5 (257b 6–13). As it appears there, however, and as Owens has pointed out, it is not part of Aristotle's effort to prove that whatever is moved is moved by something else; it is rather used to prove that motion must originate in a self-mover and that in the self-mover only one part can be the immobile mover. See "The Conclusion of the *Prima Via,*" p. 155. For Thomas's Commentary on this in the *Physics* see *In VIII Phys.,* lect. 10, p. 553, nn. 1052–1053. Note the distinction he makes there between movers which are univocal with that which they move (in that they are named and defined in the same way), and those that are not. In the former case he argues that in order for that which moves to do so it must possess that which it communicates. Thus something hot will produce heat, and only a human being will generate another human being. He distinguishes such movers from others which do not agree in name and in definition with their effects. As an example he cites the sun's role in the generation of a human being. In such cases the species of the effect is not present in the cause or mover in the same way, but in a certain fashion in a higher and more universal way. To that degree we can still say that the mover is in a certain way in actuality with respect to that which it produces, and to which the thing moved is only in potency. Another way of making this point is to distinguish between actual possession of a given perfection and virtual possession of the same. If the cause or mover does not actually possess the perfection it produces—for instance, because it (the cause) enjoys a higher level of being—it

mover or intelligence and of enabling one to reason beyond such a mover to a perfectly immobile mover. Otherwise one might conclude that Thomas's argumentation could establish no more than the existence of such a self-moving mover. In my judgment it is a more convincing way of establishing the motion principle than either of the other two ways already considered.

Thomas next turns to the second proposition—that one cannot regress to infinity in movers and things which are moved. Again he offers three arguments for this, each of which is taken from Aristotle's *Physics*. The first is based on *Physics* VII, c. 1. If we regress to infinity with movers and things which are moved, there will be an infinity of bodies; for whatever is moved is divisible and therefore a body, Thomas repeats, again referring back to *Physics* VI. (This reference indicates that in this particular argument he is once more restricting himself to corporeal or physical movers and moved movers.) But every body which moves something is moved at the same time as it moves. Therefore all of these corporeal moved movers (an infinity) will be moved when one of them is moved. But any one of them, being finite, is moved in a finite time. Therefore the infinity of movers will be moved in a finite time. But this is impossible. Therefore it is impossible for there to be an infinite regress of movers and things which are moved.[60]

The most questionable step in this reasoning, it would seem, is the claim that it is impossible for an infinity of moved movers to be moved in a finite time. It must be remembered that the argument is concerned with corporeal moved movers. In support of this claim Thomas follows Aristotle by appealing to induction and considering the different kinds of motion. If we examine these different kinds of motion, we find that the mover and that which is moved must be simultaneous with one another. (As Thomas explains in his Commentary on *Physics* VII, lect. 2, this is because each moving body moves only insofar as it is moved.) But bodies cannot be simultaneous with one another except by being continuous with or else in contact with one another. Therefore, since all of the aforementioned movers and things moved are bodies, Thomas reasons that they must form, as it were, one mobile thing either by continuity or by being in contact with one another. It will follow

---

must possess it virtually. This is to say that it must have the power to produce it. Hence Kenny's objection to this proof for the motion principle, both as it appears in SCG I, c. 13 and as in ST I, q. 2, a. 3 (the "First Way"), appears to be off the mark. Kenny argues: "The principle that only what is actually F will make something else become F does not seem universally true: a kingmaker need not himself be king, and it is not dead men who commit murders" (*The Five Ways*, pp. 21–22). Thomas was not so naive as to think that God would have to be mud in actuality in order to produce mud. For more on this see ST I, q. 4, a. 2, where Thomas explains how perfections present in effects preexist in their cause. In the case of a non-univocal (i.e., an equivocal) cause, the effect preexists virtually *(virtute)* in the efficient cause: ". . . praeexistere autem in virtute causae agentis, non est praeexistere imperfectiori modo, sed perfectiori . . ." (Leon. 4.51). On this also see MacDonald, "Aquinas's Parasitic Argument," pp. 133–35.

60. Ed. cit., p. 12. For this in Aristotle see *Physics* VII, c. 1 (242a 49–242b 53). Note that in his Commentary on this section in Aristotle, Thomas interprets the argument as being applied there by the Stagirite to local motion. See *In VII Phys.*, p. 455, lect. 2, nn. 891–892.

from this that one infinite body is moved in a finite time. But, Thomas concludes, Aristotle has shown that this is impossible in Bk VI of the *Physics*.[61]

As a second way of meeting a proposed regress to infinity Thomas turns to Aristotle's *Physics* VIII, c. 5. As Thomas phrases this argument, in movers and things moved which are strictly ordered to one another (that is, in such fashion that the motion of each one depends upon the motion of that which is prior to it), it will follow that when the first mover is removed or ceases its moving activity, none of the others will move or be moved. This follows because the first mover is a cause for the motion of all the others. But if movers and things moved are so ordered to one another to infinity, there will be no first mover; all will be, as it were, intermediary movers. Therefore none of the others will be moved and thus nothing in the world will be moved.[62]

This reasoning calls for some comments. First of all, the argument assumes a series in which each subsequent mover moves something else only insofar as it is itself moved by a prior mover, in other words, in which moved movers are ordered to one another *per se* or essentially rather than *per accidens*. Secondly, the argument has been criticized for begging the question by assuming what remains to proved—that there is a first mover. For the argument reasons that if we take away a first mover, no other moved mover will be able to exercise its moving activity. But this

61. See ed. cit., p. 12. Note: "Cum ergo omnia praedicta moventia et mota sint corpora, ut probatum est, oportet quod sint quasi unum mobile per continuationem vel contiguationem. Et sic unum infinitum movetur tempore finito. Quod est impossibile, ut probatur in VI *Physicorum*" (ed. cit., p. 12). See *Physics* VI, c. 7 (238a 20–238b 22). Also see Thomas, *In VII Phys.*, lect. 2, p. 455, n. 892: "Manifestum est autem, quod cum aliquid movet ex eo quod movetur, simul movetur movens et ipsum mobile. . . ." Both Aristotle *(Physics* VII, c. 1 [242b 53–243a 22]) and Thomas, in a belabored but not completely convincing effort, devote additional attention to showing that there cannot be an infinity of finite motions by an infinity of moved movers in a finite time. See *In VII Phys.*, lect. 2, p. 456, n. 894. Fortunately, Thomas offers better arguments against an appeal to an infinite regress, as we shall now see.

62. "Secunda ratio ad idem probandum talis est. In moventibus et motis ordinatis, quorum scilicet unum per ordinem ab alio movetur, hoc necesse est inveniri, quod, remoto primo movente vel cessante a motione, nullum aliorum movebit neque movebitur: quia primum est causa movendi omnibus aliis. Sed si sint moventia et mota per ordinem in infinitum, non erit aliquod primum movens, sed omnia erunt quasi media moventia. Ergo nullum aliorum poterit moveri. Et sic nihil movebitur in mundo" (SCG I, c. 13, p. 12). Cf. Aristotle, *Physics* VIII, c. 5 (256a 13–21). In this argument Thomas has in mind what are often referred to as "essentially ordered" *(ordinatis)* movers and things moved, or what he more frequently refers to as moved movers or caused causes which are ordered per se. For this terminology see, for instance, *In II Sent.,* d. 1, q. 1, a. 5, *in contrarium* ad 5 (Mandonnet ed., Vol. 2, p. 39): "Ad quintum dicendum, quod eumdem effectum praecedere causas infinitas *per se,* vel *essentialiter,* est impossibile; sed *accidentaliter* est possibile; hoc est dictu, aliquem effectum de cuius ratione sit quod procedat a causis infinitis, esse impossibilem; sed causas illas quarum multiplicatio nihil interest ad effectum, accidit effectui esse infinitas" (italics mine). Also see *De veritate,* q. 2, a. 10. Thomas illustrates a per se multitude with a rock which is moved by a stick and that by a hand and that by nerves and muscles and that by the soul, and a *per accidens* multitude by a number of different saws used successively as replacements by a builder of a house (Leon. 22.1.75:51–70). Also see SCG II, c. 38 ("Quod etiam quinto obiicitur . . . ," ed. cit., p. 128); and ST I, q. 46, a. 2, ad 7.

seems to miss the whole point of an infinite regress of moved movers. In such a situation there would be no first mover. How can the argument assume that the first mover is the cause of the motion of all the other movers?

The argument can be defended against this last-mentioned objection. The point is that if there is no mover which is "first" in the sense that it does not depend upon something prior for its ability to move others, there will be no satisfactory explanation for the motion of anything. The argument neither assumes nor requires that there be any numerically first mover in the series. By appealing to such a series, all we will have done is to extend indefinitely or to infinity a series of moved movers, that is, of movers which are incapable of accounting for their moving other movers. Unless there is a "first" mover, that is, a mover that does not depend upon the motion of something prior for its ability to move other things, the motion of nothing else will be accounted for. Hence there will be no motion at all. To multiply moved movers, or insufficient explanations for motion, to infinity results in nothing but that, an infinity of insufficiencies. Mere numerical (and therefore quantitative) multiplication of moved movers (of insufficient explanations) does not result in diversity in kind or quality of explanation (a sufficient explanation). To put this another way, the argument really rests on the intelligibility of being, its ontological truth, as applied to things that are moved.[63]

As Thomas himself observes, his third refutation of a regress to infinity of moved movers really reduces to the second, but with the order reversed. That which moves as an instrumental cause *(instrumentaliter)* cannot do so unless there is something which moves as a principal cause *(principaliter)*. But if one regresses to infinity in moved movers, all of these will move only, as it were, as instruments. By this Thomas means that each of these moved movers will move only insofar as it is moved. Therefore, since all will be instrumental movers, none will be a principal

---

63. In other words, the purpose of the argument is not to prove that there must be a numerically first member of the series, but only that there must be something which is first in the sense that it does not depend upon anything prior for its ability to move others. If so, this argument will hold whether the members in the series are finite or infinite in multitude. In his Commentary on *Metaphysics* II Thomas brings this point out more explicitly: ". . . concludit quod nihil ad propositum differt, utrum sit unum tantum medium, vel plura: quia omnia plura media accipiuntur loco unius, inquantum conveniunt in ratione medii.—Et similiter non differt utrum sint media finita vel infinita; quia dummodo habeant rationem medii, non possunt esse prima causa movens. Et quia ante omnem secundam causam moventem requiritur prima causa movens, requiritur quod ante omnem causam mediam sit causa prima, quae nullo modo sit media, quasi habens aliam causam ante se . . ." (Cathala-Spiazzi ed., lect. 3, pp. 86–87, n. 303). Note that Thomas finds Aristotle introducing this argumentation in order to show that a first is the cause of those which come after it, that is, of the intermediary and of the last one. For some who have criticized the argument for assuming that there is a numerical first in such a series and therefore for begging the question see C.J.F. Williams, "*Hic autem non est procedere in infinitum,*" *Mind* 69 (1960), pp. 403–5; Kenny, *The Five Ways,* pp. 26–27. For a refutation of Williams (and one which will also apply to Kenny) see Owens, "Aquinas on Infinite Regress," in *St. Thomas Aquinas on the Existence of God,* pp. 228–30. For another who realizes that the argument is not guilty of this fallacy see P. Brown, "Infinite Causal Regression," in A. Kenny, ed., *Aquinas: A Collection of Critical Essays* (Garden City, N.Y., 1969), pp. 222–23.

mover. If this is so and if, as he has stated at the beginning of this argument, that which moves as an instrumental cause cannot move unless there is something which moves as a principal cause, it will follow that nothing is moved.[64]

The major presupposition in this argument is its first premise: that which moves as an instrumental cause cannot do so unless there is something which moves as a principal cause. Thomas sometimes uses the expression "instrumental cause" strictly to signify the kind of cause which can produce an effect only because it is moved by a higher and principal cause and not because it possesses a principle for such action in its own right. It is in this way that a saw may be regarded as an instrument of a human agent so as to produce an artifact such as a bench or table. In this case the human agent would be the principal cause of the effect. At times, however, Thomas uses "instrument" in a broader way, to signify any second or caused cause, whether or not it has within itself a principle for its own action or motion. In the present case he is using it in the first and strict sense. By a principal cause, therefore, he must have in mind the kind of cause or mover that does not depend upon some other cause or mover in order to exercise its causal activity here and now, that is, something which is not a moved mover.[65] But even if all this is granted, does not this again point to a fundamental flaw in the argument itself? The premise seems to beg the question by assuming what remains to be proved—that there is some principal cause of motion.

In reply to this I would suggest that the same reasoning is operative here as was the case in the previous argument. A beginningless series of instrumental causes (i.e., of moved movers) is nothing but that, a beginningless series of moved movers. Since no one of these is capable of accounting for the motion it produces, by multiplying them to infinity one does not advance the level of explanation. If the series of moved movers (instrumental causes) is extended to infinity, there is no principal cause (unmoved mover), and there is no adequate explanation for any other motion. Therefore, there will be no motion, which, of course, is contrary to our experience.[66]

Thomas concludes his presentation of this first argument from motion by not-

---

64. Ed. cit., p. 12. Note: "Id quod movet instrumentaliter, non potest movere nisi sit aliquid quod principaliter moveat. Sed si in infinitum procedatur in moventibus et motis, omnia erunt quasi instrumentaliter moventia, quia ponentur sicut moventia mota, nihil autem erit sicut principale movens. Ergo nihil movebitur." See Aristotle, *Physics* VIII, c. 5 (256a 21–256b 3), and Thomas's exposition in *In VIII Phys.*, lect. 9, pp. 546–47, n. 1041.

65. See *De veritate*, q. 24, a. 1, ad 5: "Ad quintum dicendum quod instrumentum dupliciter dicitur: uno modo proprie, quando scilicet aliquid ita ab altero movetur quod non confertur ei a movente aliquod principium talis motus, sicut serra movetur a carpentario . . . ; alio modo dicitur instrumentum magis communiter quidquid est movens ab alio motum, sive sit in ipso principium sui motus sive non . . ." (Leon. 22.3.681:352–682:364). Cf. *De veritate*, q. 27, a. 4 (Leon. 22.3.805:285–291). See MacDonald, "Aquinas's Parasitic Argument," pp. 142–43.

66. Again I take this to mean that whether the series of instrumental movers (moved movers) is finite or infinite is irrelevant. Unless there is some unmoved mover (principal mover), there will be no motion at all.

ing that it is in this way that Aristotle has proved that there is a first immobile mover. As we have already remarked above, while he presents this as Aristotle's argument, he also accepts it as valid.[67]

With this we come to his second major argument based on motion. This is taken from *Physics* VIII. If someone holds that every mover is indeed moved, and hence that there is no first unmoved mover, this proposition is true either *per se* or *per accidens*. But if it is true only *per accidens*, it is not a necessary proposition. Therefore it follows that it could be the case that no mover is moved. But if no mover is moved, it does not move (according to the adversary's claim that every mover is itself moved). Therefore it could be the case that nothing is moved. But Aristotle regards this as impossible, i.e., that at some time there was no motion. Therefore the first statement—that every mover is moved—is not a contingent proposition. From a contingent but false proposition something false and impossible will not follow. Consequently, the claim that every mover is moved by another is not true *per accidens*.[68]

Thomas makes this same point in another way. If two things are joined in some subject only *per accidens*, and one of these is found without the other, it is probable that the latter can also be found without the former. For instance, if white and musical are both present in Socrates, and in Plato there is the quality of being musical but not that of being white, it is probable that in some other subject white may be found without musical. Hence if to be a mover and to be moved are united in a given subject only *per accidens*, and being moved is present in another subject without its being a mover, it is probable that there is a mover which is not itself moved. The point of this dialectical argument—which surely is intended by Thomas to be no more than probable—is to support the claim that the proposition "every mover is moved by another" is not true *per accidens*.[69]

Having eliminated the claim that this proposition is true *per accidens*, Thomas next attempts to show that it is not true *per se*. He argues that under that supposition, impossible consequences will still follow. For instance, the mover will be moved by the same species of motion whereby it moves something else, or else by

67. "Et sic patet probatio utriusque propositionis quae supponebatur in prima demonstrationis via, qua probat Aristoteles esse primum motorem immobilem" (p. 12).

68. Ed. cit., p. 12. Note in particular: "Ergo primum non fuit contingens quia ex falso contingenti non sequitur falsum impossibile. Et sic haec propositio, *Omne movens ab alio movetur*, non fuit per accidens vera." Cf. Aristotle, *Physics* VIII, c. 5 (256b 3–13), and Thomas's Commentary on this—*In VIII Phys.*, lect. 9, p. 547, n. 1043. As Kretzmann has remarked, in the opening statement of the proposition he is challenging, Thomas simply phrases it: "Si omne movens movetur" without adding "ab alio." Since he has added this in the concluding statement we have quoted, it seems likely that we should so interpret it throughout the argument (*The Metaphysics of Theism*, p. 68).

69. SCG I, c. 13, ed. cit., p. 12 ("Item, si aliqua duo sunt coniuncta per accidens . . ."). Cf. Aristotle, *Physics* VIII, c. 5 (256b 13–24). In his Commentary on this in the *Physics*, Thomas explicitly describes this as a probable argument: ". . . probat idem alia probabili ratione . . ." (*In VIII Phys.*, lect. 9, p. 547, n. 1044). And he concludes from this that it is probable that one may find a mover that is not moved (p. 548).

motion of another species. If it is moved by the same species of motion, that which causes alteration will itself have to undergo alteration, and that which heals will itself have to be healed. Again, one who teaches will have to be taught, and with one and the same science. Thomas rejects this as impossible. One who teaches must possess science, while one who learns must lack that which he is to be taught. Thus it would follow from this hypothesis that the same thing is had and not had by one and the same thing, which is impossible. One who teaches would have to possess science insofar as he teaches, and lack that very same science insofar as he is taught.[70]

Thomas then introduces a consideration which shows that the present argument, unlike so much of his first general argument based on motion, does not restrict itself to local motion but also can be extended to change in quality (alteration) or in quantity (increase or decrease). Suppose that someone counters that the mover is moved by a different species of motion from that whereby it moves—for instance, that a mover which causes alteration is itself moved locally, and one which moves locally is moved in terms of increase in quantity, etc. Since the genera and species of motion are only finite, it will follow that one cannot go on to infinity in postulating different species of motion and, therefore, that there must be a first mover which is not moved by anything else.[71]

Thomas observes that someone might meet this response by postulating a circle of moved movers so that when all the different genera and species of motion have been exhausted, one will then return to the first kind. Thus, if that which moves something locally is itself moved by alteration, and that which causes it to undergo alteration itself is moved by increase in quantity, then that which causes the increase in quantity will in turn be moved by local motion. Thomas rejects this and argues that we would arrive at the same impasse as before—that which moves something else according to a given species of motion must itself be moved according to the same species of motion, although mediately rather than immediately this time. Thomas would still object that this amounts to saying that the thing in question must both lack the species of motion it causes insofar as it is moved by that motion, and yet have it insofar as it causes it in something else. Although he does not explicitly state this in the immediate context, one should understand that both the proposition he is refuting ("Every mover is moved by something else") and his refutation presuppose that the mover is moved simultaneously by something else, and that this applies to all the moved movers required to explain a given motion.[72]

Given all of this, Thomas concludes that we must admit that there is some first

---

70. Ed. cit., pp. 12–13.

71. See ed. cit., p. 13. Note in particular: ". . . cum sint finita genera et species motus, sequetur quod non sit abire in infinitum. Et sic erit aliquod primum movens quod non movetur ab alio."

72. Ibid. Note: "Sed ex hoc sequetur idem quod prius: scilicet quod id quod movet secundum aliquam speciem motus, secundum eandem moveatur, licet non immediate sed mediate" (p. 13). Cf.

mover which is not moved by anything external to itself. This, he realizes, is not yet enough to show that the first mover is completely immobile. In fact, he comments that Aristotle reasons that this first mover is either completely immobile (and then we will have reached our conclusion), or else it is not, since it is moved by itself. This second possibility seems likely, observes Thomas; for that which is *per se* is always prior to that which is through something else. Therefore it is reasonable to suppose that in the order of things moved, the first thing moved is moved by itself, not by something else. But if this is so, Thomas reminds us that that which moves itself cannot be moved by itself as a whole by a whole. Such a suggestion would lead again to the aforementioned difficulties—that someone would teach and be taught simultaneously, and that something would be in act and in potency at the same time. (The reader will note the explicit reference to simultaneity here.) That which moves, continues Thomas, insofar as it moves, is in act; but that which is moved is in potency. Therefore one must rather hold that one part of our first mover serves as mover and another part as that which is moved. From this it will follow that there is something which is immobile, that is, the part of the self-mover which serves as a moving principle.[73]

Thomas comments that in self-movers which are known to us, that is to say, in animals, the moving part (the soul), while being immobile *per se,* is nonetheless moved *per accidens*. This is to say that the soul is moved indirectly when the body which it informs is moved, presumably either when the soul moves the body and thereby moves itself locally, or when the body and hence the soul is affected by something external, such as digested food. Given this, Thomas finds Aristotle going on in *Physics* VIII to show that the moving part of this first self-mover is moved neither *per se* nor *per accidens*. He notes first of all that those self-movers which are

---

Aristotle, *Physics* VIII, c. 5 (256b 27–257a 27). See Thomas's Commentary on this, *In VIII Physic.,* lect. 9, pp. 548–49, nn. 1046–1049. Kretzmann finds this particular part of Thomas's argument unsalvageable, but also seems to thinks his reference to *mediate* rather than *immediate* permits one to eliminate the simultaneity requirement *(The Metaphysics of Theism,* pp. 70–71). In light of Thomas's discussion of the motion principle in the first argument from motion, and in light of subsequent discussion in the second argument which we shall now see, it seems to me that it is essential to retain this requirement.

73. SCG I, c. 13, p. 13. Note in particular: "Non enim potest dici quod movens seipsum totum moveatur a toto: quia sic sequerentur praedicta inconvenientia, scilicet quod aliquis simul doceret et doceretur, et similiter in aliis motibus; et iterum quod aliquid simul esset in potentia et actu. . . . Relinquitur igitur quod una pars eius est movens tantum, et altera mota." Thomas also considers and rejects any suggestion that within the unmoved mover both parts are moved (so that each would be moved by the other), or that one part moves itself and the other, or that the whole moves a part, or that a part moves the whole. These would lead to the same difficulties, i.e., that something would simultaneously move and be moved according to the same species of motion, and be in act and potency at the same time. He concludes: "Relinquitur ergo quod moventis seipsum oportet unam partem esse immobilem et moventem aliam partem." See *In VIII Phys.,* lect. 10, p. 555, nn. 1060–1061.

known to us, that is, animals, are corruptible and that this accounts for the fact that in each of them their moving part is moved *per accidens*. But corruptible self-movers must be traced back to some first self-mover which is sempiternal. Therefore there must be some moving principle within this self-mover which is moved neither *per se* nor *per accidens*.[74]

Thomas remarks that Aristotle's claim that there must be some sempiternal self-mover is based on his assumption that motion is eternal. This in turn entails the perpetual generation of those self-movers which are subject to generation and corruption. No single corruptible self-mover can account for this perpetual generation of self-movers, nor can all of them taken together. This follows both from the fact that they are infinite and from the fact that they are not simultaneous with one another. Hence there must be some perpetual self-mover which causes the perpetual generation of lower self-movers. Its moving principle will be moved neither *per se* nor *per accidens*. At this point, therefore, Thomas seems to think that Aristotle has arrived at knowledge of the perpetual self-mover of the outermost heavenly sphere. Then, as additional evidence, he mentions that certain self-movers, i.e., animals, begin to be moved anew because of a motion by which they do not move themselves, as in the example of food that is digested. Hence they are moved *per accidens*. From this he again concludes that no perpetual self-mover is moved either *per se* or *per accidens*. Therefore the first self-mover is moved by a moving principle that itself is moved neither *per se* nor *per accidens*.[75]

As Thomas realizes, even such a mover need not be identified with God. Because God himself is not a part of any self-mover, continues Thomas, Aristotle goes on in his *Metaphysics* (see Bk XII, c. 7) to reason from such a self-mover to another mover which is entirely separate, and which is God. Since every self-mover is moved by desire, the mover which is still a part of a self-mover must move because it seeks some object of desire. This object will be superior to the perpetual self-mover in the order of motion, since that which moves because it desires (something else) is in some way a moved mover. (Here the argument shifts from the order of efficient causality to final causality.) But that which is desired is a mover which is

---

74. Ed. cit., p. 13. Note: "Moventia enim se quae sunt apud nos, scilicet animalia, cum sint corruptibilia, pars movens in eis movetur per accidens. Necesse est autem moventia se corruptibilia reduci ad aliquod primum movens se quod sit sempiternum. Ergo necesse est aliquem motorem esse alicuius moventis seipsum qui neque per se neque per accidens moveatur." Cf. *In VIII Phys.,* lect. 12, pp. 563–66, nn. 1069–1076. See Kretzmann, op. cit., pp. 78–79, who includes human beings among the animals considered here. For Aristotle see *Physics* VIII, c. 6 (258b 13ff.; 259b 1–31). On these texts in Aristotle see Owens, "Aquinas and the Proof from the 'Physics'," pp. 124–26. Cf. for instance, Owens's remark on p. 125: "The primary immobile movent to which the argument in *Physics* VIII leads is accordingly the soul of the first heaven." In this he is in agreement with the interpretation offered by J. Paulus, "La théorie du Premier Moteur chez Aristote," *Revue de philosophie,* n.s. 4 (1933), pp. 259–94, 394–424, especially at 267, 283, 394–407.

75. See SCG I, c. 13, pp. 13–14. On this see Owens, "Aquinas and the Proof from the 'Physics'," pp. 133–34.

completely unmoved. Therefore we must conclude to the existence of a first and separate mover which is completely unmoved and unmovable, and this is God.[76]

This procedure on Thomas's part is interesting for a number of reasons. First of all, it indicates that in his judgment the argumentation offered by Aristotle in *Physics* VIII does not necessarily arrive immediately at knowledge of God but perhaps only at a self-mover which is less than God, presumably the besouled mover of the outermost heavenly sphere, according to the Aristotelian and medieval astronomy. In order for this approach to reach God, Thomas judges it necessary to turn to the reasoning used by Aristotle in *Metaphysics* XII. Hence as Thomas here reads Aristotle, it is in the *Metaphysics* that one really reaches the absolutely immobile mover, or God. Still, this raises the question whether in Thomas's view any argument which is based on motion and which is therefore physical in its point of departure can establish the existence of God.[77]

It should be recalled that at the end of his Commentary on *Physics* VIII Thomas identifies Aristotle's First Mover with God. Moreover, Thomas's procedure in offering his first general argument from motion in SCG I, c. 13 might lead us to conclude that such an argument can directly reach God. However, as we have already pointed out, the argumentation he offers for its two key principles is in large measure restricted to corporeal movers and corporeal moved-movers. The exception is his appeal to the broader act-potency theory in his third argument to show that whatever is moved is moved by something else. This broader justification for the principle appears to be needed if one wishes to apply it, as Thomas himself does in his second argument based on motion, to a cosmic self-mover which itself is moved by something else in the order of final causality, or to put it another way, if one is to arrive at a separate and completely immobile mover.[78] Owens has dealt with the broader issue involved in interpreting Thomas's more general argumenta-

76. "Sed quia Deus non est pars alicuius moventis seipsum, ulterius Aristoteles, in sua *Metaphysica*, investigat ex hoc motore qui est pars moventis seipsum, alium motorem separatum omnino, qui est Deus. Cum enim omne movens seipsum moveatur per appetitum, oportet quod motor qui est pars moventis seipsum, moveat propter appetitum alicuius appetibilis. Quod est eo superius in movendo: nam appetens est quodammodo movens motum; appetibile autem est movens omnino non motum. Oportet igitur esse primum motorem separatum omnino immobilem, qui Deus est" (ed. cit., p. 14). For Aristotle see *Metaphysics* XII, c. 7 (1072a 23–1072b 11).

77. See Owens's comments on our text from SCG I, c. 13: "To reach God, St. Thomas realizes, the Aristotelian reasoning has to pass over to metaphysics. Aside from the identification of the Aristotelian separate primary movent with the Christian God, this is correct Peripatetic procedure" ("Aquinas and the Proof from the 'Physics'," p. 134).

78. For Thomas's concluding remark from his Commentary on the *Physics* see *In VIII Phys.*, lect. 23, p. 628, n. 1172: "Et sic terminat Philosophus considerationem communem de rebus naturalibus, in primo principio totius naturae, qui est super omnia Deus benedictus in saecula. Amen." For Owens's reflections on this see "Aquinas and the Proof from the 'Physics'," p. 143: "This seems to be the closest St. Thomas comes to saying that natural philosophy can prove the existence of God. Yet he does not say it, nor do the words necessarily imply it in the context." See SCG I, c. 13, ed. cit., p. 11 ("Tertio").

tion from motion for God's existence and suggests that for such to reach its goal, it must be shifted from the physical to the metaphysical plane. While I agree with him in large measure on this point, I have some reservations about his additional suggestion that one must interpret such arguments as accounting not only for the motion of moving bodies, but for the existence of such motion.[79] If one does this, it seems to me, one no longer has Thomas's argument based on motion but another argument based on the contingent or efficiently caused character of existence.

In SCG I, c. 13 Thomas remarks that two objections might be thought to weaken these arguments as he has borrowed them from Aristotle. First of all, they assume the eternity of motion. Secondly, they assume that the first moved thing, the heavenly sphere, is moved of itself *(ex se)*. From this it follows that it is animated, a point which many do not grant.[80]

Thomas replies to the first objection with an a fortiori kind of answer. The most effective argument for God's existence operates under the more difficult alternative—the assumption that the world is eternal. If the world and motion have begun to be, it is evident that there must be some cause which produced them *de novo*. What begins to be must derive its origin from some innovating principle; for nothing can reduce itself from potency to act, or from nonexistence to existence.[81] In this final step, therefore, the argument considers as an alternative a broader and, it would seem, metaphysical approach to which one could turn if one could prove that the world began to be.

As for the second difficulty, Thomas notes that if the first mover is not moved of itself, it must be moved immediately by something else which is totally immobile.[82] For Thomas, of course, this is God. And this would undoubtedly be his

---

79. For Owens see loc. cit., p. 144: "In his commentary on *Physics* VIII, then, St. Thomas continues to view the proof from motion against a metaphysical background that makes it lead to God, while at the same time allowing it an interpretation that takes it to the soul of the outermost sphere." Commenting on the argument from motion as he has traced it through Thomas's writings, Owens writes: "St. Thomas tends to view the whole proof in a strongly metaphysical setting, in which the principles of actuality and potentiality, first known in motion, are extended to every kind of mutability and reception of being, including the reception of being in creation." For criticism of the view that in SCG I, c. 13 (in the second argument from motion) Thomas finds Aristotle in *Physics* VIII establishing the existence of a moved and subordinate self-mover and going on only in *Metaphysics* XII to conclude to the existence of God, see A. Pegis, "St. Thomas and the Coherence of the Aristotelian Theology," pp. 67–117, especially pp. 78–86, 97–98, 108–12. Pegis's careful study not withstanding, it seems to me that the text from SCG I, c. 13 (cited above in n. 76) suggests the opposite and strongly supports the understanding of Aquinas's reading of Aristotle offered by Paulus and Owens.

80. Ed. cit., p. 14.

81. "Et ad hoc dicendum quod via efficacissima ad probandum Deum esse est ex suppositione aeternitatis mundi, qua posita, minus videtur esse manifestum quod Deus sit. Nam si mundus et motus de novo incoepit, planum est quod oportet poni aliquam causam quae de novo producat mundum et motum: quia omne quod de novo fit, ab aliquo innovatore oportet sumere originem; cum nihil educat se de potentia in actum, vel de non esse in esse" (p. 14). Cf. *In VIII Phys.*, lect. 1, p. 501, n. 970. Also see Owens, "Aquinas and the Proof from the 'Physics'," p. 141.

82. ". . . dicendum est quod, si primum movens non ponitur motum ex se, oportet quod moveatur immediate a penitus immobili" (ed. cit., p. 14).

preferred personal way of proceeding, whereby one arrives immediately at a first and separate immobile mover. He comments that even Aristotle introduces his conclusion disjunctively: either one must immediately arrive at a first and separate and immobile mover, or else at a self-mover from which one may then reason to a first and separate immobile mover.[83] Perhaps in part because Thomas is presenting these as Aristotle's arguments, he allows for either side of the disjunction. Either alternative will ultimately lead to the same conclusion, the existence of a separate and immobile mover.

Such, therefore, is Thomas's long and laborious presentation in SCG I, c. 13 of two arguments from motion for God's existence. Both arguments are explicitly drawn from Aristotle, even though Thomas has reorganized them in his own fashion. In my opinion, to some extent each runs the risk of ending at best with a besouled self-mover of the outermost heavenly sphere rather than with God, at least when each is placed within its Aristotelian and medieval physical world-view. Thomas himself explicitly recognizes this difficulty in his presentation of the second argument, but it seems that he could have raised it when dealing with the first argument from motion as well. If, as Thomas has indicated, Aristotle's argumentation in *Physics* VIII leads only to a besouled self-mover, by appealing to *Metaphysics* XII Thomas believes that he can enable it to conclude to the existence of a perfectly immobile first mover which is separate and which is God.[84] As we shall see in the following chapter, Thomas introduces a much simpler and more direct argument based on motion in ST I, q. 2, a. 3 as his first way.

Thomas concludes SCG I, c. 13 by briefly presenting three more arguments for God's existence. The first, which he takes from Aristotle's *Metaphysics* II, c. 2, focuses on the inadequacy of appealing to a regress to infinity in efficient causes and the consequent need to conclude to a first cause. It might, therefore, simply be regarded as another way of meeting that difficulty. However, it is presented by Thomas as a separate and self-contained argument for God's existence. In all essentially ordered *(ordinatis)* efficient causes, the first is the cause of the intermediary and the intermediary is the cause of the last. This holds whether the intermediary causes are one or many. And it holds for the reason that when a cause is taken away, that which it causes is also taken away. In the present case, therefore, when the first

83. "Unde etiam Aristoteles sub disiunctione hanc conclusionem inducit: quod scilicet oporteat vel statim devenire ad primum movens immobile separatum, vel ad movens seipsum, ex quo iterum devenitur ad movens primum immobile separatum" (ibid.). On Thomas's recognition of this disjunction see Owens, "Aquinas and the Proof from the 'Physics'," pp. 133–34, 136, 138, 143–44; Kretzmann, *The Metaphysics of Theism*, pp. 82–83.

84. As I have already indicated, my difficulty concerning the first general argument from motion has to do with the highly physical way in which Thomas there attempts to justify its first main premise: that whatever is moved is moved by another. Only the third justification which he offers for this—that based on the broader theory of potentiality and actuality—seems to overcome this limitation and therefore should apply to any kind of motion or change. Significantly, Thomas uses only this third approach in justifying the similar step in his first way in ST I, q. 2, a. 3.

cause is removed, there can be no intermediary cause. But if one regresses to infinity with (caused) efficient causes, there will be no first cause. Therefore all the others will likewise be eliminated, since they will be intermediary causes. Because this is clearly false, one must conclude to the existence of a first efficient cause, or God.[85]

While this argument is presented only in skeleton fashion, it calls for some comment. First of all, it is not restricted to causes of motion but simply accepts as a fact the reality of efficient causes and of essentially subordinated efficient causes. If one takes something other than motion as one's instance of something that is efficiently caused, for instance, the caused character of *esse* as following from the essence-*esse* distinction in finite beings, one may then apply the argument to that case. To put this in other terms, this kind of argument could be based on a fact accepted by physics, i.e., the reality of motion as attested to by sense experience, or on a highly sophisticated metaphysical conclusion such as the essence-*esse* distinction and composition in finite beings. Secondly, in order to protect it from the charge of assuming what needs to be proved—that there is a first cause—an interpretation such as that offered above in our discussion of Thomas's rejection of appeal to an infinite regress should again be applied here.[86]

Thomas constructs another argument from some passages in Aristotle's *Metaphysics* II, c. 1 and IV, c. 4. In the first text he notes that Aristotle has shown that those things which are true to the maximum degree are also beings to the maximum degree. In other words, here he is appealing to the convertibility between truth and being, and thus to the truth of being. In the second text he finds Aristotle arguing that there is something which is true to the maximum degree. This claim

85. "Procedit autem Philosophus alia via in II *Metaphys.* ad ostendendum non posse procedi in infinitum in causis efficientibus, sed esse devenire ad unam causam primam: et hanc dicimus Deum. Et haec via talis est. In omnibus causis efficientibus ordinatis primum est causa medii, et medium est causa ultimi: sive sit unum, sive plura media. Remota autem causa, removetur id cuius est causa. Ergo, remoto primo, medium causa esse non poterit. Sed si procedatur in causis efficientibus in infinitum, nulla causarum erit prima. Ergo omnes aliae tollentur, quae sunt mediae. Hoc autem est manifeste falsum. Ergo oportet ponere primam causam efficientem esse. Quae Deus est" (ed. cit., p. 14). For Aristotle see *Metaphysics* II, c. 2 (994a 1–19). There he argues against appealing to an infinite regress in all four orders of causality, not merely in efficient causes. Cf. Thomas, *In II Met.,* lect. 3, pp. 86–87, nn. 301–304.

86. On Thomas's second and third ways of refuting a regress to infinity in his first argument for God's existence based on motion in SCG I, c. 13 see our discussion of the texts cited in nn. 62 and 64. Reference was made in n. 63 to certain recent writers who have considered this difficulty. To these should be added C. J. Kelley, "Circularity and Contradiction in Aquinas' Rejection of Actually Infinite Multitudes," *Modern Schoolman* 61 (1984), pp. 73–100, especially pp. 74–84. Also see J. Bendiek, "Über den Gebrauch von Reihen in den Gottesbeweisen," *Franziskanische Studien* 48 (1966), pp. 75–108, esp. 80–84. There he shows that this same difficulty was recognized by a number of medieval thinkers going back at least as far as Duns Scotus. See in particular Scotus's *Lectura* I, dist. 2, pars 1, qq. 1–2 in *Opera omnia,* Vol. 16 (Vatican City, 1960), pp. 128–31. For this objection see p. 127, n. 42. Note, however, that Scotus does not present this within the context of an argument based on motion but rather as implied by an argument based on the efficient production of being which he takes from Richard of St. Victor's *De Trinitate,* I, c. 1. See p. 126, n. 41.

is based on the observation that one false statement can be more false than another. (For instance, to take an example directly from Aristotle, to say that four things are a thousand is falser than to say that four things are five.) Therefore, Thomas continues, one of these statements is truer than the other, in that it comes closer to the truth. But things can be truer than others only insofar as they approach that which is true to the maximum degree. Therefore, from this Thomas concludes that there must be something which is supremely true and, given the convertibility of truth and being, supremely being. This we call God.[87]

In evaluating this rather puzzling argument we should bear in mind that it is presented in outline form. As Van Steenberghen has pointed out, it seems to suffer from the fallacy of understanding the term truth in two different ways, that is, as ontological truth or truth of being in the first part of the argument (based on *Metaphysics* II, c. 1), and as logical truth or truth of a proposition in the second part (based on *Metaphysics* IV, c. 4). And yet it concludes to the existence of something that is supremely true in the ontological sense.[88]

Since Thomas could hardly have been so naive as to commit such a schoolboy "howler," we may give the argument a benign reading and assume that he is taking truth in the same way in both instances when he refers to that which is true to the maximum degree or supremely true, i.e., as ontological truth or truth of being. If we grant this, the justification for the argument's transition from degrees of truth in propositions to that which is (ontologically) true to the maximum degree is still not immediately evident. Here it will help to recall that, for Thomas, truth as expressed in a proposition should reflect a state of affairs that obtains in reality. However, another problem remains, one which we have already encountered when dealing with the more Platonic-Neoplatonic argumentation in Thomas's Commentary on I *Sentences:* What is the ultimate justification for the claim that where there is a more and a less there must be a maximum, especially when we apply this to the ontological order?[89] Since this argument anticipates some of the thinking found in the fourth way of ST I, q. 2, a. 3, we shall delay fuller discussion of this last-mentioned point until we take up that text in the following chapter.

87. "Potest etiam alia ratio colligi ex verbis Aristotelis. In II enim *Metaphys.* ostendit quod ea quae sunt maxime vera, sunt et maxime entia. In IV autem *Metaphys.* ostendit esse aliquid maxime verum, ex hoc quod videmus duorum falsorum unum altero esse magis falsum, unde oportet ut alterum sit etiam altero verius; hoc autem est secundum approximationem ad id quod est simpliciter et maxime verum. Ex quibus concludi potest ulterius esse aliquid quod est maxime ens. Et hoc dicimus Deum" (ed. cit., p. 14). For Aristotle see *Metaphysics* II, c. 1 (993b 26–31); IV, c. 4 (1008b 31–1009a 2).

88. Cf. Van Steenberghen, *Le problème,* pp. 123–25. For a comparison of the argumentation in SCG I, c. 13 with that in ST I, q. 2, a. 3 see M. Wagner, *Die Philosophischen Implikate der "Quarta Via." Eine Untersuchung zum Vierten Gottesbeweis bei Thomas von Aquin (S. Th. I, 2, 3c),* (Leiden, 1989), pp. 122–23.

89. See above in this chapter, Section 1, arguments 2, 3, 4.

Thomas derives his final argument in this presentation from John Damascene's *De fide orthodoxa* and notes that it is also implied by Averroes in his Commentary on II *Physics*. Things which are contrary and opposed to one another cannot cooperate so as to form one order either always or even for the most part except through the governing activity of some principle by which it is given to each of them to tend to a definite end. But in the world we see that things which differ in nature cooperate with one another so as to form one order. This happens not rarely and by chance but always or at least for the most part. Therefore, there must be someone by whose providence the world is governed, and this we call God.[90]

This argument may remind the reader of one we have taken from Thomas's *De veritate*, q. 5, a. 2, and which we have regarded as anticipating the fifth way of ST I, q. 2, a. 3.[91] However, the emphasis in the present argument seems to be more on order and design than on finality, even though there is a passing reference to an end or final cause. The emphasis in the argument from the *De veritate* is more clearly and explicitly on finality in nature. The present argument is considerably less sophisticated and less developed from the philosophical standpoint and may be regarded as a more popularized version of an argument for God's existence based on order and design. As it stands it need not be regarded as one of Thomas's major ways of demonstrating God's existence.[92]

In c. 14 of SCG I, Thomas lays down certain ground rules for his attempt to arrive at more precise knowledge of God. He strongly emphasizes the need for us to have recourse to the way of negation in doing this, since the divine substance completely surpasses any form the human intellect can grasp. It is because of this that Thomas refuses to admit that we can arrive at quidditative *(quid est)* knowledge of God in the present life. But we can achieve some knowledge of him by the way of negation, that is, by determining as precisely as possible what he is not. By thus negating of God all that is inappropriate we improve our knowledge of him. With this in mind Thomas begins to use as a working principle a conclusion he has established in c. 13, namely, that God is completely immutable. This, of course, was the conclusion of the first two arguments he offered there based on motion.[93]

90. Ed. cit., p. 14: "Ad hoc etiam inducitur a Damasceno alia ratio sumpta ex rerum gubernatione. . . ." For Damascene see his *De fide orthodoxa*, c. 3, pp. 18–19. Thomas has reworked Damascene's argument. For Averroes see *In II Phys.* cc. 75, 77, ed. cit., Vol. 4, ff. 75v–76r, 77r–77v.

91. See above in this chapter, Section 3.

92. The texts from Averroes cited in n. 90 above place more emphasis on finality than Thomas's summary argument would lead one to expect. For further discussion of the argument from SCG I, c. 13, see Van Steenberghen, *Le problème*, pp. 125–26. Neither he nor Kretzmann regards the last argument offered there by Thomas as philosophically strong, at least as it is presented in that context (see Kretzmann, *The Metaphysics of Theism*, pp. 84, 88–89).

93. Ed. cit., p. 15. Note in particular: "Ad procedendum igitur circa Dei cognitionem per viam remotionis, accipiamus principium id quod ex superioribus iam manifestum est, scilicet quod Deus sit omnino immobilis." For fuller discussion of Thomas's views on our inability to reach quidditative knowledge of God see Ch. XIII below, Section 1.

This leads him to a discussion of divine eternity in c. 15. In brief, Thomas reasons that because God is completely immutable he must be eternal.[94] In the course of developing a series of arguments for this, Thomas also offers one that is in effect another argument for God's existence, that is, one based on contingency and necessity. We will see another version of this as the third way of ST I, q. 2, a. 3 below.

In SCG I, c. 15, the argument runs as follows. In the world we see certain things which can exist or not exist (possibilia esse et non esse) or, as Thomas also puts it, which are capable of being generated and corrupted. But every being of this kind, every "possible" being, has a cause. This follows, reasons Thomas, since considered simply in itself any such thing is equally open to existing or not existing; hence, if it enjoys actual existence, this can only be owing to some cause. But one cannot regress to infinity in caused causes, continues Thomas, with a reference back to his proof of this in c. 13. Therefore we must acknowledge that there is something which is a necessary being.[95] (By a necessary being, Thomas evidently has in mind any kind of being that is not subject to generation and corruption.) Every necessary being either depends upon some other cause for its very necessity, or it does not and is necessary of itself. We cannot proceed to infinity with necessary beings which depend upon something else for their necessity, or to phrase it differently, with caused necessary beings. Therefore we must conclude to the existence of a first necessary being which is necessary of itself. And this, Thomas concludes, is God, since he is the first cause, as has already been shown (in c. 13).[96]

This argument will undoubtedly strike today's reader as unusual because of the two ways in which it takes the notion of a necessary being, that is, as a caused necessary being and then as the uncaused necessary being. In order to appreciate Thomas's thinking concerning this it is important for us to bear in mind that with which he has contrasted a necessary being, that is, a possible being. As we have just seen, by a possible being as he uses it here he has in mind any being which is capable of being generated or corrupted. Any being which is not capable of being generated and corrupted is not to be regarded as a possible being but as a necessary

---

94. See Thomas's opening argument to show that God is eternal: "Nam omne quod incipit esse vel desinit, per motum vel mutationem hoc patitur. Ostensum autem est Deum esse omnino immutabilem. Est igitur aeternus, carens principio et fine" (ed. cit., p. 15).

95. "Amplius. Videmus in mundo quaedam quae sunt possibilia esse et non esse, scilicet generabilia et corruptibilia. Omne autem quod est possibile esse, causam habet: quia, cum de se aequaliter se habeat ad duo, scilicet esse et non esse, oportet si ei approprietur esse, quod hoc sit ex aliqua causa. Sed in causis non est procedere in infinitum, ut supra probatum est per rationem Aristotelis. Ergo oportet ponere aliquid quod sit necesse esse" (pp. 15–16).

96. "Omne autem necessarium vel habet causam suae necessitatis aliunde; vel non, sed est per seipsum necessarium. Non est autem procedere in infinitum in necessariis quae habent causam suae necessitatis aliunde. Ergo oportet ponere aliquod primum necessarium, quod est per seipsum necessarium. Et hoc Deus est: cum sit causa prima, ut ostensum est." Thomas immediately goes on to show that this being, God, is eternal, since anything which is necessary of itself is eternal (ed. cit., p. 16).

being.[97] Given this, we will not be so surprised to see Thomas entertaining the notion of a caused necessary being, or a being that depends upon something else for its nature as a necessary being. By this he has in mind any being which is not subject to generation and corruption even though it may depend on something else for its very being. Any such entity—any spiritual being, for instance—enjoys its realization as a necessary being either of itself or not of itself. If it does not enjoy this of itself, it must receive it from something else and must, therefore, be caused.[98]

Another interesting feature of this argument is the fact that it raises the issue of a possible regress to infinity at two different levels. At the first level Thomas reasons that if every possible being—every being that is subject to generation and corruption—depends upon something else for its existence, there can be no infinite regress in possible beings. Since he appeals here to his earlier discussion of this in SCG I, c. 13, we may presume that he would have us apply that same reasoning to the present case. Whether or not one postulates an infinite series of such caused possible beings, one must also admit the existence of a being which is not caused in this sense, that is, which is not subject to generation and corruption. Such a being is, as we have seen, described by Thomas as a necessary being.

But even at the level of necessary beings Thomas finds it imperative to mention the issue of a regress to infinity once more. This follows from his acknowledgment that necessary (i.e., incorruptible) beings may themselves depend upon something else for their very being. Even so, he reasons, we cannot proceed to infinity with

---

97. Thomas is also familiar with another understanding of possibility, according to which anything which does not exist of itself but depends upon something else would be described as a possible being. In *De potentia,* q. 5, a. 3 he attributes such an understanding to Avicenna, but expresses his preference for another view which he there credits to Averroes, i.e., the position he adopts in our argument from SCG I, c. 15: "Avicenna namque posuit quod quaelibet res praeter Deum habebat in se possibilitatem ad esse et non esse. Cum enim esse sit praeter essentiam cuiuslibet rei creatae, ipsa natura rei creatae per se considerata, possibilis est ad esse. . . . Commentator vero . . . contrarium ponit, scilicet quod quaedam res creatae sunt in quarum natura non est possibilitas ad non esse. . . . Et haec quidem positio videtur rationabilior. Potentia enim ad esse et non esse non convenit alicui nisi ratione materiae, quae est pura potentia . . ." (Pession ed., p. 135). On the other hand, see *In I Sent.,* d. 8, q. 5, a. 2 (Mandonnet ed., Vol. I, pp. 229–30). There he notes that if we find a quiddity which is not composed of matter and form, either that quiddity will be identical with its *esse,* or it will not be. If it is, it will be the essence of God himself. If it is not, it must receive its *esse* from something else: "Et quia omne quod non habet aliquid a se, est possibile respectu illius; huiusmodi quidditas cum habeat esse ab alio, erit possibilis respectu illius esse. . . ." Cf. J. Owens, "*Quandoque* and *Aliquando* in Aquinas' *Tertia Via,*" *New Scholasticism* 54 (1980), p. 454 and n. 12.

98. See the text cited above in n. 96. Also see *De potentia,* q. 5, a. 3 (ed. cit., pp. 135–36). After noting that the possibility for nonbeing belongs to a creature by reason of its matter (see n. 97 above), Thomas comments that such a possibility may not be present in the nature of a thing in one of two ways: either because the thing is a subsisting form and lacks all matter, or because the entire *possibilitas* of the matter is filled by the form which now informs it, so that it is not in potency to receive any other form (as, he thought, is true of heavenly bodies). Since the possibility of not existing is not present in either of these kind of things, they may be described as necessary beings: "Nec tamen per hoc removetur quin necessitas essendi sit eis a Deo, quia unum necessarium alterius causa esse potest. . . ." (p. 136).

caused necessary beings. Therefore we must conclude to the existence of an uncaused necessary being. Again we may take him to mean that whether or not one multiplies caused necessary beings to infinity does not really matter. Unless we admit that there is an uncaused necessary being we will have offered no satisfactory explanation for our caused necessary beings and, therefore, for anything at all.[99]

This argument, especially in the version presented in *Summa theologiae* I, q. 2, a. 3, is often referred to as one based on contingency and necessity, and we ourselves have so described it in introducing Thomas's presentation of it in SCG I, c. 15. This parlance is acceptable, but only if one bears in mind the restricted way in which the term "possible" is used in it (meaning that which is capable of being generated and corrupted) and the correspondingly broader way in which the term "necessary" is employed (so as to apply to caused necessary beings such as human souls, angels and, for that matter, heavenly bodies according to Thomas's medieval world-view, as well as to the uncaused necessary being, the being that is necessary of itself, or God).[100]

When it comes to establishing the fact that such possible beings do exist, the argument in SCG I, c. 15 (and in ST I, q. 2, a. 3) appears to take as its point of departure the generable and corruptible character of the things we experience about us. This has led to some diversity of opinion concerning the proper way in which the argument should be interpreted. According to one approach, this argument establishes the caused or contingent character of such beings simply by appealing to the fact of change, but to substantial change in this instance. In substantial change one substantial center of existence ceases to exist as such, and another comes into existence. This, according to many, is enough to prove that any such being depends upon something else for its existence, or that it is efficiently caused.[101]

---

99. See the texts cited above in nn. 97 and 98. In SCG I, c. 13 (see n. 96 above) Thomas refers to necessary beings which have a cause of their necessity from another *(aliunde)*. One might wonder whether this means that only their necessity is caused by something else, but not their existence. Such is clearly not Thomas's understanding. If a necessary being depends upon something else for its necessity, it depends upon something else for its very *esse*. See *De potentia*, q. 5, a. 3, as cited above in n. 98.

100. In addition to the texts cited above in nn. 98 and 99 see SCG II, c. 30 (pp. 116–18). For a fuller treatment of Thomas's understanding of necessity see G. Jalbert, *Nécessité et contingence chez S. Thomas d'Aquin et chez ses prédécesseurs* (Ottawa, 1961), especially pp. 137–47. However, I do not accept Jalbert's claim that it was only in SCG II, cc. 49–55, that Thomas first defended the real distinction beween essence and existence (see pp. 136–37). On Thomas's views concerning the incorruptible character of heavenly bodies see T. Litt, *Les corps célestes dans l'univers de saint Thomas d'Aquin* (Louvain-Paris, 1963), pp. 46–90. On the movers of heavenly bodies see pp. 99–109. While Thomas constantly affirms that they are moved by created spirits, he is hesitant concerning whether such created spiritual movers are united with heavenly bodies as forms with matter.

101. See Van Steenberghen, *Le problème*, pp. 127–28; Owens, "*Quandoque* and *Aliquando*," pp. 451–55, and pp. 455–56, n. 14. Cf. pp. 465–466. Owens, however, insists that the argument is metaphysical in character, even if it starts with the fact of physical change (generation and corruption).

Other interpreters, however, see Thomas as arguing here from metaphysical contingency, that is, from the distinction between essence and *esse* in all such beings. While such an approach is attractive from the metaphysician's standpoint, and while it squares nicely with the procedure actually followed by Thomas in *De ente*, c. 4 (at least according to my reading), it does not seem to be the interpretation explicitly indicated by Thomas's words in SCG I, c. 15. There he simply writes that in the world we see certain things which are capable of existing and not existing, that is, things which are generable and corruptible. In this argument, therefore, he is content to rest his case for the caused character of such entities on their capacity to undergo generation and corruption.[102]

A word of caution is in order concerning Thomas's reference to a possible as being indifferent, as it were, to existing and to not existing. This should not be taken as implying that for him a possible entity enjoys some kind of preexisting reality in itself, and that it awaits the communication of existence from without in order to become a member of our world of actual entities at some point in the course of time. Some such interpretation would be assigned to Henry of Ghent, at least by some critics, not too long after Thomas's death, because of Henry's unusual views concerning possible being or, to use his terminology, essential being *(esse essentiae)*. But any such view is far removed from Thomas's position concerning nonexisting but possible entities.[103]

Some (Owens, for instance) have noted the Aristotelian background for Thomas's usage in the passage now under consideration. According to this view, possibility as it is employed here is closely associated with and perhaps even identified with

---

Because it starts from a possibility for being and not being, it falls under the science of being as being. See n. 14 for his criticism of others who would regard the argument as physical because of its start with physical things, for instance: T. K. Connolly, "The Basis of the Third Proof for the Existence of God," *The Thomist* 17 (1954), pp. 281–349 (who regards the argument as it appears in ST I, q. 2, a. 3 as physical, though as it is presented in SCG I, c. 15 it would be metaphysical [p. 347]); J. Bobik, "The First Part of the Third Way," *Philosophical Studies* (Maynooth) 17 (1968), pp. 142–44 (it is physical in both versions).

102. For such a reading see A. Pattin, "La structure de la 'tertia via' dans la 'Somme théologique' de saint Thomas d'Aquin," *Revue de l'Université d'Ottawa* 27 (1957), pp. 26*–35*, especially p. 30*. For a critique of this reading see Van Steenberghen, *Le problème*, p. 128, n. 30.

103. See Van Steenberghen, *Le problème*, p. 128, who sees in this way of speaking another illustration of what he calls the dialectical cast *(tournure dialectique)* which he finds to be typical of scholastics, including Aquinas. By this he has in mind their widespread tendency to express ontological relations between realities by means of the logical relations which obtain between the concepts which express these realities (see p. 42). In the present case, in the order of concepts the idea of something contingent or possible is expressed by its indifference to existing or not existing. But in the order of reality a possible enjoys no intrinsic reality in and of itself before it actually exists; therefore it cannot in itself be indifferent to exist or not to exist, since it cannot be the subject of any behavior (see p. 128). For more on Thomas's views concerning the reality to be assigned to nonexisting possibles, along with a treatment of Henry's theory (and that of Godfrey of Fontaines) see my *Metaphysical Themes*, c. VII.

matter. Thus the argument's point of departure would be the presence of matter in beings which are capable of generation and corruption, which matter is indifferent to existence and nonexistence in the qualified sense that it can receive one substantial form or receive another.[104]

While this is true enough for Aquinas, it is not quite what he actually *says* either in the present text or in its parallel in the *Summa theologiae*. What he says is that we see certain things in the world which are possibles, that is, things which are subject to generation and corruption. Taken literally, this implies that the things in question are possibles, not that their matter is possible, even though Thomas holds that their possibility (capacity to be generated or corrupted) is owing to the presence of matter in them.[105]

Finally, Thomas offers what amounts to still another presentation of this argumentation in SCG II, c. 15. There it is one of a series of arguments he develops in an effort to prove that God is the cause of being *(causa essendi)* for all other things. Again he reasons that everything which can exist and not exist has a cause. Considered in itself any such thing is indifferent to existing or not existing and must, therefore, be determined to one of these by something else. Once more Thomas rejects the viability of regressing to infinity in caused possible beings as a satisfactory explanation, and concludes that there must be some necessary being which is the cause of existing and not existing for all possibles. Again he notes that some necessary beings have a cause of their necessity. Since regress to infinity in caused necessary beings is unsatisfactory as an explanation, one must conclude to the existence of something which is necessary of itself *(per se)*. In a significant addition to his earlier version of this argumentation, he now adds that such a necessary being can only be one, as he has already shown in Bk I (see c. 42). This he identifies with God, and concludes that everything else must be reduced to God as its cause of being.[106]

This addition is important, since it suggests that Thomas does not regard any of these versions of the argument as sufficient in itself to establish the unicity or

104. See Owens, *"Quandoque* and *Aliquando,"* pp. 452–53. On this point (the identification of matter with possibility) he appears to be following D. O'Donoghue, "An Analysis of the *Tertia Via* of St. Thomas," *Irish Theological Quarterly* 20 (1953), pp. 132–44. A key Aristotelian passage supporting this is *Metaphysics* VII, c. 7 (1032a 20–22).

105. See Thomas's Commentary on the passage from *Metaphysics* VII, c. 7, cited in the preceding note: "Omne enim quod generatur vel per artem vel per naturam, est possibile esse et non esse. Cum enim generatio sit de non esse in esse mutatio, oportet id quod generatur quandoque quidem esse, quandoque non esse: quod non esset nisi esset possibile esse et non esse" [so far he is speaking of the *thing* which can be or not be, not of its matter]. He continues: "Hoc autem quod est in unoquoque in potentia ad esse et non esse, est materia" *(In VII Met.,* lect. 6, p. 343, n. 1388). I take this to mean that it is because of the presence of matter as an intrinsic potential principle that the thing itself is to be described as possible.

106. SCG II, c. 15 (ed. cit., p. 101). Note: "Hoc autem non potest esse nisi unum, ut in primo libro ostensum est."

uniqueness of the being that is necessary of itself. Additional argumentation will be required to prove that there is only one such being or only one God, as we shall see in greater detail in the following chapter after we consider the five ways.[107]

5. *Compendium theologiae* I, c. 3

While the dating of this work has been contested, for present purposes I will assume with the Leonine edition and Torrell that its first part (which includes our text) dates from ca. 1265–1267 and, therefore, between the *Summa contra Gentiles* and ST I. This is interesting because the single argument for God's existence Thomas offers there in c. 3 is an argument from motion. This particular version is much briefer and simpler than the two arguments from motion of SCG I, c. 13. This seems appropriate both in light of the seemingly broader audience for which the *Compendium theologiae* was intended, and in light of the more sophisticated if still brief version of the argument from motion presented in the slightly later ST I, q. 2, a. 3.[108]

In c. 3 Thomas introduces this argument by commenting that before taking up the unity of the divine essence, one must first hold that God exists. And this, he comments, is evident from reason. For we see that all things that are moved are moved by others. Thus lower things are moved by higher ones, such as elements by heavenly bodies. And among the elements, that which is stronger moves that which is weaker. Among heavenly bodies themselves, lower bodies are moved by a higher one. (Although these examples are all taken from the Aristotelian physics of Thomas's time, they are instances of local motion. Others could be substituted from our present-day world.)[109]

But, Thomas continues, it is impossible to proceed to infinity in things moved which are moved by others. In support he comments that what is moved by something (else) is, as it were, a certain instrument of a first mover. If there is no first mover, all the moved movers will be instruments. But if one regresses to infinity with movers and things moved, there will be no first mover. Therefore all of the movers and things moved will be instruments. Thomas counters that it is ridiculous, even among the unlearned, to hold that instruments are moved without a principal agent. To illustrate this he draws an analogy with common experience. This would be like suggesting that a bed could be built simply by appealing to an

---

107. On Thomas's argumentation in SCG I, c. 42 for the uniqueness of the necessary being *per se* see Kretzmann, *The Metaphysics of Theism,* pp. 160–65.

108. On the dating see Leon. 42.8; Van Steenberghen, *Le problème,* pp. 146–49; Torrell, *Saint Thomas Aquinas,* pp. 349–50.

109. Leon. 42.84. Note his introductory remark: ". . . primo quidem tenendum est Deum esse; quod ratione conspicuum est."

ax or a saw without any carpenter. He concludes, therefore, that there must be a first mover which is supreme over all else and which we call God.[110]

If we take the argument at face value, it simply begins with various kinds of local motion, based on our experience of different kinds of moving bodies. It does not seem that Thomas's text here would justify our broadening the argument to cover every transition from potency to act although, as we shall see below, such an application will be appropriate in the case of the first way of ST I, q. 2, a.3. Moreover, as Van Steenberghen points out, in the present version of the argument, unlike Thomas's procedure in SCG I, c. 13 and in ST I, q. 2, a. 3, he makes no attempt to offer a theoretical justification for the motion principle (that whatever is moved is moved by something else). He simply appeals to a generalization based on limited sense experience.[111]

As regards the refutation of appealing to an infinite regress as an alternative to admitting the existence of a first mover, Thomas's procedure here should be interpreted in the way we have suggested above in connection with the arguments from motion in SCG I, c. 13. If he here speaks of the need for a principal cause to account for the motion of instruments or moved movers, his point is not to show that there cannot be such a series, perhaps even infinite, of moved movers; it is rather that, without an unmoved mover or principal cause that does not depend on something else for its motion, the motion of nothing will be explained. To drive home this point here, however, he simply turns to the analogy with the carpenter's tools without a carpenter.

Finally, like some earlier arguments we have already considered, this one does not explicitly attempt to show that there can only be one first mover. However, Thomas does devote a separate chapter in the *Compendium* to this (see c. 15), as we shall note in discussing divine unicity (uniqueness) in Ch. XII below. With this background in mind, we now turn to that chapter.

---

110. Ibid. Note from his argument: "Oportet autem, si in infinitum procedatur in moventibus et motis, primum movens non esse; omnia igitur infinita moventia et mota erunt instrumenta."
111. Van Steenberghen, *Le problème*, pp. 151–52.

XII

The Five Ways

As anyone with even a casual acquaintance with Aquinas's writings is aware, it is in the *Summa theologiae* I, q. 2, a. 3 that he presents his best-known formulation of argumentation for God's existence. A number of the arguments we have considered from his earlier writings foreshadow most if not all of the "five ways" of the *Summa theologiae*. These points of similarity notwithstanding, Thomas gives a personal and particular touch to each of the five ways themselves. Because of the relatively later date of this treatment (ca. 1266–1268), because of the apparently wider readership at which the *Summa theologiae* is aimed, and because of the comprehensive way in which the five ways are fitted together, these arguments for God's existence have received more attention from Thomas's students than any of his other efforts to establish this point.[1]

At the same time, it should be remembered that the amount of space accorded to each of the five ways is relatively brief and that in certain instances, at least, familiarity with some of Thomas's most fundamental metaphysical options is presupposed by them.[2] Finally, the question has often been raised concerning whether the five ways are intended by Thomas to form one developing argument for God's existence, or five distinct and more or less independent arguments. To put this in

1. On Thomas's intention to write the *Summa* for beginners (in theology) see Ch. X above, n. 50, and the references there to Boyle, Torrell, and O'Meara. Also see Weisheipl, *Friar Thomas d'Aquino*, pp. 218–19; M-D. Chenu, *Introduction à l'étude de saint Thomas d'Aquin*, 2d ed. (Montréal-Paris, 1954), pp. 255–58. Weisheipl also observes that while Thomas managed to carry out his purpose of addressing beginning students in theology in the first part of his work, the second and third parts "are far from being a simple introduction" (pp. 222–23).

2. Some of this background has already been provided above in our consideration of earlier versions of argumentation for God's existence in Thomas's texts. At the same time, it is good to bear in mind that Thomas himself sets his five ways within the background of his own philosophy and metaphysics. This in turns suggests that it is a highly questionable procedure simply to extract the five ways from their broader setting within Thomistic metaphysics and to expect them to, as it were, "stand on their own."

other terms, how are these five proofs intended to fit together? Before making any attempt to answer this question, however, it will first be necessary for us to consider each of them in turn.

Question 2 of the First Part of the *Summa theologiae* is addressed to this issue: Does God exist?[3] In a. 1 Thomas again rejects any claim that God's existence is self-evident *(per se notum)* to us, even though he continues to hold that the proposition "God exists" is self-evident in itself. Its predicate is identical with its subject since God's essence is his act of being *(esse)*. Because we do not know of God what he is, that he exists is not known to us *per se* but needs to be demonstrated by means of things which are better known to us, i.e., his effects. As we have already seen, Thomas's denial that God's existence is self-evident to us also leads him to reject the Anselmian argument for God's existence.[4]

In a. 2 Thomas distinguishes between a demonstration which moves from knowledge of a cause to knowledge of its effect, that is, demonstration of the reasoned fact *(propter quid* demonstration), and demonstration which moves from knowledge of an effect to knowledge of its cause and is called demonstration of the fact (demonstration *quia*). This second kind of demonstration rests upon the fact that an effect depends upon its cause. If the effect is given, its cause must preexist. It is by means of this kind of demonstration that God's existence can be established.[5]

In replying to the second objection in this same a. 2, Thomas makes an interesting comment. According to the objection, the middle term in a demonstration is a thing's quiddity. But when it comes to God we cannot know what he is but only what he is not. Therefore we cannot demonstrate that God exists. In his response Thomas notes that when a demonstration moves from our knowledge of an effect to knowledge of its cause, we must put the effect in the place of the definition of the cause if we are to prove that the cause exists. This is especially true when we are dealing with God. In order to prove that something exists we need only use as a middle term a nominal definition of that which is to be demonstrated, not a real (or quidditative) definition. This follows, continues Thomas, because the question "What is it?" comes after the question "Is it?" But we apply names to God from what we discover in his effects. Therefore, in demonstrating his existence from an effect we may use as a middle term that which the name God signifies, that is, some purely nominal definition. Curiously, in each of the five ways, Thomas does not explicitly carry out this step for us, but leaves it for the reader to supply.[6]

---

3. "Circa essentiam vero divinam, primo considerandum est an Deus sit . . ." (Leon. 4.27).

4. See Leon. 4.27–28, and the text cited above in Ch. X, n. 32. For his rejection of the Anselmian argumentation see ad 2 (p. 28).

5. Leon. 4.30. Note in particular: "Ex quolibet autem effectu potest demonstrari propriam causam eius esse . . . : quia, cum effectus dependeant a causa, posito effectu necesse est causam praeexistere. Unde Deum esse, secundum quod non est per se notum quoad nos, demonstrabile est per effectus nobis notos."

6. Leon. 4.30. If we may anticipate the first way for the sake of illustration, it begins with an effect, the fact that things are moved. By using the principle that whatever is moved is moved by

1. The First Way

With this we come to a. 3: "Whether God exists." Thomas begins the corpus of this article by writing that God's existence can be proved in five ways. The first and more evident *(manifestior)* way is that which is based on motion *(motus)*. It is certain and evident to the senses that some things in this world are moved *(moveri)*. (Here, as in our previous discussion of arguments from motion in SCG I, c. 13, we shall translate this verb passively rather than intransitively.) But whatever is moved is moved by something else. In support of this claim, already familiar to us as the principle of motion, Thomas argues that nothing is moved except insofar as it is in potency to that to which it is moved. But something moves insofar as it is in actuality, since to move is nothing else but to reduce something from potency to act. And something can be reduced from potency to act only by some being in actuality. To illustrate this point Thomas notes that it is something which is actually hot (such as fire) which renders that which is only potentially hot (such as wood) actually hot and thereby moves and alters it. (This example is significant, for it indicates that if the argument starts from the fact of observable motion, motion itself is being taken more broadly than local motion; at the very least it also includes alteration.) Thomas now argues that it is not possible for the same thing to be in act and in potency at the same time and in the same respect but only in different respects. Thus what is actually hot cannot at the same time be potentially hot (with respect to the same degree of heat, we should understand), but it is at that time potentially cold. Therefore, it is not possible for something to be mover and to be moved in the same respect by one and the same motion, or for it to move itself (in this strict sense). Therefore, everything which is moved must be moved by something else.[7]

---

something else, and by eliminating appeal to an infinite regress of moved movers as an adequate explanation, it concludes to the existence of a first and unmoved mover, or God. Here the effect—motion (the fact that things are moved)—serves as the middle term in the argument as Thomas presents it. However, in order for the argument to conclude explicitly to God's existence we must supply another syllogism such as this as suggested by Van Steenberghen: By the term "God" one means a being which is the First Mover of all motions which occur in this world. But such a First Mover exists. Therefore God exists *(Le problème,* pp. 171–72; cf. p. 164). This syllogism uses a nominal definition, "First Mover," as one would expect from Thomas's reply to objection 2. But it is not this nominal definition which serves as a middle term in the first way as Thomas actually presents it, but rather an observable effect, i.e., that things are moved. Thomas's first way is really directed to establishing the minor of our supplied syllogism.

7. "Prima autem et manifestior via est, quae sumitur ex parte motus. Certum est enim, et sensu constat, aliqua moveri in hoc mundo. Omne autem quod movetur, ab alio movetur. Nihil enim movetur, nisi secundum quod est in potentia ad illud ad quod movetur: movet autem aliquid secundum quod est actu. Movere enim nihil aliud est quam educere aliquid de potentia in actum: de potentia autem non potest aliquid reduci in actum, nisi per aliquod ens in actu: sicut calidum in actu, ut ignis, facit lignum, quod est calidum in potentia, esse actu calidum, et per hoc movet et alterat ipsum. Non autem est possibile ut idem sit simul in actu et potentia secundum idem, sed solum secundum diversa: quod enim est calidum in actu, non potest simul esse calidum in potentia,

Thomas next turns to the second major part of the argument based on motion. If that by which something is moved is itself moved, this second mover must itself be moved by something else, and so on. But one cannot regress to infinity in moved movers. If there were no first mover, there would be no other mover, since second movers do not move unless they are moved by a first mover. Thus a stick does not move unless it is moved by a hand. Therefore we must arrive at some first mover which is moved by nothing whatsoever, and this everyone understands to be God.[8]

With our discussion of the two arguments from motion in SCG I, c. 13 still in mind, we are now in position to make some comments about the argument from motion in ST I, q. 2, a. 3. First of all, as we have just noted in passing, the point of departure for the argument as it is presented here now seems to be broader.[9] Motion as it is used here is not restricted to instances of local motion but, as the text explicitly indicates, is taken broadly enough so as to apply to alteration as well. Given this, one wonders whether we may apply it to any kind of motion and perhaps even to changes which are not classified by Thomas as motions in the strict sense, e.g., generation and corruption.

It should be noted that in commenting on *Physics* III, Thomas writes that in working out his definition of motion *(motus)* there Aristotle uses this term broadly so as to apply it to change *(mutatio)*. Motion, therefore (meaning thereby change), is the act of that which exists in potency insofar as it is in potency. In that context Thomas speaks of motion in terms of quantity, in terms of quality, and in terms of place, as well as in terms of substance (generation and corruption).[10] In commenting on *Physics* V Thomas follows Aristotle in dividing change *(mutatio)* into three species—generation, corruption, and motion. (Again he remarks that in Bk III Aristotle had taken the term "motion" broadly so as to apply to all the kinds of change.) In Bk V, however, he finds Aristotle using the term "motion" more strictly

---

sed est simul frigidum in potentia. Impossibile est ergo quod, secundum idem et eodem motu [for: *modo*], aliquid sit movens et motum, vel quod moveat seipsum. Omne ergo quod movetur, oportet ab alio moveri" (Leon. 4.31). Along with Van Steenberghen (op. cit., p. 167); Kenny, *The Five Ways* (p. 7, n. 1); and *Summa Theologiae. Vol. 2: Existence and Nature of God,* ([New York–London, 1964], p. 12), I have substituted *motu* for *modo* in this text. However, retention of the reading *modo* will not change the argument.

8. "Si ergo id a quo movetur, moveatur, oportet et ipsum ab alio moveri; et illud ab alio. Hic autem non est procedere in infinitum: quia sic non esset aliquod primum movens; et per consequens nec aliquod aliud movens, quia moventia secunda non movent nisi per hoc quod sunt mota a primo movente, sicut baculus non movet nisi per hoc quod est motus a manu. Ergo necesse est devenire ad aliquod primum movens, quod a nullo movetur: et hoc omnes intelligunt Deum" (Leon. 4.31).

9. For the texts from SCG I, c. 13, see ed. cit., pp. 10–11 (cited in Ch. XI above, n. 40 [for the first argument from motion]), and p. 12 (for the second argument).

10. *In III Phys.*, lect. 2, pp. 144–45, nn. 285–286. Note in particular: "Unde convenientissime Philosophus definit motum, dicens quod motus est *entelechia,* idest *actus existentis in potentia secundum quod huiusmodi*" (n. 285); "Accipit enim hic motum communiter pro mutatione, non autem stricte secundum quod dividitur contra generationem et corruptionem, ut dicetur in quinto" (n. 286).

so as to apply it to only one of these three species. When motion is taken in this restricted sense it may in turn be divided into motion in quality (alteration), motion in quantity (increase or decrease), and motion in place (local motion). Substantial change (whether generation or corruption) is not motion taken strictly; it is only change *(mutatio)*.[11]

To return to Thomas's first way, therefore, we would seem to be justified in regarding motion taken strictly in any of its three kinds as a possible starting point for the argument, i.e., alteration, local motion, and increase or decrease in quantity. If Thomas is using the term broadly so as to equate it with change, we could even use substantial change as a possible point of departure for the first way. In fact he will explicitly appeal to generation and corruption in developing his third way.

Given all of this, I am inclined to limit motion as it appears as the starting point of the first way to some form of motion taken strictly, but to suggest that in the course of justifying the principle of motion—whatever is moved is moved by something else—Thomas uses motion broadly enough to apply to any reduction from potentiality to actuality. If this is correct, it will mean that in the second part of the argument, where he considers a possible regress to infinity, he intends to eliminate any kind of moved mover or changed changer or any series of the same as an adequate explanation for the observable motion or motions with which his argument began. As we have already seen, he seems to have allowed for a similar broader understanding of motion at a certain stage in his second argument from motion in SCG I, c. 13, and perhaps also at one point in his first argument. Nonetheless, the starting point for both of those arguments appears to be motion taken strictly and, to be specific, local motion. Perhaps it is because the first way in the *Summa theologiae* begins with readily observable phenomena—local motion and alteration—that Thomas describes it as the "more manifest" way.[12]

Moreover, in his effort to justify the principle that whatever is moved is moved by something else, Thomas does not mention the first two long and involved physical approaches he had used in SCG I, c. 13. He simply builds his argument on the difference between potentiality and actuality, and develops this reasoning more fully than he had done in SCG I, c. 13. If, as we have suggested, this reasoning as it appears in the *Summa contra Gentiles* already points to a broader and more

11. *In V Phys.*, lect. 2, p. 322, n. 649: "Ubi considerandum est quod Aristoteles supra in tertio ubi motum definivit, accepit nomen *motus* secundum quod est commune omnibus speciebus mutationis. Et hoc modo accipit hic nomen *mutationis: motum* autem accipit magis stricte, pro quadam mutationis specie." See lect. 3, n. 661 (there are only three species of *motus*); n. 662 (there is no *motus* in the genus substance because motion taken strictly is between contraries, and there is no contrariety in the genus substance); lect. 4 (on the three kinds of *motus* taken strictly).

12. See my discussion above in Ch. XI, n. 54, and the texts quoted in n. 58 (from the first argument in SCG I, c. 13, and its third way of justifying the claim that whatever is moved is moved by something else); n. 76 (from the second argument in SCG I, c. 13, and its attempt to show that a perpetual self-mover of the outermost heavenly sphere, as apparently proposed by Aristotle, must still be moved in the order of final causality by a completely unmoved mover or God).

metaphysical way of justifying the principle of motion, the same holds for the present context. And if Thomas's attempt to justify this principle is valid, it should apply to any reduction from potentiality to actuality or to any kind of change, not merely to motion taken in the strict sense.[13]

Almost as a matter of definition Thomas explains that something is moved only insofar as it is in potency to that toward which it is moved. In other words, that which is moved must be capable of being moved. But something moves only insofar as it is in actuality. As we have already remarked in discussing the similar argument in SCG I, c. 13, Thomas does not mean to suggest by this that something must be or have formally that which it communicates to something else through motion. It must either be or have such formally, or else possess that characteristic virtually; this is to say, it must have the power to produce its effect. It is only with this qualification in mind that one can say of Thomas's reasoning that he means thereby that one cannot give that which one does not have (either formally or virtually).[14]

Central to Thomas's argument is the claim that something cannot be in act and in potency at the same time and in the same respect, but only in different respects. For instance, that which is actually hot cannot at the same time be potentially hot (that is, it cannot lack the same degree of heat it actually possesses); but at the same time it is potentially cold since it is capable of being cooled. This is an important part of Thomas's argument since he concludes from this that it is not possible for something to be a mover and to be moved in one and the same respect by one and the same motion, or for it to move itself (in this strict sense).[15] And if this is granted, Thomas can conclude that if something is moved, that is, if it is reduced from potentiality to actuality, this can only be because it is moved by something else. If Thomas's reasoning is valid, this principle should apply, as we have already remarked, not only to the three species of motion taken strictly, but also to change, that is, to every genuine reduction from potentiality to actuality.[16]

In the second part of the argument Thomas considers and rejects as unsatisfactory appeal to a regress to infinity in moved movers. He does so along lines which are by now familiar to us. If there is no first mover, i.e., no mover that is not moved by anything, there will be no other; for a second mover does not move except insofar as it is moved by a first mover. As before, I take this to mean not that there could not be an unending regress of moved movers but as arguing that such is

13. See Ch. XI, nn. 58 and 59 above and the corresponding part of my text.
14. See Ch. XI, n. 59 above. Cf. MacDonald, "Aquinas's Parasitic Argument," pp. 133–35.
15. As Thomas puts it: something cannot be reduced from potentiality to actuality except by some being in actuality *(ens in actu)*. Insofar as a thing is in potency to a given act, it is not yet that act. See n. 7 above.
16. Some, Van Steenberghen for instance, would take *moveri* more broadly so as to apply to *motus* in the strict sense and to generation and corruption, i.e., to change in all its forms, and apparently even at the beginning of the argument. See *Le problème,* pp. 169–70.

irrelevant: unless there is a first mover, a mover that is not moved by anything, no other motion will be possible.[17]

Thomas's first way has generated a considerable amount of discussion in the secondary literature.[18] Many of the objections raised against the argument have to do with its claim that whatever is moved is moved by something else. Already within Thomas's century there were those who denied that this applies to all cases. Exceptions should be made, it was argued, and first and foremost for spiritual activities such as human volition. Not long after Thomas's death Henry of Ghent maintained that a freely acting agent can reduce itself from a state of not acting to acting or, as he would eventually put it, from virtual act to formal act.[19] In addition, objections were at times raised at the physical level, having to do with projectile motion, the fall of heavy bodies, and the rise of those that are light (according to the Aristotelian theory of natural place). Thus a Duns Scotus would sharply restrict the application of this motion-principle even at the purely physical level.[20] And more recently, of course, it has often been urged that the principle is rendered invalid by Newtonian physics and the principle of inertia.[21]

17. See my discussion of this with reference to SCG I, c. 13 in Ch. XI above, nn. 62–64. Also see W. L. Rowe, *The Cosmological Argument* (Princeton, 1975), pp. 18–19, 32–38, where he reformulates and attempts to salvage what he regards as Thomas's question-begging formulation in the first and second ways. On the relation between God, the ultimate principal cause, and other causes see the interesting remarks by Gilson in his "Prolégomènes à la *prima via*," AHDLMA 30 (1964), pp. 64–65. In reading this one should bear in mind the two ways in which Thomas uses the notion of instrument. See Ch. XI above, n. 65.

18. See Van Steenberghen, *Le problème*, p. 180, n. 28. Others will be cited below.

19. For Henry see his Quodlibet 9, q. 5 ("Utrum voluntas moveat se ipsam"), R. Macken, ed. (Leuven, 1983), pp. 99–139; Quodlibet 10, q. 9, R. Macken, ed. (Leuven, 1981), pp. 220–55 ("Utrum subiectum per se possit esse causa sufficiens sui accidentis"). These date from Easter (i.e., during Lent) and Christmas (i.e., during Advent) of 1286. See Macken's edition of Henry's Quodlibet 1 (Leuven-Leiden, 1979), p. xvii. Henry seems to have developed his theory of virtual vs. formal willing in Quodlibet 10, or by that time. For discussion of Henry's views see Macken, "La volonté humaine, faculté plus élevée que l'intelligence selon Henri de Gand," pp. 5–51; "Heinrich von Gent im Gespräch mit seinen Zeitgenossen über die menschliche Freiheit," pp. 125–82, especially pp. 141–58; R. Effler, *John Duns Scotus and the Principle "Omne quod movetur ab alio movetur"*, pp. 15, 64–66; Wippel, *The Metaphysical Thought of Godfrey of Fontaines*, pp. 180–81, 190–91.

20. See Effler, op. cit., pp. 16–17, and throughout the rest of his study. It should be noted, however, that with Duns Scotus, Effler interprets the subject of the principle of motion to mean "everything which is in motion" rather than "whatever is moved." See pp. 33–35. This, of course, runs counter to Thomas's understanding of the principle as I read him.

21. For a helpful survey see J. Weisheipl, "Galileo and the Principle of Inertia," c. III of his *Nature and Motion in the Middle Ages*, pp. 49–63. In particular Weisheipl considers the views of William Whewell, Ernst Mach, Pierre Duhem, Alexandre Koyré, Anneliese Maier, and Stillman Drake. Each of these thinkers also assigns a greater or lesser role (considerably lesser according to Koyré) to Galileo in discovering the principle of inertia. As Weisheipl sums up his survey: ". . . all of these historians are unanimous in seeing a radical incompatibility between Aristotle's demand for causes of motion and Galileo's (and modern science's) rejection of efficient causes. From the philosophical point of view perhaps Anneliese Maier's statement of the problem is typical: Aristotle's principle 'Everything that is moved, is moved by another' had to be rejected to allow for the modern principle of inertia" (pp. 62–63).

While detailed discussion of these points would require far more attention than space will permit here, a few remarks may be made about each of them. So far as Thomas is concerned, the principle does apply universally. Whenever we are dealing with a reduction from potentiality to actuality, appeal must be made to some distinct moving principle to account for this. If our acts of volition involve any such transition from potentiality to actuality, the same will hold for them.

In the *Summa theologiae* I–II, q. 9, Thomas spells out some of his views concerning this. In a. 1 he is seeking to determine whether the will is moved by the intellect. He notes that something needs to be moved by something else insofar as it stands in potency to different things. He then distinguishes two ways in which a power of the soul can be in potency to different things: (1) simply with respect to acting or not acting (the exercise of an act); and (2) with respect to the particular kind of act, i.e., doing this or doing that (the order of specification). In the first case the focus is on a subject which sometimes acts and sometimes does not. In the second case the focus is on the object which serves to specify that act itself. In the order of exercise the will moves the other powers of the soul, including the intellect, to act. As Thomas puts it, we use the other powers of the soul when we will to do so. But he also recalls that since every agent acts for the sake of an end, the principle (the final cause) of the motion which is efficiently caused by the agent derives from the end (a particular good which falls under the object of the will, the good in general). But in the order of specification or determination of the act, the intellect moves the will by presenting a suitable object to it in the manner of a formal principle.[22]

Prior to this treatment in ST I–II, q. 9 (and the parallel discussion in *De malo*, q. 6), Thomas had identified the kind of causality exercised by the intellect with respect to the will as final rather than as formal. Under that assumption, which is not Thomas's position in these two works dating ca. 1270–1271, it would still be true that neither the intellect nor the will would move and be moved under the same aspect and in the same respect. The will would move the intellect as an efficient cause and would be moved by it in the order of final causality. Even so, in our present text where he refers to the causality exercised on the will by the object as presented by the intellect as formal causality, he is still satisfied that he has not violated the motion-principle. Indeed, in a. 3 of this same q. 9 he explicitly asks whether the will moves itself. In responding he explains that the will moves itself

22. Art. 1 is directed to this question: "Utrum voluntas moveatur ab intellectu." See Leon. 6.74–75. From this discussion note in particular: "Motio autem ipsius subiecti est ex agente aliquo. . . . Et ideo ex hac parte voluntas movet alias potentias animae ad suos actus. . . . Sed obiectum movet, determinando actum, ad modum principii formalis. . . . Et ideo isto modo motionis intellectus movet voluntatem, sicut praesentans ei obiectum suum." Also see ad 3: ". . . dicendum quod voluntas movet intellectum quantum ad exercitium actus. . . . Sed quantum ad determinationem actus, quae est ex parte obiecti, intellectus movet voluntatem. . . . Et sic patet quod non est idem movens et motum secundum idem." On Thomas's distinction between the exercise and the specification of an act see D. Gallagher, "Free Choice and Free Judgment in Thomas Aquinas," *Archiv für Geschichte der Philosophie* 76 (1994), pp. 262–70.

in this sense that, because it wills an end, it moves itself to will the means to that end. This does not mean, he points out in replying to objection 1, that the will moves and is moved in the same respect. It rather means that insofar as the will wills an end, it reduces itself from potency with respect to the means to that end so as to will them in actuality.[23]

As Thomas explains in a. 4, insofar as the will is moved by its object, it is moved by something external. (This, of course, is in the order of specification or determination and not in the order of efficient causality.) But, he continues, insofar as the will is moved to exercise its act of willing, we must also hold that it is moved by some external principle. That which is at times an agent in act and at times an agent in potency must be moved to act by some mover. Such is true of the will. As Thomas has indicated, the will can move itself to will the means to a given end. But this in turn presupposes an appropriate act on the part of the intellect, i.e., taking counsel. And the act of taking counsel on the part of the intellect presupposes still another act of the will which moves it to so act. Since we cannot regress to infinity by tracing one act of the will back to an act of the intellect and that back to another act of the will etc., Thomas concludes that the will proceeds to its first motion from an impulse *(instinctus)* given it by some external mover, and finds support for this in Aristotle's *Eudemian Ethics*.[24]

In his Disputed Questions *De malo*, q. 6, Thomas develops much of this same thinking. Here, too, he introduces the distinction between a change or motion which has to do with exercising the act of a power, and that which has to do with its specification. In dealing with the exercise of the act of the will, he observes that

23. On the development in Thomas's thinking on the causality exercised by the intellect and its object on the will, see O. Lottin, *Psychologie et morale aux XIIe et XIIIe siècles*, pp. 226–43 (on earlier writings), 252–62. For additional references concerning this see Gallagher, "Free Choice," p. 250, n. 10. Torrell dates ST I–II in 1271 and *De malo*, q. 6 around 1270. Whether one can establish the chronological priority of either of these sources over the other on the grounds of internal evidence is doubtful, in my judgment, although some have attempted this. See Gallagher, p. 261, n. 40 for references. For our purposes the teaching of these two sources is the same, but different from earlier discussions in *De veritate*, SCG, and ST I. ST I–II, q. 9, a. 3 is explicitly directed to this question: "Utrum voluntas moveat seipsam." In developing his answer Thomas draws an analogy between the will and the intellect. In knowing principles the intellect can reduce itself from potency to act as regards its knowledge of conclusions that follow from those principles. In like fashion the will, in that it wills an end, moves itself to will the means to that end. See his reply to objection 1: ". . . dicendum quod voluntas non secundum idem movet et movetur. Unde nec secundum idem est in actu et in potentia. Sed inquantum actu vult finem, reducit se de potentia in actum respectu eorum quae sunt ad finem, ut scilicet actu ea velit" (Leon. 4.78).

24. Leon. 6.78–79. Note in particular: "Sed eo modo quo movetur quantum ad exercitium actus, adhuc necesse est ponere voluntatem ab aliquo principio exteriori moveri. Omne enim quod quandoque est agens in actu et quandoque in potentia, indiget moveri ab aliquo movente. Manifestum est autem quod voluntas incipit velle aliquid, cum hoc prius non vellet. Necesse est ergo quod ab aliquo moveatur ad volendum. . . . Unde necesse est ponere quod in primum motum voluntatis voluntas prodeat ex instinctu alicuius exterioris moventis, ut Aristoteles concludit in quodam capitulo *Ethicae Eudemicae*." For Aristotle see *Eudemian Ethics*, Bk VII, c. 14 (1248a 25–32). Also see Thomas, ibid., ad 1, ad 3.

just as the will moves other powers, so does it move itself. He maintains that it does not follow from this that the will is in act and potency at the same time and in the same respect. Rather the will moves itself by moving the intellect to take counsel. Again he maintains that the act of choice on the part of the will presupposes an act of counsel on the part of the intellect, and that this in turn presupposes a prior act by the will. To avoid falling into an infinite regress, Thomas again concludes that the will is moved to its first motion by something external or exterior to it. He goes on to tell us more about this externally caused impulse which first moves the will to act. This impulse cannot be provided by a heavenly body, since the will is grounded in reason (the intellect), which is not a corporeal power. He concludes, therefore, developing a remark made by Aristotle in his *De bona fortuna* (really taken from Bk VII of the *Eudemian Ethics* as he indicates in ST I–II, q. 9), that what first moves the will and the intellect must be something above them both, i.e., God. Since God moves all things in accord with their nature as movable beings—for instance, light things upward and heavy things downward—so does he move the will in accord with its condition or nature, that is to say, not in necessary fashion but as undetermined or freely.[25]

In order to place this within its broader metaphysical context we should recall that for Thomas created agents, including those that act freely, are second causes. God alone is the first cause. Nonetheless, such created agents are true causes. In the case of a human agent, Thomas has acknowledged that it can move itself in the qualified way already mentioned—by willing the means to a given end. But like all created agents, such a freely acting agent is not the first cause of its operations, including intellection and volition. As Thomas points out in q. 3, a. 7 of his *De potentia*, God may be said to cause the actions performed by created agents in four different ways: (1) by giving to a created agent the power by means of which it acts; (2) by continuously sustaining (conserving) this created power in being; (3) by moving or applying the created operative power to its activity; (4) by serving as principal cause of that of which the created agent is an instrumental cause.[26] With

25. See *Quaestiones disputatae De malo*, q. 6 (Leon. 23.148:308–149:415). Note in particular: "Sed cum voluntas non semper voluerit consiliari, necesse est quod ab aliquo moveatur ad hoc quod velit consiliari; et si quidem a se ipsa, necesse est iterum quod motum voluntatis praecedat consilium et consilium praecedat actus voluntatis; et cum hoc in infinitum procedere non possit, necesse est ponere quod quantum ad primum motum voluntatis moveatur voluntas cuiuscumque non semper actu volentis ab aliquo exteriori, cuius instinctu voluntas velle incipiat." After concluding that it is God who first moves the will and intellect, Thomas comments: "Qui cum omnia moveat secundum rationem mobilium, ut levia sursum et gravia deorsum, etiam voluntatem movet secundum eius conditionem, non ex necessitate sed ut indeterminate se habentem ad multa" (p. 149:410–415). Also see ad 3 for this final point (p. 150:498–511).

26. Ed. cit., pp. 57–58. Thomas introduces this particular part of his discussion by observing that God does not operate in natural things in such fashion that the natural thing itself would do nothing. In order to explain just how it is that God operates in the operations performed either by a natural agent or by a created will, he then introduces the fourfold way indicated in our text. See ed. cit., pp. 57–58. In summing this up again at the end of the corpus of this same article, he makes it clear

respect to point 4 it should be noted that at times Thomas uses the language of first cause and second cause rather than that of principal cause and instrument to express this relationship between God and other agents.[27]

In the *Summa theologiae* I, q. 105, a. 5, Thomas makes this same point in slightly different fashion. God works in the activities performed by created agents: (1) by serving as the final cause of such agents; (2) by acting as an efficient cause of their operations inasmuch as second causes act by reason of the first cause which moves them to act; (3) by giving to created agents the forms which are their principles of operation and by keeping these in being. As I have indicated elsewhere, we might combine into one the third and fourth ways mentioned in the text from the *De potentia,* as Thomas himself seems to do, and view this as equivalent to the second way of the text from ST I, q. 105.[28] It is this particular form of divine causality that is of greatest interest to us here, because it shows that Thomas honors the motion principle in all cases of creaturely agency.

It is also important to note Thomas's view that if God serves as an efficient cause of creaturely operations, including human volition, he does so as the first cause. Created agents are true causes, and even true principal causes, of their appropriate operations. Moreover, although this is not our primary concern at the moment, Thomas insists that this divine causality or divine motion with respect to free human operations does not detract from their freedom. Essential to Thomas's position is the point we have just seen above—that God, the first cause, moves created agents to act in accord with their natures. If he moves natural agents to act in accord with their natures, that is, necessarily, he moves free agents to act in accord with their nature, that is, freely.[29]

My reason for introducing this discussion here is not to examine Thomas's defense of human freedom but to show that in his eyes even free human activity does

---

that he is applying this fourfold way in which God is the cause of created agents to volitions as well: ". . . sequetur quod ipse in quolibet operante immediate operetur, non exclusa operatione voluntatis et naturae" (p. 58).

27. Cf. the text from ST I, q. 105, a. 5, cited in n. 28. Cf. *De veritate,* q. 24, a. 1, ad 5, cited in Ch. XI, n. 65 above.

28. See ST I, q. 105, a. 5 (Leon. 5.476). Cf. ad 3. Here Thomas is developing his answer to the question: "Utrum Deus operetur in omni operante." See my *Metaphysical Themes,* p. 260. Also see my remark there in n. 56 about Thomas's views concerning God as the proper cause of *esse.*

29. For other texts on this correlation between created agents and God see, for instance, SCG III, c. 70 (ed. cit., p. 306). This does not mean that one part of the effect is caused by God and another by the created agent, but rather that the entire effect is to be assigned to God (as principal cause) and to the created natural agent (as an instrument). For additional texts where Thomas applies this to freely acting created agents, see SCG I, c. 68 (p. 64); SCG III, cc. 88, 89 (pp. 331–32). Note that Thomas concludes his discussion in c. 89 by appealing to the text from the *Eudemian Ethics* VII, c. 14. For texts where Thomas attempts to reconcile this theory of divine agency with human freedom see, for instance, *De potentia,* q. 3, a. 7, ad 13; ad 14 (ed. cit., p. 59); ST I, q. 19, a. 8, and ad 3 (Leon. 4.244); ST I, q. 83, a. 1, ad 3 (Leon. 5.307–8); ST I–II, q. 10, a. 4, and ad 1 (Leon. 6.89); *De malo,* q. 6 (as cited above in n. 25). For discussion see my *Metaphysical Themes,* pp. 258–63.

not violate his conviction that whatever is moved is moved by something else. At the same time, I would not recommend that one take human volition as a point of departure for Thomas's argument from motion for God's existence. This does not seem to be the kind of starting point he has in mind for his "more manifest" way, since some philosophical effort will be required to show that motion by something else is involved in volition. Moreover, the full appreciation of Thomas's views concerning the interrelationship between divine causal activity (as the first moving cause) and free human activity presupposes that one has already demonstrated God's existence and identified him as a creating, a conserving, and the first moving cause. Only then will Thomas be in position to proceed in the other direction, as it were, and view things from the standpoint of God as the First Mover.[30]

For more detailed explanation and discussion of Thomas's application of the principle of motion to purely physical motions such as those already mentioned, the reader may consult a series of studies by J. Weisheipl. If we may quickly summarize his findings, in the case of what Thomas regarded as natural motions, i.e., the fall of a heavy body or the rising of a light body, he holds that the motion of such bodies is caused by something else, that is, by the generating agent of the bodies in question. This, therefore, and not the bodies themselves, is to be regarded as the efficient cause of such motions. As for violent motions, in many instances Thomas would regard it as evident that what is moved is moved by something else—for instance, that a stick is moved by a hand, or that a heavy object is lifted upwards by someone or something in opposition to its natural tendency to fall. In the more difficult case of projectile motion, where the apparent mover is no longer in direct contact with the object which has been thrown or hurled, Thomas still thinks that his principle applies. With Aristotle he accounts for such motion by holding that what serves as a medium—air, for instance—has now been given the power to move the projectile. Even so, such a communicated power is not to be regarded as the principal cause of the motion, but only as an instrument of the true efficient cause—the one who originally threw or hurled the object.[31]

---

30. R. Garrigou-Lagrange seems to be of another opinion concerning this. In his *God: His Existence and His Nature*, Vol. 1, p. 268, after presenting Thomas's proof from motion, he comments: "This proof from motion may be exemplified in another way by considering motions of the spiritual order, as St. Thomas has done in the article of his *Summa* entitled, 'Whether the Will is Moved by any External Principle?' (Ia IIae, q. 9, a. 4)." However, Thomas does not present this kind of motion in that context as the starting point for his proof for God's existence. On the other hand, Garrigou-Lagrange makes some interesting points in his discussion of objections to the argument from motion (see pp. 270–87), although his treatment is not primarily historical.

31. Especially helpful with reference to this is Weisheipl's "The Principle *Omne quod movetur*," in his *Nature and Motion in the Middle Ages*, c. IV, pp. 75–97. Also see there c. II ("Natural and Compulsory Movement"); c. V ("The Specter of *motor coniunctus* in Medieval Physics"). For Thomas's views on the generating principle as the moving principle or cause of the natural motions of physical bodies see pp. 90–93. Among the various passages he cites from Thomas note: *In VIII Phys.*, lect. 8 (Maggiòlo ed.), p. 542, n. 1036 (an excellent summarizing passage on which also see Ch. XI above, n. 57); *In II Phys.*, lect. 1, p. 74, n. 144 (for fuller discussion see Weisheipl, p. 19,

Well and good, one may counter, but with the rise of Newtonian physics and the principle of inertia, and for that matter, already with Galileo's explanation of the motion of a body along an idealized frictionless plane, Thomas's principle of motion has been rendered invalid. And if it fails to apply in this case, one cannot claim universal validity for it or use it with any confidence in a proof for God's existence. For that matter, Aristotle's distinction between natural and violent motion also seems to have been rendered obsolete.[32]

Without attempting to enter into a full discussion of these particular questions from the standpoint of the philosophy of science or the philosophy of nature, I would recall the following points. First of all, if Thomas's explanation of natural motion is correctly understood, it does not imply that a distinct moving cause must be constantly conjoined with a body which it moves naturally. While one will hardly wish today to defend the view that light bodies tend to go up, etc., one may hold that it is because of their natures that bodies tend to behave in certain ways, for instance, to fall. If with Newton one wishes to account for this by appealing to a force exercised by another and distinct body, Thomas's general principle will not necessarily be violated. Our falling body will still be moved by something else. But as he sees things, it is the generating principle of the falling body which is the efficient cause of its tendency to fall and therefore of its actual downward motion unless it is prevented from falling by some obstacle.[33]

As for Thomas's acceptance of Aristotle's explanation of projectile motion, not too many thinkers today will be inclined to endorse their view that some moving power is communicated to the air or to some surrounding medium and that this accounts for the continuing motion of the object in question. But today's defender of Thomas's general principle of motion may still insist on searching for some efficient cause to account for the continuing motion of such a projectile, the principle

---

n. 78); *De potentia,* q. 3, a. 7 (ed. cit., p. 57). For an interesting critique of Weisheipl's interpretation of Thomas's explanation of the natural motions of physical bodies see D. B. Twetten, "Back to Nature in Aquinas," *Medieval Philosophy and Theology* 5 (1996), pp. 205–43. On Thomas's acceptance of Aristotle's account of the motion of projectiles see Weisheipl, *Nature and Motion,* p. 31, n. 30; pp. 64–66. For Thomas see *In VIII Phys.,* lect. 22, pp. 621–22, nn. 1161–1163; *In III De caelo,* lect. 7, p. 305, n. 591. For another succinct summarizing text see *De potentia,* q. 3, a. 11 (ed. cit., p. 75).

32. See n. 21 above.

33. In connection with this Kenny comments that to explain the fall of such a body by the gravitational pull of the earth (with Newton) "would seem to be more favourable to Aristotle's principle than his own mechanics are" *(The Five Ways,* p. 16, n. 1). However, this seeming support from Newtonian mechanics for the Aristotelian-Thomistic principle proves to be a mixed blessing, as Kenny also points out: "For the gravitational attraction of two bodies is mutual, whereas the Aristotelian relation of 'moving' must be an asymmetrical one if it is to lead to an unmoved mover" (p. 30). Hence it seems better, if one would defend Thomas's principle of motion, to interpret it in the case of falling bodies as he did by applying it to the generating principle and by regarding this as the mover. For another succinct exposition of Thomas's theory as applied to natural and violent motion see A. Moreno, "The Law of Inertia and the Principle *Quidquid Movetur ab Alio Movetur,*" *The Thomist* 38 (1974), pp. 316–25.

of inertia notwithstanding. This point seems to have been partially recognized by Newton himself, in that he (and Descartes) acknowledged that the principle of inertia would not explain the origin of motion in the universe.[34]

For instance, one might concede a great deal to the Newtonian theory and regard motion as a state, like rest. Then one would simply appeal to an extrinsic force, and therefore to some extrinsic mover, to account for any change in the state of rest or of uniform motion enjoyed by a given body.[35] As for the body's possession of its state (rest or motion), one would again trace this back to the generating principle which produced the body with a nature such that it will remain at rest or in motion until it is acted on by some external force. I should emphasize the point, however, that this is not the way in which Thomas and Aristotle actually accounted for projectile motion.

Or one might grant considerably less to the Newtonian theory of inertia as a philosophical explanation and insist that, in spite of its ability to offer a satisfactory physico-mathematical description of uniform motion, it leaves the philosophical search for causes unanswered.[36] In attempting to offer such an explanation one might, with certain later medieval thinkers (including some Thomists, though not Thomas himself), appeal to a theory of impetus. According to this account a transitory power would be given to the moving body by the original hurler or thrower of a given projectile. This power would continue to enable the body to move after it was no longer in direct contact with the hurler, and would serve as an instrumental cause for the motion of the projectile. The original hurler would be the principal

34. See Newton, *Optics,* Bk III, Part 1 (in Great Books of the Western World, Vol. 34, p. 540): "By this principle [*vis inertiae*] alone there never could have been any motion in the world. Some other principle was necessary for putting bodies into motion; and now they are in motion, some other principle is necessary for conserving the motion." Cited by Wallace, "Newtonian Antinomies against the *Prima Via,*" *The Thomist* 19 (1956), p. 185; and by Kenny, *The Five Ways,* p. 28. For Descartes see his *Principles of Philosophy,* II, 36: "As far as the general (and first) cause is concerned, it seems obvious to me that this is none other than God Himself, who, (being all-powerful) in the beginning created matter with both movement and rest; and now maintains in the sum total of matter, by his normal participation, the same quantity of motion and rest as He placed in it at that time" (trans. and notes by V. Rodger Miller and R. P. Miller [Dordrecht-Boston-London, 1983], p. 58). In the immediately following context, Descartes argues for this from God's immutability and constancy. See II, 37 for his "first law of nature": "that each thing, as far as is in its power, always remains in the same state; and that consequently, when it is once moved, it always continues to move" (p. 59). See II, 38 for his application of this to projectile motion (pp. 59–60). By seeking for some causal explanation for the continuation of such motion, today's defender of the Thomistic principle will be asking for a cause to account for more than the beginning of that motion.

35. For such a suggestion see J. Maritain, *Approaches to God* (London, 1955), pp. 24–27. Maritain reasons that if we do take the principle of inertia as established and if hypothetically we grant "it a meaning beyond the mere empiriological analysis of phenomena," it will be enough to take it as indicating that "Every body which undergoes a change *in regard to its state of rest or of motion* changes under the action of another thing" (p. 26). For him this will suffice to preserve Thomas's principle that whatever is moved is moved by something else.

36. See Wallace, "Newtonian Antinomies against the *Prima Via,*" pp. 173–86, especially p. 180.

efficient cause of the motion. Some students of Aquinas—including Weisheipl—regard this explanation as in accord with Thomas's principles, even though it is not the view Thomas himself defended.[37]

Finally, various writers have argued that the principle of inertia itself has never been demonstrated.[38] This is a controversy into which I am not prepared to enter. But if this claim should prove to be correct, there would be little reason for Aquinas's students today to jettison what he regarded as a demonstrated philosophical principle—that whatever is moved is moved by another—because of seeming difficulties in reconciling it with an unproved principle of Newtonian physics and mechanics. This will be especially so for those who accept Thomas's more metaphysical justification of his principle of motion, that is, the one based on the distinction between potentiality and actuality and ultimately, therefore, on the distinction between being and nonbeing. In sum, strategies such as these are available in dealing with such alleged counterexamples for one who accepts the motion principle on philosophical and metaphysical grounds. Moreover, as at least one writer has proposed, one might, unlike Thomas, simply exclude local motion as a starting-point for the argument and use another example such as alteration.[39]

This final remark brings me back to an issue already touched on: Is Thomas's first way physical or metaphysical in nature? Or to put this in different terms: Does this argument for God's existence fall under the science of being as being, or under the science that studies being as mobile? As we have now seen, the argument takes as its starting point a fact that is central to physics (philosophy of nature), i.e., motion. To that extent one might argue that it is intended by Thomas to fall within the scope of physics. Moreover, it borrows heavily from Aristotle's *Physics*, especially as it is presented in the two versions in SCG I, c. 13. Nonetheless, its most convincing effort to establish that whatever is moved is moved by something else rests on a broader (and metaphysical) point, the distinction between act and potency and the impossibility that any being might be in act and potency at the same time and in the same respect. This impossibility is by no means restricted to mobile being, but applies to the full range of being as being (the subject of metaphysics). And

---

37. See Weisheipl, *Nature and Motion in the Middle Ages*, pp. 31–33 (though it was first developed by the Franciscan Francis de Marchia, and then by Jean Buridan, presumably working independently, Thomists such as Capreolus and Domingo de Soto claimed that the impetus theory of motion was also Thomas's position); pp. 66–69, 95–96.

38. See Weisheipl, op. cit., pp. 36–42, 48, 49, 269; Moreno, "The Law of Inertia," pp. 307–13; Wallace, "Newtonian Antinomies against the *Prima Via*," pp. 178–80. Also cf. Kenny's presentation and discussion of what he describes as the "counter-attack with Mach" (op. cit., pp. 29–31).

39. Cf. E. Gilson, *Elements of Christian Philosophy*, p. 63: "To be both in act and in potency in the same respect would amount to being and not being in the same respect and at the same time." For an effort to free Thomas's argument from motion from an outmoded physical theory see MacDonald, "Aquinas's Parasitic Argument," pp. 135–38, where he overcomes projectile motion as a counterexample to the motion principle by restricting motion as used in the argument to alteration and increase and decrease in quantity. While this approach is philosophically defensible, it may grant more than is necessary to the alleged counterexample.

this justification is the only one offered for the principle of motion in the first way of the *Summa theologiae.*

Again, in presenting what appears to be primarily a physical argument from motion in SCG I, c. 13 (his second argument), Thomas has been forced to consider the possibility of a self-mover for the first heavenly sphere which is itself moved by something else in some other way, that is, in the order of desire. If such a self-mover exists, it will still be subject to his principle of motion and will depend on the unmoved mover in the order of final causality. At this point one has the impression that even this argument in SCG I, c. 13, is passing over from physics to metaphysics.

Hence my view is that the first way as it appears in ST I, q. 2, a. 3 starts from a physical fact, but that if it is to reach the absolutely unmoved mover or God, it must pass beyond this and beyond a limited and physical application of the principle of motion to a wider application that will apply to any reduction of a being from not acting to acting. In other words, the argument becomes metaphysical in its justification and application of the motion principle, and only then can it succeed in arriving at God. This means that, in its refutation of an infinite regress of moved movers as an alternative explanation, the argument concludes to a source of motion that is not itself moved in any way whatsoever and, therefore, is not reduced from potency to act in any way.

Still another way of approaching this would be to suggest that Thomas is really interested in the existence of motion from the outset and must ultimately conclude to the existence of a being that is pure actuality in order to account for the existence of the motion with which it begins. Therefore the argument would be metaphysical from beginning to end, since it would reason from the caused character of the existence of motion to an uncaused cause of the same.[40]

I would prefer to recast this suggested interpretation so that the argument would reason from the efficiently caused character of moved or changing being (rather than from the existence of motion). However, my greatest difficulty with this suggestion is historical. The argument would no longer be Thomas's first way as this appears in the text of ST I, q. 2, a. 3.

---

40. See Owens, "Immobility and Existence for Aquinas," in *St. Thomas Aquinas on the Existence of God,* pp. 219–20; "The Conclusion of the *Prima Via,*" pp. 148, 158–60, 166–68. Cf. Ch. XI, n. 79 above. Also see the discussion concerning this occasioned by T. Kondoleon's review of Knasas's *The Preface to Thomistic Metaphysics* in his "The Start of Metaphysics," *The Thomist* 58 (1994), pp. 121–30; followed by Knasas, "Thomistic Existentialism and the Proofs *Ex Motu* at *Contra Gentiles* I, c. 13," *The Thomist* 59 (1995), pp. 591–615; and Kondoleon, "The Argument from Motion and the Argument for Angels: A Reply to John F. X. Knasas," *The Thomist* 62 (1998), pp. 269–90. Knasas defends and develops Owens's position on this. For a review and critique both of what he calls the "Physical" and the "Existential" readings of the first way see D. B. Twetten's "Clearing a Way for Aquinas: How the Proof from Motion Concludes to God," in *Proceedings of the American Catholic Philosophical Association* 70 (1996), pp. 260–64. See pp. 267–71 for his proposed "Metaphysical" reading, which in various respects is close to what I am proposing here.

Before moving on to Thomas's second way, I should mention some additional questions about the first way which the presentation in ST I, q. 2, a. 3 seems to leave unanswered. First of all, is the argument based exclusively on motion as caused in the order of efficient (or moving) causality, or does it ultimately shift to the order of final causality? This issue can be raised both because of the apparent difference between Aristotle's procedure in *Physics* VII and VIII, on the one hand, and in *Metaphysics* XII, on the other, and because of Thomas's reference in SCG I, c. 13 to the possibility of reaching a self-moving first mover which would still be moved by something else in the order of desire and hence, we may conclude, as its final cause. In the text of the first way in ST I, q. 2, a. 3, however, there is no explicit reference to motion in the order of desire or to final causality. Moreover, the example mentioned at the very end of the argument—a stick which does not move unless it is moved by a hand—would make one think only in terms of efficient causality. Hence it is in that way that I prefer to read the argument.[41]

A second question may be raised, having to do with the concluding remark to the effect that all recognize this first unmoved mover as God. Has Thomas succeeded in establishing the point that there is only one such being at this point in his reasoning? If so, why does he argue explicitly for divine unicity (uniqueness) in ST I, q. 11, a. 3? Thomistic interpreters remain divided on this issue, but many recognize the fact that it is only in q. 11 that Thomas explicitly establishes divine unicity.[42] This procedure at least suggests that Thomas himself may have recognized that the claim that his unmoved mover is God needs to be supported and completed by additional argumentation.

In fact, at this point in Thomas's reasoning, one would not yet know whether the first mover is intelligent, or personal, or infinitely perfect, etc. So it is that Thomas will eventually develop each of these points in due course, along with others, in discussing the divine names. And there is, of course, the additional fact that Thomas is not content to offer only an argument from motion or a first way in ST I, q. 2, a. 3. All of this would seem to support the view that Thomas himself was aware that his demonstration of God's existence was not yet completed at the end of his first way.

At the same time, we should bear in mind Thomas's opening remark before he begins in question 3 and the following to take up the divine names or attributes. Once we have recognized that a given thing exists, it remains for us to determine how it exists in order that we may know of it what it is. But since we cannot know what God is but only what he is not, we must now consider the ways in which he

41. See n. 8 above.

42. For discussion and reference to others such as Cajetan, S. Vanni Rovighi, Garrigou-Lagrange, and M. Cocci, see Van Steenberghen, *Le problème*, pp. 178–80. Also see MacDonald, "Aquinas's Parasitic Argument," pp. 146–55, who is struck by the fact that the first way establishes the existence of an unmoved mover, but not an immovable mover. To achieve this he believes it must be completed by other ways, such as the third and the fifth.

is not. It is in the course of doing this, according to Thomas's own plan, that he establishes God's simplicity, and then his perfection, infinity, immutability, and unity. Throughout this discussion Thomas takes it as given that he has already (in his five ways) proved that God exists. With this lingering question still in mind,[43] therefore, we shall now turn to Thomas's presentation of his second argument for God's existence in ST I, q. 2, a. 3.

2. The Second Way

As Thomas himself tells us, this argument is based on efficient causality. Again it takes as its point of departure something that is given to us in the world of sensible things—the fact that there is an order of efficient causes. By this Thomas means that we find that certain things efficiently cause other things, and that they depend on prior causes in order to do so. He immediately reasons that nothing can be the efficient cause of itself, for then it would be prior to itself, and this is impossible. If we may supply the reasoning that is implied, his point is that for something to cause itself efficiently, it would have to exist in order to cause (itself), and yet would not exist, insofar as it was being caused. From this he expects us to conclude that since we do experience causes that are caused, because they cannot cause themselves they must be caused by something else.[44]

If this is granted, the possibility of a series of efficient causes which are themselves caused by something else must be faced. Thomas argues that one cannot regress to infinity in ordered efficient causes. As he explains, in such an ordered series of efficient causes, the first member is the cause of the intermediary, and that in turn is the cause of the last member in the series whether there is only one intermediary cause or whether there are many. But if there were no first among efficient causes there would be no intermediary causes and therefore no last cause; for if one takes away a cause, one also eliminates the effect. In an infinite series of caused efficient causes, there will be no first efficient cause. Hence there will be no intermediary causes and no last effect. This is enough for Thomas to reject a regress to infinity as a viable alternative to a first efficient cause.[45]

43. For Thomas see ST I, q. 3: "Cognito de aliquo an sit, inquirendum restat quomodo sit, ut sciatur de eo quid sit. Sed quia de Deo scire non possumus quid sit, sed quid non sit, non possumus considerare de Deo quomodo sit, sed potius quomodo non sit. Primo ergo considerandum est quomodo non sit; secundo, quomodo a nobis cognoscatur; tertio, quomodo nominetur" (Leon. 4.35). The lingering question is this: At this point in ST I, that is, after completing his five ways, does Thomas think that he has already demonstrated that only one God exists?

44. "Secunda via est ex ratione causae efficientis. Invenimus enim in istis sensibilibus esse ordinem causarum efficientium: nec tamen invenitur, nec est possibile, quod aliquid sit causa efficiens sui ipsius; quia sic esset prius seipso, quod est impossibile" (Leon. 4.31).

45. "Non autem est possibile quod in causis efficientibus procedatur in infinitum. Quia in omnibus causis efficientibus ordinatis, primum est causa medii, et medium est causa ultimi, sive media sint plura sive unum tantum: remota autem causa, removetur effectus: ergo, si non fuerit primum

While the terms in which this argument is cast differ from those for the first way, much of the same basic structure reappears. Again one begins with a fact which, for Aquinas, is based on undeniable data offered through sense experience: among the things we experience through the senses, some are causes of others, and some of these causes are ordered, that is, subordinated to others in the exercise of their causality. This confidence on Thomas's part is undoubtedly owing to his Aristotelianism, his own realistic theory of knowledge, and the high degree of credibility which he assigns to what we today often refer to as "common sense." Although he does not spell out particular examples for us in this argument, he would undoubtedly include substantial changes (generation and corruption of substances) as well as various instances of motion taken strictly which we have discussed above in connection with the first way, i.e., alteration, local motion, increase and decrease.[46]

For those who would prefer a more metaphysically grounded illustration of efficient causality at work, I would suggest an approach based on the efficiently caused character of any being in which essence and act of being (esse) differ as, for instance, Thomas has developed this in c. 4 of his De ente et essentia.[47] However, I hasten to add that this is not the kind of efficient causality that is immediately given to us in sense experience. In adopting such a procedure, therefore, one would now have changed the point of departure for Thomas's second way.

As I have already indicated, Thomas reasons that nothing can be its own efficient cause. Given this, by implication he is also holding that whatever is efficiently caused must be so caused by something else. This is the version of efficient causality which is at work in Thomas's second way and, as in the first way, though more briefly this time, Thomas again offers a particular justification for this within the argument itself. In other words, he does not simply assume the principle of causality as an axiom which he might apply in each and every case. For that matter, we have already seen him proceeding in similar fashion in c. 4 of the De ente. There too he had judged it necessary to show that a being in which essence and esse differ is efficiently caused.[48]

With this we may turn to the second general step in his argument—the rejection of an infinite regress of caused causes as a viable alternative to the existence of a first cause. In reasoning which recalls that which we have already seen, Thomas

---

in causis efficientibus, non erit ultimum nec medium. Sed si procedatur in infinitum in causis efficientibus, non erit prima causa efficiens: et sic non erit nec effectus ultimus, nec causae efficientes mediae: quod patet esse falsum. Ergo est necesse ponere aliquam causam efficientem primam: quam omnes Deum nominant" (Leon. 4.31).

46. See nn. 10, 11 above for references. Cf. Van Steenberghen, op. cit., p. 185.

47. For discussion of this see above in Ch. XI, Section 2.

48. In the second way, however, from the very beginning of the argument the focus is on causes that are caused rather than on effects (as in De ente, c. 4) or on things that are moved (as in the first way). In those two arguments Thomas subsequently shifts the focus to caused causes or to moved movers when he deals with the issue of an infinite regress.

makes it clear that he is dealing with what we may call essentially ordered causes (*lit.* ordered causes), that is, the case where the causal activity by a prior member of the series is required here and now for the exercise of causal activity by all subsequent members in that same series. Thomas had allowed and would continue to allow for the philosophical possibility of an infinite series of causes which are related to one another only *per accidens,* e.g., of fathers generating sons, or of a carpenter replacing one hammer with another *ad infinitum.* Once again, as I read the argument, he is not concerned here with refuting the very possibility of a beginningless series of essentially ordered caused causes, but with showing that such a series is meaningless and has no explanatory power unless one also admits that there is an uncaused cause. It is in this sense that I take his usage of the term "first."[49]

As in the first way, Thomas quickly concludes to the existence of some "first efficient cause," i.e., some uncaused cause, which is named God by everyone.[50] Once more we may raise the issue of divine unicity or uniqueness: Does this argument, simply taken in itself, prove that there is only one Uncaused Cause (God)? Might it not lead to the conclusion that there are as many first causes as there are different series or at least different kinds of series of ordered caused causes? And does the argument manage to show that the first cause whose existence it establishes is intelligent, personal, all perfect, infinite, etc.? Thomas's second way tells us no more about these issues than does his first way, it would seem, although it does make it clear that in his mind the first unmoved mover of the first way and the first efficient cause of the second way are identical and also that this being exercises efficient causality.

Before leaving the second way it may be helpful for us to compare it more fully with the argumentation for God's existence presented in c. 4 of the *De ente.* Both have in common the fact that they are based on efficient causality. Both must take into account a possible objection having to do with a regress to infinity in caused causes. But as we have already pointed out, the argument in the *De ente* begins at the level of beings in which essence and *esse* are not identical, and therefore at an explicitly metaphysical level. The second way begins with instances of causal activity which are evident to the senses, and ultimately concludes that there must be a first uncaused cause to account for such causal activity.

If, as I have suggested, the issue of divine uniqueness seems to be left unexamined by the second way, such is not true of the argument in *De ente,* c. 4. Because that argument begins, as we have seen, with the essence-*esse* distinction, it focuses on one instance of efficient causation, that of *esse* itself. It reasons to the existence of an uncaused cause of *esse* and therefore an uncaused being which is itself pure *esse.* This insight seems much closer to what the metaphysician seeks in attempting

49. See our remarks above in Ch. XI, Section 2 *(De ente,* c. 4); Ch. XI, Section 4 (first argument, from motion, second and third arguments, against infinite regress); and Ch. XII, Section 1 (first way).

50. See the final part of the text as quoted above in n. 45.

to understand something about God. Moreover, this argument anticipates our concern about divine unicity, since it has reasoned from the impossibility of there being more than one being in which essence and *esse* are identical. Because there can at most be one such being, essence and *esse* differ in all other beings. Such beings therefore are caused in terms of their very being. As already noted, this conclusion in its turn enables Thomas to show that there is in fact only one being in which essence and *esse* are identical. From all of these perspectives, therefore, the procedure in the *De ente* seems to be more satisfying to the metaphysician.[51]

But if all of this is so, why did Thomas not simply repeat the argumentation from the *De ente* as his second way in ST I, q. 2, a. 3? Perhaps, we may surmise, because of its highly metaphysical character he viewed the argument of *De ente,* c. 4 as more difficult for beginning students to grasp in its essentials. He may have realized that not all of his contemporaries, including many beginning students of theology, either understood or shared his views on the relationship between essence and *esse*. And he may not have wished to make his argumentation for God's existence dependent upon such a subtle metaphysical conclusion.

3. The Third Way

With this we come to the third of Thomas's five ways, the argument based, to use his terminology, on the possible and the necessary. We find, Thomas begins, that certain things are possibles, i.e., they have the possibility of existing and not existing. His evidence for this claim is the fact that certain things are generated and corrupted and therefore can exist and not exist. But it is impossible, Thomas continues, for all things which exist to be of this kind; for that which has the possibility of not existing at some time does not exist. If, therefore, all things are capable of not existing, at some time *(aliquando)* there was nothing in reality. But if this were so, even now there would be nothing; for what does not exist does not begin to exist except through something else that exists. Given all of this, Thomas concludes that not all beings are possible beings; there must be some necessary being.[52]

---

51. In this discussion I am assuming that my way of interpreting the general procedure in c. 4 of the *De ente* is correct. See above, Ch. V, Section 1.

52. "Tertia via est sumpta ex possibili et necessario: quae talis est. Invenimus enim in rebus quaedam quae sunt possibilia esse et non esse: cum quaedam inveniantur generari et corrumpi, et per consequens possibilia esse et non esse. Impossibile est autem omnia quae sunt, talia [omit: semper] esse: quia quod possibile est non esse, quandoque non est. Si igitur omnia sunt possibilia non esse, aliquando nihil fuit in rebus. Sed si hoc est [Van Steenberghen: esset] verum, etiam nunc nihil esset: quia quod non est, non incipit esse nisi per aliquid quod est; si igitur nihil fuit ens, impossibile fuit quod aliquid inciperet esse, et sic modo nihil esset: quod patet esse falsum. Non ergo omnia entia sunt possibilia: sed oportet aliquid esse necessarium in rebus" (Leon. 4.31). On the omission of *semper* from the text in accord with the majority of manuscripts see Van Steenberghen, *Le problème,* pp. 188–89; T. O'Brien, *Metaphysics and the Existence of God,* pp. 226–27, n. 83; J.F.X. Knasas, "Making

At this point today's reader might assume that Thomas's argument has reached its conclusion. But if we bear in mind the distinction between possible beings and caused necessary beings which we have already seen in his argument in SCG I, c. 15, we will not be surprised to find him adding a second and important step to the third way.[53] Every necessary being either depends on something else for its necessity or it does not. But it is not possible to proceed to infinity in necessary beings which depend upon something else for their necessity—just as, Thomas reminds us, he has already shown with respect to efficient causes (see the second way). Therefore there must be some being which is necessary of itself and which does not depend upon another cause for its necessity. This is the being which is the cause of the necessity present in other things, and it is referred to by everyone as God.[54]

Few other texts in Aquinas have occasioned so much controversy among interpreters as the first phase of this argument.[55] In an effort to understand Thomas's procedure here, we shall review the various steps in that phase and single out certain contested points. Once more Thomas takes as his point of departure something which we may derive from sense experience, that is, our awareness that certain beings are possible beings. As he uses the term "possible" here he means that they have the possibility of existing or not existing. As we have already seen him doing in SCG I, c. 15, here again he closely associates possible beings with their capacity to be generated and corrupted. This, in fact, is the empirical evidence with which the argument begins. Because certain things which we experience are subject to generation and corruption, we may conclude that they are possible beings, not necessary beings. As Thomas sees things, such beings are composed of matter and form. It is this composition which renders them liable to corruption; and because of such composition, they naturally come into being by being generated. However, strictly speaking, Thomas need not assume at this point in his argument that such beings are composed of matter and form. The fact that they come into being

---

Sense of the *Tertia Via*," *New Scholasticism* 54 (1980), pp. 488–89; Kenny, *The Five Ways*, p. 55. With Van Steenberghen and O'Brien, I think it should be omitted. So, too, did Godfrey of Fontaines, if one may judge from the *abbreviatio* of the third way which he himself transcribed in the margin of a manuscript in his personal library, Paris, Bibl. Nat. 15.819, fol. 226r: "Impossibile est enim omnia possibilia esse, quia quod possibile est non esse, quandoque non est."

53. See Ch. XI above, nn. 96, 97.

54. "Omne autem necessarium vel habet causam suae necessitatis aliunde, vel non habet. Non est autem possibile quod procedatur in infinitum in necessariis quae habent causam suae necessitatis, sicut nec in causis efficientibus, ut probatum est. Ergo necesse est ponere aliquid quod sit per se necessarium, non habens causam necessitatis aliunde, sed quod est causa necessitatis aliis: quod omnes dicunt Deum" (Leon. 4.31).

55. For references to many of these see J. Owens, "*Quandoque* and *Aliquando* in Aquinas's *Tertia Via*," pp. 447–75; Knasas, "Making Sense of the *Tertia Via*," pp. 476–511; Van Steenberghen, *Le problème*, p. 205, n. 37. Cf. my Ch. XI above, nn. 101, 102, 104. See T. K. Connolly, "The Basis of the Third Proof for the Existence of God," pp. 281–349, especially pp. 281–99, for a survey of much of the earlier literature concerning this.

through generation and cease to be through corruption is enough for him to make the point that they are possible beings.[56]

It is with the very next sentence that the difficulties in interpreting this argument begin: "It is impossible for all things which exist to be such [i.e., possibles], because what has the possibility of not existing at some time *(quandoque)* does not exist." Immediately one wonders how the expression "at some time" *(quandoque)* is to be taken: Does Thomas mean to say thereby that what is possible has been nonexistent at some time in the past, or that it will be nonexistent at some time in the future? Each reading continues to have its defenders.[57] Before attempting to answer this question, we should also note the following sentence: "If therefore all things have the possibility of not existing, at some time *(aliquando)* there was nothing in reality." From this Thomas concludes that if this were so, even now there would be nothing.[58] The fact that in the last-quoted sentence there is a reference to the past ("at some time there was nothing") strongly suggests that Thomas would have us interpret the previous sentence in the same sense. What he is asserting, therefore, is that if all things are possibles (capable of existing and of not existing), at some point in the past all things would have been nonexistent. Therefore at that point in the past there would have been nothing whatsoever and consequently there would be nothing now. Since this final supposition is contrary to fact, so is the assumption from which it follows, that is, that all things are possibles.[59]

If we take the argument this way, the question remains: How can Thomas move from the first disputed statement to the second one without being guilty of the fallacy of composition or a quantifier shift? It is one thing for him to say that what

56. On this see T. Miyakawa, "The Value and the Meaning of the 'Tertia Via' of St. Thomas Aquinas," *Aquinas* 6 (1963), pp. 250–51.

57. Though I have already cited the troublesome text above in n. 52, I will repeat the two troublesome sentences here and in n. 58. The first one reads: "Impossibile est autem omnia quae sunt, talia esse: quia quod possibile est non esse, quandoque non est." For some who hold that Thomas means to say that such a possible will be nonexistent at some point of time in the future see: U. Degl'Innocenti, "La validità della 'terza via'," *Doctor Communis* 7 (1954), pp. 41–70, especially 51–56; Kenny, *The Five Ways,* pp. 57–58; Gilson, *The Christian Philosophy of St. Thomas Aquinas,* p. 69. For some who take Thomas as wishing to say that any such possible being must have been nonexistent before it began to exist and who therefore see his statement as referring to the past see L. Chambat, "La 'Tertia Via' dans saint Thomas et Aristote," *Revue thomiste,* n. s. 10 (1927), pp. 334–38, especially 335; J. Bobik, "The First Part of the Third Way," pp. 142–60, esp. 144–45; J. Owens, "*Quandoque* and *Aliquando* in Aquinas' *Tertia Via,*" pp. 457–59; Van Steenberghen, *Le problème,* pp. 192–98. Still others give a nontemporal reading to *quandoque* and *aliquando* (see the following sentence in Thomas's text), meaning thereby that his purpose is rather to show that any possible being, if left to its own devices, would be incapable of existing and therefore nonexistent. See, for instance, H. Holstein, "L'origine aristotélicienne de la 'tertia via' de saint Thomas," *Revue philosophique de Louvain* 48 (1950), pp. 366–67; Knasas, "Making Sense of the *Tertia Via,*" pp. 486–89.

58. "Si igitur omnia sunt possibilia non esse, aliquando nihil fuit in rebus" (as cited in n. 52 above).

59. For some who would read the argument this way see Bobik, Owens, and Van Steenberghen as cited above in n. 57.

has the possibility of not existing did not exist at some time in the past. This statement makes sense if we emphasize the point that any such being—a possible—comes into existence by being generated, that is to say, after it has not existed. Unless we wish to suggest that some such being may have been produced from eternity by being created and thereby already also concede the existence of an eternal creative principle, it seems that we must grant Thomas's claim: if something has been generated, its existence was preceded by its nonexistence.[60]

But what of Thomas's next statement? If all things are possibles (capable of existing and not existing), at some point in the past nothing would have existed. This statement goes considerably farther than the previous one. If we suppose that every individual being is a possible and therefore has not existed at some point in the past, how does it follow from this that the totality of existing things will all have been nonexistent at the same point in the past? While some have defended Thomas against the charge of committing the fallacy of composition or a quantifier shift in this step, it is difficult to regard such defenses of his reasoning as successful.[61]

To expand upon this for a moment, suppose that we grant that every possible being—every being which comes into existence by generation—exists only after it has been nonexistent. Well and good, we may comment, but this admission hardly leads to the conclusion that the totality of possible beings will all have been nonexistent simultaneously at some point in the past. Why not rather suggest that one possible being has come into being after another, and that after another, extending backwards into a beginningless past? Under this supposition, some possible being or beings will have existed at any given point in time, although no single possible being will have existed from eternity. While Thomas himself does grant the philosophical possibility of an eternally created world, he does so ultimately only under the assumption that there is also an eternal creative cause. While this is true, he cannot assume the existence of such a being at this point in the third way.

One might appeal to some other form of reasoning at this step in order to show that the explanation just proposed will not of itself be enough to account for the existence of any given possible being, whether or not one posits a beginningless series of possible beings extending back into the past. Therefore, we must grant the existence of a being that is not a possible but which is necessary if we are to account

---

60. This point is brought out effectively by Bobik in his "The First Part of the Third Way," pp. 157–58. If a possible as Thomas here uses it is "a thing such by its nature that its non-existence both *precedes* and *follows* its existence," it is the period of preceding nonexistence which is essential for this step in the third way. Here the expression *quandoque* cannot mean "after," since the proof uses as its point of departure actually existing things which are capable of existing and not existing. "By elimination, therefore, 'quandoque' must mean *before*." Also see Owens, "*Quandoque* and *Aliquando* in Aquinas' *Tertia Via*," pp. 457–58, 472–73, n. 38.

61. See, for instance, Owens, "*Quandoque* and *Aliquando*," especially pp. 461–64, and p. 463, n. 26, for a defense and for references to other recent discussions of this. Also see L. Dewan, "The Distinctiveness of St. Thomas' 'Third Way'," *Dialogue* 19 (1980), 201–18.

for the generation of any and all possible beings.[62] This, however, would be to introduce into the third way a different kind of reasoning, based on causality, a kind which we have already seen in the first and second ways in connection with a proposed regress to infinity in moved movers or in ordered caused causes, and a kind which will reappear in the second phase of the third way itself (as applied to caused necessary beings). While such an interpretation is defensible from the metaphysical standpoint, it would entail a substantial addition to Thomas's text and a serious recasting of the first part of the third way. So true is this that one might then doubt that one was still dealing with Thomas's third way, for the temporal references in the first part would now lose their importance.[63]

In order to understand more fully Thomas's procedure in his third way, a number of recent commentators have concentrated on various possible historical sources for this argument. Aristotle, Avicenna, and Moses Maimonides have all been proposed, and not without reason. Nonetheless, careful comparison of these with the text of Thomas's third way shows that while he must have been influenced by some of them, especially by Aristotle and Maimonides, in penning his version of the argument, he has developed it in his own way.[64] In short, recourse to such

---

62. Owens appeals to the Aristotelian procedure in *Metaphysics* XII, c. 6, according to which eternal motion and time are not destructible and presuppose the existence of separate substances. "The suicidal supposition that all things are possibles excludes *ipso facto* any eternal succession" (p. 461). "In the Aristotelian series no series can go backward eternally, if all things are possibles" (p. 462). In his effort to defend the argument against the charge of a quantifier shift, he contends that the argument does not reason that because "*each* possible was non-existent at one time, therefore all things if possibles were together non-existent at one time." Rather it reasons that "universal possibility ('all have the possibility for non-existence') entails universal non-existence" (p. 464). But how is this point demonstrated? Owens argues that to propose an infinite regress in time of possible beings would presume granting the reality of something necessary. In order to establish this, however, he is introducing a different kind of reasoning which in fact leads him to view this reasoning as essentially the same as that in SCG I, c. 15 (see pp. 464–66). In my judgment, however, this reasoning is missing from the text of the third way.

63. In fact, the reformulation is so pronounced that the third way will no longer be the third way of ST I, q. 2, a. 3. Moreover, unlike Owens (pp. 465–66), I do not regard the third way as it stands in ST I, q. 2, a. 3 as essentially the same argument as that presented in SCG I, c. 15. The presence of the temporal references in the first part of the third way and their absence from the first part of the argument in SCG I, c. 15 indicate an essential distinction between the two. For additional discussion of this difficulty with the third way, i.e., an apparent quantifier shift as he describes it, see Kenny, *The Five Ways*, pp. 63–65. While I have differed with Kenny's view that *quando* should be taken as referring to some time in the future rather than to the past, his criticisms of the passage now under consideration must be taken seriously. For some others who reject the validity of this step in Thomas's procedure see Bobik, "The First Part Of the Third Way," pp. 158–59; T. Pater, "The Question of the Validity of the *Tertia Via*," in Vol. 2 of Studies in Philosophy and the History of Philosophy (Washington, D.C., 1963), pp. 137–77 (for an extended critique of both of the difficult statements in the argument in light of the defenses offered by Connolly and Degl'Innocenti). On the other hand, D. O'Donoghue seems to be oblivious to this difficulty. See his "An Analysis of the *Tertia Via* of St. Thomas," *The Irish Theological Quarterly* 20 (1953), pp. 129–52.

64. For a brief résumé of earlier twentieth-century scholarship concerning Aquinas's sources for his third way see Knasas, "Making Sense of the *Tertia Via*," pp. 477–80. For some who would see

earlier sources will not rescue the argument from this crucial weakness in its first stage. Why Thomas himself did not regard this as a serious flaw in his argument is something I have been unable to determine.

As for the remainder of the first phase of the argument, its conclusion follows naturally enough. If we concede that at some point in the past nothing whatsoever existed, there would be nothing now; for what does not exist cannot begin to exist except by reason of something which exists. While Kenny has expressed some reservations about this claim, and while David Hume rejected all attempts to demonstrate it, Thomas had no doubt about it: if something begins to exist, it must be brought into existence by something else which exists.[65] He had already argued for this in somewhat different terms in accounting for the origins of motion in his first way, and in terms of efficient causation in his second way. And as we have also seen, he had made the same point with respect to existence itself in c. 4 of his *De ente*.[66]

To repeat his reasoning in my own terms, if something begins to exist after it has not existed, this can only be owing to itself, or to nothing whatsoever, or to something else, i.e., a cause. To say that a thing is the efficient cause of its own existence is to imply that it is and yet is not at the same time and in the same respect; for it must be if it is to communicate existence (to itself) or to act as a cause, and it must not be if its existence is to be caused efficiently. To suggest that

---

Maimonides as the major source see P. Gény, "À propos des preuves thomistes de l'existence de Dieu," *Revue de Philosophie* 24 (1931), pp. 575–601, esp. 586–87; Gilson, *Le thomisme*, 6th ed. (Paris, 1965), pp. 79–81, apparently agreeing with C. Baeumker that here Thomas follows Maimonides step by step. For Baeumker see his *Witelo, Ein Philosoph und Naturforscher des XIII. Jahrhunderts* (Beiträge zur Geschichte der Philosophie des Mittelalters, III–2 [Münster, 1908]), p. 338. For Maimonides see *The Guide of the Perplexed*, S. Pines, trans. (Chicago, 1963), Bk II, c. 1, pp. 247–48; *Dux seu Director dubitantium aut perplexorum*, Bk II, c. 2, fol. 40v. While there are similarities between Maimonides' presentation of this argument and that found in Aquinas, there are also significant differences between the two versions. Hence other writers have rightly concluded that Thomas's argument is not reducible to that of Maimonides. See, for instance, L. Chambat, "La 'Tertia Via'," pp. 334, 338; Holstein, "L'origine aristotélicienne de la 'tertia via'," p. 361. Some have singled out Aristotle's *De caelo* I, c. 12 as Thomas's source. See Connolly, "The Basis of the Third Proof," pp. 312–49, with special emphasis on Thomas's procedure in his Commentary on *De caelo* I (*lectiones* 22–29); D. O'Donoghue, "An Analysis of the *Tertia Via* of St. Thomas," pp. 129–51 (*De caelo* along with some other Aristotelian texts). For criticism of this effort to interpret the third way by means of Thomas's Commentary on *De caelo* I see Knasas, pp. 480–89. Still others single out *Metaphysics* XII, c. 6. See Chambat, pp. 335–38; Holstein, pp. 361–67; Knasas, p. 489. Yet, the parallelism is by no means perfect. Hence it seems best to acknowledge that while Aristotle is surely a source, Thomas is not simply repeating either his text or that of Maimonides (or Avicenna). See Owens, "*Quandoque and Aliquando*," p. 469; and n. 31 on Avicenna. In his "The Distinctiveness of St. Thomas' 'Third Way'," p. 213, n. 5, Dewan has proposed a text from Albert the Great's Commentary on the *Metaphysics* as another possible source for Thomas. See *Metaphysica* 11.2 (Cologne, ed., 16.2, p. 482:40–71). While this is possible, the similarities between Thomas's text and Albert's can just as likely be traced back to their common sources, especially Aristotle and Maimonides.

65. For Kenny see *The Five Ways*, p. 67, and his discussion of Hume's critique in his *Treatise*. For the latter see *A Treatise of Human Nature*, L. A. Selby-Bigge, ed.; 2d rev. edition by P. H. Nidditch (Oxford, 1978), Bk I, Pt. III, Section 3 (pp. 78–80).

66. See Chapter XI above, nn. 17, 18. Cf. n. 19.

it owes its existence to nothing whatsoever is to hold that there is no explanation for its existence. Since it is not self-existent (which follows from the fact that it did not always exist but began to be), to hold that there is no explanation for its present existence is to render that existence unintelligible. For Thomas, at least, this is to fly in the face of common sense and to reject the intelligibility of being. Hence, as he sees things, only the third alternative remains. If something begins to exist after it has not existed, it must be brought into existence by something else.[67]

In the second part of the argument a line of reasoning reappears which we have already seen in SCG I, c. 15. If one grants that a necessary being does exist (to account for the coming into existence of the possible beings with which the argument began), such a being may or may not depend upon something else for its necessity (and, we may assume, for its existence). But one cannot regress to infinity in caused necessary beings (literally: "in necessary beings whose necessity is caused"), just as one cannot do so with efficient causes, as has been proved (see the second way). Therefore there must be an uncaused necessary being, which causes the necessity of the others, and which everyone calls God.[68]

This second phase of the argument is much less controversial and is, in my opinion, sound. Whether or not it succeeds in establishing the point that there is only one uncaused necessary being is, of course, another matter, and much of what we have said above about the conclusions of the first and second ways continues to apply. Additional reflection will be required to show that there is only one first and totally uncaused necessary being if we are to justify the claim that this being is God. One could, of course, reason that at this point in the argument Thomas is discussing beings that depend upon something else not only for their necessity but for their very existence. If so, one could then reason that their cause is an uncaused source of *esse* and therefore uncaused *esse* in and of itself. Even so, the argument will remain incomplete until it has been shown that there can only be one such being. One might do this by adopting Thomas's procedure in q. 11, or by introducing reasoning similar to that which he has presented in the *De ente,* c. 4.[69]

In sum, the first phase of the third way strikes me as being open to serious criticisms along the lines already pointed out. In this phase it is considerably less convincing than the argumentation from SCG I, c. 15. Why Thomas introduced this particular step into his argument in ST I, q. 2, a. 3 continues to be a matter for speculation.[70] In my opinion, no completely satisfying explanation has been

---

67. In the argumentation in *De ente,* c. 4 Thomas has already established real distinction of essence and *esse* in the beings with which he is concerned. In the third way he does not presuppose this point. For Thomas's own version of the first step in SCG I, c. 15, see Ch. XI above, Section 4, n. 95.

68. See the text as cited above in n. 54.

69. As will be seen below in Section 6, Thomas's procedure in q. 11 indicates that he was fully aware of this.

70. For a listing of various suggested explanations of this and for discussion see Van Steenberghen, *Le problème,* pp. 203–5.

forthcoming. By introducing this first step he has, of course, established the third way clearly enough as a different kind of argument from either the first or second way. But one could say the same of the much less troublesome argument offered in SCG I, c. 15. There, too, he incorporates into his argumentation the distinction between possible beings, caused necessary beings, and an uncaused necessary being and there, too, he begins with possible beings and then moves on to consider caused necessary beings in order to reason to the existence of an uncaused necessary being.

4. The Fourth Way

Thomas's fourth way is based on the varying degrees of perfection we find among beings. It immediately strikes the reader as being much more Platonic and Neoplatonic in inspiration than any of the other five ways, even though in presenting it Thomas twice refers to a passage from Aristotle's *Metaphysics*. We have already considered foreshadowings of this kind of approach in his Commentary on I *Sentences* and in *Summa contra Gentiles* I, c. 13.[71] As he develops this argument in the *Summa theologiae*, among things we find something that is more and less good, more and less true, more and less noble, and so too with respect to other perfections of this kind. But the more and less are said of different things insofar as they approach in diverse fashion something which is (such) to a maximum degree. (To illustrate this Thomas cites the example of heat: that is hotter which more closely approaches something which is hot to the maximum degree.) Therefore there is something which is truest and best and noblest and hence which is also being to the maximum degree. In support of this conclusion Thomas observes that those things which are true to the maximum degree also enjoy being to the maximum degree, and cites Bk II of the *Metaphysics*.[72] He is evidently basing this on the

---

71. See Ch. XI above, Section 1 and Section 4 (n. 87).

72. "Quarta via sumitur ex gradibus qui in rebus inveniuntur. Invenitur enim in rebus aliquid magis et minus bonum, et verum, et nobile: et sic de aliis huiusmodi. Sed *magis* et *minus* dicuntur de diversis secundum quod appropinquant diversimode ad aliquid quod maxime est: sicut magis calidum est, quod magis approximant maxime calido. Est igitur aliquid quod est verissimum, et optimum, et nobilissimum, et per consequens maxime ens: nam quae sunt maxime vera, sunt maxime entia, ut dicitur II *Metaphy.*" (Leon. 4.32). I have followed a suggestion by Van Steenberghen by assuming that the term *tale* is to be understood after *maxime est* in the third sentence. The logic of the argument demands this ("But more and less are said of different things insofar as they approach in different fashion something which is [such: inserted] to a maximum degree"). See *Le problème*, p. 213. For the text from Aristotle see his *Metaphysics* II, c. 1 (993b 30–31). Fabro notes that both here and in the reference to Aristotle's *Metaphysics* in the second stage of the argument Thomas has in mind this same general passage from *Metaphysics* II (see 993b 25–31); but in the earlier version which appears in SCG I, c. 13, Thomas had referred not only to this text in Aristotle but to another from *Metaphysics* IV, c. 4 (1008b 31–1009a 2). For Fabro see his "Sviluppo, significato e valore della 'IV Via'," *Doctor communis* 7 (1954), p. 78; cf. p. 75, n. 5. In citing Aristotle's *Metaphysics* (993b 30–31) Thomas has converted the references to *vera* and *entia*, but legitimately so in light of the convertibility of ontological truth and being.

convertible character of being and of ontological truth, a point which he had developed more fully elsewhere, especially in *De veritate*, q. 1, a. 1.[73] With this the first part of his argument comes to an end; but rather than regard his task as completed, Thomas introduces a second stage.

In this second stage he reasons that what is said to be supremely such in a given genus is the cause of all other things which are present in that genus. (In illustration he returns to the example of fire: being hot to the maximum degree, fire is the cause of heat in all other things, as Aristotle maintains in the *Metaphysics*.) Therefore, Thomas concludes, there is something which is the cause of being *(esse)* for all other beings, as well as of their goodness and every other perfection. And this we call God.[74]

In the first stage of this argument Thomas again appeals to the world as we experience it, and goes on to apply a general principle to the same. As for the world as we experience it, we note that certain things are more and less good, true, noble, etc. By referring to things as more and less good, Thomas must have in mind their ontological goodness, that is to say, their goodness of being. As we have seen, in *De veritate*, q. 1, a. 1 he had singled out goodness, along with truth and unity, as characteristics which are found wherever being itself is realized and which are convertible with being. Consequently, along with thing *(res)* and something *(aliquid)*, which he also regards as coextensive with being, these are often referred to as transcendental properties of being.[75] To say that something enjoys goodness of being is to indicate that it is an object of appetite. And to say that one thing enjoys greater ontological goodness than another is to imply that it is a more desirable object in itself. Given Thomas's hierarchical view of the universe and his conviction that ontological goodness and being are really convertible, we can understand why he would view an animal as enjoying greater ontological goodness than a mere

73. Leon. 22.1.5:161–6:200. Cf. Thomas's reply to objection 4: ". . . dicendum quod verum est dispositio entis non quasi addens aliquam naturam nec quasi exprimens aliquem specialem modum entis sed aliquid quod generaliter invenitur in omni ente, quod tamen nomine entis non exprimitur . . ." (p. 7:229–234). Cf. ad 6. Cf. Aertsen, *Medieval Philosophy and the Transcendentals*, c. 6 (pp. 243–89); Wippel, "Truth in Thomas Aquinas," pp. 307–21.

74. "Quod autem dicitur maxime tale in aliquo genere, est causa omnium quae sunt illius generis: sicut ignis, qui est maxime calidus, est causa omnium calidorum, ut in eodem libro dicitur. Ergo est aliquid quod omnibus entibus est causa esse, et bonitatis, et cuiuslibet perfectionis: et hoc dicimus Deum" (Leon. 4.32). For Aristotle see n. 72 above.

75. On Thomas's derivation of the transcendentals see Ch. VI above, Section 5. As will be recalled, goodness expresses the agreement of being with the appetitive power of the soul in that the good is that which all things desire (Leon. 22.1.5:156–159). On the transcendental character of goodness also see ST I, q. 5, a. 1 *(bonum* and *ens* are the same in reality though they differ according to reason); a. 2 (in terms of its intelligible content being [*ens*] is prior to goodness); a. 3 (every being insofar as it is being is good). On this final point also see Thomas's *In De Hebdomadibus*, lect. 3 (Leon. 50.275:40–277:143); lect. 4 (pp. 279:111–280:160). Cf. Thomas's *De malo*, q. 1, a. 1 (Leon. 23.5–6) and a. 2 (pp. 10:130–11:195); *De veritate*, q. 21, a. 1 (Leon. 22.3.592:89–594:244); a. 2 (p. 596:61–96). The whole of q. 21 is highly recommended to the reader. Also see Aertsen, *Medieval Philosophy and the Transcendentals*, c. 7, esp. pp. 299–319.

stone. The animal is endowed with life and with the power of sensation, whereas the stone is not. At the same time, an animal lacks the power of understanding which a human being enjoys and is therefore less good, ontologically speaking, than a human being.[76]

In referring to things as more and less true Thomas is thinking of truth of being or ontological truth, not of truth as it exists in the intellect (logical truth). He has in mind that quality present in any being in virtue of which it can be grasped by intellect or, to put it in other terms, the intelligibility of being. Since such truth or intelligibility is found wherever being is realized, Thomas also regards being and truth as convertible with one another. To say that one thing enjoys greater truth (of being) than another is to make the point that, viewed in itself, it is more intelligible than the other. And this in turn follows from the fact that its degree of being is greater than that present in the other. In the world as we experience it, there do seem to be varying degrees of intelligibility, or of ontological truth. Thus according to Thomas's thinking a substantial form is more intelligible than its corresponding prime matter; the essence of a human being is more intelligible than that of a rock. In sum, corresponding to the hierarchy of being is a hierarchy of ontological truth, or of intrinsic intelligibility of being.[77]

In referring to certain things as more and less noble than others, Thomas has created something of a problem for his readers. Does he intend to single out another characteristic, distinct from ontological goodness and ontological truth? If so, what does he have in mind? It is difficult to answer this question with any degree of certainty. R. Garrigou-Lagrange takes nobility as synonymous with perfection, and this suggestion may well be correct. For instance, in SCG I, c. 28 Thomas describes as universally perfect that to which no excellence (nobilitas) of any kind is lacking. He also indicates that a thing's excellence (nobilitas) follows

76. For discussion of Thomas's hierarchical view of the universe of created being see, for instance, Gilson, *The Christian Philosophy of St. Thomas Aquinas*, Part Two, pp. 147–248; J. de Finance, *Être et agir*, pp. 314–55; J. Legrand, *L'univers et l'homme dans la philosophie de saint Thomas*, Vol. I (Brussels, 1946); J. H. Wright, *The Order of the Universe in the Theology of St. Thomas Aquinas* (Rome, 1957); O. Blanchette, *The Perfection of the Universe according to Aquinas* (University Park, Pa., 1992).

77. On the convertibility of truth and being see *De veritate*, q. 1, a. 1 and ad 4 (cited in n. 73 above). Also see his reply to objection 5: ". . . concludit Philosophus quod idem est ordo alicui rei in esse et veritate, ita scilicet quod ubi invenitur quod est maxime ens, est maxime verum" (Leon. 22.1.7:242–245). For Aristotle see *Metaphysics* II, c. 1 (cited in n. 72 above). Here Thomas has not converted *ens* and *verum*. He distinguishes truth as it exists in the intellect (what we may refer to as "logical" truth) from truth of being ("ontological" truth). In addition to *De veritate*, q. 1, a. 1, see a. 2 (Leon. 22.1.9); *In I Sent.*, d. 19, q. 5, a. 1 (note in particular: ". . . verum per prius dicitur de veritate intellectus, et de enuntiatione dicitur inquantum est signum illius veritatis; de re autem dicitur, inquantum est causa. . . ." [Mandonnet ed., Vol. 1, p. 486]); SCG I, c. 60; ST I, q. 16, a. 2. See a. 3 and ad 1 on the convertible character of *verum* and *ens*. For fuller discussion see J. Vande Wiele, "Le problème de la vérité ontologique dans la philosophie de saint Thomas," *Revue philosophique de Louvain* 52 (1954), pp. 521–71, esp. 545–54; F. Ruello, *La notion de vérité chez Saint Albert le Grand et Saint Thomas d'Aquin de 1243 à 1254* (Louvain-Paris, 1969), pp. 179–227 (on *In I Sent.*, d. 19, q. 5. a. 1); Aertsen and Wippel as cited above in n. 73.

upon its mode of being *(esse)*. Accordingly, I would suggest that by this term Thomas wants to signify the varying degrees of pure ontological perfection or excellence we discover in the different beings we experience in the world about us. Just as some share more fully in ontological goodness and truth than do others, so too they may be regarded as being more perfect or more excellent, ontologically speaking, than others. Excellence *(nobilitas)* should not be regarded as a distinct transcendental.[78]

This in turn leads to another question: Does Thomas wish to restrict the starting point of the fourth way to gradation in transcendental perfections such as truth and goodness? (Interestingly enough, he does not mention ontological unity.) Or does he wish to include what we might call pure but not transcendental perfections such as life, knowledge, will, etc.? While not found wherever being is realized, such perfections also admit of degrees and, when freed from all limitation, may be applied analogically even to God, or so Thomas will maintain.[79] These perfections have the advantage of being readily recognizable in varying degrees in the world about us. But since Thomas has not explicitly singled them out in presenting the fourth way, it will be better for us not to base his argument upon them. For then one might wonder whether the general principle to which he appeals is also intended to apply to them as well as to strictly transcendental perfections. Here, therefore, I shall restrict the argument to transcendental perfections such as goodness and truth.

As Thomas expresses this principle in his text, the more and less are said of different things insofar as they approach in diverse fashion something which is such to the maximum degree. As some writers have pointed out, the example to which Thomas turns hardly proves his point. It is unnecessary for us to assume that something enjoys a maximum degree of heat in order to be aware that one kettle is hotter than another. Nonetheless, since this is only an example drawn from an outmoded medieval physics, we need not regard it as central to Thomas's argument.[80] But we may still ask: How does Thomas justify this general principle? Is it

---

78. For brief dicussions of this see Garrigou-Lagrange, *God: His Existence and His Nature*, Vol. 1, p. 306; Van Steenberghen, *Le problème*, pp. 209, 216. For SCG I, c. 28, see ed. cit., p. 29 ("Et dico universaliter"). Note that in this context Thomas also applies *nobilitas* to wisdom. While granting this, for the sake of simplicity I will restrict it within the context of the fourth way to transcendental perfections. Also see Wagner, *Die philosophischen Implikate*, pp. 95–97. He considers and rightly rejects identifying the *nobile* with the beautiful.

79. See Thomas's discussion of God's *scientia, vita,* et *voluntas* in ST I, qq. 14, 15, 18, and 19.

80. See Fabro, "Sviluppo, significato e valore della 'IV Via'," pp. 101–2; Van Steenberghen, *Le problème*, pp. 215–16. As Van Steenberghen points out, for Aristotle and his medieval followers, fire is hot of its essence and to the maximum degree. While they regarded the sun as the cause of heat in earthly things, they did not regard it as hot in itself (see n. 20, where he corrects Fabro on this detail). For fuller discussion see Wagner, *Die philosophischen Implikate*, pp. 115–21. While he concludes that this example would have been illuminating for Thomas's contemporaries who shared his world-view, Wagner denies that the controlling principle of the first part of the fourth way rests upon the example for its justification (p. 120).

immediately evident that the more and less are said of different things only insofar as they approach something which is such to a maximum degree? Even if we restrict this principle to transcendental perfections such as those named by Thomas—goodness, truth (and nobility)—it is difficult to see how he can move so quickly from our recognition of greater and lesser degrees of these perfections to the existence of something which is such perfection to the maximum degree.

In attempting to justify this step in the argument, some commentators have maintained that it should not be interpreted as resting solely on exemplar causality. Instead, they suggest, there is an implicit appeal to efficient causality in this first stage. That which possesses goodness or truth or nobility in only a greater and lesser degree must receive such perfections from some distinct efficient cause. Therefore, one may conclude to the existence of an uncaused cause of goodness, truth, and nobility, which itself is such perfection of its essence. Confirmation for this interpretation may be sought by referring to the second stage in Thomas's text. There he reasons that what is supremely such in a given genus is the cause of everything else which belongs to that genus.[81]

Any such effort, however, runs counter to the literal text of the fourth way, or so it seems to me. The first stage of the argument concludes to the existence of something which is truest and best and noblest and hence being to the maximum degree. The final point—that it is also being to the maximum degree—is based on the convertibility of ontological truth and being, and is supported by an appeal to Aristotle's *Metaphysics*, as we have noted. But until this point in the argument no reference has been made to efficient causality. It is only in the second step, after the existence of a maximum has been established, that Thomas attempts to show that this maximum is also the cause of being, goodness, etc., for all other things.[82] Hence there seems to be no justification in Thomas's text for the claim that his proof for the existence of a maximum rests on or presupposes reasoning from efficient causation. It follows, therefore, that if we wish to present the argument as

81. For Thomas's text see n. 74 above. See M. Corvez, "La quatrième voie vers l'existence de Dieu selon saint Thomas," in *Quinque sunt viae*, L. J. Elders, ed. (Vatican City, 1980), pp. 75–83, esp. pp. 77–78 (he reasons from diversity of beings in the world to the distinction of essence and existence in such beings, and from this to their efficiently caused character); Garrigou-Lagrange, *God: His Existence and His Nature*, Vol. 1, pp. 301–17. Cf. Wagner, op. cit., pp. 18–25 (on Garrigou-Lagrange's approach). For a helpful summary of some other recent approaches see J. Bobik, "Aquinas's Fourth Way and the Approximating Relation," *The Thomist* 51 (1987), pp. 17–36.

82. For the text see n. 74 above. For others who agree that in its first stage the argument is based solely on exemplar causality and is intended by Thomas to establish the existence of a really existing Maximum (or God) see L. Charlier, "Les cinq voies de saint Thomas," pp. 181–227, especially pp. 208–11; Van Steenberghen, *Le problème*, p. 211; A. Little, *The Platonic Heritage of Thomism*, pp. 62–68, 80, and c. VII (passim); Bobik, op. cit., pp. 33–36 (along with other authors cited in this article). Cf. J.-P. Planty-Bonjour, "Die Struktur des Gottesbeweises aus den Seinsstufen," *Philosophisches Jahrbuch* 69 (1962), pp. 282–97, who rather sees the entire proof as resting solely on what he calls the principle of participation through formal hierarchy, without relying on efficient causality. For discussion see Wagner, pp. 29–37.

it appears in his text, it can only be based on extrinsic formal causality, i.e., on exemplar causality.

But if this argument for the existence of a maximum is free from any reference to efficient causation, is it valid? This question is more difficult to decide. As far as Thomas himself is concerned, earlier appeals in his texts to similar argumentation have already been noted. As will be recalled, in his Commentary on I *Sentences,* d. 3, he offers two arguments based on eminence. The first is taken from eminence insofar as this applies to being. The good and the better are so named in comparison to that which is the best. Since among substances a body is good and a created spirit still better, there must be some best from which the goodness present in body and spirit derives. But as I have already noted above, Thomas offers no justification in that context for the general claim that where there is a good and a better, there must be a best.[83]

The second argument based on eminence focuses on human knowing. If we find things which are more and less beautiful, we can recognize them as such only by reason of their proximity to something which is the very principle of beauty. From this general cognitive principle Thomas quickly concludes to the existence of something from which bodies (which are beautiful) and spirits (which are more beautiful) derive their beauty. Once again, however, in the immediate context he offers no justification either for this general cognitive principle or for the ontological conclusion he draws from it.[84] While this cognitive principle makes perfect sense within an Augustinian account of human knowing, it is difficult to see how it can be granted within the terms of Thomas's own theory of knowledge and his conviction that our knowledge begins with and must in some way be derived from sense experience.[85]

Still another seeming anticipation of the fourth way is offered within this same discussion from Thomas's Commentary on I *Sentences,* an argument which Thomas describes as taken from the Dionysian way of negation *(remotionis).* Beyond everything which is imperfect there must be something which is perfect and admits of no imperfection whatsoever. Thomas goes on to apply this to bodies and then to things which are incorporeal and changeable. Beyond all of these there must be something which is completely immobile and perfect, or God.[86] Once again, however, Thomas does not see fit to justify his operative principle—that beyond that which is imperfect there must be something which is completely and

---

83. For this text see my Ch. XI above, n. 10.

84. See Ch. XI above, n. 11.

85. According to Augustine, if I am to recognize any number, or the laws of number, this can only be because the notion of number is already "impressed" on my mind. So too, if I am to recognize immutable truths such as that all men desire happiness or seek to be wise, these notions too must in some way already be impressed on my mind, presumably through divine illumination. See his *De libero arbitrio,* Bk II, c. 8, 20, 79–23, 92; c. 9, 26, 102–103 (CCSL Vol. 29, pp. 250–52, 254).

86. For the text see Ch. XI above, n. 8.

totally perfect. While antecedents may be cited for such reasoning from within the Christian Neoplatonic tradition (see, for instance, Boethius's *Consolation of Philosophy* and Anselm's *Monologium*), one wonders how Thomas can justify such a claim within his own metaphysical perspective.[87]

When we return to another foreshadowing of the fourth way in *Summa contra Gentiles* I, c. 13, our perplexity remains. As will be recalled, there Thomas reasons that if we recognize one thing as truer than another, this can only be because it comes closer to that which is true without qualification and to the maximum degree. From this he quickly draws the conclusion that there must be something which is being to the maximum degree. While this final point follows from the convertibility of ontological truth (truth of being) and of being itself, the general working principle on which the argument rests remains without justification— that the more and the less in the order of truth (and being) enables one to conclude immediately to the existence of something which is true to the maximum degree.[88]

As we return to the fourth way of the *Summa theologiae*, we wonder whether Thomas regards this general principle as self-evident. One writer has suggested that perhaps his powers of penetration were such that he immediately saw that varying degrees of transcendental perfection require a subsisting maximum to account for their imperfect realizations in the beings we experience. Within a Platonic and Neoplatonic framework, the self-evidence of such a claim might be more readily granted. But within Thomas's distinctive metaphysical approach, even though a considerable Platonic and Neoplatonic influence must be recognized, today's reader of his text may protest: the principle in question is not self-evident to him or her.[89]

One way of supplying the missing justification is to appeal to Thomas's metaphysics of participation and to regard the fourth way as an argument based on participation. This seems to be the approach adopted by C. Fabro. As he points out, there is another and later version of such an argument in Thomas's *Lectura* on St. John's Gospel, dating ca. 1270–1272.[90] As Thomas presents this argument, it is

---

87. For Boethius see his *Consolation of Philosophy*, Bk III, pr. 10, ed. cit., p. 274:9–15: "Omne enim quod inperfectum esse dicitur, id inminutione perfecti inperfectum esse perhibetur. Quo fit, ut si in quolibet genere imperfectum quid esse videatur, in eo perfectione quoque aliquid esse necesse sit. Etenim perfectione sublata, unde illud quod inperfectum perhibetur exstiterit ne fingi quidem potest." For Anselm see his *Monologium*, cc. 1, 4 (Schmitt ed., Vol. I, pp. 14–15, 17–18).

88. Ed. cit., p. 14. For this text see Ch. XI, n. 87 and our discussion there.

89. See Little, *The Platonic Heritage of Thomism*, p. 100: "But though St. Thomas obviously considers that his statement needs no proof, philosophers of lower but yet good intelligence do not find the statement in the sense just explained self-evident. . . ." Also see Van Steenberghen, *Le problème*, who notes that Thomas presents the principle as immediately evident or as *per se notum;* he does not demonstrate it. See pp. 209–10. Cf. Maritain, *Approaches to God*, pp. 40–43.

90. "Sviluppo, significato e valore," pp. 81 (for the text); 82 (on the privileged character of this presentation); 89–102 (interpretation of the argument). On the date see Torrell, *Saint Thomas Aquinas*, p. 339.

based on the nobility *(dignitas)* of God and is the way of the "Platonists." At the same time, it is clear from the context that Thomas accepts this argument as his own. Everything which is (such) by participation is reduced to something which is such of its essence as to something first and supreme. (Thus all things which participate in fire are reduced to fire which is such of its essence.) But since all things which exist participate in *esse* and are beings through participation, there must be something at the summit of all things which is *esse* of its essence in that its essence is its *esse*. This is God, the most sufficient and noblest and most perfect cause of all *esse*, from whom all things which exist participate in *esse*.[91]

This is an interesting approach and it rests on a principle frequently employed by Thomas in other contexts. That which participates in something must be traced back to something which is that perfection of its essence. Hence, that which exists by participating in *esse* must be traced back to something which is the act of being *(esse)* of its very essence.[92] Because this argument explicitly invokes participation and deals with it in the order of *esse*, it is more satisfying from a metaphysical standpoint than that offered in *Summa theologiae* I, q. 2, a. 3.

At the same time, we may ask whether this kind of argumentation can be justified without some implicit or explicit appeal to efficient causality. In fact, some such appeal seems to be involved at two levels within the argument. First of all, without stating this explicitly, the argument assumes that if something participates in a given characteristic, and especially in *esse*, it does not possess that characteristic

91. See *Lectura super evangelium Johannis*, Busa ed., Vol. 6, p. 227: "Quidam autem venerunt in cognitionem dei ex dignitate ipsius dei: et isti fuerunt platonici. Consideraverunt enim quod omne illud quod est secundum participationem, reducitur ad aliquid quod sit illud per suam essentiam, sicut ad primum et ad summum; sicut omnia ignita per participationem reducuntur ad ignem, qui est per essentiam suam talis. Cum ergo omnia quae sunt, participent esse, et sint per participationem entia, necesse est esse aliquid in cacumine omnium rerum, quod sit ipsum esse per suam essentiam, idest quod sua essentia sit suum esse: et hoc est deus, qui est sufficientissima, et dignissima, et perfectissima causa totius esse, a quo omnia quae sunt, participant esse." Note that this is one of four ways *(modi)* in which Thomas here remarks that the ancient philosophers came to knowledge of God. For all four see Fabro, pp. 79–82.

92. For some other texts see, for instance, ST I, q. 44, a. 1: "Si enim aliquid invenitur in aliquo per participationem, necesse est quod causetur in ipso ab eo cui essentialiter convenit; sicut ferrum fit ignitum ab igne." Cf. the reply to obj. 1: ". . . quia ex hoc quod aliquid per participationem est ens, sequitur quod sit causatum ab alio. Unde huiusmodi ens non potest esse, quin sit causatum . . ." (Leon. 4.455). See *De substantiis separatis*, c. 3, where Thomas is attempting to bring out points of agreement between Plato and Aristotle. After referring to Plato's theory of participation he comments: ". . . omne autem participans aliquid accipit id quod participat ab eo a quo participat, et quantum ad hoc id a quo participat est causa ipsius: sicut aër habet lumen participatum a sole, quae est causa illuminationis ipsius" (Leon. 40.D46:11–15). Also see *Compendium theologiae*, c. 68: ". . . omne quod habet aliquid per participationem reducitur in id quod habet illud per essentiam sicut in principium et causam, sicut ferrum ignitum participat igneitatem ab eo quod est ignis per essentiam suam" (Leon. 42.103:18–22). Cf. c. 123: "Item, ea quae sunt per participationem reducuntur in id quod est per essentiam sicut in causam: omnia enim ignita suae ignitionis ignem causam habent aliquo modo" (Leon. 42.127:27–30). Cf. Wagner, *Die philosophischen Implikate*, pp. 103–5.

of its essence or of itself. This follows from Thomas's general description of participation in his Commentary on the *De Hebdomadibus,* as we have seen above in Chapter IV.[93] Moreover, in various contexts he states that a participated characteristic is present in a participating subject only insofar as it is efficiently caused therein. This will follow so long as one is dealing with real or ontological participation, not merely with the logical participation of a less extended concept in one that is more extended, for instance, participation of a species in a genus.[94]

But what of participation of beings in *esse*? Thomas is convinced that this is a case of real participation, as we have also seen above in Chapter V. At times he reasons from the participated character of *esse* in particular entities to real distinction and composition therein of essence and *esse*.[95] In order to strengthen the claim that a participated being is efficiently caused, one might reason as follows. Because a participated being's essence differs from its *esse,* its *esse* must be received from without, i.e., it must be efficiently caused. As Thomas develops this in *Summa theologiae* I, q. 3, a. 4, whatever is present in a thing in addition to its essence must be caused in that thing either by the principles of its essence (as is true of a proper accident), or else by something external (as heat is caused in water by fire). If the *esse* of a thing is distinct from that thing's essence, the same will apply. It must be caused either by the essential principles of that thing or by something external. But since a given thing cannot be the efficient cause of its own *esse,* the *esse* of any such thing cannot be caused by its intrinsic and essential principles. Therefore, its *esse* must be caused by something else.[96]

The argument from participation for God's existence also seems to rest on efficient causality at a second level. One must justify the claim that what exists by

---

93. See Ch. IV above, n. 7 for the "definition" of participation offered by Thomas in his Commentary on the *De Hebdomadibus:* when something receives in particular fashion that which belongs to another in universal (total) fashion, it is said to participate in it. See n. 8 there for the third kind of participation—that whereby an effect participates in its cause. It is under this third kind, as we have seen, that participation of beings in *esse* is to be placed.

94. See the texts cited in n. 92 above on the connection between being participated and (efficiently) caused. Also see Ch. V above, Section 4, for texts where Thomas reasons directly from the participated character of *esse* in particular beings to real distinction and composition of essence and *esse* therein. A merely conceptual distinction between essence and act of being will not suffice to account for the fact that given beings really do participate in *esse*. See, for instance, the text from Quodlibet 2, q. 2, a. 1, cited in Ch. V, n. 98. This is why he can reason from the participated character of such beings to the composition of essence and *esse* within them, and thus to their being efficiently caused.

95. See Ch. V, Section 4.

96. Leon. 4.42. Note in particular: "Si igitur ipsum esse rei sit aliud ab eius essentia, necesse est quod esse illius rei vel sit causatum ab aliquo exteriori, vel a principiis essentialibus eiusdem rei. Impossibile est autem quod esse sit causatum tantum ex principiis essentialibus rei: quia nulla res sufficit quod sit sibi causa essendi, si habeat esse causatum. Oportet ergo quod illud cuius esse est aliud ab essentia sua, habeat esse causatum ab alio." Since this cannot be said of God, Thomas concludes that in him essence and act of being cannot differ.

participation is to be traced back or reduced to that which exists of its essence. In order to do this, one should again consider and eliminate as a viable alternative to the unparticipated source appeal to a series of beings which would simply participate in other and higher participating beings and these in still others *ad infinitum*. It is true that in the first stage of the fourth way of the *Summa theologiae* Thomas does not explicitly bring out either of these points, i.e., the proof that beings which participate in *esse* are efficiently caused, or the consideration of an infinite regress of participating beings. Nor does he bring out the second point in the argument in his *Lectura*. It seems to me, however, that this should be done if one is to view the fourth way as an argument based on participation and if one wishes to justify that argument within Thomas's metaphysics.[97]

In doing this, however, I must acknowledge that we will have reinterpreted the fourth way seriously, and even in its substance. It will no longer be based solely on exemplar causality in its first stage, as its text indicates that it was originally intended to be. It will now be equivalent to the argument offered in the *Lectura* on St. John's Gospel. But unless some such reinterpretation or substitution is introduced, it seems unlikely that the argument's first stage can be regarded as successful in its attempt to prove that a maximum actually exists.[98]

In discussions of the fourth way reference is some times made to Thomas's slightly earlier argumentation in *De potentia*, q. 3, a. 5. There he is attempting to show that nothing that exists apart from God is uncreated. He offers three arguments to make this point. The first may be regarded as an argument for God's existence. The remaining two, attributed by Thomas respectively to Aristotle and to Avicenna, are less clearly so. They seem to take God's existence as already established and concentrate on showing that all beings other than God receive their *esse* from him. In these latter two arguments the theme of participation is explicitly introduced.[99]

The first argument runs as follows. If one single characteristic is common to many things, it must be caused in each of them by a single cause. This common feature cannot belong to each of the different individuals by reason of that which is proper to it as an individual; for each individual, by reason of that which it is in itself, is distinct from the others, and diversity in causes results in diverse effects.

---

97. The question may be raised concerning whether he regarded these points as necessary but as implied by his texts, or whether he did not even regard them as essential for an argument based on participation. While this is difficult to determine on purely historical grounds, they seem to me to be necessary for such an argument on philosophical grounds.

98. On the other hand, if one grants that this stage succeeds in establishing the existence of a maximum in the order of ontological truth, goodness, and nobility, one should also grant its inference that a maximum exists in the order of being.

99. For this text see ed. cit., p. 49. Fabro seems to regard all three arguments as proofs for God's existence. See his "Sviluppo, significato et valore," pp. 75–78. On these texts also see Van Steenberghen, *Le problème*, pp. 140–43, who regards only the first as an argument for God's existence.

But since *esse* is common to all things and since each, when considered in itself, is distinct from the others, Thomas concludes that the *esse* realized in each must be given to it by some one cause. And this, Thomas comments, seems to be Plato's argument, since he held that before every multitude there must be some kind of unity.[100]

There is some disagreement among commentators concerning whether or not this is an argument based on participation. While Fabro concedes that the term "participation" does not appear in it, he seems to think that the notion is present therein.[101] Since the argument begins with the fact that *esse* is common to all existing things, we may, it seems to me, regard the argument as resting on the participation by the many in the perfection of *esse*. On the other hand, Van Steenberghen, while granting the argument's validity, contends that it does not start from participation but that it is based on the ontological similarity which obtains between finite beings.[102] To me this is simply another way in which Thomas makes the point that different beings merely participate in *esse (commune)*, and that no one of them is identical with it. In any event, it is another form of argumentation based on efficient causality. By reasoning that the common perfection *(esse)* cannot be accounted for in the many which share in it by an appeal to that which is proper to and distinctive of each, Thomas is in effect showing that *esse* is efficiently caused in each of them.[103] Hence this argument can hardly be regarded as one that is based on degrees of perfection, or as an equivalent of the fourth way, although it can easily be substituted for the first stage of that argument.

As for the second stage of the argument as it stands in *Summa theologiae* I, q. 2, a. 3, the point of this step is to prove that once we have established the existence of a maximum, we may also show that it is the efficient cause of the being, goodness, and other perfection present in other things. This part of the argument is much less troublesome than the first stage, or so it appears to me.[104] But it presupposes that one has already established the existence of the maximum in the argument's first stage, or else, as I have suggested, that one has substituted an argument based on participation in that stage to reach an unparticipated source. Enough has been said about this to enable us to move on now to the last of the five ways.

---

100. Ed. cit., p. 49. Note especially: "Oportet enim, si aliquid unum communiter in pluribus invenitur, quod ab aliqua una causa in illis causetur; non enim potest esse quod illud commune utrique ex se ipso conveniat, cum utrumque, secundum quod ipsum est, ab altero distinguatur; et diversitas causarum diversos effectus producit."

101. "Sviluppo," p. 77.

102. *Le problème*, p. 221. Cf. p. 140.

103. Van Steenberghen also regards this as a way of showing that *esse* is efficiently caused in finite beings by an infinite being. See *Le problème*, p. 221, n. 1.

104. For the text, see n. 74 above. This part of the proof hardly seems to be crucial if one appeals to efficient causality (or to participation) in the argument's first stage, although it will still serve to complete the overall argumentation.

5. The Fifth Way

Thomas introduces this argument by noting that it is based on the way things are governed *(ex gubernatione rerum)*. We see that certain things which lack knowledge, that is to say, natural bodies, act for the sake of an end. In support of this claim Thomas reasons that it follows from the fact that they always or at least usually *(frequentius)* act in the same way in order to attain that which is best. This shows that they reach their respective end(s) not by chance but by intention. But "things which lack cognition do not tend to an end unless they are directed [to it] by some knowing and intelligent being, as an arrow is directed [to its target] by an archer." Therefore, there is some intelligent being by which all natural things are ordered to their end, and this we call God.[105]

While the fifth way is sometimes confused with an argument based on order and design and the need for a supreme designer, Thomas's text makes it clear that he really has in mind an argument based on final causality in nature. Hence it bears much greater resemblance to the argument for divine providence in *De veritate*, q. 5, a. 2 than to the argument from design of *Summa contra Gentiles* I, c. 13.[106]

Like the other five ways, this argument begins with something which Thomas regards as evident to us from the world of everyday experience. Natural bodies, that is to say, things which are equipped with their own natures but lack the power of cognition, act for the sake of an end. Thomas knows that it is one thing for us to be aware that natural bodies act, for instance, that a heavy body tends to fall or a hot body to rise; but it is something else for us to conclude that such bodies act for an end.[107] Immediately, therefore, two possible objections come to mind. Perhaps the action of natural bodies can be accounted for merely by appealing to efficient causal activity. Or perhaps their seeming action for an end is not to be credited to the influence of any final cause but only to chance.

As regards the first objection, as we have already seen above when considering Thomas's discussion in *De veritate*, q. 5, a. 2, he had learned from Aristotle about two ancient schools of thought which left no place for final causality. Some admitted of nothing but material causes; others defended the existence of efficient causes

---

105. "Quinta via sumitur ex gubernatione rerum. Videmus enim quod aliqua quae cognitione carent, scilicet corpora naturalia, operantur propter finem: quod apparet ex hoc quod semper aut frequentius eodem modo operantur, ut consequantur id quod est optimum; unde patet quod non a casu, sed ex intentione perveniunt ad finem. Ea autem quae non habent cognitionem, non tendunt in finem nisi directa ab aliquo cognoscente et intelligente, sicut sagitta a sagittante. Ergo est aliquid intelligens, a quo omnes res naturales ordinantur ad finem: et hoc dicimus Deum" (Leon. 4.32).

106. For these see above in Ch. XI, Section 3 (and nn. 33, 34); Section 4 (n. 90), and my discussion there.

107. That Thomas is aware of this distinction is indicated by the fact that he immediately offers some argumentation to show that natural bodies act for an end, i.e., the fact that they always or at least more frequently act in the same way in order to obtain that which is best.

but still saw no need for final causes. Against such views Thomas had always defended the need for final causes, along with efficient, formal and material causes, in accounting for operations in nature such as generation.[108]

For instance, in his youthful *De principiis naturae*, c. 3, he had reasoned that while matter, form, and privation may be regarded as principles of generation, they are not sufficient of themselves to explain this process. Something which is in potency cannot reduce itself to act. Therefore an agent is required to account for this, for instance, to reduce copper from being a statue only potentially to being such in actuality by educing the form of that statue from potentiality to actuality. The form of the statue cannot do this, since it does not actually exist until the statue itself is produced. Hence in addition to matter and form there must be some efficient or moving or agent cause. But as Aristotle states in *Metaphysics* II, what acts does so only by tending toward something. Therefore, there must also be a fourth cause or principle—that which is intended by the agent. This we call the end.[109]

In developing this final point, Thomas comments that if both natural agents and voluntary agents tend toward an end *(intendit finem)*, it does not follow from this that every agent knows its end or deliberates about it. Agents whose actions are not determined, i.e., voluntary agents, must know the end if they are to determine their action to one thing rather than another. But the actions of natural agents are determined and, therefore, they need not choose means to their end. Indeed, they cannot do so, we may add. Thomas takes an example from Avicenna to show that one who plays a cithara need not deliberate about every pluck of the strings. If this were required, it would result in untimely delays and would destroy the beauty of the music. But it is surely more evident that voluntary agents deliberate than that purely natural agents do. Therefore and a fortiori, Thomas concludes that natural agents need not deliberate and that nonetheless they tend to their ends. For such an agent to tend to its end is nothing else than for it to have a natural inclination to that end, as Thomas goes on to explain.[110]

Especially important in this discussion for our immediate purpose is Thomas's claim that an agent can act only by tending toward something, i.e., an end. This applies not only to voluntary agents but to those which are determined by their natures to act in given ways. As Thomas argues in another early text *(In II Sent.*, d. 25, q. 1, a. 1), nothing acts except insofar as it is in act. Therefore every agent must be determined to one or other alternative. That which is equally open to different alternatives is, in a certain way, in potency to both, and nothing will follow from it unless it is determined to one or the other. But if an agent is to be determined

---

108. See Leon. 22.1.143:141–148 (cited above in Ch. XI, n. 31).
109. Leon. 43.41:120–42:19. For Aristotle see *Metaphysics* II, c. 2 (994b 13–16).
110. Leon. 43.42:19–41. For Avicenna see his *Sufficientia*, I, c. 14, fol. 22rb.

to a given action, this can only be through some act of knowing which presents the end for that action.[111]

Thomas speaks in much the same vein in his considerably later *Summa theologiae* I–II, q. 1, a. 2, while supporting his contention that every agent acts for an end. First among the causes is the final cause. Matter does not receive a form unless it is moved by an agent, since nothing can reduce itself from potency to act. An agent does not move except by tending to an end *(ex intentione finis)*. To prove this he reasons that if an agent were not determined to a given effect it would not produce this effect rather than any other one. Therefore, in order for it to produce a given effect, it must be determined to something which serves as its end. In sum, Thomas's view is that unless we recognize the need for an end to influence an agent in its action, we will be unable to account for the fact that the agent produces a determined effect or, indeed, that it acts at all.[112]

To return to the text of the fifth way, suppose one grants to Thomas that the actions of natural bodies cannot be fully accounted for merely by appealing to efficient causal activity. The second objection remains. Perhaps such behavior on the part of natural bodies is owing to chance. Against this suggestion he replies briefly in the fifth way by citing the fact that natural things act always or at least usually in the same way in order to attain that which is best. In other words, mere chance cannot account for a regularly repeated pattern of behavior on the part of natural entities, and especially not when this activity achieves that which is best. As we have seen above, Thomas had already made this same point and developed it somewhat more fully in his *De veritate*, q. 5, a. 2.[113]

---

111. See Mandonnet ed., Vol. 2, p. 645 (where Thomas is defending the presence of free will in God). Note from his response: "Determinatio autem agentis ad aliquam actionem, oportet quod sit ab aliqua cognitione praestituente finem illi actioni."

112. Leon. 6.9. Note Thomas's comment regarding this determination to an end: "Haec autem determinatio, sicut in rationali natura fit per rationalem appetitum, qui dicitur voluntas; et in aliis fit per inclinationem naturalem, quae dicitur appetitus naturalis." For discussion see J. Maritain, *A Preface to Metaphysics* (New York, 1948), pp. 124ff.; C. A. Hart, *Thomistic Metaphysics: An Inquiry into the Act of Existing*, pp. 65–66, 298; G. Klubertanz, "St. Thomas' Treatment of the Axiom, *Omne Agens Agit Propter Finem*," in *An Etienne Gilson Tribute*, C. J. O'Neil, ed. (Milwaukee, 1959), pp. 104–5. For this same kind of argumentation also see SCG III, c. 2, where it appears within a series of arguments intended to show that "omne agens in agendo intendit aliquem finem." Some of these are, in fact, rather aimed at showing that one cannot regress to infinity in actions. For criticism of a number of them see Kenny, *The Five Ways*, pp. 98–103. Curiously, however, Kenny omits the argument just mentioned which is, in my judgment, the most effective one offered there or elsewhere by Thomas. As it runs in the *Summa contra Gentiles*: "Item. Si agens non tenderet ad aliquem effectum determinatum, omnes effectus essent ei indifferentes. Quod autem indifferenter se habet ad multa, non magis unum eorum operatur quam aliud: unde a contingente ad utrumque non sequitur aliquis effectus nisi per aliquid determinetur ad unum. Impossibile igitur esset quod ageret. Omne igitur agens tendit ad aliquem determinatum effectum, quod dicitur finis eius" (ed. cit., p. 228).

113. See Ch. XI above, nn. 30, 31. For similar reasoning see SCG III, c. 3, where Thomas presents a series of arguments to show that "omne agens agit propter bonum." See the third argument beginning with "Adhuc." Note especially: "Videmus autem in operibus naturae accidere vel semper vel

Moreover, we should note that Thomas, following Aristotle, does not regard chance as a being or as a cause *per se* but only *per accidens*. Chance is simply our way of referring to a situation in which independently operating causes intersect or collide without any of the particular agents foreseeing that this will happen. Yet each of these agents has its particular end. An illustration is offered by Boethius. A farmer discovers buried treasure while plowing a field. Both the farmer and the one who originally buried the treasure operated for their respective particular ends, and neither intended for the farmer to discover the treasure. Because this intersection of their independently intended actions was not foreseen by either, we refer to the discovery as a chance event.[114]

If one accepts this explanation of chance events, mere chance can hardly account for the regular and beneficial activity of natural agents, whether we regard that activity as beneficial only for the agents themselves, or also for nature taken as a whole.[115] Moreover, far from excluding the influence of ends upon agents, such an account really presupposes it. If we may emphasize this point, each particular agent acts for its particular end.

This is why Thomas eliminates in his fifth way any explanation based on chance. He is convinced that particular actions cannot be rendered intelligible unless one recognizes the influence of an end upon an agent. Because of this he goes on to argue that things which lack knowledge do not tend to an end except insofar as they are directed to it by some knowing and intelligent being as, for example, an arrow is directed to its target by an archer.[116]

He says the same both in his Commentary on Bk II of the *Sentences* (d. 25, q. 1, a. 1) and in q. 1, a. 2 of the *Prima Secundae*. If we may fill in his reasoning a bit, his point is this. An agent does not act in a given way unless it is influenced by an end.

---

frequentius quod melius est. . . . Si igitur hoc evenit praeter intentionem naturalis agentis, hoc erit a casu vel fortuna. Sed hoc est impossibile: nam ea quae accidunt semper vel frequenter, non sunt casualia neque fortuita, sed quae accidunt in paucioribus. . . . Naturale igitur agens intendit ad id quod melius est . . ." (ed. cit., 229).

114. For Aristotle see *Physics* II, c. 5, passim. For Boethius see his *Consolation of Philosophy*, Bk V, pr. 1. Note in particular his definition of chance: "Licet igitur definire casum esse inopinatum ex confluentibus causis in his quae ob aliquid geruntur eventum" (*The Theological Tractates . . . The Consolation of Philosophy*, ed. cit., pp. 386–88).

115. See Thomas's Commentary on Aristotle's discussion of chance in the *Physics*, especially *In II Phys.* lect. 8, pp. 105–6, nn. 214–215. The text of the fifth way seems to leave the last point mentioned in my text unclear: Is Thomas there holding that natural agents act so as to reach that which is best for themselves, or that which is best for the whole of nature? The first alternative would be enough to support his claim that since such agents act to attain that which is best for them always or at least in the greater number of cases, such action cannot be owing to chance. The second alternative seems to be suggested by Thomas's conclusion from the fifth way that there is one intelligent being by which all natural things are ordered to their end. Hence it seems that Thomas would defend both alternatives and that they are not mutually exclusive. Cf. Van Steenberghen, *Le problème*, p. 231. But this again raises the question whether this argument succeeds in proving that there is *one* supreme intelligence, a point which we shall take up below.

116. For the text see above, n. 105.

Noncognitive agents cannot explicitly know their ends. Hence the only way of accounting for the ability of an end to influence such an agent is to appeal to an inclination which is impressed upon that agent by some intelligent being. Such an intelligent being can, of course, have in mind the end of the noncognitive agent's action.[117] This is why Thomas writes in the text from the *Prima Secundae* that agents which lack reason tend to an end through a natural inclination so as to be moved, as it were, by something else and not by themselves. Because they do not grasp the end of their action as such, they do not order themselves to that end; they are ordered to it by something else.[118]

Finally, Thomas's reference in the fifth way and in ST I–II, q. 1, a. 2 to an arrow which tends to its determined target because it is so directed by an archer might raise another question for the reader.[119] Does Thomas think that the inclination of purely natural agents to their respective ends is simply impressed on them in passing fashion, as it were, by some other intelligent being? Or does he rather have in mind a permanent inclination which is part of their very being?

The example of the archer and the arrow might lead one to believe that Thomas has in mind only the first alternative. And this would perhaps be enough for him to argue from finality in nature, though it might not be sufficient for him to show that there is only one intelligence which is responsible for such finality.

It is clear, however, from other texts that he really defends the second alternative. For instance, in the text from *In II Sent.*, d. 25, q. 1, a. 1, he had observed that the actions of natural entities are not in vain; such entities are ordered to their actions by an intellect which "constitutes" such natures. From this he goes on to conclude that the whole of nature is, in a certain fashion, the work of intelligence.[120] And on other occasions he refers to a natural body's inclination to behave in a certain way and to tend to a certain end as its natural appetite. Moreover, as he explains in ST I, q. 5, a. 5, a thing's inclination to an action follows upon its form.[121] We conclude, therefore, that what ultimately causes the form of a natural agent is also

---

117. For the text from *In II Sent.*, d. 25, q. 1, a. 1, see Mandonnet ed., Vol. 2, p. 645 (cf. n. 111 above). Note: ". . . nec aliquod agens finem sibi praestituere potest nisi rationem finis cognoscat et ordinem ejus quod est ad finem ipsum, quod solum in habentibus intellectum est. . . ."

118. See n. 112 above for ST I–II, q. 1, a. 2. The text continues: "Illa vero quae ratione carent, tendunt in finem per naturalem inclinationem, quasi ab alio mota, non autem a seipsis: cum non cognoscant rationem finis, et ideo nihil in finem ordinare possunt, sed solum in finem ab alio ordinantur" (Leon. 6.9). For a fuller discussion of natural appetite, sensitive appetite, and rational appetite (will) see *De veritate*, q. 25, a. 1. In describing natural appetite Thomas comments: ". . . nihil enim est aliud appetitus naturalis quam quaedam inclinatio rei et ordo ad aliquam rem sibi convenientem, sicut lapidis ad locum deorsum" (Leon. 22.3.729:131–136).

119. For the text from ST I–II, q. 1, a. 2, see Leon 6.9.

120. Mandonnet ed., Vol. 2, p. 645.

121. "Ad formam autem consequitur inclinatio ad finem, aut ad actionem, aut aliquid huiusmodi: quia unumquodque, inquantum est actu, agit, et tendit in id quod sibi convenit secundum suam formam" (Leon. 4.63).

responsible for that agent's inclination to its given end. Thomas says as much in *De veritate*, q. 25, a. 1.[122]

If one grants the validity of Thomas's reasoning up until this point, other questions may be raised about the fifth way. First of all, if he has shown that there is some intelligent being by whom all natural things are ordered to their end(s) and which we call God, can he show that there is only one such being? In other words, it seems once more that the question of the uniqueness of this supreme being must still be faced. Secondly, if such an intelligent being orders natural things to their appropriate end or ends by imposing a natural inclination upon them, is this not to say that this intelligence is also their efficient cause? If so, it would seem that the ultimate source of finality in the universe must be identified with the supreme efficient cause of all such beings. Thirdly and finally, this brings up the issue of the unity of the five ways themselves: Are they viewed by Thomas as five distinct arguments, each of which leads to God's existence? Or are they rather thought of as different steps in one longer and more involved argumentation for this conclusion?

6. The Uniqueness of God

In taking up the first of these questions we return to a broader issue which may be raised about each of the five ways. Do Thomas's arguments really succeed in showing that there is only one first and unmoved mover, or first efficient cause, or uncaused necessary being, or absolute maximum or, in the case of the fifth way, one supreme intelligence which is responsible for the fact that all natural agents act for an end? Or do they leave open the possibility that there might be more than one of at least some of these—for instance, more than one unmoved mover or uncaused cause? Moreover, does his argumentation show that the unmoved mover is identical with the uncaused cause, the absolutely necessary being, the supremely perfect being, and the supreme intelligence?

One may doubt whether any of these arguments, as they stand in the text of *Summa theologiae* I, q. 2, a. 3, fully establishes divine uniqueness, i.e., that there is one God and only one God. Our doubt concerning this is strengthened by the fact that in ST I, q. 11, a. 3, Thomas explicitly addresses himself to this issue. It might have been less confusing for the reader if Thomas had clearly indicated in the course of presenting the various five ways that he would eventually complete them by establishing divine uniqueness.[123] Be that as it may, it remains for us now to

---

122. See Leon. 22.3.729:141–144: "Sed haec apprehensio praeexigitur in instituente naturam, qui unicuique naturae dedit inclinationem propriam sibi convenientem."

123. According to Van Steenberghen, none of the five ways, with the exception of the fourth, establishes the uniqueness of God. And as he sees things, the fourth way is invalid as it is presented in ST I, q. 2. a. 3. See *Le problème*, pp. 235–36, 297. However, if one recasts the fourth way as we have proposed above in order to defend its validity, one may still raise the issue of divine unicity at its conclusion.

turn to his discussion of this in q. 11, and then to certain other works where he also explicitly takes up this issue.

Question 11 is addressed to the topic of divine unity. Articles 1, 2, and 4 deal with the issue of unity taken in the sense of ontological unity or the transcendental one, i.e., the undividedness of being from itself. For Thomas, since this characteristic of being is found wherever being itself is realized, it must also be present in God. But it is only in a. 3 that the question of divine uniqueness—the claim that there is only one God—is taken up explicitly.[124]

In a. 3 Thomas offers three arguments to show that there is only one God. The first of these is based on God's simplicity. That by reason of which an individual is this individual cannot be communicated to many. For example, that by reason of which Socrates is man can be communicated to many; but that by reason of which he is this man cannot be so communicated. Otherwise, just as there cannot be many Socrateses, so too there could not be many men. Because God is identical with his very nature, that by reason of which he is God and that by reason of which he is this God are one and the same. Therefore there cannot be many Gods.[125]

In order to do justice to this argumentation, one should turn back to earlier articles in the *Summa theologiae* on which it is based, that is to say, to Thomas's efforts to show that God is simple and in particular that God is identical with his nature. Thomas had devoted the whole of q. 3 to divine simplicity. As we have remarked above, he had introduced q. 3 by noting that this discussion is part of his effort to show how God is not. In this particular case he does so by arguing that all composition is to be denied of God.[126]

Thus in the opening articles of q. 3 Thomas shows first that God is not a body (a. 1); secondly that there is no matter-form composition in him (a. 2); and then in a. 3 that there is no composition in God of quiddity or essence or nature, on the one hand, and the subject which subsists *(suppositum)*, on the other—or, as Thomas also puts it, that God is identical with his essence or nature.[127]

---

124. In a. 1 Thomas asks whether unity adds anything to being. As he explains, unity does not add any real thing to being but only the negation of division of being from itself; because of this it follows that unity is convertible with being. In a. 2 he distinguishes the way in which numerical unity is opposed to numerical multiplicity from the way in which unity of being is opposed to multitude. In a. 4, while showing that God is supremely one *(maxime unus)*, he concentrates on ontological unity rather than on divine uniqueness. God is supremely one because he is supremely undivided from himself; this follows from the fact that he is perfectly simple. On the transcendental one see Aertsen, *Medieval Philosophy and the Transcendentals,* pp. 201–42.

125. Leon. 4.111. Note in particular: "Manifestum est enim quod illud unde aliquod singulare est *hoc aliquid,* nullo modo est multis communicabile. . . . Hoc autem convenit Deo: nam ipse Deus est sua natura, ut supra ostensum est. Secundum igitur idem est Deus, et hic Deus. Impossibile est igitur esse plures Deos."

126. Leon. 4.35. Cf. n. 43 in our text above.

127. See Thomas's general introduction to q. 3: "Tertio: utrum sit in eo compositio quidditatis, sive essentiae, vel naturae, et subiecti" (p. 35). In a. 3 itself Thomas begins his response this way: "Respondeo dicendum quod Deus est idem quod sua essentia vel natura" (p. 39).

Thomas develops the last-mentioned point by drawing upon his theory of the individuation of material substances and his views on the relationship between nature and the subsisting subject (supposit). In things composed of matter and form, essence or nature differs from the subject which exists (supposit). This is because essence or nature includes in itself only those things which fall within the definition of the species (as humanity includes only that which falls under the definition of human being). But individual matter and the accidents which serve to individuate it are not included within the definition of the species. For instance, this flesh and these bones and the accidents which designate this matter are not included within humanity, though they do fall under that which this human being is. Hence a human being, meaning this human being, and humanity are not completely identical; humanity is signified as a formal part of a human being. A human being (this subsisting subject) includes something which humanity considered in itself does not.[128]

In things which are not composed of matter and form and which are not rendered individuals by individual matter, forms are individuated of themselves. Hence these forms are subsisting subjects (supposits). Given this, in such beings there is no (real) distinction between nature and the subsisting subject (supposit). Therefore, since God is not composed of matter and form, concludes Thomas, it follows that God is identical with his deity, his life, and whatever else may be predicated of him. In other words, God, taken as a subsisting subject, is identical with his essence or nature.[129] If one grants this, it will of course follow that there can only be one God; for that by which deity is deity is identical with that by which deity is God.

One point remains to be examined in this argumentation. This is the assertion that in God there can be no composition of matter and form. Thomas had considered this in a. 2. In brief he had rejected matter-form composition in God: (1) because God as pure actuality excludes matter which is potentiality; (2) because every composite of matter and form is perfected by its form and is good through its form and, therefore, good only by participation, something which cannot be said of God, the first and best being; (3) because every agent acts through its form. Hence that which is the first and *per se* agent must be form primarily and *per se*. Because God is the first efficient cause, such is true of him. Being form of his essence, therefore, God is not composed of matter and form. In sum, these arguments against matter-form composition in God follow from the conclusions of the first way, i.e., that God is pure act (argument one); the second way, that God is the

---

128. ST I, q. 3, a. 3 (Leon. 4.39–40). Note in particular: ". . . sciendum est, quod in rebus compositis ex materia et forma, necesse est quod different natura vel essentia et suppositum. . . . unde id quod est homo, habet in se aliquid quod non habet humanitas." For fuller discussion of the relationship between nature and supposit see Ch. VIII, Section 1 above.

129. Leon. 4.40.

first efficient cause (argument three); and presumably the fourth way, that God is the first and best being (argument two).[130]

To return now to Thomas's defense of divine uniqueness in q. 11, a. 3, there he builds a second argument upon the infinity of divine perfection. He notes that he has already shown that God includes within himself the total perfection of being. If there were many Gods, they would have to differ from one another. Therefore something would have to belong to one which did not belong to another. If this were a privation, the God to whom it belonged would not be perfect. And if it were a perfection, that perfection would be lacking to the other God(s). Therefore there cannot be many Gods.[131]

In order to appreciate this argument we shall again have to turn back to earlier articles in the *Summa* on which it is based. Before doing this, we should mention Thomas's third argument for divine uniqueness in q. 11, a. 3. This argument appeals to the unity of the world, a unity which is manifested by the fact that different things in the world are ordered to and subordinated to one another. But if things which differ are united to form one order, they must be so united by some ordering principle. Many things are better reduced to a single order by one ordering principle than by many; for one thing is a *per se* cause of that which is one, whereas many things do not cause that which is one except *per accidens.* Since that which is first is most perfect and is such *per se* and not merely *per accidens,* the first principle which reduces the different things in the world to a single order must be one rather than many. This is God.[132]

This argument is not quite so metaphysical as the previous two and, in my judgment, not so convincing within the context of Thomas's metaphysics. It has more of an empirical base, i.e., the order we discover in the universe. If one grants that such a universal order is present, the validity of the argument rests both upon our discovery of that order and upon our inability to account for it in any other way except by appealing to one supreme ordering principle. It reminds one of an argument for God's existence based on order and design. And it strikes me as being more of an argument from fittingness than a convincing demonstration.

With this we may return to the background for the most interesting of these three arguments for divine uniqueness, the second one, which is based on the impossibility of there being more than one infinitely perfect being. Presupposed by this argument, of course, is the claim that God is infinitely perfect or, as Thomas also puts it, that God includes within himself the total perfection of being.[133]

In q. 4, a. 1 Thomas had built his case for divine perfection upon his previously

---

130. ST I, q. 3, a. 2 (Leon. 4.37–38).

131. Leon. 4.111. Note especially: "Secundo vero, ex infinitate eius perfectionis. Ostensum est enim supra quod Deus comprehendit in se totam perfectionem essendi. Si ergo essent plures dii, oporteret eos differre. Aliquid ergo conveniret uni, quod non alteri."

132. Ibid.

133. See n. 131 above.

established conclusion that God is the first efficient cause and presumably, therefore, on the conclusion of the second way. The first efficient cause, Thomas reasons, must be most perfect. Just as matter insofar as it is matter is in potency, so too, an agent insofar as it is an agent is in act. Therefore the first active principle, i.e., the first efficient cause, must be in act to the maximum degree, and therefore perfect to the maximum degree. In support of this final point Thomas reasons that something is said to be perfect insofar as it is in act; by the perfect we mean that to which nothing of its appropriate perfection is lacking.[134]

In replying to objection 3 Thomas develops this final point. The objection points out that Thomas has already argued that God's essence is identical with his *esse* (see q. 3, a. 4). But *esse* seems to be most imperfect, since it is most universal *(communissimum)* and admits of additions. In reply Thomas counters that *esse* itself is the most perfect of all; for it is related to all things as their act. And nothing enjoys actuality except insofar as it exists. Therefore *esse* itself is the actuality of all things, including forms themselves. Hence it is related to other things not as that which receives is related to that which is received, but rather as that which is received to that which receives it. When one speaks of the *esse* of a human being or of a horse, Thomas goes on to explain, *esse* is taken as that which is formal and received. Against the objection, therefore, he maintains that *esse* is the most perfect of all. If God is self-subsisting *esse,* we can easily see why Thomas regards God as perfect.[135]

If Thomas has connected perfection with actuality in the corpus of this article, in replying to objection 3 he has now just as clearly grounded actuality and therefore perfection in *esse*. As he uses the term *esse* in this discussion, he has in mind the intrinsic act of being *(actus essendi)*. It is this which is the most perfect of all, which accounts for the fact that things exist, and which is related to a creature's essence as that which is formal and received. To repeat a point just made, if God is self-subsisting *esse,* he must be self-subsisting perfection.

In q. 4, a. 2, Thomas goes on to show that the perfections of all other things are present in God, either formally or virtually, we should add. As Thomas explains, this means that God is universally perfect in the sense that no excellence of any kind is lacking to him. He offers two arguments to establish this. The first is based on the fact that whatever degree of perfection is present in an effect must be found in its efficient cause, either in the same way if we are dealing with causes and effects of the same kind (univocal causes, as Thomas sometimes describes them), or in

134. Leon. 4.50. Note: "Deus autem ponitur primum principium, non materiale, sed in genere causae efficientis: et hoc oportet esse perfectissimum. . . . Secundum hoc enim dicitur aliquid esse perfectum, secundum quod est actu: nam perfectum dicitur, cui nihil deest secundum modum suae perfectionis."

135. Ibid. ". . . ipsum esse est perfectissimum omnium: comparatur enim ad omnia ut actus. Nihil enim habet actualitatem, nisi inquantum est: unde ipsum esse est actualitas omnium rerum, et etiam ipsarum formarum."

more eminent fashion if the cause differs in kind from and is more perfect than the effect (equivocal causes, in Thomas's terminology). In proof he reasons that it is evident that an effect preexists virtually in its efficient cause. This is simply to say that the agent has the power to produce the effect. But this is for an effect to preexist not in less perfect fashion but in a more perfect way. An agent insofar as it is an agent is perfect. Because God is the first efficient cause, the perfections of all things must preexist in him in preeminent fashion.[136]

In his second argument to show that the perfections of all things are in God, Thomas recalls his earlier proof that God is self-subsisting *esse*. It follows from this that God must contain the full perfection of being within himself. For instance, if there could be such a thing as subsisting heat, nothing of the perfection of heat could be lacking to it. Because God is subsisting being *(esse)* itself, nothing of the perfection of being can be lacking to him. Given this, it follows that the perfections of all things belong to God; for the perfections of all things pertain to the perfection of being. Thomas supports this final point by reminding us once again that things are perfect insofar as they enjoy the act of being *(esse)* in some fashion.[137]

Since Thomas has explicitly referred back to his earlier proof that God is identical with his act of being *(esse)*, it will be useful now for us to turn to his discussion of this in q. 3, a. 4. In order to establish this, Thomas offers three arguments.[138] First of all, as we have already seen above in discussing a way of strengthening the fourth way, he reasons that whatever is present in a given thing in addition to its essence must be caused either by the principles of that thing's essence (as is true of proper accidents, such as the ability to laugh in a human being), or else by some external principle. Therefore, if the act of being *(esse)* of a thing differs from its essence, its act of being must be caused either by some external principle or else by that thing's essential principles. But it is not possible for a thing's act of being to be caused merely by its essential principles, since nothing can be the cause of its own act of being *(esse)*, if indeed its act of being is caused. Therefore, if the act of being of a given thing differs from its essence, its act of being *(esse)* must be caused by something else. But in his second way Thomas has already shown that God is the first efficient cause and, therefore, that his act of being is not caused. From this it follows simply by denying the consequent that essence and act of being do not differ in God.[139]

As a second argument Thomas reasons that God must be identical with his act

---

136. Leon. 4.51–52. Note that if Thomas holds that an effect preexists in a more perfect efficient cause in more perfect fashion, such is not true of the way an effect preexists in the potency of its material cause. There it preexists more imperfectly.

137. Leon. 4.52. Note: "Omnium autem perfectiones pertinent ad perfectionem essendi: secundum hoc enim aliqua perfecta sunt, quod aliquo modo esse habent. Unde sequitur quod nullius rei perfectio Deo desit."

138. As Thomas introduces his reply: "Respondeo dicendum quod Deus non solum est sua essentia, ut ostensum est, sed etiam suum esse" (Leon. 4.42).

139. Ibid. See n. 96 above.

of being *(esse)* because *esse* is the actuality of every form or nature. For instance, goodness or humanity is not said to be realized in actuality except insofar as it exists. Hence an act of being *(esse)* must be related to an essence which differs from it as act to potency. Since there can be no (passive) potentiality in God, in him essence and act of being *(esse)* do not differ. We may presume that the point that there is no potentiality in God follows for Thomas from the conclusion of the first way and also, as he indicates in q. 3, a. 1, from the fact that God is the first being.[140]

As a third argument for the identity of God with his act of being, Thomas reasons that if something merely has *esse* but is not identical with its *esse*, it is a being only by participation. If God were not identical with his act of being *(esse)*, he would be a being only by participation. He would not be the first being.[141] It is for these three reasons, therefore, that Thomas holds that essence and act of being *(esse)* are identical in God and as a consequence, that God is subsisting *esse*.

Finally, since Thomas has built his second major argument for divine uniqueness upon the infinity of divine perfection, we may ask how he establishes the infinity of God. Although Thomas develops this point on many occasions in his writings, in the *Summa theologiae* I his explicit discussion appears in q. 7, a. 1. There he distinguishes between the kind of infinity which may be ascribed to matter, and the kind attributed to form. Matter is said to be infinite (we might substitute the term "indefinite") in the sense that it can receive many forms. Because it is determined and perfected by the form it receives, the infinity assigned to matter falls on the side of imperfection. The infinity which Thomas ascribes to form is a mark of perfection. It refers to the fact that form, insofar as it is form, is common to many and is not perfected by the matter which receives it. Rather it is limited thereby in that its fullness is contracted by the matter that receives it.[142]

Thomas next recalls that the act of being *(esse)* is the most formal of all. He has shown that the divine act of being is not received by anything else and that God is identical with his act of being *(esse)*. From this he now draws the conclusion that God is infinite and perfect. In other words, in this argument Thomas appeals to his understanding of *esse* as that which is most formal and actual and by implication to his axiom that unreceived act (in this case, the act of being) is unlimited. Because God's *esse* is unreceived by anything else, it is unlimited. Therefore God himself is infinite and perfect.[143]

If we may briefly summarize this somewhat complicated background for Thom-

---

140. Leon. 4.42. In q. 3, a. 1 see corpus, arg. 2 (Leon. 4.35–36).

141. Leon. 4.42.

142. Leon. 4.72. Cf. Ch. IX above, nn. 41, 42, 43, 44, 48 on form or act as limited by matter as a potency that receives it, and the application of the axiom that unreceived act is unlimited to the issue of divine infinity.

143. Leon. 4.72. Note: "Cum igitur esse divinum non sit esse receptum in aliquo, sed ipse sit suum esse subsistens . . . ; manifestum est quod ipse Deus sit infinitus et perfectus." Central to this argument is the assumption that unreceived *esse* is unlimited. As we have already remarked above in

as's second argument for the uniqueness of God, it rests upon the following points. According to q. 3, a. 4, God is identical with his act of being. According to q. 4, a. 1, as the first efficient cause God must be in act to the maximum degree and, therefore, perfect to the maximum degree. Hence, according to q. 4, a. 2 the perfections of all other things must be present in God either formally or virtually. Finally, according to q. 7, a. 1, because the divine act of being is not received and therefore limited by anything else and because God is identical with his act of being, God's act of being is unlimited or infinite. Therefore God is infinite. Given all of this, in q. 11, a. 3 Thomas can reason that because God includes within himself the total perfection of being and because there cannot be many infinitely perfect beings, there cannot be many Gods. Therefore there is only one God.

At this juncture it may be helpful for us to consider some arguments for divine uniqueness which Thomas offers in other contexts. There is a long discussion of this in the *Summa contra Gentiles,* Bk I, c. 42. Since not all of the arguments offered there are equally convincing and since they are quite numerous, here I shall single out one which strikes me as being of considerable interest. This, the second argument offered there, reminds one of a principle used again by Thomas in his second argument in ST I, q. 11, a. 3. The argument in SCG I, c. 42 is based on divine perfection. Thomas begins by recalling that he has already shown that God is totally perfect. Therefore, if there were many Gods, there would have to be many beings which are completely and totally perfect. But this is impossible. For if no perfection is lacking to any one of them, and if no imperfection is found in any of them, there will be no way in which they can be distinguished from one another. Therefore there cannot be many such beings.[144] Again we see Thomas accepting as proved the point that God is totally perfect, and reasoning that two completely perfect beings could not be distinguished from one another and therefore cannot exist.

Since Thomas introduces this particular argument by recalling that he has already shown that God is completely perfect, we may now turn briefly to his discus-

---

Ch. V, n. 104, Thomas often appeals to this axiom in order to establish divine infinity. See, for instance, *In I Sent.,* d. 8, q. 2, a. 1 (Mandonnet ed., Vol. 1, p. 202); *In I Sent.,* d. 43, q. 1, a. 1 (p. 1003); SCG I, c. 43 (ed. cit., p. 41); SCG II, c. 52 (for which see n. 149 below); *Compendium theologiae,* c. 18 (Leon. 42.88:7–8).

144. Ed. cit., p. 38 ("Praeterea"). Kretzmann rejects this argument on the grounds that it implicitly assumes "that every characteristic must count either as a perfection or as an imperfection," which strikes him as false. I assume he envisions the possibility of a distinguishing characeric in one all-perfect being which would distinguish it from another without itself being a perfection or an imperfection. For Thomas, however, to the extent that such a characteristic is actual (there could be no passive potentiality in an all-perfect being), it must be a perfection. And if it is a privation or negation of something positive present in another all-perfect being, it would have to be counted as a lack of perfection in the first all-perfect being, i.e., an imperfection. For Kretzmann see *The Metaphysics of Theism,* p. 160. For his presentation and defense of another more extensive argument for God's uniqueness in c. 42 based on Thomas's earlier conclusion that God is a necessary being *per se,* see pp. 161–65.

sion of divine perfection in *Summa contra Gentiles* I, c. 28. There he offers a series of arguments to make his point. He begins by observing that God, who is identical with his act of being *(esse)*, is a perfect being in every way or, to translate literally, universally perfect. As Thomas explains, this means that no excellence *(nobilitas)* of any kind can be lacking to God.[145]

In his first full argument for divine perfection, Thomas reasons that a thing's excellence belongs to it in accord with its act of being *(esse)*. For instance, no excellence would be present in a man by reason of his wisdom unless it were through wisdom that he *is* indeed wise. Thus a thing's excellence is in accord with the way (mode) in which it enjoys *esse*. If a thing's *esse* is restricted to some greater or lesser specific mode of excellence, that thing is accordingly said to be more or less excellent. And if there is something to which the total power of being *(virtus essendi)* belongs, no excellence which can pertain to any thing can be lacking to it. But a thing which is identical with its act of being *(esse)* enjoys the act of being according to the total power of being. (Thomas illustrates this by calling upon one of his favorite examples. If there were a subsisting whiteness, nothing of the power of whiteness would be lacking to it because of any deficiency on the part of a receiving subject. In other words, precisely because it was a subsisting whiteness, it would not be received by any distinct subject and could not be limited thereby.) But, as Thomas reminds us, he has already shown above (in c. 22) that God is identical with his act of being. Therefore God possesses *esse* according to the total power of being *(esse)* itself. Consequently, no possible excellence can be lacking to God.[146]

Thomas builds another argument for divine perfection upon his previously established conclusion that God is pure actuality (see c. 16). But that which is in potency in no way whatsoever and which is pure actuality must be most perfect; for a thing is perfect insofar as it is in act. As pure actuality, therefore, God is most perfect.[147]

With respect to Thomas's explicit argumentation for divine uniqueness in SCG I, c. 42, we should note that he does not yet assume there that God is infinite. In fact he will take up divine infinity in the immediately following chapter 43. In this respect, therefore, his procedure in the *Summa contra Gentiles* differs from that which he would later follow in the *Summa theologiae*. Having already established divine infinity in ST I, q. 7, he can there justifiably rest part of his argumentation for divine uniqueness upon divine infinity when he takes this up in q. 11.

---

145. ". . . Deus tamen, qui non est aliud quam suum esse, est universaliter ens perfectum. Et dico universaliter perfectum, cui non deest alicuius generis nobilitas" (ed. cit., 29).

146. Ed. cit., pp. 29–30, cited in Ch. V above, n. 109. See our comments in Ch. V, Section 5 on Thomas's references to a "power of being" in this text and elsewhere. On this particular text also see Kretzmann, op. cit., pp. 133–38.

147. Ed. cit., p. 30: "Amplius. Unumquodque perfectum est inquantum est actu; imperfectum autem secundum quod est potentia cum privatione actus. Id igitur quod nullo modo est in potentia sed est actus purus, oportet perfectissimum esse."

Nonetheless, within a very different context in the *Summa contra Gentiles,* that is, in Bk II, c. 52, Thomas does offer an interesting argument for divine unicity which is based upon divine infinity. As the reader will recall from our discussion in Ch. V, there Thomas is attempting to show that in created intellectual substances *esse* (the act of being) and "that which is" (essence) differ. His first three arguments attempt to show that there can only be one being which is identical with its act of being and, therefore, that in all others essence and act of being *(esse)* differ.[148]

According to the third argument, it is impossible for there to be two completely infinite instances of the act of being *(esse).* This follows because completely infinite *esse* embraces the total perfection of being. If such infinity were present in two different things, there would be no way in which one could be distinguished from the other. But subsisting *esse* must be infinite, since it is not limited by any receiving principle. Therefore it is impossible for there to be any other case of subsisting existence *(esse)* apart from the first being.[149]

This argument ultimately rests on a by now familiar central axiom of Thomas's metaphysics: unreceived *esse* is unlimited. Thomas joins this with the point that there would be no way in which completely unlimited or infinite instances of *esse* could be differentiated from one another. At the same time, this argument's location within this particular chapter of the *Summa contra Gentiles* reminds us that other arguments offered there and elsewhere by Aquinas to show that there can only be one instance of self-subsisting *esse* may also be regarded as arguments for divine uniqueness.[150]

We shall conclude our consideration of Thomas's argumentation for divine uniqueness by turning to his presentation in the *Compendium theologiae* I, c. 15 (ca. 1265–1267), which probably precedes the discussion in ST I, q. 11 by a year or so. There he offers two major metaphysical arguments. The first reminds us of his first argument in ST I, q. 11, a. 3. That whereby a common essence is rendered individual cannot be communicated to many. Thus, while there can be many human beings, it is not possible for this individual human being to be more than one. If an essence is individuated of itself and not by reason of anything else, it cannot belong to many subjects. But the divine essence is individuated of itself, since in God there is no distinction between his essence and the subject which exists *(essentia et quod est).* In support of this Thomas harks back to his proof in c. 10 that God is identical with his essence. Therefore there can only be one God.[151]

---

148. Ed. cit., p. 145. For discussion of the first three arguments see Ch. V above, Section 2, and nn. 51–54.

149. Ed. cit., p. 145: ". . . esse enim quod omnino est infinitum, omnem perfectionem essendi comprehendit; et sic, si de duobus talis adesset infinitas, non inveniretur quo unum ab altero differret." See Ch. V, n. 54, for continuation.

150. For a number of these see Ch. V above, Section 2.

151. Note that this argument is preceded by another less persuasive one which reasons that if the term "god" is applied equivocally, to say "there are many gods" will not be to the point. If it is applied

The second argument in c. 15 is still more interesting. Thomas now maintains that there are two ways in which a form may be multiplied: either by reason of differences (as when a generic form is so divided), or by being received in different subjects. But if there is a form which cannot be multiplied in the first way, i.e., through differences, and which does not exist in a distinct subject, it cannot be multiplied at all. For instance, writes Thomas as he appeals again to his familiar example, if whiteness could subsist apart from any receiving subject, it could only be one. But the divine essence is identical with the divine act of being *(esse)*, as Thomas has shown in c. 11. Therefore, since the divine *esse* is, as it were, a form that subsists in itself, it can only be one.[152]

Notwithstanding the fact that Thomas had offered argumentation for God's existence in c. 3 of the *Compendium* and additional argumentation to show that he is unmovable, eternal, and necessary of himself (cc. 4–6), he has judged it necessary to devote a separate treatment in c. 15 to show that God is unique. This parallels his procedure in SCG I and in ST I, and also confirms our judgment that he realized that without this additional argumentation his proof that God exists would not be complete. At the same time, as we have remarked before, this additional step was not necessary in his presentation in *De ente,* c. 4, because there his proof that there could at most be one subsisting *esse* is a necessary step in his argument for distinction between essence and act of being in everything else and also, therefore, for his metaphysical argument for God's existence.

Having now considered a number of Thomas's explicit arguments for divine uniqueness, we may ask whether they are also sufficient to show that the one un-caused efficient cause of all other being must itself be identified with the ultimate source of finality in the universe. (It can more easily be granted that the unmoved mover, the being that is necessary *per se,* and even the maximum being of the fourth way may be identified with the first efficient cause of the second way.) Thomas clearly intends this. Thus he has identified as one and the same God the first efficient cause and the ultimate source of finality in the universe, i.e., the intelligent being which is responsible for the presence of finality in purely natural agents. But has he proved this point?[153]

That this is not an idle question is suggested by his earlier recognition in *Summa contra Gentiles* I, c. 13 that if by arguing from motion one arrives at a mover which is responsible for the motion in the universe, one may still ask whether that mover

---

univocally, the many gods would have to agree in genus or in species. But he has shown that God cannot be a genus or species (Leon. 42.87:1–10). For the argument analyzed in our text see p. 87:11–21. Cf. n. 125 above for ST I, q. 11, a. 3.

152. Leon. 42.87:22–35. In *De ente,* c. 4 Thomas had also mentioned reception of a form in matter as another possible way of multiplying specific forms in individuals, and rejected this as not applicable to subsisting *esse.* See Leon. 43.376:105–377:121.

153. Indeed, the conclusion established by each of the five ways he has identified with God. Compare the conclusion of the second way (and of the first and third, for that matter) with the conclusion of the fifth way.

acts for an end beyond itself. As the reader will recall, Thomas there reasoned that one must ultimately conclude to the existence of an unmoved mover which does not move for the sake of an end beyond itself. In that context he seems to have combined an argument based on efficient causation of motion with one grounded on the need for an unmoved mover in the absolute sense—that is, one that does not depend upon anything other than itself even in the order of final causality.[154]

Within the context of the fifth way and its parallels, however, Thomas's procedure is different. Here he reasons to the existence of some intelligent being in order to account for the fact that noncognitive agents act for an end. If this end is to influence them in their activity and if by definition they themselves are incapable of knowing such an end, it must preexist in cognitive fashion in some intelligence which efficiently causes such natures and imposes upon them their inclinations to their respective ends.[155] In other words, this intelligent being is also the first efficient cause of such natures. And if Thomas has successfully shown that there can be only one first uncaused efficient cause of all other things and that this being is intelligent, it will follow that there is also one supreme intelligent source responsible for the finality of natural agents precisely because the two are one and the same.[156]

Thomas offers explicit argumentation to show that God is intelligent, as we shall see below at the beginning of Ch. XIV. It will suffice here to mention *Summa theologiae* I, q. 14, a. 1. There he reasons that the immateriality of a thing determines if and to what extent it is capable of knowing. This follows from his (and Aristotle's) view that a thing is capable of knowing to the extent that it can grasp the form of some other thing in immaterial fashion. Because God is supremely immaterial, as Thomas has argued above in q. 7, a. 1, he now concludes that God is capable of knowing to the maximum degree.[157]

Moreover, as Thomas explains in replying to the first objection in q. 14, a. 1, perfections as realized in creatures are attributed to God in more perfect fashion. Therefore, when a name taken from a perfection found in a creature is assigned to God, we must negate of it all that follows from the imperfect manner in which it is realized in the creature.[158] We may presume, therefore, that Thomas would permit us to argue in this fashion as well for the presence of intelligence in God. Underlying this reasoning is Thomas's conviction that there is some kind of similar-

---

154. See Ch. XI above, n. 76 for the text and our discussion of the same.

155. Cf. *In II Sent.*, d. 25, q. 1, a. 1 (Mandonnet ed., Vol. 2, p. 645); *De veritate,* q. 25, a. 1 (Leon. 22.3.729:141–44), cited above in n. 122.

156. I am assuming here that for Thomas the ultimate efficient cause of a finite nature is the cause both of its essence and its act of being *(esse)*. See, for instance, *De potentia,* q. 3, a. 5, ad 2 (ed. cit., p. 49).

157. Leon. 4.166. For more on Thomas's view that knowledge involves possessing the form of a thing in immaterial fashion see ST I, q. 84, aa. 1–2.

158. Leon. 4.166–67.

ity, in spite of great diversity, between an effect and its first cause.[159] However, fuller discussion of Thomas's justification for our predicating certain names of God will be deferred for the following chapter.

7. The Unity of the Five Ways

In concluding this chapter concerning Thomas's five ways, I would like to return to the third issue already mentioned at the end of Section 5: Does Thomas regard the five ways as five distinct arguments for God's existence, or rather as five different versions or perhaps steps of one and the same argument? From our examination of each of them, the answer to this should now be clear. It is true that there is considerable similarity between the five ways, in that each begins with some datum based on sense experience and each, by reasoning from effect to cause, concludes to the existence of a first and uncaused cause in order to account for the effect that served as the starting point. Nonetheless, because each way begins with a different starting point and because reasoning from effect to cause is applied in different ways in each of them, each should be regarded as a distinct argument. If one grants this, however, a related question remains: Has Thomas presented the five ways in accord with some systematic organizing principle and, if so, does he regard them as the only valid ways in which God's existence can be demonstrated? There is considerable diversity of opinion among Thomistic interpreters concerning these two questions.[160]

One approach, developed by A.-R. Motte among others, holds that the grouping of the five ways is first and foremost empirical (i.e., historical) in origin. It results from Thomas's reflection upon and usage of the different historical sources he had available. He drew upon various approaches in the previous philosophical and Christian tradition which he found most suitable for his purposes. He never claimed that the five ways can be reduced to a single logical scheme or that they are the only valid ways of proving God's existence.[161]

---

159. See ST I, q. 13, a. 5: "Et sic, quidquid dicitur de Deo et creaturis, dicitur secundum quod est aliquis ordo creaturae ad Deum, ut ad principium et causam, in qua praeexistunt excellenter omnes rerum perfectiones" (Leon. 4.147).

160. For a helpful review of a number of these competing interpretations, see Van Steenberghen, *Le problème*, pp. 238–41.

161. See his "A propos des 'Cinq voies'," *Revue des sciences philosophiques et théologiques* 27 (1938), pp. 577–82. To support his case Motte cites the dependency of the five ways as they are presented in the *Summa theologiae* upon Thomas's argumentation in SCG I, cc. 13 and 15, and the explicit references in SCG to historical sources, that is, to the arguments by which philosophers and *doctores Catholici* have proved that God exists (SCG I, c. 13, ed. cit., p. 10). As we have seen, Thomas there goes on to offer two detailed arguments based on motion, each of which he assigns to Aristotle, another argument taken from Aristotle's *Metaphysics* II (to refute appeal to an infinite regress of efficient causes), one taken from both *Metaphysics* II and IV (based on degrees of truth), and one explicitly assigned to John Damascene (the argument from the way things are governed). As we have

Others have tried to reduce the five ways to a single logical scheme and/or to claim that in Thomas's mind they exclude other possible ways in which one can reason to God's existence.[162] Our examination of other forms of arguments for God's existence in Thomas's texts, including that offered in *De ente*, c. 4, to cite one of the most important, should make it unnecessary for us to devote more attention to the last-mentioned claim. The fact that he developed other arguments in other texts does not support the claim that he regarded the five ways as the only valid ways of proving God's existence. Nor do we have any textual evidence from the *Summa theologiae* or elsewhere to suggest that he later rejected those other approaches.

As for the former suggestion, that the five ways can be reduced to some single logical scheme, some have attempted to reduce all five of them in some way to the four causes.[163] Such attempts strike me as being forced. First of all, there is the obvious point that there are five ways but only four supreme kinds of causes. More-

---

also seen, one of the arguments offered for divine eternity in SCG I, c. 15 strongly foreshadows the third way. However, Motte (pp. 579–80) does not bring out sufficiently the differences between the argument from divine governance in SCG I, c. 13 and the fifth way, and between the argument based on possible and necessary being of SCG I, c. 15 and the third way. See p. 580 for his still sound conclusion that no systematic idea or scheme predetermined either the organization or the number of the five ways.

162. L. Charlier rejects the first effort (to reduce the five ways to a single proof; though they complement one another, each is a distinct proof), but supports the second claim (Thomas thought that all other valid proofs could be reduced to the five ways). See his "Les cinq voies de saint Thomas," pp. 189–90. In addition to Motte's critique of efforts to reduce the five ways to complementary aspects of a single proof (p. 577), see Van Steenberghen, *Le problème*, pp. 238–41 (especially for his résumé and critique of more recent efforts to reduce the five ways to a single organizing principle or scheme). Owens comments: "The impression that the five ways are the only ones recognized by Aquinas, and that all other variations have to be reduced in one way or another to their forms, stems from the Neoscholastic manuals." See his "Aquinas and the Five Ways," in *St. Thomas Aquinas on the Existence of God,* p. 257, n. 1.

163. See, for instance, L. Elders, "Justification des 'cinq voies'," *Revue thomiste* 61 (1961), pp. 207–25 (most surprising is his attempt to base the first way on material causality); H. Johnson, "Why Five Ways? A Thesis and Some Alternatives," in *Actes du quatrième congrès international de philosophie médiévale* (Montreal, 1969), pp. 1143–54, especially pp. 1143–45 (who would base the third way on material causality). For Elders's more recent thought concerning this see his "Les cinq voies et leur place dans la philosophie de saint Thomas," in *Quinque sunt viae,* L. J. Elders, ed., Studi tomistici 9 (Vatican City, 1980), pp. 133–46. Here he continues to reduce the five ways to the four kinds of causality, again basing the first way on material causality and basing the third way on a fifth kind of causality, God's communication of *esse* to other things (pp. 138–39). See p. 141 (for his critique of efforts by A. Kenny to link the third way to material causality); p. 145 (for his conclusion that because of the close bond between the five ways and the kinds of causality, a new proof for God's existence which would differ fundamentally from the five ways is not possible). Now also see his *The Philosophical Theology of St. Thomas Aquinas,* pp. 85–88. For Kenny see *The Five Ways,* pp. 35–37. Also see Maritain, *Approaches to God,* pp. 18–19, for the view that because the various ways start from different facts based on experience, they are specifically distinct proofs. Also see M. F. Johnson, "Why Five Ways?" in *Proceedings of the American Catholic Philosophical Association* 65 (1991), pp. 107–21, who, unsuccessfully, in my opinion, proposes still another organizing principle for the first four ways

over, as just mentioned above, it is clear that all of the five ways in some way reason from an effect, presumably one that is given to us in the world of sense experience, to an uncaused cause of the same. Common to the first three ways is an appeal to some form of efficient causation, whether in the order of motion (the first way), or in the order of caused causes (the second way), or in the order of beings subject to generation and corruption and then of beings which are not subject to generation and corruption but which are still caused (the third way). The fourth way stands out because of its different point of departure—varying degrees of perfection in the observable universe. While its first stage seems to rely exclusively on formal exemplar causality, I have suggested above that if this argument is to be regarded as valid, the participated and therefore efficiently caused character of beings which enjoy limited degrees of perfection must also be introduced in that stage. Thomas himself does not explicitly do this in the argument's first stage, but he does introduce efficient causality in its second stage. As we have also seen, the fifth way is based on final causality in purely natural entities, a phenomenon which in Thomas's judgment points to the existence of a first intelligence which efficiently causes such agents together with their inclinations to act for ends. Finally, efforts to reduce the five ways to the four causes all founder, at least in my judgment, when they attempt to reduce one or another argument to the order of material causality.

In dealing with this issue it is enough for us to acknowledge these points along with our recognition of the fact that Thomas sees fit to complete these arguments in various ways in his discussion of the divine attributes. To impose upon the five ways some overriding logical plan which would account for their supposed interlocking symmetry is to go far beyond Thomas's text, and to risk distorting his thought. And as I have already indicated, to regard the five ways as excluding in Thomas's mind all other possible ways of arguing for God's existence runs counter to his procedure in other passages. Some, H. J. Johnson, for instance, have emphasized the point that in ST I, q. 2, a. 3 Thomas explicitly states that it can be proved in five ways that God exists.[164] To me this does not indicate that Thomas therefore regarded the number five as exhaustive and/or that he must have had in mind a systematic organizing plan such as the four causes in making this selection. I would simply note that his text does not state that God's existence can be proved in *only* five ways.

On a more positive note, however, I would conclude by observing that each of the five ways does contribute something to our understanding of God, although the different perspectives which they offer do not, of course, point to any real dis-

---

based on Aristotle's discussion of actuality and potentiality in *Metaphysics* IX, while the fifth way would attain to God as the source of directed motion. He rightly regards the five ways as formally distinct proofs (pp. 110, 115). For an earlier attempt to find a key to the organization of the first four ways in Aristotle's discussion of actuality and potentiality in *Metaphysics* IX see L. Dewan, "The Number and Order of St. Thomas's Five Ways," *Downside Review* 92 (1974), pp. 1–18.

164. H. J. Johnson, op. cit., p. 1151.

tinctions within God himself. From our standpoint, however, to recognize God as the unmoved mover, the uncaused cause, the absolutely necessary being, the maximumly perfect being, and the source of finality within the universe enriches our effort to arrive at some fuller understanding of him. And this, together with the historical sources which were available to Thomas, his critical evaluation of their philosophical power, and his customary method of offering more than one argument for a given conclusion, should suffice to explain why he offered more than one way in ST I, q. 2, a. 3, and, for that matter, more than one argument for God's existence elsewhere in his writings.

XIII   Quidditative Knowledge of God and Analogical Knowledge

We have now examined Thomas's efforts to establish on philosophical grounds both the fact that God exists and that he is one. If one grants Thomas this conclusion, one may also ask what follows therefrom. In attempting to address this, we may distinguish two general questions. If one admits on philosophical grounds that God exists, what more can philosophical investigation tell us about God himself? And if one grants that God exists, what light does this cast on some of the issues concerning finite beings which we have already examined without presupposing this?

Concerning the first general question, in a number of his writings Thomas devotes considerable attention to our knowledge of the divine nature and attributes. So extensive is his treatment of this that another volume might well be written to cover that aspect of his philosophical thought. Since we cannot fully consider this topic here, in the present chapter we shall limit ourselves to two issues relating to it: the possibility of our attaining quidditative knowledge of God, and the problem of analogy insofar as this applies to our knowledge of God.

The second general question is also very broad and cannot be examined in all its fullness here. Accordingly, in the following and concluding chapter I shall return to three issues already studied above, but this time as viewed under the presupposition that God's existence has been established: (1) Thomas's argumentation for the distinction and composition of essence and act of being *(esse)* in all finite beings; (2) his application of the theory of participation to finite being; (3) the correlation between his views on quidditative knowledge of God and the subject of metaphysics.

1. Quidditative Knowledge of God

Thomas touches on this issue in a number of his texts. For instance, in the First Part of the *Summa theologiae,* after having completed his presentation of the five ways, he prefaces his discussion in q. 3 with a remark we have already noted. Once we have recognized that a given thing exists, we must determine how it exists in order to arrive at knowledge what it is. But in the case of God we cannot know what He is but only what he is not. Hence we must now consider the ways in which he is not, then how he is known by us, and thirdly, how he is named by us. Accordingly, qq. 3 through 11 in this same context are all directed to establishing ways in which God is not. In q. 12 Thomas examines how God is known by us, and in q. 13 how he is named by us. It will only be there, in q. 13, that Thomas takes up explicitly the issue of analogical predication of the divine names.[1]

This same point, that when it comes to our knowledge of God we can know that he is but not what he is, is made repeatedly by Thomas in earlier works. Here we shall briefly consider a number of these texts in chronological order in our attempt to understand precisely what Thomas means by defending this position. We shall also find that this view does not prevent him from predicating certain names of God which appear to be positive, not merely negative, in their formal meaning. At that point it will be necessary for us to move on to the second main part of this chapter, analogical predication of the divine names.

a. *In I Sent.* (1252–1256)

In his Commentary on I *Sentences,* d. 8, q. 1, a. 1, Thomas asks whether *esse* can be said of God in the strict or proper sense *(proprie).* In responding he notes that among all other names, "He who is" is the most proper name of God. Thomas offers a number of arguments to support this claim. The second is based on John Damascene's *De fide orthodoxa* to this effect. "He who is" signifies *esse* in indeterminate fashion, but does not indicate what something is. Because in this life we can only know of God that he is but not what he is, except by negation, and since we can name him only insofar as we know him, God is most properly named by us "He who is."[2]

Thomas takes another argument from Pseudo-Dionysius's *De divinis nominibus,* where this writer identifies *esse* as the first among all participations in the divine goodness. *Esse* is, as it were, the principle of the others and in a certain way contains in itself in united fashion all other participations such as to live and to understand.

---

1. Leon. 4.35. See Ch. XII above, n. 43.

2. Mandonnet ed., Vol. 1, pp. 194–95. Note especially: ". . . et quia in statu viae hoc tantum de ipso cognoscimus, quia est, et non quid est, nisi per negationem, et non possumus nominare nisi secundum quod cognoscimus, ideo propriissime nominatur a nobis 'qui est'." Cf. John Damascene, *De fide orthodoxa,* c. 9, E. Buytaert, ed., pp. 48–49. Thomas here interprets Damascene rather than cite him literally.

So too, God is the divine principle, and all other things are one in him. Thomas's implied conclusion is that, because of this similarity between *esse* and God, *esse* is the most proper name of God.[3]

Thomas derives a final argument from Avicenna. If the name "thing" is applied to something by reason of its quiddity, the name "He who is" or "being" *(ens)* is imposed by reason of the act of being *(actus essendi)*. Thomas reasons that because a creature's essence differs from its *esse,* such a thing is properly named from its quiddity and not from its act of being. But God's act of being *(esse)* and his quiddity are identical. Therefore that name which is derived from the divine act of being — "He who is"—names God properly and is his proper name.[4]

As Thomas explains in replying to the first objection, *esse* is applied to God properly, not in the sense that it cannot also belong to creatures, but in the sense that in God it is not joined or mixed with privation or potentiality.[5]

Thomas's replies to objections 3 and 4 are particularly interesting. The third objection contends that if created wisdom falls short of the uncreated wisdom, so does created *esse* fall short of the uncreated *esse.* But the name "wisdom" falls short of signifying perfectly the divine wisdom since we impose this name on God only in accord with our understanding of created wisdom. The same reasoning should apply to *esse,* it would seem, and therefore to the name "He who is." Hence the name "He who is" is not more proper than other names.[6]

In replying Thomas acknowledges that the name "He who is" does not perfectly signify the divine *esse,* for it signifies only according to the mode of something concrete and composed. But all other names signify God even more imperfectly. Thomas illustrates this with the name "wisdom." Suppose I say "God is wise." Because a form of the verb "to be" appears in this statement, a twofold deficiency applies to it. A first stems from the concrete way in which *esse* itself signifies, and this deficiency also applies to the name "He who is." A second deficiency arises from the fact that created wisdom necessarily falls short of the full intelligible content *(ratio)* of divine wisdom; because of this, greater imperfection is involved in it and in all other names than in the name "He who is."[7] While Thomas's main point here is to defend the preeminence of "He who is" among all divine names, he has also introduced an important reason for his view that all created names, including

---

3. Ed. cit., p. 195. For much of this thought in Pseudo-Dionysius's *De divinis nominibus* and in Thomas's Commentary on the same see *In librum beati Dionysii De divinis nominibus expositio,* Pera ed., c. V, 1, p. 230, nn. 266–269 (Dionysius) and c. V, lect. 1, pp. 235–37, nn. 632–641 (Thomas).

4. Ed. cit., p. 195. Note especially: "Cum autem ita sit quod in qualibet re creata essentia sua differat a suo esse, res illa proprie denominatur a quidditate sua, et non ab actu essendi, sicut homo ab humanitate. In Deo autem ipsum esse suum est sua quidditas: et ideo nomen quod sumitur ab esse, proprie nominat ipsum, et est proprium nomen eius. . . ." Cf. Avicenna, *Liber de philosophia prima,* I, c. 5 (Van Riet ed., Vol. 1, pp. 34–35). For discussion see my "The Latin Avicenna as a Source," pp. 67–69 and n. 35.

5. Ed. cit., pp. 195–96.   6. Ed. cit., 194.

7. Ed. cit., p. 196.

this most proper one, signify God imperfectly. When applied concretely, all involve some composition and therefore some imperfection in the way in which they signify. We shall see Thomas's fuller development of this point in later texts.

The fourth objection cites John Damascene to the effect that "He who is" does not signify what God is, but rather indicates a certain infinite ocean of substance. Because the infinite cannot be comprehended, it cannot be named (properly) but remains unknown. Therefore it seems that "He who is" is not a divine name.[8] Thomas replies that all other names express *esse* only in terms of some determined intelligible content. For instance, the name "wise" when taken concretely means to be something, i.e., to be wise. But the name "He who is" signifies *esse* without qualification and not as determined by any additional factor. This is why Damascene describes "He who is" as not signifying what God is but rather as indicating a certain infinite ocean of substance which is, as it were, undetermined.[9]

At this point Thomas outlines a certain progression we follow in naming God according to the way of negation. First we negate of him all that is corporeal. Secondly, we also negate of him intellectual characteristics in the way these are found in creatures, such as goodness and wisdom. Presumably by intellectual characteristics he means those that can be grasped only by the intellect. Now nothing remains in our understanding except our awareness "that God is," and our understanding remains somewhat confused. Finally, however, we negate of him even *esse* itself in the way this is realized in creatures. At this point we remain in a certain darkness of ignorance in which, in the present life, we are best united with God. This is a kind of darkness in which God is said to dwell.[10]

Thomas's recognition of the divine transcendence and ineffability is clearly evident throughout this discussion, as is his awareness of the limits of human understanding when it comes to our knowledge of the divine nature. Nonetheless, the reader may well ask for some additional precisions concerning Thomas's meaning when he denies that we can know what God is, especially since in the text just examined he has indicated that the name "He who is" is most properly said of God. Presumably, therefore, some other names may also be said of him properly.

---

8. Ed. cit., p. 194. For Damascene see *De fide orthodoxa,* c. 9, ed. cit., p. 49:16–17.

9. Ed. cit., p. 196. Note especially: ". . . sed hoc nomen 'qui est' dicit esse absolutum et non determinatum per aliquid additum; et ideo dicit Damascenus, quod non significat quid est Deus, sed significat quoddam pelagus substantiae infinitum, quasi non determinatum." For a full discussion of this passage see J. Owens, "Aquinas—'Darkness of Ignorance' in the Most Refined Notion of God," in *Bonaventure and Aquinas: Enduring Philosophers,* R. W. Shahan and F. J. Kovach, eds. (Norman, Okla., 1976), pp. 70–73. Owens comments that if Damascene does not say explicitly in the passage cited that "He who is" does not signify what God is, nonetheless Thomas appears to be justified in interpreting Damascene in that sense.

10. Ed. cit., pp. 196–97. Note especially: "Ad ultimum autem etiam hoc ipsum esse, secundum quod est in creaturis, ab ipso removemus; et tunc remanet in quadam tenebra ignorantiae. . . ." See Owens, "Aquinas—'Darkness of Ignorance'," pp. 73–81, for fuller discussion.

More light is cast on this by Thomas's discussion in distinction 22, q. 1, from this same Commentary on I *Sentences*. There in a. 1 he defends the view that God can be named, but only to the degree that he can be known. Since we can arrive at only imperfect knowledge of God, we can name him only imperfectly and, as it were, by stammering.[11] As Thomas explains in replying to the first objection, this is what Dionysius and the author of the *Liber de causis* have in mind when they refer to God as incomprehensible or unnamable. They mean to say that no name perfectly expresses God himself.[12]

In replying to the second objection, Thomas comments that when Augustine (?) refers to God as escaping from every form, he may simply be referring to corporeal forms. And it is not necessary that every thing named have a corporeal form. However, if Augustine is thinking of forms without any such restriction, he means to say that whatever form our intellect may conceive, God escapes from it by reason of His essence. For instance, God's wisdom surpasses any and all wisdom our intellect can grasp. Therefore God is not accessible to our intellect in the sense that we might approach Him perfectly by comprehending Him.[13]

Thomas's reply to the third objection is especially interesting. The objection contends that God cannot be named by a noun—or, for that matter, by a pronoun, participle, or verb. Most pertinent is the claim that God cannot be named by a noun. According to the objection, every noun signifies substance together with some quality; but in God there is no composition of substance and quality.[14]

In replying to this Thomas counters that when it is said that a noun signifies substance together with quality, we need not conclude from this that substance and quality are being used here in the strict or proper sense, as when the logician distinguishes them as two predicaments. The grammarian, on the other hand, understands the terms "substance" and "quality" with reference to the way in which they signify. From this grammatical perspective it is true that what is signi-

---

11. Ed cit., p. 532. Note: "Unde sicut Deum imperfecte cognoscimus, ita etiam imperfecte nominamus, quasi balbutiendo. . . ."

12. Ibid. Note: ". . . quod significatur in verbis Philosophi, qui dicit, lib. *De causis,* proposit. 6, quod 'linguae deficiunt a narratione eius'; et quod alibi dicit, proposit. 22: 'Causa prima superior est omni narratione, et supra omne id quod nominatur'." Note that Thomas here in the early 1250s still assumes (with the objector, see p. 531) that Aristotle is the author of the *Liber de causis*. For the passages in question see *Le Liber de causis,* Pattin ed., prop. 5(6), p. 59:22–24; prop. 21(22), pp. 93:68–69, 95:88–89. The objection also refers to a text from Pseudo-Dionysius, for which see *De divinis nominibus,* Pera ed., c. I, 5, p. 24, n. 21.

13. Ed. cit., p. 532. See p. 531, obj. 2: "Sed, sicut dicit Augustinus, Deus, qui omnem formam subterfugit, intellectui pervius esse non potest." Though Thomas attributes this same remark to Augustine in his Commentary on the *De Trinitate* and elsewhere, Decker remarks that he has not found it in Augustine's writings. See *Expositio super librum Boethii De Trinitate,* Decker ed., p. 63, n. 3. Cf. Leon. 50.83:11, note. For references to other scholastics who attributed this to Augustine cf. *De veritate,* q. 2, a. 1, obj. 10 (Leon. 22.1.38:66, note).

14. Ed. cit., p. 531.

fied by a noun is signified as if it were something which subsists. This way of signifying carries with it the grammatical consequence that something else may be predicated of it, as when for instance, we use the noun "whiteness" as the subject in a
sentence. But this does not imply that what is signified by a noun actually subsists
in itself. And it is because of this grammatical situation that the grammarian distinguishes nouns from verbs, and notes that the latter do not signify things as
subsisting.[15]

One should also take into account that by reason of which any given name, in
this case, a noun, is imposed—in other words, that which it is intended to signify;
for this serves, as it were, as the principle by which the thing becomes known. With
this in mind, Thomas grants that that by reason of which a noun is imposed may
be said to that extent to have the mode of quality; for here we are simply using the
term "quality" to refer to the principle within a thing which enables it to be known,
i.e., its form. Indeed, from this perspective, still that of the grammarian, a substantial form itself may be referred to as a quality. This usage does not imply that it is
in fact a predicamental accident.[16]

As regards the signification of a noun, it does not really matter whether the
principle which renders something knowable is identical in reality with what the
noun signifies. In fact, the two are identical in the case of an abstract noun such as
humanity, but diverse in the case of a concrete noun such as a man. (Thomas's
unexpressed point here is that a concrete noun such as a man signifies more than
the principle which renders it knowable, for instance, individuating characteristics
as well.) God can be signified by a noun which has quality as regards the intelligible
content by reason of which that noun is imposed and substance as regards that
which the noun is intended to signify. Hence with these qualifications in mind, he
concludes, we may apply nouns to God.[17]

In a. 2 Thomas explicitly defends the view that some names may be predicated
of God in the proper sense.[18] In defending this position he observes that every
perfection which is present in creatures depends upon God as upon its exemplar
cause. Since no creature can receive its perfection according to the mode in which
that perfection is present in God, every creature falls short of perfectly representing
its divine exemplar cause. There is a certain gradation among creatures, in that

15. Ed. cit., pp. 532–33.
16. Ed. cit., p. 533.
17. Ibid. "Et quia Deus seipso cognoscitur, ideo potest significari per nomen quod habeat qualitatem quantum ad rationem a qua nomen imponitur, et substantiam quantum ad id cui imponitur."
In other words, in God the principle by reason of which he is knowable is identical with that which
the noun, God for instance, signifies. For Thomas's defense of using pronouns, verbs, and participles
in speaking of God, see the remainder of this same text.
18. "Utrum aliquod nomen possit dici proprie de Deo" (ed. cit., p. 533). Here I will translate
the Latin *nomen* as "name" rather than as "noun." Because Thomas distinguished between nouns,
pronouns, verbs, and participles in replying to objection 3 in the previous article, I there rendered
nomen as "noun." Such a restriction is not necessary in the present article.

some more fully participate in the perfections they receive from God and therefore more perfectly represent Him.[19]

These ontological clarifications set the stage for Thomas to develop a distinction we have already seen him foreshadowing, i.e., that between the thing signified by a name *(res significata)*, and the mode or way in which it signifies *(modus significandi)*. Since the names we employ to signify God are taken from creatures, such names always fall short of representing God as regards the way in which they signify; for they signify divine perfections according to the manner (mode) in which such perfections are participated in by creatures.[20] Underlying Thomas's thinking here is his oft-repeated axiom to the effect that what is received is received according to the mode of the receiver. He continues, if we concentrate on that which such names are intended to signify *(res significata)*, we must draw a further distinction. Some names are imposed to signify perfections without including any mode in their meaning; in other words, they signify pure perfections. Other names are imposed to signify a perfection together with a creaturely way of participating in it. For instance, a name such as "perception" signifies knowledge together with the mode of being received *materialiter* by a power conjoined with an organ. But the name "knowledge" does not include any mode of participation in its primary meaning. Only names of the latter type, such as "wisdom," "goodness," "essence," etc., can be said of God properly as regards that which they signify *(res significata)*. Names of the former type, which do include some imperfect mode of participation in their primary meaning, cannot be said of God properly but only metaphorically. This comment is helpful since it indicates that when Thomas refers to certain names as said of God properly, he intends thereby to exclude metaphorical predication.[21]

Equally important for our purposes is Thomas's insistence that even names which signify pure perfections fall short of perfectly representing God. This is because of the creaturely way in which they signify—their *modus significandi.*[22] As Thomas implies in replying to the first objection, as regards the names we apply to

19. Ed. cit., p. 534–35.

20. Ed. cit., p. 535. Note: ". . . et ex hoc in nominibus est duo considerare: rem significatam et modum significandi. Considerandum est igitur, quod cum nomina sint imposita a nobis, qui Deum non nisi ex creaturis cognoscimus, semper deficiunt a divina repraesentatione quantum ad modum significandi. . . ."

21. Ibid. Note especially: "Si autem consideremus rem significatam in nomine, quae est id ad quod significandum imponitur nomen, invenimus quaedam nomina esse imposita ad significandum principaliter ipsam perfectionem [Mandonnet: perfectiones] exemplatam a Deo simpliciter, non concernendo aliquem modum in sua significatione; et quaedam ad significandum perfectionem receptam secundum talem modum participandi. . . ."

22. Ibid. "Unde dicendum est, quod omnia illa nomina quae imponuntur ad significandum perfectionem aliquam absolute, proprie dicuntur de Deo, et per prius sunt in ipso quantum ad rem significatam, licet non quantum ad modum significiandi. . . ." After mentioning wisdom, goodness, *essentia,* and all names of this kind, Thomas comments that they are among those which Anselm in *Monologium,* c. 15 says it is completely and without qualification better to be than not to be (Schmitt ed., Vol. 1, p. 29:29–31).

God, we must deny of him the meaning signified by such names (*res significata*), or in the case of names signifying pure perfections, at least the creaturely way in which they signify. Even with respect to the latter, something imperfect is implied by their mode of signifying.[23] This final point will be developed more fully by Thomas in Bk I of his *Summa contra Gentiles*, as we shall see below.

b. *In De Trinitate* (1257–1258/59)

Thomas develops very fully his thoughts on the human intellect's possibilities in knowing God in his Commentary on the *De Trinitate*. In q. 1, a. 2 he asks whether the human mind can arrive at knowledge of God.[24] He replies that something may be known by us in one of two ways: (1) through a form which is proper to that thing itself (as when the eye grasps a stone through the species, i.e., form of the stone), or (2) through a form of something else which is like the thing known (as when a cause is known through its likeness in its effect, or a human being through the form of a picture or image).[25] As regards the first situation, where a thing is known through its own form, this may take place through a form which is simply identical with the thing itself. So it is that God knows himself through his essence and, adds Thomas, so too does an angel know itself in this way. Or this may take place through a form which is derived from the thing itself, either by being abstracted from that thing, or by direct infusion when a form or species is directly impressed on the mind of the knower by the object known.[26]

As regards our knowledge of God in the present life, in accord with his general theory of knowledge Thomas points out that our intellect bears a determined relationship to forms it abstracts from sense experience. Hence in this life we cannot know God through that form which is identical with the divine essence itself. Such knowledge is reserved for the blessed in the life to come.[27] Even any likeness which might be directly impressed by God on the human intellect in this life would not be sufficient to make his essence known to us; for his essence infinitely surpasses every created form. And, Thomas repeats, in this life we do not know God by means of purely intelligible forms which might be likenesses of him—again because our intellect depends upon forms abstracted from phantasms.[28]

---

23. Ed. cit., pp. 535–36. Cf. E. Winance, "L'essence divine et la connaissance humaine dans le Commentaire sur les Sentences de Saint Thomas," *Revue philosophique de Louvain* 55 (1957), pp. 190–92. Also see Thomas's reply to objection 2 (ed. cit., p. 536).

24. "utrum [mens humana] possit ad Dei notitiam pervenire" (Leon. 50.80:3–4).

25. ". . . uno modo per formam propriam, sicut oculus videt lapidem per speciem lapidis, alio modo per formam alterius similem sibi, sicut cognoscitur causa per similitudinem effectus, et homo per formam suae imaginis" (Leon. 50.84:48–52).

26. Leon. 50.84:52–63. To illustrate the last-mentioned possibility, Thomas refers to Avicenna's theory according to which we know separate intelligences by a direct infusion of notions of them (*impressiones*) in our intellects.

27. Ed. cit., p. 84:64–70.

28. See p. 84:70–80.

Hence by process of elimination Thomas concludes that in this life we can only know God through the forms of his effects. But effects are of two kinds. One kind is equal to the power of its cause; knowledge of such an effect fully reveals the power and therefore the quiddity of the cause. Another kind of effect falls short of any such equality with its cause. Through knowledge of such an effect, therefore, we cannot *comprehend* the power of its agent or the *essence* of that agent. We can only know that the agent exists.[29]

Because of this Thomas reasons that knowledge of an effect may serve as a principle which enables us to know of a cause that it is, just as knowledge of the quiddity of a cause itself does when that cause is known through its own form. But every created effect falls short of the perfection of its divine cause. Because of this, in this life we can only know of God that he is. Nonetheless, Thomas adds that one person may arrive at more perfect knowledge that God is than another for this reason. A cause is known more perfectly from its effect to the extent that through knowledge of the effect the relationship of that cause to its effect is more perfectly grasped.[30]

Thomas observes that when we are dealing with effects which are not equal in perfection to their cause, three things should be taken into account: the fact that the effect comes forth from its cause; the likeness of the cause to which the effect attains; and the degree to which the effect falls short of the cause. Accordingly, he distinguishes three ways in which the human intellect can advance in its knowledge of God, but he immediately warns that none of these enables us to know what God is; they only tell us that he is. According to the first way, our knowledge is more perfect insofar as we understand more fully God's power in producing things. According to the second way, our knowledge advances insofar as we recognize God as the cause of more excellent effects; because they bear greater likeness to him, they more perfectly manifest his eminence. According to the third way, our knowledge advances insofar as we understand that God is ever more greatly removed from all that we find in his effects. These three ways correspond, of course, to the three Dionysian ways of knowing God: (1) by reasoning from his effects to him as cause; (2) by transcendence; and (3) by negation.[31]

Three points may be drawn from this discussion. First of all, here Thomas clearly acknowledges that while we can know that God is by reasoning from effect to cause, we cannot know what he is. In fact, at the end of his reply Thomas also applies this restriction to knowledge given to us through the light of faith and the

---

29. See p. 84:81–89. Note especially with respect to the second kind of effect: ". . . et per talem effectum non potest comprehendi virtus agentis et per consequens nec essentia eius; sed cognoscitur tantum de causa quod est. . . ."

30. See p. 84:89–99.

31. See pp. 84:100–85:117: "Unde dicit Dionysius in libro De divinis nominibus quod cognoscitur ex omnium causa et excessu et ablatione." See *De divinis nominibus* VII, 3 (ed. cit., p. 273, n. 321) for Dionysius's text, and for Thomas's Commentary, c. VII, lect. 4 (p. 274, nn. 729–731).

(infused) gifts of wisdom and understanding. Not even such knowledge enables us to grasp the divine essence or quiddity in this life.[32] Secondly, Thomas defends some likeness or similitude between creatures, viewed as effects, and God their cause. This likeness is greater in more perfect effects. We stress this point because, without it, Thomas's view of our capacity to know anything of God beyond asserting that he is would be very restricted indeed. Finally, Thomas's emphasis on the way of negation is quite pronounced in this discussion. And in replying to the first objection, he comments that we are said to have arrived at the summit of our knowledge of God when we know him as unknown, that is to say, when we recognize that his essence is above anything we can apprehend in this life. Thus while what God is remains unknown to us, that he is may indeed be known by us.[33]

How the point that what God is remains unknown to us can be reconciled with Thomas's acknowledgment that some positive names may be predicated of God remains to be determined. Greater clarification is still needed concerning his understanding of the quidditative knowledge of God he continues to deny to us in this life.

For some help concerning this, we may briefly interrupt our consideration of Thomas's Commentary on the *De Trinitate* and turn to another text which dates from roughly the same period, i.e., *De veritate,* q. 2, a. 1, ad 9.[34] There Thomas explains more fully his understanding of quidditative knowledge. The intellect is said to know of something what it is when it defines that thing, that is to say, when it conceives some form which corresponds to the thing itself in every respect. He observes that whatever our intellect may conceive of God, this falls short in representing him. Because of this, what God is always remains unknown to us (in this life). And this is the highest knowledge we can have of God, when we recognize that he is above all that we can know of him.[35]

---

32. Leon. 50.85:118–131.

33. See p. 85:132–138: ". . . dicimur in fine nostrae cognitionis Deum tamquam ignotum cognoscere, quia tunc maxime mens in cognitione profecisse invenitur, quando cognoscit eius essentiam esse supra omne quod apprehendere potest in statu viae; et sic quamvis maneat ignotum quid est, scitur tamen quia est."

34. Since this question appears near the beginning of the *De veritate* (1256–1259), it should probably be dated in 1256. This would place it slightly before the Commentary on the *De Trinitate* which, following Torrell, we have placed in 1257–1258/59.

35. In this article Thomas is defending our right to attribute knowledge *(scientia)* to God. He has rejected the view which restricts this to mean nothing more than that God is the cause of the knowledge we find in creatures. Against this he counters that when knowledge is attributed to God, it signifies something which is in God, as do life, essence, etc.: "Et ideo aliter dicendum est quod scientia Deo attributa significat aliquid quod in Deo est et similiter vita et essentia et cetera huiusmodi . . ." (Leon. 22.1.39:164–166). For his reply to objection 9 see p. 42:321–333. Note especially: ". . . dicendum quod tunc intellectus dicitur scire de aliquo quid est quando diffinit ipsum, id est quando concipit aliquam formam de ipsa re quae per omnia ipsi rei respondet; iam autem ex dictis patet quod quicquid intellectus noster de Deo concipit est deficiens a representatione eius; et ideo quid est ipsius Dei semper nobis occultum remanet. . . ."

In other words, in this context quidditative knowledge (knowledge what a thing is) refers to knowledge of it by means of a form which is equal or adequate to that thing in all respects. That Thomas denies such knowledge of God to us is not surprising, since no creaturely form can be adequate to its divine cause. Hence whenever we know God through a form abstracted from one of his effects, no matter how perfect that effect may be, the resulting knowledge will not tell us what God is.

If we may return to the Commentary on the *De Trinitate*, in q. 6, a. 3 Thomas considers a closely related issue: "Whether our intellect can behold the divine form itself." A number of the opening arguments eloquently state the case for a negative reply. Here I will restrict myself to the first. According to Dionysius, "If anyone of those seeing God understood what he saw, he did not see God himself but one of those things that are his," i.e., one of his creations. But the divine form is God. In other words, one who claims to have seen the divine form (God) deceives himself; for he mistakes one of God's creatures for God himself.[36] Yet as the first argument on the opposite side points out, in Romans 1:20 St. Paul writes, "The invisible things of God are seen by a creature of the world" (that is, by man, interjects Thomas), "being understood through those things which have been made, his everlasting power also and divinity."[37]

Thomas begins his reply by recalling the distinction between our knowing of something that it is *(an est)*, and our knowing what it is *(quid est)*. For us to know what it is, our intellect must be able to grasp its quiddity or essence either immediately or else by means of other things which adequately manifest its quiddity.[38] He reminds us that in this life our intellect cannot immediately grasp the essence of God or, for that matter, the essence of other separate substances. Thomas's reason for holding this continues to be based on his theory of knowledge and therefore is philosophical. In this life our intellect is immediately directed to phantasms and is therefore limited to what it can in some way abstract or infer from phantasms. If the human intellect can immediately grasp the quiddity of sensible things (at least of some), it cannot do so in the case of purely intelligible realities.[39] Still the quid-

---

36. Leon. 50.166:1–8. Note especially: "Si quis videntium deum intellexit quod vidit, non ipsum vidit, sed aliquid eorum quae sunt eius." For Dionysius see *Epistola I* (PG 3.1065A).

37. Leon. 50.166:32–35. On Thomas's awareness of different ways of interpreting this passage see above, Ch. X, n. 16.

38. Leon. 50.167:52–59. Note especially: "Ad hoc autem quod de aliqua re sciamus quid est, oportet quod intellectus noster feratur in ipsius rei quiditatem sive essentiam, vel immediate, vel mediantibus aliquibus quae sufficienter eius quiditatem demonstrent."

39. See p. 167:60–67. Note lines 64–67: ". . . et sic immediate potest concipere intellectus quiditatem rei sensibilis, non autem alicuius rei intelligibilis." This statement should be balanced against Thomas's recognition on other occasions that the essential differences of sensible things sometimes remain unknown to us. See Maurer's comment on q. 6, a. 2 *(The Division and Method of the Sciences*, 4th ed., p. 77, n. 17), and his references to *De veritate*, q. 4, a. 1, ad 8; q. 10, a. 1 and ad 6; SCG I, c. 3; and *In VII Met.*, lect. 12, p. 374, n. 1552.

dity or nature of certain invisible things is adequately manifested *(perfecte)* from the quiddities of sensible things which are known to us. Hence we can arrive at a mediate quidditative knowledge of these. For instance, by knowing what a man is and what an animal is, and by comparing the two, we can come to know what a genus is and what a species is.[40]

But when the natures of sensible things are understood, they still do not adequately express the divine essence or the essence of other separate substances. Because sensible things do not fall into the same natural genus as do separate substances, quiddity and all names of this type taken from sensible things can be predicated of sensible things and of separate substances only in what Thomas here refers to as "almost" equivocal fashion. By this we may assume he has in mind analogical predication of such names. As Thomas also explains here, if the way of similitude fails to make the essence or quiddity of God and other separate substances known to us, so does the way of causality. This is because the effects produced by such substances in our universe are not equal to the power of their causes and cannot, therefore, deliver quidditative knowledge of their causes.[41]

In sum, Thomas concludes that in this life we cannot know the "what it is" of God or of other separate substances (angels). This applies not only to natural or philosophical knowledge based on reasoning from effect to cause. It also applies to any knowledge given to us through divine revelation. Even revealed knowledge is given to us in accord with our way of knowing and uses concepts abstracted from sensible experience. Hence Thomas allows for no comfortable retreat into fideism when it comes to our knowledge of God. Since revealed knowledge depends upon likenesses and concepts derived from our experience of sensible things, it can never lead us to quidditative knowledge of God.[42]

Thomas's analysis does not come to a halt at this point. He turns to the Aristotelian view that we cannot know that something is without knowing in some way what it is, either perfectly or at least in some confused fashion. For instance, if someone knows that man exists and wishes to know what he is by defining him, that person must already know what the term "man" signifies. And this presupposes that in some way he can conceive that thing which he knows to exist even if he cannot define it. Presumably he does this by knowing some proximate or remote genus and some external accidents which apply to man. Underlying this, as Thomas also notes, is the point that in arriving at knowledge of definitions or of demonstrations, one must begin from some preexisting knowledge (precognition).[43]

---

40. Leon. 50.167:70–76.

41. See p. 167:77–93.

42. See p. 167:94–113. Note especially: "Et sic restat quod formae immateriales non sunt nobis notae cognitione quid est, sed solummodo cognitione an est, sive naturali ratione ex effectibus creaturarum, sive etiam revelatione quae est per similitudines a sensibilibus sumptas."

43. Leon. 50.167:114–168:132. Thomas has here referred to the beginning of Aristotle's *Physics*. See *Physics* I, c. 1 (184a 23–b 12).

In the case of God and of other separate substances, however, we cannot even have such obscure knowledge by appealing to a more remote genus in which they might fall. God falls into no genus, since he does not have a quiddity which is distinct from his *esse*, which membership in a genus requires. And separate substances do not belong to the same natural genus as do sensible things, even though the logician treats of them as if they did. The philosopher of nature and the metaphysician know better, since they must deal with the essences of things which exist in reality. Where they find different modes of being, as is clearly the case here, they conclude that different genera are involved. Nor can we overcome his difficulty by appealing to accidents which might be evident to us. God, of course, has no accidents, and if other separate substances do, they are not evident to us.[44]

At this point Thomas seems to have created a dilemma for himself. He continues to deny that we can know what God (or any other separate substance) is. Yet he agrees with Aristotle that we cannot know that something is unless in some way we know what it is. To resolve this dilemma he turns to the path of negation. Instead of knowing some genus for separate substances, we advance in our knowledge of them by applying negations—for instance, by noting that they are immaterial, incorporeal, etc. The more negations we can apply to them, the less vague or confused is our knowledge of them. This is because a prior negation is limited and determined by subsequent negations, just as a remote genus is limited and determined by differences. Thomas concludes that in the case of immaterial forms, including God, we know that they exist. But instead of knowing what they are, we advance in our understanding of them by appealing to negation, to causality, and to eminence—that is to say, by using the threefold Dionysian approach.[45] Thomas restates and reinforces this same general conclusion in q. 6, a. 4, of this same Commentary on the *De Trinitate*.[46]

c. *Summa contra Gentiles* (1259/60–1264/65)

Apparently not long after completing q. 6 of his Commentary on the *De Trinitate*, in Bk I of his *Summa contra Gentiles* Thomas spells out for us the details of the way of negation when it comes to our knowledge of God.[47] That Thomas himself recognized the importance of this discussion is clear from his backward

44. Leon. 50.168:133–156.

45. Ed. cit., p. 168:159–181. Both this text and that cited from q. 6, a. 4 in the following note indicate that Thomas thinks that by reasoning from effect to cause we can know that separate substances, both God and angels, exist.

46. See p. 170:96–146. Note: "Quidditas autem substantiarum separatarum non potest cognosci per ea quae a sensibus accipimus, ut ex praedictis patet; quamvis per sensibilia possimus devenire ad cognoscendum praedictas substantias esse, et aliquas earum condiciones . . . utpote quod sunt intellectuales, incorruptibiles, et huiusmodi" (p. 170:136–146). Also see ad 2 (p. 171:159–175).

47. Bk I through c. 53 dates from before the summer of 1259. Beginning in Italy in 1260 Thomas revised these chapters and by 1264–1265 completed the remainder of the work. See Torrell, *Saint Thomas Aquinas*, p. 332.

reference to it in Bk III, c. 39. There he reasons that no demonstrative knowledge of God will ever suffice to give us perfect happiness. He grants that the path of demonstration can bring us closer to proper knowledge of God than the kind of pre-philosophical knowledge he had considered in c. 38. Thus by removing or negating many things from God through demonstration, we understand more clearly how he differs from everything else. Thomas remarks that he himself has already used this approach in Bk I in proving that God is immobile, eternal, incorporeal, perfectly simple, one, and other things of this kind.[48]

Thomas now observes that we can arrive at proper knowledge of something not only by means of affirmations but also by means of negations. But there is an important difference between the kind of proper knowledge which may be gained by these two approaches. Proper knowledge based on a series of affirmations may indeed deliver knowledge of what something is, along with an understanding of how it differs from all else. But proper knowledge of a thing when grasped through succeeding negations will not yield quidditative knowledge of that thing; it will only tell us that it differs from others. It is only this second kind of proper knowledge of God which we can attain in this life by means of demonstrations.[49]

Thomas repeats much of this thinking in Bk III, c. 49, but in a different context. There he writes that a cause can be known from its effects in different ways. Accordingly, separate substances may know God either by knowing the essences of other separate substances as likenesses of God and thereby seeing their cause in his effects, or else by knowing their own essences as effects in which they see a likeness of God, their cause. In the case of separate substances, both ways of knowing God are nondiscursive. Because neither of these kinds of effects is adequate to the power of its divine cause, neither of these ways of knowing God yields knowledge of the divine essence or quidditative knowledge of God. When human beings reason from knowledge of effects to knowledge of God as their cause, they do so discursively by using their knowledge of an effect as a means for reasoning to knowledge of the existence of the cause. This knowledge is even less perfect than that reached by separate substances. Here again Thomas cites Dionysius to the effect that in this life we are joined to a God who remains, as it were, unknown. While we may know of God what he is not, what he is remains completely *(penitus)* unknown to us.[50]

---

48. Ed. Leon. man., p. 263. Note: ". . . cum per demonstrationem removeantur ab eo multa, per quorum remotionem ab aliis discretus intelligitur. Ostendit enim demonstratio Deum esse immobilem, aeternum, incorporeum, omnino simplicem, unum, et alia huiusmodi, quae in libro primo de Deo ostendimus."

49. Ibid. Note especially: ". . . per negationes autem habita propria cognitione de re, scitur quod est ab aliis discreta, tamen quid sit remanet ignotum. Talis autem est propria cognitio quae de Deo habetur per demonstrationes."

50. Ed. cit., pp. 279–80. Note especially: "Et hoc est ultimum et perfectissimum nostrae cognitionis in hac vita, ut Dionysius dicit, in Libro *De Mystica Theologia* [capp. I, II], *cum Deo quasi ignoto coniungimur:* quod quidem contingit dum de eo *quid non sit* cognoscimus, quid vero sit penitus manet ignotum" (p. 280). For discussion see A. Pegis, "Penitus Manet Ignotum," *Mediaeval Studies*

With this in mind we may turn back to Bk I of the *Summa contra Gentiles*. It will be recalled that Thomas devotes c. 13 to a series of arguments to prove that God exists. In c. 14 he wishes to begin determining how God exists *(conditiones investigare)*. He begins by reasserting his claim that we cannot know what God is. This follows from the fact that the divine substance surpasses in its immensity any form which the human intellect can grasp. Therefore we must turn to the way of negation *(via remotionis)*; for we can arrive at some knowledge concerning what God is not. The more things we can correctly deny of God, the more we approach knowledge of him. This is because we have more perfect knowledge of anything to the degree that we can mark off its differences from others.[51]

Thus in the cases of things whose definitions we can grasp, we first place them in some genus and thereby know in general fashion what they are. Subsequently we add the differences by which they are distinguished from others and thereby reach knowledge of their essence *(substantia)*. Thomas again reminds us that in the case of God, we cannot grasp any "what" *(quid)* and use this as a genus. Nor can we understand God's distinction from others through positive differences; hence we must have recourse to negative differences. But such knowledge is of value, insists Thomas, in language which reminds us of his discussion in his Commentary on the *De Trinitate*, q. 6, a. 3; for one negative difference will be contracted by another, which further differentiates God from other things. For instance, it is one thing to say that God is not an accident. By this we distinguish him from all accidents. It is another to conclude that he is not a body. In the second case we not only distinguish him from accidents but from some substances. By continuing to appeal to negations and thereby distinguishing him in ordered fashion from all that differs from him, we can arrive at a proper knowledge of his substance—i.e., when we realize that he is distinct from everything else. But such knowledge will not be perfect, since it will not tell us what God is in himself.[52]

In order to begin to develop this route of negative knowledge of God, Thomas recalls that (in c. 13) he has established that God is completely immobile. In c. 15 he proves that God is eternal, by showing, for instance, that he is not subject to change, or measured by time, or subject to generation and corruption.[53] In c. 16

---

27 (1965), pp. 212–18. Also see SCG III, c. 42, for an interesting presentation of Thomas's reasons for denying that we can in this life attain quidditative knowledge of separate substances other than God by reasoning from our knowledge of the quiddities of sensible substances (ed. cit., pp. 266–67).

51. Ed. cit., p. 15. Note especially: "Nam divina substantia omnem formam quam intellectus noster attingit, sua immensitate excedit: et sic ipsam apprehendere non possumus cognoscendo quid est. Sed aliqualem eius habemus notitiam cognoscendo *quid non est.*"

52. Ibid. Note in particular: ". . . et tunc de substantia eius erit propria consideratio cum cognoscetur ut ab omnibus distinctus. Non tamen erit perfecta: quia non cognoscetur quid in se sit." Cf. *In De Trinitate*, q. 6, a. 3 (Leon. 50.168:159–168).

53. See c. 14 (near end) and c. 15 (ed. cit., pp. 15–16). It is also in c. 15 that he introduces the argument for God's existence based on contingency, i.e., on the fact that certain things are subject to generation and corruption, as we saw above in Ch. XI.

he offers a series of arguments to show that in God there is no passive potency. In subsequent chapters he shows that in God there is no matter (c. 17), that there is no composition in him (c. 18), that God is not subject to violence, nor to anything other than the divine nature (c. 19), that God is not a body (c. 20), that God is identical with (i.e., not distinct from) his essence (c. 21), that in God *esse* and essence are identical, i.e., not distinct (c. 22), that there is nothing accidental in God (c. 23), that the divine being *(esse)* cannot be determined by the addition of any substantial difference in the way a genus is determined by differences (c. 24), that God is not a genus and cannot be defined (c. 25), that God is not to be identified with the formal being *(esse)* of other things (c. 26), and that he is not the form of any body including any self-moving mover (c. 27). In sum, Thomas continues to use the way of negation in making each of these points.[54]

In c. 28 Thomas turns to the divine perfection. If one wonders whether he will continue to appeal to the way of negation here, he quickly dispels any doubt. He explains that that being is perfect in every respect *(omnino)* to which no kind of excellence is lacking. He then develops a series of arguments to show that this is true of God, i.e., that he lacks no kind of excellence whatsoever. In addition to denying any lack of excellence or any imperfection of God, a number of these arguments also argue in negative fashion to establish this conclusion. For instance, as we saw above in Ch. XII, the first argument maintains that the excellence of a thing belongs to that thing in accord with its mode of being *(esse)*. Accordingly, insofar as a thing's act of being is limited to some greater or lesser mode of excellence, it is said to be more or less excellent. Therefore, if there is something to which the total power of being *(virtus essendi)* belongs, no excellence that can pertain to any being can be lacking to it. But the act of being pertains to that thing which is identical with its act of being according to the total power of being. Because God is his very act of being (see c. 22), he therefore possesses *esse* according to the total power of being. Hence no excellence which can belong to any being can be lacking to God. And as we shall see below, on the strength of the seemingly negative conclusion that God lacks no perfection and is therefore all-perfect, Thomas will feel justified in assigning to him certain perfections which appear to be positive in content, such as goodness, wisdom, etc.[55] Presumably this is because the negation of a negation (lack of any perfection) results in an affirmation (God is all-perfect).

54. For some interesting comments on Thomas's application of the way of negation in cc. 15–28 see Kretzmann, *The Metaphysics of Theism,* pp. 117–38, although he refers to it as the "eliminative method" and at this point in his book still applies it to what he calls Alpha rather than to God. Also see Hoping, *Weisheit als Wissen des Ursprungs,* pp. 136–58.

55. Ed. cit., pp. 29–30. Note Thomas's remark at the beginning of the chapter: "Et dico universaliter perfectum, cui non deest alicuius generis nobilitas" (p. 29). On Thomas's argumentation in c. 28 see Ch. XII above, Section 6, pp. 492–93. Also see Kretzmann, *The Metaphysics of Theism,* pp. 131–38, 140–44 (where he stresses the pivotal nature of this chapter in Thomas's discussion).

In c. 29 Thomas develops an issue which is of considerable importance for our immediate purpose, and which is also crucial for his doctrine of analogical predication of the divine names, that is to say, the likeness which does or does not obtain between creatures and God.[56] Thomas reasons that even in the case of effects which do not agree with their cause in name or in intelligible content *(ratio)*, some similarity must obtain between them and their cause. "It is of the nature of action that an agent produce something like itself, since each and every thing acts insofar as it is in act."[57] From this he concludes that the form of an effect must be present in some fashion in a cause which surpasses it in perfection (an equivocal cause), but according to another mode and with another intelligible content. As an example of what he has in mind, he turns to the case of the sun. Even though the physics of his example is outmoded, the example itself may help clarify his point. According to the physics of Thomas's day, the sun produces heat in lower bodies by acting insofar as it is in act; and heat as produced in these bodies bears some likeness to the active power of the sun which produces it here on earth; but it was also thought that heat is not present in the sun in the same way it is present in terrestrial bodies. Hence the sun was regarded as a cause of a higher order. Because of the heat it produces in terrestrial bodies, the sun may be described as hot. But heat is now being applied according to a different definition and with a different intelligible content, and so the sun may be said to be both like and unlike heat as we experience it. In similar fashion, reasons Thomas, God grants perfection to all things. By reason of this, he bears some likeness and some unlikeness to all else.[58]

Since Thomas obviously regards God as the most eminent cause and as one that infinitely surpasses everything else in perfection, one wonders what likeness can obtain between creatures and God. Even more fundamental for Thomas's position, however, is his claim that every cause produces something that is in some way like itself. How does he justify this? B. Mondin has argued that sometimes Thomas attempts to establish this principle inductively, as in SCG III, c. 69. According to Mondin this inductive effort is not a demonstration but an ostensive approach, not a proof but a taking by the hand, as it were *(manuductio)*.[59] Be that as it may,

56. "Ex hoc autem quomodo in rebus possit similitudo ad Deum inveniri vel non possit, considerari potest" (ed. cit., p. 30).

57. Ed. cit., p. 31: ". . . necesse est tamen aliquam inter ea similitudinem inveniri: de natura enim actionis est ut agens sibi simile agat, cum unumquodque agat secundum quod actu est."

58. Ibid. Note: "Unde forma effectus in causa excedente invenitur quidem aliqualiter, sed secundum alium modum et aliam rationem, ratione cuius causa aequivoca dicitur. . . . Ita etiam et Deus omnes perfectiones rebus tribuit, ac per hoc cum omnibus similitudinem habet et dissimilitudinem simul."

59. *The Principle of Analogy in Protestant and Catholic Theology* (The Hague, 1963), p. 86; "Il principio 'omne agens agit sibi simile' e l'analogia dei nomi divini nel pensiero di S. Tommaso d'Aquino," *Divus Thomas* (Piac.) 63 (1960), pp. 336–48, esp. 337. Cf. SCG III, c. 69 (p. 304): "Item. Apparet per inductionem in omnibus quod simile agat suum simile." In this context the induction is limited to the generation of matter-form composites which, the argument concludes, must be

Mondin shows that more frequently Thomas attempts to establish this principle deductively. Even so, concludes Mondin, Thomas really regards it as a self-evident principle.[60]

In the text at hand (SCG, I c. 29), Thomas reasons from the nature of action to the conclusion that every agent causes something like itself. In support he adds that each and every thing acts insofar as it is in act.[61] By this he means that if some agent is to act or produce an effect, that agent must itself be in act. Thomas probably regards this claim as intuitively certain. Nonacting agents do not produce anything. Moreover, it seems evident that if an agent is to communicate something to an effect, it must actually have or at least virtually possess what it is to communicate to its effect (and I would recall, must itself exist). It is also clear that Thomas is here thinking of principal agents, not of purely instrumental ones.[62]

Even so, if one grants this much to him, what does it establish about the similarity between an effect and a higher level or equivocal cause, especially one that is infinitely perfect? While this reasoning may show that the cause has the power to produce the effect and that the cause both acts and exists, does it prove that a perfection in the effect is similar to something that is formally present in the cause? When we are dealing with created effects and God their cause, such a conclusion should be applied to what we have called pure perfections, not to those that include or imply some participated mode of being in their definition. But even with respect to pure perfections, does such reasoning justify our concluding that there is something intrinsically and formally present in God which the produced effects resemble? Thomas believes that this is so, although he will admit that any name signifying such a perfection can be applied to God only analogically, not univocally or equivocally.[63]

---

generated by other matter-form composites. Hence this argument of itself would not justify extending the similitude claim to the divine cause. Nor does Thomas so extend it in that context.

60. *The Principle*, pp. 87–88; "Il principio," pp. 338–39. Mondin suggests that Thomas implicitly deduces the principle from the principle of sufficient reason (although not explicitly since he does not use that terminology), because he regards it as an explanation of the meaning of action and causality. P. Rosemann writes, if with some exaggeration, that the central notions of causal similarity "constitute the basic assumptions of medieval metaphysics which underlie everything that is expressed in it, while their own justification remains unexpressed." See his *Omne Agens Agit Sibi Simile: A "Repetition" of Scholastic Metaphysics* (Leuven, 1996), p. 25. Also see J. Pérez Guerrero, *La creación como asimilación a Dios* (Navarra, 1996), pp. 122–36, for discussion and criticism of different arguments taken from Thomas's texts in support of this principle.

61. See the text cited above in n. 57.

62. See Mondin, *The Principle*, p. 89. See the three restrictions which he finds Thomas applying to the principle *omne agens agit simile sibi:* (1) it applies only to *per se* causes (agents), not to causes *per accidens;* (2) it applies to principal causes, not to those that are instrumental; (3) a cause assimilates an effect to itself only to the extent that it causes that effect, and not insofar as that effect is also caused by something else.

63. See the remainder of c. 29. Central to Thomas's thinking is the point that because God grants perfections to all things, he is unlike and yet like them. Two points should be retained from this chapter: (1) Thomas never forgets that the likeness he is here defending between creatures and God

In c. 30 Thomas specifically addresses a point we have just touched on. There he singles out certain names which signify perfection without any restriction whatsoever, names such as goodness, wisdom, and being *(esse)*. These can be applied both to creatures and to God.[64] But as Thomas reminds us, even these names carry with themselves a built-in deficiency. It is true that they imply no imperfection as regards that which they are intended to signify; but they do include some deficiency in their way of signifying *(modus significandi)*. This is because our intellect derives its intelligible content from sense experience. Because sensible things are composed of matter and form, in them there is always a distinction between a form and the thing which possesses that form. A form as realized in such a thing may be simple but will be imperfect, since it does not subsist. The thing which has such a form subsists, to be sure; but it is not simple but concrete.[65]

Because of this, if we express any such name abstractly and therefore as something simple—goodness for instance—this abstract way of signifying implies that it is that whereby something subsists, not that which itself subsists. But if we express such a name concretely—a good thing—for instance, this concrete way of signifying implies some kind of composition of goodness and the thing that is good. Neither of these limitations, of course, can in fact apply to God or to the divine goodness. Hence as regards its mode of signifying, any name we apply to God implies some kind of imperfection which cannot be admitted in God. Nonetheless, the thing signified by such a name *(res significata)* applies to him in eminent fashion. Because of this, Thomas concludes, in agreement with Pseudo-Dionysius, that names of this type are to be affirmed and denied of God—affirmed because of the meaning of the name, and denied because of the way in which they signify.[66]

---

is balanced by the lack of likeness which remains between the two (see the text cited in n. 58 above); (2) it is more appropriate to say that a creature is like God than that God is like the creature. For the quality or form in the creature on which its likeness to God is based is itself present in the creature only in deficient and participated fashion when compared with its unparticipated source.

64. "Quia enim omnem perfectionem creaturae est in Deo invenire sed per alium modum eminentiorem, quaecumque nomina absolute perfectionem absque defectu designant, de Deo praedicantur et de aliis rebus; sicut est *bonitas, sapientia, esse,* et alia huiusmodi" (ed. cit., p. 31).

65. "Dico autem aliqua praedictorum nominum perfectionem absque defectu importare, quantum ad illud ad quod significandum nomen fuit impositum: quantum enim ad modum significandi, omne nomen cum defectu est. . . . Forma vero in his rebus invenitur quidem simplex, sed imperfecta, utpote non subsistens: habens autem formam invenitur quidem subsistens, sed non simplex, immo concretionem habens" (pp. 31–32).

66. See p. 32. Note especially: "Et quantum ad hoc nullum nomen Deo convenienter aptatur, sed solum quantum ad id ad quod significandum nomen imponitur. Possunt igitur, ut Dionysius docet . . . huiusmodi nomina et affirmari de Deo et negari: affirmari quidem, propter nominis rationem; negari vero, propter significandi modum." For the reference to Dionysius see his *De mystica theologia* 1, 2 (PG 3.1000), although the Leonine editors cite *De cael. hier.,* c. 2.3 and *De div. nom.* c. I, 5. For discussion of this distinction between the *res significata* and the *modus significandi* see H. Lyttkens, *The Analogy between God and the World,* pp. 375–82; "Die Bedeutung der Gottesprädikate bei Thomas von Aquin," in *Philosophical Essays Dedicated to Gunnar Aspelin on the Occasion of His Sixty-fifth Birthday,* H. Bratt et al., eds. (Lund, 1963), pp. 76–96, esp. 80–84; L. Clavell, *El nombre*

Unlike such names, Thomas notes that others include some mode which is proper to creatures even in that which they signify. Names of this type—"human being," or "stone," for instance—cannot be applied to God except metaphorically. Still other names express pure perfections together with the supereminent mode in which they are realized in God—for instance, "supreme good," or "first being." These, of course, can be applied only to God. But Thomas's qualification regarding the way in which such names signify must not be forgotten. Even such names carry with them some deficiency and limitation in their way of signifying.[67] Thomas sums up by noting that the mode of supereminence whereby pure perfections are present in God can be signified by names we impose only by negation ("eternal," "infinite," etc.), or by expressing God's relation to other things ("first cause," "supreme good"). Thomas concludes c. 30 with this well-known remark: "Concerning God we are not able to grasp what he is, but what he is not, and how other things are related to him."[68]

In c. 31 Thomas argues that the plurality of divine names does not militate against divine simplicity. He recalls from c. 29 that the perfections we find in creatures are to be attributed to God as their equivocal cause. But an effect may be said to be present in its equivocal cause virtually, in the way heat is said to be present in the sun. Thomas explains that the power to produce heat in effects must be present in the sun; but, he adds, this does not merely mean that the sun is said to be hot because it produces heat in its effects. It also means that the power by reason of which the sun produces heat is in some way like or conformed to heat.[69] He also adds that through this same single power the sun produces many other effects in creatures, such as dryness. In like fashion, the various perfections we find in creatures according to different forms must belong to God by reason of one and the same divine power (virtus). In God, of course, this power is identical with the divine essence. Consequently, God is said to be wise not merely because he produces wisdom in others; insofar as we are wise, we in some way imitate that power by means of which he makes us wise.[70]

While Thomas's primary purpose in c. 31 is to show that the plurality of divine names does not in any way compromise God's simplicity, he again has recourse to

---

propio de Dios según santo Tomás de Aquino (Pamplona, 1980), pp. 143–46; R. M. McInerny, The Logic of Analogy, pp. 156–61; Wippel, Metaphysical Themes, pp. 224–26; E. J. Ashworth, "Signification and Mode of Signifying in Thirteenth-Century Logic," Medieval Philosophy and Theology 1 (1991), pp. 39–67, esp. 50–53.

67. See c. 30, p. 31. See the text cited in n. 65.

68. See p. 32, end of c. 30: "Non enim de Deo capere possumus quid est, sed quid non est, et qualiter alia se habeant ad ipsum, ut ex supra dictis patet."

69. See c. 31 (p. 32): "Ex hac igitur virtute sol calidus dicitur, non solum quia calorem facit, sed quia virtus per quam hoc facit, est aliquid conforme calori."

70. Ibid. Note especially: "Sic igitur sapiens Deus dicitur non solum secundum hoc quod sapientiam efficit, sed quia, secundum quod sapientes sumus, virtutem eius, qua sapientes nos facit, aliquatenus imitamur."

two principles which are of central concern to us. He continues to base our ability to predicate names of God in meaningful fashion upon our discovery of perfections in creatures and our reasoning from them as effects to him as their divine cause. And he has once more argued for some minimum degree of likeness between perfections as found in creatures and the divine power which produces them. Yet this likeness cannot be so great as to enable us to know what God is. In fact, Thomas concludes that if we could understand God's essence and adapt a proper name to it, then we could express God through a single name.[71] This comment, together with Thomas's continuing denial to us of quidditative knowledge of God in this life, must be kept in mind when we turn to his discussion of univocal, equivocal, and analogical names in the immediately following chapters of the *Summa contra Gentiles*. We shall reserve discussion of this for Section 2 of this Chapter.

Before leaving this discussion in Bk I of the *Summa contra Gentiles*, we should turn to a question implied by what we have now seen in this context. To what extent has Thomas continued to follow the way of negation when he discusses divine names which imply no limitation in that which they signify? In another study I have suggested that in Bk I of this work the *via negativa* seems to be applied in three different ways. First of all, until the discussion in c. 28 the perfections Thomas assigns to God all seem to be discovered by the process of succeeding negations. Secondly, each of these names seems to include the negation of something in its formal meaning. This we have already seen above. And thirdly, while Thomas does not find anything negative in the formal meaning of names such as "goodness," "wisdom," and "being," even these carry with them a creaturely *modus significandi* when we apply them to God. This creaturely mode of signifying must itself be denied of God.[72]

In fact, as I also attempted to show in that earlier study, Thomas continues to use the path of succeeding negations even when he attempts to prove that God is good in c. 37, although in c. 30 he has also pointed out that names such as "first cause" and "supreme good" are imposed on God by reason of his relationship to other things. But he does seem to regard goodness itself as positive in content. And since he clearly defends our right on philosophical grounds to say that God is good, we may continue to ask how this claim can be reconciled with his denial that we can know what God is.[73]

71. See c. 31, end (p. 33): "Si autem ipsam essentiam prout est possemus intelligere et ei nomen proprium adaptare, uno nomine tantum eam exprimeremus. Quod promittitur his qui eum per essentiam videbunt. . . ."

72. See *Metaphysical Themes*, p. 226.

73. Ibid., p. 227, commenting on SCG I, c. 37: "Quod Deus est bonus" (ed. cit., pp. 35–36). Thomas's first argument refers back to and rests upon his proof in c. 28 that God is perfect. But he established this in large measure by using the way of negation. The second argument harks back to the proof in c. 13 that God is the unmoved mover, and therefore moves as the supreme object of appetite. But this argumentation in c. 13 showed that God is not a moved mover. The third argument to show that God is good rests on the claim that he is a being in act and not subject to potentiality

d. *De potentia* (1265–1266)

With this question still in mind we may now turn to two later sets of texts, q. 7 of the *De potentia* and the *Prima Pars* of the *Summa theologiae*.[74] In q. 7 of the *De potentia*, Thomas takes up in detail the issue of divine simplicity. In a. 1 he develops three arguments to prove that God is simple. As one would expect, each follows the way of negation.[75] In a. 2 Thomas argues that in God essence *(substantia)* and act of being *(esse)* are identical, i.e., not diverse.[76] Even though this conclusion rests on the negation of distinction of essence and *esse* in God, it also raises a question. In affirming that in God essence and act of being are identical, is Thomas not allowing for some positive and perhaps even some quidditative knowledge of God?

The first objection makes this very point. According to John Damascene, that God is is manifest to us. But what he is in terms of his substance and nature is altogether incomprehensible and unknown to us. But, continues the objection, the same thing cannot be known and not known at the same time. Therefore, God's *esse* and his substance or essence cannot be identical.[77]

To this Thomas replies by introducing a distinction we have previously seen concerning the ways in which the terms *ens* and *esse* may be used. Sometimes they are taken as referring to the essence of a thing or to its act of being; but on other occasions these terms simply signify the truth of a proposition, and can even be applied to things which do not actually exist (as when we say blindness is because it is true that a particular person is blind). Accordingly, when Damascene says that God's *esse* is manifest to us, he is using *esse* in the second way as expressing the truth of the proposition "God is," not in the first way (as the act of being). But it is only when *esse* is taken in the first way that we can say that God's essence and *esse* are the same. Hence just as his substance or essence remains unknown to us, so too does his *esse* when this is taken in the first way as act of being. Nonetheless, we can

---

of any kind. The final argument rests on the Neoplatonic axiom that the good tends to diffuse itself, but applies this to final rather than to efficient causality. Since this argument presupposes that God causes the being of all other things, it rests on the demonstration in c. 15 (not in c. 13 as the Leon. ed. indicates, and which I accepted in *Metaphysical Themes*, p. 226, n. 39) that he is not a caused cause, since he is the necessary being through himself and not through something else.

74. Limitations of space will not permit me to follow here Thomas's detailed application of "good" and similar names to God in the ensuing chapters of SCG I. For more on this see Kretzmann, *The Metaphysics of Theism*, cc. 5–8; Hoping, *Weisheit als Wissen*, pp. 168–216.

75. Pession ed., pp. 188–89. Briefly put, the first argument maintains that in God, as the first being, there can be no potentiality, whereas in every composite entity there is some admixture of potentiality and actuality. Therefore God cannot be composite and must be simple. A second argument maintains that every composite depends upon some prior agent and, therefore, that God as the first being cannot be composite. The third argument reasons that, as the first being, God is most perfect and therefore the best being. But the best can lack no goodness and cannot, therefore, be composed, for it would then lack the good of some of its parts.

76. Ed. cit., p. 191.

77. Ed. cit., p. 190. For the text from John Damascene see *De fide orthodoxa*, c. 4 (ed. cit., p. 19).

know that God is when "is" is taken in the second way; for this merely means that we know that the statement "God is" is true.[78]

In a. 4 Thomas uses three arguments based on the way of negation to show that names such as "good," "wise," "just," etc., do not predicate anything accidental in God.[79] Since names such as these do not appear to be negative but positive in that which they signify, Thomas's introduction of them easily leads him to a. 5. There he asks whether such names signify the divine substance.[80]

He begins by presenting what he himself regards as an extreme statement of the negative view. Some, most explicitly Moses Maimonides, held that names of this type may be understood in one of two ways. According to the first way, they may be taken as referring exclusively to a likeness that obtains between effects produced by God and other effects produced by us. Thus to say that God is wise is really nothing more than to indicate that he acts in the manner of one who is wise in or through his effects; this does not mean that wisdom is really something present in God himself. According to the second way of using such names, they are purely negative in meaning. When taken in this way, to say that God is living is not to describe anything actually present in God; it is only to deny of him the mode of being whereby nonliving things exist. So too, to say that God is intelligent is not to point to anything really present in God. It is only to deny of him the mode of being whereby brute animals exist.[81]

78. ". . . dicendum, quod ens est esse dicitur dupliciter, ut patet V *Metaph.* Quandoque enim significat essentiam rei, sive actum essendi; quandoque vero significat veritatem propositionis, etiam in his quae esse non habent: sicut dicimus quod caecitas est, quia verum est hominem esse caecum. Cum ergo dicat Damascenus, quod esse Dei est nobis manifestum, accipitur esse Dei secundo modo, et non primo. Primo enim modo est idem esse Dei quod est substantia: et sicut eius substantia est ignota, ita et esse. Secundo autem modo scimus quoniam Deus est, quoniam hanc propositionem in intellectu nostro concipimus ex effectibus ipsius" (pp. 191–92). Cf. my Ch. II above, n. 7 for other references to this.

79. Ed. cit., pp. 195–96. In a. 3 Thomas has offered three arguments to show that God is not in a genus. From this he concludes that God is not a species, nor an individual within a species, nor does he have any specific *differentia* (pp. 193–94). For discussion of this see M. Jordan, "The Names of God and the Being of Names," in *The Existence and Nature of God,* A. J. Freddoso, ed. (Notre Dame, Ind., 1983), p. 163. See p. 164 for his discussion of a. 4.

80. "Quinto quaeritur utrum praedicta nomina significant divinam substantiam" (ed. cit., p. 196). Cf. Jordan, *Ordering Wisdom: The Hierarchy of Philosophical Discourses,* pp. 164–67.

81. Ed. cit., p. 198. "Quidam posuerunt, quod ista nomina dicta de Deo, non significant divinam substantiam, quod maxime expresse dicit Rabbi Moyses. Dicit autem, huiusmodi nomina de Deo dupliciter esse intelligenda: Uno modo per similitudinem effectus, ut dicatur Deus sapiens non quia sapientia aliquid sit in ipso, sed quia ad modum sapientis in suis effectibus operatur. . . . Alio modo per modum negationis. . . ." For Maimonides see *The Guide of the Perplexed,* I, cc. 52–59 (pp. 114–43). Note especially c. 58 (pp. 134–37). For the medieval Latin version see *Dux seu Director dubitantium aut perplexorum* (Paris, 1520; repr. Frankfurt am Main, 1964), I, cc. 51–58 (ff. 18v–23v). For c. 57 (Latin version = c. 58 English) see ff. 22r–22v. Note the following text: "It has thus become clear to you that every attribute that we predicate of Him is an attribute of action or, if the attribute is intended for the apprehension of His essence and not of His action, it signifies the negation of the privation of the attribute in question" (English, p. 136; Latin f. 22v). For discussion of Maimonides (and Aquinas) concerning this see: H. A. Wolfson, "St. Thomas on Divine Attributes," in *Mélanges*

Thomas rejects both of these approaches as insufficient and incorrect *(inconveniens)*. Against the first he counters that there would then be no difference between our saying that God is wise, and that he is angry or that he is fire. He would be said to be angry simply because he acts in the way one does who is angry, for instance, by punishing sinners. And he would be said to be fire because he acts in the way fire acts when he purges. But such a position is opposed to the view of the saints and the prophets. When they speak of God, they approve affirming certain things of him, for instance, that he is wise or living, but reject others, for instance, that he is a body. According to Maimonides' position, at least as Thomas understands it, all things could with equal justification be affirmed and denied of God.[82]

Moreover, according to Catholic belief and, adds Thomas, according to Maimonides himself, the created world has not always existed. But if Maimonides' position were accepted, God could not be said to be wise or good before creatures actually existed. Before creation there were no effects through which God could act as one who is good or wise. Thomas finds such a claim contrary to sound faith, unless perhaps one qualifies the position to mean that before creation God *could* have acted as one who is wise, and could therefore have been called wise. But then one would be admitting that the term "wise" does point to something which actually exists in God and which is the divine substance; for whatever is present in God is identical with his substance.[83]

Thomas is equally critical of the second way of understanding divine names proposed by Maimonides. According to this view, the other names we predicate of God are to be understood as purely negative. Thomas counters that there is no name of any species by which some mode is not denied which would be inappropriate for God. For some difference is included in any specific name; and by such a difference some other species is denied. Thus the name lion includes the difference four-footed, thereby excluding bird, for instance. Hence if the names we assign to God were purely negative, just as we might call him living simply because his being is not inanimate, so we might equally well call him a lion because his mode of being is not birdlike. Moreover, Thomas reasons that every negation must be based

---

Offerts à Etienne Gilson (Paris, 1959), pp. 673–700; repr. in *Studies in Maimonides and St. Thomas Aquinas,* J. I. Dienstag, ed. (New York, 1975), pp. 1–28 (see note on p. 28); S. Feldman, "A Scholastic Misinterpretation of Maimonides' Doctrine of Divine Attributes," ibid., pp. 58–74; D. Burrell, *Knowing the Unknowable God* (Notre Dame, Ind., 1986), pp. 51–65; "Aquinas and Maimonides: A Conversation about Proper Speech," *Immanuel* 16 (1983), pp. 70–85; and the more recent but especially helpful study by A. Hyman, "Maimonides on Religious Language," in *Perspectives on Maimonides: Philosophical and Historical Studies,* J. L. Kraemer, ed. (Oxford, 1991), pp. 175–91. Unlike Aquinas Maimonides holds that there is a kind of causality in which there is no likeness between a cause and its effect(s), as in divine causality. For an earlier reference by Aquinas to Maimonides (and Avicenna) see *In I Sent.,* d. 2, q. 1, a. 3 (Mandonnet ed., Vol. 1, pp. 67–68). While Thomas's presentation of Maimonides' position is not as precise there as in *De potentia,* q. 7, a. 5, this may in part be owing to his effort in the earlier presentation to treat Avicenna and Maimonides together.
82. *De pot.,* q. 7, a. 5, p. 198.
83. Ibid.

on some affirmation. Unless the human intellect knew something positive about God, it could deny nothing of him.[84]

With these preliminaries out of the way, Thomas next presents his own position. With acknowledged dependency on Pseudo-Dionysius he counters that the names in question ("good," "just," "wise," etc.) do signify the divine substance although only imperfectly and in deficient fashion. Again he appeals to the similarity that must obtain between an effect and its cause. Since every agent acts insofar as it is in act and therefore produces something in some way like itself, the form of the effect must be present in some way in the agent cause. As Thomas well understands, it is the universality of this claim that Maimonides rejects. According to him, not every cause is like its effect, especially not God.[85]

Sometimes, continues Thomas, an effect is equal to the power of the cause. In such a case, the forms present in the agent and in the effect will be defined in the same way and belong to the same species. Such causes and effects are univocal. Sometimes the effect is not equal to the power of the cause. In these cases the form in question is not present in the same way in the cause and in the effect. It is present in more eminent fashion in the agent. Insofar as the form in question is present in the agent, the agent has the power to produce the effect. But since the agent's entire power is not expressed through its effect, the form is present in the agent in different and superior fashion than in the effect. As we have previously seen, Thomas describes such causes and effects as equivocal rather than as univocal.[86]

Thomas applies this to God's effects. No effect is equal to the divine power or God. Otherwise only one effect could proceed from that power, Thomas comments, a position he had always rejected as abhorrent. And if no effect can be equal to the power of its divine cause, it follows that the form found in any such effect cannot be understood in the same way when such a form is assigned to God. It must be present in him in a higher way. Hence the many forms realized in his different effects are united in God as in one common power. In like fashion the perfections of created things imitate God according to his unique and simple essence.[87]

Given this ontological situation, Thomas now draws his conclusion. Because our intellect takes its knowledge from created things, it is informed by the like-

---

84. Ed. cit., p. 198.

85. "Cum omne agens agat in quantum actu est, et per consequens agat aliqualiter simile, oportet formam facti aliquo modo esse in agente . . ." (ed. cit., p. 198). On Maimonides see n. 81 above and the reference to Hyman's article.

86. Ed. cit., p. 198. Note that Thomas illustrates this situation (equivocal agents) by citing the sun as the agent which generates fire. Cf. his appeal to the sun as the cause of heat in SCG I, c. 29.

87. ". . . et inde est quod omnes formae quae sunt in diversis effectibus distinctae et divisae ad invicem, in eo uniuntur sicut in una virtute communi. . . . Et similiter perfectiones rerum creatarum assimilantur Deo secundum unicam et simplicem essentiam eius" (ed. cit., pp. 198–99). Thomas was especially concerned with refuting the Avicennian theory of necessary emanation and its accompanying claim that from the supreme One only one effect can be produced immediately. See, for instance, De potentia, q. 3, a 16; De substantiis separatis, c. 10; and my "The Latin Avicenna as a Source for Thomas Aquinas's Metaphysics," esp. pp. 72–90.

nesses of perfections it discovers in creatures—for instance, likenesses or ideas of wisdom, power, goodness, and things of this type. And just as in the ontological order these creatures in some albeit imperfect way are likened to God, so too in the order of knowledge our intellect is informed by the ideas (literally: "species") of creaturely perfections.[88] As Thomas remarks, knowledge is a likening or assimilation of the intellect itself to that which is known. Therefore, he concludes, those things which the intellect thinks or says when it is informed by the likenesses of such perfections must truly exist in God. For God is the one to whom all such likenesses are similar. But if an intelligible species or idea in our intellect were adequate or equal to the divine essence in imitating it, such an idea would then comprehend the divine essence. And such a conception on the part of our intellect would give us a perfect understanding or grasp of God.[89]

Thomas reminds us, of course, that no species or idea in the human intellect is a perfect assimilation or imitation of the divine essence. Because of this, names which we apply to God to express such concepts do signify that reality which is the divine substance, but they do not signify it perfectly as it is in itself. They signify it only insofar as it is understood by us.[90]

At this point Thomas seems to be trying to reconcile his defense of some kind of positive knowledge of God's substance with his earlier claim that we cannot know what God is, but only what he is not. As Thomas now puts it, such names, i.e., names of pure perfections such as "good," "wise," "just," etc., do signify the divine substance, but not so as to enable us to comprehend it; they do so only imperfectly.[91] For this reason, he again comments that the name "He who is" is

---

88. Ed. cit., p. 199. Note: "Unde sicut res creatae per suas perfectiones aliqualiter,—licet deficienter,—Deo assimilantur, ita et intellectus noster harum perfectionum speciebus informatur."

89. Ibid.

90. Ibid. "Non autem perfecte divinam essentiam assimilat species praedicta, ut dictum est; et ideo licet huiusmodi nomina, quae intellectus ex talibus conceptionibus Deo attribuit, significent id quod est divina substantia, non tamen perfecte ipsam significent secundum quod est, sed secundum quod a nobis intelligitur."

91. "Sic ergo dicendum est, quod quodlibet istorum nominum significant divinam substantiam, non tamen quasi comprehendens ipsam, sed imperfecte. . ." (ibid.). The proper interpretation of Thomas's meaning in this context has long divided his interpreters. See, for instance J. Maritain, *Distinguish to Unite or the Degrees of Knowledge*, p. 425: "Names signifying, although ananoetically, '*id quod est divina substantia*' do indeed tell us in some manner what God is. Consequently, although on this earth we cannot in any degree or in any way know God as He is in Himself (this is exclusively reserved for the beatific vision), it is clear that we can, nevertheless, know what God is in a more-or-less imperfect, but always true, fashion." Here Maritain is criticizing a much more agnostic interpretation concerning our knowledge of the divine essence or substance proposed by A. Sertillanges. But for a critique of Maritain's reading see Gilson, *The Christian Philosophy of St. Thomas Aquinas*, p. 109, and p. 458, n. 47: "In using this text, on which Jacques Maritain bases his own interpretation . . . , we must keep in mind the exact thesis which St. Thomas is developing, namely that the divine names signify the substance of God, that is, they designate it as actually being what the names signify. It does not follow from this that these designations give us a positive conception of what the divine substance is." Also see n. 51. For critical reaction to Gilson's general position concerning this see

most fittingly applied to God since this name signifies without determining any restricting form to God. It signifies *esse* without any added determinations. So too, he again remarks, John Damascene notes that this name signifies an infinite ocean of substance.[92]

Thomas concludes his reply by citing a passage from *The Divine Names* of Pseudo-Dionysius: "The Divinity precontains in itself all existent things in simple and unlimited fashion."[93] Thomas explains that by "simple fashion" Dionysius means that the perfections present in creatures according to different forms are attributed to God according to his simple essence. And by "unlimited fashion" Dionysius means that no perfection found in a creature captures *(comprehendit)* the divine essence in such a way that by understanding that perfection our intellect might define God in himself.[94]

From all of this we may conclude that in the *De potentia* Thomas clearly defends the human intellect's capacity in this life to apply certain names to God substantially. This means that such names are not predicated of God accidentally, to be sure, but also that they do signify in some way that which God is in himself. By admitting so much, one wonders whether or not Thomas has not now allowed for some imperfect quidditative knowledge of God. He has surely allowed for some kind of positive knowledge of God when we predicate such names, since he has explicitly developed his own position against the extremely negative approach of Moses Maimonides.[95] At the same time, he has also warned us that his present position does not imply that we can comprehend or define the divine essence. Because creaturely perfections all fall short of perfectly reflecting or imitating God's essence, so do any concepts we may derive from such perfections. But, someone may still insist, has Thomas not now allowed for some quidditative knowledge of God?

The first argument for the opposed position reflects the concern we have just expressed. If *esse* can be predicated substantially of something, in that case this term

---

J.-H. Nicolas, *Dieu connu comme inconnu. Essai d'une critique de la connaissance théologique* (Paris, 1966), pp. 87–91 and the corresponding notes. Cf. p. 144 and n. 29.

92. ". . . et propter hoc, nomen *Qui est,* maxime Deo competit, quia non determinat aliquam formam Deo, sed significat esse indeterminate" (ed. cit., p. 199). For his earlier discussion in *In I Sent.,* d. 8, q. 1, a. 1, ad 4, see n. 9 above in this Chapter.

93. "Haec autem solutio confirmatur per verba Dionysii, qui dicit . . . quod quia Divinitas omnia simpliciter et incircumfinite in seipsa existentia praeaccipit, ex diversis convenienter laudatur et nominatur" (ed. cit., p. 199). Cf. *De divinis nominibus* I, 7 (Pera ed., p. 26, n. 26 [Pseudo-Dionysius] and c. I, lect. 3, p. 31, n. 101 [Thomas]) Also see *Dionysiaca. Recueil donnant l'ensemble des traductions des ouvrages attribués au Denys de l'Aréopage* (Bruges, 1937), Vol. 1, p. 50.

94. Ibid. Note especially: "*Incircumfinite* dicit, ad ostendendum quod nulla perfectio in creaturis inventa divinam essentiam comprehendit, ut sic intellectus sub ratione illius perfectionis in seipso Deum definiat."

95. Ed. cit., p. 198. In his *In I Sent.,* d. 2, q. 1, a. 3 Thomas attempts to reconcile the views of Avicenna and Maimonides, on the one hand, and those of Pseudo-Dionysius and Anselm, on the other (Mandonnet, ed., Vol. 1, p. 69). Here in the *De potentia* he attempts no such harmonization.

will signify what the thing's substance is. In other words, it will imply quidditative knowledge. But this runs counter to John Damascene's view. According to him, when such names are said of God they do not signify what he is according to his substance. Hence, runs the argument, such names cannot be predicated substantially of God as if they signify his substance.[96]

Thomas replies that Damascene means to say that such names do not signify what God is as if to define and comprehend his substance.[97] This is, of course, an important reiteration of a point Thomas has already made. If he now holds that such names may be predicated substantially of God, this does not mean that such predication yields any comprehensive or defining knowledge of him.

According to the second argument for the contrary, no name which signifies the substance of a thing can be denied of that thing. But according to Pseudo-Dionysius, with respect to the divine, negations are true, while affirmations are inexact *(incompactae)*. Hence such names do not signify the divine substance.[98]

Thomas responds by appealing once more to the distinction between the thing signified by such names *(res significata)* and the way in which they signify *(modus significandi)*. Pseudo-Dionysius did not intend to assert that such affirmations are false and inexact as regards that which they signify. On the contrary, they are truly attributed to God as regards that which they signify. What they signify is in some way present in him. But as regards the way in which they signify, this is indeed to be denied of God; for every such name signifies some definite or determined form and cannot be attributed to him in that way. Because such names do not belong to God in the way in which they are signified, they are to be denied of him. And the way in which they signify reflects the way in which they inhere in our intellects.[99]

Thomas goes on to apply to such names once more the threefold Dionysian way. According to the affirmative way, such names are to be affirmed of God. When we say that God is wise, for instance, we mean that there is in him some likeness of the wisdom which flows forth from him into creatures and which we discover in them. But according to the negative way, we understand that wisdom is not present in God in the way we understand and name it in creatures. Hence we can

96. Ed. cit, pp. 196–97. For Damascene see *De fide orthodoxa* I, c. 9 (p. 48:8–12).

97. Ed. cit., p. 199.

98. Ed. cit., p. 197. In quoting Dionysius's *De caelesti hierarchia,* c. 2 ("in divinis negationes sunt verae, affirmationes vero imcompactae") Thomas appears to fuse the translations by John Scotus Eriugena and John the Saracen. For both see Durantel, *Saint Thomas et le Pseudo-Denys* (Paris, 1919), p. 73. Cf. ST I, q. 13, a. 12, ad 1 (Leon. 4.164, 165). For an earlier reference to this see *In I Sent.,* d. 22, q. 1, a. 2 (p. 534).

99. Ed. cit., p. 199: ". . . quantum enim ad rem significatam, Deo vere attribuuntur, quae in eo aliquo modo est, ut iam ostensum est; sed quantum ad modum quem significant de Deo negari possunt. . . . modus enim significatus est secundum quod sunt in intellectu nostro. . . . unde affirmatio incompacta dicitur quasi non omnino convenienter coniuncta propter diversum modum."

say God is not wise. However, wisdom is not denied of him because his wisdom is deficient. It is present in him in more eminent fashion than can be understood or expressed by us. Therefore, according to the third Dionysian way, we say that he is superwise.[100]

But we may still ask precisely what Thomas means by denying that we can know what God is, and to what extent this claim can be reconciled with the view expressed here that certain names may be predicated of him substantially. The sixth argument for the opposite position maintains that, according to Aristotle, names signify concepts *(conceptiones)* on the part of the intellect. But we cannot understand the divine substance, since we cannot know of God what he is but only that he is. Therefore we can neither name him nor signify his substance. Thomas simply replies that this argument shows that we cannot name God by any name which would define or comprehend or be adequate to his substance. It is in this sense that we do not know what God is.[101] But is this all Thomas intends to say when he denies that we can know what God is? Would he not also deny that we can have quidditative or comprehensive knowledge of other things, such as separate substances (angels), or for that matter, of many material entities?

e. *Summa theologiae* I (1266–1268)

Before offering our final comments concerning this, we shall consider some texts from *Summa theologiae* I. As we have noted at the beginning of this chapter, in qq. 3 through 11, Thomas concentrates on different ways of showing how God is not.[102] In q. 12 he investigates how God is known by us, and finally in q. 13 how he is named by us. In qq. 3 through 11 Thomas attempts to establish God's simplicity, perfection, infinity, immutability, and unity. In this effort, as we can easily anticipate, he follows the way of negation, at least in most cases. For instance, in q. 3 he uses this approach in order to remove all composition from God, and thereby establishes the divine simplicity. Somewhat more surprisingly, perhaps, but consistent with his approach in SCG I, c. 28, in q. 4 he continues to use the way of negation to show that God is perfect. Thus in a. 1 of this question Thomas recalls that God is the first efficient cause. As such he must not be in potency (like a material cause), but must be in act to the maximum degree. And this is for him to be supremely perfect, i.e., not lacking in any perfection.[103]

---

100. Ibid.

101. For arg. 6 see p. 197. For Thomas's reply see pp. 199–200: ". . . ratio illa probat quod Deus non potest nominari nomine substantiam ipsius definiente vel comprehendente vel adaequante: sic enim de Deo ignoramus quid est."

102. See Leon. 4.35.

103. See q. 4, a. 1 (Leon. 4.50). Note especially: "Secundum hoc enim dicitur aliquid esse perfectum, secundum quod est actu: nam perfectum dicitur, cui nihil deest secundum modum suae perfectionis." Also cf. a. 2: "Respondeo dicendum quod in Deo sunt perfectiones omnium rerum.

After discussing the nature of the good in general, especially the transcendental good, in q. 5, Thomas devotes q. 6 to the goodness of God. In q. 6, a. 1 he draws upon the general notion that something is good insofar as it is an object of desire *(appetibile)*. But each and every thing desires its own perfection. And the perfection and form of an effect is a certain likeness of its agent cause. This follows because every agent produces something that is like itself, which Thomas here accepts as needing no proof. By reasoning from effect to cause, he concludes that the agent itself must be desirable, and therefore share in what we understand by the good. For what is desired of the agent is that its likeness be participated in (by others). Thomas then applies this reasoning to God. Because God is the first efficient cause of all else, he too must be good and desirable.[104]

In sum, therefore, in this argument Thomas again reasons from effects to God as their cause. If goodness is found in God's effects (which Thomas can here assume, since he has argued in q. 5, a. 3 that every being is good), and if every agent produces something that is like itself, then as the first agent, God himself must be good. At the same time, it is not immediately evident how this argument continues to follow the path of negation. Yet Thomas's earlier remarks indicate that this must be so. Perhaps he would have us remember that the discussion of God's goodness follows upon and presupposes the argumentation for God's perfection. That argument, as we have seen, turns on the denial of any kind of potentiality to God and concludes that as first efficient cause he is pure actuality. It is also aimed at showing that he does not lack any excellence of any kind. Such reasoning does follow the path of negation both in its argumentation and in its conclusion that any lack of excellence is to be denied of God.[105]

Our general interpretation of the argumentation in q. 6, a. 1 appears to be confirmed by that presented in a. 2. There Thomas wishes to show that God is the supreme good in the absolute sense, not merely within a given genus or order of things. He recalls that goodness is attributed to God as the first cause from whom all desired perfections flow. (This observation seems to connect the previous argument with that based on divine perfection.) But now Thomas adds that perfections do not flow

---

Unde et dicitur universaliter perfectus: quia non deest ei aliqua nobilitas quae inveniatur in aliquo genere . . ." (p. 51). Also see the second argument in the corpus of a. 2 (p. 51). Note: "Unde, cum Deus sit ipsum esse subsistens, nihil de perfectione essendi potest ei deesse."

104. Leon. 4.66. Note especially: "Perfectio autem et forma effectus est quaedam similitudo agentis: cum omne agens agat sibi simile. Unde ipsum agens est appetibile, et habet rationem boni: hoc enim est quod de ipso appetitur, ut eius similitudo participetur. Cum ergo Deus sit prima causa effectiva omnium, manifestum est quod sibi competit ratio boni et appetibilis."

105. See q. 4, Prologue (ed. cit., p. 50): "Post considerationem divinae simplicitatis, de perfectione ipsius Dei dicendum est. Et quia unumquodque, secundum quod perfectum est, sic dicitur bonum, primo agendum est de perfectione divina; secundo de eius bonitate." Also see q. 5, a. 3 where, while supporting the claim that every being is good, he comments: "Omne enim ens, inquantum est ens, est in actu, et quodammodo perfectum . . ." (p. 59).

from God as from an agent which is univocal with its effects, but rather as from an agent which does not agree in species or in genus with any of them. In such a cause (here again described by Thomas as equivocal) the likeness of the effect is present in more excellent fashion and, in the case of God, in most excellent fashion. Therefore God is the supreme good.[106] As Thomas clarifies in replying to the third objection, this is not to say that God belongs to a higher genus than does any creature. It is rather to say that God is outside every genus and is the principle of every genus. Hence he is related to all else by surpassing them all as the supreme good.[107]

That Thomas still believes he is following the path of negation when dealing with the divine goodness also emerges from his discussion in a. 3. In his effort to show that God alone is good through his essence, Thomas notes that everything is said to be good insofar as it is perfect. Again the use of the *via negativa* to establish the divine perfection lies in the background. After distinguishing a threefold perfection for things, Thomas argues that this threefold perfection belongs to no creature of its essence. God alone is completely perfect of his essence since in him alone are essence and act of being identical, i.e., not distinct. Therefore he alone is good of his essence.[108] We conclude, therefore, that in establishing the fact that God is good, Thomas continues to use the path of succeeding negations. This does not imply, of course, that he regards goodness itself as negative in content. But it does account for his including the discussion of divine goodness within the sequence of questions running from qq. 3 to 11 in the *Prima Pars* of the *Summa*. And as in SCG I he uses a notion that is still negative in content, divine perfection, to establish God's goodness, a positive perfection.

In taking up God's infinity in q. 7, Thomas returns to a notion which is negative in content. Hence the path of negation applies both to the method he uses in showing that God is infinite, and to the notion of infinity itself. As he puts it in a. 1, something is said to be infinite by reason of the fact that it is not finite. After distinguishing two kinds of infinity—that of matter and that of form—he concludes that only the latter type signifies perfection. The act of being *(esse)* is the most formal of all. Because the divine *esse* is not received in anything else which

---

106. Leon. 4.67. Cf. q. 4, a. 3, where Thomas distinguishes different ways in which things may be similar to one another. The least degree of similarity obtains when effect and cause do not agree either in species or in genus, but only according to some kind of analogy. It is only in this way that creatures are like God (see pp. 53–54). Note that on p. 54 Thomas again appeals to the similitude axiom. Since every agent produces something like itself insofar as it is an agent, and each thing acts in accord with its form, there must be some likeness of the form of the agent in the effect.

107. Leon. 4.67.

108. Leon. 4.68. The three kinds of perfection are (1) perfection in a thing's very being *(esse)*; (2) perfection through certain accidents which a thing needs in order to complete its operations; (3) perfection reached by attaining something else as its end. Only the first kind of perfection pertains to God, a point which Thomas establishes by eliminating the other two types in the case of God, i.e., by using the way of negation.

could limit it (for God is his own *esse*), God is infinite and perfect. Hence this argumentation is also negative, as is the conclusion established by it.[109]

In q. 8 Thomas deals with God's presence in all things. The opening remark indicates that God's omnipresence follows from his infinity; hence the proof of God's omnipresence is again based on the *via negativa* at least insofar as the proof of divine infinity was.[110] Thomas's added argument for God's omnipresence in a. 1 rests heavily on the point that all other being *(esse)* has God as its creating and conserving cause. Therefore, so long as anything other than God exists, God must be present to it.[111] In establishing the immutability of God in q. 9, Thomas is obviously dealing with a notion that is negative in content. He also follows the way or method of negation in establishing the fact that God is immutable. He does this by excluding all potentiality, composition, and internal motion from God.[112] As Thomas shows in q. 10, a. 1, the very notion of eternity rests on a negation of any limits (beginning or end) to duration, and a negation of succession.[113] And as he indicates in a. 2, it is because God is supremely immutable that he is also eternal.[114] Hence Thomas is again also following the way of negation both in his argumentation for eternity and in terms of its intelligible content.

In q. 11 Thomas takes up the issue of God's unity. As he shows in a. 1, the notion of unity or oneness of being is itself negative, since it adds nothing to being but signifies a negation of division. He goes on to show that the one and being are convertible. In a. 3 Thomas offers three arguments to establish the fact that God is

109. Leon. 4.72.: ". . . infinitum dicitur aliquid ex eo quod non est finitum. . . . Cum igitur esse divinum non sit esse receptum in aliquod, sed ipse sit suum esse subsistens . . . manifestum est quod ipse Deus sit infinitus et perfectus." On this see my "Thomas Aquinas and the Axiom That Unreceived Act is Unlimited," pp. 547–48. Also see W. J. Hankey, *God in Himself: Aquinas' Doctrine of God as Expounded in the Summa Theologiae* (Oxford, 1987), p. 76. This book rightly stresses Thomas's debt to various forms of Neoplatonism in developing his own theology, but overstates the case. It should be used with caution in its treatment of various philosophical elements in Thomas's thought—for instance, his views on the subject of metaphysics and the relationship of this subject to God (see pp. 63–67 and Endnote I, pp. 162–63). For an accurate but critical review see B. C. Bazán, *Speculum* 65 (1990), pp. 166–70.

110. See q. 8, Prologue (Leon. 4.82): "Quia vero infinito convenire videtur quod ubique et in omnibus sit, considerandum est utrum hoc Deo conveniat." Cf. q. 7, Prologue (p. 72).

111. See q. 8, a. 1 (p. 82): "Quandiu igitur res habet esse, tandiu oportet quod Deus adsit ei, secundum modum quo esse habet. . . ." This argument is not so obviously based on the way of negation except insofar as it rests on the argument from effect to cause intended to show that God is the first (and *un*caused) cause of all other *esse*.

112. See q. 9, a. 1 (ed. cit., p. 90). The first argument maintains that whatever is changed in any way is in some way in potency, something which must be excluded from God. The second maintains that there must be some composition in anything that is moved, something which likewise must be denied of God because of his simplicity. The third argument reasons that whatever is moved acquires something or reaches something it did not previously have, all of which is to be denied of God because he is infinite in perfection. For more detailed discussion and reinforcement also see a. 2, where Thomas shows that to be completely immobile is proper to God alone (pp. 91–92).

113. See q. 10, a. 1 (Leon. 4.94).

114. Ed. cit., p. 96.

one (unique), i.e., that there is only one God. Since these have been discussed in the previous chapter, I would simply note here that of these at least the first two follow the way of negation.[115] According to Thomas's announced plan, with the end of q. 11 he completes his effort to show how God is not.

Thomas had indicated that with q. 12 he would begin to show how God is known by us. At the beginning of q. 12 Thomas comments that in what has gone before (qq. 3–11) he has considered how God exists when he is simply considered in himself. Now in q. 12 he will seek to determine how God enters into our knowledge, i.e., how he is known by creatures.[116] A number of the articles in q. 12 have to do with the knowledge of God which is available to the blessed in the life to come. Nonetheless, to the extent that these discussions cast additional light on Thomas's views concerning how God may be known by us in this life, they, too, will be examined.

In a. 1 Thomas simply asks whether any created intellect can see God's essence. Thomas rejects the view of some who hold that no created intellect can ever see the divine essence. A human being's highest happiness must consist in that being's highest operation, an operation of the intellect. If the created intellect could never see God's essence, either it would never attain beatitude, or its beatitude would consist in something other than God. Thomas rejects this position as opposed to faith, because the ultimate perfection of a rational creature must be the principle of its being. (Although Thomas does not here spell this out, this appeal to faith directly eliminates the second alternative, according to which the intellect's happiness would consist in something other than God.) Thomas also rejects this as opposed to reason. He notes that there is in human beings a natural desire to know a cause once an effect is understood. If the rational intellect could never reach the first cause of all things, this natural desire to understand would remain unfulfilled. Hence on both theological and philosophical grounds Thomas concludes that the blessed do see God's essence.[117]

Even so, Thomas's replies to objections 1 and 3 indicate that not even the blessed can *comprehend* the divine essence, although they can see it. This point is important for our purposes, for it suggests that even if a creature may see God's essence, no

115. For a. 1 see Leon. 4.107. For a. 3 see p. 111. Also see above, Ch. XII, nn. 124, 125, 131, and my discussion there of these passages.

116. See q. 3, Introduction (Leon. 4.35). From q. 12, Introduction, note: "Quia in superioribus consideravimus qualiter Deus sit secundum seipsum, restat considerandum qualiter sit in cognitione nostra, idest quomodo cognoscatur a creaturis" (p. 114).

117. See q. 12, a. 1 (Leon. 4.114–15). Note in particular: ". . . si nunquam essentiam Dei videre potest intellectus creatus, vel nunquam beatitudinem obtinebit, vel in alio eius beatitudo consistet quam in Deo. Quod est alienum a fide. . . . Similiter etiam est praeter rationem. . . . Unde simpliciter concedendum est quod beati Dei essentiam videant." Hankey refers to the "immense literature on the question whether there is natural desire and capacity of man for beatitude in Aquinas" (*God in Himself*, pp. 83–84, n. 8). In addition to the references he offers there, I would recommend J. Laporta, *La destinée de la nature humaine selon Thomas d'Aquin* (Paris, 1965). For my review see *Speculum* 44 (1969), pp. 474–76.

creature will ever comprehend it. Hence it follows that when Thomas denies that we can have quidditative knowledge of God in this life, he certainly intends to deny that we can reach comprehensive knowledge of him. Indeed, we can never attain such knowledge.[118] But the quidditative knowledge he denies to us in this life is granted to the blessed in the life to come. They will see God's essence.

In a. 2 Thomas makes the point that when the divine essence is considered as an object which is to be known, it cannot be seen through any created likeness or species which would represent it as it is in itself. Any created intelligible species or likeness can only directly represent some created form. Thomas's point is that when the blessed see the divine essence, they must do so directly and not through any created likeness that might represent it. However, he concludes that some similitude is required from the side of the knowing power if God's essence is to be seen by the blessed, and refers to this as the light of glory *(lumen gloriae)*. This strengthens the intellect of the blessed so that such persons may see God. In a. 4 Thomas explains that no created intellect can see God in his essence unless God conjoins himself through his grace to that intellect and strengthens it so as to be understood by it. In other words, through its purely natural powers no created intellect, whether human or angelic, can see the divine essence.[119]

In a. 7 Thomas develops more fully the distinction between seeing God's essence and comprehending it. To comprehend something is to know it perfectly. And something is known perfectly only when it is known as fully as it is knowable. But no created intellect can ever know the divine essence as fully as it is knowable. For something is knowable insofar as it is a being in actuality. Because God's *esse* is infinite, God is infinitely knowable. It is true that one of the blessed may know God more perfectly than another insofar as the intellect of the former is filled with a greater *lumen gloriae*. But no created intellect can receive an infinite *lumen gloriae*. Hence, even though the blessed will see God, none of them can ever comprehend him.[120]

In a. 11 Thomas emphasizes the point that no mere human being can see God's essence unless he or she is separated from this mortal life. So long as we live in this mortal life our souls attain natural knowledge only of things which have forms present in matter and of other things which can be known by means of them. And as Thomas has already shown in a. 2, a knowledge of God gained by means of any created likeness is not a vision of the divine essence.[121] However, in replying to the second objection, Thomas seems to soften this a bit. He acknowledges that by

---

118. See objections 1 and 3 (Leon. 4.114), and Thomas's replies (p. 115). Note in particular ad 3: "Unde ex hoc non sequitur quod nullo modo possit cognosci, sed quod omnem cognitionem excedat: quod est ipsum non comprehendi."

119. See q. 12, a. 2 (Leon. 4.116–17). For a. 4 see pp. 120–21. Also see a. 5 and ad 2 on the role of the *lumen gloriae* as required for a created intellect to see the divine essence (p. 123).

120. See q. 12, a. 7 (Leon. 4.127).

121. For q. 12, a. 11 see Leon. 4.134–35.

operating supernaturally and beyond the normal course of events God has elevated the minds of some who were still living in the flesh but not then using their bodily senses so as to enable them to reach a vision of his essence.[122] (He points to Moses and to Paul as examples, and refers to his subsequent discussion of rapture in the *Secunda Secundae* [see q. 175, aa. 3–6]. There he explains that Paul's soul was completely elevated at the moment of rapture from dependence on phantasms and the senses.)[123]

In a. 12 Thomas returns explicitly to the issue of philosophical knowledge of God. He repeats the by now familiar point that because our natural knowledge begins with sense experience, it can extend only so far as we can be led by sensible things. But we can never move from sensible things to a direct vision of the divine essence; for sensible creatures are effects which are in no way equal to God's power. Therefore a knowledge of God based on his sensible effects can never reveal the total power of God nor, consequently, his essence. As so many times before, therefore, Thomas concludes that a knowledge of such effects is enough for us to know of God that he is, as well as those things which pertain to him insofar as he is the first cause of all else, surpassing all his effects. Hence we know of him in his relationship to creatures in that he is the cause of them all, and they all differ from him. We deny that God is any of these things he causes, not because of any deficiency on his part but because he surpasses them all. In other words, here again Thomas returns to the threefold Dionysian way of knowing God—by causality, by negation, and by supereminence or transcendence.[124]

If the discussion in a. 12 has to do with our natural or philosophical knowledge of God, in a. 13 Thomas notes that a more perfect knowledge of God is given to us by revelation based on grace even in this life. Even so, as he indicates in replying to the first objection, through revelation based on grace we still do not know what God is and are still, therefore, joined to him as it were to one who is unknown. Hence even this additional knowledge given to us by revelation, for instance, that God is three and one, does not tell us what God is.[125]

With this we turn to q. 13. As Thomas again reminds us, here he wishes to determine how God is named by us. As he comments in his opening remarks, the

---

122. Ed. cit., p. 135: ". . . dicendum quod, sicut Deus miraculose aliquid supernaturaliter in rebus corporeis operatur, ita etiam et supernaturaliter, et praeter communem ordinem, mentes aliquorum in hac carne viventium, sed non sensibus carnis utentium, usque ad visionem suae essentiae elevavit. . . ."

123. For ST II–II, q. 175, aa. 3–6 see Leon. 10.404–9.

124. Leon. 4.136: "Utrum per rationem naturalem Deum in hac vita cognoscere possimus." Note from Thomas's reply: "Unde ex sensibilium cognitione non potest tota Dei virtus cognosci: et per consequens nec eius essentia videri." See his reply to obj. 1. Human reason can never arrive at a simple form (especially God) so as to know of it what it is, but it can know of it that it is. This implies that for Thomas it is the same thing to deny that we can have quidditative knowledge of God and to deny that we can know God's essence. From this one may also conclude that if the blessed enjoy knowledge of God's essence, they also have quidditative knowledge of him.

125. Leon. 4.137–38.

way we apply names to a thing follows upon the way we know that thing.[126] Hence the discussion in q. 13 naturally follows from that offered in q. 12. In a. 1 Thomas once more defends the point that we can apply names to God. He notes that words are signs of thoughts on the part of the intellect, and thoughts are likenesses of things. Hence a word is used to signify a thing by means of some conception on the part of the intellect. It follows from this that only insofar as something can be known by the intellect can it be named by us. Thomas recalls that he has already shown that in this life God cannot be seen by us in his essence. He is known to us from creatures by reason of their relationship to him as their cause, and by the ways of negation and preeminence. Thomas repeats his long-held view that if God can be named by us from creatures, these names do not express the divine essence as it is in itself—in the way, for instance, the name "man" signifies the essence of man as it is in itself, i.e., by signifying a definition that manifests its essence.[127]

In sum, therefore, the knowledge of "what God is" which Thomas still denies to us is now equated with the kind which grasps the essence of something and expresses this through a definition. If we connect this with his discussion in q. 12 about comprehensive knowledge of God, we may conclude that Thomas denies to us in the present life not only comprehensive knowledge, but any knowledge of God's essence which would enable us to grasp that essence as it is in itself in the way we can grasp the essence of something such as a human being and define it. Hence both comprehensive knowledge and knowledge of God's essence are ruled out. As Thomas puts it in replying to the first objection, God's essence is above that which we understand of him and signify through any word or name.[128]

In replying to objection 2 Thomas returns to a distinction we have seen him making previously. The names we assign to God signify in a way or mode which is appropriate to material creatures; for we move from knowledge of creatures to knowledge of God. But because subsisting creatures of this kind are composite, and their forms are not complete subsistent entities in themselves, all the names we use to signify something as a complete subsistent entity signify concretely, and therefore in a way that is appropriate for composite entities. On the other hand, the names we use to signify simple forms do not signify something as subsisting but only as that whereby something is. Thus whiteness signifies that whereby something is white. Because God is both simple and subsisting, we assign abstract names to him to signify his simplicity, and concrete names to signify him as subsisting.

---

126. See q. 13, Introd. (Leon. 4.139): "Consideratis his quae ad divinam cognitionem pertinent, procedendum est ad considerationem divinorum nominum: unumquodque enim nominatur a nobis, secundum quod ipsum cognoscimus."

127. Ibid. Note especially: ". . . voces sunt signa intellectuum, et intellectus sunt rerum similitudines. Et sic patet quod voces referuntur ad res significandas, mediante conceptione intellectus. . . . Sic igitur [Deus] potest nominari a nobis ex creaturis: non tamen ita quod nomen significans ipsum, exprimat divinam essentiam secundum quod est. . . ."

128. Ibid.

But both ways or modes fall short of signifying him as he is in himself, just as our intellect in this life does not know him as he is in himself.[129]

Lest we draw too negative a picture about our ability to name God, Thomas turns in a. 2 to the possibility of our predicating certain names of him substantially. He immediately eliminates from this discussion those names which are negative in content, and those which simply signify God's relationship to creatures. Rather than signify his substance, the former deny something of him and the latter signify his relation to other things, or better phrased, the relation of other things to him. As for names which are said absolutely and positively of God, such as "good," "wise," etc., Thomas again notes that this issue is disputed. Some hold that even these names, though they are applied to God in affirmative fashion, in fact remove or deny something of him rather than posit anything in him. In terms reminiscent of his discussion in q. 7, a. 5 of the De potentia, he comments that according to this view, when we say that God is living, we really mean that he does not exist in the way inanimate things do. Once more he assigns this view (position 1) to Moses Maimonides. Others (position 2) hold that these names are merely intended to signify God's relationship to creatures. For instance, to say that God is good merely means that he is the cause of goodness in created things.[130]

As in the De potentia Thomas again rejects both of these views, and this time for three reasons. First of all, neither of these positions can account for the fact that certain names may be said of God in preference to others. Thus God is the cause of bodies as well as of goodness. According to the second position, therefore, one could with equal justification describe God as a body and refer to him as good. And according to the first position, one might say that God is a body in order to deny that he is pure potency, i.e., prime matter. As a second criticism, Thomas reasons that all names would be said of God in secondary fashion, just as "healthy" is said of medicine in that way because medicine causes health in an animal. Thirdly, Thomas appeals to the intention of those who speak about God. They have something more in mind when they refer to him as living than merely to say that he is the cause of life in us, or that he differs from nonliving things.[131]

Against such positions Thomas concludes that names of this kind do signify the divine substance, and are predicated of God substantially. Nonetheless, they fall short of representing him. For they can only signify God in the way the human intellect can know him. And because our intellect knows God by reasoning from creatures, it can only know him in the way creatures represent him. Therefore such names signify the divine substance imperfectly, just as creatures imperfectly represent him. When we say that God is good, our meaning is not that God is the cause

129. Leon. 4.139–40. See ad 3 for more on the grammatical limitations of the names we may apply to God.

130. "Utrum aliquod nomen dicatur de Deo substantialiter" (Leon. 4.141). In De potentia, q. 7, a. 5 he attributes both views to Maimonides. See above, n. 81.

131. Leon. 4.141.

of goodness, as position 2 would have it, or that he is not evil, as position 1 holds. We mean that what we call goodness in creatures preexists in God in higher fashion. Hence we should not think that because God causes goodness he is good. It is because he is good that he causes goodness in things.[132]

In replying to objection 1 Thomas comments on a text taken from John Damascene which also appeared in an objection in *De potentia*, q. 7, a. 5. Those things which are said of God do not signify what he is according to his substance but what he is not, or a certain relationship, or one of those things which follow upon his nature or operation. Thomas again counters that by saying that none of these names signifies what God is, Damascene means that "what God is" is not perfectly expressed by any of them. Each signifies him imperfectly, just as creatures imperfectly represent him. And in his reply to objection 3, Thomas repeats the point that we cannot know God's essence in this life as it is in itself, but we can know it insofar as it is represented by created perfections.[133]

In sum, therefore, as in the *De potentia*, Thomas now explicitly defends the possibility of our predicating the names of pure perfections of God in substantial fashion. At the least, this means that they do signify the divine substance and do, therefore, signify something which is really present in God. They do so only insofar as they express concepts derived from our experience of perfections present in creatures. Because of the imperfect way such perfections represent God, names based on such perfections only imperfectly signify the divine substance. Moreover, they always carry with them the liability of the way in which they signify, their *modus significandi*, a liability which applies in one way to names which are predicated abstractly, and in another to names which are predicated concretely.

Awareness of these points may help us understand why Thomas continues to insist that such names do not give or imply any quidditative knowledge of God on our part and, even less so, any comprehensive knowledge of God. Comprehensive knowledge of God's essence is not even possible for the blessed, whether human or angelic. Quidditative knowledge, or essential knowledge, would enable us to grasp the divine essence as it is in itself, in the way we can grasp the essence of man and define it. Such quidditative or essential knowledge, while granted to the blessed, is not possible for us in this life. But given these qualifications, Thomas does defend the possibility of our reaching an imperfect positive knowledge of God in this life,

---

132. Leon. 4.141–42. Note especially: "Et ideo aliter dicendum est, quod huiusmodi quidem nomina significant substantiam divinam, et praedicantur de Deo substantialiter, sed deficiunt a repraesentatione ipsius. . . . Sic igitur praedicta nomina divinam substantiam significant: imperfecte tamen, sicut et creaturae imperfecte eam repraesentant. Cum igitur dicitur *Deus est bonus*, non est sensus, *Deus est causa bonitatis*, vel *Deus non est malus*: sed est sensus, *id quod bonitatem dicimus in creaturis, praeexistit in Deo*, et hoc quidem secundum modum altiorem. . . ." Cf. *In I Sent.*, d. 2, q. 1, a. 3 (Mandonnet ed., Vol. 1, p. 71). But there Thomas does not say that such names can be predicated of God substantially, although he does state that they are truly and properly said of him.

133. Leon. 4.141–42. For the reference in *De potentia*, q. 7, a. 5, obj. 1 and reply see ed. cit, pp. 196–97, 199. For John Damascene see *De fide orthodoxa*, c. 9 (ed. cit., p. 48:9–12).

a knowledge which may be philosophical, and a knowledge which enables us to apply certain names to him substantially.

With this background in mind, we are not surprised to find Thomas also defending in q. 13, a. 3 the possibility of our applying certain names to God properly, a position he had maintained since his Commentary on I *Sentences*. He again appeals to the distinction between what such names are intended to signify and the way in which they signify *(modus significandi)*. As regards that which they signify, such names are properly applied to God; but as regards the way in which they signify, they are not properly said of God. For they retain a mode of signifying which pertains to creatures.[134] In a. 4 Thomas indicates that even those names which signify the divine substance in the imperfect way he has defended are not synonymous with one another. This is because each name expresses a concept of a particular perfection as it is realized in creatures. These various perfections as found in creatures represent in varied and manifold ways the one and simple divine principle. Hence they enable the human intellect to form different concepts which it may apply to the divine being.[135]

In a. 5 Thomas explicitly takes up the issue of univocal, equivocal, and analogical predication of names of God. Since we shall devote the following part of this chapter to that issue, we may bypass it here. We should note that in a. 6 Thomas refers to the fact that names of pure perfections not only tell us that God is the cause of goodness, for instance, or whatever perfection is at issue. Such names are also said of God essentially *(essentialiter)*. This is simply another term for his earlier defense of substantial predication of such names.[136]

In a. 11 Thomas asks whether the name "He who is" is most proper (or appropriate) for God. Consistent with his earlier discussion in *In I Sent.*, d. 8, q. 1, a. 1, he replies that it is, and this for three reasons. First of all, this name does not signify any particular form but the act of being *(esse)* itself. Because God's act of being is identical with his essence, and because this is true of no other being, this name most properly applies to him. Secondly, all other names are either less common than this or, if they are convertible with it, they add something to its meaning and in a certain way inform and determine it (here Thomas is thinking of the relation of the other transcendentals to being). Again he notes that our intellect cannot know God's essence in this life as it is in itself. But whatever determined mode it applies to what it understands of God must fall short of the mode whereby God is in himself. Therefore the less determined such names are, and the more universal

---

134. Leon. 4.143: "Quantum igitur ad id quod significant huiusmodi nomina, proprie competunt Deo, et magis proprie quam ipsis creaturis, et per prius dicuntur de eo. Quantum vero ad modum significandi, non proprie dicuntur de Deo: habent enim modum significandi qui creaturis competit."

135. Ed. cit., pp. 144–45.

136. Leon. 4.150. Note: "Sed supra ostensum est quod huiusmodi nomina non solum dicuntur de Deo causaliter, sed etiam essentialiter."

and unqualified, the more properly they may be applied to God. The name "He who is" determines no mode of being but stands indeterminately with respect to all. For this reason, as he again reminds us, John Damascene refers to God as having *esse* as if it were a certain infinite and undetermined ocean of substance. Thirdly, this name is most proper because of what it consignifies; for it signifies to exist, to be sure, but also to exist in the present, and this is most properly said of God, for whom there is neither past nor future.[137]

Until this point Thomas's treatment of "He who is" as the most appropriate or proper divine name is consistent with his earlier discussions. But in his reply to objection 1 he argues that this name "He who is" is more proper than the name "God" with respect to that by reason of which it is imposed, i.e., *esse,* and also with respect to its mode of signifying and consignifying. However, as regards that which the name is imposed to signify, the name "God" is more proper, since it is intended to signify the divine nature. And viewed from this perspective, in terms of that which the name is imposed to signify, the name "Tetragrammaton" (YHWH) is even more proper; for it is imposed to signify the incommunicable and, if one may so speak, singular substance of God.[138]

In summing up this lengthy discussion of Thomas's views on whether or not we can know what God is, I would now like to recall the following. From the beginning to the end of his career Thomas has consistently denied to us in this life quidditative knowledge of God. We can know that God is, and what God is not, but not what God is. He has also consistently defended the possibility of some kind of nonmetaphorical predication of divine names, and one which we may describe as proper.

Secondly, I have not found in his earlier treatments within similar contexts any explicit admission that certain names may be predicated of God substantially or essentially, although this is clearly defended in the *De potentia* and in the *Summa theologiae.* As I have suggested in an earlier study, this seems to me to be owing, at least in part, to a greater concern on Thomas's part to avoid in these later works the extremely negative view he has associated with Moses Maimonides in particular, and

---

137. Ed. cit., p. 162.

138. Ibid. For a helpful discussion see A. Maurer, "St. Thomas on the Sacred Name 'Tetragrammaton'," *Mediaeval Studies* 34 (1972), pp. 275–86, repr. in his *Being and Knowing: Studies in Thomas Aquinas and Later Medieval Philosophers* (Toronto, 1990), pp. 59–69 (cited here). Maurer concludes that this view that the name "Tetragrammaton" is in one sense more proper to God than the name "He Who is" is unique to the *Summa Theologiae* (p. 65) and identifies Maimonides' *Guide* as Thomas's source for this late precision (pp. 66–69). Cf. L. Clavell, *El nombre propio de Dios,* pp. 143–46. It should also be noted that in a. 12 Thomas explains that affirmative propositions can be formed about God without doing any violence to the divine simplicity. This follows from the fact that our intellect must use different notions or ideas *(conceptiones)* in understanding God, since it does not see him as he is in himself. Even so, in using these different notions, the human intellect recognizes that it is one and the same divine reality which corresponds to all of them. The intellect expresses this conceptual plurality by using a distinct subject and predicate. And it expresses the underlying real unity by composing the subject and predicate in a judgment (Leon. 4.164).

with others who remain unnamed.[139] At the same time, he always remains true to his acceptance of the threefold Dionysian approach to the divine names, based on reasoning from effect to cause, negation, and transcendence or supereminence.

Thirdly, in our efforts to determine precisely what Thomas denies when he rejects quidditative knowledge of God for us in this life, it is clear from what we have seen that he eliminates comprehensive knowledge. At least as he has defined this in q. 12 of the *Summa,* such knowledge would imply that we could know God as fully as he is knowable, or to an infinite degree. Such knowledge is impossible, according to Thomas, for any created intellect, even when possessing the beatific vision.

Fourthly, since Thomas does admit in this discussion that with the aid of the *lumen gloriae* the blessed can see God's essence in itself, he is distinguishing between comprehensive knowledge and quidditative knowledge. As he has explained in q. 12 of the *Summa,* quidditative knowledge would enable us to define God, or to grasp his essential intelligibility, much in the way we can define man as a rational animal, etc. Such knowledge would not necessarily be comprehensive, but is nonetheless denied to us in this life. This applies both to philosophical knowledge of God based on reasoning from effect to cause and to knowledge given to us through scriptural revelation. This distinction between comprehensive knowledge and a quidditative and defining knowledge is helpful, and seems to advance the discussion beyond that found, for instance, in *De veritate,* q. 2, a. 1, where quidditative knowledge is simply presented as that which is equal or adequate to a thing in every respect.[140] Be that as it may, it is now clear that both comprehensive knowledge and defining or quidditative knowledge of God are denied to us in this life.

---

139. See *Metaphysical Themes in Thomas Aquinas,* pp. 229–34, 236–37, 240; also "Thomas Aquinas on What Philosophers Can Know about God," *American Catholic Philosophical Quarterly* 66 (1992), pp. 286–88. T.-D. Humbrecht has recently suggested that Thomas already defended substantial attribution of some divine names (goodness, wisdom) in *In I Sent.* d. 22, q. 1, *expositio textus* (Mandonnet ed., Vol. 1, pp. 543–44). See his "Dieu a-t-il une essence?" in *Revue thomiste* 95 (1995), pp. 7–18, esp. p. 15. However, in that context, where Thomas is summarizing Peter's text after having already offered his more personal views on the divine names in q. 1, aa. 1–4, he finds the Lombard distinguishing between names that may be said of the one divine essence and others that may be said only of individual persons within the Trinity. Peter lays down certain rules for dealing with each type, which Thomas here briefly summarizes. To mention but the first two, names pertaining to the one divine essence (1) are predicated absolutely and only with respect to themselves *(ad se),* and (2) "significant substantiam," i.e., the one divine essence or nature. Names pertaining to particular persons within the Trinity (1) are predicated relatively, and (2) do not signify the divine substance (or essence). This is consistent with Peter's own text (see p. 529), where he states that names signifying the one divine essence are said *ad se* and therefore not relatively but substantially. But this usage and meaning is very different from that which Thomas has in mind in our passages from ST I and the *De potentia* where he writes that certain names can be said of God *substantialiter* and in one passage, *essentialiter.* It is this latter usage of this terminology stemming from Thomas's concern to offset (Maimonides') excessive agnosticism in dealing with divine names of pure perfections that I do not find in his earlier works.

140. See n. 35 above.

Finally, in all of his later discussions Thomas continues to distinguish between what is signified by such names, and the way in which they signify. Even names dealing with pure perfections carry with them some creaturely mode of signifying. And this must be denied of God even when such names are applied essentially or substantially.

Before leaving this discussion, we should consider one remaining point. Does not Thomas frequently recognize that it is difficult if not impossible for us to arrive at knowledge of the essence of many material things? Indeed he does, as we have noted above. But if this is true, what is distinctive about his denial that we can have quidditative knowledge of God in this life? If we must settle for a knowledge of some purely corporeal things which is purely descriptive and based only on a number of accidents we may have grasped about such things, is our knowledge of God, nonquidditative though it may be, any less satisfactory?[141]

As for Thomas's answer to this, he would first point out that when it comes to our knowledge of God and his essence, there are no accidents in God to which we can appeal. Hence while knowledge of a particular material thing when based on accidents may be less than essential or quidditative, it at least tells us something positive and something unique about that thing as it exists in this place and at this time. Moreover, in SCG I, c. 3, after mentioning this limitation in our knowledge of many properties of material things, he has, as it were, turned the tables on any such argument by observing that it is much more the case that human reason is incapable of investigating the intelligible depths of God.[142]

Finally, the deficiency involved in applying names to God either abstractly or concretely does not apply to our knowledge of corporeal entities based on our

141. On Thomas's recognition in certain passages of our inability at times to grasp the specific difference of a thing and therefore our need to substitute knowledge of accidents (or of effects) see n. 39 above. Note especially *De veritate,* q. 4, a. 1, ad 8: ". . . sed quia differentiae essentiales sunt nobis ignotae, quandoque utimur accidentibus vel effectibus loco earum, ut in VIII Metaphysicae dicitur, et secundum hoc nominamus rem. . ." (Leon. 22.1.121:337–341). See also q. 10, a. 1 (Leon. 22.2.296:112–297:116), where Thomas writes that because the essences of things are unknown to us, frequently we use the names of powers to designate the essences. In such cases an essence should be designated through its proper power. In replying to obj. 6 (p. 299:280–283) Thomas comments that in such cases accidents sometimes manifest or designate an essence in the way proper effects make known their cause. In SCG I, c. 3, Thomas also remarks that the properties of many sensible things remain unknown to us, and the natures of many properties which we do apprehend through sense experience are not perfectly grasped by us (ed. cit., p. 3).

142. See SCG I, c. 3 (ed. cit., p. 3): "Adhuc idem." For a difficulty somewhat similar to the one I have raised in the preceding paragraph, see J. F. Ross's review of my *Metaphysical Themes in Thomas Aquinas,* in *Journal of the History of Philosophy* 25 (1987), pp. 593–94. He refers to one's knowing what a dog is, or what metal is, or what blood is, and to a lesser extent, what electricity is or what gravity is, without having a "comprehensive and defining knowledge." Ross believes that according to Aquinas "even *that* sort of real quidditative knowledge of God is not available to us." While I agree with Ross on this point, I do not think that Thomas would describe such knowlege as "real quidditative knowledge." For another interesting effort to explain what Thomas means when he denies that we can know what God is see B. Davies, "Aquinas on What God Is Not," *Revue internationale de philosophie* 52 (1998), pp. 207–25.

awareness of some of their accidents. For instance, if I find certain accidents realized in a corporeal substance, I can apply a concrete mode of signifying to the accidents and to the substance, since in reality substance and accidents are really composed. Thus I can say "Fido is white" without having to deny of Fido the concrete way in which "white" signifies in this statement.

In conclusion, therefore, when Thomas denies that we can in this life know "what God is," he is recognizing a greater limitation in our knowledge of God than any which applies to our knowledge of purely corporeal entities. This is evidently so in the case of those material things about which we can have defining and essential knowledge, such as human beings; but it also applies to those corporeal entities about which we can have at best a descriptive knowledge based on accidents.

2. Analogical Knowledge of God

As we have now seen, Thomas defends the human intellect's capacity to arrive at knowledge that God exists by reasoning from effect to cause. And while Thomas continues to deny that we can ever reach quidditative knowledge of God in this life, he defends our ability to predicate certain names of him in positive fashion. When carried out correctly such predication may be proper and in some instances—at least according to Thomas's later treatments—a kind he also describes as substantial or essential. Yet Thomas will not admit that this delivers a knowledge of God on our part which is comprehensive or defining or adequate to the divine essence. Even the names of pure perfections carry with them some creaturely mode of signifying which we must always deny of the divine.

We may now ask whether what the names of pure perfections signify is exactly the same when they are applied to God and when they are applied to creatures. To phrase this in another way, is there some minimum content or meaning which remains exactly the same when such names are applied to creatures and to God? Or to express it in still another way, are such names univocal regarding that which they signify when they are affirmed of God and of creatures?

Raising the question in this final way of course brings us back to the problem of analogy of being which we already encountered in Chapter III.[143] There we distinguished two levels at which this issue might be investigated—the predicamental (or horizontal) and the transcendental (or vertical). We deferred treatment of this problem at the transcendental level, at least insofar as it applies to God, until after we had examined Thomas's argumentation for God's existence. Since we have now completed that task, we are in position to take up this issue.

Throughout Thomas's various discussions of this question we shall see that he retains the distinction between univocal, equivocal, and analogical predication. We should also note that at least in his more mature discussions of analogical predica-

143. See Ch. III above, Section 2.

tion of the divine names, he takes up this issue only after he has examined and rejected our ability in the present life to reach quidditative knowledge of God. In sum, his later discussions of the issue of quidditative knowledge of God presuppose that he has made his case for God's existence by reasoning from effect to cause. And his explicit discussions of analogical predication of the divine names presuppose that he has already addressed the issue of quidditative knowledge of God. This is why we have chosen to follow that same order of exposition in our own text.[144]

As we approach this topic, we should also recall that for Thomas metaphysics has as its subject being as being. God himself is not the subject and not even included under the subject of metaphysics. God enters into its consideration only insofar as he is a principle or cause of its subject (or of what falls under its subject).[145] Given this position and given Thomas's rejection of any kind of quidditative knowledge of God on our part in this life, we will not be surprised to find that he rejects univocal predication of any divine name. Even so, it is interesting to see how he arrives at his defense of analogical predication of such names, and how he understands this. Accordingly, we shall now single out for special consideration a series of key texts taken once again in chronological order.

a. *In I Sent.* (1252–1256)

In his Commentary on I *Sentences,* d. 35, q. 1, a. 4, Thomas asks whether God's knowledge *(scientia)* is univocal with ours. In examining the issue of God's knowledge, Thomas is evidently dealing with a pure perfection. In earlier articles he has just established that knowledge is present in God, that God knows things other than himself, and that he has a knowledge of such things which is both certain and proper.[146] Thomas begins his response to a. 4 by observing that something can be

---

144. In the *Summa contra Gentiles* I, c. 30, Aquinas concludes with the remark about our not knowing what God is but only what he is not and how other things are related to him (cited above in n. 68). Only in cc. 32–34 does Thomas explicitly take up the issue of univocal, equivocal and analogical predication of the divine names. It is only in a. 7 of q. 7 of the *De potentia* that Thomas turns to this same issue, that is to say, after his discussion of quidditative knowledge and his defense of the view that some names express the divine substance *substantialiter* in earlier articles of the same q. 7. And as we have just seen, in ST I Thomas devotes qq. 3–11 to showing how God is not, q. 12 to how God is known by us, and q. 13 to how he is named by us. In q. 13, it is not until a. 5 that he takes up the issue of analogical predication of the divine names, and again only after having defended predication of certain divine names substantially in a. 2. Even in the *Compendium theologiae* I, where he explicitly devotes little attention to the issue of quidditative knowledge of God, he follows this same order. In c. 24 he remarks that because the human intellect cannot grasp the divine essence in itself, we must reason from perfections we find in creatures to knowledge of God as their source. Hence we need to employ many names in doing this (Leon. 42.90). In c. 25 he argues that these different names are not synonymous, and in c. 26 that, since our intellect cannot perfectly capture the divine essence through any of them, we cannot define that which is in God. Finally in c. 27 he rejects univocal and equivocal predication of such names of God and decides for analogy.

145. See our discussion of this above in Ch. I and also Ch. III, n. 64.

146. In a. 1 Thomas asks: "Utrum in Deo sit scientia" (Mandonnet ed., Vol. 1, pp. 807–13). In a. 2 he defends God's knowledge of things other than himself (pp. 813–15) and in a. 3 makes the point

common to other things in one of three ways—univocally, equivocally, or analogically. As he will continue to do in his later major discussions of this same issue, he proceeds by eliminating both univocal and equivocal predication of knowledge (or of any pure perfection) of God and of creatures.[147]

To show that nothing can be said univocally of God and of a creature, Thomas builds his argument on his metaphysics of essence and act of being *(esse)*. In all cases where univocal predication is appropriate there must be some kind of commonness in the order of nature (or essence), but not in the order of the act of being. This follows because only one (substantial) act of being can be found in any one substantial entity. Thus the condition of humanity is not realized with the same act of being in two different human beings. Therefore, whenever the form signified by a name is *esse* itself, that name cannot be predicated univocally. Given this, neither can being *(ens)* be predicated univocally, since, as Thomas often reminds us, the name being *(ens)* is derived from the verb *esse*.[148] What we have so far is a general argument against predicating *esse* univocally at any level. And this in turn is broadened so as to apply to being *(ens)* as well. Underlying all of this, of course, is Thomas's conviction that in creatures essence and act of being *(esse)* cannot be identified.

Thomas immediately goes on to apply this thinking to the case of the divine names. The nature or form of whatever is affirmed of God must be identical with the divine act of being. This is so because God's act of being and nature (essence) are identical. Therefore nothing can be predicated univocally of God and of any creature. Implied here of course is Thomas's unwavering conviction that there can be no composition in God. Also assumed is his previous conclusion that the act of being *(esse)* can never be predicated univocally of any two creatures. Hence neither it nor anything else can be predicated univocally of a creature and God; for in God any other perfection must itself be identical with the divine *esse*.[149] Again we see that the difference in ontological situations—identity vs. composition of essence and *esse*—grounds the distinction between God and any creature, and the resulting impossibility of our univocally predicating any name of both.

In assessing the general argument against univocal predication of *esse* I am reminded of one of the ways in which Thomas argues for the distinction and composition of essence and *esse* in substances other than God, i.e., the genus argu-

---

that God's knowledge of things other than himself is proper and certain (pp. 815–18); also see ad 4 (p. 818).

147. In a. 4 he asks: "Utrum scientia sua sit univoca nostrae scientiae" (p. 818). Thomas's response begins on p. 819. See p. 807 for Thomas's initial phrasing of this question.

148. See p. 819. Note especially: "Huius ratio est quia cum in re duo sit considerare: scilicet naturam vel quidditatem rei, et esse suum, oportet quod in omnibus univocis sit communitas secundum rationem naturae, et non secundum esse, quia unum esse non est nisi in una re . . . et ideo quandocumque forma significata per nomen est ipsum esse, non potest univoce convenire, propter quod etiam ens non univoce praedicatur."

149. "Et ideo cum omnium quae dicuntur de Deo natura vel forma sit ipsum esse, quia suum esse est sua natura, . . . ideo nihil de Deo et creaturis univoce dici potest" (pp. 819–20).

ment.[150] Central to such reasoning and to the present argument is the view that wherever univocal predication obtains (or membership in a genus, according to the genus argument), there must be some kind of commonness in the order of nature or essence, but not in the order of *esse*. In the genus argument Thomas reasons that the common feature which is predicated of things belonging to the same genus must be asserted of them in quidditative fashion. But the act of being *(esse)* does not pertain to a quiddity except insofar as that quiddity is received in this or that individual. Because the quiddity or nature is common to all members of a genus and an individual act of being is not common, the two cannot be identified. According to the present reasoning, univocal predication requires commonness in the order of nature or essence, but not in the order of *esse;* for one act of being can be found in only one being. Because of this, the form signified by *esse* cannot be predicated univocally; and neither therefore can being *(ens)* be so predicated.[151]

In Ch. V above I expressed some reservations about the validity of the genus argumentation for real composition and distinction of essence and *esse*. Does it succeed in establishing anything more than a distinction between a being when it is considered abstractly and universally, on the one hand, and as an actual and individual existent, on the other?[152]

Whatever the merits of that criticism of the genus argument, it does not apply to the present case. If one grants real distinction between essence and *esse* in created entities for any reason whatsoever, Thomas will contend that univocal predication of *esse* is not possible. Univocal predication of essence of members of the same genus (or species) will be possible precisely because essentially the same kind of nature or essence is present in each. But because the act of being is individual and unique to a given individual, we cannot abstract a universal notion of the act of being *(esse)* which could still be applied univocally to the individuals in which it is realized. And if *esse* cannot be predicated univocally, neither can *ens* (being). But if being cannot be predicated univocally of two distinct finite entities, much less so can it be predicated univocally of any finite entity and of God. Hence, no other pure perfection such as knowledge can be predicated univocally of any creature and God. For in God, every such perfection is really identical with the divine being and the divine act of being *(esse)*.

In a. 4 Thomas next turns to the opposite extreme position. If knowledge (and other pure perfections) cannot be predicated univocally of God and creatures, one

150. See Ch. V above, Section 3. Note that in several presentations of this argument, Thomas is attempting to show that God does not fall into any genus (see *In I Sent.*, d. 8, q. 4, a. 2; SCG I, c. 25; *De potentia*, q. 7, a. 3; ST I, q. 3, a. 5).

151. The major difference between the two ways of arguing is this: The genus argument does not presuppose but attempts to establish distinction of essence and act of being in all members of a genus; the present argument simply accepts real distinction or composition of essence and act of being as established and concludes that because of this, univocal predication of *esse*, and therefore of *ens,* is not possible. On this argument see Montagnes, *La doctrine de l'analogie*, p. 68.

152. See Ch. V above, Section 3, and n. 75 for additional discussion.

might conclude that names can only be said of them in equivocal fashion. Against this Thomas argues that in the case of names which are predicated purely equivocally because of chance or fortune, as when, for instance, the same name happens to be applied to two human beings, we cannot reason from our awareness of one to awareness of the other. But we can reason from our awareness of knowledge in a creature to some awareness *(cognitionem)* of knowledge *(scientia)* in God. Therefore the name knowledge *(scientia)* is not itself purely equivocal.[153]

Central to this argument is a point already familiar to us and one we shall see again. Thomas is convinced that we can reason from our awareness of a pure perfection such as knowledge as it is realized in created beings to some awareness of it in God. Because of this, equivocal predication of such names is to be ruled out. This would not preserve the element of similarity presupposed by such reasoning.[154]

By process of elimination, therefore, Thomas concludes that knowledge is said analogically of God and of a creature. And the same will hold for other names of this kind. At this point he introduces a distinction we have already touched on above in our Ch. III. Thomas distinguishes two kinds of analogy. One kind involves a sharing in some single factor which is prior to all the entities that share in it. This kind of analogy cannot apply to God and any creature, just as univocity cannot. But there is another kind of analogy according to which one thing imitates another insofar as it can, without ever perfectly attaining to it. This is the kind of analogy which obtains between a creature and God.[155] In anticipation of Thomas's usage in later texts, I shall refer to the first kind as the analogy of "many to one" and to the second as the analogy of "one to another."[156]

In replying to objection 6 within this same a. 4, Thomas again rejects any similarity between a creature and God based on the claim that both would share in some common factor or perfection. (This would follow if one applied the analogy of many to one to God and a creature.) He counters that the similarity between a creature and God is rather based on the claim that a creature imitates God. He adds that if the creature can be said to be similar to God, the converse is not true.[157] Already at the beginning of his Commentary on I *Sentences* (Prologue, q. 1, a. 2, ad 2) Thomas had commented that an analogical commonness or community may

153. Ed. cit., p. 820. Cf. Thomas's argumentation for the presence of *scientia* in God in q. 1, a. 1 of this same d. 35 (pp. 808–10). There he builds three arguments on the threefold Dionysian approach.

154. To put this in other terms, a theory of purely equivocal predication of the divine names would result in agnosticism on our part about any knowledge of God's nature and attributes. Cf. Montagnes, *La doctrine*, p. 69.

155. See p. 820: "Et ideo dicendum, quod scientia analogice dicitur de Deo et creatura, et similiter omnia huiusmodi. Sed duplex est analogia." See Ch. III above, n. 68, for the remainder of this text.

156. By doing this I do not wish to imply that Thomas's later understanding of the analogy of many to one and one to another is completely identical with his view in the present text.

157. "Ad sextum dicendum, quod inter Deum et creaturam non est similitudo per convenientiam in aliquo uno communi, sed per imitationem; unde creatura similis Deo dicitur, sed non convertitur . . ." (p. 821).

be based on the fact that a number of things participate according to priority and posteriority in something that is one, or it may be based on the fact that one thing receives its existence *(esse)* and its intelligibility *(ratio)* from another. There, too, he had opted for the second kind of analogical commonness in the case of creatures and God, i.e., the analogy of one to another.[158]

Before turning to Thomas's *De veritate* for his next major treatment of analogical predication of the divine names, we should consider another frequently discussed passage from his Commentary on I *Sentences*. In distinction 19, q. 5, a. 2 Thomas defends the view that there is one divine truth by reason of which all other things are true; for they depend upon the divine truth as upon their efficient and exemplar principle. Nonetheless, distinct truths are also present in created entities by reason of which each of them may be said to be true in the formal sense.[159]

Against this claim the first objection argues that truth is said analogically of the different things in which there is truth, just as health is said of all healthy things. But in the case of health it is by reason of numerically one and the same health that an animal is said to be healthy as its subject, medicine as its cause, and urine as its sign. Hence it seems there is only one truth by which all things are said to be true. In other words, the objection would deny that truth is intrinsically present in creatures. It would be intrinsically present only in God.[160]

In replying Thomas notes that something may be said analogically in one of three ways. (1) The analogy may apply to the order of meaning only, but not to the order of existence *(esse)*. The meaning, for instance, of health, is applied to different analogates, e.g., animal, diet, urine, in different fashion, and according to priority and posteriority. But this diversity applies only to the order of meaning, not to the order of existence. Health actually exists or enjoys real being only in an animal, not in the other cases.[161] (2) The analogy may apply only to the order of existence but not to the order of meaning. To illustrate this Thomas turns to a very medieval example, "body" as it is predicated of terrestrial and heavenly bodies. Because all

---

158. Mandonnet ed., Vol. 1, p. 10, cited above in Ch. III, n. 68. The text concludes: ". . . creatura enim non habet esse nisi secundum quod a primo ente descendit, nec nominatur ens nisi inquantum ens primum imitatur; et similiter est de sapientia et de omnibus aliis quae de creatura dicuntur."

159. Mandonnet ed., Vol. 1, pp. 491–92. Note: "Unde dico, quod sicut est unum esse divinum quo omnia sunt, sicut a principio effectivo exemplari, nihilominus tamen in rebus diversis est diversum esse, quo formaliter res est; ita etiam est una veritas, scilicet divina, qua omnia vera sunt, sicut principio effectivo exemplari; nihilominus sunt plures veritates in rebus creatis, quibus dicuntur verae formaliter." In another context I have argued that in this passage Thomas does not restrict his conclusion to truth of the intellect but applies it to truth of being as well. See my "Truth in Thomas Aquinas," pp. 303–7. Cf. pp. 317–21 for additional precisions drawn from the *De veritate*. In brief, if we take truth broadly *(improprie)*, Thomas holds that it is intrinsically and formally present in things; but if we take truth in the strict sense *(proprie)*, it is intrinsically and formally presen: only in some intellect.

160. For obj. 1 see ed. cit., p. 491.

161. See p. 492. Note: "Ad primum igitur dicendum, quod aliquid dicitur secundum analogiam tripliciter: vel secundum intentionem tantum, et non secundum esse; et hoc est quando una intentio refertur ad plura per prius et posterius, quae tamen non habet esse nisi in uno. . . ."

bodies share in the notion of corporeity, body is defined in the same way in its various applications. Hence the logician, who considers meanings only and not the order of being, says that the name "body" is predicated univocally of all bodies, including the terrestrial (corruptible) and the celestial (incorruptible). But the metaphysician and the natural philosopher must also take into account the existence *(esse)* of any nature. They realize that the existence *(esse)* of corporeity is not the same in terrestrial (or corruptible) and celestial (incorruptible) bodies and therefore deny that the name "body" or anything else is predicated univocally of the corruptible and the incorruptible. Even for them, however, this analogy applies only to the order of existence, not to the order of meaning.[162] (3) Finally, the analogy may apply both to the order of meaning and the order of existence. This happens when there is no perfect equality either in meaning or in existence. It is in this way that being *(ens)* is said of substance and accident. In such cases the common nature or perfection must enjoy some existence *(esse)* in each of the things of which it is predicated, but one that differs in terms of a greater or lesser degree of perfection. It is also in this way that truth, goodness, and names of this kind (i.e., pure perfections) are said analogically of God and of creatures. Whence it follows that all of these are really present in God and in creatures, each with its appropriate existence, and at the same time, that they are present in varying degrees of perfection. Thomas concludes from this that there are different truths, and each of these must have its appropriate existence.[163]

Important for our purposes is the fact that Thomas explicitly applies to the case of the divine names the third kind of analogy he has here distinguished—that which applies to both the order of meaning and the order of existence. Without dwelling at length on this passage, therefore, we may assume that in other passages

---

162. Ibid. Note: "Vel secundum esse et non secundum intentionem; et hoc contingit quando plura parificantur in intentione alicuius communis, sed illud commune non habet esse unius rationis in omnibus, sicut omnia corpora parificantur in intentione corporeitatis. . . . Unde quantum ad metaphysicum et naturalem, qui considerant res secundum suum esse, nec hoc nomen, corpus, nec aliquid aliud dicitur univoce de corruptibilibus et incorruptibilibus. . . ."

163. "Vel secundum intentionem et secundum esse; et hoc est quando neque parificatur in intentione communi, neque in esse; sicut ens dicitur de substantia et accidente; et de talibus oportet quod natura communis habeat aliquod esse in unoquoque eorum de quibus dicitur, sed differens secundum rationem maioris vel minoris perfectionis. Et similiter dico, quod veritas, et bonitas, et omnia huiusmodi dicuntur analogice de Deo et creaturis. Unde oportet quod secundum suum esse omnia haec in Deo sint, et in creaturis secundum rationem maioris perfectionis et minoris; ex quo sequitur, cum non possint esse secundum unum esse utrobique, quod sint diversae veritates" (ibid.). This passage has been subject to considerable commentary on the part of Thomistic commentators, both classical and contemporary. It was central to Cajetan's interpretation as set forth in his *De nominum analogia*. See Ch. III above, n. 87 for criticism of his interpretation of this text and his way of applying it to Thomas's other discussions of analogy. On Thomas's text see Montagnes, *La doctrine*, p. 61 and n. 100; McInerny, *The Logic of Analogy*, pp. 97–125; *Aquinas and Analogy*, pp. 5–14 (on Cajetan's misreading of the text); S. M. Ramirez, "En torno a un famoso texto de santo Tomás sobre la analogía," *Sapientia* 8 (1953), pp. 166–91 (also of interest for the point discussed above in my n. 159), especially pp. 169–76.

dealing with our predicating knowledge or other pure perfections of God and creatures, Thomas would have us make use only of the third kind of analogy he has just distinguished. To repeat, according to that kind of analogy the perfections signified by analogical names are realized in creatures and in God according to an analogy which applies both to the order of meaning and to the order of *esse*. This means that the predicated perfection is to be understood differently when it is applied to God and to any creature, but not so much so as to remove all similarity. And it means that the predicated perfection is intrinsically present, i.e., *secundum esse* both in God and in creatures, but in differing degree of perfection.[164]

b. *De veritate* (1256–1259)

In q. 2, a. 11 of the *De veritate* Thomas again takes up the issue of the predication of the divine names. This time he asks whether knowledge *(scientia)* is predicated in purely equivocal fashion of God and of us.[165] It is interesting to observe that a number of the opening arguments in support of purely equivocal predication of such names of God and of us rest on the denial that there is any real similarity or likeness between creatures and God (see arguments 1, 2, 3, 4).[166] And the two opening arguments against purely equivocal predication make the case for some kind of similarity between creatures and God.[167]

Thomas begins his reply by restating his argument against univocal predication of anything of a creature and of God. In the case of univocals, the meaning or intelligible content *(ratio)* of a name is common to both things of which that name is predicated univocally. Hence as regards the meaning of the name, univocals are equal, even though in the order of existence *(secundum esse)* one may be prior or posterior to the other. For instance, in terms of their definition as number all numbers are equal, even though according to the nature of things one number is naturally prior to another.[168] The point Thomas is making here is important, for it means that diversity in the order of existence does not necessarily rule out univocal predication, so long as the meaning attached to a name remains the same.

But, Thomas continues, no matter how much a creature may imitate God, it can never reach the point where anything will belong to it and to God with exactly the same meaning or intelligible content. To prove this point Thomas again introduces his metaphysics of essence and act of being *(esse)*. Those things which are found in different things with the same meaning or intelligible content are common to them from the standpoint of substance or quiddity but are distinct in terms

164. See the text quoted in the previous note.

165. "Undecimo quaeritur utrum scientia aequivoce pure dicatur de Deo et nobis" (Leon. 22.1.77).

166. Ibid.

167. See p. 78:78–92: "Sed contra . . ." The first argument is philosophical and the second scriptural (Gen. 1:26).

168. Leon. 22.1.78:93–103. Note especially: ". . . et sic quantum ad illius nominis rationem univocata in aliquo aequalia sunt, quamvis secundum esse unum altero possit esse prius vel posterius. . . ."

of their acts of being *(esse)*. But all that is present in God is identical with the divine act of being. Just as God's essence is identical with his act of being *(esse)*, so too God's knowledge is identical with his actually knowing. But the act of being which is proper to one thing cannot be communicated to another. And just as it is impossible for a creature to possess the divine act of being, so is it impossible for a creature to reach the point where it would possess something with the same meaning or intelligible content with which God possesses it.[169]

If this argument against univocal predication is essentially the same as the one we have just seen from his Commentary on I *Sentences*, d. 35, q. 1, a. 4, Thomas introduces a new consideration into his argumentation against purely equivocal predication of the divine names. Unless there were some agreement or similarity between a creature and God, the divine essence would not be a likeness for creatures. Consequently, in knowing his essence God would not know creatures. (Thomas can take the fact that God knows individual creatures as given, since he has already argued for this in previous articles of q. 2 [see especially aa. 3 and 5]. In a. 4, ad 2 and in a. 5 Thomas stresses the role of the divine essence in that, by knowing his essence, God knows the likeness which all other things imitate and which is productive of those things. Therefore God knows each of those things.) To repeat Thomas's present argument, if there were no likeness between creatures and God, in knowing himself God would not know other things. Just such a lack of likeness is implied by a theory of purely equivocal predication of the divine names and, therefore, what we might call a divine agnosticism would result.[170]

Moreover, continues Thomas, if there were no similarity between creatures and God, we could not reason from created things to any knowledge of God. Nor among the various names we apply to creatures would any one name be more fittingly applied to God than another. Agnosticism on our part concerning God would result. Thomas, however, here assumes that we can reason from creatures to some knowledge of God, and that some names of created perfections are more fittingly applied to God than others. We have seen his views concerning this in the

---

169. Leon. 22.1.78:103–118: "Creatura autem quantumcumque imitetur Deum non tamen potest pertingere ad hoc ut eadem ratione aliquid sibi conveniat qua convenit Deo . . . unde cum esse quod est proprium unius rei non possit alteri communicari, impossibile est ut creatura pertingat ad eandem rationem habendi aliquid qua habet Deus sicut impossibile est quod ad idem esse perveniat." Note that at the end Thomas comments that if in our case there were no difference between a man, on the one hand, and for a man to exist, on the other, man could not be predicated univocally of Socrates and of Plato; for *esse* in each of them is diverse (lines 118–122).

170. "Nec tamen potest dici quod omnino aequivoce praedicetur quicquid de Deo et creaturis dicitur, quia nisi esse aliqua convenientia creaturae ad Deum secundum rem, sua essentia non esset creaturarum similitudo et ita cognoscendo suam essentiam non cognosceret creaturas . . ." (lines 122–128). For a. 3 see Leon. 22.1.50–52 (see also Thomas's replies to objections 1, 2, and 3). For a. 5 see especially pp. 62:246–63:313. For more on Thomas's discussion of divine knowledge in the *De veritate*, especially of the divine ideas, see my *Thomas Aquinas on the Divine Ideas*, pp. 12–23. And for a detailed discussion of the whole of q. 2 see S.-T. Bonino, *Thomas d'Aquin. De la verité ou la science en Dieu* (Fribourg, 1996). For his commentary on a. 11 see pp. 499–513.

preceding section of this chapter, and in those chapters where we considered his argumentation for God's existence. Given this, he quickly concludes that a theory of purely equivocal predication of the divine names will not suffice.[171]

As in his discussion in *In I Sent.*, d. 35, Thomas moves by process of elimination to the conclusion that the name "knowledge" is predicated of God's knowledge and knowledge in ourselves neither univocally nor purely equivocally but according to analogy. He adds that the expression "according to analogy" really means "according to a proportion." And he now introduces a new distinction. Agreement in terms of proportion may be of two types and, corresponding to this, analogical community may also be twofold. One kind of agreement obtains between those things which are so proportioned to one another that they have a determined distance or other relationship to one another. For instance, the number two is so related to the unit as to serve as its double. Another kind of agreement obtains between two things which do not have a determined relationship to one another and is rather based on the agreement or similarity of two proportions with another. Thus the number six agrees with the number four because, just as six is the double of three, so is four the double of two. Thomas describes the first kind as an agreement of proportion, and the second type as an agreement of proportionality.[172]

Thomas then goes on to apply this distinction to analogy. Something is said analogically of two things in the first way (by agreement of proportion) when one of these things bears a relationship to the other. Thus being is predicated of substance and of accident because of the relationship accident has to substance. So too, healthy is said of urine and of an animal because urine bears some relationship to the health of the animal (by serving as a sign of the same). But something may also be said analogically in the second way (by agreement of proportionality). It is in this way that the name "sight" is said of corporeal vision and of understanding: just as sight is to the eye, so is understanding to the mind.[173]

And then Thomas draws a rather surprising conclusion. When a name is predicated analogically in the first way, there must be some determined relationship between those things to which something is analogically common. Because of this it is impossible for anything to be said analogically of God and of creatures in this fashion. Thomas's reason for saying this is that no creature has (or can have) a relationship to God in such fashion that the divine perfection could be determined by it.[174] As Thomas here presents this kind of analogy, therefore, it is based on a determined

171. Leon. 22.1.78:128–79:134.

172. Leon. 22.1.79:135–153. Note especially: "Convenientia autem secundum proportionem potest esse dupliciter et secundum quam haec duo attenditur analogiae communitas . . . prima ergo convenientia est proportionis, secunda autem proportionalitatis."

173. P. 79:153–165.

174. P. 79:165–172: "Quia ergo in his quae primo modo analogice dicuntur oportet esse aliquam determinatam habitudinem inter ea quibus est aliquid per analogiam commune, impossibile est aliquid per hunc modum analogice dici de Deo et creatura quia nulla creatura habet talem habitudinem ad Deum per quam possit divina perfectio determinari. . . ."

and mutual relationship between the analogates. What is surprising, however, is the fact that earlier in his Commentary on the *Sentences,* he had defended an analogy based on a direct comparison or relationship of a creature to God. And as we shall see below, in subsequent treatments he will again defend what he then calls the analogy of one to another when predicating names of creatures and of God.[175]

Moreover, even in the present context he notes in replying to the first objection that it is true that God cannot be regarded as similar to creatures. But creatures may be said to be similar to God in some fashion. This notion that a creature may be similar to God without implying that God must therefore also be similar (or related, we may add) to the creature would seem to be enough for Thomas to overcome the objection he has raised against using an analogy of proportion in the case of the divine names. Nonetheless, here he does not pursue that path.[176]

Instead he concludes that because no determined relationship is implied by the other kind of analogy (proportionality), there is nothing to prevent us from using that type when we predicate something of God and a creature.[177] This decided preference for what is sometimes called the analogy of proper proportionality has heavily influenced one Thomistic school of interpretation, that begun by Cardinal Cajetan.[178] Most more recent scholars regard this particular discussion of Thomas as uncharacteristic of his earlier and later thinking on analogical predication of the divine names, and hence as not reflecting his definitive position. As will appear from what follows below, the weight of the texts strongly supports this view. But it must be acknowledged that at least for a short time in the year 1256 Thomas defended the analogy of proportionality in the case of predication of divine names, and rejected analogy of proportion.[179] Not unexpectedly, he also defends the same

175. See *In I Sent.,* d. 35, q. 1, a. 4 (Mandonnet ed., Vol. 1, p. 820); and the Prologue, q. 1, a. 2, ad 2 (p. 10). Cf. notes 155, 157, and 158 above.

176. Leon. 22.1.79:194–80:213. Note: ". . . Deus nullo modo creaturis similis dicendus est, sed creaturae possunt similes Deo dici aliquo modo." My point is that while any creature is really related to God and determined by that relationship, God is not really related to the creature and, strictly speaking, not really similar to the creature so as to be determined by that relationship. For the point that creatures are really related to God see *De potentia,* q. 7, a. 9, end of corpus (ed. cit., p. 208). For the denial that God is really related to creatures see a. 10 (p. 210). In the latter context also see ad 5 (p. 211).

177. ". . . sed in alio modo analogiae nulla determinata habitudo attenditur inter ea quibus est aliquid per analogiam commune, et ideo secundum illum modum nihil prohibet aliquod nomen analogice dici de Deo et creatura" (Leon. 22.1.79:172–177).

178. See n. 163 above in the present Chapter and Ch. III, n. 87 for references to Cajetan's general position. For his identification of analogy of proportionality (to the exclusion of analogy of proportion [attribution]) with Thomas's analogy *secundum esse et secundum intentionem* see par. n. 30 of his *De nominum analogia.* See nn. 23ff. for his description of it, and n. 29 for his decided preference for it as the only kind capable of making known to us the intrinsic entities, goodnesses, and truths of things—in other words, as the only intrinsic analogy (see p. 29). Cf. n. 21 (p. 21) for his identification of analogy of proportion (for Cajetan, analogy of attribution) with Thomas's analogy *secundum intentionem et non secundum esse,* and hence as exclusively extrinsic.

179. Concerning this historical shift see Klubertanz, *St. Thomas Aquinas on Analogy,* p. 94; Montagnes, *La doctrine,* pp. 72–93; Bonino, *Thomas d'Aquin,* pp. 508–9.

view in a. 11 in replying to some of the objections. For instance, in his reply to objection 4 he speaks of three kinds of likeness, only one of which he admits between a creature and God, i.e., that based on an agreement of proportions (proportionality).[180] His overriding concern throughout much of this discussion seems to be to protect divine transcendence. His theory of analogy of proportionality is not equally successful, however, in protecting him against the kind of agnosticism on our part which he associates with a theory of purely equivocal predication of the divine names.

We should also note that in a somewhat later discussion in *De veritate*, q. 23, a. 7, ad 9, Thomas again appeals to proportionality as an alternative way of explaining the similarity or likeness between a creature and God. Here Thomas wants to defend the point that man is conformed to God since he was made according to his image and likeness. Because of the infinite distance between man and God, there can be no mathematical proportion between the two in the way proportion is found between different quantities. But insofar as the name proportion is transferred to signify any relationship of one thing to another, there is nothing to prevent us from speaking of some proportion of man to God. Thus, insofar as man was created by God and is subject to him, man stands in some relationship to God. This first explanation on Thomas's part does not necessarily commit him to rejecting analogy of proportion and defending only proportionality.[181]

But he then proposes another possible solution. It might be said that while there can be no proportion properly speaking between the finite and the infinite, still there can be the kind of proportionality which consists of a likeness of two proportions. As in q. 2, a. 11, he cites the case of six being like four because four is related to two as six is related to three. In this way we may say that just as the infinite is to the infinite, so is the finite to the finite. Hence there is this kind of likeness between a creature and God, since just as God has those things which belong to him, so does a creature have those things which belong to it.[182]

---

180. Leon. 22.1.80:231–244. Thomas comments that a likeness based on the fact that two things participate in something that is one, or on the fact that one thing has a determined relation to the other would diminish the infinite distance between creatures and God. But this is not true of a likeness based on an agreement of proportions.

181. According to Weisheipl, this question was disputed in 1258–1259. See *Friar Thomas d'Aquino*, p. 363. See Leon. 22.3.672:305–321. Note especially: ". . . secundum tamen quod nomen proportionis translatum est ad quamlibet habitudinem significandam unius rei ad rem aliam—utpote cum dicimus hic esse proportionum similitudinem, sicut se habet princeps ad civitatem, ita gubernator ad navim—, nihil prohibet dicere aliquam proportionem hominis ad Deum, cum in aliqua habitudine ad ipsum se habeat, utpote ab eo effectus et ei subiectus." The example cited here might lead one to believe that even this first solution is restricted to proportionality: as a ruler is to a state so is a pilot to a ship. But the application rather indicates a direct relation of a human being to God as created by him and subject to him. On this text see Klubertanz, *St. Thomas Aquinas on Analogy*, pp. 91–94.

182. See p. 672:321–335. Thomas clearly regards this second alternative as based on proportionality: "quae est duarum proportionum similitudo." The text concludes: ". . . et per hunc modum est similitudo inter creaturam et Deum, quia sicut se habet ad ea quae ei competunt, ita creatura ad sua

In this text there is neither a decisive rejection of analogy of proportion, nor an exclusive acceptance of analogy of proportionality. Proportionality is proposed as an alternative way of accounting for a creature's similitude or likeness to God. Even so, Klubertanz is surely correct when he writes that "the absence of any subsequent text which teaches proper proportionality between God and creatures constitutes strong evidence that St. Thomas quietly abandoned this doctrine after 1256."[183] At the very least, by the time of *De veritate*, q. 23 Thomas no longer regards proportionality as the only way of accounting for a creature's likeness to God.[184]

c. *Summa contra Gentiles* I (1259/60–1264/65)

With this we may return to Thomas's discussion of the divine names in the *Summa contra Gentiles*. As we saw in the previous section of this Chapter, in Bk I, c. 31, Thomas defends the point that a plurality of divine names is not repugnant to God's simplicity.[185] In cc. 32 and following he explicitly takes up the issue of univocal, equivocal, and analogical predication of the divine names. In c. 32 itself he offers a number of arguments to show that nothing can be predicated univocally of God and of creatures.

The first argument maintains that if the form an effect receives from its cause is not the same in species as the form through which that cause acts, a name taken from that form in the effect cannot be predicated univocally of the cause. For instance, according to Thomas's medieval world-view, fire as generated by the sun and the sun itself are not both said to be hot univocally. But no form which is caused by God can attain to the species of the divine power itself, for that which creatures receive in divided and partial fashion is present in God in simple and total fashion. Therefore nothing can be said univocally of God and of other things.[186]

This argument is interesting because it maintains that specific likeness between the form present in an effect and in its cause is required for univocal predication of a name of both. And because Thomas has previously denied that God belongs to any genus or that he can be designated by any substantial difference (and belong to any species), it will follow that the form of no effect can agree in species with its divine cause. Moreover, as Thomas's argument here assumes, in c. 28 he has just

---

propria." On this see Klubertanz as cited in the preceding note. His remarks on p. 94 indicate that he dates this disputed question (q. 23) ca. 1256, i.e., at roughly the same time as q. 2, a. 11. As I have indicated in n. 181, Weisheipl places q. 23 in 1258–59, and this seems to me to be much more likely, since this question naturally falls into Thomas's third year as Regent Master (1258–1259). It seems most unlikely that Thomas would have conducted the first 23 questions of the *De veritate* in one year.

183. Op. cit., p. 94. See my remarks in the preceding note about the date for q. 23. Since it presents proportionality as only the second of two possible solutions, it already marks some advance over q. 2, a. 11.

184. However, unlike Klubertanz's apparent view (see pp. 92, 94), I do not see the text from q. 23, a. 7, ad 9 as indicating an exclusive choice for proportionality.

185. Ed. Leon. man., pp. 32–33.

186. Ed. cit., p. 33.

shown that God is totally *(universaliter)* perfect. Since this can be true of no effect, no effect can be specifically the same as God. Hence univocal predication of any name of God and his effects is precluded.[187]

The second argument continues along the same general line, but in a fortiori fashion. Even if an effect does belong to the same species as its cause, univocal predication of a name of the cause and the effect will still not be possible unless the effect receives specifically the same kind of form according to the same mode of being. For instance, the name "house" is not predicated univocally of a house which exists in the mind of a builder and of the material form of the house itself, because the two modes of being differ. Even if created things could attain to some form which is completely like that of their divine cause, they would not possess it according to the same mode of being. There is nothing in God which is not identical with the divine act of being *(esse)*; but this is not true of anything else. Once again, therefore, univocal predication of anything of creatures and God is ruled out. According to this more metaphysically based argument, therefore, diversity in mode of being precludes univocal predication.[188]

In the third argument Thomas reasons that whatever is predicated univocally of a number of things must be a genus, or species, or difference, or accident, or property. But he has shown in c. 24 that nothing can be predicated of God as a substantial difference, or as a genus (c. 25). It follows from this that neither a definition nor a species can be predicated of him, since a species consists of a genus and a difference. Thomas has shown in c. 23 that there are no accidents in God. Hence he now concludes that nothing can be predicated of God as an accident or as a property, for a property falls into the genus of accidents. If one agrees with Thomas that this exhausts the list of possible candidates for univocal predication, it will again follow that nothing can be predicated univocally of God and other things.[189]

Thomas's fourth argument reasons that if something is predicated univocally of a number of things, it is simpler than any of them, at least in the order of thought, i.e., conceptually. But nothing can be simpler than God either in the order of thought or in the order of reality. Hence nothing can be predicated univocally of God and of other things.[190]

That Thomas holds that nothing can be simpler than God in the order of reality is not a surprising claim, of course, since this follows from the divine simplicity.

187. See cc. 24 and 25 for the points that God cannot be designated by any substantial difference (and fall into a species), and that he is not in any genus.

188. Ed. cit., p. 33. Note the controlling statement: "Si aliquis effectus ad speciem causae pertingat, praedicationem nominis univoce non consequetur nisi secundum eundem essendi modum eandem specie formam suscipiat. . . ."

189. Ibid. In other words, this argument rests on our inability to apply any of the predicables to God. Hence it is more a logical than a metaphysical argument.

190. Ibid. Note especially: "Quod univoce de pluribus praedicatur, utroque illorum ad minus secundum intellectum simplicius est."

But he also maintains that nothing, including our understanding of being, presumably, is simpler than God even in the order of thought. This may be one more reason why he refuses to admit that God and creatures somehow share in being, even in the notion of being that serves as the subject of metaphysics; for that would mean that, even as realized in God, being would have to be differentiated and that it would therefore be prior even to God, at least conceptually.[191]

Thomas's fifth argument rests on the claim that if something is predicated univocally of a number of things, it belongs to each of those only by participation. In support he notes that a species is said to participate in a genus, and an individual in a species. But nothing is said of God by participation, for whatever is participated is limited *(determinatur)* according to the mode of the participant. Hence it is possessed only in particular or partial fashion and not according to every mode of perfection. It follows once more that nothing can be predicated univocally of God and other things.[192]

One might counter that participation of a species in a genus and of an individual in a species are cases of logical participation rather than real participation, according to Thomas's own division in his Commentary on the *De Hebdomadibus*.[193] But unlike real participation, logical participation does not require real composition of the participant and that in which it participates. Thomas would counter, however, that even logical participation is inappropriate in the case of God, for this would suggest that he is in some way conceptually subordinated to that in which he participates. I stress this because this may well be one of Thomas's most fundamental reasons for rejecting univocal predication of anything of God and creatures. If he were to admit that any perfection could be so predicated, he would thereby subordinate God to that perfection in which both God and creatures shared.[194]

Finally, argues Thomas, whatever is predicated of different things according to priority and posteriority is certainly not predicated of them univocally. That which is prior is included in the definition of that which is posterior—as for example, substance is included in the definition of accident insofar as the latter enjoys being. If being were said univocally of substance and accident, substance would also have to be included in the definition of being insofar as being is applied to substance, since it is included in being's definition when being is applied to an accident. This, of course, is impossible. But everything predicated of God and other things is said of them according to priority and posteriority; for all things are said of God essen-

191. See my discussion of this above in Ch. I and again in Ch. III, n. 64.

192. Ibid. Note: "De Deo autem nihil dicitur per participationem: nam omne quod participatur determinatur ad modum participantis [conjectural reading for *participati*], et sic partialiter habetur et non secundum omnem perfectionis modum. Oportet igitur nihil de Deo et rebus aliis univoce praedicari."

193. For this text see Ch. IV above, n. 8.

194. See my comments immediately above concerning Thomas's fourth argument against univocal predication.

tially and predications are made of other things by participation. Therefore nothing can be predicated univocally of God and of other things.[195]

Against this argument a defender of univocal predication might counter that what makes possible such predication of certain perfections of God and of creatures is the fact that we can abstract pure perfections from both the participated way in which they are realized in creatures and the essential way in which they are realized in God. Hence we can think of such a perfection without also thinking of it in terms of priority and posteriority, even though it will never be realized except in one way or the other way, i.e., as participated or essentially. Thomas would reply that this would be to regard such a perfection as in some way superior to creatures and to God, at least as conceptually superior, and that this simply cannot be admitted.[196]

In sum, these arguments against univocal predication of divine names in SCG I, c. 32 are different from those we have seen in the Commentary on I *Sentences* and in *De veritate,* q. 2, a. 11. Interesting also is the omission in this text of the argument based on the claim that a member of a genus (or species) must have an essence which differs from its *esse.* However, I should point out that some of that reasoning does appear in c. 25 as part of Thomas's effort to show that God is not included in any genus. In that chapter the third argument maintains that whatever is included in a genus differs in terms of its act of being *(esse)* from the others in that genus. But things in the same genus must also agree in terms of their generic quiddity. Hence the act of being of everything which is present in a genus is different from the generic quiddity, something which cannot be true of God. Therefore God is in no genus.[197] I mention this to show that Thomas has not forgotten his earlier reasoning.

In c. 33 Thomas considers the opposite position and endeavors to show that not all names said of God and of creatures are purely equivocal, i.e., equivocal by chance. The first argument reasons that in the case of names which are purely equivocal (equivocal by chance), it is purely accidental when one name is applied to different things. More importantly, Thomas also notes that in such cases the fact that a name is imposed on one thing does not imply that that thing bears any relationship to another thing which happens to receive the same name. But Thomas flatly denies that this is true of certain names which are predicated of God and creatures. An order or relationship between an effect and a cause is implied when such names are said of creatures and of God. Because of this, Thomas

---

195. Ed. cit., p. 33. Note in particular: "Quod praedicatur de aliquibus secundum prius et posterius, certum est univoce non praedicari. . . . Nihil autem de Deo et rebus aliis praedicatur eodem ordine, sed secundum prius et posterius: cum de Deo omnia praedicentur essentialiter . . . ; de aliis autem praedicationes fiunt per participationem. . . ."

196. Again we return to the thinking behind Thomas's fourth argument.

197. See ed. cit., p. 26.

concludes that they are not applied to God and creatures in purely equivocal fashion.[198]

To put this another way, it is the ontological relationship between a creature viewed as an effect and God viewed as its cause which justifies our predicating the name of a pure perfection of God and of the creature. For such predication to be meaningful, this cause-effect relationship must in some way be preserved in our application of the name to creatures and to God. This relationship alone grounds the minimum degree of similarity or likeness which must obtain between the two, as Thomas has argued, for instance, in c. 29. And such similitude or likeness in turn renders inadequate any theory of purely equivocal predication of the divine names.[199]

Thomas's second argument explicitly brings out this very point. Where pure equivocation obtains, no likeness between the things named is expressed, but merely the unity of a name or term. But Thomas reminds us that he has already shown that there is some kind of likeness of creatures to God (see c. 29). This very likeness again rules out as inadequate a theory of merely equivocal predication of the divine names.[200]

The third argument returns to the more epistemological approach characteristic of his earlier treatments in *In I Sent.*, d. 35, and *De veritate*, q. 2, a. 11. When one name is predicated of different things in purely equivocal fashion, we cannot move from our knowledge of one to knowledge of the others. But we can move from perfections we find in other things to some knowledge of God, as Thomas is convinced he has now shown in the *Summa contra Gentiles*. Once again purely equivocal predication of the divine names is eliminated.[201]

As the fourth argument shows, pure equivocation prevents us from making any progress in building an argument. If nothing could be said of God and of creatures except equivocally, no argumentation could be developed which reasons from creatures to God. Against this Thomas cites the practice of all who speak about divine things. And against this he could just as easily again cite his own development of such argumentation in this same work.[202]

---

198. Ed. cit., pp. 33–34. Note especially: ". . . sed omnino per accidens est quod unum nomen diversis rebus attribuitur: non enim nomen impositum uni significat ipsum habere ordinem ad aliud. Sic autem non est de nominibus quae de Deo dicuntur et creaturis. Consideratur enim in huiusmodi nominum communitate ordo causae et causati. . . ."

199. Again we are reminded of the crucial role in Thomas's theory of the divine names of his view that every agent produces an effect that is in some way like itself.

200. Ed. cit., p. 34. "Amplius. Ubi est pura aequivocatio, nulla similitudo in rebus attenditur, sed solum unitas nominis. Rerum autem ad Deum est aliquis modus similitudinis, ut ex supra dictis patet. Relinquitur igitur quod non dicuntur de Deo secundum puram aequivocationem."

201. Ibid. See especially: "Item . . . Ex his autem quae in rebus aliis inveniuntur in divinorum cognitionem pervenimus, ut ex dictis patet."

202. Ibid.

Finally, Thomas reasons that there would be no point in predicating a name of a thing unless we could understand something about that thing through the name. But if all the names applied to God and creatures were purely equivocal, such names would tell us nothing about God; for the meanings of such names are known to us only insofar as they are said of creatures. It would then be useless for us to say or to prove of God that he is a being, or good, or anything else of this kind.[203] Against this one might reply that through names of this kind we only know what God is not. To describe him as living would mean that he does not belong to the class of inanimate things. In response Thomas counters that in that event a name such as "living" would at least have this in common when it is applied to God and to creatures, i.e., the negation of being inanimate. Even this is enough to show that it is not purely equivocal, he concludes.[204]

In sum, the added contribution of this series of arguments against purely equivocal predication of the divine names is to show that it fails to express the likeness that obtains between creatures and God. This likeness itself has been established, Thomas maintains, by reasoning from created things viewed as effects to God as their cause. And because that reasoning presupposes that in some way every effect is like its cause, the success of such reasoning itself undercuts, in Thomas's eyes, any theory of merely equivocal predication of such names of creatures and of God.[205]

Having now eliminated to his own satisfaction both theories of univocal and purely equivocal predication of the divine names, Thomas concludes in c. 34 that such names can only be predicated analogically of creatures and of God. As he here explains, this means that they are applied according to an ordering or relationship to some one thing. But analogical predication based on an ordering or relationship to some one thing may happen in two different ways. In the first way, this is based on the fact that many different things all bear a relationship to something that is one. For instance, it is in relationship to one and the same health that an animal is said to be healthy as its subject, medicine as its efficient cause, food as that which preserves it, and urine as its sign. In the second way, an analogical name is predicated of two things not because they are both related to some third thing, but because one of them is related to the other. Thus being *(ens)* is said of substance and accident because an accident bears a relationship to substance, not because substance and accident are both related to some third thing. Thomas concludes that names are not said analogically of God and other things in the first way, be-

---

203. Ibid. Hence arguments 3, 4, and 5 are all based on the unacceptable agnosticism that would result from a theory of the purely equivocal character of divine names. Not appearing here is the argument from agnosticism on God's part that would also result, which Thomas had used in *De veritate*, q. 2, a. 11.

204. Ed. cit., p. 34. Note especially: ". . . ad minus oportebit quod *vivum* de Deo et creaturis dictum conveniat in negatione inanimati. Et sic non erit pure aequivocum."

205. Montagnes (p. 70), after quoting arg. 1 from our text, remarks that the "noetic" argumentation has now been reinforced by a metaphysical argument. He also comments that this metaphysical approach first appears in the *Summa contra Gentiles*. Also see p. 70, n. 13.

cause this would imply that something is prior to God. Only the second kind of analogical predication is admissible in the case of the divine names.[206]

In other words, Thomas has now clearly defended his preference for an analogy of "one to another" in the case of divine names. He has just as clearly rejected any kind of analogy of "many to one," because this would in some way subordinate God along with creatures to some third "one" in which both would share. His thinking here is clearly at odds with his rejection of analogy of proportion in *De veritate* q. 2, a. 11, since that too was an analogy of one to another. And his option there for analogy of proportionality as the only kind to be used in predicating names of God has simply disappeared. The present text brings him back to a position which is fairly close to and develops the view he had espoused in his Commentary on I *Sentences*.[207] But the theory presented in SCG I, c. 34 is more coherent, more unified, and more fully developed. Here analogy of "one to another" is applied at the level of both predicamental and transcendental analogy.[208] And it is this theory we shall find Thomas defending in his later major treatments in the *De potentia* and in *Summa theologiae* I.

Before turning to those texts, however, we should note that Thomas introduces another distinction in SCG I, c. 34. After having selected analogical predication of the second kind (the analogy of one to another) for the case of the divine names, he notes that in this kind of analogy it sometimes happens that the order of naming corresponds to the order that obtains in reality; but sometimes these two orders differ. The order of naming follows upon the order of knowledge, since a name is a sign of an intelligible conception. Therefore when that which is prior in reality is also prior in the order of discovery, the order of naming and the order in reality are the same. Thus substance is prior to accident in nature, because substance serves

206. Ed. cit., p. 34. Note in particular: "... praedicantur neque univoce neque aequivoce, sed analogice: hoc est secundum ordinem vel respectum ad aliquid unum. Quod quidem dupliciter contingit. Uno modo, secundum quod multa habent respectum ad aliquid unum. . . . Alio modo, secundum quod duorum attenditur ordo vel respectus, non ad aliquid alterum, sed ad unum ipsorum: sicut ens de substantia et accidente dicitur secundum quod accidens ad substantiam respectum habet, non quod substantia et accidens ad aliquid tertium referantur."

207. However, in his Commentary on I *Sentences*, Thomas depicts both substance and accident as participating in unequal fashion *(secundum prius et posterius)* in a common *ratio (ens)* which would be prior to both. See Prologue, q. 1, a. 2, ad 2 (Mandonnet ed., Vol. 1, p. 10). There he notes that analogical community may be twofold: "Aut ex eo quod aliqua participant aliquid unum secundum prius et posterius, sicut potentia et actus rationem entis, et similiter substantia et accidens; aut ex eo quod unum esse et rationem ab altero recipit . . ." (see n. 158 above for continuation). Also see obj. 2 (p. 9) where the same point is made, a point which Thomas does not reject in replying to that objection. Cf. Montagnes, *La doctrine*, p. 73, n. 17.

208. See Montagnes, pp. 80–81. For predicamental analogy, note how being is said of substance and accident in SCG I, c. 34, and at the transcendental level, how names are predicated of God and creatures. For close similarities between Thomas's presentation in *In I Sent.* and some texts of Albert the Great *(In I Sent.*, and his Commentary on the *Divine Names)* see Montagnes, pp. 73–75, n. 20. For a much broader treatment of analogy in Albert which brings out the originality of his personal position see de Libera, *Albert le Grand*, pp. 89–101.

as a cause of accident. And substance is also prior in the order of knowledge, because substance is included in the definition of an accident. In this case, therefore, the two orders correspond. Therefore being is said of substance before it is said of accident according to both orders.[209]

But if that which is prior in reality is posterior in the order of knowledge or discovery, then in the case of analogical predication the order of naming differs from the order of reality. For instance, the power of healing in a healing medicine or food is prior in nature to the health of the animal just as a cause is prior to its effect. But because we know of this power through its effect, we name the power from the effect, i.e., we call it health-giving only because we have already named an animal healthy. In the case of our knowledge of God we reason from knowledge of other things to knowledge of him. As Thomas puts it, "he is said to be named from his effects." Therefore the names we apply to God have first been assigned to other things and then to God, even though the reality signified thereby first belongs to God. In this case, therefore, the order of naming does not correspond to the order of reality.[210]

d. *Compendium theologiae* I (1265–1267)

As we have already seen, contemporary scholars have encountered difficulty in dating this work. Here I am following the Leonine edition, Van Steenberghen, and Torrell in placing its first part ca. 1265–1267. This makes it more or less contemporary with the *De potentia,* which we shall take up next.[211]

In Part I, c. 27 Thomas argues that names are not said of God and other things either purely univocally or purely equivocally. Against univocal predication of such names he briefly reasons that the definition of that which is said of a creature is not identical with the definition of that which is said of God. But such is required for univocal predication.[212]

Against purely equivocal predication of such names of God and other things, Thomas reasons that when names are applied in that way, a name is imposed on one thing without any reference or relationship (of that thing) to another to which the name is also applied. Because of this, we cannot reason from one application of the name to any knowledge about some other thing to which the name is also applied. But in the case of the names we predicate of God and creatures, we assign them to God according to some order he bears to those things in which we first consider the meaning of the names. Because of this we can move from knowledge

---

209. Ed. cit., p. 34. As Thomas expresses his conclusion: "Et ideo ens dicitur prius de substantia quam de accidente et secundum rei naturam et secundum nominis rationem."

210. Ed. cit., pp. 34–35. Note Thomas's concluding remarks: "Sic igitur, quia ex rebus aliis in Dei cognitionem pervenimus, res nominum de Deo et rebus aliis dictorum per prius est in Deo secundum suum modum, sed ratio nominis per posterius. Unde et nominari dicitur a suis causatis."

211. See Ch. XI above, n. 108.

212. Leon. 42.90:1–7. For the general context within which c. 27 appears, see n. 144 above.

of those other things to knowledge about God. And this is enough to eliminate purely equivocal predication of such names.[213] In other words, here Thomas rests his case against purely equivocal predication of names of God on a counterfact: we can and do reason from certain perfections we find in creatures to some knowledge of God.

Thomas concludes again by process of elimination that such names are predicated of God and creatures according to analogy, that is, according to their proportion (or relation) to some one thing. It is because we compare other things to God as their first source that we attribute to him names which signify perfections in other things. From this Thomas concludes that these names are first said of creatures as regards our imposing such names, and we move from this usage to apply them to God. But as regards the reality they signify (secundum rem significatam), these names are first said of God, from whom perfections "descend" to other things.[214] This distinction reminds us of one we have just seen Thomas making in Summa contra Gentiles I, c. 34. And here again Thomas has opted for the analogy of one to another when dealing with divine names and makes no mention of analogy of proportionality. Apart from these points, this text does not contribute significantly to our understanding of Thomas's theory of analogical predication of divine names.

e. De potentia, q. 7 (1265–1266)

In the preceding section of this Chapter we have already examined in some detail earlier articles in q. 7. There we found Thomas defending the view that names of pure perfections such as "good," "wise," "just," etc., are predicated of God in such fashion that they signify the divine substance imperfectly and in deficient fashion, although they do not imply any kind of comprehensive knowledge on our part and do not yield quidditative knowledge of God.[215]

In a. 7 Thomas explicitly faces the issue of univocal, equivocal, and analogical predication of such names. He begins his reply by emphatically rejecting the possibility of univocal predication of anything of creatures and of God. First of all, every effect of an univocal agent is equal to the power of its efficient cause. But no creature, since it must be finite, can be equal to the power of the first agent, for this is infinite. Therefore no likeness of God can be received in a creature in univocal fashion.[216] Although Thomas does not explicitly state this here, he expects us to

---

213. Leon. 42.90:7–17. Note especially: "Haec autem nomina quae dicuntur de Deo et de aliis rebus, attribuuntur Deo secundum aliquem ordinem quem habet ad istas res in quibus intellectus significata eorum considerat, unde et per alias res ratiocinari de Deo possumus. . . ."

214. Leon. 42.90:18–91:29. In this text too we see a combination of reasoning based on our ability to reason from creatures to God (the noetic factor) and that based on the ontological dependence of creatures on God which justifies this (the metaphysical approach).

215. See above, Section 1–d.

216. Pession ed., p. 203. To bring out this reasoning more clearly, we may insert an implied step. If no creature or created perfection can be equal to the power of God, no creature or created perfec-

conclude that because no perfection can be received in a creature in the same way it is present in God, no name which signifies such a perfection can be applied univocally to God.

Moreover, even if a given kind of form is defined in the same way in a cause and in an effect, different modes of existing for that form will still prevent univocal predication. As in SCG I, c. 32 Thomas cites the example of the form of a house as it is present in the mind of a builder and in its proper matter. This diversity in modes of being (immaterial vs. material) prevents the name "house" from being predicated univocally of both. Accordingly, even if, *per impossibile,* goodness as realized in creatures and in God had the same definition or intelligible content *(ratio),* goodness still could not be predicated univocally of creatures and of God. For what is present in God in immaterial and simple fashion is realized in the creature in material fashion and in different ways. Moreover, being is not said univocally of substance and accident. A substance is a being which enjoys existence *(esse)* in its own right *(per se),* whereas an accident is that whose existence *(esse)* is to exist in something else. Again these different relationships to *esse* preclude univocal predication of being.[217]

But God's relationship to *esse* is different from that of any creature, since he is his *esse* (act of being). This is true of no creature. Therefore *esse* cannot be said univocally of God and a creature and, as a consequence, neither can anything else which is predicated of the two; for the first of all of these is being *(ens).*[218]

Thomas next turns to those who would deny that anything can be predicated analogically of God and creatures and who would limit all such predications to the purely equivocal. He comments in passing that this was the view of Moses Maimonides and, as we have seen, he has already dealt with this position at some length in q. 7, a. 5. Against any such theory Thomas here counters that in the case of purely equivocal predication something is not said of one thing in terms of its relationship to another when the same term is applied to both. But all things which are said of God and creatures are said of God according to some relationship God has to creatures or which creatures have to God. Because of this, purely equivocal predication of such terms must be rejected.[219] Moreover, since all our knowledge of God is drawn from creatures, if such predications were purely equivocal, we

---

tion can be a perfect or adequate likeness of God. Therefore, no likeness of God can be received in a creature univocally, i.e., as a perfect or adequate likeness of its divine cause.

217. Ed. cit., pp. 203–4. Note especially: ". . . etsi una sit ratio formae existentis in agente et in effectu, diversus tamen modus existendi impedit univocam praedicationem. . . .Ex quo patet quod diversa habitudo ad esse impedit univocam praedicationem entis."

218. Ed. cit., p. 204. "Deus autem alio modo se habet ad esse quam aliqua alia creatura; nam ipse est suum esse, quod nulli alii creaturae competit. Unde nullo modo univoce de Deo [et] creatura dicitur; et per consequens nec aliquid aliorum praedicabilium inter quae est ipsum primum ens. . . ." Understood in this text is Thomas's often repeated point that the name being *(ens)* is taken from *esse.* *Esse* as it is used in this text should be taken in the sense of act of being.

219. Ibid. On Thomas's discussion of Maimonides see Section 1–d of this Chapter, pp. 523–25.

would know nothing about God beyond the empty names themselves. They would tell us nothing about the divine reality. And it would follow from this that all the demonstrations offered by the philosophers about God would be sophistical because of the fallacy of equivocation. In addition, comments Thomas, an effect must in some way be like its cause. Therefore nothing should be predicated in purely equivocal fashion of an effect and its cause.[220]

Having now eliminated both univocal and purely equivocal predication of names of God and creatures, Thomas concludes that names of this type, i.e., pure perfections, are predicated analogically. He distinguishes two kinds of analogical predication. According to one type, something is predicated of two things because both are related to a third. It is in this way that being is predicated of both quality and quantity, because both are related to substance. According to the other type of analogical predication, something is predicated of two things because one of them is directly related to the other. It is in this way that being is predicated of substance and quantity, because of quantity's relationship to substance.[221]

According to the first kind of analogical predication, something must be prior to the two things which are both related to it. It is in this way that substance is prior to both quantity and quality, and their relationship to it justifies applying the name being to each of them as well. According to the second kind of analogy there is no need for something else to be prior to the two things of which the analogical name is predicated; but one of them must be prior to the other. Thomas concludes that because nothing is prior to God, and God is prior to every creature, the second kind of analogical predication is to be employed when we predicate names of God and of any creature. In other words, he again rejects the analogy of many to one (two to a third, as it is named here) and accepts the analogy of one to another to account for our predicating names of God and of creatures.[222]

In defending the analogy of one to another, Thomas's position in the *De potentia* is perfectly consistent with his view in *Summa contra Gentiles* I, c. 34. It is true that his argumentation against univocal predication and against purely equivocal predication is much briefer here than that presented in the *Summa contra Gentiles*, but there is no inconsistency between the two sets of arguments. Most of the arguments presented in the *De potentia* were already developed in the *Summa contra Gentiles*. We might also note that in replying to the fourth opening argument in support of univocal predication, Thomas again brings out his decided preference for the analogy of one to another. As he explains, when we say that God is better

220. Ed. cit., p. 204.
221. "Huius autem praedicationis duplex est modus. Unus quo aliquid praedicatur de duobus per respectum ad aliquod tertium, sicut ens de qualitate et quantitate per respectum ad substantiam. Alius modus est quo aliquid praedicatur de duobus per respectum unius ad alterum, sicut ens de substantia et quantitate" (ibid.). It is interesting to note that here he uses the predication of being to illustrate both the analogy of two to a third and the analogy of one to another.
222. Ibid. Note: "Et ideo cum Deo nihil sit prius, sed ipse sit prior creatura, competit in divina praedicatione secundus modus analogiae, et non primus."

than any creature or that he is the supreme good, we do not mean that he participates in the same genus along with creatures, as a species participates in a genus.
We rather mean that he is, as it were, the principle (or cause) of the genus in which
creatures participate.[223] And as Thomas explains in replying to the third opening
argument in support of equivocal predication of the divine names, God is not said
to be like creatures, but creatures are like God. To illustrate this he notes that we
do not say that a man is like his image or portrait, but that the portrait is like the
man.[224] As Thomas comments in q. 7, a. 10, in God there is no real relation to
creatures, but there is a real relation in creatures to God, that of effect to cause.[225]

f. *Summa theologiae* I (1266–1268)

With this we turn to Thomas's chronologically last major discussion of analogy
at the transcendental level, in the *Prima Pars*, q. 13. In the previous section of this
chapter we have already examined some of his efforts there to show that God can
be named by us from creatures. Thus he maintains that these names do not signify
the divine essence as it is in itself (a. 1), and yet that certain names can be predicated
of him substantially albeit imperfectly (a. 2), and properly (a. 3). In a. 3 he again
appeals to the distinction between what the names of pure perfections are intended
to signify and the way in which they signify (their *modus significandi*). As regards
that which they signify, such names are properly applied to God, but not as regards
the way in which they signify. After explaining why these names are not synonymous with one another in a. 4, Thomas turns in a. 5 to the issue of univocal,
equivocal, and analogical predication of such names.[226]

As in his other major discussions of this, Thomas begins by eliminating univocal
and equivocal predication of the divine names. His single argument against univocal predication recalls reasoning we have already seen. Any effect which is unequal
to the power of its cause receives a likeness of that cause in deficient fashion, and
not according to the same definition or intelligible content. Hence what exists in
divided and multiple fashion in the effects is realized in the cause in simple fashion
and in only one way. So it is through its one power that the sun can produce many
and varied forms in lower bodies. In like fashion, all perfections present in created

223. The argument maintains that there is some comparison between God and a creature, for it
is said that God is supremely good, and that a creature is good. Therefore they both belong to one
genus, and something can be said of them univocally (ed. cit., p. 203). For the reply see p. 204,
ad quartum.

224. For this argument see p. 203, *sed contra*, 3. In brief, it maintains that where there is no
likeness, nothing can be predicated in common except equivocally. But between a creature and God
there is no likeness. For Thomas's reply to this see p. 205, *ad tertium*.

225. See p. 210. Note: "Unde relinquitur quod in eo non est aliqua relatio realis ad creaturam,
licet sit relatio creaturae ad ipsum, sicut effectus ad causam." Note that Thomas there criticizes
Maimonides for rejecting any relationship between God and creatures.

226. Leon. 4.146: "Utrum ea quae de Deo dicuntur et creaturis, univoce dicantur de ipsis." In
his Introduction to q. 13 Thomas phrases it: "Quinto: utrum nomina aliqua dicantur de Deo et
creaturis univoce, vel aequivoce" (p. 139).

things in divided and multiple fashion preexist in God in united fashion or as one.[227]

When a name of a perfection is applied to a creature, it signifies that perfection as distinct in definition from the other perfections of that creature. For example, when the name "wise" is said of a human being, we signify thereby a perfection which is distinct from that person's essence, active powers, act of being, etc. But when we apply the name "wise" to God, we do not want to signify something distinct from his essence or his power or his act of being. So too, when the name "wise" is said of a human being, in a certain way it circumscribes and comprehends the thing signified. This is not so when such a name is applied to God, for it then leaves the thing signified as something which is not comprehended and something which surpasses the meaning of the name. From this Thomas concludes that the name "wise" is not applied to God and to a human being with the same intelligible content (ratio), nor is any other name. Therefore no name is predicated univocally of God and creatures.[228]

Two things should be noted about this argument. First of all, it brings out the point that in a creature there is a fundamental distinction between the perfection signified by a name such as "wise," and that creature's essence or active powers or act of being. This follows, of course, from Thomas's theory of a real distinction between the substantial essence of any created entity and its accidents, including any active powers, not to mention its act of being.[229] Secondly, Thomas here stresses the point that as regards the thing signified by a name such as wise, the name does in a way circumscribe and comprehend that which it signifies. In the case of God, however, this name, like any other we may apply to him, leaves the thing signified as something which we do not comprehend and something which surpasses any meaning we may give to the name. This will be true of any pure perfection we apply to God and to creatures.[230] Hence on both counts, univocal predication is excluded.

In this discussion Thomas devotes relatively little attention to purely equivocal predication of divine names. It is to be rejected because, if it were accepted, nothing could be known or demonstrated about God without our falling into the fallacy of equivocation. We have seen Thomas making this point before; but he now rejects

227. Leon. 4.146. Note: "Quia omnis effectus non adaequans virtutem causae agentis, recipit similitudinem agentis non secundum eandem rationem, sed deficienter: ita ut quod divisim et multipliciter est in effectibus, in causa est simpliciter et eodem modo. . . ."

228. Ibid. Note especially: "Et sic, cum hoc nomen sapiens de homine dicitur, quodammodo circumscribit et comprehendit rem significatam: non autem cum dicitur de Deo, sed relinquit rem significatam ut incomprehensam, et excedentem nominis significationem. Unde patet quod non secundum eandem rationem hoc nomen sapiens de Deo et de homine dicitur. . . . Unde nullum nomen univoce de Deo et creaturis praedicatur."

229. Here I am taking potentia as referring to a human being's operative powers.

230. See the text cited above in n. 228. This, of course, is consistent with his rejection of quidditative knowledge of God on our part. See Section 1 of this Chapter.

such a consequence as opposed to the philosophers who proved many things about God in demonstrative fashion, and to St. Paul's dictum in Romans 1:20 to the effect that the "invisible things of God are seen, being understood through those things which have been made."[231] In other words, such a theory would run counter both to philosophical reason and to faith. We might add that here Thomas can justifiably give short shrift to the theory of equivocal predication, since in a. 2 he had criticized two theories which seem to border on this, one which would reduce all positive names of God to those that are purely negative, and one which would hold that they tell us nothing about God but only something about his relationship to or actions with respect to creatures.[232]

As in his previous discussions of this, Thomas now concludes that such names (names of pure perfections) are said of God and creatures according to analogy, that is, according to proportion. And once more he distinguishes two kinds of analogical predication. One kind takes place when many things to which the name is applied are ordered and related to one. For example, it is in this way that healthy is said of medicine and of urine, because both have an ordering and relationship to the health of an animal. Another kind of analogical predication occurs because one thing to which the name is applied has a direct relationship to the other. Health may also be used to illustrate this kind of analogy, as when we refer to medicine and to an animal as healthy because medicine causes health in the animal.[233]

In other words, here again Thomas distinguishes between the analogy of many to one and the analogy of one to another. As in previous texts, here too he indicates that it is only according to the second kind of analogy—the analogy of one to another—that certain names are applied to God and to creatures. In support he comments that we cannot name God except from creatures. Hence whatever is said of God is based on some ordering or relationship of the creature to God as to its principle and cause, in which cause, he adds, the perfections of all things preexist in preeminent fashion.[234]

Once more, therefore, Thomas makes it perfectly clear that it is the ontological situation which provides the foundation for analogical predication. Because a creature is ordered to God as its principle and cause, the name of certain pure perfections insofar as they are realized in creatures may be applied to God, but only analogically, not univocally and not equivocally. This entire procedure presupposes

---

231. Leon. 4.146.

232. See Leon. 4.141–42. Cf. our previous discussion in Section 1–e of this Chapter.

233. Leon. 4.146–47. Note: "Dicendum est igitur quod huiusmodi nomina dicuntur de Deo et creaturis secundum analogiam, idest proportionem. Quod quidem dupliciter contingit in nominibus: vel quia multa habent proportionem ad unum. . . . vel ex eo quod unum habet proportionem ad alterum. . . . "

234. Leon. 4.147: "Et hoc modo aliqua dicuntur de Deo et creaturis analogice, et non aequivoce pure, neque univoce. Non enim possumus nominare Deum nisi ex creaturis. . . . Et sic, quidquid dicitur de Deo et creaturis, dicitur secundum quod est aliquis ordo creaturae ad Deum, ut ad principium et causam, in qua praeexistunt excellenter omnes rerum perfectiones."

the validity of Thomas's previous philosophical demonstration of God's existence. And it also assumes the truth of his claim that every effect is in some way like its cause, the great diversity between God and any of his effects notwithstanding.[235]

Thomas adds another precision in this discussion in a. 5. After commenting that this kind of community (analogical) is intermediary between pure equivocation and univocity, he notes that in the case of names predicated analogically there is no single intelligible content (ratio), as is true of univocals; nor is the intelligible content totally diverse, as is true of the purely equivocal. In the case of analogy, the name which is applied in different ways signifies different relationships to something that is one. He illustrates this with his familiar example. "Healthy," for instance, when said of urine signifies a sign of the health of an animal. When said of medicine it signifies a cause of health in the animal. But he applies this to all kinds of analogy, including the analogy of divine names, which is under discussion.[236]

This view that the intelligible content (ratio) corresponding to an analogous term is not simply one and yet not totally diverse corresponds with similar statements Thomas makes elsewhere about analogy at the predicamental level. For instance, as we saw above in Ch. III, in commenting on *Metaphysics* IV, c. 2 he remarks that in analogical predication something is affirmed of different things according to intelligible contents (rationes) which are partly diverse and partly not diverse. Because each of the secondary analogates to which such a term applies is related in different fashion to one primary thing, the various intelligible contents will vary when the name is applied to these different things. Because it is to one thing that the various secondary analogates are ordered, their intelligible contents are partly not diverse or partly the same.[237] In his *De principiis naturae*, c. 6, Thomas refers to a term as predicated analogically when it is applied to things which differ in intelligible content, but which are attributed (or ordered) to one and the same thing. Although the language in those two descriptions is slightly different, the underlying position is fundamentally the same.[238] Hence we may

235. To put this another way, Thomas's conclusion about analogical predication of such names in a. 5 builds upon his discussion in a. 2 (see p. 142).

236. "Neque enim his quae analogice dicuntur, est una ratio, sicut est in univocis; nec totaliter diversa, sicut in aequivocis; sed nomen quod sic multipliciter dicitur, significat diversas proportiones ad aliquid unum . . ." (ibid.).

237. See *In IV Met.*, lect. 1, Cathala-Spiazzi ed., p. 151, n. 535: "Quandoque vero secundum rationes quae partim sunt diversae et partim non diversae: diversae quidem secundum quod diversas habitudines important, unae autem secundum quod ad unum aliquid et idem istae diversae habitudines referuntur; et illud dicitur 'analogice praedicari', idest proportionaliter, prout unumquodque secundum suam habitudinem ad illud unum refertur." See Ch. III above, p. 81.

238. See Leon. 43.46:33–41. Note: "Analogice dicitur praedicari quod praedicatur de pluribus quorum rationes diversae sunt, sed attribuuntur uni alicui eidem, sicut sanum dicitur de corpore animalis et de urina et de potione, sed non ex toto idem significat in omnibus: dicitur enim de urina ut de signo sanitatis, de corpore ut de subiecto, de potione ut de causa. Sed tamen omnes istae rationes attribuuntur uni fini, scilicet sanitati." As we noted in Ch. III, there is a slight difference between this text and that cited in n. 237 from *In IV Met.* According to this text the *rationes* of the

conclude that at both the transcendental and the predicamental levels, the intelligible content corresponding to an analogical term is partly the same and partly not the same when that term is applied to different analogates. Simply to describe the intelligible content as diverse would run the risk of reducing analogous predication to pure equivocation. Simply to describe it as one and the same would reduce analogy to univocity.

In the case of analogy at the predicamental level, we noted in Ch. III that Thomas often appeals to what we might describe, in his later terminology, as the analogy of many to one. We also found some instances of his usage at that level of an analogy based on proportionality. But more fundamental, especially in the case of the predication of being at the predicamental level, is the analogy of many to one. This, of course, closely reflects Aristotle's views about the πρὸς ἕν predication of being in his *Metaphysics* IV, c. 2. But as we also noted in Ch. III, it seems that one could reduce the analogy of many to one to a still more fundamental analogy of one to another, especially in the case of the predication of being of different accidents, and then of an accident and of substance.[239] In fact, we find further support for this in *De potentia,* q. 7, a. 7, where Thomas applies both the analogy of many to one and the analogy of one to another in predicating being at the predicamental level.[240] And as we have now seen, at the transcendental level Thomas has very decisively opted for the analogy of one to another.

different analogates are diverse, but all are attributed (or ordered) to some one thing, e.g., to one end, health. According to the text from the Commentary on the *Metaphysics,* the *rationes* themselves are partly diverse because they include the different relationships, and partly not diverse because each of these relationships is ordered to one thing. Unlike the text from the *De principiis,* the text from *In IV Met.* suggests that the different relationships *and* the one thing to which they are ordered are included in the *rationes.* See Ch. III above, n. 65, and the related discussion. The text from ST I (see n. 236 above) is closer to that from *In IV Met.* Klubertanz *(St. Thomas Aquinas on Analogy,* pp. 23–24) cites three early texts wherein he finds Thomas defending a single intelligibility *(una ratio)* in the case of analogy, and concludes that Thomas changed his position on this point, since he defends a plurality of intelligibilities in all other texts. However, in two of the troublesome texts Thomas speaks of a *ratio* which is one *secundum analogiam.* See *In I Sent.,* d. 22, q. 1, a, 2, ad 3 (Mandonnet ed., Vol. 1, p. 536); *In II Sent.,* d. 1, q. 1, a. 1 (Vol. 2, pp. 12–13). This is to say that the intelligibility or *ratio* is one only analogically, and hence not one in the univocal sense. Hence it does not necessarily have to be regarded as contradicting Thomas's later references to analogous *rationes* as being partly the same and partly not the same, or his equally early reference in the *De principiis* to the *rationes* as diverse. Klubertanz's third text is taken from *In I Sent.,* d. 22, q. 1, a. 3, ad 4: "Omnia enim huiusmodi dicuntur de Deo et creaturis non aequivoce, sed secundum unam rationem analogice" (Mandonnet ed., Vol. 1, p. 539). Here again the term *analogice* qualifies the reference to one *ratio.* Much the same may be said for the two sets of texts juxtaposed by R. McInerny which at first sight seem respectively to reject a *ratio communis* and then to accept it. The texts which seem to accept it are all qualified in one way or another, some by showing that the *ratio communis* is properly or perfectly present only in one of the analogates. See his *Studies in Analogy* (The Hague, 1968), pp. 2–12. For his solution see pp. 61–66.

239. See *De principiis naturae,* c. 6, as discussed above in Ch. III. See n. 48 and my corresponding text. Cf. notes 49, 50.

240. See above in this Chapter, n. 221.

In concluding this discussion of analogy at the transcendental level, I would like to ward off a possible misunderstanding. An oversimplified view of Thomas's position might infer from what we have seen that the intelligible content *(ratio)* signified by an analogous name such as "good" or "true" or "being" remains exactly the same when we abstract it from the participated way in which it is realized in creatures and the unparticipated way it is present in God. If so, we might then speak of a common intelligible core or content which is retained by such an abstracted concept of an absolute perfection. This would remain exactly the same and would be applied to God or to creatures by the simple addition on our part of the appropriate mode of being, unparticipated and unlimited, on the one hand, or participated and limited, on the other.

And indeed a long-standing school of Thomistic interpretation seems to view matters more or less this way, as Montagnes has pointed out. Whether such writers refer to this abstracted concept as a perfection in itself, or as an absolute perfection, or as a transcendental analogue, the theory seems to be the same. There is some fundamental intelligible core which we can abstract in the case of pure perfections. This common core serves as a bridge, as it were, which enables us to move from knowledge of perfections in their finite and participated state to such a pure perfection considered in itself, and from this to its application to the infinite and unparticipated source of all being.[241]

However, our examination of Thomas's texts on analogy does not support such an approach. In his presentation both of the analogy of many to one (at the predicamental level) and of the analogy of one to another (at both the predicamental and transcendental levels), Thomas's texts indicate that the *rationes* involved, the intelligible contents, are partly the same and partly not the same. The perfection in question belongs to one analogate in primary fashion and to the other or others in secondary fashion. Our understanding of such a perfection as it is realized in a secondary analogate, e.g., an accident or a creature, also carries with it an awareness of it as ordered to, as related to, and as dependent upon the primary analogate, whether this be a substance or whether it be God himself.

Thus at the predicamental level, if being is said of an accident such as quantity and of substance by the analogy of one to another, this is because our understanding of the accident necessarily includes an understanding of it as ordered to and dependent upon substance. And the same will hold if we predicate being of two different accidents, because both are related to and depend upon substance (analogy of many to one). It is in substance, of course, that being is realized in primary

241. See Montagnes, *La doctrine de l'analogie,* pp. 94–103, for a good exposition and critique of this way of viewing an analogical concept. Note especially his citation from M.T.-L. Penido, *Le rôle de l'analogie en théologie dogmatique,* pp. 189–90. See Montagnes, p. 97, n. 57. The usefulness of Penido's book is badly compromised by its uncritical acceptance of Cajetan's rejection of analogy of proportion as always purely extrinsic.

fashion. So too, at the transcendental level, if being or goodness or any pure perfection is predicated of a creature and of God, in the order of reality it belongs to God first and foremost as the uncaused and unparticipated source of its presence in others. In the order of discovery, however, after one has demonstrated the existence of God, one's full understanding of it as present in creatures carries with it an awareness of its relationship of dependence upon its unparticipated source.[242]

In sum, according to Thomas's thinking we should not view an analogical intelligible content as something we grasp simply by abstracting it from the participated way it is realized in creatures so as to view it in itself, as it were, and then predicate it of God according to his mode of being. Such an approach would subordinate both created beings and God himself to this abstracted absolute perfection in itself. And it would in effect reduce such abstracted analogical concepts to univocal concepts. For Thomas, when we recognize such a perfection in a creature as analogical and as participated, we recognize it as ordered to something else. After demonstrating God's existence we recognize that to which it is ordered as its unparticipated source. The perfection in question is either participated and finite and ordered to its source, or it is unparticipated and infinite and subsistent in itself. There is no common *tertium quid* or absolute perfection in itself which might serve as a bridge between the two.

3. Conclusions on Our Knowledge of God

Both in his discussions of quidditative knowledge of God and in his treatment of analogical predication of the divine names, Thomas has been deeply concerned with respecting the divine otherness and transcendence. Hence he has strongly argued against any claim that we can arrive at quidditative knowledge of God or predicate names of him univocally. At the same time, we have also found Thomas consistently rejecting the opposite extreme by opposing any theory of purely equivocal predication of divine names. Frequently when arguing against such a position he has appealed to the principle that every agent produces something like itself. While we have already considered his argumentation for this principle in SCG I, c. 29, I would like to return briefly to his discussion of it before concluding this chapter.[243]

Reference was made above to Mondin's conclusion that while Thomas sometimes argues inductively for this principle, this approach is not really a demonstration. While Mondin also found him attempting to establish the principle in deductive fashion, he concluded ultimately that Thomas regards it as self-evident in the sense that it follows from the principle of sufficient reason. Mondin recognizes that

242. See Montagnes, pp. 95–97.
243. See Section 1–c above in this Chapter, pp. 517–18.

Thomas never so named any such principle. For my part, I would prefer to say that for Thomas it follows from the intelligibility of being insofar as this is applied to the causal activity of agents.[244]

As will be recalled from Section 1 of the present chapter, in SCG I, c. 28 Thomas argues that God is all-perfect by showing that no excellence of any kind is lacking to him. This sets the stage for his effort in c. 29 to show that there is some likeness between creatures and God their cause. Even in this case, where we are dealing with what he calls an equivocal cause or agent, "it is of the nature of action that an agent produce something like itself, since each and everything acts insofar as it is in act." Therefore the form of an effect must be present in some way in its cause, even in the case of a higher-order or equivocal cause such as God, who does not fall into the same species or genus as any of his effects. In this instance the form of the effect will be present in God according to another mode and with a different intelligible content *(ratio)*. As we have seen, Thomas illustrates this by appealing to the example of the sun and the heat it causes here on earth. But he really grounds his claim on the philosophical point that God grants perfections to all of his effects as their efficient cause. It is because of this that there is some likeness as well as unlikeness between them and God.[245]

This argumentation is more or less paralleled in ST I, q. 4. As we saw above in Ch. XII, there in a. 1 Thomas argues for the divine perfection because, as the first efficient cause, God must be in act to the maximum degree and therefore perfect to the maximum degree.[246] In a. 2 he repeats his efforts in SCG I, c. 28 to show that God is universally perfect in the sense that no excellence of any kind can be lacking to him. Again he reasons that whatever perfection is found in an effect must be present in its efficient cause, either according to the same intelligible content if that agent is univocal with its effect, or more eminently if the agent is equivocal. Even in the latter case the effect must preexist in the cause virtually, which is to say that the agent has the power to produce it. This is for the effect to preexist not in a more imperfect way, but in one that is more perfect. Therefore, concludes Thomas, because God is the first efficient cause of all else, the perfections of all things must preexist in him in preeminent fashion.[247] Thomas also offers another argument, which reasons that because God is self-subsisting *esse*, he must contain within himself the total perfection of being. Because the perfections of all things fall

244. For references to Mondin see above, nn. 59, 60. The discussions by Mondin should be supplemented by Kretzmann's helpful treatment in *The Metaphysics of Theism*, pp. 140–53. The immediately following section in Kretzmann's book is also interesting, although I do not think Thomas would describe divine causation as partly univocal and partly equivocal, as Kretzmann seems to suggest (pp. 154, 157).

245. Ed. cit., pp. 30–31, partially quoted in notes 57 and 58 above.

246. Leon. 4.50, discussed above in Ch. XII, Section 6, and partially quoted there in n. 134.

247. Leon. 4.51–52.

under the perfection of being, the perfection of no other thing can be lacking to him.[248]

In a. 3 Thomas attempts to prove that a creature is like God. He begins by distinguishing different degrees of likeness in accord with the different ways in which a form may be shared. (1) The most perfect likeness obtains between things which share in the same form both according to the same intelligible content and the same mode (degree)—as, for instance, two equally white things. (2) Less like one another are things which share in the same form according to the same intelligible content (ratio) but not in the same degree—e.g., the less white and the whiter. He calls this an imperfect likeness. (3) Still less like one another are those which share in some form, but not according to the same intelligible content, as is true of nonunivocal agents and their effects. Even in this third case, insists Thomas, because every agent produces something like itself insofar as it is an agent, and because every agent acts in accord with its form, there must be some likeness of the form of the agent in the effect.[249]

Thomas goes on to apply these different kinds or degrees of likeness to cause-effect relationships. (1) If agent and effect fall within the same species, the likeness between the two will be in terms of specifically the same intelligible content, as when one human being generates another. Thomas does not explicitly here consider the second degree of likeness he had just distinguished above, presumably because that is also still specific, even though it allows for difference in degree. (2) A lesser degree of likeness obtains when an agent and its effect do not fall into the same species (as, for instance, between things generated by the power of the sun and the sun itself, where the likeness is only generic). (3) In the case of God, however, because he falls into no genus or species, the degree of likeness between his effects and himself is even less. This likeness is neither specific nor generic but only analogical in the way the act of being (esse) itself is common to all things. It is in this way that God's effects, insofar as they are beings (entia), are like or similar to him as the first and universal principle of all (other) being (esse).[250]

Consequently, while he has defended the possibility of our arriving at some kind of knowledge of God which is not purely negative but which may be described as proper, substantial, and analogical, Thomas would have us never forget the considerable limitations to which such knowledge is subject. It will of course never be comprehensive or, in this life, quidditative. It will always be subject to the need to

248. Leon. 4.52, partially quoted in Ch. XII above, n. 137.

249. Leon. 4.53–54. Note: "Cum omne agens agat sibi simile inquantum est agens, agit autem unumquodque secundum suam formam, necesse est quod in effectu sit similitudo formae agentis." Rather than offer a proof for the similitude principle, here Thomas uses it to establish the likeness of a creature to God.

250. Leon. 4.54. Note especially: ". . . non tamen quod participent similitudinem formae agentis secundum eandem rationem speciei aut generis, sed secundum aliqualem analogiam, sicut ipsum esse est commune omnibus. Et hoc modo illa quae sunt a Deo, assimilantur ei inquantum sunt entia, ut primo et universali principio totius esse."

deny of God the creaturely *modus significandi* we employ in predicating names of him. It will never enable us to apply names univocally to God and creatures but only analogically, at best. These limitations ultimately follow from the ontological situation, the fact that in the order of reality effects are not like God either specifically or generically but only "according to some kind of analogy in the way the act of being itself is common to all (beings)."[251]

251. Ibid.

XIV   Concluding Remarks

In our effort to reconstruct the fundamental features of Thomas's metaphysics of finite being, we have now reached his assessment of what we can hope to know about God on philosophical grounds. This, of course, is in accord with the methodology he himself laid down for metaphysics. Like any other theoretical science, it has a given subject, being as being, and it is its business to arrive at knowledge of the causes and principles of that subject. In this case, this means that one must arrive at knowledge of the existence of God.[1] Thomas spends a great amount of time in filling in what it is we can know about God by following the path of reason, once he is viewed as the uncaused cause of all other being, as well as what additional light this perspective may cast upon our analysis of finite being when it is in turn viewed as created by God and as ultimately ordered to return to him. Limitations of space (and time) will prevent me from following Thomas's fuller development of these themes here, as this could easily fill another volume.[2]

At this point I would like to return to a few of the themes involved in Thomas's analysis of finite being which may benefit from being revisited, as it were, from the perspective of their depending on God, their uncaused cause. Presupposed for this discussion is the philosophical conclusion that God exists, understanding thereby that he is the unmoved mover, the uncaused cause of all other being, the uncaused necessary being, the maximumly perfect being, and the ultimate source of finality in nature. Also presupposed for this will be Thomas's philosophically established

---

1. See the Prooemium to his Commentary on the *Metaphysics,* ed. cit., p. 2, and our discussion of this above in Ch. I, Section 2.

2. For some interesting contributions which treat of the universe insofar as it comes forth from God and is ordered to return to him as its ultimate final cause see J. Legrand, *L'univers et l'homme dans la philosophie de saint Thomas;* de Finance, *Être et agir,* 2d ed., cc. 4–9; J. H. Wright, *The Order of the Universe in the Theology of St. Thomas Aquinas;* and Kretzmann's effort to set forth Thomas's natural theology as he presents it in SCG I, II, and III. The first volume *(The Metaphysics of Theism),* already cited above, concentrates on SCG I. The second volume, completed before its author's untimely death, did not appear in time for me to use it in this study.

conclusions that God is unique, perfectly simple, all-perfect, and all-good. And although we have not yet singled this out for extended consideration, also presupposed for this should be the fact that God is intelligent, a point for which Thomas argues philosophically on repeated occasions. Without pausing here to review all of his argumentation for this conclusion, I would note that one would expect it to follow both from his claim that God is all-perfect, and from his proof that God is the ultimate source of final causality in nature.[3]

And indeed he does use these approaches on various occasions. For instance, in his Commentary on I *Sentences,* d. 35, q. 1, a. 1, he presents argumentation based on divine perfection at two points, first in the *sed contra* as a supporting introductory argument for the position he himself defends here (that knowledge [*scientia*] pertains to God), and then in the corpus of his response as one of three ways of establishing this point, i.e., by the way of eminence. The argument in the *sed contra* is very brief. No perfection can be lacking to that being which exists most perfectly. But science is a most excellent *(nobilissima)* perfection. Therefore science cannot be lacking to God, in whom perfections of all kinds are united.[4] The argument from eminence reasons that if something is present in many different things in increasing degree as they more closely approach some one (principle), it must be found in that one principle to a maximum degree. But as various entities more closely approach the first being, they participate in knowledge more perfectly— for instance, human beings more so than brute animals, and angels more so than human beings. Therefore the most excellent kind of knowledge is present in God.[5]

In the *Compendium theologiae* I, c. 28, immediately after rejecting univocal and equivocal predication of divine names and opting for analogy in the preceding chapter, Thomas offers three brief arguments to prove that God is intelligent. The first begins with Thomas's already established conclusion in c. 21 to the effect that all perfections found in all other things must be present in God as their source in superabundant fashion. But among those perfections understanding seems to excel, since intellectual things are more powerful than all others. Therefore God must be intelligent.[6]

In light of his defense of God as all-perfect in SCG I, c. 28, we would expect to see Thomas drawing upon this conclusion in his efforts there in c. 44 to prove that

3. See our discussion above in Ch. XIII, Section 1-c, pp. 516–17 (argumentation for divine perfection in SCG I, c. 28), our examination of the fifth way in Ch. XII, Section 5, pp. 480–85, and of divine intelligence in ST I, q. 14, a. 1 in Ch. XII, Section 6, pp. 496–97.

4. Mandonnet ed., Vol. 1, p. 808: "Praeterea, nulla perfectio deest ei qui perfectissime est. Sed scientia est nobilissima perfectio. Ergo Deo, in quo omnium generum perfectiones adunantur . . . scientia deesse non potest."

5. Ed. cit., p. 810. Note how he phrases his conclusion: ". . . unde oportet quod in Deo nobilissima cognitio inveniatur."

6. See Leon. 42.91:1–7. For c. 21 see p. 89:1–24. There he concludes that if the divine essence is infinite, it is impossible for it to have only the perfection of some genus or species and to be deprived of others. The perfections of every genus and species must exist in it.

God is intelligent. And he does include such an approach along with a series of other arguments. He recalls from c. 28 that no perfection that can be found in any kind of being can be lacking to God.[7] To ward off a possible objection, he remarks in passing that this does not imply any kind of composition within God himself. And as we have just seen him claiming in his later *Compendium theologiae,* here, too, he comments that among perfections the most powerful is for something to be intellective; for it may therefore be said in a certain way to be all things and, therefore, to possess within itself the perfection of all things. Here, of course, he is simply reechoing the Aristotelian theme that a cognitive being becomes in some way that which it knows when it cognizes it, and hence that by reason of its intellect the soul can in some way become all things, i.e., all intelligible objects. Most important for the argument is its claim that to be intelligent is to enjoy a perfection and indeed a pure perfection, the kind that does not necessarily entail a limited or imperfect mode of being. Given this, Thomas quickly concludes that God is intelligent.[8]

As we have suggested above, Thomas's argumentation for God's existence based on finality in nature (the fifth way) would also lead us to expect him to use this as another way of establishing the point that God is intelligent, and so he does. In his Commentary on I *Sentences,* d. 35, q. 1, a. 1, he introduces this approach as the second of three ways in which he there argues for knowledge in God, the way of causality. Every agent has some intention and desire for an end. But some knowledge on the part of one who establishes the end and directs things to it is presupposed if there is to be desire for that end. Agents which tend to an end but lack knowledge must be directed to their end by some prior agent, just as an arrow tends to its target owing to some determination by an archer. So it is with agents which act out of natural necessity. Their operations must be determined by some intellect which constitutes nature itself. Hence the first agent must not act by necessity, for then it would not really be first but would itself have to be directed to its end by some still prior being. Therefore the first agent must act with intellect and will and must be intelligent and knowing.[9]

As we have seen above in Ch. XI, Section 3, Thomas argues in similar fashion in *De veritate,* q. 5, a. 2 in his effort to show that the world is governed by providence. He had already drawn upon such reasoning at an earlier point within the same work (q. 2, a. 3) in making the case for God's knowledge of other things.[10]

---

7. Ed. cit., p. 43: "Adhuc. Deo nulla perfectio deest quae in aliquo genere entium inveniatur, ut supra ostensum est. . . ."

8. Ibid. Note: "Inter perfectiones autem rerum potissima est quod aliquid sit intellectivum: nam per hoc ipsum est quodammodo omnia, habens in se omnium perfectionem." For full discussion see Kretzmann, *The Metaphysics of Theism,* pp. 184–96.

9. Mandonnet ed., Vol. 1, pp. 809–10.

10. For q. 5, a. 2 see Leon. 22.1.144:163–177. For q. 2, a. 3 see pp. 50:211–51:228. For some useful notes on this last-mentioned discussion see Bonino, *Thomas d'Aquin,* pp. 409–12 (although I disagree with his statement on p. 412 that the fifth way is an argument based on order rather than on finality).

And as we saw in Ch. XII, Section 5, such thinking is central to Thomas's fifth way in ST I, q. 2, a. 3. Moreover, he had already included it in his series of arguments to show that God is intelligent in SCG I, c. 44[11]

We shall presuppose still another point in this concluding chapter, for which Thomas explicitly argues on various occasions, namely, that God is a creative principle. This has already been implied by his demonstrations that God is the uncaused cause of the *esse* or act of being enjoyed by everything else, especially since according to Thomas's metaphysics this means that in the case of any finite being its essence and its corresponding act of being *(esse)* are simultaneously produced by God and depend upon him for their continuing being. Indeed, it is really the finite being itself which is created, including both its essence and its act of being.

Even so, since Thomas does offer specific arguments to show that God is a creative principle, we shall examine some of them now. Thus in his Commentary on II *Sentences*, d. 1, q. 1, a. 2, Thomas develops argumentation to show that not only is creation possible but it is a fact; it has indeed occurred. He explicitly states that the fact that there is creation not only is held on faith but also can be demonstrated by reason. Everything which is imperfect within a given genus arises from something in which the nature of that genus is found in primary and foremost fashion. But since every thing (with the exception, of course, of the first being), including all that is found in every such being, participates in *esse* in some way and is also mixed with imperfection, every such being in terms of all that it is in itself must arise from the first and perfect being. In stating that every thing in terms of all that is found within that thing itself arises from the first being, Thomas is already making the case that creation involves the production of such things in terms of their total being or, as he also puts it, in terms of their total substance. Therefore, he concludes, it follows that all things must proceed from the first being by way of creation.[12]

He goes on to explain that the act of creation presupposes nothing which pre-exists in the thing that is created and therefore differs in this respect from all other changes, which presuppose some matter or some subject. In the case of generation or alteration the causality of the generating or altering principle does not extend to all that is found in a thing, but only to a form which is educed from potentiality to actuality. The causality of the creative principle, on the other hand, extends to everything present in what is created. Therefore creation can be described as a production of something from nothing *(ex nihilo)*, which is to say that nothing is presupposed for a creative act which itself would not be created. Moreover, he remarks that in

---

11. For SCG I, c. 44 see ed. cit., p. 43: "Item. Omne quod tendit determinate in aliquem finem. . . ." Also cf. SCG III, c. 64, where Thomas uses it as one of a series of arguments to prove that God governs or rules the universe by his providence (ed. cit., p. 296): "Item. Probatum est quod corpora naturalia moventur et operantur propter finem, licet finem non cognoscant. . . ."

12. Mandonnet ed., Vol. 2, pp. 17–18. Note: "Hoc autem creare dicimus, scilicet producere rem in esse secundum totam suam substantiam. Unde necessarium est a primo omnia per creationem procedere."

the case of creation the nonexistence of the thing created is prior to its existence in the order of nature, although not necessarily so in the order of time. This means that if the thing that is created were simply left to its own devices, it would not exist. Hence creation may be said to be *ex nihilo* in two senses: (1) the thing created is not produced from any preexisting subject; (2) when simply viewed in itself apart from its creating cause, the created thing's nonexistence is prior to its existence.[13]

When creation is understood this way, it can be demonstrated, repeats Thomas, and it is in this sense that philosophers have defended it. But if we also add to it the notion that what is created must have previously been nonexistent in the order of duration, when taken in this sense it cannot be demonstrated nor is it defended by the philosophers. Understood in this way it can be held only on the grounds of religious faith. In other words, here Thomas already defends what would be one of his most controverted positions, that it cannot be demonstrated that the world (meaning the universe) ever began to be. This can only be accepted on the strength of religious belief. While I cannot pause here to discuss this issue more fully, I would simply recall, as I have shown elsewhere, that throughout his career Thomas defended the view (1) that the noneternity of the world has not been demonstrated; and (2) that it cannot be demonstrated. Only in a very late discussion of this issue in his *De aeternitate mundi* did he explicitly defend an even stronger view (3) that an eternally created world is possible.[14]

Before leaving this early discussion of creation in his Commentary on the *Sentences,* however, I would like to mention another point. In a. 3 of this same d. 1, q. 1, Thomas asks whether the ability to create can pertain to any being other than God. He mentions the view of philosophers according to which only one first effect is immediately caused by God, and others by means of this, and soul by means of intelligence, and corporeal nature by means of spiritual nature, so that there are other creative principles. He probably has in mind some Neoplatonic emanation scheme such as those proposed by Algazel or Avicenna or the *Liber de causis.*[15]

13. Ed. cit., p. 18.
14. Ibid. Note: "Si autem accipiamus tertium oportere ad rationem creationis, ut scilicet etiam duratione res creata prius non esse quam esse habeat, ut dicatur ex nihilo, quia est tempore post nihil, sic creatio demonstrari non potest, nec a philosophis conceditur, sed per fidem supponitur." Cf. my "Thomas Aquinas on the Possibility of Eternal Creation," in *Metaphysical Themes in Thomas Aquinas,* c. 8 (pp. 191–214). On a key passage from his *De aeternitate mundi,* see pp. 205–12. For other discussions of this in Thomas and in other medieval thinkers see: *The Eternity of the World in the Thought of Thomas Aquinas and His Contemporaries,* J.B.M. Wissink, ed. (Leiden, 1990); R. C. Dales, *Medieval Discussions of the Eternity of the World* (Leiden, 1990); *Medieval Latin Texts on the Eternity of the World,* R. C. Dales and O. Argerami, eds. (Leiden, 1991).
15. Ed. cit., p. 21. See Ch. VI above, nn. 9, 10, for references to the emanation schemes proposed by Algazel and Avicenna. In the present text, however, I would not rule out the likelihood that Thomas is referring to the *Liber de causis,* as I did in my more detailed presentation of an emanation scheme in his Commentary on the *De Trinitate,* q. 4, a. 1. See my reference in Ch. VI, n. 9 to Weidemann's "Tradition und Kritik."

After rejecting this position as heretical, Thomas mentions two other positions. According to one view (to which he himself would later clearly subscribe), the power to create can belong to God alone and cannot be communicated to any creature; for it requires infinite power which cannot be so communicated. Others, however, held that even though in fact God has not communicated creative causality to any creature, he could do so. Thomas finds this position defended by Peter the Lombard in Bk IV, d. 5. Somewhat surprisingly in light of his later discussions of this, Thomas here sees some plausibility in this position if one views things simply from the side of what is created; for no part of what is created would pre-exist, and the first cause might communicate to a second cause the power to produce being in the unqualified sense *(esse simplex)* or matter and therefore to create. However, Thomas also points out that if one views this from the side of God, the creative principle, creation is an action which does not presuppose the action of any prior cause. Hence just as no second cause or creature can become the first cause, so too, one may argue, the ability to create cannot be communicated to it. Nonetheless, unlike his later treatments, here, perhaps out of deference to Peter the Lombard, he leaves the theoretical issue somewhat open.[16]

In the *Summa contra Gentiles,* after having considered God's operations *ad intra* from c. 44 onward throughout the latter half of Bk I, Thomas turns in Bk II to his operations *ad extra.* In c. 6 he argues from points he has already established in Bk I to show that God is the efficient cause of being for other things. Among the various arguments he assembles, the first reasons that because an efficient cause brings its effects into being, God is the cause of being for other things. The fourth argument maintains that among lower things it is a sign of perfection for them to be able to produce things similar to themselves. But God is supremely perfect, as he has shown in Bk I. Therefore it pertains to God to make some beings similar to himself in actuality and thus to cause the being of other things.[17]

---

16. Ed. cit., pp. 21–22. Note especially: "Si autem sumatur ex parte creati, sic illius proprie est creatio cui non praeexistat aliquid in re. Et hoc est esse. . . . et ex parte ista accipiendo creationem, potuit communicari creaturae, ut per virtutem causae primae operantis in ipsa, aliquod esse simplex, vel materia produceretur. . . ." For discussion of this see de Finance, *Être et agir,* pp. 142–44. As he points out, while Thomas is somewhat more inclined to reject Peter's opinion when commenting on Bk IV, d. 5, q. 1, a. 3, he still hesitates (see ad 5). For Peter see *Sententiae in IV Libris distinctae,* T. II, *Liber III et IV* (Grottaferrata [Rome], 1981), Bk IV, d. 5, c. 3, p. 267:6–17. For Thomas's Commentary see Moos ed., Vol. 4, p. 209 (where he notes that according to the common opinion the power to create cannot be given to any creature, since this requires infinite power). But see ad 5 (pp. 210–11) where Thomas observes that Peter might respond that in the case of creation the distance between being and nonbeing need not necessarily be regarded as infinite and hence as requiring infinite power. For Thomas's firm rejection of this possibility in more mature texts see *De potentia,* q. 3, a. 4; SCG II, cc. 20, 21; *Compendium theologiae* I, c. 70; ST I, q. 45, a. 5.

17. On Thomas's application of the distinction between God's immanent operations and his operations *ad extra* to the structure of the *Summa contra Gentiles* see II, c. 1 (ed. cit., p. 93). For c. 6 see p. 96.

In c. 15 Thomas extends his effort to show that God is the cause of being for all other entities or, as he puts it, that nothing other than God exists without being produced by him. While the first argument is fairly lengthy, one may reduce it to its essentials. It is impossible for something to be predicated of two different things in such a way that it is caused in neither of them. Rather, either one will cause it in the other (as fire causes heat in a mixed body so that both may be said to be hot), or some third principle will cause it in both (as fire causes heat in two different candles). But the act of being *(esse)* is said of everything that exists. Therefore it is impossible for there to be two entities, neither of which would have a cause of its being; either both must be caused by something else, or one must be the cause of being for the other. Therefore everything which exists in any way whatsoever must derive from something which itself does not depend on anything else for its being. But Thomas has shown in Bk I that God's being has no cause (since he is the uncaused cause). Therefore everything else which exists in any way whatsoever must depend on him for its being *(esse)*.[18]

In another argument he reasons that what is predicated essentially is the cause of things predicated only by participation. But God is a being essentially because he is identical with his act of being. Every other being is a being only by participation, since there can only be one being which is identical with its act of being. Therefore God is the cause of the being of all other things.[19]

And in still another argument Thomas introduces reasoning which we have already examined above in the context of arguments for the existence of God. As the reader will recall, there he reasons that everything which is capable of existing and not existing *(possibile)* must have some cause, because when such a thing is simply considered in itself it is open to both and must be determined to one of these (existing) by something else. But since one cannot regress to infinity in caused possible beings, there must be some necessary being that causes the being of the possibles. And since a regress to infinity in caused necessary beings is likewise unacceptable, one must conclude to the existence of a being that is necessary of itself. And since this can only be unique, and is God, all other things must be traced back to him as the cause of their being.[20]

So far Thomas's argumentation in SCG II has developed the implications that follow from his earlier demonstration that God is the uncaused cause of the being *(esse)* of all other things and that, because he is unique, everything else must depend upon him for its being. Still, in order to complete his case for God as the creative principle, he turns in c. 16 to a series of arguments intended to show that God produces things in being from no preexisting subject such as matter. In the interests of brevity, here I will limit myself to Thomas's last philosophical argument in that

18. Ed. cit., p. 100.
19. Ed. cit., p. 101 (the first "Item").
20. Ibid. See Ch. XI above, Section 4, final argument, pp. 439–40.

context. Prime matter exists in some way because it is being in potency. But God is the cause of things that are in any way, as Thomas has shown in the preceding chapter. Therefore God is the cause of prime matter, and for this there is no pre-existing subject. Therefore the divine causal action requires no preexisting matter or subject.[21]

In q. 3 of the *De potentia* Thomas devotes nineteen articles to various matters relating to creation. In a. 1 he simply wants to show that God can create something from nothing. Again he draws a contrast between God and any purely natural agent. The latter does not produce being as such but only preexisting being which is determined to this or that. Such an agent acts by moving and therefore requires matter to serve as a subject for change or motion. For this reason it cannot produce something from nothing. God, however, is pure actuality, both with respect to himself, since he is totally free from any mixture of potentiality, and with respect to other things which actually exist, since he is the origin or cause of all other beings. Therefore by his action he can produce an entire subsisting being without presupposing anything. He is the principle of all caused being *(esse)* and can produce something from nothing.[22]

In q. 3, a. 5 Thomas offers three metaphysical arguments to demonstrate that nothing exists that is not created by God, excepting, of course, God himself. Since we have already considered the first argument in another context, here we may immediately turn to its conclusion. Because the act of being *(esse)* is common to all things and because, simply considered in themselves they are distinct from one another, *esse* cannot belong to them of themselves but must be given to them by one single cause. This, remarks Thomas, seems to be the argumentation used by Plato.[23]

In a second argument, which he attributes to Aristotle, Thomas notes that if something is participated in by many things in different fashion, it must be given to each of them in which it is found imperfectly by something in which it is realized most perfectly. For things which are said positively in greater or lesser degree owe this to their greater or lesser proximity to something that is one. But we must grant

21. Ed. cit., p. 103 ("Item").

22. Pession ed., p. 39. Thomas had prepared for the argument we have reported in our text by noting that every agent acts insofar as it is in act. Therefore action is to be attributed to an agent in accord with the way actual being pertains to it. But individual things exist in particular fashion, first in relation to themselves, since their entire substance is not actuality, and second, with respect to other things which exist in actuality. Thus each particular thing only has an act that is determined to one genus or species, and no such thing can produce being as being but only insofar as it is this being, determined to this or that species. At this point Thomas moves on to the argument we have just presented.

23. Ed. cit., p. 49. Note how Thomas introduces these arguments: "Et hoc triplici ratione demonstrari potest. . . ." See our Ch. XII above n. 100, where we cite this argument while discussing the fourth way. It also recalls the first argument we analyzed above in this Chapter from SCG II, c. 15, where it is used to establish the same conclusion as in the present context (see n. 18).

the existence of one being which is the truest and most perfect being (which follows from the fact that there is some completely immovable and most perfect mover, as the philosophers have proved). Therefore all less perfect things must receive their acts of being *(esse)* from it.[24]

Thomas's third argument reasons that what exists through something else must be traced back as to its cause to that which exists of itself. But we must grant the existence of some being which is its own act of being. This follows from the fact that there must be a first being which is pure actuality and completely free from composition, i.e., perfectly simple. Therefore all other things which are not identical with their act of being but only participate in *esse* must derive from that one first being. Thomas credits Avicenna with this argument.[25]

In replying to the second objection, in a text we have mentioned before, Thomas remarks that by reason of the fact that the act of being is given to a quiddity or essence, not only the act of being but the essence or quiddity itself is said to be created. Before it actually exists the quiddity is nothing, except perhaps in the intellect of the Creator, and there it is not a creature but the creative essence. This is important because it shows that, in accord with Thomas's theory of essence and act of being, to hold that the act of being of a given entity is produced from nothingness amounts to holding that the entire being, including its essence and its act of being, is created. This is because the act of being *(esse)* does not exist without its correlative essence principle, nor does an essence exist without its corresponding act of being.[26]

In concluding this brief survey of Thomas's views on creation, I would simply note that in the *Compendium theologiae* I, c. 68, Thomas again attempts to show that everything other than God that exists in any way whatsoever depends upon him. He offers arguments we have seen in earlier texts, one based on the claim that God, as the first and most perfect being, must be the cause of *esse* for all lesser entities, and another which essentially repeats the argument based on participation as we have just seen it in SCG II, c. 15. In c. 69 he argues that God does not presuppose matter in creating things. Rather matter, too, is created by God.[27]

And in ST I, q. 44, a. 1 he again turns to the argument from participation to show that all things other than God, which participate in being to a greater or lesser degree, must be caused by the one perfect being which exists most perfectly. In a. 2 he reasons that what causes things insofar as they are beings causes them not merely insofar as they are such and such by reason of accidental forms, or insofar as they are these things by reason of their substantial forms, but also in

---

24. Ed. cit., p. 49.   25. Ibid.

26. Ibid. Cited above in Ch. IV, n. 93.

27. Leon. 42.103. Note from his first argument in c. 69 to show that God need not presuppose matter in creating: "Necesse est autem materiam produci per [Leonine: par] actionem Dei, cum ostensum sit quod omne quod quolibet modo est Deum habeat causam essendi . . ." (p. 103:8–10).

terms of all that pertains to their being *(esse)* in any way whatsoever. Therefore even prime matter is caused by the universal cause of beings.[28]

With these presuppositions concerning God in mind, I would now like to return to a few of the themes we have already examined in Thomas's metaphysics without assuming God's existence as already demonstrated: (1) his argumentation for distinction and composition of essence and act of being in finite or created beings; (2) his application of his metaphysics of participation to finite or created being; (3) the correlation between his views on the subject of metaphysics and quidditative knowledge of God.

1. God-to-Creatures Argumentation for Essence-*Esse* Composition and Distinction

In Ch. V above, Section 2, we considered a number of Thomas's arguments for distinction and composition of essence and act of being in finite beings based on the claim that it is impossible for there to be more than one being in which essence and act of being are identical. In that context I noted that if in these discussions Thomas usually takes God's existence as already established and moves from this to distinction and composition of essence and act of being in other things, in many of these texts he would not have to make that assumption. It would be enough for him to show that in one being at most can there be identity of essence and act of being and, therefore, that in everything else the two are distinct and composed with one another. In that context I set aside arguments which do seem to require as one of their working principles prior knowledge of God's existence. It is to some of these arguments that we now turn.[29]

Thomas presents two such arguments in his Commentary on I *Sentences*. In d. 8, q. 5, a. 1 he attempts to determine whether any creature is simple. He begins his response by commenting that everything that proceeds from God so as to differ from him in essence also falls short of his simplicity. However, Thomas immediately issues a caveat. For something to fall short of the divine simplicity, it does not necessarily have to be composed. Consequently he distinguishes between two types of creatures. One kind enjoys complete being within itself, such as a human being and things of this type, in other words, substances. Another kind does not exist in itself but only in something else, such as prime matter, or a form, or even a universal.[30]

---

28. For q. 44, a. 1 see Leon. 4.455. For a. 2 see p. 458. Cf. also his reply to objection 3, which reinforces his conclusion: "Unde oportet quod etiam illud quod se habet ex parte potentiae, sit creatum, si totum quod ad esse ipsius pertinet, creatum est."

29. As the reader will recall, in Ch. V, Section 1 above I maintained that Thomas's argumentation in *De ente*, c. 4 does not presuppose knowledge of God's existence in order to establish distinction of essence and act of being in other entities, even though in phase two he does reason from the impossibility of there being more than one being in which essence and *esse* are identical to this conclusion.

30. Mandonnet ed., Vol. 1, pp. 226–27. Cf. Ch. V above, n. 103.

According to Thomas, creatures of the first type do fall short of the divine simplicity by being composed. This is because in God alone are act of being and quiddity identical. Therefore in every created substance, whether corporeal or spiritual, there must be both a quiddity or nature, and an act of being, which is given to it by God. Therefore it will be composed of the act of being *(esse* or *quo est)*, on the one hand, and of "that which is" or essence on the other.[31] If this argument is to stand on its own, however, it still needs to prove that only in God are act of being and quiddity identical.

In this same d. 8, q. 5, Thomas directs a. 2 to establishing the simplicity of the human soul. After rejecting matter-form composition of the soul, he reasons that if we find a quiddity which is not composed of matter and form, either that quiddity is identical with its act of being or it is not. If it is identical with its act of being it will be the very essence of God himself, which is his act of being, and it will be completely simple. But if it is not identical with its act of being, it must have received its act of being from something else, as is true of every created quiddity. And because everything which does not have something of itself is potential *(possibile)* with respect to it, and since a quiddity of this kind receives its act of being from another, it will be potential with respect to that act of being. Therefore potentiality and actuality will be present in it, since the quiddity itself is potential and the act of being is its very act. It is in this way, he explains, that he understands the act-potency composition of angels and of the separated soul.[32]

Important for Thomas's reasoning here is his claim that if some quiddity is identical with its act of being, it is God himself and perfectly simple. If one grants this, one can easily reason that if something is not God himself, it is not identical with its act of being, which is an almost perfect illustration of God-to-creatures argumentation for nonidentity of essence and act of being in such entities. Not fully justified in this text, however, or in the previous one, is the claim that if some quiddity is identical with its act of being, it is God himself and perfectly simple or, as the previous text puts it, that only in God are act of being and quiddity identical.[33]

Thomas addresses this issue in a different way in a text from his Commentary on II *Sentences,* d. 3, q. 1, a. 1. There he is rejecting matter-form composition of angels and must, therefore, show that there is still some other kind of composition within them. He notes that it is not essential to quiddity insofar as it is quiddity to be composed. If it were, no simple nature could ever be found, which is false at least in the case of God. Nor is it essential to quiddity taken as such that it be

---

31. Ibid. Note Thomas's final remark with reference to the second kind of creature. It falls short of the divine simplicity either because it is divisible in potency or per accidens, or "quia est componibile alteri . . ." (p. 227). Cf. Ch. VI above, n. 24.

32. Ed. cit., pp. 229–30.

33. Note in particular: "Si illa quidditas sit esse suum, sic erit essentia ipsius Dei, quae est suum esse, et erit omnino simplex" (p. 229).

simple, since composite essences are readily at hand. But the act of being insofar as it is that by reason of which things actually exist is related to different natures or quiddities in different ways. One kind of nature or quiddity does not include within its intelligible content its actual existence, as is evident from the fact that one can understand what such a thing is—for instance, a phoenix or an eclipse—without knowing that it is. But there is another kind of nature or essence whose intelligible content does include its actual existence *(esse)*. Indeed its *esse* (act of being, presumably) is identical with its nature or quiddity. An *esse* (act of being) of this kind cannot be caused by something else, since that which something has by reason of its quiddity or essence it has of itself. But everything other than God has an *esse* (act of being) that it receives from something else. Therefore, concludes Thomas, in God alone is his act of being *(esse)* identical with his nature or quiddity. In all other things *esse* (act of being) differs from the quiddity to which that *esse* is given. He concludes that because that which receives something from something else is "possible" or in potency with respect to it, the quiddity of such a thing is related to the act of being it receives as potency to act. Therefore an intelligence (angel) is composed of potency and act.[34]

The assumption that God exists enters into this argument at two levels. First, Thomas appeals to it to make the point that there is one kind of quiddity which is not composed, since at least God is perfectly simple. Second, there is a nature or quiddity whose intelligible content does include its *esse* (existence) and which is identical with its *esse* (act of being, presumably). Such a thing is uncaused. By contrast, everything other than God has an *esse* (act of being) that it receives from something else. Therefore, because God alone is identical with his quiddity or nature, in all other things act of being and quiddity or essence or nature differ. Thomas's point here seems to be that because only God's *esse* is uncaused, everything else receives its *esse* from something else. Because it receives its act of being from something else and is caused, its *esse* (act of being) is distinct from its quiddity or nature.[35]

This argument employs what we have above referred to in discussing the *De ente et essentia*, c. 4 as the *intellectus essentiae* argument, but does not immediately use it to prove that essence and act of being are distinct in the case of entities which do not include existence within their intelligible content. Rather, after drawing support from the contrast with that unique being whose essence does include its

---

34. Mandonnet ed., Vol. 2, pp. 87–8.

35. See p. 87: "Quaedam enim natura est de cuius intellectu non est suum esse, quod patet ex hoc quod intelligi potest [omit: esse, with Parma] cum hoc quod ignoretur an sit, sicut phaenicem, vel eclipsim, vel aliquid huiusmodi. Alia autem natura invenitur de cuius ratione est ipsum suum esse, immo ipsum esse est sua natura. Esse autem quod huiusmodi est, non habet esse acquisitum ab alio; quia illud quod res ex sua quidditate habet, ex se habet. Sed omne quod est praeter Deum habet esse acquisitum ab alio. Ergo in solo Deo suum esse est sua quidditas vel natura; in omnibus autem aliis esse est praeter quidditatem, cui esse acquiritur."

esse within its intelligible content and which is uncaused, the argument concludes that in everything else *esse* is received from something else or efficiently caused. And this in turn leads to the conclusion that in all such beings essence and act of being differ.[36]

This is not one of Thomas's more finished and convincing arguments for a more than conceptual distinction and composition of essence and act of being in things other than God. As in phase 1 of the argumentation in *De ente*, c. 4, it moves too quickly from understanding *esse* as referring to the fact that things exist (in the examples of the eclipse and the phoenix) to taking it as signifying the act of being (in the case of God, and then by contrast, also in other things). But it is of considerable interest in that it gives us a fuller understanding of one of Thomas's early ways of arguing from God to creatures for this composition and distinction.[37]

Another brief version of "God-to-creatures" argumentation appears in Thomas's only slightly later Quodlibet IX of Christmas 1257. There in q. 4, a. 1 he was asked whether an angel is composed of matter and form. After arguing at some length against this position, Thomas wants to show that there is act-potency composition in angels nonetheless. He counters that because the substance of an angel is not identical with its act of being, something which is true of God alone to whom *esse* belongs of himself and not from something else, we find in an angel both a substance or quiddity, which subsists, and its act of being, by means of which it subsists or exists. Because the substance of an angel viewed in itself is in potency to the act of being it receives from something else, there is a composition of potency and act therein.[38]

Most interesting for our immediate purpose is Thomas's briefly stated reason for holding that the substance of an angel is not identical with its act of being. This, he says, is true of God alone to whom *esse* belongs of himself and is not derived from something else. In other words, he reasons from the fact that God's act of being is uncaused to the conclusion that in him essence and act of being are identical, and from this to the contrast with all other things. In all of them essence and act of being differ and are therefore composed. Presumably this is because, unlike God, they receive their *esse* from something else and therefore enter into composition with it. Thomas does not explicitly state this, however. It could be

36. Hence, strictly speaking, I do not regard it as a direct or immediate *intellectus essentiae* argument for real distinction of essence and *esse,* even though I have cited it along with some other texts in Ch. V, n. 31 above.

37. See the text quoted in n. 35. As I indicate in presenting this argument in my text, at some point the meaning of the term *esse* must shift from existence (or existing) to the act of being. Otherwise the argument will not show that in things other than God *esse* differs from quiddity and enters into act-potency composition with it. I have indicated in my text where I think the shift in meaning occurs.

38. Leon. 25.1.102:115–103:127. Note: "Sed quia substantia angeli non est suum esse, hoc enim soli Deo competit cui esse debetur ex se ipso et non ab alio, invenimus in angelo et substantiam sive quidditatem eius, quae subsistit, et esse eius, quo subsistit, quo scilicet actu essendi dicitur esse. . . ."

that he simply protects the divine simplicity by immediately concluding to the necessarily composed character of things other than God. In any event, the argument accepts God's existence as granted along with the fact that his act of being is uncaused and is, therefore, identical with his essence.[39]

Here I would simply recall in passing three arguments taken from SCG II, c. 52, which we have reviewed above in Ch. V, Section 2. In each of these Thomas offers philosophical reasons for holding that because there can only be one instance of subsisting *esse*, in everything else essence and act of being differ. While all three of these understandably take God's existence as already proved in Bk I of this work, I included them in our previous discussion as arguments which would not have to make this assumption. Even so, I mention them again here because they do explicitly address the key point that there can at most be only one instance of self-subsisting being, in which essence and act of being are identical.[40]

In a later text from ST I, q. 44, a. 1 Thomas wants to show that everything other than God is created by him. Thomas comments that earlier in this same work, while dealing with divine simplicity, he showed that God is self-subsistent being (see ST I, q. 3, a. 4). Moreover, he notes that he has also already shown that self-subsisting being can only be one. This seems to be a reference to q. 7, a. 1, ad 3, since he now recalls basically the same reasoning he had employed there. As he reasoned there, insofar as the divine *esse* is not received in something else and is therefore infinite, it is distinguished from all other instances of *esse*, and they are distinguished from it, just as, if there were such a thing as subsisting whiteness, then by reason of the fact that it was not received in something else it would be distinguished from all instances of whiteness that do exist in subjects.[41] The reader will recognize this familiar example. From this he now concludes that things other than God are not identical with their acts of being, but only participate in *esse*. And from this he also concludes that things that differ in their respective degrees of participating in *esse* must all be caused by one first being, which is most perfectly.[42]

This argument for distinction of essence and act of being is based on the uniqueness of self-subsisting *esse*, and this uniqueness itself is grounded on the point that the divine act of being is not received in any subject and must therefore as self-

---

39. Because Thomas introduces this argumentation almost as an *obiter dictum* to support distinction of essence and *esse* in angels and his refutation of matter-form composition in them, we should not expect him to develop it fully for its own sake here. Brief though it is, it does move from identity of essence and *esse* in God alone to their otherness or distinction in everything else.

40. For the arguments from SCG II, c. 52 see ed. cit., p. 145, and Ch. V above, notes 51–54.

41. For q. 44, a. 1 see Leon. 4.455. For q. 7, a. 1 see Leon. 4.72. There in the corpus of his response Thomas concludes that since the divine *esse* is not received in something and God is his own subsisting *esse*, he is infinite and perfect. Then in replying to obj. 3 he draws upon this to reason as we have just explained in our text.

42. Q. 44, a. 1 (p. 455): "Relinquitur ergo quod omnia alia a Deo non sint suum esse, sed participant esse. Necesse est igitur omnia quae diversificantur secundum diversam participationem essendi, ut sint perfectius vel minus perfecte, causari ab uno primo ente, quod perfectissime est."

subisting be infinite and perfect. By contrast, other instances of *esse* must be received in some subject and such subjects must be distinct from their acts of being and only participate in being. In this argument Thomas understandably can and does take God's existence as established, since he has dealt with this in offering his five ways in q. 2, a. 3.[43]

Finally, in order to appreciate fully Thomas's God-to-creatures approach to establishing composition and distinction of essence and act of being in created entities, it may be helpful for the reader to review the texts we considered above in Ch. V, Section 2. While granting that in those texts Thomas also takes God's existence as given, I argued that he does not have to assume this in order for those particular arguments to reach their conclusion. Even so, those texts may now be reread under the assumption that God has been proved to exist, in accord with the methodology we have been following.

As for the additional God-to-creatures arguments we have now considered, they are not necessarily more compelling than (or, in the case of some, perhaps not even as compelling as) others we have previously examined. But by considering them we now have some fuller insight into how Thomas at times moves from knowledge of God's existence to a composition and distinction of essence and act of being in all other substances.

2. From Unparticipated to Participated Being

As we saw in Ch. IV above, Thomas distinguishes three different types of participation: (1) logical participation (whether of a species in a genus, or of my understanding of an individual in a species); (2) real predicamental participation (of a substance in an accident, or of matter in form); (3) real participation of an effect in its cause. Because our primary interest in this study of Thomas's metaphysics has been in his explanation of the participation of beings in being *(esse)*, we compared this with the first two kinds of participation just mentioned. We concluded that participation of beings in *esse* does not fall under either of them, but should rather be placed under the third member, whereby an effect participates in its cause.[44]

Further exploration of Thomas's understanding of the participation of beings in *esse* led us to distinguish three different ways in which he understands that *esse* in which they are said to participate. (1) At times by this he means that finite beings participate in the act of being viewed in general *(esse commune)*. (2) On other occa-

---

43. One might suggest that even in this argument Thomas could merely claim that there can at most be one instance of self-subsisting being and therefore that in everything else essence and act of being must differ, whether or not that one instance of self-subsisting being is actually realized. However, in light of the context I would not interpret this argument that way, especially since it is a stage in Thomas's effort to prove that everything else is caused by a really existing first being, God.

44. See Ch. IV above, Section 1, esp. pp. 103–6.

sions he means that finite beings participate in self-subsisting *esse* (God). (3) On still other occasions he simply means that they participate in their own acts of being.

So far as the philosophical order is concerned, after one has arrived at a metaphysical understanding of being as being through the process of separation, one should be in position to realize that no given finite being exhausts the fullness marked out by one's understanding of being as such. Without yet relating particular beings to an unparticipated source as their first efficient cause, the philosopher should be able to think of each of them as only participating in being as such without exhausting it and, if one shares Thomas's understanding of *esse* as the intrinsic act by reason of which each individual entity exists, as participating in this actuality viewed in general, i.e., in *esse commune*.

As we saw in Ch. V, Thomas uses this approach, along with a number of others, to conclude to composition of an essence principle and an intrinsic act of being *(esse)* within every finite being. According to my reading of his texts, many of his efforts to make this point do not presuppose prior knowledge of God's existence. As we remarked above, on some occasions Thomas refers to a given entity as participating in its own act of being. This application likewise does not presuppose prior knowledge of God's existence. Once Thomas has proved God's existence, of course, and shown that in him alone are essence and act of being identical, he has thereby also eliminated any possibility of maintaining that God himself participates in his own act of being or, I would now add, in *esse commune*.

This brings us back to the remaining way in which finite beings participate in *esse*, i.e., in self-subsisting *esse* (God), their unparticipated source. It goes without saying that this usage of participation does presuppose God's existence. And given the immediate context for many of the passages in which Thomas employs this application of participation, he could and did legitimately assume that God exists—either because of the theological nature of the particular treatise and/or because he had already offered argumentation in that work to make that point. In our effort to follow the philosophical order in presenting Thomas's metaphysical thought, we noted that until we had considered his formal argumentation for God's existence we would regard his references to finite beings as participating in subsisting being as putative rather than as yet definitively established.[45] Since we have now completed our examination of that argumentation, we may remove the putative or hypothetical characterization we have assigned to such references. Moreover, we may now ask what this way of referring to participation in *esse* adds to Thomas's general theory of participation.

First of all, it heightens the need for him to distinguish clearly between *esse commune* and *esse subsistens*. We have already emphasized the importance of this distinction in Ch. IV.[46] It should be recalled again here, however, if we are to avoid

45. See Ch. IV above, p. 109.
46. See Ch. IV above, section 2, passim.

a fatal misreading of Aquinas's thought. Precisely because *esse commune* and *esse subsistens* are not to be identified, to be aware that something is participating in the former is not yet to be aware that it is participating in the latter. In the order of philosophical discovery we reach the former before we discover the latter. But in the order of reality the orders are reversed. The fact that creatures are created by God accounts for their dependency upon him as upon the unparticipated source of their being—including, of course, both their essences and their respective acts of being. This in turn accounts for the fact that they can and do participate in *esse commune,* as well as in their own acts of being.

Secondly, for us to think of God as subsisting being enables us to bring out more fully the distinction between creatures and God himself. Thomas uses this approach on different occasions. For instance, in ST I, q. 3, a. 4 he offers a series of arguments to show that God's essence is identical with his act of being. The third reasons that just as something which simply has fire without being identical with it only participates in it, so too that which has *esse* and is not identical with it is a being *(ens)* only by participation. If God were not identical with his act of being, he would only be a being by participation and not of his essence. But then he would not be the first being, which Thomas rejects as absurd and which would, of course, run counter to the conclusion of his five ways.[47] While his explicit aim here is to show that God is identical with his act of being, this text also shows that, as the first being, God is being itself or being of his essence, not being by participation.

Thirdly, as I have already anticipated to some extent in my discussion in Ch. IV above, Geiger's emphasis on the importance of participation by similitude in Thomas's metaphysics can only be justified under the assumption that God exists. Thus, in the order of philosophical discovery, only after one has established God's existence is one justified in regarding participation in divine being as philosophically established. At this point one may turn to participation by similitude in order to help account metaphysically for the procession of participated beings from God. This is especially useful in explaining God's knowledge and production of the essence principle of each created entity and in showing how any created being depends upon God as its formal exemplar cause. Because of this it may be said to participate in him by imitating him or being likened to him according to its appropriate degree. This is so because it imitates its appropriate divine idea, which divine idea itself is simply God's way of viewing his essence as capable of being imitated by a creature. But appeal must also be made to God's exercise of his creative efficient causality. Only because of this does the participated being, including both its essence and its act of being, actually exist and hence actually imitate the divine being.[48]

47. Leon. 4.42.
48. See Ch. IV above, section 3.

3. Quidditative Knowledge of God and the Subject of Metaphysics

In Ch. I we considered Thomas's views concerning the subject of metaphysics. In agreement with Avicenna and with most of his thirteenth-century contemporaries, he denies that God is to be regarded as the subject of this discipline. Its subject is being as being or, as he at times phrases it, being in general *(ens commune)*. But unlike most if not all other thirteenth-century writers, he also denies that God falls under the notion of being that serves as the subject of this science. God enters into its field of consideration only indirectly, as the cause or principle of its subject, being as being.[49]

We have seen how this solution enables Thomas to defend the unity of the science of being as being and the philosophical science of the divine. Indeed, he holds out knowledge of the divine (knowledge of the ultimate cause or principle of its subject) as the end or goal of metaphysical inquiry. We have also seen how Thomas applies his distinction between the two kinds of things that are separate from matter and motion in the order of existence to this issue. The subject of metaphysics, being as being, falls under what we have called the negatively or neutrally immaterial. God, as the primary instance of positively immaterial being, enters into its field of investigation only indirectly, as a cause or principle of that which falls under its subject.[50]

In Ch. IV I suggested that this distinctive claim by Aquinas—that God is not included within the subject of metaphysics—fits together very well with his refusal to include God under *esse commune*. Even so, it is not *esse commune* but *ens commune* or being insofar as it is being that constitutes its subject. Hence it would not be correct to describe its subject as existence in general.[51]

What I would now like to suggest is that an additional reason for Thomas's refusal to include God within the subject of metaphysics or under *ens commune* may be his denial that we can reach quidditative knowledge of God in this life. We have examined Thomas's views concerning this at some length in Ch. XIII. Suffice it to say here that if he had allowed for some kind of imperfect quidditative knowledge of God, he might then have been more open to the possibility of including God within the notion of being that is the subject of metaphysics. But since he consistently rejects the possibility of such knowledge throughout his career, this makes it unlikely that he would include God within or under the subject of metaphysics. To do so might lead to the inference that if God can serve as the subject of a purely human philosophical discipline, then we should be able to reach some imperfect knowledge concerning what he is. Since allowing us any quidditative

49. See Ch. I, Section 2. For some other thirteenth-century views concerning this see Ch. I, n. 56.
50. See the texts from Thomas's Commentary on the *De Trinitate* and the Prooemium to his Commentary on the *Metaphysics* cited above in Ch. I, nn. 53, 54, 55, 63.
51. See Ch. IV above, pp. 122–23 and nn. 75–78.

knowledge of God in this life would compromise the divine transcendence in Thomas's eyes, so too would including him under the subject of metaphysics.

As I have also noted in Ch. XIII, one of Thomas's reasons for rejecting predication of anything of creatures and God according to the analogy of many to one is his view that nothing, including the notion of being itself presumably, can be simpler than or prior to God.[52] Once again we can see how closely this fits together with his denial that God falls under the subject of metaphysics. If God were included under the notion of being that serves as its subject, this would seem to make the notion of being in some way prior to God and to all else that falls under it.

4. Epilogue

In the Introduction to this study I indicated that in my effort to reconstruct the essential elements of Thomas's metaphysical thought I would be guided by his own remarks concerning the division of the theoretical sciences, the subject of metaphysics, the intellectual processes involved in arriving at that subject, and the philosophical order as he defines this as distinguished from the theological order. While acknowledging that he did not write a *Summa metaphysicae,* I have now presented the kind of metaphysical book he might have written had he chosen to do so, in accord with the philosophical order and methodology as he himself defines this. It is my hope that it will prove useful to today's readers who are trained in philosophy and interested in Aquinas's metaphysical thought, without their necessarily being trained as theologians or, for that matter, without their necessarily sharing his Christian religious belief. In other words, I have not presented this as a study of Aquinas's theology, or of his "Christian Philosophy" when this is defined in the Gilsonian sense, but of his metaphysics.

Throughout this exposition I have taken chronology into account wherever this seemed to be necessary or helpful. This was to allow shifts and developments in Thomas's thought concerning particular issues to become manifest when such seem to have occurred. I would now offer two thoughts concerning the issue of development in his thought. On the one hand, Aquinas's metaphysics shows development and change on a number of points over the more than twenty years of his professional career. This, of course, is only to be expected from such a gifted and original thinker who was constantly enriching his intellectual reservoir, as it were, by eagerly studying newly translated philosophical literature as quickly as it became available to him in Latin translation, and who was also often required by the very nature of his work as a professional teacher to revisit many of the positions he had already treated in earlier writings. Some of these developments are much more significant than others, of course, such as his gradually deepening awareness of

---

52. See SCG I, c. 34 (cited above in Ch. XIII, n. 206); *De potentia,* q. 7, a. 7 (cited in Ch. XIII, n. 222).

the implications of participation for his metaphysics of *esse*, or his later defense of substantial predication of some divine names notwithstanding his rejection of quidditative knowledge of God in this life, or his shifts concerning the use of analogy of proportionality in predicating divine names, or, to mention an issue I have explored in another study, his claim in his *De aeternitate mundi* that an eternally created world is possible.

At the same time, I have also been impressed by the fact that the greater part of his fundamental metaphysical choices already appear, at least in some form, in his earliest writings such as his *De ente et essentia* and his Commentary on the *Sentences*, especially on Bk I. This is not to deny that his way of exposing and defending many of these points would deepen and develop considerably over the years. Nonetheless, there is a fundamental metaphysical core upon which he will often subsequently draw in both his philosophical and theological discussions throughout his career. As illustrations of some of these fundamental choices I would mention his views on the nature and subject of metaphysics, his consistent rejection both of univocity and of the equivocal character of being, his defense of analogy of being on both the predicamental and transcendental levels, his recognition of the primacy of *esse*, his defense of composition and distinction of essence and act of being in all finite beings, his application of the metaphysics of act and potency to the compositions of essence and act of being, substance and accidents, and matter and form, his acceptance and adaptation of the Aristotelian theory of substance and accident to his metaphysics of *esse*, his defense of a real distinction between the soul and its powers, the purely potential character of prime matter, unicity of substantial form, the essentials, at least, of his theory of individuation in spite of certain variations concerning the role of dimensions, his continual appeal to a posteriori argumentation for God's existence, and his rejection of quidditative knowledge of God.

I readily acknowledge that more could be written about Thomas's treatment of the various elements of his metaphysics examined here, and that still other topics could also be investigated with considerable profit (for instance, the nature and attributes of God, and the procession of the universe from him along with his providential governance of the same and its return to him as the ultimate final cause). Hopefully enough has been said to give the reader a good general grasp of his metaphysical thought. Whether or not one should describe it as a system is, I think, a matter of semantics. I would note that in Thomas's mind all of the parts and elements singled out for consideration here are closely interconnected and naturally influence one another. It seems clear that Thomas had this underlying metaphysics in his mind throughout most of his career and that in addition to proving him to be a great and creative metaphysician, this underlying metaphysics also made it possible for him to be the great and creative theologian he also was.

Bibliography

Printed Sources

Adams, M. M. *William Ockham*. Vols. 1, 2. Notre Dame, Ind., 1987.

Aertsen, J. A. *Medieval Philosophy and the Transcendentals: The Case of Thomas Aquinas*. Leiden–New York–Cologne, 1996.

———. "Method and Metaphysics: The *via resolutionis* in Thomas Aquinas." *New Scholasticism* 63 (1989), pp. 405–18.

———. *Nature and Creature: Thomas Aquinas's Way of Thought*, trans. H. D. Morton. Leiden–New York, 1987.

———. "Die Thesen zur Individuation in der Verurteilung von 1277, Heinrich von Gent und Thomas von Aquin," in *Miscellanea Mediaevalia* 24: *Individuum und Individualität im Mittelalter* (Berlin–New York, 1996), pp. 249–65.

———. "Was heißt Metaphysik bei Thomas von Aquin?" in *Miscellanea Mediaevalia* 22.1: *Scientia und Ars im Hoch- und Spätmittelalter* (Berlin–New York, 1994), pp. 217–39.

Albert & Thomas: Selected Writings, ed. S. Tugwell. New York–Mahwah, 1988.

Albert the Great. *B. Alberti Magni . . . Opera omnia*. Vol. 1, incl. *De praedicamentis tractatus VII, De sex principiis . . . tractatus VIII*, ed. A. Borgnet. Paris, 1890.

———. *Sancti Doctoris ecclesiae Alberti Magni Opera omnia*, Cologne ed., Münster, 1951– . Vol. 4, *Physica;* Vols. 16.1, 16.2, *Metaphysica*.

Albertson, J. "The *Esse* of Accidents according to St. Thomas." *Modern Schoolman* 30 (1953), pp. 265–78.

Allen, R. E. "Participation and Predication in Plato's Middle Dialogues," in *Plato I: Metaphysics and Epistemology: A Collection of Critical Essays*, ed. G. Vlastos (Garden City, N.Y., 1971), pp. 167–83.

———. *Plato's Parmenides: Translation and Analysis*. Minneapolis, 1983.

Anonymous. *L'existence de Dieu*. Cahiers de l'actualité religieuse 16. Tournai-Paris, 1961.

———. *Le Liber de causis*, ed. A. Pattin. *Tijdschrift voor Filosofie* 28 (Leuven, 1966), pp. 90–203.

———. Review of *La controverse de 1270 . . .* by E.-H. Wéber. *Rassegna di letteratura tomistica* 5 (1973), pp. 65–72.

Anselm. *Sancti Anselmi cantuariensis archiepiscopi opera omnia*, ed. F. S. Schmitt. Stuttgart-Bad Canstatt, 1968.

Aristotle. *Aristotelis De anima*, ed. W. D. Ross. Oxford, 1956; repr. 1979.

597

————. *Aristotelis Metaphysica,* ed. W. Jaeger. Oxford, 1957.

————. *Aristotelis opera,* Vols. 1 and 2, ed. I. Bekker. Berlin, 1831.

————. *Aristotle's Metaphysics,* 2 vols., ed. W. D. Ross. Oxford 1953.

————. *Aristotle's Physics,* ed. W. D. Ross. Oxford, 1936; repr. 1998.

————. *The Complete Works of Aristotle. The Revised Oxford Translation.* Two vols., ed. J. Barnes. Princeton, N.J., 1984.

Ashley, B. M. "St. Albert and the Nature of Natural Science," in *Albertus Magnus and the Sciences: Commemorative Essays 1980,* ed. J. A. Weisheipl (Toronto, 1980), pp. 73–102.

Ashworth, E. J. "Signification and Mode of Signifying in Thirteenth-Century Logic." *Medieval Philosophy and Theology* 1 (1991), pp. 39–67.

Augustine. *De libero arbitrio,* in *Aurelii Augustini opera* (CCSL 29). Turnhout, 1970.

Averroes. *Aristotelis opera cum Averrois commentariis,* 10 vols. Venice, 1562–74; repr. Frankfurt, 1962.

————. *Averroes' De substantia orbis,* ed. A. Hyman. Cambridge, Mass., and Jerusalem, 1986.

Avicenna. *Liber de anima seu sextus de naturalibus: IV-V,* ed. S. Van Riet. Louvain-Leiden, 1968.

————. *Liber de Philosophia prima sive Scientia divina: I-IV,* ed. S. Van Riet. Louvain-Leiden, 1977.

————. *Liber de Philosophia prima sive Scientia divina: V-X,* ed. S. Van Riet. Louvain-Leiden, 1980.

————. *Sufficientia.* Venice, 1508.

Baeumker, C. *Witelo, Ein Philosoph und Naturforscher des XIII. Jahrhunderts.* Beiträge zur Geschichte der Philosophie des Mittelalters, III-2. Münster, 1908.

Baisnée, J. A. "St. Thomas Aquinas's Proofs of the Existence of God Presented in Their Chronological Order," in *Philosophical Studies in Honor of the Very Reverend Ignatius Smith, O.P.,* ed. J. K. Ryan (Westminster, Md., 1952), pp. 29–64.

Balas, D. L. "A Thomist View on Divine Infinity." *Proceedings of the American Catholic Philosophical Association* 55 (1981), pp. 91–98.

Bañez, D. *Scholastica Commentaria in Primam Partem Summae Theologicae S. Thomae Aquinatis.* Madrid-Valencia, 1934; repr. Dubuque, Iowa, n.d.

Bassler, W. "Die Kritik des Thomas von Aquin am ontologischen Gottesbeweis." *Franziskanische Studien* 55 (1973), pp. 97–190; 56 (1974), pp. 1–26.

Baumgartner, H. M., G. Gerhardt, K. Konhardt, and G. Schönrich. "Kategorie, Kategorienlehre. 4: Thomas von Aquin," in *Historisches Wörterbuch der Philosophie,* ed. J. Ritter and K. Gründer, Band 4 (Basel-Stuttgart, 1976), cols. 722–723.

Bayerschmidt, P. *Die Seins- und Formmetaphysik des Heinrich von Gent in ihrer Anwendung auf die Christologie.* Münster i. W., 1941.

Bazán, B. C. "La corporalité selon saint Thomas." *Revue philosophique de Louvain* 81 (1983), pp. 369–409.

————. "Le dialogue philosophique entre Siger de Brabant et Thomas d'Aquin. A propos d'un ouvrage récent de E. H. Wéber, O.P." *Revue philosophique de Louvain* 72 (1974), pp. 53–155.

————. "Les questions disputées, principalement dans les facultés de théologie." Part I of B. C. Bazán, J. F. Wippel, G. Fransen, and D. Jacquant, *Les questions disputées et les questions quodlibétiques dans les facultés de théologie de droit et de médecine* (Turnhout, 1985).

————. "Préface," in *Quaestiones disputatae de anima,* Leonine edition, Vol. 24.1.

————. Review of *God in Himself: Aquinas' Doctrine of God as Expounded in the Summa Theologiae* by W. J. Hankey. *Speculum* 65 (1990), pp. 166–70.

————. "The Human Soul: Form and Substance? Thomas Aquinas' Critique of Eclectic Aristotelianism." *AHDLMA* 64 (1997), pp. 95–126.

Beierwaltes, W. *Identität und Differenz*. Frankfurt am Main, 1980.

Bendiek, J. "Über den Gebrauch von Reihen in den Gottesbeweisen." *Franziskanische Studien* 48 (1966), pp. 75–108.

Bérubé, C. *La Connaissance de l'Individuel au Moyen Âge*. Montreal, 1964.

Blanche, F. A. "Sur la langue technique de saint Thomas d'Aquin." *Revue de philosophie* n.s. 1 (1930), pp. 7–30.

Blanchette, O. *The Perfection of the Universe according to Aquinas*. University Park, Pa., 1992.

Bobik, J. *Aquinas on Being and Essence*. Notre Dame, Ind., 1965.

———. "Aquinas's Fourth Way and the Approximating Relation." *The Thomist* 51 (1987), pp. 17–36.

———. "Dimensions in the Individuation of Bodily Substances." *Philosophical Studies* (Maynooth) 4 (1954), pp. 60–79.

———. "La doctrine de saint Thomas sur l'individuation des substances corporelles." *Revue philosophique de Louvain* 51 (1953), pp. 5–41.

———. "The First Part of the Third Way." *Philosophical Studies* (Maynooth) 17 (1968), pp. 142–60.

Boethius. *In Categorias Aristotelis libri quattuor*. Migne PL 64.

———. *In Isagogen Porphyrii Commenta*, ed. S. Brandt. CSEL 48. Vienna, 1906.

———. *The Theological Tractates with an English Translation; The Consolation of Philosophy*, trans. H. F. Stewart, E. K. Rand, and S. J. Tester. Cambridge, Mass.–London, 1978.

Boland, V. *Ideas in God According to Saint Thomas Aquinas: Sources and Synthesis*. London–New York–Cologne, 1996.

Bonaventure. *Doctoris seraphici S. Bonaventurae . . . opera omnia*. Quaracchi, 1882–1902.

Bonino, S.-T. *Thomas d'Aquin: De la verité ou la science en Dieu*. Fribourg, 1996.

Bonnette, D. *Aquinas' Proofs for God's Existence. St. Thomas Aquinas on: "The Per Accidens necessarily implies the Per Se."* The Hague, 1972.

Bougerol, J. G. *Introduction à Saint Bonaventure*. Paris, 1988.

Boyle, L. *The Setting of the Summa Theologiae of Saint Thomas*. Étienne Gilson Series 5. Toronto, 1982.

Breton, S. "La déduction thomiste des catégories." *Revue philosophique de Louvain* 60 (1962), pp. 5–32.

Brown, B. F. *Accidental Being: A Study in the Metaphysics of St. Thomas Aquinas*. Lanham, Md., 1985.

———. "Accidental *Esse:* A Confirmation." *New Scholasticism* 44 (1970), pp. 133–52.

Brown, P. "Infinite Causal Regression," in *Aquinas: A Collection of Critical Essays*, ed. A. Kenny (Garden City, N.Y., 1969), pp. 214–36.

Brown, S. "Avicenna and the Unity of the Concept of Being." *Franciscan Studies* 25 (1965), pp. 117–50.

———. "Godfrey of Fontaines and Henry of Ghent: Individuation and the Condemnation of 1277," in *Société et Église. Textes et discussions dans les universités d'Europe centrale pendant le moyen âge tardif*, ed. S. Wlodek (Brepols, 1995), pp. 193–207.

———. "Henry of Ghent (b. ca. 1217; d. 1293)," in *Individuation in Scholasticism. The Later Middle Ages and the Counter-Reformation*, ed. J.J.E. Gracia (Albany, N.Y., 1994), pp. 195–219.

Brunner, F. *Platonisme et Aristotélisme. La critique d'Ibn Gabirol par saint Thomas d'Aquin*. Louvain-Paris, 1965.

Burrell, D. *Aquinas: God and Action*. Notre Dame, Ind., 1979.

———. "Aquinas and Maimonides: A Conversation about Proper Speech." *Immanuel* 16 (1983), pp. 70–85.

————. *Knowing the Unknowable God.* Notre Dame, Ind., 1986.

Cajetan, Thomas de Vio. Commentary on *Summa theologiae.* In *Sancti Thomae de Aquino Opere Omnia,* Leonine edition, Vols. 4–12.

————. *De nominum analogia,* Eng. trans. E. Bushinski and H. Koren. Pittsburgh, 1953.

————. *De nominum analogia. De conceptu entis,* ed. P. N. Zammit. Rome, 1934.

————. *In De ente et essentia D. Thomae Aquinatis commentaria,* ed. M.-H. Laurent. Turin, 1934.

Callus, D. A. "The Origins of the Problem of the Unity of Form," in *The Dignity of Science,* ed. J. A. Weisheipl (Washington, D.C., 1961), pp. 121–49.

Capreolus, J. *Defensiones theologiae Divi Thomae Aquinatis,* Vol. 2. Turin, 1900.

Carlo, W. E. "The Role of Essence in Existential Metaphysics," in *Readings in Metaphysics,* ed. J. Rosenberg (Westminster, Md., 1963), pp. 278–81; orig. publ. in *International Philosophical Quarterly* 2 (1962), pp. 584–89.

————. *The Ultimate Reducibility of Essence to Existence in Existential Metaphysics.* The Hague, 1966.

Chambat, L. "La 'Tertia Via' dans saint Thomas et Aristote." *Revue thomiste,* n.s. 10 (1927), pp. 334–38.

Charlier, L. "Les cinq voies de saint Thomas: Leur structure métaphysique," in *L'existence de Dieu.* Cahiers de l'actualité religieuse 16 (Tournai-Paris, 1961), pp. 181–227.

Châtillon, J. "De Guillaume d'Auxerre à saint Thomas d'Aquin: l'Argument de saint Anselme chez les premiers scolastiques," in *D'Isidore de Séville à saint Thomas d'Aquin* (London, 1985), pp. 209–31.

Chenu, M-D. *Introduction à l'étude de saint Thomas d'Aquin.* 2d ed., Montreal-Paris, 1954.

Chevenal, F., and R. Imbach. *Thomas von Aquin. Prologe zu den Aristoteles-Kommentaren.* Frankfurt am Main, 1993.

Chossat, M. "Dieu," in *Dictionnaire de théologie catholique* (Paris, 1899–1950), Vol. 4, pt. 1, col. 1180.

————. "L'Averroïsme de saint Thomas. Notes sur la distinction d'essence et d'existence à la fin du XIIIe siècle." *Archives de philosophie* 9 (1932), pp. 129[465]–177[513].

Clarke, W. N. "Commentary on the 'Being of Creatures'," in *Readings in Metaphysics,* ed. J. Rosenberg (Westminster, Md., 1963), pp. 273–76; orig. pub. in *Proceedings of the American Catholic Philosophical Association* 31 (1957), pp. 128–32.

————. *Explorations in Metaphysics: Being—God—Person.* Notre Dame, Ind., 1994.

————. "The Limitation of Act by Potency in St. Thomas: Aristotelianism or Neoplatonism?" *New Scholasticism* 26 (1952), pp. 167–94; repr. in *Explorations in Metaphysics: Being—God—Person* (Notre Dame, Ind., 1994), pp. 65–88.

————. "The Meaning of Participation in St. Thomas." *Proceedings of the American Catholic Philosophical Association* 26 (1952), pp. 147–57; repr. in *Explorations in Metaphysics: Being—God—Person* (Notre Dame, Ind., 1994), pp. 89–101.

————. "The Platonic Heritage of Thomism." Review of *The Platonic Heritage of Thomism* by A. Little. *Review of Metaphysics* 8 (1954), pp. 105–24.

————. "What Cannot Be Said in St. Thomas' Essence-Existence Doctrine." *New Scholasticism* 48 (1974), pp. 35–38.

Clavell, L. *El nombre propio de Dios según santo Tomás de Aquino.* Pamplona, 1980.

Collins, J. *The Thomistic Philosophy of the Angels.* Washington, D.C., 1947.

Connolly, T. K. "The Basis of the Third Proof for the Existence of God." *The Thomist* 17 (1954), pp. 281–349.

Corvez, M. "La quatrième voie vers l'existence de Dieu selon saint Thomas," in *Quinque sunt viae* ed. L Elders (Vatican City, 1980), pp. 75–83.

Cosgrove, M. R. "Thomas Aquinas on Anselm's Argument." *Review of Metaphysics* 27 (1974), pp. 513–30.

Courtès, C. "Cohérence de l'être et Premier Principe selon saint Thomas d'Aquin." *Revue thomiste* 70 (1970), pp. 387–423.

———. "L'être et le non-être selon saint Thomas d'Aquin." *Revue thomiste* 66 (1966), pp. 575–610; 67 (1967), pp. 387–436.

———. "Participation et contingence selon saint Thomas d'Aquin." *Revue thomiste* 69 (1969), pp. 201–35.

Cunningham, F. "Distinction according to St. Thomas." *New Scholasticism* 36 (1962), pp. 279–312.

———. *Essence and Existence in Thomism: A Mental vs. The "Real Distinction"?* Lanham, Md., 1988.

———. "Textos de Santo Tomás sobre el *esse* y *esencia*." *Pensamiento* 20 (1964), pp. 283–306.

———. "The 'Real Distinction' in John Quidort." *Journal of the History of Philosophy* 8 (1970), pp. 9–28.

Dales, R. C. *Medieval Discussions of the Eternity of the World.* Leiden, 1990.

———, and O. Argerami, eds. *Medieval Latin Texts on the Eternity of the World.* Leiden, 1991.

d'Ancona, C. *Recherches sur le Liber de causis.* Paris, 1995.

Davidson, H. A. *Proofs for Eternity, Creation and the Existence of God in Medieval Islamic and Jewish Philosophy.* New York–Oxford, 1987.

Davies, B. "Aquinas on What God Is Not." *Revue internationale de philosophie* 52 (1998), pp. 207–25.

———. *The Thought of Thomas Aquinas.* Oxford, 1993.

de Finance, J. *Être et agir dans la philosophie de Saint Thomas.* 2d ed., Rome, 1960.

De Guzman Vicente, L., "De notione subsistentiae apud sanctum Thomam." *Divus Thomas* (Piac.) 71 (1968), pp. 397–422.

de Libera, A. *Albert le Grand et la philosophie.* Paris, 1990.

De Raeymaeker, L. *Metaphysica generalis.* Vol. 1. Louvain, 1931.

———. *The Philosophy of Being.* St. Louis–London, 1954.

de Vaux, R. *Notes et textes sur l'Avicennisme latin aux confins des XIIe-XIIIe siècles.* Paris, 1934.

de Vries, J. "Das 'esse commune' bei Thomas von Aquin." *Scholastik* 39 (1964), pp. 163–77.

Degl'Innocenti, U. (H.) "Capreolo d'accordo col Gaetano a proposito della personalità?" *Euntes docete* 7 (1954), pp. 168–203.

———. "La distinzione reale nel 'De ente et essentia' di S. Tommaso." *Doctor communis* 10 (1957), pp. 165–73.

———. "De nova quadam ratione exponendi sententiam Capreoli de constitutione ontologica personae." *Divus Thomas* (Piac.) 53 (1950), pp. 321–38.

———. "Il pensiero di San Tommaso sul principio d'individuazione." *Divus Thomas* (Piac.) 45 (1942), pp. 35–81.

———. "La validità della 'terza via'." *Doctor Communis* 7 (1954), pp. 41–70.

del Prado, N. *De veritate fundamentali philosophiae christianae.* Fribourg, 1911.

Denis, P. "Le premier enseignement de saint Thomas sur l'unité de la forme substantielle." *AHDLMA* 21 (1954), pp. 139–64.

Descartes, R. *Principles of Philosophy,* trans. V. R. Miller and R. P. Miller. Dordrecht-Boston-London, 1983.

Dewan, L. "The Distinctiveness of St. Thomas' 'Third Way'," *Dialogue* 19 (1980), pp. 201–18.

———. "The Number and Order of St. Thomas's Five Ways," *Downside Review* 92 (1974), pp. 1–18.

———. "Saint Thomas, Joseph Owens, and the Real Distinction between Being and Essence." *Modern Schoolman* 61 (1984), pp. 145–56.

Dod, B. G. "Aristoteles latinus," in *The Cambridge History of Later Medieval Philosophy,* ed. N. Kretzmann et al. (Cambridge, 1982), pp. 45–79.

Doig, J. *Aquinas on Metaphysics: A historico-doctrinal study of the Commentary on the Metaphysics.* The Hague, 1972.

———. "Science première et science universelle dans le 'Commentaire de la métaphysique' de saint Thomas d'Aquin." *Revue philosophique de Louvain* 63 (1965), pp. 73–82.

Dolan, S. E. "Resolution and Composition in Speculative and Practical Discourse." *Laval théologique et philosophique* 6 (1950), pp. 9–62.

Driscoll, J. A. "EIΔH in Aristotle's Earlier and Later Theories of Substance," in *Studies in Aristotle,* ed. D. J. O'Meara (Washington, D.C., 1981), pp. 129–59.

Dümpelmann, L. *Kreation als ontisch-ontologisches Verhältnis. Zur Metaphysik der Schöpfungstheologie des Thomas von Aquin.* Freiburg-Munich, 1969.

Dunphy, W. "Maimonides and Aquinas on Creation: A Critique of Their Historians," in *Graceful Reason: Essays in Ancient and Medieval Philosophy Presented to Joseph Owens, CSSR,* ed. L. Gerson (Toronto, 1983), pp. 361–79.

Durantel, J. *Saint Thomas et le Pseudo-Denys.* Paris, 1919.

Düring, I. *Aristoteles. Darstellung und Interpretation seines Denkens.* Heidelberg, 1966.

Effler, R. *John Duns Scotus and the Principle "Omne quod movetur ab alio movetur."* St. Bonaventure, N.Y., 1962.

Elders, L. J. "Les cinq voies et leur place dans la philosophie de saint Thomas," in *Quinque sunt viae,* ed. L. Elders. Studi tomistici 9 (Vatican City, 1980), pp. 133–46.

———. *Faith and Science. An Introduction to St. Thomas' 'Expositio in Boethii De Trinitate.'* Rome, 1974.

———. "Justification des 'cinq voies'." *Revue thomiste* 61 (1961), pp. 207–25.

———. *The Philosophical Theology of St. Thomas Aquinas.* Leiden, 1990.

———, ed. *Quinque sunt viae.* Studi tomistici 9. Vatican City, 1980.

———. "St. Thomas Aquinas' Commentary on the 'Metaphysics' of Aristotle." *Divus Thomas* (Piac.) 86 (1983), pp. 307–26.

Fabro, C. "The Intensive Hermeneutics of Thomistic Philosophy: The Notion of Participation." *The Review of Metaphysics* 27 (1974), pp. 449–91.

———. "Un itinéraire de saint Thomas. L'établissement de la distinction réelle entre essence et existence." *Revue de philosophie* 39 (1939), pp. 285–310; repr. in his *Esegesi tomistica* (Rome, 1969), pp. 89–108.

———. *La nozione metafisica di partecipazione secondo S. Tommaso d'Aquino.* Milan, 1939; 2d revised ed., Turin, 1950.

———. *Partecipazione e causalità.* Turin, 1960.

———. *Participation et causalité selon s. Thomas d'Aquin.* Louvain-Paris, 1961.

———. "Platonism, Neo-Platonism and Thomism: Convergencies and Divergencies." *New Scholasticism* 44 (1970), pp. 69–100.

———. "Sviluppo, significato e valore della 'IV Via'." *Doctor communis* 7 (1954), pp. 71–109.

———. "The Transcendentality of *Ens-Esse* and the Ground of Metaphysics." *International Philosophical Quarterly* 6 (1966), pp. 389–427.

Feldman, S. "A Scholastic Misinterpretation of Maimonides' Doctrine of Divine Attributes," in *Studies in Maimonides and St. Thomas Aquinas,* ed. J. I. Dienstag (New York, 1975), pp. 58–74.

Flasch, K. "Die Beurteilung des Anselmianischen Arguments bei Thomas von Aquin." *Analecta Anselmiana* IV, 1 (1975), pp. 111–25.

Forest, A. *La structure métaphysique du concret selon saint Thomas d'Aquin.* 2d ed., Paris, 1956.

Gallagher, D. "Free Choice and Free Judgment in Thomas Aquinas." *Archiv für Geschichte der Philosophie* 76 (1994), pp. 247–77.

Garceau, B. *Judicium: Vocabulaire, sources, doctrine de saint Thomas d'Aquin.* Montreal-Paris, 1968.

Garrigou-Lagrange, R. *God: His Existence and His Nature,* Vol. 1. St. Louis–London, 1949.

Geiger, L.-B. "Abstraction et séparation d'après s. Thomas *In de Trinitate,* q. 5, a. 3." *Revue des sciences philosophiques et théologiques* 31 (1947), pp. 3–40.

———. "Les idées divines dans l'oeuvre de S. Thomas," in *St. Thomas Aquinas 1274–1974. Commemorative Studies,* ed. A. Maurer et al. (Toronto, 1974), Vol. 1, pp. 175–209.

———. *La participation dans la philosophie de s. Thomas d'Aquin.* Paris, 1942; 2d ed., 1953.

Gèny, P. "À propos des preuves thomistes de l'existence de Dieu." *Revue de Philosophie* 24 (1931), pp. 575–601.

Georgiadis, C. "Two Conceptions of Substance in Aristotle," in *Substances and Things: Aristotle's Doctrine of Physical Substance in Recent Essays,* ed. M. L. O'Hara (Washington, D.C., 1982), pp. 172–87.

Geyer, B. "Albertus Magnus und die Entwicklung der scholastischen Metaphysik." *Miscellanea Mediaevalia* 2: *Die Metaphysik im Mittelalter* (Berlin, 1963), pp. 3–13.

Giles of Rome. *Errores philosophorum,* ed. J. Koch. Milwaukee, 1944.

———. *Quaestiones disputatae de esse et essentia.* Venice, 1503.

Gilson, E. *Being and Some Philosophers.* Toronto, 1949; 2d ed. 1952.

———. *The Christian Philosophy of St. Thomas Aquinas.* New York, 1956.

———. "Éléments d'une métaphysique thomiste de l'être." AHDLMA 40 (1973), pp. 7–36.

———. *Elements of Christian Philosophy.* Garden City, N.Y., 1960.

———. *History of Christian Philosophy in the Middle Ages.* New York, 1955.

———. *Introduction à la philosophie chrétienne.* Paris, 1960. English trans. by A. Maurer: *Christian Philosophy: An Introduction* (Toronto, 1993).

———. *Jean Duns Scot. Introduction à ses positions fondamentales.* Paris, 1952.

———. "La notion d'existence chez Guillaume d'Auvergne." AHDLMA 15 (1946), pp. 55–91.

———. *The Philosopher and Theology.* New York, 1962.

———. *La philosophie de Saint Bonaventure.* 3d ed., Paris, 1953.

———. "La preuve du 'De ente et essentia'." *Acta III Congressus Thomistici Internationalis: Doctor communis* 3 (Turin, 1950), pp. 257–60.

———. "Prolégomènes à la *prima via.*" AHDLMA 30 (1964), pp. 53–70.

———. "Propos sur l'être et sa notion," in *San tommaso e il pensiero moderno.* Studi tomistici 3 (Vatican City, 1974), pp. 7–17.

———. "Quasi Definitio Substantiae," in *St. Thomas Aquinas 1274–1974: Commemorative Studies,* ed. A. Maurer et al. (Toronto, 1974), Vol. 1, pp. 111–29.

———. *The Spirit of Medieval Philosophy.* London, 1936; repr. 1950.

———. "Thomas Aquinas and Our Colleagues," in *A Gilson Reader,* ed. A. C. Pegis (Garden City, N.Y., 1957), pp. 278–97.

———. *Le thomisme.* 6th ed., Paris, 1965.

———. "Trois leçons sur le problème de l'existence de Dieu." *Divinitas* 5 (1961), pp. 23–87.

Godfrey of Fontaines. *Les Quatre premiers Quodlibets de Godefroid de Fontaines,* ed. M. de Wulf and A. Pelzer. Les Philosophes Belges 2. Louvain, 1904.

———. *Le huitième Quodlibet, Le neuvième Quodlibet, Le dixième Quodlibet,* ed. J. Hoffmans Les Philosophes Belges 4. Louvain, 1924, 1928, 1931.

Goichon, A.-M. *La distinction de l'essence et de l'existence d'après Ibn Sina (Avicenne).* Paris, 1937.

Grabmann, M. "Doctrina S. Thomae de distinctione reali inter essentiam et esse ex documentis ineditis saeculi XIII illustratur," in *Acta Hebdomadae Thomisticae Romae celebratae 19–25 Novembris 1923 in laudem S. Thomae Aquinatis* (Rome, 1924), pp. 131–90.

Guérard des Lauriers, M. L. *La preuve de Dieu et les cinq voies.* Rome, 1966.

Guttmann, J. *Das Verhältniss des Thomas von Aquino zum Judenthum und zur jüdischen Litteratur.* Göttingen, 1891.

Hadot, P. "La distinction de l'être et de l'étant dans le *De Hebdomadibus* de Boèce," in *Miscellanea Mediaevalia* 2: *Die Metaphysik im Mittelalter* (Berlin, 1963), pp. 147–53.

Hall, D. *The Trinity. An Analysis of St. Thomas Aquinas' Expositio of the De Trinitate.* Leiden–New York–Cologne, 1992.

Hankey, W. J. *God in Himself: Aquinas' Doctrine of God as Expounded in the Summa Theologiae.* Oxford, 1987.

Hart, C. A. *Thomistic Metaphysics: An Inquiry into the Act of Existing.* Englewood Cliffs, N.J., 1959.

Hartshorne, C. *Anselm's Discovery: A Re-Examination of the Ontological Proof for God's Existence.* La Salle, Ill., 1965; repr. 1991.

Hegyi, J. *Die Bedeutung des Seins bei den klassichen Kommentatoren des heiligen Thomas von Aquin. Capreolus—Silvester von Ferrara—Cajetan.* Pullach bei München, 1959.

Henle, R. J. *Saint Thomas and Platonism: A Study of the "Plato" and "Platonici" Texts in the Writings of Saint Thomas.* The Hague, 1956.

Henninger, M. G. *Relations: Medieval Theories 1250–1325.* Oxford, 1989.

Henry of Ghent. *Henrici de Gandavo opera omnia.* Vol. 5, *Quodlibet I,* ed. R. Macken. Leuven-Leiden, 1979.

———. *Henrici de Gandavo opera omnia.* Vol. 13, *Quodlibet IX,* ed. R. Macken. Leuven, 1983.

———. *Henrici de Gandavo opera omnia.* Vol. 14, *Quodlibet X,* ed. R. Macken. Leuven, 1981.

———. *Quodlibeta . . . cum duplici tabella.* Paris, 1518.

Hernandez-Pacheco, J. *Acto y substancia. Estudio a través de Santo Tomás de Aquino.* Seville, 1984.

Hissette, R. "Albert le Grand et Thomas d'Aquin dans la censure parisienne du 7 mars 1277," in *Miscellanea Mediaevalia* 15: *Studien zur mittelalterlichen Geistesgeschichte und ihren Quellen* (Berlin–New York, 1982), pp. 226–46.

———. *Enquête sur les 219 articles condamnés à Paris le 7 mars 1277.* Louvain-Paris, 1977.

———. "L'implication de Thomas d'Aquin dans les censures parisiennes de 1277." *Recherches de théologie et philosophie médiévales* 44 (1997), pp. 3–31.

Hoenen, P. *Cosmologia.* 5th ed., Rome, 1956.

Holstein, H. "L'origine aristotélicienne de la 'tertia via' de saint Thomas." *Revue philosophique de Louvain* 48 (1950), pp. 354–70.

Honnefelder, L. *Der Begriff des Seienden als solchen als Gegenstand der Metaphysik nach der Lehre des Johannes Duns Scotus.* Münster, 1979.

———. "Der zweite Anfang der Metaphysik. Voraussetzungen, Ansätze und Folgen der Wiederbegründung der Metaphysik im 13./14. Jahrhundert," in *Philosophie im Mittelalter. Entwicklungslinien und Paradigmen,* ed. J. P. Beckmann, L. Honnefelder, G. Schrimpf, G. Wieland (Hamburg, 1987), pp. 164–86.

Hoping, H. *Weisheit als Wissen des Ursprungs. Philosophie und Theologie in der "Summa contra gentiles" des Thomas von Aquin.* Freiburg im Breisgau, 1997.

Hopkins, J. *A Companion to the Study of St. Anselm.* Minneapolis, 1972.

Humbrecht, T.-D. "Dieu a-t-il une essence?" *Revue thomiste* 95 (1995), pp. 7–18.

Hume, D. *A Treatise of Human Nature,* ed. L. A. Selby-Bigge; 2d ed., rev. by P. H. Nidditch. Oxford, 1978.

Hyman, A. "Maimonides on Religious Language," in *Perspectives on Maimonides: Philosophical and Historical Studies,* ed. J. L. Kraemer (Oxford, 1991), pp. 175–91.

Imbach, R. "Averroistische Stellungnahmen zur Diskussion über das Verhältnis von *esse* und *essentia.* Von Siger von Brabant zu Thaddaeus von Parma," in *Studi sul XIV secolo in memoria di Anneliese Maier,* ed. A. Maierù and P. Bagliani (Rome, 1981), pp. 299–339.

Jalbert, G. *Necessité et contingence chez S. Thomas d'Aquin et chez ses prédécesseurs.* Ottawa, 1961.

James of Viterbo. *Jacobi de Viterbio, O.E.S.A., Disputatio prima de quolibet,* ed. E. Ypma. Würzburg, 1968.

John Damascene. *De fide orthodoxa: Versions of Burgundio and Cerbanus,* ed. E. M. Buytaert. St. Bonaventure, N.Y., 1955.

John Duns Scotus. *Opera omnia.* Vol. 16, *Lectura in librum primum Sententiarum.* Vatican City, 1960.

John of Saint Thomas. *Cursus Philosophicus Thomisticus.* Vol. I: *Ars logica,* ed. B. Reiser. Turin, 1930.

John Pecham. *Quodlibeta Quatuor,* ed. G. Etzkorn. Grottaferrata, 1989.

John, H. J. *The Thomist Spectrum.* New York, 1966.

Johnson, H. J. "Why Five Ways? A Thesis and Some Alternatives," in *Actes du quatrième congrès international de philosophie médiévale* (Montreal, 1969), pp. 1143–54.

Johnson, M. F. "Why Five Ways?" *Proceedings of the American Catholic Philosophical Association* 65 (1991), pp. 107–21.

Jordan, M. "The Names of God and the Being of Names," in *The Existence and Nature of God,* ed. A. J. Freddoso (Notre Dame, Ind., 1983), pp. 161–90.

———. *Ordering Wisdom: The Hierarchy of Philosophical Discourses in Aquinas.* Notre Dame, Ind., 1986.

———. "Theology and Philosophy," in *The Cambridge Companion to Aquinas,* ed. N. Kretzmann and E. Stump (Cambridge, 1993), pp. 232–51.

Judy, A. "Avicenna's *Metaphysics* in the *Summa contra gentiles* (III)." *Angelicum* 53 (1976), pp. 185–216.

Kant, I. *Immanuel Kant's Critique of Pure Reason,* trans. N. Kemp Smith. London, 1964.

Kelley, C. J. "Circularity and Contradiction in Aquinas' Rejection of Actually Infinite Multitudes." *Modern Schoolman* 61 (1984), pp. 73–100.

Kelly, M. "Action in Aquinas." *New Scholasticism* 52 (1978), pp. 261–67.

Kenny, A. *The Five Ways: St. Thomas Aquinas' Proofs of God's Existence.* Notre Dame, Ind., 1980.

Kleineidam, E. *Das Problem der hylomorphen Zusammensetzung der geistigen Substanzen im 13. Jahrhundert, behandelt bis Thomas von Aquin.* Breslau, 1930.

Klinger, I. *Das Prinzip der Individuation bei Thomas von Aquin.* Vier-Türme, 1964.

Klubertanz, G. P. *The Discursive Power: Sources and Doctrine of the 'Vis Cogitativa' According to St. Thomas Aquinas.* St. Louis, 1952.

———. *Introduction to the Philosophy of Being.* 2d ed., New York, 1963.

———. "St. Thomas and the Knowledge of the Singular." *New Scholasticism* 26 (1952), pp. 135–66.

———. *St. Thomas Aquinas on Analogy: A Textual Analysis and Systematic Synthesis.* Chicago, 1960.

———. "St. Thomas on Learning Metaphysics." *Gregorianum* 35 (1954), pp. 3–17.

———. "St. Thomas' Treatment of the Axiom, *Omne Agens Agit Propter Finem,*" in *An Etienne Gilson Tribute,* ed. C. J. O'Neil (Milwaukee, 1959), pp. 101–17.

———. "The Teaching of Thomistic Metaphysics." *Gregorianum* 35 (1954), pp. 187–205.

Knasas, J.F.X. "Making Sense of the *Tertia Via.*" *New Scholasticism* 54 (1980), pp. 476–511.

———. *The Preface to Thomistic Metaphysics.* New York–Bern–Frankfurt am Main–Paris, 1990.

———. "Thomistic Existentialism and the Proofs *Ex Motu* at *Contra Gentiles* I, c. 13." *The Thomist* 59 (1995), pp. 591–615.

Kondoleon, T. "The Argument from Motion and the Argument for Angels: A Reply to John F. X. Knasas." *The Thomist* 62 (1998), pp. 269–90.

———. "The Start of Metaphysics" (review of *The Preface to Thomistic Metaphysics* by J.F.X. Knasas). *The Thomist* 58 (1994), pp. 121–30.

König, E. "Aristoteles' erste Philosophie als universale Wissenschaft von den APXAI." *Archiv für Geschichte der Philosophie* 52 (1970), pp. 225–46.

Kosman, L. "Aristotle's First Predicament," in *Substances and Things: Aristotle's Doctrine of Physical Substance in Recent Essays,* ed. M. L. O'Hara (Washington, D.C., 1982), pp. 19–42.

Krapiec, A. M. "Analysis formationis conceptus entis existentialiter considerati." *Divus Thomas* (Piac.) 59 (1956), pp. 320–50.

Kremer, K. *Die Neuplatonische Seinsphilosophie und ihre Wirkung auf Thomas von Aquin.* Leiden, 1966.

Krempel, A. *La doctrine de la relation chez saint Thomas; exposé historique et systématique.* Paris, 1952.

Kretzmann, N. *The Metaphysics of Theism: Aquinas's Natural Theology in Summa Contra Gentiles I.* Oxford, 1997.

———, and E. Stump, eds. *The Cambridge Companion to Aquinas.* Cambridge, 1993.

Künzle, P. *Das Verhältnis der Seele zu ihren Potenzen. Problemgeschichtliche Untersuchungen von Augustin bis und mit Thomas von Aquin.* Freiburg-Schweiz, 1956.

Langevin, G. "L'action immanente d'après s. Thomas d'Aquin." *Laval théologique et philosophique* 30 (1974), pp. 251–66.

Laporta, J. *La destinée de la nature humaine selon Thomas d'Aquin.* Paris, 1965.

Lefèvre, C. A. "Siger de Brabant a-t-il influencé saint Thomas? Propos sur la cohérence de l'anthropologie thomiste." *Mélanges de science religieuse* 31 (1974), pp. 203–15.

Legrand, J. *L'univers et l'homme dans la philosophie de saint Thomas.* 2 vols. Brussels-Paris, 1946.

Leroy, M.-V. "*Abstractio* et *separatio* d'après un texte controversé de saint Thomas." *Revue thomiste* 48 (1948), pp. 328–39.

———. Review of *Metaphysical Themes in Thomas Aquinas,* by J. F. Wippel. *Revue thomiste,* n.s. 4 (1984), pp. 667–71.

Litt, T. *Les corps célestes dans l'univers de saint Thomas d'Aquin.* Louvain-Paris, 1963.

Little, A. *The Platonic Heritage of Thomism.* Dublin, 1949.

Lloyd, A. C. *Form and the Universal in Aristotle.* Liverpool, 1981.

Lohr, C., ed. "*Logica Algazelis,* Introduction and Critical Text." *Traditio* 21 (1965), pp. 223–90.

Lottin, O. *Psychologie et morale aux XIIe et XIIIe siècles.* Vol. 1. Louvain-Gembloux, 1942.

Lotz, J. B. *Ontologia.* Barcelona, 1963.

Lyttkens, H. *The Analogy between God and the World: An Investigation of Its Background and Interpretation of Its Use by Thomas of Aquino.* Uppsala, 1952.

———. "Die Bedeutung der Gottesprädikate bei Thomas von Aquin," in *Philosophical Essays*

Dedicated to Gunnar Aspelin on the Occasion of His Sixty-fifth Birthday, ed. H. Bratt et al. (Lund, 1963), pp. 76–96.

MacDonald, S. "Aquinas's Parasitic Cosmological Argument." *Medieval Philosophy and Theology* 1 (1991), pp. 119–55.

————. "The *Esse/Essentia* Argument in Aquinas's *De ente et essentia.*" *Journal of the History of Philosophy* 22 (1984), pp. 157–72.

Macken, R. "Les diverses applications de la distinction intentionnelle chez Henri de Gand." *Miscellanea Mediaevalia* 13.2: *Sprache und Erkenntnis im Mittelalter* (Berlin, 1981), pp. 769–76.

————. "Heinrich von Gent im Gespräch mit seinen Zeitgenossen über die menschliche Freiheit." *Franziskanische Studien* 59 (1977), pp. 125–82.

————. "Le statut de la matière première dans la philosophie d'Henri de Gand," *Recherches de Théologie ancienne et médiévale* 46 (1979), pp. 130–82.

————. "Le statut philosophique de la matière selon Bonaventure." *Recherches de Théologie ancienne et médiévale* 47 (1980), pp. 188–230.

————. "Subsistance de la matière première selon Henri de Gand," in *San Bonaventura, Maestro di Vita Francescana e di Sapienza Cristiana (Atti del Congresso internazionale per il VII centenario di San Bonaventura da Bagnoregio),* Vol. 3 (Rome, 1976), pp. 107–15.

————. "La volonté humaine, faculté plus élevée que l'intelligence selon Henri de Gand." *Recherches de Théologie ancienne et médiévale* 42 (1975), pp. 5–51.

Mahoney, E. P. "Metaphysical Foundations of the Hierarchy of Being according to Some Late-Medieval and Renaissance Philosophers," in *Philosophies of Existence: Ancient and Medieval,* ed. P. Morewedge (New York, 1982), pp. 169–82.

Manser, G. M. *Das Wesen des Thomismus.* 3d ed., Fribourg, 1949.

Mansion, A. "L'objet de la science philosophique suprême d'après Aristote, Métaphysique, E, I," in *Mélanges de Philosophie Grecque offerts à Mgr Diès* (Paris, 1956), pp. 151–68.

————. "Philosophie première, philosophie seconde et métaphysique chez Aristote." *Revue philosophique de Louvain* 56 (1958), pp. 165–221.

Maritain, J. *Approaches to God.* London, 1955.

————. *Distinguish to Unite or The Degrees of Knowledge,* trans. G. Phelan. New York, 1959.

————. *Existence and the Existent.* New York, 1948.

————. *A Preface to Metaphysics.* New York, 1948.

————. "Reflexions sur la nature blessée et sur l'intuition de l'être." *Revue thomiste* 68 (1968), pp. 5–40.

Markus, R. A. "Augustine: Reason and Illumination," in *The Cambridge History of Later Greek and Early Medieval Philosophy,* ed. A. H. Armstrong (Cambridge, 1967), pp. 362–73.

Matthews, G. "Aquinas on Saying That God Doesn't Exist." *The Monist* 47 (1963), pp. 472–77.

Maurer, A. "Dialectic in the *DE ENTE ET ESSENTIA* of St. Thomas Aquinas," in *Roma, magistra mundi. Itineraria culturae medievalis.* Mélanges offerts au Père L. E. Boyle à l'occasion de son 75e anniversaire, ed. J. Hamesse (Louvain-la-Neuve, 1998), pp. 573–83.

————. "Form and Essence in the Philosophy of St. Thomas." *Mediaeval Studies* 13 (1951), pp. 165–76; repr. in his *Being and Knowing. Studies in Thomas Aquinas and Later Medieval Philosophers* (Toronto, 1990), pp. 3–18.

————. "St. Thomas on the Sacred Name 'Tetragrammaton'." *Mediaeval Studies* 34 (1972), pp. 275–86; repr. in his *Being and Knowing: Studies in Thomas Aquinas and Later Medieval Philosophers* (Toronto, 1990), pp. 59–69.

————, trans. and intro. *St. Thomas Aquinas: On Being and Essence.* Toronto, 1968.

————, trans. and intro. *St. Thomas Aquinas: The Division and Methods of the Sciences* (Questions V and VI of his Commentary on the *De Trinitate* of Boethius). Toronto, 1953; 4th ed., 1986.

McGill, A. C. "Recent Discussions of Anselm's Argument," in *The Many-Faced Argument,* ed. J. H. Hick and A. C. McGill (New York, 1965), pp. 33–110.

McGovern, M. "Prime Matter in Aquinas," in *The Metaphysics of Substance. Proceedings of the American Catholic Philosophical Association* 61 (1987), pp. 221–34.

McInerny, R. *Aquinas and Analogy.* Washington, D.C., 1996.

———. *Boethius and Aquinas.* Washington, D.C., 1990.

———. "Boethius and Saint Thomas Aquinas." *Rivista di Filosofia neo-scolastica* 66 (1974), pp. 219–45.

———. *The Logic of Analogy: An Interpretation of St. Thomas.* The Hague, 1961.

———. *Studies in Analogy.* The Hague, 1968.

McMahon, F. E., and J. Albertson. "The Esse of Accidents: A Discussion." *Modern Schoolman* 31 (1953–54), pp. 125–32.

———, and G. B. Phelan. "The *Esse* of Accidents." *New Scholasticism* 43 (1969), pp. 143–48.

McMahon, W. E. "Albert the Great on the Semantics of the Categories of Substance, Quantity, and Quality." *Historiographia Linguistica* (Amsterdam) 7:1/2 (1980), pp. 145–57.

———. "The *Liber sex principiorum,* A Twelfth-Century Treatise in Descriptive Metaphysics," in Studies in the History of Linguistics, Vol. 20: *Progress in Linguistic Historiography,* ed. K. Koerner (Amsterdam, 1980), pp. 3–12.

Meehan, F. X. *Efficient Causality in Aristotle and St. Thomas.* Washington, D.C., 1940.

Miller, M. "The Problem of Action in the Commentary of St. Thomas Aquinas on the *Physics* of Aristotle." *Modern Schoolman* 23 (1945–46), pp. 135–67.

Minio-Paluello, L., ed. *Aristoteles Latinus.* I.6–7: *Categoriarum supplementa: Porphyrii Isagoge et Liber sex Principiorum.* Bruges-Paris, 1966.

Miyakawa, T. "The Value and the Meaning of the 'Tertia Via' of St. Thomas Aquinas," *Aquinas* 6 (1963), pp. 239–95.

Mondin, B. "Il principio 'omne agens agit sibi simile' e l'analogia dei nomi divini nel pensiero di S. Tommaso d'Aquino." *Divus Thomas* (Piac.) 63 (1960), pp. 336–48.

———. *The Principle of Analogy in Protestant and Catholic Theology.* The Hague, 1963.

Montagnes, B. *La doctrine de l'analogie de l'être d'après saint Thomas d'Aquin.* Louvain-Paris, 1963.

Moody, E. A. *The Logic of William of Ockham.* New York, 1965.

Moreno, A. "The Law of Inertia and the Principle *Quidquid Movetur ab Alio Movetur.*" *The Thomist* 38 (1974), pp. 316–25.

———. "The Nature of Metaphysics." *The Thomist* 30 (1966), pp. 109–35.

Morewedge, P. "Philosophical Analysis and Ibn Sina's 'Essence-Existence' Distinction." *Journal of the American Oriental Society* 92 (1972), pp. 425–35.

Moses Maimonides. *Dux seu Director dubitantium aut perplexorum.* Paris, 1520; repr. Frankfurt, 1964.

———. *The Guide of the Perplexed,* trans. S. Pines. Chicago, 1963.

Motte, A.-R. "A propos des 'Cinq voies'." *Revue des sciences philosophiques et théologiques* 27 (1938), pp. 577–82.

Muckle, J. T., ed. *Algazel's Metaphysics.* Toronto, 1933.

Mullaney, T. U. "Created Personality: The Unity of Thomistic Tradition." *New Scholasticism* 29 (1955), pp. 377–85.

Muñiz, F. "El constitutivo formal de la persona creada en la tradición tomista." *La Ciencia tomista* 68 (1945), pp. 5–89; 70 (1946), pp. 201–93.

Muskens, G. L. *De vocis* ἀναλογίας *significatione ac usu apud Aristotelem.* Groningen, 1943.

Nardi, B. "La dottrina d'Alberto Magno sull' 'inchoatio formae'," in *Studi di filosofia medievale* (Rome, 1960), pp. 69–101.

Neumann, S. *Gegenstand und Methode der theoretischen Wissenschaften nach Thomas von Aquin aufgrund der Expositio super librum Boethii De Trinitate.* Münster, 1965.

Newton, I. *Optics,* Bk III, Part 1, in Great Books of the Western World, Vol. 34. Chicago, 1952.

Nicolas, J.-H. "Chronique de Philosophie." *Revue thomiste* 48 (1948), pp. 538–91.

———. *Dieu connu comme inconnu. Essai d'une critique de la connaissance théologique.* Paris, 1966.

Noone, T. "Albert the Great on the Subject of Metaphysics and Demonstrating the Existence of God." *Medieval Philosophy and Theology* 2 (1992), pp. 39–52.

O'Brien, T. *Metaphysics and the Existence of God: A Reflexion on the Question of God's Existence in Contemporary Thomistic Metaphysics.* Washington, D.C., 1960.

O'Donoghue, D. "An Analysis of the *Tertia Via* of St. Thomas." *Irish Theological Quarterly* 20 (1953), pp. 132–44.

O'Hara, M. L., ed. *Substances and Things: Aristotle's Doctrine of Physical Substance in Recent Essays.* Washington, D.C., 1982.

O'Meara, T. F. *Thomas Aquinas: Theologian.* Notre Dame, Ind., 1997.

O'Rourke, F. *Pseudo-Dionysius and the Metaphysics of Aquinas.* Leiden–New York–Cologne, 1992.

Owens, J. "The Accidental and Essential Character of Being in the Doctrine of St. Thomas Aquinas," in *St. Thomas Aquinas on the Existence of God. The Collected Papers of Joseph Owens,* ed. J. Catan (Albany, N.Y., 1980), pp. 52–96.

———. "Aquinas and the Five Ways," in *St. Thomas Aquinas on the Existence of God. The Collected Papers of Joseph Owens,* ed. J. Catan (Albany, N.Y., 1980), pp. 132–44.

———. "Aquinas and the Proof from the 'Physics.'" *Mediaeval Studies* 28 (1966), pp. 119–50.

———. "Aquinas as Aristotelian Commentator," in *St. Thomas Aquinas 1274–1974: Commemorative Studies,* ed. A. Maurer et al. (Toronto, 1974), Vol. 1, pp. 213–38.

———. "Aquinas—'Darkness of Ignorance' in the Most Refined Notion of God," in *Bonaventure and Aquinas: Enduring Philosophers,* ed. R. W. Shahan and F. J. Kovach (Norman, Okla., 1976), pp. 69–86.

———. "Aquinas' Distinction at *De ente et essentia* 4.119–123." *Mediaeval Studies* 48 (1986), pp. 264–87.

———. *Aquinas on Being and Thing.* Niagara, N.Y., 1981.

———. "Aquinas on Infinite Regress," in *St. Thomas Aquinas on the Existence of God. The Collected Papers of Joseph Owens,* ed. J. Catan (Albany, N.Y., 1980), pp. 228–30.

———. "Aquinas on Knowing Existence." *Review of Metaphysics* 29 (1976), pp. 670–90; repr. in *St. Thomas Aquinas on the Existence of God. The Collected Papers of Joseph Owens,* ed. J. Catan (Albany, N.Y., 1980), pp. 20–33.

———. "Being and Natures in Aquinas." *Modern Schoolman* 61 (1984), pp. 157–68.

———. "The Conclusion of the *Prima Via*," in *St. Thomas Aquinas on the Existence of God. The Collected Papers of Joseph Owens,* ed. J. Catan (Albany, N.Y., 1980), pp. 143–55.

———. *The Doctrine of Being in the Aristotelian Metaphysics.* 3d ed., Toronto, 1978.

———. "The Doctrine of Being in the Aristotelian *Metaphysics*-Revisited," in *Philosophies of Existence, Ancient and Medieval,* ed. P. Morewedge (New York, 1982), pp. 33–59.

———. *An Elementary Christian Metaphysics.* Milwaukee, 1963.

———. "Immobility and Existence for Aquinas," in *St. Thomas Aquinas on the Existence of God: The Collected Papers of Joseph Owens,* ed. J. Catan (Albany, N.Y., 1980), pp. 208–27.

————. *An Interpretation of Existence*. Milwaukee, 1968.

————. "Judgment and Truth in Aquinas." *Mediaeval Studies* 32 (1970), pp. 138–58; repr. in *St. Thomas Aquinas on the Existence of God: The Collected Papers of Joseph Owens*, ed. J. Catan (Albany, N.Y., 1980), pp. 34–51.

————. "Metaphysical Separation in Aquinas." *Mediaeval Studies* 34 (1972), pp. 287–306.

————. "*Quandoque* and *Aliquando* in Aquinas' *Tertia Via*." *New Scholasticism* 54 (1980), p. 447–75.

————. "Quiddity and Real Distinction in St. Thomas Aquinas." *Mediaeval Studies* 27 (1965), pp. 1–22.

————. *St. Thomas and the Future of Metaphysics*. Milwaukee, 1957.

————. *St. Thomas Aquinas on the Existence of God: The Collected Papers of Joseph Owens*, ed. J. Catan. Albany, N.Y., 1980.

————. "Stages and Distinction in *De ente:* A Rejoinder," *The Thomist* 45 (1981), pp. 99–123.

————. "The Starting Point of the *Prima Via*," in *St. Thomas Aquinas on the Existence of God: The Collected Papers of Joseph Owens*, ed. J. Catan (Albany, N.Y., 1980), pp. 169–91.

————. "Thomas Aquinas (b. ca. 1225; d. 1274)," in *Individuation in Scholasticism: The Later Middle Ages and the Counter Reformation*, ed. J.J.E. Gracia (Albany, N.Y., 1994), pp. 173–94.

————. "Thomas Aquinas: Dimensive Quantity as Individuating Principle." *Mediaeval Studies* 50 (1988), pp. 279–310.

Pater, T. "The Question of the Validity of the *Tertia Via*," in Vol. 2 of Studies in Philosophy and the History of Philosophy 2 (Washington, D.C., 1963), pp. 137–77.

Patfoort, A. *L'unité d'être dans le Christ d'après s. Thomas*. Tournai, 1964.

Patt, W. "Aquinas's Real Distinction and Some Interpretations." *New Scholasticism* 62 (1988), pp. 1–29.

Pattin, A. "La structure de la 'tertia via' dans la 'Somme théologique' de saint Thomas d'Aquin." *Revue de l'Université d'Ottawa* 27 (1957), pp. 26*-35*.

Paulus, J. *Henri de Gand. Essai sur les tendances de sa métaphysique*. Paris, 1938.

————. "La théorie du Premier Moteur chez Aristote." *Revue de philosophie*, n.s. 4 (1933), pp. 259–94, 394–424.

Pegis, A. "Penitus Manet Ignotum." *Mediaeval Studies* 27 (1965), pp. 212–26.

————. "St. Thomas and the Coherence of the Aristotelian Theology." *Mediaeval Studies* 35 (1973), pp. 67–117.

Peifer, J. F. *The Concept in Thomism*. New York, 1952.

Penido, M.T.-L. *Le rôle de l'analogie en théologie dogmatique*. Paris, 1931.

Pérez Guerrero, J. *La creación como asimilación a Dios*. Navarra, 1996.

Peter Lombard. *Magistri Petri Lombardi . . . Sententiae in IV Libris distinctae*. Grottaferrata (Rome), 1971–81.

Phelan, G. B. "The Being of Creatures," in *Readings in Metaphysics*, ed. J. Rosenberg (Westminster, Md., 1963), pp. 265–72; orig. pub. in *Proceedings of the American Catholic Philosophical Association* 31 (1957), pp. 118–25.

Planty-Bonjour, J.-P. "Die Struktur des Gottesbeweises aus den Seinsstufen." *Philosophisches Jahrbuch* 69 (1962), pp. 282–97.

Plato. *Platonis Opera*, ed. J. Burnet. Vol. 1. Oxford, 1900, 18th imprint, 1902. Vol. 2. Oxford, 1901, 21st repr., n.d.

Porro, P., trans. *Tommaso d'Aquino, Commenti a Boezio*. Intro. by the translator. Milan, 1997.

Prufer, T. *Sein und Wort nach Thomas von Aquin*. Munich, 1959.

[Pseudo-] Dionysius. *De caelesti hierarchia*. Migne PG 3.

———. *De divinis nominibus.* Greek text and Latin trans. in Thomas Aquinas, *In Librum beati Dionysii De divinis nominibus Expositio,* ed. C. Pera. Turin-Rome, 1950.

———. *De mystica theologia.* Migne PG 3.

———. *Dionysiaca. Recueil donnant l'ensemble des traductions des ouvrages attribués au Denys de l'Aréopage.* Vol. 1. Bruges, 1937.

———. *Epistola I.* Migne PG 3.

Putallaz, F.-X. *Le sens de la réflexion chez Thomas d'Aquin.* Paris, 1991.

———, and R. Imbach. *Profession: Philosophe Siger de Brabant.* Paris, 1997.

Quarello, E. "Discussioni nell'interpretazione di Capreolo sul problema della persona." *Salesianum* 18 (1956), pp. 297–310.

———. "Il problema scolastico della persona nel Gaetano e nel Capreolo." *Divus Thomas* (Piac.) 55 (1952), pp. 34–63.

Quinn, J. M. *The Thomism of Etienne Gilson: A Critical Study.* Villanova, 1971.

Rabeau, G. *Species. Verbum. L'activité intellectuelle élémentaire selon S. Thomas d'Aquin.* Paris, 1938.

Rahman, F. "Essence and Existence in Avicenna." *Mediaeval and Renaissance Studies* 4 (1958), pp. 1–16.

———. "Ibn Sina," in *A History of Muslim Philosophy,* Vol. 1, ed. M. M. Sharif (Wiesbaden, 1963), pp. 480–506.

Ramirez, S. M. "En torno a un famoso texto de santo Tomás sobre la analogía." *Sapientia* 8 (1953), pp. 166–91.

Régis, L.-M. "Analyse et synthèse dans l'oeuvre de saint Thomas," in *Studia Mediaevalia in honorem admodum reverendi Patris Raymundi Josephi Martin* (Bruges, 1948), pp. 303–30.

———. *Epistemology,* trans. I. M. Byrne. New York, 1959.

———. "Un livre: *La philosophie de la nature.* Quelques 'Apories'." *Études et recherches* 1 (1936), pp. 127–56.

Renard, H. "What Is St. Thomas' Approach to Metaphysics?" *New Scholasticism* 30 (1956), pp. 64–83.

Robert, J.-D. "La métaphysique, science distincte de toute autre discipline philosophique, selon saint Thomas d'Aquin." *Divus Thomas* (Piac.) 50 (1947), pp. 206–22.

———. "Le principe: 'Actus non limitatur nisi per potentiam subjectivam realiter distinctam.'" *Revue philosophique de Louvain* 47 (1949), pp. 44–70.

———. "Note sur le dilemme: 'Limitation par composition ou limitation par hiérarchie formelle des essences.'" *Revue des sciences philosophiques et théologiques* 49 (1965), pp. 60–66.

Roland-Gosselin, M.-D., ed. *Le "De ente et essentia" de s. Thomas d'Aquin.* Paris, 1948; orig. pub. 1926.

Rosemann, P. *Omne Agens Agit Sibi Simile: A "Repetition" of Scholastic Metaphysics.* Leuven, 1996.

Rosenberg, J. *The Principle of Individuation: A Comparative Study of St. Thomas, Scotus, and Suarez.* Ph.D. dissertation, The Catholic University of America, Washington, D.C., 1950.

———, ed. *Readings in Metaphysics.* Westminster, Md., 1963.

Ross, J. F. "Aquinas on Belief and Knowledge," in *Essays Honoring Allan B. Wolter,* ed. W. A. Frank and G. J. Etzkorn (St. Bonaventure, N.Y., 1985), pp. 245–69.

———. Review of *Metaphysical Themes in Thomas Aquinas* by J. F. Wippel. *Journal of the History of Philosophy* 25 (1987), pp. 592–94.

Rowe, W. L. *The Cosmological Argument.* Princeton, 1975.

Ruello, F. *La notion de vérité chez Saint Albert le Grand et Saint Thomas d'Aquin de 1243 à 1254.* Louvain-Paris, 1969.

Schmidt, R. W. "L'emploi de la séparation en métaphysique." *Revue philosophique de Louvain* 58 (1960), pp. 373–93.

———. "The Evidence Grounding Judgments of Existence," in *An Etienne Gilson Tribute,* ed. C. J. O'Neil (Milwaukee, 1959), pp. 228–44.

Schmitz, K. "Analysis by Principles and Analysis by Elements," in *Graceful Reason. Essays in Ancient and Medieval Philosophy Presented to Joseph Owens, CSSR,* ed. L. P. Gerson (Toronto, 1983), pp. 315–30.

Schneider, T. *Die Einheit des Menschen. Die anthropologische formel "anima forma corporis" in sogennanten Korrektorienstreit und bei Petrus Johannis Olivi.* Münster, 1973.

Schrimpf, G. *Die Axiomenschrift des Boethius (De Hebdomadibus) als philosophisches Lehrbuch des Mittelalters.* Leiden, 1966.

Schulze, M. *Leibhaft und Unsterblich: Zur Schau der Seele in der Anthropologie und Theologie des Hl. Thomas von Aquin.* Freiburg, Switzerland, 1992.

Schweizer, O. *Person und hypostatische Union bei Thomas von Aquin.* Freiburg, Switzerland, 1957.

Siger of Brabant. *Ecrits de logique, de morale et de physique,* ed. B. Bazán. Louvain-Paris, 1974.

———. *Quaestiones in Metaphysicam,* ed. W. Dunphy. Louvain-la-Neuve, 1981.

———. *Quaestiones in Metaphysicam,* ed. A. Maurer. Louvain-la-Neuve, 1983.

Sillem, E. *Ways of Thinking about God: Thomas Aquinas and the Modern Mind.* New York, 1960.

Silvester of Ferrara. Commentary on *Summa contra Gentiles,* in *Sancti Thomae Opera omnia,* Leonine edition, Vols. 13–15.

Simon, Y. *Introduction à l'ontologie du connaître.* Paris, 1934.

Smith, V. *The General Science of Nature.* Milwaukee, 1958.

———. "The Prime Mover: Physical and Metaphysical Considerations," in *Proceedings of the American Catholic Philosophical Association* 28 (1954), pp. 78–94.

Snyder, S. C. "Albert the Great, *Incohatio Formae,* and the Pure Potentiality of Matter." *American Catholic Philosophical Quarterly* 70 (1996), pp. 63–82.

Speer, A. " *Yliathin quod est principium individuandi.* Zur Diskussion um das Individuationsprinzip im Anschluss an prop. 8[9] des 'Liber de causis' bei Johannes de Nova Domo, Albertus Magnus und Thomas von Aquin," in *Miscellanea Mediaevalia* 24: *Individuum und Individualität im Mittelalter* (1996), pp. 271–85.

Sweeney, E. "Individuation and the Body in Aquinas," in *Miscellanea Mediaevalia* 24: *Individuum und Individualität im Mittelalter* (1996), pp. 178–96.

Sweeney, L. "Bonaventure and Aquinas on the Divine Being as Infinite," in his *Divine Infinity in Greek and Medieval Thought* (New York, 1982), pp. 413–37.

———. "Existence/Essence in Thomas Aquinas's Early Writings." *Proceedings of the American Catholic Philosophical Association* 37 (1963), pp. 97–131.

———. *A Metaphysics of Authentic Existentialism.* Englewood Cliffs, N.J., 1965.

———. "Presidential Address: Surprises in the History of Infinity from Anaximander to George Cantor." *Proceedings of the American Catholic Philosophical Association* 55 (1981), pp. 3–23.

Synave, P. "La révélation des vérités naturelles d'après saint Thomas d'Aquin," in *Mélanges Mandonnet,* Vol. 1 (Paris, 1930), pp. 327–70.

Taylor, R. "St. Thomas and the *Liber de causis* on the Hylomorphic Composition of Separate Substances." *Mediaeval Studies* 41 (1979), pp. 506–13.

te Velde, R. A. *Participation and Substantiality in Thomas Aquinas.* Leiden–New York–Cologne, 1995.

Théry, G. "L'Augustinisme médiévale et le problème de l'unité de la forme substantielle," in *Acta Hebdomadae Augustinianae-Thomisticae* (Rome, 1931), pp. 144–200.

Thomas Aquinas. *Sancti Thomae de Aquino Opera omnia,* Leonine edition. Rome, 1882– . Vol. 1*.1, *Expositio Libri Peryermenias.* Vol. 1*.2, *Expositio Libri Posteriorum.* Vols. 4–12, *Summa theologiae.* Vols. 13–15, *Summa contra Gentiles.* Vols. 22.1, 22.2, 22.3, *Quaestiones disputatae De veritate.* Vol. 23, *Quaestiones disputatae De malo.* Vol. 24.1, *Quaestiones disputatae De anima.* Vols. 25.1, 25.2, *Quaestiones de quolibet.* Vol. 40, *De substantiis separatis, etc.* Vol. 42, *Compendium theologiae, etc.* Vol. 43, *De principiis naturae, De aeternitate mundi, De mixtione elementorum, De unitate intellectus contra Averroistas, De ente et essentia, etc.* Vol. 45.1, *Sentencia libri De anima.* Vol. 45.2, *Sentencia libri De sensu et sensato* (incl. *De memoria et reminiscencia*). Vol. 47.2, *Sententia libri Ethicorum.* Vol. 50, *Super Boetium De Trinitate, Expositio libri Boetii De ebdomadibus.*

———. *Sancti Thomae de Aquino Expositio super librum Boethii De Trinitate,* ed. B. Decker. 2d ed., Leiden, 1955; repr. 1959.

———. *In duodecim libros Metaphysicorum Aristotelis expositio,* ed. M.-R. Cathala and R. M. Spiazzi. Turin-Rome, 1950.

———. *In Libros Aristotelis De caelo et mundo expositio,* ed. R. M. Spiazzi. Turin-Rome, 1952.

———. *In librum beati Dionysii De divinis nominibus expositio,* ed. C. Pera. Turin-Rome, 1950.

———. *Thomas von Aquin, In librum Boethii de Trinitate, Quaestiones Quinta et Sexta,* ed. P. Wyser. Fribourg-Louvain, 1948.

———. *In octo libros Physicorum Aristotelis Expositio,* ed. P. M. Maggiòlo. Turin-Rome, 1954.

———. *S. Thomae Aquinatis doctoris angelici in omnes S. Pauli Apostoli Epistolas Commentaria,* Vol. 1. Turin, 1929.

———. *In quattuor libros Sententiarum,* in *S. Thomae Aquinatis opera omnia,* Vol. 1, ed. R. Busa. Stuttgart–Bad Cannstatt, 1980.

———. *Lectura super evangelium Johannis,* in *S. Thomae Aquinatis opera omnia,* Vol. 6, ed. R. Busa. Stuttgart–Bad Cannstatt, 1980.

———. *On the Truth of the Catholic Faith. Summa Contra Gentiles, Book Two: Creation.* Trans. J. F. Anderson. Garden City, N.Y., 1956.

———. *Quaestiones disputatae.* Vol. 2, incl. *De potentia* (ed. M. Pession), *De spiritualibus creaturis, De unione verbi incarnati* (ed. M. Calcaterra and T. S. Centi), *De virtutibus . . . etc.* (ed. A. Odetto). Turin-Rome, 1953.

———. *Questions on the Soul* [*Questiones de anima*], trans. J. Robb. Milwaukee, 1984.

———. *Scriptum super libros Sententiarum.* Vols. 1 and 2, ed. P. Mandonnet. Paris, 1929.

———. *Scriptum super Sententiis.* Vols. 3 and 4, ed. M. F. Moos. Paris, 1933 and 1947.

———. *Summa contra Gentiles.* Editio Leonina manualis. Rome, 1934.

———. *Summa theologiae Prima Pars, Pars IaIIae,* ed. P. Caramello (Turin-Rome, 1950); *Pars IIaIIae, Pars IIIa et Suppl.,* ed. De Rubeis, Billuart, P. Faucher (Turin-Rome, 1948).

———. *Summa Theologiae. Vol. 2: Existence and Nature of God,* ed. T. McDermott. New York–London, 1964.

———. *Sancti Thomae de Aquino Super Librum de causis expositio,* ed. H. D. Saffrey. Fribourg-Louvain, 1954.

Sancti Thomae Aquinatis Tractatus De spiritualibus creaturis, ed. L. W. Keeler. Rome, 1959.

Torrell, J.-P. *Initiation à saint Thomas d'Aquin. Sa personne et son oeuvre.* Fribourg, 1993; Eng. trans., *Saint Thomas Aquinas.* Vol. 1, *The Person and His Work.* Washington, D.C., 1996.

Trapp, D. "Aegidii Romani de doctrina modorum." *Angelicum* 12 (1935), pp. 449–501.

Tugwell, S., ed. See *Albert & Thomas: Selected Writings.*

Twetten, D. B. "Back to Nature in Aquinas." *Medieval Philosophy and Theology* 5 (1996), pp. 205–43.

————. "Clearing a Way for Aquinas: How the Proof from Motion Concludes to God." *Proceedings of the American Catholic Philosophical Association* 70 (1996), pp. 259–78.

Valbuena, I. "De significatione specialis praedicamenti 'habitus' apud philosophum et divum Thomam." *Angelicum* 22 (1945), pp. 172–77.

Van Steenberghen, F. "Etienne Gilson, historien de la pensée médiévale," *Revue philosophique de Louvain* 77 (1979), pp. 487–508.

————. *Maître Siger de Brabant.* Louvain-Paris, 1977.

————. *La philosophie au XIIIe siècle.* 2d rev. ed., Louvain-la-Neuve, 1991.

————. *Le problème de l'existence de Dieu dans les écrits de s. Thomas d'Aquin.* Louvain-la-Neuve, 1980.

————. *Thomas Aquinas and Radical Aristotelianism.* Washington, D.C., 1980.

Vande Wiele, J. "Le problème de la vérité ontologique dans la philosophie de saint Thomas." *Revue philosophique de Louvain* 52 (1954), pp. 521–71.

Verbeke, G. "La structure logique de la preuve du Premier Moteur chez Aristote." *Revue philosophique de Louvain* 46 (1948), pp. 137–60.

————. "Substance in Aristotle." *Proceedings of the American Catholic Philosophical Association* 51 (1987), pp. 35–51.

Wagner, M. *Die Philosophischen Implikate der "Quarta Via." Eine Untersuchung zum Vierten Gottesbeweis bei Thomas von Aquin (S. Th. I, 2, 3c).* Leiden, 1989.

Wallace, W. A. "Newtonian Antinomies against the *Prima Via.*" *The Thomist* 19 (1956), pp. 151–92.

————. *The Role of Demonstration in Moral Theology.* Washington, D.C., 1962.

Wéber, E.-H. *La controverse de 1270 à l'Université de Paris et son retentissement sur la pensée de s. Thomas d'Aquin.* Paris, 1970.

————. "Les discussions de 1270 à l'Université de Paris et leur influence sur la pensée philosophique de s. Thomas d'Aquin," in *Miscellanea Mediaevalia* 10: *Die Auseinandersetzungen an der Pariser Universität im XIII Jahrhundert* (Berlin, 1976), pp. 285–316.

Weidemann, H. *Metaphysik und Sprache. Eine sprachphilosophische Untersuchung zu Thomas von Aquin und Aristoteles.* Freiburg-Munich, 1975.

————. "Tradition und Kritik: Zur Auseinandersetzung des Thomas von Aquin mit dem ihm überlieferten Platonismus in der 'Expositio super librum Boethii de Trinitate,'" in ΠΑΡΑ-ΔΩΣΙΣ: Studies in Memory of Edwin A. Quain, ed. H. G. Fletcher and M. B. Schulte (New York, 1976), pp. 99–119.

Weisheipl, J. A. "Albertus Magnus and Universal Hylomorphism: Avicebron," in *Albert the Great Commemorative Essays*, ed. F. J. Kovach and R. W. Shahan (Norman, Okla., 1980), pp. 239–60.

————. "The Concept of Matter in Fourteenth Century Science," in *The Concept of Matter in Greek and Medieval Philosophy*, ed. E. McMullin (Notre Dame, Ind., 1965), pp. 147–69.

————. *Friar Thomas d'Aquino: His Life, Thought and Work.* Garden City, N.Y., 1974; 2d rev. ed., Washington, D.C., 1983.

————. "Galileo and the Principle of Inertia," in *Nature and Motion in the Middle Ages,* ed. W. E. Carroll (Washington, D.C., 1985), pp. 49–63.

————. "The Life and Works of St. Albert the Great," in *Albertus Magnus and the Sciences. Commemorative Essays 1980*, ed. J. A. Weisheipl (Toronto, 1980), pp. 13–51.

————. "Natural and Compulsory Movement," in *Nature and Motion in the Middle Ages,* ed. W. E. Carroll (Washington, D.C., 1985), pp. 25–48.

————. *Nature and Motion in the Middle Ages,* ed. W. E. Carroll. Washington, D.C., 1985.

————. "The Principle *Omne quod movetur ab alio movetur* in Medieval Physics." *Isis* 56 (1965), pp. 26–45; repr. in *Nature and Motion in the Middle Ages,* ed. W. E. Carroll (Washington, D.C., 1985), pp. 75–97.

——. "The Relationship of Medieval Natural Philosophy to Modern Science: The Contribution of Thomas Aquinas to Its Understanding." *Manuscripta* 20 (1976), pp. 181–96.

——. Review of *Metaphysical Themes in Thomas Aquinas* by J. F. Wippel. *Review of Metaphysics* 38 (1985), pp. 699–700.

——. "The Specter of *motor coniunctus* in Medieval Physics," in *Nature and Motion in the Middle Ages,* ed. W. E. Carroll (Washington, D.C., 1985), pp. 99–120.

White, K. "Aquinas on the Immediacy of the Union of Soul and Body," in *Studies in Thomistic Theology,* ed. P. Lockey (Houston, 1995), 209–80.

——. "Individuation in Aquinas's *Super Boetium De Trinitate,* Q. 4." *American Catholic Philosophical Quarterly* 69 (1995), pp. 543–56.

Wilhelmsen, F. "Existence and *Esse.*" *New Scholasticism* 50 (1976), pp. 20–45.

William de la Mare. *Le Correctorium Corruptorii "Quare" (Les premières polémiques thomistes* I), ed. P. Glorieux. Le Saulchoir, Kain, 1927.

Williams, C.J.F. "*Hic autem non est procedere in infinitum.*" *Mind* 69 (1960), pp. 403–5.

Winance, E. "L'essence divine et la connaissance humaine dans le Commentaire sur les Sentences de Saint Thomas." *Revue philosophique de Louvain* 55 (1957), pp. 171–215.

Winandy, J. "Le Quodlibet II, art. 4 de saint Thomas et la notion de suppôt." *Ephemerides theologicae Lovanienses* 11 (1934), pp. 5–29.

Winiewicz, D. "A Note on *Alteritas* and Numerical Diversity in St. Thomas Aquinas." *Dialogue* 16 (1977), pp. 693–707.

Wippel, J. F. "Aquinas's Route to the Real Distinction: A Note on *De ente et essentia,* c. 4." *The Thomist* 43 (1979), pp. 279–95.

——. "Bishop Stephen Tempier and Thomas Aquinas: A Separate Process against Aquinas?" *Freiburger Zeitschrift für Philosophie und Theologie* 44 (1997), pp. 117–36.

——, trans. and intro. *Boethius of Dacia. On the Supreme Good. On the Eternity of the World. On Dreams.* Toronto, 1987.

——. "The Condemnations of 1270 and 1277 at Paris." *Journal of Medieval and Renaissance Studies* 7 (1977), pp. 169–201.

——. "Essence and Existence in the *De ente,* ch. 4," in *Metaphysical Themes in Thomas Aquinas* (Washington, D.C., 1984), pp. 107–32.

——. "Essence and Existence," in *The Cambridge History of Later Medieval Philosophy,* ed. N. Kretzmann et al. (Cambridge, 1982), pp. 385–410.

——. "Godfrey of Fontaines and the Act-Potency Axiom." *Journal of the History of Philosophy* 11 (1973), pp. 299–317.

——. "The Latin Avicenna as a Source for Thomas Aquinas's Metaphysics." *Freiburger Zeitschrift für Philosophie und Theologie* 37 (1990), pp. 51–90.

——. *Mediaeval Reactions to the Encounter between Faith and Reason.* The Aquinas Lecture 1995. Milwaukee, 1995.

——. *Metaphysical Themes in Thomas Aquinas.* Washington, D.C., 1984.

——. *The Metaphysical Thought of Godfrey of Fontaines: A Study in Late Thirteenth-Century Philosophy.* Washington, D.C., 1981.

——. "The Possibility of a Christian Philosophy: A Thomistic Perspective." *Faith and Philosophy* 1 (1984), pp. 272–90.

——. "Presidential Address: Substance in Aquinas's Metaphysics," in *Proceedings of the American Catholic Philosophical Association* 61 (1987), pp. 2–22.

——. "Quodlibetal Questions, Chiefly in Theological Faculties." Part II of B. C. Bazán,

J. F. Wippel, G. Fransen, and D. Jacquart, *Les questions disputées et les questions quodlibétiques dans les facultés de théologie, de droit et de médecine* (Turnhout, 1985), pp. 151–222.

———. "The Relationship between Essence and Existence in Late-Thirteenth-Century Thought: Giles of Rome, Henry of Ghent, Godfrey of Fontaines, and James of Viterbo," in *Philosophies of Existence, Ancient and Medieval,* ed. P. Morewedge (New York, 1982), pp. 131–64.

———. Review of *Aquinas on Metaphysics . . .* by J. Doig. *Speculum* 52 (1977), pp. 133–35.

———. Review of *La destinée de la nature humaine selon Thomas d'Aquin,* by J. Laporta. *Speculum* 44 (1969), pp. 474–76.

———. "Thomas Aquinas and Participation," in *Studies in Medieval Philosophy,* ed. J. F. Wippel (Washington, D.C., 1987), pp. 117–58.

———. "Thomas Aquinas and the Axiom That Unreceived Act Is Unlimited." *Review of Metaphysics* 51 (1998), pp. 533–64.

———. "Thomas Aquinas and the Condemnation of 1277." *Modern Schoolman* 72 (1995), pp. 233–72.

———. "Thomas Aquinas on Demonstrating God's Omnipotence." *Revue internationale de philosophie* 52 (1998), pp. 227–47.

———. "Thomas Aquinas on the Distinction and Derivation of the Many from the One: A Dialectic between Being and Nonbeing." *Review of Metaphysics* 38 (1985), pp. 563–90.

———. "Thomas Aquinas on the Divine Ideas." *Etienne Gilson Series* 16. Toronto, 1993.

———. "Thomas Aquinas on Substance as a Cause of Proper Accidents," in *Philosophie im Mittelalter. Entwicklungslinien und Paradigmen,* ed. J. P. Beckmann, L. Honnefelder, G. Schrimpf, G. Wieland (Hamburg, 1987), pp. 201–12.

———. "Thomas Aquinas on What Philosophers Can Know about God," *American Catholic Philosophical Quarterly* 66 (1992), pp. 279–97.

———. "Thomas Aquinas's Derivation of the Aristotelian Categories," *Journal of the History of Philosophy* 25 (1987), pp. 13–34.

———. "Truth in Thomas Aquinas." *Review of Metaphysics* 43 (1989/1990), pp. 295–326, 543–67.

Wissink, J.B.M., ed. *The Eternity of the World in the Thought of Thomas Aquinas and His Contemporaries.* Leiden, 1990.

Wittmann, M. *Die Stellung des hl. Thomas von Aquin zu Avencebrol (Ibn Gebirol).* Beiträge zur Geschichte der Philosophie des Mittelalters 3, 3. Münster, 1900.

Wolfson, H. A. "St. Thomas on Divine Attributes," in *Mélanges Offerts à Etienne Gilson* (Paris, 1959), pp. 673–700; repr. "with corrections and an Appendix" in *Studies in Maimonides and St. Thomas Aquinas,* ed. J. I. Dienstag (New York, 1975), pp. 1–28.

Wolter, A. "The Ockhamist Critique," in *The Concept of Matter in Greek and Medieval Philosophy,* ed. E. McMullin (Notre Dame, Ind., 1965), pp. 124–46.

Wright, J. H. *The Order of the Universe in the Theology of St. Thomas Aquinas.* Rome, 1957.

Zavalloni, R. *Richard de Mediavilla et la controverse sur la pluralité des formes.* Louvain, 1951.

Zimmermann, A. *Ontologie oder Metaphysik? Die Diskussion über den Gegenstand der Metaphysik im 13. und 14. Jahrhundert.* 2d rev. ed., Leuven, 1998.

———, ed. *Ein Kommentar zur Physik des Aristoteles aus der Pariser Artistenfakultät um 1273.* Berlin, 1968.

Manuscripts

Leipzig, Universitätsbibliothek 482
Paris, Bibl. Nat. lat. 15.819
Vatican Library 808

Index of Names

Index of Topics

The Metaphysical Thought of Thomas Aquinas: From Finite Being to Uncreated Being was composed in Adobe Garamond by Graphic Composition, Inc., Athens, Georgia; printed on 50-pound Natural Smooth and bound by Sheridan Books, Ann Arbor, Michigan; and designed and produced by Kachergis Book Design, Pittsboro, North Carolina.